Let's Go:
Alaska
& the Pacific Northwest

"Its yearly revision by a new crop of Harvard students makes it as valuable as ever." —*The New York Times*

"Value-packed, unbeatable, accurate, and comprehensive." —*The Los Angeles Times*

"A world-wise traveling companion—always ready with friendly advice and helpful hints, all sprinkled with a bit of wit." —*The Philadelphia Inquirer*

"Lighthearted and sophisticated, informative and fun to read. [Let's Go] helps the novice traveler navigate like a knowledgeable old hand." —*Atlanta Journal-Constitution*

"All the essential information you need, from making a phone call to exchanging money to contacting your embassy. [Let's Go] provides maps to help you find your way from every train station to a full range of youth hostels and hotels." —*Minneapolis Star Tribune*

"Unbeatable: good sight-seeing advice; up-to-date-info on restaurants, hotels, and inns; a commitment to money-saving travel; and a wry style that brightens nearly every page." —*The Washington Post*

▓ Let's Go researchers have to make it on their own.

"The writers seem to have experienced every rooster-packed bus and lunar-surfaced mattress about which they write." —*The New York Times*

"Retains the spirit of the student-written publication it is: candid, opinionated, resourceful, amusing info for the traveler of limited means but broad curiosity." —*Mademoiselle*

▓ No other guidebook is as comprehensive.

"Whether you're touring the United States, Europe, Southeast Asia, or Central America, a Let's Go guide will clue you in to the cheapest, yet safe, hotels and hostels, food and transportation. Going beyond the call of duty, the guides reveal a country's latest news, cultural hints, and off-beat information that any tourist is likely to miss." —*Tulsa World*

▓ Let's Go is completely revised each year.

"Up-to-date travel tips for touring four continents on skimpy budgets." —*Time*

"Inimitable.... Let's Go's 24 guides are updated yearly (as opposed to the general guidebook standard of every two to three years), and in a marvelously spunky way." —*The New York Times*

Let's Go Publications

Let's Go: Alaska & The Pacific Northwest
Let's Go: Britain & Ireland
Let's Go: California
Let's Go: Central America
Let's Go: Eastern Europe
Let's Go: Ecuador & The Galápagos Islands
Let's Go: Europe
Let's Go: France
Let's Go: Germany
Let's Go: Greece & Turkey
Let's Go: India & Nepal
Let's Go: Ireland
Let's Go: Israel & Egypt
Let's Go: Italy
Let's Go: London
Let's Go: Mexico
Let's Go: New York City
Let's Go: Paris
Let's Go: Rome
Let's Go: Southeast Asia
Let's Go: Spain & Portugal
Let's Go: Switzerland & Austria
Let's Go: USA
Let's Go: Washington, D.C.

Let's Go **Map Guide:** Boston
Let's Go **Map Guide:** London
Let's Go **Map Guide:** New York City
Let's Go **Map Guide:** Paris
Let's Go **Map Guide:** San Francisco
Let's Go **Map Guide:** Washington, D.C.

LET'S GO

The Budget Guide to
Alaska
& the Pacific Northwest

1997

Elizabeth M. Angell
Editor

Sara K. Smith
Associate Editor

St. Martin's Press ≈ New York

HELPING LET'S GO

If you want to share your discoveries, suggestions, or corrections, please drop us a line. We read every piece of correspondence, whether a postcard, a 10-page e-mail, or a coconut. All suggestions are passed along to our researcher-writers. Please note that mail received after May 1997 may be too late for the 1998 book, but will be retained for the following edition. **Address mail to:**

Let's Go: Alaska & the Pacific Northwest
67 Mt. Auburn Street
Cambridge, MA 02138
USA

Visit Let's Go at **http://www.letsgo.com,** or send e-mail to:

Fanmail@letsgo.com
Subject: "Let's Go: Alaska & the Pacific Northwest"

In addition to the invaluable travel advice our readers share with us, many are kind enough to offer their services as researchers or editors. Unfortunately, the charter of Let's Go, Inc. enables us to employ only currently enrolled Harvard-Radcliffe students.

Maps by David Lindroth copyright © 1997, 1996, 1995, 1994, 1993, 1992, 1991, 1990, 1989, 1988 by St. Martin's Press, Inc.

Map revisions pp.2, 3,56, 57, 61, 63, 119, 133, 189, 203, 205, 235, 275, 277, 301, 311, 313, 316, 317, 361, 409, 411, 493, 509 by Let's Go, Inc.

Distributed outside the USA and Canada by Macmillan.

ISBN: 0-312-14644-2

First edition
10 9 8 7 6 5 4 3 2 1

Let's Go: Alaska & the Pacific Northwest is written by Let's Go Publications, 67 Mt. Auburn Street, Cambridge, MA 02138, USA.

Contents

About Let's Go

Back in 1960, a few students at Harvard University banded together to produce a 20-page pamphlet offering a collection of tips on budget travel in Europe. This modest, mimeographed packet, offered as an extra to passengers on student charter flights to Europe, met with instant popularity. The following year, students traveling to Europe researched the first, full-fledged edition of *Let's Go: Europe*, a pocket-sized book featuring honest, irreverent writing and a decidedly youthful outlook on the world. Throughout the 60s, our guides reflected the times; the 1969 guide to America led off by inviting travelers to "dig the scene" at San Francisco's Haight-Ashbury. During the 70s and 80s, we gradually added regional guides and expanded coverage into the Middle East and Central America. With the addition of our in-depth city guides, handy map guides, and extensive coverage of Asia, the 90s are also proving to be a time of explosive growth for Let's Go, and there's certainly no end in sight. The first editions of *Let's Go: India & Nepal* and *Let's Go: Ecuador & The Galápagos Islands* hit the shelves this year, and research for next year's series has already begun.

We've seen a lot in 37 years. *Let's Go: Europe* is now the world's bestselling international guide, translated into seven languages. And our new guides bring Let's Go's total number of titles, with their spirit of adventure and their reputation for honesty, accuracy, and editorial integrity, to 30. But some things never change: our guides are still researched, written, and produced entirely by students who know first-hand how to see the world on the cheap.

HOW WE DO IT

Each guide is completely revised and thoroughly updated every year by a well-traveled set of 200 students. Every winter, we recruit over 120 researchers and 60 editors to write the books anew. After several months of training, Researcher-Writers hit the road for seven weeks of exploration, from Anchorage to Ankara, Estonia to El Salvador, Iceland to Indonesia. Hired for their rare combination of budget travel sense, writing ability, stamina, and courage, these adventurous travelers know that train strikes, stolen luggage, food poisoning, and marriage proposals are all part of a day's work. Back at our offices, editors work from spring to fall, massaging copy written on Himalayan bus rides into witty yet informative prose. A student staff of typesetters, cartographers, publicists, and managers keeps our lively team together. In September, the collected efforts of the summer are delivered to our printer, who turns them into books in record time, so that you have the most up-to-date information available for *your* vacation. And even as you read this, work on next year's editions is well underway.

WHY WE DO IT

At Let's Go, our goal is to give you a great vacation. We don't think of budget travel as the last recourse of the destitute; we believe that it's the only way to travel. Living cheaply and simply brings you closer to the people and places you've been saving up to visit. Our books will ease your anxieties and answer your questions about the basics—so you can get off the beaten track and explore. Once you learn the ropes, we encourage you to put Let's Go away now and then to strike out on your own. As any seasoned traveler will tell you, the best discoveries are often those you make yourself. When you find something worth sharing, drop us a line. We're Let's Go Publications, 67 Mt. Auburn St., Cambridge, MA 02138, USA (e-mail: fanmail@letsgo.com).

HAPPY TRAVELS!

Maps

Acknowledgements

Thanks to Sara, my little Rhody, without whose incredible commitment and unfailing patience this book would not exist. She cheered up, poked fun, prodded on, and generally kept me as sane as I'm going to get. Our five RWs were copy zealots, sending back pages of incredible finds and perfect prose. I couldn't have asked for more. Thanks to Amanda for maps and a smile on every page, to the DR for putting up with me, to Mike for his giggle and for our giant mechanized tail, to Amina for eleventh hour proofing and 4am talks, to JY for being bigger than anyone imagined, and to Tim and the rest of my block for taking care of me. My heartfelt appreciation goes to everyone who took the time to read and reread. Thanks to KcM and Andrew for their phone skills and a damned good time; to team UGH for helping to tame the beast. My final round goes to my family for pushing me on and holding me up. Thank you Dad for taking me to breakfast; Mom for cheering me up and letting me return the favor; Mags for taking me home with you; and my brother Keefer for being the only boy I know who calls when you want him to. I love you all.—**EMA**

To Liz: thanks for the t-shirts, the hysterical laughing jags in the wee small hours, and the extended analysis of the ones who weren't cute enough to get away with it. And for being an incredibly capable editor and having a work ethic more insane than my own. To our mascot Li Xiaoshuang, for bringing honor to *chez domestique;* to Amanda for the gentle prods; to Jen for being my "outside" friend; to Jesse for the trips to McDonald's and for sticking around; to Jane O'Donnell for the help I should have accepted; to Amber for leaving the light on for me; to Kate for the tea, the sympathy, and the kickin' 4th of July; to KcM for the education in techno; to the London Boys for perking up an otherwise lackluster August; to Dan H. for the no-utensils luncheon; to Andy for the rides home from the station; to Mom and Rich for always listening. To RI: you don't exist solely for the sake of comparison to other, bigger states (or even bigger national parks). Some people actually live there.—**SKS**

Editor	Elizabeth M. Angell
Associate Editor	Sara K. Smith
Managing Editor	Amanda K. Bean
Publishing Director	Michelle C. Sullivan
Production Manager	Daniel O. Williams
Associate Production Manager	Michael S. Campbell
Cartography Manager	Amanda K. Bean
Editorial Manager	John R. Brooks
Editorial Manager	Allison Crapo
Financial Manager	Stephen P. Janiak
Personnel Manager	Alexander H. Travelli
Publicity Manager	SoRelle B. Braun
Associate Publicity Manager	David Fagundes
Associate Publicity Manager	Elisabeth Mayer
Assistant Cartographer	Jonathan D. Kibera
Assistant Cartographer	Mark C. Staloff
Office Coordinator	Jennifer L. Schuberth
Director of Advertising and Sales	Amit Tiwari
Senior Sales Executives	Andrew T. Rourke
	Nicholas A. Valtz, Charles E. Varner
General Manager	Richard Olken
Assistant General Manager	Anne E. Chisholm

Researcher-Writers

Robyn Kali Bacon   *Southern British Columbia, Alberta*
Robyn claims to be from Berkeley, but we know this can't be so. Deep down, she hails from the land of Yoho and the maple leaf. Between the singular experience of watching the Olympics in a Calgary pub and rescuing her long-suffering truck, Robyn had her hands full. Her effortless and hilarious prose was always a joy in the home office, reminding us all that haiku and dedicated research make a winning combination. We owe her special thanks for her diligently phat proofreading. Though her future lies in publishing, we know she left her heart in Tofino.

Brian Ericson   *Southcentral Alaska, Northern British Columbia*
A Colorado native, Brian was no stranger to the slings and arrows of outrageous scenery. Weathering everything from the extremes of Dutch Harbor and Unalaska, to "dry" 3am ferries, to a rude awakening about the affable "hot dog" guy in Anchorage, Brian took on Alaska like the veteran researcher that he is. A master of the superlative, he never gave up his search for the best, the most mind-boggling, and the cheapest the Alaskan coast has to offer. He researched with heretofore unseen gusto and a truly democratic flair, not resting until the last stone was turned.

Mary S. Hatcher   *Oregon*
Despite a love-hate relationship with her $10-a-day vehicle and a rocky start in Portland, Maggie never failed to come through with copious prose and dozens of new ideas. A lover of culture high and not-so-high, she shared her infectious enthusiasm for the Shakespeare Festival and the Country Fair, the wineries and the dives. Her unflagging eye for detail was as impressive as her candor. Ever the trooper (she is, after all, a rugby player), she never let a little transmission trouble get in the way of a new restaurant and a better "lemony fresh" motel.

Raymond D. Heary   *Alaska, Northern British Columbia*
Ray leapt into the driver's seat and kept his foot to the pedal for 11,000 miles, two months, and some of the most bone-jarring, car-stalling roads on the continent. (Our apologies to Hertz.) He covered everything from Seattle to Prudhoe Bay and back again, bringing revolutionary zeal to his route. Even with an unfailing eye for detail, Ray never lost sight of the big picture. We wish him luck at Med school and in his crusade against the ravages of our material culture. (Special thanks to Howie, who played Queequeg to Ray's Ishmael.)

Lindsey M. Turrentine   *Washington*
She knew she had a big challenge. She was up for it. She called early and often. She went on marathon writing jags, taking her own seasoned and caffeinated editor's pen to every town intro she could lay her hands on. She attacked everything from the metropolitan giant of Seattle to the wilds of Olympic National Park with equal aplomb. Whether frolicking with nuns on Shaw Island or gorging herself on cherries in Yakima, Lindsey proved that this job *can* be fun. "Just one more greybox," quoth she, and pressed ever onward.

Theodore K. Gideonse   *Redwood National Forest, CA*
Deus ex machina, or was it just Ted? Two years running, he has dedicated himself unflinchingly to the pages of *Let's Go: Alaska and the Pacific Northwest*. Thanks.

How to Use This Book

As the Bible of the budget traveler, *Let's Go: Alaska and the Pacific Northwest* preaches a simple faith. Commandment 1: Things change, people change. Call ahead. Commandment 2: The best way to travel is tough and cheap. You can buy luxury, but you can't buy the joys of an out-of-the-way budget find. Press on and you will be rewarded. Commandment 3: Thou shalt plan ahead. Any good trip begins with a healthy dose of planning: never fear, we're here to help you. Commandment 4: This hallowed volume covers a tremendous portion of North America. We do not pretend to do it all. You will sometimes have to forge into unknown territory. Commandment 5: Buy a map. Use it a lot. Commandment 6: The faithful follower's best tool is, in the end, not her trusty yellow volume. It is her sense of adventure which will take her off the beaten path and into uncharted waters.

That said, we've tried to give you the straight smack. No need to interpret this pup; just follow these easy directions. **Essentials,** at the beginning of the book, provides information on trip planning, how to come and go from the grand old U.S. of A. (and Canada of course), and how to get around once you're there.

Our Alaskan journey begins in the urban sprawl of **Anchorage,** in **Southcentral Alaska,** and includes glaciers, fjords, oceanfront mountain ranges and tremendous marine life. In the second chapter, the **Interior,** you'll find Alaska's infamous highway system. These roads are not for the timid, but along them you can access **Denali,** the tallest peak in North America, and the city of **Fairbanks,** a major stopping point for those planning a trip in Alaska's rugged inland wilderness. Chapter three follows **Southeastern Alaska,** better known as the Panhandle, north from **Ketchikan** to **Skagway,** including **Juneau,** the Alaskan capital. Chapter four is the final chapter on Alaska and covers the massive Alaskan **Bush.** The path to budget nirvana is rocky and steep, and it probably won't include the expensive and inaccessible Bush. Chapters five through seven cover Western Canada. **Southern British Columbia** begins with the Province's most accessible destination, **Vancouver,** and proceeds north through **Vancouver Island.** If you have a taste for the open road and the company of Winnebagos, head for **Northwestern Canada,** the birthplace of the **Alaska Hwy.,** and the home of the **Yukon Territory.** Chapter seven delves deep into the badlands of **Alberta** and the Canadian Rockies, including **Banff** and **Jasper National Parks.** The last two chapters of our hallowed tome will lead you back to the States. The chapter on **Washington** begins with **Seattle,** and chapter eight finishes up with **Oregon,** starting with **Portland.**

For each specific area, the guide lists Practical Information and Orientation, Accommodations, Food, Sights, and Entertainment. Coverage of the outdoors follows Sights when appropriate. It may be useful to flip through a few sections to familiarize yourself with the book; understanding its structure will help you make the most of the wealth of information it contains.

A NOTE TO OUR READERS

The information for this book is gathered by *Let's Go*'s researchers during the late spring and summer months. Each listing is derived from the assigned researcher's opinion based upon his or her visit at a particular time. The opinions are expressed in a candid and forthright manner. Other travelers might disagree. Those traveling at a different time may have different experiences since prices, dates, hours, and conditions are always subject to change. You are urged to check beforehand to avoid inconvenience and surprises. Travel always involves a certain degree of risk, especially in low-cost areas. When traveling, especially on a budget, always take particular care to ensure your safety.

ESSENTIALS

PLANNING YOUR TRIP

▨ When to Go

Traveling is like comedy—timing is everything. In Alaska and the Pacific Northwest, your competing concerns will be the tourist season and the weather. In general, summer is high season; between June and August expect to share the warm weather with crowds of fellow tourists. If you prefer to experience the region as the natives do, go during the off-season when crowds are smaller and rates are lower. However, some of the sights and attractions you come to see may be closed durin the off-season and winter travel can be treacherous and unpleasant—snow, icy roads, and prohibitively cold weather (especially in northern Canada and Alaska) will limit both your movement and your desire to be outdoors.

Major holidays may also affect your travel plans. On some holidays, such as Independence Day in the U.S. and Canada Day in Canada, nearly every town has a celebration of some sort. On many major holidays, businesses and services are closed, and transportation, whether by road, rail, or air, can be crowded (see **Appendix** for **Holidays and Festivals**).

CLIMATE

In **Alaska,** the weather varies from the coast inland. In general, summer and early fall are the warmest and sunniest times of year. However, wet, windy, and cold days even during the summer should be no real surprise. In Alaska's interior, the temperature ranges from the 70s in summer to the -30s in winter. As you progress farther north, summer days and winter nights become longer. In Alaska and the Yukon, certain summer days will last from 6am to 2am.

In **Alberta,** the north and south of the province differ in temperature, although the entire area tends to be dry and cool. In January, the average temperature is around 15°F in the south, and closer to -20°F in the north; in the summer, both regions warm up to around 70°F.

In **British Columbia, Washington,** and **Oregon,** the key weather-making factor is the **mountains.** West of the mountains it rains quite a bit; to the east it is relatively dry. In general, temperatures west of the mountains are cooler in the summer and warmer in the winter than east of the mountains (see **Appendix** for temperatures).

▨ Useful Information

GOVERNMENT INFORMATION OFFICES

Each state and province has its own travel bureau (listed below) which can refer you to other useful organizations, send you brochures and maps, and answer your questions about the region. Contact the tourist bureau (often called the "Visitors Information Center") in any city you plan to visit for more than a few days. They can provide invaluable last-minute advice about special deals on accommodations, tours, or newly opened establishments. Some will even make reservations for you. Addresses for local tourist offices throughout Alaska and the Pacific Northwest can be found in the Practical Information section for each town or region.

Alaska Division of Tourism, P.O. Box 110801, Juneau, AK 99811-0801 (907-465-2010; fax 465-2287).

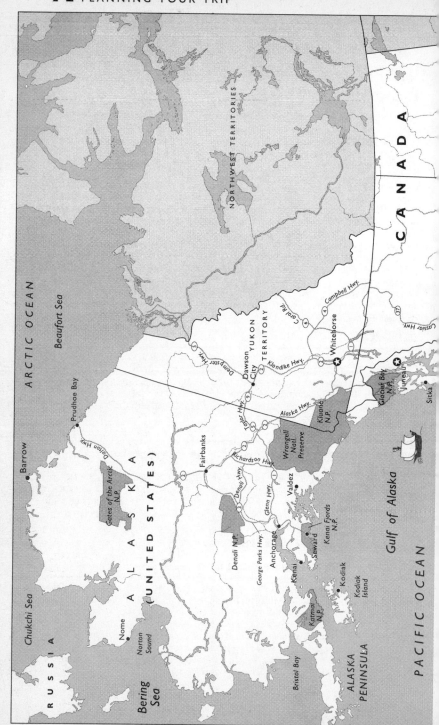

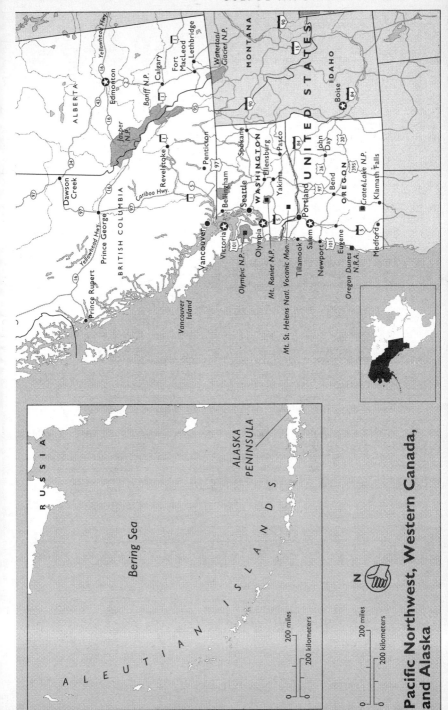

Pacific Northwest, Western Canada, and Alaska

Travel Alberta, Commerce Place, 10155-102 St. 3rd floor, Edmonton, AB T5J 4G8 (800-661-8888 or 403-427-4321; fax 427-0867).

Tourism British Columbia, 1117 Wharf St., Victoria, BC V8W 2Z2. (604-387-1642 for Ministry of Tourism and Small Business; http://www.tbc.gov.bc.ca/tourism/tourismhome.html) Call 800-663-6000 for travel information and accommodations reservations throughout British Columbia.

Oregon Tourism Commission, 775 Summer St. NE, Salem, OR 97310 (800-547-7842; fax 503-234-6762).

Washington State Tourism, Dept. of Community, Trade and Economic Development, P.O. Box 42500, Olympia, WA 98504-2500. Call 800-544-1800 for a general state tourism travel packet or 206-586-2088 to reach the State Department of Tourism with questions.

Yukon Department of Tourism, P.O. Box 2703, Whitehorse, YT Y1A 2C6 (403-667-5340; fax 667-3546).

General information for foreigners planning to travel to the U.S. is provided by the **United States Travel & Tourism Administration,** Department of Commerce, 14th St. and Constitution Ave. NW, Washington, DC, 20230 (202-482-4003 or 202-482-3811). The USTTA has branches in Australia, Canada, and the United Kingdom; contact the Washington office for details on the branch in your country.

TRAVEL ORGANIZATIONS

Council on International Educational Exchange (Council), 205 East 42nd St., New York, NY 10017-5706 (888-COUNCIL/268-6245; fax 212-822-2699; e-mail info@ciee.org; http://www.ciee.org). A private, nonprofit organization, Council administers work, volunteer, and academic programs around the world. They also offer identity cards, including the ISIC and the GO25, and a range of publications, including the magazine *Student Travels* (free). Call or write for more information.

Federation of International Youth Travel Organizations (FIYTO), Bredgade 25H, DK-1260 Copenhagen K, Denmark (tel. (45) 33 33 96 00; fax 33 93 96 76; e-mail mailbox@fiyto.org), is an international organization promoting educational, cultural and social travel for young people. Member organizations include language schools, educational travel companies, national tourist boards, accommodation centers and other suppliers of travel services to youth and students. FIYTO sponsors the GO25 Card.

International Student Travel Confederation, Herengracht 479, 1017 BS Amsterdam, The Netherlands (tel. (31) 20 421 2800; fax 20 421 2810; http://www.istc.org; e-mail istcinfo@istc.org) The ISTC is a nonprofit confederation of student travel organizations whose focus is to develop, promote, and facilitate travel among young people and students. Member organizations include International Student Rail Association (ISRA), Student Air Travel Association (SATA), ISIS Travel Insurance, and the International Association for Educational and Work Exchange Programs (IAEWEP).

TRAVEL PUBLICATIONS

On the road, knowledge is power. The mail-order travel shops listed below offer books with the scoop on specific travel issues. Some sell travel supplies as well.

Adventurous Traveler Bookstore, P.O. Box 1468, Williston, VT 05495 (801-860-6776; fax 860-6607, or both at 800-282-3963; e-mail books@atbook.com; http://www.gorp.com/atbook.htm). Free 40 page catalogue upon request. Specializes in outdoor adventure travel books and maps for the U.S. and abroad. Their World Wide Web site offers extensive browsing opportunities.

Bon Voyage!, 2069 W. Bullard Ave., Fresno, CA 93711-1200 (800-995-9716, from abroad 209-447-8441; e-mail 70754.3511@compuserve.com). Annual mail order catalog offers a range of products for everyone from the luxury traveler to the diehard trekker. Books, travel accessories, luggage, electrical converters, maps, videos, and more. All merchandise may be returned for exchange or refund within 30 days of purchase, and prices are guaranteed (Lower advertised prices will be matched and merchandise shipped free).

Rand McNally, 150 S. Wacker Dr., Chicago, IL 60606 (800-333-0136), publishes one of the most comprehensive road atlases of the U.S., Canada, and Mexico, available in their stores throughout the country, and most other bookstores for $9. Phone orders are also available.

Specialty Travel Index, 305 San Anselmo Avenue, Suite 313, San Anselmo, CA 94960 (415-459-4900; fax 459-4974; e-mail spectrav@ix.netcom.com; http://www.spectrav.com). Published twice yearly, this is an extensive listing of "off the beaten track" and specialty travel opportunities. One copy $6, one-year subscription (2 copies) $10.

Superintendent of Documents, U.S. Government Printing Office, P.O. Box 371954, Pittsburg, PA 15250-7954 (202-512-1800; fax 512-2250). Open Mon.-Fri. 7:30am-4:30pm. Publishes *Your Trip Abroad* ($1.25), *Health Information for International Travel* ($14), and "Background Notes" on all countries ($1). Postage is included in the prices.

Travel Books & Language Center, Inc., 4931 Cordell Ave., Bethesda, MD 20814 (800-220-2665; fax 301-951-8546; email travelbks@aol.com). Sells over 75,000 items, including books, cassettes, atlases, dictionaries, and a wide range of specialty travel maps, including wine and cheese maps of France, Michelin maps, and beer maps of the U.S. Free comprehensive catalog upon request.

U.S. Customs Service, P.O. Box 7407, Washington, DC., 20044 (202-927-5580). Publishes 35 books, booklets, leaflets, and flyers on various aspects of customs. *Know Before You Go* tells everything the international traveler needs to know about customs requirements; *Pockets Hints* summarizes the most important data from KBYG. *Hints for Visitors* tells everything a foreign traveler visiting the U.S. for a year or less needs to know about customs requirements; *Customs Tips for Visitors* summarizes the most important information from *Hints for Visitors* (available in more than a dozen languages).

Wide World Books and Maps, 1911 N. 45th St., Seattle, WA 98103 (206-634-3453; fax 634-0558; e-mail travelbk@mail.nwlink.com; http://nwlink.com/travelbk). A good selection of travel guides, travel accessories, and hard-to-find maps.

INTERNET RESOURCES

Along with everything else in the '90s, budget travel is moving rapidly into the information age. Most of this information can be yours with the click of a mouse. There are a number of ways to access the **Internet.** Most popular are commercial internet providers, such as **America Online** (800-827-6394) and **Compuserve** (800-433-0389). Many employers and schools also offer gateways to the Internet, often at no cost (unlike the corporate gateways above). The Internet itself can be used in many different forms, but the most useful to 'net-surfing budget travelers are the World Wide Web and Usenet newsgroups.

Dr. Memory's Favorite Travel Pages (http://www.access.digex.net/~drmemory/cyber_travel.html) is a great place to start surfing. Dr. Memory has links to hundreds of different web pages of interest to travelers of all kinds.

Rent-A-Wreck's Travel Links (http://www.rent-a-wreck.com/raw/travlist.htm) are, surprisingly, very good and very complete.

Big World Magazine (http://boss.cpcnet.com/personal/bigworld/bigworld.htm), a budget travel 'zine, has a web page, also with a great collection of links to travel pages.

Shoestring Travel (http://www.stratpub.com) is a budget travel e-zine, with feature articles, links, user exchange, and accommodations information.

The Student and Budget Travel Guide (http://asa.ugl.lib.umich.edu/chdocs/travel/travel-guide.html) is just what it sounds like.

In addition to the web sites above, we also list relevant web sites throughout different sections of the Essentials chapter. Remember that web sites come and go very rapidly; a good web site one week might disappear the next, and a new one might quickly take its place.

■ Documents and Formalities

When you travel, *always carry on your person two or more forms of identification, including at least one photo ID.* A passport combined with a driver's license or birth certificate usually serves as adequate proof of your identity and citizenship. Most establishments require several IDs before cashing traveler's checks. Never carry your passport, tickets, ID, money, traveler's checks, insurance, and credit cards all together; one instance of absentmindedness or thievery could leave you broke with no ID. If you plan an extended stay, you might want to register your passport with the nearest embassy or consulate.

PASSPORTS

Be sure *before you leave* to photocopy the page of your passport that contains your photograph and identifying information; this will help prove your citizenship and facilitate the issuing of a new passport if your old one is **lost** or **stolen**. Carry this photocopy in a safe place apart from your passport, and leave another copy at home. Consulates recommend you also carry an expired passport or an official copy of your birth certificate. If you do lose your passport, notify the local police and the nearest embassy or consulate of your home government *immediately*. If you have the information that was on your passport, identification, and proof of citizenship, some consulates can issue a new passport within two days; of course, it may take weeks. In an emergency, ask for immediate temporary traveling papers which will permit you to return to your home country.

U.S. and Canadian citizens may cross the U.S./Canada border with only proof of citizenship (e.g. a birth certificate or a voter's registration card along with a photo ID; a driver's license alone will not be enough). U.S. citizens under 18 need the written consent of a parent or guardian; Canadian citizens under 16 need notarized permission from both parents.

Australian citizens must apply for a passport in person at either a post office, a passport office, or an Australian diplomatic mission. An appointment may be necessary. A parent may file an application for a child who is under 18 and unmarried. Application fees are frequently adjusted. For more info, call toll-free (in Australia) 13 12 32.

British citizens can apply in person or by mail to a passport office for a full passport, which is valid for 10 years (five years if under 16). The fee is UK£18. Children under 16 may be included on a parent's passport. Processing by mail usually takes four to six weeks. The London office offers same-day, walk-in rush service; arrive early.

Irish citizens can apply for a passport by mail to either the **Department of Foreign Affairs,** Passport Office, Setanta Centre, Molesworth St., Dublin 2 (01 671 16 33), or the Passport Office, 1A South Mall, Cork (021 627 25 25). Obtain an application at a local Garda station or request one from a passport office. The new Passport Express Service offers a two week turn-around and is available for an extra IR£3. Passports cost IR£45 and are valid for 10 years. Citizens under 18 or over 65 can request a three-year passport that costs IR£10.

New Zealand citizens can obtain passport application forms from travel agents or the **Department of Internal Affairs Link Centre.** Completed applications may be lodged at Link Centres and at overseas posts, or forwarded to the Passport Office, PO Box 10-526, Wellington, New Zealand. Processing time is 10 working days from receipt of a correctly completed application. The application fee for an adult passport is NZ$80 in New Zealand, and NZ$130 overseas. An urgent passport service is also available.

South African citizens can apply for a passport at any **Home Affairs Office.** Two photos, either a birth certificate or an identity book, and a SAR80 fee must accompany a completed application. Passports are valid for 10 years.

EMBASSIES AND CONSULATES

To obtain information concerning visas, passports, and other specific information about traveling to Canada and the U.S. you should contact the U.S. or Canadian consulate in your home country. If the embassy is closer, you may want to go there; embassies usually have consular hours.

U.S. Embassies and Consulates

U.S. Embassy: Australia, Moonah Place, Canberra, ACT 2600 (011 61 6 270-5000); **Canada,** 100 Wellington St., Ottawa, Ontario, K1P 5T1 (613-238-5335); **Ireland,** 42 Elgin Rd., Ballsbridge, Dublin 4 (011 353 1 668 7122); **New Zealand,** 29 Fitzherbert Terr., Thorndon, Wellington (011 64 4 472 2068); **South Africa,** 225 Pretorius St., PO Box 9536, Pretoria (011 27 12 342 1048); **United Kingdom,** 24 Grosvenor Sq., London W1A 1AE (011 44 171 499 9000).

Consulate: Australia, MLC Centre, 19-29 Martin Place, 59th Fl., Sydney NSW 2000 (011 61 2 373 9200); Canada, 1155 Saint Alexandre St., Montreal, Quebec, PO Box 65 Station Desjardins, H5Z 1Z1 (514-398-9695); **New Zealand,** 4th Fl., Yorkshire General Bldg., corner of Shortland and O'Connell St., PO Box 42022 Auckland 1 (011 64 9 303 2724); **South Africa,** PO Box 6773, Roggebaai 8012 (011 27 21 25 4151); **United Kingdom,** Queen's House, 14 Queen St., BT1 6EQ, Belfast, N. Ireland (011 44 123 232 8239).

Canadian Embassies and Consulates

Embassy in Australia, Commonwealth Ave., Canberra ACT 2600 (011 61 6 273 3844); **Ireland,** Canada House 65 St. Stephen's Green, Dublin 2 (011 353 14 78 19 88); **New Zealand,** 61 Molesworth St., Thorndon, Wellington (011 64 4 473 9577); **South Africa,** 5th Floor, Nedbank Plaza, Corner of Church and Beatrix St., Arcadia, Pretoria 0083, (011 27 12 324 3970); **United Kingdom,** McDonald House, 38 Grosvenor Square, W1X 0AA (011 44 171 258 6600); **United States,** 501 Pennsylvania Ave., Washington D.C., 20001 (202-682-1740).

Consulate in Australia, Level 5 Quay West, 111 Harrington St., Sydney NSW, 2000 (011 612 364-3000); **New Zealand,** Princes Court, 2 Princes St., Auckland (011 54 9 309 3690).

U.S. AND CANADIAN ENTRANCE REQUIREMENTS

Travelers who are not citizens of either the U.S. or Canada will need a visa to cross the border. Mexican citizens may cross into the U.S. with an I-186 form. Foreign visitors to the United States are required to have a passport, visitor's visa, proof of intent to leave (an exiting plane ticket, for example), and proof of financial support. To work or study in the U.S. or Canada, you must obtain special documents (see **Alternatives to Tourism,** p. 17).

U.S. Visas

Travelers from certain nations may enter the U.S. without a visa through the **Visa Waiver Pilot Program.** Visitors qualify as long as they are traveling for business or pleasure, are staying for 90 days or less, have proof of intent to leave (e.g., a returning plane ticket), a completed I-94W, and enter aboard particular air or sea carriers. Participating countries are Andorra, Austria, Belgium, Brunei, Denmark, Finland, France, Germany, Iceland, Italy, Japan, Liechtenstein, Luxembourg, Monaco, the Netherlands, New Zealand, Norway, San Marino, Spain, Sweden, Switzerland, and the UK. Contact the nearest U.S. consulate for more information; countries are added frequently.

Most visitors obtain a **B-2,** or "pleasure tourist," visa, usually valid for six months. Don't lose your visa. If you do lose your I-94 form (arrival/departure certificate attached to your visa upon arrival), you can replace it at the nearest **U.S. Immigra-**

tion and **Naturalization Service** office, though it's very unlikely that the form will be replaced within the time of your stay. If you need information on visa extensions, call the local INS office, listed in your local telephone directory.

Canadian Visas

Citizens of Australia, Ireland, Mexico, New Zealand, the U.K., and the U.S., may enter Canada without visas, as long as they plan to stay for 90 days or less and carry proof of intent to leave. South Africans do need a visa to enter Canada. Citizens of all other countries should contact their Canadian consulate for more information.

CUSTOMS: ENTERING

Passing customs should be routine, but take it seriously; don't joke around with customs officials or airport security personnel. It is illegal to transport perishable food like fruit and nuts, which may carry pests. In addition, officials may seize articles made from protected species, such as certain reptiles and the big cats. See **Health** (p.14) for information on carrying prescription drugs.

U.S. Customs: You may bring the following into the U.S. duty free: $200 in gifts; 200 cigarettes (1 carton) or 100 cigars; and personal belongings such as clothes and jewelry. Travelers ages 21 and over may also bring up to one liter of alcohol, although state laws may further restrict the amount of alcohol you can carry. Cash or travelers checks can be transported, but amounts over $10,000 must be reported. Customs officers may ask how much money you're carrying and your planned departure date to ensure that you'll be able to support yourself in the U.S. The **U.S. Customs Service,** 1301 Constitution Ave., Washington, D.C. 20229 (202-927-5580), publishes a helpful brochure entitled, *Know Before You Go* (KBYG). It details everything the international traveler needs to know about customs requirements.

Canadian Customs: besides personal items, the following items may be brought in free of duty: up to 1.14L of alcohol or a 24-pack of beer (as long you are of age in the province you are visiting), 50 cigars, 200 cigarettes (1 carton), 1kg of manufactured tobacco, and gifts valued less than CDN$60. As in the U.S., if you exceed the limited amounts, you will be asked to pay a fine. Canadian officials will also inquire about your means of support while there. For detailed information on Canadian customs and booklets on other Canadian travel information, write Revenue Canada, Customs, Excise and Taxation, Communication Branch, Ottawa, Ont., Canada K1A 0L5 (613-954-7125; fax 957-9039).

CUSTOMS: RETURNING HOME

Upon returning home, you must declare all articles you acquired abroad and must pay a duty on the value of those articles that exceed the allowance established by your country's customs service. Goods and gifts purchased at duty-free shops abroad are not exempt from duty or sales tax at your point of return; you must declare these items, as well. Restrictions generally apply to items such as alcohol, tobacco and tobacco products, and perfume. Contact the authorities listed below for your own country's specifics.

Canada: Canadian Customs, 2265 St. Laurent Blvd., Ottawa, Ontario K1G 4K3 (613-993-0534).
Great Britain: Her Majesty's Customs and Excise, Custom House, Nettleton Road, Heathrow Airport, Hounslow, Middlesex TW6 2LA (011 01 81 910 3744; fax 910 3765).
Ireland: The Revenue Commissioners, Dublin Castle (011 01 679 27 77; fax 671 20 21; e-mail taxes@ior.ie; http:\\www.revenue.ie) or The Collector of Customs and Excise, The Custom House, Dublin 1.
Australia: Australian Customs Service, GPO Box 8, Sydney NSW 2001 (02 213 2000; fax 213 4000).

New Zealand: Consult the New Zealand Customs Guide for Travelers, available from customs offices, or contact New Zealand Customs, 50 Anzac Ave., Box 29, Auckland (011 09 377 35 20; fax 309 29 78).

South Africa: Commissioner for Customs and Excise, Private Bag X47, Pretoria 0001, distributes the pamphlet *South African Customs Information,* for visitors and residents who travel abroad. South Africans residing in the U.S. should contact the Embassy of South Africa, 3051 Massachusetts Ave., NW, Washington DC 20008 (202-232-4400; fax 202-244-9417).

YOUTH, STUDENT, AND TEACHER I.D.

Many U.S. establishments will honor an ordinary university student ID for student discounts. Still, two main forms of student and youth identification are extremely useful, especially for the insurance packages that accompany them.

International Student Identity Card (ISIC) The 1997 card is valid from Sept. 1996-Dec.1997 and costs $18. Flashing this card can procure you discounts for sights, theaters, museums, accommodations, train, ferry, and airplane travel, and other services. Present the card wherever you go, and ask about discounts even when none are advertised. Applicants must be at least 12 years old and degree-seeking students of a secondary or post-secondary school. Because of the proliferation of phony ISICs, many airlines and some other services require other proof of student identity: a signed letter from the registrar attesting to your student status and stamped with the school seal and/or your school ID card. The card provides accident insurance of up to $3000 with no daily limit, as well as $100 per day of in-hospital care for up to 60 days. In addition, cardholders have access to a toll-free **Traveler's Assistance hotline** (800-626-2427 in U.S. and Canada, elsewhere call collect 713-267-2525) whose multilingual staff can provide help in medical, legal, and financial emergencies overseas. When you apply for the card, ask for a copy of the *International Student Identity Card Handbook,* which lists some available discounts. Most budget travel agencies (see p. 23) issue the ISIC. The **International Teacher Identity Card (ITIC)** is $19 and offers similar but limited discounts, as well as medical insurance coverage. For more info on these handy cards consult the organization's new web site (http:\\www.istc.org).

International Youth Discount Travel Card or **GO25 Card;** issued by the **Federation of International Youth Travel Organizations (FIYTO),** Bredgade 25H, 1260, Copenhagen K, Denmark, (45 33 33 96 00; fax 45 33 93 96 76). A discount card for travelers under 26 but not students. This 1-year card offers many of the same benefits as the ISIC, and most organizations that sell the ISIC also sell the GO25 Card. A brochure that lists discounts is free when you purchase the card. US$10, CDN$15, UK£5 (without travel insurance), US$16 (with insurance); prices subject to change.

■ Money Matters

Staying in the cheapest accommodations possible and preparing your own food from time to time, you should expect to spend anywhere from $20 to $60 per person per day, depending on the local costs of living and your own needs. Transportation will increase these figures. Don't sacrifice your health or safety for a cheaper tab though—no trip is fun if you're always hungry, tired, or getting mugged.

CURRENCY AND EXCHANGE

You'll get better exchange rates for U.S. and Canadian dollars in their place of origin, and wholesale rates offered at banks will be lower than those offered by other exchange agencies. If the bank has a surcharge for every exchange, you'll lose money with every transaction, so convert in large sums. It's a good idea to buy enough U.S. dollars before you leave to last a couple of days; this prevents finding yourself stuck with no money upon an arrival after banking hours or on a holiday. If you are planning to visit a little-touristed area, where bank tellers may not recognize or be willing to exchange foreign currencies, carry U.S. dollars. Most international airports in the U.S. have currency exchange booths.

The Greenback (The U.S. Dollar)

CDN$1 = US$.73	US$1= CDN$1.37
UK£1 = US$1.54	US$1 = UK£0.65
IR£1 = US$1.58	US$1 = IR£0.63
AUS$1 = US$0.79	US$1 = AUS$1.26
NZ$1 = US$0.67	US$1 = NZ$1.48

The main unit of currency in the U.S. is the dollar; the dollar is divided into 100 cents. The color of paper money is green in the U.S; bills come in denominations of $1, $5, $10, $20, $50, and $100. The U.S. has 1¢ (penny), 5¢ (nickel), 10¢ (dime), and 25¢ (quarter) coins.

The Loony (The Canadian Dollar)

US$1 = CDN$1.37	CDN$1 = US$0.73
UK£1 = CDN$2.10	CDN$1 = UK£0.48
IR£1 = CDN$2.15	CDN$1 = IR£0.46
AUS$1 = CDN$1.08	CDN$1 = AUS$0.93
NZ$1 = CDN$0.92	CDN$1 = NZ$1.09

The main unit of currency in Canada is the **dollar,** which is identical to the U.S. dollar in name only. You will need to exchange money when you go over the border, although in many places you may be able to use American currency. Paper money comes in denominations of $2, $5, $10, $20, $50, and $100, which are all the same size but color-coded by denomination. Coins come in denominations of 1¢, 5¢, 10¢, 25¢, and $1. Many years ago, the Canadian government phased out the $1 bill and replaced it with a $1 coin, known as the **loony** for the loon which graces its reverse.

SALES TAX AND TIPPING

The U.S. **sales tax** is the equivalent of the European Value-Added Tax. Expect to pay 6-9% in Oregon and Washington; in these states, groceries are not taxed. Prices tend to be higher in Canada than in the U.S., as are taxes; you'll quickly notice the 7% **goods and services tax (GST)** and an additional **sales tax** in some provinces. Visitors can claim a rebate of the GST they pay on accommodations of less than one month and on most goods they buy and take home, so be sure to save your receipts and pick up a GST rebate form while in Canada. The total claim must be at least CDN$7 of GST (equal to $100 in purchases) and must be made within one year of the date on which you purchased the goods and/or accommodations for which you are claiming your rebate; further goods must be exported from Canada within 60 days of purchase. A brochure detailing restrictions is available from local tourist offices or through **Revenue Canada, Customs, Excise, and Taxation, Visitor's Rebate Program,** 275 Pope Rd., Summerside, Prince Edward Island, Canada C1N 6C6 (800-668-4748 in Canada, 613-991-3346 outside Canada).

In the U.S., it is customary to **tip** waitstaff 15% on sit-down meals and cab drivers 15% on the fare. Tip more for unusually good service, less for unusually bad. At the airport, try to carry your own bags; porters expect a customary $1 per bag tip. Tipping is less compulsory in Canada, and a good tip signifies remarkable service. **Bargaining** is generally frowned upon and fruitless in both the U.S. and Canada.

TRAVELER'S CHECKS

Traveler's checks are the safest way to carry large sums of money; small denominations ($10 or $20) are safest and most convenient. Traveler's checks are widely accepted and refundable if lost or stolen, and some even come with perks such as travel insurance. Several agencies and banks sell traveler's checks (e.g., American

Express or Bank of America), usually for a 1% commission. In less-touristed regions, have some cash on hand; smaller establishments may not accept traveler's checks.

You should expect a fair amount of red tape and delay in the event of theft or loss of traveler's checks. Ask for a list of refund centers when you buy your checks. To expedite the refund process, keep your check receipts separate from your checks and store them in a safe place; record check numbers when you cash them and leave a list of check numbers with someone at home. Keep a separate supply of cash or traveler's checks for emergencies. Be sure never to countersign your checks until you're prepared to cash them. The following companies sell traveler's checks denominated in U.S. and Canadian dollars:

American Express: 800-221-7282 in the U.S. and Canada; in the U.K. 011 0800 52 13 13; in New Zealand 011 0800 44 10 68; in Australia 011 008 25 19 02. Elsewhere, call U.S. collect 801-964-6665. American Express traveler's cheques are now available in 11 currencies including: Australian, British, Canadian, and U.S. They are the most widely recognized worldwide and the easiest to replace if lost or stolen. Checks can be purchased for a small fee at American Express Travel Service Offices, banks, and American Automobile Association (AAA) offices. Cardholders can also purchase checks at American Express Dispensers at Travel Service Offices at airports, by ordering them via phone (800-ORDER-TC/67337-82), and through America OnLine. American Express offices cash their checks commission-free, although they often offer slightly higher rates than banks. You can also buy **Cheques for Two** which can be signed by either of two people traveling together.
Citicorp: Call 800-645-6556 in the U.S. and Canada; in the U.K. 01144 181 297 4781; from elsewhere call U.S. collect 813-623-1709. Sells both Citicorp and Citicorp Visa traveler's checks in US, Australian, Canadian, and U.S. dollars, and British pounds. Commission is 1-2% on check purchases. Check holders are automatically enrolled for 45 days in the Travel Assist Program (hotline 800-250-4377 or collect 202-296-8728) which provides travellers with English-speaking doctor, lawyer, and interpreter referrals as well as check refund assistance and general travel information. Citicorp's World Courier Service guarantees hand-delivery of traveler's checks when a refund location is not convenient. Call 24hrs a day, seven days a week.
Thomas Cook MasterCard: Call 800-223-9920 in the U.S. and Canada; elsewhere call U.S. collect 609-987-7300; from the U.K. call 011 0800 622 101 free or 011 1733 502 995 collect or 011 44 1733 318 950 collect. Offers checks in U.S., Canadian, and Australian dollars, British pounds, and ECUs. Commission 1-2% for purchases. Try buying the checks at a Thomas Cook office; if you cash your checks there they will not charge you commission.
Visa: Call 800-227-6811 in the U.S.; in the U.K. 011 0800 895 492; from anywhere else in the world call 011 01733 318 949 and reverse the charges. If you give your zip code to the operator at any of the numbers, they will tell you where their closest office is. All Visa traveler's checks can be reported lost at these numbers.

CREDIT CARDS

Credit cards can be invaluable in the U.S. and Canada, and are sometimes expected or required (for example, many car rental agencies require that you have a credit card). Credit cards are also useful when an emergency, such as an unexpected hospital stay, leaves you temporarily without other resources. In addition, some cards carry services for users which may range from personal or car rental insurance to emergency assistance. Major credit cards can be used to instantly extract cash advances from associated banks and ATM machines; this can be a great bargain for foreign travelers because credit card companies get the wholesale exchange rate, which is generally 5% better than the retail rate used by banks.

MasterCard (outside North America, "EuroCard" or "Access") and **Visa** ("Carte Bleue" or "Barclaycard") are the most widely accepted. Both sell credit cards through banks. For lost or stolen cards call Visa (800-336-8472); Mastercard (800-999-0454). **American Express** cards carry a hefty annual fee ($55), unless you are a student, in which case you have the option of obtaining the free Optima card. Both of these

American Express cards offer extensive travel-related services. For a lost or stolen card, call 800-CASH-NOW/528-4800).

ATM CARDS

There are tens of thousands of ATMs (automatic teller machines) everywhere in the U.S. and Canada, offering 24-hour service in banks, airports, grocery stores, gas stations, etc. ATMs allow you to withdraw cash from your bank account wherever you are, and get the same favorable exchange rate as credit cards. Two major ATM networks in the U.S. are **Mastercard/Cirrus** (800-4-CIRRUS/424-7787) and **PLUS/Visa** (800-843-7587), slightly more common in Western Canada. Inquire at your bank about fees charged for ATM transactions. **American Express** also offers Express Cash, with over 100,000 ATMs located in airports, hotels, banks, office complexes, and shopping areas around the world. Express Cash withdrawals are automatically debited from the cardmember's specified bank account or line of credit. Green card holders may withdraw up to $1000 in a seven day period. There is a 2% transaction fee for each cash withdrawal with a $2.50 minimum. To enroll in Express Cash, Cardmembers may call 1-800-CASH NOW/2274-669. Outside the U.S. call collect (904) 565-7875.

EMERGENCY CASH

If you run out of money on the road, you can have more mailed to you in the form of traveler's checks bought in your name, a certified check, or through postal money orders, available at post offices (85¢ fee; $600 limit per order; cash only). Certified checks are redeemable at any bank, while postal money orders can be cashed at post offices upon display of two IDs (one of which must be a photo ID). Keep receipts, since money orders are refundable if lost. **Personal checks** from home will probably not be acceptable no matter how many forms of identification you have.

Wiring money can cost from around $15 (for domestic service) to $35 (international), depending on the bank, plus there will be a fee ($7-15) for receiving the money. Once you've found a bank that will accept a wire, write or telegram your home bank with your account number, the name and address of the bank to receive the wire, and a routing number. Also notify the bank of the form of ID that the second bank should accept before paying the money. As a very last resort, consulates will wire home for you and deduct the cost from the money you receive.

Western Union (800-CALL-CASH/225-5227) is a well-known and expensive service that can be used to cable money with your Visa or MasterCard within the domestic United States. You or someone else can phone in a credit card number or bring cash to a Western Union office for pick-up at another Western Union location. The rates for sending cash are generally $10 cheaper than with a credit card. Rates to send cash from a local office are $29 to send $250, $40 to send $500, and $50 to send $1000. You will need ID to pick up the money.

American Express is one of the easiest ways to get money from home. AmEx allows green card holders to draw cash from their checking accounts at any of its major offices and many of its representatives' offices, up to $1000 every 21 days (no service charge, no interest). Unless using the AmEx service, avoid cashing checks in foreign currencies; they usually take weeks and a $30 fee to clear.

■ Safety and Security

HELP LINES

United States Department of State (202-647-5225) issues travel advisories on the U.S. and/or Canada, including crime and security, on their 24-hr. hotline.

Travel Assistance International by Worldwide Assistance Services, Inc. (1133 15th St. NW, Ste. 400, Washington, D.C. 20005-2710; 800-821-2828 or 202-828-5894; fax 202-331-1530) provides its members with a 24-hr. hotline for emergen-

For emergencies in the U.S. and Canada, dial **911**. This number works in most places. If it does not, dial 0 for the operator and request to be connected with the appropriate emergency service (i.e., police, fire, ambulance, etc.).

cies and referrals. Their year-long frequent traveler package ($226) includes medical and travel insurance, financial assistance, and lost documents.

United States Center for Disease Control (404-332-4559, fax 332-4565; http://www.cdc.gov) is an excellent source of general information on health for travelers, and maintains a travelers hotline (see **Health**, p. 14).

American Automobile Association (AAA), 1050 Hingham St., Rocklin, MA 02370 (800-AAA-HELP/800-222-4357), offers members emergency road service in the U.S. and free towing (for more on membership benefits see **By Car** p. 30).

Traveler's Assistance Hotline (800-626-2427 in U.S. and Canada, elsewhere call collect 713-267-2525) is available to International Student Identity Card holders (see **Youth, Student, and Teacher I.d.,** p. 9).

STREET SMARTS

Trust your instincts—they are your most valuable assets. Try to look like you know what you are doing and where you are going, even if you don't. Do not keep money or anything precious in your back pocket or a fanny pack; use a neck pouch or money belt instead. Always keep an eye on your belongings; on trains and buses, put a leg through the straps of your bag if you can. Walking directly into a cafe or shop to check your map beats checking it on a street corner; better still, look over your map before leaving the hotel room so that you can act as if you know where you are going. Walking with nervous, over-the-shoulder glances can be a tip that you have something valuable to protect. Be aware of your surroundings; in cities, a single block can separate safe and unsafe areas. Do not respond or make eye contact with people who harass you. Carry a whistle to scare off attackers or attract attention. Finally, sleeping in a car or van parked in the city is *extremely* dangerous—even the most dedicated budget traveler should not consider it an option.

A good self-defense course will give you more concrete ways to react to different types of aggression. **Model Mugging**, a national organization with offices in several major cities, teaches a very effective, comprehensive course on self-defense. Contact Lynn S. Auerbach on the East Coast (617-232-7900); Alice Tibits in the Midwest (612-645-6189); and Cori Couture on the West Coast (415-592-7300). Course prices vary from $400-500. Women's and men's courses offered. Community colleges frequently offer self-defense courses at more affordable prices.

ALCOHOL AND DRUGS

If you carry **prescription drugs** while your travel, it is vital to have a copy of the prescriptions themselves readily accessible at the U.S. and Canadian borders. The importation of **illegal substances** into Canada or the U.S. is, not surprisingly, illegal, and a punishable offense. Away from borders, police attitudes towards drugs vary widely across the region. Drugs are illegal in every state. If you are arrested for drug possession in the U.S. or Canada you can be subject to a wide range of charges.

In Oregon, Washington, and Alaska, the **drinking age** is 21 years of age. British Columbia and the Yukon Territory prohibit drinking below the age of 19, while in Alberta you can drink at 18. In both the U.S. and Canada, the law is strictly enforced. Particularly in the U.S., be prepared to show a photo ID (preferably some government document—driver's license or passport) if you look under 30. Some areas of the country are still "dry" meaning they do not permit the sale of alcohol at all, while other places do not allow it to be sold on Sundays. Officials at both the United States and Canadian borders take **drunk driving** very seriously.

■ Health

BEFORE YOU GO

Prevention is the best way to stay healthy, but be prepared if something unexpected happens. A compact **first-aid kit** should suffice for minor problems on the road. The following items are advisable: bandages of several sizes, aspirin, antiseptic soap or antibiotic cream, a thermometer with a sturdy case, tweezers, moleskin, a decongestant, motion sickness remedy, medicine for diarrhea or stomach problems, sunscreen, insect repellent with DEET, burn ointment, and an elastic bandage.

In your **passport** or other document, write the names of any people you wish to be contacted in case of a medical emergency and list any allergies or medical conditions of which doctors should be aware. Bring any **medication** you regularly take and may need while traveling, as well as a copy of the **prescription** and a statement of any preexisting medical conditions you may have, especially if you will be bringing insulin, syringes, or any narcotics into the USA or Canada. If you wear **glasses** or **contact lenses,** carry an extra prescription and arrange to have your doctor or a family member send a replacement pair in an emergency. A good rule of thumb: if you can't live without something, bring a spare or make a backup plan. The following organizations may be of some help:

American Diabetes Association, 1660 Duke St., Alexandria, VA 22314 (800-232-3472). Call or write to receive a copy of *Travel and Diabetes*, and a diabetic ID card.

American Red Cross, 285 Columbus Ave., Boston, MA 02116-5114 (800-564-1234). Call to purchase the Red Cross's invaluable *First-Aid and Safety Handbook* ($15), The American Red Cross also offers many well-taught and inexpensive first-aid and CPR courses.

International Association for Medical Assistance to Travelers (IAMAT) offers a membership ID card, and a directory of doctors. Membership is free, though donations are appreciated and used for further research. In the **United States,** 417 Center St., Lewiston, NY 14092 (716-754-4883; fax 519-836-3412; e-mail iamat@sentex.net; http://www.sentex.net/iamat). In **Canada,** 40 Regal Road, Guelph, Ontario, N1K 1B5 (519-836-0102) or 1287 St. Clair Avenue West, Toronto, M6E 1B8 (416-652-0137; fax 519-836-3412).

Medic Alert Foundation, 2323 Colorado Ave., Turlock, CA, 95382 (24-hr. hotline 800-432-5378). For travelers with medical conditions that cannot be easily recognized (diabetes, epilepsy, heart conditions, allergies to antibiotics, etc.). Membership provides the internationally recognized Medic Alert Identification Tag and an annually updated wallet card. Lifetime membership is $35 the first year, and $15 annually thereafter.

COMMON AILMENTS

Many travelers experience fatigue, discomfort, or mild diarrhea upon arriving in a new area; allow time for your body to adjust before becoming worried. *Be especially aware of your health if you are camping and hiking.* Stay hydrated no matter where you are or what you're doing there. If you suffer from any of the following ailments in a severe or prolonged form, seek medical help as soon as possible.

Altitude: Allow your body a couple of days to adjust to the lower atmospheric oxygen levels before engaging in a strenuous activity like hiking. Expect some drowsiness. The effects of alcohol may be amplified.

Bee Stings: Can be potentially fatal if you are allergic. Always be prepared if you are. If you suffer from restricted breathing after a sting, seek medical attention.

Diarrhea: The most dangerous side effect of any diarrhea is dehydration. Traveler's diarrhea is common. Many people take over-the-counter remedies to counteract it (such as Pepto-Bismol or Immodium), but be aware that such remedies can complicate serious infections. If your diarrhea is severe, bloody, accompanied by fever or chills, or lasts more than a few days, seek medical help.

Frostbite: Skin affected by frostbite turns white, then waxy and cold. Victims should drink warm beverages, stay dry, and *gently and slowly* warm the frostbitten area with dry fabric or, better, with steady body contact. *Never rub or pour hot water on frostbite;* skin is easily damaged when frozen.

Giardia: Found in many rivers and lakes, *giardia lamblia* is a bacteria which causes gas, painful cramps, loss of appetite, and violent diarrhea. It can stay in your system permanently, and often does not cause any symptoms until weeks after it is ingested. To protect yourself, bring your water to a rolling boil for several minutes, or purify it with iodine tablets before drinking or cooking with it.

Heat exhaustion: Characterized by dizziness and nausea due to loss of water and salt, the best remedy is (surprise!) rest, water, and salty foods. Not a life threatening condition, but it may take a day to recover.

Heatstroke: In the early stages of heatstroke, sweating stops, body temperature rises, and an intense headache develops, which if untreated can be followed by mental confusion and, ultimately, death. Cool the victim off immediately with liquids, wet towels, and shade. Seek medical attention immediately, no matter where you are.

Hypothermia: Hypothermia results from exposure to cold and can occur even in the middle of summer, especially in rainy or windy conditions or at night. The signs are easy to detect: body temperature drops rapidly, resulting in the failure to produce body heat; you may shiver, lose coordination, feel exhausted, or have slurred speech, sleepiness, hallucinations, or amnesia. *Do not let victims of advanced hypothermia fall asleep*—their body temperatures will drop further, and if they lose consciousness they may die. To avoid hypothermia, keep dry and out of the wind. Dress in layers; wool keeps insulating even when wet; pile fleece jackets and Gore-Tex rain gear are also excellent choices. Never rely on cotton for warmth; this "death cloth" is actually harmful when wet.

Lyme Disease: Tick-borne diseases, such as Lyme disease, can be very serious. Lyme disease may be a problem for travelers in the Pacific Northwest, but is not known to exist in Alaska. Lyme, carried by dear ticks, is characterized by a circular rash of two inches or more which looks like a bull's eye. Other symptoms are flu-like: fever, headache, fatigue, or aches and pains. Untreated, Lyme disease is very dangerous. There is no vaccine, but Lyme can be treated with antibiotics if caught early. Removing a tick within 24hrs greatly reduces the risk of infection. While hiking, periodically stop and check for ticks; deer ticks are brownish and about the size of the head of a pin.

Poison Ivy, Poison Oak, Poison Sumac: These three-leafed plants secrete oils that can cause unbearable itchiness, hives, and sometimes inflammation of the infected areas. Some people have allergic reactions that cause serious asthma-like symptoms; find medical help if this occurs. If you think you have come into contact with one of these plants, wash your skin in soap and cold water (heat dilates the pores, driving the poison deeper). An excellent soap is **Fels Naptha,** available at any well stocked drug store. If rashes occur, calamine lotion, topical cortisones (like Cortaid©), or antihistamines may stop the itching. *Never scratch the affected area;* this will only spread the oil to other locations.

Rabies: If you are bitten by any animal, clean your wound thoroughly and seek medical help. Although the danger of rabies is greater in rural areas, the threat exists in the city as well.

Sunburn: Carry sunscreen with you and apply it liberally and often. Sunscreens of SPF (**S**un **P**rotection **F**actor) 20 are strong enough for the fairest skin; higher ratings won't help and are more expensive.

AIDS, HIV, and STDs: AIDS presents a particular threat, because it is fatal and not as well understood as other sexually transmitted diseases (STDs). Of the estimated 1 million people in the U.S. who are infected with HIV, the virus believed to be the cause of AIDS, 80% do not realize that they are infected. To lessen your chances of contracting any STD, use a latex condom every time you have sex. Condoms are widely available in the U.S. and Canada, but it doesn't hurt to stock up before you set out. Opt for water-based lubricants over oil-based formulas which render latex useless in preventing viral transfer. Council's brochure, *Travel Safe: AIDS and International Travel,* is available at all Council Travel offices (see **Travel Organizations,** above).

Let's Go should not be your only information source on common health problems while traveling, hiking, or camping. The **United States Centers for Disease Control and Prevention,** Travelers' Health, 1600 Clifton Rd. NE, Atlanta, GA 30333 (404-332-4559 for traveler's hotline; 404-639-3311 for public inquiries; 800-227-8922 for STD hotline; 800-342-2437 for AIDS/HIV hotline; 800-243-7889 for TTY; fax 332-4565; http://www.cdc.gov) is an excellent source of information for travelers around the world. The CDC publishes the booklet "Health Information for International Travelers" ($14), an annual global rundown of disease, immunization, and general health advice, including risks in particular countries.

■ Insurance

Beware of unnecessary coverage—your current policies might well extend to many travel-related accidents. **Medical insurance** (especially university policies) often cover costs incurred abroad. Canadians are protected by their home province's health insurance: check with the provincial Ministry of Health or Health Plan Headquarters. Your **homeowners' insurance** often covers theft during travel.

   ISIC and **ITIC** provide $3000 worth of accident and illness insurance and $100 per day for up to 60 days of hospitalization. They also offer up to $1000 for accidental death or dismemberment, up to $25,000 if injured due to an airline, and up to $25,000 for emergency evacuation due to an illness. The cards also give access to a toll-free **Traveler's Assistance hotline** (in the U.S. and Canada 800-626-2427; elsewhere call collect to the U.S. 713-267-2525) whose multilingual staff can provide help in emergencies. To supplement ISIC's insurance, **Council** (see **Travel Organizations,** above) offers the inexpensive Trip-Safe plan with options covering medical treatment and hospitalization, accidents, baggage loss, and charter flights missed due to illness; **Council Travel** and **STA** also offer more comprehensive and expensive policies. **American Express** (customer service 800-528-4800) cardholders receive automatic car rental (required to decline collision insurance) and travel accident insurance on flight purchases made with the card.

   Insurance companies usually require a copy of the police report for thefts, or evidence of having paid medical expenses (doctor's statements, receipts) before they will honor a claim and may have time limits on filing for reimbursement. Always carry policy numbers and proof of insurance. Check with each insurance carrier for restrictions and policies. Most of the carriers listed below have 24hr. hotlines.

   Access America, 6600 West Broad St., PO Box 11188, Richmond, VA 23230 (800-284-8300; fax (804) 673-1491). Covers trip cancellation/interruption, on-the-spot hospital admittance costs, emergency medical evacuation, sickness, and baggage loss. 24-hr. hotline.

   The Berkeley Group/Carefree Travel Insurance, 100 Garden City Plaza, P.O. Box 9366, Garden City, NY 11530-9366 (800-323-3149 or 516-294-0220; fax 516-294-1096). Offers two comprehensive packages including coverage for trip cancellation/interruption/delay, accident and sickness, medical, baggage loss, bag delay, accidental death and dismemberment, and travel supplier insolvency. Trip cancellation/interruption may be purchased separately at a rate of $5.50 per $100 of coverage. 24-hr. worldwide emergency assistance hotline.

   Globalcare Travel Insurance, 220 Broadway Lynnfield, MA 01940 (800-821-2488; fax 617-592-7720); e-mail global@nebc.mv.com; http://www.nebc.mv.com/globalcare). Complete medical, legal, emergency, and travel-related services. On-the-spot payments and special student programs, including benefits for trip cancellation and interruption GTI waives pre-existing medical conditions with their Globalcare Economy Plan for cruise and travel, and provides coverage for the bankruptcy or default of cruiselines, airlines, or tour operators.

Travel Guard International, 1145 Clark St., Stevens Point, WI 54481 (800-826-1300 or 715-345-0505; fax 345-0525). Comprehensive insurance programs starting at $44. Programs cover trip cancellation and interruption, bankruptcy and financial default, lost luggage, medical coverage abroad, emergency assistance, accidental death. 24hr. hotline.

▓ Alternatives to Tourism

Finding a job is often a matter of timing and luck. Job leads may come from local residents, hostels, employment offices, and chambers of commerce. Temporary agencies often hire for non-secretarial placement as well as for standard typing assignments. Marketable skills, i.e. touch-typing, dictation, computer knowledge, and experience with children will prove very helpful in your search for a temporary job. Consult newspapers and bulletin boards on college campuses for job listings.

STUDY OPPORTUNITIES

If you are interested in studying in the Pacific Northwest or Alaska. You can contact universities (listed below) directly for information about enrolling. But as a first step, soliciting information from a clearinghouse is sensible. An excellent source of information on studying in the U.S. and Canada is the **Institute of International Education (IIE)** (809 United Nations Plaza, New York, NY10017-3580; 212-984-5413 for recorded information; fax 212-984-5358), which administers many exchange programs. IIE publishes *Academic Year Abroad,* which details over 2300 semester and academic-year programs offered worldwide ($43, plus $4 shipping), and *Vacation Study Abroad,* with information on over 1800 short-term programs including summer and language schools ($37, plus $4 shipping).

Colieges and Universities

Lewis & Clark College, 0615 SW Palatine Hill Rd., Portland, OR 97219-7899 (503-768-7040 or 800-444-4111; fax 503-768-7055; e-mail admissions@lclark.edu; http://www@lclark.edu).

Oregon State University, 104 Kerr Administration, Corvallis, OR 97331-2106 (541-737-4411; fax 541-737-2482; http://www.orst.edu).

Simon Fraser University, Burnaby, BC V5A 1S6 (604-291-3224; fax 291-3929; http://www.sfu.ca); branch downtown at Harbor Center, 515 West Hastings, Vancouver, BC V6B 5K3 (604-291-5040).

University of Alaska Anchorage, 3211 Providence Dr., Anchorage, AK 99508 (907-786-1480; fax 786-4888; http://www.uaa.alaska.edu).

University of Alaska Fairbanks, P.O. Box 757480, Fairbanks, AK 99775-7480 (907-474-7500; fax 474-5379; e-mail fyapply@aurora.alaska.edu).

University of Alberta, 120 Administration Bldg., Edmonton, AB T6G 2M7 (403-492-3113; fax 492-7172; e-mail registrar@ualberta.ca; http://www.registrar.ualberta.ca).

University of British Columbia, Office of the Registrar 2016-1874 East Mall, Vancouver, BC V6T 1Z1 (604-822-3159; fax 604-822-5945).

University of Calgary, 2500 University Dr. NW, Calgary, AB T2N 1N4 (403-220-6645; fax 289-1253; http://www.ucalgary.ca).

University of Oregon, Office of Admissions, 1217 University of Oregon, Eugene, OR, 97403-1217 (541-346-3201; fax 346-5815; e-mail uoadmit@oregon.uoregon.edu; http://www.uoregon.edu/home.html).

University of Victoria, P.O. Box 3025, Victoria, BC V8W 3P2 (604-721-8111).

University of Washington, Office of Admission, 1410 N.E. Campus Parkway, Room 320, Box 355840, Seattle, WA 98195-5840 (206-543-9686; fax 685-3655; http://www.washington.edu)

Washington State University, 370 Lighty Student Services Bldg., Pullman, WA 99163-1067 (509-335-5586; fax 335-4902; e-mail admiss@wsu.edu; http://www.wsu.edu).

U.S. Student Visas

Foreign students who wish to study in the United States must apply for either a J-1 visa (for exchange students) or an F-1 visa (for full-time students enrolled in an academic or language program). For information on how to obtain and submit the proper forms, and how to acquire an on-campus job, contact the international student office at the institution you will be attending.

Canadian Student Visas

To study in Canada you will need a **Student Authorization** in addition to any entry visa you may need. To obtain one, contact the nearest Canadian consulate or embassy. Be sure to apply at least four months ahead of time; it can take a long time to go through, and there is a processing fee. You will also need to prove to the Canadian government that you are able to support yourself financially. A student authorization is good for one year. If you plan to stay longer, it is extremely important that you do not let it expire before you apply for renewal. Canadian immigration laws do permit full-time students to seek on-campus employment. For specifics, contact a Canadian Immigration Center (CIC) or consulate.

WORKING IN THE U.S.

Volunteer (unpaid) jobs are readily available throughout the Pacific Northwest and Alaska. Some jobs provide room and board in exchange for labor. You nearest U.S. embassy or consulate will help you get specific information on the jungle of paperwork surrounding **work visas.** Write to **Council see Budget Travel Agencies,** p. 23. Council also runs a summer travel/work program which provides students with the opportunity to spend their summers working in the U.S.; university students from the following countries are eligible: **Australia,** NUS Services, 220 Faraday St., 1st floor, Carlton, Melbourne, Victoria 3053 (61 3 348 1777); **Canada,** Travel CUTS, 187 College St., Toronto, Ontario M5T 1P7 (416-979-2406); **Costa Rica:** OTEC, Calle 3, Avenida ly 3, Edificio Ferencz, 275m norte del Teatro Nacional, San Jose (506 222-866); **France,** Council Travel, 22, rue des Pyramides, 75001 Paris (33 1 44 55 55 44); **Germany,** Council Travel, Graf Adolph Strasse 64, 40210 Dusseldort (49 211 32 9088); **Ireland,** Usit, Aston Quay 19, O'Connell Bridge, Dublin 2 (353 1 6798833); **New Zealand,** STA Travel Ltd, 10 High St., P.O. Box 4156, Auckland (64 9 309 0458); **Spain,** TIVE, Jose Ortega y Gasset, 71, 3rd floor, 28006 Madrid (34 1 347 7778); **United Kingdom,** BUNAC Travel, 16 Bowling Green Lane, London EC1R OBD (44 171 251 2472).

Foreign university-level students can get on-the-job technical training in fields such as engineering, computer science, agriculture, and natural and physical sciences from the **International Association for the Exchange of Students for Technical Experience** (10400 Little Patuxent Pkwy. #250, Columbia, MD 21044-3510; 410-997-3068 or 3069; http://www.softaid.net/aipr/html). The **IAESTE** operates 8- to 12-week programs for college students having completed two years of study in a technical field. non-refundable $50 application fee; apply by Dec. 10 for summer placement.

U.S. Work Visas

You **must** apply for a work visa. Working or studying in the U.S. with only a B-2 (tourist) visa is grounds for deportation (see **U.S. and Canadian Entrance Requirements,** p. 7). The first step toward acquiring a work visa begins at the U.S. consulate or embassy nearest you (see **Embassies and Consulates,** p. 7).

WORKING IN CANADA

Most of the organizations and the information discussed above are also useful for Canada. Contact individual organizations and write for the publications which interest you most. **Travel CUTS** can also help you see **Budget Travel Agencies,** p. 23

Canadian Work Visas

If you intend to work in Canada, you will need an **Employment Authorization,** obtained before you enter the country; visitors are not ordinarily allowed to change status once they have arrived. A processing fee applies. Your potential employer must contact the nearest **Canadian Employment Centre (CEC)** for approval of the employment offer. For more information, contact the consulate or embassy in your home country. Residents of the U.S., Greenland, and St. Pierre/Miquelon may apply for Employment Authorization at a port of entry.

CANNERIES

Seafood harvesting and processing jobs are no bed of roses. While it is possible to earn a lot of cash in a little time, you must be willing to put in long, hard hours at menial and unrewarding tasks. As the Alaska Employment Service eloquently states, "Most seafood processing jobs are smelly, bloody, slimy, cold, wet, and tiring because of manual work and standing for many hours. The aroma of fish lingers with workers throughout the season. Most get used to it. Those who can't generally leave…" If you're still interested, the following **Alaska Employment Service** (part of the Department of Labor) offices are a good source of information: Kodiak 486-3105, Anchorage 269-4800, Petersburg 772-3791, Sitka 747-3347, Ketchikan 225-5500, Homer 235-7791, Kenai 283-4304, Dillingham 842-5579, Seward 224-5276, Valdez 835-4910. Area code 907.

■ Packing

Pack lightly…that means you. Even if you have a car. The more you bring, the more you have to worry about. A good general rule is to pack only what you absolutely need, then take half the clothes and more money.

THE BACKPACK

If you plan to cover most of your itinerary by foot, a sturdy backpack is invaluable. Many packs are designed specifically for travelers, while others are for hikers; consider how you will use the pack before purchasing one or the other. Some convert into normal-looking suitcases. In any case, get a pack with a strong, padded hip-belt to transfer weight from your shoulders to your hips; it is a common error to carry the weight of these packs on your shoulders. When carried correctly, a pack's weight should rest entirely on your hips. Avoid excessively low-end prices—you get what you pay for. Quality packs cost anywhere from $150 to $420.

DRESS FOR SUCCESS

The clothing you bring will, of course, depend on when and where in the U.S. you're planning to travel. In general, **dressing in layers** is best when traveling; if you're hot, peel off a shirt, and if you're cold, add a warmth layer (see **Camping and the Outdoors,** p. 43).

Summer: Stick to natural fibers and lightweight materials. Start with a few t-shirts; they take up virtually no space and you can wear a sweatshirt or sweater over them on a chilly night. Pack a couple of pairs of shorts and jeans, as well as underwear, socks, a towel, and swimwear.

Winter: Bring heavier layers, including at least one that insulates while wet, such as polypropylene, polarfleece, or wool.

Rain: Rain ponchos tear easily and are cumbersome to wear, but light and compact to carry. Rain gear can be had cheaply, but the best by far is a rain jacket made with Gortex. Premium protection is worth the higher price.

Footwear: For extensive walking, get good **athletic shoes** or **lace-up leather shoes.** Your whole foot should be covered. Leather-reinforced nylon **hiking boots** are good for general walking and essential for hiking: they're lightweight, rugged and dry quickly. A pair of light **flip-flops** provides protection against fungal floors. *Break in your shoes before you leave home.* Two pairs of socks—light absorbent cotton inside and thick wool outside—will cushion feet, keep them dry, and help prevent blisters.

Random Useful Stuff: umbrella, ressealable plastic bags (for damp clothes, soap, food), plastic trash bags (for rain protection), alarm clock, strike-anywhere matches, sun hat, sunglasses, needle and thread, safety pins, whistle, pocketknife, notebook and pens, water bottle, tweezers, flashlight, string, clothespins, padlock, earplugs, compass, deodorant, razors, condoms, tampons, maps, and a lead-lined pouch (for protecting film from airport x-rays).

Sleepsacks: If planning to stay in **youth hostels,** make the requisite sleepsack (instead of paying the hostel's linen charge). Fold a full size sheet in half the long way, then sew it closed along the open long side and one of the short sides.

■ Specific Concerns

WOMEN TRAVELERS

Women exploring any area on their own inevitably face additional **safety concerns.** You may want to consider staying in hostels which offer single rooms which lock from the inside or religious organizations which offer rooms for women only. Stick to centrally located accommodations and avoid late-night treks or metro rides. Remember that hitching is *never* safe for lone women, nor even for two women traveling together. Choose train compartments occupied by other women or couples. If you spend time in cities, you may be harassed no matter how you're dressed. Look as if you know where you're going (even when you don't) and ask women or couples for directions if you're lost or if you feel uncomfortable. Your best answer to verbal harassment is no answer at all. Don't hesitate to seek out a police officer or a passerby if someone gives you a hard time. In emergencies, a toll-free call to 911 from any pay phone should result in immediate assistance; always carry enough extra money for a bus or taxi. Carry a whistle or an airhorn on your keychain, and *use it* in an emergency, or any time you feel unsafe; calling strident attention to yourself may be embarrassing, but potential attackers want nothing less than a noisy, conspicuous situation. A **Model Mugging** or other self-defense courses (see p. 13) will not only prepare you for a potential mugging, but will also raise your level of awareness of your surroundings as well as your confidence. For more information and resources, consult the following organizations:

Handbook For Women Travelers by Maggie and Gemma Moss (UK£9). Encyclopedic and well-written. From Piaktus Books, 5 Windmill St., London W1P 1HF (tel. (0171) 631 07 10).

A Journey of One's Own, by Thalia Zepatos, (Eighth Mountain Press $17), The latest thing on the market, interesting and full of good advice, plus a specific and manageable bibliography of books and resources.

Women Going Places, a women's travel and resource guide emphasizing women-owned enterprises. Geared towards lesbians, but offers advice appropriate for all women. $14 from Inland Book Company, 1436 W. Randolph St. Chicago, IL 60607 (800-243-0138) or order from a local bookstore.

OLDER TRAVELERS

Senior citizens are eligible for a wide range of discounts on transportation, museums, movies, theaters, concerts, restaurants, and accommodations. If you don't see a senior citizen price listed, ask and you may be surprised (for information on the Golden Age Passport, see **Camping and the Outdoors: National Parks** p.44).

AARP (American Association of Retired Persons), 601 E St., NW, Washington, DC 20049 (202-434-2277). Members 50 and over receive benefits and services including the AARP Motoring Plan from AMOCO (800-334-3300), and discounts on lodging, car rental, and sight-seeing. Annual fee $8 per couple; lifetime membership $75.

Elderhostel, 75 Federal St., 3rd Fl., Boston, MA 02110-1941 (617-426-7788, fax 426-8351; http://www.elderhostel.org). For those 55 or over (spouse of any age). Programs at colleges, universities, and other learning centers in over 50 countries on varied subjects lasting one to four weeks.

National Council of Senior Citizens, 1331 F St. NW, Washington, DC 20004 (202-347-8800). Memberships are $12 a year, $30 for three years, or $150 for a lifetime. Individual or couple can receive hotel and auto rental discounts, a senior citizen newspaper, use of a discount travel agency, supplemental Medicare insurance (if you're over 65), and a mail-order prescription drug service.

Unbelievably Good Deals and Great Adventures That You Absolutely Can't Get Unless You're Over 50, by Joan Rattner Heilman. After you finish reading the title page, check inside for some great tips on senior discounts and the like. Contemporary Books, $10.

BISEXUAL, GAY, AND LESBIAN TRAVELERS

Generally, in the larger cities of the Pacific Northwest, you need not compromise your freedom to enjoy your trip. Be warned, however, that some communities may not be so receptive to openly gay and lesbian travelers. The most open atmospheres can be found in large cities and tourist and college towns. Wherever possible, *Let's Go* lists local gay and lesbian information lines and community centers. The **International Gay Travel Association,** Box 4974, Key West, FL 33041 (800-448-8550; fax 305-296-6633; e-mail IGTA@aol.com; http://www.rainbow-mall.com/igta), is an organization of over 1100 companies serving gay and lesbian travelers worldwide.

Damron Travel Guides, PO Box 422458, San Francisco, CA 94142 (415- 255-0404 or 800-462-6654). Publishers of the *Damron Address Book* ($15), which lists bars, restaurants, guest houses, and services in the United States, Canada, and Mexico which cater to gay men. The *Damron Road Atlas* ($15) contains color maps of 56 major U.S. and Canadian cities and gay and lesbian resorts and listings of bars and accommodations. *The Women's Traveller* ($12) includes maps of 50 major U.S. cities and lists bars, restaurants, accommodations, bookstores, and services catering to lesbians. *Damron's Accommodations* lists gay and lesbian hotels ($19). Mail order available; add $5 shipping.

Ferrari Guides, PO Box 37887, Phoenix, AZ 85069 (602-863-2408; fax 439-3952; e-mail ferrari@q-net.com). Gay and lesbian travel guides: *Ferrari Guides' Gay Travel A to Z* ($16), *Ferrari Guides' Men's Travel in Your Pocket* ($14), *Ferrari Guides' Women's Travel in Your Pocket* ($14), *Ferrari Guides' Inn Places* ($16). Available in bookstores or by mail order (postage/handling $4.50 for the first item, $1 for each additional item mailed within the US. Overseas, call or write for shipping cost.)

Gayellow Pages, PO Box 533, Village Station, New York, NY 10014. (212-674-0120; fax 420-1126). An annually updated listing of accommodations, resorts, hotlines, and other items of interest to the gay traveler. USA/Canada edition $16.

Women Going Places (Inland Book Company, $14) An international women's travel and resource guide emphasizing women-owned enterprises, geared toward lesbians. Available in bookstores.

TRAVELERS WITH DISABILITIES

Hotels and motels in Alaska and the Pacific Northwest have become increasingly accessible to disabled persons, and many national parks are trying to make exploring the outdoors more feasible (see **National Parks,** p. 44). Call ahead to restaurants, hotels, parks, and other facilities to find out about accessibility.

Hertz, Avis, and National **car rental agencies** have hand-controlled vehicles at some locations (see **By Car: Renting,** p. 32). Amtrak **trains** and all **airlines** can better serve disabled passengers if notified at least 72 hours in advance. Greyhound buses will also provide free travel for a companion; if you are without a fellow traveler, call

Greyhound (800-752-4841) at least 48 hours but no more than one week before you plan to leave and they will make arrangements to assist you. For transportation information in individual U.S. cities, contact the local chapter of the Easter Seals Society.

American Foundation for the Blind, 11 Penn Plaza, New York, NY 10011 (212-502-7600), open Mon.-Fri. 8:30am-4:30pm. Provides information and services for the visually impaired. For a catalogue of products, contact Lighthouse Y, 10011 (800-829-0500).

Facts on File, 11 Penn Plaza, 15th Floor, New York, NY 10001 (212-967-8800). Publishers of *Disability Resource*, a reference guide for travelers with disabilities ($45 plus shipping). Available in retail bookstores or by mail order.

Mobility International, USA (MIUSA), P.O. Box 10767, Eugene, OR 97440 (514-343-1284 voice and TDD; fax 343-6812). International Headquarters in Brussels, rue de Manchester 25, Brussels, Belgium, B-1070 (332 410 6297, fax 410 6874). Contacts in 30 countries. Information on travel programs, international work camps, accommodations, access guides, and organized tours for those with physical disabilities. Membership $25 per year, newsletter $15. Sells the periodically updated and expanded *A World of Options: A Guide to International Educational Exchange, Community Service, and Travel for Persons with Disabilities* ($14, nonmembers $16). In addition, MIUSA offers a series of courses that teach strategies helpful for travelers with disabilities. Call for details.

Society for the Advancement of Travel for the Handicapped (SATH), 347 Fifth Ave., #610, New York, NY 10016 (212-447-7284; fax 725-8253). Publishes quarterly travel newsletter *SATH News* and information booklets (free for members, $13 each for nonmembers) with advice on trip planning for people with disabilities. Annual membership $45, students and seniors $25.

Twin Peaks Press, PO Box 129, Vancouver, WA 98666-0129 (360-694-2462, orders only MC and Visa 800-637-2256; fax 360-696-3210). Publishers of *Travel for the Disabled,* which provides travel tips, lists of accessible tourist attractions, and advice on other resources for disabled travelers ($20). Also publishes *Directory for Travel Agencies of the Disabled* ($20), *Wheelchair Vagabond* ($15), and *Directory of Accessible Van Rentals* ($10). Postage $3 for first book, $1.50 for each additional book.

Organizations that arrange tours or trips for disabled travelers:

Directions Unlimited, 720 N. Bedford Rd., Bedford Hills, NY 10507 (800-533-5343; in NY 914-241-1700; fax 241-0243). Specializes in arranging individual and group vacations, tours, and cruises for the physically disabled.

Flying Wheels Travel Service, 143 W. Bridge St., Owatonna, MN 55060 (800-535-6790; fax 451-1685). Arranges trips in the USA and abroad for groups and individuals in wheelchairs or with other sorts of limited mobility.

The Guided Tour Inc., Elkins Park House, Suite 114B, 7900 Old York Road, Elkins Park, PA 19027-2339 (800-783-5841 or 215-782-1370; fax 635-2637). Organizes travel programs for persons with developmental and physical challenges and those requiring renal dialysis. Call, fax, or write for a free brochure.

KOSHER AND VEGETARIAN TRAVELERS

Travelers who keep kosher should contact synagogues in larger cities for information on kosher restaurants; your own synagogue or college Hillel should have access to lists of Jewish institutions across the nation. **The Jewish Travel Guide** ($12, postage $1.75) lists synagogues, kosher restaurants, and Jewish institutions in over 80 countries. It is available in the U.S. from Sepher-Hermon Press, 1265 46th St., Brooklyn, NY 11219 (718-972-9010; $13.95 plus $2.50 shipping).

Vegetarian food is gaining acceptance in even the staunchest ranching communities in Alaska and the Pacific Northwest. *Let's Go* often notes restaurants with good vegetarian selections in city listings. The **North American Vegetarian Society,** P.O. Box 72, Dolgeville, NY 13329 (518-568-7970) sells several titles related to travel in the U.S. and Canada.

GETTING THERE AND GETTING AROUND

■ Budget Travel Agencies

Council Travel (http://www.ciee.org/cts/ctshome.htm), the travel division of Council, is a full-service travel agency specializing in youth and budget travel. They offer railpasses, discount airfares, hosteling cards, guidebooks, budget tours, travel gear, and student (ISIC), youth (GO25), and teacher (ITIC) identity cards. U.S. offices include: Emory Village, 1561 N. Decatur Rd., **Atlanta**, GA 30307 (404-377-9997); 2000 Guadalupe, **Austin**, TX 78705 (512-472-4931); 273 Newbury St., **Boston**, MA 02116 (617-266-1926); 1138 13th St., **Boulder**, CO 80302 (303-447-8101); 1153 N. Dearborn, **Chicago**, IL 60610 (312-951-0585); 10904 Lindbrook Dr., **Los Angeles**, CA 90024 (310-208-3551); 1501 University Ave. SE, **Minneapolis**, MN 55414 (612-379-2323); 205 E. 42nd St., **New York**, NY 10017 (212-822-2700); 953 Garnet Ave., **San Diego**, CA 92109 (619-270-6401); 530 Bush St., **San Francisco**, CA 94108 (415-421-3473); 4311½ University Way, **Seattle**, WA 98105 (206-632-2448); 3300 M St. NW, **Washington, D.C.** 20007 (202- 337-6464). **For U.S. cities not listed**, call 800-2-COUNCIL (226-8624). Also 28A Poland St. (Oxford Circus), **London**, W1V 3DB ((0171) 437 7767).

STA Travel, 6560 North Scottsdale Rd. #F100, Scottsdale, AZ 85253 (800-777-0112). Student and youth travel organization with over 100 offices worldwide, including 16 U.S. locations. Offers discount airfare for young travelers, railpasses, accommodations, tours, insurance, and ISIC. Offices include: 429 S. Dearborn St., **Chicago,** IL 60605 (312-786-9050); 4341 University Way NE, **Seattle,** WA 98105 (206-633-5000); 10 Downing St., Suite G, **New York,** NY 10003 (212-627-3111); 297 Newbury St., **Boston,** MA 02115 (617-266-6014); 3730 Walnut St. **Philadelphia,** PA 19104 (215-382-2928); 2401 Pennsylvania Ave., **Washington, DC** 20037 (202-887-0912); 7202 Melrose Ave., **Los Angeles,** CA 90046 (213-934-8722); 51 Grant Ave., **San Francisco,** CA 94108 (415-391-8407); **UK:** Priory House, 6 Wrights Ln., London W8 6TA, (tel. (0171) 938 4711). **New Zealand:** 10 High St., Auckland, (tel. (09) 309 9723). **Australia:** 222 Faraday St., Melbourne VIC 3050, (tel. (03) 349 6911).

Let's Go Travel, Harvard Student Agencies, 67 Mt. Auburn St., **Cambridge,** MA 02138 (617-495-9649 or 800-5-LETS GO/553-8746). Offers railpasses, HI-AYH memberships, ISIC, ITIC, FIYTO cards, guidebooks (including all of the *Let's Go* books and Map Guides), maps, bargain flights, and a complete line of budget travel gear. All items available by mail; call or write for a catalog.

Campus Travel, 52 Grosvenor Gardens, **London** SW1W OAG (http://www.campustravel.co.uk). 41 branches in the U.K. Student and youth fares on plane, train, boat, and bus travel. Flexible airline tickets. Discount and ID cards for youths, travel insurance for students and those under 35, and maps and guides. Puts out travel suggestion booklets. Telephone booking service: in Europe call (0171) 730 3402; in North America call (0171) 730 2101; worldwide call (0171) 730 8111; in Manchester call (0161) 273 1721; in Scotland call (0131) 668 3303.

Travel CUTS (Canadian University Travel Services, Ltd.), 187 College St., Toronto, Ont. M5T 1P7 (416-979-2406; fax 979-8167; e-mail mail@travelcuts). Canada's national student travel bureau; its version of Council, with 40 offices across Canada. In the **U.K.,** 295-A Regent St., London W1R 7YA, (tel. (0171) 637 3161). Discounted domestic and international flights; ISIC, FIYTO, GO25, HI hostel cards; and railpasses. Special fares with valid ISIC or FIYTO cards. Free *Student Traveller* magazine, and info on Student Work Abroad Program (SWAP).

USIT Youth and Student Travel, 19-21 Aston Quay, O'Connell Bridge, Dublin 2 (tel. (01) 602 1200; fax 671 2408). In the USA: New York Student Center, 895 Amsterdam Ave., New York, NY, 10025 (212-663-5435). Specializes in youth and student travel. Offers low-cost tickets and flexible travel arrangements all over the world. Sells ISIC, FIYTO-GO25 cards.

■ By Air

When dealing with any commercial airline, buying in advance is best. Periodic **price wars** may lower prices in spring and early summer months, but they are unpredictable; don't delay your purchase in hope of catching one. To obtain the cheapest fare, buy a round-trip ticket, stay over at least one Saturday, and travel during off-peak times (Mon.-Thurs. morning) and off-peak hours (overnight **"red-eye"** flights can be cheaper and faster than primetime flights). Chances of receiving discount fares increase on competitive routes. Fees for changing flight dates range from $25 (for some domestic flights) to $150 (for many international flights). Most airlines allow children under two to fly free on the lap of an adult.

Since travel times peak June to August and around holidays, reserve a seat several months in advance for these times. Call the airline the day before your departure to confirm your flight reservation, and get to the airport early to ensure you have a seat; airlines often overbook. (Of course, being "bumped" from a flight doesn't spell doom if your travel plans are flexible—you will probably leave on the next flight and receive a free ticket or cash bonus. If you would like to be bumped to win a free ticket, check in early and let the airline officials know.) The following programs, services, and fares may be helpful for planning a reasonably-priced airtrip, but always be wary of deals that seem too good to be true:

APEX (Advance Purchase Excursion Fare): The commercial carriers' lowest regular offer; specials advertised in newspapers may be cheaper, but have more restrictions and fewer seats. APEX fares provide you with confirmed reservations and often allow "open-jaw" tickets (landing and returning from different cities). Call as early as possible; these fares often require a two- to three-week advance purchase. Be sure to inquire about any restrictions on length of stay.

Frequent Flyer Tickets: These are great when you finally earn them. If you have a frequent flyer account, make sure you're getting credit when you check in. Frequent flyer tickets are not transferrable.

Air Passes: Many major U.S. airlines offer **Visit USA** air passes to international travelers. You must purchase these passes outside of North America, paying one price for a certain number of flight vouchers. Each voucher is good for one flight on an airline's domestic system; typically, all travel must be completed within 30-60 days. The point of departure and destination for each coupon must be specified at the time of purchase, and once in the U.S., changes carry a $50-$75 fee. Dates of travel may be changed once travel has begun, usually at no extra charge. **USAir** offers packages for the East coast (from $199) and for all 48 states (from around $359). **United, Continental, Delta, Air Ontario, Air BC,** and **TWA** sell vouchers as well. TWA's **Youth Travel Pak** offers a similar deal to students 14-24 years of age, including North Americans. **Canadian Regional Airlines** (England office tel. 011-44-1737-555300; fax 01737 555300) offer unlimited air passes to Western Canada (one-week WestPass $249, two-week $349); and the Canadian Regional network (one-week NationalPass $325, two-week $425).

WITHIN NORTH AMERICA

Given the large distances between points within the United States and Canada, North Americans travel less on buses and trains and more in airplanes or cars when traversing long distances. Buses and trains take much longer and do not always confer a savings equal to the added trouble (a cross-country trip will take three to five days, compared with seven hours by plane).

Major Airlines

Air Canada, (800-776-3000). Discounts for ages 12-24 on stand-by tickets for flights within Canada; still, advance-purchase tickets may be cheaper.

Alaska Airlines, P.O.B. 68900, Seattle, WA 98168 (800-426-0333).

America West, 4000 E. Sky Harbor Blvd. Phoenix, AZ 85034 (800-235-9292). Serves primarily the western United States.

American, (800-433-7300).
Continental, 2929 Allen Parkway, Houston, TX 77210 (800-525-0280; fax 713-590-2150).
Delta, Hartsfield International Airport, Atlanta, GA 30320 (800-241-4141).
Northwest, 5101 Northwest Dr., St. Paul, MN 55111-3034 (800-225-2525).
Northwestern Air Lease Ltd., P.O. Box 23, Fort Smith, NWT X0E 0P0, Canada (800-661-0789, outside Canada 403-872-2216; fax 872-2214). Scheduled service within Northwest Territory.
Southwest, P.O. Box 36611, Dallas, TX 75235-1611 (800-435-9792).
TWA, 1 City Center, 515 N. 6th St., St. Louis, MO 63101 (800-221-2000).
United, P.O. Box 66100, Chicago, IL 60666 (800-241-6522).
USAir, Crystal Park Four Dr., Arlington, VA 22227 (800-428-4322).

FROM ELSEWHERE

From Europe Travelers from Europe will experience the least competition for inexpensive seats during the off-season; but "off-season" need not mean the dead of winter. Peak-season rates generally take effect on either May 15 or June 1 and run until about September 15. You can take advantage of cheap off-season flights within Europe to reach an advantageous point of departure for North America. (London is a major connecting point for budget flights to the U.S.; New York City is often the destination.) Once in the States, you can catch a coast-to-coast flight to make your way out West; see **Within North America,** above for details.

If you decide to fly with a commercial airline rather than through a charter agency or ticket consolidator (see below), you'll be purchasing greater reliability, security, and flexibility. Many major airlines offer reduced-fare options, such as three-day advance purchase fares: these tickets can only be purchased within 72 hours of the time of the departure, and are restricted to youths under a certain age (often 24). Check with a travel agent for availability. Seat availability is known only a few days before the flight, although airlines will sometimes issue predictions. The worst crunch for leaving Europe takes place from mid-June to early July, while August is uniformly tight for returning flights.

Some airlines with cheaper international flights are: **British Airways** (800-247-9297), **Continental, Northwest, TWA,** and **United.** Smaller, budget airlines often undercut major carriers by offering bargain fares on regularly scheduled flights. Competition for seats on these smaller carriers can be fierce—book early. Other trans-Atlantic airlines include **Virgin Atlantic Airways** (800-862-8621) and **IcelandAir** (800-223-5500).

From Asia, Africa, and Australia Whereas European travelers may choose from a variety of regular reduced fares, Asian, Australian, and African travelers must rely on APEX (see p. 25). A good place to start searching for tickets is the local branch of an international budget travel agency (see **Budget Travel Agencies,** p. 23). **STA Travel,** with offices in Sydney, Melbourne, and Auckland, is probably the largest international agency you will find.

Qantas (800-227-4500), **United,** and **Northwest** fly between Australia or New Zealand and the United States. Advance purchase fares from Australia have extremely tough restrictions. If you are uncertain about your plans, pay extra for an advance purchase ticket that has only a 50% penalty for cancellation. Many travelers from Australia and New Zealand take **Singapore Air** (800-742-3333) or other Far East-based carriers for the initial leg of their trip.

Delta Airlines (800-241-4141), **Japan Airlines** (800-525-3663), **Northwest** (800-225-2525) and **United Airlines** (800-538-2929) offer service from Japan. **South African Airways** (800-722-9675), **American** (800-433-7300), and **Northwest** connect South Africa with North America.

CHARTER FLIGHTS AND TICKET CONSOLIDATORS

Charters save you a lot of money on peak-season flights if you can be flexible. Companies reserve the right to change the dates of your flight or even cancel the flight a mere 48 hours in advance. Delays are not uncommon. Restrictions on the length of your trip and the time frame for reservations may also apply. To be safe, get your ticket as early as possible, and arrive at the airport several hours before departure time. Think carefully when you book your departure and return dates; you will lose all or most of your money if you cancel your ticket. Prices and destinations change markedly from season to season, so be sure to contact as many organizations as possible in order to get the best deal. Try **Interworld** (305-443-4929); **Travac** (800-872-8800) or **Rebel**, Valencia, CA (800-227-3235) or Orlando, FL (800-732-3588).

Ticket consolidators sell unbooked commercial and charter airline seats for very low prices, but deals include some risks. Tickets are sold on a space-available basis which does not guarantee you a seat; you get priority over those flying stand-by but below regularly-booked passengers. The earlier you arrive at the airport the better, since passengers are seated in the order they checked in. Consolidators tend to be more reliable on domestic flights, both in getting you on the flight and in getting you exactly where you want to go. Consolidators come in three varieties: wholesale only, who sell only to travel agencies; specialty agencies (both wholesale and retail); and "bucket shops" or discount retail agencies. As a private consumer, you can only deal directly with the latter, but you have access to a larger market if you use a travel agent, who can also get tickets from wholesale consolidators. Look for bucket shops' tiny ads in weekend papers—the *Sunday New York Times* is best. Be wary and if possible, deal with consolidators close to home so you can visit in person if necessary. Get the company's policy in writing: insist on a receipt that gives full details about the tickets, refunds, and restrictions, and record who you talked to and when. For more information and a list of consolidators, consult Kelly Monaghan's *Consolidators: Air Travel's Bargain Basement* ($7 plus $2 shipping) from the Intrepid Traveler, P.O. Box 438, New York, NY 10034 (e-mail intreptrav@aol.com).

1-800-FLY-ASAP, 1001 28th St., Fargo, ND 58103 (9800-FLY-ASAP/359-2727); fax 602-956-6414. A travel agency which only negotiates with major carriers. Flights within U.S., Canada, and Mexico only; call one to two weeks in advance of trip.

Cheap Tickets, (800-377-1000). Offices in Los Angeles, CA (310-645-5054), San Francisco, CA (415-896-5023), Honolulu, HI (808-947-3717), Overland Park, KS, and NYC (212-570-1179).

Mr. Cheap's Travel, (800-636-3273 or 800-672-4327). Offices in El Cajon, CA (619-442-1100), Denver, CO (303-758-3833) and Clackamas, OR (503-557-9101).

STA Travel, Los Angeles, CA (213-934-8722, fax 213-937-6008) or San Francisco, CA (415-391-8407, fax 415-391-4105). Also has offices in Berkeley, Santa Monica, and Westwood, CA. Specializes in student travel.

Unitravel, St. Louis, MO (800-325-2222 or 314-569-0900). Wholesale only.

COURIERS

Courier travel works like this: you are a traveler seeking an inexpensive ticket to a particular location; the courier service is a company seeking to transport merchandise to a particular location. If your destinations and schedules coincide, the courier service will sell you a cheap ticket in exchange for use of the luggage space which accompanies it. Courier services offer some great prices, but schedules may be confining and luggage is limited to carry-on bags only. For a practical guide to the air courier scene, check out Kelly Monaghan's *Insider's Guide to Air Courier Bargains* ($15 plus $3 shipping), available from Upper Access Publishing (UAP), P.O. Box 457, Hinesburg, VT 05461 (800-356-9315), or consult the *Courier Air Travel Handbook* ($10 plus $3.50 shipping), published by Bookmasters, Inc., P.O. Box 2039, Mansfield, OH 44905 (800-507-2665; fax 419-281-6883). **NOW Voyager,** at 74 Varick St. #307, New York, NY 10013 (212-431-1616), offers courier service: 70% off a ticket, but remember, only carry-on luggage (one item). You are subject to stays of very limited duration on roundtrip flights. Flights originate primarily in NYC. They also do reliable consolidation. Phones open Mon.-Fri. 10am-5:30pm, Sat. noon-4:30pm, EST. **Air Tech** (see **Flying Standby,** below) also arranges courier flights.

FLYING STANDBY

Standby brokers sell no tickets but they promise that you will get to a destination near where you want to go, within a window of time (usually 5 days), from a location in a region you've specified. Call in before your date-range to hear all of your flight options for the next seven days and your probability of boarding; then decide which flights you want to try for. At the airport, present a voucher at the airport which grants you the right to board a flight on a space-available basis. This procedure must be followed again for the return trip. Flexibility of schedule and destination is often necessary, but all companies guarantee you a flight or a refund if the available flights that fit your date and destination range were full.

Airhitch, 100 North Sepulveda Blvd. 903, El Segundo, CA 90245 (800-326-2009 or 212-864-2000 on the East Coast; 800-397-1098 or 310-726-5000 on the West Coast), offers flights to and from a greater number of cities than most standby brokers, but you must often list three cities within a given region to which you are willing to fly; Airhitch guarantees that you will get to one of them. You must also give a 5-day travel window for domestic flights. Be sure to read *all* the fine print. The "USA-hitch" program connects the northeastern United States with the West (NYC to Seattle or Baltimore to L.A. $129), and California to Hawaii ($129). "Sunhitch" program offers round-trip tickets from the East coast to the Caribbean or Mexico for $189. Programs change frequently; call for the latest information.

Air Tech, 584 Broadway #1007, New York, NY 10012 (212-219-7000). Space available flights and last-minute confirmed flights at discounts. Domestic travelers must give a 2-day travel window. Flights primarily from NYC (Boston departures possible). One way to L.A. or San Francisco $129; West Coast to Hawaii $129. To Europe $169 each way with a 5-day window. One-year open tickets to Europe (NYC-Paris $595).

■ By Train

Amtrak (800-872-7245, or 800-USA-RAIL) is the main provider of train service in the U.S. Most cities have Amtrak offices which directly sell tickets, but tickets must be bought through an agent in some small towns. **Discounts on full rail fares:** senior citizens (15% off); travelers with disabilities (15% off); children under 15 accompanied by a parent (50% off); children under age two (free); current members of the U.S. armed forces, active-duty veterans, and their dependents (25% off). Circle trips, and holiday packages can also save money. Call for up-to-date info and reservations. Although Amtrak serves Washington and Oregon, it does not run to Alaska. Amtrak offers a wide range of special tickets, promotions, and packages, but these are generally large in scope and will not save travelers much money on relatively short routes such as those within the Pacific Northwest. However, if your aim is to see a lot of the U.S. on your way to the Pacific Northwest, Amtrak's special promotions may be a good deal; call for details. **VIA Rail** (800-561-3949) is Amtrak's Canadian analogue. Regular fare tickets are discounted 40% with 7-day advance-purchase, and fares vary with seasons. Discounts on full fares for students, youths under 24, and seniors (10% off); children ages two to 15, accompanied by an adult (50% off); and children under two (free on the lap of an adult). Reservations are required for some tickets. Traveling to and from the region can usually be accomplished more cheaply by air than by Amtrak.

USA Rail Pass: a discount option available only to those who aren't citizens of North America; allows unlimited travel and unlimited stops over a period of either 15 or 30 days. A 30-day nationwide travel pass sells for $440 during peak season (June 17-Aug. 21) and $350 during the off-season (except late Dec.); a 15-day nationwide pass is $355/$245. A 30-day pass limited to travel in the western region (as far east as Denver) is $330/290; the 15-day pass for the west is $265/$215; a 30-day pass to the eastern region (as far west as Chicago) is $265/$240; and the 15-day version is $205/$185.

Great American Vacations, 1220 Kensington, Oakbrook, IL 60521 (800-437-3441). An Amtrak-affiliated travel agency which offers packages in conjunction with airlines and hotel chains and, occasionally, discounts not to be found anywhere else.

Canrail Pass, on **Via Rail,** Place Ville Marie, lobby Level, Montreal, Québec H3B 2G6, allows unlimited travel on 12 to 15 days within a 30-day period. Between early June and late September, a 12-day pass costs $420, senior citizens and youths under 24 pay $377. Off-season passes cost $287, seniors and youths pay $258. Add $35 for each additional day of travel desired

For Alaskans in the most isolated regions, the **Alaska Railroad** may be the only link to civilization. North America's northernmost railroad covers 470 mi. of land—connecting Seward and Whittier in the south with Anchorage, Fairbanks, and Denali National Park farther north. In 1984, the railroad, one of the last nationally owned railroads in the country, was sold into private hands, changing its name to the **Alaska Railroad Corporation (ARRC),** P.O. Box 107500, Anchorage, AK 99510-7500 (800-544-0552; fax 907-265-2323 e-mail akrr@alaska.net). See specific locations for fares, details and additional rail options.

■ By Bus

Buses generally offer the most frequent and complete service between the cities and towns of the Pacific Northwest and Alaska. Often a bus is the only way to reach smaller locales without a car. *Russell's Official National Motor Coach Guide* ($14.45 including postage) contains schedules of every bus route (including Greyhound) between any two towns in the United States and Canada. Russell's also publishes two semiannual *Supplements,* one which includes a Directory of Bus Lines and Bus Stations ($6), and one which offers a series of Route Maps ($6.45). To order any of the above, write Russell's Guides, Inc., P.O. Box 278, Cedar Rapids, IA 52406 (319-364-6138; fax 364-4853).

Greyhound (800-231-2222), operates the largest number of routes the U.S., though local bus companies may provide more extensive services within specific regions. Schedule information is available at any Greyhound terminal or by calling the 800 number. Reserve with a credit card over the phone at least ten days in advance, and the ticket can be mailed anywhere in the U.S. Otherwise, reservations are only available up to 24 hours in advance. You can buy your ticket at the terminal, but arrive early. *Advance purchase is cheaper, so make reservations early.* **Discounts on full fares:** senior citizens (15% off); children ages two to 11 (50% off); travelers with disabilities or special needs and their companions ride together for the price of one (call 800-752-4841 for more information). If **boarding at a remote "flag stop,"** be sure you know exactly where the bus stops. It's a good idea to call the nearest agency and let them know you'll be waiting and at what time. Catch the driver's attention by standing on the side of the road and flailing your arms wildly—better to be embarrassed than stranded. Whatever you stow in compartments underneath the bus should be clearly marked; be sure to get a claim check for it, and watch to make sure your luggage is on the same bus as you.

Ameripass: Allows adults unlimited travel for 7 days ($179), 15 days ($289), 30 days ($399), or 60 days ($599). Prices for students with a valid college ID, and senior citizens are slightly less; 7 days ($159), 15 days ($259), 30 days ($359), or 60 days ($359). Children's passes are half the price of adults. The pass takes effect the first day used. Before purchasing an Ameripass, total up the separate bus fares between towns to make sure that the pass is really more economical, or at least worth the unlimited flexibility it provides. Most bus companies in the U.S. honor Ameripasses, but check for specifics.

International Ameripass: For travelers from outside North America. Primarily sold in foreign countries, they can also be purchased in either of Greyhound's International Offices, located in New York City and Los Angeles (800-246-8572). A 4-day pass, which can not be used during a weekend, is $99, 5-day pass $119, 7-day pass $159, 15-day pass $219, 30-day pass $299, 60-day pass $499.

Greyhound Lines of Canada (800-661-8747 in Canada or 403-265-9111 in the United States) is a Canadian bus company with no affiliation with Greyhound. **Alaskon Express,** 745 W. 4th Ave. Suite 200, Anchorage 99501 (907-277-5581), which is operated by Gray Line of Alaska, runs four buses per week to a variety of cities in Alaska and the Yukon, including Whitehorse, Tok, and Skagway; also offers daily service to Seward and Valdez. **Seward Bus Lines,** 5430 B Street, Anchorage, AK 99518 (907-563-0800) is a small, affordable bus company that runs to Seward ($30 one way, $60 roundtrip). They also make reservations and sell tickets for **Home Stage Lines,** with service to Homer ($45 one way, $80 roundtrip).

Green Tortoise, 494 Broadway, San Francisco, CA 94133 (415-956-7500 or 800-867-8647), has "hostels on wheels" in remodeled diesel buses done up for living and eating on the road; meals are prepared communally. Green Tortoise's charm lies in its price and its personality, not in its luxury. Cost includes transportation, sleeping space on the bus, and tours of the regions through which you pass. Deposits ($100 most trips) are generally required since space is tight.

■ By Car

BEFORE YOU STEP ON IT

American Automobile Association (AAA), 1050 Hingham St., Rocklin, MA 02370 (800-AAA-HELP/222-4357). The best-known of the auto clubs. Offers free trip-planning services, road maps and guidebooks, discounts on car rentals, emergency road service anywhere in the U.S., free towing, and commission-free traveler's cheques from American Express. AAA has reciprocal agreements with the auto associations of many other countries which often provide you with full benefits while in the U.S. There are two types of membership, basic and plus, but the two services do not differ greatly; basic memberships are $54 for the first year with $40 yearly renewal; $23 per yr. for associate (a family member in household).

AMOCO Motor Club, P.O Box 9041, Des Moines, IA 50368 (800-334-3300). Trip planning and travel information, 24hr towing (free for 5mi. or back to the tower's garage), emergency road service, and car rental discounts. $50 annual membership enrolls you and one other household member. Premier membership ($75) entitles you to 50mi. free towing.

Mobil Auto Club, 200 N. Martingale Rd., Schaumbourg, IL 60174 (800-621-5581). Benefits include locksmith, towing (free up to 10mi.), roadside service, and car-rental discounts. $52 annual fee covers you and one person of your choice.

Montgomery Ward Auto Club, 200 N. Martingale Rd., Schaumburg, IL 60173-2096 (800-621-5151). Provides 24-hr. emergency roadside assistance in any car, whether owned, rented, or borrowed, unlimited trip routing, and up to $1500 for travel emergencies. $79 monthly membership fee. Associate memberships available for driving-age children 16-23 for $24 annually.

UNDER THE HOOD AND ON THE INTERSTATE

If you are driving in America, a **road atlas** is your best friend. **Rand McNally's Road Atlas,** covering all of the USA and Canada, is one of the best resources for maps (available at bookstores and gas stations, $10).

Learn a bit about minor automobile maintenance and repair before you leave, and pack an easy-to-read manual—it may at least help you keep your car alive long enough to reach a reputable garage. Your trunk should contain the following **necessities:** a spare tire and jack, jumper cables, extra oil, flares, a blanket (several, if you're traveling in winter), extra water for you and your car, and a flashlight. If there's a chance you may be stranded in a remote area, keep emergency food and water on hand. Always have plenty of gas and check road conditions ahead of time when possible, particularly during the winter. **Gas** is generally cheaper in towns than at interstate service stops. The enormous travel distances of North America will require you to spend more on gas than you might at first expect. Tune up your car, make sure the tires have enough air, check the oil, and avoid running the air-conditioner unnecessarily and your car will burn less fuel. Be sure to **buckle up**—it's the law in many regions of the U.S. and Canada.

In the 1950s, President Eisenhower envisioned an **interstate system,** a federally funded network of highways designed primarily to subsidize American commerce. There is a simple, consistent system for numbering interstates. Even-numbered interstates run east-west and odd ones run north-south, decreasing in number the farther south and west they are. If the interstate has a three-digit number, it is a branch of another interstate (i.e., I-285 is a branch of I-85), and is often a bypass skirting around a large city. An *even* digit in the *hundreds* place means the branch will eventually return to the main interstate; an *odd* digit means it won't. North-south routes begin on the West Coast with I-5 and end with I-95 on the East Coast. The southernmost east-west route is I-4 in Florida. The northernmost east-west route is I-94, stretching from Montana to Wisconsin.

Let's Go lists U.S. highways in this format: "I" (as in "I-90") refers to Interstate highways, "U.S." (as in "U.S. 1") to United States Highways, and "Rte." (as in "Rte. 7") to state and local highways. For Canadian highways, "TCH" refers to the Trans-Canada Highway, "Hwy." refers to standard autoroutes (see **Appendix** for mileage).

DRIVING PERMITS AND INSURANCE

Although not required in the U.S. or Canada, the International Driving Permit (IDP) can smooth out difficulties with American and Canadian police officers and serves as an additional piece of identification. A valid driver's license from your home country must always accompany the IDP. An IDP must be issued in your own country before you depart; check with your national automobile association. Some foreign driver's licenses are valid in the U.S. for up to one year; check before you leave.

Canadian license holders can obtain an IDP (CDN$10) through any **Canadian Automobile Association (CAA)** branch office in Canada, or by writing to CAA Central Ontario, 60 Commerce Valley Drive East, Thornhill, Ontario L3T 7P9 (416- 221-4300).

Proper insurance is required by law. Most credit cards cover standard insurance. If you rent, lease, or borrow a car, you will need a **green card,** or **International Insurance Certificate,** to prove that you have liability insurance. Most car rental agencies include coverage in their prices. If you lease a car, you can obtain a green card from the dealer. Some travel agents offer the card, and it may be available at the border. Verify whether your auto insurance applies abroad; even if it does, you will still need a green card to certify this to foreign officials.

RENTING

While the cost of renting a car for long distances is often prohibitive, renting for local trips may be reasonable. National chains usually allow cars to be picked up in one city and dropped off in another (for a hefty charge). By calling a toll-free number you can reserve a reliable car anywhere in the country. Drawbacks include steep prices and high minimum ages for rentals (usually 25). If you're 21 or older and have a major credit card in your name, you may be able to rent where the minimum age would otherwise rule you out. **Alamo** (800-327-9633) rents to ages 21-24 with a major credit card for an additional $20 per day. **Avis** (800-331-1212) and **Hertz** (800-654-3131) enforce a minimum age of 25, unless the renter has a corporate account. Some branches of **Budget** (800-527-0700) rent to ages 21-24 with a credit card, but it's not the norm. Most **Dollar** (800-800-4000) branches and some **Thrifty** (800-367-2277 or 703-658-2200) locations allow ages 21-24 to rent for an additional daily fee of about $20. **Rent-A-Wreck** (800-421-7253) specializes in supplying vehicles that are past their prime for lower-than-average prices. Most branches rent to ages 21-24 with an additional fee, but policies and prices vary from agency to agency. Most packages allow you a certain number of miles free before the usual charge of 30-40¢ a mile takes effect; if you'll be driving a long distance (a few hundred miles or more), ask for an unlimited-mileage package.

There are also local agencies which serve a specific city or region, and these sometimes offer better deals. When dealing with any car rental company, be sure to ask whether the price includes insurance against theft and collision. There may be an additional charge for the collision and damage waiver (CDW), which is about $12-15 per day. If you use **American Express** to rent the car, they will automatically cover the CDW; call AmEx's car division (800-338-1670) for more information.

AUTO TRANSPORT COMPANIES

These services match drivers with car owners who need cars moved from one city to another. Would-be travelers give the company their desired destination and the company finds a car which needs to go there. The only expenses are gas, tolls, and your own living expenses. Some companies insure their cars; with others, your security deposit covers any breakdowns or damage. You must be at least 21, have a valid license, and agree to drive about 400 mi. per day on a fairly direct route. Companies regularly inspect current and past job references, take your fingerprints, and require a cash bond. Cars are available between most points, although it's easiest to find cars for traveling from coast to coast; New York and Los Angeles are popular transfer points. If offered a car, look it over first. Think twice about accepting a gas guzzler since you'll be paying for the gas. With the company's approval you may be able to share the cost with several companions.

Auto Driveaway, 310 S. Michigan Ave., Chicago, IL 60604 (800-346-2277; e-mail jsonl@aol.com; http://www.autodriveaway.com).

A. Anthony's Driveaway, 4391 NW 19th Ave., Pompano Beach, FL 33064 (305-970-7384; fax 970-3881).

Across America Driveaway, 3626 Calumet Ave., Hammond, IN 46320 (800-964-7874; 310-798-3377 in L.A.; 312-889-7737 in Chicago).

NORTHCOUNTRY DRIVING

Many major roads in Alaska and Northwestern Canada are still in **desperately bad shape.** Dust and flying rocks are major hazards in the summer, as are the road construction crews, which interrupt long-distance trips with miserable 10- to 30-mi. patches of gravel as they repave the road. Many of the worst roads in Alaska have been treated with calcium chloride to minimize the dust flying up from the road. It can be very hard on your car's paint, though, and you should take every opportunity to wash your car. *Drive slowly*, it will make the trip much easier on your car. Melting and contracting permafrost in the north causes "frost heaves," creating dips and Dali-esque twists in the road. Radiators and headlights should be protected from flying rocks and swarming bugs with a **wire screen** and/or plastic **headlight covers;** good **shocks** and a functional **spare tire** are absolutely essential. Wintertime snow cover can actually smooth your ride a bit: the packed surface and the thinned traffic can create easier driving (although the dangers of avalanches and driving on ice offer a different set of concerns). Check **road conditions** before traveling.

Two guides which include maps, and detailed routes are available from **Vernon Publications, Inc.,** 3000 Northup Way, #200, Bellevue, WA, 98004 (800-726-4707; fax 206-822-9372). *The MILEPOST* is an exceptional guide to Alaska and northwestern Canada ($19), and, for off-the-road travel in Alaska, *The Alaska Wilderness Guide* covers bush communities and remote areas ($16.95).

■ On Two Wheels

If you're willing to make a substantial initial investment and don't mind moving much more slowly for much more effort, bicycling can be a great way to take in a region at a leisurely pace. Remember that safe and secure cycling requires a helmet (usually about $40) and a U-shaped Kryptonite or Citadel lock (about $30). Information about cycling in the Northwest is available from tourist bureaus, which often distribute free maps. Some cities, like Seattle, are very bike-friendly and allow bicycles on public transportation.

BIKE BOOKS

Bike Nashbar, 4111 Simon Rd., Youngstown, OH 44512 (800-627-4227; fax 330-782-2856), is the leading mail-order catalog for cycling equipment. They will beat any nationally advertised in-stock price by 5¢, and will ship anywhere in the U.S. and Canada. They also have a techline (330-788-6464; open Mon.-Fri. 8am-midnight, Sat.-Sun. 8am-4pm) to answer questions about repairs and maintenance.

Rodale Press, 33 E. Minor St., Emmaus, PA 18098-0099 (800-8484735; 610-967-5171), publishes a number of publications for the intrepid cyclist. *Bike Touring* ($11, Sierra Club) discusses how to equip and plan a bicycle trip.

The Mountaineers Books, 1011 SW Klickitat Way #201, Seattle, WA 98134 (800-553-4453; fax 206-223-6306; e-mail mbooks@mountaineers.org), publishes *Bicycle Gearing: A Practical Guide* ($9) which discusses in lay terms everything you need to know.

Ten-Speed Press, Box 7123, Berkeley, CA 94707 (510-559-1600), publishes *Anybody's Bike Book* ($10 plus $3.50 shipping), which provides vital information on repair and maintenance during long-term bike sojourns.

Umbrella Books, a subsidiary of Epicenter Press, at P.O. Box 82368 Kenmore, WA 98028 (206-485-6822), sells a number of regional guides, including *Bicycling the Oregon Coast,* by Robin Cody ($11), and *Alaska's Wilderness Highway, Traveling the Dalton Road,* by Mike Jensen.

ESSENTIALS

CYCLING TOURS AND ASSOCIATIONS

Adventure Cycling Association, P.O. Box 8308-P, Missoula, MT 59807 (406-721-1776; fax 721-8754; e-mail acabike@aol.com), is a national non-profit organization that researches and maps long-distance routes and organizes bike tours for members. Membership costs $128 in the U.S., $35 in Canada and Mexico.

The Canadian Cycling Association, 1600 James Naismith Dr., #212A, Gloucester, Ont. K1B 5N4 (613-748-5629; fax 748-5692; e-mail cycling@cdnsport.ca), distributes *The Canadian Cycling Association's Complete Guide to Bicycle Touring in Canada* (CDN$20), plus guides to specific regions of Canada, Alaska, and the Pacific Coast. Also sells maps and books.

Rocky Mountain Cycle Tours, Box 1978, Canmore, AB T0L 0M0 (403-678-6770 or 800-661-2453; fax 403-678-4451), organizes summer bicycle tours in Alberta and B.C. for groups of fewer than 20 ($680-1200 for 6 days, 5 nights)

Backroads, 801 Cedar St., Berkeley, CA 94710-1800 (800-462-2848; fax 510-527-1444; http://www.backroads.com), offers biking, hiking, running, camping, and skiing tours in 23 states, including Alaska and parts of British Columbia. Trips range from a weekend excursion ($239) to a 9-day extravaganza ($978).

Another two-wheel option, motorcycling is cheaper than driving a car, but it takes a tenacious soul to pull off the trip. Contact the **American Motorcyclist Association** (800-AMA-JOIN/262-5646), the linchpin of U.S. biker culture. A full membership ($29 per year) includes a subscription to the extremely informative *American Motorcyclist* magazine and a kick-ass patch for your riding jacket. Also, try getting in touch with the **Motorcycling Safety Foundation,** 2 Jenner St., Suite 150, Irvine, CA 92718-3800 (800-447-4700).

■ By Ferry

Along the Pacific coast, ferries are an exhilarating and often unavoidable way to travel. Some Alaskan towns can only be reached by water or air. In addition to basic transportation, the ferry system gives travelers the chance to enjoy the beauty of the water and the coast, one of the Northwest's finest outdoor experiences. Ferry travel, however, can become quite expensive when you bring a car along. In Alaska, schedule an overnight ferry ride and sleep free in the Solarium, on the top deck, or in the lounge. Free showers are also a bonus on all but the smallest boats.

ALASKA MARINE HIGHWAY

The **Alaska Marine Highway,** P.O. Box 25535, Juneau, AK 99802-5535 (800-642-0066) consists of two completely unconnected ferry systems administered by one bureaucracy. The **southeast** system runs from Bellingham, WA and Prince Rupert, BC up the coast to Skagway, stopping in Juneau, Ketchikan, Haines, and other towns. The **southcentral/southwest** network serves Kodiak Island, Seward, Homer, Prince William Sound, and, occasionally, the Aleutian Islands. For both systems, the ferry schedule is a function of tides and other navigational exigencies. **Stopovers** are encouraged. There is a slight additional charge for stopovers, and should be reserved at the same time as the rest of your itinerary. Write ahead for all schedules, rates, and information. Practically none of southeast Alaska (the Panhandle) is accessible by road; most of this area can be reached only by plane or on the Marine Highway ferry from Bellingham, WA or Prince Rupert, BC. Connections can also be made from most towns via **Alaska Airlines,** or overland from Haines and Skagway (see **Alaskon Express** under **By Bus** on page 29).

Those who intend to hit the ground running, and keep running, would be smart to check out the **AlaskaPass.** The pass offers unlimited access to Alaska's railroad, ferry, and bus systems; a 15-day pass sells for $649, a 30-day pass for $899. A pass allowing travel on 21 non-consecutive days over a 45-day period costs $949. The fare may seem expensive, but with a network that extends from Bellingham, WA to Dutch Harbor on the Aleutian Islands, the pass is a good deal for those who want to see a lot of Alaska in a short amount of time. If you're interested, call 800-248-7598, 7am-7pm (Alaska time).

The full trip from Bellingham to Skagway takes three days—an adventure in itself, peppered with whales, bald eagles, and the majesty of the Inside Passage. (**The Love Boat's** notorious Alaskan voyages took this same route.) All southeast ferries have free showers, cafes, and a heated top-deck "solarium" where passengers without cabins can sleep (bring a sleeping bag); selected sailings also offer lectures on history and ecology.

PLANNING YOUR FERRY TRIPS

The **Alaska Northwest Travel Service, Inc.,** 3303 148th St. SW, Suite 2, Lynnwood, WA 98037 (206-787-9499 or 800-533-7381, fax 206-745-4946), is an agent for Alaska and British Columbia ferries, as well as a full service travel agency specializing in Alaska; they can book ferries, cruise ships, and airline reservations. They will also plan individualized itineraries. Ferry scheduling information can also be found in *The Milepost,* published by Vernon Publications. For information on how to obtain a copy see **By Car: Northcountry Driving,** p. 33.

Information about fares, reservations, vehicles, and schedules varies greatly throughout the year (see sections on Seattle, southwestern BC, and Alaska). Be sure to consult each ferry company when constructing your itinerary in order to clear up any additional questions before finalizing your plans.

BC Ferries, 1112 Fort St., Victoria, BC V8V 4V2 (schedules, general information 888-223-3779 within British Columbia, 604-669-1211 outside of BC; fax 604-381-5452; http://bcferries.bc.ca/ferries) Passenger and vehicle ferry service on 25 routes throughout coastal British Columbia. Service areas include Mainland-Vancouver Island (three major routes), Sunshine Coast, Northern and Southern Gulf Islands, and northern services (Inside Passage between Port Hardy and Prince Rupert, Prince Rupert to Queen Charlotte Islands, and Discovery Coast Passage, between Port Hardy and Bella Coola). Special facilities for passengers with disabilities. No reservations, except on the following routes: Tsawwassen/Gulf Islands, Inside Passage, Discovery Coast Passage, and Queen Charlotte Islands; call the above numbers to reserve.

Black Ball Transport, Inc., 430 Belleville St., Victoria, BC. V8V 1W9 (604-386-2202); Foot of Laurel, Port Angeles 98362 (360-457-4491 fax 604-386-2207). Ferries daily between Port Angeles, WA and Victoria, with a crossing time of 95 min. Fare for an adult $6.50 each way; for car and driver, $27 each way; for a motorcycle and driver, $16.50 each way. Bicycles $3.25 extra. All prices in U.S. funds. Advance reservations not accepted.

Washington State Ferries, 801 Alaskan Way, Seattle, WA 98104 (1-800-84-FERRY/ 33779 for schedule information; http:www.wsdot.wa.gov/ferries/). Ferries to Sidney, BC, and throughout Puget Sound. Reservations are usually unnecessary, except for travel to the San Juan Islands or British Columbia. Service is frequent, especially in summer. Schedules change seasonally. Fares fluctuate, but are reasonable. Ferries run approximately between 5am and 1:30am. Waits of several hours to board a ferry during the summer are not uncommon.

■ By Thumb

> *Let's Go* urges you to consider the risks and disadvantages of hitchhiking before thumbing it. Hitching means entrusting your life to a stranger who happens to stop beside you on the road. While this may be comparatively safe in some areas of Europe and Australia, it is **NOT** so in the United States. We do **NOT** recommend it. We strongly urge you to find other means of transportation. Do not put yourself in a situation where hitching is the only option.

If you feel you have no other alternative, if you *insist* on ignoring our warnings, and decide to hitchhike anyway, there are many precautions that must be taken. First, assess the risks and your chances of getting a ride. **Women traveling alone should never, ever, ever hitch in the United States. Never.**

Never hesitate to refuse a ride if you will feel at all uncomfortable alone with the driver. If at all threatened or intimidated, experienced hitchers ask to be let out no matter how uncompromising the road looks, and they know *in advance* where to go if stranded and what to do in emergencies. Near metropolises like New York and Los Angeles, hitching is tantamount to suicide. In rural areas, hitching is reportedly less risky. All states prohibit hitchhiking while standing on the roadway itself or behind a freeway entrance sign; hitchers more commonly find rides near intersections where many cars converge. The information provided below is not intended as an endorsement of hitching.

HITCHING IN ALASKA

Many people hitchhike instead of depending on buses in Alaska, but it is not unusual to find yourself stranded on a sparsely traveled route. A wait of a day or two between rides is not unusual on certain stretches of the Alaska Hwy., especially in Canada. Alaska state law prohibits moving vehicles from not picking up stranded motorists, as the extreme weather conditions can be life-endangering. However, hitchhiking backpackers may only legally thumb for rides on the on-and-off ramps of major highways—not on the highways themselves.

Carrying a large cardboard sign clearly marked with your destination can improve your chances of getting a ride. Drivers may not want to stop if they don't know where you're going. When it gets particularly tough, hitchers add "SHARE GAS."

Catching a ride from Canada into Alaska on the Alaska Hwy. involves passing the **Alaska-Yukon "border" check,** which is a series of questions about citizenship, insurance, contraband, and finances, followed by an auto inspection. Hitchers should walk across the border to avoid hassle.

ONCE THERE

▓ Embassies and Consulates

Embassies in U.S.: Australia, 1601 Massachusetts Ave. NW, Washington, D.C. 20036 (202-797-3000); **Canada,** 501 Pennsylvania Ave. NW, Washington, D.C. 20001 (202-682-1740); **Ireland,** 2234 Massachusetts Ave. NW, Washington, D.C. 20008 (202-462-3939); **New Zealand,** 37 Observatory Circle NW, Washington, DC 20008 (202-328-4800); **South Africa,** 3051 Massachusetts Ave. NW, Washington, DC 20008 (202-232-4400); **United Kingdom,** 3100 Massachusetts Ave. NW, Washington, DC 20008 (202-462-1340).

Consulates in U.S.: Australia, 630 5th Ave., New York, NY 10111 (212-408-8400); Century Plaza Towers, 19th floor, 2049 Century Park East, Los Angeles, CA 90067 (310-229-4800); **Canada,** 1251 Ave. of the Americas, Exxon Building, 16th Floor, New York, NY 10020-1175 (212-596-1600); 300 S. Grand Ave.,10th floor, California Plaza, Los Angeles, CA 90071 (213-346-2700); **Ireland,** 345 Park Ave., 17th Floor, New York, NY 10154 (212-319-2555); 44 Montgomery St., Suite 3830, San Francisco, CA 94101 (415-392-4214); **New Zealand,** 12400 Wilshire Blvd., Suite 1150, Los Angeles, CA 90025 (310-207-1605); **South Africa,** 333 E. 38th St., 9th Floor, New York, NY 10016 (212-213-4880); 50 N. La Cienega Blvd., Suite 300, Beverly Hills, CA 90211 (310-657-9200); **United Kingdom,** 845 3rd Ave., New York, NY 10022 (212-745-0200); 11766 Wilshire Blvd., Suite 400, Los Angeles, CA 9002-6538 (310-477-3322).

Embassies in Canada: Australia, 50 O'Connor St., suite 710, Ottawa, Ontario K1P 6L2 (613-236-0841); **Ireland,** 130 Albert St., suite 1105, Ottawa, Ontario K1P 5G4 (613-233-6281); **New Zealand,** 99 Bank St., suite 727, Ottawa, Ontario K1P 6G3 (613-238-5991); **Mexico,** 45 O'Connor St., Suite 1500, Ottawa, Ontario, K1P 1A4 (613-233-8988); **South Africa,** 15 Sussex Dr., Ottawa, Ontario K1M 1M8 (613-744-0330); **United Kingdom,** 80 Elgin St., Ottawa, Ontario K1P 5K7 (613-237-1530); **United States,** 100 Wellington St., Ottawa, Ontario K1P 5T1 (613-238-5335).

Consulates in Canada: Australia, 175 Bloor St. East, suite 314, Toronto, Ontario M4W 3R8, (416-323-1155), World Trade Center office complex, suite 602, 999 Canada Place, Vancouver, British Columbia V6C 3E1 (604-684-1177); **New Zealand,** 888 Dunsmuir St., suite 1200, Vancouver, British Columbia V6C 3K4 (604-684-7388); **South Africa,** 1 Place Ville Marie, suite 2615, Montreal, Québec H3B 4S3 (514-878-9217); Stock Exchange Tower, suite 2300, 2 First Canadian Place, Toronto, Ontario M5X 1E3 (416-364-0314); **United Kingdom,** 1000 de la Gauchetiere West, Suite 4200, Montreal, Québec H3B 4W5 (514-866-5863); 1111 Melville St., suite 800, Vancouver, British Columbia V6E 3V6 (604-683-4421); **United States,** 2 Place Terrasse Dufferin, CP 939, Québec, G1R 4T9 (418-692-2095); 1095 Pender St. West, Vancouver, British Columbia V6E 2M6 (604-685-4311). For U.S. visa and immigration services, call 900-451-6663 (open Mon.-Fri. 7am-8pm); to schedule an appointment with the U.S. consulate, call 900-451-2778.

▓ Accommodations

Always make reservations, especially if you plan to travel during peak tourist seasons. If you find yourself in dire straits, don't spend the night under the stars in an unsupervised campground; it's often uncomfortable, unsafe, and sometimes illegal, even in national parks and forest areas. The local crisis center hotline may have a list of persons or groups, as well as local shelters, who will house you in an emergency.

HOSTELS

Youth hostels offer unbeatable deals on indoor lodging ($5-25 per night), and they are great places to meet traveling companions from all over the world. Many hostels even have **ride boards** to help you hook up with other hostelers going your way. As a rule, hostels are dorm-style accommodations where the sexes sleep apart, often in large rooms with bunk beds. (Some hostels allow families and couples private rooms, often for an additional charge.) You must bring or rent your own sleep sack (see **Packing**, p. 19). Sleeping bags are often not allowed. Hostels frequently have kitchens and utensils available, and some have storage areas and laundry facilities. Many also require you to perform a communal chore daily.

The Hostel Handbook for the U.S.A. & Canada (Jim Williams, Ed.; available for $3 from Dept: IGH, 722 Saint Nicholas Ave., NY, NY 10031; email Hostel@aol.com) lists over 500 hostels. If you have Internet access, check out the **Internet Guide to Hostelling** (http://hostels.com). Reservations for HI hostels may be made via the International Booking Network (IBN), a computerized system which allows you to book to and from HI hostels months in advance for a nominal fee. If you plan to stay in hostels, consider joining one of these associations:

Hostel Membership

Hostelling International-American Youth Hostels (HI-AYH), 733 15th St. NW, Suite 840, Washington, DC 20005 (202-783-6161; fax 202-783-6171;http://www.taponline.com/tap/travel/hostels/pages/hosthp.html). Maintains 34 offices and over 150 hostels in the U.S. Memberships can be purchased at the national office in Washington, DC and at many travel agencies (see p. 23). 1-year membership $25, under 18 $10, over 54 $15, family cards $35; includes *Hostelling North America: The Official Guide to Hostels in Canada and the United States*. Make reservations directly or through the International Booking Network (IBN), a computerized reservation system which lets you book from other HI hostels worldwide up to six months in advance.

Hostelling International-Canada (HI-C), 400-205 Catherine St., Ottawa, Ontario K2P 1C3, Canada (613-237-7884; fax 237-7868). Maintains 73 hostels throughout Canada. IBN booking centers in Edmonton, Montreal, Ottawa, and Vancouver; expect CDN$9-22.50 per night. Membership packages: 1-yr, under 18 CDN$12; 1-yr., over 18 CDN$25; 2-yr., over 18 CDN$35; lifetime CDN$175.

Youth Hostels Association of England and Wales (YHA), Trevelyan House, 8 St. Stephen's Hill, St. Albans, Hertfordshire AL1 2DY, England (tel. (01727) 855215; fax 844126). Enrollment fees are: UK£9.30; under 18 UK£3.20; UK£18.60 for both parents with children under 18 enrolled free; UK£9.30 for one parent with children under 18 enrolled free; UK£125.00 for lifetime membership.

An Óige (Irish Youth Hostel Association), 61 Mountjoy St., Dublin 7 (tel. (01) 830 4555; fax 830 5808; http://www.touchtel.ie). One-year membership is IR£7.50, under 18 IR£4, family IR£7.50 for each adult with children under 16 free.

Youth Hostels Association of Northern Ireland (YHANI), 22 Donegall Rd., Belfast BT12 5JN, Northern Ireland (tel. (01232) 315435; fax 439699). Prices range from UK£6.50-10. Annual memberships UK£7, under 18 UK£3, family UK£14 for up to 6 children.

Scottish Youth Hostels Association (SYHA), 7 Glebe Crescent, Stirling FK8 2JA (tel. (01786) 45 11 81; fax 45 01 98). Membership UK£6, under 18 UK£2.50.

Australian Youth Hostels Association (AYHA), Level 3, 10 Mallett St., Camperdown NSW 2050 (tel. (02) 565 1699; fax 565 1325; e-mail YHA@zeta.org.au). AUS$42, renewal AUS$26; under 18 AUS$12.

Youth Hostels Association of New Zealand (YHANZ), P.O. Box 436, 173 Gloucester St., Christchurch 1 (tel. (643) 379 9970; fax 365 4476; e-mail hostel.operations@yha.org.nz; http://yha.org.nz/yha). Annual membership fee NZ$24.

Hostel Association of South Africa, P.O. Box 4402, Cape Town 8000 (tel. (21) 419 1853; fax 216937). Membership SAR45; Students SAR30; Group SAR120; Family SAR90; Lifetime SAR225.

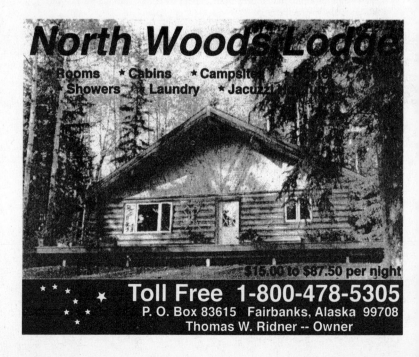

Rucksackers North America, 1412 Cerrillos Rd., Santa Fe, NM 87505 (505-988-1153); ask for Preston Ellsworth.

Backpackers Hostels Canada, a very helpful service, can be reached by sending an e-mail message to ljones@mail.foxnet.net.

HOTELS AND MOTELS

Many visitors centers, especially ones off major thoroughfares entering a state, have hotel coupons that can save you a bundle; if you don't see any, ask. Budget motels are usually clustered off the highway several miles outside of town, but the carless may do better to try the hostels, YMCAs, YWCAs, and dorms downtown. The annually updated *National Directory of Budget Motels* ($6, plus $2 shipping), from **Pilot Books,** 103 Copper St., Babylon NY 11702 (516-422-2225 or 422-2227; fax 422-2227), covers over 2200 low-cost chain motels in the U.S. Pilot Books also publishes *The Hotel/Motel Special Program and Discount Guide* ($6, plus $2 shipping), which lists hotels and motels offering special discounts. Also look for the comprehensive *State by State Guide to Budget Motels* ($13), from Marlor Press, Inc., 4304 Brigadoon Dr., St. Paul, MN 55126 (800-669-4908 or 612-484-4600; fax 612-490-1182; e-mail marlor@ix.netcom.com).

It is fortunate that the **Canadian hostel system** is somewhat more extensive than that of the U.S. because that country's dearth of cheap motels puts most Canadian hotels and motels beyond the means of most budget travelers. Budget motel chains in the U.S. cost significantly less than the chains catering to the next-pricier market, such as Holiday Inn. Chains usually adhere more consistently to a level of cleanliness and comfort than locally operated budget competitors; some even feature heated pools and cable TV. Contact these chains for free directories:

Motel 6 (800-466-8356)

Super 8 Motels (800-800-8000, 605-229-8708; fax 605-229-8900; http://www.super8motels.com/super8.html; call for their International Directory.)

Choice Hotels International (800-453-4511).

Best Western International (800-528-1234, 602-957-4200; fax 602-957-5505; inquire about discounts for seniors, families, frequent travelers, groups, or government personnel).

BED AND BREAKFASTS

As alternatives to impersonal hotel rooms, bed and breakfasts (private homes with spare rooms available to travelers, abbreviated B&Bs) range from the acceptable to the sublime. B&Bs may provide an excellent way to explore an area with the help of a host who knows it well, and some go out of their way to be accommodating—accepting travelers with pets or giving personalized tours. Often the best part of your stay will be a home-cooked breakfast (and occasionally dinner). Many B&Bs do not provide phones or TVs, and bathrooms must sometimes be shared.

Prices vary widely. B&Bs in major cities are usually more expensive than those in out-of-the-way places. Doubles can cost anywhere from $20-300 per night; most are in the $30 to $50 range. Some homes give special discounts to families or seniors. Reservations are almost always necessary, although in the off-season (if the B&B is open), you can frequently find a room on short notice.

For more information on B&Bs, consult *Bed & Breakfast, USA* ($16), from Tourist House Associates, Inc., RR 1, Box 12-A, Greentown, PA 18426, *The Complete Guide to Bed and Breakfasts, Inns and Guesthouses in the U.S. and Canada* ($17), which lists over 11,000 B&Bs plus inns (available through Lanier Publications, P.O. Box D, Petaluma, CA 94952, 707-763-0271; fax 707-763-5762; e-mail lanier@travelguides; or CompuServe ["Go B&B"] or America Online ["Bed & Breakfast Guide Online"]), and *America's Favorite Inns, B&Bs, and Small Hotels* ($20, CDN$27). All three can be found in bookstores. In addition, check local phone books, visitors' bureaus, and information at bus and train stations. The following services book rooms in B&Bs throughout the U.S. and Canada:

Bed and Breakfast International, P.O. Box 282910, San Francisco, CA 94128-2910 (800-872-4500 or 415-696-1690; fax 415-696-1699). Rates range $60-$150 per night per room and include breakfast; 2-night min. stay. Discounts for singles, families with children, and stays over one week.

Bed and Breakfast: The National Network (TNN) of Reservation Services, Box 4616, Springfield, MA 01101 (800-884-4288; fax 401-847-7309; email anna's@wsii.com; http://www.bandbnet.com) can book reservations at over 7000 B&Bs throughout America and Canada. A travel kit will be mailed upon request.

YMCAS AND YWCAS

Not all **Young Men's Christian Association (YMCA)** locations offer lodging; those that do are often located in urban downtowns, which can be convenient but a little gritty. YMCA rates are usually lower than a hotel's but higher than a hostel's and may include use of libraries, pools, air conditioning, and other facilities. Many YMCAs accept women and families (group rates often available), and some will not lodge people under 18 without parental permission. All reservations must be made and paid for in advance, with a traveler's check (signed top and bottom), U.S. money order, certified check, Visa, or Mastercard. Call the local YMCA in question for fee information. For information or reservations (reservation fee $3), contact **Y's Way International,** 224 E. 47th St., New York, NY 10017 (212-308-2899; fax 212-308-3161; http://www.ymca.org/ for links to branches worldwide).

Most **Young Women's Christian Associations (YWCAs)** accommodate only women or, sometimes, couples. Nonmembers are often required to join when lodging. For more information or a world-wide directory ($10), write **YWCA-USA,** 726 Broadway, New York, NY 10003 (212-614-2700). For Y's in **Canada,** contact the Montreal YMCA at 1450 Stanley St., Montreal, PQ H3A 2W6 (514-849-8393; fax 514-849-8017) or YMCA Canada, 2160 Yonge St., Toronto, Ontario M4S 2A9 (416-485-9447; fax 417-485-8228).

The network of YMCAs and YWCAs extends to many larger **Canadian** cities. You will generally find the same type of clean and affordable rooms as those offered in the States, mostly in downtown areas. For Y's in **Canada,** contact the Montréal YMCA at 1450 Stanley St., Montréal, PQ H3A 2W6 (514-849-8393; fax 849-8017) or the YMCA Canada, 2160 Yonge Street, Toronto, Ontario M4S 2A9 (416-485-9447; fax 417-485-8228).

ALTERNATIVE ACCOMMODATIONS

Many **colleges and universities** in the U.S. and Canada open their residence halls to travelers when school is not in session—some do so even during term-time. No general policy covers all of these institutions, but rates tend to be low, and some schools require that you express at least a vague interest in attending their institution. College campuses can be some of the best sources for information on things to do, places to stay, and possible rides out of town. To contact colleges and universities in Alaska and the Pacific Northwest, see **Study Opportunities,** p. 17. Also try:

Willing Workers on Organic Farms, Postfach 615, CH-9001 St. Gallen, Switzerland (e-mail fairtours@gu.apc.org.), compiles a list of organic farms worldwide which provide beds and meals in exchange for labor. Send two international reply coupons for more information.

Barclay International Group, 150 West 52nd Street, New York, NY 10022 (800-845-6636 or 212-832-3777; fax 212-753-1139), arranges hotel alternative accommodations (apartment, condo, cottage, B&B or villa rentals) in over 20 countries, including the U.S. and Canada. Most are equipped with kitchens, telephones, TV, and concierge and maid service. Rentals are pricey, starting around $500/week off-season. Generally less expensive than hotels with comparable amenities, these accommodations may suit families with children, business travelers, or Kosher or vegetarian travelers.

Intervac U.S., International & USA Home Exchange, PO Box 590504, San Francisco, CA 94159 (415-435-3497 or 800-756-HOME/4663; fax 415-435-7440; e-mail IntervacUS@aol.com). Part of a worldwide home-exchange network. Publishes four catalogs per year, containing more than 9000 homes in 34 countries on 6 continents. Members contact one another directly. $70 will get you three of the company's catalogs and inclusion of your own listing in one.

The Invented City: International Home Exchange, 41 Sutter St.-Suite 1090, San Francisco, CA 94104 (800-788-CITY/2489 in US or 415-252-114; fax 415-252-1171; e-mail invented@aol.com). Listing of 1700 homes worldwide. For $50, you get your offer listed in one and receive three catalogs. It works via a simple swap; details are worked out between members.

Homestay/USA, 25 Bay State Rd., Boston, MA 02215 (East Coast office: 800-662-2967 or 617-247-0350, fax 247-2967; West Coast Office: 800-858-0292 or 415-288-1380, fax 288-1381). World Learning's Homestay/USA arranges homestays with U.S. families for both groups and individuals for all times of the year. The East Coast office handles placements in the Northeast and Southeast United States while the West Coast office handles other regions.

▓ Camping and the Outdoors

USEFUL PUBLICATIONS

A variety of publishing companies offer hiking, biking, and camping guidebooks to meet the educational needs of novice or expert. For information about camping, hiking, and biking, write or call the publishers listed below to receive a free catalog.

Family Campers and RVers/National Campers and Hikers Association, Inc., 4804 Transit Rd., Bldg. #2, Depew, NY 14043 (716-668-6242); fax same). This all volunteer conservation group publishes *Camping Today,* which comes with the $20 membership fee.

Sierra Club Bookstore, 85 2nd St. 2nd Fl., San Francisco, CA 94109 (415-977-5600 or 800-935-1056; fax 923-5500). Books on many national parks, several series on different regions of the U.S., as well as *Learning to Rock Climb* ($14), *The Sierra Club Family Outdoors Guide* ($12) and *Wildwater* ($12).

The Mountaineers Books, 1001 SW Klickitat Way, Ste. 201, Seattle, WA 98134 (800-553-4453 or 206-223-6303; fax 223-6306; http://mbooks@mountaineers.org). Many titles on hiking (the *100 Hikes* series), biking, mountaineering, natural history, and conservation.

Wilderness Press, 2440 Bancroft Way, Berkeley, CA 94704-1676 (800-443-7227 or 510-843-8080; fax 548-1355). Publishes over 100 hiking guides and maps for the western U.S. including *Backpacking Basics* ($11, including postage), and *Backpacking with Babies and Small Children* ($11).

REI, P.O. Box 1700, Sumner, WA 98352–0001 (800-426-4840), publishes *European Camping and Caravanning* ($20), an annually updated catalog of European campsites, and *The U.S. Outdoor Atlas* ($17), a similar book for the U.S. Few of their books are offered via mail-order, so check their retail stores.

Woodall Publications Corporation, P.O. Box 5000, 13975 W. Polo Trail Dr., Lake Forest, IL 60045 (800-323-9076 or 847-362-6700; fax 362-8776). Covering the U.S., Mexico, and Canada, Woodall publishes the ever-popular and annually updated *Woodall's Campground Directory* ($20) and *Woodall's Plan-it, Pack-it, Go!: Great Places to Tent, Fun Things To Do* ($13) which are generally available in American bookstores.

Go Camping America Committee, (800-47-SUNNY/78669). Ask for a free catalog of RV camping publications and state campground associations.

For topographical maps of the U.S., write the **U.S. Geological Survey,** Branch of Information Services, P.O. Box 25286, DFC, Denver, CO 80225 (800-435-7627; fax

303-202-4693); or the **Canada Map Office,** 130 Bentley Ave., Ottawa Ont., K1A 0E9 (613-952-7000; fax 613-957-8861), which distributes geographical, historical, and topographical maps as well as aeronautical charts. All maps are less than $15.

NATIONAL PARKS

National parks protect some of America and Canada's most spectacular scenery. Alaska's crowning Denali (Mt. McKinley), Oregon's stone-still Crater Lake, and Alberta's Banff and Jasper are treasures that will remain intact for generations. Though their primary purpose is preservation, the parks also make room for recreational activities such as ranger talks, guided hikes, skiing, and snowshoe expeditions. Most national parks have backcountry camping and developed tent camping; others welcome RVs, and a few offer opulent living in grand lodges. A mixed blessing, internal road systems allow you to reach the interior and major sights even if you are not a long-distance hiker.

Entry fees vary from park to park. Pedestrian and cyclist entry fees tend to range from $2-4, while vehicles go from $4-10. Most national parks offer discounts such as the annual **Golden Eagle Passport** ($25), which allows the bearer and family free entry into all parks. Visitors ages 62 and over qualify for the **Golden Age Passport,** ($10), entitling them to free entry and a 50% discount on basic fees like camping. Ask for details at the entrance station of parks. The **Golden Access Passport** offers free access to travelers with disabilities. Visitors centers at parks offer excellent free pamphlets and information, and the U.S. Government Printing Office publishes *National Parks: Lesser-Known Areas* ($1.75).

The Western Canadian equivalent to the Golden Eagle Passport is the **Great Western Pass.** The pass costs CDN$35, can be purchased at any Canadian National Park in western Canada, and covers entrance fees for a year. A Park permit is $5 per day, $10 if there are two or more people in a vehicle. The annual fee is $35. Parks also require backcountry camping permits ($6 per person per night, $35 per person per year), available at a Parks office. Fines are steep if you don't have a permit, so be wary. Write for information on camping and recreational opportunities:

Washington: Forest Service/National Park Service, Outdoor Recreation Information Center, 915 2nd Ave. #442, Seattle, WA 98174 (206-220-7450).

Oregon: Nature of the Northwest, 800 NE Oregon St., Room 177, Portland, OR 97232 (503-872-2750) for a list of national campgrounds in Oregon and Washington.

Alberta and **British Columbia:** Parks Canada, 220 4th Ave. SE, #552, Calgary, AB T2G 4X3 (800-748-7275 or 403-292-4401).

Alaska: Alaska Public Lands Information Center, 605 W. 4th Ave. Suite 105, Anchorage, AK 99501 (907-271-2737; fax 907-271-2744). The National Parks Main Headquarters number is 202-208-4747.

STATE AND PROVINCIAL PARKS

In contrast to national parks, the primary function of **state and provincial parks** is recreation. Prices for camping at public sites are almost always better than those at private campgrounds. Don't let swarming visitors dissuade you from seeing the large parks—these places are huge, and even at their most crowded they offer many opportunities for quiet and solitude. Reservations are absolutely essential at the more popular parks in the Pacific Northwest; make them through **DESTINET** (800-388-2733, outside the U.S. 619-452-8787). While DESTINET handles park reservations, the number for National Forest campgrounds reservations is 800-280-2267. In the U.S. contact the State Division of Parks for information and brochures; find their addresses and phone numbers listed in the states' **Practical Information** sections. Most campgrounds are strictly first-come, first-camped. Arrive early: many campgrounds, public and private, fill up by late morning. Some limit your stay and/or the number of people in a group.

NATIONAL FORESTS

If the national parks are too developed for your tastes, **national forests** provide a purist's alternative. While some have recreation facilities, most are equipped only for primitive camping—pit toilets and no running water are the rule. Fees range from $10-20. Forests are well marked and accessible, but can often get crowded, especially in the summertime. Backpackers can take advantage of specially designated **wilderness areas,** which are even less accessible due to regulations barring all vehicles. **Wilderness permits,** required for backcountry hiking, can usually be obtained (generally free to enter, but occasionally a reservation fee) at parks; check ahead. Adventurers who plan to explore some real wilderness should always check in at a USDA Forest Service (202-205-1706) field office before heading out. Write ahead to **USDA Forest Service,** PAO 2 Central, P.O. Box 96090, Washington, DC 20090-6090, for maps and the free *Guide to Your National Forests*. Try regional offices as they are more helpful and less busy than the central office.

The USDA Forest Service oversees more than 200 scenic and well-maintained wilderness **log cabins** for public use, scattered throughout the southern and central regions of Alaska. User permits are required along with a fee of $25 per party (of any size) per night. Reservations are usually necessary several months in advance. Most cabins have seven-day use limits (hike-in cabins have a three day limit May-Aug.) and are usually accessible only by air, boat, or hiking trail. For general information, contact the Forest Service's regional office in the **Pacific Northwest** (503-326-5640) or **Alaska** (907-586-8751). The **U.S. Fish and Wildlife Service,** 1011 E. Tudor Rd., Anchorage 99503 (907-786-3487), maintains numerous campgrounds within the National Wildlife Refuges of the Alaska, including the **Kenai National Wildlife Refuge** (907-262-7021; 15 campgrounds with sites from $6-10; max. stay of either 3 or 14 days depending on the campground). Any remaining questions that you have can probably be answered by the **Alaska Public Lands Information Center** (907-271-2737), which also mails out maps, brochures, and other information.

The U.S. Department of the Interior's **Bureau of Land Management (BLM),** Public Affairs, Rm. 5600, 1849 C St. NW, Washington DC, 20240 (202-209-3100 at Department of the Interior; 202-208-5717 fax at BLM), offers a wide variety of outdoor recreation opportunities—including camping, hiking, mountain biking, rock climbing, river rafting, and wildlife viewing—on the 270 million acres it oversees in ten western states and Alaska. These lands also contain hundreds of archaeological artifacts and historic sites like ghost towns. The BLM's many **campgrounds** include 20 sprinkled throughout Alaska, all free (except for the Delta BLM campground on the Alaska Hwy).

CAMPING AND HIKING EQUIPMENT

If you purchase **equipment** before you leave, you'll know exactly what you have and how much it weighs. Whether buying or renting, taking the time to find sturdy, light, and inexpensive equipment is a must. Peruse catalogs and talk to knowledgeable salespeople. Mail-order firms are, for the most part, reputable and cheap—order from them if you can't do as well locally.

Sleeping bags: At the core of your equipment is the **sleeping bag.** What kind you should buy depends on the time of year you plan to use it. Most of the better sleeping bags are rated according to the lowest outdoor temperature at which they will still keep you warm. Bags are sometimes rated by season rather than temperature: keep in mind that "summer" translates to a rating of 30-40°F, "three-season" means 20°F, and "four-season" or "winter" means below 0°F. Sleeping bags are made either of down (warmer and lighter, but miserable when wet) or of synthetic material (cheaper, heavier, more durable, and useful even when wet).

Pads: If you're using a sleeping bag for serious camping, you should also have either a foam pad or an air mattress for comfort and to insulate you from the ground. An excellent alternative is a **Therm-A-Rest,** an air-mattress which inflates when you unroll it.

Tents: The best tents are free-standing, with their own frames and suspension systems; they set up quickly and require no staking, though staking will keep your tent from blowing away. Low profile dome tents are the best all-around. When pitched their internal space is almost entirely usable, which means little unnecessary bulk. If you're traveling by car, go for the bigger tent; if you're hiking, stick with a smaller tent that weighs no more than 3.5 lbs. For especially small and light-weight models, contact **Sierra Design,** which sells the "Clip Flashlight," a two-person tent that weighs less than 1.4kg (3 lbs.). Be sure your tent has a rain fly and remember to seal the seams of your tent with waterproofer.

Backpacks: If you intend to do a lot of hiking, you should have a **frame backpack.** Buy a backpack with an internal frame if you'll be hiking on difficult trails that require a lot of bending and maneuvering—internal-frame packs mold better to your back, keep a lower center of gravity, and can flex adequately to follow you through a variety of movements. In addition, internal frame packs are more manageable on crowded planes, trains, and automobiles, and are less likely to be mangled by rough handling. Make sure your pack has a strong, padded hip belt. Any serious backpacking requires at least 4000 cu. inches, while longer trips require around 5000. This is one area where it doesn't pay to economize—cheaper packs may be less comfortable, and the straps are more likely to fray or rip quickly. Test-drive a backpack for comfort before you buy it: walk around with it on, imagine walking a few miles up a rocky incline with a full pack. For more information, see **The Backpack** (p. 19).

Other: Rain gear should come in two pieces, a top and pants, rather than a poncho. Ponchos turns into sails when the wind kicks up. **Synthetics** are of the essence in any climate: polypropylene tops, socks, and long underwear, along with a pile jacket, will keep you warm when wet. When camping in autumn, winter, or spring, bring along a **"space blanket"** for emergencies, a technological wonder that helps you to retain your body heat ($3.50-13; doubles as a ground-cloth) but don't expect it to do the work of several good wool sweaters. Don't go anywhere without a **canteen** or water bottle. Plastic models keep water cooler in the hot sun than metal ones do, and are virtually shatter- and leak-proof. Large, collapsible **water jugs** will significantly improve your lot in primitive campgrounds and weigh practically nothing when empty, though they can get bulky. Bring **water-purification tablets** for when you can't boil water. Though most campgrounds provide campfire sites, you may want to bring a small **metal grate** or **grill** of your own. For those places that forbid fires or the gathering of firewood, you'll need a **camp stove** (Coleman, the classic, starts at about $30). Consider GAZ-powered stoves, which come with bottled propane gas that is easy to use and widely available in Europe. Make sure you have **waterproof matches,** or your stove may do you no good; it's always a good idea to have a lighter on hand. A **camp knife, insect repellent,** and **calamine lotion** are also essential camping items. Last but not least, **always** have a warm hat that covers your ears. Other necessities include: **battery-operated lantern** (gas is inconvenient and dangerous), **plastic groundcloth** for the floor of your tent, **nylon tarp** for general purposes, **waterproof backpack cover** (although you can forego the cover by storing your belongings in plastic bags inside your backpack), **"stuff sack"** or plastic bag to keep your sleeping bag dry. Finally, a First Aid kit is essential!

WHERE TO GET IT

Shop around locally before turning to mail-order firms; this allows you to get an idea of what the different items actually look like (and weigh), so that you know what to expect if you order by mail. The mail-order firms listed below offer lower prices than those you're likely to find in stores, and they can also help you determine which item you need.

Campmor, P.O. Box 700, Saddle River, NJ 07458-0700 (800-526-4784; http://www.campmor.com). Has a wide selection of name brand equipment at low prices. One year guarantee for unused or defective merchandise.

Recreational Equipment, Inc. (REI), 1700 45th St. E, Sumner, WA 98390 (800-426-4840; http://www.rei.com). Stocks a wide range of the latest in camping gear and holds great seasonal sales. Many items guaranteed for life (excluding normal wear and tear).

L.L. Bean, Freeport, ME 04033-0001 (Customer service 800-341-4341; U.S. orders 800-221-4221, Canadian and International, 207-552-6878; U.S. fax 207-552-3080, Canadian and International fax 207-552-4080). Monolithic equipment and outdoor clothing supplier favored by northeastern Americans; high quality and chock-full of information. Call or write for their free catalog. The customer is guaranteed 100% satisfaction on all purchases; if it doesn't meet your expectations, they'll replace or refund it. Open 24hrs per day, 365 days per year.

Sierra Design, 1255 Powell St., Emeryville, CA 94608 (510-450-9555; fax 510-654-0705) has a wide array of especially small and lightweight tent models. You can often find last year's version for half the price.

Sierra Trading Post, 5025 Campstool Rd., Cheyenne WY 82007-1802 (307-775-8000; fax 307-775-8088). Savings on name brand outdoor clothing and equipment. Mail order and two locations in Cheyenne and Reno, NV.

WILDERNESS CONCERNS

The three most important things to remember when hiking or camping are **stay warm, stay dry,** and **stay hydrated.** The vast majority of life-threatening wilderness problems stem from a failure to follow this advice. If you are going on any hike, over-night or just a day hike, you should pack enough equipment to keep you alive should disaster occur. This includes rain gear and warm layers (not cotton!). You should never be forced to rely on cotton for warmth. This "death cloth" will be absolutely useless should it get wet. Instead wear synthetic materials designed for the outdoors, or wool. Pile fleece jackets and Gore-Tex® rain gear are excellent choices (see **Camping and Hiking Equipment,** p. 45) especially hat and mittens, a first-aid kit, high energy food, and water. *All of these items are vital.*

Be sure to wear hiking boots with good ankle support appropriate for the terrain you are hiking. Twisted or sprained ankles can be very serious, and could keep you from walking for hours or days. Be sure that the boots are broken in. A bad blister will ruin your hike. If you feel a "hot-spot," treat it with moleskin immediately.

Always check weather forecasts and pay attention to the skies when hiking. A bright blue sky can turn to rain—or even snow—before you can say "hypothermia." If on a day hike and weather turns nasty, turn back. If on an overnight, start looking immediately for shelter. The most important thing about camping safely no matter where you are is to protect yourself from the environment. This means having a proper tent with rain-fly, warm sleeping bag, and proper clothing (see **Camping and Hiking Equipment,** p. 45). Another major concern is safe water. Many rivers and lakes are contaminated with *giardia* (see **Common Ailments,** p. 14). To protect yourself from this invisible trip-wrecker, bring your water to a rolling boil for at least five minutes, or purify it with iodine tablets. A portable water purification system also works well and though you'll find it a little bit more expensive than a fire, you'll save valuable cooking fuel by not using your stove. A good guide to outdoor survival is *How to Stay Alive in the Woods,* by Bradford Angier (Macmillan, $8). For information about basic medical concerns and first-aid, see **Health,** p. 14. If possible you should let someone know that you are going hiking, either a friend, your hostel, a park ranger, or some local hiking organization. Above all, do not attempt a hike beyond your ability—you will be endangering your life.

For the sake of those who follow you, try to practise **"minimum impact camping"** techniques. This essentially means leaving no trace of your presence when you leave a site. Don't unnecessarily trample vegetation by walking off established paths. Some rules to remember: make small fires using only dead branches or brush; using a camp-stove is the more cautious and efficient way to cook. Don't cut vegetation, and don't

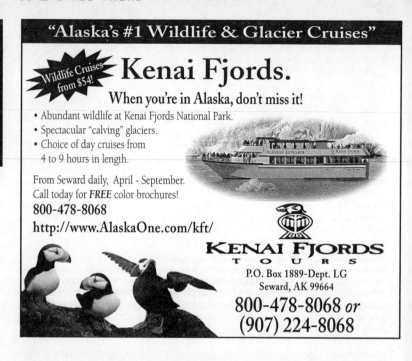
clear new campsites. Make sure your campsite is at least 150 feet from water supplies or bodies of water. If there are no toilet facilities, bury human waste at least four inches deep and 150 feet or more from any water supplies and campsites. Always pack your trash in a plastic bag and carry it with you until you reach the next trash can.

BEAR IN MIND

The aggressiveness of bears varies from region to region. Rangers and other local authorities will always be your best resource for learning the details of bear behavior (and how best to deal with it) in a particular region. Ask local rangers for information before entering any park or wilderness area. The one rule that stands for any area: no matter how tame a bear appears, don't be fooled—they're dangerous and unpredictable animals. If you're close enough for a bear to be observing you, you're too close. To avoid a grizzly experience, *never feed a bear* or tempt it with such delicacies as open trash cans; contact with food can make them hungry for more and you may end up as dessert. What's more, your action could force the rangers to put to death a previously harmless animal. Keep your camp clean, and don't cook near where you sleep. Do not leave trash or food lying around camp. If you're near a beach, it's a good idea to eat in a tidal zone so that traces of food can be washed away at high tide. The best way to keep your toothpaste from becoming a condiment is to **bear-bag.** This amounts to hanging your edibles from a tree, out of reach of hungry paws. This is a challenging technique, ask a salesperson at a wilderness store or a park ranger to show you how.

Avoid greasy foods, especially bacon and ham. Grease gets on everything, including your clothes and sleeping bag, and bears find it an alluring dressing for whatever or whomever is wearing it. Bears are attracted to perfume smells; do without cologne, scented soap, and hairspray while camping, and be sure to bear-bag any odorous items you do bring. Park rangers can tell you how to identify bear trails. Don't camp on them.

Wear bells or sing loudly when wandering through areas populated by bears, and shine a flashlight when walking at night; bears will avoid you if given sufficient warning. If you stumble upon a sweet-looking bear cub, leave immediately, lest its overprotective mother stumble upon you. And stay away from dead animals and berry bushes—these are *le menu* for bears.

Given the amount of popular wisdom on the subject, it might seem that there are more ways to fend off a bear attack than there are to brush your teeth. If you see a bear at a distance, calmly walk (don't run) in the other direction. If it seems interested, some old hands recommend waving your arms or a long stick above your head and talking loudly; the bear's dull vision gives it the impression that you're much taller than a person, and it may (if you're lucky) decide that *you* are threatening to *it* and flee. A bear standing on its hind legs is not necessarily going to attack; growling is a more reliable danger sign. If you're charged, some recommend trying to stand your ground. If the bear attacks, assuming the fetal position with your hands clasped behind your neck may provide some protection. Always ask rangers for info and advice before camping and hiking in bear country, and obey any posted warnings.

ORGANIZED ADVENTURE

Begin by consulting tourism bureaus, which can suggest parks, trails, and outfitters as well as answer more general questions. **Outside Magazine,** Outside Plaza, 400 Market St., Santa Fe, NM 87501 (505-989-7100; fax 505-989-4700; http://www.outside.starwave.com), provides listings of organized outdoor events and publishes an Active Travel directory in each issue. **Sierra Club Outings,** 85 Second St., San Francisco, CA 94105 (415-977-5630; fax 415-977-5745; e-mail national.outings@sierraclub.org; http://www.sierraclub.org/outings), plans over 350 outings throughout North America. Activities include backpacking, cross-country skiing, rafting, family trips, bike tours, service trips, and more. Outings are also available through the local Sierra Club chapters, located throughout the U.S. and Canada. **TrekAmerica,** P.O. Box 189, Rockaway, NJ 07886 (800-221-0596; fax 201-983-8551; e-mail treka-mnj@ix.netcom.com; http://www.trekamerica.com) organizes small group adventure camping tours for ages 18-38; activities include hiking, biking, horseback riding, canoeing, kayaking, and rafting. Trips range from seven days to nine weeks. **Footloose,** an outfit run by TrekAmerica, plans adventure tours in small international groups for all ages and levels of hiking experience; trips can go from seven days to three weeks throughout the U.S. and Canada. **Alaska Wilderness Journeys,** P.O. Box 220204, Anchorage, AK 99522 (800-349-0064, fax 907-344-6877, e-mail akwildj@alaska.net) organizes up to 10-day combination and trekking tours through Alaska as well as Africa, Australia, and the Russian Far East.

OUTDOOR SPORTS

Water Sports

The latticework of fast-flowing rivers in the Pacific Northwest is ideal for canoeing, kayaking, and whitewater rafting. Boating opportunities are suggested in the Activities sections throughout the book. Travel agents and tourism bureaus can recommend others.

The **River Travel Center,** P.O. Box 6, Pt. Arena, CA 95468 (800-882-RAFT/7238; fax 707-882-2638), can place you in a whitewater raft, kayak, or sea kayak with one of over 100 outfitters. Trips range in length from one to 18 days and range in price from $80 (one day) to $2000 (extended). **Sierra Club Books** publishes a kayaking and whitewater rafting guide entitled *Wildwater* ($12). The club offers kayaking trips to the Pacific Northwest and Alaska every year. *Washington Whitewater* ($18.95) and *Canoe Routes: Northwest Oregon* ($12.95), published by The Mountaineers Books, might also interest you.

Snow Sports

Tourism bureaus can help you locate the best sports outfitters and ski areas. *Let's Go* suggests options in the Activities sections throughout the book. For Oregon and Washington skiing guides and information (both downhill and cross-country), write the **Pacific Northwest Ski Areas Association,** P.O. Box 2325 Seattle, WA 98111-2325 (206-623-3777; fax 447-5897). The Sierra Club publishes *The Best Ski Touring in America* ($10.95), which also includes British Columbia and Quebec.

Pay attention to cold weather safety concerns. Know the symptoms of hypothermia and frostbite, and bring along warm clothes and quick energy snacks like candy bars and trail mix (see **Common Ailments,** p. 14). Drinking alcohol in the cold can be dangerous: even though you *feel* warm, alcohol can slow your body's ability to adjust to the temperature, and thus make you more vulnerable to hypothermia.

Fishing

Should you wish to take advantage of the regions' well-stocked lakes and streams, contact the appropriate department of fisheries for brochures that summarize regulations and make sport fishing predictions. Some fishing seasons are extremely short, so be sure to ask when the expected prime angling dates occur. Licenses are available from many tackle shops, or you can purchase them directly from the state or provincial department of fisheries. Consult the appropriate departments of game to purchase licenses and receive regulations pamphlets.

Alaska: Department of Fish and Game: Licensing Section, P.O. Box 25525, Juneau, AK 99802-5525 (907-465-2376; fax 465-2440; open Mon.-Fri. 8:30am-5pm). Nonresident fishing license $10 for 1 day, 1 day "salmon sticker" additional $10, $15 for 3 days, 3 day "salmon sticker" additional $15, $30 for 14 days, $50 for a year.

Alberta: Natural Resources Service, Licensing and Vendor Services, 9945 108th St., Edmonton, AB T5K 2G6 (403-427-6729; fax 422-9558; http: www.gov.ab.ca/dept/env.html). Nonresident fishing license CDN$18 for Canadians, CDN$36 for non-Canadians. CDN$24 limited 5-day fishing license for non-Canadians.

British Columbia: Fish and Wildlife Information, Ministry of Environment, 780 Blanshard St., Victoria, BC V8V 1X4 (604-387-9739). Non-Canadian angling license CDN$25 for 8 days, CDN$40 for 1 year, CDN$20 for steelhead tags.

Oregon: Department of Fish and Wildlife, 2501 SW 1st Ave., P.O. Box 59, Portland, OR 97207 (503-872-5275). Nonresident 1-year fishing license $40.50, plus tags for salmon ($10.50), sturgeon ($6), and halibut ($6). One-day license covers all tags ($6.75; also 2, 3, 7 day licenses).

Washington: Department of Fish and Wildlife, 600 Capitol Way, Olympia, WA 98501-1091 (360-902-2200). Nonresident game fishing license, good for 1 year, under age 14 $20, over 14 $48. Nonresident Personal Use Food Fish License $20. Nonresident Shellfish/Seaweed License $20.

Yukon Government, Department of Renewable Resources, Fish and Wildlife Branch, 10 Burns Rd., P.O. Box 2703, Whitehorse, YT Y1A 2C6 (403-667-5221). Non-Canadian license CDN$5 for 1 day, CDN$20 for 6 days, CDN$35 for 1 year.

Hunting

Regulations on hunting in Alaska and the Pacific Northwest are extensive. Certain animals may not be hunted, and others require special trapping licenses and permits. Since rules are often specific to a region, your best bet may be to start with an organization like the **Alaska Public Lands Information Center,** 605 W. 4th Ave. #105, Anchorage AK 99501 (907-271-2737; fax 271-2744). In the state of Alaska, all nonresident hunters must have a license. Residents take precedence over nonresidents in the event of a game shortage—that is, nonresidents will be eliminated or restricted first when there isn't enough game to allow everyone to hunt. Since many regulations are not simple common-sense rules, and since (in the words of the State of Alaska) "ignorance is no excuse," would-be hunters should take a look at state hunting regulations before they pick up a gun.

■ Keeping in Touch

MAIL

U.S. Mail Individual offices of the **U.S. Postal Service** are usually open Monday to Friday from 9am to 5pm and sometimes on Saturday until about noon; branches in many larger cities open earlier and close later. All are closed on national holidays. **Postcards** mailed within the U.S. cost 20¢; letters cost 32¢ for the first ounce and 23¢ for each additional ounce. To send mail to Canada from the U.S., it costs 40¢ to mail a postcard, 52¢ to mail a letter for the first ounce, 72¢ for two ounces, 95¢ for three ounces, and 19¢ for each additional ounce. It costs 35¢ to mail a postcard to Mexico; a letter is 46¢ for an ounce, 86¢ for two ounces, and 40¢ for each additional ounce up to 12 ounces. The U.S. Postal Service now requires that **overseas** letters be mailed directly from the post office and accompanied by a customs form. **Overseas rates:** postcards 50¢, ½oz. 60¢, 1oz. $1, 40¢ per additional ounce. **Aerogrammes,** sheets that fold into envelopes and travel via air mail, are available at post offices for 50¢. Domestic mail generally takes 3-5 days; overseas mail, 7-14 days. Write **"AIR MAIL"** on the front of the envelope for speediest delivery.

The U.S. is divided into postal zones, each with a five-digit **ZIP code** particular to a region, city, or part of a city. Some addresses have nine-digit ZIP codes, used primarily to speed up delivery for business mailings. Writing the ZIP code on letters is essential for delivery. The normal form of address is as follows:

Jonathan Edwards
Fire 'N Brimstone Inc. (title and/or name or organization, optional)
123 4th Avenue, Apt.#456 (address, apartment #)
New York, New York 10021 (city, state, zip code)
USA (country, if mailing internationally)

Canadian Mail In **Canada** mailing a letter (or a postcard, which carries the same rate as a letter) to the U.S. costs CDN$0.52 for the first 30 grams and CDN$.77 for 31-50 grams. To every other foreign country, a 20-gram letter costs CDN$0.90, a 50-gram letter CDN$1.37, and a 51- to 100-gram letter CDN$2.25. The domestic rate is CDN$0.45 for a 30-gram letter, and CDN$0.71 for a letter between 31 and 50 grams. Aerogrammes cost CDN$0.90. Letters take from seven to ten days to reach the U.S. and about two weeks to get to an overseas address by air. Canada Post's most reliable and pricey service is **Priority Courier,** which offers speedy delivery (usually next-day) to major American cities (CDN$23.50 for a document). Delivery to overseas locations usually takes two days; to Europe CDN$35.50 for a document; to the Pacific CDN$40; International CDN$69. Guaranteed next-day domestic delivery exists between any two Canadian cities and starts at CDN$8.70 plus tax; cost varies depending on location.

In Canada, **postal codes** are the equivalent of U.S. ZIP codes and contain letters as well as numbers (for example, H4P 1B8). The normal form of address is nearly identical to that in the U.S.; the only difference is that the apartment or suite number can *precede* the street address along with a dash. For example, 23-40 Sherbrooke St. refers to Room #23 at 40 Sherbrooke St.

General Delivery and Other Services Depending on how neurotic your family is, consider making arrangements for them to get in touch with you. Mail can be sent **General Delivery** to a city's main branch of the post office. Once a letter arrives it will be held for at least 10 days; it can be held for longer if such a request is clearly indicated by you or on the front of the envelope. Customers should bring a passport or other ID to pick up General Delivery mail. Family and friends can send letters to you labeled like this:

Mr. Gus "Zippy" <u>Van Sant</u> (underline last name for accurate filing)
c/o General Delivery
Main Post Office
Seattle, WA 98101

American Express offices throughout the U.S. and Canada will act as a mail service for cardholders if you contact them in advance. Under this free **"Client Letter Service,"** they will hold mail for 30 days, forward upon request, and accept telegrams. The last name of the person to whom the mail is addressed should be capitalized and underlined. Some offices will offer these services to non-cardholders (especially those who have purchased AmEx Travellers' Cheques), but you must call ahead to make sure. For "Traveler's Companion," a free list of offices and instructions on how to use the service, call 800-528-4800.

Other alternatives include a variety of private mail services. **DHL** (800-225-5345 in USA and Canada) will send mail to almost anywhere in Western Europe in two to three days for approximately $30. **Federal Express** (800-463-3339 in USA and Canada) will send mail express to Western Europe in two business days, also for about $30; other destinations are more variable.

TELEPHONES

Most of the information you will need about telephone usage—including area codes for the U.S., foreign country codes, and rates—is in the front of the local **white pages** telephone directory. The **yellow pages,** published at the end of the white pages or in a separate book, lists the numbers of businesses and other services alphabetically by the service or merchandise they provide. Federal, state, and local government listings are provided in the **blue pages** at the back of the directory. To obtain local phone numbers or area codes of other cities, call **directory assistance** at 411. Dialing "0" will get you the **operator,** who can assist you in reaching a phone number and provide you with general information. You can reach local directory assistance and the operator free from any pay phone. For long-distance directory, dial 1-(area code)-555-1212. All area codes are listed at the end of the **Practical Information** for a section.

Country codes are as follows for English-speaking countries: the **United Kingdom** (44 1); **Ireland** (353); **Australia** (61); **New Zealand** (64); **South Africa** (27). Country codes and city codes may sometimes be listed with a zero in front (e.g. 033), but when using the international dialing code, required to place a call outside of the U.S. (011), drop successive zeros (e.g. 011-33). In some areas you will have to give the operator the number and he or she will place the call.

You may want to consider getting a **calling card** if you plan to make a lot of international calls. The calls (plus a small surcharge) are billed either collect or to a calling card. Some companies will be able to connect you to numbers only in your home country; others will be able to provide other worldwide connections. For more information, call AT&T about its **AT&T Direct** services (800-331-1140, from abroad 412-553-7458), **Sprint** (800-877-4646), or **MCI WorldPhone** and **World Reach** (800-996-7535). MCI's WorldPhone also provides access to MCI's Traveler's Assist, which gives legal and medical advice, exchange rate information, and translation services. For similar services for countries outside the U.S., contact your local phone company. In Canada, contact Bell Canada **Canada Direct** (800-565-4708); in the U.K., British Telecom **BT Direct** (800 34 51 44); in Ireland, Telecom Éireann **Ireland Direct** (800 250 250); in Australia, Telstra **Australia Direct** (13 22 00); in New Zealand, **Telecom New Zealand** (123); and in South Africa, **Telkom South Africa** (09 03).

Phone rates tend to be highest in the morning, lower in the evening, and lowest on Sunday and late at night. Also, remember **time differences** when you call. See **Appendix** for time zones in Alaska and the Pacific Northwest. Toll free U.S. numbers (those that begin with 800) do not work from Canada.

Let's Go Picks

We started our journey in Seattle, sipping coffee and tripping off to the San Juan Islands. From there, we ranged far and wide, from the Redwood forests of Northern California to the mighty glaciers of the Kenai Fjords. The following is a whirlwind tour of our favorites. Remember, this is just the tip of the iceberg.

Best Hiking: Anaktuvuk Pass, YT had truly indescribable tundra hiking. If you're ever in the neighborhood—which you probably won't be—it's an experience like no other (p. 175); we discovered that the **Granite Creek Trail, Juneau, AK** (p. 158) had an exceptional view in a town with nothing but exceptional trails. The **AB Mountain/ Skyline Trail, Skagway, AK** was a brutal climb, and we almost killed ourselves getting there, but at least we would have died happy (p. 169). The hike up to and around **Crater Lake** was almost as stunning as the lake itself (p. 490). Of course, none of us can deny the appeal of standbys like **Mt. St. Helens** in Washington (p. 377), and **Denali** (p. 107), and **Wrangell-St. Elias** in Alaska (p. 103).

Best Museums: We leapt with the collared lizards and made like a simulated desert habitat in the **High Desert Museum** near Bend, OR (p. 496); we felt like pieces of parsley stuck in the teeth of human history next to the massive sculptures which grace the halls of the **Museum of Anthropology** at UBC in Victoria, BC (p. 208); we had a healthy dose of modern North American "culchah," and some African coffin-maker's masterpieces thrown in, at the **Seattle Art Museum** (p. 325); we visited the creative refuges of the biggest, baddest, and only literary talents to come out of the far North—the **Jack London** and **Robert Service** cabins in Dawson City, YT (p. 272); finally, we still thirsted for a decent First Nations exhibit and some BC history, so we went back to the **Royal British Columbia Museum** in Victoria, BC (p. 208).

Best Way to Cut Loose: When hiking and camping got mundane, we took the leap and went **bungee jumping** in Nanaimo, BC (p. 210); tore it up on **dune buggies** in Reedsport, OR (p. 451); chartered a plane in Talkeetna, AK and went on the **flightseeing** tour of our lives over Denali National Park (p. 115); escaped on a romantic **horseback-riding** jaunt down the beach in Bandon, OR (p. 457); scooted up to Tenakee Springs, AK, to soothe our saddle-sore rumps in the natural **hot springs** (p. 151); and had a chat with the locals before taking a day trip to Metlakatla, AK so that we could ride the **float plane** (p. 137). On the seventh day we rested.

Best View: When the car's A/C broke down and we had to cool off in a hurry, we stopped at the **Eagle Quality Center** in Homer, AK. Imagine our surprise at discovering one of the best views in the state—from the parking lot (p. 83). Getting there was half the fun on the **Mt. Vestovia Trail** in Sitka, AK (p. 150). We ran out of words to describe our experience atop **Ballyhoo Mtn.,** Dutch Harbor, AK (p. 181), and found them again at **Volunteer Park** in Seattle, WA (p. 325). No sooner had we caught our breath then the view of the ocean from **Battle Rock** in Port Orford, OR (p. 422) promptly took it away.

Best Meat and Mead: And of course we had to eat. **El Erradero** in Baker City, OR, had the best Mexican food this side of the border (p. 506); the **Cow Bay Café** in Prince Rupert, BC (p. 243) was a creative restaurant in a completely unexpected place; the **Phnom Penh Noodle Soup House** in Seattle, WA held up our plans to journey to Southeast Asia (p. 323); we washed it all down with a glass of chocolate orange wine from the **Shallon Winery** in Astoria, OR (p. 435) and took off for **Klondike Kate's** in Dawson City, YT (p. 270) when we just wanted some cheap eats. After that, it was time to celebrate at the **Rose and Crown** in Banff, AB (p. 292); of course, when it was all over, we had to celebrate again on cheap drink night on **Electric Ave.** in Calgary, AB (p. 303).

ALASKA

Alaska's beauty and intrigue are born of extremes: North America's highest mountains and broadest flatlands; windswept tundra and lush rainforests; underwater salmon runs and overland caribou herds; virgin spruce forests in the southeast and oil pumps at the top of the world. Harsh weather and a ruthless landscape left the Interior untouched until the 19th century, and even today the state remains largely undeveloped. But the hand of humanity has left its mark: logging, overfishing, and oil drilling have stripped forests, emptied streams, and drawn a jagged pipeline across the belly of the tundra. In less than a century, the exploitation of natural resources brought Alaska to the brink of environmental collapse, and both the state and federal governments were forced to confront the devastating effects of the logging, fishing and oil industries. It remains to be seen whether Americans will step in to save their last great wilderness.

To the native Aleuts, who thrived for millennia on the rugged Aleutian islands, the spectacular and enormous expanses to the northeast were "Alyeska," or "the Great Land." To the Europeans and followers of "manifest destiny" who journeyed into the northwestern hinterlands, Alaska was the "Last Frontier." To summertime tourists, this region is the "Land of the Midnight Sun." Only to the ignorant is Alaska merely a "frozen wasteland." For half of the year, all but the northernmost reaches of the state explode in a riot of vegetation.

As geographically impressive as it may be, Alaska remains vulnerable to the whim of a temperamental Mother Nature. The Aleutian Islands, perched on the "Ring of Fire" at the edge of the Pacific Plate, are perpetually wracked by earthquakes and active volcanoes. In 1964, the Good Friday quake, centered in Miner's Lake (located between Whittier and Valdez), registered 9.2 on the modern Richter Scale and lasted eight terrible minutes. Its aftershocks continued for several days. Many coastal towns, including Kodiak and Whittier, were demolished by the tsunami which followed the earthquake; Valdez was completely destroyed and rebuilt on a new site.

Although the wounds of disaster linger, Alaska still entices nature lovers. Photographers find a wilderness teeming with caribou, bear, moose, Dall sheep, and wolves. Anglers are lured by millions of spawning salmon, huge off-shore halibut, and the trophy-sized grayling and trout that churn in countless interior lakes. With only one quarter of Alaska's land accessible by highway, hikers and campers can find unparalleled opportunities for a truly solitary wilderness experience. But you needn't be a hardcore outdoorsperson to see much of the state's beauty—even stunning glaciers can be reached by road.

Geography

Physically, Alaska truly is "The Great Land." The state contains 586,412 square miles, more than one-fifth of the land mass of the United States. The 33,000-mi. coastline stretches 11 times the distance from New York to San Francisco. Four major mountain ranges cross the state: the Wrangell Mountains, the Chugach Mountains, the Brooks Range, and the Denali-topped Alaska Range. Alaska is also home to Wrangell-St. Elias, the largest national park in America, which covers an area of 13 million acres, twice the size of Massachusetts. Nineteen Alaskan peaks reach over 14,000 ft., 94 lakes have a surface area of more than 10 sq. mi., and a glacial icefield larger than the state of Rhode Island.

On the archipelago of the **Southeastern Panhandle,** the isolated state capital of Juneau rests among numerous fjord-scarred islands, verdant rainforests, and sub-arctic swamps known as *muskeg.* **Southcentral Alaska** is the home of Kodiak Island, the Kenai Peninsula, Prince William Sound, and the Kodiak brown bear. The 20,320-ft.-tall Denali dominates the interminable flatlands of the **Interior,** the area north and east of Anchorage. The **Bush** encompasses the vast and empty areas north and west of the Interior, including the Brooks Range and the Arctic Circle, the Seward Peninsula, and all of western Alaska along the Bering Sea. The Alaska Peninsula and the storm-swept **Aleutian Islands** extend into the extreme southwestern reaches of the Bush, offering tenuous purchase to a handful of hardy humans.

Early and Native History

The first Alaskans arrived in the region 20,000 years ago, migrating over the Bering Land Bridge from Siberia to Alaska. Today, four distinct native groups inhabit Alaska. The Southeast is home to the Tlingit and Haida peoples, renowned for their exquisitely carved totem poles and the formidable wooden forts from which they almost staved off Russian invaders in the 19th century. The Interior and Southcentral regions harbor the once-nomadic Athabasca nation. The Aleutian Island Chain is populated largely by the Aleuts, who were enslaved by the Russians for their skill as fur trappers. The Inuit (commonly given the misnomer of "Eskimos" or "raw meat-eaters") reside almost exclusively within the Arctic Circle, and share a common language and heritage with the native Siberians across the Bering Strait.

Under orders from Peter the Great to find a route from the Arctic to the Pacific, Russian seafarers lead by Admiral Vitus Bering landed on Kayak Island off Prince William Sound in 1733. Bering's expedition brought the fur of sea otters back to Russia, and began an intense competition for control of the lucrative trade in this "soft gold." Russians based their colonization of the Alaskan wilderness in the southern coastal region, which even today retains an unmistakably Slavic imprint. By the mid-1800s, the once-bountiful supply of fur-bearing animals was nearly exhausted, and the Aleut population had diminished through forced labor. The Russians welcomed an American bid for the "dead land," and Alaska became the U.S.'s last frontier.

Statehood

The United States bought Alaska for $7,200,000, or about 2¢ per acre, on October 18, 1867. Critics mocked the purchase, popularly called "Seward's Folly" after the Secretary of State who negotiated the deal under President Johnson. At this time, Native Alaskans restated their claims to their ancestral lands. The issue went unresolved, and titles were held in abeyance for more than a century.

James Seward was vindicated a scant 15 years after the purchase, when large deposits of gold were unearthed in the Gastineau Channel. Juneau, the northern Eldorado, was born. As gold-panning prospectors exhausted deposits on the Gastineau, they found other rivers such as the Yukon, the Charley, the Fortymile, and the Klondike, and hundreds of millions of dollars in gold made their way to the continental U.S. But it wasn't until 1959 that Alaska became the 49th state, decades after the last major gold deposits were mined. Throughout the 1960s, native Alaskans watched with growing frustration as the federal and state governments divvied up vast tracts of land. The discovery in 1968 of huge oil deposits beneath the shore of the Beaufort Sea in the Arctic Ocean brought matters to a head. Natives increased the pressure for settlement of the claims which had been so long ignored and sought a share in the anticipated economic boom.

In December of 1971, the federal government finally made its peace with the native peoples, state and federal courts, and environmental groups by passing the Alaska Native Claims Settlement Act. Natives, who then numbered around 60,000, received a total of $1 billion and 40 million acres of land; unfortunately these riches did not come without a price. "No trespassing" signs have shot up all over, and native corporations have been compelled to sell off natural resources in exchange for the almighty dollar. Native-held land displays some of the state's ugliest logging scars, including the ragged moonscape of Prince of Wales Island.

Oil Comes to Alaska

In 1973, the Alyeska Pipeline Service Company received official permission to build a pipeline from Prudhoe Bay to Valdez—800 mi. through the heart of the Alaskan wilderness. This single pipeline has had a revolutionary effect on the state's political,

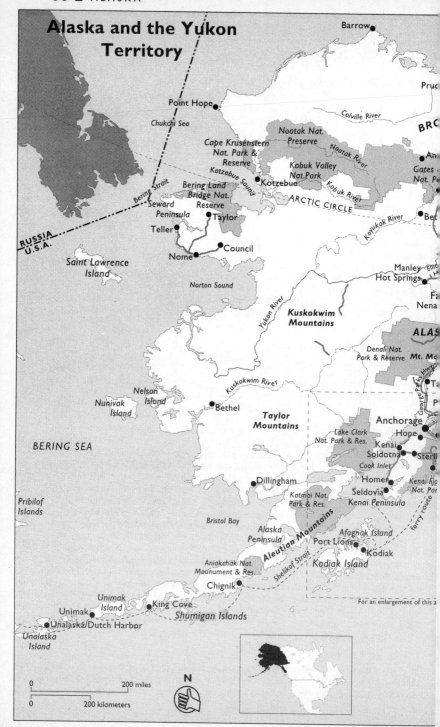

Alaska and the Yukon Territory

Barrow

Prus

Point Hope

Chukchi Sea

Colville River

BRO

Noatak Nat. Preserve

Noatak River

Ana

Cape Krusenstern Nat. Park & Reserve

Kobuk Valley Nat. Park

Gates Nat. Pe

Kotzebue Sound

Kotzebue

ARCTIC CIRCLE

Kobuk River

Bering Strait

Bering Land Bridge Nat. Reserve

Seward Peninsula

Taylor

Koyukak River

Bet

RUSSIA U.S.A.

Teller

Nome

Council

Saint Lawrence Island

Norton Sound

Manley Hot Springs

Eme

Fa

Nena

Yukon River

Kuskokwim Mountains

ALAS

Denali Nat. Park & Reserve

Mt. Mc

Ta

Nelson Island

Kuskokwim River

Bethel

Taylor Mountains

P

George Parks Hwy.

Nunivak Island

Anchorage

Hope

Lake Clark Nat. Park & Res.

Kenai

Soldotna

Sterli

BERING SEA

Cook Inlet

Dillingham

Homer

Seldovia

Kenai Fjo Nat. Par

Pribilof Islands

Katmai Nat. Park & Res.

Kenai Peninsula

Bristol Bay

Alaska Peninsula

Afognak Island

Port Lions

Kodiak

ferry route

Aniakchak Nat. Mounument & Res.

Shelikof Strait

Kodiak Island

Chignik

For an enlargement of this a

Unimak Island

King Cove

Unimak

Shumigan Islands

Unalaska/Dutch Harbor

Unalaska Island

0   200 miles

0   200 kilometers

N

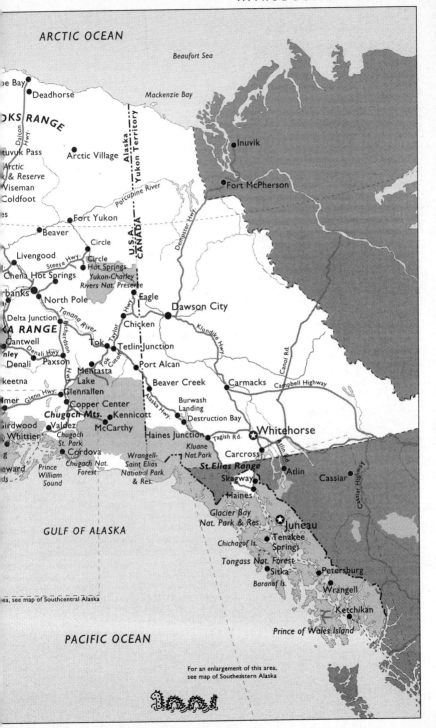

ARCTIC OCEAN

Beaufort Sea

Mackenzie Bay

e Bay

Deadhorse

OKS RANGE

Dalton Hwy.

tuvuk Pass

Arctic Village

Arctic
& Reserve

Viseman

Coldfoot

Inuvik

Alaska
Yukon Territory

Porcupine River

Fort McPherson

Fort Yukon

Beaver

Circle

U.S.A.
CANADA

Livengood

Steese Hwy.

Circle
Hot Springs

Chena Hot Springs

Yukon-Charley
Rivers Nat. Preserve

banks

North Pole

Eagle

Dawson City

Delta Junction

Tanana River

Chicken

KA RANGE

Cantwell

Richardson Hwy.

Tok

Taylor Hwy.

nley

Denali Hwy.

Paxson

Denali

Tok Cutoff

Tetlin Junction

Port Alcan

Klondike Hwy.

Canol Rd.

keetna

Mentasta
Lake

Beaver Creek

Carmacks

Campbell Highway

mer

Glenn Hwy.

Glennallen

Burwash
Landing

Chugach Mts.

Copper Center

Kennicott

Alaska Hwy.

Destruction Bay

irdwood

Valdez

McCarthy

Haines Junction

Tagish Rd.

Whitehorse

Whittier

Chugach
St. Park

Kluane
Nat.Park

Carcross

Cordova

Chugach Nat.

eward

Forest

Wrangell-
Saint Elias
National Park
& Res.

St. Elias Range

Atlin

Cassiar

ds

Prince
William
Sound

Skagway

Cassiar Highway

Haines

GULF OF ALASKA

Glacier Bay
Nat. Park & Res.

Juneau

Chichagof Is.

Tenakee
Springs

Tongass Nat. Forest

Sitka

Petersburg

Baranof Is.

Wrangell

ea, see map of Southcentral Alaska

Ketchikan

Prince of Wales Island

PACIFIC OCEAN

For an enlargement of this area,
see map of Southeastern Alaska

ALASKA

social, and economic landscape. By 1981, four years after the Trans-Alaska pipeline was installed, $7,200,000 worth of crude oil—the exact price Seward had paid for the state more than 100 years before—flowed from the Arctic oil field every 4½ hours. State revenues from oil taxation have created a trust fund in the name of the people of Alaska, and eliminated state sales and income tax.

In addition to jobs and wealth, the pipeline has brought pollution, overcrowding, profligate spending, and, in some cases, tragedy. Twenty-five years to the day after the Good Friday earthquake of 1964 leveled the port city of Valdez, the Exxon oil tanker *Valdez* ran aground on Bligh Reef, spilling over 250,000 barrels (11 million gallons) of syrupy crude into the blue waters of Prince William Sound and onto shores as far away as Kodiak Island, several hundred miles to the south. Thousands of marine mammals and birds succumbed to the thick black tide that swept the Sound. Clean-up crews were unprepared and could do little to control the damage caused by the spill. A full 10% of the Sound was poisoned by oil, and 2% of Alaska's total coastline was polluted. By the summer of 1990 no oil was visible to the casual observer, but the long-term effects of the spill are uncertain at best; in addition to poisoning thousands of marine mammals and birds, the oil has disrupted feeding cycles in the Sound and threatened the communities whose livelihoods come from the sea.

Exxon has spent $2.5 billion to clean up the spilled oil, and in October 1991 the company agreed to pay an additional $900 million over the next 11 years for future clean-up operations, plus $100 million in restitution to the state and federal governments and $25 million in criminal fines. Hundreds of lawsuits filed against Exxon by private individuals, including native Alaskans, are still pending. Recent federal and state environmental reports have revealed that marine biologists (and the courts) may have underestimated the extent of the damage caused by the spill.

The tremendous uproar surrounding the spill underscored the present shift taking place within the Alaskan economy. Even as the pipeline's profits are divided among the oil companies, native corporations, and the state and federal governments, the oil rush has begun to subside. Alaskans are starting to realize that the vast expanses of unspoiled land, not to be found anywhere else in the U.S., are their most marketable commodity. The astounding sum of Exxon's payment attests to the growing political clout of the proponents of preservation and ecotourism.

Recent Events

For years, oil barons have been clamoring to perform exploratory drilling in the Arctic National Wildlife Refuge (ANWR), an enormous swath of land in the northwestern part of the state virtually untouched by anyone but a few Aleuts, several thousand caribou, and billions of mosquitoes. The oil companies claimed that added federal and state revenue, as well as new jobs produced by a major oil strike, would be a great economic boon. However, environmentalists were afraid that the drilling would disrupt the pristine wilderness and the animals that depend on it. In the fall of 1994, a Republican Congress swept into Washington, much to the glee of Alaska's pro-oil interests. Despite presidential vetoes of bills designed to hand over the ANWR to oil companies, open Tongass National Forest to logging, and weaken the Environmental Protection Agency, the ultimate fate of Alaska's resources remain in the balance.

Literature

A good primer on Alaska is John McPhee's *Coming Into the Country*, which sketches a fascinating overview of Alaskan issues and wilderness lifestyles. Jack London's *The Call of the Wild* is a classic in these parts. *Village Journey,* by Thomas Burger, gives a first-hand perspective on emerging Native corporations, tribal organizations which broker for the economic and political rights of Natives. A depiction of Eskimo culture and heritage can be found in Lael Morgan's *Art and Eskimo Power*. Walter Hickel's *Who Owns America* outlines the Governor's plans for future development of the state. In his monster epic *Alaska*, James Michener takes quite a few historical liberties, but does justice to the scope of the region itself and its recent history. Edna Ferber's *Ice Palace* depicts an Alaska on the verge of statehood and economic boom.

Going to Extremes by Joe McGinniss and *Alaska: The Sophisticated Wilderness* by Jon Gardey both acquaint the reader with Alaskan settlers seeking refuge from the lower 48. Finally, the venerable Native newspaper *Tundra Times,* founded in part by the legendary Eskimo journalist Howard Rock, publishes out of Anchorage and provides the most up-to-date discussions of current Native American issues without glossing over internal diversity and factionalism.

PRACTICAL INFORMATION

Capital: Juneau.

Visitors Information:

Alaska Division of Tourism, 33 Willoughby St., 9th Floor; P.O. Box 110801, Juneau 99811-0801 (465-2010; fax 465-2287). Open Mon.-Fri. 8am-5pm.

Alaska Public Lands Information Center and **National Park Service,** 605 W. 4th Ave. #105, Anchorage, 99501 (271-2737), in the Old Federal Bldg. Help in crossing any and all wilderness areas. Extensive audio-visual displays and other resources. Branch offices in Fairbanks, Ketchikan, and Tok. Open daily 10am-5:30pm.

Alaska State Division of Parks, 3601 C St., Suite 200, Anchorage 99510 (269-8400). Information on camping and other activities at all state parks. Open Mon.-Fri. 11am-5pm.

United States Forest Service, 101 Egan Dr., Juneau 99801 (586-8751). General information regarding national parks and reserves. Open daily 8am-5pm, winter Mon.-Fri. 9am-5pm.

Alaska Department of Fish and Game, 1255 West 8th St., P.O. Box 25526, Juneau 99802-5526 (465-4112/4100). Information on hunting and fishing regulations available here. Open Mon.-Fri. 8am-5pm.

Alaska State Employment Service, 10002 Glacier Highway Suite #200, Juneau 99801 (465-4562). Information on jobs. Open Mon.-Fri. 8am-5pm.

Legislative Information Office, 716 W. 4th Ave. Suite 200, Anchorage 99501-2133 (258-8111). For the scoop on Alaska's juicy political debates. Or call the **Alaska State Government General Information** service at 269-7460.

United States Customs Service: 202-927-6724. This Washington, DC office will connect you with the Canadian Customs and Excise office for information regarding the rules and regulations of traveling through Canada on your way to Alaska.

Payphones: In many towns, phones will not return coins, even if the party you're calling doesn't answer. Dial, wait until the party picks up, and *then* deposit coins. They will understand the lag.

Population: 603,617. **Nicknames:** The Last Frontier; Land of the Midnight Sun. **Motto:** North to the Future. **Flower:** Forget-Me-Not. **Bird:** Willow Ptarmigan. **Fish:** King Salmon. **Tree:** Sitka Spruce. **State Holiday:** Alaska Day, Oct. 18. **Land Area:** 586,412 sq. mi.

Emergency: 911.

State Troopers: 269-5511; 269-5722 in Anchorage, 451-5100 in Fairbanks.

Time Zones: Alaska (most of the state; 4 hr. behind Eastern); Aleutian-Hawaii (Aleutian Islands; 5 hr. behind Eastern).

Postal Abbreviation: AK.

Sales Tax: None.

Drinking Age: 21.

Area Code: 907.

GETTING AROUND

The cost of travel both to and through Alaska is exorbitant no matter how you go. Bringing a car is not necessarily the wisest plan—if at all feeble, the car may not survive the rocky drive up the largely unpaved **Alaska Highway.** Even if you and your car do arrive safely, there often aren't enough usable roads to justify the time and expense of driving (gas is expensive, breakdowns are common, and traveling with a car on the ferry is costly). Many people do venture onto Alaska's roads despite the difficulties, and are rewarded with stunning views and access to true wilderness. (See

Northcountry Driving, p. 33.) Most of Alaska's major highways are known by their name, rather than their number. The Dempster Hwy., for instance, is officially Highway 5, but no one refers to it as such.

Alaska's road and rail networks cover little of the massive state, and it is no mystery why one in 36 Alaskans has a pilot's license. Air travel is often a necessity, albeit an exorbitantly expensive one (the hourly rate usually exceeds $100). Several intrastate airlines, almost exclusively based at the Anchorage airport, transport passengers and cargo to virtually every village in Alaska: **Alaska Airlines** (to larger Bush towns and Cordova; 800-426-0333); **ERA Aviation** (southcentral; 243-6633); and **Reeve Aleutian Airways** (Aleutians; 243-4700). Many other charters and flight-seeing services are available. Write **Ketchum Air Service Inc.,** P.O. Box 190588, Anchorage 99519 (243-5525), on the North Shore of Lake Hood, to ask about their charters. One-day flights and overnight or weekend trips to isolated lakes, mountains, and tundra usually range from $165 up.

Those who intend to conquer all of Alaska should check out the **AlaskaPass.** The pass offers unlimited access to Alaska's railroad, ferry, and bus systems; a 15-day pass sells for $649, a 30-day pass for $899. A pass allowing travel on 21 non-consecutive days over a 45-day period costs $949. The fare may seem expensive, but with a network that extends from Bellingham, WA to Dutch Harbor on the Aleutian Islands, the pass is a good deal for those who want to see a lot of the Pacific Northwest in a short amount of time. If interested, call 800-248-7598, 7am-7pm (Alaska time).

Southcentral Alaska

Southcentral Alaska stands on the threshold of Alaska's future. Anchorage, Prince William Sound, the Kenai Peninsula, and Kodiak Island are becoming less isolated as economic opportunities and an expanding network of well-maintained roads draw more and more people up from the Lower 48. The cost of living is slowly declining and Alaska's isolation, while in no danger of ending shortly, is gradually eroding.

This region has developed several different competing, and probably incompatible, models for the state's next century. Anchorage is rapidly becoming the Strip Mall That Ate Alaska, and might reasonably be mistaken for suburban Los Angeles with some moose mixed in. Kodiak has gone the way of the dollar, as its industrial docks, pricey motels, and cultural desiccation attest. In contrast, in much of the Kenai Peninsula and Prince William Sound, locals and newcomers alike enjoy a slow-paced lifestyle enriched by a cornucopia of cultural and artistic pursuits. In Cordova, residents have staunchly refused to be joined by road to Anchorage, and a coalition of fishermen and environmentalists recently elected a Green Party mayor to defend the town's blissful isolation. Homer, though accessible by road, has maintained a distinct character and a remarkable population of artists, actors, and aging hippies. Last but not least, Valdez, the southern terminus of the Alaska Pipeline, attracts heavy tankers racing to pump themselves full.

Massive and challenging peaks, rivers churning with fish, and a diverse cast of animal life can be reached in less than a day from Anchorage. But as the state makes itself more presentable to guests and export industries, the pristine and untouched expanses devoid of human presence that to many people define Alaska, are receding into a distance open only to the most diligent.

■ Anchorage

Only 80 years ago, cartographers wasted no ink on the modest tent city that is now Alaska's foremost metropolis. Approximately half the state's population, about 250,000 people, lives in the unflatteringly nicknamed "Los Anchorage." The city achieved its comparatively monstrous size by serving as the headquarters of three

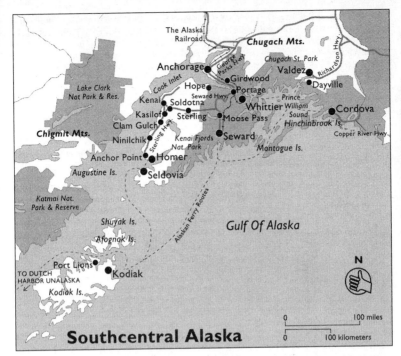

Southcentral Alaska

The Alaska Railroad
Chugach Mts.
Anchorage
Girdwood
Valdez
Chugach St. Park
Richardson Hwy.
Dayville
George Parks Hwy.
Hope
Portage
Prince
Cook Inlet
Seward Hwy.
Kenai
Soldotna
Whittier William
Cordova
Kasilof
Sterling
Moose Pass
Sound
Hinchinbrook Is.
Clam Gulch
Chigmit Mts.
Ninilchik
Kenai Fjords Nat. Park
Seward
Montague Is.
Copper River Hwy.
Sterling Hwy.
Anchor Point
Homer
Augustine Is.
Seldovia
Katmai Nat. Park & Reserve
Shuyak Is.
Afognak Is.
Gulf Of Alaska
Alaskan Ferry Routes
Lake Clark Nat. Park & Res.
Port Lions
Kodiak
TO DUTCH HARBOR UNALASKA
Kodiak Is.

N

0   100 miles
0   100 kilometers

ALASKA

economic "projects": the railroad, the war, and the pipeline. Anchorage today has an air of prefabrication. Writer John McPhee has called it "condensed, instant Albuquerque." Extremely spread out, the low buildings of Anchorage sprawl for miles along highways and side-streets, leaving the traveler looking in vain for a city at the heart of the suburbs. But in addition to a jumble of fast-food joints and discount liquor stores, Anchorage supports a full range of popular culture: semi-professional baseball and basketball teams, performances by internationally known orchestras and music stars, theater, and opera. In any other state, this might make for a well respected city; in Alaska, however, Anchorage doesn't stand a chance against her physically stunning sisters. While the wilderness occasionally encroaches on the city it cannot save Anchorage from being, in the end, an eyesore with a bad rap.

PRACTICAL INFORMATION AND ORIENTATION

Visitors Information: Log Cabin Visitor Information Center, W. 4th Ave. (274-3531), at F St. The Log Cabin is usually crammed with visitors and a staff of volunteers. A new building behind the cabin is typically less crowded and has more brochures. Lots of maps, including the 25¢ **Bike Trails** guide. Open June-Aug. daily 7:30am-7pm; May and Sept. 8am-6pm; Oct.-April 9am-4pm. Smaller visitors info outlets are at the **airport** (274-3531); in the domestic terminal near the baggage claim (terminal open daily 9am-4pm), and in the international terminal in the central atrium (terminal open during flight arrivals 8am-4pm), as well as in the **Parkgate Building** (696-4636), 11723 Old Glenn Hwy. Call 276-3200 for a **recorded calendar** of weekly events. **Alaska Public Lands Information Center,** Old Federal Bldg., 605 W. 4th Ave., (271-2737 or 258-7295 for recorded info), between F and G St. 8 state and federal offices (including the **Park Service, Forest Service, Division of State Parks, State Fish and Game,** and the **Fish and Wildlife Service**), all under one roof, provide the most current info on the entire state. Popular **topographic maps,** a computerized **sportfishing map,** an interactive trip-planning video unit, and live presentations on Alaska's outdoor attractions. Films daily at 10am, noon, 2 and 4pm. Open daily 9am-5:30pm.

Fishing Information: Alaska Department of Fish and Game, 333 Raspberry Rd. (344-0541 or 349-4687 for recorded info). Open Mon.-Fri. 8am-5pm.

Employment: Alaska Employment Service, P.O. Box 107224, 3301 Eagle St. (269-4746). Take bus #3 or 60. Open Mon.-Fri. 8am-4:30pm.

Currency Exchange: Thomas Cook, 311 F St. (278-2822 or 800-CURRENCY/287-7362) in the Hilton Hotel. Open Mon.-Fri. 9am-5pm, Sat. 10am-2pm.

Airport: Anchorage International Airport, P.O. Box 190649-VG, Anchorage 99519-0649 (266-2525). Serviced by 8 international and 15 domestic carriers, including **Delta** (249-2110 or 800-221-1212), **Northwest Airlines** (266-5636 or 800-225-2525), **United** (800-241-6522), and **Alaska Airlines** (800-426-0333). Smaller airlines like **Reno Air** (800-736-6247) and **American West** have cheap deals. Nearly every airport in Alaska can be reached from Anchorage, either directly or through a connecting flight in Fairbanks. An entire section of the classified ads in the *Daily News* lists secondhand tickets. **The Ticket Exchange,** 505 W. Northern Lights (274-8153), also buys and sells tickets at reduced rates. Open Mon.-Fri. 9am-6pm and Sat. 10am-4pm. Call ahead. See also **Essentials: Charter Flights and Ticket Consolidators,** p. 27.

Trains: Alaska Railroad, 411 W. 1st Ave., Anchorage 99510-7500 (265-2494, 800-544-0552 out of state). To: Denali ($95), Fairbanks ($135), and Seward ($50). In winter, 1 per week to Fairbanks; no service to Seward. A summertime "flag-stop" also runs between Anchorage and Hurricane (between Talkeetna and Denali) on Sat. and Sun. ($88). The train will make unscheduled stops anywhere along this route. Just wave it down with a white cloth and wait to be acknowledged with a whistle. For more information write to Passenger Service, P.O. Box 107500, Anchorage. Ticket window open Mon.-Fri. 5:30am-5:30pm, Sat.-Sun. 5:30am-1:30pm.

Buses: Alaskon Express (800-544-2206) sends buses daily to Seward ($39), Valdez ($65), and Portage train station ($29). Buses every other day to Haines ($185) and Skagway ($205). **Homer Stage Lines** (272-8644). To Homer ($45) Mon., Wed., and Fri. **Alaska Direct** (277-6652). To Whitehorse, YT (3 per week, $145).

Public Transportation: People Mover Bus (343-6543), in the Transit Center, on 6th Ave. between G and H St., just up the street from the Anchorage Youth Hostel. Buses leave from here to all points in the Anchorage area, 6am-10pm; restricted schedule on weekends. Cash fare $1, tokens 90¢, day pass $2.50 (the latter two can be purchased in the Transit Center). The downtown region, bordered by 5th Ave., Denali St., 6th Ave., and K St., is a **free fare zone** Mon.-Fri. 9am-3pm and 6-8pm, Sat. 9am-8pm, and Sun. 11am-6pm. The Transit Center office is open Mon.-Fri. 8am-5pm and has a free transit **map.** Service is only hourly to most spots, so plan ahead.

Ferries: Alaska Marine Highway, 333 W. 4th St. (272-7116), in the Post Office Mall. No terminal, but ferry tickets and reservations. Open Mon.-Fri. 8am-4:30pm.

Taxi: Yellow Cab, 272-2422. **Checker Cab,** 276-1234. **Alaska Cab,** 563-5353. About $13 from airport to downtown hostel. All 24hr. Cabs will gladly go downtown for $12-13. The **Valley-Airport Shuttle** (373-7933) offers a more affordable ride; 24hr. advanced reservations required.

Car Rentals: Affordable Car Rental, 4707 Spenard Rd. (243-3370), across from the Regal Alaskan Hotel. $35 per day, unlimited mi. Must be at least 21 with major credit card. Ask about a free drop-off and pick-up from downtown or the airport.

Ride Board: At Anchorage Youth Hostel (see **Accommodations,** below).

Bicycle Rental: Downtown Bicycle Rental (279-5293 or 279-8337), on 5th St., near C St. 7 blocks from the Coastal Trail. $10 per 4hr., $16 per 24hr. Lock, helmet, map, and gloves included. Also rents tennis equipment. Must have a major credit card. Open daily 9am-10pm.

Camping Equipment: Recreational Equipment, Inc. (REI), 1200 Northern Lights Blvd. (272-4565), near Spenard, at Minnesota. High-quality packs, clothing, tents, stores, and dried foods. Open Mon.-Fri. 10am-9pm, Sat.-Sun. 10am-6pm. The **Army-Navy Store** (279-2401), on 4th Ave. across from the Post Office Mall. Good prices, but caters mostly to hunting and fishing. Open Mon.-Fri. 9am-8pm, Sat. 10am-7pm, Sun. 10am-5pm. For buying or selling **used equipment,** try **Play It**

Anchorage

N

0 |————| 1/2 mile

0 |————| 1/2 kilometer

Knik Arm

E. Whitney Rd.

Ship Creek

Viking Dr.

W. 1st Ave. E. 1st Ave.

Post Rd.

W. 2nd Ave.

W. 3rd Ave. E. 3rd Ave.

W. 4th Ave. E. 4th Ave.

W. 5th Ave. E. 5th Ave.

Free Fare Zone

E. 6th Ave.

Memorial
Cemetery E. 7th Ave.

E. 8th Ave.

W. 8th Ave. E. 9th Ave.

W. 9th Ave.

Delaney Park E. 10th Ave.

W. 10th Ave. E. 11th Ave.

W. 11th Ave.

W. 12th Ave. E. 12th Ave.

E. 13th Ave.

W. 13th Ave. E. 14th Ave.

W. 14th Ave. E. 15th Ave.

W. 15th Ave.

TO HUMANA
HOSPITAL

W. 16th Ave. E. 16th Ave.

17th Ave.

Westchester
Lagoon Chester
Creek
Greenbelt

19th Ave. Chester Creek

20th Ave.

E. 21st St.

Spenard Rd.

Minnesota Dr. W. Fireweed La.

Arctic Blvd.

TO EARTHQUAKE PARK,
WORZENOF POINT W. 27th Ave. TO UNIVERSITY
OF ALASKA

Northern Lights Blvd. E.

Benson Blvd.

Redwood St.

Anchorage

Basics
Anchorage Public Lands
 Information Center, 2
City Bus Station, 7
Eagle Crest, 10
Log Cabin Visitor Information
 Center, 4
Post Office, 3
Alaska Railroad Depot, 1
Anchorage Youth Hostel, 8

Nonessentials
Anchorage Museum of History
 and Art, 9
Heritage Library and Museum, 14
Imaginarium, 5
Loussac Public Library, 17
Midtown Lodge, 13
Mulcahy Stadium, 11
Old City Hall, 4
Performing Arts Center, 6
Qupqugiac Inn, 16
Sears Mall, 15
Sullivan Arena, 12
University Center, 18
Visual Arts Center, 5

TO
GLENN HWY.
AND FAIRBANKS

32nd Ave.

W. 34th Ave. E. 33rd Ave.

TO
CHUGACH
STATE
PARK

W. 36th Ave. E. 36th Ave.

Old Seward Hwy.

Seward Hwy.

W. 40th Ave.

Cedar Union Drive

Bering St.

Eureka St.

Denali St.

TO ANCHORAGE
INTERNATIONAL
AIRPORT, LAKE HOOD,
LAKE SPENARD

Tudor Rd.

TO
ALASKA
ZOO

Gambell Hyder St. Juneau Karluk St. Latouche St. Medfra St.

Barrow Cordova St. Denali Eagle Fairbanks St. Ingra Gambell

C St. D St. E St. F St. K St. N St. P St. H St. G St. L St. B St. A St.

Again Sports (278-7529), at 27th and Spenard near REI. Rotating inventory of quality fishing and camping equipment at discount prices. Open Mon.-Thurs. 10:30am-9pm, Fri. 10:30am-8pm, Sat. 10:30am-6pm, Sun. 11:30am-5pm.

Bookstore: Cook Inlet Books, 415 W. 5th Ave. (258-4544). Claims to offer the largest selection of Alaska books anywhere. Terrific collection of cheap classics as well. Open daily 8:30am-10pm. For a dog-eared copy of *White Fang,* try **C&M Used Books,** 215 E. 4th Ave. (278-9394). Open Mon.-Tues. and Thurs.-Fri. 10am-7pm, Wed. and Sat. 10am-6pm. **Title Wave,** 1068 W. Fireweed Lane (278-9283). A tsunami of used tomes. Open Mon.-Sat. 10:30am-6:30pm, Sun. noon-5pm.

Library: ZJ Loussac Library (261-2975), at 36th Ave. and Denali St. Take bus #2 or 60. The massive $40 million building devotes an entire wing to Alaskan material. Open Mon.-Thurs. 11am-9pm, Fri.-Sat. 10am-6pm; winter also Sun. 1-5pm.

Laundromat: K-Speed Wash, 600 E. 6th St. (279-0731). Wash $1.50, 7½-min. dry 25¢. Open Mon.-Sat. 7am-10pm. **Anchorage Youth Hostel** (see **Accommodations,** below) has laundry facilities. Wash and dry $1. Laundry open 5pm-10pm.

Weather: 936-2525. **Motorists and Recreation Forecast:** 936-2626. **Road Conditions Report:** 273-6037. **Marine Weather Forecast:** 936-2727.

24hr. Crisis Line: 272-4048. **24hr. Rape Crisis Line:** 563-7273.

Disabilities Access Line: Challenge Alaska (563-2658). The Log Cabin Visitors Center (see listing above) is equipped with a **TTY** for people with communications disabilities.

Gay and Lesbian Helpline: 258-4777.

Hospital: Alaska Regional Hospital, 2801 DeBarr Ave. (264-1224).

STD Information: 343-4611. **HIV/AIDS Information: Alaska AIDS Assistance Association,** 276-4880 or 800-478-2437.

Emergency: 911. **Police:** 786-8400.

Post Office (279-3062), W. 4th Ave. and C St. on the lower level in the mall. Open Mon.-Fri. 10am-5:30pm, Sat. 10am-4pm. Stamp machine in lobby open Mon.-Sat. 6am-9pm, Sun. 6am-3pm. **General Delivery ZIP Code:** 99510. The **state's central post office** (266-3259) is next to the international airport. It does *not* handle general delivery mail, but is open 24hr.

Area Code: 907.

From its seat 114 mi. north of Seward on the Seward Hwy., 304 mi. west of Valdez on the Glenn and Richardson Hwy., and 358 mi. south of Fairbanks on the George Parks Hwy., Anchorage serves as the transportation hub of Southcentral Alaska.

Military bases to the north, the Chugach Mountains to the east, and the Knik and Turnagain Arms of the Pacific to the west and south frame the **Anchorage Bowl,** within which the city sprawls across some 50,000 acres. The **downtown area** of Anchorage is laid out in a grid. Numbered avenues run east-west, and addresses are designated East or West from **C Street.** North-south streets are lettered alphabetically west of **A Street,** and named alphabetically east of A Street. The rest of Anchorage spreads out along the major highways. The **University of Alaska, Anchorage** campus lies on 36th Ave., off Northern Lights Blvd.

ACCOMMODATIONS

Anchorage is blessed with a multitude of hostel and quasi-hostel accommodations, but hotels and B&Bs—especially downtown—are extremely expensive. Even most so-called "budget" motels start at $75. Try **Alaska Private Lodgings,** 1010 W. 10th Ave. (258-1717), or **Stay With a Friend,** 3605 Arctic Blvd. #173 (278-8800). Both can refer you to B&Bs farther away with singles from $50 and doubles from $55.

Anchorage International Youth Hostel (HI-AYH), 700 H St. (276-3635), at 7th, 1 block south of the city bus station. Fantastic location on the edge of downtown. Somewhat unsocial, but you can't beat the facilities: kitchens, TVs, balconies, and laundry. Frequently filled to the rafters in summer; write or call at least a day ahead for reservations. Wheelchair accessible. Lockout noon-5pm. Curfew 1am; watchman can check you in until 3am. 3-night max. stay in summer. Pay by 11am or lose your spot. $15, nonmembers $18; photo ID required. Weekly and monthly rates during the off season's "winter community" program.

Spenard Hostel, 2845 W. 42nd Pl. (248-5036). Take bus #7 or 36 out Spenard to Turnagain Blvd. 42nd Pl. is the 1st left from Turnagain. This spacious, comfortable hostel provides a more intimate alternative to the gargantuan downtown facility. Ideal departure point for the airport or a nice spot for a few days' stay. Three kitchens, free local phone calls, common rooms with TV, bike rental to guests ($5). No curfew, no lockout. Chore requested. 6-day max. stay. Beds $12.

Qupqugiaq Inn, 640 W. 36th Ave. (563-5634) between Arctic Blvd. and C St. Take bus #36 or 7. Combines the privacy of a hotel with the community of a hostel. Common lounge and kitchen areas, but private rooms with locks on the doors. Tastefully furnished. Rooms face the occasionally noisy street. No smoking or alcohol, common areas closed at 10pm. Singles start at $26, doubles $32.

Eagle Crest (276-5913), 9th Ave. and Eagle St. Atmosphere similar to a hostel, but with many long-term residents. Clean and well managed by the Salvation Army. Common kitchen and laundry. Free coffee. No curfew. Backpackers are welcome and should feel fairly comfortable. Bed in 4-person room $15, chore required. Private rooms available, mostly by the week (around $80) or month ($220-300).

Midtown Lodge, 604 W. 26th (258-7778), off Arctic Blvd. Take bus #9. Simple, spotless cubicles with shared bath. Fridges, cable TVs, and phone with free local calls. Call for free airport shuttle. Free continental breakfast; free soup and sandwiches in the lobby for teatime snack. Singles $44. Doubles $55. Weekly $175.

Camping

Two camping areas maintained by the city welcome tents and RVs. Excellent camping opportunities await in nearby **Chugach State Park** (354-5014). Two of the best areas are **Eagle River** (688-0998; $15) and **Eklutna** (EE-kloot-nah; 694-2108; $10), respectively 12.6 mi. and 26½ mi. northeast of Anchorage along Glenn Hwy. Both are very popular with city residents, so show up early—especially on weekends.

Centennial Park, 5300 Glenn Hwy. (333-9711), north of town off Muldoon Rd. Look for the park sign. Take bus #3 or 75 from downtown. 90 sites for tents and RVs. Showers, dumpsters, fireplaces, pay phones, and water. 7-day max. stay. Noon check-out. Sites $13, Alaskans or Golden Age $11. Open May 1-Sept. 30.

Lions' Camper Park, 800 Boniface Pkwy. (333-9711), is only open as needed for overflow from Centennial. 50 sites with similar amenities at identical prices.

John's Motel and RV Park, 3543 Mt. View Dr. (277-4332). Only 2 mi. from downtown. 50 RV sites. Full hookups $20.

FOOD

Being the large city that it is, Anchorage presents budget travelers with the most affordable and varied culinary fare in the state. Natch.

Check out **Nordstrom's Café** (279-7622), on the second floor of the department store on 603 D St., for a bottomless 25¢ cup of coffee (open Mon.-Sat. 9:30am-9pm, Sun. 11am-6pm). The affable **sausage guy** who sets up shop at 4th Ave. and G St. not only serves an amazing reindeer dog with chips and a drink for $3; he's also a friend to half the city (don't be fooled by the cheap imitations patronized by the *other* half of the city). The **Great Harvest Bread Company,** 570 E. Benson Blvd. (274-3331), stocks great bread (open Mon. 10am-6pm, Tues.-Fri. 7am-6pm, Sat. 7am-5pm). For a wide selection of brand name groceries, the 24-hour **Carr's** (272-4574), at 13th and Gambell, is a 1-mi. walk from the hostel. At night, take bus #11; this neighborhood is tough for the six months of the year it's actually dark.

Maharaja's, 328 G St. (272-2233), between 3rd and 4th Ave. The gilded decor and spicy lunch buffet provide a feast for all the senses at this authentic Indian restaurant. All-you-can-eat buffet ($8) served Mon.-Fri. 11:30am-2pm. Dinner service can be painfully slow, but the terrific entrees ($8-12) are well worth the wait. Served Sun.-Thurs. 5:30-9:30pm, Fri.-Sat. 5:30-10pm.

Twin Dragon, 612 E. 15th Ave. (276-7535), near Gambell. Standard American decor masks one of the town's finest treats: a lunch buffet of marinated meats and vegetables, lightly barbecued on a giant, circular grill ($6.25). This new spot has become a favorite among Anchorage's knowledgeable diners. Buffet served Mon.-Sat. 11am-3:30pm, Sun. 1-3:30pm. Open daily 11am-midnight.

Blondie's Café (279-0698), at the corner of 4th and D St. Bizarre combination of neon-pink zebra carpeting and Iditarod memorabilia suggests the gold rush in drag. If the inside freaks you out, just sit outside and watch the endless parade of pedestrians. All-day breakfast includes 3 hotcakes for $4.25. Ham and cheese sandwich $5. Open daily 5am-midnight.

Thai Cuisine, 444 H St. (277-8424). Therrific Thai fare. 19 vegetarian dishes ($7-9) include the alarmingly titled *Lard Nar.* Lunch specials include entree, rice, soup, and salad ($6.50-8). Open Mon. 11am-9pm, Tues.-Sat. 11am-10pm, Sun. 4-10pm.

Kumagoro Restaurant, 533 4th Ave. (272-9905). The combination of Alaskan fish and Japanese expertise make for excellent sushi. Skip the pricey dinners; daily lunch specials (served 11:30am-2pm) include such dishes as halibut teriyaki with soup, rice, and vegetables ($6). At night, karaoke crooners ham it up at the mike. Bar and restaurant open daily 11am-10pm. Sushi bar open 5-10pm.

White Spot Café, 109 W. 4th Ave. (279-3954). A fine cheeseburger with homecut fries ($3.50) has made this tiny establishment an Anchorage favorite since 1959. Sparse interior is decorated only with condiments and a cramped pinball machine. Two eggs, potato, toast, and coffee ($2.75). Open daily 6:30am-6:30pm.

Legal Pizza, 1034 W. 4th Ave. (274-0686). Just down the street from the courthouse. Offers a buffet deal even the public defenders can afford: all-you-can-eat pizza, salad bar, soup, and beverages ($6) served Mon.-Fri. 11:30am-3pm. Arrive by 12:30pm for the best selection of pizzas. You can catch leftovers later on for $1 a slice. If you're not a trough feeder, try the caeser salad ($7) or share a huge 18-in. veggie pizza ($20). Open Mon.-Fri. 10am-11pm, Sat.-Sun. 5-11pm.

Muffin Man, 529 I St. (279-6836). Absolutely stunning muffins come in 9 regular varieties and countless daily creations. Try the raspberry ripple or apple crumble (75¢, jumbo $1.50). They also offer bagels (75¢), breakfast sandwiches ($4-5), and tantalizing salads and sandwiches. Creativity runs rife in this establishment! Open Mon.-Fri. 6am-3pm, Sat. 6:30am-3pm.

Side Street Espresso, 428 G St. (258-9055). A gathering spot for the hip and the yup, this mellow place offers weekly political salons, frequent acoustic music, a decent book exchange, and bound copies of local writers' efforts. Sip a cappuccino ($2) or espresso ($1.50) beneath Anchorage artists' more abstract meanderings. Open Mon.-Fri. 7am-7pm, Sat.-Sun. 8am-5pm.

Firehouse Café (562-5555), on the corner of Spenard and Benson with a flamingo-pink, can't-miss-it exterior. A converted warehouse that doesn't hide its past. No salons here, but wisecracking counter boys and an alternateen crowd complemented by hippies on acoustic evenings and the homesick on Irish Jig night. Recently expanded menu includes pasta and other "real food." Killer drinks. Tall latté ($2.15), hot chocolate ($2). Open Mon.-Fri. 6am-11pm, Sat.-Sun. 8am-11pm.

Alaska Flapjacks, 1230 W. 27th Ave. (274-2241). The best breakfast spot in town advertises itself as a family restaurant, possibly because you could almost feed a family with one of their morning specials. Three eggs, bacon, biscuit and gravy, and hash browns $6. Open daily 6am-8pm.

SIGHTS AND ACTIVITIES

Watching over Anchorage from Cook Inlet is **Mt. Susitna,** known to locals as the "Sleeping Lady." Legend has it that it marks the resting spot of an Athabascan maid who dozed while awaiting her lover's return from war. When peace reigns in the world, the stories say, she will awake. Closer to town off Northern Lights Blvd., **Earthquake Park** recalls the 1964 Good Friday earthquake. The quake was the strongest ever recorded in North America, registering 9.2 on the Richter scale. You can walk, skate, or bike to the **Tony Knowles Coastal Trail,** an 11-mi. paved track that skirts Cook Inlet on one side and the backyards of Anchorage's upper-crust on the other. When it was built for a million dollars per mile, critics complained that the trail would only be an expensive invitation for burglars to prey on wealthy homeowners. Fears have proved unfounded, though, and the heavily-traveled trail is arguably one of the best urban bike paths in the country. In the winter it is groomed for **cross-country skiing.**

The **Anchorage Museum of History and Art,** 121 W. 7th Ave. (343-6173), at A St., is the best museum in town. It features permanent exhibits of Native Alaskan artifacts and art, as well as national and international art exhibits for those who have already seen their share of indigenous works. A traditional dance series runs three times per day in summer ($4), and a summer film series shows at no extra cost. The gallery gives free tours daily at 10am, 11am, 1pm, and 2pm ($5, seniors $4.50, under 18 free; open daily May 15-Sept. 15 9am-6pm; Sept. 16-May 14 Tues.-Sat. 10am-6pm, Sun. 1-5pm). The **Alaska Aviation Heritage Museum,** 4721 Aircraft Dr. (248-5325), provides a fun look at Alaska's pioneer aviators. The collection includes 22 rare planes, dated 1928-1952, some salvaged from remote Bush areas. The museum also houses a theater where rare footage is shown continuously. Take bus #6 to the airport; the museum is within easy walking distance ($5.75, seniors $4.50, youths $2.75; open daily 9am-6pm, winter Tues.-Sat. 10am-4pm).

The **Imaginarium,** 725 5th Ave. (276-3179), across from the Westmark, a hands-on "science-discovery center," recreates Arctic marine environments, glacier formation, and other scientific peculiarities of the North ($5, seniors $4, under 12 $4; open Mon.-Sat. 10am-6pm, Sun. noon-5pm). The Imaginarium is primarily for kids, but the young-at-heart might enjoy it as well.

Just in case you haven't glimpsed any of Alaska's animals in the wild, you're guaranteed to spot them at the **Alaska Zoo,** Mile 2 on O'Malley Rd. (346-3242). Take bus #91. **Binky the polar bear** mauled an Australian tourist here in 1994 and became a local hero ($6, seniors and 12-18 $4, under 12 $3; open daily 9am-6pm). He has since, regrettably, passed away. (*Let's Go* does not recommend attempting to endear yourself to locals by maiming tourists.)

SHOPPING

For an unconventional shopping experience, head to the non-profit gift shop at the **Alaska Native Medical Center,** 255 Campbell (257-1150), at 3rd St. Many native Alaskans pay for medical services with their own arts and handicrafts, and the Alaska State Museum in Juneau has sent buyers here to improve its exhibitions. Walrus bone *ulus* (knives used by Native Alaskans, $27-85), fur moccasins, parkas, and dolls highlight the selection (open Mon.-Fri. 10am-2pm, and occasionally Sat. 11am-2pm).

Works from the Alaskan Bush, similar to those on display at the Museum of History and Art (see above), are sold at the **Alaska Native Arts and Crafts Showroom,** 333 W. 4th Ave. (274-2932). Birch baskets (from $25), beadwork and other jewelry ($3-50), and ivory carvings (from $30) tempt you here (open Mon.-Fri. 10am-6pm, Sat. 10am-5pm). More made-in-Alaska products, as well as fresh produce and fish, are available for your purchase and consumption at the **Saturday Market** (276-7207), at the Lower Bowl Parking Lot at the corner of 3rd and E. The outdoor market is held Saturdays late May through early Sept., 10am-6pm.

ENTERTAINMENT

Trek to the **Alaska Experience Theater,** 705 W. 6th Ave. (276-3730), to vicariously experience a flightseeing trip to Denali, a river-rafting trip that will make you gasp for air, and other Alaskan adventures on the inner surface of a hemispherical dome. The 70mm film (40min.) will make your head spin ($7, children $4; every hr. 9am-9pm). An earthquake exhibit at the theater will cost you another $5, $4 for the kids. The earth quakes for 35 minutes each time between 9am and 8:30pm. The **Capri Cinema,** 3425 E. Tudor Rd. (275-3799), runs a mix of art flicks and second-run mainstream works. Take bus #75 (shows $4). On a rainy day, park yourself at the **Denali Theater,** 1230 W. 27th St. (275-3106), at Spenard, where double-features of popular movies in limbo between the big screen and video release show for $1.01.

If you're yearning for a touch of Arctic Broadway, the **4th Avenue Theatre,** 630 4th Ave. (257-5678), one block west of the Log Cabin Visitors Center (see **Practical Information,** above), has been faithfully restored to its original 1940s decor. The neon-clad building now contains a small grocery and gift shop, and is home to a dinner show (19.95). Live entertainment can also be found at nearby **Cyrano's Off Center Playhouse,** at 413 D St. (274-2599). Mark Muro puts on a terrific "one-guy" comedy show called *Alaska: Behind the Scenery,* featuring witty insights into what the tour guides don't tell you.

NIGHTLIFE

The brew-pub revolution has finally hit Anchorage. In the last year, no fewer than four beer-brewing restaurants have sprung up in the area. **Railway Brewing Company** (277-1996), in the railroad depot on 421 W. 1st., offers six tasty creations at affordable prices (pints $3.25, 6-beer sampler $4.50). Try the bizarre chili flavored beer or an excellent foccacia sandwich ($6.50). The popular **Glacier Brewhouse,** 737 W. 5th (274-BREW/2739), pours a smaller selection of more expensive brews (pints $4) in a mammoth restaurant. The food is even pricier (nachos $7). If you're not in the mood for a local brew, head to **Humpy's,** where you can get one from just about anywhere else. A relatively young and loud crowd enjoys over 40 draft beers as well as excellent halibut tacos ($7).

Anchorage's leading gay and lesbian bar is the **Blue Moon,** 530 E. 5th Ave. (277-0441), near the Sheraton. A mellow bar area accompanies a dance space with disco every night and a drag show on Wednesdays and alternating Saturdays. Patrons have adopted the streets surrounding a nearby church affiliated with homophobic minister Jerry Prevo and perform upkeep with vigor (bar open Mon.-Thurs. 1pm-2am, Fri. 1pm-3am, Sat. 3pm-3am, Sun. 3pm-2am).

In midtown, Alaskans party at **Chilkoot Charlie's,** 2435 Spenard Rd. (272-1010), at Fireweed. Take bus #7 or 60. Six bars fill this huge space, in addition to a rockin' dance floor and a quiet lounge. Ask about the nightly drink specials, or you'll pay an outrageous price (Negra Modelo is a steal at $3). Two different bands at each end of this behemoth "log cabin" play nightly from 9:30pm (open Mon.-Thurs. 10am-2:30am, Fri.-Sat. 10am-3am, Sun. noon-2:30am).

Less overwhelming and more intriguing is **Mr. Whitekey's Fly-by-Night Club,** 3300 Spenard Rd. (279-SPAM/7726). Take bus #7. Mr. Whitekey's serves "everything from the world's finest champagnes to a damn fine plate of Spam." The house special promises you anything with Spam at half-price when you order champagne (free with Dom Perignon). Try Spam nachos or Spam and cream cheese on a bagel ($3-7). Nightly music ranges from rock to jazz to blues. They also feature *The Whale Fat Follies,* a new anti-tourist tourist attraction of "musical off-color follies," nightly at 8pm (bar open Tues.-Sat. 4pm-2:30am).

EVENTS

The **Anchorage Music Festival** has been held from mid-June through early July since 1956. For information and tickets for this mostly classical festival, call 263-2787. The summer solstice (June 21) brings dancing to the streets and runners from all over the world to the inspirational **Mayor's Marathon** (343-4474). The **Fur Rendezvous,** held the second week of February, revives the era when fur trappers gathered to whoop it up. Today, affectionately referred to as "Fur Rondy," it includes the world sled-dog championship races, a grand prix, and snowshoe softball games. The Anchorage **Bucs** (272-2827) and **Pilots** (274-3627), the city's two **semi-professional baseball** teams, wear the more traditional cleats for their summertime games. Watch them slug it out at Mulcahy Park on 16th Ave. and A St.; call ahead for times and ticket prices. Call the visitors information center (274-3531) or their recorded **events hotline** (276-3200) for info on these and other happenings.

Does The Word "Mush" Mean Anything To You?

Charlie Darwin would have liked these odds: snow, wind, and frigid cold, separating the women from the girls. The infamous **Iditarod** begins in Anchorage in the first weekend in March. Dogs and mushers alike traverse the trail over two mountain ranges, along the mighty Yukon, and over the frozen Norton Sound to Nome. Alaskan state pride holds that the route is 1049 mi. in honor of Alaska's status as the 49th state. The distance is actually closer to 1100 mi. and takes top finishers about two weeks to complete.

The race commemorates the 1925 rescue of Nome when sled dog mushers ferried 300,000 units of life-saving diptheria serum from Nenana (near Fairbanks) to Nome. The first Iditarod was a 27-mi. jaunt in 1967 organized by historian Dorothy G. Page. By 1973, the first full race was run in 20 days. Today, an average of 57 mushers race each year. The Iditarod record is held by Susan Butcher, who finished in less than 11 days and won the race in 1986, '87, '88, and '90.

Once **a rollicking good time Alaska-style,** the race has come under fire by animal-rights activists in recent years because of the hardships of sled dogs, some of whom inevitably die en route to Nome. Still, the city turns out in force for the ceremonial start of the race in Anchorage on March 3 (just outside town, the teams are unceremoniously loaded onto trucks and shuttled to the actual starting line). For more information, contact the **Iditarod Trail Committee,** Dept. M - P.O. Box 870800, Wasilla, AK 99687 (376-5155; see **Wasilla,** p. 73).

OUTDOORS

To counteract urban claustrophobia, hike to the summit of **Flattop Mountain** in the "Glenn Alps" of the Chugach Range near Anchorage. The excellent view of the city and (if it's clear) sun-soaked Denali is well worth the 2-mi. (1-2hr. one way) climb. The most frequently climbed trail in Alaska is deceptively difficult due to its steepness and slippery shale, but even novices will find it manageable. Wear long pants, as you may find yourself sliding down. To reach the trailhead, jump on bus #92 to the intersection of Hillside Rd. and Upper Huffman Rd. From there walk ¾ mi. along Upper Huffman Rd., then go right on Toilsome Hill Dr. for 2 mi. Trail signs at the park entrance point the way up the 4,500-ft. mountain.

A cornucopia of less crowded trails branch from the **Powerline Trail,** which is accessible from the same parking lot as Flattop Trail. The **Middle Fork Loop** provides a 7½-mi. roundtrip to **Little O'Malley Peak,** a taller cousin of Flattop with similarly splendid views and considerably fewer hikers. An offshoot from Middle Fork just past Campbell Creek leads leftward to **Williwaw Lakes,** a breathtaking region at the base of Mt. Williwaw. The roundtrip on this gentle trail runs 13 mi. and makes either a rigorous day hike or a leisurely overnight journey. Camping is permitted throughout the area, although open fires are forbidden.

Glacier tours are an excellent way to spend what might otherwise be hours of aimless wandering through the mean streets of Anchorage. **Philips' 26 Glacier Cruise** (276-8023 or 800-544-0529) actually departs from Whittier, but most folks wisely choose not to spend the night there, and opt for a roundtrip journey from Anchorage instead. The five-hour voyage travels 110 mi. through College and Harriman Fjords and brings you intimately close to six impressive and frequently active tidewater glaciers (the other 20 are worshiped from afar). While there are no guarantees, given the sheer number of glaciers the tour visits, it's one of the best opportunities in the state to witness the amazing spectacle of huge chunks of ice plummeting into the ocean. Lesser tour highlights include the frisking of sea otters and harbor seals, and a salute from the occasional whale. The 26 Glacier Tour is far from cheap. In addition to the $119 for the tour itself, you also have to fund the roundtrip to Whittier. If you're traveling on your own, the best option may be to take the bus which the company provides for $60. Otherwise, renting a car to get to Portage and taking the train to Whittier ($16 roundtrip) is the cheapest route. In addition to being pricey, the tour is far from personal: the boat typically carries well over 200 passengers. Despite these faults, however, the remarkable fields of ice, and the gorgeous scenery that surrounds them, will quickly make you forget the tourists and the monumental dent the trip will put in your wallet. Tickets can only be picked up at the company's office at 509 W. 4th Ave. in Anchorage.

■ Near Anchorage

SEWARD HIGHWAY: ANCHORAGE TO PORTAGE

For heart-stopping scenery, just point your wheels south on the Seward Hwy. from Anchorage, and aim your gaze out the window. The highway runs south along the **Turnagain Arm** of the Cook Inlet. English explorer Captain Cook named it in 1778 while looking for the Northwest Passage. Cook left disappointed, having had to turn, again. The Turnagain Arm is known for its dramatic tidal fluctuations. Miles of the arm are temporarily uncovered at low tide, only to be inundated by 10-ft. high "bores," walls of water created as the 15 mph riptide races in. Bald eagles feed atop the dozens of sandbanks that form, and the bore tide is worth the wait. Be careful not to walk on the exposed sand at low tide.

About 15 mi. down the arm, at the Seward Hwy. Mile 117.4 (mileposts give the distance from Seward), is **Potter Marsh,** created when the Alaska Railroad bed dammed the surface run-off from nearby mountains and further enhanced when the 1964 earthquake caused the land to drop a few feet. Potter Marsh was declared a wetlands bird and wildlife sanctuary in the mid-70s. The marsh's boardwalk, one of the state's best centers for wildlife photography, is an ideal place for viewing. Bring binoculars and try to time your visit between the frequent tour bus arrivals.

Two mi. farther south, you'll find the **Potter Section House Historical Site** (345-5014), the last of the Alaska Railroad's original roadhouses. The site exhibits displays on railroad history and has a vintage snowplow engine with 9-ft. rotor blades. The roadhouse itself doubles as the headquarters for **Chugach State Park** (see p. 71; open Mon.-Fri. 8am-4:30pm). To catch a glimpse of an incoming bore tide or a pod of Beluga whales chasing salmon up the inlet, pull over at **Beluga Point,** at Mile 110.3. The bore tides generally reach Turnagain Arm two hours after the low tide in Anchorage; consult the *Daily News* for a tidal report.

Dall sheep often appear in the rocky crevices of **Bird Ridge,** 9 mi. down the highway at Mile 102. Sheep even wander down to the roadside in summer. A convoy of RVs pulled over beside the ridge is usually the first giveaway that something is astir.

At Mile 90 is the turnoff for the small community of Girdwood. Immediately to the left after leaving the highway is the **Chugach National Forest Service Visitors Center** (open summers Mon.-Fri. 8am-5pm; call 783-3242 for winter hours). The rangers at the visitors center can provide information on hikes within the protected lands that stretch from just south of Anchorage to Prince William Sound. The most spectacular short hike in the vicinity of Anchorage can be reached along **Crow Creek Road.** Hike the **Old Iditarod Trail** which stretches from Girdwood in the Chugach National Forest to Crow Creek in Chugach State Park, or to an impressive gorge and the base of **Raven Glacier** on the Crow Pass. It is a steep 3½ mi. day hike.

Three mi. from Seward Hwy. Mile 90, on the Alyeska Access Rd., lies the **Alyeska Ski Resort** (783-2222), boasting seven chair lifts and a 3934-ft. vertical drop. The resort is open November through April for skiing (a full-day lift ticket runs about $40). While in Alyeska, stay at the **Girdwood-Alyeska Home Hostel, HI-AYH** (783-2099), run by the same folks who manage the Anchorage Hostel. To get there, turn left onto the Alyeska Access Rd., go 2 mi., take a right on Timberline Dr., and a right on Alpina after ¼ mi. The hostel has 11 beds and a sauna but no hot showers ($10, nonmembers $13). Winter or summer, it's worth the detour into Alyeska just to visit the **Bake Shop** (783-2831), an outstanding restaurant below the Alyeska Resort. People from across the state sing the praises of its bottomless bowls of soup ($4) and sourdough ($3 per loaf; open Mon.-Fri. and Sun. 7am-7pm, Sat. 7am-8pm).

Several miles up pothole-ridden Crow Creek Rd. is the **Double Musky Inn** (783-2822), set back from the road in the trees ¼ mi. from the junction. The Musky deserves its reputation as one of the best restaurants in Alaska; it's where Anchorage residents take their out-of-town guests. If you can't swing a spicy Cajun-style dinner ($16-30), at least treat yourself to a drink or dessert (about $4). The double musky pie and the coconut salmon appetizer ($8) both deserve special attention (open Tues.-Thurs. 5-10pm, Fri.-Sun. 4-10pm).

PORTAGE

The town of Portage, little more than a train and bus stop, is 45 minutes from downtown Anchorage at Mile 80 of the Seward Hwy. The **Alaska Backpacker Shuttle** (344-8775 or 800-266-8625) runs buses between the train station and Anchorage for $20. Hitchers report that rides are easy to find.

The Portage Hwy., beginning at Seward Hwy. Mile 78.9, leads you through magnificent **Portage Valley,** where you can get your fill of glaciers without taking a pricey boat tour. Four roadside glaciers sit staunchly along the Portage Valley. The glaciers imperceptibly grind against each other, causing spectacular blue ice chunks to "calve" off the glaciers and fall into Portage Lake. The best way to see the region's glaciers is not with a tour but on the Whittier-Valdez Ferry ($65; see **Valdez,** p. 96).

On the lakeside, the **Begich, Boggs Visitors Center** (783-2326) houses what are perhaps the most modern displays of any Alaskan information outlet. Unfortunately, Portage Glacier is no longer visible from the visitors center. It has receded about 2000 ft.—almost half a mile—since the center's construction. You must now take a $21 boat tour to see the glacier and watch it calve into Portage Lake. The center is still impressive, presenting glacial exhibits, a free 20-min. glacier movie, and guided hikes (open daily 9am-6pm; winter Sat.-Sun. 11am-4pm). To reach the center, take the 5-mi. detour off Seward Hwy., south of Alyeska, along the well paved **Portage Hwy.** The cheapest official tour may be the one given by **Gray Line** (277-5581), which conducts the seven-hour mother-of-all-tours of Portage Glacier, including stops at the **Visitor Center** and **Alyeska Ski Resort** ($55, under 12 $28; daily tours at 9am and noon). Tours run from May 16 to September 21.

Two state-run **campgrounds** on Portage Hwy. have excellent sites with panoramic glacial views. **Black Bear** ($9) and **Williwaw** ($10) provide water and toilets; Williwaw also has a short hiking trail and a viewing ledge overlooking salmon-spawning areas (salmon run from early July to late Aug.). For more information on the hikes and trails in the area, call the Anchorage office of the **Chugach National Forest** (271-2500) or write them at 3301 C St., Anchorage 99503. **Alaska Public Lands Information,** 605 W. 4th, Anchorage 99501 (271-2737) has information on the Chugach as well.

GLENN HIGHWAY: ANCHORAGE TO PALMER AND WASILLA

The Glenn Hwy. departs Anchorage at the end of 5th Ave. and stretches through Glennallen, 189 mi. northeast of Anchorage, to Tok and the Richardson Hwy. The first 37 mi. also serve as the "beginning" of the George Parks Hwy., which connects Anchorage to Denali and Fairbanks. Leaving Anchorage, the highway traces the western edge of the Chugach State Park, 770 sq. mi. of park north, east, and south of Anchorage. The first access point to the park is at the exit for Eagle River, 13 mi. from Anchorage. Leaving the highway, a right turn onto Eagle River Rd. will lead you into the park and to magnificent views of the Eagle River Valley and the glaciers which feed it. Trails into the park, including the popular Crow Pass Trail (a 2- to 3-day 26-mi. hike across the park to Girdwood), leave from the **Eagle River Nature Center** (694-2108). A variety of interesting shorter trips also leave from the center. Even if the center is closed, maps posted outside give ample info. The Nature Center itself is a worthwhile stop ($1, Tues.-Sat. 10am-7pm, Sun. noon-8pm). Exhibits include comprehensive collections of butterflies, animal furs, horns, and skulls. The Nature

Center also offers excellent guided hikes with local experts and professors on geology, birds, butterflies, or other topics every weekend.

A second entrance to Chugach State Park is located at Mile 26 of the highway, at the exit for Eklutna. Just off the highway is the trailhead to Thunderbird Falls, a leisurely 1-mi. hike to the overlook for a gorge and falls. Eklutna Lake Rd. also begins just off the highway and, after a short paved stretch, winds its way 10 mi. to glacial silt-filled, blue-green **Eklutna Lake,** the largest lake in Chugach State Park. Several interesting hikes, including the **Twin Peaks Trail,** leave from the west end of the lake. This trail is a fantastic moderate-to-difficult 3½ mi. hike which leads above treeline to views of the lake and the glaciers beyond. Other trails trace the northeastern edge of the lake and head into the heart of the park, offering travelers the opportunity to stretch their legs for an hour or two or take a longer trip up to the glacier which feeds the lake.

Also at Mile 26, off the Eklutna exit, is **Eklutna Village Historical Park** (688-6026), an Athabascan village dating back to 1650 ($3.50; open mid-may to Sept. daily 10am-6pm). The restored village is home to **St. Nicholas Russian Church,** a small log structure built in 1830 and still used for local services, which is the oldest standing building in greater Anchorage. The community is a glimpse into the mingling of Russian Orthodox religion and traditional Athabascan culture. Many of the spirit houses outside the church are also adorned with crosses.

From here, the Glenn Hwy. heads into the **Matanuska Valley,** as famous for its mountain backdrop as for its gargantuan produce. Farmers who settled the area in the 1930s watched in astonishment as the long summer daylight turned garden-scale vegetables into cabbages and potatoes big enough to feed a ship. Today the valley is still widely known for its produce, legal and illegal: those in the know claim that **Matanuska Valley Thunderfuck** is some of the world's best marijuana. (*Let's Go* does not recommend getting thunderfucked.)

Near the entrance to the Matanuska Valley is the turn-off for the George Parks Hwy. Staying on the Glenn Hwy. quickly leads into the agricultural hamlet of **Palmer.** Get down at the **Alaska State Fair** (745-4827 or 800-850-FAIR/3247), on the fairgrounds at Mile 40.2 on Glenn Hwy. The 11-day event ends on Labor Day and includes parades, rodeos, and an agricultural sideshow starring the aforementioned cabbages ($6, seniors $3, ages 6-12 $2; open daily 10am-10pm). The prize in 1996 for the largest cabbage was a whopping $2000. Learn more about Palmer's history at the **visitors center,** 723 South Valley Way (745-2880), across the railroad tracks (open May to mid-Sept. daily 8am-6pm). Next to the visitors center, a garden and greenhouse provide samples of the region's mammoth fruits and legumes.

Four blocks from the visitors center is the artsy alternative to Palmer's agricultural side, **Vagabond Blues,** 642 S. Alaska (745-2233). Featuring a library, couches, plenty of espresso and soup, and a friendly clientele, Vagabond Blues features an "open wall," where upstart artists display their work.

A few miles off Parks Hwy., at Mile 50.1 of the Glenn Hwy., lies the **world's only domesticated musk-ox farm.** Descendents of a herd from Greenland that was introduced to Alaska in 1934, Palmer's domesticated oxen are prized for their fleece, called *qiviut*. Finer than cashmere, *qiviut* does not shrink and is eight times warmer than regular wool. This wonder fleece, gathered when the oxen shed, supports a healthy cottage industry for traditional Inuit weavers under the auspices of a statewide organization ($7, seniors and students $6, under 6 free; open daily 9am-7pm). You can visit their cousins, the friendly reindeer, at the **Reindeer Farm** (745-4000), on the Bordenburg Butte Loop Rd. off the Old Glenn Hwy., 11 mi. from its southern junction with Glenn Hwy. Visitors can hand-feed the affable beasts and pet their babies ($5, seniors $4, ages 3-11 $3; open daily 10am-6pm). Just south of the reindeer farm, a turn-off leads to a trail up Bordenburg Butte. A steep 30- to 45-min. hike will leave you gasping for air as you gaze, speechless, over the entire valley and surrounding mountains.

Campers should continue south toward Anchorage and turn east on Eklutna Rd., at Glenn Hwy. Mile 26.3, for 10 mi. to **Eklutna Campground,** a state-run spot with water and toilets ($10, at the same turnoff for Thunderbird Falls and Eklutna Lake). For more information on the area, contact the **Wasilla Chamber of Commerce, #C18** Cottonwood Creek Mall, Wasilla 99687 (376-1299; open Mon.-Fri 8am-5pm).

On the George Parks Hwy. about 15 mi. from Palmer, lies **Wasilla,** a town which shares Palmer's overgrown agricultural heritage. Wasilla is a boon to strip mall devotees, but the outlying areas do have some worthwhile stops. The **Dorothy Page Museum** (373-9071) and the town's **visitors center** are on Main St., off the Parks Hwy. (museum $3, $2.50 seniors and students, under 18 free; open daily 9am-6pm).

Relive the days when dogsleds carried medicine across endless frozen tundra at the **Knik Museum and Mushers Hall of Fame,** Mile 13.9 on Knik Rd. (376-7755), which begins as Wasilla's Main Street. A veritable Cooperstown, the museum features mushing memorabilia and famous dog sleds ($2, seniors $1.50, under 18 free; open June-Aug. 31 Wed.-Sun. noon-6pm). The **Iditarod Race Headquarters,** Mile 2.2 on Knik Rd. (376-5155), is the best place to start that career you've always wanted as a musher. You can try sled-dog racing here, except in the spring or fall when it's too muddy. Call or write Raymie Redington, P.O. Box 5420, Wasilla 99654 (376-6730) for details. Dog sled demos cost $20 for a four-person sled (see p. 69).

Anchorage's **Stay-With-A-Friend B&B** (344-4006), a B&B booking company, projects its sphere of influence north to Wasilla (singles start at $50, doubles at $55). **Big Lake** (head onto Big Lake Rd. from Mile 52.5 on Parks Hwy.) and **Nancy Lake** (Mile 66.5 and 67.3 on Parks Hwy.) for camping ($10 per site), lodging, canoeing, and fishing (day-use parking $3). Nancy Lake (495-6273) also rents 12 spacious public-use cabins on the lake for $30; call 745-3975 in advance for reservations or information on the Big Lake campgrounds. Or splash in whitewater with **NOVA Riverrunners** (745-5753). NOVA suits you up and takes you rafting down the Matanuska Valley's rivers, with day trips ranging from easy floats to heart-stopping plunges through unforgiving class V rapids ($60-125). NOVA also organizes multi-day adventures. For more information on the area, go to **Matanuska Visitors Center** at Mile 35.5 on the George Parks Hwy. (746-5000; open daily 8:30am-6:30pm).

KENAI PENINSULA

■ Hope

The only town on the southern side of Turnagain Arm, Hope is the twinkle of lights that can be seen across the water from the Seward Hwy. Without a major salmon run or ferry terminal, this minuscule former gold rush town of 200 remains untrampled, unlike other communities within a daytrip of Anchorage.

The first gold discovered in Alaska was found here by Russians as early as 1849, but they kept it secret for fear of losing their claim. The first major strike was made by American prospectors in 1889, and the town grew to 3000 people years before Anchorage even existed. The boom was short-lived, but many of its relics and, more importantly, the view of the Turnagain Arm, remain. Much of the federal land around Hope is still open to recreational mining, but more people visit Hope for its pink salmon fishing and its peaceful setting. Hope lies near the end of the scenic 18-mi. Hope Hwy. This road joins the Seward Hwy. 71 mi. outside of Anchorage, just where it turns sharply south down the Kenai (KEEN-eye) Peninsula toward Seward.

Practical Information and Events The Hope **visitors center** (782-3268) sits ¼ mi. out on Palmer Creek Rd., just before the townsite (open mid-April to mid-Sept. daily 8am-8pm; mid-Sept. to mid-April Sat.-Sun. noon-6pm). The center provides information on mining and hiking near Hope; maps of the Resurrection Trail and other excellent hikes are available only in Seward.

Resurrection Creek, at the edge of town, supports a healthy run of **salmon** in July and August. The annual **Hope Pink Salmon Derby** runs July to mid-August and awards an ounce of gold to the angler who bags the biggest fish (no entry fee; entrants must register at the visitors center to win). During the third weekend in July, Hope puts on a series of community events, including a bazaar, a raffle, a square dance, and a 5km fun run. If you've had a bad day, hurl away your frustrations at Hope's municipal horseshoe pit across from the Seaview (free). The **post office** (782-3352) sits across from the museum on the way into town (open Mon.-Fri. 8:30am-4:30pm, Sat. 10am-2pm; **General Delivery ZIP Code:** 99605).

Accommodations, Camping, and Food Although Hope's indoor accommodations are not as outrageously priced as those of other peninsula towns, camping is still the best way to go. Camp for free at **Coeur d'Alene Campground,** just 7 mi. past the visitors center up Palmer Creek Rd. (free; pit toilets and no water). **Porcupine Campground,** at the end of the Hope Hwy. is closer to town (1.3 mi.) and features roomy sites, some overlooking Turnagain Arm (sites $8; water and pit toilets). If you just can't stand camping (what the hell are you doing in Alaska?), **Henry's One-Stop Grocery and Motel,** Mile 15.8 of the Hope Hwy. (782-3222), has motel rooms ($50), showers ($2), full RV hookups ($15), groceries, and laundry facilities (wash $1, dry 75¢; open Mon.-Thurs. 8am-6pm, Fri.-Sun. 8am-7pm). In town, the **Seaview Motel** (782-3364) occupies a choice location near the mouth of Resurrection Creek. Rooms with separate baths are $35 for singles, $45 for doubles. They also have tent and RV sites ($7, electrical hookups $12).

In the late afternoon, the sun slants into the peaceful **Seaview Café** (782-3364). Gorge yourself on the all-you-can-eat ribs, chicken, and pork chop barbecue with baked beans, potato salad, and a sourdough roll ($11). The pie, however, is their pride and joy ($3; open daily 9am-6pm).

Outdoors The Forest Service permits **amateur gold mining** along Sixmile Creek from Mile 1.5 to 5.5 on the Hope Hwy. Closer to town, another 20-acre claim (beginning at the Resurrection trailhead foot bridge of Resurrection Creek Rd.) is also open to weekend panners, and, several times in the last few years, amateurs have taken home healthy sized nuggets. Hope also presents a range of enjoyable day hikes and is at the northern end of a 70-mi. series of trails crossing the Kenai Peninsula from Seward to Hope.

The **Resurrection Pass Trail,** originally a 19th-century gold miner byway, leads 39 mi. through the Chugach National Forest from Hope to the Sterling Hwy. This four- to five-day hike traverses mountain passes and lake shores and offers excellent wildlife viewing. Of all the hikes in the Kenai Peninsula, this one best combines wilderness, wildlife, and accessibility. Many people even take a week or more just to enjoy the varied scenery. To reach the Resurrection Pass trailhead in Hope, turn south onto Palmer Creek Rd. at Mile 16.2 of the Hope Hwy. and take the immediate right fork to reach Resurrection Creek Rd. The trail begins 4 mi. down the road at a parking area. No less than seven Forest Service **cabins** punctuate this hike. They can be reserved for $20 a night in Anchorage (and usually have been, long before you arrived in Alaska) and at the **Seward Ranger Station** in Seward. Fine fishing in Juneau and Trout Lakes rewards you near the end of the trail. The southern trailhead lies on the Sterling Hwy. near Cooper Landing, 106 mi. south of Anchorage and 53 mi. east of Soldotna.

If you have less time, a two- to three- day hike to the **Devil's Creek Trail** cutoff leaves from Mile 18 of the Seward Hwy. and intersects the trail in one of its most scenic stretches, about half the distance from Hope to the Sterling Hwy. For more information on the Resurrection Pass Trail and the extension to Seward, contact the U.S. Forest Service's Seward Ranger District, 334 4th Ave., Seward 99664 (224-3374; open Mon.-Fri. 8am-5pm).

Beginning from the Porcupine Campground, the **Hope Point Trail** is a more challenging hike up to a peak above treeline. This 5-mi. roundtrip initially follows Porcupine Creek, then climbs steeply to the treeline and on to Hope Point, delivering a stunning view of the Turnagain Arm and the surrounding mountains.

The **Gull Rock Trail,** an easy 5-mi. trek along Turnagain Arm, affords fine views of the water, the shore, and, on an exceptionally clear day, Denali. The trek initially follows an old wagon road out of the Porcupine Campground at the end of the Hope Hwy. It passes the remains of a sawmill and a homestead along the way to the rock. There is no camping, so allow four to six hours for the roundtrip.

Resurrection Creek is an excellent place to fish and usually far less crowded than other streams so close to both the Turnagain Arm and the beaten path. The creek is home to dolly varden and every type of salmon except sockeye, so fishermen can catch worthwhile suppers anytime between June and September. Getting to the creek is easiest near the Old Hope Townsite or off Resurrection Creek Rd. about 5 mi. from the Hope Hwy.

■ Seward

Seward's steep snowcapped mountains slant to the edge of Resurrection Bay, making it one of the most scenic towns in Alaska. But Seward holds paramount importance as the gateway to the world-famous **Kenai Fjords National Park,** and the tidal glaciers and icefields are more scenic than the town itself. Seward also commands respect for surviving the 1964 earthquake that rang in at 9.2 on the Richter scale and sent six successive tsunamis sweeping across the peninsula. Today, Seward has worked hard to preserve its "charming seaside town" demeanor and is a stopover for most major cruise lines. Historic downtown Seward is walkable, and the Golden Arches and strip malls that blight its peninsular neighbors, Soldotna and Kenai, are thankfully missing. Anchorage, 127 mi. north, is connected to Seward by the scenic **Seward Hwy.**

PRACTICAL INFORMATION AND ORIENTATION

Visitors Information: Chamber of Commerce, Mile 2 on the Seward Hwy. (224-8051). Encyclopedic knowledge of Seward. Computerized directory of accommodations and restaurants. Open daily 9am-5pm. Also operates a **railroad car,** 3rd and Jefferson St., where you can pick up a self-guided walking tour and mark your home town on the world map. Another information center is located in the small boat harbor. Both are open daily in summer 11am-5pm. **National Park Service Visitors Center,** 1212 4th Ave. (224-3175), also at the small-boat harbor. Info and maps for the spectacular Kenai Fjords National Park. Nature talks at 5:30pm (daily Memorial day-Labor day), slide shows upon request. Open in summer daily 8am-7pm; winter Mon.-Fri. 8am-noon and 1-5pm. **Seward Ranger Station, Chugach National Forest,** 334 4th Ave. (224-3374), at Jefferson. Extensive trail info, maps, and detailed advice on trails close to town. Cabin reservations for the Seward Ranger District. $25 per night, 7-day max. stay for all cabins (see **Hope: Outdoors,** p.74). Open Mon.-Fri. 8am-5pm.

Employment Office: Seward Employment Center, P.O. Box 1009 (224-5276), 5th and Adams, on the 2nd floor of the City Building. Open Mon.-Fri. 9am-noon and 1-4:30pm.

Airport: 2 mi. north of town on Seward Hwy. **F.S. Air Service** (478-9575) flies to Anchorage 3 times daily in the summer (roundtrip $130). **Scenic Mountain Air** (288-3646) offers 1-hr. flightseeing trips over the fjords ($99 per person, 2 person min.) and a fly-in, hike-out package leaving from Moose Pass at Seward Hwy. Mile 29 ($99 per person, 2 person min.).

Trains: Alaska Railroad (264-2494). Depot at the northern edge of town, across from the visitors center. Nightly service to Anchorage (May 12-Sept. 2; $50).

Buses: Seward Bus Lines, 1914 Seward Hwy. (224-3608). To Anchorage (1 per day, 9am; $30, $5 extra for service to the airport).

Ferries: Alaska Marine Highway (224-5485, 800-642-0066 for reservations). Ferry dock at 4th and Railway Ave. Served by the *Tustumena*. About 1 per week in summer to: Kodiak ($54), Valdez ($58), and Homer ($98). No service during one week of every month. Call for schedule.

Trolley: Just wave it down and it will take you anywhere on its route through town ($1.50). Operates daily 10am-6pm. Group tours available.

Taxi: Independent Cab (224-5000). **PJ's Taxi** (224-5555). Both 24hr.
Car Rental: Seward Tesoro, Mile 1.9 of the Seward Hwy. (224-8611). $44 per day with unlimited free mileage. Must be at least 25 with credit card.
Winter Road Closure Information: 800-478-7675.
Kayak Rental: Adventures and Delights (224-3960), next to the National Park Visitors Center. Singles $30 for the first day, $15 per day thereafter, $10 per day after a week. Doubles $55 first day, $45 thereafter, $15 after a week. $200 deposit or credit card imprint per boat. Rents to experienced kayakers only; thorough skills demonstration required. Guided day trips start at $95 per day. Open daily 9am-6pm; off season 9-10am and 4:30-6pm.
Laundromat and Showers: Seward Laundry (224-5727), 4th and C St. Wash, dry, and fold $1.35 per lb. Showers $3.50 (no time limit). Open daily 9am-9pm, last wash at 7:30pm. Showers also at the Harbormaster Bldg. (5-min. shower $1).
Bookstore: Reader's Delight, 222 4th Ave. (224-2665). Mostly paperbacks, but has a collection of used books-on-tape so you can finally quit listening to that Steely Dan tape you found on your car floor. Open daily 10am-7pm.
Pharmacy: Seward Drug, 224 4th Ave. (224-8989). Open daily 10am-7pm.
Fishing Supplies: The Fish House (224-3674), across from the Harbormaster. Rent rods ($10), buy tackle. Tips and instructions free. Fishing licenses available (see **Fishing,** p. 50). Wide selection. Open daily 6am-10pm.
Crisis Line: 224-3027. 24hr.
Hospital: Seward General (224-5205), 1st Ave. and Jefferson St.
Emergency: 911. **Police:** 224-3338.
Post Office: 224-3001, 5th Ave. and Madison St. Open Mon.-Fri. 9:30am-4:30pm, Sat. 10am-2pm. **General Delivery ZIP Code:** 99664.
Area Code: 907.

ACCOMMODATIONS AND CAMPING

Seward offers a number of cheap camping and room options, though some of them are a trek from Seward itself. Seward's municipal campground, **Waterfront Campground,** is clean and inexpensive, while private alternatives offer more solitude. At Mile 29 on Seward Hwy., the nearby town of **Moose Pass** has four campgrounds with excellent fishing to boot: **Primrose** at Mile 18, **Ptarmigan Creek** at Mile 23, **Trail River** at Mile 24, and **Wye** at Mile 36. All are run by the **Chugach National Forest;** for information, contact Alaska Public Lands Information, 605 W. 4th, Anchorage 99501 (271-2737).

Snow River International Home Hostel (HI-AYH), Mile 16 of Seward Hwy. No phone; call the central hosteling number in Anchorage (276-3635). Beautiful new house in a scenic but inconvenient location with 10 beds, showers, sauna, and kitchen facilities. $15, nonmembers $18. Open May to mid-Sept.
Municipal Waterfront Campground, along Ballaine Rd. between Railway Ave. and D St. One of the most scenic spots you'll ever spend the night, if you can get a grassy spot. Gravel lot hosts plentiful RVers. Toilets are scattered throughout the campground; restrooms and showers at the Harbormaster Bldg. 2-week max. stay. Check-out 4pm. Sites $8 for tents, parking spots $8. Open May 15-Sept. 30.
Saltwater Sportsmen's Lodge (224-5271), ½ mi. up Exit Glacier Rd. off Sterling Hwy. Mile 3.7. Soak in the sauna, roast marshmallows, fall asleep in your small cabin on the creek, rise early, use the pit toilets and showers, and beat the crowds to Exit Glacier. Cabins $55-75 for 2, $10 for each additional person. Walk-in tent sites $15 for 3, $3 for each additional person.
Ballaine House Lodging, 437 3rd Ave., Box 2051 (224-2362). Travelers weary of wildlife can sink into the couch and watch some cable TV or take a 2-block walk to downtown. A clean and well-furnished B&B. Singles $50. Doubles $72.
Exit Glacier Campground, 8½ mi. down Exit Glacier Rd., off Seward Hwy. Mile 3.7. All budget tenters should come here: water, pit toilets, secluded sites, and a ½-mi. walk to Exit Glacier. Stroll to your walk-in tentsite and fall asleep to the far-off ring of the cash register at the fee-charging campgrounds.

FOOD

Seward offers a decent variety of affordable food, but you'll be glad you didn't come for the cuisine. Stock up on groceries at the **Eagle Quality Center,** 1907 Seward Hwy. (open 24hr.). It's a hike from downtown, but you can reward yourself with a $1 ice cream cone at the in-store soda fountain. At night, the younger crowd's bar-hopping usually begins at the **Yukon Bar,** 4th and Washington (224-3065), where you can pin a dollar to the ceiling and leave your mark in Alaska. Pool tables and live rock Thurs.-Sat. (open daily noon-1:30am).

Don's Kitchen (224-8036), at 4th Ave. and Washington St. A popular lunch spot and good place to eavesdrop on fishing stories. Their biscuits-and-gravy plate ($4) is available in ½ portions ($3). Sandwiches and fries from $6. Open 24hr.

Peking, 338 4th Ave. (224-5444), at Jefferson St. Tasty lunch specials with rice and soup ($6.25-7.95) served 11:30am-3pm. Well decorated, clean interior is Alaska's closest thing to an Asian art museum. Open daily 11:30am-10:30pm.

Christo's Palace (224-5255), at 4th Ave. and Railway Ave. Cavernous pizza joint and bar. 14-in. pizza $12. Wide variety of Italian and Mexican fare; $9 fetches a hearty chimichanga plate. Dinner served until 11pm, pizza and sandwiches until 1:30am. Open daily 11am-1:30am.

Resurrect Art Coffee House Gallery, 320 3rd Ave. (224-7161). Kenai's only coffee shop, located in a converted Lutheran church. Food is limited to plastic-wrapped muffins and sweets, but you can sip espresso or Italian soda ($1.50) at the altar-turned-art display or in the balcony-turned-loft. Art books available for browsing; Luther's Small Catechism is notably missing. Occasional live music and poetry readings. Open daily 7:30am-10:30pm.

SIGHTS AND EVENTS

The self-guided **walking tour** of Seward, detailed on the **map** available at the visitors center, passes many turn-of-the-century homes and businesses. A complete tour takes two to three hours. The **Resurrection Bay Historical Society Museum,** in the Senior Center building at 3rd and Jefferson St., exhibits traditional Alaskan artifacts, including a fine collection of woven baskets ($1, children 50¢; open Memorial Day-Labor Day daily 10am-5pm; extended hours when cruise ships are in town). From June 15 to Labor Day, you can see the "Earthquake Movie" at the **Seward Community Library** (224-3646), 5th Ave. and Adams St., daily at 2pm. The movie shows actual footage of the 1964 Good Friday earthquake. With a supporting cast of fires and tsunamis, the quake destroyed much of Seward and Southcentral Alaska ($2 donation requested, 12 and under free; library open Mon.-Fri. noon-8pm, Sat. noon-6pm). The 40-year-old **Liberty Theater,** 304 Adams St. (224-5418), projects current films ($5, $3 for matinees). In the spring of 1994, the Liberty began to release films on their national release date (a source of community pride).

The **Silver Salmon Derby** opens each year on the second Saturday in August and closes eight days later. In 1995 the city upped the prize for the elusive tagged fish to $100,000. No one has caught the fish since 1980, when Japanese tourist Katsumi Takaku nabbed it from the city docks.

The other annual event that gets Seward hopping is the **Mountain Marathon** on the 4th of July. Alaska's oldest footrace, the marathon began when a sourdough challenged a neighbor to run up and down the 3022-ft. Mt. Marathon in less than an hour. The current record is 43 minutes for men and 50 minutes for women. The race has been joined by a parade while the governor and hundreds of enthusiasts run, slide, fall, and bleed down the steep mountainsides to the shores of Resurrection Bay. Thousands of sadistic spectators set up lawn chairs in town and watch the painful spectacle with binoculars. The annual **Seward Silver Salmon 10K Run** takes off during the Labor Day weekend, and the **Exit Glacier 5K and 10K Run** happens in mid-May. While these races may sound tough, Seward's truest test of physical endurance comes in the third weekend of January when the three-day **Seward Polar Bear Jump** plunges participants into the frigid water.

OUTDOORS

Seward is the point of entry into the incredible **Kenai Fjords National Park.** (The **Park Service Visitors Center** is near the small-boat harbor; see **Practical Information.**) The park's coastal mountain system is packed with wildlife and glaciers, but is largely inaccessible to novice kayakers unless they care to spend a considerable amount of money. It is totally inaccessible to hikers without mountaineering equipment and experience. However, if you feel the urge to stretch your Alaska budget for wildlife viewing, Seward is the place to do it. Boat cruises are the easiest and most popular way to see the park. The best and most expensive cruises access either **Aialik Bay,** for more forested terrain and wildlife, or **Northwestern Lagoon,** which offers views of tidal glaciers and spectacular geological formations. You are likely to see bald eagles, humpback whales, sea otters, Steller's sea lions, and Dall's porpoises playing near the bow of your boat. **Kenai Fjords Tours** (224-8030 or 800-478-8068) runs to the Lagoon for $129, $59 children; to Aialik Bay for $99, $49 children. **Major Marine Tours** (224-8030 or 800-764-7300) offers the best tour to Aialik. For $99 you get a ranger on board to explain wildlife and glacier facts, and an excellent salmon, halibut, and shellfish dinner. There are a variety of tours within Resurrection Bay as well, including overnight trips, and it is best to shop around for the type of trip you want. The cheapest start at $59. Pick up the list of charters at the Chamber of Commerce (see **Practical Information**) or from shops along the boardwalk next to the harbormaster's office.

Seward also offers great day hikes. **Exit Glacier** is 9 mi. west on the road that starts at Mile 3.7 of the Seward Hwy. Kenai Fjords Tours runs 2½-hr. tours of Exit Glacier for $19 (under 12, $9.50). Tours depart daily at 2pm, May-Sept., from the small boat harbor. The ranger station maintains a variety of hiking trails ranging from a leisurely ½-mi. stroll to an amazing, if grueling, 3000 ft. climb up to the glacier and the **Harding Ice Field.** Allow six to seven hours for the 8-mi. roundtrip. The rangers will prevent you from getting within 50 ft. of the glacier face, as chunks of ice weighing several tons are continually breaking off, or "calving." Rangers lead one-hour **nature walks** daily at 10am and 2pm, leaving from the Exit Glacier Ranger Station (free). The Exit Glacier Campground is ½ mi. from the ranger station (see **Accommodations and Camping,** above).

Travelers who want to stay closer to the water can hike in Caines Head State Recreation Area, at the mouth of Resurrection Bay along the **McGilvrey Trail.** One and a half mi. into the 7-mi. trail, there is a 3-mi. stretch negotiable only at low tide. Most people stay overnight before returning in order to wait for another low tide. Consult the newspaper, the Chamber of Commerce, the coast guard, or any commercial fisherman for tide information. The last 2½ mi. lead along sand, ending at South Beach, where camping is free. Nearby **Mt. Marathon** offers a view of the city and ocean. From 1st and Jefferson St., take Lowell St. to reach the trail, which begins with a steep ascent up a rocky stream bed. Once above vegetation, a network of trails continues up the rocky ledge to the left. Another route climbs through the scree to the right. The route provides better footing for the ascent, and the scree can be fun to run through on the way down. Unless you're training for the race, plan on a two-hour climb to the top and a 45-minute hop-and-slide to come down. There is no final peak at the end of the trail, but the **views** over Resurrection Bay are worth it. Salmon and halibut fill the bay, and grayling and dolly varden can be hooked right outside of town. Charters are available for both halibut and salmon throughout the summer; prices run from $95-145, with all gear provided. Call **The Fish House** (800-257-7760; see **Practical Information**), the largest charter-booking service in Seward. You can also fish for free from the shore or docks.

■ Sterling Highway to Kenai

The Sterling Hwy. begins 37 mi. north of Seward at Tern Lake and continues south along Cook Inlet to Homer. Shortly after its intersection with the Seward Hwy., it passes **Kenai Lake,** which stretches in a giant Z-shape through the Chugach Range. The Sterling continues along the Kenai River to the town of **Cooper Landing.** The Kenai offers several places to whitewater raft without risking life and limb. Some of these floats are as scenic as you can get on a class III river. Rafting and fishing tour companies generally supply lunch and gear on full-day trips, but anglers should buy their own licenses beforehand. Try **Alaska Wildland Adventures** (800-478-4100) in Cooper Landing for a variety of full and half day rafting or fishing trips for $42-185. The **Alaska River Co.** (595-1226) offers hiking as well as rafting and fishing tours for $35-150. Another far less pricey option is the $3 ferry trip to the opposite bank of the Kenai River. The boat uses cables and current to carry it across and is frequented by anglers. The ferry can be found at Mile 55 on the Sterling.

Anglers rejoice: you have reached the Promised Land of salmon fishing, a land flowing with kings, silvers, reds, and pinks. During the summer runs, the town and surrounding campgrounds take on a carnival-like atmosphere as eager fisherfolk line up on the banks of the Kenai River to try their luck. It won't be unusual for you to see anglers standing shoulder to shoulder and filling their baskets with fish.

The Kenai River area also offers extensive hiking opportunities. The Southern Resurrection Pass trailhead is a long and beautiful trek through the surrounding wilderness. The trail is in excellent condition and extremely flat, beginning in Hope and climbing gradually to Resurrection Pass. It then descends gently into a valley with several lakes and lovely beaver-dammed creeks. The Devil's Pass Trail then continues south to Seward. The hike from Seward to the Sterling is 26.7 mi. and can take from two to five days depending on your pace. The trail is popular and USFS cabins can be reserved six months in advance.

The highway parallels the Kenai River until it enters the **Kenai National Wildlife Refuge.** This stretch of the Peninsula is prime moose territory (the 1,730,000 acres of land were designated the Kenai National Moose Refuge in 1941) and offers excellent canoeing opportunities. In 1980, the refuge grew to 1.97 million acres and was redesignated the Kenai National Wildlife Refuge. To get to the Kenai National Wildlife Refuge **Visitors Center** (P.O. Box 2139, Soldotna; 262-7021) from the Soldotna visitors center at 44790 Sterling Hwy. between Miles 95 and 96, go left on Funny River Rd., and right onto Ski Hill Rd. Pick up a copy of *Refuge Reflections*, which gives you detailed fishing, hiking, and canoeing tips. There are several nearby nature trails with free guided walks Saturday at 11am and 1:30pm and Sunday at 11am (open Mon.-Fri. 8am-5pm, Sat.-Sun. 9am-6pm). The Swanson and Moose Rivers meander into the Kenai National Wildlife Refuge, offering one to seven day canoe trips through the refuge's remote forests and lakes. The **Sports Den** (262-7491) has fishing supplies and canoes for $35 per day, $25 per day for three or more days (open Mon.-Sat. 8am-7pm, Sun. 9am-6pm). Boats are sometimes available alongside the highway; residents put their vessels in their front yards and hang "for rent" signs. Boat rentals aren't cheap, but both the Swan Lake and the Swanson River Routes offer pristine wilderness and an exceptional variety of wildlife. For free **canoe route maps** drop by the visitors center, or write or call the refuge manager (also at the visitors center address and phone).

Camp anywhere along the Sterling Hwy. The sites are too numerous to name and in the high season you may have to go to several before you can find a spot. Grab a meal at **Sal's Klondike Diner,** 44619 Sterling Hwy. (262-2220), ½ mi. from the river and several hundred miles from the Klondike. A model train circles overhead. Menu "loded" with gold rush trivia. Chicken fried steak with mashed potatoes, vegetable, roll, and salad is a favorite ($8). Open 24hr.

Call 262-9228 for **road conditions** and 911 for an **ambulance** or in an **emergency.** Call 260-FIRE/3473 in case of a **fire.** The nearest **hospital** is **Central Peninsula General,** 250 Hospital Pl. (262-4404). The **post office** (262-4760), Binkley St., downtown, is open Mon.-Fri. 8:30am-5pm, Sat. 10am-2pm. **General Delivery ZIP Code:** 99669. The **area code** is 907.

■ Kenai

Perched on a bluff overlooking the Cook Inlet, Kenai has a magical view of the Aleutian-Alaska Range and its prominent volcanoes, Mt. Redoubt and Mt. Augustine. Fueled by commercial fishing, offshore oil drilling, and a huge fertilizer plant, Kenai has become the peninsula's largest and fastest growing city. The Dena'ina people lived here until Russian fur traders colonized the area in 1791; the U.S. military later established a fort in what is now Old Kenai. Kenai's fast-paced industrial growth has been a mixed blessing: larger population has brought the peninsula's best variety of restaurants and services, but the hurried expansion spared few traces of the city's history and left a forgettable cityscape of RV parks and strip malls. Kenai's natural environment has thankfully not been entirely wrecked. The pristine Captain Cook State Recreation Site lies 30 mi. away, and the mouth of the Kenai remains a good place to catch salmon or watch beluga whales do the same.

PRACTICAL INFORMATION AND ORIENTATION

Visitors Center: Visitor and Cultural Center, 11471 Kenai Spur Hwy. (283-1991), just past the corner of Spur and Main St. An Alaska-sized reservoir of information, erected for the town's 1991 bicentennial. Usual array of pamphlets is supplemented by a room full of stuffed native wildlife, an area dedicated to traditional Alaskan artifacts, and a small theater with films on the area's development. Open Mon.-Fri. 9am-8pm, Sat.-Sun. 10am-7pm; winter Mon.-Fri. 9am-6pm. **National Park Service,** 502 Overland Dr., P.O. Box 2643, Kenai 99611 (283-5855). Best source of info on **Lake Clark National Park and Preserve,** across Cook Inlet from Kenai. Hours vary.

Airport: 1 mi. north of downtown. Take Kenai Spur Rd. to Willow St.; follow signs for Airport Loop. **ERA** (800-426-0333) service to Anchorage (rates start at $35, reserve in advance for lowest rates).

Taxi: Alaska Cab, 283-6000. **Inlet Cab,** 283-4711. Both 24hr.

Car Rental: Hertz (283-7979), at the airport. $45 per day, unlimited mi. Must be 21 with credit card. Several other companies also at the airport.

Buses: Kenai Peninsula Bus Lines (563-0800). 1 per day to Anchorage ($30) and Homer ($19).

Library: 163 Main St. Loop (283-4378). Open Mon.-Thurs. 8:30am-8pm, Fri.-Sat. 8:30am-5pm.

Laundromat and Showers: Wash-n-Dry (283-8473), Lake St. and Kenai Spur Rd. Wash $1.50, dry $1. 20-min. shower $4.20. Open daily 8am-10pm.

Pharmacy: Carr's (283-6300), at Kenai Spur Hwy. and Airport Way. Open Mon.-Sat. 9am-9pm.

Crisis Line: 283-7257. 24hr.

Women's Resource Center: 325 S. Spruce St. (283-9479). 24hr.

Hospital: Central Peninsula General Hospital, 250 Hospital Pl. (262-4404).

Emergency: 911. **Police:** 283-7879.

Post Office: 140 Bidarka (283-7771). Open Mon.-Fri. 8:45am-5:15pm, Sat. 9:30am-1pm. **General Delivery ZIP Code:** 99611.

Area Code: 907.

Kenai, on the western Kenai Peninsula, is about 158 mi. from Anchorage and 96 mi. north of Homer. Kenai can be reached via **Kalifornsky Beach Rd.,** which joins the Sterling Hwy. from Anchorage just south of Soldotna, or via **Kenai Spur Hwy.,** which runs north from Soldotna and west to Kenai. Kalifornsky mile markers measure distance from Kenai, while the Kenai Spur mile markers measure distance from Soldotna. Both roads provide access to the peninsula's lakes and peaks; on a clear day, you can see the 10,000-ft. **Mt. Redoubt Volcano** across Cook Inlet.

ACCOMMODATIONS AND CAMPING

The annual invasion of tourists and anglers has launched Kenai's hotel rates into orbit. Check the visitors center (see **Practical Information**) for listings of local bed and breakfasts, starting at $45. Backpackers used to stay in a free municipal camp-ground that has since been moved to the park at Kenai Spur Hwy. and Marathon Rd. As if the decentralized location weren't enough, campers now must pay $8 for grav-elly sites (water, pit toilets). This leaves not a single legal budget accommodation in Kenai. Although camping down by the beach (take Spruce Dr. from the Kenai Spur Hwy.) is illegal, hard-core budget travelers are reportedly not harassed.

Beluga Lookout RV Park and Lodge, 929 Mission St. (283-5999 or 800-745-5999 in Alaska). Take Main St. toward the water and go right on Mission. Prime location and unbeatable view, but no tent sites. You can scan the sea for belugas from the viewing benches or from the lounge. Full hookup $15-20, $25 for bay view.

Katmai Hotel, 10800 Kenai Spur Hwy. (283-6101), 1 block from downtown. Small rooms with nice decor and cable TV. Singles $49. Doubles $59.

North Star Lodge, Mile 21 Kenai Spur Hwy. (776-5259). A hotel and restaurant 9 mi. north of town with space for 12 men in a bunkhouse. Water, shared bath. $15 in the bunkhouse. Showers $3. Rooms from $65.

FOOD

Carr's Quality Center (283-7829), in the Kenai Mall next to the K-Mart on Kenai Spur Rd. and Airport Way, is the city's largest grocery store. They have a bakery, fruit and juice bar, natural foods section, pharmacy, and fast food (open 24hr.).

Little Ski-Mo's Burger-n-Brew (283-4463), on Kenai Spur Rd. across from the visi-tors center. Staggering array of burgers offered in a dimly lit lodge-like interior, complete with fireplace. Try the Twin Cities ($6.50), with egg, bacon, cheddar cheese, and sprouts, served with fries. Surprise, surprise: Ski-Mo's also serves *udon,* Japanese wheat noodles (3 varieties $6.50 each). Burger and fries $4.40. Open Mon.-Sat. 11am-10:30pm, Sun. 11:30am-9:30pm.

New Peking, 145 S. Willow St. (283-4662), off Kenai Spur Rd. Savor a $5 lunch spe-cial (served daily 11:30am-3pm) or all-you-can-eat lunch buffet ($6) amid the pot-ted plants and lush oriental setting. Dinner entrees, including vegetarian options, $8 and up. Open Mon.-Fri. 11am-10pm, Sat.-Sun. noon-10pm.

Kitchen Express, 115 S. Willow St. (283-5387), across from the Merit Inn. A tasty way to get your lips around some well prepared seafood without breaking the bank. Oyster, shrimp, and salmon entrees $11-12; bowl of clam chowder with bread is $3. Open Mon.-Fri. 6am-7pm, Sat. 10am-5pm.

Thai Lotus, 106 S. Willow St. (283-7250). A little pricey, but you'll forget about the tile floor and white walls once you taste Top of the World Chicken Cashew Nut ($10) or devour one of many lunch specials ($6.50-8.50). All-you-can-eat lunch buf-fet $6.95. Open Mon.-Fri. 11am-10pm, Sat. 4pm-10pm, Sun. 11am-8pm.

SIGHTS AND ACTIVITIES

The most breathtaking sight in Kenai is **Cook Inlet,** framed by smooth sand, two mountain ranges, and volcanic **Mt. Augustine** and **Mt. Redoubt.** Take in the magic of the inlet and its beluga whales, salmon runs, and eagles as you stroll the beach at the end of Spruce Dr. The best time to see whales is two hours before or after high tide. If you coordinate your visit with the arrival of the fishing boats, you may see a free-loading sea lion or seal as well.

Better yet, travel the 30 mi. out to **Captain Cook State Recreation Area** at the northern end of the Kenai Spur Rd. The excellent views of the inlet and the Alaska-Aleutian Range beyond can make for a lovely picnic on a bluff or a boulder strewn beach (you can also camp here; $10; water and pit toilets). Canoeing opportunities are so plentiful you could trip over them. Bald eagle sightings are especially common as well. A small **caribou** herd, often spotted trotting along Kenai Spur Hwy. or Bridge Access Rd., roams the flatlands between Kenai and Soldotna.

The **Holy Assumption Russian Orthodox Church,** on Mission St. off Overland, offers a look at Kenai's Russian heritage and an excellent view of the inlet. Originally built in 1846 and rebuilt in 1896, this National Historic Landmark contains 200-year-old icons (open in summer Mon.-Fri. 11am-4pm; tours upon request).

Recreational opportunities in the Kenai area are everywhere. Check at the Chamber of Commerce for fishing charter information (prices are comparable to those in Soldotna) or with the Forest Service (see **Practical Information**) for canoeing and hiking activities. The majority of fishing takes place in the **Kenai River,** of course. The best place to look for fish is in the slower eddies where fish like to rest. You are allowed to fish anywhere along the river that is not privately owned. Inexperienced fisherfolk should ask at fishing shops for recommended locations so they do not damage the banks of the river and jeopardize the fish habitat. You can fish for free at the mouth of the Kenai River if you have a license and rod (park at the end of Spruce Dr. and hike to the mouth). **Swanson River** and **Stormy Lake,** in the vicinity of the Captain Cook recreation area, offer chances at rainbow trout, silver salmon, and arctic char. Contact the State Division of Parks for regulations. **Nikiski,** 12½ mi. north of Kenai at Mile 23.4 of the Spur Rd., is home to an alien spacecraft cleverly disguised as a **geodesic-domed pool** (776-8472) behind the school. Located near the pool, a hockey rink, ski/running trail, and picnic area await the playful Earthling ($3, seniors $2, $6 buys use of the waterslides; open Tues.-Thurs. 7am-5pm and 6-9pm, Fri.-Sun. 1-5pm).

■ Sterling Highway: Kenai to Homer

From Kenai, the Sterling Hwy. winds through short, shoreline forest on a bluff overlooking the Cook Inlet. This stretch of road looks across the inlet to the Alaska-Aleutian Range. In particular, there are fantastic views of **Mt. Redoubt** and **Mt. Iliamna,** both volcanoes that rise over 10,000 ft. and have erupted in the last 50 years. The Hwy. continues into the town of **Ninilchik,** another hamlet with spectacular fishing, fantastic scenery, a strong Russian heritage, and an excellent clamming beach. The **visitors center** (567-1028) sits in the Ninilchik Village, in the Village Cache Store at the end of Village Rd. (turn off at Sterling Hwy. Mile 135.1; open Mon.-Sat. 6am-10pm), and the nearby parking lots are a good stopping point for exploring the area. Other than the unmatched views of Mt. Iliamna and Mt. Redoubt and the Aleutian-Alaska Range across the inlet, the only attractions are the old **Russian fishing village** on Village Rd. and the **Holy Transfiguration of Our Lord Orthodox Church,** built in 1901. Both overlook Cook Inlet, and the church, high up on a bluff, offers an unparalleled view of the two volcanoes. To get there, hike up the trail beginning next to the visitors center. The church and cemetery are still in use, but the Russian village is abandoned and dilapidated.

If you decide to stay in town for the night, head for the **Beachcomber Motel and RV Park** (567-3417), on Beach Access Rd. Each of the motel's four rooms has a shower, full kitchenette, TV, and unimpeded views of Mt. Redoubt across the Cook Inlet (singles $50, doubles $60, full hookups for RVs $15). For campers the obvious choice is to stay at one of the **state campgrounds** near town, each complete with water and toilets. The sites cater to RVs, but tenters can set up camp in the grass and still be within a short walk of the beach and clamming (sites $10). Superb sites in the **Ninilchik State Recreation Area,** some overlooking the inlet from a bluff, are less than 1 mi. north of town (sites $10). The nearby, beach-level **Deep Creek Recreation Area** is one of the most popular places to camp on the peninsula. Locals claim that it has the world's best saltwater king salmon fishing; dolly varden and steelhead trout as well (sites $10; day-use parking $5; boat launching available). **Clamming** on the beaches bordering the village is Ninilchik's main attraction when the tides are low. You can rent a shovel and pail ($5) and get tide information at the visitors center. RV hookups rattle and hum closer to town at **Hylea's Camper Park,** Mile 135.4 of Sterling Hwy. (567-3393; full hookup $19; fish cleaning station and smoker available; showers $2 for 10min.; $1.50 wash, $1.50 dry).

Buy groceries and fishing supplies at the **General Store** (567-3378) on Sterling Hwy. (open daily 6am-midnight). On the east side of the Sterling, a long, low restaurant and bar sit back on a gravel plot. The **Inlet View Café**, Mile 135.4 on Sterling Hwy. (567-3337), offers a sterling view of the Cook Inlet and hearty sandwiches named for the mountains you can see across the water: the Redoubt, Iliamna, and others ($5.50-8). A halibut basket, cole slaw, and fries is $8 (open daily 5:30am-midnight). The bar is a laid-back local hangout (open daily 10am-5am).

The Sterling Hwy. continues from Ninilchik along the western edge of the peninsula until it turns east toward **Homer.** Views of the Aleutian volcanoes dot the horizon from the Kenai Fjords National Park to Homer.

▦ Homer

In a state where the unique is commonplace and gorgeous is the norm, Homer's eclectic culture and idyllic setting still stand out. Although the population's mainstays are fisherfolk and aging counterculturalists, Homer is also home to many artists, several Russian Orthodox colonies, a fabulous public radio station, folk singer Jewell, and 1980s commercial celebrity Dom DeLuise. Moderate temperatures and a mere two feet of annual rainfall have resulted in this area's nickname, the "banana belt" of coastal Alaska. The beautiful weather provides plenty of opportunity for these diverse elements to mix against a spectacular backdrop. One end of the town rises up on bluffs above Kachemak Bay with wide views of the blue mountains and pale glaciers across the water. Homer supports its own theater group, scores of galleries stocked with the work of local artists, and one of the best small newspapers in Alaska.

The town extends into the bay along the improbable 4½-mi. tendril of sand and gravel known as the **Spit.** The ruggedly beautiful island and wilds of **Kachemak State Park** lie across the Kachemak Bay, where the southern end of the **Kenai Mountains** reaches the sea. Also on the south side of the bay are the artist/fishing colony of **Halibut Cove,** the scantly populated **Yukon Island,** the **Gull Island** bird rookery, and the Russian-founded hamlet of **Seldovia.**

PRACTICAL INFORMATION AND ORIENTATION

Visitors Information: Homer Chamber of Commerce and Visitor Information Center, 135 Sterling Hwy. (235-7740), near Main St. All the necessary info and pamphlets. Staff will help you find a room in the area. Open June-Labor Day daily 9am-8pm, Labor Day-mid-Dec. and mid-Jan-May 9am-5pm.

Park Information: Alaska Maritime National Wildlife Refuge Visitor Center, 509 Sterling Highway (235-6961), next to the Best Western Bidarka Inn. Wildlife exhibits, marine photography, and helpful advice on backcountry adventures in Kachemak Bay. They also lead **bird walks** on the Spit twice a week. Open daily 9am-6pm. **Southern District Ranger Station,** Kachemak Bay State Park, P.O. Box 321 (235-7024), 4 mi. outside town on the Sterling Hwy. **Fishing Licenses:** $15 for 3 days, available at local sporting goods stores and charter offices, or contact the **Alaska Dept. of Fish and Game,** 3298 Douglas St. (235-8191), near Owen Marine. Open Mon.-Fri. 8am-5pm.

Bank: First National Bank, on Homer Bypass at Heath St. 24-hr. ATM. Open Mon.-Thurs. 10am-5pm, Fri. 10am-6pm.

Employment Service: 601 E. Pioneer Ave. #123 (235-7791). Open Mon.-Fri. 8am-noon and 1-4:30pm.

Airport: Competing airlines have terminals on opposite sides of the runway. **Southcentral Air,** on Kachemak Dr. off Homer Spit Rd. (800-478-2550 or 283-3926). $65 for all 50-min. flights to Anchorage (4-6 per day), plus daily flights to Seldovia and Kenai. **Era Aviation** is in the actual airport; follow signs from Ocean Dr. just before it becomes the Spit Rd. (800-866-8394). $64 to Anchorage if you reserve early, otherwise $79 (6 per day). Also 1 per day to Kenai. **Homer Air** (235-8591) has service to Seldovia ($26).

Buses: Homer Stage Line, 424 Homer Spit Rd. Make reservations through **Central Charters** (235-7847). Infrequent and expensive bus service makes flying a far more tempting option. To: Soldotna ($25, 1 every other day), Anchorage ($45, 1 every other day). $5 extra for drop-off at Anchorage Airport. Runs Memorial Day to Labor Day only.

Ferries: Alaska Marine Highway, P.O. Box 166, (235-8449 or 800-382-9229). Office and terminal just before the end of the Spit. Open Mon.-Fri. 8:30am-4pm and when ferry is in. To: Seldovia ($18), Kodiak ($48), Seward ($96), Cordova ($138), and once a month to Dutch Harbor Aleutian Islands ($242).

Taxi: Chux Taxi, 235-2489. **Maggie's Taxi,** 235-2345. To downtown from the airport ($4) or ferry ($8). **Day Breeze Shuttle** (399-1168) runs between Spit and town twice daily ($2), cruises up and down the Spit the rest of the day ($1).

Share-A-Ride: KBBI Public Radio, AM 890. Serves as an on-air bulletin board several times daily. Will broadcast requests for those both seeking and offering rides. Entertaining listening even if you're not in the ride market. Call 235-7721.

Car Rental: Polar Car Rental, 4555 Sterling Hwy. Suite B (235-5998). $47 per day, 30¢ per mi. after 100 free mi. $5 extra for unlimited miles (open daily 8am-9pm, winter 8am-5pm, but available 24hr.). **Payless,** at airport (235-8280) is also $52 with unlimited mi. (open 7:30am-7:30pm). Must be 21 with a credit card for both.

Bike Rental: Homer Saw and Cycle, 1532 Ocean Dr. (235-8406). Top-of-the-line Trek mountain bikes, $15 ½day, $25 for 24hr. Open 9am-5pm Mon.-Fri., Sat. 11am-4pm. They also rent through **Trips** (235-0708), closer to downtown at 158 W. Pioneer (open Mon.-Sat. 11am-7pm). Biking is a great way to get around this rather spread out town, but be forewarned—there are lots of hills.

Bookstore: The Bookstore, 436 Sterling Hwy. (235-7496), next to the Eagle Quality Center. Open Mon.-Sat. 10am-7pm, Sun. noon-5pm.

Library: Homer Public Library, 141 Pioneer Ave. (235-3180), near Main St. Computer available for free internet access. Open Tues. and Thurs. 10am-8pm, Mon.,Wed., and Fri.-Sat. 10am-6pm.

Laundromat and Showers: Homer Cleaning Center (235-5152), on Main St. downtown. Wash $1, 6-8min. dry 25¢. Last load 1hr. before closing. Shower $2.50 for unlimited time, or shower together in a private room, 2 for $5.51, towel included. Open Mon.-Sat. 8am-10pm, Sun. 9am-9pm.

Women's Crisis Line: 235-8101. 24hr.

Hospital: South Peninsula Hospital, 4300 Bartlett (235-8101), off Pioneer.

Emergency: 911. **Police:** 235-3150.

Post Office: 3261 Wadell Rd. (235-6125), off Homer Bypass. Open Mon.-Fri. 8:30am-5pm, Sat. 10am-1pm. **General Delivery ZIP Code:** 99603.

Area Code: 907.

Surrounded by 400 million tons of coal, Homer rests on **Kachemak ("Smoky") Bay,** named after the mysteriously burning deposits that greeted the first settlers. Homer is on the southwestern Kenai Peninsula, on the north shore of the bay. **The Sterling Hwy.** links it with Anchorage (226 mi. away) and the rest of the Kenai Peninsula. The heart of Homer lies in a triangle defined by the shoreside Homer Bypass, downtown drag Pioneer Ave., and cross-cutting Lake St. Homer Bypass becomes Sterling Hwy. west of town, while east of town it becomes Ocean Dr. and veers right to follow the spit as Homer Spit Rd.

ACCOMMODATIONS AND CAMPING

Homer further endears itself to budget travelers with lots of cheap accommodations. Contact the **Homer Referral Agency** for B&Bs starting at $50 per night (235-8996), or check with the visitor's center.

Sunspin Guest House, 358 E. Lee Dr. (235-6677 or 800-391-6677). From Pioneer Ave. take Kachemak Way toward the bluff to Lee Dr. on left. Convenient location, though little atmosphere. Free rides to airport, the Spit, and the ferry. High-class bunkroom $25, private rooms $50 and up.

Driftwood Inn, 135 W. Bunnell (235-8019 or 800-478-8019 in AK), a short walk from downtown. Take the Homer Bypass, turn toward the ocean on Main St., then right on Bunnell. Spotless, ease-inducing, ultra-modern rooms in a rustic building.

Laundry and luggage storage for guests. Free local calls, continental breakfast. Homey guest lounge and a great view. Singles $54. Doubles $64.

Seaside Farm, 58335 East End Rd. (235-7850), 4½ mi. out of town. An amazingly beautiful but inconvenient ($12 cab ride to the airport) location. Hostel facilities, while bearable, are not nearly as appealing as the view across the bay. Camping out in the clover field is the much better bet. Mossy, the friendly, crunchy matron, runs a semi-commune of transient and semi-permanent sorts. Enjoy a roofed, outdoor common area and seaside strolls. Farm work for lodging deals available. Also rents bikes for $15 per day. Bunks $15 with shower. Tent sites $6, showers an additional $3. Private cabins with kitchenettes available at a discount to backpackers: $30 single, $40 double, otherwise $55 for double.

Spit Municipal Camping, 3735 Homer Spit Rd. (235-3160), across from the Fishing Hole, near the beginning of the Spit. The city controls 2 areas for RVs, 1 for tents and RVs. A once beautiful area that is now a giant gravel parking lot. Extremely popular and crowded nonetheless. Terrific views if you don't have someone camped in front of you. 2 permanent city restrooms with fresh water near the office. Tents $3. RVs $7.

Karen Hornaday Park, office at Public Works Dept., City Hall, 491 E. Pioneer (235-3170). From Pioneer, go uphill on Bartlett St. to Fairview, left to Campground Rd., then right to the park. Water, pit toilets, and nice view of the bay. Tent sites $3. RVs $7.

Kachemak Bay State Park, 7 water mi. across from the Spit. Gorgeous, secluded and free, but it will probably cost $50 per person to get there. Most locals vehemently maintain that it's well worth the expense. Spend a couple days and enjoy the hiking trails. For further info, stop by or call the Southern District Ranger Station (see **Practical Information**). A public use cabin is also available ($35 for first 4, $10 each additional person up to a total of 8).

FOOD

Homer has one of the best collections of restaurants in the state. If for some reason you decide not to take advantage of these exceptional offerings, the town also has an excellent selection of grocery stores. The huge, 24-hr. **Eagle Quality Center,** 436 Sterling Hwy. (235-2408), has a stunning array of options. **John's Corner Market,** on Lake St. at Pioneer Ave. sells fantastic produce (open Mon.-Sat. 10am-7pm).

On the Spit, you can usually hook or snag a salmon from the **Fishing Hole.** Buy fresh seafood directly from fishermen or at one of the retail outlets: **Katch Seafoods,** 765 Fish Dock Rd. (235-7953 or 800-368-7400), offers salmon and halibut for $3 per lb. **The Coal Point Trading Co.,** 4306 Homer Spit Rd. (235-3877 or 800-235-3877), will sell it to you raw, or vacuum-pack and deep-freeze your catch for 70¢ per lb. (open 6am-after 11pm). Wash down your cooked catch with locally brewed beer from the **Homer Brewing Company,** 1562 Homer Spit Rd. (235-FOAM/3626).

Downtown

Red Pepper Kitchen, 475 Pioneer (235-8362). So popular with the locals, it's hard to find a seat after 9:30pm. Deluxe burritos with homemade beans $4.50, Mediterranean pizza slice $3.50. Don't miss the locally made Snap Dragon Ginger Brew ($2). Open daily till 10pm.

Two Sisters Bakery, 106 W. Bunnell (235-2280). Take Main St. toward the water. Conventional but excellent bakery/café by day turns into a world culinary tour by night. Four evenings per week, the sisters concoct masterpieces from 1 of over 10 countries. Pricey ($10-14), but where else in Alaska can you find amazing Turkish or Moroccan food? Fri. and Sat. always feature Indian and Thai. Lunch treats include focaccia sandwiches ($4.50) and salmon chowder ($3). Open Mon.-Sat. 7am-3pm, world tour served Wed.-Sat. 6-10pm.

Café Cups, 162 Pioneer Ave. (235-8330). A gathering place for artists and young travelers. Feels like the best of a big-city café successfully hybridized with Homer's offbeat charm. Try the tasty, unusual sandwiches ($6.50-8 with salad), and espresso milkshake ($4.50). Outdoor seating. Open daily 7am-10pm.

The Thai and Chinese Restaurant, 601 E. Pioneer (235-7250). The front runner in the race for champion of the Asian lunch buffet. Passable Chinese and Thai entrees and sushi, all-you-can-eat, for $6 (served 11am-3pm). Much of the same appears again for the dinner buffet ($7; served 5-9pm). Open daily 11am-9pm.

On the Spit

Alaska's Italian Bistro, 4241 Homer Spit Rd. (235-6153). Magnificent ocean views in a tastefully unaffected space. Dinners aren't cheap, but lunch beckons with a tapas bar of clams casino ($8) or oysters bistro ($9). Open daily noon-10pm.

Glacier Drive-In, 3789 Homer Spit Rd. (235-7148), next to the Spit Campground. Spit tourists and an airborne mix of sea salt and grill grease evoke every boardwalk in America. You can't drive in, but you can take out or sit down in the classic fast food interior. Cajun dog ($2.30), hamburger ($3.90) and milkshakes ($2.10). Grab a 50¢ cup of coffee. Open daily 11am-8pm.

SIGHTS AND EVENTS

The **Pratt Museum,** 3779 Bartlett St. (235-8635), is the best museum on the peninsula. Recently remodeled, the Pratt houses a gallery of local art and historical exhibits of Kenai artifacts. "Eclectic" doesn't quite capture it; displays range from homesteader cabins to artifacts of the Inuit and Denali peoples, and include some great exhibits on marine mammals. View the skeleton of the Bering Sea beaked whale, or take part in the feeding frenzy in the salt water aquarium (fish frenzied Tues. and Fri. 4-5pm. Admission $3, seniors and under 18 $2; open daily 10am-6pm; Oct.-April Tues.-Sun. noon-5pm).

Homer has a great collection of **galleries,** including **Ptarmigan Arts,** 471 Pioneer Ave. (235-5345; open Mon.-Sat. 10am-7pm, Sun. 10am-5pm), with the work of over 40 Alaskan artists and craftspeople. The **Bunnell Street Gallery,** 106 W. Bunnell (235-2662), features innovative contemporary art (open summer daily 10am-6pm; winter 11am-5pm). The visitors center offers a complete list of area galleries. The town's active theater group performs at **Pier One Theater,** P.O. Box 894 (235-7333), near the start of the buildings on the Spit. You can catch plays there on the mainstage throughout the summer. (Tickets $9, seniors $8, children $6, Thurs. $1 off night shows; Thurs. and Sun. at 7:15pm, Fri.-Sat. at 8:15pm.) A series of other performances take place Sunday through Thursday, many featuring Homer's most famous son, Tom Bodett, of National Public Radio and Motel 6 ("We'll leave the light on for ya") fame. Check the *Homer News* for up-to-date schedules. **Homer Family Theater** (235-6728), at Main St. and Pioneer Ave., features current blockbusters and feel-good movies. Tickets are $5; get advance tickets at The Bookstore or at the door 30 minutes before showtime.

Homer never sleeps in the summer. Nightlife ranges from beachcombing at low tide in the midnight summer sun to hanging at the tourist trap and sometimes local joint, **Salty Dawg Saloon,** under the log lighthouse toward the end of the Spit (open 11am-whenever, as the sign says). **Alice's Champagne Palace,** 196 Pioneer Ave. (235-7650), is a wooden barn with diverse live music. Many young locals drop in as the midnight sun creeps along the horizon (Tues.-Sat. from 2pm into the morning).

Since Homer is often billed as the halibut capital of the world, it should come as no surprise how much hoopla is attached to the **Homer Jackpot Halibut Derby.** The competition runs from May 1-Labor Day and offers a grand prize in the neighborhood of $30,000. Every year several would-be winners are left crying at the scales after they land prize-winning fish with no ticket. Tickets are available in local charter offices on the Spit ($7). For those who prefer feathers to fins, the **Homer Shorebird Festival** (May 9-11 in 1997) offers birding tours, educational workshops, an arts fair, and 8-10,000 migrating birds. Last year, the event drew over 1000 registered participants and guerilla ornithologists. On the second Sunday in August, KBBI, the local public radio station, stages a fabulous fundraising **concert** on the town commons, featuring blues, rock, and bluegrass from 11am-8pm. The annual **Winter Carnival,** held during the first week in February, features sled dog races and snow machine competitions.

OUTDOORS

Nearly everyone who comes to Homer spends some time on the **Homer Spit.** Don't feel obligated to follow the crowds; this 5-mi. strip of sand is one of the most heinous tourist traps in the state. While there is no denying the Spit offers some great views, the utter lack of greenery and the concentration of vehicles makes the area a virtual parking lot. Even if you get off the pavement, there seems to be no escape from the RVs and crowded tents that litter the beach. To actually get a patch of sand to yourself, head to Bishop's Beach (take Main St. toward the water, and follow the signs to the left on Bunnell Ave.).

About the only good justification for visiting the Spit is to leave it via one of the many boats in the harbor. The vast majority of them are halibut charters; on a particularly good day, as many as 90 of them may set off in search of big, ugly fish. Choosing a charter, like fishing itself, is something of a crap shoot. Although most charter companies are reputable businesses, there are a few that strip their customers more cleanly than a filleted halibut. Many of the boats are booked through **Central Charters** (235-7847), located near the middle of the Spit's buildings. Full-day trips start at $150. All tackle and bait are included, and there is a refund policy for foul weather. A fishing license (3 days $15) earns you a daily one-fish limit. Check with the tourist office for a list of companies; not every reliable business will necessarily be a member, but those that are should be reputable.

If you don't have enough cash to chase after the big sea monsters, consider heading to the **Fishing Hole** near the start of the Spit, where anyone who can hold a rod can probably catch a salmon. A vigorous stocking program plants salmon fry in this tidal lagoon, which return years later to spawn. The lagoon is unsuitable for spawning, and anglers manage to hook or snag most of the fish that return.

For those only interested in catching great views, **bikes** are your best bet. If you're feeling brave, consider biking up the killer **East Hill Rd.** (predictably to the east of town off East End Rd.) for a panorama of the Kenai Mountains. The road levels out to quiet, flat gravel and fields of fireweed and other wildflowers. If you're traveling on foot, you can either take to the beach or check out the 6-mi. **Homestead Trail** just to the west of town. The trail has three different access points; check the *Homer Tourist Guide* for details.

■ Near Homer

KACHEMAK BAY

Locals are vocal in their praise of **Kachemak Bay State Park:** most maintain a visit to Homer is not complete without a trip across the bay. One of the largest coastal parks in the country, the area contains roughly 375,000 acres of beaches and tide pools, mountains and glaciers, and includes one of the northernmost temperate rainforests in the world. Stop by the **Southern District Ranger Station** (see **Practical Information**) for information on the park's myriad hiking and camping opportunities. **St. Augustine's Charters** offers regularly scheduled water-taxi service to the park, at 9am and 4pm daily, for $50 roundtrip. Personalized service is also available. Call **Inlet Charters** (235-6126 or 800-770-6126) for reservations. **Mako's Water Taxi** (399-4133) and **Rainbow Tours** (235-7272) offer similar services for about the same price, but price varies depending on the number of people and your destination. If you're just looking for an excuse to cruise and don't care to land anywhere, **Rainbow Tours** offers a 1½ hour cruise to Gull Island where you'll see murres, cormorants, guillemots, other birds with unpronounceable names, a few puffins, and about sixteen bijillion gulls. Tours depart the Spit at 9am and 4:30pm and cost $15 (under 12 $10, seniors $12.50). If you want to cruise the bay in style, go for a sailing tour on the 1930s-era **St. Augustine's Fire,** a gorgeous wooden sailing yacht. Two hours in the lap of nautical luxury costs $35 per person. Call **Inlet Charters** for a booking (see above). For a self-powered water adventure, consider a full-day kayak trip with **True**

ALASKA

North Kayak Adventures, P.O. 2319 (book through **Trips,** 235-0708, or **Central Charters,** 235-7847). Enthusiastic guides will lead you to some amazingly secluded and beautiful spots. The tour, although expensive, comes with a great lunch and lots of sea otters ($140, including roundtrip water taxi).

HALIBUT COVE

Yet another great way to spend an afternoon is with **Danny J. Tours** (235-7847 or 296-2223) visiting the colorful artist/fishing colony of Halibut Cove, and its few dozen residents. The trip leaves the Spit daily at noon and makes a short visit to Gull Island before dropping you off at the village for two and a half hours (roundtrip $35, seniors $28, children $17.50). On land, head to the **Saltry** (296-2223), the cove's only restaurant, for a lunch of raw and cooked fish. Try the halibut salad ($8), or the *nori maki* ($9; open 1-5pm, 6-9pm). Walk the raised boardwalk village to the **Halibut Cove Art Gallery** and view a collection of works by residents. Explore octopus-ink paintings at **Diana Tillion's Cove Gallery.** Diana herself extracts ink from stranded octopi with a hypodermic needle, eats the octopi, and then paints with their body fluids. If you tire of the galleries, several hiking trails surround the town. Reboard the Danny J. at 4pm, and arrive back at the Spit by 5pm.

■ Seldovia

Virtually untouched by the tourist mania rampant on the rest of the peninsula, this isolated hamlet combines southwestern marine charm with Homer's rolling terrain and funky ambience. The Russians named Seldovia for its herring, and the fishing industry has kept the town afloat for centuries. Seldovia is also blessed with unique geological surroundings. The town overlooks four active volcanoes: **Augustine, Iliamna, Redoubt,** and **Spur.**

Practical Information **Synergy Artworks,** Main St. (234-9901), across from the boat harbor, is home to the Chamber of Commerce and rooms stacked to the rafters with visitor information, including a free and detailed **map** (open Memorial Day- Labor Day daily 10am-6pm; shorter hours during the off season). Linger to enjoy striking art that far outdoes the meager stock of pamphlets. The **airport** is less than 1 mi. out of town on Airport Ave. Seldovia is served by **Homer Air** (235-8591; to Homer $27, roundtrip $50). The **ferry** M/V Tustumena chugs from Homer to Seldovia twice a week (Tues. 12:30pm, Sun. 3am; $18, roundtrip $36). You have the choice of spending either four hours (while the Tustumena refuels) or a few days (until the next ferry arrives) in Seldovia.

Once in town, the **Seldovia Taxi** (234-7675) will shuttle you about (open 8am-2am), or you can rent a bike at **The Buzz,** on the harbor side of Stamper's Market on Main St. (234-7479). The cost is $15 for a half-day (6am-noon or noon-6pm), $20 for a full day (6am-6pm), or $25 for 24hr. (license or credit card deposit required). They also rent fishing tackle for $15 per day, with a $25 deposit (open daily 6am-6pm). Stock up on books for the long ferry ride at **Magistrate Library,** on Seldovia St. near Main St. (open Tues. 2-4:30pm and 7:30-9:30pm, Thurs. 3:30-6pm and 7:30-9:30pm, Sat. 11:30am-4:30pm). For kayak rental, call **Kayak'atak** (234-7607 or 234-7425; singles $40 per day, doubles $70 per day). The phone at the **Seldovia Medical Clinic** is 234-7825 (open Mon., Wed., Fri. 9am-5pm); in an **emergency** call 911. The **police** can be reached at 234-7640. Call the **fire hall** at 234-7812. The **post office** (234-7831) is at Main St. and Seldovia St. and is open Mon.-Fri. 9am-5pm. The general delivery **ZIP Code** is 99663; the **area code** is 907.

Accommodations, Camping, and Food The **Dancing Eagles Lodge** (234-7627), at the end of Main St. by the boardwalk, offers rustic cabins, a private extension of the town's boardwalk, and a terrific view of the bay. Rates start at $45 per person per night. Less attractively situated cabins overlook the airport at **Seldovia**

Seaport Cottages, 313 Shoreline Dr., Box 118 (234-7483). Pleasant interiors offer kitchenettes and double or twin beds (singles or doubles $60, each additional person $10). The Chamber of Commerce keeps a list of Seldovia's B&Bs, most of which cost $60-85 (234-9901). RV camping is available for $8 at **Wilderness Park,** as are additional and more secluded tent spots for $5. The park is approximately half a mile past the marked turnout for **Outside Beach** on Anderson Way. **Stamper's Market** (234-7633), on Main St., stocks a modest supply of groceries, hardware, tackle, pharmaceuticals, and liquor (open Mon.-Sat. 9am-8pm, Sun. noon-5pm). Frozen dairy treats, hot showers, and laundry services combine in a bizarre but happy matrimony at the **Harbor Laundromat** (234-7420), also on Main St. (10min. shower $4, towel and soap included; laundry is $2-4 to wash, 25¢ per 5min. dry). Enjoy a delicious cone ($1.43) or a smacktastic milkshake ($2.86) as you towel off or fold your clothes (open daily 10am-9pm; last shower 8:30pm).

The Buzz (234-7479) serves coffee and espresso and provides a good place to loiter on a rainy afternoon. Linger with great food, including a $5.75 calzone and $4.25 slice of quiche. The cappuccino ($2) and raspberry rhubarb tart ($2.75) are a delectable combination (open daily 6am-6pm). The cheapest eats in town (during the season) are at the **Seaport Sandwich Shop,** next to the Harbormaster's Office overlooking the harbor. Their outside deck is a perfect location for a sound chomping of their $3.50 turkey sandwiches, $2 slices of pizza, and a $1.50 tacos (open daily noon-8pm).

Sights and Entertainment Stop by the small **museum,** 328 Main St. (234-7898), sponsored by the Seldovia Native Association (open Mon.-Fri. 8am-5pm). The adjacent **Berry Kitchen/Museum Gift Shop,** 328 Main St., in the Seldovia Native Association Building (234-7898), whips up a mean blueberry jam—don't be afraid to ask for a sample (open daily 10am-5pm). On a hill overlooking the water, the beautiful **St. Nicholas Orthodox Church** was built in 1891. It's a beautiful place to poke around, and tours are given daily at 9:10am, 1:10, and 6:10pm for $4.50 a head.

The **Otterbahn Hiking Trail,** starting at the Susan B. English School, near Winifred Ave., and winding a mile to Outside Beach, takes you up to a small lighthouse perched above cliffs that plunge into the bay. On a clear day, the **view** of the volcanoes is magnificent. There is also a 6-mi. hike up the bay on the dirt extension of Rocky St.; consult the **Seldovia Map** on how to get there. If getting back to nature grows stale, you can head to the **Linwood Bar** (234-7857) in town, or to the bar at the **Seldovia Lodge** for a tall cold one.

Seldovia triples in size on **Independence Day.** An old-fashioned celebration draws hundreds of visitors from all over the peninsula and includes parades, log-rolling, the 5K "Salmon Shuffle" race, a horseshoe tournament, greased pole climbing, and a pancake feed at the fire hall.

KODIAK ISLAND

Kodiak Island is the strikingly beautiful victim of astonishingly hard luck. In this century, Kodiak has been rocked by earthquakes, washed over by tsunamis, doused in the oil of the Exxon *Valdez,* and blanketed in nearly two feet of volcanic ash. Rain falls 180 days each year, but it doesn't seem to bother the wildlife. The island shelters the **Kodiak National Wildlife Refuge,** home to about 2600 Kodiak brown bears, the largest carnivorous land mammals in the world. The refuge's 800 mi. of coastline surround the island's sharp peaks. As for Kodiak's human population, the rich waters around the island have made its fishing and crabbing fleet the state's most productive, drawing floods of young people each summer to work its canneries. Islanders take their seafood seriously, and until recently, tourism has been only an afterthought.

■ Kodiak

Kodiak was the first capital of Russian Alaska before Alexander Baranov moved the Russian-American Company headquarters to Sitka. The glittering ladies of St. Petersburg achieved a new level of fur-fashion opulence, thanks to Russian enslavement of the indigenous Alutiia people, who were forced to hunt Kodiak Island's sea otters to near extinction.

The nearby **Novarupta Volcano**, on the other hand, is anything but extinct. It erupted in 1912 with a force 10 times greater than the 1980 eruption of Mt. St. Helens, spewing so much ash into the air that for two days residents could not see a lantern held at arm's length (only one eruption in human history displaced more volcanic matter). In 1964, the biggest earthquake ever recorded in North America (9.2 on the new Richter Scale) shook the area, causing $24 million in damage, and creating a tsunami that destroyed much of downtown Kodiak. The swamped fishing port was rehabilitated by the Army Corps of Engineers; one 200-ft. vessel, *The Star of Kodiak,* was cemented into the ferry dock and converted into a cannery.

Local color is hard to find—if it exists at all. Unless you fancy waiting for the next natural disaster to liven things up, come for the outdoors or not at all. Keep in mind that the gorgeous shorelines to the north and south are virtually inaccessible without a car, and that no one on the island rents to travelers under 25.

PRACTICAL INFORMATION AND ORIENTATION

Visitors Information: Kodiak Island Convention and Visitors Bureau, 100 Marine Way, (486-4782; fax 486-6545), in front of the ferry dock. Hunting and fishing info, charter and accommodations arrangements, and an inconveniently enormous map. Open Mon. 8am-10pm, Tues.-Fri. 8am-5pm, Sat. 9am-5pm, Sun. 1-9pm, and for most ferry arrivals; winter Mon.-Fri. 8am-noon and 1-5pm. **Fish and Wildlife Service and Wildlife Refuge Visitor Center,** 1390 Buskin River Rd. (487-2600), just outside Buskin State Recreation Site, 4 mi. southwest of town on Rezanof Rd. Wildlife displays, stuffed brown bears, films on the island's wildlife, and info on Kodiak National Wildlife Refuge and its cabins. Open Mon.-Fri. 8am-4:30pm, Sat. noon-4:30pm. **State Department of Parks,** SR Box 3800, Kodiak 99615; 1200 Abercrombie Dr. (486-6339), at Fort Abercrombie. Info on local state parks and campgrounds. Open Mon.-Fri. 8am-5pm.

Fishing Information: Alaska Department of Fish and Game, Box 686, Kodiak, at 211 Mission Rd. (486-1880, 486-4559 for 24-hr. recorded info). Info on regulations and seasons. No licenses. Open Mon.-Fri. 8am-4:30pm.

Employment: Alaska State Employment Service, 305 Center St. (486-3105), in Kodiak Plaza. Open Mon.-Fri. 8am-noon and 1-4:30pm. First stop for fish canners.

Airport: 5 mi. southwest of town on Rezanof Dr. Served by **Era Aviation** (800-866-8394). To: Anchorage (5-7 per day, $159). **Pen Air** serves Karluk ($150 roundtrip) and Larsen Bay ($120 roundtrip). Call daily 5am-10pm.

Ferries: Alaska Marine Highway. Terminal next to the visitors center (800-562-6731; fax 486-6166 or 486-3800). The *Tustumena* docks in Kodiak May-Sept., 1 to 3 times per week; less frequently in winter. To: Homer ($48), Seward ($54), Valdez ($98), Cordova ($98). 5-day run to Dutch Harbor (Aleutian Islands) once every month ($202). Terminal open Mon.-Fri. 8am-5pm, Sat. 8am-4pm, and when boats are in.

Car Rental: Budget, 516 Marine Way (486-8500), airport (487-4001), or downtown. Starting at $43, base prices are higher than its partner, **Rent-a-Heap** (486-5200), but unlimited free mi. make Budget a better deal. Must be 25 with a credit card. Downtown open Mon.-Fri. 9am-7pm, Sat. 9:30am-7pm, Sun. noon-7pm. Airport open daily 6:30am-10pm.

Taxis: A&B Taxi (486-4343) and **AAA Ace Mecca Taxi** (486-3211). $3 plus $2 per mi. $13 to the airport. 24hr. **Custom Tours of Kodiak** (486-4997) offers a $5 shuttle to the airport from downtown. Call ahead.

Camping and Fishing Equipment: Mack's Sports Shop, 117 Lower Mill Bay (486-4276), at the end of Center Ave. Open Mon.-Sat. 7am-7pm, Sun. 9am-6pm. **Cy's**

Sporting Goods, 202 Shelikof St. (486-3900), near the harbor. Mostly hunting and fishing gear. Open Mon.-Fri. 8am-8pm, Sat. 8am-7pm, Sun. 9am-5pm.

Library: 319 Lower Mill Bay Rd. (486-8686). Open Mon.-Fri. 10am-9pm, Sat. 10am-5pm, Sun. 1-5pm. Periodicals section is an ideal escape from rainy streets.

Laundromat and Showers: Ernie's, 218 Shelikof (486-4119), across from the harbor. Wash $3, 4-min. dry 25¢. 20-min. shower $4. Drop-off available. Open daily 8am-8pm. Last shower 7:30pm, last wash 6:30pm.

Weather: Local forecasts, 487-4313. **Marine forecasts,** 487-4949.

Pharmacy: Wodlinger Drug and Photo, 312 Marine Way (486-4035), across from the harbormaster. Pharmacy open Mon.-Fri. 10am-6pm. Store open Mon.-Sat. 9:30am-6:30pm, Sun. noon-4pm. Photo development $8-10.

Hospital: Kodiak Island Hospital, 1915 E. Rezanof Dr. (486-3281).

Crisis Line: 486-3625. **Women's Crisis Line:** 422 Hillside Dr. (486-6171). **AIDS Helpline:** 800-478-2437.

Emergency: 911. **Police:** 217 Lower Mill Bay Rd. (486-8000). **Fire:** 219 Lower Mill Bay Rd. (486-8040).

Post Office: 419 Lower Mill Bay Rd. (486-4721). Open Mon.-Fri. 9am-5:30pm. **Downtown Contract Station** in the AC Grocery is open Mon.-Sat. 10am-6pm. **General Delivery ZIP Code:** 99615.

Area Code: 907.

The city of Kodiak is on the eastern tip of Kodiak Island, roughly 250 mi. south of Anchorage. One hundred mi. of paved and rutted gravel roads follow the scenic coastlines north and south of the city; Chiniak Rd., which heads south for 42 mi., is an especially worthwhile trip. In town, the main drag is Center St., which starts at the ferry terminal and heads inland. It ends at the intersection with Rezanof Dr. to the left, and Lower Mill Bay Rd. to the right.

ACCOMMODATIONS AND CAMPING

Kodiak has no hostel and no true budget accommodations. The available alternatives present a dilemma: you can get a cheap motel room in a convenient location or a room in a B&B (with a few more bells and whistles) that will be far, far away. Many B&B owners also frown on renting to unmarried couples. Finding a room becomes almost impossible when, as often happens, the airport shuts down due to bad weather. Watch for Kodiak's brutal 11% hotel tax.

Backpackers can head for **Gibson Cove,** 2 mi. west off Kodiak on Rezanof. Built by the city for transient cannery workers, Gibson Cove looks and feels like a gravel parking lot and stinks of fish, but at $2 per night with free hot showers, who can quibble? Better scenery and more breathable air can be found slightly farther away at two pleasant state-run facilities.

Lakeview Terrace B&B, 2426 Spruce Cape Rd., P.O. Box 3107 (486-5135), 2½ mi. northeast of town on Rezanof. Large, spotless rooms with comfortable queen beds, cable TV, private sinks, semi-private bath, and breakfast. Born-again hostess offers free Bibles to guests upon departure. Singles $45. Doubles $55.

Russian Heritage Inn, (486-5657), 119 Yukon, off Lower Mill Bay Rd. near Mark's Sports Shop. Nothing Russian about this place other than the little blue domes on the doors. Very congenial owner offers recently remodeled rooms. About ½ have fridges. Big cable TVs. Laundry: $1.50 wash, same to dry. One tiny room rents for $50. Bigger ones are $65-75, regardless of number of occupants.

Shelikof Lodge, 211 Thorsheim Ave. (486-4141; fax 486-4116), a small street to the right of McDonald's. A remodeling job has perked up this otherwise generic motel. Comfortable green rooms with cable TV. Courtesy van to the airport Mon.-Fri. 8:30am-4:30pm (summers only). Singles $60. Doubles $65.

Fort Abercrombie State Park Campground (486-6339), 4 mi. northeast of town on Rezanof-Monashka Rd. Water, shelters, and toilets. No RV hookups; designed for backpackers. World War II ruins, trails, a trout-fishing lake, and spectacular sunsets. 13 sites for $10. 7-day max.

Buskin River State Recreation Site (486-6339), 4½ mi. southwest of the city, off Rezanof Dr. Water and pit toilets, RV dump station, 15 sites. Feels like a genuine campground rather than a commandeered gravel pit. Over 50% of Kodiak's sport fish are caught on the nearby Buskin River. 14-night max. Sites $10.

FOOD

Dine out at lunch, when specials keep things affordable. Stock up on groceries at the convenient **AC Grocery,** downtown at 111 Rezanof (486-5761; open Mon.-Sat. 7am-10pm, Sun. 7am-9pm). Two mi. from downtown, the Chinese deli at **Safeway,** 2685 Mill Bay Rd. (486-6811) has attained heretofore unheard-of levels of popularity (open daily 6am-midnight). **Cactus Flats Natural Foods,** 338 Mission St. (486-4677; open Mon.-Sat. 10am-6pm) does vitamins, too.

The 2nd Floor, upstairs from the Peking House (486-8555). One of the only places in town locals get excited about. Lunch specials include miso soup, rice, and salad. Chicken teriyaki ($9.25), vegetable tempura ($7), great sushi ($7-10). Open Mon.-Thurs. 11am-2:30pm and 5-10pm, Fri. 11:30am-2:30pm and 5-11pm, Sat. 5-11pm, Sun. 5-10pm.

Henry's All-Alaskan Sports Café (486-8844), in the mall on Marine Way. Surprisingly swank for Kodiak. Pasta entrees $10 and up, but burgers and other excellent sandwiches are only $6-9. Good place to catch up on your favorite teams and kick back with a beer. Drink slowly, though (Alaskan Amber, $4.50 a pint). Open Mon.-Thurs. 11am-10:30pm, Fri.-Sat. 11am-11:30pm, Sun. 1:30-9:30pm.

El Chicano, 103 Center Ave. (486-6116). Pinkish stucco and ultra-padded booths. Good, but not great, Mexican offerings. Try a bowl of black-bean soup with home-made Mexican bread ($4.75) or an enormous "license plate" burrito ($8.25). Open Sun.-Thurs. 7am-9:30pm, Fri.-Sat. 7am-10pm.

Beryl's, 202 Center Ave. (486-3323), to the right of the First National Bank. Attractive wooden furniture and an array of crafts bring Beryl's as close to earthy as Kodiak comes. $6 sandwiches, plus a variety of ice cream and sweets. Try a pineapple or creme de menthe milkshake ($2.75). Open Mon.-Fri. 6:30am-6pm, Sat. 8:30am-6pm, Sun. 10am-4:30pm.

SIGHTS AND EVENTS

Built in 1808 as a storehouse for sea otter pelts, the **Baranov Museum,** 101 Marine Way (486-5920), is housed in the **oldest Russian structure standing in Alaska** and the oldest wooden structure on the U.S. West Coast. The museum displays a great collection of Russian and traditional Alaskan artifacts, and includes a library with period photos and literature ranging from the Russian period to the present. ($2, under 12 free; open Mon.-Fri. 10am-4pm, Sat.-Sun. noon-4pm; Labor Day-Jan. and March-Memorial Day Mon.-Wed. and Fri. 11am-3pm, Sat. noon-3pm.) The **Holy Resurrection Russian Orthodox Church** (486-3854), just in front of the museum, houses the oldest parish in Alaska. Built in 1794 and rebuilt after a fire shortly before World War II, its elaborate icons date back to the early 19th century, and its church bells are still rung by hand. While no longer open to the public, you might try stopping by 15 minutes before vespers (Sat. and Thurs. at 6:30pm) to chat with the priest and take in the beautiful interior.

The **Alutiia Museum and Archaeological Repository,** 215 Mission Rd. (486-7004), built with Exxon money from the Valdez oil spill, houses displays and artifacts documenting the 7000-year-old culture of the Alutiia. The replicas are cool, even if most of the museum is not. (Open Mon.-Sat. 10am-4pm, Sun. noon-4pm.) The **Kodiak Alutiia Dancers** ($15; shows Mon.-Wed., and Fri., 3:30pm) provide a more animated glimpse of native culture at the Tribal Council Barbara (486-4449).

Across the bridge on Near Island, engineers at the **Fisheries Industry Technology Center,** 900 Trident Way (486-1500), rack their brains inventing new fish products. Stop by to tour their laboratories and sample tomorrow's fish products (open Mon.-Fri. 8am-5pm; call ahead to arrange a tour).

ALASKA

Beautiful **Fort Abercrombie State Park** (486-6339), 3½ mi. north of town, was the site of the first secret radar installation in Alaska. The fort is also the site of a World War II defense installation; after Attu and Kiska in the Aleutian chain were attacked and occupied by the Japanese in 1942, Kodiak became a major staging area for the lesser known North Pacific Campaign. Both installments are in severe disrepair. Check them out along one of the park's beautiful **hiking trails.** Bunkers and other reminders of the Alaskan campaign remain elsewhere as well, including an old naval station 6½ mi. southwest of Kodiak.

The five-day **Kodiak Crab Festival** (486-5557), held just before Memorial Day, celebrates a bygone industry with parades, fishing derbies, and kayak, bike, foot, crab, and "survival suit" (don't ask) races, and a blessing of the fleet. The event culminates with the **Chad Ogden Ultramarathon,** a superhuman race along 43 mi. of hilly roads from Chiniak to Kodiak. **St. Herman's Days** (486-3854), held on the weekend closest to August 9, honors the first saint of the Russian Orthodox Church in North America (canonized 1970). On one of these days, depending on the weather, visitors are welcome to join the faithful in an annual pilgrimage to St. Herman's former home on Spruce Island. The Thursday evening service at the Resurrection Church also relates the life of St. Herman.

OUTDOORS

The sheer number of fish in the island's rivers and surrounding waters will send you reeling. The 100-mi. road system permits access to good **salmon streams.** In Kodiak, surfcasting into Mill Bay at high tide often yields a pink or silver salmon. **Red salmon,** running from early June to early August, appear in the Buskin and Pasagshak Rivers. **Pink salmon** run up the Buskin, Russian, American, and Olds Rivers in astounding numbers from mid-July to mid-September. Better-tasting but scarcer **silver salmon** run up the same rivers from late August until early October. **Dolly varden,** the most frequently hooked fish on Kodiak, can be plucked year-round from the Pasagshak and Buskin Rivers.

On the rare clear day, **hikers** can obtain a commanding view stretching from the Kenai Peninsula to the Aleutian Peninsula atop **Barometer Mountain.** To reach the trailhead, go west out of town on Rezanof, then take the first right past the end of the airport runway (about 5 mi. from town). After a stand of thick alders, the trail climbs steadily and steeply along a grassy ridge before arriving at the summit. Most hikers require about two hours to make the 5-mi. climb to the top, and usually descend in half that time. The trail up **Pyramid Mountain,** beginning from the parking lot at the pass on Anton Larsen Bay Rd., is another popular hike about 11 mi. from town. Pause near the top shoulder of alpine tundra to admire the view before attempting the rugged final ascent. The hike covers 4 mi. in all, and takes two to four hours. Ask at the visitors center (see **Practical Information** above) about a $5 *Trail Guide* prepared by local outdoors folk. The friendly visitors center staff may recommend and xerox the descriptions of particular hikes.

On a guided **sea kayaking trip,** you can come eye-to-eye with sea otters, puffins, bald eagles, and if you're lucky, even view the giant Kodiak bear from a comfortable distance. **Wavetamer,** P.O. Box 228 (486-2604), offers two-hour tours of Near Island and Mill Bay ($40) and a five-hour coastal trek ($85). All gear is provided, and there is a two-person minimum for the two and four-hour trips. Two-hour tours are available in the evenings (Mon.-Thurs.); both trips are available during the day Friday to Sunday. **Kodiak Kayak Tours** (486-2722) offers two daily trips, which spend about three hours exploring much of the same territory. Trips typically start at 9am and 2pm, but they're flexible. Experience is not necessary. Call at least one day in advance ($45).

If you have a vehicle, the 42-mi. coastal drive to Chiniak offers the chance to see beautiful seascapes with small coastal islands muted in fog (and dozens of mufflers lying along the j-j-jarringly rough road). If the potholes haven't rearranged your dental work, stop in for a deluxe high-rise hamburger with fries ($5) at the **Road's End Restaurant and Bar** (486-2885), 42 Roads End in Chiniak. They also serve a generous grilled-cheese sandwich with fries ($3.50) and premier pies ($3.50 per slice) of many varieties (open Tues.-Wed. 2-10pm, Thurs.-Sun. noon-10pm).

KODIAK NATIONAL WILDLIFE REFUGE

Kodiak National Wildlife Refuge encompasses the western two-thirds of Kodiak Island. Kodiak bears share the region with red foxes, land otters, weasels, brown bats, and a variety of other mammals. Since this is a refuge rather than a park, the area is maintained to accommodate the wildlife, not the tourists. Human recreational use is a secondary concern at best; no trails, much less roads, lead into the refuge, and there are no official campgrounds. While there are eight public use cabins within the refuge, only three can be reached by boat—the others require a prohibitively expensive float plane ride (somewhere in the $450 per person range). Even the numerous "guaranteed" brown bear viewing tours are not such a great deal—most companies' three to four-hour float plane tours will run you $350-400, which is why you won't see too many price quotes in their brochures.

Ultimately, the closest you're probably going to get to the refuge is the **visitors center,** 4 mi. southwest of Kodiak (see **Practical Information**), where you can experience this remarkable area through an impressive archive of videos and a collection of stuffed bears. Kodiak is a beautiful place, but you can visit other beautiful places (such as Denali or Wrangell-St. Elias) on the same type of sightseeing tours without taking out a second mortgage on your house.

PRINCE WILLIAM SOUND

■ Whittier

Flanked by massive glaciers and waterfalls, Whittier enjoys incredible natural beauty. Its gorgeous setting contrasts starkly with a remarkably unattractive town. Over half of the population lives in the hulking, concrete, 14-story Begich Towers. The similarly designed Buckner Building, once an Army outpost, is another eyesore. The harbor area is the most pleasant place in town, home to restaurants, boats, and the exit to **Portage** via the Alaska Railroad. Whittier is a strategically located port of transfer and a gateway to the Sound; frequent rail and ferry connections won't strand you in Whittier for long. Consider lingering for a few hours, though, if you're in the mood for a terrific short hike.

Practical Information The **Visitors Center,** P.O. Box 604 (472-2329), is in the center of town, slyly camouflaged in a refurbished railroad car next to the tracks. Get information on hiking, boating, camping, or fishing (open daily 11am-noon and 1-6pm). Learn how to leave Whittier from the **Alaska Railroad,** P.O. Box 107500, Anchorage, 99510 (265-2494 or 800-544-0552; 265-2607 recording), which runs four to six trips between Whittier and Portage daily ($13). From Portage, catch an **Alaska Backpacker Shuttle** (344-8775) bus that meets the train three times per day and runs to Anchorage ($20, $35 roundtrip). Call ahead. To leave by water, call the **Alaska Marine Highway** (472-2378; fax 472-2381), ½ mi. east of town, by the small boat harbor. Ferries run to Valdez ($58) and Cordova ($58).

Take a **shower** at the **Harbormaster Office** (472-2320), in the small boat harbor ($3; open Sat.-Wed. 8am-9pm, Thurs.-Fri. 8am-7pm). There are trained EMTs in Whittier, but **no doctor** or full-time clinic. A **part-time medical clinic** is in Begich Towers Apt. 302 (472-2303; open Thurs.-Mon. 10am-6pm). Over-the-counter **pharmaceuticals** are available at the Anchor Inn Grocery (see below). The **emergency** number is 911. Reach the **police** at 472-2340 and the **fire** department at 472-2560. The **post office** (472-2552) is on the first floor of Begich Towers (open Mon., Wed., and Fri. 11:30am-5:30pm). The **General Delivery ZIP Code** is 99693. The **area code** is 907.

Whittier, Portage, Billings, and Maynard Glaciers surround Whittier, 63 mi. southeast of Anchorage and 105 mi. west of Valdez. At the head of nearby College Fjord, **Harvard and Yale Glaciers** loom. Harvard Glacier is, of course, larger than its secondrate neighbor. Yale Glacier is widely regarded as a poor excuse for a glacier and an embarrassment to Harvard Glacier. Like other towns in the Sound, Whittier is no stranger to rain. More than 21 ft. drips on this soggy hamlet each year.

Accommodations, Camping, Food, and Sights If you must spend the night, there is one public campground in Whittier, the **Whittier Campgrounds,** behind Begich Towers next to the Whittier Glacier Falls, which have water and toilets. Don't keep food in your tent; the summer bear trail passes right through camp. Sites are $5 on the honor system; no maximum stay.

Whittier's few restaurants offer standard Alaskan fare. The **Anchor Inn** (472-2354) is the best place to buy groceries. Don't hold out for a bargain: a box of cereal can run a nightmarish $6.35! (Open daily 9:30am-9:30pm.) Babs, the piemaker at the **Hobo Bay Trading Company** (472-2374), in the Harbor Area, presides over a political salon that doubles as a first-rate short-order restaurant. A ray of sunshine, Babs creates the most welcoming atmosphere in Whittier. Try a hearty taco ($2.50) or a piece of fresh-baked pie with ice cream ($4; open Tues.-Sun. 11am-7pm). Food comes at surprisingly reasonable prices at the **Tsunami Café** (472-2452), at the harbor, where locals line the counter sipping cold beer ($2.50). The house specialty is pizza—an 8-in. personal size pie runs $6.75, and a 12-in. vegetarian pie runs $13.50 (open daily 11am-9pm).

Whittier is a popular departure point for glacier boat tours ranging from **Renown Charters'** (800-655-3806) relatively soothing three-hour tour ($59) to **Phillips Cruises'** (800-544-0529) insane 26-glacier, six-hour extravaganza ($119). Your best chance for amusement is to quickly pack off to the beautiful areas that surround the town. **Hiking** opportunities abound; the best dayhike climbs the 2½-mi. **Portage Pass Trail** to the stunning Portage Glacier overlook in about one to one and a half hours. To reach the trailhead, take W. Camp Rd. out of town along the railroad tracks and cross the tracks toward the airstrip; the trail forks off to the left.

■ Valdez

The most difficult decision for many travelers headed for Valdez is whether to come by boat or car. Either choice is rewarding. Those who come by ferry will pass through magnificent fjords and glacial valleys. Those on wheels pass views of the major peaks of the Wrangell-St. Elias range, over a scenic alpine pass, and finally through waterfall-filled canyons before descending into Valdez.

Historically, Good Friday has been anything but good to Valdez. The 1964 Good Friday Earthquake leveled the entire town, which was rebuilt on its present site; 25 years later, on Good Friday, the infamous Exxon *Valdez* rammed into nearby Bligh Reef and spilled 11 million gallons of oil over 1640 sq. mi. of Prince William Sound. The port of Valdez itself was spared, but Exxon used Valdez as the staging point for the clean-up, causing the town's population to triple and prices to skyrocket. Yet today, as for the past 20 years, oil continues to provide Valdez with its wealth. As the northernmost ice-free port in Alaska, Valdez was chosen as the terminus for the Alaska pipeline, and oil now runs the show.

In the summer, Valdez's bountiful waters and gorgeous natural setting attract a peculiar mix of visitors. College-aged adventurers seek their fortunes in canneries (called "slimehouses" locally) and charter boats while living in a crowded tent city on a hill. Below them, fleets of RVs rest in three downtown parks as their owners pump money into the fishing, charter, and cruise industries. A handful of backpackers pass through, camping in the hills outside the city and exploring the beautiful surroundings. Locals toil long hours in the fishing, construction, and tourism industries and save up for the winter. During winter, income is scarce but the snow brings a whole new set of outdoor sports. Locals wait for the spring, when the fish again head upstream and the tourists down-highway.

PRACTICAL INFORMATION AND ORIENTATION

Visitors Information: Valdez Convention and Visitors Bureau, P.O. Box 1603 (800-770-5954 or 835-2984), at Fairbanks and Chenega St. Information on sights, accommodations, hiking, and camping. Showings of the 1964 Earthquake film at the college every few hr., $3. Open daily 8am-8pm; winter Mon.-Fri. 8:30am-5pm. Free local phone. **Parks and Recreation Hotline:** 835-3200.

Job Service: 835-4910 or 800-495-5627, on Meals Ave. in the State Office Bldg. Info on canneries and fish processors in Valdez. Visit the office or send a self-addressed stamped envelope to P.O. Box 590, Valdez. Open Mon.-Fri. 8am-noon and 1-4:30pm.

Fishing Information: Get the free pamphlet *Valdez Fishing Facts and Hints* from the visitors center or check with one of the many sporting goods stores in town. The visitors center also publishes a guide to fishing charter services.

Airport: Valdez Airport, 4 mi. out of town on Airport Rd. off Richardson Hwy. **ERA Aviation** (835-2636) flies 4 times daily to Anchorage ($74 in advance, $89 or $99 later depending on availability).

Buses: Gray Line of Alaska (800-544-2206) runs from the Westmark Hotel in Valdez to Anchorage daily ($65).

Ferries: Alaska Marine Highway, P.O. Box 647 (835-4436 or 800-642-0066), at the city dock at the end of Hazelet Ave. To: Whittier ($58), Cordova ($30), and Seward ($58). The Whittier run makes a stop at Columbia Glacier and has been called "the best tour deal in Alaska."

Taxis: Valdez Yellow Cab (835-2500). The 4-mi. trip to the airport will cost you $7, each additional person $1. 24hr.

Car Rental: Valdez-U-Drive, P.O. Box 852 (835-4402), at the airport. $35 per day; rates fluctuate. Must be 25 with a major credit card.

Camping Supplies: The Prospector (835-3858), beside the post office on Galena Dr. One of the best places in the state. Immense supply of clothing, shoes, tarps, freeze-dried food, and fishing tackle. Open Mon.-Fri. 8am-10pm, Sat. 8am-8pm, Sun. 10am-7pm.

Kayak Rental: Anadyr Adventures, 203 N. Harbor Dr. (835-2814). Single kayak $45 per day, doubles $65. Rents to experienced kayakers only. 2-hr. orientation class ($10), damage deposit ($200-300) or credit card required. 3-hr. tours $50.

Bike Rental: Beaver Sports (835-4727), across from the post office on Galena. Bikes $5 per hr.; $20 24hr. Open Mon.-Fri. 10am-7pm, Sat. 9am-6pm, Sun. 1-6pm.

Library: 200 Fairbanks Dr. (835-4632). Outstanding 3-floor modern library, with well-stocked "Alaska Room" and a selection of free books. Open Mon. and Fri. 10am-6pm, Tues.-Thurs. 10am-8pm, Sat. noon-5pm.

Laundromat: Like Home Laundromat, 121 Egan (835-2913). Wash $1.50, 7-min. dry 25¢. Open daily 8am-9pm.

Public Showers: $3 for 10min. at the Harbormaster, or cough up an additional $1 at the **Bear Paw RV Park** (see below) for spotless private bathrooms with sinks, plus all the time you want.

Weather: 835-4505.

Crisis Line: 835-2999. 24hr.

Pharmacy: Village Pharmacy (835-3737), adjacent to Eagle Quality Center at Pioneer and Meals. Open Mon.-Thurs. 9am-6pm, Fri. 9am-7pm, Sat. 11am-2pm.

Hospital: Valdez Community Hospital, 911 Meals Ave. (835-2249).

Emergency/Ambulance: 911. **Police:** 835-4560.

Post Office: 835-4449, at Galena St. and Tatitlek St. Open Mon.-Fri. 9am-5pm, Sat. 10am-noon. **General Delivery ZIP Code:** 99686.

Area Code: 907.

Valdez lies 304 mi. east of Anchorage at the top of the Valdez Arm, in the northeast corner of Prince William Sound. From Valdez, the spectacular **Richardson Hwy.** runs

115 mi. north to Glenallen, where it intersects with the Glenn Hwy., heading southeast to Anchorage and northeast to Tok.

ACCOMMODATIONS AND CAMPING

The visitors bureau (see **Practical Information**) lists over 70 bed and breakfasts that charge about $65 for singles and $75 for doubles (about $30 less than a hotel room). The **free reservation center** (835-4988) for Valdez will set you up with B&Bs, glacier tours, rafting trips, and helicopter tours. Although Valdez prohibits camping in non-designated areas, insolvent sojourners sometimes camp on the banks of **Mineral Creek** (a 15-min. walk from downtown; take Mineral Creek Dr. from Hanagita St.). Twenty-four mi. up the Richardson Hwy. from town is the astoundingly beautiful **Blueberry Lake State Recreation Site** (sites $6).

Sea Otter Campground (835-2787), at the end of South Harbor Dr. Offers beautiful sites along the water for RVs and a few grassy tent sites inside the windblock formed by RVs. Very friendly management. Sites $14 non-waterfront, $16 waterfront, full hookups $20.

Valdez Glacier Campground (835-2531), 5½ mi. from town, 1½ mi. past the airport. Look for small sign on the left. 101 campsites, first-come, first-served. So-so view of an unimpressive glacier, but the sites are big and chock full o' trees. Bears aplenty, so be careful to keep a clean camp. This campground is difficult to reach without a car or bicycle, although rides are reportedly easy to find given the steady stream of traffic. Water and pit toilets. 15-day max. stay. Sites $10.

Bear Paw Camper Park, P.O. Box 93 (835-2530), in the small boat harbor downtown. Like all downtown parks, it's mainly a gravel parking lot with hookups, but Bear Paw is well groomed and in a prime location. RV sites $14, with hookups $20. A separate colony of tent sites covers a small hill, $15 for 2 people, $2.50 per additional person. Free showers for guests.

Raven Berth and Breakfast, P.O. Box 2581, Boat Harbor Slip C-21 (835-5863). A floating B&B! Take a stroll on the docks to see the day's catches, hear about the big one that got away, and dream of a 300-lb. halibut in your small (but comfortable) berth. Singles $45-55. Doubles $55-65. Call ahead.

FOOD

For those who must stick to a tight budget, there's always the **Eagle Quality Center** (835-2100), at Meals Ave. and Pioneer Dr. (open 24hr.); or the **Red Apple Market,** 113 Egan St. (835-4496), where the deli offers a three-piece chicken dinner for $4 (open daily 7am-11pm).

Mike's Palace (also called the **Pizza Palace**), 201 N. Harbor Dr. (835-2365). Locals and tourists alike line up for the great Greek, Italian, Mexican, and American fare. Gyros ($6) for lunch and Halibut Olympia ($13) for dinner are big sellers. Baklava $3.25. Open daily 11am-11pm.

Fu Kung, 207 Kobuk St. (835-5255). Like the mirror room in Bruce Lee's *Enter the Dragon*, Fu Kung's ugly Quonset hut exterior is deceiving. Inside you'll find a clean, well decorated Chinese restaurant with lunch specials ($6-7) and savory almond chicken ($9.50). Open daily 11am-11pm.

Totem Inn Restaurant (835-4443), at Richardson Hwy. and Meals Ave. A dark horse in the town race for breakfast supremacy. Roomy and homey. Stretch out your legs and try a stack of cakes ($3.75; with sausage, bacon, or ham, and 2 eggs $5.75). Nurse your coffee while admiring the taxidermy. Open daily 5am-10pm.

Valley Christian Book and Coffee Shoppe, 126 Pioneer Dr. (835-5881). Believers and pagans alike can partake in the soup-in-a-sourdough-bowl ($4.95; free refills). Blessed are the budget travelers, for they shall inherit croissants ($1.25) and bagels with cream cheese ($1.20). Open Mon.-Fri. 9am-6pm, Sat. 10am-5pm.

SIGHTS AND EVENTS

The **Valdez Museum,** 217 Egan Dr. (835-2764), packs an informational punch that is impressive given its small size. Inside, you'll see Valdez's original 1907 steam fire engine, and exhibits on both Good Friday disasters ($3, seniors $2.50, under 18 free; open Mon.-Sat. 8am-7pm, Sun. noon-7pm).

On midsummer weekends, travelers looking to yuk it up should hit the **Civic Center** (835-3200), on Clifton Ave. for "Valdez on the Light Side" (835-3200). The show is a song and dance history of Valdez, written and performed by locals ($7, under 12 $3; intermittently on Fri.-Sun. eves.). The **Salmon Gulch Hatchery** (835-4874), on Dayville Rd., 14 mi. out of town off the Richardson Hwy., offers guided tours (6 per day, $1). Half a mile outside of town on the Richardson Hwy., there's a pullout at Cripple Creek where a strong run of silver salmon battle upstream in July.

After an 800-mi. journey from the fields of Prudhoe Bay, the **Alaska Pipeline** deposits a quarter of America's domestic oil into tankers that wait in Valdez. Unfortunately for penny-pinchers, the price of the two-hour tour of the **Valdez Marine Terminal** recently jumped from free to $15 (ages 5-12 $7.50, under 5 free). If you can't spring for the tour, at least drop by Alyeska's **visitors center** (835-2686) at the airport, where you'll see plenty of pipeline exhibits and free movies about its construction and the surrounding natural environment.

The **Gold Rush Days** celebration (slated to take place during the first week in Aug.) can mean feast or famine for budget travelers, depending on their shrewdness and cunning. The visitors center hosts a free salmon and halibut fry (with hot dogs for the kids) in addition to the fashion show, dance, and ugly-vehicle contest. However, financial ruin may await those caught by the **traveling jail.** To be freed, you must "donate" the same amount "donated" by the person who ordered your arrest (call 835-4247 for information). Valdez makes the most of its massive snowfall and alpine setting by hosting the **World Extreme Skiing Championship** (late March) and the **King of the Hill Snowboard Competition** (first weekend in April).

OUTDOORS

Valdez has few developed hiking trails, but those it has are a good way to take in the city's beautiful surroundings. Begin at the 1.2-mi. **Mineral Creek Trail,** just north of downtown, which follows a magnificent gorge through uninhabited backcountry (look out for bears). The trail begins 8 mi. down a gravel road at the end of Mineral Creek Dr. and winds up at a turn-of-the-century gold mine. Mineral Creek Dr. passes dozens of waterfalls, and the numerous cross-country ski trails that branch off it double as mountain-bike trails in the summer. The 1.3-mi. **Solomon Gulch** trail starts 150 yd. northeast of the hatchery on Dayville Rd. near Valdez's hydro-electric plant and ends at breathtaking **Solomon Lake.** The **Goat Trail** follows a Native Alaskan footpath that was the only route from Valdez to the Interior prior to the opening of the Richardson Hwy. Unmaintained and full of heavy brush, it begins near Mile 13.5 of the highway and accompanies the Lowe River for 5 mi.

Fishing is the big draw for many of Valdez's summertime visitors. Fishing charter services outnumber even RV parks and gift shops (compare prices at the visitors center), but some fish, especially pink salmon, are as close by as the town docks. Thanks to its coastal location, Valdez doesn't get nearly as cold as Interior cities in winter (average January temperature is 25°), so you can cruise around area trails without losing any appendages to frostbite. Downhill skiers often drive or hitchhike up to Thompson Pass and ski down to the townsite. For more detailed information, pick up the free guide *Snowcountry* from the visitors center.

By boat, helicopter, or plane (and for the right price), you can investigate two of the Sound's most prized possessions and most popular tourist destinations: **Columbia** and **Shoup Glaciers.** Several boat tour companies offer competitively priced trips, but it is still best to shop around either along the waterfront or through the brochures at the visitors center. The best economy option is the **Alaska Marine Highway,** which pauses in front of the face of the 3-mi. wide Columbia Glacier for about 10 minutes on its way to and from Whittier ($58). If you've driven to Valdez and hope to stay overnight, **Stan Stephens Charters** (800-478-1297 or 835-4731) offers a 5½-hour economy cruise to Columbia ($66.50 per person, ages 6-12 $46.50, 5 and under free). **Captain Jim's Charter Company** (800-997-6722) also offers a five-hour Columbia Glacier trip, a nine-hour Meares Glacier trip, and wildlife cruises at similar prices to those at Stan Stevens.

The **Chapel of the Sea** allows the pious and penniless to board the *Lu-Lu Belle* cruise boat for a one-hour non-denominational church service in Prince William Sound. Show up Sunday at 7:30am at the dock adjacent to the Westmark Hotel for the 8am departure; seats are limited and the cruise's breathtaking scenery inspires a religious awakening among tourists each Sunday (free; offering collected).

▓ Cordova

Cordova lies in one of the most spectacular and unblemished regions in the state. Accessible only by sea or air, it has preserved its intense natural beauty in a relatively tourist-free setting. If it weren't for the handful of motels with cars in their lots, you might not know there were any tourists here at all.

Proposals to connect Cordova with the road network of Alaska's interior have met with opposition from this idiosyncratic and contentious community. Cordovans would rather admit visitors in a manner compatible with its independent and low-key style. Residents have recently begun a four-year program aimed at designing a sustainable tourist industry that will focus on low-impact eco-tourism rather than cruise ships and T-shirt kiosks. Among the players is a former mayor who, until a narrow defeat in 1994, was the nation's highest elected official from the Green Party, and is now the owner of the Orca Book Store (see below).

Cordova is within easy reach of **Childs Glacier,** one of the least visited and most spectacular sights accessible by road in all of Alaska. Fortified by rugged mountains of volcanic rock and salmon-filled waters, Cordova has been known to lure visiting nature-lovers and anglers, and never let them go. **Hiking** and **fishing** are both among the best in Alaska. The area's only drawback is the weather: there's a reason the hills are so amazingly lush and green. Lots of cloudy days and 150 in. of precipitation make for a somewhat damp paradise. June is the best month for staying dry.

PRACTICAL INFORMATION AND ORIENTATION

Visitors Information: Cordova Historical Museum, P.O. Box 391, 622 1st St. (424-6665). Friendly staff people, including an original Hippie Cove resident, have all the details. Open Tues.-Sat. 1-5pm. **Cordova Chamber of Commerce,** P.O. Box 99 (424-7260), on 1st Ave. next door to the National Bank of Alaska. Plenty of pamphlets on local attractions. Open Mon.-Fri. 8am-4pm. **Chugach National Forest,** Cordova Ranger District, Box 280 (424-7661), on 2nd St. between Browning and Adams on the second floor. Excellent information on hiking trails and fishing. Reserve any of the 17 Forest Service **cabins** here. Most cabins provide no water. Open Mon.-Fri. 8am-5pm.

Banks: First National Bank of Anchorage (424-7521) and **National Bank of Alaska** (424-3258). Both on 1st St., with 24hr. **ATMs**.

Fishing Information: Alaska Dept. of Fish and Game, Box 669 (424-3215; recorded information, 424-7535). **Licenses** available at Davis' Super Foods on 1st St. (open Mon.-Sat. 7:30am-9pm, Sun. 9am-8pm) or A.C. Company (424-7141) in the Small Boat Harbor (open Mon.-Sat. 7am-10pm, Sun. 8am-9pm).

Airport: 13 mi. east of town on the Copper River Hwy. Serviced by **Alaska Airlines** (424-3278 or 800-426-0333). To: Juneau ($176) and Anchorage ($50-112).

Shuttle: The **Airport Shuttle** (424-5356) meets all flights and runs to town for $9. Call ahead.

Ferries: Alaska Marine Highway, P.O. Box 1689, Cordova 99574 (800-642-0066 or 424-7333), 1 mi. north of town on Ocean Dock Rd. off 1st Ave. One way to: Valdez ($30), Whittier ($58), Seward ($58), Kodiak ($98), and Homer ($138).

Taxis: Wild Hare Taxi Service (424-3939). 24hr.

Car Rental: Imperial Car Rentals (424-5982, 424-7440 Sun. and after hours), at the airport. $55 per day with unlimited free mileage. Must be 25 with a major credit card.

Bike and Kayak Rental: Wannabe's, 503 2nd St. (424-5696). Terrific deals on bikes: $2 per hr., $20 per day, $24 for 24hr. Includes helmet and lock. Rubber inflatable kayaks with paddles and vests $20 per day. Owner has great advice on where to go. Mountain bikes, hard-shell kayaks, and boats also available from **Cordova Coastal Adventures** (424-3842).

Camping Equipment: Flinn's Clothing & Sporting Goods Store (424-3282), on 1st St. Open Mon.-Sat. 9am-6pm, Sun. 10am-1pm.

Bookstore: Orca Book Store (424-5305), on 1st St. Not a huge selection, but the cappuccino bar in the back is a nice touch. Ask the owner, a Green Party member and former mayor, about local politics. Open Mon.-Sat. 8am-5pm.

Library: 424-6667, on 1st St., next to the museum. Open Tues.-Sat. 1-9pm.

Laundromat: Whirlwind Laundromat, 100 Adams St. (424-5110), at 1st St. Wash $3.25, 5-min. dry 25¢. Open Mon.-Sat. 8am-8pm, Sun. 8am-5pm; winter daily 10am-6pm.

Showers: Harbormaster's, 602 Nicholoff Way (424-6400). $3 for 5min. Tokens available Mon.-Fri. 8am-5pm. Showers open 24hr.

Public Pool: Bob Korn Memorial Swimming Pool (424-7200), on Railroad Ave. Open daily, complicated schedule. Call ahead. Swim and shower, $5.

Pharmacy: Cordova Drug Co., P.O. Box 220 (424-3246), on 1st St. Open Mon.-Sat. 9:30am-6pm.

Hospital: Cordova Community Hospital, 602 Chase Ave. (424-8000), off Copper River Hwy.

Emergency and **Ambulance:** 911. **Police:** 424-6100, next to the post office on Railroad Ave. **Fire:** 424-6117.

Post Office: 424-3564, at Council St. and Railroad Ave. Open Mon.-Fri. 10am-5:30pm, Sat. 10am-1pm. **General Delivery ZIP Code:** 99574.

Area Code: 907.

Cordova is on the east side of Prince William Sound on **Orca Inlet.** Airline rates to Cordova from Juneau or Anchorage can, with advance purchase, be reasonable. Flying can be cheaper than taking a bus from Haines or Skagway to Valdez, and you'll have a faster, more pleasant trip.

Like most Alaskan coastal towns, Cordova starts at the shore and ascends rapidly. Streets parallel the ocean, with Railroad Ave. at water level and numbered streets increasing in number up the hillside. First St. is the downtown shopping district and leads out of town to the ferry terminal. Railroad Ave. becomes Copper Bay Hwy. out of town toward the airport and Childs Glacier.

ACCOMMODATIONS AND CAMPING

Cordova's isolated beauty comes at a price. Thankfully, a beautiful bed and breakfast makes the expense bearable. If camping is your game, there's always **"Hippie Cove,"** a bizarre place where you can crash for free. Unsanctioned tents often spring up near the reservoir at the top of a rocky trail off Whitshed Rd., and near the ski area behind town. You can access the ski area using an unmaintained trail at the end of Browning.

Hippie Cove, ¾ mi. north of the ferry terminal on Orca Inlet Dr.; cross a few small streams to get there. Hippie Cove serves as an unofficial city campground and an arboreal flophouse. Although the area takes its name from the squatters who moved in during the early 70s, today's residents are chiefly a mix of cannery workers and ramshackle alcoholics. There is a wood stove **sauna,** where townspeople and Cove dwellers gleefully roast, then soak themselves in an icy stream-fed bath. Sauna dress code suggests a birthday suit. There is no charge to stay at the Cove for the time being, and it has flush toilets and drinking water. *The city has threatened unlicensed campers with eviction, and the future of Hippie Cove is uncertain; ask around before packing off to Orca Inlet Dr.*

Northern Nights Inn (424-5356), 3rd St. and Council Ave. Run by an enthusiastic and generous hostess, this meticulously restored home of a copper-era millionaire, now adorned with period antiques, is worth the cost. Private baths, cable TV, VCRs, microwaves, and fridges. Singles $45. Doubles $50. Provides referrals to Cordova's other B&Bs.

Alaskan Hotel and Bar, P.O. Box 484 (424-3299), on 1st St. The only building on the street with a fresh coat of paint. Overall air of long-decayed elegance. Clean, simple rooms occupy the upper floors. Rooms above the bar a bit noisy at night. Singles and doubles $35 with shared bath, $55 with private bath. Add $10 for more than 2 people.

FOOD

By small-town Alaskan standards, Cordova has a terrific variety of affordable lunch options. The dinner scene is not as pleasant, since many of the restaurants close at mid-afternoon. The best selection of groceries at the most reasonable prices is in the colossal **A.C. Company** (424-7141), on Nicholoff St. in the small boat harbor (open Mon.-Sat. 7am-10pm, Sun. 7am-9pm).

The Cookhouse Café, 1 Cannery Row (424-5926), ¼ mi. south of the ferry terminal. Good eats and bright, clean decor make this one of Cordova's top spots. A fine place to meet younger, talkative, and cheerful workers. Killer breakfast, served all day, includes 4 hotcakes for $4. Try the *rigatoni al forno* ($7)...mmm. Open Mon.-Fri. 6am-3pm, Sat. 6am-11pm, Sun. 9am-2pm.

Baja Taco (424-5599), in a red bus by the Small Boat Harbor. A rolling taco stand whose owner goes south of the border in winter for research and development. Big 'n' tasty chicken burrito $5.75, breakfast burrito $5.75, espresso 50¢. Open Mon.-Fri. 7:30am-4pm, Sat.-Sun. 9:30am-4pm.

Club Restaurant (424-3405), on 1st St., behind the Club Bar. The angler's breakfast spot of choice. Somewhere between nautical authenticity and unforgivable kitsch, the Club strikes an entertaining balance. A ship's prow, complete with life-size lady of luck, emerges from one wall. "Hot and Hearty Breakfast Specials" include the sausage and muffin for $2.25. Deli sandwiches cost $3.50 at the take-out window. Open Mon.-Sat. 6am-9pm, Sun. 7am-5pm.

Killer Whale Café (424-7733), on 1st St. in the back of the groovy Orca Bookstore. It seems that every Alaskan town, no matter how tiny, has an earthy espresso-laden café. This is one of the better ones. Eat in light-washed, wood-lined splendor on one of two inside decks overlooking the book-filled ground floor. A favorite hangout for the hip of all ages and from all over. Killer sandwiches ($5.50-8) and cappuccino ($2). Open Mon.-Sat. 8am-4pm.

SIGHTS AND EVENTS

If it's raining (since this area averages 150 in. a year, it probably is), dry off in the **Cordova Historical Museum,** P.O. Box 391, 622 1st St. (424-6665), in the same building as the library on 1st St. Inside the museum you'll find real iceworms (*Mesenchytraeus solifugus*) that live inside the glaciers. Bigger and more exciting is Prince Willie, an erratic leatherback turtle who strayed several thousand miles and wound up in a local fisherman's net. The museum also boasts an old printing press, the reconstructed business end of a lighthouse, and an Inuit kayak ($1 donation suggested; open Tues.-Sat. 1-5pm).

For the past 32 years, Cordova residents have held an **Iceworm Festival** in winter to honor the semi-legendary creature and to relieve cabin fever. The celebration breaks loose the first weekend in February and includes the parade of a 100-ft. iceworm propelled by Cordova's children down frozen 1st St. and the crowning of Miss Iceworm Queen. Like most coastal towns in Alaska, Cordova also hosts an annual **Salmon Derby,** P.O. Box 99 (424-7260), the last weekend in August and the first weekend of September. For those who prefer watching to hooking wildlife, the **Copper River Delta Shorebird Festival** hosts educational lectures, guided excursions, and a gaggle of excited ornithologists during the first week of May. At other times of the year, locals seek solace from the rainy nights at the **Alaskan Hotel and Bar** (424-3288), housing the original oak bar front from 1906 (open Mon.-Thurs. 8am-2am, Fri.-Sat. 8am-4am, Sun. 10am-2am). Live blues and rock bands from 10pm until closing, four nights a week including Friday and Saturday.

OUTDOORS

All along the Copper River Hwy. runs the vast **Copper River Delta,** a preserve covering over 1100 sq. mi. A simple drive or pedal along the highway reveals stunning vistas of mountains, wetlands, and glacial deltas. A single vantage point in this diverse land may display granite peaks, sodden muskeg, and 50-ft. sand dunes. The Delta swarms with bears, moose, wolves, coyotes, eagles, swans, and sea otters.

Childs Glacier, at the end of the 50-mi. highway, is almost as accessible and far more impressive than its famous cousin in Juneau (Mendenhall). Under the heat of the summer sun, the glacier calves 20-story chunks of ice, which fall hundreds of feet before crashing into the Copper River's silty water. The largest icefalls are capable of sending 20-ft. waves over the observation area on the opposite bank of the river, ¼ mi. from the glacier. Splintered trees and boulders strewn throughout the woods are evidence of the awesome power of this water. Although falls of this size happen perhaps once a season, they are unpredictable events and, as several alarming signs suggest, viewers should be prepared to run. Another set of signs prohibits harvesting the salmon flung into the woods by the waves and left high and dry. The Childs Glacier provides a rare chance to watch geological change. If you spend much time in Cordova and don't see this glacier, you are missing the point.

While you're at the glacier, explore the **Million Dollar Bridge** only a few hundred yds. from the glacier viewing area. Built in 1910, the bridge was considered an engineering marvel because of its placement between two active glaciers. One has retreated, but Childs is now less than ½ mi. away. The structure was heavily damaged in the 1964 earthquake and a primitive patch job keeps it standing today; many people drive safely across the span, but officially at their own risk. Legend has it that if you watch an iceberg float under the upstream side of the bridge, then dash across in time to drop a penny onto its icy back as it emerges, you will be granted a wish. (*Let's Go* does not recommend toying with the supernatural.)

The combined splendor of the delta and the glacier make the somewhat expensive trip worthwhile. If you're traveling with a group, rent a car from Imperial (see **Practical Information**), pack a lunch (there's no food anywhere on the highway), and make a glorious day of it. Travelers have been known to hitchhike and get stranded, since Childs is not a major tourist attraction. If you're traveling alone or can't get a rental car, **Copper River and North West Tours** (424-5356) meets ferries and offers an informative narrative and a comfy roundtrip bus ride. The "Million Dollar" tour lasts five to six hours and includes a delicious lunch spread during the three hour stop at Childs ($35).

Within biking distance of town (about 15 mi.), the **Sheridan Glacier** lets hikers get up close and personal with an icy monolith. Follow Sheridan Glacier Rd., left of the Copper River Hwy. just past the airport, to its end and pick up a marked trail. If you choose to walk out onto the glacier, you take your life into your own hands: icefields often contain crevasses, which can swallow walkers without a trace, and are sometimes covered with a seemingly solid crust of snow. Nonetheless, scores of locals and tourists venture onto Sheridan's broad back every summer. Another good biking spot is Whitshed Rd., which begins just east of town and provides some of the most photogenic views of the state.

Hiking in the Delta is often wet and tough, but the neighboring **Chugach Mountains** provide dry trails and excellent climbing opportunities. An easy hike from town is the 2.4-mi. **Crater Lake Trail,** reachable by Power Creek Rd., 1½ mi. north of Cordova. From Crater Lake cradled high in an alpine bowl, there are excellent views across the sound, delta, and mountains. For a more strenuous hike, continue among mountain goats along a 5½-mi. ridge to connect with the **Power Creek Trail.** The ridge-route meets the Power Creek Trail midway on its 4.2-mi. ascent to one of the most spectacular Forest Service **cabins** in the state (one of three in the area accessible by foot). The Power Creek Trail begins at the end of Power Creek Rd., 7 mi. from town. The loop combining the Crater Lake and Power Creek trails is a 12-mi. hike. Other, shorter trails branch off the Copper River Hwy.; check with the **Forest Service** (see **Practical Information**) for an excellent **pamphlet** on hiking around Cordova.

Fishing here is superb, as all five species of Pacific salmon spawn seasonally in the Copper River. You can catch salmon and halibut right off the city dock, but the fishing is usually better along Orca Inlet Road, on the Eyak River, or at Hartney Bay. It's possible to fish during a major run almost all year. King salmon run in the winter; sockeye and pink run in the mid- and late summer; dolly varden in the summer and early fall; and coho salmon in late summer and fall.

▒ Wrangell-St. Elias National Park

Wrangell-St. Elias National Park and Preserve elicits the same awe-struck praise so many of its Alaskan brethren do: vast, beautiful, pristine, wild, and so on. But Wrangell is unique, even in Alaska, because it is little known and uncrowded, features spectacular wilderness and wildlife, and can be enjoyed on a tight budget.

The **largest national park in the U.S.,** Wrangell-St. Elias is so vast that the 22 largest National Parks from the lower 48 states could all fit within its boundaries (Yellowstone, Glacier, Grand Canyon, Grand Teton, Yosemite, Everglades...). Four major mountain ranges converge here: the Wrangell, St. Elias, Chugach, and Alaska Ranges. Nine peaks tower more than 14,000 ft. within the park, including the second highest mountain in the U.S. (18,008 ft. **Mt. St. Elias**). The heights are covered in constant snow and ice: the Bagley Icefield is the largest non-polar icefield in North America, and the Malaspina Glacier, a piedmont glacier near the coast, is larger than the state of Rhode Island. Mountain sheep populate the jagged slopes within the park, and moose and bear are commonly sighted in the lower elevations.

The park is in the southeast corner of Alaska's mainland and is bordered by the Copper River to the west and Kluane National Park in the Yukon to the east. Two roads provide park access: the **McCarthy Rd.** and the **Nabesna Rd.,** which enters from the northern park boundaries. The towns of Chitina, McCarthy, and Kennicott remain supply centers and part of the region's colorful copper mining history. In spite of its fascinating human history and unbeatable natural setting, the majority of tourists don't even know Wrangell-St. Elias exists; only 52,000 people visited the park in 1994 (compared to 489,000 in Denali).

The **visitors center** (822-5234) can be found 1 mi. off Richardson Hwy. Mile 105.1 on the side road toward **Copper Center** (open in summer daily 8am-6pm; winter Mon.-Fri. 8am-5pm). Informed rangers will give you maps and the low-down on all the to-dos and to-sees in the park. There are also **ranger stations** in **Chitina** (CHITna; 823-2205; open daily 10am-6pm) and in **Slana** on the northern park boundary (822-5238; open daily 8am-5pm).

FROM THE PARK PERIMETER TO MCCARTHY

Most travelers head into the park via the Edgerton Hwy., eventually arriving in McCarthy. To reach McCarthy, the hub of the park, and its sister town Kennicott, turn onto the Edgerton Hwy. at its junction with the Richardson Hwy. (33 mi. south of Glenallen) and follow the Edgerton east. On a clear day along the Edgerton Hwy., look north to see 12,010 ft. Mt. Drum and 16,237 ft. Mt. Sanford. On exceptionally clear days, steam can be seen rising from the flat summit of 14,113 ft. Mt. Wrangell, Alaska's tallest active volcano. After 33 mi. of blessed pavement you'll reach **Chitina.** Once the largest town in Alaska and heralded as a future capital, Chitina bucked the yoke of greatness. The town was a transport hub for the Kennicott Railway and when the copper mine closed, the town virtually disappeared. Today it remains a sleepy town of 300 with a single café, the **It'll Do Café,** where big cinnamon rolls are $2.50

and the sign in the parking lot that says "Caution: Old Fisherman Crossing" is only half-joking (open daily 6am-10pm). Chitina also has a general store (823-2111; open daily 7am-8pm), a saloon, and a ranger station (see above).

If you haven't stocked up on groceries yet (you should have), do it in Chitina, since there is no grocery store in McCarthy. Penniless campers will delight in the spacious Dept. of Transportation **campground** just across the Copper River from Chitina (free; pit toilets; no water). Across the highway from the campground you can witness Chitina's famous fishwheels and dipnets in the Copper River. Because its turbid, silt-ridden waters make fishing with conventional tackle impossible (fish can't eat what they can't see), the Copper River is one of only four rivers in Alaska where the use of dipnets and fishwheels is legal.

From Chitina, the **McCarthy Road** follows the old roadbed of the **Copper River and Northwestern Railway** for 58 mi. to the Kennicott River. This is arguably the roughest state road in Alaska (Dalton Hwy. included). Severe washboard, rocks, pot-holes, and even an occasional railroad spike in the road make this a rough three-hour one way trip which necessitates a spare tire. The key is to take it slow; with normal tires, any speed over 20 mph dramatically increases your chances of a blow-out. If you want to preserve your car, take a shuttle or even the surprisingly affordable flight from Chitina (see **McCarthy: Practical Information,** below). If you decide to drive it, enjoy the scenery and stop at Mile 17 for the **Kuskulana Bridge.** The 525-ft. long bridge (a former railroad trestle) passes 238 ft. above the Kuskulana River and was the greatest thrill of the McCarthy Rd. before it was upgraded and guard rails were added in 1988. Thrill-seekers can still get their fix of adrenaline here thanks to **Club Way North,** P.O. Box 1003, Girdwood 99587 (783-1335). The club organizes bun-gee jumps from here in the summer ($50, **free if you jump naked;** call or write for times and reservations).

After jolting and rattling for 41 more mi., the road terminates on the western edge of the Kennicott River. You can park ($5) or camp ($10) at the lot on the river, but beware of glacial water releases which can cause the river to suddenly rise and sub-merge the parking lot. Half a mile back from the river on McCarthy Rd. is another lot that offers free parking and camping. Just past this lot, a narrow, rocky state-owned road leads the opposite way to several roadside campsites (free; no facilities). The only way across the raging river is by a hand-operated **tram** (a metal "cart" with two seats, running on a cable). It is far easier to have somebody pull you across, so return the favor if somebody helps you out. A foot bridge to replace the tram is reportedly in the works; it will be more convenient but much less fun. McCarthy is an easy ½-mi. walk from the opposite side of the river.

▓ Kennicott and McCarthy

In the early 1900s, the richest copper ore ever discovered was found in the nearby mountain ridge on the east side of the Kennicott Glacier. The find attracted Stephen Birch, a young mining engineer who, backed by the Guggenheim brothers and J.P. Morgan, formed the Kennecott Copper Corporation. (Misspelled, the company and mine's name remained Kennecott while the town and glacier are named Kennicott.) To transport the ore, the Copper River and Northwest Railway was constructed between 1908 and 1911. The CR&NW (jokingly called "Can't Run and Never Will") did run for 196 mi. from the Kennecott mines to the warm-water port of Cordova until 1938 when falling copper prices forced the mine to close. The town of **Kenni-cott,** whose centerpiece is a 14-story building where ore was processed, was known for maintaining strict conduct rules. Amazingly, much of Kennecott remains remark-ably intact, earning the name "America's largest ghost town." Visitors are free to roam the streets, but the buildings are private property and closed to the public. It is worth saving your energy for better hikes and taking the $8 roundtrip shuttle from McCar-thy (see below).

McCarthy, 5 mi. closer to the river than Kennicott, sprouted up as a free-wheeling alternative to its stick-in-the-mud neighbor. Brothels and alcohol made the town more attractive to miners. Today's McCarthyites seem satisfied with the steady trickle of tourists to their isolated town, and maintain many of the old buildings along with a quiet, mellow charm.

Practical Information and Sights Walking up from the river, the first building you'll encounter houses the **McCarthy-Kennecott Historical Museum,** with artifacts and documents from mining days (free; open daily 9am-6pm). This is a good place to get general information about the area and pick up a map for a walking tour of Kennicott and McCarthy ($1 donation).

Getting to McCarthy isn't very difficult. Drive on your own if you want to test your car's suspension. **Backcountry Connections** (822-5292 or 800-478-5292 in Alaska) offers similar service as well as a Glennallen-McCarthy route ($49 one way, $70-88 roundtrip; $35 one way from Chitina, $60-70 roundtrip). Vans depart Monday through Saturday from Glenallen (7am) and Chitina (8am), depart from McCarthy (4pm), then go back through to Chitina (7:30pm) and Glenallen (8:30pm). **Wrangell Mountain Air** (see **Sights and Outdoors**) flies here daily from Chitina for those who would rather not tackle the highway ($60 each way). Relatively regular traffic makes hitchhiking *one* possibility, though getting stranded is another. (*Let's Go* does not recommend hitchhiking.) The McCarthy Lodge has **showers** for $5. There is no **post office;** local mail is flown in bi-weekly.

Accommodations, Camping, and Food Rooms at the **McCarthy Lodge** (554-4402), in downtown McCarthy, are expensive ($95 single, $105 double). **Camping** is $10 in the lot just west of the river (before you cross to go to McCarthy) and free at the lot half a mile farther back toward Chitina (pit toilets, no water). Because almost all of the land around McCarthy and Kennicott is privately owned and local drinking water comes from nearby creeks, camping is prohibited in all areas on the eastern side of the Kennicott River except on land north of Kennicott.

The town has no general store, though the **Nugget Gift Shop** has some snacks and camping supplies (open daily 9am-6pm). **Tailor-Made Pizza** (554-4000) serves hearty calzones for $9. Try the Erie, a vegetarian extravaganza with ingredients too numerous to list (open daily 8am-10pm). The **McCarthy Lodge** (see above) serves breakfast ($5-8) and dinner ($12-23) in a rustic dining room with wooden floors and antique-covered walls (open daily 7am-10pm).

Sights and Outdoors If you go **flightseeing** anywhere in Alaska, do it here. Because of the proximity of 16,390-ft. Mt. Blackburn and the spectacular glaciers, a short flight can offer views of incredible scenery. On **Wrangell Mountain Air** (800-478-1160 for reservations), based in downtown McCarthy, a 35-minute flight takes you over Kennicott and the amazing icefalls of the Kennicott and Root Glaciers ($40). The best bargain, a 70-minute trip, will take you up the narrow **Chitistone Canyon** to view the thundering **Chitistone Falls** and over 15 glaciers and five mountain peaks ($75). You can also fly out to see 18,000-ft. Mt. St. Elias and 19,800-ft. Mt. Logan in a longer 90-minute flight ($110). There is a three-person minimum on all flights. **McCarthy Air** (800-245-6909), also in McCarthy, offers similar flights and rates. The two companies are very competitive, so make sure to compare rates before you sign on.

Mountain biking is an excellent way to explore the area. You'll see much more than you would walking and have more flexibility than a guide or shuttle service can give. At **St. Elias Alpine Guides** (277-6867) you can rent bikes ($30 per day, $35 with shocks) and take the Old Wagon Trail to Kennicott (5 mi.), then continue on a trail that takes you alongside Root Glacier and within view of the Erie Mine (4 more mi.). **Copper Oar** (522-1670), at the end of the McCarthy Rd., offers a two-hour whitewater trip down the Kennicott River for $45.

Most **hikers and trekkers** use the McCarthy Road or McCarthy as a base. The park maintains no trails, but miners and other travelers from decades past have established various routes and obscure roads that follow the more exciting pathways. Rugged ter-

ALASKA

rain and harsh, unpredictable weather require extra precaution. Be sure to consult with the visitors center or a ranger station before you set out. The most common route is a hike out past Kennicott to the Root Glacier, which follows road-bed and glacial moraine with three moderate stream crossings. The 16-mi. roundtrip makes a long day trip or an easy two-day hike. A hike to **Dixie Pass** has the advantage of accessibility (it starts from Mile 13 on the McCarthy Road); hikers should allow three to four days for the 24-mi. roundtrip. Those with a little more money and strong hiking expertise should consider the **Goat Trail** (fly-in required). The trail is a 25-mi. one way trek from Lower Skolai Lake to Glacier Creek and traverses the ridge high above **Chitistone Canyon and Falls,** one of the park's more spectacular features. Access is only available by air taxi. Allow between $150-200 per person for the drop-off and pick-up. Though only 25 mi., the extremely rugged terrain and many stream crossings make this a four- to eight-day trek for expert hikers only. For any overnight trip, the park service requests a written itinerary; though it's not required, it's in your own best interest. Pick up topographical maps from the ranger station or the visitors center. Be aware that this is bear country.

For those on a serious shoe-string and without much time, just walking around McCarthy and Kennicott is interesting. Across the street from McCarthy's abandoned general store, you'll find a tiny **art gallery** featuring the work of local artist Loy Green. The gallery houses memorable, if a bit unorthodox, paintings such as "The Spirit of Man and Bear within a Harmonic Ray of Creation." A **shuttle bus** runs to Kennicott from McCarthy on a regular schedule ($8 roundtrip). It's a 5-mi. hike between the two towns. If you walk to Kennicott, take the Old Wagon Trail and not the main road (look for the sign on the left side of the road shortly after turning toward Kennicott at the "Y"). The trail leads through the forest, away from the dusty road. Or explore the old, obscure mining roads that surround the town. St. Elias Alpine Guides (see above) also organizes guided hikes ($55 for a half-day excursion onto Root Glacier) and fly-in hikes (starting at $105 per person).

THE NABESNA ROAD

The Nabesna Road, running southeast for 42 mi. from the town of **Slana,** offers vehicular access to the park's interior. The turnoff for Slana is on the Glenn Hwy., 65 mi. southwest of Tok. Another route into Wrangell-St. Elias, the Nabesna road is a gentler drive except when the water level is high in the three or four streams your car will have to pass over. Conditions permitting, the drive takes one and a half hours, versus three bumpy hours on the McCarthy; moreover, ATV and hiking trails are accessible from the road. However, the Nabesna Road's terminus is the uninspiring, abandoned mining town of **Nabesna.** There's little to see here and it's best to stay away from the privately owned, abandoned gold mine here. All Nabesna travelers should check with the staff at the Slana Ranger Station before entering the park. They'll provide trail information, ATV permits, water levels, and road conditions.

Interior Alaska

Alaska's vast Interior sprawls between the Alaska Range to the south and the Brooks Range to the north, covering 166,000 sq. mi. of the nation's wildest and most stunning terrain. Most of the Interior alternates between flat forest and marshy, treeless tundra, punctuated by immense mountain ranges. The Yukon River, the Tanana River, and hundreds of other major and minor rivers have created the sloughs, inlets, lakes, and bogs that sustain a huge waterfowl population. The unofficial state bird, the mosquito, outnumbers all other animals by over a thousand to one in summer. Larger mammals, including moose, grizzlies, wolves, caribou, Dall sheep, lynx, beavers, and hares, roam the parks and wild country of the Interior. Few people live here; outside Fairbanks, Alaska's second-largest city, the region is sparsely inhabited.

Interior Alaska is the home of the Athabascan Native people, many of whom still trap, hunt, and fish within the Interior's network of waterways. These nomadic hunters' traditional domain followed the migration of caribou and the spawning cycles of salmon. Unlike the Native Americans in the Lower 48, Athabascans have not been confined to reservations; instead, they own title to their own land, a result of the Alaska Native Land Claims Settlement Act of 1971. Although many have left their remote villages and traditional lifestyle for modern living in Fairbanks and Anchorage, Alaskan native heritage is alive and well across the state in cultural institutions and an active native political movement.

▓ Denali National Park

Denali National Park is the home of the highest mountain in North America. Despite the blundering audacity of the Princeton-educated prospector who renamed the 20,320-ft. peak after Republican Presidential nominee William McKinley in 1896, locals and visitors alike call it Denali or simply "the mountain." The pure-white upper reaches of Denali, visible from over 10 mi. away, dominate this region like a second sun. From base to summit, Denali boasts the greatest vertical relief in the world; even Mt. Everest rises only 10,000 ft. from its base on the Plateau of Tibet. Denali's 18,000 ft. of rock and ice scrape toward the sky with hardly a hill intervening. It's so big that it manufactures its own weather: when moist air from the Pacific collides with the cold mountaintop, sudden storms encircle the peak. As a result, Denali's face is only visible about 20% of the time in the summer, and a large number of the park's visitors never actually see the mountain. Despite the fact that postcard photographers are obsessed with this majestic mountain, there is much more to see in the park than its centerpiece—for example, the remarkable wildlife. Visitors regularly spot grizzly bears, caribou, and Dall sheep, and the park also supports significant populations of black bears, moose, and wolves. Campgrounds are relatively small and quiet, and a trek into easily accessible backcountry leaves humanity entirely behind. With a little planning, it's easy to avoid the overwhelming crowds.

PRACTICAL INFORMATION AND ORIENTATION

Denali National Park commands respect. If you land in the park unprepared, you'll probably lose a day or more just getting your bearings. Moving through the park can be a complex, time-consuming, and highly confusing process. Because most park privileges are distributed on a first-come, first-served basis, its a good idea to conduct all administrative business at the Visitor's Center *as early in the day as possible*. If at all possible, make reservations in advance. Forty percent of campsites and shuttle-bus tickets can be reserved by calling 800-622-7275 (272-7275 from Anchorage), at least *five days before* your visit.

The reason for all the confusion is that only the first 14 mi. of the park are accessible by private vehicle; the remaining 71 mi. of dirt road can be reached only by shuttle or camper bus. If you go no farther than Mile 14 of the park road, you'll be missing out on 98% of the park's landscape and wildlife. You need no permit for driving or dayhiking in the first 14 mi., but must pay a $3 registration fee ($5 per family) that applies to all visitors. To go beyond Mile 14, you'll need to take a shuttle bus (see **Buses within the park,** p. 109), unless you're driving to Teklanika campground, which requires a special permit. The restrictions on driving along the Denali Park Road may seem inconvenient, but they limit traffic, keep the park in more pristine condition than would otherwise be possible, and make the park extraordinarily accessible to those without cars. One needs only witness the alternative in traffic-clogged Yellowstone or Yosemite to appreciate the system.

Regardless of how much you plan, you will still have to deal with crowds. The masses flock to Denali between mid-June and mid-August. Unfortunately, the shuttle bus only runs from late May to mid-September, so the window of relatively crowd-free access is small. By mid- to late August, spectacular fall colors peak, mosquito season is essentially over, and the snows of September have not yet arrived—all of which make the last half of August an excellent time to visit. No matter when you go, be prepared for wet, cool weather.

Summer Visitors Information: Denali Visitor Center (683-1266), 0.7 mi. from Rte. 3. All travelers stop here for orientation. The headquarters of the **shuttle-bus** service (see **Buses within the Park,** p. 109). Registration or park entrance fee $3, families $5. **Maps,** shuttle-bus schedules, and **permits** for campground ($6-12) and backcountry camping (free permit; you will need to take the $15 bus if you have a permit for beyond Mile 14). Info on campsites, wildlife tours, sled-dog demonstrations, and campfire talks. Denali Park's indispensable publication *Alpenglow,* including event schedules and rates as well as park history, is also available (free). The center has installed a "backcountry simulator" which provides useful info for wilderness hikers. Open in summer daily 7am-8pm; lines often start forming by 6:30am. Shuttles depart as early as 5am in peak season. Lockers outside 50¢. **Eielson Visitors Center,** 66 mi. into the park, is accessible by shuttle bus. Staffed by helpful rangers who lead tundra walks. No food available here. None. Open daily in summer 9am-early evening. Write to **Denali National Park and Preserve,** P.O. Box 9, Denali Park 99755 (683-1266) for information on the park; or consult one of the **Public Lands Information Centers** (see page 45 or page 117).

Winter Visitors Information: Skiing and sled-dog racing are popular wintertime activities in Denali. Visit the Park Headquarters (683-9500) at Mile 3.5, on the left side of the park road.

Banks: None in the park or immediate vicinity. Tempermental **ATM** at a gas station in Healy. Most places accept credit cards.

Buses: The **Riley Creek Loop Bus** runs the 30-min. loop to the visitors center, the Denali Park Hotel, the Alaska Railroad station, and the Riley Creek campground daily from 5:30am to 9:15pm. A tan **courtesy bus** is owned by the chalets and makes runs from the Denali Park Hotel to the chalet near Lynx Creek Pizza.

Taxi: Denali Taxi Service, 683-2504.

Bike Rental: Denali Mountain Bike, P.O. Box 448, Denali (322-0716). 21-speed Mongooses $7 per hr., $25 per day. Unlike private vehicles, bikes *are* permitted on all 85 hilly, bus-crowded miles of the park road.

Kayak Rental: Denali Outdoor Center, P.O. Box 1171 (683-1925). $35 per day, $45 with equipment, $55 including dry suit. Call at least one week in advance. Must have prior experience.

Laundromat and Showers: McKinley Campground, P.O. Box 340, Healy 99743 (683-1418), 12 mi. north of park entrance. Showers ($2.50 for 7½ minutes) and the only public laundromat in the area (wash $2, dry $1). **McKinley Mercantile,** 1½ mi. into the park. Unlimited showers $3, with a $5 key deposit. Showers open daily 8:30am-1:30pm, 2:45-8:30pm.

Medical Clinic: 683-2211, in Healy. Open Mon.-Fri. 9am-5pm. Registered nurse on call 24hr.

Emergency: 683-910, in the park (24hr.); 911, from nearby Healy.

Post Office: 683-2291, next to Denali National Park Hotel, 1 mi. from the visitors center (see above). Open Mon.-Fri. 8:30am-5pm, Sat. 10am-1pm; Oct.-May Mon.-Sat. 10am-1pm. **General Delivery ZIP Code:** 99755-9998.
Area Code: 907.

Transportation to the Park

The park can be easily reached by road or rail. The **George Parks Hwy.** (Rte. 3), the road connecting Anchorage (240 mi. south of Denali) and Fairbanks (120 mi. north), offers direct access to the Denali Park Rd. Leading east away from Denali is Rte. 8, the gravel **Denali Hwy.**, between Cantwell and Paxson. Closed in winter, the Denali Hwy. is breathtaking, skirting the foothills of the Alaska Range amid countless lakes and streams teeming with grayling, trout, and Arctic char.

Several bus companies have service connecting Denali with Anchorage and Fairbanks. **Parks Highway Express** (479-3065) charges $20 per person from Anchorage (about 5hr.) or Fairbanks (about 3hr.) to Denali. Call for departure times. **Moon Bay Express** (274-6454) has one bus daily to Anchorage ($35, $60 roundtrip, bikes $10 each). **Fireweed Express** (452-0251) provides daily van service to Fairbanks ($25 one way, bikes $5).**Alaska Direct** (277-6652) runs from Fairbanks to Denali ($30; Wed., Fri., and Sun. 4pm) and from Anchorage ($50; same days 7am). The **Alaska Backpacker Shuttle** runs a bus one way from Anchorage to Denali ($35, bikes $10). The **Alaska Railroad,** P.O. Box 107500, Anchorage 99510 (683-2233, out of state 800-544-0552), makes regular stops at Denali station (open daily 10am-5pm), 1½ mi. from the park entrance, but is slower than the shuttle services. The railroad runs to Fairbanks (1 per day, 4pm; $47); and Anchorage (1 per day, 12:30pm; $88). Bikes $20. Check bags at least a half-hour before departure. With all, call for reservations.

Buses within the Park

If you're going beyond Savage River at Mile 14, and aren't camping at Teklanika, you must take a bus. The park's concessionaire recently took over the **bus system** within the park, expanding both the number of available seats and the fee you'll have to pay for one. Costs range from $12-26, depending on how far into the park you plan to go. A **3-day pass** is available, costing double the price of a single ticket for your destination. Tickets can be purchased by phone (800-622-7275; Mon.-Fri. 7am-4pm, Sat. 10am-4pm), or in person at the visitors center within two days of departure. Calling ahead is strongly recommended. If you wait until you get to the park to purchase tickets, arrive at the visitors center as close to opening as possible (7am). Space on buses leaving in two days begins to get tight in late afternoon.

There are two different bus services into the park interior. **Shuttle buses** leave the visitors center daily (5am-2:30pm). Go for the less frequent Wonder Lake bus if you can, as the best views of Denali are beyond Eielson. The 11- hour roundtrip to Wonder Lake sounds grueling, but if the sun and the wildlife are out, you'll be glad you went. If it's cloudy on the day of the trip, Wonder Lake can be an utter washout. You're better off getting off at Eielson and spending the three hours you'd spend on the bus hiking instead. The eight-hour roundtrip to Eielson is the next best bet for a cloudy day. It allows you to see a wide array of terrain while still leaving adequate time for a day hike (shuttle to Toklat, Mile 48, $12; to Eielson Visitor Center, Mile 65, $20; to Wonder Lake, Mile 85, $30). **Camper buses** ($15) move faster, transporting *only* people with **campground permits** and **backcountry permits.** However, camper buses will stop to pick up dayhikers along the road. Camper buses leave the visitors center five times daily. The final bus stays overnight at Wonder Lake and returns at 7am the next morning.

ACCOMMODATIONS AND CAMPING

With one exception, accommodations and campgrounds within the park are open in the summer only. Any hotel room in or near the park will be prohibitively expensive. For a more "civilized" camping experience, check out the local KOA (Kampground

ALASKA

The Shuttle Bus: An Approach

Getting a **window seat** is critical. Nobody wants to stare at another passenger's head for upward of five hours in a vain attempt at spotting romping caribou. With this in mind, show up about half an hour early for your bus so that you can catch a decent seat. Your second priority on an outbound bus is to get a seat on the same side as the driver. This side enjoys fabulous views down into river valleys and out to the Alaska range, while the other side spends much of the time staring at a hillside right next to the bus. Finally, it's best to sit toward the front, where you can more easily see wildlife the driver has stopped for, and ask questions without having to yell. The **Denali Road Guide** ($5; available at the visitors center and the hotel bookshop) and **binoculars** (the hotel gift shop rents for $6 per 24hr.) are two highly valuable investments.

of America). The beautiful hostel is about the only option that can shelter without breaking the bank.

Denali Park Resorts, 825 W 8th Ave., #240, Anchorage 99501 (800-276-7234), runs the park's tourist services, including the **Denali National Park Hotel** (683-2215), which is centrally located near the railroad station, airstrip, trails, park headquarters, a grocery store, and a gas station, but you'll choke on the cost (singles $135). Since you have better things to do with $135, plan to stay at the hostel or camp at one of the park's wonderful campgrounds.

Campers need a **permit,** which can be obtained at the visitors center (40% of the sites at 4 of the park's 7 campgrounds may be reserved by calling 800-622-7275). Remaining sites are distributed at the visitors center on a first-come, first-served basis. Get to the visitors center early to enhance your chances of getting a site, but a wait of several days to get a permit is not uncommon. Backpackers who lack vehicles and who are waiting for a backcountry or campground permit can find a $6 space in **Morino Campground,** next to the hotel (no reservations). Many people find it helpful to set up camp in Morino the first day while they take the shuttle bus in and preview potential campsites within the park. You can camp a total of 14 days in park campgrounds. The park's first two campgrounds are effectively adjuncts of the visitors center and serve mostly as bases for daytrips deeper into Denali. **Savage, Sanctuary,** and **Teklanika** are in high, dry country with access to dramatic views. **Igloo Creek** is low and wooded. **Wonder Lake** is low and wet but has an amazing direct-line view of the mountain. All are clean and well maintained.

Hardsiders are going to have a hard time in Denali. Since realizing that the larger specimens of the Winnebago tribe compete with The Mountain in dominating skylines and affecting local weather patterns, park officials have clamped down. There are no hookups and only one dump station, at Riley Creek. RV drivers can pay $12 per night to park at **Riley Creek, Savage River,** and **Teklanika River Campgrounds,** or they can head to the numerous RV parks huddled near the park entrance.

Denali Hostel, P.O. Box 801 (683-1295), Denali Park. Drive 9.6 mi. north of park entrance, turn left onto Otto Lake Rd., drive 1.3 mi. The second house on the right (log house with blue trim) is the hostel. Beautiful location (o, the sunsets!). Nice beds by hostel standards, full kitchen, TV room. Morning shuttles to the park, daily pick-ups from the visitors center at 5pm and 9pm, and from the Alaska Railroad (Anchorage train only). Open May-Sept., check-in 5:30-10pm. No curfew. Beds $22 plus tax. Cash or travelers cheques only. Reserve, we implore you.

Riley Creek, Mile ¼ Denali Park Rd. The only year-round campground in Denali (no water in winter). All sites are assigned at the visitors center. Often has the only sites still open at mid-morning. Piped water, flush toilets, and sewage dump. Reservations are available. 100 sites, $12.

Morino Creek, Mile 1.9 Denali Park Rd., next to the train tracks. 60 sites for backpackers without vehicles. Water, chemical toilets. Self-registered sites $6 per person. Nearest showers at the Mercantile, ¼ mi. back up the road.

Savage River, Mile 13 Denali Park Rd. Flush toilets and water. Last area accessible by car without a permit. 33 sites, $12.

Sanctuary River, Mile 23 on Denali Park Rd. Chemical toilets but no water. Accessible only by shuttle bus. No fires; stoves only. 7 tent sites, $6.

Teklanika River, Mile 29 Denali Park Rd. Piped water and chemical toilets. Accessible only by shuttle bus or by a vehicle with a permit. 53 tent and RV sites, $12.

Igloo Creek, Mile 34 Denali Park Rd. Pit toilets but no water. No open fires. Accessible only by shuttle. 7 tent sites, $6.

Wonder Lake, Mile 85 Denali Park Rd. You are a happy camper indeed if you happen to end up at Wonder lake on a clear day. Spectacular, soul-searing views of Denali. Piped water, flush toilets. No vehicles allowed. About a bizillion mosquitoes (give or take a few trillion). 28 tent sites, $12.

McKinley Campground, P.O. Box 340, Healy 99743 (683-1418), 11 mi. north of park entrance. Grass, trees, and picnic tables. Good showers and the only public laundromat in the area (see **Practical Information**). Tent sites for 1-2 people $16.75, any larger tent $19.25; full hookup $27.50.

FOOD

Food in Denali is expensive. Try to bring groceries into the park with you. Meager provisions in the park are available at **McKinley Mercantile** (683-2215), 1½ mi. along Denali Park Rd. A monster cinnamon roll can be had for $2 (open daily 7am-10pm). The **Lynx Creek Grocery** (683-2548) has similarly priced items 1 mi. north of the park entrance (open daily 7am-midnight). Be aware that once you get on a park bus, there is no food available. Anywhere.

Lynx Creek Pizza, (683-2547) 1 mi. north of park entrance. Imposing portions of Italian and Mexican favorites ($7-8.25) and good pizza (16 in. from $15.75). Lodge decor. Pass on the Mexican, which has picked up massive salt deposits on its journey north, in favor of the easier-travelling Italian. Go for the slice-salad-soda-scoop lunch special ($7.50). Open daily 11am-11pm.

Denali Park Hotel (683-2215). Offers the only sit-down options in the park. In the **Dining Room:** breakfast and lunch around $6-7; dinner starts at $10.50 (open daily 7am-2:30pm and 5-9:30pm). In the **Whistle Stop Snack Shop:** mediocre, pre-fab burgers, $6; cold sandwiches, $6.50 (open daily 5am-11pm, hot breakfast till 7am). Small **Espresso Station** has muffins for $2, small cappuccino for $2.25.

McKinley/Denali Steak and Salmon Bake Restaurant, (683-2733) 1 mi. north of park entrance. Tacky signs out front guide you to a reasonably priced tourist magnet. Pounds of food doled out in a picnic setting. Try the Sourdough Breakfast (scrambled eggs, ham, reindeer sausage, potatoes, juice, coffee, and all-you-can-eat blueberry or sourdough pancakes) for $9. All-you-can-eat soup, salad, rolls, and pudding available all day for $9.50. Open daily 5am-11pm.

EXPLORING THE BACKCOUNTRY

Although dayhiking is unlimited and requires no permit wherever there are no wildlife restrictions, only two to 12 backpackers can camp at one time in each of the park's 43 units. Overnight stays in the backcountry require a free permit, available one day in advance at the backcountry desk at the visitors center. Folks start waiting outside as early as 6:30am in order to get their top picks. Come to the desk, look at the **quota board,** and research your choices using the handy *Backcountry Description Guides.* Also thumb through *The Backcountry Companion,* available in the visitors center bookstore. The rangers will usually leave two or three zones open to unlimited backcountry camping, but these areas tend to be undesirable, thick with mosquitoes, and set back from the road behind other quadrants. Some quadrants are temporarily closed after a fresh wildlife kill or a "bear encounter." **Sable Pass,** a romping ground for bears, is closed to hikers.

The quadrants contain diverse terrain. **Taiga** is low-lying, forested country. **River bars** are level, rocky areas by rivers; these offer very good footing for hikers, but be prepared to get wet fording the rivers. **Low tundra** means brushy, wet areas above the treeline; the soggy terrain is not easily navigable and makes for difficult, exasperating hiking under buggy conditions. **Alpine tundra** or **dry tundra** is high, dry ground above the treeline. The higher elevation means fewer mosquitoes. Generally, the southern reaches of the park contain dry tundra and river bars, opening wide vistas of Denali. The North is more brushy, but contains high points with incredible views of the mountain. The first few units along the park road consist of spongy tundra and dense taiga forest with a small bear population. Walking on soggy natural mattresses quickly loses its novelty. Some of the most enjoyable hiking and wildlife-viewing is in the middle of the park, near the **Toklat River** and **Polychrome Pass.**

Denali's backcountry operations are guided by the conviction that independent wandering provides more rewards than guided trekking. With this in mind, and in an effort to disperse hikers as widely as possible, rangers will not recommend specific areas, although many will suggest areas that meet hikers' desires. Except near the park entrance, no trails in the park are formally maintained.

No matter where you camp, keep within the zone for which you signed up. Pitch your tent completely out of sight of the road. To keep from getting lost, pick up **topographic maps** ($2.50) at the visitors center. Before you leave the visitors center, rangers will give you a short introduction to bear management, and you must watch five brief **backcountry simulator programs.** Most zones require that you carry a black, cylindrical **bear-resistant food container,** available free at the backcountry desk. These are bulky, so be sure to leave extra space in your backpack. To alert bears of your presence when in low-visibility situations, it is recommended that you sing, shout, or make other loud noises. Using your voice is best, since bears recognize it as human and will be disinclined to investigate (see **Bear in Mind,** p. 48). The Rangers recommend that visitor's read Stephen Herrero's book, *Bear Attacks: Their Cause and Avoidance.*

DAYHIKING AND OTHER ADVENTURES

You can dayhike in the heart of the park by riding the shuttle bus to a suitable embarkation point and asking the driver to let you off. Don't feel obligated to get off at one of the designated rest stops (about every 1-1½hr. along the routes). The drivers are happy to drop you off anywhere that isn't restricted due to wildlife activity. Once you have wandered to your heart's content, head back to the road and flag down a shuttle bus heading in your direction. The first couple of buses that pass may be full, but it's rare to have to wait more than a half hour or so to find a ride. Many of the buses stop running fairly early, so be sure to check with your driver regarding when the last buses will be passing your area.

If you're seeking a more structured hiking experience, park rangers organize one hour **tundra walks** daily from Eielson. Check with the visitors center about what bus you should take to get there in time. Guided hikes also leave twice daily from the visitors center. The **discovery hikes** are more strenuous three- to five-hour hikes, which leave in the afternoon from the visitors center. The treks are limited to 15, and require advance sign-up. A ranger will lead you through a "cross-country scramble" or a moose trail excursion. Many other talks and naturalist programs are also posted at the visitors center. The **sled-dog demonstrations** are another worthwhile free offering. The dogs play a critical role in the winter, when the park is accessible only to sled-dog teams, skiers, and snowmobiles. Buses leave the visitors center for demonstrations at 9:30am, 1:30, and 3:30pm.

Don't despair if you're trapped in limbo waiting for your hot date with a shuttle bus. There are a number of worthwhile **trails** which snake around the visitors center and the Denali Hotel. The beautiful **Rock Creek Trail** runs 2.3 mi. from the hotel to near Park Headquarters where the sled-dog demonstrations are held. The more challenging **Mt. Healy** overlook trail climbs steeply for 2½ mi. to an impressive view of the valley. If you're feeling particularly ambitious, you can continue up the ridge to the 5700-ft. summit.

Several rafting companies run the rapids of Denali's **Nenana River.** Look for a company that offers equipment to stay dry and warm; the water temperature hovers around 37° F (3° C). The best deal in town is at **McKinley Raft Tours,** P.O. Box 138, Denali National Park (683-2392), which offers six daily two hour tours ($40) ranging from mere float trips to significant whitewater action. **Alaska Raft Adventures,** P.O. Box 87 (683-2215 or 800-276-7234), **Denali Rafting Adventures,** Drawer 190 (683-2234), and **Denali Park Resorts** (800-276-7234) offer similar trips at somewhat higher prices. While flightseeing in Denali is a rewarding investment, this is, ironically, not the best spot to do it. Talkeetna, to the south of the park, offers much more affordable trips (see p. 115).

■ Denali Highway

Fortunately for solitary sorts, the Denali Hwy.'s 112 mi. of gravel scare away most tour buses and RVs. This makes the highway a scenic leg on the road-less-traveled to Denali, and the wonderful free campgrounds and unique geological formations make it a worthwhile destination in itself. The road stretches west to east from Paxson (80 mi. south of Delta Junction on the Richardson Hwy.) to Cantwell (27 mi. south of the Denali park entrance). Bullet-riddled road signs attest to the popularity of hunting in this area, but mountain bikers, hikers, fishermen, birders, and archeologists also frequent the region. You'll see vast tundra and the snow-capped Alaska Range to the north and the Wrangell Mountains to the southeast. Glaciers and permafrost have been up to geological mischief, creating bizarre mounds, ridges, and basins all along the highway. For explanations of these features and general highway information, pick up the Bureau of Land Management's *Denali Highway Points of Interest* pamphlet, available at most local roadhouses, visitor centers, and pit stops.

Except for the 21 mi. west of Paxson, the Denali Hwy. is entirely gravel. Rocks and potholes vigorously assert their presence along some stretches, but the road is for the most part well-maintained. At Mile 21 (heading west), the **Tangle Lakes Campground** (water, toilets) and, ¼ mi. farther on, the **Tangle River Campground** (water, toilets) are both scenic and free. Both campgrounds provide easy access to the **Delta River Canoe Route** (a 35-mi. canoe route with one difficult stretch of class III rapids) and the **Upper Tangle Lakes Canoe Route** (an easier paddle beginning at Tangle River and ending at Dickey Lake, 9 mi. to the south). Topographic **maps** are necessary for both routes. If you crave the great indoors, the **Tangle River Inn,** Mile 20 (822-7304, 895-4439 in winter), right across the highway from the boat launch, has bunkhouse beds for $23 (shared bath, common room with pool table and TV) and rooms for $42.50 (single or double). The folks at the Inn also rent canoes ($3 per hr., $24 for 24hr.).

The Tangle Lakes area serves as a base for mountain bikers, ATVers, and birders. Pick up the BLM's free *Trail Map and Guide to the Tangle Lakes National Register District* at the Tangle River Inn for detailed trail information. The area is fragile because of the 400 local archeological sites. For more information on the area, write the Bureau of Land Management at Box 147, Glennallen. Birders and flora fans should continue to the **Tangle River Lodge** (688-9173) at Mile 22, where the owners have the lowdown on the area's fowl, flowers, and canoe routes.

On a clear day, spectacular mountain scenery lines the rest of the highway, interrupted by an occasional roadhouse or café. At Mile 80, the highway crosses the beautiful Susitna River. At Mile 95, pull into an unmarked turnoff and jog an easy 600 yd. up the hill for a prime view of Mt. Deborah and the valley below. The turnoff at Mile 130 provides an excellent view of Denali on rare clear days.

■ George Parks Highway

The George Parks Highway links Anchorage and Fairbanks, Alaska's two largest cities. It passes through some of Alaska's finest, most mountainous country. All 358 mi. of the two-lane highway are paved and, except for a few sections with frostheaves, in excellent condition. **Denali National Park** and the hub of **Talkeetna** are located on this route, and for that reason most tourists who use a car in Alaska will drive the Parks Highway.

From **Wasilla** (see also p. 71), the highway runs north past a number of scenic state campgrounds and state recreation areas. The parks offer unlimited canoeing opportunities, though many of the lakes are also open to jet skis and motorboats. The highway then passes the town of **Willow** (look back, you missed it) which has the notable distinction of having been passed up for the site of a new Alaskan capital. A state referendum defeated the crucial bill that would have funded the move.

■ Talkeetna

Talkeetna, at the confluence of the Talkeetna, Susitna, and Chulitna Rivers, is the most popular flight departure point for some 1200 annual climbers of **Denali,** only 60 air mi. to the north. Every year between May and July, climbers from across the globe converge on Talkeetna, creating an international village in an unlikely place. From the town, climbers are flown to a base camp on the Kahiltna Glacier at 7200 ft.; from there it's all uphill. The Denali climb is one of the world's most demanding tests for a mountaineer: in the spring and summer of 1992, a record 13 climbers lost their lives on its unforgiving slopes.

With a small population of 500, including climbers, Bush pilots, and miners, Talkeetna is widely known for its local personalities. The wayward traveler may meet an amputee craftsman whose wheelchair is pulled by a huskie, a woman who boasts of having skinned and cleaned 27 moose in a single winter, or a young man who recently scaled Denali at age 12. The town is just far enough off the beaten path to remain relatively quiet and escape the deluge of tourists. Most of those who come here do so because of the incredible outdoor opportunities.

Practical Information Visitors Information (733-1686) for Talkeetna, including pamphlets about local air charters and walking tours, is located in the **Three German Bachelors Cabin** at Main St. and Talkeetna Spur (open mid-May-Labor Day daily 10am-5:30pm). If it's closed, **Talkeetna Gifts and Collectibles** (733-2710) next door has most of the same information (open daily 8am-7pm). The **Talkeetna Ranger Station** (733-2231) is on D St. While the facility is primarily used by climbers on their way to the mountain, it's also a tranquil place to plan a trip to the park (open April-Sept. Mon.-Fri. 8am-4:30pm). There are **no banks** of any kind in town. The closest **ATM** is 14 mi. away where the Spur Rd. leaves the Parks Hwy.

Talkeetna is 113 mi. north of Anchorage, 280 mi. south of Fairbanks, and 14 mi. off the Parks Hwy. on Talkeetna Spur Rd. (Mile 98.5). The **Alaska Railroad Station,** P.O. Box 107500, Anchorage 99510 (733-2268 or 265-2615), is near the Bachelors Cabin. There is one train per day to: Denali ($48), Anchorage ($45), and Fairbanks ($85). Call 800-544-0552 for ticket information. A far cheaper, and equally pleasant, transportation option is the **Parks Highway Express** shuttle bus (479-3065) which stops in Talkeetna every day but Tuesday and charges $20 to Anchorage, $40 to Fairbanks. **Alaska Backpacker Shuttle** and **Moon Bay** offer similar services: $35 to Anchorage or Denali.

The **library** (733-2359) is 1 mi. from town on Talkeetna Spur Rd. (open Tues. noon-8pm, Wed. and Fri. 11am-6pm, Thurs. 10am-6pm, Sat. 11am-5pm). The **Sunshine Community Health Clinic** (733-2273) is 8 mi. farther on the same street. The **Three Rivers Tesoro Gas Station** (733-2620), on Main St., has a **laundromat** (wash $1.50, 10-min. dry 25¢) and **showers** ($2; open Mon.-Sat. 8am-9pm, Sun. 9am-7pm). The **emergency number** is 911. Reach the **fire** department at 733-2443. The **Post Office** (733-2275) is in town on the Spur (open Mon.-Fri. 9am-5pm, Sat. 10am-2pm; **General Delivery ZIP Code:** 99676).

Accommodations and Camping The town's undisputed top spot is the **K2 Bunkhouse,** a hostel geared to climbers. The Bunkhouse offers a clean, cheerful, lodge-style ambience and a full kitchen brimming with tales of Denali. Laundry (wash

$1.25, dry $1.25), hot showers, toilets, and 18 beds in a co-ed dorm. To register, drop by the **K2 Aviation** office, Box 545-B (733-2291; fax 733-1221), ½ mi. south of town on the spur. The bunkhouse is in town, at the end of the dirt trail leaving Main St. at the Deli (see **Food,** below). Reservations are essential during the climbing season (mid-May to mid-July). A good deal for private rooms hides up the street at the **Fairview Inn** (733-2423), P.O. Box 645. Singles are $32, doubles $42; accepts reservations. Cheap, bunk-style accommodations are also available for $21 at the **Talkeetna Roadhouse** (733-1351 or 733-2341), at Main and C St. This comfortable establishment also offers private rooms with shared baths (singles $45, doubles $60, cabin $75; an additional $15 per person after 2 people). Make reservations well in advance for stays during the climbing season.

Camping is convenient at the **River Park Campground** at the end of Main St. The town hopes to install flush toilets soon, and plans to start charging a fee. While beautiful, the area is a popular late-night hangout for local teens, and may not be particularly serene. Potentially quieter spots are available at **Talkeetna Boat Launch and Camping.** Turn left from the spur road at the airport and follow the signs (sites $6). The area is wooded and clean and has water, outhouses, and easy river access. Several paths beginning at the railroad tracks across from the waiting booth make a convenient shortcut to town.

Food A sparse selection of groceries populates the shelves at **Nagley's Store** (733-FOOD—that's 733-3663 for those of you keeping score at home), on Main St. A latté, ice cream cone, or hot dog will only set you back 99¢. (Open daily 7am-10pm, winter 7am-8pm.) For a sit-down meal, go straight to the **Roadhouse Café** (see **Accommodations,** above), where lunch hovers around $6 (open daily 6:30am-9pm). Talkeetna's spot for pizza, sandwiches, and espresso is the **McKinley Deli** (733-1234), at Main and C St. The $7.50 spaghetti dinner with bread and salad is a tasty deal. If you're really lucky, they might be grilling fresh halibut and salmon on the BBQ outside (open daily 6am-11pm).

Sights, Events, and Entertainment If it's raining, check out the **Museum of Northern Adventure** (733-3999), on the Talkeetna Spur, which offers lighthearted exhibits on everything from climbing McKinley to "cabin fever" ($2.50, under 12 $1.50; open in summer daily 11am-7pm, but somewhat flexible). The more somber **Talkeetna Historical Society Museum** (733-2487), off C St., has high-quality displays on Alaskan transportation and mountaineering, including a 12 ft. x 12 ft. x 2 ft. model of Denali ($1; open in summer daily 10am-5pm).

The second weekend in July brings the **Moose Dropping Festival,** capped off by the infamous "gilded moose-dropping toss," which will be an experimental sport in the 2000 Sydney Olympics. January brings the **Wilderness Women Contest,** which includes events like fish-gutting and tree-chopping, and the associated **Bachelor's Ball.** A local theatrical group called **Denali Drama** is in the process of converting a hangar into a playhouse. Ask around to find out if they're up and running.

Outdoors You may not be able to climb the mountain, but at least you can look at it. The Denali **overlook,** 1 mi. down the Talkeetna Spur, boasts one of the state's best car-accessible views of Denali. If the clouds cooperate, you will be treated to a view of nearly 4 mi. of rock and ice climbing straight to the sky. This perspective pales in comparison, however, to the views accessible by plane. Flightseeing tours might cost less than you think, and to see the mountain from such a distance—not to mention the countless other sheer peaks and marine glaciers you'll pass along the way—is a truly incomparable experience. Talkeetna's air services are actually closer to the mountain than services at the park entrance, so they can get you there cheaper and faster. **Doug Geeting Aviation,** P.O. Box 42 (800-770-2366 or 733-2366) and **Hudson Air Service,** P.O. Box 648 (800-478-2321 or 733-2321) offer one-hour tours of the mountain starting at $55 and $59, respectively. An hour is plenty of time to be overwhelmed by the view, but for another $30-45, you can extend the trip by half an hour and fly all the way around the summit, taking in all 14,000 feet of **Wickersham Wall,** the longest uninterrupted slope in the world. Most services also offer **glacier landings** near the base of the peak for anywhere from $30-45 extra. Be wary of companies offering landings far into July, though, as snow conditions then are unsafe. **McKinley Air Service** (800-564-1765 or 733-1765) and **K2 Aviation** (see **Accommodations,** above) offer virtually identical trips. If you come to Talkeetna intent on flightseeing, plan on staying for a couple of days. The clouds frequently fail to cooperate.

Fishing opportunities and river tours abound in the waterways around town. **Talkeetna River Guides,** P.O. Box 563 (800-353-2677 or 733-2677), offers a two hour float trip with views of Denali and frequent wildlife sightings for $39 per person, $15 for children under 15. A five hour sport-fishing trip costs $99 per person, an eight hour trip $150. **Mahay's Riverboat Service,** P.O. Box 705 (733-2223), also offers access to the wet 'n' wild wilderness. Their two hour jet boat trips are significantly louder and a little less expensive. They also have a one hour "sunset cruise" ($19.50, under 12 $9.75). An alternative is to rent a canoe from **Alaska Camp and Canoe** on Railroad Ave. (733-CAMP/2267). They also rent out fishing equipment.

■ George Parks Highway: Denali to Fairbanks

From Talkeetna, the highway begins a gradual ascent into the Alaska Range and offers some of the best views of Mt. McKinley available. Towering over the 6000-ft. molehills which surround it, Denali has the greatest total altitude gain of any mountain in the world. It is literally the biggest peak on earth. The **South Denali Viewpoint,** located near the entrance to the park, offers one of the most spectacular profiles of the 20,000-ft. peak. The turnoff to the Viewpoint is just a few miles from the Ruth Glacier. Widely considered the best view of Denali, the clearest moment is usually between 10pm and 4am. **Denali State Park** offers a few nice campgrounds ($12 per site) and hiking trails, and is much less crowded than the national park.

A second fantastic viewpoint is the **Denali Viewpoint,** 10 minutes farther north. From here, the road winds northward through the Alaska Range, passing over a few surprisingly steep creek canyons and through Broad Pass, the scenic high point of the road. From here, most of what you see to the west is Denali National Park. The Parks Hwy. soon passes the turnoff for the Denali Hwy., an incredibly scenic drive through the basins which drain the Alaska Range. From here, it is less than 20 minutes to the park (see **Denali Hwy.,** p. 113).

Leaving Denali, the road winds its way along the **Nenana River** and out of the Alaska Range for about 10 mi. After passing the town of Healy, near the park's northern border, the highway follows the Nenana River into the Tanana River Basin for 60 mi. until it meets the town of Nenana. Fifty-three mi. south of Fairbanks, Nenana was once the terminus of the Alaska Railroad, and until the railroad was extended to Fairbanks, supplies were hauled overland or floated up the Tanana to Fairbanks. Today, Nenana is most famous for the **Nenana Ice Pool,** in which residents of Alaska and the Yukon, bored out of their skulls during the winter, bet on the precise minute when the river will thaw in the spring and dislodge a ceremonially placed tripod. The pot has recently amassed $300,000. Today, this tradition is just one of the events at the **Nenana Ice Classic.** For more information, write P.O. Box 272, Nenana 99760 (832-5446). While in town, check out the **Alaska State Railroad Museum,** at the end of the main street in the Nenana Train Depot, which displays memorabilia and exhibits on the railroad's construction, a truly Herculean feat ($1).

Since Nenana is the only major town between Denali and Fairbanks, it makes a great spot to camp or have lunch. The best place to eat is **The Little Cabin,** just off A St. on 3rd Ave., where $2.25 will buy you a piece of pie and a cup of coffee and $5 will get you a great submarine sandwich. You can find an inexpensive dinner at the **Depot Café and Bar** until the bar closes daily at 5am. Campers should head to **Nenana Valley RV Park** which offers large grassy sites, laundry services, nice bathrooms, and free showers (tents $10, RVs $14, full hookups $17, wash $2, dry $1). The cheapest motel in town is the aptly named **Tripod Motel,** at Milepost 304 (832-

The Northern Lights

Aurora borealis, for many as emblematic of the far north as Denali or the grizzly bear, will be missed by summer visitors to Alaska's Interior. Because the sun barely dips below the horizon, the curtains of white, green, and sometimes red light cannot be seen from early April to mid-August. If you want to see the lights when they first start to appear in the second week of August, you'll have to be awake at 2am. Fall and early spring are the best times to see the northern lights, which are caused by showers of particles emitted from sunspots. Fairbanks is one of the premier sites in the world for viewing the aurora. Around Fairbanks, the phosphorescent light show happens as many as 240 nights a year, whereas at the North Pole, you'd be lucky to see it 100 nights a year.

9800), where rooms start at $37.50 and move up from there depending on the room size and number of people. A bit nicer but still a bargain is the **Finnish Alaskan Bed and Breakfast,** at Mile 302 (832-5628), where a small room for one or two people will cost you $50 (shared bath).

From Nenana, the Parks Hwy. winds into the foothills around Fairbanks, offering a last glimpse south toward the Alaska Range. Seven mi. south of Fairbanks, the highway passes a short side road leading to the one-time gold camp of Ester. Every night (except Sunday) things pick up considerably when the popular **Malamute Saloon** opens for dinner. The vaudeville shows, which offer everything from Robert Service readings to song and dance numbers, are popular with tourists from Fairbanks and occur Mon.-Fri. at 9pm and 7pm in July ($11, children 3-12 $5). Complimentary bus service is available from Fairbanks (call 479-2500).

■ Fairbanks

Had E.T. Barnette not run aground with his load of goods near the junction of the Tanana and Chena Rivers and decided haphazardly to set up a trading post, and had Felix Pedro, an Italian immigrant-turned-prospector, not unearthed a golden fortune nearby, Fairbanks might never have existed. But they did, and today Fairbanks stands unchallenged as North American civilization's northernmost hub (witness the signs for "world's northernmost Woolworth's," "northernmost Southern barbecue," "world's northernmost Denny's" etc., etc.). As such, Fairbanks' appeal to visitors stems from its role as gateway to the Arctic. From here you can drive, fly or float to the Arctic Circle and into the tundra. But do not make the long and arduous trip merely to visit this outpost. Your time would be better spent at any of the stunning parks which litter Alaska. That said, Fairbanks' university, its omnipresent tourism industry, and its endless strip malls can't hide the rough-and-ready flavor of this frontier town. Men noticeably outnumber women, the streets are filled with 4WD steeds, and any of the roads leading out of town will take you to utter wilderness in minutes. Through frigid winters and swarms of vicious hybrid mosquitoes, Fairbanks residents persevere and enjoy everything from Shakespeare in the Park one minute to moose hunting the next.

PRACTICAL INFORMATION AND ORIENTATION

Visitors Information: Convention and Visitors Bureau Log Cabin, 550 1st Ave., Fairbanks 99701 (456-5774 or 800-327-5774), distributes the free *Visitor's Guide,* which lists tourist offices, transportation services, annual events, activities, and shops, and includes maps. Free local calls. Open daily 8am-8pm; Labor Day-Memorial Day Mon.-Fri. 8am-5pm. **Fairbanks Information Hotline** (456-4636) has a 24-hr. recording for upcoming events. **Alaska Public Lands Information Center (APLIC),** 250 Cushman St. #1A, Fairbanks 99707 (456-0527), has exhibits and info on different parks and protected areas of Alaska. Free daily films. Staff welcomes requests for advice on hiking. Open daily 9am-6pm; in winter Tues.-Sat. 10am-6pm. Fairbanks is also home to the headquarters of the **Gates of the Arctic National**

Park, 201 1st Ave. (456-0281; open Mon.-Fri. 8am-5pm) and the **Arctic National Wildlife Refuge,** 101 12th Ave., Room 266 (456-0250), in the U.S. District Court Building (open Mon.-Fri. 8am-4:30pm). You should visit these headquarters if you are considering a trip to either park; the staff gives thorough, indispensable advice on how to navigate these immense expanses of wilderness.

Airport: Located 5mi. from downtown on Airport Way. Served by: **Delta** (1-800-221-1212), to the lower 48; **Alaska Air** (452-1661), to Anchorage ($39) and Juneau ($268); **Frontier Flyer Services** (474-0014) flies to smaller Bush towns such as Bettles ($113). Cheaper fares are sometimes possible with advance purchase. A number of other carriers also serve Fairbanks including **Northwest**, **United**, and **Reno Air.**

Trains: Alaska Railroad, 280 N. Cushman St. (456-4155), next to the *Daily News-Miner* building. An excellent way to see the wilderness. From mid-May to mid-Sept., 1 train daily to: Nenana ($36), Anchorage ($135), and Denali National Park ($50). Prices are substantially cheaper during the off-season. Ages 2-11 ½-price. Depot open Mon.-Fri. 7:30am-4:30pm, Sat.-Sun. 7:30am-noon. In winter, a train leaves for Anchorage every Sun. ($70).

Buses: Parks Highway Express (479-3065) runs 6 buses per week to Denali ($20, roundtrip $40) and Anchorage ($40, roundtrip $75). Alaskon Express (800-544-2206; 4 per week to Haines, $174). **Alaska Direct** (800-780-6652; 3 per week to Denali, $30). **Fireweed Express** (452-0521) runs daily van service to Denali ($25, roundtrip $45), with pick up at Billie's Backpackers Hostel (see **Accommodations**, below); call for times and reservations.

Public Transportation: the **Municipal Commuter Area Service (MACS)** (459-1011), at 6th and Cushman St. Two routes (red and blue) through downtown Fairbanks and the surrounding area. Fare $1.50; seniors, high school students, and disabled 75¢; under 5 free. Day pass $3. Transfers good within 1hr. of stamped time. Pick up a schedule at the Convention and Visitors Bureau (see above).

Taxi: King Cab, 452-5464. **Fairbanks Taxi,** 452-3535. Both 24hr.

Car Rental: Nearly all of the national companies offer packages with free mileage, however, they will *not* allow you to drive on dirt roads. Many of the smaller companies, on the other hand, charge hefty fees for extra mileage. **Rent-a-Wreck,** 2105 Cushman St. (452-1606). $30 per day, 30¢ per mi. after 100mi.; must be 21 with credit card. **U-Save Auto Rental,** 3245 College Rd. (479-7060). $37 per day, 26¢ per mi. after 100mi.; must be 21 and credit card "preferred."

Road Conditions: 456-7623 or 800-478-7675.

Bike and Canoe Rental: Beaver Sports, 3480 College Rd. (479-2494), across from College Corner Mall. Mountain bikes $16 for 6hr., $20 overnight, $94 weekly. $250 deposit required (cash or credit). Canoes $24 per day, $17 per day for 3-6 days, $80 per week; paddles and life jackets included. $500 per boat deposit required. Open Mon.-Fri. 10am-8pm, Sat. 9am-7pm, Sun. 1-6pm.

Camping Equipment: Rocket Surplus, 1401 Cushman St. (456-7078). Fine camping fashions and gear. Open Mon.-Sat. 9am-6pm. **Apocalypse Design, Inc.,** 101 College Rd. (451-7555), at Illinois. Speedy repairs on zippers and straps. Open Mon.-Fri. 9am-6pm, Sat. 10am-4pm. (Also see **Beaver Sports** above.)

Laundromat and Showers: B & C (479-2696), at University and College, in Campus Mall. $2 wash, 8-min. dry 25¢. Showers $2.50. Open Mon.-Sat. 7am-10:30pm, Sun. 9am-10:30pm. **B & L** (452-1355), at 3rd and New St. on Eagle Rd. Wash and dry each $1.50. Showers $2.50 for 20min. Open daily 8am-11pm.

Bookstore: Gulliver's New and Used Books, 3525 College Rd. (474-9574), in College Corner Mall. Open Mon.-Fri. 10am-8pm, Sat. 10am-6pm, Sun. noon-6pm. Also in the Shopper's Forum, 1255 Airport Way (456-3657). Open Mon.-Fri. 10am-9pm, Sat. 10am-6pm, Sun. noon-6pm.

Library: Noel Wien Library, 1215 Cowles St. (459-1020). Open Mon.-Wed. 10am-9pm, Thurs.-Fri. 10am-6pm, Sat. 10am-5pm.

Weather: 452-3553.

Crisis Line: 452-4357; also provides contacts with gay and lesbian groups. **Rape Crisis:** 452-7273 and 800-478-7273. **Poison Control Center:** 456-7182.

Pharmacy: Payless Drugstore, 38 College Rd. (452-2072), in the Bentley Mall. Open Mon.-Sat. 9am-10pm, Sun. 10am-6pm.

ALASKA

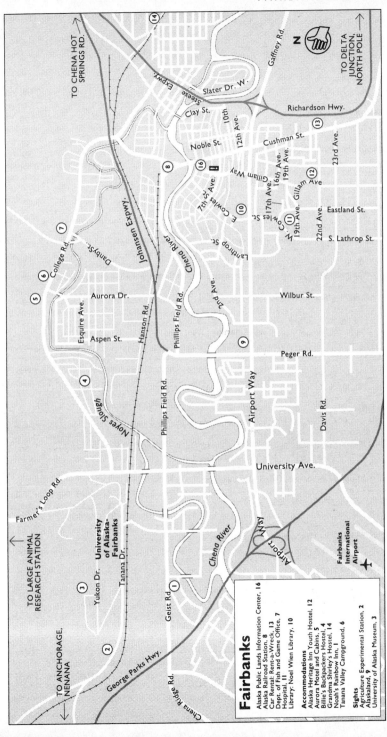

TO CHENA HOT SPRINGS RD.

TO DELTA JUNCTION, NORTH POLE

N

Gaffney Rd.

Steese Expwy.

Slater Dr. W.

Clay St.

Richardson Hwy.

10th Ave.

12th Ave.

Noble St.

Cushman St.

16th Ave.

19th Ave.

23rd Ave.

Gillam Way

17th Ave.

Cowles St.

E. Cowles St.

5th Ave.

Eastland St.

19th Ave.

22nd Ave.

Lanthrop St.

S. Lathrop St.

Chena River

Wilbur St.

Aurora Dr.

Danby St.

College Rd.

Esquire Ave.

Aspen St.

Hanson Rd.

Johansen Expwy.

Phillips Field Rd.

2nd Ave.

Peger Rd.

Airport Way

Davis Rd.

Noyes Slough

Phillips Field Rd.

University Ave.

Farmer's Loop Rd.

TO LARGE ANIMAL RESEARCH STATION

University of Alaska-Fairbanks

Yukon Dr.

Tanana Dr.

Chena River

Airport Way

Fairbanks International Airport

TO ANCHORAGE, NENANA

George Parks Hwy.

Geist Rd.

Chena Ridge Rd.

Fairbanks

Alaska Public Lands Information Center, 16
Alaska Railroad Station, 8
Car Rental: Rent-a-Wreck, 13
Dept. of Fish and Game Office, 7
Hospital, 11
Library: Noel Wien Library, 10

Accommodations
Alaska Heritage Inn Youth Hostel, 12
Aurora Motel and Cabins, 5
Billie's Backpackers Hostel, 4
Grandma Shirley's Hostel, 14
Noah's Rainbow Inn, 1
Tanana Valley Campground, 6

Sights
Agriculture Experimental Station, 2
Alaskaland, 9
University of Alaska Museum, 3

Hospital: Fairbanks Memorial, 1650 Cowles St. (452-8181), off Airport Hwy.
Emergency: 911. **Alaska State Troopers:** 452-2114.
Post Office: 315 Barnette St. (452-3203). Open Mon.-Fri. 9am-6pm, Sat. 10am-2pm.
General Delivery ZIP Code: 99707.
Area Code: 907.

Anchorage is 358 mi. south via the **George Parks Hwy.,** and Prudhoe Bay is 480 mi. down dangerous, gravelly **Dalton Hwy.** Be warned: locals guarantee a flat tire and towing may cost more than your car is worth. Delta Junction is 97 mi. southeast of Fairbanks on the **Richardson (Alaska) Hwy.** Fairbanks itself can be a confusing city to navigate as it is difficult to identify "downtown" in the maze of urban sprawl. Nearly every tourist destination lies on one of four thoroughfares: **Airport Way, College Rd., Cushman Blvd.,** and **University Way.** The city center lies in the vicinity of South Cushman, north of Airport Way. Fairbanks also features an extensive **bike trail** system. None of the urban trails are particularly scenic, but it's a lot quicker than walking. Pick up a guide to Fairbanks' bike trails and pamphlets mapping out self-guided walking and driving tours at the visitor's center.

ACCOMMODATIONS AND CAMPING

For info on bed and breakfasts, go to the visitors bureau, or call or write **Fairbanks B&B,** 902 Kellum St., Anchorage (452-4967). The visitors bureau also stocks flyers listing all the local hostel services and plenty of campground brochures.

Grandma Shirley's Hostel, 510 Dunbar St. (451-9816). Shirley's beats out all other hostels to earn the title of überhostel of Fairbanks. Take the Steese Expressway to Trainor Gate Rd., go right and follow to E St., take a left, and finally right onto Dunbar St. Grandma fixes you up with bedding, a spectacular kitchen, showers (soap, shampoo and towels included), a common room with TV, a big backyard, and free use of three old but road-worthy bikes. Men and women share a room with 9 beds. $15.

Alaska Heritage Inn Youth Hostel (AAIH), 1018 22nd Ave. (451-6587). Big with the international crowd, this hostel has a common room with TV and a picnic area. 15 beds. $12, non-members $15, plus $3 linen charge first night.

Billie's Backpackers Hostel, 2895 Mack Blvd. (479-2034). Take Westwood Way 1 block off College to Mack Rd. Look for the "Billie's B&B" sign. Billie's leaves something to be desired, but if you have a hankering for European bunkmates, he can satisfy. Hot showers and kitchen. $14.50, plus $5 for a full breakfast or dinner.

Aurora Motel and Cabins, 2016 College Rd. (451-1935). Not the Ritz, but cheap by Fairbanks standards. TVs and baths, but no phone. Small cabins for rent ($40) fit 2 adults comfortably. Call for reservations.

Tanana Valley Campground, 1800 College Rd. (456-7956), next to the Aurora Motel and Cabins. Somewhat noisy, but surprisingly grassy and secluded given its in-town location. 5 spots with power hookup available. Free showers, laundromat ($2 wash and dry). Sites $12. Tentsites for travelers with no vehicle $6.

Chena River State Campground, off of Airport way on University Ave. With two or more people, this place is worth the $15 per night fee. Its well-landscaped, clean, and situated on a particularly quiet stretch of the Chena River.

FOOD

For an artery-blocking good time, look no further than Airport Way or College Rd., and you'll find almost every fast-food chain in existence. Groceries are available 24 hours at **Carr's,** 526 Gaffney (452-1121), and at **Safeway,** 3627 Airport Way (479-4231), or 30 College Rd. (850-1907). If you're really stocking up, **Sam's Club,** 48 College Rd. (451-4800), will let non-members buy in bulk for an additional 5% of the low total price (open Mon.-Sat. 9am-8pm, Sun. 11am-7pm). Catch some bizarre yet strangely delicious flavors of homemade ice cream at **Hot Licks** (479-7813), located in the Campus Corner Mall at the intersection of College and University (open Mon.-Fri. 7am-11pm, Sat. 11am-11pm, Sun. noon-10pm). The **Farmers Market,** at the fair-

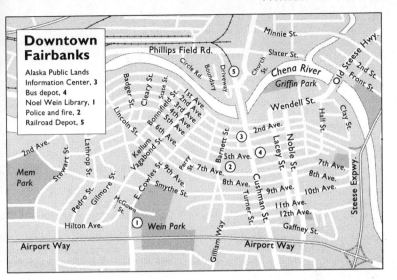

Downtown Fairbanks

Alaska Public Lands
Information Center, **3**
Bus depot, **4**
Noel Wein Library, **1**
Police and fire, **2**
Railroad Depot, **5**

grounds at Aurora and College, is the place for fresh produce (Wed. noon-5pm; Sat. 9am-4pm).

Souvlaki, 112 N. Turner (452-5393), across the bridge from the visitors center. You can almost get your fill on the heavenly aroma alone. Succulent stuffed grape leaves (3 for $1.15). Salad in a pita ($3). Take-out. Open Mon.-Fri. 10am-9pm, Sat. 10am-6pm; in winter Mon.-Sat. 10am-6pm.

Sam and Sharon's Sourdough Café, 3702 Cameron Street (479-0523). A local favorite. The best sandwiches in town start at $7, dinner entrees at $9.

Gambardella Pasta Bella, 706 2nd Ave. (456-3417). This superb, family-run Italian restaurant is nestled in a garden of potted plants. The lunch menu (served 11am-5pm) offers subs from $4 and excellent eggplant parmesan or pasta à la carte for $6.50. Dinner entrees run $10-14. Open daily 11am-5pm and 5:30-10pm.

Little Saigon, 1753 College Rd. (452-4327). Look for the "Foong's" sign just east of Aurora Dr. The few locals who have discovered it can't stop raving about this small Vietnamese restaurant. Service is slow since the owner makes everything fresh herself, but you'll be glad you waited after tasting the Goi Chon spring rolls ($3 for 3 big rolls) or the Bún Thit Nuong (a hearty serving of pork with vermicelli, $4.25). Open noon-10pm.

The Whole Earth, 1157 Deborah St. (479-2052), behind College Corner Mall. A health food store and restaurant in one. Sit among potted plants and enjoy a cup of organic coffee and Anna's Hummus Sandwich ($3.75). Locals praise the giant No Bull Burger and the Vegetarian Sandwich (both meatless, of course, $4.25). All sandwiches served on fresh homemade whole-wheat rolls. Store and seating open Mon.-Sat. 8am-8pm, Sun. noon-6pm. Hot food served 11am-7pm.

Rosey & Son Barbeque, 617 27th Ave. (452-3827), off S. Cushman St. You'll forget you ever left 'Bama. Cornbread and black-eyed peas (big portions, $4.50) or pork ribs ($5.20); pig feet and pig ears are available for the brave at heart. Small, family-run, and friendly. Open Sun., Tues.-Thurs. 11am-8pm, Fri.-Sat. 11am-10pm.

Thai House, 528 5th Ave. (452-6123). The planet's northernmost Thai restaurant never advertises, but is jam-packed. Lunch entrees start at $8. Don't say "spicy" unless you *mean* it. Open Mon.-Sat. 11am-4pm and 5-10pm.

India Rose, 500 Old Steese Hwy. (452-1155). Buffets are the best buy here. Consume your fill of pizza and salad ($4 lunch, $5 dinner) or pizza and 15-plus Indian dishes ($7 lunch, $10 dinner). The atmosphere is pure pizza joint with Indian wall hangings, but the food is excellent, and the $1 soda is bottomless. Open Mon.-Sat. 11:30am-10pm.

Food Factory, 44 College Rd. (452-3313), also at 18th and Cushman St. (452-6348) and the North Pole. Watch sports on the big screen as you try in vain to finish your foot-long hoagie ($5-8). A dizzying array of beer, 106 international varieties and 14 microbrews. Open Mon.-Thurs. 10:30am-11pm, Fri.-Sat. 10:30am-midnight, Sun. noon-10pm.

The Pumphouse Restaurant and Saloon, Mile 1.3 Chena Pump Rd. (479-8452). The food is expensive, but if a night on the town is what you're after, head to the Pumphouse. This place is so cool that one of the city's bus lines goes out of its way to drop you here. Lunches for $10. Dinner entrees average $18. Open daily 11:30am-2pm and 5-10pm. Bar open weekends until 2am.

SIGHTS

One of Fairbanks's proudest institutions and main attractions is the **University of Alaska-Fairbanks (UAF),** at the top of a hill overlooking the flat cityscape. Both bus lines stop at the **Wood Campus Center** (474-7034), which has pool tables, lots of video games, and flyers advertising campus goings-on. The **Student Activities Office** (474-6027), located in the Wood Center, has information on movies, music and campus activities during the school year, and on excellent and very affordable outdoor trips run by the university during the summer (Open Mon.-Fri. 8am-5pm). The **University of Alaska Museum** (474-7505), a ten minute walk up Yukon Dr., features exhibits on Natural History from each of Alaska's five regions, ranging from displays on the aurora borealis to tales of the Russian involvement in Alaska to indigenous crafts; an extremely rare 36,000 year-old bison recovered from the permafrost is perhaps the most impressive display ($5, seniors $4.50, 13-18 $3, families $12.50; open daily 9am-7pm; May and Sept. 9am-5pm; Oct.-April noon-5pm). Weekdays at 10am, the university offers free, two hour tours of the campus beginning in front of the museum. Even if you are in town for only a few days, try to stop by the University's **Geophysical Institute**, where displays explain the aurora borealis and current research being conducted on volcanoes and plate tectonics. Free tours and a slide show are also offered Thurs. at 2pm (474-7798).

Travelers can tiptoe through the tulips in the **Georgeson Botanical Gardens** (474-1959; best viewing time is July or August) or ogle the resident porcine population at the university's **Agriculture Experimental Station.** The garden and station are both on West Tanana Dr. The **Large Animal Research Station** is also worth a visit, and its tours offer a rare chance to see baby musk ox and other animals up close; Tuesday and Saturday at 11am and 1:30pm, and on Thursday at 1:30pm only ($5, seniors, $4, students $2, families $10). If you miss the tour, grab your binoculars and view the musk ox, reindeer, and caribou from the viewing stand on Yankovitch Rd.

Alaskaland, P.O. Box 1267, Fairbanks 99707, on Airport Way, is a small-scale, would-be Arctic Disneyland, but rides are limited to a train and merry-go-round. Overrun by kids, Alaskaland is a tourist trap of woolly mammoth proportions. But at least there's no general admission charge, and the gates are open 11am-9pm, making for great late-night picnicking. (The park's rides and museums charge nominal fees: Air Museum $1, boat tour $3.) If hokey is what you're after, check out the **Fairbanks Ice Museum** for a look at what a Fairbanks winter will do to your average sculptor; around the corner from the visitors center ($6, seniors $5, 13-18 $3). Another local museum is the **Dog Mushers Museum,** 535 2nd Ave., Suite 211 (456-6874), on 2nd Ave. in the Coop Plaza, the museum itself is little more than a room full of sleds and other mushing paraphernalia, but some cool videos are screened in the theater (free; donations accepted; open Mon.-Sat. 9:30am-4:30pm).

Well worth the 9 mi. trip north along the Steese Hwy., **Gold Dredge #8** is only $10 for a day of panning. Not only do you have a good chance of earning your money back in gold, but fossilized fragments of mammoths, mastodons and Keith Richards abound.

ENTERTAINMENT

With nothing but black spruce to keep them company in the surrounding tundra, Fairbanks residents turn eagerly to the bars at night. Come carouse with boisterous, rugged types fresh from the North Slope oil fields. UAF students and everyone else head for the legendary **Howling Dog Saloon** (457-8780), 11½ mi. down Steese Hwy., at the intersection of the Old and New Steese Highways, for live rock-and-roll (except Tues. and Wed. nights). Look for a colorful wooden structure in the middle of nowhere encircled by pickup trucks. The summer crowd is especially diverse, described by management as "rough, tough, and good-lookin'." Volleyball, pool, and horseshoe games go on until 4am or so, as does the band (open May-Oct. daily 9pm-5am).

Blues Breakers, 1705 S. Cushman (452-9999). High-energy blues for a mostly 30-something audience. Features tequila "on tap" (the tap is homemade). Get your motorcycle gear and step into an Easy Rider crowd. Open daily 8am-5am.

The Marlin, 3412 College Rd. (479-4646). Fairbanks' only jazz bar. Live music Tues.-Sat., jazz on Thurs.; at other times sit next to the portrait of your favorite musician and enjoy the laid-back atmosphere. Open daily 5pm-5am.

Senator's Saloon, Mile 1.3 on Chena Pump Rd. (479-8452), in the Pump House Restaurant. Yuppies and Oysters. Take drinks out to the deck and watch float planes land and river boats whiz by. Open Sun.-Thurs. 11:30am-1am, Fri.-Sat. 11:30am-2am.

Crazy Loon Saloon, 2949 Parks Hwy. (455-4487), 5mi. out of town on the George Parks Hwy. Modeled after the Howling Dog, the Crazy Loon plays live rock and draws a mixed crowd. The building, huge even by Fairbanks standards, looks like an enormous quonset hut. Crowd and cover charge depend on the band; a typical weekend cover is $2, and hippies, military-types, and college students all show up if the music is right. Open Tues.-Sat. 4pm-4am.

EVENTS

The best time to visit the city is in mid-July; citizens don Gold Rush duds and throw parades, sales, and many other gala events for **Golden Days,** a celebration of the Felix Pedro discovery which sparked the gold rush. Watch out for the traveling jail; if you haven't purchased the silly-looking pin commemorating the event, you may be taken prisoner and forced to pay a steep price to spring yourself. (Most stores and businesses in town sell the pins.) The budget traveler might want to stay on board the paddywagon; it's a free ride and goes all over Fairbanks. For details, contact the Fairbanks Chamber of Commerce (see **Practical Information**). Be warned, though: Fairbanks teems with tourists at this time. Make hotel reservations several months in advance if you're coming to town during Golden Days.

The **Tanana Valley Fair** (452-3750), in the second week of August, is a traditional country fair with rides, lots of food, and "biggest cabbage" and "cutest baby" competitions (suggestions for replacing them with "biggest baby" and "cutest cabbage" have so far been ignored). Follow the line of cars down College Rd. to the fairgrounds ($7, seniors $3, ages 6-17 $5).

For a sports spectacular with native flavor, see the **World Eskimo-Indian Olympics,** P.O. Box 2433, Fairbanks (452-6646). Held at the **Big Dipper,** 1901 Lathrop at 19th Ave. in late July, Inuit and other Native people from all over Alaska compete in shows of strength and endurance such as the knuckle hop and ear weight, and celebrate folklore and traditional dance (nightly pass $10, seniors and children $8.00; season passes $20, seniors and children $15).

Some of the wildest events occur around the summer solstice. The **Yukon 800 Marathon Riverboat Race** sends some high-horsepower people in low-slung powerboats on an 800-mi. quest up the Tanana and Yukon Rivers to the town of Galena and back. A few days before the solstice, the 10km **Midnight Sun Run** happens on a well-lit Saturday night, beginning at 10pm. The annual **Midnight Sun Baseball Game** occurs on the summer solstice. Featuring the Fairbanks Goldpanners, the game begins at 10:30pm, as the sun dips, features a short pause near midnight for the celebration of the midnight sun, and ends as the sun rises. The Goldpanners play more than 30 home games throughout the summer and have won five minor league national championships since 1970. Barry Bonds and Dave Winfield have played here. Games are played at **Growden Memorial Park** near Alaskaland (451-0095; $4).

Enjoy **bluegrass** at the **Fairbanks Folk Festival,** usually held in mid-July. In winter, February's **Yukon Quest Dog Sled Race** runs between Fairbanks and Whitehorse, starting in Fairbanks in even years, and in Whitehorse in odd. The Quest is far more rigorous than the more famous Iditarod: fewer dogs, fewer stops, and less compassion for the human condition. For information, visit the Yukon Quest Business Office, 558 2nd Ave. (452-7954), or the Yukon Quest Store at 2nd and Cushman (open Mon.-Sat. 9am-8pm).

■ Near Fairbanks

In any direction, a scant 20 minute drive will bring you to bona fide Alaskan wilderness. In the vicinity of Fairbanks, you can soak your feet in hot spring lakes, look for wildlife in a river basin, or hike up a ridge for a view of the Brooks or Alaska Range, both over 200 miles away.

CHENA HOT SPRINGS ROAD

The **Chena River Recreation Area** (451-2695) spills across both sides of Chena Hot Springs Rd. (which branches off the Steese Hwy. at Mile 5) from Miles 26 through 51, and encompasses almost 400 sq. mi. of wilderness. The area offers outstanding fishing, hiking, canoeing, and camping on the Upper Chena River and in the surrounding basin. Tent sites convenient to Chena Hot Springs Rd. are available at quiet, secluded **Rosehip Campground** (Mile 27) and **Tors Trail Campground** (Mile 39). Both cost $8 and offer pit toilets and water.

The **Granite Tors Trail,** across the street from the Tors Trail Campground, is a 15-mi. loop up to the "Tors," which begins in boreal forest at river level and runs above treeline to a peak topped by giant granite pillars. The summit makes an excellent site for an overnight camp-out. A two-day trip begins in the boreal forest on the **Angel Rocks Trail** (look for signs near Mile 49) which follows the Chena River before turning up to the top of Angel Rocks, prominent granite slabs that offer excellent views of the river valley. This 3½ mile loop through exquisite wilderness makes for a wonderful afternoon hike, but be sure to bring bug juice. This is serious mosquito country. The **Chena Dome Trail** is the most spectacular trail in the park, a more remote 29-mi. adventure which follows the rim of the Angel Creek Valley, almost 23 mi. of which is above treeline. This 3-day adventure, beginning and ending in boreal forest, offers excellent views of the Chena River and the Alaska Range.

Chena Hot Springs

Fifty-seven mi. northeast of Fairbanks on Chena Hot Springs Rd. lies the **Chena Hot Springs Resort** (in Fairbanks 452-7867, at the resort 369-4111), an extremely popular destination with Fairbanks residents and travelers in the winter. The large covered pool is filled with mineral water and offers a welcome escape from the bitter cold. In the winter, scores of Japanese travelers shiver their way to the resort for its prime Northern Lights viewing. In the summer, the resort is still a nice place to relax and lower 48ers and Europeans alike are frequent guests in rooms at relatively reasonable summer rates (singles $85 and doubles $95). An even better deal are the **Trapper's Cabins** ($35) which fit two adults comfortably (no water). All guests have free access to the pools. Expect fine fishing near this inn once the water level has dropped from the spring snow melt. Non-patrons may use the hot pool for $8, ages 5-12 and seniors $6. Handsome hiking trails and riverside tent and RV campsites ($10, with electricity $12) are nearby. The resort's **restaurant** serves pricey but excellent food; budget options include a reindeer burger ($7) and pasta primavera ($8.75; open daily 8am-4:30pm and 5-10pm).

STEESE HIGHWAY

The **Steese Hwy.** heads northeast out of Fairbanks 162 mi. to the town of **Circle** on the **Yukon River.** Just outside Fairbanks, the Steese meets Chena Hot Springs Rd. and a right turn will bring you towards Chena River Recreation Area and the Chena Hot Springs. The **Elliot Highway** comes hard on the heels of the Chena Hot Springs Rd. Be sure to make a right turn at the intersection to stay on the Steese. For the next 20 mi., the Steese winds through boreal forest, past two ski resorts and into a region of coniferous forests dominated by stunted spruce and fir trees known as **taiga**. At Mile 16.5 is the **Felix Pedro Monument**, a plaque honoring Pedro's discovery of gold in the creek across the highway.

Campgrounds at Mile 39 and 60 provide access to the **Chatanika River Canoe Trail,** which parallels the Steese for nearly 30 mi. The stream is clear and class II, and the only treacherous paddling obstacles are low water and overhanging trees. **Cripple Creek Campground**, at Mile 60, allows recreational goldpanning, and offers good fishing. The road begins to climb consistently at about Mile 70, and heads towards the highway's nicest scenery. The **White Mountain Recreation Area** and the **Steese National Conservation Area** lie side-by-side to the north. At Mile 86 is the trailhead for the **Pinnell Mountain Trail,** the most spectacular—and popular—hike in the vicinity of Fairbanks. The 27 mi. trail is entirely above treeline, passing through alpine tundra flora. Watch for the spectacular display of wildflowers in June and early July. Allow three days for the entire trip; two cabins are well spaced along the trail for both nights. With proper timing you can bask in the midnight sun (June 18-24) or watch the migration of caribou in the valleys below (July-Sept.). The trail intersects the highway again at Mile 107 where most hikers hitch back to their cars. (*Let's Go* does not recommend hitchhiking.) Even if you don't have time to do the entire hike, a half hour scramble up either end of the trailhead is worthwhile, rewarding hikers with wonderful views of the surrounding White Mountains. For white-water enthusiasts, White Mountain Recreation Area's **Birch Creek,** with several entry points between Mile 94.5 and 147, offers a 127-mi. course including several class III rapids. At Mile 108, the highway passes over **Eagle Summit,** offering beautiful views to all, even drivers. For more information on the region, call the Fairbanks office of the **Bureau of Land Management** (474-2350). Detailed topographic maps of the area are available at APLIC or at the U.S. Geological Survey (USGS) (456-0244), in the Federal Building at the end of 12th Ave. in Fairbanks, or write USGS Map Distribution, Box 25296, Building 810, Denver Federal Center, Denver, CO 80225.

Central (Mile 127), a small town of about 400 summer residents, is the highway's only real pit stop. The **Circle District Museum** ($1 adults, 50¢ children, open daily noon-5pm, Memorial Day-Labor Day) is an excellent place to stretch your legs. The impressive collection includes beautiful native beadwork commissioned by miners, samples of local gold and a pipe organ that was carried over the Chilkoot Trial and floated down the river to Circle for entertainment at Miller's Roadhouse. The **Central Motor Inn** (520-5228) serves fairly inexpensive meals (sandwiches $6, dinner from $9) and offers laundry and shower facilities (showers $3, wash and dry $2 each). Circle Hot Springs Rd. leads 8 mi. out of town to the **Arctic Circle Hot Springs Resort** (520-5113). The resort offers pricey cabins and suites, but budget travelers can opt for the "indoor camping," where you bring your own sleeping bag and bunk in small cubbyholes on the 4th floor (singles $20, $15 each additional person; guests have free use of the warm, outdoor mineral water-filled pool and poolside showers). For those not staying at the resort, a dip in the warm, mineral-rich water costs $7, children 5-15 $4.50, seniors and military $5.

From Central, the road gets considerably worse and winds its way down towards the **Yukon River Flats Basin.** Unless you are planning to float the mighty **Yukon River** or urinate into its great waters (an unsavory activity favored by some tourists) there is little reason to drive the highway's final 34 mi. to **Circle**. For those who make the trek to see the river, the **Yukon Trading Post** (773-1217) sells groceries and serves meals at Bush prices, and runs a café that isn't much cheaper (open daily 9am-

---

The North Pole

The town of North Pole is a shrine to Christmas. St. Nicholas Drive runs into Santa Claus Lane and the town has coordinated efforts to develop new bus stops, lampposts, and shopping malls, all in the merry theme. Santa officially moved to the North Pole in 1953, and the once sleepy little town of Moose Crossing underwent a dramatic transformation. The U.S. Postal Service redirected his mail to the newly christened "North Pole," and now St. Nick receives 20,000 letters each year; so many letters, in fact, that the jolly old man has recruited North Pole schoolchildren to help answer his mail.

The town's gimmick was originally conceived in an effort to woo toy manufacturers. Town planners hoped that corporations would rush to display "made in the North Pole" on their products, but no one came. Today, most of the 1700 residents of this otherwise unremarkable town are military personnel stationed at nearby Fort Wainwright who have happily adopted year-round holiday cheer. You can eat Mexican at Santa's Tortilla Factory, do your duds at Santa's Suds, or go on a ride at Santaland Caravan Park. Best of all, you can have the old geezer write you, or a young friend of your choice, a personalized letter. Just send $5, the recipient's name, age, sex, full mailing address, brothers' and sisters' names (or pets), favorite hobby, and something special you would like Santa to write. His official address is 325 S. Santa Claus Lane, North Pole, AK 99705.

9pm). Camping alongside the river is free (pit toilets) and water is available at the Washeteria (showers $2 for 5min., $3 wash, $3 dry).

There is a **post office** (773-1220), Mile 161 on the Steese Highway (open Mon., Wed., Fri. 10am-3pm; Tues.-Thurs. 10am-2:30pm; **ZIP Code:** 99733).

RICHARDSON HIGHWAY

Accessible from the south on the Richardson Hwy., **Harding Lake** (Mile 321.4 on Richardson Hwy.), **Birch Lake** (Mile 305.5 on Richardson Hwy.), and **Quartz Lake** (Mile 277.8 on Richardson Hwy.) are Sunday anglers' dreams. The state stocks the lakes with salmon and trout for that extra-tough fishing challenge. Boat ramps ($3) and campsites ($6) are provided at Harding and Quartz Lake. Birch Lake has primitive camping facilities.

■ Alaska Highway: Tok to Delta Junction

Tok lies at the junction of the **Tok Cutoff** and the **Alaska Highway,** and only 12 mi. from **Tetlin Junction**. The town exists as a spot to rest and stock up at the intersection of the Alaska Highway and the Taylor highway. From here it is 208 mi. northwest to Fairbanks on the **Alcan**, 138 mi. southwest to **Glenallen** on the Tok Cutoff and 387 mi. (619km) southeast to Whitehorse, YT, along the Alcan. The Tok Cutoff also offers access to **Wrangell-St. Elias National Park** (see p. 103). Tok is noteworthy both for its magnificent view of the Alaska range and for its obscenely high concentration of gift shops and RV parks. Those agonizing over which direction to head can do some deep thinking at the recently constructed, cavernous **visitors center** (883-5775). This glorified brochure distribution center is the **largest single-story building in Alaska** (open mid-May to mid-Sept. Mon.-Fri. 7am-9pm, Sun. 9am-7pm). Just east of the visitors center and adjacent to the state trooper building is the extremely helpful **Public Lands Information Center** (883-5667), which has information regarding all national and state parks, monuments, and preserves. Stop by to use the excellent trip-planning service (open daily 8am-8pm; winter Mon.-Fri. 8am-4:30pm). The **Tetlin National Wildlife Sanctuary** is a haven for birds sandwiched between the Alaska Highway and Wrangell-St. Elias National park south of Tok. The headquarters can offer information on this largely inaccessible preserve.

Check out **Burnt Paw Northland Specialties** (883-4121), on the Alaska Highway next to the Post Office, which offers nightly sled-dog demonstrations Monday through Saturday at 7:30pm (open June to late-Sept., daily 7am-9pm). There is a **laundromat** at the Northstar RV Park (see below; wash $1.25, 7-min. dry 25¢). In an **emergency,** dial 911. Other important numbers are: **health clinic/ambulance,** 883-5855; **police,** 883-5111; **fire,** 883-2333. The **post office** (883-5880) is near the intersection of the Glenn Hwy. and the Alaska Hwy. (Open Mon.-Fri. 8:30am-5pm, Sat. 11:30am-3pm; **ZIP Code:** 99780.)

Hitchhikers report having a hard time catching a ride out of town. If you're stuck, **Alaska Direct** (800-770-6652) runs buses leaving from the front of Northstar RV Park at 3pm. Buses go to Fairbanks (Wed., Fri., Sun., $40), Anchorage (Tues., Fri., Sun., $65), and Whitehorse, YT (Wed., Fri., Sun., $80).

The **Tok Youth Hostel (HI-AYH)** (883-3745), is an incredibly inconvenient 9 mi. west of town on Pringle Dr. in a huge canvas tent reminiscent of *M*A*S*H.* (Members $7.50, non-members $10.50; open May 15-Sept. 15; kitchen facilities, no showers or phones.) If you're looking to pitch a tent, the better-situated **Northstar RV Park** (883-4502), ½ mi. east of the visitors center on the Alaska Highway, has tent sites for $5, though a shower will cost you another $3.50. A site with a full hookup comes with two free showers for $18. If you fill up your gas tank, you'll get a free cup of coffee and car wash (open daily 6am-11pm). Also cheap is the **Tok River State Recreation Area Campground,** 4 mi. south of town, which offers sites for $10 and an outstanding view of the Alaska Range. The cheapest place to stay indoors is the **Snowshoe Motel** (883-4511), at Mile 1314 across from the visitors center and next to Frontier Foods (singles $60, doubles $65, free breakfast, cable TV, phone and free local calls included).

Tok offers plenty of expensive, forgettable roadside food, but one notable exception is the **Northstar World Famous Restaurant** (863-4631 in summer, 663-5233 in winter), at Mile Post 1313 on the east side of town. Even Texans homesick after months in the RV swear that the $11 all-you-can-eat rib special is unbelievable (served after 4pm, including Texas toast, baked beans, and potato salad; restaurant open daily 6am-10pm). If it's a sugar rush you need, scare up some quarters and find the **Valley Bakery** (883-2501), ½ mi. east of the visitors center at Mile 1313. Donuts run 60-95¢ (open June 1-Sept. 1, Mon.-Sat. 5am-6pm). Tok's answer to wholesale shopping, **Frontier Foods,** is across from the visitor center; non-restaurant-eaters will rejoice in reasonably priced bulk items and fresh fruit (open daily 7am-11pm, winter until 10pm).

DELTA JUNCTION

Like Tok, **Delta Junction** exists because it lies at the intersection of two main highways. The town is aptly called "the crossroads of Alaska." The Alaska Hwy. leads back 108 mi. southeast to Tok, while the Richardson Hwy. extends 151 mi. northwest to Fairbanks and 266 mi. south to Valdez. Though Fairbanks argues otherwise, the huge post in front of the visitor center declares Delta Junction to be the terminus of the Alaska Hwy. For $1 you can buy a macho certificate stating that you've successfully reached its end.

The **visitors center** (895-5063) is found (you guessed it) at the intersection of the two highways (open mid-May to mid-Sept. daily 8am-7:30pm). The **post office** (895-4601) is just north of the highway on the east side of the highway. (Open Mon.-Fri. 9:30am-5pm, Sat. 10:30am-noon; **General Delivery ZIP Code:** 99737.) Important phone numbers: **police,** 911 or 895-4344; **health clinic,** 895-5100.

Tenters should head to **Delta State Recreation Site,** ½ mi. from the visitor center towards Fairbanks, where roomy, well-protected sites with drinking water and pit toilets cost $8. No one has ever accused Delta Junction cuisine of being distinctive or unpredictable, but two restaurants near the visitors center give a fair deal to wayward travelers. At the **Pizza Bella Restaurant,** the highest nourishment-to-dollar ratio is found in the tasty subs, served on fresh toasted rolls ($4-7; open Sun.-Thurs. 11am-10pm, Fri.-Sat. 11am-11pm). **Big Top Drive-In** (895-4055) serves up standard burgers 'n' shakes with Top-40 tunes. You can celebrate Alaska's bond with the other non-contiguous state by ordering a Hawaiian Burger ($4.75), a juicy patty with cheese, pineapple, and Canadian bacon (open May 1-Aug. 31 daily 11am-10pm). Gung-ho grocery grabbers should hit the **Delta Shop-Rite** (895-4653), just north toward Fairbanks (open Mon.-Sat. 7am-9pm, Sun. 8am-7pm).

Attractions in the area include a **buffalo** ranch. To catch a glimpse, go 7 mi. toward Tok on the Alaska Hwy. and turn left on Clearwater Rd. After 4 mi., turn left just past the Clearwater Fire Station and drive up to the fence for a view of the herd. Towards Fairbanks, 10 mi. north of town is **Big Delta Historic Park,** home of **Rika's Roadhouse** (895-4201), a restored roadhouse complete with live barnyard animals (free walking tour by request). Travelers thirsty for an engineering marvel can go on a tour of **Alyeska Pump Station #9,** the only pump station on the Trans-Alaska Pipeline open to the public. One hour tours run every two hours from June-Sept. 9am to 5pm daily (869-3165; reservations strongly encouraged). Less motivated types can simply drive past Rika's and observe the pipeline impressively suspended over the Tanana River.

If you stumble into town on the first weekend in August, then welcome to the **Deltana State Fair!** The most exciting event of the fair is undoubtedly the **Great Alaskan Outhouse Race** which gives new meaning to "the runs." The race features numerous outhouses on wheels, pulled or pushed by four competitors, while one lucky individual sits on the "throne" for the length of the race. The winners receive the coveted "Golden Throne Award" (2nd place, "The Silver Plunger;" 3rd place, "The Copper Snake").

■ Taylor Highway

The Taylor Hwy. stretches 160 mi. northeast across increasingly dry landscape from **Tetlin Junction** to the picturesque town of **Eagle** on the Yukon River. The road is narrow and the drive is a difficult one: boulders, frost heaves, and sections of washboard interrupt lengths of the highway, making this a long and bumpy, albeit beautiful, ride. Ninety-six mi. north of Tetlin Junction at **Jack Wade Junction** the highway meets the **Top-of-the-World Hwy.,** which heads east toward **Dawson City, YT** (see p. 270). No scheduled bus service follows this route; those without a car could hitchhike, but it can be difficult since traffic is sparse and dominated by RVs and campers with gear-stuffed cars. Most hitchers have a good book handy and start early in the morning. (*Let's Go* does not recommend hitchhiking.) Travelers headed on to Dawson City should keep in mind that the **border** is open only from 8am to 8pm Alaska time, and that Canadian customs officials can be tough on hitchhikers. Moreover, the border station is on a high mountain pass in the middle of nowhere: entertainment is scarce and the nights can be extremely cold for those bedding down at the border.

From **Mile 0,** the Taylor Hwy. climbs to over 3500 ft. as it winds toward 5541-ft. Mt. Fairplay. A sign just past the summit at Mile 35 explains the history of the Taylor Hwy. and offers a good opportunity to stretch your legs and view alpine flora. At Mile 49, the Bureau of Land Management (BLM) operates the **West Fork Campground,** with 32 sites, pit toilets, and water. As with all BLM sites, camping is free.

The megalopolis of **Chicken,** rumored to have received the name after local miners couldn't spell their first choice, "Ptarmigan," lies at mile 66. Each summer Chicken's population burgeons from its winter level of 11 to upwards of 100, and the **Chicken Creek Saloon** throws the wildest pre-solstice, solstice, and 4th of July parties in the region. Free walking tours of historic Chicken leave daily at 1pm from the parking lot in front of the saloon and are the only way to see the original mining cabins. Next to the Saloon, the **Chicken Creek Café** will flip you three weighty flapjacks for $4.25 (served until noon) or a burger with potato salad for $6 (open daily 8am-5pm). If passing through in the evening, you might want to check out the nightly Salmon Bake (summer). Tent campers and RVs can set up on the lawn next to the café in Chicken for free, although the parking lot is less than ideal for tents. The **Chicken Mercatile Emporium** houses souvenirs aplenty and is the official headquarters of the Chicken chapter of the **Far From Fenway Fan Club** ($18 gets you a t-shirt and an official membership card, in case anyone asks for proof).

The **Jack Wade Dredge,** a huge machine used for placer mining, lies rusting away right next to the highway at Mile 86. The dredge has deteriorated considerably and its safety is dubious, but that doesn't stop most people from wandering around its hollow insides. At Jack Wade Junction the road forks: north for 64 mi. to Eagle and east for 79 mi. via the Top-of-the-World Hwy. to Dawson. Make sure you have proof of funds or you might fall victim to an arbitrary decision at the border and get stuck in Alaska 120 mi. from the nearest settlement (see border-crossing above). For the last 64 mi. from the junction to Eagle the road often narrows and snakes along mountainsides and canyons of 40 Mile River, another popular, though difficult, spot for river runners; all drivers, especially RVers, should enjoy spectacular views and slow down to avoid head-on collisions.

■ Eagle

The small town of **Eagle**, pop. 160, stands alone at the end of the Taylor Hwy. on the banks of a beautiful bend in the Yukon River and on the brink of vast stretches of wilderness. From the east, the Yukon river flows from jagged peaks, and it is a four to five day float from Dawson City. To the northwest, the river continues into the **Yukon-Charley Rivers National Preserve** and to Circle, a four to six day float along what is perhaps the most beautiful and popular stretch of the Yukon. The Yukon is the fourth longest river in North America and has the fifth largest flow volume of any river on earth. No other American river is as undeveloped and laced with frontier history and floating the entire river has become a cult experience. The trip takes four months and ends in the river delta near Nome (for more on the Yukon River, see **Whitehorse: Sights and Activities,** p. 265).

Like most towns along the Yukon River, Eagle exists because of the Klondike gold rush. Established in 1898 as a permanent mining community, Eagle's central location in the Interior led the Secretary of War to establish an adjacent military base, Fort Egbert, here in 1899. In 1901, Eagle became the interior's first incorporated city. The end of the Gold Rush marked the beginning of Eagle's decline as a military and mining center, but extensive restoration work by the BLM and Eagle Historical Society have returned many of the town's buildings to their original condition. The town is of limited historical interest but is an extraordinarily scenic and friendly launching point for trips down the Yukon.

Practical Information and Sights The Department of the Interior **Visitor Center** (547-2233), located on the westernmost edge of 1st St., is a good place to browse for an hour or so and can provide detailed information on the geography and wildlife of the region (open daily 8am-5pm). The best way to access the towns incredible historic offerings is through the daily 3-hr. walking tour ($3, under 12 free), which leaves at 9am from the **Courthouse Museum** on Berry St. The courthouse, one of the first in Alaska, is open to the general public throughout much of the day. **Amundsen Park,** on 1st St. at Amundsen, honors the Norwegian explorer who hiked several hundred miles across Northern Canada into Eagle from the Arctic Ocean in the winter of 1905. Two months after using Eagle's telegraph—the cable to Valdez was an engineering feat as remarkable as the construction of the Alaska Highway—to inform the world that he had successfully navigated the Northwest Passage, Amundsen mushed back to his ship, frozen in the ice floes of the Arctic Ocean. In the space of nine months, he had successfully completed the first northward journey from the Atlantic to the Pacific.

In case of a **medical emergency** call 547-2300. The **post office** (547-2211) is on 2nd St. at Jefferson (open Mon.-Fri. 8:30am-4:30pm). The **ZIP Code** is 99738.

Camping, Accommodations, and Food Campers will rejoice upon finding the **Eagle BLM Campground,** a 1-mi. hike from town past Fort Egbert (no water, pit toilets). Several short hiking trails start at the campground. The unremarkable looking **Yukon Adventure Bed and Breakfast** (547-2221), about ½ mi. east of town, sets a new standard for B&B amenities with a sun deck, TVs, VCRs in doubles, and a nice movie selection. With your back to the river, take a left on 1st Ave., past the Village Store, and follow the signs for the boat launch (singles $50, doubles $60). The **Eagle Trading Co.** (547-2220) on Front St. has it all: gas, groceries, showers ($4), laundromat ($4 per load), RV hookups ($15), and rooms for rent (singles $50, doubles $60). (Open daily 9am-8pm; no credit cards accepted.) The adjacent **Riverside Café** (547-2250) serves standard hotel fare at reasonable (by Bush standards) prices (burgers with fries or salad, $5; open daily 7am-8pm).

Floating from Eagle to Circle The **Visitors center** (see above) is the place to begin for detailed information on the popular 158-mi. float through the **Yukon-Charley Rivers National Preserve** from Eagle to Circle. Plan on spending four to six days, depending on how many hours you plan to paddle or camp on the river. The trip passes through some of Alaska's wildest country. Bear, moose, and beaver abound, as do mosquitoes, though campers can generally avoid them by camping on the numerous gravel bars in the river. **Eagle Canoe Rentals** (547-2203) sets you afloat for a five-day trip to Circle for $160 (paddles, life jackets, and canoe return included) or bargain with Bill Elmore, owner of **Eagle Commercial** (547-2355), just behind the Riverside Café on First St., for rentals. You can get information in advance from the Park Service by writing Superintendent, P.O. Box 167, Eagle, AK 99738.

Southeastern Alaska

Southeastern Alaska (also known as the Panhandle or just Southeast) encloses the waters of the Inside Passage, spanning 500 mi. north from the breathtaking Misty Fjords National Monument, past Juneau, to Skagway at the foot of the Chilkoot Trail. This network of islands, inlets, and saltwater fjords hemmed in by mountains is distinguished by a cold-temperate rainforest climate, over 60 major glaciers, and 15,000 bald eagles.

Some communities of the Interior and Southcentral Alaska have experienced what Alaskans consider urban sprawl, but towns along the Panhandle cling to narrow pockets of coast. Isolation amid steep coastal mountains has helped these towns to maintain both their size and their unique personalities. Gold Rush days are alive and well in Skagway, while Sitka preserves artifacts of Russian occupation. Petersburg, Wrangell, and smaller communities prosper with the logging and fishing industries, while surprisingly cosmopolitan Juneau derives most of its revenue from the government.

The Alaskan Marine Highway system provides the cheapest, most exciting way to explore the Inside Passage. In order to avoid the high price of accommodations in towns without hostels, plan your ferry trip at night so you can sleep on deck.

SOUTHERN PANHANDLE

▓ Ketchikan

Ketchikan is the first stop in Alaska for northbound cruise ships and ferries that expel flocks of ambitious tourists and would-be cannery workers. One might conclude that the crowds and notoriously bad weather (the town averages nearly 14 ft. of rainfall a year) would make Ketchikan an unpleasant place to visit. Its location is the key: the city provides access to Prince of Wales Island, Metlakatla, and most notably, Misty Fjords National Monument. Access to the Monument does not come cheap. Even though it's only 20 mi. from Ketchikan at its nearest point, transportation to the soaring cliffs and crashing waterfalls of this spectacular region will cost you at least $125.

Over 3 mi. long and several hundred yd. wide, Ketchikan has the classic shape of Alaskan coastal cities. The town is Alaska's fourth largest, with 15,000 residents, and is divided between a tourist-filled historic district and long chains of weather-beaten stores and homes. Refugee artists from the lower 48 and indigenous carvers dwell chiefly within the narrow confines of the historic district and nearby Saxman Village, while the rest of the community is left to loggers and fisherfolk.

PRACTICAL INFORMATION AND ORIENTATION

Visitors Information: Ketchikan Visitors Bureau, 131 Front St. (225-6166 or 800-770-3300), on the cruise ship docks downtown. For info on Ketchikan proper. Maps and access to local charter and touring companies. Open May-Sept. daily 7am-5pm; limited winter hours. **Southeastern Alaska Visitors Center (SEAVC)** (228-6214), on the waterfront next door to the Federal building. Info on public lands around Ketchikan and throughout the Panhandle, including Tongass and Misty Fjords. Inquire about local trails, make reservations for area campsites. Open May-Sept. daily 8:30am-4:30pm; Oct.-Apr. Tues.-Sat. 8:30am-4:30pm.

Airport: Across from Ketchikan on Gravina Island. A small ferry runs from the airport to just above the state ferry dock every 15min. summer, every 30min., otherwise ($2.50). The **Airporter** (225-5429) carries people and bags between the airport and the ferry terminal. **Alaska Airlines** (225-2145 or 800-426-0333), in the mall on Tongass Ave., provides flight info from Ketchikan. Daily flights to Juneau ($124). Open Mon.-Fri. 9:30am-5pm.

Ferries: Alaska Marine Highway (225-6181), at the far end of town on N. Tongass Hwy. Ferries to: Wrangell ($24), Petersburg ($38), Sitka ($54), Juneau ($74), Haines ($88), and Skagway ($92). Turn right from the terminal to reach the city center. Buses to town until 6:45pm; after that split the $8 cab fare with a pal.

Public Transportation: Local bus fare $1, seniors and anyone under 11 75¢. Buses run every 20min., Mon.-Sat. 6:40am-7pm. The main bus route runs a loop with turnaround points at the airport parking lot near the ferry terminal at one end and Dock and Main St. downtown at the other. Stops about every 3 blocks.

Taxi: Sourdough Cab, 225-5544. **Alaska Cab,** 225-2133. **Yellow Taxi,** 225-5555. Don't try to flag them down; call ahead. All run 24hr.

Air Taxis and Tours: Taquan, 225-8800. **Ketchikan Air Service,** 225-9888. **Misty Fjords Air and Outfitters,** 225-5155. Tours $125 (90min.) and $169 (2hr.) per person. Shop Around.

Car Rental: Alaska Rent-A-Car, at the airport (225-2232) or 2828 Tongass Ave. (225-5000 or 800-662-0007). Free local pick-up and delivery. $7 per hr., $43 per day, with unlimited free mileage. Must be 21 or older to rent. Open Mon.-Sat. 8am-5pm, Sun. 8am-3pm.

Bike Rental: The Pedalers (723-1088), near the visitors center. $8 per hr., $40 per day.

Kayaking: Southeast Exposure, 507 Stedman St. (225-8829). Required 1½-hr. orientation class ($30). Singles $35 per day, 6 or more days $30 per day. Doubles $50 per day, 6 or more days $45 per day. $200 damage deposit. Office empty on good kayaking days. Open daily 8am-5pm.

Bookstore: Parnassus (Ms. Lillian's), 5 Creek St. (225-7690). An upstairs special-subject book shop with an eclectic selection of used and new books. Discernible emphasis on women's studies. Open daily 8:30am-6pm; winter closed Mon.

Showers: Seamen's Center (225-6003) on Mission St. next to St. John's. A warm, dry lounge where workers and others can clean up and watch television. Although oriented to Ketchikan's down and out, the Seamen's Center welcomes backpackers and other travelers. Showers $1.50, laundry 75¢. Open daily 3-10pm; Sept.-May Wed. and Sat.-Sun. 6-9pm. Volunteers can help cook or clean for 2hr. any evening. **The Mat** (225-0628), about ¾mi. from downtown at 989 Stedman, offers TV and a play area as well as showers.

Public Radio Station: KRBD 105.9, 123 Stedman St. (225-9655).

Weather: 874-3232. Ketchikan airport weather report.

Laundromat: Highliner Laundromat, 2703 Tongass (225-5308). Wash $1.75, 7-min. dry 25¢. Showers ($2 for 10min.). Open 6:30am-9:30pm.

Pharmacy: Downtown Drugstore, 300 Front St. (225-3144). Open Mon.-Fri. 8am-6:30pm, Sat. 8am-6pm, Sun. 10am-4pm.

Hospital: Ketchikan General Hospital, 3100 Tongass Ave. (275-5171). **Clinic:** 3612 Tongass (225-5144). Open Mon.-Fri. 7:30am-6:30pm.

Fire Dept.: 225-9616, Main St. near Dock St. **Police Station:** 225-6631, at Main St. and Grant St., across from the hostel.

Post Office: 225-9601, next to the ferry terminal. Open Mon.-Fri. 8:30am-5pm. Substation at corner of Race and Tongass (225-4153). Open Mon.-Fri. 9am-6pm, Sat. 9am-5pm. Another substation (225-2349) is in The Trading Post, at Main and Mission St. Open Mon.-Sat. 9am-5:30pm. **General Delivery ZIP Code:** 99901.

Area Code: 907.

Ketchikan rests on Revillagigedo Island, 235 mi. southeast of Juneau, 90 mi. northwest of Prince Rupert, BC, and 600 mi. northwest of Seattle, WA. Upon reaching Ketchikan from Canada, you should **roll back your watch** by an hour. If you're flying in, a shuttle ferry ($2.50) will bring you to the main island, dropping you near the ferry terminal. Catch a bus ($1) or walk the 2 mi. downtown from the ferry terminal to avoid a hefty cab fare.

ACCOMMODATIONS

Besides hostels, rooms here are expensive. The **Ketchikan Reservation Service** (225-3273) provides info on B&Bs (singles from $50-75).

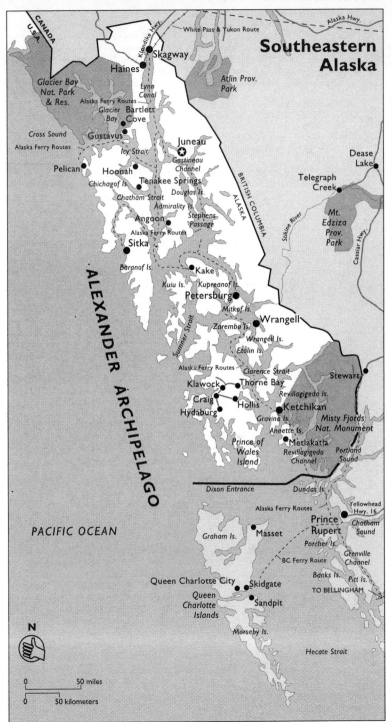

Southeastern Alaska

CANADA
U.S.A.

White Pass & Yukon Route

Alaska Hwy.

Klondike Hwy.

Skagway

Haines

Atlin Prov.
Park

Glacier Bay
Nat. Park
& Res.

Lynn
Canal

Alaska Ferry Routes

Glacier
Bay

Bartlett
Cove

Cross Sound

Gustavus

Alaska Ferry Routes

Juneau

Dease
Lake

Telegraph
Creek

Icy Strait

Gastineau
Channel

Pelican

Hoonah

Tenakee Springs

BRITISH COLUMBIA

Chichagof Is.

Douglas Is.

ALASKA

Mt.
Edziza
Prov.
Park

Chatham Strait

Admiralty Is.

Angoon

Stephens
Passage

Stikine River

Alaska Ferry Routes

Sitka

Cassiar Hwy.

Baranof Is.

Kake

Kuiu Is.

Kupreanof Is.

Petersburg

Mitkof Is.

Wrangell

Zaremba Is.

Summer Strait

Wrangell Is.

Etolin Is.

Alaska Ferry Routes

Clarence Strait

Klawock

Thorne Bay

Stewart

Revillagigedo Is.

Craig

Hollis

Ketchikan

Hydaburg

Gravina Is.

Misty Fjords
Nat. Monument

Annette Is.

Metlakatla

ALEXANDER ARCHIPELAGO

Prince of
Wales
Island

Revillagigedo
Channel

Portland
Sound

Dixon Entrance

Dundas Is.

PACIFIC OCEAN

Alaska Ferry Routes

Yellowhead
Hwy. 16

Prince
Rupert

Chatham
Sound

Graham Is.

Masset

Porcher Is.

Grenville
Channel

BC Ferry Route

Banks Is.

Pitt Is.

Queen Charlotte City

Skidgate

TO BELLINGHAM

Queen
Charlotte
Islands

Sandpit

Morseby Is.

Hecate Strait

N

0   50 miles

0   50 kilometers

Ketchikan Youth Hostel (HI-AYH), P.O. Box 8515 (225-3319), at Main and Grant St. in the basement of the First Methodist Church. Not a rollicking social scene. No beds, but foam mats on the floor are reasonably comfortable if you have a sleeping bag. Clean kitchen, common area, 2 showers, tea and coffee. Strict lockout 9am-6pm. Lights out at 10:30pm, on at 7am. Curfew 11pm. Call ahead if arriving on a late ferry. 3-day max. stay subject to availability. Overflow sleeps in the sanctuary. Baggage storage during lockout. Open June 1-Sept. 1. $8, nonmembers $11. Reservations advisable.

Innside Passage B&B, 114 Elliot St. (247-3700), located on the stairway just above Tongass Ave., about ½mi. from downtown. Beautiful rooms in a convenient location share a bath with jacuzzi. Reservations strongly recommended and require that you mail in a check in advance (no credit cards). Singles $60, doubles $70.

New York Hotel and Café, 207 Stedman St. (225-0246). A painstakingly restored 8-room hotel beside the Creek St. boardwalk. Stocked exclusively with high-quality, turn-of-the-century antiques. Cable TV, queen-size beds, and luxurious bathtubs. Singles $69, doubles $79; Oct.-April $55-59. Reserve 3 weeks in advance.

CAMPING

If you plan in advance, camping can be an escape from high accommodation prices. Keep in mind that Ketchikan's infamous rain can sometimes make camping miserable. Check out **The Outfitter,** 3232 Tongass (225-6888; open Mon.-Fri. 8am-7pm, Sat. 8am-6pm, Sun. 8am-4pm), or **Plaza Sports,** in the Plaza Mall (225-1587; open Mon.-Fri. 8am-8pm, Sat. 7am-8pm, Sun. 7am-6pm), for supplies before you set out. Campgrounds usually have time limits of a week or two, but cannery workers tent up in the public forests for up to a month. There is no public transportation to the campgrounds, so plan on hiking, biking, or paying the exorbitant cab fare. SEAVC (228-6214) provides information and reservations for all the campgrounds listed, as well as information about cabins with stoves ($25) in remote locations of the **Tongass National Forest.** Spaces fill rapidly in the summer; reservations are advisable.

A number of similar campgrounds lurk in the area. **Signal Creek Campground,** 6 mi. north of the ferry terminal on Tongass Hwy. 25, features attractive views and lakeside nature trails. **Last Chance Campground,** 2 mi. north of Ward Lake's parking lot entrance, is a good choice for RVs. Fully accessible to the handicapped. **Three C's Campground,** ½ mi. north of Signal Creek, has four units for backpackers with few assets but privacy. All three campgrounds run between $8-10 per site and have water, pit toilets, and a 2-week max. stay. Anyone can camp for up to 30 days in Tongass National Forest. Sites are not maintained, but any clearing is free. After 30 days, campers may not return for six months.

FOOD

The restaurant scene here follows a typical pattern—one or two worthwhile semi-creative establishments and a heap of mediocre "standard fare" joints. Stock up on groceries at **Super-Valu,** 3816 Tongass Ave. (225-1279; open daily 24hr.). The supermarket most convenient to downtown is **Tatsuda's,** 633 Stedman, at Deermount St., just beyond the Thomas Basin (225-4125; open daily 7am-11pm). The freshest seafood swims in Ketchikan Creek; anglers frequently hook King salmon from the docks by Stedman St. in the summer; if you luck out, **Silver Lining Seafoods,** 1705 Tongass Ave. (225-9865), will custom smoke your catch for $2.45 per pound (open Mon.-Fri. 9am-6pm, Sat. 10am-5pm, Sun. 11am-4pm). Look for boats along the waterfront selling shrimp.

5 Star Café, 5 Creek St. (247-7827). One of those worthwhile, semi-creative restaurants. Smoked salmon with herbal cream cheese $5.75, daily soup $2.50, delicious scones $2. The bright, wood-lined interior is low-key and welcoming and an art gallery in back gives you an excuse to linger. Open Mon.-Sat. 7:30am-5:30pm, Sun. 9am-5pm.

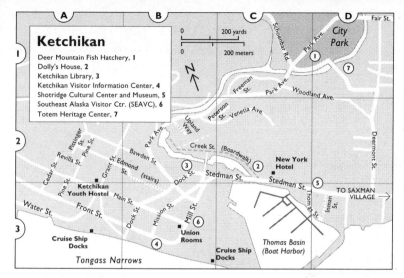

Ketchikan

Deer Mountain Fish Hatchery, 1
Dolly's House, 2
Ketchikan Library, 3
Ketchikan Visitor Information Center, 4
Shotridge Cultural Center and Museum, 5
Southeast Alaska Visitor Ctr. (SEAVC), 6
Totem Heritage Center, 7

ALASKA

Papa's Pizza (247-7272) on Front St. above the Totem Bar. A local favorite. Fine toppings on excellent crusts, including several vegetarian offerings. Woody and airy, with a clear view of the bay. Personal pizza $6, mighty big one $20. Open Sun.-Thurs. 11am-9pm, Fri.-Sat. 11am-10pm.

Sea Breeze Café, 1287 Tongass Ave. (247-3082). Escape the cruise ship chaos about ½mi. from downtown, tucked in among the float plane docks. Surprising machaca burrito for $8, along with traditional halibut and chips for $9 and an array of $6 sandwiches. Planes land noisily nearby for your viewing pleasure.

Jimbo's Café, 307 Mill St. (225-8499), across from the cruise ship docks. Try a 1-lb. Alaskan burger for $9. Stack of 3 pancakes $3.75. Where the inebriated stagger after the bars have closed. The rest of the time, tourists slip into the semi-circular lunch counter in search of local color. Colorful locals willingly oblige. Offers a phone for free local calls. Open daily 6am till "very, very late."

SIGHTS AND ENTERTAINMENT

Too many of Ketchikan's offerings are kitschy tourist-lures. Entrance fees to attractions are almost universally $3 and not worth it. Skip the official walking tour, which makes no distinction among good, bad, and ugly and check out Ketchikan's high points on your own.

When you say "Ketchikan" you might as well say "totems galore." The **Saxman Native Village,** 2½ mi. southwest of Ketchikan on Tongass Hwy ($8 by cab), is the largest totem park in Alaska. Founded at the turn of the century in an effort to preserve indigenous culture, the village has a traditional house, dancers, and an open studio where artisans carve new totems. The poles on display mix recent and old work, some dating back as far as 150 years (open weekdays 9am-5pm and on weekends when a cruise ship is in).

The **Totem Heritage Center,** 601 Deermount St. (225-5900), on the hill above downtown, houses 33 well-preserved totem poles from Tlingit, Haida, and Tsimshian villages. It is the largest collection of authentic, pre-commercial totem poles in the U.S. Only a handful are on display ($3, under 13 free, Sun. afternoon free; open daily 8am-5pm). Across the creek, at the **Deer Mountain Fish Hatchery** (225-6760), a self-guided tour explains artificial sex, salmon style. Unfortunately, visitors can only peer at the goings-on from a small centrally located deck. Best to seek your jollies elsewhere (open daily 8am-4:30pm). The **Ketchikan Library,** overlooking a waterfall and rapids, is the best place to pass a rainy day. The library's impressive periodicals collection enables road-weary sophisticates to catch up on *The Nation, The New Yorker,* and the Sunday *New York Times* (open Mon.-Wed. 10am-8pm, Thurs.-Sat. 10am-6pm, Sun. 1-5pm). The **city dump** up Park St. is (sadly) a perennial favorite among the locals for bear and eagle watching.

While most of "historic downtown" is unremarkable, the colorful stretch of houses perched on stilts along **Creek Street** is worth a look. This picturesque area was once a thriving red-light district where, as tour guides quip, sailors and salmon went upstream to spawn. Women in black fishnets and red-tasseled silk still beckon passersby into **Dolly's House,** 24 Creek St. (225-6329), a brothel turned museum. Antiques are set amid secret hideaways where Dolly kept money, bootleg liquor, and respectable customers during police raids. Hours vary with cruise ship arrivals; typically open 'til 2:30 or 4:30pm. Call ahead ($3).

The town is chock full of drinking establishments. Downtown is lined with tourist-oriented pubs, while every third building on Water St. contains a bar. Fishermen crowd into **The Potlach,** on the docks off of Stedman St., just south of downtown. Uprooted railroad car seats provide a place to sip a beer and a blackboard bears messages from one boatman to another (open daily 10am-midnight or 2am, depending on the crowd). A younger, more diverse crowd gathers at the **First City Saloon** (225-1494), on Water St. toward the ferry terminal. First City serves Guiness, St. Pauli Girl, and a variety of microbrews starting at $2-3 for domestics. Killer blues by the local Emerald City All-Stars on Tuesdays (open daily 9am-2am, with a meat and potatoes kitchen open from 11am-2am).

But like Mom always said, you don't have to drink to have a good time. Ketchikan's **First City Players** present an intriguing variety of plays to sell-out crowds Thursday through Saturday at 8pm. On Fridays in July and August, check out the bawdy *Fish Pirate's Daughter,* a melodrama about Prohibition Ketchikan. Shows ($8) are performed at the **Main Street Theatre,** 338 Main St. (225-4792). The annual **Timber Carnival,** a spirited display of speed-chopping, axe-throwing virtuosity, coincides with Ketchikan's boisterous 4th of July celebrations. The second Saturday in August brings crafts, food, and live music to the streets along with a fiercely contested **slug race** at the **Blueberry Festival.**

OUTDOORS

Although Ketchikan offers boundless hiking and kayaking opportunities within the nearby Misty Fjords National Monument (see below), you barely have to go beyond the city limits to find a trailhead leading into the hills. A good dayhike from Ketchikan is 3001-ft. **Deer Mountain.** Walk up the hill past the city park on Fair St.; the marked trailhead branches off to the left just behind the dump. A steep but manageable ascent leads up the mountain. If you have the luck to be hiking on a clear day, the walk provides exceptional views of the town and sea beyond. While most hikers stop at the 2½ mi. point, a longer route leads over the summit and past an A-frame overnight shelter that can be reserved at the SEAVC. The trail runs above treeline along a steep ridge, where snow and ice may remain into the summer. At the peak, clear skies open upon a mountain-and-lake vista extending into Misty Fjords. **Blue Lake,** an alpine pond stocked with trout, is in the middle of the ridge walk.

At the summit of the 3237-ft. John Mountain, the **John Mountain Trail** descends from the ridge, passing the **Stivis Lakes** on its way down to the **Beaver Falls Fish Hatchery** and the **South Tongass Highway,** 13 mi. from Ketchikan. This section of the hike is poorly marked and may test hikers' ability to read topographic maps. The entire hike, manageable by experienced hikers in a full day, is 10 mi. long and requires a pick-up at the end of the route. A less strenuous and equally accessible outing is the trek along a boardwalk built over muskeg up to Perseverance Lake. The **Perseverance Trail,** beginning 10 mi. north of the city just before the Three C's campground, climbs 600 ft. over 2.3 mi. to an excellent lake for **trout-fishing.**

Fishing begins with a license purchase at the outfitter or Plaza Sports (see above). Licenses cost $10 per day, $15 for 3 days, $30 for 2 weeks, and $50 for the season. In addition to fishing from the docks, you can avoid high charter prices by **renting** a boat and equipment from **Mountain Point Charter and Boat Rental** 5660 S. Tongass Hwy., Ketchikan (225-1793 or 1-800-634-6878; fax 225-7994).

■ Near Ketchikan

METLAKATLA

Metlakatla (Tsimshian for "salt water channel passage") lies 15 mi. southwest of Ketchikan on Annette Island in the Tsimshian Reservation (sim-SHEE-an). The community was founded in 1887, when Anglican lay minister William Duncan led 800 Tsimshians here from British Columbia after difficulties with Canadian religious authorities. Until recently, this village of 400 has made little effort to attract tourists, but locals are hopeful that a new tour package from Ketchikan will attract tourists.

Staying for more than a day trip may be difficult, as it requires a separate permit. Thankfully, a one day visit is plenty. If nothing else, it's a good, low-priced excuse to escape the Ketchikan crowds and charter a float plane to get a bird's eye view of some incredible scenery.

Pro-Mech Air (225-3845 in Ketchikan, 886-3845 in Metlakatla) offers safety-conscious float plane service for $17 ($32 roundtrip, 4 flights per day; trip takes 15min.). **Taquan Air** (886-6868) offers comparable service for a slightly higher price. The **Alaska Marine Highway** (800-624-0066) makes 6 trips a week to the island, including 2 on Saturdays. Scheduling can be inconvenient. The trip takes about 1¼ hours and costs $14. Obtain a visitor's permit at the **Municipal Office Building** (on Upper Milton St., though street names mean little here), open Mon.-Fri. 9am-3pm.

If you insist against all reason on staying here, your cheapest bet will be the **Annette Inn** (886-5360) on Kate St., which offers large rooms, private baths, and cable TV for $60; doubles go for $95. Food options are predictably limited. The hungry snacker should head to the **Mini Mart** (886-3000) at the south end of Upper Milton St. for egg rolls ($2.25) or mammoth cinnamon rolls ($1.75; open daily 8am-10pm). The friendly owners of the **Pizza Place** (886-5360), downstairs from the Annette Inn, serve up small pizzas from $8 and great subs for $6.50. (Open Mon.-Fri. 11am-7pm, Sat. noon-7pm.)

There's always the beach, but if you must hike, a trail up **Yellow Hill** offers great views of the island's west side and takes about a half hour. The trail starts about 1½ mi. south of town on Airport Rd. Look for the boardwalk on the right. Even more impressive is the route leading to **Purple Lake.** Reach the trailhead by taking Airport Rd. south for 2.7 mi., then continuing another 1.8 mi. on Purple Mountain Rd. You can ask the airline with whom you fly in if they can take you to the trailhead. This steep 3-mi. trail leads up a rocky mountainside gushing with waterfalls.

The new official tour costs $89. The more worthwhile alternative is a $17 salmon or halibut **barbeque** and a **tribal dance performance.** The only things you miss out on are the roundtrip plane ride and a short tour of the area—to see *what* is unclear. Stop by the Long House down Western Ave. from Leasks Market or call 247-8737 or 800-643-4898 to find out if the show is on for the day.

If you're not a fish fan and need some culture, the **Duncan Museum** (886-7363) is a free alternative. The museum, once the home of founding father William Duncan, features a collection of his personal effects and old photographs of the village. Look for the bright yellow cottage at the south end of town. Call Laverne, the curator, to schedule a visit. The museum doesn't keep regular hours.

MISTY FJORDS NATIONAL MONUMENT

The incredible **Misty Fjords National Monument** lies 20 mi. east of Ketchikan and is accessible by kayak, power boat, or float plane. This 3420-sq.-mi. park offers great camping, kayaking, hiking, and wildlife viewing. Walls of sheer granite, scoured and scraped by retreating glaciers, rise up to 3000 ft. from saltwater bays. More than 12 ft. of annual rainfall and runoff from large icefields near the Canadian border feed the streams and waterfalls which empty into two long fjords, **Behm Canal** (117 mi. long) and **Portland Canal** (72 mi. long), on either side of the monument. Four first-come, first-serve shelters (free) and 14 Forest Service cabins ($25) dot the preserve, most require a chartered floatplane to reach. Always ask ahead at SEAVC.

Although seasoned kayakers prepared to navigate the difficult currents between Ketchikan and Behm Canal can paddle straight into the park, another option is **Alaska Cruises,** 220 Front, Box 7814 (225-6044). They will bring you and your boat on one of their four sightseeing tours per week. They drop off and pick up paddlers anywhere along their route for $225, $175 at the entrance or head of Rudyard Bay. **Walker Cove, Punchbowl Cove,** and **Rudyard Bay,** off Behm Canal, are several choice destinations for paddlers. These waters are frigid and extended stretches of coast have no good shelter or dry fire wood.

A slew of charter operations visit the monument; plan on spending at least $125 for a visit. Alaska Cruises offers an 11-hour **boat tour** with three meals ($140). An **air tour** of the park costs more than $1 for every minute in the air. **Combination** boat and flight tours last six hours and cost about $185. Call the Ketchikan Visitors Bureau (see **Ketchikan: Practical Information**) for more information.

■ Prince of Wales Island

Prince of Wales Island sits less than 30 mi. west of Ketchikan. The island lies beneath a dense rainforest broken only by mountain peaks, patches of muskeg, and large clear-cuts. Most of the island is managed by Tongass National Forest and Native American Tribal Groups. The road system was built to facilitate logging and shows the industry's scars. Even so, a great deal of Prince of Wales Island remains covered in virgin forest.

Prince of Wales is a favorite destination of hunters and sport fishermen. Canoers, kayakers, and scuba-divers also flock here for some of the best opportunities in the region. Numerous, expensive charter companies wait happily to greet them. The prices of accommodations and transportation follow suit: although it's cheap enough to *get* here, it's prohibitively expensive to *stay* here. Car rentals on the island are ridiculous and it costs $41 to take a car on the ferry from Ketchikan. Not surprisingly, navigating the island by car is difficult and thumbing it is usually fruitless and time-consuming. Float planes are an option—try **Promech** (800-860-3845 or 826-3845), **Ketchikan Air** (826-3333), or **Taquan Air** (826-8800).

CRAIG

Craig, on the west coast of Prince of Wales, is home to most of the island's tourist resources: charter services, the district ranger station, a number of very nice hotels you probably can't afford, and one excellent restaurant. Outside of these few things, there's little reason to linger. The surrounding area is heavily clear-cut and there are no convenient hiking trails.

For information on caves, camping, and the 19 wilderness cabins on Prince of Wales Island, drop by the **Forest Service Office** (826-3271) at 9th Ave. and Main St. (open Mon.-Fri. 7am-5pm). **Ketchikan Air Island Travel,** on Front St., sells fishing and hunting licenses (open Mon.-Sat. 7am-7pm, Sun. 9am-7pm); **JT Brown,** next to Ruth Ann's, handles tackle (open Mon.-Sat. 8am-7pm). The **Craig Health Clinic** (826-3257) is on 3rd St. (open Mon.-Tues. and Thurs.-Fri. 9am-1pm and 2-6pm; Sat. 10am-12:30pm and 1:30-4pm). The **police** (826-3330) are across from the library on 3rd St. Send pictures home from the **Craig Post Office** (826-3298) on Craig-Klawock St. next to Thompson House (open Mon.-Fri. 8am-5pm, Sat. noon-2pm; **General Delivery ZIP Code:** 99921).

Almost anybody in Craig will point you in the direction of **Ruth Ann's** (826-3376; open daily 6:30am-10:30pm), on Front St., for an affordable and creative breakfast or lunch (about $6-8) options. Dinner prices go through the roof; the cheapest entree goes for $18. **Thompson House Groceries** (826-3394), on Craig-Klawock St., might be your best bet for an evening meal. In addition to a good selection of groceries, they have a salad bar and a deli.

Though most of Prince of Wales Island falls within the **Tongass National Forest,** allowing free unimpaired camping, Craig is surrounded by private tribal lands where camping is prohibited. The **TLC Laundromat and Rooms** (826-2966), on Cold Storage Rd. behind the supermarket, offers a slumber space that is both affordable and legal. Singles $42, doubles $50. The laundromat ($1.75 wash, 25¢ dry) also has showers ($1.50 for 5min.; open daily 7am-9pm).

Craig lies about 30 mi. west of Hollis, where the ferry docks. If you're carless, check to see if the **Prince of Wales Transporter** (755-2348) are still in business. They used to meet almost every ferry and roll on to Craig ($20). **Jackson Cab** will drive to Craig for around $23 (755-2557) and **Wilderness Rent-a-Car** (826-2205 or 755-2205) rents at truly outrageous rates ($45 per day, 30¢ per mi.). Locals report that between Hollis and Craig, hitchhikers are rarely seen waiting long for rides. Light traffic on logging roads can make for significant waits elsewhere. (*Let's Go* does not recommend hitchhiking.)

THORNE BAY

A narrow, dusty logging road cuts northeast across the island from **Klawock,** 4.3 mi. north of Craig, to Thorne Bay (**Hospital:** 828-3906; **Police:** 828-3905; **Fire:** 828-3313), an unpretentious town recently created by the incorporation of a logging camp. The area provides attractive waters for kayaking and its tributary rivers win the praise of anglers. Unlike Craig, Thorne Bay lies within **Tongass National Forest** and campers may pitch tents for up to one month, limiting themselves to two weeks on any site. Call or stop by the **Forest Service Station** (828-3304) for more information. Locals recommend the **Eagles Nest Campground,** 12 mi. north of Thorne Bay; a camp unit ($5) includes access to bathroom, water, cooking grates, a canoe launch, picnic tables, and RV parking. Two reasonable indoor accommodations are also available. **Marilyn Black's B&B,** in a double-wide trailer on Sandy Beach Rd., offers $50 singles and continental breakfasts, but is no place for adamant non-smokers. **Brenda's Beehive B&B** (828-3945) on Bayview Ct. offers two comfortable beds ($55, $70 with dinner). The **Thorne Bay Market,** where a gallon of milk goes for $4, lies in a cove beyond the docks (open Mon.-Sat. 8am-8pm, Sun. 9am-6pm). **Some Place to Go** (828-8888), an outdoor hamburger stand on the road out of town, serves a tasty cheeseburger for $3 (open 10am-7pm).

SIGHTS AND OUTDOORS ON THE ISLAND

Perhaps the most distinctive of the Island's attractions is **El Capitan Cave,** North America's deepest cavern. The cave bores into the limestone that underlies Prince of Wales and is adorned with striking marble outcrops. Recently, speleologists (not to be confused with amateurish "spelunkers") uncovered the remains of a 12,000-year-old grizzly bear deep within the cave. The Forest Service has installed a gate 150 ft.inside the cave to reduce damage to El Capitan's delicate interior. Free two-hour tours start behind the gate (June-Aug., Thurs.-Sun. at 8am, 10am, 1pm and 6pm) and require a hard-hat. Off-season tours are available with 14-day advance notice. Make reservations at the **Thorne Bay Ranger District** (828-3304). The cave is about a two-hour drive from either Craig or Thorne Bay.

The **Craig Dive Center** (826-3481 or 800-380-DIVE/3483), at 1st and Main in Craig, rents canoes for $25 per day and kayaks for $20 per day. Kayak rental requires previous experience. The Dive Center also offers a two tank boat dive for a group of four ($125 per person). **Log Cabin Campgrounds** (755-2205 or 800-544-2205) in Klawock rents canoes for $20 per day. The Forest Service can provide maps for a number of established **canoe trails** and reserve you a spot at one of the **wilderness cabins** that line these routes ($25 per night).

■ Wrangell

Wrangell is the only place in Alaska to have been ruled by four different nations. The Russian-American Company ousted a Tlingit village near the mouth of the Stikine River in 1834 to build a fort which they leased to the British-owned Hudson Bay Company in 1840. Soon after the United States purchased Alaska from Russia in 1867, Britain turned over control of the fort to the Americans. As the only gateway to Canada's interior between Prince Rupert and Skagway, the Stikine River became a crucial transportation corridor during the three gold rushes of the next four decades. Wrangell exploded as a tramping ground for miners traveling to and from the goldfields. Explorer and ecologist John Muir passed through the town and was duly unimpressed: "It was a lawless draggle of wooden huts and houses, built in crooked lines, wrangling around the boggy shores of the island."

Now an orderly, prosperous, lumber and fishing town with a picturesque harbor, Wrangell's attractions are convenient enough to allow a brief visit during a ferry layover and plentiful enough to merit a night's stay. While the town cannot offer the spectacular vistas of a Juneau or a Sitka, it doesn't have the mob mentality of heavily touristed Ketchikan, either. Locals take their day of rest very seriously (grocery stores, the museum, and the tourist office are all **closed on Sunday**).

PRACTICAL INFORMATION

Visitors Center: Chamber of Commerce Visitors Center (874-3901 or 800-FOR-WRGL/367-9745) in the Stikine Inn near the City Dock. Friendly, knowledgeable staff. Open Mon.-Fri. 9am-5pm, Sat. hours vary based on cruise ship schedules. **Forest Service,** 525 Bennett St., ¾mi. east of town (874-2323). Open Mon.-Fri. 8am-5pm. Reserve cabins here.

Fishing: Alaska Dept. of Fish and Game (874-3822) in the green Kadin Building on Front St. Provides info on fishing and hunting seasons and regulations.

Bank: National Bank of Alaska on Front St. Only place in town with an **ATM.** Open Mon.-Fri. 9:30am-5:30pm.

Airport: Alaska Air (874-3309; 874-3308 for recorded flight info) makes daily stops in Wrangell: once on a flight to Petersburg and Juneau and, again, on a flight to Ketchikan and Seattle. $90 to Ketchikan.

Ferries: Alaska Marine Highway (874-2021) at Stikine Ave. and McCormack St. Frequent service to Sitka ($38), Juneau ($56), and Ketchikan ($24). 24hr. recording of arrivals and departures, 874-3711. Open 1½hr. before arrivals. Luggage lockers 25¢.

Taxi: Porky's Cab Co., 874-3603; **Star Cab,** 874-3622; both open 24hr. Both provide shuttle service to area trails.

Car Rental: Practical Rent-A-Car (874-3975), Airport Road near the airport. Compact car $42 per day, van $46, unlimited mileage.

Air Charter Services: Sunrise Aviation, P.O. Box 432 (874-2319). **Ketchikan Air Service,** P.O. Box 874 (874-2369). **Temsco Helicopters,** P.O. Box 5057 (874-2010).

Public Library: 874-3535, on 2nd St. Good Alaska section, including many rare and out-of-print volumes. Open Mon. and Fri. 10am-noon and 1-5pm, Tues.-Thurs. 1-5pm and 7-9pm, Sat. 9am-5pm.

Laundromat: Thunderbird Laundromat at 233 Front St. Wash $2, dry 25¢. Open daily 6am-8pm.

Public Swimming Pool: 874-2444, indoors at Wrangell High School on Church St. Also weight room, racquetball, and showers. Hours vary; closed Sun. Pool, weight room, gym $1.50, under 18 $1. Racquetball: two players $6.

Showers: in **Hungry Beaver Pizza,** 299 Shakes St. Unusual location but clean. $3.

Pharmacy: Wrangell Drug, 202 Front St. (874-3422). Open Mon.-Sat. 9am-6pm, Sun. 11am-6pm.

Hospital: 874-3356, at Bennett St. and 2nd Ave.

Emergency: 911. **Police** (874-3304) and **Fire** (874-3223) both in the Public Safety Building on Zimovia Hwy.

Post Office: 874-3714, at the north end of Front St. The town rejected home delivery in 1983 in favor of the ritual of coming in to check P.O. boxes. Open Mon.-Fri. 8:30am-5pm, Sat. 11am-1pm. **ZIP Code:** 99929.
Area Code: 907.

ACCOMMODATIONS AND CAMPING

First Presbyterian Church Hostel, 202 Church St. (874-3534), 5 blocks from the ferry terminal. Just look for the groovy neon cross. A surprisingly underutilized resource—you may end up having the entire place to yourself. Sleep on foam mats, bring your own sleeping bag. Showers, kitchen, and piano. Daytime luggage storage, access available if necessary. Capacity 20. Curfew 10pm unless you're on a late ferry; call ahead. Open mid-June-Labor Day daily 5pm-9am. $10.

Harbor House B&B, 645 Shakes Ave. (874-3084 or 800-488-5107), just before the bridge to Shakes Island. Three terrific rooms creatively decorated with antiques, including an intimate Ship Room decked out in yellow cedar. Share common bath and small kitchen and ride around town on complimentary, if slightly dated, bikes. Continental breakfast included. Singles $55, doubles $70.

Rooney's Roost B&B (874-2026) on the corner of 2nd St. and McKinnon. Other B&Bs may come and go, but Rooney's perseveres. Mrs. Rooney and her breakfasts have a following. Rooms are well kept and have nice (if bland) views. Reserve several weeks in advance for July and August. Rooms $50-55 for 1or 2 people.

City Park, 1 mi. south of town on Zimovia Hwy. (2nd St. changes names several times before becoming Zimovia Hwy. south of town), immediately beyond the cemetery and baseball field. Picnic tables and shelters, drinking water, toilet, bumpy tent spots, and a beautiful view of the water. A bit close to the sewage treatment plant. 24hr. max. stay. Free. Open Memorial Day-Labor Day.

Shoemaker Bay RV Park, 5 mi. south of town on the Zimovia Hwy. 29 RV sites, 8 wooded tent sites, picnic tables, water tap, flush toilet. ¾mi. trail to Rainbow Falls across the highway. RV sites $5 without power, $8 with power. Tents free!

FOOD

The cuisine scene in Wrangell went from bad to worse when one of the few decent sit-down restaurants in town inexplicably closed. If you're looking for anything other than pizzas and burgers, head to **Benjamin's Groceries** (874-2341) on Outer Dr., which offers tasty deli sandwiches (open Mon.-Sat. 8am-8pm). The huge **stump** at the corner of Grief and Church St. is a lovely lunch spot.

J&W's, 120 Front St. (874-2120). A safe bet, standard fare. Good, messy burgers from $3.50, fried mini-burritos for $1.65. More creative alternatives include salmon and shrimp burgers ($5) and 13 flavors of shakes ($2.65 for medium). Open Mon.-Sat. 11am-7pm, Sun. noon-7pm.

Hungry Beaver Pizza/Marine Bar, 274 Shakes St. (874-3005), near the island. Where drinkers and high school grease lovers mix. One-person pizzas from $5.50. Waterfront bar is low-key and a last refuge for late-night eaters. Capricious bar menu. Kitchen open daily 4-10pm. Bar open daily 10am-2:30am.

SIGHTS AND OUTDOORS

If the ferry schedule permits you to spend only 45 minutes of your life in Wrangell, a walk out to **Shakes Island** might be the best use of your time. Follow Front St. to Shakes St., where a short bridge leads out to the island in the middle of Wrangell's snug harbor. Outdoor totems guard the **Shakes Tribal House,** a meticulous replica of the communal home of high-caste Tlingits. A Civilian Conservation Corps work team built the house during the Depression without the aid of a sawmill or a single nail. Inside, finely carved totems on a sunken floor stand below large timbers scarred by the original adze marks. The house is open during the summer whenever a ship or ferry docks for more than one hour. Also open by appointment (874-3747) for a donation of $10 or more; regular donation $1.

Stone carvings by the region's first inhabitants are strewn across **Petroglyph Beach**, ¾ mi. north of the ferry terminal on Evergreen Ave. Although some are simple circles and spirals, others describe complex facial patterns, usually thought to represent spirits or totem animals. Archaeologists remain uncertain about the age of these petroglyphs. Local Tlingit tradition maintains that the petroglyphs were in place before the Tlingit reached the harbor, but is silent about their source.

Previously owned by the first all-female corporation in America, the mine at **Wrangell Garnet Ledge** was deeded to the Boy Scouts and children of Wrangell in 1962. Children now chip garnets out of the rock by hand and line up to hawk their wares whenever a ship arrives. The mine, by the mouth of the Stikine River, can only be reached by boat. The museum sells permits for $10 per day and 10% of the garnets must be left with the Scouts. A charter tour to the Ledge is unlikely to run less than $135. It's cheaper to restrain your mining bug and buy a garnet at the dock.

Hikers can follow in John Muir's footsteps and scramble up nearby **Mt. Dewey** to an observation point with a commanding view of town and the Stikine River flats. Walking down 2nd St. toward the center of town, McKinnon St. is on the left. Follow McKinnon St. to a left on 3rd St. and look for a white sign marking the trailhead. The trail is primitive and not regularly maintained. Three mi. beyond City Park on Zimovia Hwy., the **Rainbow Falls Trail** runs .7 mi to the top of a forty-ft. waterfall. Unfortunately, the only frontal view of the fall is from a significant distance. Far more rewarding is the **Institute Creek Trail,** which breaks off from the Rainbow Fall Trail just before the top of the falls. The result of a Herculean trail-building effort, the route follows a nearly continuous boardwalk for 2.7 mi. It parallels a series of impressive waterfalls (50min. from trailhead) before breaking into several muskeg openings on a ridgetop. A three-sided Forest Service shelter (available for overnight stays on a first-come first-serve basis) sits on the ridge at the end of the trail. Plan on a two-to two and a half hour trip up and a one and a half-to two-hour trip down. Both taxi services in town will take you to the trailhead for $7-8 if you don't want to walk. The **Wrangell Ranger District,** Box 51 (874-2323; open Mon.-Fri. 8am-4:30pm), has more information on the trails, campsites, and cabins in the Wrangell area.

The Stikine River is the fastest navigable river in the Northwest. Charter boat operations regularly run up the Stikine and over to Garnet Ledge. There are six Forest Service cabins throughout the Stikine delta and two bathing huts at **Chief Shakes Hot Springs,** a few mi. up river. The only developed black bear observatory in Southeast Alaska, the **Anan Bear Observatory,** is also accessible by boat. Here you can watch rapacious bears feast on the pink salmon that climb the falls to spawn. Call **Stickeen** *(sic)* **Wilderness Adventures,** Box 934, 107 Front St. (874-2085 or 800-874-2085, fax 874-2285) for information; they will schedule departures around your ferry schedule (open Mon.-Fri. 9am-5pm). A day trip to the Anan Observatory or up the Stikine River runs $125 per person. For a listing of charter boat services (Wrangell has over 24 of them), contact the **Wrangell Chamber of Commerce (see Practical Information,** above). The Chamber of Commerce also provides information on scuba-diving tours, whale-watching, fishing and hunting trips, and sightseeing outings. Several charter organizations transport rafts and kayaks up the river.

The **Wrangell Museum** (874-3770) temporarily occupies the basement of the community center on Church St. Besides the interesting but predictable collections of Native American artifacts, the museum houses a communications and aviation room and an exhibit on the region's natural history. ($2, under 16 free; open May-Sept. Mon.-Fri. 10am-5pm, Sat. 1-5pm, and Sun. when ferries are in port longer than 1hr; hours different Oct-April, call ahead.)

For a real dose of Wrangell culture, visit on the 4th of July for the logging show and hotly contested **4th of July Queen competition,** as well as the traditional parade and fireworks; or drop by during Memorial Day weekend for the "special derby days" of the Salmon Derby. The derby's biggest fish nets a $5000 prize.

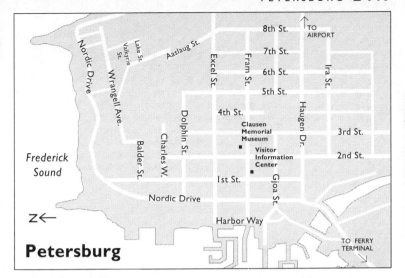

Petersburg

ALASKA

■ Petersburg

In 1897, Norwegian immigrant Peter Buschmann saw opportunity in the natural harbor, abundant fish, and convenient glacier ice and built a cannery here. Petersburg now claims the world's largest halibut fleet and a strong Scandinavian legacy. Fishing is the mainstay of the local economy and Petersburg draws a horde of summer workers. Its isolation from the path of large cruise ships has lent the island community an uncommon cohesiveness: a few years ago when one of the canneries found itself understaffed with a heap of salmon to process, the management went through the phone book calling for extra hands. Retirees, housewives, and people just home from work all rallied to help.

Unfortunately, Petersburg's strong sense of community has made it somewhat cool towards strangers. The polite townsfolk evince no hostility, but make little effort to accommodate budget travelers. Students and backpackers who plan to stay should be forewarned that there are no hostels and no storage facilities for packs.

PRACTICAL INFORMATION AND ORIENTATION

Visitor Information Center: P.O. Box 649, Petersburg 99833 (772-4636), at 1st and Fram St. Home of a replica of the **world-record 126½lb. king salmon.** Co-administered by Chamber of Commerce and Forest Service. Reserve Forest Service cabins here. Helpful, informed staff. Open Mon.-Fri. 9am-5pm, Sat. 10am-4pm, Sun. noon-4pm; winter Mon.-Fri. 10am-noon and 1-3pm. **Forest Service** (722-3871), P.O. Box 1328, above the post office. Info on hiking and fishing. Reserve cabins here, too. Open Mon.-Fri. 8am-5pm.

Flights: Alaska Airlines, 1506 Haugen Dr. (772-4255), 1 mi. from the Federal Bldg. To: Juneau ($105), Seattle ($346, $181 with 2-week advance purchase). **Haines Air,** next door (772-4200) offers 3 daily flights to Juneau and often beats Alaska's prices. For sightseeing, contact **Temsco Air** (772-4220).

Ferries: Alaska Marine Highway (772-3855), terminal at Mile 0.9 on the Mitkof Hwy., 1 mi. from the center of town. To: Ketchikan ($38), Sitka ($26), Wrangell ($18), and Juneau ($44). Open 1½hr. before ferry arrivals.

Employment: Petersburg Employment Service (772-3791) at Haugen Dr. and 1st St. Fish-steeped staff. Provides info on all 3 canneries in town. Call to request the lyrically succinct pamphlets *Alaska Job Facts* and *Seafood Processing Jobs in Alaska.* Open Mon.-Fri. 9-11am and noon-8pm, Sat.9-11am and noon-3pm.

Taxi: City Cab, 772-3003. Rates start at $4. Open 24hr.

Car Rental: Allstar Car Rentals (772-4281) at the Scandia House Hotel. $45 per day with unlimited mileage. Credit card required. Also rents 18-ft. **boats** ($150 per day, $125 for guests of the hotel).

Bike Rental: Northern Bikes, 114 Harbor Way (772-3978). Seize the deal: $3 per hr., $20 for the day. Try out a tandem at $5 per hr.

Laundromat: Glacier Laundry (772-4400), downtown at Nordic and Dolphin. Sleeping bags dry cleaned for $14. Wash $1.75, 7-min. dry 25¢. Open daily 6am-10pm. Also at **LeConte RV Park** (772-4680) at 4th and Haugen.

Showers: LeConte RV Park (see below), **Tent City** (see below), **Gym** (see below), and **Glacier Laundry** ($2, towels for $1).

Pharmacy: Rexall Drug, 215 Nordic Dr., downtown. Open Mon. and Fri. 9am-9pm, Tues.-Thurs. and Sat. 9am-6pm, Sun. noon-6pm.

Gym: Petersburg Gymnasium (772-3392) at the end of 2nd Ave. by the high school. Pool $2.50, weight room $1.50, basketball and racquetball available, shower $2. Exceptionally clean and inviting. Open Mon., Wed., Fri. 8am-9:30pm, Tues. and Thurs. 6:30am-9:30pm, Sat. 8am-9:30pm, Sun. 1-9:30pm.

Library: at Haugen and Nordic above the Fire Hall. Open Mon.-Thurs. noon-9pm, Fri.-Sat. 1-5pm.

Bookstore: Sing Lee Alley Books, 11 Sing Lee Alley (772-4440). Open Mon.-Sat. 10am-5pm, Sun. noon-4pm. Classics and popular/mid-brow contemporary.

Hospital: Petersburg Medical Center (772-4291) at Fram and N. 1st St.

Emergency: Police, 16 S. Nordic Dr. (772-3838). **State Troopers,** 772-3100.

Post Office: 772-3121, at Haugen and Nordic Dr. Open Mon.-Fri. 9am-5:30pm, Sat. 11am-2pm. Lobby has stamp machine and is open Mon.-Fri. 7am-8pm, Sat. 8am-6pm. **General Delivery ZIP Code:** 99833.

Area Code: 907.

If you're looking for Nordic Drive, Main St., or Mitkof Hwy., you're probably on it. The main drag goes by several names. The ferry drops you off 1 mi. south of downtown, but it's a painless walk. Cabs to the center run about $4, $6 out to Tent City.

ACCOMMODATIONS AND CAMPING

The only two places within city limits for backpackers are often packed with summer cannery workers. By virtue of price, Tent City is the best budget option. Camping on your own is impossible because wet, untentable muskeg covers the area; the next nearest campground to Petersburg is 22 mi. away. However, an 8-mi. journey gets one into the Tongass National Forest and its free, month-long camping. Many cannery workers camp illegally in the woods beyond the muskeg. Contact the visitors center (see **Practical Information**) for more comprehensive bed and breakfast listings, though prices are appalling compared to **Sitka.**

Nordic House B&B, 806 Nordic Dr., Box 573 (772-3620), ¼ mi. north of ferry terminal. Three lovely rooms, a common kitchen and bath, and sitting space with a fine harbor view. Continental breakfast. Singles start at $60. Doubles start at $70. Be sure to make reservations for July and Aug.

Narrows Inn, Box 1048 (772-4284). Mile 1 of Mitkof Hwy., across from the ferry. Generic motel with generic rooms right across the street from the ferry. Overpriced for what you get, but still the cheapest bed in town. Private baths and cable TV. Kitchenettes in many rooms. 25 units. Singles from $55, doubles from $65. Call before June for summer reservations.

Tent City (772-9864), on Haugen Dr. past the airport, 2 mi. from the ferry. Established by the city and administered by Parks and Recreation in a sort of cannery workers' apartheid, this ramshackle collection of tarps and wooden platforms rests atop muskeg swamp and is home to most of Petersburg's transient workers. Camp manager Charlie Freeman has added several amenities (pay phone, griddle, hotplate, refrigerator, and a shelter) and a dose of order to what used to be largely self-governed. The new no-alcohol policy has mellowed things out a bit, but Tent City is generally not considered the friendliest or safest place in the world. Several sites are set aside for tourists and short-term visitors. Water, toilet, 4 showers (50¢), and pit fires with wood. Quiet hours 10pm-noon. Open May-Sept. $5 per night, $30 per week, and $100 per month.

Ohmer Creek Campground, Mile 22 of Mitkof Hwy. Maintained by the Forest Service. 10 sites. 14-day max. stay. Gravel trail takes you to choice fish-watching venues. Water, pit toilets. Free.

LeConte RV Park, P.O. Box 1548 (772-4680), at 4th and Haugen. 1 mi. from ferry, 3 blocks from downtown. Limited space for tent sites ($6); rates vary from $15-20 for RV hookups. Essentially a butt-strewn parking lot with a few grassy corners. A camp of last resort. A **coin-op laundry** (wash and dry both 75¢) and **showers** ($1.25 per 5min.) are open to the public (bring shower shoes!).

FOOD

Even though it's swimming in fish, Petersburg still charges a bundle for seafood. **The Trading Union** (772-3881), on Nordic Ave. downtown, offers a selection of both sea and land-dwelling groceries (open Mon.-Sat. 8am-7pm, Sun. 9am-7pm).

Helse-Health Foods and Deli (772-3444) on Sing Lee Alley off Nordic Dr. With flowers, little wooden stools, and plenty of reggae, this place offers refuge from typical Alaskan *bourgeois cuisine.* Soup and bread ($5), "Cheese Breeze": avocado, shrimp, mushrooms, and havarti ($6.75). Lots of juices. Open Mon.-Fri. 7:30am-6pm, Sat. 8:30am-6pm; winter Mon.-Fri. 7:30am-3pm, Sat. 10am-3pm.

Pellerito's Pizza (772-3727) across from the ferry. Good if you're at this end of town. Try the chicken primavera on noodles with garlic bread ($6.65) or, if you're really hungry, order a football-sized calzone ($9). Pizza by the slice $2.50. Open Tues.-Sun. 11am-11pm.

Harbor Lights Pizza, 201 Sing Lee Ave. (772-3424). Brobdingnag slices at Lilliput prices ($3.25). Big pizzas don't cost much, either. Pasta and standard pizza place alternatives. Convenient to downtown, great view. Open daily 11am-10pm.

Homestead Café (772-3900), Nordic Dr. at Excel, across from the general store. Run by fishermen's wives who understand large appetites and frequented by fishermen who know how to eat. The good ol' boys of Petersburg play dice on the tables and chat at the counter. Waitresses are tough and sometimes desultory, but are known to treat cannery workers kindly. Go ahead and try to finish their stack of pancakes ($3.50). We dare you. Prodigious plate of biscuits and gravy $5.50. Hearty Viking burger and fries $8. Open Mon.-Sat. 24hr. Lunch starts at 11am.

SIGHTS AND ENTERTAINMENT

This is one of the best places on the Panhandle to see a fishing town at work, as long as the fish are biting. Only one of the town's three canneries is open to the public: Patty Norheim leads groups of four or more on three-hour tours (watch out, Gilligan) through the shrimp cannery next to the harbormaster's office, through the rest of the city and a hatchery, and finally back to her home for cocktails. Find out about the **"Patty Wagon"** ($25) at 772-4837 or stop in at the Tides Inn.

Petersburg's colorful array of homes and flower-lined streets often induces mindless wandering. If your brain feels like exercise, take it to the **Clausen Memorial Museum,** P.O. Box 708 (772-3598), at 2nd Ave. and Fram St., which displays native artifacts and an inspiring history of fishing techniques ($2, under 12 free; open Mon.-Sat. 9:30am-4:30pm, Sun. 12:30-4:30pm). Outside the museum is the bizarre **Fisk Fountain,** a hulking metal monolith featuring an abstract array of **fish.**

On the third full weekend in May, Petersburg joins its international brethren in joyous celebration of Norwegian independence (1905) from Sweden. During the **Little Norway Festival,** mock Vikings dance, sing, parade, hunt their own furs, wear horns, sail in long boats, and violently "board" a plane at the local airport. Memorial Day weekend brings the **Salmon Derby.** The search for a specially tagged fish, and the accompanying $10,000 prize, has been sadly unsuccessful in recent years. Several years ago a local caught the tagged fish, thought he had won, and celebrated publicly only to be reminded that one must catch the fish *during the derby* to win. Hold your nose and stay away from open spaces on the **4th of July** in Petersburg. Celebrations feature a **competitive herring toss.**

OUTDOORS

The island's fishing sites yield salmon, halibut, crab, shrimp, dolly varden, and cutthroat trout, while the land teems with black bears, deer, moose, and waterfowl. For more information, or to obtain Alaska state sportfishing and hunting licenses, contact the **Alaska Dept. of Fish & Game** (see **Essentials: Outdoor Sports,** p. 49). Contented amateurs will discover that **jigging** for herring from the docks is alarmingly fun. Morning and evening are the best times to glimpse the island's wildlife.

While the Petersburg area offers a multitude of hiking opportunities, only a couple of trails are readily accessible by foot. The **Raven's Roost Trail** leads to a Forest Service cabin by the same name ($25 per night; call well in advance for reservations). After starting out near the large orange and white tanks behind the airport, the trail crosses a section of muskeg and climbs steeply to an alpine region with excellent views of Petersburg and the Wrangell Narrows. The cabin, with a second story sleeping loft, sits at the end of the 4-mi. trail.

Another popular walk follows what locals call the **Loop;** from Nordic Drive, walk past the Eagle's Roost Picnic Area and Sandy Beach Park, onto the Frederick Pt. Boardwalk (Sandy Beach has indigenous petroglyphs which are visible at low tide), and back on Haugen Drive. The Loop takes about one and a half hours to complete, unless you linger to watch the boats and floatplanes on Frederick Sound. Pick up the *Petersburg Map* at the ferry terminal or visitors center (see **Practical Information**) for a complete illustration of the trails and logging roads on Mitkof Island.

The planked **Petersburg Creek Trail,** ½ mi. across the Wrangell Narrows on neighboring Kupreanof Island, runs 11½ mi. up to Petersburg Lake through a wilderness area to another Forest Service cabin. If the tide is high enough, you can also go up the creek a few miles by boat to make a 6½-mi. hike to the lake. Although many charter operators in town ferry people across the narrows and rent skiffs, this can cost more than $100. Try asking at the harbormaster's office about boats making the crossing with space for an extra passenger. A small number of people also live across the narrows and make the afternoon commute home. (*Let's Go* does not recommend skiffhitching.)

Several area outfitters offer reasonably priced outdoor adventures. Scott Roberge at **Tongass Kayak Adventures,** 106 N. Nordic Dr., P.O. Box 707 (772-4600), offers guided sea kayak tours up Petersburg Creek. (Five-hour tours daily June-Aug., $45 per person, children under 12 $30; includes gear.) Or do it yourself: kayak rentals are $40 per day for a single, and $50 per day for a double with a three day minimum. Skipper Stephen Berry offers four-hour boat tours of Le Conte Bay and Glacier for $85 per person and six-hour whale-watching expeditions for $135 per person at **Sights Southeast,** P.O. Box 934 (772-4503). **Terry's Unforgettable Expeditions,** P.O. Box 114 (772-2200), offers an $80 excursion to Le Conte Glacier, a $120 whale-watching float, and a $150 full-day expedition through area waters (all prices per person).

Contact the **Forest Service** for advice on necessary equipment, safety considerations, Forest Service Recreation Cabin reservations, and the pamphlet *Hiking Trails: Petersburg Ranger District, Tongass National Forest.* Most information and all reservations are also available at the visitors center (see **Practical Information**).

■ Sitka

The only major Panhandle town with direct access to the Pacific Ocean, Sitka was settled by Russians in 1799. The native Tlingit grew to resent the Russian presence. In 1802, they burned and razed the settlement, massacring nearly all the Russian inhabitants. In 1804, the manager of the Russian-American Company, Alexander Baranov, returned with a fleet and began a naval bombardment of the Tlingit fort. After a bloody 10-day battle, the Tlingit ran out of ammunition and withdrew under cover of

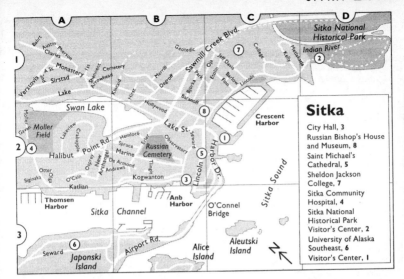

Sitka

City Hall, 3
Russian Bishop's House and Museum, 8
Saint Michael's Cathedral, 5
Sheldon Jackson College, 7
Sitka Community Hospital, 4
Sitka National Historical Park Visitor's Center, 2
University of Alaska Southeast, 6
Visitor's Center, 1

darkness. Baranov declared "New Archangel" the capital of Russian America. The fur trade made it a wealthy cultural center preeminent in the Northwest; Seattle and San Francisco were mere fishing villages compared to Sitka. Though Russia eventually sold Alaska to the U.S. in 1867 for $7.2 million, the Russian legacy lives on in Sitka's fascinating historical buildings.

Sitka has managed to avoid being overrun by flocks of visitors. College students mix with leather-faced fishermen, paint-spattered artists, and the occasional refugee intellectual from Northern California. The town has benefited from an influx of urbane ex-urbanites, who add a fresh tone to the usual Alaskan demographic mix.

PRACTICAL INFORMATION AND ORIENTATION

Visitors Information: Sitka Convention & Visitor's Bureau, P.O. Box 1226 (747-5940). The bureau's most convenient booth is in the Centennial Bldg. at 330 Harbor Dr. Surprisingly few brochures, but a helpful volunteer staff. Open Mon.-Fri. 8am-5pm, weekends only when cruise ships are in and when the Centennial Bldg. hosts events. **Forest Service: Sitka Ranger District,** Tongass National Forest, 201 Katlian, #109 (747-6671). Open Mon.-Fri. 8am-5pm. Pick up a copy of *Sitka Trails.* Also distributes pamphlets about cabins ($25 per night). Ask the irrepressible Rhonda for insight into the virtues of local hikes.

Flights: Alaska Airlines, 800-426-0333 or 966-2266. Service to Juneau ($87) and Ketchikan ($124). Also flies to Seattle, Anchorage, Wrangell, and Petersburg.

Ferries: Alaska Marine Highway, 7 Halibut Rd. (747-8737 or 800-642-0066), 7 mi. from town. To: Ketchikan ($54), Petersburg ($26), and Juneau ($26). Open from 2hr. before arrival until departure.

Shuttle: Sitka Tours (747-8443) offers convenient, affordable rides to both the ferry terminal and airport, as well as tours around town. Call ahead (7am-5pm) for a pickup at your accommodation. $3 one way, $5 roundtrip.

Luggage Storage: The **fire station** on Halibut Point Rd. near downtown stores backpacks for free, as does the **Centennial Bldg.** when space is available. The ferry terminal has 25¢ lockers with a 24hr. max.

Taxis: Sitka Taxi, 747-5001. $12.50 from Sitka to the ferry dock, plus 50¢ per additional person. Runs 24hr.

Car Rental: Advantage Car Rental (747-7557) at the airport terminal. From $31 per day with unlimited mileage. Must be 21 with credit card.

Bike Rental: J&B Bike Rental (747-8279) on Lincoln St. in **Southeast Diving & Sports.** Mountain bikes $5 per hr., $15 per day, $25 overnight. Open Mon.-Sat. 10am-5:30pm.

Kayak Rental: Baidarka Boats (747-8996) on Lincoln St. above Old Harbor Books. Single $25 per ½-day, $35 per day. Double $35 per ½-day, $45 per day. Rates less with longer rentals. Required 1-hr. instructional class for novices ($25). Open Mon.-Sat. 10am-6pm, earlier and Sun. by appointment.

Bookstore: Old Harbor Books, 201 Lincoln (747-8808). Superb Alaska section and info on local arts events. Marine charts and **topographical maps.** Free copies of the *New York Review of Books,* the *New York Times Book Review,* and the *Bloomsbury Review.* Open Mon.-Fri. 9am-6pm, Sat.-Sun. 9am-5pm.

Library: Kettleson Memorial Library, 320 Harbor Dr. (747-8708). Stunning view of the harbor. Open Mon.-Thurs. 10am-9pm, Fri. 1-6pm, Sat.-Sun. 1-5pm.

Laundromats and Shower Facilities: Homestead Laundromat, 713 Katlian Ave. (747-6995). Wash $1.75, 30-min. dry $1.25. Showers $2. Open Mon.-Sat. 8am-8pm, Sun. 8am-5pm. **Duds 'n Suds Laundromat,** 906 Halibut Point Rd. (747-5050), near the hostel. Wash $1.75, 10-min. dry 50¢. Shower $2 for 10 min. Open Mon.-Fri. 7am-8pm, Sat.-Sun. 8am-8pm.

Public Pool: Hames P.E. Center, 801 Lincoln St. (747-5231), at Sheldon Jackson College. One day's access to the gym, weights, and pool $3, seniors and children under 12 $2. Racquetball an extra $10 per hr. Pool open Mon.-Fri. 6-8am, noon-1pm, and 6-8:30pm; Sat.-Sun. 3-4:30pm and 6-7:30pm. Other facilities open Mon.-Fri. 7am-10pm, Sat.-Sun. 2-8pm.

Pharmacy: Harry Race Pharmacy, 106 Lincoln St. (747-8006), near Castle Hill. Also has 1-hr. photo. Open Mon.-Sat. 9am-6pm; Sun. 9am-1pm.

Hospital: Sitka Community Hospital, 209 Moller Dr. (747-3241), near the intersection of Katlian and Halibut.

Post Office: For all General Delivery mail, go to the **Pioneer Station,** 201 Katlian Ave. (747-5525), inside the Westmark Hotel Annex across from Pioneer Home, open Mon.-Sat. 8:30am-5:30pm. **ZIP Code:** 99835.

Area Code: 907.

ACCOMMODATIONS AND CAMPING

Camping facilities are at least 8 mi. from town though decent. Cannery workers practice renegade camping closer to town along the Indian River and Gavon Hill trails. Sitka also has 20 **B&Bs** from $40 per night. The visitors bureau lists rates and numbers. The youth hostel is probably your budget's best bet.

Sitka Youth Hostel (HI-AYH), 303 Kimshan St., Box 2645 (747-8356). In the United Methodist Church at Edgecumbe and Kimshan St. Find the McDonald's 1 mi. out of town on Halibut Point Rd. and walk 25 yd. up Peterson St. to Kimshan. 20 cots, kitchen facilities, VCR with several movies, and a worn pool table. Sleeping bags required. Free showers. Lockout 9:30am-6pm but enforcement is lax. Will store packs during the day. Curfew 11pm. 3 day max. stay. $7, nonmembers $10. Open June-Aug.

Sitka Hotel, 118 Lincoln St. (747-3288; fax 747-8499). Posh lobby. A great bet if you're not into the hosteling scene. Rooms with shared baths $40 single, $50 double, but fill quickly. Private baths $10 extra, mini-kitchens $10 extra. Free local calls, cable TV, laundry facilities. Reserve 3 weeks in advance and request a view.

Abner's B&B, 200 Seward St. (747-8779). Clean, pleasant room in a modest house listed on the National Register of Historic Places. One min. from the heart of downtown. Full breakfast. Friendly, liberal hosts. Single $40. Double $50.

Starrigaven Creek Campground, at the end of Halibut Point Rd., 1mi. from the ferry terminal, 8mi. from town. A Forest Service campground. 32 sites for tents and RVs. Water, pit toilets, picnic shelter. Secluded sites, good fishing from shore. Near a scenic estuary trail. 14-day max. stay. No access after 10pm. Sites $8. Reserve for an additional $7.50 by calling the Forest Service at 800-280-2267.

Sawmill Creek Campground, 8½ mi. south of town. Take Halibut Point Rd. to Sawmill Creek Rd. junction in Sitka. Follow Sawmill Creek Rd. to pulp mill, then take the left spur for 1.4 mi. Unmaintained 10-unit campground. Picnic tables, fireplaces, pit toilets. Great scenery and decent fishing in nearby Blue Lake. Quiet hours 10pm-6am. 14-day max. stay. Free.

FOOD

Restaurants in town are frustratingly expensive. Splurge, or fend for yourself at **Lakeside Grocery,** 705 Halibut Point Rd. (747-3317; open daily 6am-midnight). You can pick up fresh seafood along the docks or at **Seafood Producers Coop,** at 507 Katlian Ave. (747-5811). Halibut and salmon run $2-3 per lb. (open daily, 9am-5pm). Good bulk food and snacks are available at **Evergreen Natural Foods,** 101 American Way (747-6944), where 1lb. of granola runs $2.50 (open Mon.-Fri. 9am-6pm, Sat. 10am-5pm).

Channel Club, 2906 Halibut Point Rd. (747-9916), 3 mi. from downtown. Call from town or the hostel for a courtesy van. The restaurant every Sitkan recommends. Crowded with locals and informed tourists who ignore the unremarkable decor and concentrate on their food. Fantastic salad bar with over 30 individual salads ($12), each a culinary delight. Open Sun.-Thurs. 5-10pm, Fri.-Sat. 5-11pm.

The Backdoor, 104 Barracks St. (747-8856), behind Old Harbour Books. An amiable coffee shop and popular hostelers' hangout, with attractive local art on display and unpredictable poetry readings. Some nights feature live accordion music. Double-shot 12oz. Buzzsaw (coffee with espresso) $2.25, big-ass cookies $1, scones $1. Open Mon.-Sat. 7am-5pm, but open frequently after hours.

The Bayview Restaurant, 407 Lincoln St. (747-5440), upstairs in the Bayview Trading Company. Upscale decor with yet another great view. Food is well-prepared, but portions are more modest than prices. Chow on *pirogies* (Russian dumplings with salad and borscht, $7.50). More than 25 variations on the hamburger theme. Open Mon.-Sat. 6:30am-8pm, Sun. 6:30am-3pm; winter Mon.-Sat. 7am-8pm, Sun. 7:30am-2pm.

King Fisher Café in the Totem Square building at 201 Katlian (747-4888). An otherwise unremarkable coffee shop distinguishes itself with a grilled focaccia sandwich filled with tasty meats and cheeses. Open Mon.-Fri. 7am-5pm, Sat. 9am-4pm.

The Pioneer Bar (747-3456) on Katlian St. is clearly the nightspot of choice for both permanent and transient Sitkans. Photos of fishing boats line the walls and long-hairs and rednecks mix easily. (Domestic beer $2.75, imports $3.25, Alaska Amber on tap $4 per pint; open Mon.-Sat. 8am-2am, Sun. noon-2am.)

SIGHTS, EVENTS, AND ENTERTAINMENT

Sitka is one of the few cities in the Southeast whose indoor attractions are more than just an excuse to get out of the rain. The onion-domed **St. Michael's Cathedral,** built in 1848 by Bishop Innocent, is a reminder of Sitka's Slavic heritage. The cathedral was rebuilt in 1966 after a fire claimed the original structure. Today haunting icons gleam on its walls along with neo-Baroque paintings from a movement supported by Catherine the Great. Services are open to the public and are conducted in English, Tlingit, and Old Slavonic. ($1 donation; hours vary with cruise ship schedules, generally open Mon.-Sat. 11am-3pm., Sun. noon-3pm.)

Two blocks down Lincoln St. is the meticulously refurbished **Russian Bishop's House,** one of four remaining Russian colonial buildings in America. Upstairs is a magnificent chapel dedicated to the Annunciation of the Virgin Mary and adorned with beautiful gold and silver icons. (Free; photography is allowed; open 8:30am-4:30pm, tours every ½hr. except 12:30pm; call 747-6281 for tour reservations.) At the east end of Lincoln St., **Castle Hill,** at one time the site of Baranov's Castle, the seat of Russian administration in Alaska, and Tlingit forts, provides an accessible and stunning view of the cathedral and the Sound (open daily 6am-10pm).

The **Sheldon-Jackson Museum** (747-8981), on the tidy Sheldon-Jackson College campus at the east end of Lincoln St., is one of Alaska's best museums for Native artifacts and history. The collections date back to the 1880s and represent Athabascan, Aleut, Inuit, and Northwest Coast artistic styles. Displays include costumes, weaponry, and stunning argillite carvings. Pull-out drawers hold Inuit children's toys and the raven helmet worn by Chief Katlean, the Tlingit hero in the 1804 battle. Give yourself a good hour here. ($3, free with student ID; open daily 8am-5pm.)

The broken cone of **Mt. Edgecumbe** dominates the view across Sitka Sound. Dormant for 11,000 years, the volcano was the site of an infamous prank by an eccentric millionaire. About 20 years ago, a huge pile of burning tires was dumped into the crater and spewed clouds of dense black smoke, nearly causing the town's evacuation. The offender was fined.

The manicured trails of the **Sitka National Historic Park,** a.k.a. "Totem Park" (747-6281), lie a few minutes' walk down Lincoln St., ½ mi. east of St. Michael's. The trails pass by 15 masterfully replicated totems placed along the shoreline among old-growth trees. At one end of the 1-mi. loop stands the site of the **Tlingit Fort,** where the hammer-wielding chief Katlean almost held off the Russians in the battle for Sitka in 1804. The park **visitors center** offers an audio-visual presentation of the battle and the opportunity to watch traditional artists at work in the **Southeast Alaskan Native American Cultural Center** (747-8061; open daily 8am-5pm). Demonstrations include woodcarving, silver carving, costume making and weaving.

The **Alaska Raptor Rehabilitation Center** (747-8662), on Sawmill Creek Rd., has a fantastic collection of recovering bald eagles and owls. On most summer days when ships are in town, there are guided tours for $10. Schedule varies; call ahead to confirm (open daily 8am-5pm and with cruise ships).

The June **Sitka Summer Music Festival** ranks as one of the state's most popular events and draws world-renowned musicians to play chamber music. The concerts, held in the Centennial Building on Tuesday, Friday, and some Saturday evenings, can be crowded. Reservations are a good idea. Rehearsals, however, are free and rarely crowded. (All shows $14, under 18 $7; order tickets by calling 277-4852 or 747-6774; send a request to the Sitka Summer Music Festival, P.O. Box 3333; or stop by MacDonald's Bayview Trading Co., 407 Lincoln St., open Mon.-Fri. noon-1pm and 4:30-6pm, Sat. 1-3pm; contact the visitors bureau at 747-8601 for information.)

If you're in town in October, check out the **Alaska Day** celebrations which mark the sale of Alaska to the U.S. on Oct. 18, 1867 (it's a statewide holiday). Castle Hill is the site of a reenactment of the transfer ceremony, which takes place at 3pm. A road race, the Baranof Ball, concerts, teas, a parade, and beard-judging contests (men are encouraged to cultivate circa 1867-style facial hair) are among the highlights.

OUTDOORS

The Sitka area offers excellent **hiking** opportunities. Rain gear and a copy of *Sitka Trails* (pick up at the forest service information booth or office) will prove invaluable on almost any hike. **Gavin Hill** provides relatively easy access to sensational views of the Sound. The trailhead is near downtown, at the end of Baranof St. While steep, the majority of the 2500-ft. ascent is a boardwalk trail and the three to four-hour climb is pleasant. The ridge along the top leads to **Harbor Mountain.** A road also goes almost all the way to the top of the peak, so you can avoid backtracking by arranging a ride back down in advance. The Harbor Mountain trailhead is about 10 mi. from downtown on Harbor Mountain Rd. Bring along lots of water, since little is available along either trail.

Play Indiana Jones as you bushwhack through **Mount Verstovia Trail,** which provides challenging access to incredible panoramas. You will encounter numerous trees laying across the trail and a multitude of unmarked paths. The shoulder of Mt. Verstovia is about 2½ mi. along the route, although you can continue on farther to the actual peak. This route is hard work and not particularly safe (do not take it alone), but it is a rewarding challenge. The trailhead is about 2 mi. east of town right next to Rookie's Sports Bar and Grill on Sawmill Creek Hwy. The sign has long since been overgrown by trees; just look for a little bridge to the left of the building.

A great rainy day hike is the gentle and intimately beautiful **Indian River Trail,** a 5½ mi. riverside trek to the base of Indian River Falls. Follow the main gravel road for about ¾ mi. until you reach a blue pump house. From there, the trail branches off into the old growth forest and meanders through muskeg and tall trees alongside the clear pools of the Indian River. The rocky Three Sisters Mountains occasionally come into view, as do spawning salmon in early fall. The trail gains about 250 ft. in elevation; plan on a four to five-hour roundtrip.

The forest service also maintains a number of **remote trails** in the Sitka region, most accessible only by boat or floatplane, and many leading to **wilderness cabins** ($25 per night). Perhaps the most striking of these is the **Mt. Edgecumbe Trail**, a full-day (8-12hr.), 6.7-mi. one-way clamber to the summit crater of Sitka's dormant volcano. The trailhead lies behind Fred's Creek Cabin, a half-hour skiff journey from Sitka. A shelter for exhausted hikers sits 3 mi. up the trail. The end of the hike offers stunning views of the Sitka region and of red volcanic ash covering the ground. Contact the forest service (see above) for complete lists of remote trails and cabins.

In addition to kayak and bicycle rental services, over 30 **charter operators** vie to separate you from Sitka and your money. **Bare Island Charters,** 709 Lincoln St. (747-4900), charges $80 per person for a half-day wildlife-watching journey. **Sitka Secrets,** 500 Lincoln St. #641 (747-5089), offers a comparable full-day service for $160 per person. Contact the visitors bureau for a complete list of operators.

NORTHERN PANHANDLE

■ Tenakee Springs

Vacationing can be hard work and this is bad. Vacationing in Tenakee Springs is not hard work and this is good. Life is easier at a slower pace and Tenakee residents have mastered the art of living slowly. The population hovers around 100 and is a mix of fishermen and loggers, retired and vacationing professionals, artists, and counterculture loyalists. The community sincerely welcomes visitors, even those heavy in pack and light in wallet. Tenakee's main street is a dirt path beside a row of houses along the shore of Tenakee Inlet. An oil delivery truck and a fire truck make rare appearances as the only automobiles in town. The city provides no water, sewer, or sanitation services—hence the outhouses extending out over the beach.

Practical Information To get to the **library** (736-2248), which is located in the same building as the **city office** (736-2207), take a left from the ferry, continue about ¼ mi., and enter the big wooden building on your right (open Tues., Thurs., and Sat. 11am-3pm). Check out the decent selection of "trade 'em" paperbacks. The **post office** (736-2236; open from Mon.-Fri., 8am-noon and 12:30-4:30pm, Sat. 8am-noon) has a **General Delivery ZIP Code** (99841). The **area code** is 907.

Tenakee is on Chichagof Island. **Bring cash.** There are **no banks** on this island and no one accepts credit cards. Residents value their isolation and are adamantly opposed to forest service proposals to construct a road link with neighboring **Hoonah.** The state ferry *LeConte* makes a half-to one-hour stopover in Tenakee on its route between Juneau and Sitka. About one hour is all you'll need to survey the town, but a day's stay is worth it if the ferry schedule allows. The one-way fare to Tenakee from either Sitka or Juneau is $22. For more scheduling flexibility, both **Loken Aviation** (736-2306 or 800-478-3360) and **Wings of Alaska** (736-2247) fly from Juneau six or seven days a week ($60-65 one way).

The Hot Spring Tenakee's namesake, a natural sulfuric hot spring that feeds the public bath house, is the town's epicenter. Miners and fishermen have been soaking out their aches and worries in these therapeutic 106°F (41°C) waters for more than a century and the Tlingit maintained a winter settlement at the spring long before European conquest. Since few homes have showers, this is where most of modern Tenakee's retirees and urban refugees take their daily baths.

You won't find this small, unglamorous yellow bathhouse on any postcards. It sits at the end of the ferry dock and, if you're ambitious, you can even get in a good soaking during a layover—assuming that members of your gender happen to be bathing at the time. Men and women have separate bathing hours (men 2-6pm and 10pm-9am, women 9am-2pm and 6-10pm), largely because bathers are required to be nude. They are also required to be clean before entering, so bring your soap. The bath is free, but donations are welcome at Snyder Mercantile across the street.

To reach an even higher plane of relaxation, follow the bath with a visit to **Moon Feather Therapeutic Massage,** P.O. Box 44. Diane Ziel runs this business out of her home just around the corner from the bath beside the Blue Moon Café. Sign up for appointments on her door (½hr. $20, 1hr. $35, 1½hr. $50).

Accommodations, Camping, and Food   There are exactly two places to stay in town and one of them has a price tag in the thousands (for a week). The only affordable option is to rent one of six available cabins from **Snyder Mercantile** (736-2205). The smaller, more basic cabins sleep one to two people comfortably (from $40). A larger cabin sleeps four to five people (from $45). Both have outhouses and cooking facilities; bring your own towels and bedding. A $65 cabin sleeps seven, with carpet, fireplaces, and (a rare find in Tenakee) a flush toilet. Reservations are essential in summer. (Local, regional, and international art is on display and for sale next door to Snyder's at **The Shamrock.** Hours are posted monthly and accommodate most ferry visits.) The more adventurous can brave the bears (Chichagof Island has about one bear per sq. mi.; only Admiralty Island has a denser population) and head for the woods. Walking from the ferry dock to town, a right turn on the dirt path points you east. After about ¾ mi. walking east, the path leads into a wooded area with several free, primitive **campsites.** Another ¾ mi. along the trail, the free **Indian River Campground** provides tent sites, a shelter, and a picnic table beside the Indian River, a spot favored by bears in summer.

Other than the berries along the main path, food in Tenakee can be difficult to find. Snyder Mercantile stocks a decent supply of groceries including vegetables and fruit flown in weekly (open Mon.-Sat. 9am-noon and 1-5pm, Sun. 9am-2pm). A great bet for breakfast or lunch is **The Bakery** (736-2262) in the Shamrock, which offers great cinnamon rolls ($2) and fresh bread ($2 for small loaves), as well as a variable lunch menu (open daily 8am-2pm). The **Blue Moon Café,** unassuming as it may appear, is a Tenakee institution. If Rosie is there, and if she feels like cooking, try the french fries. Ham and eggs are $7.25, a chicken dinner, $8.50. Arrange in advance for anything other than a cheeseburger; Rosie needs time to thaw her ingredients.

Sights and Outdoors   Tenakee's only street extends several mi. in either direction from town and is closed off to motor vehicles after a short distance. To the west the street leads along the water past a communal saw mill and small homesteads lying farther and farther apart. Tread carefully around private land here; not everyone loves wanderers. Several mi. from town the path turns out onto the shore of the inlet, where silver salmon leap from the water in midsummer and smooth rocks make good footing for an extended walk along the beach. Avoid shore walks in town; outhouses and garbage make the beach unappealing. To the east, the wide beach may make for better walking than the faint path that parallels the shore through the woods.

An excellent **paddling** adventure begins in Hoonah and follows the long inlet of Port Frederick back to its end. From there, a 100-yd. portage leads to the upper region of Tenakee Inlet. Paddlers can explore the unbroken shores and hidden coves of the inlet on their way out to Tenakee Springs. The 40-mi. trip could also be made in the reverse direction, but the hot springs are probably best savored at the end. **Mother Truckers** (736-2323) will rent bicycles ($20) and kayaks (single: ½-day $40, full day $65; double: ½-day $50, full day $75; open daily 8am-5pm). Or, rent a kayak in Juneau and bring it over on the ferry for $9.

For **chartered expeditions** to fish, view wildlife, and learn the intricacies of the inlet from someone who has been on the water around Tenakee all his life, contact

Jason Carter (736-2311). Jason runs ½-day and full-day trips as well as transporting kayaks, all for reasonable prices.

■ Juneau

In October 1880, in a move he probably regretted later, Tlingit Chief Kowee led Joe Juneau and Richard Harris to the gleaming "mother lode" in the hills up from Gold Creek. The next summer would bring boatloads of prospectors to dig in the mines. Harris's irritating habit of staking multiple claims extended to his desire for the town's name, but angry miners vetoed "Harrisburg."

Juneau today is arguably the most spectacular capital city in the United States. Victorian mansions crowd against log cabins, and hulking state office buildings compete for space with simple frame houses. Monolithic Mt. Juneau looms large over the city. Accessible only by water and air, Juneau thankfully retains a small-town friendliness, and has avoided the urban sprawl that plagues Anchorage.

The tourist industry, however, has no problem making its presence felt. Juneau is the second busiest cruise ship port in the U.S. (after Miami), and downtown is often filled with souvenir-hungry tourists.

PRACTICAL INFORMATION AND ORIENTATION

Visitors Information: Davis Log Cabin Visitors Center, 134 3rd St., Juneau 99801 (586-2201 or 586-2284; fax 586-6304), at Seward St. Excellent source for pamphlets on walking tours, sights, and natural wonders. Open Mon.-Fri. 8:30am-5pm, Sat.-Sun. 9am-5pm; Oct.-May Mon.-Fri. 8:30am-5pm. **National Forest and National Park Services,** 101 Egan Dr. (586-8751), at Willoughby, in Centennial Hall. Helpful staff and extensive pamphlets provide info on hiking and fishing in the Juneau area, as well as info on, and reservations for, Forest Service **cabins** in **Tongass National Forest.** Also pick up a copy of the valuable *Juneau Trails* booklet ($4) listing many 5-12 mi. hikes. Free, informative 20-min. films on 16 topics, from wildlife to Glacier Bay, shown upon request. Open daily in summer 8am-5pm; winter Mon.-Fri. 8am-5pm.

Fishing Licenses: Alaska Dept. of Fish and Game (465-4112; licensing 465-2376). **Fishing Information Hotline** (465-4116). Up-to-date reports on weather, seasons, and fish locations.

Airport: Juneau International Airport, 9 mi. north of Juneau on Glacier Hwy. Served by Alaska Air, Delta Airlines, and local charters. **Alaska Airlines** (789-0600 or 800-426-0333), on S. Franklin St. at 2nd St., in the Baranov Hotel. To: Anchorage ($99-222), Sitka ($87), Ketchikan ($124), and Gustavus ($65). Open Mon.-Fri. 8:30am-5pm. Check the Davis Log Cabin Visitors Center for schedules and routes of all airlines. **Island Waterways** provides transportation to downtown if you don't feel like dealing with the bus ($7, $12 roundtrip).

Buses: Capital Transit (789-6901). From downtown to Douglas, the airport, and Mendenhall Glacier, Mon.-Sat. 7am-10:30pm, Sun. 9am-5:30pm. Hourly express service downtown, Mon.-Fri. 8:30am-6pm. The closest stop to the ferry is at Auke Bay, 1½ mi. from the terminal. Fare $1.25; drivers cannot make change. **Schedules** available at municipal building, library, Davis Log Cabin, and on buses. **MGT Ferry Express** (789-5460). Meets all ferries and runs to downtown hotels or airport ($5). Call between 6-8pm a day in advance to reserve a ride from any major hotel to the airport or ferry (whether you're staying at a hotel or not). Rides $5. From the hostel, the Baranov is the closest hotel. Also offers a 2½-hr. guided tour of Mendenhall Glacier ($12.50). Tour times vary; call ahead.

Ferries: Alaska Marine Highway, 1591 Glacier Ave., P.O. Box 25535, Juneau 99802-5535 (800-642-0066 or 465-3941; fax 277-4829). Ferries dock at the Auke Bay terminal 14 mi. from the city on the Glacier Hwy. To: Bellingham, WA ($226), Ketchikan ($74), Sitka ($26), and Haines ($20). Lockers (25¢ for 48hr.) are limited and fill quickly.

Taxis: Capital Cab (586-2772) and **Taku Taxi** (586-2121). Both run a 1-hr. charter to Mendenhall Glacier for about $45, to the ferry about $25. Exact services differ slightly; both let you split charter cost. Call and inquire.

Car Rental: Rent-A-Wreck, 9099 Glacier Hwy. (789-4111), next to the airport. $30 per day with 100 free mi. plus 15¢ per extra mi. Must be at least 21 with a credit card or piles of cash.

Bike Rental: Mountain Gears, 210 N. Franklin St. (586-4327). Mountain bikes $6 per hr., $25 for 24hr. Prices include helmet and lock. Open Mon.-Fri. 10am-6pm, Sat. 10am-5pm. Call to find out about informal group rides or for advice on area trails. **Cycle Alaska** (364-3377) will deliver a bike to your door. $30 for an 8-hr. day. Also rent from the depot on Marine Way across from Marine Park (open 9am-4pm daily).

Kayak Rental: Juneau Outdoor Center (586-8220), on Douglas Island. Will deliver kayaks anywhere in Juneau. Single $35 per day, double $45. Experience required, but instruction happily provided.

Camping Equipment: Foggy Mountain Shop, 134 N. Franklin St. (586-6780), at 2nd. High-quality, expensive gear. Open Mon.-Sat. 9am-6pm. Less expensive equipment is available at **Western Auto** (780-4909), 3 mi. toward the ferry terminal on Lemon Creek Rd., 300 yd. off the Glacier Hwy. Open Mon.-Fri. 7am-9pm, Sat. 7am-8pm, Sun. 7am-7pm.

Luggage Storage: At the hostel (free if you're staying there, otherwise $1 per bag). Lockers at the ferry terminal (see above). Also try the counter at the **Alaskan Hotel** (see below). In theory they charge $1.56 (includes tax) per bag, but they'll often store them for free. 24hr. access.

Bookstore: Big City Books, 100 N. Franklin St. (586-2130). Open Mon.-Fri. 9am-8pm, Sat. 9am-6pm, Sun. 10am-6pm. **The Observatory,** 235 2nd St. (586-9676). A used and rare bookstore with many **maps** and prints. Open Mon.-Fri. 10am-5:30pm, Sat. noon-5:30pm; winter Mon.-Sat. noon-5:30pm.

Library: 586-5249, over the parking garage at Admiral Way and S. Franklin St. It's worth coming up just for the views and a great stained-glass window. Open Mon.-Thurs. 11am-9pm, Fri.-Sun. noon-5pm. The **State Library** and the **Alaska Historical Library** hold large collections of early Alaskan photographs. Both are on the 8th floor of the State Office Building and are open Mon.-Fri. 9am-5pm.

Currency Exchange: Thomas Cook, 127 N. Franklin. (586-5688). Open Mon.-Fri. 9am-5:30pm, Sat. 10am-4pm, Sun. 10am-2pm.

Laundromat: The Dungeon Laundrette (586-2805), at 4th and Franklin St. Wash $1.50, dry $1.50. Open daily 8am-8pm. Also at the **hostel** (see below): wash $1.25, dry 75¢.

Public Showers: The Alaskan Hotel (see below), $3.12.

Events Hotline: 586-5866.

Weather: 586-3997.

Pharmacy: Juneau Drug Co., 202 Front St. (586-1233). Open Mon.-Fri. 9am-9pm, Sat. 9am-6pm, Sun. 10am-7pm.

Suicide Prevention Hotline: 586-4357.

HIV/AIDS Information and Counseling: AIDS Helpline (800-478-2437). **Alaskans Living With HIV** (463-5688), on N. Franklin St. Upstairs from Heritage Coffee. Provides conversation and information. Friendly gay staffers will also provide advice on being gay in Juneau. Open Mon.-Fri. 8am-4pm.

Gay/Lesbian Information: Southeast Alaska Gay and Lesbian Alliance (586-GAYS/4297). 24hr. hotline.

Hospital: Bartlett Memorial (586-2611), 3½ mi. north off Glacier Hwy.

Emergency and Ambulance: 911. **Police:** 210 Admiral Way (586-2780), near Marine Park. Visitors can pick up a permit here to allow 48-hr. **parking** in a 1hr. zone. Open for permits Mon.-Fri. 8am-4:30pm.

Post Office: Main Office, 709 W. 9th St. (586-7987). Open Mon.-Fri. 9am-5pm, Sat. 6am-3pm for parcel pick-up only. **ZIP Code:** 99801. A **Substation** (586-2214) for outgoing mail is located at 221 S. Seward St. Open Mon.-Fri. 9:30am-5pm, Sat. 9:30am-2pm.

Area Code: 907.

Juneau sits on the Gastineau Channel opposite Douglas Island, 650 mi. southeast of Anchorage and 900 mi. northwest of Seattle. Franklin St. is the main street down-

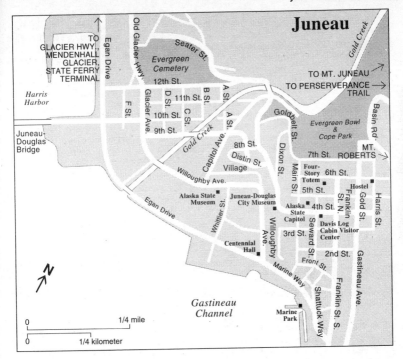

town. **Glacier Hwy.** connects downtown, the airport, the residential area of the Mendenhall Valley, and the ferry terminal.

ACCOMMODATIONS AND CAMPING

The few establishments aside from the hostel that have semi-affordable options have them in very limited quantities, so phone ahead. One of the best sources for rooms is the **Alaska Bed and Breakfast Association,** P.O. Box 3/6500 #169, Juneau 99802 (586-2959), which can help you find a room downtown from $65. Less convenient locations start around $55. While the forest service offers two great campgrounds, neither are easily accessible without a car.

Juneau International Hostel (HI-AYH), 614 Harris St. (586-9559), at 6th atop a steep hill. A beautiful facility in a prime location with an astoundingly rigid management. The minutes till morning lockout are barked out at regular intervals and chores are assigned rather than selected. Not bad enough to justify the extra money to stay elsewhere, but be prepared. Kitchen available 7-8:30am and 5-10:30pm. Common area with comfy couches. Coin-op laundry (wash $1.25, dry 75¢); small charges for sheets, towels, soap, and detergent. Strict lockout from 9am-5pm and non-negotiable 11pm curfew. All 48 beds $10. Frequently fills, but you can make reservations with a $10 deposit mailed in advance. They don't take phone reservations. 3-day max. stay if they're full.

Inn at the Waterfront, 455 S. Franklin (586-2050), over the Summit Restaurant. Don't be scared off by the classy looking restaurant downstairs—this place was once a Gold Rush brothel. 14 clean, comfortable rooms. A few have shared bath and go for $51 single, $60 double. Continental breakfast included.

Alaskan Hotel, 167 Franklin St. (586-1000 or 800-327-9347 from the lower 48). A very handsome hotel built of dark wood, right in the center of downtown. Has been meticulously restored to original 1913 decor. Bar on 1st floor features live tunes and dancing. Rent your own hot tub with a radio for $10.40 per hr. noon-

4pm, $20.80 per hr. 4pm-2am. Free luggage storage for guests. Laundry ($1 wash, $1 dry). Kitchenettes and TVs available. Singles $55, with bath $70. Doubles $65, with bath $80. Rates lower in winter.

Mendenhall Lake Campground, on Montana Creek Rd. Take Glacier Hwy. north 9 mi. to Mendenhall Loop Rd.; continue 3½ mi. and take the right fork. If asked, bus driver will let you off within walking distance (2 mi.) of camp (7am-10:30pm only). About 6 mi. from ferry terminal. View of the glacier, with trails that can take you even closer. 60 sites. Fireplaces, water, pit toilet, picnic tables, free firewood. 14-day max. stay. Sites $8, Golden Age $4. Reserve for an extra $7.50 by calling 800-280-CAMP/2267.

Auke Village Campground, on Glacier Hwy., 15 mi. from Juneau. Near a scenic beach. 1½ mi. west of ferry terminal. 12 sites. Fireplaces, water, flush toilets, picnic tables. No reservations. 14-day max. stay. Sites $8, Golden Age $4.

FOOD

Juneau accommodates seekers of anything from fresh salmon to filet-o'-fish sandwiches. The **Juneau A&P Market,** 631 Willoughby Ave. (586-3101; fax 586-6775), near the Federal Building, is one of the best grocery stores in the region, with a terrific salad bar ($3.29 per lb.), and big deli sandwiches ($3.39; open daily 24hr.). Find costlier health-food items at **Rainbow Foods** (586-6476), at 2nd and Seward St. (open Mon.-Fri. 10am-7pm, Sat. 10am-6pm, Sun. noon-6pm). The corner of Front St. and Seward is home to Juneau's fast food huts.

Armadillo Tex-Mex Café, 431 S. Franklin St. (586-1880). Fantastic food. Always packed with locals and tourists alike. Authentic Southwest paintings and a few kitschy plastic armadillos make this one of the few Tex-Mex places not decorated by Plastic Sombreros, Inc. Hunker down to a heaping plateful of T. Terry's nachos ($8). The *chalupa,* a corn tostada heaped with chicken, beans, guacamole, and cheese, goes for $8. Two enchiladas $6. Excellent free chips and salsa. Open Mon.-Sat. 11am-10pm, Sun. 4-10pm.

Fiddlehead Restaurant and Bakery, 429 W. Willoughby Ave. (586-3150), ½ block from the State Museum. Fern-ishings for affluent sprout-lovers. Salads, seafood, exquisite desserts, and fresh Alaskan sourdough. Great sandwiches and burgers on fiddlehead buns with soup or salad $7-10. Open daily 6:30am-10pm, winter until 9pm. The **Fireweed Room** upstairs serves more expensive fare with evening jazz in the summer. Pay a $5 cover just to listen. Open daily 6-10pm.

Channel Bowl Café (586-6139), across from Juneau A&P on Willoughby Ave. A small spot with blaring blues and professional thespians manning the grill. A spirited, sometimes manic stopping place for hip locals and ferry castaways. Try the pancakes with berries, pecans, and real maple syrup ($5.50) or "cheeburg" ($6). Breakfast served "as long as we're vertical." Open daily 7am-2pm.

Heritage Coffee Co., 174 S. Franklin St. (586-1087). A popular place to escape for an hour or two from Juneau's often wet and tourist-ridden streets. Easygoing staff assembles large sandwiches ($6.25) and pours excellent cups of coffee (espresso $1, cappuccino $1.75). Open Mon.-Fri. 6:30am-7pm, Sat.-Sun. 7am-6pm.

Thane Ore House Salmon Bake, 4400 Thane Rd. (586-3442). A few mi. outside of town, but "Mr. Ore" will pick you up at your hotel. All-you-can-eat salmon, halibut, ribs, and fixings ($18.50). Open May-Sept. daily 11:30am-9pm.

SIGHTS

The **Alaska State Museum,** 395 Whittier St. (465-2901), leads you through the history, ecology, and culture of Alaska's four major indigenous groups (Tlingit, Athabascan, Aleut, and Inuit) with excellent exhibits. The museum also houses the famous "First White Man" totem pole, a carved likeness of Abraham Lincoln. ($3, seniors and students free; open Mon.-Fri. 9am-6pm, Sat.-Sun. 10am-6pm; Sept. 18-May 17 Tues.-Sat. 10am-4pm.) The **Juneau-Douglas City Museum,** 114 W. 4th St. (586-3572), has displays on mining, hand-woven quilts, and traditional crafts. ($1, students and children free; open Mon.-Fri. 9am-5pm, Sat.-Sun. 11am-5pm; winter Thurs.-Sat. noon-4:30pm; closed Jan.-Feb.)

The **House of Wickersham,** 213 7th St. (586-9001), was home to one of Alaska's founding fathers, Judge James Wickersham. As a U.S. District Court judge, Wickersham steamed and sledded around Alaska to oversee a region extending from Fort Yukon to the Aleutian Islands when he wasn't busy founding the Alaska Railroad, establishing the University of Alaska, or pushing for statehood ($2; open May 15-Oct. 1 daily 9am-4pm).

The hexagonal, onion-domed 1894 **St. Nicholas Russian Orthodox Church** on 5th St. between N. Franklin and Gold St. holds rows of icons and a glorious altar. Services, held Saturday at 6am and Sunday at 10am, are conducted in English, Old Slavonic, and Tlingit. Tours are open to the public ($1 donation requested; open daily 9am-5pm). The **State Office Building** (the S.O.B.) on Willoughby has an 8th-floor **observation platform** overlooking Douglas Island and the channel. A large atrium on the same floor contains a totem pole and a pipe organ fired up for a free **concert** every Friday afternoon.

If you're visiting town between mid-July and September, trek to **Gastineau Salmon Hatchery** (463-5113 or 463-4810), 2697 Channel Dr. off Egan Dr. When the salmon are running, thousands pack into the spawning ladder. While the most impressive spectacle and a brief talk are both available outside for free, you have to pay $2.75 ($1 for children) for access to the small aquarium inside. (Open Mon.-Fri. 10am-6pm, Sat.-Sun. noon-5pm.)

While you're in the neighborhood, head farther to the **Alaska Brewing Co.,** 5429 Shaune Dr. (780-5866). The company offers free tours complete with a free sample of its excellent award-winning brews. Given the price of beer in Alaska, it's hard to turn down the free samples. Thursday and Friday are bottling days with the most to see. To reach the brewery, take the hourly city bus to Lemon Creek, turn onto Anka Rd. from the Glacier Hwy., and Shaune Dr. is the first on the right. (Tours available on the ½-hr. Tues.-Sat. 11am-4:30pm; Oct.-April Thurs.-Sat. 11am-4:30pm.)

ENTERTAINMENT

The doors swing and the cash registers ring at the **Red Dog Saloon,** 278 S. Franklin (463-9954). Juneau's most popular tourist trap hosts live music on weekends. In the winter, locals return to their customary stools between walls lined with bear pelts and money ("tourist pelts"). Beer will set you back $3.50-4.50 (open Sun.-Thurs. 10am-midnight, Fri.-Sat. 10am-1am; off-season Sun.-Thurs. noon-midnight, Fri.-Sat. noon-1am). The **Alaskan Hotel,** 167 Franklin St., hosts frequent live Cajun and blues and manages to retain its local crowd year-round despite the shocking cost of beer. (Bar open daily noon-midnight; bands start playing at 9pm.) The gay-friendly **Penthouse** (463-4141), on the 4th floor of the Senate Building, features a dance floor and flocks of hard-partying young people. (Must be 21; $2 cover on the weekends; open Sun.-Thurs. 9pm-1am, Fri.-Sat. 9pm-3am.)

Two new establishments have added even more options to Juneau's happenin' nightlife. **The Galleon Bar,** 544 S. Franklin (586-4712), is a huge ship subtly disguised as a bar. Eight draft beers are on tap for $4 per pint. Nightly music, including blues, reggae, and an open mic night, guarantee an entertaining night at sea (open 11am to "the wee hours"). **The Hanger on the Wharf** on Marine Way is the current youth magnet, and offers a huge selection of micro-brews and great views of the Channel. (Open Mon. 4-11pm, Tues.-Wed. 11:30am-11pm, Thurs.-Sun. 11:30am-1am.) Catch the latest blockbusters at the **20th Century Theater** downtown at 222 Front St. or **The Glacier Cinema** in Mendenhall Valley at 9091 Cinema Dr. Both theaters have two nightly shows and weekend matinees. Check a paper or call 463-FLIX/3549 for information.

ALASKA

A Stellar Money-Spending Opportunity

Everywhere you go in Alaska, you will find tour companies who want your money. Don't pass up a tour of **Tracy Arm** simply because you don't wish to subsidize another crackpot tour operation. The $99 you spend on a tour is one of the best investments you can make in Alaska. If you can come up with the funds to get to the region, you owe it to yourself to take the trip. Fondly known as **"the poor man's Glacier Bay,"** Tracy Arm offers much of the same spectacular beauty and wildlife as its cousin at well under half the cost. On a typical day, you can count on seeing humpback and killer whales (about 75% of the time), hundreds of seals, bald eagles, and an assortment of other furred or wingèd critters. Even if you don't see a single animal, the trip is incredible. It passes by the **Sawyer Glaciers,** which frequently calve large chunks of ice into the sea. If you don't catch them in the act, you can still admire the massive icebergs glowing blue in the water.

Three primary tour companies offer these eight and a half-hour cruises. The biggest of these is **Auk Nu Tours** (800-820-2628), 76 Egan Dr. The tour is cheap ($99), but the huge boats and resulting impersonality might detract from the joy of an included free lunch. **Bird's Eye Charters** (790-2510), whose small boats take only 16 passengers, is on the opposite end of the spectrum. $140 buys you breakfast, lunch, snacks, and all the personal attention and friendliness money can buy. The happy medium lies near **Adventure Bound** (463-2509 or 800-228-3875), 245 Marine Way. Friendly owner Steve personally pilots a midsized boat with a maximum of 28 passengers. There's no free food, but reasonably priced snacks and simple sandwiches are available (probably best just to bring your own). The list price is $99 ($49 for those under 18), but they've been known to charge as little as $70 for advance reservations.

OUTDOORS

Juneau's trail system is the most extensive in the southeast, and undoubtedly one of the most spectacular in the state. If you're looking for the best view of Juneau and are willing to sweat for it, go to the end of 6th St. and head up the trail to the summit of **Mt. Roberts** (3576 ft.). It's a steep, 4-mi. climb, but worth it. Higher elevations reveal stunning, panoramic views up the Gastineau Channel and west toward the Pacific, as well as a look at nearby Mt. Juneau. The recent addition of a **tramway** means that you'll have to deal with many who didn't sweat for the view. The trams run every half hour from a terminal on the cruise ship dock (463-3412; $16).

A number of excellent trails start at the end of Basin Rd. The **Perseverance Trail,** which leads to the ruins of the Silverbowl Basin Mine and booming waterfalls, is one of the most popular. The **Granite Creek Trail** branches off the Perseverance Trail and follows its namesake to a beautiful basin 3.3 mi. from the trailhead. The summit of Mt. Juneau lies 3 mi. farther along the ridge and, predictably, offers terrific views. The shorter, steeper **Mt. Juneau Trail,** which departs from Perseverance Trail about 1 mi. from the trailhead, offers similar panoramas. The 9½-mi. **Montana Creek Trail,** near Mendenhall Glacier, is a local favorite. For more details on this and other area hikes, drop by the visitor center or any local bookstore to pick up *Juneau Trails,* published by the Alaska Natural History Association ($4). Rangers provide free copies of maps from this book at the Centennial Building (see **Practical Information**). Mountain biking is excellent but often restricted. Check with Mountain Gears (see **Practical Information**) for specifics. Whatever your mode of transport, be sure to keep the bears in mind.

In winter, the slopes of the **Eaglecrest Ski Area,** 155 S. Seward St., Juneau 99801 (586-5284 or 586-5330), on Douglas Island, offer decent alpine skiing. ($24 per day, children grades 7-12 $17, up to 6th grade $12; full equipment rental $20, children $14). The Eaglecrest ski bus departs from the Baranov Hotel at 8:30am and returns at 5pm on winter weekends and holidays (roundtrip to the slopes $6). In the summer, the Eaglecrest **"Alpine Summer"** trail is a good way to soak in the mountain scenery of virtually untouched Douglas Island.

The best excuse to spend $100 in town is on an incredible boat tour of **Tracy Arm.** It will without a doubt be one of the best days you spend in Alaska. However, if you've rented a kayak (see **Practical Information,** above) and want to go beyond Gastineau Channel, **Kayak Express,** 4107 Blackberry St. (780-4591) will drop you off and pick you up at Gustavus, Hoonah, or Port Adolphus for $210 (one way $125), or at Oliver's Inlet, Port Couverden, St. James Bay, or Funter Bay for $120 (one way $75). Other drop-off points can be arranged. **Alaska Discovery,** 5449 Shuane Dr. (780-6226 or 800-586-1911), provides both equipment and guides for its daily kayak trips through the inside passage north of Juneau ($125 per person, transport from downtown $18). If you prefer the skies, **Temsco Helicopters,** Juneau Airport (789-9501; fax 789-7989), offers a one-hour flight to the Mendenhall Glacier, including a one and a half-hour glacier landing ($142 per person).

■ Glacier Bay National Park

Glacier Bay National Park was once referred to by lesser known French explorer Jean François de Galaup as "perhaps the most extraordinary place in the world." Glacier Bay is indeed awe-inspiring. Massive crystal monoliths broken off from its namesake glaciers float peacefully in its fjords, while humpback whales glide through the icy blue depths. **Glacier Bay National Park** encloses 16 tidewater glaciers, and is backed by the Fairweather Mountains, the highest coastal range in the world. Charter flights, tours, and cruise ships all make the spectacular voyage into Glacier Bay, offering close-up views of glaciers, rookeries, whales, and seals. The Bay is divided into two inlets, Tarr and Muir, which extend westward and eastward, respectively. Tarr Inlet advances as far as the Grand Pacific and Margerie Glaciers, while Muir ends at the Muir and Riggs Glaciers.

Glacier Bay provides a rare opportunity to see geological and ecological processes radically compressed into a short time period. A mere two centuries ago, the **Grand Pacific Glacier** covered the entire region under a sheet of ancient ice. Severe earthquakes separated the glacier from its terminal moraine—the silt and debris that insulates advancing ice from the relatively warm seawater that surrounds it—and the glacier retreated 45 mi. in 150 years (somewhere approaching light speed in glacial term). As a result, the uncovered ground is virgin territory, colonized by pioneering vegetation, which visitors can observe progressing gradually up the bay.

Any visit to this park is expensive. **Air Excursions** (697-2376) flies one way to Gustavus from Juneau for $60, roundtrip $100. **Alaska Airlines** (800-426-0333) offers the same service for slightly less (with 7-day advance purchase, one way $49, roundtrip $98). **Auk-Nu Tours** (800-820-2628) runs a ferry service from Auke Bay, near Juneau. The beautiful route takes about two hours and costs $45 ($85 roundtrip). Gustavus is 6 mi. from Bartlett Cove, where information and accommodations cluster. A bus ride between the two sites costs $8. Anyone with time can enjoy the walk along shaded dirt roads. An **information center** (697-2230, winter 789-0097) is maintained by the park service in Bartlett Cove (open June-Sept. daily 9am-5:30pm; winter Mon.-Fri. 8am-4:30pm). Once at Bartlett Cove, backpackers can stay in the free campground, which has 25 sites and is rarely full. Sightings of humpback whales and orcas are common from the beach-level sites. Those without a tent can collapse in comfortable dorm beds at **Glacier Bay Lodge** (800-622-2042) for $28 a night. Reservations are advisable. **Puffin Travel, Inc.** (697-2260) runs a bed and breakfast and provides free bicycles, as well as transportation to and from the airport (cabins with private bath $85-125).

The only reasonably priced food in Glacier Bay comes from **Bear Track Mercantile** (697-2358), at the crossroads of Gustavus (open daily 9am-7pm). **Medical assistance** in the area can be found at the **Gustavus Community Clinic** (697-3008). In an **emergency,** dial 911. **Kayak Rental** is available at **Glacier Bay Sea Kayaks,** P.O. Box 26, Gustavus 99826 (697-2257). Double kayaks rent for $50 per day for one to three days,

$40 per day for five to nine days, and $35 per day for 10 days or more. The area is rapidly becoming one of the most popular places in the state for extended kayak trips.

There are several trails around Bartlett Cove, the most substantial of which is the 3-mi. **Park River Trail,** featuring frequent bear sightings. The lodge and information center offer several daily ranger-led walks and presentations. After having paid to reach Glacier Bay, however, you will likely crave the wild slopes and coves beyond Bartlett. Wilderness camping and hiking are permitted throughout the park. Tour-boat skippers drop passengers off at points designated by the Park Service; you'll have to arrange to be picked up later. The four drop-off areas, any three of which are open at most times, provide access to hiking and kayaking. Drop-off and pick-up, and an unavoidable but spectacular tour, cost $178 on the *Spirit of Adventure* (see below). Visitors should contact the **Glacier Bay National Park** at P.O. Box 140, Gustavus 99826 (697-2230) for assistance with planning a backcountry trip.

Seeing the most impressive part of the park, the **West Arm,** means taking a boat tour. Your best bet is to find a buddy with a thick billfold. The *Spirit of Adventure* is owned by the Glacier Bay Lodge (800-622-2042), next to Bartlett Cove, and offers six different **sightseeing packages** for the glaciers. They range in price and niceties from a $74, half-day whale-watching trip to a $379 package including flights to and from Juneau, a night at the B&B and an eight-hour glacier tour. Puffin Travel (see above) also operates a travel-booking service for sightseeing, fishing, photography tours, and other accommodations. For more information, write to Box 3-LG, Gustavus 99826. They also sell package trips, including a roundtrip flight or one way ferry and return trip by plane between Juneau and Gustavus, one night at the Puffin B&B, and a one-day tour of the park on the *Spirit of Adventure* ($333 per person for flight option; $318 for flight/ferry combo).

■ Haines

Haines occupies one of the most strikingly beautiful settings of any city on the Southeast Coast, with clear blue water, snow-covered coastal peaks, glaciers, sunny days, and breathtaking trails winding in and out of beaches, forests, and mountains. The area's star attraction arrives in late fall or early winter, when warm upwellings in the Chilkat River encourage an out-of-season salmon run that draws as many as 4000 bald eagles, more than double the town's human population, to the Chilkat Peninsula's "Council Grounds" for a feast.

Over the past twenty years, Haines's economy has shifted dramatically from timber, logging, and mining to tourism. The town has weathered the transition well. Haines relies on its natural beauty to support a flourishing outdoor recreation industry. While the town itself is friendly, it lacks the historical intrigue of Skagway. It is because of this that it has managed to avoid attracting big cruise ships.

PRACTICAL INFORMATION AND ORIENTATION

Visitors Information: Haines Visitors Information Center (766-2234 or 800-458-3579), 2nd Ave. near Willard St. Worth stopping by just for a chat with the enthusiastic director, Tyson. Info on accommodations, hiking around town, and surrounding parks. Make sure to pick up the free pamphlet *Haines is for Hikers.* Free tea and coffee inside. Open Mon.-Fri. 8am-8pm, Sat.-Sun. 10am-1pm and 2-7pm. **State Park Information Office,** 259 Main St., P.O. Box 430 (766-2292), above Helen's Shop between 2nd and 3rd Ave. Legendary Ranger Bill Zack can tell you everything about hiking in the area, the dangers of bears, and the Chilkat Bald Eagle Preserve. Officially open Tues.-Sat. 8am-4:30pm, but call ahead: Bill patrols the region in the daytime, and is usually out 8:30am-3:30pm.

Bank: First National Bank of Anchorage, on Main St. Only bank in town. 24hr. ATM. Open Mon. 10am-5pm, Tues.-Fri. 10am-4pm.

Air Service: Haines Air (766-2646), and **LAB Flying Service** (766-2222 or 800-426-0543) both on Main St., offer comparable rates on flights to Juneau (about $100 roundtrip), Skagway, and Glacier Bay.

Buses: Alaskon Express; make reservations through **Ft. Seward Tours** (766-2000) in the lobby of the Hotel Halsingland. Buses depart from same location traveling north on Tues., Thurs., and Sun., with an overnight stop in Beaver Creek, YT, near the Alaskan border. To: Anchorage ($185), Fairbanks ($180), and Whitehorse, YT ($82). Open daily 9am-8pm.

Ferries: Alaska Marine Highway (766-2111). Terminal on Lutak Rd., 4 mi. from downtown. Hitchers report they can usually get into town. A taxi runs $5. Daily to Juneau ($20) and Skagway ($14). The **Water Taxi** (766-3395) runs to Skagway twice daily in summer ($18, roundtrip $29).

Taxi: Other Guy's Taxi (766-3257). $6 from ferry to downtown. Long-term ferry parking for ferry passengers $5 per day, $25 per week. 24hr.

Car Rental: Thunderbird Hotel (766-2131). $45 per day, 30¢ per mi. after 100 mi. **Eagle's Nest Car Rental** (766-2891), at Eagle's Nest Motel, offers identical rates. **Avis** (766-2733), at Hotel Halsingland, grudgingly offers an 8hr. time limit deal for $40 with unlimited mileage. Must be 25 with a credit card. Don't be late, or you'll pay the regular $63 per day. Call ahead to reserve.

Bike Rental: Sockeye Cycle (766-2869), Portage St. in Ft. Seward. $6 per hr., $20 per ½-day, $30 per 8hr. Helmets and locks included. Open Mon.-Sat. 9am-6pm.

Kayak Rental: Tanani Bay Kayak and Canoe Rentals (766-2804), near corner of Union and Front St. Single kayaks and canoes $16 per day, double kayaks $26 per day. Life vests and paddles included. **Deishu Expeditions** (766-2427), on Portage St. near the cruise ship dock. Single $35 per day, double $55 per day. All gear included. Open daily 9am-6pm, call to arrange pick up or drop off at other times.

Bookstore: The Babbling Book (776-3356), on Main St. near Howser's Supermarket. Good collection of Alaskan and Native Alaskan culture and politics, current fiction and non-fiction. Open Mon.-Sat. 10am-6pm, Sun. noon-6pm.

Library: 766-2545, 3rd Ave. Open Mon. and Wed. 10am-9pm, Tues. and Thurs. 10am-4:30pm and 7-9pm, Fri. 10am-4:30pm, Sat. 1-4pm, Sun. 2-4pm.

Laundromat and Showers: Port Chilkoot Camper Park (766-2000), across from the Halsingland Hotel. Wash $2, 7-min. dry 25¢. Showers $1.50. Open daily 7:30am-9pm. **Susie Q's** (766-2953), on Main St. near Front St. Wash $2, dry 50¢. Showers $2. Open daily 8am-8pm; winter 8am-6pm.

Health Center: 766-2521.

Emergency and Ambulance: 911. **Police:** 766-2121.

Post Office: On Haines Hwy., between 2nd Ave. and Front St. Open Mon.-Fri. 9am-5:30pm, Sat. 1-3pm. **General Delivery ZIP Code:** 99827.

Area Code: 907.

Most of the Haines business district lies in a rectangle outlined by Main St. and the Haines Hwy., which run toward the water, and their perpendiculars, 2nd and 3rd Ave. The post office and police station lie outside the rectangle along the Haines Hwy., which runs to Fort Seward, an eight- to ten-minute walk. Haines lies on a thin peninsula between the Chilkat and Chilkoot Inlets. Below this narrow neck of land, the two inlets merge into **Lynn Canal.** Both the U.S. (767-5511) and Canada (767-5540) have customs offices at Mile 42 of the Haines Hwy. (open daily 7am-11pm). Travelers must have at least $200 cash (although the requirement varies based on destination), a credit card, and valid proof of citizenship to cross into Canada.

ACCOMMODATIONS AND CAMPING

Since the weather in Haines is better than almost anywhere else in Southeast Alaska, there are few good reasons not to pitch a tent. In addition to the private campgrounds listed below, there are several state campgrounds in and around Haines that compete for budget travelers. **Chilkat State Park,** 7 mi. south on Mud Bay Rd. by the sea, has good king salmon and halibut fishing, guided nature walks, and is near the hiking trail to **Seduction Point** (35 sites; $8). **Chilkoot Lake,** 10 mi. north of town on Lutak Rd., provides views and sockeye salmon fishing (32 sites; $10). **Mosquito Lake,** 27 mi. north on Haines Hwy., is a small spot which earns its name in late summer (5 sites; $8). All state campgrounds have water and toilets.

Bear Creek Camp and International Hostel, Box 1158 (766-2259), on Small Tracts Rd. 2 mi. outside of town. From downtown, follow 3rd Ave. out Mud Bay Rd. to Small Tracts Rd. A ring of basic cabins, 2 of which are hostel dorms. Each building has its own unique odor. Spartan furnishings—a roof and a bed (actually foam pads on bunks). No coed social space other than kitchen. The lack of curfew means that you don't have to spend much time here. Location is convenient to nothing. Call ahead for ferry terminal pickup. Though Bear Creek is not affiliated with AYH, it gives member discounts: $14, nonmembers $15, family cabins $37. Tent sites for $8.50 have access to kitchen and showers, but there's better camping at Portage Cove.

Hotel Halsingland, Box 1589 MD, Haines 99827 (766-2000, 800-542-6363 in the lower 48, 800-478-2525 in AK and Canada). Play soldier in old Ft. Seward officers' quarters. Has several small economy rooms with sinks and shared bath ($39, doubles $49). Call ahead for cheap rooms—a bath more than doubles the price.

The Officers' Inn Bed and Breakfast (same number as Halsingland), replicates the look of the Halsingland, to which it is adjacent. Singles $50, doubles $55 (shared bath, more for private baths). Continental breakfast and afternoon tea included. Courtesy shuttle will pick up/drop off all over Haines.

Fort Seward Lodge, Box 307, Haines 99827 (766-2009 or 800-478-7772). Another historic Fort Seward building. A bit dark, but clean and attractive, with hand-finished furniture. 10 rooms at reasonable rates. Singles with shared bath $45. Doubles from $55. Private bath $15 more. Oct.-April $10 off.

Portage Cove, ¾ mi. from town on Beach Rd., accepts only backpackers and cyclists (sites $8).

Port Chilkoot Camper Park, Box 41589 (766-2000 or 800-542-6363), across from Hotel Halsingland. A few trees provide some protection from the road, but hardly a natural setting. Gravelly in places, but well maintained. Convenient to downtown. Laundromat and showers ($1.50). Summer only. 60 sites. Tents $6.75. RVs with full hookup $15.

Salmon Run RV Campground (766-3240), at Lutak Inlet, ½ mi. from the ferry terminal, away from town. Half of the sites overlook the beach. Wooded, with streams on grounds. Restrooms. Sites $10. Open year-round.

FOOD

Haines restaurants are limited in variety but high in quality. Groceries are expensive, so try to stock up in Juneau before you come. Of the two markets in town, most locals prefer **Howser's Supermarket** (766-2040), on Main St. (open daily 8am-9pm). For fresh seafood head to **Bell's Seafood** (766-2950), on 2nd Ave., under the "Old City Jail and Firehouse" sign. Try salmon for $7 per lb., or prawns for $13 per lb. (open Sun.-Tues. and Thurs.-Sat. 9am-6pm, Wed. 9am-10pm).

Chilkat Restaurant and Bakery (766-2920), on 5th Ave., near Main. Family-style restaurant with healthy portions. Fantastic baked goods available for takeout. All-you-can-eat soup-and-salad bar ($9). Basic sandwiches $5, "creative" ones around $8. Popular Mexican night on Fridays. Open Mon.-Sat. 7am-9pm, Sun. 9am-9pm.

Porcupine Pete's (766-9999), at Main St. and 2nd Ave. Authenticity freaks, repent! Haines's leading tourist trap also serves some of the city's tastiest fare in a low-key, split-level setting. Hamburger pita, a tasty sourdough-calzone concoction, fills your plate ($6.25). Good sourdough pizza ($2.50). Open daily 11am-10pm.

Bamboo Room (776-2800), on 2nd Ave. near Main St., next to the Pioneer Bar. No bamboo in sight. This unpretentious diner is a favorite breakfast spot, crowded until 3pm with fisherfolk downing the buckwheat hotcakes and coffee ($4.25). Lunch specials $6, dinner specials $9-10. Open daily 6am-10pm.

Port Chilkoot Potlatch (766-2040), at the Tribal House in Ft. Seward. Not the cheapest salmon bake in the region, but one of the better ones. All-you-can-eat BBQ salmon and ribs, plus salad bar and cheesecake. One free beer or wine. You'll be forced to mingle with the cruise ship crowds, but it's probably worth it. Reservations recommended. Operates daily through summer, 5-8:30pm.

SIGHTS AND ENTERTAINMENT

Fort William Seward, on the west side of town, was established in 1901 to assert an American presence during a border dispute with Canada. With little to do other than shovel snow and watch for fires, the colonial-style post quickly became known as a gentle assignment. Boredom was the soldiers' only enemy: "Even among men with the most modern arms, time is the hardest thing to kill," lamented one observer in a 1907 newspaper. After it was declared surplus following World War II, five veterans bought the entire 400-acre compound with plans of making a commune out of the old fort. Their utopian venture never succeeded, but most of these settlers became free-enterprising members of the community. Today Fort Seward lies at the center of Haines's tourist activity. In the middle of the grounds sits a replica of a **Totem Village** (766-2160), complete with a tribal house.

The **Chilkat Dancers** perform traditional Tlingit dances with interpretive narration at the **Chilkat Center for the Arts.** Performances are usually at 8pm, but revolve around cruise ship and ferry schedules. Call the Hotel Halsingland (766-2000) for tickets ($10, under 18 $5, under 5 free). The village is also home to **Sea Wolf Studio-Gallery** (766-2540), where you can watch artist Tresham Gregg carve Tlingit masks (open Mon.-Fri. 10am-5pm with some variance for cruise ships and whim). Crossing to the far side of the parade grounds takes you to the **Alaska Indian Arts Center** (766-2160). Visitors can watch artisans in their workshops and marvel at the craft of totem pole carving (open Mon.-Fri. 9am-noon and 1-5pm).

Originally in an unheated room over the grocery store, the **Sheldon Museum,** 25 Main St. (766-2366), now calls a two-story building home. While the collection is impressive, considering its origins, it is not nearly as extensive as the Sheldon Jackson Museum in Sitka or the State Museum in Juneau. It does, however, provide a comprehensive overview of both native cultures and town history, without being overwhelming ($3, under 18 free; open daily in summer 1-5pm, often later).

Check out the works of local artists near the visitors center. The **Northern Arts Gallery** (766-2318; open daily 10am-5pm), and **Chilkat Valley Arts** (766-2990; open daily 10am-6pm), in the adjoining building, are noteworthy. Equally good is **Inside Passage Artisans** (766-2539), next door, which features work by Native Alaskan artists from across the region (open daily 9am-5pm, later when cruise ships are docked). Galleries here offer high quality craft work in fur, wood, and on film rather than the usual tourist cache.

The wooden **American Bald Eagle Association Center,** P.O. Box 49 (766-3094) at the intersection of Haines Hwy. and 2nd Ave., offers an indoor look at Haines's wildlife. Stuffed fauna of all shapes and sizes, notably a grizzly bear, a moose, several wolves, and a lot of eagles, bedeck the display room. The center also screens a film of the November bald eagle occupation (free; open Mon.-Sat. 10am-6pm, Sun. 1-4pm, and to accommodate cruise ships).

Wildlife of a different sort hits Haines in early July (July 4-6 in 1997), when the **Haines Rodeo** brings the **Hats, Boots, and Buns Cowboy Beauty Contest,** line dancing, multiple barbecues, and of course, rodeo riding galore. Call the visitors center (see **Practical Information**) or the Chamber of Commerce (766-2202) for details. Another traditional event, the **Southeast Alaska State Fair,** lights up the fairground here in mid-August, bringing the usual mix of rides, sales booths, and displays to the area. At the same time, blues and bluegrass artists strut their stuff at the **Alaska Bald Eagle Music Festival.** Complementing these old time favorites is a long list of events that puts most other towns in the region (Juneau included) to shame. Haines becomes Party Central in May with a **craft beer and home-brew festival** (May 16-18 in 1997), a **Bald Eagle Run** and **Harley Davidson Rodeo** (May 23-25 in 1997), and an Alaskan version of Mardi Gras (May 30-June 1). The new **Alaska Bald Eagle Festival** welcomes masses of eagles to town in mid-November (Nov. 15-17 in 1997) with speakers and naturalist-guided trips to the preserve (800-246-6268 or 766-2202 for more info).

OUTDOORS

The **Haines Hwy.** winds 40 mi. from Haines through the **Chilkat Range** north through the Yukon. The views are guaranteed to blow you through the back of your Winnebago. **Chilkat Bald Eagle Preserve,** a 19-mi. drive up the highway, protects the feeding grounds where as many as 4000 eagles may gather in November—the world's largest annual concentration. While the reserve is the year-round home for a number of eagles, the pictures you'll see of hundreds of birds perched in birch woods or sitting in the river are all taken during late fall and winter. Don't be disappointed if you only see a handful on a summer visit.

Three main **trails** head into the wilderness around Haines. The **Mt. Riley Trail** starts in several places and ends on a 1760-ft. summit with a fantastic 360° view of the Lynn Canal, the Chilkoot and Chilkat inlets, and everything else within 30 mi. The primary trailhead is marked by a large sign about 3½ mi. from town, 1½ mi. down Mud Bay Rd. past the hostel. This route is steep for the majority of its 2.1 mi. Another trailhead, more difficult to find, is behind the fort. This route covers about 3.8 mi. one way and is fairly flat (and fairly uninteresting) for the first couple of miles before meeting up with the main trail. A copy of *Haines is for Hikers,* available at the visitors center, can help you locate trailheads.

For more ambitious view-seekers, **Mt. Ripinsky,** the 3920-ft. mountain looming over town to the north, provides a challenging hike over two summits connected by an alpine ridge. On a clear day, the view from the ridge extends all the way to Juneau. On partly cloudy days, however, the summit is often shrouded, while the shorter Mt. Riley continues to provide excellent views. To reach Mt. Ripinsky's trailhead, follow 2nd Ave. north to Lutak Rd. Branch off Lutak onto Young St. at the hill, then turn right along a buried pipeline for 1 mi. After cresting the 3610-ft. **North Summit,** the trail dips down along the ridge where it may be difficult to follow in poor weather. At the end of the ridge, it climbs again to the 3920-ft. peak, and descends steeply to its end at Mile 7 of the Haines Hwy. This strenuous 10-mi. hike makes for a long day of walking or a relaxed overnight trip.

The more relaxing **Seduction Point trail** offers 6¾ mi. of birds, beaches, ocean bluffs, berry picking, wildflowers, and views of Davidson Glacier. Take Mud Bay Rd. out of Haines 7 mi. to Chilkat State Park and look for the trailhead. Try to time the last part of the hike along David's Cove to coincide with low tide. The trail also makes an excellent shorter hike if you're not up to a full day outdoors.

While a variety of raft, boat, and nature tours compete for tourist dollars, none of them are unique or long enough to justify the cost. If you really want to get out on the water, consider renting a very affordable kayak from Tanani Bay Kayak (see **Practical Information**).

■ Skagway

In August 1896, a Tlingit man named Skookum Jim was washing a pan in a tributary of the Klondike River when he discovered strips of gold so thick they looked "like cheese in a sandwich." One of the greatest adventures in North American history was on. By the next October, Skagway, which provided one of the cheapest (though hardly easiest) access points to the Yukon Rush, was a thriving town of 20,000. (A town of 20,000 in Alaska would be large *today.*) From Skagway, the stampeders drove their pack horses mercilessly along the rocky but relatively gradual White Pass Trail. Over 3000 horses perished along this route in the winter of 1897-98, earning it the name **Dead Horse Trail.** The shorter **Chilkoot Trail,** starting in the nearby ghost town of **Dyea,** climbs too steeply for pack animals, but was just as popular. On the other side of the mountains, miners built boats on Lake Bennett and floated north on the Yukon River to the diggings. To prevent food riots, the Canadian Mounties would not let prospectors into the Yukon without half a ton of food and supplies; to carry this much, a person might make 30 or 40 trips over the pass. When the Nome gold

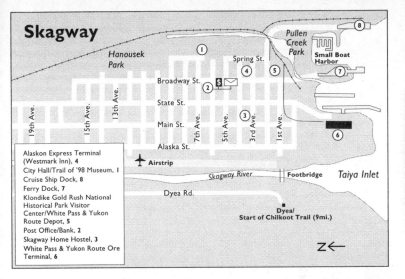

Skagway

Hanousek
Park

Spring St.

Pullen
Creek
Park

Small Boat
Harbor

Broadway St.

State St.

Main St.

Alaska St.

19th Ave.

15th Ave.

13th Ave.

7th Ave.

5th Ave.

3rd Ave.

1st Ave.

Airstrip

Skagway River

Footbridge

Taiya Inlet

Dyea Rd.

Dyea/
Start of Chilkoot Trail (9mi.)

Cruise Ship Dock, **8**

Alaskon Express Terminal
(Westmark Inn), **4**
City Hall/Trail of '98 Museum, **1**
Cruise Ship Dock, **8**
Ferry Dock, **7**
Klondike Gold Rush National
Historical Park Visitor
Center/White Pass & Yukon
Route Depot, **5**
Post Office/Bank, **2**
Skagway Home Hostel, **3**
White Pass & Yukon Route Ore
Terminal, **6**

ALASKA

rush began in about 1900, Skagway dwindled, surviving only as a port and the terminus of a railway over White Pass.

The railroad still runs today, but carries tourists rather than miners and supplies. Much of the town of Skagway has been brilliantly restored by the National Park Service to its original 1898 condition, right down to the wooden sidewalks. While cruise ship tourists enjoy the town's golden history, surprisingly few take advantage of its wide array of hiking opportunities. Most visitors stick to the heavily hiked Chilkoot Trail, undoubtedly the most popular backpacking route in the Southeast. A scant 29 in. of annual rainfall means that hikers are almost always rewarded with clear views. The town's spectacular setting, entertaining history, and terrific hostel make it worth battling the summer crowds for a visit.

PRACTICAL INFORMATION AND ORIENTATION

Visitors Information: Klondike Gold Rush National Historical Park Visitor Center (983-2921), 2nd and Broadway. This should be your first stop in town regardless of your plans. Walking tours 4 times daily. An excellent introduction to Skagway's history is the free ½-hr. film *Days of Adventure, Dreams of Gold,* shown on the hour. Also the place to go for updated info on the Chilkoot Trail and other hikes. Open May-Sept. daily 8am-8pm. **Skagway Convention and Visitors Bureau** (983-2855), on 5th Ave. just off Broadway. Comparatively unhelpful. Little to offer that can't be found at the visitors center. Open Mon.-Wed. 8am-5pm, Thurs.-Sun. 8am-noon and 1-5pm. The **Forest Service's** Skagway Office (983-3088) on 2nd St. near Spring Ave., in a yellow building. Hours vary widely, and are posted. To reserve a cabin call the Juneau office (586-8751).

Bank: National Bank of Alaska. The one and only. 24hr. ATM. Open Mon.-Fri. 9:30am-5pm. Currency exchange available at a **Thomas Cook** booth on 2nd Ave. near the railroad tracks.

Air Service: Skagway Air Service, 983-2218. 6-7 flights per day to Haines ($30) continuing on to Juneau ($70). Also several flights to Gustavus ($81) and tours of Glacier Bay ($110). Open daily 7am-9pm.

Trains: White Pass and Yukon Route, P.O. Box 435 (983-2217 or 800-343-7373), 1 block off Broadway on 2nd. 3-hr. roundtrip excursion to White Pass Summit, on one of the steepest and most scenic railroad grades in North America. Trains run May 16-Sept. 22, leaving daily at 8:45am and 1:15pm ($75, under 13 $38). Can also be used to access remote hiking trails along the route (see **Outdoors**). Combined train and bus service to and from Whitehorse, YT leaves daily at 12:40pm ($95 one way, under 13 $48). All trains wheelchair accessible.

Buses: Alaska Direct (800-770-6652) runs vans from the hostel and hotels to Whitehorse ($35) daily, with connections on Wed., Fri., and Sun. to Fairbanks ($120) and Anchorage ($145). Requires an overnight stay in Whitehorse. **Alaskon Express** (983-2241 or 800-544-2206), in the Westmark Inn, 3rd Ave. between Broadway and Spring. Buses Sun., Tues., and Thurs. to Anchorage and Fairbanks ($200). Trips include an expensive overnight stop near the Alaska border in Beaver Creek, YT. 1 per day in summer to Whitehorse, YT ($54, at 7:30am).

Ferries: Alaska Marine Highway, 983-2941. Ferries daily to Haines ($14) and Juneau ($26). **Water Taxi,** 776-3395. 2 per day to Haines ($18, roundtrip $29).

Taxi: Pioneer Taxi, 983-2623. Tour of Dyea ($15), to Chilkoot Trailhead ($10). Tour of town, waterfront, and White Pass ($24). **Klondike Tours** (983-2075) also runs to the Chilkoot Trailhead 5-6 times per day ($10); call for schedule.

Car Rental: Sourdough Van & Car Rentals (983-2523 or 800-478-2529), at 6th Ave. and Broadway, is cheapest, starting at $30 per day. 100 free mi. for each day you rent, 30¢ per additional mi. **ABC Rentals** (983-3222 or 800-421-7456), next to the Corner Café (see below), charges $35 per day for a compact; mopeds $10 per hr. or $40 for 24hr.

Bike Rental: Sockeye Cycle (983-2851), on 5th Ave. off Broadway. Rates begin at $6 per hr., $30 per day, including helmet and lock. Open daily 9am-6pm. **Bike Rental** (983-2643 or 2687), on 4th Ave. at State St. $4 per hour or $20 per day. Helmets included. Open daily 9:30am-5pm, closed in foul and cold weather.

Library: 983-2665, 8th Ave. and State St. Open Mon.-Fri. 1-9pm, Sat. 1-5pm.

Laundromat: Services Unlimited Laundromat (983-2595), at 2nd Ave. and State St. Wash $2, 5-min. dry 25¢. Open daily 8am-6:30pm.

Hospital: Skagway Medical Service, 983-2255 or 983-2418.

Post Office: 983-2320, at Broadway and 6th, next to the bank. Open Mon.-Fri. 8:30am-5pm. Lobby open 24hr. for postage machine. **General Delivery ZIP Code:** 99840.

Area Code: 907.

At the northernmost tip of the Inside Passage, Skagway is the terminus of the Alaska Marine Hwy. From here, travelers on wheels can connect to the Alaska Hwy. by taking the **Klondike Hwy.** (Rte. 98 in AK; Hwy. 2 in YT) to Whitehorse. Haines is 12 mi. away by water. Hitchers say they do better by spending $14 on the ferry to Haines and trying the more heavily traveled Haines Hwy. to Kluane and interior Alaska.

The ferry drops you off right on the edge of downtown. Skagway's main drag, Broadway, runs inland from the docks. Broadway is paralleled by Spring St. to the right as you leave the docks, and State and Main St. to the left. The four streets are intersected by numbered avenues, beginning at the docks and increasing in number as you go inland. Only about 700 people spend the winter in Skagway. Another 1500 arrive for summer jobs in the tourist industry, and on a busy day 3000 visitors may spill off the cruise ships and ferries.

ACCOMMODATIONS AND CAMPING

Its hostel is reason enough to visit Skagway. If you're not a hosteler, it's wise to make reservations at least one month in advance at all Skagway hotels. Also see the **Forest Service cabins** in the Outdoors section below.

Skagway Home Hostel, P.O. Box 231 (983-2131), at 3rd and Main, ½ mi. from the ferry. In a comfy old house, you're invited to become part of a friendly, idiosyncratic family. Kitchen and other facilities shared by owners and guests alike. Sign up for dinner before 4:30pm ($5, free if you help cook). No lockout, curfew 11pm, free showers, kitchen. $3 for wash, dry, and detergent. 19 beds and 2 rooms for couples, overflow in nearby church ($13). Chore required. Will store packs. Sheets and towels $1. Check-in 5:30-9pm or call ahead.

Golden North Hotel, P.O. Box 431 (983-2294), at 3rd Ave. and Broadway. The coolest affordable hotel in the Southeast. Also the oldest hotel operating in the state (since 1898). Each room maintains period style in unique fashion. Many have canopy beds, claw-footed bathtubs, and the like. Singles $45, with private bath $60. Doubles $50, with bath $75.

Gramma's B&B (983-2312), at 7th Ave. and State St. Clean, comfortable, modern. No frontier pretensions here. Satellite TV, shared bath, continental breakfast, hearing-impaired phone. Singles $55. Doubles $65. Triples $75.

Skagway Inn, P.O. Box 500 (983-2289), on Broadway at 7th. Built in 1897 as a brothel, the inn is now respectably refurbished. Many rooms contain original or restored antique furniture. Transport to Chilkoot Trail with advanced (1-day) notice. Pickup and delivery to ferry and airport. Shared baths. Hearty breakfast included. Expensive restaurant below. Singles $55-60. Doubles $75.

Hanousek Park (983-2768), on Broadway at 14th, 1½ mi. north of the ferry. Privately run. Clean and wooded, but a bit close to population centers for the inspired outdoorsperson. Drinking water, modern bathrooms with showers (25¢ for 2min.), fire rings. Sites $8, with RV hookup $15.

Dyea Camping Area, 9 mi. northwest of Skagway on the Dyea Rd. Near the start of the Chilkoot Trail. 22 sites. Pit toilets, fire rings, no drinking water or showers. 2-week max. stay. Free.

FOOD

The one area in which Skagway is sorely lacking. Groceries and film are beyond expensive, so stock up before you get here. If you must shop in Skagway, try the **Fairway Supermarket** (983-2220), at 4th and State (open daily 8am-9pm).

Corner Café, 4th and State (983-2155). Where the locals head for basic, affordable grub. Open-air seating lets you avoid the smoke. Listen to that fryer sizzle! Stack of sourdough pancakes ($3.25); biscuits and gravy ($3.75). Burgers and sandwiches ($4.50-7). Open daily 6am-9pm.

Prospector's Sourdough Restaurant (983-2865), on Broadway between 4th and 5th Ave. Local high-school sports trophies adorn the walls for that hometown feel. Portions are sizable even when you're not helping yourself. All-you-can-eat soup and salad bar is one of the best deals in town ($8). Open daily 6am-10pm.

Mabel G. Smith's, 342 5th Ave. between Broadway and State. The counter in back serves up terrific baked goods (muffins $1.25) and a variety of ways to satisfy your caffeine addiction. Open Mon.-Thurs. and Sat.-Sun. 6am-6pm, Fri. 6am-11pm.

Broadway Bistro (983-6231), on Broadway between 3rd and 4th St. About the fastest food you can find in town. Pizza slices $2, all-you-can-eat spaghetti $10, and a surprising variety of beverages including beer, wine, and Starbucks coffee. Open daily 8am-2pm, 5pm-8pm, coffee from 6:30am.

SIGHTS AND EVENTS

Most of Broadway (which *is* downtown) is preserved in pristine 1898 form as the **Klondike Gold Rush National Historical Park.** The Park Service owns and operates 15 downtown buildings and has assembled a small museum beside the visitors center. A restored vintage saloon on Broadway and many other period pieces have been leased by the Park Service to local businesses. Check out the worthwhile hourly film at the park's visitors center (see **Practical Information**).

Polish up on your gold rush trivia at the **Trail of '98 Museum,** housed in the 1899 **Arctic Brotherhood Hall.** A testament to the state's dearth of interesting architecture, the driftwood-covered façade of the hall is Alaska's most photographed building. Among the treasures in the museum's collection are the world's only duck-neck robe and the bloodstained tie that local con-man Soapy Smith wore on the day of his death. For a more lively taste of history, head next door to the **Red Onion Saloon,** Skagway's first bordello. A century ago, the bartender marked each lady's availability by placing one of the dolls on the rack downstairs in the appropriate position: upright or prostrate. Now the Red Onion is a bar with an enviable collection of bed pans adorning one wall. Come for live afternoon jazz or for the open jam Thursday nights, when the locals come out to play (open daily 10am-12:30; no cover).

> ## The Cleanest Con Man in the North
>
> Skagway's most notorious ne'er-do-well, Jefferson "Soapy" Smith, acquired his improbable name as a result of his favorite con, the "soap game." He would sit on a street corner selling bars of soap for the outrageous price of $5. There were, of course, few takers. Eventually, Soapy would take out a number of $50 and $100 bills and wrap them up with a few of the bars of soap before mixing them up with the others in the basket. A crowd quickly gathered, and a number of the braver members would step forward to buy bars. As luck would have it, those first two or three bars would invariably hold very large bills, and triggered a buying frenzy. Luck seemed to end abruptly at that point, and most people just ended up with a very pricey bar of soap. The two or three lucky fellows (otherwise known as accomplices) would meet up with Soapy later in the day and return the planted bills in exchange for a handsome payoff. Ultimately, though, **Soapy Smith** wasn't a bad sort: he bought the community a new church with much of the money he had conned. In appreciation of his peculiar brand of philanthropy, the town named him Grand Marshall of the 4th of July parade in 1898. Just a few days later, Soapy met his untimely end in a shootout with Frank Reid when Soapy attempted to storm a town meeting. Skagway's lovable antihero was buried outside the limits of the town cemetery, while Frank was given a choice plot and a tombstone inscribed with the words "He gave his life for the honor of Skagway."

Skagway's history is almost overshadowed by its souvenir shops. One of the most intriguing is the **Corrington Alaskan Ivory Co.** (983-2580), 5th and Broadway, which contains a display of expensive carved bone and ivory pieces both in the showroom and in a free museum (open daily 9am-8pm). **Inside Passage Arts** (983-2585), Broadway and 4th St., sells quality work by local Native artists. Come in to view even if you can't buy (open daily 8am-5pm; later when cruise ships are in).

Once you've gotten your fill of Broadway and the accompanying crowds, head down State St. until it meets 23rd Ave. and look for the sign pointing to Soapy Smith's grave across the railroad tracks just outside the **Gold Rush cemetery.** More respectable folk like Frank Reid can be found *inside* the cemetery. A short trail nearby leads to booming **Reid Falls,** which cascades 300 ft. down the mountainside and provides a spectacle no walker can or should miss.

Rabid Soap-o-philes go to the **Skagway Days of '98** show in the Eagles Dance Hall (983-2234), 6th and Broadway. For decades the show has featured song and dance, play-money gambling by the audience, and audience-actor interaction. It's definitely worth the money ($14, kids $7). While the matinee performances are a little cheaper ($12, kids $6), the evening ones tend to be better, and include play-gambling (daily in summer; 7:30pm gambling, 8:30pm show).

Dyea, near the head of the Chilkoot Trail, lies 9 mi. out of Skagway on the unpaved Dyea Rd. The town crashed after the gold rush, and scavengers quickly moved in to dismantle houses, banks, hotels, and other buildings for scrap wood. Today the only evidence of Dyea's former glory are scattered foundations, the remnants of wooden pilings that once supported a large wharf, and **Slide Cemetery,** where more than 50 victims of an 1898 avalanche on the crowded Chilkoot Pass are buried. The Park Service runs walking tours of Dyea during the summer at varying times. They will explain, among other things, why the wharves are now hundreds of feet from the water. Taxi fare to Dyea is roughly $10, but views of the inlet on the way to Dyea are better seen from a rented bike. The friendly, knowledgeable folk at **Klondike Tours,** P.O. Box 320 (983-2075), give a three-hour tour of Skagway and Dyea (with an Alaskan Sled Dog Show at the end) for $30.

OUTDOORS

If you're in Skagway, chances are you'll venture onto the Chilkoot trail. Before you go, pick up the complete *Hiker's Guide to the Chilkoot Trail,* a joint publication of the U.S. and Canadian National Park Services, before attempting the rewarding hike. Both the pamphlet and a mandatory, free overnight camping permit are available at the Dyea Ranger Station, less than ½ mi. from the trailhead.

Park officials patrol the trail and rangers are also usually at the trailhead in Dyea. If you're planning to continue into British Columbia, be sure to call **Canadian customs** (403-667-3943) before leaving Skagway (Dyea has no phones), and have proof of solvency ($150 and a credit card, plus a valid photo ID and birth certificate or passport) before crossing the border. According to rangers, these requirements are enforced at will and whim, but are most likely to trip up the scruffy and potentially indigent. (For more on the trail, see p. 267.)

Although the Chilkoot Trail is the marquee name in Skagway hiking, excellent shorter hikes have inspiring views and fewer people around you to block them. The **Dewey Lake Trail System** provides some of the best hikes near town, ranging from a 20-minute stroll to a strenuous climb up to two alpine lakes at 3700 ft. To reach the trail system, walk east toward the mountains along 2nd. Ave. Follow the dirt path just before the railroad tracks to the left, and look for signs pointing out the trail on the right. **Lower Dewey Lake,** a long, narrow pond surrounded by woods, lies less than a mile up the trail. Here one trail branches out around the lake (about 2 mi.), and another toward **Icy Lake** and Upper Reid Falls (about 1½ mi.). Both of these walks are gentle, with little change in elevation.

A third trail to **Upper Dewey Lake** branches off the Icy Lake trail near the northern end of Lower Dewey Lake. The first section of the 2¼-mi. trail is brutal, but the climb mellows out somewhat and switchbacks its way to the lake. Upper Dewey rests in a stunning amphitheater of serrated peaks. A small **cabin** with cramped space for four and a permanent smoky odor sits by the lake. It is available on a first-come, first-served basis. The best **camping sites** are along the opposite shore. You need a permit for overnight camping anywhere in the forest surrounding Skagway; get one free at the **Skagway Police Station** at 7th and Broadway. An extension of the Upper Dewey trail leads south from the lake 1 mi. across a rocky alpine bench to the limpid waters of the **Devil's Punchbowl.** Excellent views of the inlet below make this side trip worthwhile. Keep an eye out for rock cairns marking the way, as the trail is often difficult to find. Also, since this exposed area can be cold even on sunny summer days, don't forget a jacket. Plan on a two- to three-hour trip one way from town to Upper Dewey, and a three- to four-hour trip to the Punchbowl.

A.B. Mountain, named for the pattern created by the melting snow on its side each spring, dominates the skyline on the west side of town. The **Skyline Trail** leads up this mountain. Both the directions to the trailhead and the challenging trail itself are confusing, so pick up a **Skagway Trail Map** at the park visitor center or Skagway Visitors Bureau to avoid getting lost. If you walk from town, it's about 4.8 mi. to the spectacular 3500-ft. summit. While the summit takes about 3½ hours to reach, the route provides terrific views early in the climb. Two other hikes near Skagway combine cabins, glaciers, and the White Pass and Yukon Route railroad. The trail to the **Denver Glacier** begins just short of milepost 6 on the Railroad. This trail passes below the towering walls of the Sawtooth Range and winds down in the brush of the Denver Glacier moraine. The 3½-mi. hike begins at a Forest Service **caboose** beside the railroad tracks (which doubles as a cabin). Inquire at the forest service office (586-8751) about the availability of the cabin. Don't chance a walk out to the trailhead along the tracks, as tunnels and bridges offer no escape from swift trains. The WP&YR train will deposit hikers at the trail on its two daily trips to White Pass (leaves at 8am and 12:40pm) and make a flag stop to bring them back to town (roundtrip $25; pickup daily at 11:25am, 4pm; confirm times when purchasing ticket). The clearly marked **Laughton Glacier Trail,** beginning at milepost 14 along the train tracks to White Pass, makes an easy 1½-mi. ascent to a more conventional forest service cabin. From there, it's another 1½ mi. to an immense wall of hanging glaciers. The roundtrip train fare to and from the trailhead is $50 (leaves daily at 8am, 12:40pm, pickup daily at 11am, 3:30pm).

The Bush

Known variously as the Country, the Wilderness Rim, and the Bush, this vast expanse of frozen tundra and jagged coastline overwhelms the small settlements and narrow landing strips which constitute the area's human presence. The Bush towns of **Nome** and **Prudhoe Bay** are places few Alaskans have ever seen. Polar bears ride ice floes and hundreds of thousands of caribou roam freely across the tundra. Native Alaskan settlements are few and far between, accessible only by plane, boat, or dogsled. Cannery workers and oil drillers swarm to remote settlements for the big money, knowing it's theirs to save because there's nowhere to spend it.

Each area of the Bush has distinctive features. The **Southwest** includes the flat, soggy, buggy terrain of the Yukon-Kushkowin delta, the mountainous Alaska Peninsula, and the **Aleutian Islands,** a volcanic archipelago with some of the worst weather on earth. **Western Alaska** includes the **Seward Peninsula,** a treeless, hilly expanse of tundra. **Nome,** at the end of a peninsula on the coast of the Bering Sea, is frequently swept by harsh storms. The **Brooks Range,** Alaska's Arctic crown, stretches from the northwest to the Canadian border, while the flat, endless expanses of tundra on the **North Slope** spread northward from the Brooks to the Arctic Ocean, where oil companies employ thousands of Alaskans. The town of **Barrow** on the Arctic Ocean is the world's largest Inuit village and the northernmost point of the United States. A sense of adventure and self-reliance are characteristics anyone who hopes to travel in the Bush must have; most towns won't expend energy entertaining guests. Revel in the isolation and be prepared to rough it.

Transportation in the Bush is not cheap. Tour outfitters abound, ready and willing to lead you out into the wilds to fish, hunt, hike, kayak, canoe, or photograph for a steep price. **Alaska Airlines** (800-426-0333) services Nome, Kotzebue, Barrow, and Prudhoe Bay. Smaller companies like **Larry's Flying Service** (474-9169 in Fairbanks) and **Frontier Flying Services** (474-0014 in Fairbanks) fly to the more remote spots like Anaktuvuk Pass ($268 roundtrip from Fairbanks) and Fort Yukon. Chartering a plane costs over $250 per hr., but it's the only way to get into the middle of the wilderness, away from even the most remote communities.

NORTHEAST ALASKA

▓ Dalton Highway

The Dalton Hwy. reaches all the way to the gates of Prudhoe Bay, the second northernmost settlement in Alaska. But before you consider driving, check your wallet to see if you can afford a tour, as it is by far the best way to see the region. If you have no interest in preserving your car, or cannot afford a tour, the highway is well worth the trip. Just be sure you and your automobile make it back in one piece. The visitors center in Fairbanks tries to discourage ignorant yokels from attempting the 500 mi. of extremely tough, dangerous road to Deadhorse, the gateway to oil-drilling operations at **Prudhoe Bay** and the northernmost point the oil companies will let you reach if you're not on a tour.

The breathtaking drive parallels the pipeline from Fairbanks over the Arctic Circle to Deadhorse, where you can arrange to have a tour of Prudhoe Bay. The entire highway was opened to the public on January 1, 1995. Truckers driving 36-wheel rigs spitting rocks and dust dominate the highway; a tiny number of RVs, a handful of 4WD vehicles, and an occasional crazy motorcyclist constitute the tourist traffic. It is passable, however, in a standard passenger car. Some hitchers proceed on the logic that no one will leave someone stranded in the middle of nowhere, but truckers, the vast majority of the traffic, almost never stop for hitchers. (*Let's Go* does not recommend hitchhiking.) Simply put, it is not a smart choice to make the drive in your own vehicle. Rocks, boulders, ditches, and mud—often so deep that you are lucky to reach the other side—interrupt a dangerously sharp gravel road. Your suspension will be wrecked, and if you drive more than 50 mph, you are likely to end up with at least one flat tire and no services in sight. The trip takes approximately 24hr. roundtrip in perfect weather and at safe speeds, which usually means below 45 mph on the good stretches and often no more than 30 mph.

The key to this spectacular drive is good preparation and a healthy dose of patience. The visitor's center in Fairbanks recommends bringing two spare tires. Bring at least one, extra gas, tools, extra clothing, and food supplies. You do not want to pay to be towed back to Fairbanks, since it costs around $7 *per mile*.

If you're determined to go north but don't want to test your car's threshold for pain, the **Northern Alaska Tour Company** (474-8600) offers a day trip to the Arctic Circle boundary, and a three-day trip to Prudhoe Bay. The packages are pricey (starting at $99), but comprehensive, and a single flat tire halfway up the Dalton Hwy. could put you in far worse financial and emotional condition. Given that comprehensive tours of Prudhoe Bay itself start at $60, and that you will pay at least $30 for gas to get there, the tours are by far the best means of travel.

FROM FAIRBANKS TO THE ARCTIC CIRCLE

A drive up the Dalton Hwy. begins with an 83-mi. jaunt from Fairbanks along the **Elliot Hwy.** to Mile 0 of the Dalton Highway. Enjoy the 40 mi. of pavement as you head out from Fairbanks; it's the last you'll see for almost 900 mi. At Mile 49.5, sojourners pining for a glimpse of homestead life should stop at the **Wildwood General Store.** This homestead's owners are raising 23 children and keep the store open "whenever someone's around." If your timing is right you can get a tour.

At Dalton Hwy. Mile 56 (139mi. from Fairbanks) you will encounter the **Yukon River.** On the north side of the river is one of the highway's two **service stations.** You can get unleaded gas at **Yukon Ventures** (655-9001) for $1.81 per gallon or rent a room for $50 per person. The gas station is open daily 7am-11pm, and the café is open daily 7am-9pm.

The road next winds through its first alpine region as it gains elevation and passes **Finger Rock** (to the east at Mile 97.5) and **Caribou Mountain** (to the west). The rest area just past Finger Rock is an ideal place to calm your pothole-jarred nerves and enjoy the view of the **Brooks Range.** You'll soon pass over several steep hills with names like "Happy Man" and "Beaver Slide."

Next comes the **Arctic Circle,** the southernmost point at which the sun does not set on the longest day of the year. A recently constructed pulloff has several picnic tables and presents the visitor with four placards on the Arctic seasons (summer, winter, winter, and winter). The enormous "Arctic Circle" sign is a great photo opportunity, and the spot is good for free camping. If you're satisfied with reaching the Arctic Circle, you might camp here and retreat to Fairbanks come morning; the road only gets worse.

FROM THE ARCTIC CIRCLE TO DEADHORSE

Continuing north, over 1500-ft. **Gobblers Knob,** past Prospect Camp and Pump Station No. 5, over the Jim River and the South Fork of the Koyukuk River, you'll rattle along to the town of **Coldfoot,** which has the last services available before Prudhoe Bay (240 mi. away). Coldfoot, "the northernmost truck stop in North America," was originally a mining town which, at its peak, boasted "one gambling hall, two road houses, seven saloons, and 10 prostitutes." Its name originated in 1898, when a group of timid prospectors got "cold feet" about wintering above the Arctic Circle and headed south again. "Downtown" is a huge and muddy parking lot. Around the perimeter of the field is the **Coldfoot Café** (678-5201) with good, hot, and (surprise!) expensive food: burgers and fries start at around $7 (open 24hr.). The **general store** is open daily noon-9pm and has limited supplies (mostly to feed your car; for supplies

ALASKA

to feed yourself continue to Wiseman). Gas will cost you about $1.81 per gallon for unleaded. The **Arctic Acres Inn** (678-5224) maintains several RV sites (electrical hookups $20), but if you just hike one mi. out of town in any direction and stay out of sight, nobody will care where you pitch your tent, as long as you leave no evidence of your stay. Eight mi. north of Coldfoot, the BLM-administered **Marion Creek Campground** has sites in muskeg forest with water and pit toilets for $6. You can take a **shower** at the hotel for $3 or do a load of **laundry** for $4.

Just north and around the corner is the **Coldfoot Visitor Center** (678-5209), managed jointly by the National Park Service, Bureau of Land Management, and the Dept. of Fish and Wildlife. This is an excellent source of information if you're planning on doing intense trekking or paddling in the Brooks Range (open daily 1-10pm, nightly slide presentations 8:30pm). For a bit of history, walk across the highway and down the road. On your way to historic **Coldfoot,** you'll pass by the **Coldfoot Cemetery** on the banks of the Koyukuk River, which consists of two weather-worn, broken-down cabins dating from the turn of the century. The **post office** is next to the general store. (Open Mon., Wed., and Fri. 1:30-6pm; **ZIP Code:** 99790.)

Twelve mi. north of Coldfoot at Mile 188.6 is the junction for the village of **Wiseman,** truly the last frontier and worth the short side trip. Three mi. off the beaten path, this town was immortalized by Robert Marshall in his 1933 book, *Arctic Village*. Perhaps the wildest frontier town accessible by road in Alaska, Wiseman is home to many of the dogs who appeared in the Walt Disney movie *White Fang* (including White Fang himself). The **Wiseman Trading Post** (796-9001), at the end of the road to Wiseman over a narrow footbridge, is the quintessential frontier general store. You can pitch a tent behind the store for $2.50.

From Wiseman, the highway continues into the heart of the Brooks Range. Keep your eyes open for moose, Dall sheep, bear, caribou, hawks, ground squirrels, and other animals. At Mile 235, **the last tree** found along the highway—a surprisingly tall and majestic spruce—is posted with a sign, and marks the beginning of the steep and awe-inspiring ascent toward **Atigun Pass** (4752ft.). The highway cuts steeply into the mountainside as it approaches the pass and offers spectacular views of the Dietrich River Valley. Check out the glacial **cirque** (an amphitheater-shaped depression) on the mountainside east of the highway. Once the mountains are breached, the long descent toward the **Arctic Ocean** begins.

In the final stretch of the highway, the mountains gradually flatten into a broad expanse of monotonous tundra. The tundra is perpetually brown except for a short month-long summer in July-August. Although it looks easy, walking on the tundra in this area is a nightmare. It is filled with bumps and lumps of moss called tussocks, and is underlaid by tremendous amounts of water unable to escape through the frozen ground. Try a tundra walk and you're guaranteed a wet, soggy, difficult hike. Despite the rough terrain, you may see **caribou, foxes, and multitudes of birds** roaming freely and without difficulty throughout the North Slope. Even with the perpetual sun, the temperature is noticeably cool, typically about 43 °F (5 °C) for much of the summer.

Approximately 10 mi. from the end of the highway, the land becomes enshrouded in a layer of coastal fog, blocking the sun and causing the temperature to plummet. **Deadhorse** suddenly appears on the horizon at the end of the highway, and 3 mi. beyond is Prudhoe Bay, accessible only to officially sanctioned tours.

And then you're there. At the **Arctic Ocean.** The northernmost point accessible by road in North America. Fun, wasn't it? Now you just have to get back.

■ Prudhoe Bay

Named in 1826 by English Arctic explorer Sir John Franklin after the fourth Duke of Northumberland, Baron Prudhoe, Prudhoe Bay may not be enough of a reward for those who've endured the grueling 500 mi. trek up the Dalton Hwy. Oil was discovered here in 1968 and it took less than 10 years for full-fledged oil extraction to begin. The pipeline itself—reaching 800 mi. from Prudhoe Bay to the warm-water port of

Old Pilots And Bold Pilots, But No Old Bold Pilots

Most Alaskans say that Bush pilots are one or the other, but never both. The state has the highest per capita ownership of small planes, the greatest number of pilots, the greatest number of float planes, and one of the nation's most heavily used airports (in Anchorage). In much of the Interior and the Bush, small planes aren't simply the best way to get there; they're the only way to get there. Some of the state's most colorful lore is based in aviation—for example, the story of the third governor of Alaska who broke both ankles crash landing his small plane rather than endanger the children playing in the landing field. Tales of unusual cargo are as common as tales of unusual landings: bush pilots have been know to transport canoes, beer, furniture, even moose to the farthest reaches of the state.

Valdez—was built in less than three years, employed more than 30,000 people, and cost $8 billion. Extraction continues today, and more than two million barrels of oil are contained within the length of the pipeline at any given time, moving south at a rate of 6 to 7 mph. The entire oil-drilling operation at Prudhoe Bay is built on gravel pads designed to protect the underlying tundra; when the oil runs out (probably within the next 30 years), everything in Prudhoe Bay and Deadhorse, including the gravel, will be removed as required by law.

The weather is wretched. Covered by fog and swept by Arctic winds, the temperature can drop below freezing any day of the year, and, with windchill, the temperature is usually below freezing. In winter, the official record low wind-chill factor was recorded at -167°F (-110°C). Prudhoe Bay receives nine weeks of perpetual daylight and eight of eternal night each year. In winter, the land is blanketed with snow and ice, and the Beaufort Sea freezes solid. It is common for polar bears to wander into town off the Arctic ice floes in search of seals or a hapless oil employee.

This is not a normal community. Everything exists for and because of oil. Every building and structure contributes in some manner to oil production. No permanent residents, extremely limited tourist facilities, and no "town proper" can be found in Prudhoe Bay. The camp of **Deadhorse** on the southern perimeter of **Lake Colleen,** at the terminus of the Dalton Hwy., is the closest thing to a town around here. Deadhorse owes its name to the gravel company who brought the first road-building materials north, and whose motto was: "We'll haul anything, even a dead horse."

Sights and Practical Information Prudhoe Bay's visitor center (659-5748), run by the Atlantic Richfield Co. (ARCO), can only be accessed during a tour, but any of the hotel desks or travel agencies can supply you with information. Although more than 255 mi. of roads run through the oil fields, very little is publicly accessible. The roads are privately owned by the oil companies and access is controlled by two guarded check points. The only way to see the oil fields is from Deadhorse, where you can check them out aboard a tour. **Arctic Caribou Inn** (659-2368) offers excellent four-hour tours for $60. You'll stand next to Mile 0 of the pipeline, check out the interior of the worker's bunkhouses (surprisingly nice), and dip your fingers into the icy waters of the Arctic Ocean, among other things. There is also a "shuttle" tour which costs $25 and lasts one hour. This abbreviated version is mostly a driving tour of the fields, but still affords you the chance to leap into the Arctic Ocean. Shuttle tours are only given at 8am and 11:30am, so arrive in the morning if you want to take one. (Ted, the tour operator, can be convinced to run shuttles at other times, if he's in the mood.)

Deadhorse's airport is served by **Alaska Airlines** (800-225-2752). A one-way flight from Fairbanks costs $248. In an emergency, call the ARCO operator at 659-5900, as there are no "public" emergency services. Keep in mind that Prudhoe Bay is a "dry" community. No alcohol or firearms are allowed. The **post office** (659-2669) is located in the general store. (Open daily 1-3:30pm and 6:30-9pm; **ZIP Code:** 99734.) The **area code** is 907.

Accommodations and Food The only gas station in Prudhoe Bay is run by the Northwest Alaska Native Corporation (NANA). Ask at one of the hotels for directions. The **Prudhoe Bay Hotel** (659-2520) has singles for $75 and doubles for $130 (shared bath, 3 meals included). A converted bunkhouse with a spacious rec room, the Prudhoe Bay even has its own **cafeteria,** which serves breakfast for $12, lunch for $15, and dinner for $20. The **Arctic Caribou Inn** also serves meals at the same prices, and has doubles available at $175. If you're thinking of camping, you may be able to pitch a tent on a luxuriously soft gravel pad out by the airport—ask at the Arctic Caribou Inn for directions.

For other necessities, the **Prudhoe Bay General Store** (659-2425), next to the Arctic Caribou Inn, is like a miniature mall with a post office and the prices aren't all that steep, considering where you are (open daily 8am-9pm).

■ Brooks Range

Defining Alaska's north coast, the magnificent **Brooks Range** describes a tremendous semicircle from the Chuchki Sea in the west, through the Noatak National Preserve and **Gates of the Arctic National Park,** to the **Arctic National Wildlife Refuge (ANWR)** and the Canadian border in the east. Too far from Fairbanks to draw tourists, too isolated (with the exception of Anaktuvuk Pass) to support human habitation and too huge to be patrolled by park rangers, the Brooks Range is the last stretch of virgin wilderness in U.S. possession. A few remote settlements and the thin trail of the Dalton Hwy. are the only signs of humanity's encroachment.

Accessing the Brooks Range, and the parks which encompass it, is both difficult and expensive. It's possible to hike into the Brooks Range from the Dalton Hwy. near Wiseman, but to get to the best parts of the range, or to get even more than 10 mi. from the highway, most people fly into the park. Talk to park officials before planning a trip into the Brooks (the headquarters for both the Gates and ANWR are located in Fairbanks; see **Fairbanks: Practical Information** on p.107). The **Coldfoot Visitors Center** (678-5209) can give you specific information on where to hike into the range from the Dalton Hwy.

ANAKTUVUK PASS

Literally translated, "Anaktuvuk" means **"caribou crap."** Twice a year, swarms of caribou descend upon Anaktuvuk in their migratory grazings. It comes as no surprise, then, that the Nunamiut (NOON-ah-myoot) are making their last stand here. North America's last true nomads, this inland Inuit people only began to make permanent settlements in the last 50 years. Surrounded by **Gates of the Arctic National Park** and nestled in a wide, mirage-like mountain pass in the tundra of the Arctic Divide, the Nunamiut struggle to maintain their subsistence lifestyle amid the pressures and developments of the 20th century.

Though Anaktuvuk and the surrounding land is within the park and protected by U.S. law, it is actually private land owned by the Nunamiut. Until recently, the Nunamiut have been wary of opening up their land to tourist use. They manage it, as well as hunt and trap aboard motorcycles and ATVs. They are careful not to overrun the land, though the trail of ATV tracks around town is initially startling to visitors. Travelers are quite welcome, but residents politely and steadfastly request the following: if you come, do not litter or interrupt the activities of the Nunamiut; use low impact camping techniques (see **Camping and the Outdoors: Wilderness Concerns,** p. 47), and absolutely never take pictures of the local people without permission. There are other requests about wilderness travel as well, but these are best learned by speaking to a ranger.

The mountain backdrop encircling the pass is one of the world's most beautiful. The jagged **Brooks Range** is treeless and the relief doesn't stop for over 1000 mi. beginning with the Bering Straight and reaching well into Canada. The only pass wide enough for a town is in Anaktuvuk, but this is also the only place large enough for the caribou. The pass itself is actually a "col"; to the north and south of the pass, two different river basins drain the nearby peaks and valleys. Flowing south, the headwaters of the John River flow through town into the Tanana, on into the Yukon, and finally the Pacific. A small creek in summer, the headwaters of the Anaktuvuk River eventually flow some 300 mi. toward Prudhoe Bay.

Hiking the tundra is probably unlike anything you have experienced before. The tundra is extraordinarily challenging to navigate and potentially dangerous. You are likely to encounter snow walls, hidden crevasses, and wild animals, even the rare wolf. The terrain is best if you enjoy the process of hiking itself, as it can be difficult to reach any fixed destination. Beware of potentially frigid weather all year round. The rangers are the best source of information, but they advise calling ahead since they do not keep regular hours.

Larry's Flying Service (474-9169), one of the most well-respected Bush airlines, offers flights to Anaktuvuk Pass from Fairbanks (Tues. and Fri. $250 roundtrip), as do several others. If you can stop your stomach from staging a coup, the flight over the tops of the awe-inspiring Brooks Range is worth the money. Wilderness so pristine and beautiful is found few places on earth. If stuck in town, visitors should head to the **Simon Panaek Museum** (661-3413), which has extensive displays on traditional Nunamiut culture. The **Hans van der Laan Brooks Range Library** also houses a huge collection of material on the people and land of Alaska's Far North. (Both free; both open June 1-Aug. 31 Mon.-Thurs. 10am-5pm, Fri. 10am-4:30pm, Sat.-Sun. 1-5pm; Sept. 1-May 31 Mon.-Fri. 8:30am-5pm.)

The town has no rooms for rent, but visitors can camp anywhere just outside of town. The hills on the other side of the John River offer good camping spots. The **Nunamiut Corporation Store** (661-3327) has groceries at steep Brooks Range prices (open Mon.-Fri. 10am-6pm, Sat. noon-6pm). A hole-in-the-wall restaurant, the **Nunamiut Corp. Camp Kitchen** (661-3123), on the south end of town, has breakfast ($6), burgers ($5) and halibut dinners ($16). (Open Mon.-Sat. 7am-1pm and 3-7pm.) The **washeteria** (661-9713), next to the enormous blue-roofed school, has **showers** (free!) and **laundry** facilities (wash $1, 10min. dry 50¢. Open Mon.-Tues. and Sat. 1-5pm and 6-9:30pm, Wed. and Fri. 8:30am-8:30pm, Sun. 10am-noon and 1-6:30pm). **Emergency numbers** include: **police,** 911; **medical/fire,** 611; **public safety officer,** 661-3911; **health clinic,** 661-3914. The **post office** (661-3615) is next to the airstrip (open Mon.-Fri. 8:30-11:30am, 12:30-5:30pm; **ZIP Code:** 99721).

GATES OF THE ARCTIC NATIONAL PARK AND THE ARCTIC NATIONAL WILDLIFE REFUGE

With over 11,200 sq. mi. of protected wilderness, Gates of the Arctic National Park is designed to preserve the central Brooks Range. Six National Wild and Scenic Rivers run through the park and provide excellent floating opportunities. Heavy glaciation has carved huge U-shaped valleys throughout the park that are great for hiking and route-finding. Covering a huge swath of northeast Alaska, the Arctic National Wildlife Refuge (ANWR) encompasses more than 31,100 incredibly remote sq. mi., an area larger than Maine. The calving ground of the porcupine caribou herd and the Brooks Range's highest mountains are here. Oil companies are close to winning their battle to move in for exploration, and this may soon alter the area forever. The only—and very expensive—way in is by chartered plane, so keep dreaming.

The park is most accessible to the decidedly wealthy and the powerfully determined. Budget backpackers sometimes hitch up the Dalton Hwy. and hike in from several access points along the road. (*Let's Go* does not recommend hitchhiking.) Those with a bit more money can fly commercially into Anaktuvuk Pass and head out from there. Those with still more cash to spare can charter a plane and immerse themselves in true isolation. The town of **Bettles** lies south of the mountains on the Middle Fork of the Koyukuk River and is the jumping-off point for those chartering a plane. Several companies offer charter service (see above). Ask around for the best deal, and expect to pay several hundred dollars an hour for a plane.

Facility with a compass, bear awareness, and other backcountry skills are necessary for any backpacker heading into the park. A sudden drop in temperature can quickly lead to hypothermia. If you have any doubts about your preparedness, simply *do not go.* This is extreme wilderness and only a healthy respect for Mother Nature and a good deal of experience will get you through it. For more information, contact **Park Headquarters, 201 1st Ave.** (456-0281), in Fairbanks, or write Superintendent, Gates of the Arctic National Park, P.O. Box 74680, Fairbanks, 99707-4680. The Park Service operates a **Gates of the Arctic Field Station** (692-5494) in Bettles for those seeking information (open daily 8am-5pm). In Bettles, **Sourdough Outfitters** (692-5252) offers guided and unguided adventures in the Brooks Range. Canoes and other kinds of equipment are available for rent, and guides are extremely knowledgeable about the park. Stop by for tips before venturing out.

Ask around about good places to pitch a tent, or stay in the **Bettles Lodge** (800-770-5111 or 692-5111). The lodge has a bunkhouse ($15, sleeping bag required), which is a better deal than regular rooms (singles $85, doubles $115). The lodge's **restaurant** has good cheeseburgers ($6.25; open daily 8-10am, noon-2pm and 6-10pm). The **Bettles Trading Post** (692-5252) sells expensive groceries (open Mon.-Sat. 9am-6pm, Sun. noon-4pm).

At the lodge, you can also take a **shower** ($3.50) or do some **laundry** ($7.50 per load). The **post office** (692-5236) is at the northern end of town (open Mon.-Fri. 8am-noon and 1-4pm, Sat. "for a few hours"). The **ZIP Code** is 99726.

■ Fort Yukon

Fort Yukon lies at the convergence of the Porcupine and Yukon Rivers, eight mi. north of the Arctic Circle. It is the largest Native Alaskan community and has long been an outpost of the Hudson's Bay Company. The town is rich in relics of Native history. The town's walking-tour pamphlet (available at the **Native village** or the **Sourdough Hotel**) details a collection of sights: a ghost town, St. Stephen's Church with its beaded moose-skin altar cloths, the Fort Yukon replica, a museum, and the small town center. Check out the Fort Yukon branch of the **University of Alaska,** which primarily educates Native Alaskans from the surrounding towns of Arctic Village, Beaver, Birch Creek, Central Chalkyitsik, Circle, Circle Hot Springs, Rampart, Stevens Village, and Venetie. **Frontier Flying Services** (474-0014) flies three times a day Mon.-Fri., and once on Sat. and Sun. in the summer from Fairbanks to Fort Yukon ($154 roundtrip, $120 seniors and children). Home-cooked meals are available for $8-15 at the time-warped **Sourdough Hotel** (662-2402). It's a bit musty, but spacious and clean (singles or doubles $65 per person with shared bathroom).

NORTHWEST ALASKA

■ Nome

The Klondike's counterpart in Alaska, Nome owes its existence to the "three lucky Swedes" who discovered gold on nearby Anvil Creek in 1898. Despite the climatic misfortunes of arctic temperatures and Bering Sea storms, Nome supports a population of 4000, half of which is native Alaskan. Built almost entirely on permafrost, buildings are elevated on pilings to prevent the ground from thawing beneath them, and most have extremely ramshackle exteriors. Those who can afford to get here will find untamed wilderness surprisingly accessible by road, refreshingly non-commercialized relics of mining history, and some famously wild saloons.

PRACTICAL INFORMATION

Visitors Center: P.O. Box 240 (443-5535), located on Front St. Free nightly presentations at 7pm. Don't miss the uproariously funny video "No Place Like Nome." Open in summer daily 9am-9pm; off-season 9am-6:30pm.

Airport: Located about 2 mi. west of town. The airport is served by **Alaska Airlines** (800-426-0333); roundtrip from Fairbanks $460. **Alaska Airlines Vacations** (800-468-2248) offers circuit tours from Anchorage to Nome to Kotzebue. **Frontier Flying Services** (474-0014 in Fairbanks) flies from Fairbanks (roundtrip $506, seniors and children $436).

Taxis: Checker Cab, 443-5211. **Nome Cab,** 443-3030. Both 24hr. Standard fare is $3 per person for places in town, $5 to the airport.

Car Rental: Bonanza (443-2561), 187 Front St. $65 per day for a pickup truck, van $85 per day, both with unlimited mileage (credit card required). **Stampede** (443-3838), 4WD pickup, Bronco, or van $75 per day, unlimited mileage (credit card or $100 cash deposit required). All renters must be 21. **Gas** sells for around $2.10 per gallon.

Books: Arctic Trading Post (443-2686), across from the Nugget Inn, has the most extensive selection of local literature. Open daily 7am-11pm.

Library: Kegoayah Kozga Library (443-5133), above the museum on Front St. Open summers Mon.-Fri. noon-8pm, Sat.-Sun. noon-6pm.

Laundromat: Nome Washeteria (443-5335), at Seppala St. and C St. The only laundromat in town. Wash $4, dry $4. Open Mon.-Sat. 11am-8pm.

Shower: Rec center (443-5431) at the northern edge of town on East Sixth Ave. Free with the $4 admission price.

Weather: 443-2321, or check the box outside the visitors center.

Hospital/Pharmacy: Norton Sound Hospital (443-3311), at the end of Bering St.

Emergency: 911. **Police:** 443-5262.

Post Office: 240 E. Front St. (443-2401). Open Mon.-Fri. 9am-5pm. **ZIP Code:** 99762.

Area Code: 907.

ACCOMMODATIONS

Beds in Nome are costly, but camping is permitted (free) on Nome's flat, sandy beaches, about a one mi. walk east along Front St. past the sea wall. Gold miners dot the beaches, so enjoy the company. If you have a car, head for **Salmon Lake,** at Mile 38 of the Taylor Hwy., or **Pilgrim Hot Springs,** seven mi. off the Taylor Hwy. at Mile 53.6 (see **Outdoors,** below).

Ocean View Manor B&B (443-2133), on the beach about 1 block from the bank, on Front St. Offers a deck-side view across Norton Sound and the Bering Sea. TV, phones, refrigerators, shared or private bath. Prices include continental breakfast and kitchen privileges. Singles $50-55, with private bath $60; doubles $55-60, with private bath $65.

Betty's Igloo, P.O. Box 1784 (443-2419), at the eastern edge of town on 1st Ave. and K St. Clean and comfortable with kitchen facilities, a spacious common room, and friendly hosts. Shared bath. Children not allowed. Breakfast included. Singles $55, doubles $70. Reservations strongly recommended.

Weeks Apartments (443-3194), at 3rd. Ave. and G St. A mother lode of amenities: TV, maid service, kitchen, private bath, and private washer and dryer. Clean and nondescript. Singles $50-60, doubles $70-80.

FOOD

Don't be alarmed by the often dilapidated exteriors of Nome's restaurants—almost all the buildings look like that. Stock up on groceries and supplies at **Hanson's Trading Company** (443-5454) on Bering St. (open Mon.-Sat. 7:30am-10pm, Sun. 10am-7pm). The rowdy bars in town are grouped together on Front St.

Fat Freddie's (443-5899), next to the visitors center. Popular tour destination because it's clean, well-lit, and overlooks the ocean. Soak in the blue expanses of the Bering Sea while you chow down on the soup and all-you-can-eat salad bar for $8. Breakfast omelettes for $6.50. Open daily 6am-10pm.

Pizza Napoli (443-5300), at the corner of Front St. and Lanes Way. Join the local crowd for burgers (from $4.50) or pizza (from $10). Booths offer privacy and dim lighting—this might be the best place in Nome to make a romantic move. Open daily 11am-11pm.

Twin Dragon (443-5552), at the corner of Front St. and Steadman. Avoid the tackiness and grease that plague lesser Chinese joints. Unbelievably fresh vegetables—how'd they do that? The bright, well decorated interior makes the Almond Chicken or Sweet and Sour Pork (both $11.95) taste all the better. Look for lunch specials. Open Mon.-Fri. 11am-11pm, Sat. noon-11pm, Sun. 3-11pm.

The Glue Pot (443-5474), on Front St., diagonal from the visitors center. Not for those seeking a refined atmosphere. But the hamburgers ($3.95) or breakfast specials ($8.75-9.85) will fill you up; then play some pinball or pawn your necklace (the Glue Pot brokers gold and jewelry on the side). Nome's only after-bar hangout. Open Mon.-Sat. 11am-3:30am, Sun. 1pm-2am.

EVENTS

Isolation from the rest of the world seems to make residents do strange things. The **Bering Sea Ice Golf Classic** is held in March on the frozen Bering Sea. Standard golf rules apply (with some interesting exceptions) on this six-hole course. Contestants' bright orange balls skirt the course's unique hazards: crevasses, ice chunks, bottomless snow holes, and frost-leafed greens. Extremity-warmers (whisky and rum) are provided with contestants' entry fee. Course rules dictate: "If you hit a polar bear (Endangered Species List) with your gold ball, you will have three strokes added to your score. If you recover said ball, we will subtract five strokes." The biggest event of the winter, however, is the **Iditarod dogsled race.** The world's foremost dogsled race finishes in mid-March beneath the log "banner" visible year-round next to City Hall. Thousands of spectators journey in, and it isn't uncommon for all local accommodations to be booked nearly a year in advance. Tardy room-seekers can contact the visitors center, which assists with overflow housing.

Summer festivities include the **Midnight Sun Festival** on the weekend closest to the solstice (June 21st). After a parade and a BBQ, the **Nome River Raft Race,** the city's largest summer event, commences. Home-made contraptions paddle their way down the three to four mi. course, hoping to clinch the prestigious fur-lined Honey-Bucket. On Labor Day, the **Bathtub Race** sends tubs mounted on wheels down Front St. The bathtub must be full of water at the start and have at least 10 gallons remaining by the finish. Teammates outside the tub wear large brim hats and suspenders while the one in the tub totes a bar of soap, towel, and bath mat.

OUTDOORS

Branching out into the surrounding wilderness, Nome's three highways are a godsend for the adventurous traveler. All are entirely gravel, but are generally well-main-

---

Pannin' fer Gold

It's a bit like shampooing: lather, rinse, repeat. Scoop up some likely-looking beach sand and gravel. Swirl water, sand, and gravel in a tilted gold pan, slowly washing materials over the edge. (Repeat.) Eventually you'll be down to black sand, and—hopefully—gold. Gold is shinier than brassy-looking pyrite (Fool's Gold), and it doesn't break down upon touch, like mica, another common glittery substance. You can try *panning à la Nome* on the beaches one mi. east of the visitors center. Panning on the beaches is free, but you have to bring your own pan. If your scale can take it, try the **Alaska Commercial Company** (443-5559), on Front St., next to the museum, for $8.50-12 pans.

tained and navigable in a rental car. According to the visitors center, hitching a ride up the **Taylor** or **Council Hwy.** is fairly easy on weekends, when many Nome residents head that way. (*Let's Go* does not recommend hitchhiking.) There are excellent **fishing** rivers along the highways, including the **Nome** and **Pilgrim Rivers,** both accessible via the Taylor Hwy. Bring mosquito repellent or you will curse the day you ever heard of Nome.

The **Taylor Hwy.** (also known as the Kougarok Rd.) heads north from Nome for 86 mi., though it peters out without reaching a destination of note. Along the way is **Salmon Lake,** near Mile 40. Popular with locals, the lake offers excellent fishing and primitive campsites. At Mile 53.6, an unmarked 7-mi. road leads to the **Pilgrim Hot Springs** area. The Catholic Church ran an orphanage here from 1917 to 1941, and, surprisingly, many of the buildings are intact and undisturbed. After soaking in the natural hot springs, you can wander around the abandoned church, which still contains original statues, paintings, and stained glass. A private company has a lease on the property until October 31, 2068 and plans to develop it eventually, but for now you can camp, soak, and explore for free. The **Kigluaik Mountains** are accessible via this highway and offer some good hiking and wildflower viewing.

The **Council Hwy.** travels 76 mi. from Nome to **Council,** a ghost town and summer home for Nome residents (it's appealingly below the treeline). En route, the highway goes around Cape Nome, passing the fascinating **"Last Train to Nowhere,"** a failed railroad immortalized by the engine and cars that sit slowly rusting on the tundra. The **Nome-Teller Hwy.** winds west from Nome for 76 mi. to the small and nondescript Native village of **Teller.**

Nome's outskirts are home to the remnants of over 40 abandoned gold dredges, as well as a handful that still operate. The closest non-operating dredge is about 1.6 mi. from downtown on Front St., on the way to the Taylor Hwy.

ALEUTIAN ISLANDS

This is no place to go on a budget. At the fiery boundary between two tectonic plates, the string of snow-capped volcanoes that make up the Alaska Peninsula and the Aleutian Islands stretches more than 1000 mi. into the stormy North Pacific. The Aleutians are one of the most remote locations on earth; the westernmost islands are within a few hundred miles of Kamchatka, Russia. The lava-scarred cones on these green but treeless isles are abused by some of the world's worst weather. Vicious storms packing winds of over 100mph can blow in any time.

Russia used the islands as stepping stones into Alaska. In June 1942, the Japanese tried to divert the American forces from the southern Pacific by occupying the outer islands of Attu and Kiska, and bombarding the Aleutian town of Unalaska. A year later, the U.S. military stormed Attu, touching off a bloody, obscure battle which left thousands of American and Japanese soldiers dead on the wind-swept tundra.

The Peninsula and the islands are home to Aleut villages, small military installations, and larger towns dedicated to serious deep-sea fishing. In the summer, a few hundred tourists come here, despite the cost and time involved, to explore the natural beauty of this volcanic wilderness and to view the millions of migratory seabirds that stop here. Several species of aves found here nest nowhere else.

GETTING THERE

The only two methods of getting to the Aleutian Islands are both prohibitively expensive. A one way flight from Anchorage to **Dutch Harbor,** the largest town on the Aleutians, costs around $350 and lasts about two to three hours. A roundtrip ferry on the **Alaska Marine Hwy.** costs $400 and takes five days. The ferry is the better choice, as the whole point of traveling to the Peninsula and the Aleutians is not merely the destination (there is really nothing there) but instead to spend time enjoying the unique panoramas and wildlife. The ship is hardly a cruiseliner, and it's probably a

Location, Location, Location

And you thought that all of the action during World War II was in Europe and the South Pacific. The Aleutian Islands, due to their extreme westerly location, were the site of many (or at least several) tussles between the Japanese and the U.S. Beyond providing a fertile ground for military confrontation away from the tender eyes of American citizens, the Aleutian chain was also a convenient spot for unsavory practices like nuclear testing. Take, for example, the idyllic Amchitka Island. The U.S. military built a base on Amchitka during the war, and then from 1965 to 1973 conducted underground nuclear testing under the auspices of the Atomic Energy Commission. In the late 80s the Navy took advantage of Amchitka's location (closer to Russia than it is to any city in the U.S.) to build a radar station there. The military installation folded by the end of the Cold War, and now there's little in the way of action on Amchitka. It seems that proximity to the enemy is really only an advantage when there's an enemy to be near. With all quiet on the (far) Western front, strategic defense points are of little use.

good idea to try it out on a day trip before committing yourself to the boat's confines for five days. If you are serious about a ferry voyage to the Aleutians, consider purchasing the **AlaskaPass,** which might make the trip more affordable (see p. 35). The Alaska Marine Highway makes this trip only seven times per year between April and September, and it is best to go in July, when the weather is mildest. Make reservations at least two weeks in advance; boats often fill in summer.

The *M/V Tustamena* serves the Aleutian chain from Kodiak. It features a dining room with limited hours and decent food (bringing some of your own from Kodiak is a very good idea), showers, and a lounge where an on-board naturalist regularly gives slide shows on the plants and wildlife seen from the ship. Cabinless passengers can sleep above decks. The solarium is (cough) right next to the (ack) exhaust tower. If you want to splurge for the trip, spend the extra $470 for a four-person cabin (about $23.50 per person per night).

Most of your companions for the trip will be seniors taking advantage of the $200 they save on discount tickets, with a scattering of families, students, fisherfolk, and maniacal birdwatcher types who run around with binoculars the size of small children screaming, "It's a Whiskered Auklet!"

The ferry stops briefly at several small towns, ranging from quaint fishing villages to prefabricated cannery quarters, before reaching Dutch Harbor, the most interesting town in the Aleutians. Unfortunately, it only stops here about five hours before turning around and heading back, so you're not left with much time to explore. Stock up on Dramamine or another seasickness remedy before you leave. You'll be weathering 5- to 15-ft. seas; they don't call the *M/V Tustamena* the "Vomit Comet" for nothing.

■ Unalaska and Dutch Harbor

Isolated in the Pacific Ocean, at the western limit of the extensive Alaska Marine Hwy. ferry service, Dutch Harbor and Unalaska are about as remote a community of 4300 as you'll find in North America. In 1942, the Japanese began their ill-fated Aleutian campaign with a bombing raid on Unalaska, then a heavily fortified stronghold.

Unalaska (OO-na-las-ka) and Dutch Harbor are at the head of stunning Unalaska Bay, on Unalaska and Amaknak Islands respectively. For years, the name Dutch Harbor only referred to the port harbor itself, but recently a town, complete with its own zip code, has arisen 1 mi. from the old town of Unalaska.

Unalaska is hardly a haven for the budget traveler. Remoteness and unusually high incomes (over $130 million in seafood passes through this port every year) keep prices high. Take heart: the view of treeless, snow-capped mountains soaring thousands of feet from Unalaska Bay's chilly blue waters is always free.

Practical Information and Orientation Unalaska lies about 300 mi. from the tip of the Alaska Peninsula. It is in the same time zone as the rest of Alaska. The twin towns have a refreshing lack of concern for the tourist trade. The big money here is in seafood—you'll find mighty few tacky t-shirt shops. Dutch Harbor and Unalaska are connected by a short bridge. For general information, go to the **Unalaska Convention and Visitors Bureau,** P.O. Box 545 (581-2612), in the Grand Aleutian Hotel. They are open Mon.-Fri. 8am-5:30pm and occasionally on weekends. **Alaska Marine Highway** (800-642-0066) ferries dock at the City Dock about 1½ mi. from Dutch Harbor and 2½ mi. from Unalaska. The *M/V Tustamena* arrives about once every three to four weeks in the summer (one way to Kodiak, $202). The **airport,** located about ¼ mi. from City Dock on the main road into town, is served by several carriers, including **Reeve Aleutian** (800-548-2248 or 581-3382; to Anchorage $355 one way), the comparable **Pen Air** (581-1383), and **Alaska Airlines** (266-7700). **Taxi** service is available from five companies (locals are as baffled by that number as you are), including **Harbor Express** (581-1381) and **Alaska Taxi** (581-2129). Rent a bike at the **Community Center** (581-1297) at 5th and Broadway, in Unalaska. Mountain bikes rent for only $10 per day, $15 on weekends ($75 deposit). The **clinic** in town is **Iliuliuk Family and Health Services** (581-1202), in a big green building around the corner from the police station (open Mon.-Fri. 8:30am-6pm, Sat. 9am-5pm; for after-hours assistance call 581-1233). In an **emergency** dial 911. The **Post Office** in **Unalaska** (581-1232) is open Mon.-Fri. 8am-5:30pm, Sat. 1-5pm. The **ZIP Code** for Unalaska is 99685 and for Dutch Harbor 99692. The **Area Code** is 907.

Accommodations and Camping Once again: it ain't cheap. The visitors bureau (see **Practical Information,** above) keeps a list of accommodations including several guest houses. Most land in the area, with the notable exception of Summer Bay, is owned by native corporations, and a fee must be paid to camp there. Contact the **Ounalashka Corporation** (581-1276) for details. Camp for free at **Summer Bay.** From the City Dock or the airport, hike 2½ mi. through Dutch Harbor and Unalaska. Follow Summer Bay Rd. along the shore for another 2 mi. to Summer Bay. A bridge, some sand dunes, and a few picnic tables and barbecues mark the spot, though there are no other facilities. Set your tent in a sheltered location, or the vicious wind gusts will introduce your possessions to Iliuliuk Bay. **The Bunkhouse,** P.O. Box 598, Dutch Harbor, 99692 (581-4357), offers respectable rooms with shared baths, a lounge with TV, fridge and microwave, and laundry facilities. Singles $40, doubles $50. Weekly rates much cheaper.

Food Two enormous grocery stores, with enough square footage to comfortably house most of the town's residents, compete for town-wide supremacy. **Eagle Quality Center** (581-4041) in Dutch Harbor has a good selection, plus a tempting salad bar and hot deli items. **Ziggy's** (581-2800), next door to the Eagle, is a favorite local hang-out. Full stack of sourdough pancakes $5. Sandwiches and burgers $6-8. Mexican dinners $9-16. Open daily 6am-11pm. **Stormy's Pizza** in Unalaska has a multi-cultural lunch buffet featuring Mexican, Chinese, Japanese, pizza, and a salad bar for only $8.95. (Buffet available Mon.-Sat. 11am-2pm. Open Mon.-Sat. 11am-2am, and Sun. 5pm-midnight.)

Sights If you have the good fortune to have your ferry layover in Unalaska on a sunny day, you would be utterly foolish not to hike to the top of **Mt. Ballyhoo**, just behind the airport. The summit affords one of the most mind-bogglingly beautiful, amazingly awe-inspiring sights in the entire universe. (Superlative overkill is not possible here.) Amazing gold, red, and black rock formations jut out of the sheer cliff that plummets 1634 ft. to the translucent green water of the ocean below. While the winners of an annual race make the roundtrip to the summit in 26 minutes, a slightly more sane pace will get you to the top in 45 minutes to an hour. You can wander along the ridge for another 20-30 minutes past the summit, and still easily make it back to catch the ferry.

ALASKA

If the weather is lousy, or the thought of climbing 1600 ft. makes you cringe, then get a cab (see **Practical Information**) to drive you the 3 mi. to the **Unalaska Cemetery and Memorial Park** on the eastern edge of Unalaska. These two sights include a description of the Japanese air attacks of June 1942. You can still see the bow of the *USS Northwestern,* sunk during the attack, slowly rusting in the bay.

Heading back toward Unalaska on Beach Front Rd., you will soon reach the impressive **Holy Ascension Orthodox Church,** built 1824-27 and expanded 1894, the oldest standing Russian-built church in the U.S. The once dilapidated church has recently been restored to its former splendor. This area was once the thriving (if misguided) center of Orthodox missionary activity in Alaska.

Right after you cross the "bridge-to-the-other-side" on the way back to the ferry, you will come to **Bunker Hill,** which was heavily fortified during World War II. A quick 420-ft. climb gets you to a large concrete bunker and a great view of the surrounding bays and mountains.

Those planning to stay longer than three to four hours should ask locals or the visitors bureau about the numerous trails and military artifacts strewn across the local countryside. Check with **Aleutian Adventure Sports** (581-4489) for information on kayaking and other outdoor activities. If you happen to be in Unalaska on any night except Sunday, join commercial fishermen fresh from the open sea at the **Elbow Room Bar** (581-1470), between 2nd and 3rd on Broadway. Once voted the second rowdiest bar in the world, things have calmed down considerably.

WESTERN CANADA

Western Canada's vast expanses of wilderness contain a broad spectrum of ecological wonders, and some of the most idyllic urban areas in the Pacific Northwest. British Columbia is home to spongy arctic tundra in the north, lush coastal forests in the west, and a high, arid plateau in the east. Alberta's endless prairies, and the unadulterated sweep of the Yukon seem a world away from the big-city bustle of Vancouver. Six thousand miles from its colonial rulers in Britain and France, Western Canada has always taken pride in its spirit of self-reliance.

Native History

Western Canada's natives are among the most important and least recognized participants in its history. Bands culturally similar to Indians of the United States began to form along the coast about 10,000 years ago. Coastal societies were linguistically diverse, complex in organization, and blessed with an abundance of salmon and cedar. They are perhaps best known for the traditional ceremony of the potlatch, in which chiefs give away their possessions in a display of wealth and generosity that affirmed their privileged status within a group. Further inland, the nomadic horsemen of the plains followed bison migration patterns throughout the long, harsh winter. Though natives served as indispensable guides and translators for the French and English during the fur boom, many tribes were crippled by the onslaught of white settlers. After several centuries of European domination, the natives of Western Canada have begun to reclaim their lands and their autonomy.

The British Invasion

For white settlers, Western Canada's earliest claim to fame rested on the backs of small furry animals. On his third visit to Nootka Sound in 1778, English explorer James Cook traded some rusty nails for a few ragged sea otter pelts from the native Nuu-chah-nulth. The furs fetched a fortune in China during Cook's return trip, and the fur frenzy was on. The fur trade of the late 1700s was among the most lucrative and highly developed industries of its time. The English Hudson's Bay Company engaged in cutthroat competition with the Montreal-based North West Company. These warring fortune-hunters were linked by the trading language of the native Chinook, who served as mercenary go-betweens in the Northwest. In 1821, the North West Company was absorbed by its competitor and the fur-trade became both less frenzied, and less dependent on Indian aides.

Miners struck gold near Vancouver in 1856, and prospectors swarmed up the coast from Northern California. Where revenue went, government followed; the governor of Vancouver Island enlarged his jurisdiction to establish a real provincial administration over the mainland in Canada. In 1866, the arrangement was official, and the coastal colony above what remained of the Oregon territory—later known as Washington State—became British Columbia. The region's population boomed along with the Canadian Pacific Railroad. In 1896, a white man from California and his two Indian brothers-in-law fatefully struck gold near Dawson, in the Yukon. This territory, where caribou now outnumber people five to one, became host to a boom town of mythic proportions for a few harried decades before receding back into comfortable anonymity. The Yukon became a Canadian territory in 1898 but has not yet achieved provincehood. Alberta, whose fertile agricultural plains would later yield valuable oil, became a Canadian province in 1905.

Recent Events

Like so many economies founded on the plunder of natural resources, the provinces of Western Canada are now struggling with conversion economies that prove reluctant to convert. While Washington and Oregon continue to sop up the technology overflow from California's Silicon Valley, a province like British Columbia has no such recourse. Though the logging industry has prospered as restrictions on U.S. logging drive business north, its primary-resource economy is still vulnerable to economic shocks. Under the pressure of environmental groups, tourists, and native peoples, many areas have turned to a new brand of environmental exploitation: ecotourism. Today, capitalist instincts and good intentions together motivate environmental preservation.

The pattern of recent Western Canadian affairs is typical of developed nations. The government must find ways to cope with a history of exploitation of native people and resources. In 1995, the government admitted wrongdoing in a 1950s "relocation" project which moved 100 Inuit north of the Arctic Circle. Native bands have begun push more aggressive for autonomy and land, and their activism has recently paid off. In March 1996, after three years of talks between government officials and the Nisga'a band in northern British Columbia, representatives reached an agreement granting the Nisga'a greater control over their resources and the right to limited self-government. Though non-natives fear discrimination, and logging interests feel slighted; natives feel that their victories are hard-won and overdue. Canadians have also had to pay for mistakes they made in the early plundering their forests and lakes. At about the time the Nisga'a pact was finalized, Canadian Fisheries Minister Fred Mifflin announced that the commercial salmon-fishing fleet must be halved in the summer fishing season to protect against future shortages.

Arts and Literature

In the centuries before European settlement, the Kwakiutl tribe of the present-day Canadian coast enacted "world-renewal" ceremonies with such harrowing and theatrical effects as tunnels, trapdoors, ventriloquism, and bloody sleight-of-hand beheadings, all while costumed in fantastical cedar masks. Spectators today favor music over bloodshed, and the performing arts still dazzle audiences across the Northwest. For the diligent Native culturophile, the Provincial Museum in Victoria, B.C. is a good place to start, with an impressive showcase of Native American art.

The entertainment industry also continues to grow in Western Canada's urban centers. Vancouver is a popular location for filming movies and television shows when producers need lovely scenery and cooperative city officials. The cost of filming in large cities in the U.S. is astronomical, and municipal red tape can potentially derail an entire shoot. Not so in Canada: the runaway FOX hit *The X Files* calls Vancouver home. *Little Women* was shot here when Massachusetts proved too cold in April, and *Rumble in the Bronx* was actually a rumble in—you guessed it—Vancouver. Native art is popular and prevalent.

The literature of the region is often heavily influenced by Native cultures and the physical beauty of the land (the exception being, of course, the sci-fi *oeuvres* of Vancouver resident William Gibson). Novelist Jack London and poet Robert Service kept the Yukon mystique alive long after the decline of Dawson. *Notes from the Century Before: A Journal of British Columbia,* by Edward Hoagland, are just that. *I Heard the Owl Call My Name* and *Again Calls the Owl,* by Margaret Craven, *Trees are Lonely Company,* by Howard O'Hagan, and *Fencepost Chronicles,* by W.P. Kinsella are all good bets for a better picture of the western Canadian experience. Jean Craighead George's *Julie of the Wolves* is perfect for younger readers.

Southern British Columbia

British Columbia attracts so many visitors that tourism has become the province's second-largest industry after logging. Despite excellent year-round skiing, most tourists arrive in the summer and flock to the beautiful cities of Vancouver and Victoria and to the pristine lakes and beaches of the warm Okanagan Valley. Heading north, thick forests, low mountains, and occasional patches of high desert are interrupted only by supply and transit centers, such as Prince George and Prince Rupert. Still farther north, even these outposts of civilization defer to thick spruce and fir forests stretching to the horizon, intermittently logged or blackened by lightning fires. This chapter covers only the southern part of the province; for coverage of northern British Columbia, including the Cariboo Highway, Yellowhead Highway 16, the Queen Charlotte Islands, the Cassiar and Alaska Highways, and the Yukon Territory, see the following chapter.

British Columbia's parks are popular with hikers, mountaineers, cyclists, rafters, and skiers. On Vancouver Island, the coastal rainforests of Strathcona and Pacific Rim Parks are beautiful and largely untrammeled. In the southeastern part of the province, Glacier, Yoho, and Kootenay Parks allow visitors to escape into some of Canada's most amazing outdoor country. Here, you can enjoy country just as beautiful as Alberta's Jasper and Banff without the tourist mobs.

PRACTICAL INFORMATION

Capital: Victoria.
Visitors Information: Tourism British Columbia, 1117 Wharf St., Victoria V8W 2Z2 (387-1642 or 800-663-6000).
Park Information: Parks Canada, 220 4th Ave. SE #552, Calgary, AB T2G 4X3 (403-924-2200). **BC Parks,** 1610 Mt. Seymour Rd., North Vancouver, V7G 1L3 (666-0176).
Motto: *Splendor sine Occasu* (Splendor Undiminished). **Year of Royal Naming:** 1858, by Queen Victoria. **Year to Join Confederation:** 1871. **Provincial Holiday:** British Columbia Day, 1st Mon. in Aug. **Provincial Flower:** Pacific Dogwood. **Provincial Tree:** Douglas Fir. **Provincial Bird:** Stellar Jay.
Emergency: 911 in most areas; some rural areas may not have 911 service.
Time Zone: Mostly Pacific (1hr. behind Mountain, 2 behind Central, 3 behind Eastern). Small eastern part is Mountain (1hr. behind Central, 2 behind Eastern).
Postal Abbreviation: BC.
Provincial Sales Tax: 7%.
Drinking Age: 19.
Traffic Laws: Mandatory seatbelt law.
Area Code: 604.

GETTING AROUND

British Columbia is Canada's westernmost province, covering over 890,000 sq. km, bordering four U.S. states (Washington, Idaho, Montana, and Alaska) and three Canadian jurisdictions (Alberta, the Yukon Territory, and the Northwest Territories). Vancouver, on the mainland, can be reached by interstate highway from Seattle; Victoria, on Vancouver Island to the southwest of Vancouver, requires a ferry trip (for ferry information, see p. 35) from Anacortes, Port Angeles, Seattle, or the **Tsawwassen Terminal** near Vancouver. However you travel, get used to thinking of distances in terms of kilometers in three digits.

The **Coquihalla Hwy.** (Hwy. 5) was completed in 1986 to carry tourists comfortably from Hope to Jasper National Parks. The Coquihalla Hwy. costs $10 to ride, but is a much more direct route and constitutes a substantial time savings. If you don't think your car is capable, you can always enjoy the Fraser River Canyon's scenery via the Trans-Canada Hwy. from Hope to Banff. Much of British Columbia is served by **Greyhound** (662-3222 in Vancouver; 800-231-2222 from the U.S.).

■ Vancouver

Western Canada's largest city is quickly joining the post-industrial age. The unemployment rate has fallen by half in recent years, and electronics and international finance are supplanting timber and mining as the city's economic base. A growing wave of Chinese immigration is directing Vancouver's culture and economy toward the Far East. Cynics say their city is becoming "Hongcouver" and fear future racial tensions, while others argue that Vancouver is a modern multi-ethnic metropolis.

The number and range of Vancouver's offerings is astounding. You can go for nature walks among stands of 1000-year-old virgin timber, windsurf, take in a modern art exposition, or get wrapped up in a flick at one of the most technologically advanced movie theaters in the world, all without leaving downtown. Filled with beaches and parks, the cultural vortex of Vancouver has swallowed many an unsuspecting vacationer.

PRACTICAL INFORMATION

Visitors Information: Travel Infocentre, 200 Burrard St. (683-2000). Full info on accommodations, tours, and activities spanning much of BC. Courtesy phones for reservations. Open daily 8am-6pm. **Parks and Recreation Board,** 2099 Beach Ave. (257-8400). Open Mon.-Fri. 8:30am-5pm.

Tours: The Gray Line, 255 E. 1st Ave. (879-9287). City tours with several package options. Basic 3½-hr. tours leave daily at 9:15am and 1:45pm. $32, seniors $28, ages 5-12 $20. Reservations required.

VIA Rail, 1150 Station St. (in Canada 800-561-8630, in U.S. 800-561-3949). Sky Train stop. Trains to: Jasper (3 per week, $147), Edmonton (3 per week, $204). Open Mon. and Thurs. 8am-8pm, Tues.-Wed., Fri., and Sun. 8am-3:30pm, Sat. 12:30pm-8pm.

BC Rail, 1311 W. 1st St. (651-3500), just over the Lions Gate Bridge at the foot of Pemberton St. in North Vancouver. Take the BC Rail Special Bus on Georgia St. or the SeaBus to North Vancouver, then bus #239 west. Daily trains to: Garibaldi ($26), Whistler ($30), Williams Lake ($115), Prince George ($171), and points north. Open daily 6am-8:30pm, phones on 8am-8pm.

Greyhound, 1150 Station St. (662-3222), in the VIA Rail Station. Bus service to the south and across Canada. To: Calgary (6 per day, $98), Banff (5 per day, $96), Jasper (3 per day, $86), and Seattle (5 per day, $30). Open daily 5:30am-12:30am.

Pacific Coach Lines, 1150 Station St. (662-7575). Buses serve southern BC, including Vancouver Island, in conjunction with Greyhound. Service to Victoria ($22.50, $42 roundtrip) includes ferry and service into downtown Victoria.

Public Transportation: BC Transit Information Centre (521-0400). Fare $1.50, rates rise during rush hour; students, seniors, and children 75¢. Day passes ($4.50, students, seniors, and children $2.25) available at all 7-11 and Safeway stores, from ticket machines at Skytrain stations, or at the Travel Infocentre.

BC Ferries (669-1211 for general info, 685-1021 for recorded info, 943-9331 for Tsawwassen ferry terminal). Ferry goes to Victoria, the Gulf Islands, Sunshine Coast, Mainland, and Vancouver Island ($6.50, ages 5-11 $3.25, car and driver $31.50-33.50, motorcycle and driver $20, bicycle and rider $9). Ferries to Nanaimo on Vancouver Island leave from Horseshoe Bay, approximately 10km northwest of Vancouver.

Taxis: Yellow Cab (681-3311). **Vancouver Taxi** (255-5111). Both 24hr.

Car Rental: ABC Rental, 255 W. Broadway (873-6622). $35 per day, unlimited mileage. $209 per week; $13 per day for collision coverage. Must be 21 with credit card. Open Mon.-Fri. 7:30am-6:30pm, Sat.-Sun. 7:30am-5pm.

Bicycle Rental: Bayshore Bicycles, 745 Denman St. (680-2453). Convenient to Stanley Park. Practically new bikes $5.60 per hr., $20 for 8hr., $25 overnight. Open May-Sept. daily 9am-9pm. Winter hours vary with daylight hours.

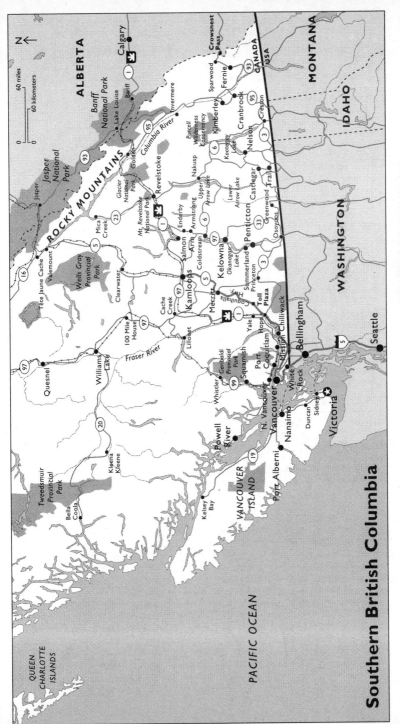

Southern British Columbia

Camping Equipment Rental: Recreation Rentals, 2560 Arbutus St. (733-7368), at Broadway. Take bus #10 or #14 from Granville Mall. Backpacks ($9 per day, $25 per week), 2-person tents ($15 per day, $45 per week), and every kind of camping and sports equipment. Open daily 8am-7pm.

Scuba Rental: The Diving Locker, 2745 W. 4th Ave. (736-2681). Complete outfit $80, $50 if you have your own gear. Open Mon.-Thurs. 9am-9pm, Fri. 9:30am-7pm, Sat. 9:30am-5:30pm.

Public Library: 350 W. Georgia St. (331-3600). Brand new and beautiful. Open Mon.-Wed. 10am-9pm, Thurs.-Sat. 10am-6pm.

Arts Hotline: 684-2787. 24hr.

Weather: 644-9040.

Road Conditions: 660-2800.

Crisis Line: Vancouver Crisis Center (872-3311). 24hr.

Women's Services: Rape Crisis Center (255-6344). 24hr. **Women's Resource Center,** 1144 Robson St. (482-8585), in the West End between Thurlow and Bute St. Open Mon.-Thurs. 10am-2pm; Sept.-June Mon.-Fri. 10am-5pm.

Senior Services: Senior Citizen's Information and Support Network, 301-555 6th St. (524-0516 or 525-2000). Open Mon.-Fri. 8:30am-4:30pm.

Services for the Disabled: BC Coalition of People with Disabilities, 204-456 W. Broadway, Vancouver V54 1R3 (875-0188). Open Mon.-Fri. 9am-5pm.

Gay and Lesbian Information: Gay and Lesbian Switchboard, 1170 Bute St. (684-6869). Counseling and info. Very helpful staff. Open daily 7-10pm.

AIDS Information: AIDS Vancouver (687-2437). Open Mon. and Thurs.-Fri. 10am-5pm, Tues.-Wed. 10am-6pm.

Public radio: CBC Radio, 690 AM.

Poison Control: 682-5050.

Pharmacy: Shoppers Drug Mart, 2979 W. Broadway (733-9128), at Carnarvon. Open Mon.-Sat. 8am-11pm, Sun. 10am-6pm.

Hospital: UBC Hospital (822-7121).

Emergency: 911. **Police:** 312 Main St. (665-3535), at Powell.

Post Office: Main branch, 349 W. Georgia St. (662-5725). Open Mon.-Fri. 8am-5:30pm. **Postal Code:** V6B 3P7.

Area Code: 604.

GETTING THERE

Vancouver is in the southwestern corner of the British Columbia mainland, across the Georgia Strait from Vancouver Island and the city of Victoria. **Vancouver International Airport** is on Sea Island, 23km south of the city center. To reach downtown from the airport, take BC bus #100 to the intersection of Granville and 70th Ave. Transfer there to bus #20, which arrives downtown by heading north on the Granville Mall. The private **Airport Express** (244-9888) bus leaves from airport level #2 and heads for downtown hotels and the bus station (4 per hr., $9, seniors $7, ages 5-12 $5; runs 6am-midnight).

Greyhound makes several runs daily between Seattle and Vancouver. The downtown bus depot provides access to the city's transit system. **VIA Rail** runs trains east. The **BC Rail** station in North Vancouver sends trains toward northern British Columbia. **BC Ferries** connects the city of Vancouver to Vancouver Island and the Gulf Islands. Ferries leave from the **Tsawwassen Terminal,** 25km south of the city center. To reach Vancouver from Tsawwassen, take bus #640 to the Ladner Exchange and transfer to bus #601, which arrives downtown on Seymour St.

Bicyclists will find many excellent routes in and near Vancouver, including routes in the Fraser River Canyon, along the shore of the Strait of Georgia, on the Gulf Islands, and on Vancouver Island. Call **Cycling BC** (737-3105) for more information. **Tourism British Columbia** (see **Practical Information,** above) publishes a thorough pamphlet on cycling. Note that the George Massey Tunnel on Hwy. 99, under the Fraser River—which you must use to get to and from the Tsawwassen terminal—is closed to bicycles. A shuttle service transports cyclists through the tunnel. Call the

WESTERN CANADA

Vancouver

Police, 9
SeaBus Terminal, 8
Travel Infocentre, 6
VIA Rail and Greyhound
Station, 11

Sights
Aquarium, 1
Aquatic Centre, 17
BC Place Stadium, 13
Brockton Oval, 2
Canada Place, 7
Granville Mall, 14
Kitsilano Beach, 21
Lost Lagoon, 5
Malkin Bowl, 3
Maritime Museum, 20
Robson Square, 15
Science World, 12
Sunset Beach Park, 16
Vancouver Museum
and H. R. MacMillan
Planetarium, 19
Vanier Park, 18
Zoo, 4

Accommodations
Paul's Guest House, 23
Vancouver International
Hostel, 22
Vincent's Backpackers
Hostel, 10

Boundary Rd.
TO SIMON FRASER U.
Trans-Canada Hwy.
Cassiar St.
Second Narrows Bridge
Main St.
Rupert St.
Grandview Hwy.
CITY OF NORTH VANCOUVER
Exhibition Park
Renfrew St.
Broadway
Renfrew St.
McGill St.
3rd St.
Nanaimo St.
1st Ave.
Nanaimo St.
Hastings St.
John Hendry Park
Skytrain
Burrard Inlet
Commercial Dr.
Victoria Dr.
Venables St.
Knight St.
Clark Dr.
Skytrain
Fraser St.
Prior St.
Terminal Ave.
Kingsway
Powell St.
Main St.
Main St.
King Edward Ave.
CHINATOWN
GAS TOWN
Pender St.
Cambie Bridge
2nd Ave.
TO QUEEN ELIZABETH PARK
SeaBus
Skytrain
Dunsmuir St.
Cambie St.
Cambie St.
DOWN TOWN
Georgia St.
Howe St.
Granville Bridge
False Creek
6th Ave.
Oak St.
TO VANCOUVER INTERNATIONAL AIRPORT
Lions Gate Bridge
TO BC RAIL STATION
WEST END
Davie St.
Granville Island
Granville St.
Fir St.
Stanley Park
Denman St.
Beach Ave.
Burrard Bridge
Pacific Blvd.
KITSILANO
Arbutus St.
English Bay
10th Ave.
N
4th Ave.
Broadway
MacDonald St.
Alma St.
Dunbar St.
Strait of Georgia
POINT GREY
10th Ave.
16th Ave.
TO UNIVERSITY OF BRITISH COLUMBIA
Jericho Beach Park

Bicycling Association of British Columbia for information on times and fares. The shuttle service operates daily in the summer but less frequently in winter.

ORIENTATION AND GETTING AROUND

Vancouver looks like a mitten with the fingers pointing west (brace yourself for a never-ending metaphor) and the thumb to the north. South of the hand flows the Fraser River and beyond the fingertips lies the Georgia Strait. Downtown is on the thumb. At the thumb's tip lie the residential **West End** and **Stanley Park.** Burrard Inlet separates downtown from North Vancouver; the bridges over False Creek (the space between the thumb and the rest of the hand) link downtown with **Kitsilano** ("Kits"), **Fairview, Mount Pleasant,** and the rest of the city. East of downtown, where the thumb is attached, lie **Gastown** and **Chinatown.** The **airport** lies south, at the pinkie-tip; the University of British Columbia lies on top of the fingers at **Point Grey.** Kitsilano and Point Grey are separated by the north-south **Alma Ave.** The major highway approaches, Hwy. 99 and the Trans-Canada Hwy., enter the city from the south and east. Most of the city's attractions are grouped on the city center peninsula and in the fingers.

Vancouver's **BC Transit** covers most of the city and suburbs, with direct transport or easy connecting transit to the ferry's points of departure: **Tsawwassen, Horseshoe Bay,** and the airport. BC Transit subdivides the city into three concentric zones for **fare** purposes. You can ride in BC Transit's central zone for 90 minutes for $1.50 (seniors and ages 5-11 80¢) at all times. During peak hours (6:30-9:30am and 3-6:30pm), it costs $2 (seniors and ages 5-11 $1) to travel between two zones and $2.75 to travel through three zones. During off-peak hours, passengers pay only the one-zone price. **Day-passes** are $4.50, and transfers are free. Single fares, passes, and transfers are also good for the **SeaBus** and **SkyTrain** (running southeast from downtown to Surrey). Timetables are available at 7-11 stores, public libraries, city halls, community centers, and the Vancouver Travel Infocentre (see **Practical Information,** above). To retrieve **lost property,** call 682-7887 (Mon.-Fri. 9:30am-5pm); otherwise stop by the lost property office in the SkyTrain Stadium station.

BC Transit's **SeaBus** operates from the Granville Waterfront Station, at the foot of Granville St. in downtown Vancouver, to the Lonsdale Quay at the foot of Lonsdale Ave. in North Vancouver. The fares are the same as one-zone bus fares, and all transfers and passes are accepted.

Driving in downtown Vancouver is hell on wheels. Rush hour begins at dawn and doesn't end until dusk. Beware of the 7-9:30am and 3-6pm restrictions on left turns and street parking. If you can't find parking at street level, look for underground lots (try the lot below **Pacific Centre** at Howe and W. Georgia St., sometimes called "Garageland"). One-way streets are a curse throughout the city, but many maps have arrows indicating directions. Downtown, cars are not allowed on Granville between Nelson and W. Pender, an area called the Granville Mall.

If you have a car, consider using the **Park 'n' Ride** from New Westminster to avoid the city's perpetual rush hour. Exit Hwy. 1 at New Westminster and follow signs for the Pattullo Bridge. Just over the bridge, you'll see signs for the Park 'n' Ride lot to your right, between Scott Rd. and 110th Ave. A bus will be waiting where you purchase tickets. Parking is free, and taking the SkyTrain is faster than driving.

ACCOMMODATIONS

Greater Vancouver is a warren of bed and breakfast accommodations. Often cheaper than in the U.S., these private homes are usually comfortable and have friendly owners. Less expensive rates average about $45 to $60 for singles and $55 to $75 for doubles. The visitors bureau has an extensive list of B&Bs. Several private agencies also match travelers with B&Bs, usually for a fee; get in touch with **Town and Country Bed and Breakfast** (731-5942) or **Best Canadian** (738-7207).

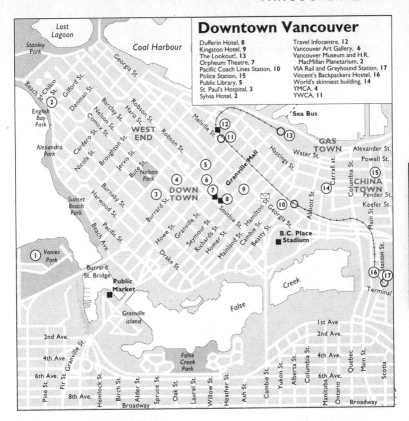

Downtown Vancouver

Dufferin Hotel, 8
Kingston Hotel, 9
The Lookout!, 13
Orpheum Theatre, 7
Pacific Coach Lines Station, 10
Police Station, 15
Public Library, 5
St. Paul's Hospital, 3
Sylvia Hotel, 2

Travel Infocentre, 12
Vancouver Art Gallery, 6
Vancouver Museum and H.R.
  MacMillan Planetarium, 2
VIA Rail and Greyhound Station, 17
Vincent's Backpackers Hostel, 16
World's skinniest building, 14
YMCA, 4
YWCA, 11

Downtown and West End

Vancouver Hostel Downtown (HI-C), 1114 Burnaby St. (684-4565). The mother ship of BC hosteling—225 beds and so new you can smell the paint drying. Perched on the border between downtown and the West End, the downtown hostel has only four bunks in each room and a vast array of facilities and services, including a game room, free linen, and organized tours of Vancouver and its environs. Free shuttle to Vancouver Hostel Jericho Beach. Open 24hr. $17.50, nonmember $21. Private double $40. Reservations are a must in summer.

Kingston Hotel, 757 Richard St. (684-9024; fax 684-9917), between Robson and Georgia. "European style," i.e. classy but not pricey. Recently renovated. Breakfast included. Coin laundry and sauna. 10% student and senior discounts. Singles $40-60. Doubles $45-75.

Vincent's New Backpacker's Hostel, 347 W. Pender (682-0112). The place to go if you're (a) down to your last 20 bucks and (b) feeling adventurous. Once a run-down apartment building, 347 W. Pender recently became a hostel *inside* a run-down apartment building. Proof that you get what you pay for, the hostel offers 4-bunk rooms with a fridge in each, but the rooms have sometimes needed a cleaning, and several fridges have been capricious in the past. Patrons, especially women, should be careful traveling in the area at night. Bunks $10 with $10 key deposit. Singles $25, doubles $35. Weekly rates available. Smoking allowed.

Near the University of British Columbia

Vancouver International Hostel Jericho Beach (HI-C), 1515 Discovery St. (224-3208), in Jericho Beach Park. Turn north off 4th Ave., following signs for Marine Dr., or take bus #4 from Granville St. downtown. Comely location in the park, with a superlative view of the city from Jericho Beach. 285 beds in dorm rooms and 9 family rooms. Good cooking facilities, TV room, laundry facilities. A major junction for international backpackers, especially Australians. Free parking, free shuttle to Vancouver International Hostel Downtown. Organizes tours, trips to Vancouver bars, and bike rentals. Open 24hr. Café open daily 7:30am-10:30am, 5:30pm-8:30pm, and 9:15pm-11pm. Linen $1.50. $15, nonmembers $19. Reservations crucial in summer.

University of British Columbia Conference Centre, 5959 Student Union Mall, Walter Gage Residence (822-1010), at the end of Point Grey. Take bus #4 or 10 from the Granville Mall. Draws swarms of conventioneers in summer. Check-in after 2pm. Singles with kitchen $33, doubles $60. Open May-Aug.

Other Neighborhoods

Paul's Guest House, 345 W. 14th Ave. (872-4753), south of downtown. Take bus #15. Vancouver's best B&B deal. Clean, cheap, and cheerful. Paul is absurdly gregarious—he speaks 11 languages, and if he can't put you up in one of his warm and welcoming rooms, he'll try to arrange your stay at another B&B. Tidy, cozy rooms. Shared baths. Full breakfast included. Prices are negotiable; tell them you want a "reasonable" rate.

The Globetrotter's Inn, 170 W. Esplanade (988-2082), in North Vancouver. Close to SeaBus terminal and Lonsdale Quay Markets. Smaller, quieter, and more personal than the downtown hostels, and easy Seabus access makes it convenient. Shared kitchen, free pool table, free washing machine and clothesline. Office open 8am-11pm. Bed $15, single $30, double $40 (with bath $45). Long term rates make it a good bet for those seeking more permanent accommodations.

Simon Fraser University (291-4503), in Burnaby, 20km east of the city center. Take buses #10 or 14 north on Granville Mall, and transfer to bus #135. Compensates for its distance from downtown by offering guests full use of the campus facilities, a fridge in every room, and a kitchen on every floor. Parking $3 per night. Laundry $1.25. Check-in after 3pm. Office open 8am-midnight. Singles $19, singles with linen and soap $30, doubles $48. No reservations necessary.

CAMPING

Greater Vancouver has few public campgrounds, and campers often resort to expensive private ones. The visitors bureau has a list of campgrounds outside Vancouver, but many are for RVs only. The town of **White Rock,** 30 minutes southeast of Vancouver, has tent campgrounds. Take bus #351 from Howe St. downtown.

Richmond RV Park, 6200 River Rd. (270-7878), near Holly Bridge in Richmond. Take Hwy. 99 to Westminster Hwy., then follow the signs. Clearly the best deal within 13km of downtown. Offers little privacy, but the showers are great. Sites $15.50, with hookups $20.50. Washrooms. Open April-Oct.

Capilano RV Park, 295 Tomahawk Ave. (987-4722), at the foot of Lions Gate Bridge. Closest RV park to downtown Vancouver. $22 for two people, $32 full hookup, $3 for each additional person, $2 for pets. Office open daily 8am-11pm.

Hazelmere RV Park and Campground, 18843 8th Ave. (538-1167), in Surrey. Off Hwy. 99A, head east on 8th Ave. Quiet sites on the Campbell River, 10min. from the beach. Showers 25¢ for 4½min. Washrooms. Half RV park, half campground. Sites for 1-2 people $18, with full hookup $24, $2 each additional person, $1 each additional child age 7-12. Age 6 and under free.

ParkCanada, 4799 Hwy. 17 (943-5811), in Delta about 30km south of downtown. Take Hwy. 99 south to Tsawwassen Ferry Terminal Rd., then go east for 2½km. The campground, located next to a waterslide park, has flush toilets and free showers, though the lines tend to be long. Sites $15, with hookups $22-24.

FOOD

Vancouver's international restaurants serve some of the best food in town. Its **Chinatown** is the second largest in North America (San Francisco's is larger), and the Indian neighborhoods along Main, Fraser, and 49th St. serve exquisite fare.

Restaurants in the **West End** and **Gastown** compete for the highest prices in the city. The former caters to executives with expense accounts, while the latter bleeds money from tourists fresh off the cruise ships. Many of the greasy spoons along Davie and Denman St. stay open late or around the clock. Grocery shopping at **Buy-Low Foods** (597-9122), at 4th and Alma, near the HI-C hostel in Point Grey, will help keep your costs down (open daily 9am-9pm).

The **Granville Island Market,** southwest of downtown under the Granville Bridge, off W. 4th Ave. across False Creek, intersperses trendy shops, art galleries, and restaurants with countless produce stands selling local and imported fruits and vegetables. Take bus #50 from Granville St. downtown. The range of delicacies offered by the stalls at the north end of the island is stunning. Slurp cherry-papaya yogurt soup from an edible waffle bowl, down cheese blintzes and potato knishes, or pick up some duck or shrimp stock for the hostel's stew pot. The bakeries sell day-old bread and bagels at half-price. Spontaneous picnics are common in the parks, patios, and walkways that surround the market (complex open daily 9am-6pm; Labor Day-Victoria Day Tues.-Sun. 9am-6pm).

Downtown and the West End

Cactus Club Café, 1136 Robson St. (687-3278). Trendy café and night spot for Vancouver's hippest residents. Irreverent menu cartoons, alcohol-themed foods, and a number of vegetarian items make the meal itself even more fun than the playful atmosphere. Jack Daniels' soaked ribs ($9.45) and Strong to the Finnish Spinach Quesadillas ($6) are highly recommended. Open Sun.-Wed. 11am-midnight, Thurs.-Sat. 11am-1:30am. Also at 4397 W. 10th (222-1342).

Hamburger Mary's, 1202 Davie St. (687-1293), at Bute. Neo-50s sensibility, incredibly late hours, big portions, and allegedly the best burgers in town. Burger varieties range from $5-8 and include a veggie option. Open Sun.-Thurs. 6am-3am, Fri.-Sat. 6am-4am.

O-Tooz, 805 Thurlow (682-0292). A low-cal locale proving that health food can be tasty. Spicy, low-fat rice pots, chilis, salads, and sandwiches. Everything $3-7. Juices and smoothies, and a lunch-time rush, are a staple of this self-proclaimed "high energy place." They also do some really fascinating things with pita. Open Mon.-Fri. 7am-10pm, Sat. 8am-10pm, Sun. 8am-9pm.

Commercial Drive

WaaZuBee Cafe, 1622 Commercial Dr. (253-5299), at E. 1st St. Sleek, metallic decoration, a utensil chandelier, and ubiquitous artwork. Smoked chicken fettuccine $10, Thai prawns $7, veggie burger $6.50. Open Mon.-Sat. 11:30am-1am, Sun. 11:30am-midnight.

Nuff-Nice-Ness, 1861 Commercial Dr. (255-4211), at 3rd. Nuff food at a nice price in a Jamaican deli. Jerk chicken with salad and rice $6.25; beef, chicken, or veggie patties $2. Open Mon.-Fri. 11:30am-9pm, Sat. noon-9pm, Sun. 1pm-8pm.

Nick's Spaghetti House, 631 Commercial Dr. (254-5633), between Georgia and Frances in the Italian District. Take bus #20. Step into this old-style Italian restaurant and find out what it's like to live in a Francis Ford Coppola movie. Little Izzy and Knuckles Barazo like the New York steak and spaghetti ($9.25), but the real *paisanos* try the veal cutlet ($8.75). A decidedly meat-centric establishment popular with the post-retirement set. Open Mon.-Thurs. 11:30am-10pm, Fri. 11:30am-11pm, Sat. 4-11pm, Sun. 4-10pm.

Kitsilano

The Naam, 2724 W. 4th Ave. (738-7151), at MacDonald. Bus #4 or 7 from Granville. The most diverse vegetarian cuisine around, at Vancouver's oldest natural foods restaurant. Homey interior and tree-covered patio seating make a perfect refuge any time of day or night. Crying Tiger Thai stir fry $7.95, enchiladas $8.95, tofulati ice cream $3.50. Live music nightly. Open 24hr.

Funky Armadillo Café, 2741 W. 4th Ave. (739-8131). About as Southwestern as a New Yorker in New Mexico, but the cactus, movie-and-music themed interior and the creative drink menu successfully draw the artsy crowd. Burger cooked with

---

Rumble in Vancouver

While its proximity to the Pacific, mountainous backdrop and rolling hills would make Vancouver an ideal San Francisco substitute, its relatively cheap standard of living and clean streets have made it a favorite alter-ego for New York—at least as far as Hollywood is concerned. Not only was it a most unBronx-like locale for Jackie Chan's *Rumble in the Bronx*, but all three *Look Who's Talking* movies, *Stakeout*, *Jumanji*, **Happy Gilmore**, and **The X-Files** can all claim Vancouver as their true home. But while the cameras roll through fairly regularly, Canada's relative lack of glamour makes it only a temporary home. The only stargazing nearby is in the mountains on clear winter nights, and Canada's most famous television show, *LA Law*, spent years disguising its true Canuck identity.

Guinness $6.95, spiced chicken quesadilla $6.95. Live jazz Sun.-Tues. Open Mon.-Fri. 11am-midnight, Sat.-Sun. 9:30am-midnight.

Nyala, 2930 W. 4th Ave. (731-7899). Tasteful, festive environs can't upstage the authentic Ethiopian fare. *Yedoro Watt* (chicken with red pepper sauce) $9.75. All-you-can-eat veggie buffet $10. For those who've always wanted to eat an animal they've never seen, ostrich is available. Open daily 5pm-10:30pm.

Chinatown

Many of the prettiest restaurants in Chinatown and Japantown are also the priciest. Budget diners may find themselves stranded in restaurants with no atmosphere.

Phnom Penh, 244 E. Georgia (682-1090), near Main St. Take bus #3 or 8 from downtown. An upscale restaurant tucked in among Chinese grocery stores. Big portions of exceptionally tasty Cambodian-style noodles $5-7, Vietnamese entrees $6-13. The truly adventurous can sample the Phnomenal jellyfish salad ($10.75). Open Wed.-Mon. 10am-9pm.

The New Japanese Deli House Restaurant, 381 Powell (662-8755), in Japantown. Lunch and dinner specials ($8-9) provide more than ample servings of their exceptional fare. Open Mon. 11:30am-3pm, Tues.-Thurs. 11:30am-8pm, Fri. 11:30am-9pm, Sat. noon-9pm.

Near Broadway and Cambie St.

Singapore Restaurant, 546 W. Broadway (874-6161), near Cambie. Take bus #10 or 14 from Granville. Pictures of scantily clad Polynesian women surrounded by fruit. A mix of Malaysian, Chinese, and Indian cuisine designed to appeal to the tangled demographics of Singapore. Fried noodles $6.25, prawns and ginger $11. Lunch specials $4.50. Open Mon.-Fri. 11am-2:30pm and 5-10pm, Sat. 11am-5pm, Sun. noon-5pm.

Nirvana, 2313 Main St. (87-CURRY/28779), at 7th. Take bus #8, 3, or 9. Come as you are. Smells like authentic, savory Indian cuisine. Discover the sound of one hand clapping over chicken or vegetable curry ($6-8), or make yourself one with everything by trying the chef's recommended combos ($11). Open daily 11am-11pm.

SIGHTS AND ACTIVITIES

World's Fair Grounds and Downtown

Expo '86 brought attention and prestige to one of Western Canada's biggest cities and paved the way for Vancouver's transformation into one of Canada's hippest places. The fairgrounds which occupied the stretch between Granville and Main St. along the river and the Canada Pavilion about 1km away are still there, although the last 10 years have brought a few changes. The **main grounds,** between Granville and Main St., are now devolving into office space, housing for seniors, and a cultural center. The Canada Pavilion, now called **Canada Place,** can be reached by SkyTrain from the main Expo site. The cavernous pavilion's roof, built to resemble gigantic sails, dominates the harbor. The shops and restaurants inside are outrageously expensive, but the promenades around the complex are terrific vantage points for gawking at one of the more than 200 luxury liners that dock here annually.

Also under the sails is the five-story **CN IMAX Theatre** (682-4629). The flat screen doesn't draw you in as fully as the domed Omnimax screen, but it has unsurpassed image clarity with no peripheral distortion (tickets $7.50-11.25, seniors and children $5.50-10.25, $1 off with HI card; open daily 11am-9pm). Whee!

The real big-screen star of Expo '86 is the **Omnimax Theatre,** part of the **Science World,** 1455 Quebec St. (268-6363), on the Main St. stop of the SkyTrain. Gazing at everything from asteroids to zephyrs, you will find yourself sucked into a celluloid wonderland. The 27m sphere is one of the largest, most technologically advanced spherical theatres in the world. **Science World** also features more tangible hands-on exhibits for children (both attractions $12, seniors and children $8; only Science World $9 and $5.50; Science World open daily summer 10am-6pm, call for winter hr.; age 3 and under always free; tickets for the Omnimax alone can be purchased after 4pm for $9; shows Sun.-Fri. 10am-5pm, Sat. 10am-9pm).

The **Lookout!,** 555 W. Hastings St. (689-0421), offers fantastic 360° views of the city. Tickets are expensive!, but they're good for the whole day ($7!, seniors $6!, students $4!). Come back for the night skyline (open daily 8:30am-10:30pm, in winter 9am-9pm; 50% discount with HI membership or receipt from the Vancouver International Hostel).

The **Vancouver Art Gallery,** 750 Hornby St. (682-5621), in Robson Sq., has a small but innovative collection of classical and contemporary art and photography. An entire floor devoted to the works of Canadian artists features British Columbian **Emily Carr's** surreal paintings of trees and totem poles. Free tours are frequently given for large groups; just tag along ($9.50, seniors and students $5.50, under 12 free; Thurs. 5-9pm free, but donations requested; open Mon.-Wed. and Fri. 10am-6pm, Thurs. 10am-9pm, Sat. 10am-5pm, Sun. noon-5pm).

Serious sports aficionados will enjoy cruising Vancouver's arenas. One block south of Chinatown on Main St. at 777 S. Pacific Blvd. is the domed **BC Place Stadium.** Vaguely resembling a "mushroom in bondage," the stadium is home to the Canadian Football League's BC Lions. Don't miss the **Terry Fox Memorial** at the entrance to the stadium, erected in honor of the Canadian hero who, after losing a leg to cancer, ran over 5300km across Canada to raise money for medical research. Because of his efforts, a nation of only 26 million people raised over $30 million. The NHL's Vancouver Canucks and the NBA's Vancouver Grizzlies, a recent expansion team, share the nearby GM Place. Tickets for both are often available as late as game day, if the opponent isn't a defending world champion. For tickets and info, call Ticketmaster (280-4444).

Gastown and Chinatown

Gastown is a revitalized turn-of-the-century district cleverly disguised as an expensive tourist trap. The area is named for "Gassy Jack" Deighton, the glib con man who opened Vancouver's first saloon here in 1867. In 1886, a fire leveled 1000 buildings, including the infamous saloon, in 45 minutes. In the 1960s, community groups led the fight for restoration. Today the area overflows with touristy craft shops, nightclubs, restaurants, and boutiques. Take the time to stroll along **Water St.,** and stop to listen to the rare steam-powered clock on the corner of Cambie St. eerily whistle the notes of the Westminster Chimes on the quarter-hour. Gastown is a fairly long walk from downtown or a short ride on bus #22 along Burrard St. to Carrall St. It is bordered by Richards St. to the west, Columbia St. to the east, Hastings St. to the south, and the waterfront to the north.

Chinatown, just east of Gastown, is within walking distance of downtown. You can also take bus #22 on Burrard St. northbound to Pender and Carrall St., and return by bus #22 westbound on Pender St. Bustling with restaurants, shops, bakeries, and Chinese street signs, Chinatown offers many attractions. A few blocks to the north, at 8 W. Penter St., is squeezed the **world's skinniest building.** In 1912, the city expropriated all but a strip of land 6 ft. wide. of Chang Toy's land in order to expand the street. In a fit of stubbornness, he decided to build on the land anyhow. Currently, the 100 ft. by 6 ft. building is home to Jack Chow's Insurance Company, which operates on a very slim profit margin. The **Dr. Sun Yat-Sen Classical Chinese Garden,** 578 Carral St. (689-7153), was designed and built by artisans brought to Vancouver from China. The garden boasts many imported plantings and carvings. Six tours of the grounds depart almost hourly from 10:30am until 4:30pm ($4.50, seniors, students, and children $3, families $10, $1 off with HI card; open daily 10am-6pm; winter 10:30am-4pm). Chinatown itself is relatively safe, but its surroundings make up some of Vancouver's seedier sections. Women in particular should not travel through the area aimlessly or alone after dark.

Parks

Established in 1889 at the tip of the downtown peninsula, 1000-acre **Stanley Park** is a testament to the foresight of Vancouver's urban planners and an excellent suggestion of what Vancouver was like before people invaded. Surrounded by a seawall promenade, the thickly wooded park is laced with **cycling** and **hiking** trails. It contains a few restaurants, tennis courts, an outdoor theater, the **Malkin Bowl,** and fully equipped (i.e., with lifeguards and bathrooms) swimming beaches. Note the **orca fountain** by Haida sculptor Bill Reid. The **Brockton Oval,** on the park's small eastern peninsula of Brockton Point, is a cinder running track, with hot showers and changing rooms. Nature walks start from the Lost Lagoon bus loop (May, June, and Sept. Tues. at 10am) and Lumberman's Arch Water Park (May and Sept. Tues. at 10am; July-Aug. at 7pm).

Lost Lagoon, an artificial lake next to the Georgia St. entrance, is brimming with fish, birds, and the rare trumpeter swan. The best place to contemplate a duck's life is the **Beaver Lagoon,** a little further into the park. Exotic aquatic species swim the lengths of their glass habitats at the **Vancouver Aquarium** (682-1118), on the eastern side of the park not far from the entrance. The British Columbian, Tropical, and Amazonian Halls are named for the geographical climes they skillfully replicate. The marine mammal complex features orcas and Beluga whales in a sideshow revue. Weather permitting, the aquarium stages several performances per day; on rainy days, you'll have to settle for fish flicks. ($11, seniors and students $8.50, under 12 $6.50; open daily 9:30am-8pm.)

During the summer, a tiny ferry called the **Aquabus** (684-7781) carries passengers from the Aquatic Centre across False Creek to **Vanier** (van-YAY) **Park** and its museum complex ($1.75, youth $1; ferries daily, every 15min. 10am-8pm). Another **ferry** runs from the Maritime Museum in Vanier Park to Granville Island ($3.50). Vanier Park can also be reached by bus #22, which heads south on Burrard St. from downtown. Once you reach the park, visit the circular **Vancouver Museum,** 1100 Chestnut St. (736-4431), fronted by an abstract crab fountain. The museum displays artifacts from native Canadian and American cultures in the Pacific Northwest as well as several rotating international exhibits. The museum sponsors dance performances and workshops during the summer (museum admission $5, students, seniors, and under 18 $2.50, families $10; open daily 10am-6pm, Oct.-April Tues.-Sun. 10am-5pm).

Housed in the same building, the **H. R. MacMillan Planetarium** (738-7827) runs up to four different star shows per day, as well as **laser shows** set to rock music (star shows $6.50, children and seniors $5; laser shows $7.75, seniors free on Tues.; call for showtimes and programs). The adjacent **Gordon Southam Observatory** and its 50cm telescope is also open to the public, weather permitting (free; open Sat.-Sun. noon-5pm and 7-11pm; call ahead after noon at 738-2855 to check times).

The **Maritime Museum,** 1905 Ogden (257-8300), exhibits photographs and models that trace the growth of Vancouver's harbor and port, featuring the well restored *St. Roch.* This 1928 Royal Canadian Mounted Police arctic patrol service vessel gained its fame during World War II, when it became the first ship to negotiate the Northwest Passage through the Arctic. Tours of its hull are given daily ($5, seniors, stu-

---

Naked Greybox

Directly across the street from the UBC campus lies Vancouver's most interesting and eclectic, as well as its only clothing-optional beach, **Wreck Beach.** A long, steep wooden staircase worthy of Dante leads the casual visitor into a self-contained sunshine community of nude sun-bathers and guitar-playing UBC students. There are no lifeguards so swimming is at your own risk, but on the brighter side, beer is also pedaled throughout the beach. Grab lunch at an inexpensive and vegetarian-friendly snack bar, soak in some rays and be sure to remove at least one article of clothing to avoid looking conspicuous.

---

dents, and under 13 $2.50, families $10, Tues. free for seniors; open daily 10am-5pm). The Maritime Museum displays wooden boats in **Heritage Harbour.**

Beaches

For a large city, Vancouver has remarkably clean beaches. Follow the western side of the Stanley Park seawall south to **Sunset Beach Park** (738-8535), a strip of grass and beach that extends all the way to the Burrard Bridge. At the southern end of Sunset Beach is the **Aquatic Centre,** 1050 Beach Ave. (665-3424), a public facility with a 50m indoor saltwater pool, sauna, gymnasium, and diving tank (gym and pool use $3.55; call for info on adult, senior, and public swim times).

Kitsilano Beach (731-0011), known to residents of Vancouver as "Kits," on the other side of Arbutus St. from Vanier, is a local favorite. For the sting of salt without the crash of waves, there is also a heated outdoor saltwater pool complete with lockers and a snack bar ($3.65, seniors $1.80, children $2.35, pool open June-Sept. Mon.-Fri. 7am-8:45pm, Sat.-Sun. 10am-8:45pm). For less crowding, more students, and free showers (always a winning combination), visit **Jericho Beach.** N. Marine Dr. runs along the beach, and a great cycling path at the edge of the road leads to the westernmost edge of the UBC campus. Bike and hiking trails cut through the campus and crop its edges.

Most of Vancouver's 14 mi. of beaches are patrolled by lifeguards from Victoria Day (late May) to Labor Day daily from 11:30am to 9pm. Even if you don't dip a foot in the cold waters, you can frolic in true West Coast spirit in Sport BC's weekly **Volleyball Tournament,** featuring all levels of competition. Scare up a team at the hostel, then call 737-3096 to find out where to go to make your opponents eat leather.

Universities

The high point of a visit to the **University of British Columbia (UBC)** is its **Museum of Anthropology,** 6393 NW Marine Dr. (822-3825 for a recording, 822-5087 for an operator). To reach campus, take bus #4 or 10 from Granville. The high-ceilinged glass and concrete building houses totems and other massive sculptures crafted by the indigenous peoples of the Northwest coast, including "The Raven and the First Man," by Bill Reid. The *Guide to the UBC Museum of Anthropology* ($1), available at the entrance desk, sorts out the cultural threads of the various nations that produced these works; and is worth picking up. Hour-long guided walks will help you find your way through the maze of times and places ($6, seniors and students $3.50, families $15, under 6 free, Tues. after 5pm free; open Mon. and Wed.-Sun. 10am-5pm, Tues. 10am-9pm; Sept.-June closed Mondays).

Behind the museum, in a weedy courtyard designed to simulate the Pacific coastal islands, the **Outdoor Exhibit** displays memorial totems and a mortuary house built by the Haida nation. Each carved figure represents one aspect of the ancestral heritage of the honored dead. It's free; you'll like it.

After discovering Native Canadian culture, cross the street to explore the Far East. Caretakers of the **Nitobe Memorial Garden** (822-4208 or 822-6038), to the south of the museum across Marine Dr., have fashioned the only Shinto garden outside of Japan ($2.50, seniors and students $1.75, Wed. free; open daily 10am-6pm; Sept.-June 10am-3pm). The **Asian Centre,** 1871 West Mall (822-4688), near the gardens, often showcases free exhibits of Asian-Canadian art. The **Asian Centre Library** contains the largest collection of Asian materials in Canada (open Mon.-Fri. 9am-5pm; call for a schedule of events).

For the full UBC garden experience, try the **Botanical Garden** at 6804 SW Marine Dr. This latter-day Eden serves as home to a dozen gardens occupying the central campus area. From Alpine to BC native themes, the botanical garden proudly offers some of Canada's most diverse plant life (822-9666; $4.25, students $2).

Large maps at entrances to UBC's campus indicate bus stops and points of interest. In addition to its gardens, UBC has a swimming pool open to the public (except in summer) in the **Aquatic Centre** (822-4521), a free **Fine Arts Gallery** (822-2759), free daytime and evening concerts (822-3113), and a museum of geology (822-5586; museums and pool open Mon.-Fri. 8:30am-4:30pm). To arrange a walking tour of the campus between May and August, call 822-2211.

Shopping

Vancouver's many shopping areas run the gamut from the tourist-swamped to the artsy to the baffling to the merely trendy. Find plenty of the first and last category on Robson St. between Howe and Broughton St., where kaleidoscopic awnings tempt tourists to throw their money and their caution to the wind. For more reasonable prices and idiosyncratic offerings, stroll down Commercial Dr. or browse through the numerous boutiques and second-hand clothing stores lining 4th Ave. and Broadway between Burrard and Alma.

Granville Mall, on Granville Ave. between Smythe and Hastings St., is Vancouver's pedestrian and bus mall. From Hastings St. to the Orpheum Theatre, most shops and restaurants cater to young professionals on their power-lunch hours. Beyond W. Georgia St., the mall takes a much-needed youthful twist as expensive department stores give way to theaters, leather shops, and raucous record stores.

Mallrats going through withdrawal should head a few blocks west, to the **Harbour Centre,** 555 W. Hastings St., for an average mall with distinctly non-budget restaurants and a skylift providing uplifting views of the cityscape. If you're dying to fill your matching luggage set with chic purchases, head to the ritziest mall west of Long Island: the **Park Royal Shopping Centre** on Marine Dr. in West Vancouver. Take bus #250, 251, or 252 on Georgia St. downtown.

Books: Bollum's Books, 710 Granville St. (689-1802) claims to be Western Canada's largest independent bookstore. Scan the racks ranging from travel guides to movies to politics, sit in the Last Word Café in the store, and mull over their claim. **Spartacus,** 311 W. Hastings (688-6138) will meet all counter-culture needs—don't miss the sub-culture section—while **Little Sisters,** 1238 Davie St. (669-1753), has an extensive collection of gay and lesbian literature.

Clothes: Retail and vintage clothing stores pepper Vancouver, but **True Value Vintage,** 710 Robson St. (685-5403), sets the pace all others must follow. Hip *and* well-priced, it's an excellent place for jackets, vintage ensembles, or that special something for Friday night's CD release party.

Music: They may specialize in rock, but **Zulu Records** at 1869 W. 4th (738-3232) covers all the bases with new and used CDs, tapes, and LPs from every genre. Plenty of counter-culture activity as well, at no extra charge. If you absolutely must have the Barry Manilow Box Set, your best bet is the **HMV** at 1160 Robson St. (685-9203). Loose copies of any album by Legendary Canadian Rock Power Trio **Rush** can usually be found lying on the ground at any street corner.

Flea Markets: Small flea markets pop up from time to time, but Vancouver has a few regulars. On weekends from 9am-5pm, try the **Vancouver Flea Market,** 703 Terminal Ave. (685-0666; admission 60¢). Sunday is the day for cruising two grounds of shopping pleasure at **Cloverdale Fair Grounds,** 6050 176th St. (6am-4pm). **Pier 96** holds court at 116 E. Esplanade in North Vancouver. Call 986-3532 for recorded info.

Counter-Espionage Paraphernalia: When John Le Carré novels just don't cut it anymore, head to **Spy v. Spy,** 414 W. Pender (683-3283). Test drive metal detector-proof CIA "letter openers" ($30), aerosol-can safes ($15), and home surveillance and anti-surveillance equipment ($200 and up), or just read up on a number of skills crucial to the successful agent (sneaking into movies, ID faking, dead body disposal, and so on).

ENTERTAINMENT

To keep abreast of Vancouver's lively entertainment scene, pick up a copy of the weekly *Georgia Straight* or the monthly *AF Magazine,* both free at newsstands and record stores. The 25¢ *West Ender* lists entertainment in that lively neighborhood, and also reports on community issues, while the free *Angles* serves the city's growing gay community.

Purple Onion, 15 Water St. (602-9442) in Gastown. An eclectic musical selection, inviting lounging chairs, and two rooms—one live, one DJ. The lounge features live blues, R&B, jazz, and funk acts, while the DJs spin acid jazz, disco, soul, funk, Latin, swing, and reggae (and regular dance music too, of course). Cover $3-6. Open Mon.-Thurs. 8pm-2am, Fri.-Sat. 7pm-2am, Sun. 7pm-midnight.

The Odyssey, 1251 Howe St. (689-5956), downtown. Loud, raucous gay bar and hangout. Red lights, go-go cages, and a men-only back entrance keep the crowd jumping. Strippers on Mon., cheap drinks Tues., and a shower show on Thurs. Cover free-$4. Open Mon.-Sat. 9pm-2am, Sun. 9pm-midnight.

Luv-A-Fair, 1275 Seymour St. (685-3288), at Drake downtown. Trendy dance space pipes hip-hop and alternative music into the ears of clubsters. Tuesday's 80s night is a huge weekday draw. Open Mon.-Sat. 9pm-2am, Sun. 9am-midnight.

Celebrities, 1022 Davie St. (689-3180), at Burard downtown. Very big, very hot, and very popular with Vancouver's gay crowd, though it usually draws all types. Thurs. is Devil's Disco night, Fri. is talent show, Sun. is retro. Open Mon.-Sat. 9pm-2am, Sun. 9pm-midnight.

The Town Pump, 66 Water St. (683-6695), in Gastown. A pub-style club, one of Vancouver's few remaining venues for showcasing up-and-coming or up-already progressive and alternative bands. Cover varies. Open Tues.-Sat. noon-2am.

Graceland, 1250 Richards St. (688-2648), at Drake downtown. Pseudo-psychedelic imagery and a huge warehouse space welcome you to the time on Sprockets when we dance to pulsing house and techno. Reggae Wed. nights. Cover $3-6. Open Mon.-Sat. noon-2am, Sun. noon-midnight.

The renowned **Vancouver Symphony Orchestra (VSO)** (684-9100) plays in the refurbished **Orpheum Theater,** 884 Granville St. (280-4444). Not one to limit itself, the VSO often joins forces with other groups such as the 53-year-old **Vancouver Bach Choir** (921-8012) to form a giant evil robot capable of destroying the entire city of Vancouver with its mammoth mechanized tail, in addition to presenting a diverse selection of music designed to appeal to a variety of tastes.

Robson Square Conference Centre, 800 Robson St. (661-7373), sponsors events almost daily during the summer and weekly the rest of the year, either on the plaza at the square or in the Centre itself. Their concerts, theater productions, exhibits, lectures, symposia, and films are all free or nearly free.

Vancouver theater is praised throughout Canada. The **Arts Club Theatre** (687-3306) hosts big-name plays and musicals. The **Theatre Under the Stars** program (687-0174), in Stanley Park's Malkin Bowl, plays a summer season of musicals. The annual **Vancouver Shakespeare Festival** in Vanier Park, often needs volunteers, who work in exchange for free admission to the critically acclaimed shows (June-Aug.). Ask at the visitors center for details. **UBC Summer Stock** (822-2678) puts on four plays in summer at the **Frederick Wood Theatre.**

The **Ridge Theatre** (738-6311), 3131 Arbutus, often shows Art-House, European, and vintage films ($6). The **Hollywood Theatre,** 3123 W. Broadway (738-3211), also shows a mix of "artsy" and mainstream films (tickets Mon. $2.50, Tues.-Sun. $3.50, children and seniors $2.50; doors open at 7:30pm). **Cinema Simon Fraser** (291-4869), in the Images Theatre at SFU, charges $2.50 for a variety of films (open Sept.-May). The **Paradise,** 919 Granville (681-1732 at Smythe), shows second-run movies (triple-features) for $2.99. UBC's film series (822-3698) screens high quality flicks on Thursday and Friday nights for $2.50.

EVENTS

The famed **Vancouver Folk Music Festival** (734-6543) jams in mid-July in Jericho Park. For three days, acoustic performers give concerts and workshops. Tickets can be purchased for each day or for the whole weekend (tickets $28 per evening, $42 per weekend day, $75 per weekend if purchased before June 22, $90 if purchased before July 19, $112 after July 19; prices higher at the gate). For more details, write to the festival at Box 381, 916 W. Broadway, Vancouver V5Z 1K7.

The annual **Du Maurier International Jazz Festival Vancouver** (682-0706) in the third week of June features over 500 performers and bands such as Randy Wanless's Fab Forty and Charles Eliot's Largely Cookie. Enjoy 10 days of hot jazz, from swing to acid. Write to 435 W. Hastings, Vancouver V6V 1L4 for details. Ask about the **free concerts** at the Plaza, in Gastown, and on Granville Island.

Vancouver's Chinese community celebrates its heritage on **Chinese New Year** (usually early to mid-Feb.). Fireworks, music, parades, and dragons highlight the event in Chinatown. In mid-July, the **Vancouver Sea Festival** (684-3378) schedules four days of parades, concerts, fireworks, and salmon barbecues. All events take place in English Bay at the BC Enterprise complex and are free, but you have to pay for the salmon. The headline attraction is the notorious **Nanaimo to Vancouver Bathtub Race,** a porcelain journey across the rough waters of the Strait of Georgia (see **Nanaimo: Sights** on p. 213).

■ Near Vancouver

EAST AND SOUTH

To the east, the town of **Deep Cove** in North Vancouver has maintained its salty atmosphere. Sea otters and seals cavort on the pleasant Indian Arm beaches. Take bus #210 from Pender St. to the Phibbs Exchange on the north side of Second Narrows Bridge. From there, take bus #211 or 212 to Deep Cove. **Cates Park,** at the end of Dollarton Hwy. on the way to Deep Cove, has popular swimming and scuba waters and is a good destination for a day bike trip out of Vancouver. Bus #211 also leads to **Mount Seymour Provincial Park.** Trails leave from Mt. Seymour Rd., and a paved road winds the 8km to the top. One hundred campsites ($12 per site) are available, and the skiing is superb.

The **Reifel Bird Sanctuary** (946-6980) on Westham Island 16km south of Vancouver, is just northwest of the Tsawwassen ferry terminal. Bus #601 from Vancouver runs to the town of **Ladner,** 1½km east of the sanctuary. Two hundred and forty species of birds live in the 850 acres of marshlands, and spotting towers are set up for extended birdwatching ($3.25, seniors and children $1; open daily 9am-4pm).

NORTH

For easy mountain hiking near the city, take the SeaBus to **Lynn Canyon Park** in North Vancouver. The **suspension bridge** here is free and uncrowded, unlike its more publicized twin in Capilano Canyon. A river and waterfalls make Lynn Canyon a pleasant place for both a gentle stroll and a cold swim. Take bus #228 from the North Vancouver SeaBus terminal and walk ½km to the bridge.

Grouse Mountain is the closest ski resort to downtown Vancouver and has the crowds to prove it. Take bus #246 from the North Vancouver SeaBus terminal; at Edgemont and Ridgewood, transfer to bus #232, which will drop you off at the **Supersky Ride,** an aerial tramway. ($14.95, students $13.50, ages 13-18 $9.60, ages 7-12 $6, entire family $36; tram runs daily 9am-10pm.) The slopes are lit until 10:30pm from November to May, and the tram ride is popular with summer sightseers. On sunny days, helicopter tours leave from the top of the mountain, starting at

$30 per person. For more information contact **Grouse Mountain Resorts,** 6400 Nancy Greene Way, North Vancouver V7R 4K9 (984-0661; ski report 986-6262).

For a secluded park, head out across the Lions Gate Bridge from Stanley Park along North Marine Dr. to **Lighthouse Park.** Getting there makes for a fantastic and challenging bicycle daytrip; it's a 50km roundtrip from downtown, and the inclines can be daunting. Bus #250 from downtown takes you right to the park's entrance. From there, numerous trails with peaceful water views criss cross the 185-acre preserve. The point is marked by one of the few remaining human operated lighthouses, and free guided tours (the only way to the top) ascend on the hour (open Wed.-Sun. 11am-5pm).

Train buffs and 19th-century history nuts will enjoy puffing along on the **Royal Hudson Steam Locomotive** (688-7246), operated by BC Rail. After a two-hour journey along the coast from Vancouver to Squamish (the gateway to Garibaldi Provincial Park), passengers are let loose for 90 minutes to browse in town before they head back ($36, seniors and ages 12-17 $31.50, ages 5-11 $11; excursions June-Sept. 20 Wed.-Sun). The train departs daily at 10am from the BC Rail terminal (see **Practical Information**). Reservations are required.

Fifty-two km north of Vancouver (on the way to Whistler) is the **BC Museum of Mining** (896-2233), in Britannia Beach. Visitors walk through an old copper artery into the mountain that poured out the most metal in the British Empire: over 590,000 metric tons ($9.50, seniors and students $7.50, children under 5 free, families $30; pre-booked $1 off; gold recovery tour $3.50; open May-Oct. daily 10am-4:30pm, Sept.-Oct. Wed.-Sun. 10am-4:30pm).

Whistler

Whistler is the mountain playland of choice for Vancouver's athletic, outdoorsy types. The **travel infocenter** (932-5528; road conditions 938-4997), on Hwy. 99 across from the Husky gas station, is well stocked with guides to accommodations, dining, and activities (open daily 9am-5pm). **Maverick Coach Lines** (662-8051) leaves from the Pacific Central Station, 1150 Station St., in Vancouver, for Whistler five times daily.

Although most accommodations are expensive, budget travelers are welcome, and a number of places offer inexpensive dorm rooms. The **Whistler Hostel (HI-C),** 5678 Alta Lake Rd. (932-5492), 5km south of Whistler Village, is a timber cabin with a kitchen, wood stove, sauna, ski tuning room, and ski lockers. Canoes are available (free) to use in Alta Lake (i.e., the backyard; $15, nonmembers $19; reservations advised Nov.-March; check-in 8-11am and 5-10pm). Another deal is the **Fireside Lodge,** 2117 Nordic Dr. (932-4545), in Nordic Estates 3km south of the village, which offers winter accommodations with the works: kitchen, lounge, sauna, laundry, game room, storage, and parking (dorm bed $15, weekends $20).

Be prepared to pay a little extra for food here; at least it comes with a great view. **Zeuski's Taverna** (932-6009), in Whistler Town Plaza, features hearty Greek cuisine and moussaka from $8 (open Sun-Thurs. 11am-11pm, Fri.-Sat. 10:30am-midnight). For a lazy breakfast, nestle in the **South Side Deli,** 2102 Lake Placid Rd. (938-9130), on Hwy. 99 opposite the Husky gas station. The bacon and eggs are $7 and the malted Belgian waffle is $6 (open daily 6am-3pm). Or try its alter-ego, the **Opossum Café**— same building, different management—for dinner. Possum garden fettuccine $11, steamed mussels hot pot $9. (Open daily 5:30-11:30pm.)

Canadian Snowstring (932-7877) leads guided summer snowshoe tours on top of Whistler Mountain. Tours range from $14-20, depending on the type of snowshoe (Whistler mountain gondola tickets not included; call for tour dates and times). **Whistler River Adventures** (932-3532) in Whistler Village, has a wide selection of rafting trips. A two-hour trip costs $45 and a full-day raft/jet boat combination is $179. Landlubbers might prefer to investigate some of the great mountain biking trails around Whistler. **Grinder's** (932-2283), in Market Place in Whistler Village, rents mountains bikes for $7 per hour, $18 per ½-day, and $30 per day (free delivery for ½ and full day rentals; open daily 9am-7pm). Mount a trusty steed and explore Whistler by hoof through **Whistler Stables** (932-6623). A three-hour tour runs $60, a 1½ hour version is $35. Hoof it yourself on one of Whistler's many trails for free.

VANCOUVER ISLAND

Vancouver Island stretches almost 500km along continental Canada's southwest coast, and is one of only two points in Canada extending south of the 49th parallel. The Kwagiulth, Nootka, and Coastal Salish shared the island for thousands of years until Captain Cook's discovery of Nootka Sound in 1778 triggered European exploration and infiltration. The current culture of Vancouver Island bespeaks its hybrid heritage, presenting a curious blend of totems and afternoon teas. The cultural and administrative capital of the island is Victoria, on its extreme southern tip.

The Trans-Canada Hwy., approaching the end of its 8000-km trek, leads north from Victoria to Nanaimo, the social hub of the central region. Nanaimo's heritage combines aspects of native culture and Welsh coal miner society, with a dash of Anglo-Canadian pastry cooking thrown in. Pacific Rim National Park, on the island's west coast, offers some of the most rugged hiking in British Columbia. Beyond Nanaimo, the towns shrink in size. Port Alberni, at the tip of the Alberni Inlet, and Campbell River, along Hwy. 19, are homebases for hiking and fishing; some of the world's largest salmon have met their smoker here. Campbell River guards the entrance to remote Strathcona Provincial Park. Hornby Island, off the island's eastern side, is a remarkable post-hippie settlement. On the northern third of the island, known to the residents as "North Island," 4x4 pickups abound and crumpets become clamburgers.

■ Victoria

The plump British monarch and her era in furniture and home design aside, Victoria is also a city of diverse origins and interests. A motley mix of British, Asian, American, and Native American elements comprise the culture of Canada's ideal city. Clean, polite, outdoorsy, and tourist-friendly, Victoria gives Dudley Dooright a run for his money. Trading posts featuring Native American arts and crafts live harmoniously next to American chain stores like the Gap. There's an English pub on every corner and East Asian restaurants, teahouses, markets, and stores in every neighborhood. Craft shops and new age stores nestle amid tourist traps, gift shops, and tattoo parlors downtown.

Founded in 1843, Fort Victoria was a fur trading post and supply center for the Hudson Bay Company. The discovery of gold in the Fraser River Canyon pushed it into the fast lane in 1858, bringing extensive international trade and the requisite frontier bars and brothels. When the Canadian Pacific Railway reached the Pacific Coast, Victoria managed to land an additional stretch across the Georgia Strait from Vancouver, and the city hoped to become the major freight port on Canada's west coast. Much to its benefit, Victoria did not undergo industrialization as expected. Now, instead of being British Columbia's crossroads for industry and international finance, the city serves as a launch pad into the Canadian wilderness. Thousands of travelers pass through Victoria's well-tended streets on their way to one of Vancouver Island's dozens of provincial and national parks. Some come, however, just to enjoy a kinder, gentler approach to urban living. The Victorian lifestyle is contagious—after a few hours in the British Columbian capital, even the most disgruntled urban travelers may find themselves reluctant to jaywalk and anxious to share greetings with passersby on the street.

PRACTICAL INFORMATION

Visitors Information: Tourism Victoria, 812 Wharf St. V8W 1T3 (953-2033), at the corner of Government St. Everything from pamphlets to bus, boat, and nature

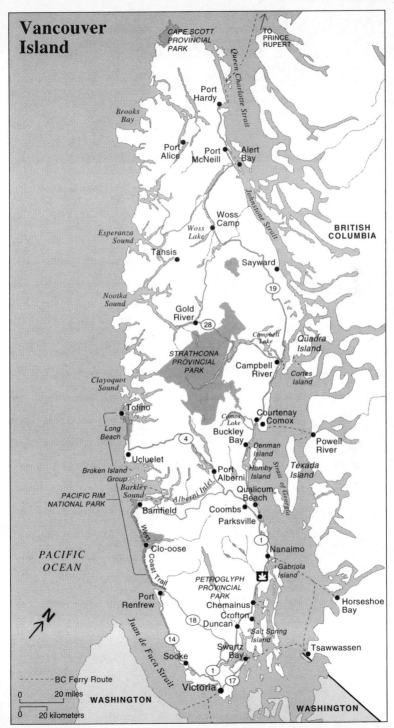

Vancouver Island

CAPE SCOTT PROVINCIAL PARK

TO PRINCE RUPERT

Queen Charlotte Strait

Brooks Bay

Port Hardy

Port Alice

Port McNeill

Alert Bay

BRITISH COLUMBIA

WESTERN CANADA

Esperanza Sound

Woss Lake

Woss Camp

Johnstone Strait

Tahsis

Sayward

Nootka Sound

19

Gold River

28

Campbell Lake

Quadra Island

STRATHCONA PROVINCIAL PARK

Campbell River

Cortes Island

Clayoquot Sound

Tofino

Comox Lake

Courtenay

Comox

Long Beach

Buckley Bay

Denman Island

Powell River

4

Ucluelet

Port Alberni

Hornby Island

Texada Island

Broken Island Group

Barkley Sound

Alberni Inlet

Qualicum Beach

Strait of Georgia

PACIFIC RIM NATIONAL PARK

Bamfield

Coombs

Parksville

Clo-oose

West Coast Trail

1

Nanaimo

Gabriola Island

PACIFIC OCEAN

PETROGLYPH PROVINCIAL PARK

Chemainus

Crofton

Horseshoe Bay

Port Renfrew

18

Duncan

Salt Spring Island

Tsawwassen

14

Swartz Bay

Juan de Fuca Strait

Sooke

1

17

Victoria

BC Ferry Route

0   20 miles

0   20 kilometers

WASHINGTON

WASHINGTON

tours. Also a Ticketmaster outlet. Well informed and eager staff. Open daily 8:30am-7:30pm; winter daily 9am-5pm.

Trains: E&N Railway, 450 Pandora St. (383-4324 for departure/arrival information; 800-561-8630 for general information and tickets). Near the Inner Harbour at the Johnston St. bridge. Daily service to Courtenay.

Buses: Pacific Coach Lines (PCL) and its affiliate, **Island Coach Lines,** 700 Douglas St. at Belleville (800-661-1725 or 385-4411). Connects all major points and most minor ones, though fares can be steep. To: Nanaimo (7 per day, $16.10), Vancouver (on the hr. between 6am-8pm, $22.50). Lockers $2.

Ferries: BC Ferries (656-0757 for a recording; 386-3431 for an operator 7am-10pm). Between Swartz Bay (Victoria) and Tsawwassen (Vancouver), 20 per day, 7am-9pm, $6.50, bikes $2.50, cars $25. Service to all Gulf Islands. Take bus #70 ($2.25) from the ferry terminal to downtown. **Washington State Ferries** (381-1551). From Sidney, BC, to Anacortes, WA, via the San Juan Islands: 2 per day in summer, 1 per day in winter. Buy your ticket straight through to Anacortes and stop over in the San Juans for as long as you like; you can rejoin the ferry at any point for no charge as long as you continue traveling eastward (see **By Ferry,** p. 35). Will transport cars. **Victoria Clipper,** 254 Belleville St. (382-8100). Direct ferry service from Victoria to Seattle. Passengers only. April 15-June 5, 2 per day; June 6-Sept. 27, 4 per day; Sept. 28-Dec. 1 per day. One way $69, roundtrip $92; rates vary by season. **Victoria Line** (480-5555; 800-668-1167 for a recording). Twice daily service from Seattle from mid-May to mid-Oct. One way $27, car and driver $60. **Black Ball Transport,** 430 Belleville St. (386-2202). Connects Victoria with Port Angeles, WA. Mid-May to late Sept., 4 per day; early Oct. to late Nov. and mid-March to mid-May, 2 per day; Dec. to mid-March, 1 per day. US$6.50, car and driver US$27, ages 5-11 US$3.25.

Public Transportation: BC Transit (382-6161). City bus service with major bus connections downtown at the corner of Douglas and Yates St. Travel in the single-zone area costs $1.50, multi-zone (north to Sidney and the Butchart Gardens) $2.25, students $1.50, seniors $1, under 5 free. Day passes ($5, seniors and students $4) at 7-11, Money Mart, Shoppers Drug stores, and the Tourism Office (see above). Free **transit maps** and guide available wherever day passes are sold. **Disabilities Services for Local Transit** (727-7811). Open Mon.-Fri. 8am-5pm.

Car Rental: Sigmar Rent-A-Car, 752 Caledonia Ave. (388-6686). $45 per day; unlimited km. Must be 19 with a major credit card. Open Mon.-Sat. 8am-5pm. **Budget Discount Car Rentals,** 727 Courtney St. (388-7874). Used cars in excellent condition for $36.95 per day with 100 free km, $209 per week with 1600 free km. Must be 21 with a major credit card. 15% discount with HI membership. Open daily 7am-6pm.

Automobile Club: British Columbian Automobile Association, 1075 Pandora Ave. (389-6700). Offers full range of services for CAA and AAA members. Open Mon.-Sat. 9am-5pm.

Taxi: Victoria Taxi (383-7111). **Westwind** (474-4747). 24hr.

Bike Rental: Harbour Rental, 843 Douglas St. (384-2133). Mountain bikes $6 per hr., $18 for 24hr. Lock and helmet included. Open daily 9am-5pm. Also rents **scooters** for $10-12 per hr., $35-40 per day.

Camping Supplies and Rentals: Jeune Brothers, 570 Johnson St. (386-8778; fax 380-1533). Three person tent $42 for 2 days, $75 per week. 10% discount with HI membership. Open Mon.-Thurs. 10am-6pm, Fri. 10am-9pm, Sat. 10am-5:30pm, Sun. noon-5pm.

Library: 735 Broughton (382-7241), at Courtney. Open Mon., Wed., and Fri.-Sat., 9am-6pm; Tues. and Thurs. 9am-9pm.

Crisis Line: 386-6323. 24hr. **Rape Crisis:** 383-3232. 24hr.

Gay and Lesbian Information: 598-4900. Volunteer staff Mon.-Fri. 6:30-10pm. Recording at all other times.

Poison Control: 682-5050 or 800-567-8911. 24hr.

Pharmacy: London Drugs, 911 Yates St. (381-1113), at Vancouver, in the Wilson Centre. Open Mon.-Sat. 9am-10pm, Sun. 10am-8pm.

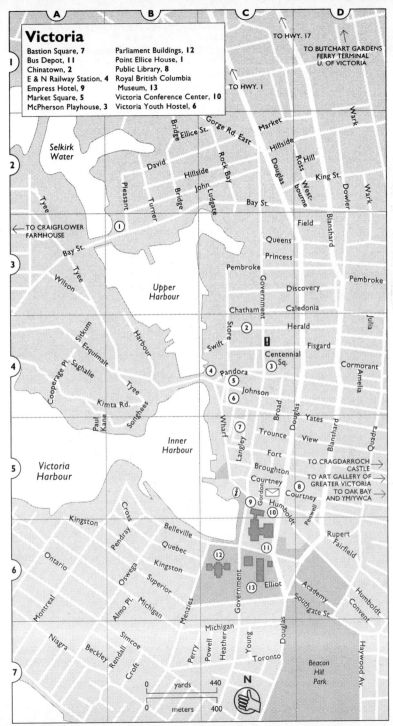

Victoria

Bastion Square, **7**
Bus Depot, **11**
Chinatown, **2**
E & N Railway Station, **4**
Empress Hotel, **9**
Market Square, **5**
McPherson Playhouse, **3**

Parliament Buildings, **12**
Point Ellice House, **1**
Public Library, **8**
Royal British Columbia
  Museum, **13**
Victoria Conference Center, **10**
Victoria Youth Hostel, **6**

TO HWY. 17
TO BUTCHART GARDENS
FERRY TERMINAL
U. OF VICTORIA

TO HWY. 1

Selkirk
Water

Gorge Rd East
Bridge Ellice St.
Market
Hillside
Rock Bay
Hill
David
Ross
King St.
Hillside
Douglas
Westbourne
Pleasant
John
Turner
Bridge
Ludgate
Bay St.
Wark
Dowler
Wark

TO CRAIGFLOWER
FARMHOUSE

Bay St.
Tyee
Wilson

Field
Blanshard

Queens
Princess
Pembroke
Pembroke

Upper
Harbour

Government
Discovery

Chatham
Caledonia

Store
Herald
Julia

Swift
Fisgard

Sitkum
Esquimalt
Saghalie
Harbour

Cooperage Pt.

Centennial
Sq.

Pandora

Johnson

Tyee
Kimta Rd.
Songhees
Paul Kane

Road
Douglas
Yates

Wharf
Trounce
View
Blanshard

Langley

Fort
Quadra

Inner
Harbour

Broughton

Courtney
Gordon
Courtney
Pembroke

TO CRAGDARROCH
CASTLE
TO ART GALLERY OF
GREATER VICTORIA
TO OAK BAY
AND YM/YWCA

Victoria
Harbour

Humboldt
Rupert
Fairfield

Kingston
Cross
Belleville

Pendray
Quebec
Kingston

Ontario
Oswega
Superior
Government

Montreal
Almo Pl.
Michigan
Menzies
Elliot
Academy
Southgate St.
Humboldt
Convent
Haywood Av.

Niagra
Beckley
Rendall
Croft
Simcoe
Perry
Powell
Heather
Young
Michigan
Toronto
Douglas

Beacon
Hill
Park

0   yards   440
0   meters   400

N

Emergency: 911. **Police:** 625 Fisgard (384-4111 for non-emergency), at Government St. Staff sergeant on duty 24hr.
Post Office: 905 Gordon St. V8W 3P9 (381-6114). Open Mon.-Fri. 9am-5:30pm, Sat. 9:30am-5pm. **Postal Code:** V8W 1L0.
Area Code: 604.

ORIENTATION AND GETTING AROUND

While the Seattle and Port Angeles **ferries** dock downtown, the ferry from the San Juan Islands docks at **Sidney,** 28km north on **Hwy. 17,** and the Vancouver/Gulf Islands ferry docks at **Swartz Bay,** 32km north. **Hwy. 1,** the **Trans-Canada Hwy.,** leads north and reaches the rest of Vancouver Island; **Hwy. 14** leads west to **Port Renfrew** and **Pacific Rim National Park.**

Parking downtown is difficult and expensive. Meters charge $1 for 48 minutes while most lots cost $1-1.50 for an hour. Parking in residential neighborhoods, however, is free. Cross the Johnson St. bridge and turn at the first right to find a free lot by the shipyards, a mere 10-minute walk from downtown. If the meter expires, don't panic. Victorian police seem reluctant to ticket cars with out-of-town plates.

Victoria enfolds the Inner Harbour; **Government St.** and **Douglas St.** are the main north-south thoroughfares, running through all of downtown. Residential neighborhoods, wealthier in the east, form a semicircle around the Inner Harbour.

ACCOMMODATIONS

Victoria Youth Hostel (HI-C), 516 Yates St. V8W 1K8 (385-4511), at Wharf St. downtown. 108 beds in the remodeled Victoria Heritage Building. Big, modern, and spotless; the pinnacle of hostel living. Staff and volunteer concierges offer a wealth of information, including valuable tips on where to find free parking. Extensive kitchen and laundry facilities. Ping pong, video games. Laundry $1.75 per load. Linen rental $1.50. Family rooms available. Desk open from 7am-midnight; curfew 2:30am. $15, nonmembers $19.

Renouf House Bunk & Breakfast, 2010 Stanley Ave. (595-4774; fax 598-1515), take bus #10 or walk down Johnson to Fernwood St. Stanley Ave. is one block west of Fernwood and two blocks north from Johnson. B&B or hostel? You decide: Renouf house offers both private rooms and bunks. Built in 1912 and full of antique furniture, dark wooden staircases. No TV. Large continental breakfast featuring homemade granola and breads. Staff organizes kayaking tours of the islands. Kitchen and laundry. Bunk $18.25. Singles with shared bath $33.25, with private bath $55. Doubles with shared bath $45, with private bath $65.

Victoria Backpackers Hostel, 1418 Fernwood Rd. (386-4471), take bus #10 to Fernwood and Douglas. 36 beds with coed and female-only rooms. Imagine your elderly aunt has turned her house—the one with the huge, well-kept garden out front and the Johnson-era furniture—into a hostel. Kitchen and lounge. Laundry $2 per load. Linen $1. Free parking in back. Bunks $12, private doubles $35.

University of Victoria (721-8395), 20min. northeast of the Inner Harbour by bus #4 or 14. From Hwy. 17, take MacKenzie to Sinclair. Housing office is in lot five. Private rooms with shared baths. Coin-op laundry machines. Play with the wild rabbits living under the buildings on campus. Registration after 3pm, reservations advised. Open May-Aug. Singles $37, doubles $52. Cafeteria breakfast included. Cheaper long-term rates available.

YM/YWCA, 880 Courtney St. (386-7511), at Quadra, within walking distance of downtown. Residence is women only; other Y facilities are coed. Heated pool and new gym. Private rooms with shared baths, free use of the facilities. Reception 7am-9pm. Check-out 7-11am. Dorm beds $19, singles $37, singles $56.

Battery Street Guest House, 670 Battery St. (385-4632). Between Douglas and Government St. The owner will talk your ear off in English or Dutch, but the conversation is pleasant, the rooms welcoming, and the ocean a mere block away. No smoking. Singles from $45, doubles from $65.

CAMPING

The few campgrounds on the perimeter of Victoria cater largely to wealthy RV drivers. Many campgrounds fill up in July and August; reservations are a good idea.

Goldstream Provincial Park, 2930 Trans-Canada Hwy. (391-2300; 800-689-9025 for reservations). A forested area along a river, 20km northwest of Victoria. Great short hiking trails and swimming. In Nov., the river is crowded with spawning salmon. Flush toilets and firewood available. 150 gorgeous, gravelly sites ($15.50). The nearby **Freeman King Visitor Centre** gives the history of the area from the Ice Age to the welfare state. Roam a self-guided trail, or have a naturalist take you for a walk. Open daily 9:30am-4:30pm; winter, open weekends only.

Thetis Lake Campground, 1938 Trans-Canada Hwy. (478-3845), 10km north of the city center. Sites are peaceful and removed. Metered showers and a laundromat. Sites $19 for 2 people, 50¢ per additional person.

Fort Victoria Camping, 340 Island Hwy. (479-8112; fax 479-5806), 7km northwest of downtown. Take bus #14 or, from Victoria, turn left onto Helmcken Rd. from the Trans-Canada Hwy., then turn right on Island Hwy. Both RV and tent sites available, though RVers might do better to try the cheaper, more scenic campground further down the Trans-Canada. Free hot showers. Laundromat. Sites $20 for 2 people, full hookups $25.

FOOD

The variety and high quality of the food in Victoria undermines the tourism industry's attempts to pass off the city as the North American equivalent of Jolly Old England. The abundance of coffee shops crawling with in-house baked pastries is a reminder of Victoria's proximity to Seattle. A stroll along **Government** and **Wharf Streets** offers countless restaurants, but *caveat emptor*—some raise their prices for the summer tourists and are dutifully avoided by locals. **Chinatown,** beginning at Fisgard and Government St. and continuing to the northwest, contains the expected range of Chinese cuisine. Also, **Fernwood Village,** three blocks north from Johnson and accessible by bus #10, provides creative restaurants scattered in among craft shops and a respite from the tourist-swarmed downtown.

If you feel like cooking, head down to **Fisherman's Wharf** at the corner of Harbour and Government St. On summer mornings, you can buy the day's catch as it flops off the boats. For large scale grocery shopping, try **Thrifty Foods,** 475 Simcoe (544-1234), six blocks south of the Parliament buildings (open daily 8am-10pm).

John's Place, 723 Pandora St. (389-0711), between Douglas and Blanshard. Only John's portions can match its reputation among locals. Complete with jukebox and Marilyn pinups, John's offers Canadian fare with a Thai twist and a little Mediterranean thrown in. Savory fresh herb bread and butter. Try John's favorite *Goong Nam Prik Pow* (sautéed tiger prawns in curry sauce; $10.95). Open Mon.-Thurs. 7am-10pm, Sat. 7am-11pm, Sun. brunch 8am-3pm, Sun. dinner 5-10pm.

Milky Way, 128-560 Johnson St. (360-1113). Breakfast, lunch, and dinner specials ranging from $2.95-9.95 for a multi-course meal make this one of the better bargains in town, while the star-studded decor makes it one of the more entertaining. Live music weekend nights. Open daily 7am-11pm.

Pluto's, 1150 Cooke St. (385-4747). Judy Jetson meets the 1950s in a wacky gas station. Blessed by the budget fairy, Pluto's lies farther from the bustle of downtown. Open Sun.-Thurs. 8am-11pm, Fri.-Sat. 8am-midnight.

Ferris' Oyster and Burger Bar, 536 Yates St. (360-1824), near the hostel. Boasting a menu far more extensive than its name would suggest, from tofu hot dogs ($4) and burgers ($5) to the $3 oyster shooter (a raw oyster with salsa and a half-shot of vodka or tequila to kill any bacteria). Open Mon.-Thurs. noon-10pm, Fri.-Sat. noon-11pm, Sun. noon-10pm. HI members discount.

El Rancho Restaurant, 1600 Bay St. (595-7422). Bus #2 to Bay St. Or, take Johnson to Quadra, turn left, then turn right on Bay St. One of the only places in Victoria where "South of the Border" doesn't mean Washington State, El Rancho specializes in "Latino" food—a mix of Mexican, Spanish, Tex-Mex, and Californian cooking. Free parking, and the only tourists there are usually lost. Steak, chicken, seafood, and vegetarian fajitas $11.95. Sunday is chef creation night: a 3-course meal is $16.95. Catch the early bird specials on weekends. Open Sun.-Thurs. 5:30-10pm, Fri.-Sat. 5:30-11pm.

The Sally Café, 714 Cormorant St. (381-1431). Great for lighter fare and heavier conversation, the Sally Café is so vegetarian friendly even the menus are green. (That was a joke.) Curried chicken and apricots $5.95, sandwiches from $4.75. Open Mon.-Fri. 7am-5pm, Sat. 8am-5pm.

The Blethering Place, 2250 Oak Bay Ave. (598-1413), at Monterey St. in upright Oak Bay. Take bus #2 or drive west on Fort St. and turn right on Oak Bay. Only the wealthy Oak Bay neighborhood lives up to Victoria's British hype. Despite the Anglophilia, live music is diverse, ranging from Celtic folksongs to flamenco. High tea (the Victorian way) with appropriate pastries baked on the premises is $11. Ploughman's lunch ($7.95) is a cheesier, meatier alternative. Dinners from $9. Open daily 8am-9pm.

Bennie's Bagelry, 132-560 Johnson St. (384-3441), between Wharf and Pandora. Creative bagel sandwiches are a meal in themselves. Whole-grain, environmentally safe bagels 65¢. Brie melt $4.25. Open Mon.-Thurs. 7am-7pm, Fri.-Sat. 7am-11pm, Sun. 10am-5pm.

Zombies Pizza, 1219 Wharf St. (389-2226). Cheerfully morbid decor and $2 slices make this a good, quick stop. Open Mon.-Sat. 11am-3am for those post-pub-closing munchies, Sun. 11am-1am.

SIGHTS AND ACTIVITIES

If you don't mind becoming one with the flocks of tourists hurling themselves lemming-like toward the shores of Victoria, wander along the **Inner Harbour** and watch the boats come in as the sun sets behind the neighboring islands. A trip through the **Royal British Columbia Museum,** 675 Belleville St. (387-3014 recording; 387-3701 operator) will remind you of why you came to Canada in the first place. Excellent, intense, and extensive exhibits on the biological, geological, and cultural history of the province from protozoans to the present. The First Nations exhibit features a totem pole room and a transplanted native house. (Admission $5.35, seniors $3.21, youth $2.14, under 5 free; open daily July 1-Sept. 8 9:30am-7pm, Sept. 9-June 30 10am-5:30pm). **Thunderbird Park** and its many totems loom large behind the museum. Tours available after July 1. **The Art Gallery of Greater Victoria,** at 1040 Moss (384-4101), houses a rotating collection of 10,000 pieces from contemporary Canada, traditional and contemporary Asia, North America, and Europe, as well as **the only Shinto shrine outside of Japan.** (Adults $4, seniors and students $2, under 12 free; admission free on Mondays. Open Mon.-Sat. 10am-5pm, Sun. 1-5pm.) The tourist office has pamphlets on the historic houses and parks in Victoria.

Across the street from the museum stand the imposing **Parliament Buildings,** 501 Belleville St. (387-3046), home of the Provincial government since 1898. The 10 story dome and Brunelleschi-esque vestibule are gilded with almost 50oz. of gold. At night, over 300 lights line the façade. Free tours leave from the main steps daily 9am to 5pm (about 20-23 times a day in summer, winter on the hour; open Mon.-Fri. 8:30am-5pm, on weekends open for tours only).

Just north of Fort St. on Wharf is **Bastion Square,** which earned Victorians the Vincent Massey Award for Excellence in Urban Environment in 1971. The **Maritime Museum,** 28 Bastion Sq. (385-4222), exhibits ship models, nautical instruments, and a modified 13m native canoe that shoved off from Victoria in 1901 on a daring but unsuccessful trip around the world (open daily 9:30am-4:30pm).

Since the end of the legal opium trade, **Chinatown,** entered through the "Gate of Harmonious Interest" on Fisgard St. at Government St., has diminished substantially, but its many restaurants and intriguingly inexpensive **Market Square** shops make for a worthwhile excursion. Market Square, the bulk of which lies on Johnson St. four blocks south of Fisgard, is a collection of countless stores, restaurants, and wooden walkways and is home to a popular public fair on summer Sundays.

Beacon Hill Park, off Douglas St. south of the Inner Harbour, is a flowering oasis just blocks from downtown that pleases walkers, bikers, and the picnic-inclined. More adventurous mountain bikers can try tackling the **Galloping Goose Trail,** a 60km trail beginning in downtown Victoria and continuing to the west coast of the island through cities, rainforests, and canyons. The trail is open to cyclists, walkers, and horses. Horses on bicycles strongly discouraged.

By sea, Victoria is a hub for a number of the sailing, kayaking, and whale-watching tours available on Vancouver Island. But for a more active aquatic experience, **Oak Bay Marine Group** at the Oak Bay Marina (598-3369) rents deep sea fishing charters for $6 per hour, minimum 4 hours. Group rates, much like the hungry seals who sun themselves along the Marina, are always plentiful. After a few days of hiking, biking, and visiting museums, unwind with a tour of the **Vancouver Island Brewery** at 2330 Government St. (361-0007). Tours start at 1 and 3pm Wednesday through Saturday and include free samples. The free tour is educational as well as alcoholic.

EVENTS AND ENTERTAINMENT

Those crazy Canooks may be on the metric system, but the best deal for beer is still the pint. And Victoria is lousy with pubs. For pints that come with live music, **Harpo's Cabaret,** 15 Bastion Sq. (385-5333), at Wharf St. brings in an eclectic array of bands ranging from blues and jazz to neo-hippie rock acts. Two blocks away, **Steamer's Public House,** 570 Yates (381-4340), ships in both local acts and world beat grooves. The free weekly *Monday Magazine* (inexplicably released every Wednesday), available at the hostel, hotels, and most places downtown, provides an exhaustive listing of who's playing where. For even more up-to-the-minute information, check the telephone poles and light posts downtown—posted fliers are often the best source for what's happening.

Nightlife in Victoria doesn't really start jumping until Thursdays, but once the weekend comes, the whole city seems ready to party. Most clubs offer weekday drink specials to draw crowds—cheap beer nights have the highest success rates.

Drawing Room, 751 View St. (920-7797). A club considerate enough to offer a lounge, with easy chairs, pool tables, and a wall-to-wall carpet for dancers fleeing the frenzied techno/alternative/house music playing on the dancefloor next door. Fresh fruit bar for mixed drinks and vitamins. Cover $2-3, weekends $4. Open Tues.-Thurs. 8pm-2am, Fri.-Sat. 9pm-2am.

Rumors, 1325 Government St. (385-0566). Gay and lesbian clientele; drinking, dancing, and one of Victoria's more inviting dancefloors. Drag shows on alternate Sundays, male strippers on Thursdays. Every third Friday is women's night. Open Mon.-Sat. 9pm-2am, Sun. 9pm-midnight.

Sticky Wicket, 919 Douglas St. (383-7137). Seven bars and a club all in one building, next door to the Strathcona Hotel. The Roof Top Bar, cleverly located on the roof, even has its own beach volleyball court available for rent. The club, **The Forge,** specializes in mid-70s rock with a wattage that could vaporize tungsten. The Forge charges a $3 cover on weekends, but the pubs are cover-free and serve food until 1am. Open Mon.-Sat. 11:30am-2am, Sun. 11:30am-midnight.

Scandals, 770 Yates (389-0666). Explore the wonders of a low drinking age in this second home for Victoria's swinging under-25 set. Laser beams shoot across the floor with reckless abandon (watch out). Mostly alternative music with Tuesday and Wednesday retro nights. Sunday is a mellower disco night. Cover $1-3. Open Mon.-Sat. 9pm-2am, Sun. 9pm-midnight.

Spinnakers, 308 Catherine (386-2739). Across the Johnson St. bridge. Plentiful tourists and seafood specials. Beer brewed on site. Live music featured on weekends. Open daily 7am-11pm.

The **Victoria Symphony Society,** 846 Broughton St. (385-6575), performs regularly under conductor Peter McCoppin. The highlight of its year is the Symphony Splash, a free concert on the first Sunday in August played on a barge in the Inner Harbour that concludes with fireworks and usually draws 40-50,000 international listeners. For the last week and a half of June, Victoria oozes jazz during **JazzFest,** as over a dozen performers play venues throughout the city (388-4423).

On Tuesdays, first-run movies at **Cineplex** Odeon theaters are half-price ($4.50). For more off-beat and foreign films, head to the University of Victoria's **Cinecenter** (721-8365) in the student union (bus #4 and 14). **Phoenix Theaters** at the University of Victoria (721-8000) has productions in June, as well as term-time live theater performances. And from mid-July to mid-August, Victoria goes Elizabethan/Jacobean when the **Annual Shakespeare Festival** lands in the Inner Harbour (360-0234).

■ Near Victoria

SOOKE

West of Victoria on Hwy. 14 lies the town of Sooke, named for the T'sou-ke people and host to the logging events and festivities of **All Sooke Day** on the third Saturday in July. The **Sooke Region Museum** (642-6351), just off Hwy. 14 at 2070 Phillips Rd., delivers an excellent history of the area (open daily July-Aug. 9am-6pm, Sept.-June 9am-5pm; free). The museum also houses a **travel infocenter.** Next to the park where All Sooke Day takes place, on Phillips Rd. past the museum, is the **Sooke River Flats Campsite** (642-6076), with a phone, showers, toilets, and running water (gates locked 11pm-7am; sites $10). To get to Phillips Rd. from the city, take bus #50 to the Western Exchange and transfer to #61. Turn right at Sooke's only stop light to find **Camp Barnard,** 3130 Young Lake Rd. (642-5924), a former Boy Scout camp with cabins that sleep eight ($35) and tent sites ($10) as well as fire pits, hot showers, and swimming. Reservations required.

Sooke is a haven for wealthier Victorians, making cheap indoor accommodations scarce. Try the **Blackfish B&B** (642-6864), 7 mi. west of the stop light (singles $35, doubles $50-60). Large groups should ask about the great **bungalow** down on the pebble beach with free laundry and a full kitchen (sleeps 9; $125 per night).

North of Sooke lie some of the best opportunities for beachcombing on the southern island. Hwy. 14 continues along the coast, stringing together two provincial parks: **Juan de Fuca,** home to **China Beach** and **Loss Creek** (both day use), and **French Beach,** with tent sites (May-Oct. $9.50). Camping is free at the **Jordan River Recreation Area** ten minutes past French Beach.

GULF ISLANDS

Just off the southeastern coast of Vancouver Island lies British Columbia's stunningly beautiful **Gulf Island Archipelago.** Five islands are accessible by BC Ferries (call 386-3431 or pick up a schedule for info). The three principle members of the chain are Salt Spring, Mayne, and Pender. For information on the five main islands, call the **Tourist Information Centre** in Salt Spring (537-5252) or Victoria (382-3551). On Salt Spring, the elusive **HI-C hostel** at 640 Cusheon Lake Rd. (537-4149) has its own hiking trails ($14, nonmembers $17). **Maxine's Boardwalk Cafe,** #2-104 Fulford Ganges Rd. (537-5747) on Salt Spring, sports a reasonably priced breakfast and lunch menu with colorful daily specials and a waterfront view. Salt Spring offers the largest population and widest activities of the five islands. Options range from climbing **Mt. Maxwell** for a panoramic view of BC and Washington to playing golf at **Blackburn Meadows,** 269 Blackburn Rd. (537-1707), a farm converted into an organic golf course right next to an Audobon sanctuary (9 holes $11, club rental $10). Or just play with the mounties at the **Royal Canadian Mounted Police** outpost on the outskirts of Ganges. (*Let's Go* does not recommend taunting or sassing national police forces.)

■ Nanaimo

As seen from the highway, Nanaimo is a strip of motels, gas stations, and greasy spoons gracelessly protruding from the forests and mountains surrounding it. An excursion off the highway, however, reveals why it has become a crossroads for the outdoors enthusiasts who flock to the island every summer. Boasting 25 parks and a beach in town as well as several provincial parks nearby, Nanaimo can be a destination in itself as well as a pit stop on the way to the rainforests on the northern and western parts of Vancouver Island.

PRACTICAL INFORMATION AND ORIENTATION

Visitors Information: Travel Infocentre, 266 Bryden St. (754-8474), off Terminal Ave., just northwest of downtown. Information on all of Vancouver Island. Accommodations directories available. Open daily 8:30am-7:30pm; winter Mon.-Fri. 9am-5pm, Sat.-Sun. 10:30am-4:30pm.

Trains: VIA Rail, 321 Selby St. (800-561-8630). To: Victoria (2 per day, $19.26; with 7-day advance purchase $12). Student and senior discounts.

Buses: Laidlaw, 753-4371. At Comox and Terminal, behind Tally Ho Island Inns. To: Victoria (7 per day, $16), Port Hardy (daily at 9am, in summer alternate days at 3pm, $69). Tofino and Ucluelet (4 per day, $29 and $26).

Ferries: BC Ferries, (753-6626 for recorded info, 753-1261 for an operator). To: Vancouver (approx. 8 per day between 7am and 9pm; passenger $6.50, car and driver $31.50). Also to **Horseshoe Bay** on the mainland and **Gabriola Island,** with connections to **Bowen Island** and **Langdale.** Terminal at the northern end of Stewart Ave. Take the ferry shuttle from Gordon St. Exchange downtown.

Car Rental: Rent-A-Wreck, 111 Terminal Ave. S. (753-6461). Used cars start at $30 per day, first 100km free, 16¢ for each additional km. Must be at least 21 with a major credit card. Open Mon.-Fri. 8am-6pm, Sat. 9am-4pm, Sun. 10am-4pm. **Budget,** 17 Terminal Ave. S. (754-7368). An infinite number of rate and free km packages available. Must be at least 19. Free pickup in most parts of town.

Bus Information: 390-4531. Gordon Street Exchange, at Front St. and Gordon St. 12 bus routes serve the area. Fares $1.30, seniors $1.05.

Laundromat: 702 Nicol St. (753-9922), at Robins in **Payless Gas Station.** 24hr.

Crisis Line: 754-4447. 24hr.

Gay and Lesbian Information: Gayline (754-2585). Call Mon.-Fri. 6-9pm.

Pharmacy: London Drugs (753-5566), in Harbour Park Mall at Terminal Ave. Open Mon.-Sat. 9am-10pm, Sun. 10am-8pm.

Hospital: 1200 Dufferin Crescent (754-2141).

Emergency: 911.

Police: 303 Pridaux St. (754-2345), at Fitzwilliam. **Fire:** 666 Fitzwilliam St. (753-7311/7344), at Milton.

Post Office: (741-1829). Harbour Park Mall, at Terminal. Open Mon.-Fri. 8:30am-5pm. **Postal Code:** V9R 5E2.

Area Code: 250.

Nanaimo lies on the eastern coast of Vancouver Island, 111km north of Victoria on **Hwy. 1,** the **Trans-Canada Hwy.,** and 391km south of **Port Hardy** via **Hwy. 19,** the **Island Hwy.** Hwy. 1 transforms into Hwy. 19 in Nanaimo but only after three successive name changes: Nicol St., Terminal Ave. S., and finally Terminal Ave. N. The **ferry** terminal is 2km north of downtown on **Stewart Ave.**

ACCOMMODATIONS AND CAMPING

Thompson's Hostel, 1660 Cedar Rd. (722-2251), off the Cedar Hwy. about 5km south of downtown. The best camping near town—right on the Nanaimo River with refrigerator and 4-burner gas stove at the sites. Indoor accommodations are almost as pleasant. House has 12 beds, free pool, darts, ping-pong, and a piano. Free parking and linen. No curfew. Laundry $3. Beds $13, sites $6.

Nicol St. Hostel, 65 Nicol St. (753-1188), 7 blocks southeast of the Island Bus Lines Depot. With more beds than the house seems capable of holding and tent sites in the back yard, the Nicol St. Hostel houses a surprising number of travelers. Registration from 4-11pm. Beds $17. Tent sites $8. Laundry $2.

Big 7 Motel, 736 Nicol St. (754-2328). Nightmarish decor circa 1986. As compensation, all rooms have cable *and* HBO. Desk open 24hr. Singles $34, winter $28; doubles $40, winter $34.

Brother (XII), Can You Spare A Dime?

The new age-ism common on Vancouver island started early in Nanaimo when a man calling himself **Brother XII** heralded the coming of the Age of Aquarius in the 1920s. He developed his own theology and organized a large cult following among Islanders, especially the wealthy. Brother XII (or simply XII to his friends) and his followers left Nanaimo in 1927 to form Utopia at Cedar-by-Sea on the nearby DeCourcy Island. The more conservative Nanaimo-ites earned a chance to combat XII and his teachings when people began fleeing the island, telling stories of Brother XII's greed, his nasty habit of forcing the elderly to commit suicide once they'd left their money to him and, of course, his network of sex slaves. He was put on trial in 1932 and fled to Europe where he died in 1934. When he disappeared, Brother XII supposedly left $1.4 million in gold buried somewhere around Cedar-by-Sea. In 1982, the Nanimo paper ran a story of an unemployed 35-year-old steam fitter who found the gold but only after facing death three times at the hands of Brother XII's lingering magic. The article, as it turns out, was an elaborate April Fool's joke. These days, though, most residents steer clear of magic and Nanaimo's mystical side has toned itself down. While the area once sported a witch-run coffee shop and is rumored to have a pagan church, the most popular cult these days is nature worship.

Westwood Lake, 380 Westwood Rd. (753-3922), west of town off Jingle Pot Rd. Take bus #5. Only 200yds. from the trout-stocked lake. Foot path of giant concrete footprints leads to the office. Full facilities. 66 sites. $15, $18 with hookups.

Brannen Lake Campsite, 4220 Biggs Rd. (756-0404), 6km north of ferry terminal. Follow the signs from Hwy. 19. On a ranch and definitely worth the trip. Clean bathrooms with hot showers ($1). Free hayrides every night, and you can help with the animals. Hike to a nearby waterfall. Sites $14, with hookup $16.

FOOD

Nanaimo supports a multitude of budget eateries. Cafés and restaurants speckle the downtown area, while the highway hosts an endless party of little dives, many open late or 24 hours. Those more inclined to greaseless spoons can seek refuge in the massive **Thrifty Foods** in the Harbour Park Mall (754-6273; open daily 8am-10pm).

Filthy McNasty's, 14 Commercial St. (753-7011). An eclectic oasis of multi-media wall art, gourmet food, and tantalizing desserts. Simple Salmon (was a pizza; $8). All-you-can-eat pasta $5, Sun.-Thurs. 5-9pm. Live jazz on weekend nights. Open Sun.-Wed. 9am-9pm, Thurs.-Sat. 9am-6pm and 9:30pm-midnight.

Gina's Mexican Café, 47 Skinner St. (753-5411), up the hill off Front St. A self-proclaimed "Tacky but Friendly Place," Gina's lives up to its billing with wild bright colors, a "Gringo card" to help with menu translation, and dishes that have won "countless gringo awards." Combo plates $8.95, nachos starting at $5.75. Open Mon.-Thurs. 11am-9pm, Fri. 11am-10pm, Sat. noon-10pm, Sun. 2-8:30pm.

Pagliacci's, 7 Old Victoria Rd. (754-3443), across from Nicol St. Hostel. Classy dining starring movie-themed dishes served with exquisite focaccia bread. Seafood, vegetable, and meat pastas, starting at $7.50. If this next meal is to be your last, consider indulging in one of the pricier 5-course entree meals ($13.95-19.95). Open Sun.-Thurs. 11:30am-10pm, Fri.-Sat. 11:30am-11pm.

The Scotch Bakery, 87 Commercial St. (753-3521). Nanaimo Bar (a chocolaty local confection) seekers come here for a fix (80¢). Don't ignore the apple fritters (85¢) or sausage rolls ($1.29) either. Open Mon.-Sat. 8am-4:30pm.

SIGHTS

The **Nanaimo District Museum,** 100 Cameron Rd. (753-1821), has a full-scale walkthrough model of a coal mine as well as a semi-interactive exhibit on the native Snunēmuxw. The small museum makes a particular effort to pay tribute to the Chinese presence in Nanaimo ($2, students and seniors $1.50, under 12 50¢; open Mon.-

Fri. 9am-6pm, Sat.-Sun. 10am-6pm; after Labor Day Tues.-Sat. 9am-5pm). Only 300m from the museum is the **Bastion** (754-1631), built by the Hudson's Bay Company as a storehouse and fort against native attacks. A six-lb. cannon booms daily at noon (free; open Mon.-Fri. 9am-5pm, Sat.-Sun. 10am-5pm; summer only).

About 2.5km west of town is the **Nanaimo Art Gallery,** 900 5th St. (755-8790), which features various rotating exhibitions of local and international art and culture. Bus #6 will save you the 30-minute walk uphill (open Mon.-Sat. 10am-5pm and Sun. noon-5pm). About 1km farther west on Nanaimo Lakes Ave. by the city reservoir, the **Morrell Nature Sanctuary** provides tranquil trails, a perfect place to write haiku and digest lunch.

Three km south of town on Hwy. 1, the **Petroglyph Provincial Park** protects the carvings of hundreds of generations of Salish shamans. A menagerie of animals and mythical creatures decorates the soft sandstone. Rubbings can be made from concrete replicas at the base of the trail leading to the petroglyphs.

Farther south, the ever-expanding **Bungy Zone,** P.O. Box 399, Station A, Nanaimo, BC V9R 5L3 (753-5867), stretches a dimension of sight, sound, and giant rubber bands. Thrill seekers from all over the continent make a pilgrimage here to drop 140 feet into a narrow gorge, secured against certain death only by a thick elastic bungee cord. The short but exhilarating trip down costs $95 (2 for 1 if you rent a car from Budget; discount with HI card; group rates available). Three new activities—the Flying Fox, Ultimate Swing, and Rap Jumping—are coming soon. Watch for package deals. To reach the Zone, take Hwy. 1 south to Nanaimo River Rd. and then follow the signs.

Departure Bay washes onto a pleasant beach in the north end of town off Stewart Ave. **North Island Water Sports,** 2755 Departure Bay Rd. (758-2488), rents kayaks ($30 per day, $70 for a double) and scramblers (like kayaks, but you sit on top of them; $8 per hr., $20 for 3hr.). The week-long **Marine Festival** is held during the second week of July. Highlights include the **Silly Boat Race** and the renowned **Bathtub Race.** Bathers from all over the continent race porcelain tubs with monster outboards from Nanaimo to Vancouver across the 55km Georgia Strait. They hand out prizes to everyone who makes it across, and ceremoniously present the "Silver Plunger" trophy to the first tub that sinks. The organizer of this bizarre but beloved event is the **Royal Nanaimo Bathtub Society,** 51A Commercial St., Nanaimo V9R 5G3 (753-7223).

■ Near Nanaimo

PORT ALBERNI

Port Alberni is the only pit stop on Hwy. 4, about 25km west of Hwy. 19 and a third of the way from Nanaimo to Pacific Rim National Park. The town bills itself as the "Salmon Capital of the World" and hosts an annual **Salmon Festival** each Labor Day weekend. Brochures and advice on the general area are at the Port Alberni **Infocentre** (724-6535), on Hwy. 4 (open daily 8am-8pm; in winter closes at 5pm). **Naesgaard's,** a farmer's market off Hwy. 4 just west of town, overflows with farm-fresh fruit, flowers, and vegetables (open Mon.-Sat. 9am-8:30pm, Sun. 10am-8:30pm; winter Mon.-Sat. 9am-6pm, Sun. 10am-6pm). **Sproat Lake Provincial Park** (723-2952), 13km west of Port Alberni off Hwy. 4, offers space to explore mysterious petroglyphs, boat, swim, fish, and camp (sites from $12). Less well-known is **Stamp Falls Provincial Park,** on the way to Sproat Lake. Originally World War II troop carriers, the **Martin Mars Bombers,** moored on Sprout Lake in the summer, are the last two working flying boats of their kind. Today, they are used to fight fires.

CHEMAINUS

About 30km south of Nanaimo on Hwy. 1 lies the town of Chemainus. When the closing of the town's sawmill threatened economic disaster in 1980, an ambitious revitalization program, centered on a series of more than 30 striking murals, helped turn things around. The murals which depict the town's history now rival Madonna in self-promotion.

In mid-July, **Chemainus Daze** offers arts, crafts, and a chance to meet with the mural artists. In addition to its novel public art scene, a deep-water port and proximity to both Duncan (City of Totems!) and Nanaimo makes a stay in Chemainus a worthwhile alternative to a night in one of Vancouver Island's bigger cities.

The **Horseshoe Bay Inn,** 9576 Chemainus Rd. (246-3425), at Henry, has singles for $28, doubles for $40, with private bath $46. The **Chemainus Hostel,** 9694 Chemainus Rd. (246-2809), is not only a good place to find a bed, a kitchen and laundry facilities, but is also a source of information on activities across the island. Experience local culture by stopping by the **Senior Drop-In Centre,** on the corner of Willow and Alder (246-2111), for 25¢ coffee and homemade scones (open daily 10am-4pm). Call the **Chemainus Arts and Business Council** at 246-4701 for more information on town activities.

HORNBY ISLAND

In the 1960s, large numbers of draft-dodgers fled the U.S. to settle peacefully on quiet Hornby Island, halfway between Nanaimo and Campbell River. Today, Hornby Island and **Denman** comprise a fitting mix of inhabitants: the descendants of the pioneering families that came here around 1850 and hippie-holdovers who offer spiritual awareness readings. At the center of all activities on Hornby sits **The Co-op** (335-1121) at the end of Central Rd. by Tribune Bay. Home to Hornby's only **tourist information** and **post office,** the Co-op is also a well stocked grocery store and deli (open daily 9am-7pm).

With its light traffic and paved roads, Hornby Island is easily explored on two wheels. You can rent bikes ($7 per hr., $25 per day, $30 overnight) from **Hornby Island Off-Road Bike Shop** (335-0444) at the Co-op (see above; open daily 10am-5pm). For kayak rentals, try Hornby Ocean Kayak, 3150 Shingle Spit Rd. (335-2726). Kayaks are $25 for four hours, $40 per day. Low tide at Tribune Bay and Whaling Station Bay uncovers over 300m of the finest sand on Vancouver Island. **Tribune Bay,** at the base of Central Rd., is the more accessible of the two beaches. The alternative, **Whaling Station Bay,** is about 5km farther north. On the way there from Tribune Bay, Helliwell Rd. takes you to stunning **Helliwell Provincial Park.** A well groomed trail leads you on a one-hour **jaunt** through old-growth forest to bluffs overlooking the ocean. **Cormorants** dive straight into the ocean to surface moments later with trophy-quality fish, while **bald eagles** cruise on the sea breezes.

The **Hornby Festival** draws musicians, comedians, and artists from all over Canada for ten days in early August. Call the Hornby Festival Society (335-2734) for details. For more information, contact **Denman/Hornby Tourist Services,** at the Denman General Store (335-2293), or ask at the Co-op.

If you plan on spending more than a day here, bring a tent and food. The **Hornby Island Resort** (335-0136), right at the ferry docks, is a pub/restaurant/laundromat/hotel/campground. The pub fare is standard but reasonably priced; the restaurant has breakfast plates from $6 (restaurant open daily 9:30am-9pm; sites $17 per night, with hookup $18). **Bradsdadsland Country Camp,** 1980 Shingle Spit Rd. (335-0757), offers standard plots for your tent (sites for 2 people $18.50 per night; $1.50 per additional person, $1.50 per pet; full hookup $3). **Jen's Café,** 578 Central Rd. (335-1487), serves soup and salad for $5-6, and sandwiches and burgers for $5 (open daily 8am-8pm).

Laidlaw has a flag stop at **Buckley Bay,** on Hwy. 19, where the ferry docks. **BC Ferries** sails nine times daily (roundtrip $3, car and driver $8.25). It's a 10-minute ride from Buckley Bay to Denman; disembark and make the 11km trek across the island to the Gravely Bay docks for another 10-minute ride to Hornby. Once on Hornby, there are only two roads to worry about: **Shingle Spit Rd.** (try saying that 10 times fast) and **Central Rd.,** separated by the docks. Central Rd. extends to the eastern shore where all the "action" is. However, it's 15km away, and there's no public transit.

This area is difficult to cover without a bike or car, so some foot-travelers ask friendly faces for lifts at Denman or on the ferry. (*Let's Go* does not recommend hitch-hiking.) If you need a **taxi**, call 285-3598. Some useful numbers are: **emergency,** 911; **police,** 338-1321. A **post office** (335-1121) is at the Co-op at the terminus of Central Rd., on the eastern shore of the island (**Postal Code:** V0R 1Z0). The **area code** is 250.

▨ Pacific Rim National Park

The three regions of Pacific Rim National Park vary so greatly in landscape and sea-scape that only a government could have combined them under the same jurisdiction. The park, a thin strip of land on Vancouver Island's remote Pacific coast, can be reached in three distinct ways. To reach the south end of the park, the **West Coast Trail** at **Port Renfrew,** take Hwy. 14 to its end. Hwy. 14 runs west from Hwy. 1 not far from Victoria. The middle section—the **Broken Group Islands** in **Barkley Sound** and **Bamfield**—is far more difficult to reach. The Broken Islands can only be reached by water and the trip to Bamfield requires a 100km drive over bone-jarring logging roads from either Hwy. 18 or through Port Alberni. Hwy. 18 connects to Hwy. 1 at Duncan about 60km north of Victoria. For access to **Long Beach,** at the Park's northern reaches, take the spectacular drive across the center of Vancouver Island on Hwy. 4 to the Pacific Rim Hwy. This stretch connects **Ucluelet** (yoo-CLOO-let) to **Tofino** (toe-FEE-no). Hwy. 4 branches west of Hwy. 1 about 35km north of Nanaimo and leads through **Port Alberni** on the way to the Pacific coast.

Each spring, around 22,000 **gray whales** stream past the park. Orcas, sea lions, black-tailed deer, bald eagles, and black bears also frequent the area. The park is part of the second largest temperate rainforest in North America, and it is wise to be prepared for frequent downpours.

WEST COAST TRAIL: PORT RENFREW & BAMFIELD

Port Renfrew is the most easily accessible of the three gateways into the **West Coast Trail,** a.k.a. the Katmandu of North American backpacking. The trail extends through the southern third of the Pacific Rim National Park between Port Renfrew and Bamfield, weaving through 77km of forests and waterfalls, scaling steep wooden ladders and rocky slopes, and tracing the treacherous shoreline that has been the graveyard of many ships. Only **experienced hikers** should attempt this slick trail, and never alone. Gray whales, sea otters, and black bears along the route may provide company, but they can't help you in an accident. The trail is regulated by a strict quota system and reservations are necessary to hike it. For information on the legendary trek, call the Park Superintendent at 800-663-6000 or write to Box 280, Ucluelet V0R 3A0. The Park Super can send maps, tide tables, ferry information, and trail safety brochures as well. Hikers end up paying about $100 in fees, including a reservation fee, a trail use fee, and a ferry crossing fee. The trail is only open from April 15-Sept. 30, but you can (and probably should) make reservations by March 1.

Both Port Renfrew and Bamfield are somewhat isolated. Trucks and boats are the best vehicles to get you where you're going. A long winding drive down Hwy. 14 lands you in Port Renfrew, while hours of logging roads and the Pacific are the only two ways into Bamfield. Because Bamfield lies on two sides of an inlet, water transit is necessary to cross town. The **Kingfisher Marina** (728-3228) operates a water taxi service just for such occasions.

If you only want to spend an afternoon roughing it, you can visit Port Renfrew's **Botanical Beach Provincial Park.** Nature enthusiasts will delight in the many varieties of intertidal life, as well as sandstone, shale, quartz, and basalt formations. And not to be outdone by its national park neighbor, the Botanical Beach offers a hiking trail of its own, connecting Port Renfrew to the nearby **Juan de Fuca Provincial Park** and **China Beach.**

Seek out **maps** and information on the area and registration information for the West Coast Trail at the **Trail Information Center** (647-5434) in Port Renfrew (open

May-Sept. daily 9am-5pm). Or try the one in Pachena Bay, at the northern trailhead, 5km from Bamfield (728-3234). The **Pacheenaht Band Bus Service** (647-5521) provides transportation from Port Renfrew to Bamfield ($40) and points between. To get to either Port Renfrew or Bamfield from elsewhere on the island, try the **West Coast Trail Port Renfrew Connector** (361-9080, reservations required) which runs twice daily between Victoria and Port Renfrew ($25). **West Coast Trail Express** (477-8700) travels to Bamfield from Victoria ($47) and Nanaimo ($47). Reservations encouraged. The local hospital is the **Bamfield Red Cross Outpost Hospital** (728-3312). The **post office** is in Bamfield, across the inlet near the Bamfield Inn, next to the General Store (open Mon.-Fri. 8:30am-5pm). The **postal code** is V9P 2G2. The **area code** is 250.

Accommodations in town are limited, making camping in the park your best bet. Campgrounds pop up in both towns and some locals rent tent sites on their property. Near Port Renfrew, the **Pacheenaht Campground** offers campsites ($8) and RV sites ($13). The **Seabeam Fishing Resort and Hostel** (728-3286) in Bamfield sports the area's cheapest indoor accommodations ($15, nonmembers $20) complete with full kitchen and laundry facilities. Head to **Camp Ross** (337-5935) at the West Coast Trailhead for an amazing shoreside location (free; outhouses, pay phone, 3-day max). To wash the trail dust off in Port Renfrew, most hikers and campers use the public **shower** ($1) and **laundry** ($2), available at the **Port Renfrew Hotel** (647-5541).

Almost all the restaurants in both towns are inexpensive, but campers and hikers might prefer the convenience of shopping at Port Renfrew's **General Store** (647-5587) and Bamfield's **Kamshee Store** (728-3411). Both are open daily 9am-9pm, winter 9am-7pm. Dinner out is likely to disappoint.

LONG BEACH: UCLUELET AND TOFINO

At the northern end of the Pacific Rim National Park lie Ucluelet and Tofino. Thirty km apart at opposite ends of the Pacific Rim Hwy. and on either side of the park, the two towns also stand at either end of the range of small town atmospheres. Ucluelet retains its fishing-village attitude until it floods every July and August with Long Beach travelers. Meanwhile, Tofino may have sold its soul to the commercial devil, but it remains Canada's best answer to California (it even has its own surfing subculture), making it the more popular of the two destinations. Both towns provide ample access to Pacific Rim's many trails and to the surrounding waters.

Find **visitor information** 3km into the Long Beach unit off Hwy. 4, close to the **Port Alberni** junction (726-4212; open mid-April to mid-Oct. daily 9:30am-5pm); in **Tofino** at 351 Campbell St. (725-3414; open daily 9am-8pm; March-June and Sept.-Oct. Sat.-Sun. 9am-5pm; Nov.-Feb. closed); and in **Ucluelet** at 227 Main St. (726-4641; open daily 10am-5pm; Sept.-June Mon.-Fri. 10am-3pm).

Laidlaw, 700 Douglas St. (385-4411 in Victoria, 724-1266 in Port Alberni, 725-3101 in Tofino, 726-4334 in Ucluelet) connects Victoria and Nanaimo with Tofino and Ucluelet through Port Alberni. Four buses leave daily: Victoria to Tofino, $45, to Ucluelet $42. **Alberni Marine Transportation, Inc.,** P.O. Box 188, Port Alberni V9Y 7M7 (800-663-7192), operates the ferry *Lady Rose* year-round from Port Alberni to Bamfield ($19, roundtrip $38), Ucluelet ($22, roundtrip $44), and Gibraltar Island in the Broken Group Islands ($20, roundtrip $40).

The laundromat in Ucluelet is **Koin Laundrette** in Davison's Shopping Plaza on Peninsula St. In Tofino try the **Tofino Laundromat** at 448 Campbell (open 24hr.). The **hospital** is at 261 Neill St., Tofino (725-3212). Reach the **police** at 725-3242 in Tofino. The **post office**, 161 1st St., (725-3734) is at 1st and Campbell in Tofino (open Mon.-Thurs. 10am-3pm, Fri. 10am-5pm). The **area code** is 250.

Even in the off season, a bed in Tofino can be pricey, and once summer rolls around camping becomes expensive too. Reservations can make or break a July-August visit, as those without can easily find themselves shut out of the handful of reasonably priced accommodations and instead forced into a motel room, all of which start at $75 for a single.

Recently reopened and under new management, the **Tofino Hostel,** 241 Campbell (725-2288 or 725-3309), has beds for $20 and a private double for $45, as well as a clean kitchen, laundry, and a backyard deck. Many of the B&Bs in town offer better rooms and rates than the motels. **Stephanie's,** 420 Gibson St. (725-4230) has almost unconscionably reasonable rates (for Tofino) with three rooms $45-60 in July and Aug., off season $35-50. Kids are a fixture at Stephanie's, so if you don't want to hang with the under-10 set, look elsewhere. In Ucluelet, the **Ucluelet Hotel** (726-4234), on Main St., provides inexpensive rooms and a bar downstairs (singles and doubles $29 with shared bath, $40 with private bath). **Agapé,** 246 Lee St. (726-7073), 4km before Ucluelet, is a treasure at $35-40 for a single, $50-65 for a double, including a gourmet hot breakfast.

While there are a number of campgrounds between the park and Tofino, they average at least $20 to camp and almost $30 for a hookup. It costs $5 per day to remain in the park; annual passes are also available ($35). The **Park Superintendent** can be contacted year-round for advance information at Box 280, Ucluelet V0R 3A0 (726-7721). Locals can often provide tips on free camping in the area. The only campground in the park itself is **Green Point Campground** (726-4245), 10km north of the park information center. Green Point has 94 sites equipped with hot water, flush toilets, fireplaces, and (in July and August) swarms of campers and mosquitoes ($20; reservations required, call 800-689-6025). **Ucluelet Campground** (726-4355), off Pacific Rim Hwy., offers sites with showers and toilets ($17, full hookup $20, showers $1 for 4min.; open March-Oct.).

Ucluelet and Tofino's budget dining reflects their slightly hipper interpretation of the West Coast lifestyle. If the vegetables were any fresher at **Matterson's Tea House,** 1682 Peninsula Rd. in Ucluelet (726-2200), they'd be in the ground. If you're tired of grilled fish, try eating yesterday's halibut catch burger-style ($7.50; open daily 7:30am-9pm). For the early morning angler and the late night bowler in all of us, **Smiley's Family Restaurant,** 1992 Peninsula Rd. (726-4213) is open 21 hours per day and has a bowling alley ($2.84 per game), a pool table, and an arcade to help you burn off the calories from their fish and chips ($5.50) and homemade pies (open daily 4am-1am; winter 7am-10pm). More than just a restaurant and bakery offering some of the finest eats in Western Canada, the **Common Loaf Bake Shop,** 131 1st St. (725-3915), is also Tofino's social center. A slice of gourmet pizza goes for $3.75. The colorful **Alleyway Café,** 305 Campbell (725-3105), is hard to find (it's literally in an alleyway), but offers veggie burgers ($6.25), salmon quesadillas ($7), and burritos ($4.85) to those who make it.

Orcas and **gray whales** migrate past the park and the neighboring **Clayoquot Sound** every spring. The grays stay in the area all summer at the feeding grounds in the Sound. Local boatsmen will gladly take you on a three-hour ride for close observation ($50-60). Smooth rides in large boats are available, but the daring venture out in **Zodiacs,** hard-bottomed inflatable rafts with huge outboards that ride the swells at 30 knots. **Remote Passages** (725-3330) offers Zodiac adventures supplemented by a discussion of the coastal environment ($50, students and seniors $46, under 12 $30). For a longer excursion, Remote Passages also runs day trips to **Hot Springs Cove,** a six- to seven-hour trip which includes an hour of whale watching, a tour of the Sound and its bird, marine, and wildlife, and three hours at the Hot Springs themselves, a series of pools of progressive warmth that eventually open into the ocean ($75, $70 off season). **Subtidal Adventures,** 1956 Peninsula Rd. in Ucluelet (726-7336), offers cruises to the Broken Group Islands ($45, ages 6-12 $25, under 6 $15) and leads kayaking trips around and on nearby islands ($38 for 2.5 hr., $50 for 4 hr.). **Majestic Ocean Kayaking** (726-2868) in Tofino has kayaks for $75 per day.

Radar Hill, a few km north of Green Point and connected to the highway by a short paved road, allows you to see far and wide. Learn about the indigenous wildlife and culture at the **Wickaninnish Centre** (726-4212), 3km off Hwy. 4 just past the park entrance (free; open daily mid-May to Labor Day).

Most visitors take advantage of the park's magnificent **hiking trails.** Pick up a *Hiker's Guide* at the visitors center for a list of nine hikes ranging from 100m to 5km in length along the Long Beach stretch. When the rain finally overwhelms you, seek refuge in the art galleries in Ucluelet and Tofino. Ucluelet's **Du Quah Gallery,** 1971 Peninsula Rd. (726-7223), is more modest than Tofino's **Eagle Aerie Gallery,** 350 Campbell St. (725-3235), which houses paintings behind its striking and unusual carved wooden doors.

■ Comox Valley

Billing itself as the "recreation capital of Canada," the Comox Valley area includes the towns of Courtenay, Comox, and Cumberland and boasts the highest concentration of artists in Canada, along with many museums and galleries. The discovery of the 80-million-year-old "Courtenay Elasmosaur" in 1989 has transformed the valley into a minor mecca of paleontology as well. With Strathcona Provincial Park's southern regions just a llama's trot away, outdoor adventure abounds in both summer and winter. Its year-round tourist season, its "artsy" population, and its farm animals combine to move the Comox Valley to a rhythm distinct from the summer-oriented remainder of the island.

Practical Information The **tourist office** in Courtenay is at 2040 Cliffe Ave. (334-3234). **Laidlaw** (334-2475), at Fitzgerald and Cumberland Rd. in Courtenay, connects the area to points north and south along Hwy. 19. **BC Ferries** (339-3310) connects Comox with Powell River on the mainland. Some useful numbers in the Comox Valley: **Emergency,** 911; **Weather,** 339-5044; **Police,** 338-1321; **Hospital,** 339-2242. The **post office** is at 4-2401 Cliffe Ave. (334-0875), across from the museum in Courtenay (open Mon.-Thurs. 9am-4pm, Fri. 9am-5:30pm; **postal code** V9N 7G3). The **area code** is 250.

Accommodations, Camping, and Food Pricey motels line the highway south of Courtenay. B&Bs abound and are a better bet. The **Mountain View Bed and Breakfast,** 605 Ellcee Pl. (338-0157), in Courtenay offers spotless bathrooms, a TV lounge area, and a view from the balcony (singles from $25, doubles from $40; reservations recommended). Campers should try **Kin Beach** (339-4079), on Astra Rd. in Comox, where $7.50 buys one of 16 sites, a beach 100m away, and tennis courts. **Miracle Beach** (337-5720), on Miracle Beach Dr. in Black Creek, has more facilities than Kin Beach, but is harder to reach ($14.50; showers, flush toilets). For a spectacular view of the Georgia Strait and the Coastal Mountains, lodge at the **Bed and Breakfast By the Sea,** 650 Hutton Rd., Comox V9M 3U5 (339-0492). A sundeck, the beach, and a home-cooked breakfast make for a pleasant stay (singles $35, doubles $45). For those who want the comfort of sleeping in or near doors without the hassle of being in town, the **North Comox Lake Hostel,** 4787 Lake Trail Rd. (338-1914), about 10km from town, trades a bed for $15, a tent site for $8, and linen for a smile. The hostel is within a day's hike of Strathcona, and has its own log pyramid that hostelers and locals use for meditation.

The many **farmer's markets** in the area tend to be more appealing than most restaurants. The most comprehensive and conspicuous market is **Farquharson Farms,** 1300 Comox Rd. (338-8194), in Courtenay. Not satisfied with fresh fruit and vegetables alone, Farquharson also sells gardening supplies and patio furniture for those determined to settle the nearby beaches (open daily 9am-6pm). The **Bar None Cafe,** 244 4th St. (334-3112), off Cliffe Ave. in Courtenay, stocks exceptional all-vegetarian fare. Choose your own rice and pasta dishes, salads, and fresh salsas, and pay $1.85 per 100 grams. Espresso and juice bar, too. (Open Mon.-Sat. 8am-7pm; Sun. brunch 11am-3pm.) The **Old House Restaurant,** 1760 Riverside Ln. (338-5406), features luxurious, lodge-style architecture and a menu big enough for sushi (from $5), pizza ($3.75 per slice), organic coffee, and fresh muffins. (Open Tues.-Thurs. 8am-7pm, Fri. 8am-8pm, Sat. 9am-5pm.) **Safeway** (open daily 8am-10pm) and **Shopper's Drug Mart** (open Mon.-Fri. 9am-9pm, Sat. 9am-6pm, Sun. 9am-5pm) are both on 8th St. in Courtenay.

Sights and Activities The **Arts Alliance**, 367 4th St. (338-6211), in Courtenay, a focal point for the local arts community, houses craft galleries (open Tues.-Sat. 10am-5pm). The **Courtenay District Museum**, 360 Cliffe Ave. (334-3611), holds permanent exhibits on pioneer life, native culture and art, industry, and geology. A paleontology annex, next to the museum, stores the bevy of dinosaur bones uncovered in the area (open daily 10am-4:30pm; in winter Tues.-Sat. 10am-4:30pm). The **Comox Air Force Museum** (339-8162), at the Canadian Forces Base, Ryan and Little River Rd. in Comox, will tell you everything you ever wanted to know but were afraid to ask about the Royal Canadian Air Force. (Open daily 10am-4pm; Sept.-May Sat.-Sun and holidays 10am-4pm.) **Horne Lake Caves Provincial Park,** south of Courtenay on Horne Lakes Rd., opens its caves to the public. Several guided tour programs are offered at ranging levels of difficulty ($7-59, under 12 $5-10).

▒ Strathcona Provincial Park

Elk, deer, marmots, and wolves all inhabit the more than 2000 sq. km. of Strathcona, one of the best preserved and most beautiful wilderness areas on Vancouver Island. The park's two visitors centers are on **Buttle Lake,** on Hwy. 28 between Gold River and Campbell River, and **Mt. Washington/Forbidden Plateau**, outside Courtenay off Hwy. 19. The two official **campgrounds,** sharing 161 campsites between them, are Buttle Lake and Ralph River, both on the shores of Buttle Lake, accessible by Hwy. 28 and secondary roads (follow the highway signs). **Buttle Lake,** closer to Campbell River, has comfortable sites, a playground, and sandy beaches on the lake ($12). Less crowded **Ralph River** provides convenient access to the park's best hiking trails ($9.50). From Ralph River, the difficult 12km **Phillips Ridge** hike takes about five hours roundtrip, passing two waterfalls in a 790m climb and ending atop a wildflower-strewn mountain by an alpine lake.

Visitors who wish to explore Strathcona's **backcountry areas** must camp 800m from main roads. To minimize environmental impact, camp at least 30m away from water sources as well. Backcountry campers are rewarded by lakes, waterfalls, ancient cedar and fir forests, and wildflower meadows. Campfires are discouraged in the park. Those entering the undeveloped areas of the park should notify the park service of their intended departure and return times, and should be well-equipped (**maps** and **rain gear** are essential). The **Forbidden Plateau** and **Mt. Washington,** lying just outside the park boundaries, hit their high-seasons in the winter with a heavy influx of skiers. For information on the park, contact BC Parks, District Manager, Box 1479, Parksville, BC V9P 2H4 (604-954-4600).

▒ Campbell River

A large rock covered with aquatic-themed graffiti welcomes you to Campbell River, another of BC's many self-proclaimed "Salmon Capitals of the World." It also sports the best beaches, kayaking, and whale watching on the eastern shore of the island, as well as scuba diving which is "second only to the Red Sea," according to National Geographic. The abundance of gas stations illustrates Campbell River's role as the transportation hub of the Northern Island, providing easy access to Strathcona, Port Hardy and its Alaskan ferry, and Quadra, Cortes and Discovery Islands.

Practical Information The **Travel Infocentre,** 923 Island Hwy. (287-4636), has a helpful staff and brochures (open daily 8am-6pm; Sept.-May Mon.-Fri. 9am-5pm, Sat. 10am-5pm). **Laidlaw** (287-7151) is at 13th and Cedar. **BC Ferries** runs from Campbell River to Quadra Island (15 daily; $3, cars $8.50, ages 5-11 $1.50, under 5 free). Find **Rent-a-Wreck** (287-8353) at 1891 Island Hwy. in the Esso station (open Mon.-Tues. and Sat.-Sun 8am-5pm, Wed.-Fri. 8am-9pm). A local laundromat is **Sunrise Laundry Ltd.** (923-2614) in Sunrise Sq. (open Sun.-Fri. 8am-9pm, Sat. 8am-6pm). Useful numbers are: **emergency, 911; crisis hotline,** 287-7743; **hospital,** 375 2nd Ave. (287-7111); **poison control,** 800-567-8911; **police,** 286-6221.

Accommodations, Camping, and Food Finding inexpensive lodging here is like swimming upstream in spawning season. The best bet is camping in **Strathcona Provincial Park** (see above). But if you still insist on shelter, the **Lighthouse Bed and Breakfast** practically gives away its rooms, a full morning meal, and an exceptional view of the harbor. (Singles $40. Doubles $50.)

Budget food and local color flourish at **Banner's** (286-6711) in the Tyee Mall on Island Hwy. Breakfast is served all day (pancakes $5.25). If the bright pink and green of the restaurant clash with your appetite, **Overwaitea Foods** at 13th and Elm provides relief in the form of groceries and its own deli (open daily 9am-9pm).

Sights and Activities Sockeye, coho, pink, chum, and chinook **salmon** are hauled in by the boatload each year from the waters of the Campbell River. The savvy can reap deep-sea prizes from **Discovery Pier** in Campbell Harbour (fishing charge $1; rod rentals $2.50 per hr., $6 per ½-day). The pier has 200m of boardwalk plants and an artificial underwater reef built to attract astigmatic fish.

Scuba-gear rentals can be pricey, but **Beaver Aquatics,** 760 Island Hwy. (287-7652), offers a $25 package that includes suit, mask, snorkel, and fins (open Mon.-Sat. 9am-5pm, Sun. 10am-2pm). A tour of the **Quinsam River Salmon Hatchery,** 4217 Argonaut Rd. (287-9564) also provides you with a chance to see the fishies up close. An audio-visual extravaganza introduces you to shiny, happy little fish, blissfully unaware of the rods and reels lying ahead. Nature trails and picnic tables sit on the hatchery grounds (open daily 8am-4pm).

■ Alert Bay

Its centrality to the cultural legacy of the Kwakiutl, one of the many coastal native nations, sets the fishing village of Alert Bay (pop. 600) apart from its aquatourist brothers. One of the richest repositories of native culture on Vancouver Island, Alert Bay boasts a 173-ft. totem pole, the second largest in the world, that tells the story of the Kwakiutl. The pole towers near the **U'Mista Cultural Center** (974-5403), 2km north of the ferry terminal. The center houses breathtaking bronzes and masks as well as other cultural artifacts reclaimed from Canadian museums (open Mon.-Fri. 9am-5pm, Sat.-Sun. noon-5pm; winter Mon.-Fri. 9am-5pm).

Practical Information Find **travel information** in **Port McNeil** by the ferry dock. In **Alert Bay,** there's information galore at 116 Fir St. (974-5213; open daily 9am-6pm). **BC Ferries** (956-4533) operates a ferry from Port McNeill to Sointula and Alert Bay ($4, car $10.75; daily 8:40am-9:50pm). **Laidlaw** runs one from Port McNeil to Victoria (1 per day, $76; departs from the Dalewood Inn). You can grab a **shower** at the pool on Campbell Way past the skating arena (956-3638; $2.50, ages 14-19 $2, under 14 $1). Some useful numbers in Alert Bay are: **emergency,** 911; **St. George's Hospital,** 182 Fir St. (974-5585). In Port McNeill: **police,** 974-5544. The **area code** is 250.

Sights and Accommodations The island straits near Alert Bay and Port McNeill support the continent's highest concentration of orcas. Expensive sighting charters are everywhere, but catch a glimpse of the pods surfacing in synchronicity while you're on the ferry or from the harbor at Alert Bay. When marine life grows tiresome, trade in the ocean for a swamp and explore the cedar trees, bald eagles, and ravens of the **Gator Gardens,** off Orca Way.

At the fabulous **Pacific Hostelry (HI-C),** 349 Fir St. (604-974-2026), play the piano and enjoy the bay view ($17, non-members $19). Reservations are recommended, as group programs sometimes fill the beds; to quote a hostel authority, "if the beds are full, you're just screwed." Restaurants are limited and most are expensive, so you may want to stock up at the **Blueline Supermarket,** 257 Fir St. (974-5521; open Mon.-Fri. 9am-9pm, Sat. 9am-6pm, Sun. 10am-5pm).

The U'Mista Cultural Centre

The traditional gift-giving ceremony of the **potlatch,** held by many Northwest Coast natives, was outlawed by Canada's Dominion Government in 1884. In 1921 police officers stumbled upon a ceremony held on Village Island and twenty men and women were briefly sent to prison for their participation in the event. The ceremonial gear from the potlatch was confiscated and sent to museums and private collections (including that of the officer responsible for the raid and the Superintendent General of Indian Affairs). It was not until the late 1960s that a serious effort was made to repatriate the lost objects.

The Board of Trustees of the National Museum agreed to return a portion of the confiscated artifacts on the stipulation that museums be built in Cape Mudge and Alert Bay to house the collections. The **U'Mista Cultural Centre** now holds one of the richest repositories of Native culture on Vancouver Island. The center takes its name from the traditional term for the return of a loved one taken captive by raiding parties. The return of the Kwakiutl's treasures is, therefore, a form of *u'mista.* (974-5403; open Mon.-Fri. 9am-5pm, Sat.-Sun. noon-5pm; winter closed weekends.)

■ Port Hardy

Port Hardy was content to be a quiet logging and fishing community until BC Ferries made it the southern terminus for ferries carrying passengers from Prince Rupert and Alaska. Virtually overnight, the unassuming town etched a name for itself as a major transportation port, complete with a chainsaw-carved welcome sign. A mild coastal town, Port Hardy remains an excellent (as well as the only) place for ferry passengers to spend the night.

Practical Information Pick up a restaurant guide and tour **maps** at the **Travel Infocentre,** 7250 Market St. (949-7622). Take Hardy Bay Rd. off Hwy. 19 to Market St. (open Mon.-Sat. 8am-9pm, Sun. 9am-9pm; winter Mon.-Fri. 9am-5pm). **Laidlaw** (949-7532), on Market St. across from the Travel Infocentre, connects Port Hardy to Victoria through Nanaimo (1 per day, $80 from Victoria, $69 from Nanaimo). The **BC Ferry** terminal (949-6722) is 3km south at Bear Cove. (Service between Prince Rupert and Port Hardy every other day; one way $93, with car $289.) **North Island Taxi** can be reached at 949-8800. **North Star Cycle and Sports** (949-7221), at Market and Granville St., rents bikes for $10 per hour or $25 per day. Other outdoor equipment needs may be taken care of at **Smyth's True Value,** 7070 Market St. (949-7155). Clean those stinkin' socks for $4-5 in the machines at **Payless Gas Co.** (949-2366), on Granville St. (open 24hr.). Some helpful phone numbers in Port Hardy are: **emergency,** 911; **crisis line,** 949-6033; **police,** 7355 Columbia Ave. (949-6335); **hospital,** 949-6161. Port Hardy's **postal code** is V0N 2P0. The **area code** is 250.

Accommodations and Camping The demand for hotel rooms is as high as you would expect in any port town, especially on ferry nights. Trot to the **Pioneer Inn** (949-7271), off Hwy. 19 on Old Island Hwy., 2km south of town, for rooms next to a salmon hatchery. The Pioneer has laundry facilities and a dining room (singles $56, doubles $60). The many B&Bs in the area are often less expensive (singles run $40-55) and more available. The infocenter operates a free reservation service. For a quiet, wooded setting, pitch your tent at **Quatse River Campground,** 5050 Hardy Bay Rd. (949-2395), across from the Pioneer Inn. Toilets come in a choice of flush and pit (*Let's Go* recommends the flush toilet); showers and laundromat available (sites $14, full hookups $18, $1 discount for seniors). The campground shares its grounds with a **fish hatchery** (949-9022); a visitor viewing area is accessible, and tours are available October through June. **Wildwoods Campsite** (949-6753), on the road from the ferry within walking distance of the terminal, has comfortable sites strewn with pine needles. Despite their close proximity, sites maintain reasonable privacy. There

are hot showers, but expect a line in the morning (sites $11, with hookup $16, hiker/
biker $5).

Food Their half of the legendary 400-lb. carrot may lie buried by the Welcome to
Port Hardy sign, but **Giant Foods** (949-6532) is still big enough for most grocery
needs (open 6am-10pm). A brigade of superb budget restaurants serve dinners for
under $10. **Sportsman's Steak & Seafood House** (949-7811), on Market St. across
from the infocenter, offers lunch sandwiches stuffed with meat from $6-7. A 6 oz.
steak runs $8.25 (open daily 11am-11pm). The **Roadhouse,** a family restaurant at the
Pioneer Inn on Old Island Hwy., has sandwiches ($4-7) and pasta entrees ($7-10). Several **markets** line the aptly named Market St.

■ Cape Scott Provincial Park

Sixty km of logging roads (watch for trucks) lead through wild and wet Cape Scott to
parking lots near trailheads. Most begin from the lot on **San Josef Rd.,** near the
entrance to the park, although Cape Scott will soon have a 100km trail connecting
Port Hardy to the depths of the park.

Camping in the park is not restricted to primitive sites. Fresh water is available at
popular **San Josef Bay** and **Nels Bight.** Good **topographic maps** help enterprising
trekkers (available from **Maps BC,** Ministry of Environment, Parliament Bldgs., Victoria BC V8V 1XS). For more detailed information on the park, pick up the Cape Scott
Provincial Park pamphlet at one of the travel infocenters elsewhere in the region,
since none exist anywhere near the park, or write to BC Parks, District Manager, Box
1479, Parksville, BC V9P 2H4 (604-954-4600). And finally, while the scenery may
vary, the constant rain will not. Bring **rain gear.**

SOUTHEASTERN BRITISH COLUMBIA

■ Fraser River Canyon

The Fraser River courses down from the Rocky Mountains and hurls itself through
1300km of plateaus and steep canyons on its journey to the Pacific. From the comfort
of puncture-proof rafts, visitors today may not appreciate the audacity of Simon
Fraser's 1808 expedition down the river from Mt. Robson to Vancouver. Today's
slightly easier route from Cache Creek to Hope (the Trans-Canada Hwy.) makes
Fraser's trailblazing somewhat unnecessary. The Fraser's 200km of coiling rapids are
not quite as exciting as the infocenter's pamphlets would have you believe, but the
sheer size of the towering, pine-covered canyon walls makes it a striking scene.

HOPE

The biggest thing happening in **Hope** is the intersection of several highways. **Hwy. 1,**
the Trans-Canada Hwy, leads west into Vancouver and bends north at Hope, running
to Yale and Cache Creek where it joins **Hwy. 97,** the Cariboo Hwy., and heads to
northern British Columbia. **Hwy. 7** runs west to Vancouver's suburbs along the north
bank of the Fraser River. **Hwy. 3,** the Crowsnest Trail, winds east through breathtaking country, close to the U.S. border, to Osoyoos near Penticton, through Kootenay
Country to Nelson, Crowsnest Pass, and into Alberta. Finally, **Hwy. 5,** the Coquihalla
Hwy., is a new toll road ($10) running north to Kamloops with good access to the
Okanagan country.

The staff at the **Travel Infocentre** in Hope, 919 Water Ave. (869-2021), are unofficial experts on the filming in Hope of the original Rambo blockbuster, *First Blood,*
but are knowledgeable on other subjects as well. Besides providing the riveting
"Rambo Walking Tour," the infocenter also has information on the Fraser River Canyon (open daily 8am-8pm; Oct.-May 9am-5pm).

Buses arrive at the **Greyhound station,** 833 3rd Ave. (869-5522), and make connections further east in Chiliwack for destinations throughout Western Canada. Many people try hitching north on Hwy. 1 where rides are reputedly easy to find. (*Let's Go* does not recommend hitchhiking.) Rent a car at **Gardner Chev-Olds,** 945 Water St. (869-9511), next to the infocenter ($40 per day, $240 per week; 13 ¢ per km after 100km; open Mon.-Sat. 8am-6pm). The **police** in Hope (869-7750) are at 670 Hope-Princeton Hwy. off Hwy. 3. The **post office** is at 777 Fraser St., across from the Cariboo Restaurant (open Mon.-Fri. 8:30am-5pm).

If you must stay overnight, trek a block north from the bus station to Wallace St. and hang a left. The **Hope Motor Hotel,** 272 Wallace St. (869-5641), rents singles from $40 and doubles from $46-55. Be sure to request one of the recently renovated rooms. Breakfast is included in the price of the room, except during July and August. Campers can try **Telte Yet Campsite,** 600 Water Ave. (869-9481), which has a luscious river view and tent sites for $12, hookups for $17.

Try the **Suzie Q Family Restaurant,** 2591 Wallace St. (869-5515), a block north of the Greyhound station, which serves both cheap Western *and* Japanese cuisine (open daily 7am-10pm). For groceries, there's **Save-On Foods,** on Old Hope-Princeton Way (open Sat.-Thurs. 9am-8pm, Fri. 9am-9pm).

OUTDOORS

For a better look at the Fraser River, try one of the moderately difficult **hikes** that start from trailheads near Hope. The short, lush **Rotary Trail** starts at Wardle St. and runs to the confluence of the Fraser and Coquihalla Rivers. A more challenging hike is the two-hour climb to the summit of **Thacker Mountain.** To reach the foot of this trail, cross the Coquihalla River Bridge, take a left on Union Bar Rd., and then go left again on Thacker Mountain Rd. The car park at the road's end marks the beginning of a 5km gravel path to the peak, which provides clear views of Hope and the Fraser River. Pause for a pleasant diversion at **Kawkawa Creek** off Union Bar Rd., recently "enhanced" to aid the mid- and late-summer salmon spawnings. The boardwalk along the creek leads to a swimming hole and popular picnicking spot.

The **Coquihalla Canyon Recreation Area** is a five- to ten-minute drive out of Hope along Kawkawa Lake Rd. Here, the **Othello Quintet Tunnels** provide mute evidence of the impressive engineering that led to the opening of the Kettle Valley Railway in 1916. Blasted through solid granite, these rough tunnels overlook the Coquihalla River. Turn right on Othello Rd. off Kawkawa Lake Rd., and right again on Tunnel Rd. Allow half an hour to walk through the tunnels.

For an even closer view of the river, head 36km north on Hwy. 1 to the small town of Yale. Take the first right after the stoplight, then follow the gravel road about 1km; you'll find a close-up view of the majestic **Lady Franklin Rock,** which splits the Fraser into two sets of heavy rapids. If you're interested in getting *on* the river, **Fraser River Raft Expeditions** (800-363-RAFT/7238), just south of town, is undoubtedly the way to go. Although the $95 fee for a full-day trip might seem as steep as the canyon walls, those who can pull together the funds shouldn't miss the heart-pounding, body-drenching thrills. One-day and multi-day **rafting trips** down the Fraser, Thompson, Nahatlatch, and Coquihalla Rivers are available, and the friendly guides serve up great meals. Trips leave almost daily; call ahead to reserve.

When Simon Fraser made his pioneering trek down the river, he likened one particularly tumultuous stretch of rapids to the "Gates of Hell." Yale lies just beyond **Hell's Gate** on the Fraser. The white foaming waters, 25km north of Yale on Hwy. 1, make the success of Fraser's journey seem miraculous. When melting snow floods the river in spring, the 60m-deep water rushes through the narrow gorge with incredible force. A cluster of gift shops and eateries are now embedded in the precipitous cliffs where Fraser once advised "no human beings should venture." The gondolas of **Hell's Gate Airtram,** 43111 Hwy. 1 (867-9277), will "fly" you 502 ft. across the canyon in four minutes ($9, seniors $8, ages 6-14 $6, families $24). The timid usually opt for the free **hike** down to the river.

■ Penticton

Close your eyes and imagine Florida. Now replace the ocean with a large lake, change the palm trees into Douglas fir, add mountains and make sure all the locals are avid hockey fans with snow tires. Okay, now open your eyes, and voilà, you're in Penticton. Indigenous peoples named the region between Okanagan and Skaha Lakes *Pentak-tin,* "a place to stay forever," but their eternal paradise was long ago transformed by heated pools and luxury hotels into one of Western Canada's biggest vacation towns. Hot weather, sandy beaches, and proximity to Vancouver, Seattle, and Spokane have ushered in the Tourist Age, and it may strain your budget to spend a weekend here—let alone eternity.

PRACTICAL INFORMATION AND ORIENTATION

Visitors Information: Penticton Visitors Information Centre, 185 Lakeshore Dr. (493-4055 or 800-663-5052), at the end of Main Street. Located next to a giant peach. A fountain of travel brochures and an attentive staff. Open daily 8am-8pm; Sept.-June Mon.-Fri. 9am-5pm, Sat.-Sun. 10am-4pm. **Information Centre** on Hwy. 97, 7km south of downtown. Smaller than the main office, but carries a number of brochures. Open June-Sept. daily 9am-5pm, winter weekends only.

Buses: Greyhound, 307 Ellis (493-4101). To: Vancouver (2 per day, $45), Kelowna (4 per day, $9).

Public Transportation: Penticton Transit System, 301 E. Warren Ave. (492-5602). Bus service $1.25, seniors and students $1, under 5 free. Day pass $3, students $2.50. All drivers carry complete schedules. Many of the routes converge at Wade and Martin St. Transit office open Mon.-Fri. 8am-5pm. Buses run Mon.-Fri. 6:30am-10pm, Sat. 8:30am-6:30pm; June-Sept. also Sun. 9:40am-7:30pm.

Taxi: Klassic Kabs (492-6666). 24hr.

Car Rental: Budget Rent-A-Car (493-0212), in the main terminal at the Penticton Airport. $42 per day during the week, $24 on weekends. 100km free, 15¢ per additional km. Must be at least 21 with major credit card.

Bike Rental: The Penticton Hostel (492-3992) has two bikes to rent to anyone for $15 per day; call ahead to reserve. **Sun Country Cycle,** 533 Main St. (493-0686). $25 per day, helmet included. Open Mon.-Sat. 9am-5:30pm.

Laundry: Plaza Laundromat, 417-1301 Main St. (493-8710), in the Plaza Shopping Mall. Wash $1.50, 6-min. dry 25¢. TV on premises. Open daily 8am-10pm.

Weather: 492-6991.

Crisis Line: 493-6622. **Women's Shelter:** 493-7233.

Hospital: Penticton Regional, 550 Carmi Ave. (492-4000).

Emergency: 911. **Police:** 1103 Main St. (492-4300).

Post Office: Westminster Postal Outlet, 701-1301 Main St. (493-3133), at Plaza Card and Gift. Open Mon.-Fri. 9am-5pm. **Postal Code:** V2A 5M0.

Area Code: 250.

The warmest, driest town in the region, Penticton lies 400km east of Vancouver on **Hwy. 3,** at the southern extreme of the Okanagan Valley. Lake Okanagan borders the north end of town, while smaller Skaha Lake lies to the south. Main St. bisects the city from north to south.

ACCOMMODATIONS AND CAMPING

Because Penticton is a year-round resort city, hotels here charge more than those in the surrounding towns. The hostel charges less per night the longer you stay, making it the best deal in town. Since you'll still be paying through the nose even if you camp, you might as well try to find a campground on the shores of one of the lakes. Make reservations; vacant sites can be scarce in July and August.

Penticton Hostel (HI-C), 464 Ellis St. (492-3992). Best bet in Penticton. Conveniently located ½ block from the Greyhound stop and 10min. from the beach. Comfortable lounge and patio, kitchen, laundry facilities, gas grill. Frequented by a diverse, international crowd. Fills in July and Aug. Accommodates 45. Linen $2. $14.50, nonmembers $18.50, under 10 ½price. Cost per night decreases with every additional night you stay.

Riordan House, 689 Winnipeg (493-5997). More elegant than the neon-bedecked concrete-box motels on Lakeshore Dr., and costs not a penny more. The gorgeous Victorian-style mansion was built in 1921. Three impeccably decorated, enormous rooms include plush carpeting, TV, and VCR. The house even has a library. Mr. Ortiz makes a knockout breakfast (included in the room fee) of luscious local fruits and fresh-baked scones. Rooms $55-75.

Wright's Beach Camp (492-7120). Directly off Hwy. 97 on the shores of Skaha Lake at the south end of town. Nearby traffic is often noisy. Small, reasonably priced pizza joint on the grounds. Washrooms, showers. Sites $20, with hookups $24-30. Crowded; reserve at least 2 weeks in advance.

South Beach Gardens, 3815 Skaha Lake Rd. (492-0628). Across the street from the beach, east of the Channel Parkway. 280 sites sprawled over 18 acres. Closely cropped willows provide shade. Unserviced sites $16. Serviced sites $18-22.

Okanagan Lake Provincial Park (494-0321). 50km north of Penticton on Hwy. 97. 168 sites packed between the highway and the lake in 2 separate units. Stay in the north park, where sites are roomier. Good beach swimming. No reservations; always full in summer. Cruise for sites early (8-10am). Sites $15.50.

FOOD

A few local sandwich shops provide the only decent inexpensive food in town. Stockpile in preparation for a nuclear winter at **Super Valu Foods,** 450 Martin St., one block west of Main (492-4315; open Mon.-Sat. 9am-9pm, Sun. 9am-6pm).

Whole Food Market (493-2855)**,** in Creekside Plaza on Main St. A true supermarket of health food, with lots of organic produce, bulk grains and pastas, and herbs. Best of all, the deli counter in the back slaps together fantastic sandwiches for $2.50-3. Open Mon.-Fri. 9am-8pm, Sat. 9am-6pm, Sun. 10am-5pm; Sept.-June Mon.-Wed. 9am-6pm, Thurs.-Fri. 9am-9pm, Sat. 9am-6pm, Sun. 10am-5pm.

Judy's Deli, 129 W. Nanaimo (492-7029). Take-out only. Sit atop a large, splinter-free bench in front of the radio station next door. Beach-goers stop for hearty home-made soups ($1.65-2) and butter-laden sandwiches ($2.80-3.30). Browse the herbs and homeopathic medicines. Open Mon.-Sat. 9am-5:30pm.

Spotted Dog Coffee Bar, 320 Martin (493-2050). Soda-fountain atmosphere meets espresso bar menu. Go figure. Light food choices and yummy cookies (2 for $1). Open Mon.-Fri. 7am-10pm, Sat. 8am-10pm, Sun. 10am-4pm.

SIGHTS AND EVENTS

Known throughout Canada for its bountiful fruit harvests, the **Okanagan Valley** lures visitors with summer blossoms, sleepy towns, and tranquil lakes. Tourists with cars should explore Hwy. 97 and Hwy. 3A south of Penticton; camp in an orchard bursting with newly ripened cherries, eat the fruit at a family stand, sample the wines at a local vineyard, or fish in one of the pristine lakes.

The Penticton tourist trade revolves around **Okanagan Lake.** Long, hot summers and the sport facilities on the lake make Okanagan a popular hangout for the young. **California Connection** (490-7844), on the beach next to the Coast Lakeside Hotel, rents out jet skis (from $35 per ½hr.) and paddleboats ($10 per hr.). Although renting equipment can blast a hole through your pocket, basking in the plentiful sun and swimming in the warm waters are both free.

For a sample of local culture, take a trip to the **Art Gallery of the South Okanagan,** 11 Ellis St. (493-2928), at Front St. This lovely beachfront gallery exhibits local and international artists and just recently is free (open Tues.-Fri. 10am-5pm, Sat.-Sun. 1-5pm). The **Penticton Museum** (also known as the **R.N. Atkinson Museum**), 785 Main St. (490-2452), presents one artist's interpretation of the region's history with native artifacts and wildlife displays (free; open Mon., Wed., and Fri.-Sat. 10am-5pm, Tues. and Thurs. 10am-8:30pm; Sept.-June Mon.-Sat. 10am-5pm). In the park on Main

St. across the road from the lake, the town sponsors free **summer evening concerts** at the Gyro Bandshell that usually begin around 7:30pm.

Looking suspiciously like an East African wildlife preserve, the **Okanagan Game Farm** (497-5405), on Hwy. 97 south of Penticton, covers 560 acres and protects 130 animal species from crazy summer life on the lake. Zebras, rhinos, gnus, **aoudads,** and ankoli frolic free of fences and bars. Cars can drive throughout the park, and animal checklists should keep the kiddies entertained ($10, ages 5-15 $7; open daily 8am-dusk). The **Skaha Bluffs,** southeast of town on Valley View Rd., have developed into a popular **rock climbing** venue, offering pitches of varying difficulties. For information about the area, stop in at **Ray's Sports Den,** 215 Main St. (493-1216). The shop also organizes reasonably priced classes—if you've been thinking about learning to climb, this might be the place to do it (open Mon.-Fri. 9:30am-6pm, Sat. 9:30am-5pm, Sun. 10am-4pm).

Travelers in extremely dire straits may consider signing on to **pick fruit** at one of the many orchards stretching south from Penticton to the U.S. border along Hwy. 97. Pickers are usually allowed to camp free in the orchards, and are paid a per-quart wage; the faster you move, the more you're paid. Daily earnings of more than $40 are common. Different fruits reach ripeness from mid-June (cherries) through mid-September (pears). Contact the Penticton Chamber of Commerce for more information, or cruise Hwy. 97 or Hwy. 3A until you see a "Pickers Wanted" sign.

The colorful **Blossom Festival** in April welcomes the fresh flowers blooming in the hundreds of apple, peach, and cherry orchards. The city shifts into full gear with the **Peach Festival** and the hellacious **Ironman Canada Triathlon** in mid-August. The Peach Festival offers recreational and aquatic activities for all ages, including a volleyball tournament and sand castle contest, while the triathlon subjects true athletes to 4km of swimming, 180km of bicycling, and 45km of running.

The mists and mellow fruitfulness of fall mark the ripening of the wine season. There are several wineries within easy driving distance of Penticton. **Hillside Cellars Winery** (493-4424), at the junction of Vancouver and Naramata Rd. northeast of Penticton, has a winery shop offering tastings and tours (open April 1-Oct. 31 daily 10am-6pm; Nov.-March by appointment only). North of Summerland, **Sumac Ridge Estate Winery** (494-0451) also offers tours daily at 10am, 2, and 4pm in the summer (open daily 9am-6pm; Nov.-April Mon.-Fri. 9am-5pm, Sat.-Sun. 11am-5pm). The **Okanagan Wine Festival** (490-8866), in early October, is fun for those fond of feeling thick pulp squish between their toes. Nearby, **Apex Alpine,** P.O. Box 1060 (492-2880), provides winter diversion with six ski lifts, 44 runs, and a 670m vertical drop (open Nov.-late April).

The hills running throughout the Okanagan Valley are more than just pretty to look at. Heavy winter snowfalls make for excellent skiing and Penticton smoothly transforms from summer beach resort to winter mountain playland. **Apex Mountain Resort** sports a mix of downhill, cross-country, and night skiing within easy reach of town. Republicans will enjoy the commitment to family values (their words, not ours). Call 800-387-APEX/2739 for more information.

■ Salmon Arm

Salmon Arm is a backwoods honky-tonk town like thousands of others, but its setting is extraordinary. Lake Shuswap is sublime, and the mountains cradling the town are breathtaking, especially when the leaves turn in autumn.

Practical Information The **Travel Infocentre,** 751 Marine Park Dr., Box 999 (832-2230), has brochures for you and your grandmother. Follow the **"?"** signs from the Trans-Canada Hwy. (Hwy. 1) across the train tracks (open daily 9am-7pm; Labor Day-May Mon.-Fri. 9am-5pm).

The **Salmon Arm Transit System** (832-0191) has regular service Monday to Saturday and door-to-door service Monday to Friday. Call for prices and to arrange a ride. You can wash out your grubby clothes at the **B-Line Laundromat,** 456 Trans-Canada

Hwy. (832-5500), in Smitty's shopping center (wash $1.50, 12-min. dry $1; open daily 6am-11pm). If you need an **ambulance,** call 833-0188; the **hospital** is at 601 10th St. NE (832-2182). The **police** are at 501 2nd Ave. NE (832-6044). The **post office** is at 370 Hudson St. NE (832-3093; open Mon.-Fri. 8:30am-5pm; **General Delivery Postal Code:** V1E 4M6). The **area code** is 250.

Accommodations, Camping, and Food

When in Salmon Arm, your best option is to stay at the **Cindosa Bed and Breakfast,** 930 30th St. SE (832-3342), where the Moores will pamper you with comfy beds and fantastic, home-cooked breakfasts. They'll even pick you up at the bus station, or bus #2 will take you right by (singles $45, doubles $55). For a beautiful lake view and warm British hospitality, try **Ducks Galore** (832-8906) on 16th St., where a double with its own bath will only set you back $50-65. If you're mobile, it's worth the trek out to the **Squilax General Store Hostel** (675-2977), 50km west of Salmon Arm on the Trans-Canada Hwy., for a unique hosteling experience—the sleeping quarters are on board three Canadian National Railway cabooses, specially procured and outfitted for the purpose with showers, phone, and laundry. The mellow and friendly proprietor, Blair, is a well-spring of information about the area. The sign on the front of the store is home to the remnants of an enormous **bat colony** displaced when its former haunt, a nearby church, burned down ($12.50, $17 nonmembers). It is an unofficial flag stop for **Greyhound,** so ask the driver to drop you off there. **Glen Echo Resort,** 6592 Trans-Canada Hwy. NW V1E 4M2 (832-6268), 5 mi. west on Hwy. 1, is smack on Lake Shuswap, with a sandy beach, excellent swimming all summer long, and a gregarious owner (open Victoria Day-Sept.; 65 sites; $19, lakeside $22, hookups free, showers 25¢).

Despite its name, Salmon Arm's culinary establishments showcase neither fish nor limbs. Stop in at **Golden Pantry Foods,** 452 Trans-Canada Hwy. (832-7910), for healthy foods in bulk (open Mon.-Sat. 9am-5:30pm). Or check out the classy track lighting over the produce section at **Safeway,** 360 Trans-Canada Hwy. (832-8086; open daily 8am-10pm). Restaurants offer standard fare. Try your luck at the **Farmer's Market** every Tuesday and Friday morning at the **Picadilly Mall,** 1151 10th Ave. SW (832-0441). Vegetables, fruit, and handicrafts are the main ware. The hippest food in town is at the veggie-friendly **Planet Bistro,** 331 Hudson Ave. NE (832-4932). An extensive number of light dishes go for under $5. Black bean quesadillas are $7, burgers (gulp) $7.25. (Open Mon.-Fri. 11am-7pm, Sat. 4-11pm.)

Sights

Learn what curds and whey really are at **Gort's Gouda Cheese Factory,** 1470 50th St. SW (832-4274). The free tours only last a few minutes, getting you to the tasty cheese samples all the faster (tours Mon. and Fri. at 2pm; call to arrange tours at other times). Even if there's no tour, you can stock up on bargain cheeses and watch the cheesemaking process through viewing windows.

The Salmon Arm area teems with wildlife. **McGuire Park,** on Hwy. 1 next to the hospital, is the spot to view Canadian geese, muskrats, turtles, and ducks. Catch kokanee or rainbow trout in **Lake Shuswap,** swim or whitewater raft on nearby **Adams River,** or hike out to **Margaret Falls,** just west of town. Follow the signs off Hwy. 1 for **Heral Park.** A 10km detour and a short hike on the slopes bring you to the striking falls.

The **Caravan Farm Theatre** (546-8533) presents top-notch performances during the summer (Sat.-Thurs., 8pm). The Farm, 5 mi. northwest of Armstrong, is bursting with leftover hippie charm, including great organic produce and musical instruments dangling from the trees ($15, students and seniors $12, children $8; tickets available at the Squilax General Store).

Every four years in October, the Salmon Arm area experiences two runs: the famous **salmon run** on the Adams River 46km west of Salmon Arm, where more than a million sockeye salmon desperately thrash their way up from the Pacific Ocean to spawn, and the less famous **tourist run,** in which thousands of bystanders cram into tiny Roderick Haig-Brown Provincial Park and strain to catch a glimpse of the colorful

---

This Horse Talks

The beloved life companion of Salmon Armer Phyllis Olson, **Shag-ra** the horse has earned fame and fortune through appearances on *America's Funniest Home Videos* and David Letterman's Stupid Pet Tricks. He opens cabinets, he answers phones, he stirs pots, and, most importantly, he sings. Well, sort of. A cross between Milli Vanilli and Mr. Ed, Shag-ra is the newest lip synching sensation to hit the scene. In the face of skepticism and plagued with an unappetizing tooth discoloration, Shag-ra perseveres undaunted. For more information and cute personal mementoes from Shag-ra, contact the Chamber of Commerce.

---

fish. The sight of salmon at the end of a 600km journey from the sea, packed tightly into the river, is truly awe-inspiring.

■ Revelstoke

In the 19th century Revelstoke was a town straight out of a Sam Peckinpah Western, complete with dust-encrusted megalomaniacs maiming each other amid the gold-laden Selkirk Mountains. The town now attracts an older, wiser Winnebago-driving crowd, but it has set its sights on young skiers and hikers. A major expansion of the ski resort at Mt. Mackenzie, 5km south of town, was recently proposed.

PRACTICAL INFORMATION AND ORIENTATION

Visitors Information: Travel Information Centre (837-3522), at the junction of Hwy. 1 and Hwy. 23 N. Open May-June daily 9am-5pm; July-Aug. 9am-8pm. **Chamber of Commerce,** 204 Campbell Ave. (837-5345), downtown. Open Mon.-Fri. 8:30am-noon and 1-4:30pm. **Canadian Parks Service** (837-7500), at Boyle Ave. and 3rd St. Open Mon.-Fri. 8:30am-noon and 1-4:30pm.
Buses: Greyhound, 1899 Fraser Dr. (837-5874), 1 block below and parallel to Hwy. 1. To: Calgary ($50), Vancouver ($61), Salmon Arm ($13.50). Open Mon.-Sat. 7am-7pm and 10-11:30pm, Sun. 10am-1pm, 3-7pm, and 10-11:30pm.
Taxi: Johnnie's, 314 Townley St. (837-3000). **R Taxi,** 857-4000. Both 24hr.
Car Rental: Tilden Car Rental, 301 W. 1st St. (837-2158). New cars at decent rates. $37 per day with 100km free, 15¢ per additional km. Must be 19 with a credit card. Open Mon.-Sat. 8am-6pm.
Bicycle Rental: Spoketacular Sports, 2220 MacKenzie (837-2220). $5 per hr., $25 per day. Open Tues.-Sat. 9am-5pm.
Ambulance: 837-5885. **Police:** 320 Wilson St. (837-5255).
Post Office: 307 W. 3rd St. (837-3228). Open Mon.-Fri. 8:30am-5pm. **Postal Code:** V0E 2S0.
Area Code: 250.

Revelstoke is situated on the Trans-Canada Hwy., 410km west of Calgary and 575km east of Vancouver. The town can be easily covered on foot or by bicycle. **Mount Revelstoke National Park** is much larger, covering 263 sq. km.

ACCOMMODATIONS AND CAMPING

Revelstoke has indeed sold out to The Man. This is primarily evidenced by the sky-rocketing cost of accommodations. An average motel room now runs at least $55 and most local campgrounds favor the more lucrative RV sites to tent sites.

Smokey Bear Campground (837-9573), on Hwy. 1, 5km west of Revelstoke. Close to the noisy highway. Clean bathrooms, metered showers, laundromat, and stocked store. 35 ft. Smokey Bear statue out front. RVs and tents welcome. Management seems to be absent on occasion. Sites $10-18, extra for water, electric.
Frontier Motel (837-5119), at Hwy. 1 and Hwy. 23 N next to the infocenter. Also sports a popular restaurant, a gas station, and a 24hr. convenience store. 28 small but pleasant rooms. Color TV. Popular restaurant next door is run by the same

management (breakfast before 8am included in room rate). Singles $35-45. Doubles $41-51. Prices drop $4 in winter.

FOOD

Food prices are on the rise as well, but there are still some good deals to be found in town. Cook for yourself courtesy of **Cooper's Supermarket** (837-4372) in the Alpine Village Centre at 555 Victoria St. (open Mon. 9am-6pm, Tues.-Thurs. and Sat. 8am-7pm, Sun. 8am-9pm).

Chalet Deli (873-5552), across the parking lot from Cooper's, is the best place in town to grab lunch. Try a personal pizza with your choice of sauce for $2.75. Or settle for a meaty sandwich on fresh bread for $4 (open Mon.-Sat. 5am-6pm).

Frontier Restaurant (873-5119), at the junction of Hwy. 1 and Hwy. 23N. Offers the "Ranchhand," a ½lb. cheeseburger with the works ($7.60) and saloon-inspired decor (open daily 5am-9pm).

Alphaus, 604 W. 2nd St. (837-6380), at Garden Ave. Meat Galore. Sandwiches on homemade rye $3.50-6.25. Authentic German specialties $8-12.50 (open Tues.-Sat. 8:30am-8pm).

SIGHTS

The guiding light of tourism in town is the **Revelstoke Dam** (837-6515 or 837-6211), 5km north of Hwy. 1 on Hwy. 23. The visitors center illustrates the dam's mechanical marvels with a free tour via "talking wand." Extensive videos and exhibits outline the construction, operation, and environmental impact of the dam from a surprisingly even-handed perspective. Ride the elevator to the top of the dam for an impressive view (open daily 8am-8pm; mid-Sept. to late Oct. 9am-5pm; mid-March to mid-June 9am-5pm; wheelchair accessible).

The **Revelstoke Railway Museum,** 719 W. Track St. (837-6060) off Victoria Road, a shrine to the Iron Horse, features old photographs and story-board exhibits outlining the construction of the first Canadian transcontinental lines. The museum preserves a steam locomotive and Canadian Pacific Railway office-on-wheels in an enormous hangar. Upstairs, an observation deck provides a bird's-eye view of the heavy traffic on the main C.P.R. line right outside ($5, seniors $3, ages 7-17 $2, under 7 free; open daily 9am-5pm; winter daily 10am-8pm).

Mt. Revelstoke National Park (837-7500) teems with all sorts of animals that eat, drink, walk, and copulate right in front of you. Thirty-five km of established trails lead to spectacular high-alpine lakes. At the summit of Mt. Revelstoke are some of the few vehicle-accessible alpine meadows in western Canada. **Summit Rd.** branches off from the Trans-Canada Hwy. one and a half km east of Revelstoke and takes an hour to drive roundtrip. Two special **boardwalks** just off Hwy. 1 on the east side of the park allow exploration of the local brush. The "skunk cabbage" trail leads through "acres of stinking perfection": brambles of skunk cabbage plants grow to heights of over 1½m. Some of the majestic cedars on the "giant cedars trail" are over 1000 years old.

Revelstoke has tried some curious variations on **downhill skiing** to spice up its winter season. **Mt. Mackenzie,** P.O. Box 1000 (call collect at 837-5268), 5km outside of town, gives you a chance to climb deep bowls of powdered snow in motorized snow cats. For the less adventurous (or less wealthy), the mountain also maintains 21 trails with a 2000-ft. vertical drop. **Cross-country** skiers will find more than enough snow and trails in the nearby national parks to keep them busy all winter. The big game guides at **Monashee Outfitting,** 825 Olhausen (837-3538) are willing and able to organize hiking, fishing, horse rides, canoeing, cross-country skiing, and anything else your little heart desires.

WESTERN CANADA

■ Glacier National Park

Major A.B. Rogers won a $5000 salary bonus and immortality when he discovered a route through the Columbia Mountains, finally allowing Canada to build its first transcontinental railway. Completed in 1885, the railway was a dangerous enterprise; more than 200 lives were lost to avalanches during its first 30 years of operation. Today, **Rogers Pass** is at the center of Glacier National Park, and 1350 sq. km of national park commemorate old A.B.'s efforts, as well as those of the other explorers who bound British Columbia to the rest of Canada. Canada's most appropriately named national park, Glacier hosts over 400 of the big guys.

Practical Information The Trans-Canada Hwy.'s many **scenic turn-offs** offer picnic facilities, bathrooms, and historical plaques. For a detailed description of the park's 19 hiking trails, talk to the Parks Canada staff or buy a copy of *Footloose in the Columbias* ($1.50) at the **Rogers Pass Information Centre** (837-6274), on the highway in Glacier. The center has enough computerized information, scale models, and exhibits to warrant a visit. Don't miss the free 25-minute movie *Snow War,* which includes a chilling scene from an actual avalanche rescue (open daily 7am-9pm; winter hours vary). **Park passes** are required if you don't drive straight through ($4 per day, $35 per year, good in all Canadian national parks). Prices in the park often change; for updates or general information about Glacier National Park, write the Superintendent, P.O. Box 350, Revelstoke V0E 2S0, or call 873–7500.

Glacier lies on the Trans-Canada Hwy., 350km west of Calgary and 723km east of Vancouver. **Greyhound** (837-5874) makes four trips daily from Revelstoke to Glacier ($10). In an emergency, call the **Park Warden Office** (837-6274; open daily 7am-5pm; winter daily 7am-11pm; 24hr. during avalanche control periods). The **area code** is 250.

Accommodations, Camping, and Food There are two campgrounds in Glacier: **Illecillewaet** (ill-uh-SILL-uh-watt) and **Loop Brook.** Both offer flush toilets, kitchen shelters with cook stoves, and firewood (sites for both $13; open mid-June-Sept.). Illecillewaet stays open in winter without plumbing; winter guests must register at the Park Administration Office at Rogers Pass. **Backcountry campers** need a backcountry pass ($6), and must register with the Administration Office beforehand, and pitch their tents at least 5km from the pavement. You'd do well to drop by a supermarket in Golden or Revelstoke before you enter the park; choices are limited and unappealing in the park.

Outdoors A century after Rogers's discovery, Glacier National Park remains an unspoiled and remote wilderness. The jagged peaks and steep, narrow valleys of the Columbia Range prevent development, even along the highway corridor. One would literally have to move mountains to build here. The Trans-Canada Hwy. cuts a thin ribbon through the center of the park, affording spectacular views of over 400 glaciers. More than 140km of challenging trails lead from the highway, inviting rugged mountain men and women to penetrate the near-impenetrable. Try to visit the park in late July or early August, when brilliant explosions of mountain wildflowers offset the deep green of the forests. Glacier receives measurable precipitation every day in summer, but the clouds of mist that encircle the peaks and blanket the valleys only add to the park's astonishing beauty. Unless you're directly descended from Sir Edmund Hilary or Tenzing Sherpa, avoid exploring the park in winter, as near-daily snowfalls and the constant threat of avalanches often restrict travel to the Trans-Canada Hwy.

Eight popular **hiking trails** begin at the Illecillewaet campground, 3.4km west of Rogers Pass. The easy 1km **Meeting of the Waters** trail leads to the impressive confluence of the Illecillewaet and Asulkan Rivers. The 4.2km **Avalanche Crest** trail offers spectacular views of Rogers Pass, the Hermit Range, and the Illecillewaet River Valley; the treeless slopes below the crest testify to the destructive power of winter snowslides. From early July to late August, the park staff run daily **interpretive hikes** beginning at 9am (for information contact the center). Come prepared for a four- to six-hour tour with a picnic lunch, a rain jacket, and a sturdy pair of walking shoes. Regulations prohibit biking on the trails in Glacier. The park's glacial meltwaters—a startling milky-aqua color due to sediment suspended in the current—do not support many fish; determined anglers can try their luck with the cutthroat in the Illecillewaet River (get a permit, $6 for 7 days, at the information center).

For nearby **Kootenay** and **Yoho National Parks,** see pages 295 and 297.

■ Nelson

Nestled in the forested hills at the foot of Kootenay Lake in the Kootenay mountains, Nelson has been spared much of the onslaught of BC tourism. Frequented primarily by other British Columbians, Nelson offers visitors a break from the crowds and a chance to mingle with an eclectic mixture of locals and seasonal transplants. Every summer is a summer of love as the neo-hippies and New Agers mix peacefully with the more down-to-earth Nelsonites.

Nelson's scenic beauty is not an undiscovered asset. Bequeathed a large number of landmark buildings by a long, undisturbed history, Nelson welcomed the lights, camera, and action of Hollywood when it served as the backdrop for the 1986 romantic comedy *Roxanne* starring Steve Martin. But the grace with which this small town accepted the fast-paced camera crews is only further testimony to its melting pot capabilities. Whether you drink mineral water, beer, whiskey, or herbal tea, you'll fit right in here.

PRACTICAL INFORMATION

Visitors Information: Nelson and District Infocentre, 225 Hall St. (352-3433). The staff will shower you with info on how to keep busy. Open daily 9am-6pm; Sept.-June Mon.-Fri. 10am-6pm.

Buses: Greyhound, 1112 Lakeside (352-3939), in the Chako-mika Mall. To: Vancouver ($81), Calgary ($77), and Banff ($60).

Public Transportation: Nelson Transit Systems, 352-2911. 3 lines cover the city, a fourth travels on the North Shore of Kootenay Lake to Balfour. Exact fare required. Within the city, adults $1, students and seniors 80¢. The North Shore route is more expensive, depending on how far you go. Buses run Mon.-Fri. 6:30am-11:30pm, Sat. 8:30am-7:30pm.

Taxi: Kootenay Kabs (354-1212).

Car Rental: Rent-A-Wreck, 301 Nelson St. (352-5122), at the Shell station. $20 per day plus 12¢ per km, or $199 per week with 1000 free km. Must be 19 with a credit card. Open daily 7:30am-9:30pm.

Bike Rental: Gerick Cycle, 702 Baker St. (354-4622). $15 per day, $25 for a weekend. Open Mon.-Thurs. and Sat. 9am-5:30pm, Fri. 9am-9pm.

Pharmacy: Pharmasave, 639 Baker St. (352-2313). Open Mon.-Thurs. 9am-6pm, Fri. 9am-9pm, Sat. 9am-5:30pm, Sun. 10am-4pm.

Hospital: Kootenay Lake District, 3 View St. (352-3111). If you break your leg, don't try to walk; it's way up the hill in the southeast part of town.

Ambulance: 352-2112. **Fire:** 352-3123. **Police:** 352-2266.

Post Office: 514 Vernon St. (352-3538). Open Mon.-Fri. 8:30am-5pm. **General Delivery Postal Code:** V1L 5P3.

Area Code: 604.

Nelson lies in Kootenay County, at the junction of Hwy. 6 and 3A. From Nelson, Hwy. 3A heads west 41km to **Castlegar.** Hwy. 6 leads south 65km to the U.S. border, where it becomes Washington Rte. 31, continuing 110 mi. south to Spokane.

ACCOMMODATIONS AND CAMPING

Dancing Bear (HI-C), 171 Baker St. (352-7573, fax 352-7573). Wooden lodge complete with library, fireplace, kitchen, and laundry. One of the finest hostels in western Canada. The small rooms have one bed or bunk each. Clean. No curfew. Check-in 4-10pm. $17, nonmembers $20, ages 6-10 half-price, under 5 free.

Kokanee Creek Provincial Park (825-4212), 5km beyond Chinook Park on Hwy. 3A. On the shores of Kootenay Lake. Wheelchair-access sites available. No reservations; fills early. 132 sites, $12.

Nelson City Tourist Park, on High St. Take Vernon to its eastern terminus and follow the signs. Packed like sardines. Still, it's the best place to crash if you're unable to get out of town. 40 sites, $13. Showers for non-campers $2.

FOOD

The diverse population of Nelson supports a variety of restaurants, most of them cafés. Whatever your style, you can get the supplies you need at **Super Valu,** 708 Vernon St. (352-2815; open Mon.-Wed. and Sat. 9am-6pm, Thurs.-Fri. 9am-9pm, Sun. 10am-6pm). Stock up on fresh bread at one of the many bakeries downtown; great cookies can be found at the **Kootenay Baker,** 295 Baker St. (352-2274).

Book Garden Café, 556 Josephine St. (352-1812). A sunny, green hangout for hippies, artists, and intellectuals who chat on the garden patio and read books from the adjoining bookstore. Unbelievable eggplant-basil sandwich $5.95. Soup $2.95, tortilla chips with red pepper pesto $3.95. Open Mon.-Sat. 9am-5:30pm, Sun. brunch 10am-4pm.

Zocalo Café, 802 Baker St. (352-7223). Huge dance hall-like building with eclectic art. Patio dining gives a great view of the lake. Trio of quesadillas: leek with goat cheese, brie and sundried tomatoes, and chef's selection $6.95. Chilled gazpacho $4.23. Frozen margarita $4.50. Open Mon.-Sat. 11am-11pm, Sun 4am-10pm.

The Outer Clove, 536 Stanley St. (352-6800). A red-walled garlic-themed interior (even the Mona Lisa print is sporting a few cloves) welcome you into a cozy European-styled eatery. Dinner is a little pricey, but the lunch specials and tapas ($3-7, really just pretentious appetizers) are both excellent and economical. Polenta $6.75, Fritatta $5.75, Buddha's Feast $7. Open Mon-Sat. 11:30am-10pm.

SIGHTS AND OUTDOORS

Pick up the free brochure *Architectural Heritage Walking Tour* at the Chamber of Commerce and examine the buildings that made Nelson into a movie backdrop. Extend your tour behind the wheel through the homes of the **Uphill District.** The Chamber of Commerce also hands out a free guide to a walking tour of sites filmed in *Roxanne,* but the narrative refers extensively to events in the movie, so if you don't remember it, you'll be lost.

The West Arm of Kootenay Lake, bordering Nelson on the north, may look huge, but its just a tiny part of the enormous lake. Abundant fish, notably **dolly varden, rainbow trout** (up to 30lb. according to local legend), and **kokanee** cruise the lake. **Sturgeon** of up to 1½m in length prowl the Kootenay River.

Twenty-five km east of Nelson on Hwy. 3A, the **West Kootenay Visitor Centre** (825-4723), in Kokanee Creek Provincial Park, displays a range of exhibits on local human and natural history, with hands-on displays that will delight the small fry. Behind the visitors center, a spawning channel fills up with bright red kokanee in late August and early September, as they struggle upstream to spawn and then drift back downstream, dead. The visitor center is also a great place to get information about outdoor recreation in the area (open July-Aug. daily 9am-9pm).

Forty km northeast of Nelson, Hwy. 3A crosses Kootenay lake on a **ferry.** The 6km crossing takes 45 minutes, making it the longest free ferry ride in the world (ferry runs daily 6am-midnight).

The Kokanee Creek Rd., heading north from Hwy. 3A, 21km northeast of Nelson, is a major access to **Kokanee Glacier Provincial Park,** 320 sq. km of rugged peaks

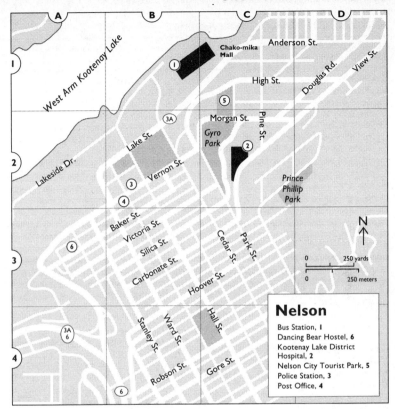

Nelson

Bus Station, 1
Dancing Bear Hostel, 6
Kootenay Lake District
Hospital, 2
Nelson City Tourist Park, 5
Police Station, 3
Post Office, 4

and alpine lakes. The park contains several glaciers, numerous dayhiking opportunities, and North America's last remaining Sasquatch. From Gibson Lake at the end of Kokanee Creek Rd., a spectacular four-hour hike leads one way past Kokanee and Kaslo Lakes to the Slocan Chief Cabin. Pick up the **park pamphlet** at the Nelson Chamber of Commerce, or call the Ministry of Parks District Manager at 825-9509.

The gentle but isolated and densely forested hills of the Kootenay Country are ideal for **mountain biking.** Thousands of kilometers of abandoned roads are accessible to the intrepid explorer. Pick up *Mountain Bike Adventures in the Kootenay* at the Chamber of Commerce. One popular route begins at the top of Silver King Rd. in the southwest part of town, and proceeds through a lush forest to an abandoned mine about a two-hour ride from town.

During the winter, the phenomenal powder of **Whitewater Ski Area** (354-4944), 35km southeast of town, attracts skiers from far away, and Nelson slips comfortably into the role of ski-resort town. The resort maintains 32 trails and slopes with a 1300 ft. vertical drop (lift tickets $34, seniors and ages 13-18 $27, ages 7-12 $21; snow report, 352-7669).

■ Crowsnest Pass

Crowsnest Pass, a convenient stop for travelers driving between Alberta and British Columbia, was the site of multiple cataclysmic mining disasters, frequent shootouts, and train robberies during the wild rum-running days of the 1920s. The grim history of Crowsnest Pass prompts many visitors to overlook its natural beauty, though

Dall sheep, and bears stroll among the area's stately pines and brilliant mountain wild-flowers.

CAMPING AND FOOD

Chinook Lake Campground (Alberta Forest Service, 800-661-8888). Follow Hwy. 3 west from Coleman for 9km, then follow the signs up Allison Creek Rd. Virtually inaccessible to the traveler on foot. 70 sites. $7-9.

Lost Lemon Campground (562-2932), just off Hwy. 3A near Blairmore. More commercial than most in the Pass, this campground offers hot showers, a hot tub, a heated pool, laundry facilities, and 64 sites for RVs or tenters. Great fishing in the Crowsnest River. Sites $16, full hookups $20.

Chris and Irvin's Cafe, 7802 17 Ave. (563-3093), in downtown Coleman. This classic diner serves up the Miner's Deluxe ($3.25). Fantastic fries. Open Mon.-Fri. 6am-10pm, Sat. 7am-10pm, Sun. 8am-7pm.

Gramma's Cookie Box (562-2777), on Main Street in Blairmore. Don't leave Blairmore without stopping in for delicious baked goods of every conceivable variety. Try the poppy seed bun (55¢). Fresh, homemade bread ($7 for 11 loaves; smaller quantities available). Or, have Gramma slap together a sandwich ($3.75-4.25) or sub ($4.50-5.25) for you.

SIGHTS AND ACTIVITIES

A small town near Crowsnest Pass ran afoul of the mining gods when one tunnel too many sent Turtle Mountain tumbling like a giant sandcastle. Ninety million cubic feet of stone spilled into the town of Frank, burying 70 people and their houses in less than two minutes. The **Frank Slide Interpretive Centre** on Hwy. 3 details the dramatic collapse of the still-unstable mountain. The staff is knowledgable on the local great outdoors—Joey has written several books on nearby **hiking** ($4, seniors $3, children $2, information is free, open daily 9am-8pm, winter 10am-4pm).

The Pass offers a host of diversions more cheerful than mining-disaster sites. The **trout fishing** in the **Crowsnest River, Castle River,** and **Oldman River** is reputed to be among the best in the Rockies. Crowsnest Pass is also home to the **Gargantua Cave,** the second longest and deepest cave in all of Canada. Known simply as "The Cave," Gargantua is located near the Alberta-British Columbia border at the site of Old Man River's spill into Crowsnest Lake. (Sadly for Rabelais fans, there is no Pantagruel Cave to be found.) Drop by the Frank Slide Interpretive Centre (above) for a look at topographic maps and for information on how to safely explore the cave.

If you are heading west, take Hwy. 3 into the beautiful Kootenay country of British Columbia. If heading north into **Kananaskis** and **Banff,** consider taking the scenic but bumpy **Forestry Trunk Rd.,** which meets Hwy. 3 near Coleman. The drive offers spectacular vistas of mountains colored in vibrant hues of green, red, brown, and purple. The road is lined with Forest Service campgrounds such as **Dutch Creek, Old Man River,** and **Cataract Creek** (sites $7-9). Call 562-7307 for information. An **Alberta Tourism Information Centre** (563-3888) is located 8km west of Coleman on Hwy. 3 and can provide further information on sights in the area. (Open May 15-Labor Day daily 9am-7pm.)

Northwestern Canada

Northern British Columbia, the incredible Queen Charlotte Islands, and the Yukon Territory remain among the most remote and sparsely inhabited regions of North America. Averaging one person per 15 sq. km, the land's loneliness and its sheer physical beauty are overwhelming. Native peoples have lived here for thousands of years, adapting their lifestyle and culture to the patterns of animal migration and the uncompromising climate. Gradually white settlers migrated West, attracted by the wealth of natural resources. The first were fur traders looking for faster new routes through the area. Several major gold rushes, beginning in the Fraser Valley in 1858, brought stampeders who eventually settled permanently. Since then, the lumber and mining industries have brought many others.

Despite the tell-tale signs of the logging and mining industries, Northwestern Canada remains a bountiful, beautiful, and almost entirely unspoiled region. Sadly, many Alaska-bound travelers blow through British Columbia and the Yukon without appreciating their far less crowded attractions. Muttering "Must...get...to...Alaska," these zombies drive on, without exploring the prime fishing of the Lakes Region, the untouched hiking terrain of Mt. Edziza Provincial Park, and the colorful history of Dawson City. Travel infocenters give abundant and indispensable council on where to go and what to find there. If you're looking for immense forests, stark mountains, yawning canyons, roaring rivers, clear lakes, abundant wildlife, and freedom from summer crowds, savor Northwestern Canada.

A word to the wise: it can be very cold in Northwestern Canada, even in the summer and especially at night. If you plan on spending more than a couple of nights outdoors, you will need at least an excellent tent, an ensolite pad, and a warm sleeping bag for extra warmth. A wool hat and long underwear, and perhaps an extra blanket, won't hurt either. It can easily snow during the summer anywhere north of Prince George. For more information, see **Camping and the Outdoors,** page 43.

NORTHERN BRITISH COLUMBIA

▓ Cariboo Highway (97)

The **Cariboo Highway** is the portion of Highway 97 which runs south for approximately 450km between Cache Creek and Prince George. From there, Highway 97 continues north to Dawson Creek (402km) and the start of the Alaska Highway (p. 259). Due to the surrounding region's mammoth cattle industry, you'll see many more cows along the highway than you will "cariboo." Still, the scenery is impressive, with small lakes nestled among rocky hills and patchy forest. A visit to one of the 12 Provincial Parks in the area is well worth a brief departure from the highway. Two of the nicest of the Parks, both close to the Cariboo, are Green Lake, a series of glacial kettle lakes, and Pinnacle, where an eight-minute walk will lead you to an unexpected view of a steep sandstone canyon carved into the surrounding plateau. Nearly all of the Provincial Parks, even those farther from the highway, deserve a visit if you're not in a hurry.

Many of the small towns along Hwy. 97 are slowly becoming more than just pit stops en route to Prince George. **Cache Creek,** at the junction of the Cariboo Hwy. and the Trans-Canada Highway (Hwy. 1), does not have much to offer tourists in the way of sight-seeing, but weary campers can stay at the **Cache Creek Campground,** perched scenically along Cache Creek, 1km north of town on Hwy. 97. The campground offers a pool and a spa free to campers (sites $13, full hookups $18, coin showers, laundry, wash and dry both $1.50). Travelers can take a half-hour nature walk on one of the 35 trail-filled acres. Hard-core budgeters might opt instead for the

Brookside Campsite (459-2519), located 1km west of town toward Kamloops on Hwy. 1 East, which offers free showers, cheaper laundry ($1.25 each wash and dry), and costs $11 at one of 16 tent sites or $17 for one of 77 full hookups.

From Cache Creek on, gold rush-era roadhouses have grown into towns along Hwy. 97. **100 Mile House,** 153km north of Cache Creek, offers services and groceries, and proudly displays the **world's largest pair of cross-country skis,** a fitting tribute to the cross-country skiers who flock to Cache Creek every winter. The **Travel Infocentre** (395-5353), located at the Chamber of Commerce next to the towering skis, is another helpful stop (open summer daily 8am-5pm; winter Mon.-Fri. 9am-5pm). The highway's biggest pit stops are the towns of **Williams Lake,** at Mile 155, and **Quesnel** (kwuh-NEL), halfway between Williams Lake and Prince George. The **Travel Infocentre** (392-5025) in Williams Lake is on the highway and can give you the scoop on activities and events in the area (open Sat.-Sun. 8am-6pm; Mon.-Fri. 9am-4pm). You can secure a roof over your head and polish your mini-golf game at the **Lakeside Resort Motel** (392-4181), on Hwy. 97 near the south end of town. Singles are $47, doubles are $53, and rooms come with 18 holes of free putt-putt pleasure. If you're looking for a swim, try the **Slumber Lodger** (800-663-2831), located at 27 7th Ave. downtown. Rooms are $45 for a single, $49 for a double, and swimming, cable, and local calls are free. As with most of the motels in Williams Lake, kids under 12 stay free. For campers who can tolerate 14 more miles up the road, **Whispering Willows Campground** beckons northward. Free showers and firewood come with a $10 site; RVers also pay $10 but miss out on free firewood.

Williams Lake is home to the province's most active cattle marketing and shipping industry. The town celebrates its cowboy heritage over Canada Day Weekend, usually in the first week of July, with the four-day **Williams Lake Stampede.** The festivities include a rodeo, parade, and "pony chuckwagon races." Beware the jump in motel prices during Stampede weekend.

Immense, wild **Tweedsmuir** and **Ts'il?Os** (SIGH-loss) **Provincial Parks** can be reached on Hwy. 20 west from Williams Lake. Tweedsmuir is home to grizzlies, all five species of Pacific salmon, the Atnarko River, Hunlen Falls, Monarch Glacier, and the colorfully streaked shield volcanoes of the Rainbow Mountains. Rugged Ts'il?Os is home to Canada's first grizzly bear refuge. Currently, highways to each park are half paved but easily navigable, except in foul weather. For general park information and to make campground reservations, call **BC Parks** in Williams Lake (800-689-9025). About 50km north of Williams Lake on Hwy. 97 the **Marguerite Ferry** shuttles both cars and passengers across a narrow stretch of the rambling Fraser River (free 7am-7pm); off-road enthusiasts can stay on the other side and take a mostly gravel road to Quesnel. Ask the ferry captain for directions. Even more scenic is the gravel road from Williams lake to the ferry, but be sure to ask at the infocenter for directions beforehand—it's very easy to get lost.

In Quesnel, the **Travel Infocentre,** 703 Carson Ave. (992-8716), is just off Hwy. 97 in Le Bourdais Park (open May-Aug. daily 8am-6pm, Labor Day-Victoria Day Mon.-Fri. 8:30am-4:30pm). Stretch your weary limbs on the **River Walk,** a paved trail along the river dotted with tidbits of information about Quesnel's history. You can visit **Pinnacle Provincial Park,** a scant five minutes away (just cross the river on Marsh Rd., then turn right on Baker Drive), and take a short walk to impressive viewpoints. The **Wheel Inn** (992-8975), on Carson and Front Streets, directly across from the foot bridge that spans the Fraser River, offers basic accommodations at $35 for singles and $38 for doubles. **Roberts Roost Campground,** 3121 Gook Rd. (747-2015), is 8km south of town. Open April to October, this landscaped, lakeside campground has coin showers, laundry, fishing, and rowboat and canoe rentals ($4 per hour).

For those beyond hard-core and off the deep end, the **Alexander Mackenzie Heritage Trail** might be the ultimate challenge. The over-250km trail begins from Hwy. 97 just north of Quesnel and stretches across western British Columbia to **Bella Coola** on the Pacific, tracing the final leg of Mackenzie's 1793 journey across Canada to the western coast (allow 14-21 days for the trip). Mackenzie reached the Pacific

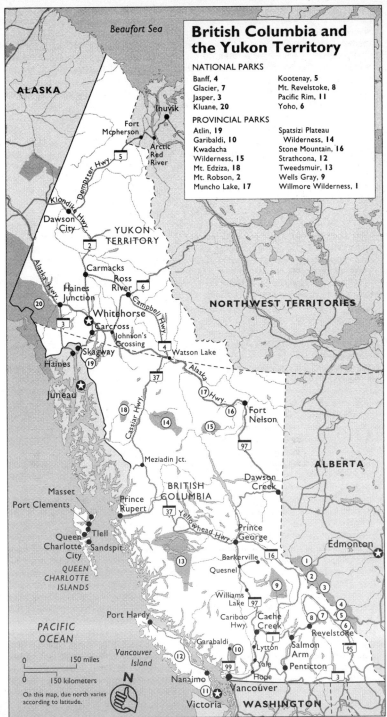

British Columbia and the Yukon Territory

NATIONAL PARKS

Banff, 4
Glacier, 7
Jasper, 3
Kluane, 20

Kootenay, 5
Mt. Revelstoke, 8
Pacific Rim, 11
Yoho, 6

PROVINCIAL PARKS

Atlin, 19
Garibaldi, 10
Kwadacha
Wilderness, 15
Mt. Edziza, 18
Mt. Robson, 2
Muncho Lake, 17

Spatsizi Plateau
Wilderness, 14
Stone Mountain, 16
Strathcona, 12
Tweedsmuir, 13
Wells Gray, 9
Willmore Wilderness, 1

WESTERN CANADA

before Lewis and Clark, though they continue to hog all the glory. For history and trail guides on the Mackenzie Trail, visit the **Quesnel Public Library** (992-7912).

Anyone traveling north to Prince George on Hwy. 97 will live a better life for having stopped at **Cinema Second Hand General Store** (998-4774), 83km south of Prince George on Hwy. 97. Cash-strapped road warriors will find everything they need here (except an actual cinema), plus a wide variety of things they could never possibly need, such as a full selection of disco LPs (open daily 9am-9pm). Cinema also offers **free camping**, handily equipped with **pit toilets.**

■ Prince George

At the confluence of the **Nechako** and **Fraser** Rivers, Prince George's magnificent riverbanks are slowly succumbing to the pulp and lumber mills which infest the valley floor. Even with more than 100 parks, several pleasant museums, and 73,000 friendly residents, Prince George is unfortunately fighting an uphill battle to become more of a destination and less of a stopover. Recent additions to the town include a civic center, a national university, and the Cougars, a Western League Hockey Team.

Practical Information You can pick up a useful free map of Prince George at either of the two **Travel Infocentres** in town (800-668-7646 for general information). The first is at 1198 Victoria St. (562-3700), at 15th Ave. (open Mon.-Fri. 8:30am-5pm); the second (563-5493) is at the junction of Hwy. 16 and 97 (open May-Sept. daily 9am-8pm), just look for the giant "Mr. P.G." log man—you can't miss him. **BC Rail** (561-4033), at the end of Terminal Blvd., 2km south off Hwy. 97, runs trains to Vancouver (3 per week, $177 with meals included; station open Mon.-Fri. 8am-noon and 1-9pm). **VIA Rail,** 1300 1st Ave. (564-5233 or 800-561-8630), serves Prince Rupert (3 per week, with 7 day advance purchase $50, $42 children and students, otherwise $83, $75 students). **Greyhound,** 1566 12th Ave. (564-5454), across from the Victoria St. infocenter, offers service to Edmonton, AB (1 per day, $87), Vancouver (3 per day, $85), Prince Rupert (2 per day, $82), and other points. Lockers are available for $1 for the first 24hr., $1.60 each additional 24hr. (station open Mon.-Sat. 5:30am-midnight, Sun. 6:30-9:30am, 3:30-5:30pm, and 9pm-midnight. Call ahead for ticket counter hours).

The **public library** is at 887 Dominion (563-9251; open Mon.-Thurs. 10am-9pm, Fri.-Sat. 10am-5:30pm, Sun. 1-5pm). If you are traveling north, make a point to stop at **Centre City Surplus,** 1222 Fourth Ave. (800-661-3773 or 564-2400), for any last minute items at extremely competitive prices (open Mon.-Sat. 9am-6pm, Fri. 9am-9pm). You can do your laundry at that nameless place at 231 George St., $1.25 each wash and dry. **Prince George Regional Hospital** is at 2000 15th Ave. (565-2000, emergency 565-2444). The **police** are at 994 Brunswick St. (562-330; 24hr.). The **post office** is at 1323 5th Ave. (561-2568; open Mon.-Fri. 8:30am-5pm). The **Postal Code** is V2L 4R8. The **area code** is 604.

Accommodations and Camping If you're only stopping in Prince George to get a good night's sleep and stock up on provisions, a good bet is the **Queensway Court Motel,** 1616 Queensway at 17th Ave. (562-5068), close to downtown. Singles are $32, doubles $37, and the well-kept rooms come with fridges, cable TV, and free local calls. Campers can head for the **Log House Restaurant and RV Park,** (963-9515), located on the shores of pristine Tabor Lake. Sites $12, full hookups $18, cabins with no amenities $35 for singles, and $40 for doubles. To get there, head out of town on 16W, turn right on "Old Cariboo Hwy.," and then left on Giscome Rd. This excellent but expensive steak restaurant and RV park is an attraction for European vacationers exploring British Columbia. Offers waterskiing ($15 for 20min.), and hunting and fishing trips via seaplane. Rowboat, canoe, and pedalboat rentals are $5, $8, and $8 per hr. respectively. If you're in a hurry or just looking for a low-key overnight spot, choose the **Bee Lazee Campground** (963-7263), 15km south of town on Hwy. 97. Plenty of amenities encourage you to bee lazee: outdoor pool, free showers, laundry ($1.25 each wash and dry), and car wash ($1 for 4min.). Sites can be had for $11, with full hook-up $17. Sample the Bee Lazee's fresh honey, and don't worry: the bees are instructed not to bother campers.

Food Cruelty or coincidence? The oddly named **Overwaitea's,** 1666 Spruce St. (564-4525), is a grocery store a short walk from the downtown infocenter (open daily 8am-10pm). Basic restaurant fare can be had at **Nick's Place,** 363 George St. (562-2523), where a large plate of good spaghetti costs $5 as a luncheon special (open Mon.-Sat. 11am-3:30am, Sun. 4-10:30pm). After lunch, venture across the street to the hip, traveler-happy **Javva Mugga Mocha Café** for dessert or coffee (espresso, muffins both $2). The café also runs a used book exchange, $2 paperback, $3 hardcover, with more titles than the Hapsburgs. **Jade Garden Restaurant,** 1533 3rd Ave. (562-6110), just off Victoria St., has an all-you-can-eat lunch smorgasbord for $6.25, dinner $9.25. Entrees $7.

Sights and Events Fishing is excellent near Prince George, with more than 1500 stocked lakes within a 150km radius, and the closest to downtown is **Tabor Lake,** where the rainbow trout all but jump into your boat in spring and early summer. The lake is 10km east on Hwy. 16; take a right onto "Old Cariboo Hwy." and a left onto Giscome Rd. For a complete listing of lakes and information on licenses, contact the infocenters.

For a bird's eye view of this industrial city, climb atop Connaught Hill Park, where you'll find picnic tables and ample frisbee throwing space. To reach the park, scale the yellow metal staircase behind the visitor's center or take Connaught Dr. off Queensway. **Forests for the World,** a wildlife preserve on nearby Cranbrook Hill, is only a 15-minute drive from town and one of the prettiest parts of Prince George. To get there, take Hwy. 97 north, turn left on 15th Ave., right on Foothills Rd., and left onto Cranbrook Hill Rd., and finally left on Kueng Rd.

Fort George Park, on the banks of the Fraser River off 20th Ave., offers expanses of lawn, picnic tables, and barbecue pits. Lurking inside the park is **Fort George Regional Museum** (562-1612), which houses frontier artifacts, including several primitive chain saws (open daily 10am-5pm; call for winter hours; $3, children $2, families $6). For a thorough introduction to Canadian rail history, head to the **Prince George Regional Railway and Forest Industry Museum** (563-7351) on River Rd. Visitors can climb aboard and explore the growing collection of rolling stock (pretentious railway-speak for train cars); the highlight of the museum is an original 1914 Grand Trunk Railroad Station, one of only three that remain in Canada (open Victoria Day-Labor Day Thurs.-Mon. 10am-5pm; $3.50, students $2.50). The Railway museum is just outside **Cottonwood Island Nature Park,** which has plenty of leisurely riverside walking trails along the banks of the Nechako River.

Mardi Gras, which lasts for 10 days in late February, features events such as snow gold, dog-pull contests, and jousting with padded poles, and is worthwhile if you're in town anyway. For information call 564-3737. Summertime events include the **Canadian Northern Children's Festival** held in Fort George Park, a four-day event held in mid-May, which features live theater, vaudeville, and plenty of music. **Sandblast,** on the third Sunday in August, sends a group of daring skiers down the steep, sandy, snowless Nechako Cutbanks. Prince George's **Oktoberfest** is held on an early October weekend. Enjoy traditional Bavarian oom-pah-pah music while taking in plenty of beer, bands, and bratwurst.

■ Yellowhead Highway (16): Mt. Robson to Prince George (319km)

In British Columbia, Hwy. 16 passes dramatic scenery as it continues west. Eighty km west of Jasper stands **Mt. Robson.** At 3954m, it is the highest peak in the Canadian Rockies. Climbers conquered her in 1913 after five unsuccessful attempts. Wimps can appreciate Robson's beauty from the parking lot beside the **park headquarters**

(566-4325; open May-Aug. daily 8am-8pm; Sept. daily 8am-5pm; Oct.-April closed). Visitors can choose from five nearby hiking trails ranging from 8½km dayhikes to 70km treks. Vacillators can stew in the campground at **Mt. Robson Provincial Park** ($14.50 with flush toilets and hot showers).

Just west of Mt. Robson is **Tête Jaune Cache** where Hwy. 16 intersects **Hwy. 5** leading south to Kamloops (339km) and the Okanagan country. Hwy. 5 is the fastest route from Jasper to Vancouver. Between the Rockies and Cariboo Mountains, 63km west of Tête Jaune Cache, lies the hamlet of **McBride.** Travelers not driving wood-burning vehicles are advised to fill up in McBride, since 205km of timber separate it from Prince George, the next significant town to the west. Huddled masses unwilling to negotiate the steep, winding grades to Prince George can find refuge (including flush toilets, showers, and laundry) at the **Beaver View Campsite** (569-2513) in McBride, 1km east of McBride on Hwy. 16 (sites $12; partial hookup $14-$16). Or stop at scenic **Purden Lake Provincial Park** (565-6340) for fishing or camping (sites $12 with flush toilets).

The woodchips littering Hwy. 16 from McBride to Prince George are proof of the heavy local logging activity. This region produces over six million cubic meters of lumber annually. Visitors tempted to chain themselves to trees or condemn the practices of the timber industry are invited to read the brochure *Don't Believe Everything That Greenpeace Tells You,* available at tourist information counters. Remember that here, as in much of the rural Northwest, terms like "deforestation" and "clear-cutting" are ways of describing how people make a living.

■ Yellowhead Highway (16): Prince George to Prince Rupert (724km)

West of Prince George, the steep grades and towering timbers of the forest region gradually give way to the gently rolling pastures and tiny towns of British Columbia's interior Lakes District. If late-night highway-induced munchies kick in, stop at the 24hr. PetroCan station in **Fort Fraser** (690-7542), where the "restaurant" will fix you up with a plate of hash browns ($2). Inhale secondhand smoke and vicariously experience the ebb and flow of life in a small town in northern British Columbia. Thanks to a drunken surveyor, Hwy. 16 takes a turn at the town of **Burns Lake** where virtually every building is adorned with the likeness of a trout. The **infocenter** is the best place to stop for info on fishing (692-3773; open daily 9am-7pm). However, before wetting a line, puffing a hackle, or seating a reel, visitors should consult British Columbia's *Provincial Angling* regulation synopsis, a guide replete with vivid prose and page-turning witticisms. Those wishing to savor the guide at length should consider hunkering down at the **Wanakena Motel** on Hwy. 16 (692-3151; singles start at $45, doubles at $55; continental breakfast included).

Eighty km west of Burns Lake is **Houston** and its Texas-scale contribution to the rampant superlativism of the late 20th century: the **world's largest flyrod** (60 ft. long and over 800lb.). Houston's infocenter (845-7640; open daily 8am-7pm, closed weekends in winter) offers a guide explaining how to "realize your fishing fantasies"—indulge these fantasies at one of more than 25 area lakes and streams. Sixty-four km northwest of Houston, **Smithers** offers skiing on the slopes of Hudson Bay Mountain and, in late August, the **Bulkley Valley Days** festival. In early September, travelers frustrated with their vehicles can strap on their helmets and enter the **Demolition Derby** in hopes of garnering fame and cash prizes. Or they can limit their participation to the coinciding **Telkna Barbecue.** The **information center** (847-5072) is in a converted railway car.

Forty-four km west of the town of **New Hazelton** is the **junction** with the **Cassiar Hwy. (Hwy. 37)** leading north 733km to the Yukon and the Alaska Hwy. (see p. 254). For the remaining 97km to **Terrace,** Hwy. 16 winds along the base of the Hazelton Mountains and follows the thundering Skeena River. There is no gas available along the 144km stretch of Hwy. 16 between Terrace and Prince Rupert.

■ Terrace

In 1944, an MIT-esque male-to-female ratio and an extended spell of bad weather caused 3,000 Canadian Army troops stationed in Terrace to mutiny. For three weeks, disgruntled enlisted men ruled Terrace and officers took refuge in Prince Rupert, 144km to the west. In the years since the mutiny, Terrace has calmed down considerably. Today on the banks of the Skeena River, fishing has replaced armed rebellion as the most popular means of easing boredom.

Practical Information The **Visitors Center** is at 4511 Keith St. (635-2064; open daily 9am-8pm), off Hwy. 16. Bus connections are offered by **Greyhound,** 4620 Keith St. (635-3680). Two westbound and two eastbound buses leave each day. To catch a train, contact **VIA Rail** (800-561-8630), which runs trains to Prince George and Prince Rupert. Do your duds at **Richard's Cleaners,** 3223 Emerson (635-5119; open Mon.-Sat. 7am-9pm, Sun. 10am-9pm). Suds yourself at the **public showers** at the **Terrace Aquatic Center,** 3220 Kalum Ave. (638-4755). Pool, hot tub, and gym facilities ($4, seniors $2.10, children $1.60). Mills Memorial **Hospital** is at 4720 Hangland Ave. (635-2111). The **police** are at 3205 Eby St. or call 635-4911. Phone 638-1102 for an **ambulance.** The **public library** is at 4610 Park Ave. (open Tues.-Fri. 10am-9pm, Sat. 10am-5pm). Mail your letters from 3232 Emerson (open Mon.-Fri. 8:30am-5pm). The **postal code** is V86 4A1. The **area code** is 604.

Accommodations, Camping, and Food The **Alpine House,** 4326 Lakelse (635-7216), is clean, and happily removed from the noisy downtown area (singles $50, doubles $55, single or double with kitchenette $65). Campers should head to **Ferry Island Municipal Campground** (638-4750) just east of Terrace on Hwy. 16, in a surprisingly natural setting given its close-to-downtown location. After a short walk from your wooded campsite, you'll emerge from the forest at the island's prime fishing spot along with a legion of eager anglers who got there first (sites $8.50, hookup $11). The community pool is half-price if you stay at Ferry Island. **Kleanza Creek Provincial Park** (847-7320), is the site of an abandoned gold mine 19km east of the city on Hwy. 16. Sites are a little cramped, but the tall trees and riverside picnic area compensate (sites $9.50).

Terrace offers a handful of welcome breaks from the dreariness of highway diner cuisine. **Safeway,** 4655 Lakelse Ave., is the cheapest place to buy food (open Mon.-Fri. 9am-9pm, Sat.-Sun. 9am-6pm). At **Bert's Deli** (635-5440), at Kalum and Park St., order a meatloaf sandwich ($2.40) and gape in amazement as they pile on the meat (open Mon.-Thurs. and Sat. 9am-7pm, Fri. 9am-9pm, Sun. noon-7pm). **Don Diego's,** 3212 Kalum St. (635-2307), is a small, laid-back joint that serves Mexican, Greek, and whatever's in season. Lunch specials go for $6-8; dinners go for $9-19. Try the house iced tea ($1; open daily 11:30am-9pm).

Sights **Heritage Park** (635-4546), at Kalum and Herby St., is a must-see for impoverished history buffs. Its 11 original cabins house countless artifacts from the pioneer era, including a working pump organ and an elaborate wreath made from human hair—perfect for seekers of the grisly side of kitsch (open Wed.-Sat. 10:30am-5pm; $1.50, children $1, family $4). **Gruchy's Beach** is 8km south of Terrace on Hwy. 37. It's a 1½km hike from the parking lot and it's big, sandy, and begging to be picnicked on. Those looking for more solitude and a little adventure should check out **Humphrey Falls,** where you can cliff-jump in between sandwiches (ask for directions at the infocenter). The **Tseax Lava Beds,** Canada's youngest lava flow and British Columbia's newest provincial park, is 80km north of Terrace. To reach this 54 sq. km swath of lunarscape, follow Kalum Lake Drive through the scenic valleys of the Tseax and Nass Rivers.

Before the **Grand Pacific Trunk Railway** joined Terrace with the rest of humanity in 1914, paddle-wheel boats on the Skeena were the city's primary contact with the outside world. **Riverboat Days** celebrates Terrace's pioneer and paddleboat heritage every year in late July. During the **Wild Duck Race,** 5000 rubber duckies race down the Skeena River.

Amble, sashay, skip, run, or walk along Terrace's 11 well-maintained **trails.** Hikers with a little more time should check out the **Redsand Lake Demonstration Forest,** 26km north on West Kalum Forest Road. The Forest Service is developing a network of trails around beautiful Redsand Lake and through a variety of forested areas. Grab an interpretive pamphlet at the infocenter. Anglers can strap on their hip-waders and try their luck on the east shore of **Ferry Island,** or ask for hot tips at the **Misty River Tackle Shop,** 5008 Agar Ave. (638-1269; open daily 7am-midnight).

■ Prince Rupert

In 1910, a nationwide contest was held to determine the name for the new city at the western terminus of the Grand Trunk Pacific Railway. The winning entry from among 12,000 was the shockingly bland "Prince Rupert"—the name of a 17th century British-Canadian business magnate. Even today, there is little of note in or about Prince Rupert. Despite its location at the base of tree-covered hills overlooking an island-speckled bay, the city's downtown is not much to look at. A few small museums and a handful of totem poles are about the only attractions the town has to offer, and the closest hiking rails are several kilometers outside of town. Nevertheless, most of the locals are friendly, and despite the fact that the city is notorious in Canada for its rainy weather (which has earned it the euphemistic nickname "The City of Rainbows"), it's not a bad place to get stuck for a day or so.

PRACTICAL INFORMATION AND ORIENTATION

Visitors Information: Traveler's Information Centre (624-5637), at 1st Ave. and McBride St. (open May 15-Labor Day daily 9am-9pm; winter Mon.-Fri. 10am-5pm). Stacks of info and a less-than-riveting self-guided tour. More impressive is the small **Museum of Northern British Columbia** that shares the same building (open summers 9am-8pm).

Banks: Plenty to choose, but the only one open on Sat. **Northern Savings Credit Union** at 1st St. and 3rd Ave. Open Mon.-Fri. 8:30am-5:30pm, Sat. 9am-3pm.

Airport: Prince Rupert Airport, on Digby Island. A ferry and bus connection to downtown costs $11 and takes about 45 min. **Air BC,** 112 6th St. (624-4554), flies to Vancouver ($349, standby $125). **Canadian Airlines** (624-9181), on the ground floor of the mall on 2nd Ave. W, offers the same service at $300 and $210 respectively, with special $105 youth fares for those under 25. Standby flights can be cheaper than the bus or train.

Trains: VIA Rail (800-339-8752 from BC, 800-663-8238 outside of BC, 984-5246), toward the water on Bill Murray Way. Trains to Prince George (3 per week, $50 with 7-day advance purchase, $42 students). **BC Rail** continues to Vancouver from Prince George ($177, $159 students), but an overnight stay is required (see **Essentials: By Train,** p. 29).

Buses: Greyhound, 822 3rd Ave. (624-5090), near 8th St. Runs buses twice daily to Prince George ($81), Vancouver ($165). Open Mon.-Fri. 8:30am-12:30pm and 3-8:15pm, Sat.-Sun. 9-11:15am and 6-8:15 pm.

Public Transportation: Prince Rupert Bus Service (624-3343) provides local service downtown Mon.-Sat. ($1, seniors 60¢, day pass $2.50, seniors $2). The #52 bus runs about every ½hr. 7am-10pm, from 2nd Ave. and 3rd St. to within a 5-min. walk of the ferry terminal.

Ferries: Alaska Marine Highway (627-1744), at the end of Hwy. 16 (Park Ave.). Runs ferries north from Prince Rupert along the Alaskan panhandle, including Ketchikan (US$38, car US$75) and Juneau (US$104, car US$240). **BC Ferries** (624-9627), next door, serves the Queen Charlotte Islands (6 per week; in peak season, $22.25, car $85) and Port Hardy (every other day, $100, car $206). Vehicle reservations required 3 weeks in advance. Ferry-goers may not leave cars parked on the streets of Prince Rupert. Some establishments charge a daily rate for storage; check with the ferry company or the information center (see above).

Shuttle: Seashore Charter Services (624-5645) is cheap and convenient. Call ahead and they'll take you to the ferry terminal for $3. Look for their minibus at the terminal when you arrive.

Taxi: Skeena Taxi (624-2185). Open 24hr. A ride from town to the ferry port costs from $6-8.

Car Rental: Tilden Auto Rental (624-5318), in the mall at 2nd Ave. and 5th St. During the week $47 per day, on weekends $30 per day. 25¢ per km, must be over 21 with a credit card.

Bike Rental: Vertical Cycles (627-1766), on 3rd Ave. near 1st St. $18 for 3hr., $25 for 24hr. High quality; includes lock and helmet. Open daily 9:30am-5:30pm.

Public Library: McBride St. and 6th Ave. (627-1345). Open Mon. and Wed. 1-9pm, Tues. and Thurs. 10am-9pm, and Fri.-Sat. 1-5pm; in winter also open Sun. 1-5pm.

Bookstore: Star of the West Books, 518 3rd. Ave. (624-9053), stocks a fine collection of regional titles. Open Mon.-Fri. 9am-9pm, Sat. 9am-6pm; Jan.-April Mon.-Sat. 9am-6pm.

Laundromat: Mommy's Laundromat, on 6th St. between 2nd and 3rd Ave. She won't do the laundry for you, but her machines are cheap. Wash 75¢, dry 75¢ for 15min. Open daily 9am-9pm.

Emergency: 911. **Hospital:** 1305 Summit Ave. (624-2171). **Police:** 100 7th Ave. (624-2136).

Post office: 624-2136, on 2nd Ave. and 3rd. St. You can receive general delivery mail at the main office (open Mon.-Fri. 8:30am-4:30pm), but only **substations** sell stamps and postal supplies. The most convenient substation is in the **Shoppers Drug Mart** at 3rd Ave. and 2nd. St. (open Mon.-Fri. 9:30am-9pm, Sat. 9:30am-7pm, Sun. 11am-6pm). **Postal code:** V8J 3P3.

Area code: 604.

The only major road into town is **Hwy. 16,** also known as McBride St. at the city limits. At the north end of downtown, Hwy. 16 makes a sharp left and becomes 2nd Ave. Downtown, avenues run north-south and increase in number from west to east; streets run east-west and increase in number from north to south. McBride St. is one block north of 1st St. At the south end of downtown, Hwy. 16 becomes Park Ave., continuing to the ferry docks.

From the ferry docks, the walk downtown takes 30 minutes, 45 with a heavy pack. Hitching is feasible, but inconsistent. A safer bet is the Seashore Charter Services Shuttle (see above) or a cab to downtown. (*Let's Go* does not recommend hitchhiking.)

ACCOMMODATIONS AND CAMPING

Nearly all of Prince Rupert's hotels are within the six-block area defined by 1st Ave., 3rd Ave., 6th St., and 9th St. Everything fills when the ferries dock, so call a day or two ahead. Unfortunately, most motels are pricey; you'll have to shell out at least $55 for a single.

Pioneer Rooms, 167 3rd Ave. E (624-2334). Well kept and clean interior. Noise until late could be a problem for singles blocked off only by curtains ($20). Single with a door $25, doubles $30. Laundry facilities ($5 wash and dry, including soap), microwave, and TV downstairs. Showers $3 for non-guests.

Rose's Bed and Breakfast, 942 1st Ave. W. (624-5539). Glowing white rooms inside a bright pink exterior. Shared lounge area with big couches and a mammoth TV. Full kitchen and a view of the harbor. Hostess speaks French, provides complimentary bikes, and serves up a lovely breakfast. Singles $40, doubles $50.

Eagle Bluff Bed and Breakfast, 201 Cow Bay Rd. (627-4955 or 800-833-1550), on the waterfront. Very attractive rooms in a prime location overlooking the dock. Private deck for sunset watching. $45 singles, $50 doubles, both with shared bath; $10 extra for private bath.

Park Ave. Campground, 1750 Park Ave. (624-5861 or 800-667-1994). Less than 2km east of the ferry terminal via Hwy. 16. The only campground in Prince Rupert. Some sites are forested, others have a view of the bay, and all are well maintained.

WESTERN CANADA

Populous RV crowd. Sites $9. RV sites $16. Reservations recommended. Accepts Visa and MasterCard.

FOOD

The best budget-food options in Prince Rupert begin in the bulk food department at the colossal **Safeway** (624-2412) at 2nd. St. and 2nd Ave. (open daily 9am-9pm). Most other food options are unexceptional and overpriced. Take locals' recommendations with a grain of salt—no place is fantastic.

Cow Bay Café, 100 Cow Bay Rd. (627-1212), around the corner from Eagle Bluff B&B. Local patrons and a mercurial menu. Such diverse delights as smoked salmon tarts ($6.50), jambalaya ($7.50), or a shrimp quesedilla ($8) will keep you on your toes. Gaze out at the harbor and thank your lucky stars that you found this place. Open Tues. noon-2:30pm, Wed.-Sat. noon-2:30pm, and 6-9pm.

Galaxy Gardens, 844 3rd Ave. W. (624-3122). A standout in the surprisingly large Chinese restaurant crowd. Enjoy very good *chow meins* ($7.50) and Cantonese entrees ($11 and up) in an attractive setting. Open daily 11am-10pm.

Rodho's (624-9797), on 2nd Ave. near 6th St. Head to Rodho's for Italian and Greek fare. Hellenic art lines the walls. A large Greek salad costs $7, pasta dishes $7-9, and Greek entrees $11-13. Licensed for liquor. Open daily 4pm-1am.

Lambada's Cappucino & Espresso, 101 3rd Ave. (624-6464). Tasteful New York ambiance and a mixed clientele of backpackers, local fishermen, and semi-urban professionals. Join them for a gigantic cream cheese cinnamon bun ($2), a scrumptious scone ($1), or a cappucino ($2.15). Open Mon.-Fri. 7:30am-9pm, Sat. 7:30am-5pm, Sun 12pm-5pm.

ENTERTAINMENT

Well, there's always the movies. The cinema at 2nd Ave. and 6th St. shows three features twice a night. While drinking establishments abound, kicking back with a beer may prove alarmingly expensive. Two clubs compete for dockers, but those accustomed to big-city entertainment may prefer watching paint dry.

The Commercial Inn, 901 1st Ave. (624-6142), on the Waterfront. Authentic local color in the form of tipsy fishermen and other down-to-earth folks. Quiet during the week, but things pick up with live cover bands on weekends. Comfortable, spacious setting with free billiards. Occasionally rowdy, so watch your step. $2.75 beer on tap. Sell your soul or your first-born and splurge on a premium bottle ($4.75). Open 11am-1am weekdays, 12pm-2:30am weekends.

Breaker's Pub, 117 George Hills Way in Cow Bay (624-5990). The "no rollerblades" sign on the door is a good indication of the kind of crowd this place attracts. Pool tables, nice view, vintage 80s tunes and expensive beers ($4 for a pint on draft). Bar open Mon.-Thurs. 11:30am-12am, Fri-Sat. 11:30am-1am, Sun. noon-midnight; kitchen closes earlier.

Bogey's (624-6711), on 3rd Ave. near Rodho's. You guessed it: lots of *Casablanca* posters, but Rick would be alarmed by the black lighting that bathes the interior and sets the big white stars on the carpet aglow. An enthusiastic and notably older crowd of drinkers and dancers. Drinks around $4. Open daily 9am-2am.

SIGHTS AND OUTDOORS

Few visitors realize that Prince Rupert Harbor has the highest concentration of archaeological sites in North America. Three-hour **archaeological boat tours** leave from the **Traveler's Information Centre** daily. A local expert will escort you to several sites, including the modern village of **Metlakatla,** in addition to pointing out many more from the boat. Sadly, some of the most intriguing sites are also the farthest away. Tours depart June 19-30 daily 12:30pm, July-early-Sept. daily 1pm; $20, children $12, under 5 free.

A number of attractive small parks line the hills above town and are a nice place for a short walk. Tiny **Service Park,** off Fulton St., offers panoramic views of downtown (which isn't any more attractive from above) and the harbor beyond. Take in an even broader view from a trail leading up the side of **Mt. Oldfield,** to the east of town. The trailhead is about 6km from downtown on Hwy. 16—consider renting a bike to get there if you don't have a car. The **Butze Rapids** and **Tall Trees** trails depart from the same location. Ambitious bikers can cycle 16km down the road to **Diana Lake Park,** which features a picnic area set against an enticing lake.

QUEEN CHARLOTTE ISLANDS

Sometimes called the "Canadian Galapagos," the remarkable Queen Charlotte Islands evolved in semi-isolation and, in addition to a plentiful assortment of more common wildlife, contain several plant species found nowhere else. Located in the Pacific Ocean about 130km west of Prince Rupert, the islands form an archipelago made up of two principal islands, Graham and Moresby, and 148 surrounding islets. Graham, the northern island, is home to all but one of the islands' peaceful communities, the world's only known Golden Spruce tree, a particularly potent (and illegal) strain of hallucinogenic mushroom, and the world's largest black bears. Hot springs steam in the mists of mountainous Moresby Island and its smaller neighbors to the south. The massive wooden totem poles of the islands' first inhabitants decay on the shores of the Pacific Ocean in Canada's newest national park.

The timber industry is the islands' main employer, narrowly beating out the Canadian government. In the 1980s the islands attracted global attention when environmentalists from as far away as Germany joined the Haidas and other locals in demonstrations to stop logging on parts of Moresby Island. In response to the protests, the Canadian government established the **Gwaii Haanas/South Moresby National Park Reserve** in 1988. The park, which is only accessible by boat or plane, covers the southern third of the Queen Charlottes and protects them from logging and development. Perhaps not coincidentally, the area's steep terrain and modest trees make it unsuitable for logging.

The creation of the park sparked a significant amount of media attention and tourist activity in the area rose. This free publicity was relatively short-lived, however, and the islands today are once again quiet and uncrowded. The lack of public transportation and exorbitant cost of car rentals help to deter the faint of heart, but residents are rumored to be generous in picking up hitchhikers. (*Let's Go* does not recommend hitchhiking. And traffic, even on the highway, is light.)

The BC Ferry from Prince Rupert docks at **Skidegate Landing,** between **Queen Charlotte,** 4km west of the landing, and the village of **Skidegate,** 2km to the northeast. Most visitors stay and eat in Queen Charlotte, the largest town in the islands, but all of the island communities have at least some tourist facilities. Many of the best accommodations and attractions lie farther to the north off Hwy. 16 in **Tlell, Port Clements,** and **Masset.** To the south sits Moresby Island and the town of **Sandspit.** From Skidegate Landing, 12 daily ferries make the 20 minute crossing between the islands. Locals refer to Queen Charlotte City as "Charlotte," Port Clements as "Port," and Tlell as "Tuh-LEL."

■ Queen Charlotte City

Queen Charlotte City's central location and size make it a great starting point for exploration of the two major islands by car. Don't be fooled by the name, though; this community of just over 1,000 is no city. Charlotte grew around a sawmill and logging is still its foremost industry, though fishing and the government also supply a significant number of jobs. While the location is pleasant, there's little to do here besides enjoy the view of the waterfront. Many businesses, including most grocery stores, are closed on Sundays and Mondays. Try to visit on a Tuesday.

WESTERN CANADA

PRACTICAL INFORMATION

Visitors Information: Visitor Reception Centre, Wharf St., on the east end of town. Beautiful new facility provides information both on Gwaii Hannas National Park and the islands as a whole. Nifty 3D map of the islands and a creative natural-history presentation. A copy of the *Guide to the Queen Charlotte Islands* is $3.95; detailed maps of the towns are worth it. Open May 1-16 daily 8am-noon, May 17-Sept. 2 8am-5pm.

Banks: Northern Savings Credit Union, Wharf St. (559-4407). One of two banking locations on the island (also a branch in Masset). ATM on 3rd Ave. is a lifesaver since many businesses don't take credit cards. Closed Mondays. Open Tues.-Thurs. 10am-5pm, Fri. 10am-6pm, Sat. 10am-3pm.

Parks Canada: Gwaii Haanas Park Information (559-8818), 2nd Ave. off of 2nd St. Try the Visitor Reception Centre for information during the summer. Register here during the rest of the year. Open Mon.-Fri. 8am-4:30pm.

Ministry of Forests: 559-6200 or 559-8324, on 3rd Ave. in a blue building at the far west end of town. Information on free campsites maintained by the Forest Service on Graham and Moresby Islands. Open Mon.-Fri. 8:30am-noon and 1-4:30pm.

Fishing Licenses: Obtain a saltwater license at **Meegan's Store,** 3126 Wharf St., (559-4428), or at the **Sea Raven Hotel,** 3301 3rd Ave. (559-4423). Freshwater licenses are available only from the **Government Agent** (559-4452 or 800-663-7674). Prices vary depending on how long the license lasts.

Ferries: BC Ferry, terminal in Skidegate Landing (559-4485 or 800-663-7600), 4.5km east of Queen Charlotte City. To Prince Rupert (July-Aug. 6 per week, Sept. 5 per week, Oct.-June 4 per week; $22.25, car $84.75, bike $6). If you have a car, reserve at least 3 weeks in advance. Car fares do not include driver. Also runs between Skidegate Landing on Graham Island and Alliford Bay on Moresby Island (12 trips per day, $3 roundtrip, car $8.50, off-season car $7.50).

Taxi: Eagle Cabs, 209 3rd Ave. (559-4461). $7-10 from Charlotte to the ferry terminal. Runs daily 8am-2pm.

Car Rental: Rustic Rentals (559-4641), west of downtown at the Charlotte Island Tire. Another office at 3922 3rd Ave. (559-8865), at Jo's Bed and Breakfast by the ferry. Will rent to 18-yr.-olds with a credit card. Reliable if unimpressive collection of used cars. $39 per day plus 15¢ per km over 50. Office open Mon.-Fri. 8:30am-6pm, Sat. 9am-5:30pm, but available 24hr. Will pick up at the ferry terminal in Skidegate. **Twin Services** (559-8700) provides more affordable short-term rentals: 8hr. for $35, 24hr. for $60, no charges for mileage. Limited selection, so reserve early. Also offers 24hr. towing and a garage. Open Mon.-Fri. 8:30am-8:30pm, Sat. 8:30am-7pm, Sun. 9am-7pm.

Bike Rental: Surplus Culture (559-4653) rents bikes out of a decrepit-looking shop on 3rd Ave. $15 for 4hr., $20 for 24hr. Open Tues.-Sat. 10am-6pm.

Books: Bill Ellis Books (559-4681) on 3rd Ave. at the far west end of Charlotte. A remarkable collection of works about and by the Haida and other Native American peoples. Open Mon.-Fri. 8:15am-4pm.

Laundromat: 121 3rd Ave. (559-4444). Wash $1.50, dry 25¢. Open daily 9am-9pm.

Pharmacy: 559-4310, downstairs in the hospital building. Open Mon.-Tues. and Thurs.-Fri. 10:30am-12:30pm and 1:30-5:15pm, Wed. 1:30-5:15pm.

Hospital: 559-4300, on 3rd Ave. at the east end of town.

Emergency: Police (RCMP), 3211 Wharf St. (559-4421). **Ambulance,** 800-461-9911. **Fire,** 559-4488.

Post Office: 559-8349, in the City Centre Bldg. on 3rd Ave. Open Mon.-Fri. 8:30am-5:30pm, Sat. noon-4pm. **Postal code:** V0T 1S0.

Area Code: 604.

ACCOMMODATIONS AND CAMPING

The small hotels of Queen Charlotte City are clean, cozy, friendly, and for the most part expensive. During the summer, make reservations or arrive early in the day to secure a room. The cheaper options are in very limited supply.

Jo's Bed and Breakfast, 4813 Ferry Loop Rd. (559-8865). Follow the road from the ferry terminal up the hill to the white house with blue trim. Convenient to the ferry, but a significant distance from anything else. Some rooms are skylit and feature sweeping ocean views. Others enjoy a communal kitchen and lounge, as well as communal noise. Comfy beds with fluffy comforters make getting up in the morning a challenge, but Jo's generous continental breakfasts will persuade you. Free local calls, and a shed to store bags in. Singles $30, doubles $40, campsite on lawn $5 including use of bathroom. Cash only. Reservations a good idea.

Spruce Point Lodge (559-8234), on the little peninsula across from the Chevron station at the west end of town. Six hostel beds in a co-ed dorm for $17.50 with your own bedding, $20 if they provide the sheets. Singles $55. Doubles $65. Reservations strongly recommended. Dorm reservations accepted for groups only.

The Premier Hotel, 3101 3rd Ave. (888-322-3388 or 559-8415; fax 559-8198). This low-key hotel has been attractively renovated with a veranda and balcony. Rooms in the un-renovated back hall are a bit dated and small, but only $30 with shared bath. Newer balcony rooms with a view start at $60, and can serve as doubles at no extra charge. The cheaper rooms go quick, so reserve early.

Gracie's Place, 3113 3rd Ave., Box 447 (888-244-4262 or 559-4262). Pay a little bit more for a significant step up in atmosphere. Gracie's attractive rooms are adorned with antique furniture and down quilts. Singles $50, doubles a deal at $60. Kitchen units $20 extra.

Joy's Island Jewellers, 3922 3rd Ave., Box 819 (559-4742; fax 559-8188), at the east end of town. A few campsites available in the yard, with some of the islands' best drinking water from a private spring. Gorgeous ocean views. No toilet facilities. Tents $5, RVs $8, full hookups $10.

Haydn Turner Park Campsite, at the west end of 4th Ave. A 25-min. walk from the town center. Sites include free firewood taken from the towering spruces that dwarf tents (and campers). A few spots at the end overlook the water. Toilets and water (boil before drinking). Tents $5, RVs $7.

FOOD

Most locals save their eating out for trips to the mainland, and will direct visitors to the grocery store for *haute cuisine à la Charlotte.* Buy your own grub at **City Center Stores Ltd.** (559-4444), in the City Center Building (open Tues.-Fri. 9:30am-9pm, Mon. and Sat. 9:30am-6pm). On nights and Sundays try **Yee's Autobody and Groceries,** on 7th St. at the west end of town (open daily 7:30am-10:30pm).

Hummingbird Café, 2600 3rd Ave. (559-8583), on the second floor of the Misty Harbor Inn. Upscale for Charlotte, the Hummingbird offers an airy, sun-washed dining area, stellar ocean view, and entrees ranging from a $5.25 burger to an $8 plate of spaghetti. Provides sizable salads to vegetarians and the health-conscious. Open for breakfast Mon. 11:30am-2:30pm, Tues.-Thurs. 11:30am-2:30pm and 5-9pm, Fri. 11:30am-2:30pm, Sat. 8am-2:30pm, Sun. 8am-1pm.

Pizza Factory, 3rd Ave. (559-8940), just west of Hummingbird. Tawdry and tasty. Pizzas start at $9, burgers $5, and great potato wedges at $2.75. Also a popular spot for ice cream. Open daily till 10pm.

Oceana Restaurant, 3rd Ave. (559-8683), next door to the Pizza Factory. Suspected to be the better of the town's two Chinese restaurants, Oceana serves up the traditional assortment of *chow meins* and *chop sueys* for about $10. Open Mon.-Sat. 11:30am-3pm and 5-10pm.

Isabel Creek Store, 3219 Wharf St. (559-8623), next to Margaret's Café. Organic fruits and vegetables, juices, and some excellent home-baked breads. A break from fried food and a good place to drop by before a backpacking trip. Open Mon.-Sat. 10am-5:30pm, and they guarantee, "during power outages."

Hanging by a Fibre (559-4463; fax 559-8430), on Wharf St. underneath the Pub. Meet local hipsters and the occasional artist. Store and gallery specializing in paper-art and basketry. Cappuccino $2, café latte $3, regular coffee $1, muffins and cookies 50¢. Open Sat.-Weds. 9am-7pm, Thurs.-Fri. 9am-9pm.

SIGHTS AND OUTDOORS

Displays of contemporary Haida artwork sparkle at **Rainbows Art Gallery and Gift Shop,** (559-8420) on 3rd Ave. at Alder, a gallery brimming with silver, gold, and argillite (black shale) carvings and gorgeous ink-drawings on traditional Haida themes (open Mon.-Sat. 10am-6pm, Sun 11am-5pm).

Skidegate Mission, known as "the Village," is a cluster of small, worn houses on Rooney Bay, 2km east of the ferry landing, along Hwy. 16 leading north. Skidegate has been a Haida village for centuries; today's community of 530 is a nexus of Haida art and culture. Residents are resigned to tourists, but they still hope visitors will be discreet and respectful. Visit the **Skidegate Band Council Office** (559-4496), in a Haida longhouse built in 1979 according to ancient design specifications. The totem pole in front is a favorite perch of bald eagles. Ask the receptionist for permission to view the artwork and old photographs inside (office open Mon.-Fri. 9am-noon and 1-4:30pm). Halfway between Skidegate Landing and Skidegate Mission is the **Queen Charlotte Islands Museum** (559-4643), housing totem poles from remote village sites, an extensive collection of stuffed birds, and contemporary Haida prints and carvings. The shed next door protects the 50-ft. cedar canoe carved for Vancouver's Expo '86 by renowned Haida artist Bill Reid. ($2.50, children free. Open May-Sept. Mon.-Fri.10am-5pm, Sat.-Sun. 1-5pm; closed Sun. and Tues. Oct.-April.)

Unlike most mountains allegedly in the shape of something, **Sleeping Beauty Mountain** actually resembles snoozing royalty. Ask a local to point out her distinct facial features. The challenging climb up the Beauty starts about 12km west of town off a logging road (follow the signs after 3rd Ave. turns to gravel) and takes about three hours to the top. The peak offers stunning views in every direction. A natural attraction requiring significantly less effort is **Balance Rock,** which sits on a roadside beach 1km north of Skidegate. A group of brawny loggers recently failed in an attempt to dislodge the mighty boulder, so don't fret about it falling from its precarious perch. The scenic and virtually traffic-free roads throughout the islands beckon seductively to cyclists.

■ Sandspit

The only permanent community on Moresby Island, Sandspit lies about 13km east of the ferry dock at Alliford Bay on a thin strip of land. With neatly trimmed houses and yards, endless ocean views, and bald eagles in seaside trees, the town is the Charlottes' most attractive residential area. Homes line Beach Road and Copper Bay Road, perpendicular to the beach. While Sandspit has limited culinary options, reasonably priced accommodations are plentiful, and tend to fill up less quickly than those on Graham Island. The town serves as one of the major launch points for kayak and boat trips to Gwaii Hannas/South Moresby National Park Reserve, and also provides access to logging roads that venture into the isolated interior.

Practical Information The **Parks Canada** office is in the airport at the north end of town (627-5362, open daily May 1-16 8am-noon, May 17-Sept. 2 8am-5pm). Register here or at their office in Queen Charlotte City before venturing into the park. Further information can be obtained from the **TimberWest Information Centre** (637-5436), on Beach Rd. (open Mon.-Fri. 9am-5pm). The friendly staff provides local information as well as access to the free, primitive **campsites** that the company maintains in several locations on the island. This stop is essential for anyone planning to travel local logging roads, which are open to the public when free of gargantuan trucks. Schedule available here.

Sandspit is 13km east of the Alliford Bay ferry landing on Moresby Island. There's not much traffic on the connecting road; those hitching from Sandspit to catch a late ferry often have a hard time finding a ride and recommend getting an early start. (*Let's Go* does not recommend hitchhiking.) **Inter-Island Ferry** (559-4485) runs between Skidegate Landing on Graham Island and Alliford Bay on Moresby Island (12 trips per day between 7am and 10:30pm; $3 roundtrip, car $10). **Budget Rent-A-Car,** 383 Beach Rd. (637-5688), rents cars at luxury prices ($47 per day plus 30¢ per km. Must be 21 with a credit card). Another office is at the airport.

The **library,** 383 Alliford Bay (637-2247), sits at the north end of town (open Tues. 2:30-6:30pm, Thurs. 3-5pm and 7-9pm). The **health clinic** (637-5403) is on Copper Bay Rd. in the school building. (Open Mon.-Fri. 10am-noon; after hours, call the **Queen Charlotte City Hospital** at 559-8466.) In an **emergency** call: **ambulance,** 1-559-4506 or 800-461-9911; **fire,** 637-2222; **police,** 559-4421 in Queen Charlotte City. The **Post Office** (637-2244) is at Beach and Blaine Shaw Rd. (open Mon.-Fri. 8:30am-5:30pm, Sat. 12:30-3:30pm). The **postal code** is V0T 1T0. The **area code** is 604.

Accommodations, Camping, and Food Rooms in town are more afford-able and less crowded than most on the islands. The **Seaport Bed and Breakfast** (637-5678), just up the road toward Spit Point, offers island hospitality with guest pick-up at the airport, plush couches, cable TV, and a breakfast of fresh eggs and home-baked goods. The newly added studio space is bright and beautifully deco-rated. The original rooms are nice, but suffer by comparison. Reservations are essen-tial in summer (singles $30, doubles $40). The **Moresby Island Guest House** (637-5300), on Beach Rd. next to the post office, provides eight rooms with shared wash-rooms, kitchen, and coin-operated laundry facilities. In the morning, they provide the ingredients for you to make breakfast. Kitchen use after breakfast costs $10. (Singles $30, doubles start at $55, overflow cots $15.) Trail-weary explorers can spend an extra $10 on the outdoor hot tub at the **Gwaii Hanaas Bed and Breakfast,** 368 Cris-tina Pl., (637-5312), off Copper Bay Rd. Enjoy spacious, comfortable rooms decorated with the hostess's own ceramic creations, hot breakfasts, and communal lounge. (Sin-gles $40, doubles $50.)

Ramble to **Dick's Wok Inn,** 388 Copper Bay Rd. (637-2275), where a heaping plate of fried rice costs $9 and up (open daily 5-10pm). Locals give Dick mixed reviews, but he's the only game in town for sit-down meals, aside from burgers at one of the bars. Try the mango pudding with soft ice-cream ($3) for a cross-cultural treat. Also offers a limited selection of very expensive groceries. A more affordable option is the **Bun Wagon,** 396 Copper Bay Rd. (635-5722). Customers can sit at picnic tables next to the road-side stand and enjoy delicious $2.50 dogs or big burgers with fries from $5.50 (open Mon.-Wed. 11am-2pm and 4-7pm, Fri.-Sun. 11am-7pm). The **Supervalu Supermarket,** 383 Alliford Bay (637-2249), resides in the mini-mall near the spit (open Mon.-Tues. and Thurs.-Sat. 9:30am-6pm, Wed. 9:30am-7:30pm).

Sights and Outdoors Stroll to the end of the spit for spectacular sunrises and sunsets. Anglers can cast for silver salmon in the surf. Well-maintained dirt logging roads lead south and west of town into some remarkably scenic areas. Rocky shores line the ocean north of **Copper Bay,** a haven for bald eagles (10km south), while **Grey Bay** (20km south) offers a virtually uninterrupted expanse of sand. Twenty free, primitive campsites line the beach, but the area is popular with locals so arrive early on weekends. A few km down the road from the campsites, a 4.5km trail follows the shore south to **Cumshewa Head.** Check with the TimberWest Information Centre (see **Practical Information,** above) to find out when the roads are open to the public. The roads are perfect for mountain biking, but the closest rental place is in Charlotte. Bikes are allowed on the ferry.

In the summer, **TimberWest** will take you out to see the trees (and stumps) on an informative and free 4½-hour **logging tour.** Get a view of an active logging site and the rare chance for a frank discussion of logging practices. While some may wince at the sight of glorious spruce trees being reduced to 2x4s, a great deal of environmen-tal forethought goes into modern logging. At the very least, the tour is a great way to venture into the backcountry if you're without transportation. Tours leave from the office on Beach Rd. at noon on Wednesday and Friday.

WESTERN CANADA

■ Yellowhead Highway(16): Tlell and Port Clements

Two small towns dot the quiet highway between Charlotte and Masset. The tiny community of Tlell, 40km north of Queen Charlotte City, is mostly houses and farms spread thinly along a 7km stretch of Hwy. 16. The town enjoys some of Graham Island's best beach vistas and a hefty population of urban refugees who earn the town a reputation as the Charlottes' "hippie" zone. Here the rocky beaches of the south give way to sand, and the Tlell River offers excellent trout fishing and water warm enough for swimming.

Port Clements, 20km north of Tlell, is a gritty logging community. Although blessed with an enticing harbor and a few nearby curiosities, the town has little to hold the footloose traveler. A tangled network of logging roads stretches inland from the port; these bumpy byways are open to public use and provide access to the heavily forested interior. Port Clements faces west onto Masset Inlet, and has some of the best sunsets in the Charlottes.

Practical Information Both communities boast a **post office.** The one in Tlell is on Hwy. 16, 2km south of Wiggins Rd. (557-4551, open Mon.-Sat. 2-5pm; **Postal code:** V0T 1Y0). Port Clements' lies between Hemlock and Spruce Ave. (open Mon.-Fri. 8:30am-12:30pm and 1:30-5:30pm, Sat. 1:30-5:30pm; **Postal code:** V0T 1R0). Port, as it is fondly known, also offers a **Village Office** (557-4295), on Cedar Ave. between Tingley and Pard St., which provides information and free **maps** of the logging roads (open Mon.-Fri. 1-5pm). You can browse for more information at the **Port Clements Islands Regional Library** (557-4402) at Tingley St. and Cedar Ave. (open Wed. 3-5pm and 7-9pm, Fri. 2-6pm). There is a **health clinic** in Port on Park St. (557-4478) next to the elementary school, with variable hours. Call **Island Taxi** in Port at 557-4230, 24hr. In an **emergency,** call 557-4355 (fire) or 800-461-9911 (ambulance). The **area code** for both towns is 250.

Accommodations and Camping Near Tlell, travelers can pitch a tent or park an RV at **Misty Meadows Campground,** just south of the Tlell River Bridge. Pit toilets, picnic tables, and water grace 30 sites (call Naikoon Provincial Park Headquarters at 557-4390). Or sink into the lap of luxury at **Hltunwa Kaitza Bed and Breakfast** (557-4664), just north of Richardson Ranch on the oceanside of the road nestled against the dunes, just seconds from the beach. This may be the islands' nicest B&B, and is certainly its most distinctive. The hostess, Cecilia, oversees a flock of friends and relations who are likely to drop by for tea in the evening. A common living space is adorned with lovely driftwood furniture, including hanging chairs that descend from giant spruce beams. Rooms are skylit, immaculate, and comfortable. (Singles $30, mat on the floor $15, laundry free.) The new owner at **Pezuta Lodging** (557-4250), just north of the Tlell River, has fixed things up nicely. A new hardwood deck complements a big cozy lounge with TV and wood stove. In addition to hosting individual travelers, the owner also takes on big groups (12-15), and for $60 per day will provide lodging and all meals. Otherwise, a shared hostel-type bedroom costs $18, while private singles go for $30 (doubles $35, all rates include breakfast). Those seeking a more traditional motel experience can try the **Golden Spruce Motel,** 2 Grouse St. (557-4325), in an uninspiring location in Port Clements. Singles start at $40, doubles at $45, renovated rooms $5 more, kitchenettes $5 extra.

Food Options here are extremely scarce. The only restaurant is the **Yakoun River Inn** on Bayview Dr. in Port Clements (557-4440). This classically rural establishment features a country music jukebox and serves up some damn good burgers starting at $5.75. Enjoy the autographed $2 bill collection adorning the walls, and think of how many pints of beer it could buy (not many at $4.50 a pint). Just don't try to hustle the locals at a game of pool (open Mon.-Sat. noon-2am, Sun. noon-midnight). Very near the opposite end of the Tlell dining spectrum is the **Body Currents Cappuccino Bar** (557-2089), 1km south of Richardson Ranch on Richardson Rd. off Wiggins Rd., which serves great chocolate chip cookies and cappuccino. The adjacent **gallery** exhibits and sells handmade local jewelry and crafts (both open Tues.-Sun. 10am-5pm). **Riverworks Farm & Store** (557-4363), on Hwy. 16, 2km south of Wiggins Rd. next to the post office, peddles island-grown produce and eggs (open daily 10am-5:30pm). More traditional groceries lurk in the **Bayview Market** (557-4331), on Bayview Dr. (open Tues.-Sat. 10am-6pm). Given the mediocre selection, you'd be better off shopping in Charlotte or Masset. Or stop by **Golden Spruce Farms,** 1km south of town on Bayview Dr. (557-4583). An astonishing variety of fresh vegetables (considering it's nearly impossible to grow potatoes here) available.

Sights and Outdoors One of the most popular trails around Tlell leads to the **Pezuta shipwreck,** the hulking remains of a 246-foot lumber barge that ran aground during a gale in 1928. The 2hr. hike to the site leaves from the Tlell River picnic area off Hwy. 16 just north of the river. The trail spends equal time wandering through lush forest and across sand dunes and agate-strewn beaches. Keep an eye out for land and water otters just before the wreck.

If you're feeling truly adventurous, consider continuing on past the wreck and embarking on a multi-day expedition along **East Coast Beach.** The highway cuts inland just north of Tlell, so backpackers have the only access to over 90km of incredibly pristine beach. A number of wooden shelters punctuate the beach, but you'll still need a tent or tarp. Expect to take between four and six days to reach the road access at the north end of the route 25km east of Masset. Adventurers are required to register at **Naikoon Provincial Park Headquarters** before setting out.

Oddity-seekers will be delighted in Port Clements, home of the world's only known **Golden Spruce.** A rare mutation causes the tree's needles to be bleached by sunlight. To reach the albino tree, drive 5½km south of town to a roadside pullover; from there it's a 10-min. walk to the banks of the **Yakoun River.** Eight km south of the pullover, a trail leads to an unfinished **Haida canoe.** The would-be boat was uncovered by loggers and remains in its original site. Nearby stumps are full of test holes where the early builders sampled other trees for their canoe potential.

▓ Masset

Sitting at Western Mile Zero of the Yellowhead Highway, Masset presents an underwhelming façade to visitors. But hidden among this rather drab collection of tired buildings are some surprisingly eccentric establishments and truly eccentric eccentrics (keep an eye out for the bearded old man paddling around in his handmade canoe). The majority of travelers who make their way to Masset come for the spectacular scenery that surrounds the town. Tow Hill and the Blow-hole to the east of town in Naikoon Provincial Park more than justify the northern trek.

PRACTICAL INFORMATION AND ORIENTATION

Visitors Information: Tourist Information Centre, Old Beach Rd. (626-3300), at Hwy. 16. Plenty of local history and trail maps for choice birdwatching. Open daily July-Aug. 9am-8pm.

Bank: Northern Savings Credit Union (626-5231), on Main St. north of Collison. The only bank and ATM on the islands outside of Queen Charlotte City. Open Tues.-Thurs. 10am-5pm, Fri. 10am-6pm, Sat. 10am-3pm.

Car Rental: Tilden Rentals, 1504 Old Beach Rd. (626-3318), at the Singing Surf Inn. New cars from $40 per day, plus 25¢ per km. Must be 25. Open Mon.-Sat. 7am-10pm, Sun. 8am-10pm. Better to rent in Queen Charlotte City or Sandspit than to have to hitch to get to your rental car in Masset.

Taxi: Jerry's Taxi, 626-5017.

Laundromat: Raven & Eagle Gifts & Cleaners, 2132 Collison Ave. (626-3511), at Orr St. Wash $1.50, 35-min. dry for $1.25. Open Mon. 10am-4pm, Tues.-Sat. 10am-5pm.

Public Library: 626-3663, at Collison Ave. and McLeod St. Open Tues. and Sat. 2-6pm, Thurs. 2-5pm and 6-8pm.
Emergency: Ambulance, 800-461-9911; **Fire,** 626-5511; **Police** (626-3991), on Collison Ave. at Orr St.
Post Office: 626-5155, on Main St. north of Collison. Open Mon.-Fri. 8:30am-5:30pm, Sat. 8:30am-12:30pm. **Postal code:** V0T 1M0.
Area Code: 250.

ACCOMMODATIONS AND CAMPING

A friendly budget god has finally smiled on Masset and created cheap accommodations. Expensive options are generally more appealing. There is free **beach camping** on North Beach, 1km past Tow Hill (about 30km east) in the provincial park. Watch for signs indicating you are no longer on Indian Reserve property.

Naikoon Park Motel (626-5187), on Tow Hill Rd. about 8km east of town. A difficult but not impossible place to reach for travelers thumbing it. New laid-back owners have spruced up the place with an extremely bright paint job and cheap hostel rooms. Sleep on not-particularly-comfy-lookin' foam mats for $17. Traditional singles $40. Kitchen units for 2-3 are $55. Beach is right across the road.

Copper Beech House, 1590 Delkatla Rd. (626-5441), at Collison. A B&B that looks more like an eclectic private museum. Sumptuous rooms and a diverse collection of artifacts offer comfort and endless fascination. Owner David Phillips knows a lot about a lot of things, and is more than willing to share. Dig deep in your wallet and find a way to come here. Singles $50, doubles $75. Longer-term visitors can arrange to exchange 4hr. a day of work for free room and board.

Harbourview Lodging, 1618 Delkatla Rd. (626-5109 or 800-661-3314), just north of Collison. Gracious owner oversees a comfy B&B right on the harbor. Everything in the clashing interior is in good shape. Downstairs singles have TVs, and share a bath and dry sauna. Two big upstairs rooms, each with living room, kitchen, free laundry facilities, and private deck. Fresh muffins in the morning. Singles $40. Doubles $45. Call for reservations in summer.

Masset-Haida Lions RV Site and Campground (626-3788) on Tow Hill Rd., next to the wildlife sanctuary. Unexceptional but functional. On-site office open 7pm-10pm. 22 gravelly sites, toilets, pay showers. Sites $8, with electricity $10.

Agate Beach Campground, 26km east of town in Naikoon Provincial Park, at the base of Tow Hill. Gorgeous if you can get there. 32 beachfront sites with an area reserved for tenters. Picnic shelter, firewood, water, flush toilets. Free clamming. Sites May-Sept. $9.50 for party up to 4; winter free. For more information call Park Headquarters (557-4390).

FOOD

Free and potentially toxic razor clams on Agate and North Beach! Call the red-tide hotline (666-3169) before you start gathering the ingredients for what could be a vomit-inducing cup of chowder. Stop by the **Department of Fisheries and Oceans** on Christie St. to pick up a free permit and tips on how to harvest your favorite bivalve. Lemons and other seafood garnishes sold at **Delmos Co-op** on Main St., south of Collison Ave. (626-3933, open Mon.-Sat. 10am-6pm).

The Sanctuary Café, (626-5140) sits on the beach around the corner from the pier at the east end of Collison Ave. A literally and figuratively colorful menu includes such options as Indian *samosas* ($8), homemade chips and salsa ($4), and chocolate espresso muffins ($2). Even if you don't come for a meal, at least drop by for a huge glass of herbal iced tea ($1.50) and some people-watching.

Café Gallery, 2062 Collision (626-3672). Lots of private dining spaces in a restaurant hung with local artists' work. A good way to escape the weary, dreary streets of Masset. The owners happily *sprechen Deutsch* with homesick Germans. Chicken burger with ham and cheese $8.95. Open Mon.-Sat. 8:30am-9pm.

Pearls, Main St. south of Collison (626-3223). The local choice for Chinese food. Chicken *chow mein* ($8), shrimp fried rice ($9). Open Mon.-Sat. 11:30am-9pm.

SIGHTS AND ACTIVITIES

The area's premier attraction is **Tow Hill,** an incredible outcrop of volcanic basalt columns that rises out of nowhere at the far end of Agate Beach, about 34km east of town. An easy boardwalk trail leads up the back of the hill to a fabulous overlook. You can see miles of virgin beach, and on a clear day, the southern reaches of Alaska. Sunsets are gorgeous. Footpaths lead away from the observation deck (about ½hr.) toward even more breathtaking vistas and a view of the rocky shoreline over 100m below. On the way back down, take a detour to the **Blow Hole,** a small cave that erupts with 10-15ft.-high sprays of water when the tide comes in. Over the centuries, innumerable pools and mini-canyons have been carved out of the rocky cliffs. It's a good idea to coordinate your visit with mid-tide, when the hole is active.

Two other excellent hikes depart from the Tow Hill Viewpoint parking lot: a four-hour beach walk to **Rose Spit** at the northeast corner of the island and a 3½-hour hike on the **Cape Fife** trail, which provides access to the East Coast Beach and the multiday backpacking route of Tlell (see **Tlell and Port Clements,** p. 250). Across the Hiellen River, **North Beach** is the site of the Haida creation myth, where Raven discovered a giant clam full of tiny men.

Closer to town, red-breasted sapsuckers, orange-crowned warblers, glaucous-winged gulls, great blue herons, and binocular-toting tourists converge on the **Delkatla Wildlife Sanctuary,** off Tow Hill Rd. in Masset. The best paths for observing the 113 airborne species begin at the junction of Trumpeter Dr. and Cemetery Rd. Continue on Cemetery Rd. past the sanctuary to reach **Oceanview Cemetery,** a remarkably lively place set in a lush green forest right on the beach.

With over 600 residents, **Old Massett,** 2km west of town, is the largest Haida village on the Charlottes. Unfortunately, outside of a few modern totem poles, there's not much to look at. Hold out for the **Haida Gawaii Museum** in **Skidegate** (see p. 248). You can apply for permits to visit abandoned Haida villages on Graham Island at the **Masset Band Council Office** (626-3337), in the large cedar-and-glass building at the east end of town (open Mon.-Fri. 8:30am-noon and 1-4:30pm).

■ Gwaii Haanas/South Moresby National Park Reserve

Arguably the most tranquil region of Canada's Western Coast, Gwaii Haanas was born of controversy. The territory was provincially-owned Crown Land until the late 1980s, and was disturbed by humans only through sporadic logging and occasional visits to a few deserted Haida villages. In the mid-80s, a dispute over logging on one of the area's islands embroiled the timber industry, the Haida nation, environmentalists, and the government of British Columbia. The federal government interceded in 1988, purchasing the southern third of the Queen Charlotte Islands and declaring the region a Park Reserve. The Canadian Parks Ministry administers and patrols the islands, while Haida representatives, known as **watchmen,** inhabit key locations, guide visitors, and collect fees for visits to Haida sites.

A journey into Gwaii Haanas begins with registration at the **Parks Canada** offices in Sandspit (at the airport) and Queen Charlotte City, downtown on 2nd Ave. (559-8818) or with the **Haida Gwaii Watchmen** at Second Beach, 1km north of Skidegate Landing (559-8225). Write to: Superintendent, Gwaii Haanas National Park Reserve, Box 37, Queen Charlotte, B.C. V0T 1S0; or to Haida Gwaii Watchmen, P.O. Box 609, Skidegate, Haida Gwaii V0T 1S0. Be sure to ask about appropriate camping locations. The Haida forbid camping in their traditional sites, and require a $25 fee (good for a full year) for day visits.

Entry into the park reserve usually starts at **Camp Moresby,** near Gray Bay (see **Sandspit,** p. 248). Check with **TimberWest** (637-5436) in Sandspit on Beach Rd. before traveling these sometimes hazardous logging roads. Two companies dominate the market for kayak rentals and charter trips into the Park Reserve. **Moresby Explor-**

ers (637-2215 or 800-806-7633), run by the energetic and competent Doug Gould, offers $110 day trips, $140 overnight trips to Doug's floating cabin off Juan Perez Sound, and $250 week-long kayak rentals which include transportation to the cabin and back. While the charters are fun and hit many of the high points, kayak rental is a more affordable option for experienced kayakers. If you're short on cash, give Doug a call and see what he's got planned—prices can be flexible if you are. Doug's business sits on Beach Rd. in Sandspit, just south of Copper Bay Rd. **Queen Charlotte Adventures** (559-8990 or 1-800-668-4288) run by Mary Kellie and Barb Rowsell, sits outside Queen Charlotte City on the road to Skidegate, and offers sea kayak rentals ($60 per day, $310 per week), marine transport ($120 from Queen Charlotte to Juan Perez Sound), and guided kayak, powerboat, and sailboat tours. Keep in mind that it may take several days to reach places in the reserve by kayak.

Only a few thousand visitors each summer make the long ocean journey south from Moresby Camp (no roads penetrate the reserve). Those who do enjoy a region of remarkable beauty and diverse plant and animal life. Old-growth forest stands tall in **Hlk'Yaak** (Windy Bay). Chains of lakes and waterfalls span the breadth of southern Moresby Island. At **Gandla K'in** (Hotsprings Island), several seaside pools steam at a year-round 100°F (37°C). The **San Christoval Mountains** thrust up semi-alpine peaks, which bear snow well into summer. The waters of **Juan Perez Sound** teem with jellyfish and enormous orange and purple starfish.

The artifacts of several eras and cultures also rest in Gwaii Haanas. Deserted logging camps from the 1930s display Dr. Seuss-like, steam-driven logging devices, ancient, decaying trucks, and highways built entirely of wood. Clan totem poles slowly decay at **Skedans** and **Ninstints,** Haida villages deserted after epidemics of smallpox and tuberculosis in the late 19th century. These settlements are being permitted to "return to the land" in keeping with Haida tradition. In 1982, Ninstints was declared a UNESCO World Heritage Site.

ALASKA APPROACHES

■ Cassiar Highway (37)

A growing number of travelers prefer **Hwy. 37,** the **Cassiar Hwy.,** to the Alaska Hwy., which has become an institution among RV drivers. Any waitress or hotel owner along the highway's 733km will readily list its advantages over the Alaska Hwy.—less distance, better scenery, and fewer crowds. Built in 1972, the highway slices through extremes of charred forests, untouched wilderness, and logged wastelands, and passes scores of alpine lakes on its way from Hwy. 16 in British Columbia to the Alaska Hwy. in the Yukon. Three evenly spaced provincial parks offer scenic camping right off the highway, and the Cassiar's services, while sparse, are numerous enough that you'll be fine if you fill up your car and yourself when you have a chance. *North to Adventure,* available at most BC infocenters (free), offers a partial list of facilities and campgrounds on the route. Since the Cassiar has less traffic, hitchhiking is less popular than on the Alaska Highway.

JCT. HWY. 16 TO MEZIADIN JCT.

Just north of the junction of Hwy. 37 and Hwy. 16 stand the totem poles of **Gitwengak,** which relate the history of the Native fort that stood on nearby **Battle Hill** until 1800. Four km farther, the **Kitwanga Loop Road** leads through Kitwanga and to the National Historic Park where Battle Hill is located. The hill served as a stronghold and base for the mighty warrior **Nekt.** It was once equipped with an extensive tunnel system and spiked logs that would roll down on intruders; fortunately for unarmed travelers, these have since given way to stairs and interpretive panels.

The totem poles of **Kitwancool,** or "place of reduced number," lie another 17km to the north. The village was originally called **Gitenyow,** "the place of many people"; after extended warfare, however, the indigenous peoples, sticklers for accurate nomenclature, changed its name.

Meziadin Lake Provincial Park (meh-zee-AD-in) lies 155km north of the 16/37 junction, with free firewood and fishing on Meziadin Lake (sites $9.50; water and pit toilets). Grab gas and shoot the bull with truckers at **Meziadin Junction. Whitehorse,** YT lies 953km to the north. Sixty-two km west, along Hwy. 37A, are **Stewart,** BC and **Hyder,** AK. The road to Stewart and Hyder offers stunning views of gaping canyons and immense glaciers.

■ Stewart and Hyder

The Alaska ferry *Aurora* heads south weekly from Ketchikan to the natural Portland Canal and threads its way north through the turquoise waters of this scenic fjord to the twin towns of Stewart, BC, and Hyder, AK. The towns lie within 1½ mi. of each other at the terminus of the fjord and the end of Rte. 37A, a well paved highway that cuts through magnificent canyons and makes the area an excellent side trip for Cassiar travelers. With the mining and timber industries facing an uncertain future, the tiny towns are teaming up to recruit tourists, armed with attractions like the world's fourth-largest glacier and a prime bear-viewing location. Most events in this little international community (including the ferry arrival) happen in Stewart. With about 900 people, Stewart is 10 times the size of Hyder. Hyderites deal in Canadian currency (except at the post office), use the British Columbia area code, and send their children to school in Stewart. From July 1-4, the two communities erupt in a kinship extravaganza. The only thing separating them for these precious few days is the Canadians' irritating tendency to call infocenters "infocentres." Ultimately, this practice is pretentious, impractical, and not very North American-sounding.

Practical Information and Sights A left turn from the ferry terminal takes you to Hyder; a right turn, to Stewart. Hyder's **information center** displays the *Hyder Weekly Miner* from 1919-1934 on microfiche for free (open Thurs.-Tues. 10am-2pm). The major tourist activity in Hyder is to sidle up to the bar in the historic **Glacier Inn** and ask to be "Hyderized." About $30,000 in signed bills line the walls of this bar, where early miners would tack up cash as insurance against ever returning to town too broke to buy a drink. In Stewart, the recently constructed **information center** (636-9224) is open daily from 9am to 7pm. A recently renovated **museum** ($2, under 12 free) offers, among other things, an exhibit on the Great Avalanche of '65 and a disturbing collection of photos documenting the 1981 filming of *The Thing,* starring Kurt Russell. **Fish Creek,** 5 mi. from Hyder, is an excellent place to view bears, if you don't mind the company of other tourists. Each year during the salmon spawning season (late July), bears emerge from the bushes *en masse* to feed on bloated, dying salmon and tourists set up camp on the riverbank, as though it were a Dead show, with lawn chairs and a battery of recording devices. Travelers hoping to watch the bears in a more peaceful setting should come early in the morning for an unimpeded view.

Salmon Glacier, 18 mi. from Hyder on the road past Fish Creek, is the fourth largest glacier in the world, an unimaginably vast and surprisingly accessible ice sheet. Starting at Mile 19, the road creeps along a ridge almost directly above the glacier for several miles, providing spectacular views. The rocks above the road make for good hiking, and at night the sun sets behind the immense glacier, creating a golden photo-op. The road is poor enough that you might not want to drive it; ask at the visitors center about taking a tour. **Bear Glacier,** 30 mi. east of Stewart in British Columbia, sits in plain view of Hwy. 37A and is also a noteworthy stop. Ask the rangers at the **Forest Service** (636-2367; open *Alaska time* Fri.-Sun. 9-10am and 1-2pm, Mon. 9am-noon and 1-2pm) about trails in the area. Look into the spectacular **Titan Trail,** a 7-

mi., one-way hike up from the valley. It becomes rocky and difficult after 5 mi. and gains over 4000 ft. of elevation.

Hyder's municipal building burned down on July 3, 1995, and until a new one is built, the post office, library, and Forest Service are in temporary locations. The **Hyder post office** (636-2662) accepts only US currency (open *Pacific time* Mon.-Fri. 9am-1pm and 2-5pm, Sat. 10:30am-12:30pm) and is currently in a trailer near the start of Fish Creek Rd. **Stewart's post office** is at Brightwell St. and 5th Ave. (open *Pacific time* Mon.-Fri. 9:30am-6:30pm, Sat. 9:30am-1:30pm). The **police** (636-2233) are posted at 8th Ave. and Conway St. in Stewart. The **area code** is 604.

Many visitors never stay overnight in Hyder because if they're traveling by **ferry**, spending one night means spending a week. The *Aurora's* weekly roundtrip from Ketchikan to Stewart/Hyder ($40) includes a three-hour layover that gives pedestrians just enough time to see both towns. Inquire at the Cornell Travel Agency in Stewart about **bus service** east to Terrace, BC.

Camping, Accommodations, and Food Both towns have campgrounds. Stewart's **Lion's Campground** (636-2537) is orderly and quiet, with tent sites ($10 for 2 people, $3 per additional person), sites with electricity ($15), and incredibly clean showers ($1). Hyder's **Camp Runamuck** borders a horse pasture and is within earshot of the Glacier Inn saloon (tent sites $8; "sleeping rooms" $28 with shared bath). The **Sealaska Inn** (636-2486) offers cheap rates (singles or doubles $48). If you can handle the eye strain, the **King Edward Hotel** (636-2244) on 5th Ave. and Columbia in Stewart provides reasonably priced hotel accommodations. Rooms are decorated with at least four different fabric patterns, each chosen carefully to clash with the others. Rooms start at $55, double with kitchenette $65.

Cut-Rate Foods (636-2377) on 5th Ave. in Stewart fulfills its calling with scores of cheap no-name products (open Mon.-Sat. 9am-8pm, Sun. 9am-6pm). The **Bitter Creek Café** (636-2166), also on 5th Ave., allows you to admire historic pictures while they flip you three hotcakes ($4; open daily 8am-9pm). In Hyder, the **Border Café** has a "naked burger" with fries for $3.50, and a "Hamburger Steak" with hash browns, veggies, tossed salad, or bread for $8. They also do breakfast all day (open Tues. and Thurs.-Fri. 8:30am-7pm, Wed. 8:30am-6pm, Sat. 8:30am-4pm).

CASSIAR HIGHWAY (37): MEZIADIN JCT. TO JCT. ALASKA HWY.

Ninety-five km north of Meziadin Junction is **Bell II Crossing,** an oasis of civilization in the Cassiar wilderness. Bell II houses a **restaurant** (638-9020; open daily 7am-8pm) and a **gas station** (open daily 6am-11pm). Minor car and tire repair is available. The food is standard highway fare, and RV parking is available ($9.50).

After about 65km, the immense Iskut burn area becomes interspersed with new growth—mostly fireweed and what is rumored by locals to be the largest huckleberry patch in British Columbia. Fifty-three km beyond the patch is **Kinaskan Lake Provincial Park** (847-7320), where campsites are $9.50. The campground includes a boat launch into the spectacular lake, where rainbow, cutthroat, and lake trout thrive. At the far end of the lake is the head of a 24km hiking trail to Mowdade Lake in **Mount Edziza Provincial Park** (see below). Twenty-six km north on the Cassiar is the **Ealue Lake** turnoff, which leads to a trailhead pointing deep into the virgin backcountry of the **Spatsizi Wilderness Plateau** (see below).

Even the most discriminating hostel connoisseurs will heartily approve of the **Red Goat Lodge** (234-3261), just south of **Iskut** (354km north of Meziadin Junction). The **hostel (HI-C)** in the basement of this regal lodge boasts a full kitchen, spacious common room, and wood stove ($12, non-members $15). At the equally impressive **B&B,** singles are $65, doubles $85; tent sites are $10. Shower and laundry facilities are available (open May 20-Sept. 5). **Canoe** rental starts at $10 for an evening on **Eddontenajon Lake** (ed-un-TEN-a-jon). Rentals for trips on the Stikine and Spatsizi Rivers start at $30 per day.

At the small Native village of **Iskut,** fill the tank and grab some groceries at the **Co-op** (234-3241), which doubles as the **post office** (open Mon., Wed., and Fri. 9am-4pm, Tues. 1-4pm; **postal code** V0J 1K0). If you and your vehicle can stick it out a little longer, only 84km separate you from Dease Lake.

Dease Lake

In 1874, during the peak of the Cassiar gold rush, William Moore cut a trail connecting Telegraph Creek on the Stikine River with Dease Lake, a remote interior trading post. Dease Lake has grown into a simple roadside community and a popular base for exploring the vast and rugged **Mount Edziza** or **Spatsizi Wildernesses** nearby.

The **Dease Lake Tourist Information Office** is in the Northern Lights College (771-5500; open Mon.-Fri. 8:30am-noon and 1-5:30pm). The **Stikine Health Center,** at the north end of town, accepts cash or check for medicine (walk-in Mon.-Fri. 8:30am-noon and 1-4:30pm). The **doctor** can be reached at 771-3171. For information on local trails or campsites, **British Columbia Parks** (771-4591) and the **Forest Service** (771-4211) share the building next door to the tourist office. The **Shell station** (771-5600) has showers ($4) and a laundromat (wash $2, 10-min. dry 25¢; open daily 7am-11pm). Reach the **police** at 771-4111. The **post office** is in the Shell station (771-5600; open Mon.-Fri. 8:30am-5:30pm). The **postal code** is V0C 1L0.

The closest free, forest service campsite to town is scenic **Allen Lake.** Luckily for tipsy tenters, the lake is a short stumble from the Tanzilla Bar (from Boulder St., go left on 1st Ave. and follow to its end; no water, pit toilets). Be sure not to drive your car to the campground's parking lot. The extremely steep gravel driveway is likely to hold your car hostage until a tow truck can winch it out. For a complete listing of campgrounds, get a Forest Service map at the tourist information center or from the Forest Service (see above). Dease Lake's only motel, the **Northway Motor Inn** (771-5341), offers clean and simple rooms (singles $64, double occupancy $68, double beds $76). There are two year-round restaurants in Dease Lake. **Northway Country Kitchen** (771-4114), known locally as "the restaurant," offers decent food in a clean, spacious setting. Tickle your palate with "pirogies & smokies," cheese-filled potato dumplings accompanied by four sizable sausages ($9.25; open daily 6:30am-10pm). The other place is called **The Other Place** (771-3667), and many locals say it has bigger portions and lower prices than "the restaurant." A burly clubhouse sandwich and fries goes for $7.50 (open daily 7am-10pm). Groceries and gas are available at the **Goodacres Store** (open Mon.-Sat. 7am-9pm, Sun. 10am-9pm).

Visitors to Dease Lake have four options: drive the remaining 237km to the Alaska Hwy. junction, explore the Spatsizi Wilderness Plateau, hike through the volcanic wasteland called Mount Edziza Provincial Park, or follow the **Telegraph Creek Road,** an excellent scenic sidetrip for the intrepid who tire of highway driving. The Dease Lake Tourist Office requires all travelers planning to go into the wilderness to fill out a trip itinerary. The back copy of the itinerary goes to the police, who will be dispatched to retrieve lost or injured travelers.

Spatsizi Plateau Wilderness Park and Mount Edziza Provincial Park

Long a major hunting ground for the Tahltan people, **Spatsizi Wilderness Plateau** became a provincial park and wildlife reserve in 1975. Supporting one of the largest populations of **Woodland Caribou** in British Columbia, Spatsizi is home to an extensive range of wildlife species. **Ealue Lake Road,** near the **Tatogga Lake Junction,** 25km north of Kinaskan Lake Provincial Park, offers the only vehicle access to trucks leading into Spatsizi Wilderness Plateau. To reach the trailheads, follow the so-called road for 22km until it joins with the BC Rail grade, a tertiary road of variable quality described by BC Parks as "rough, but driveable for most vehicles." Because of its isolation, British Columbia Parks strongly recommends that only experienced hikers explore Spatsizi.

The stunning volcanic corners and brilliantly colored volcanic rock of **Mount Edziza Provincial Park** are sights to behold, but only for the most experienced hikers. Weather in both parks is highly variable. In the summer, daytime temperatures may climb as high as 30°C and then plummet to below freezing at night; snow flurries are not uncommon in mid-summer. As with Spatsizi Plateau Wilderness Park, there is no vehicle access. Most people visit Mt. Edziza by plane, bypassing the grueling week-long trek into the park along the **Klastine River,** or find a boat from **Kinaskan Lake Provincial Park** to do the **Mowdade Trail.** For a donation, a comprehensive **trail guide** is available at the Stikine Riversong (see below). All hikers, regardless of previous wilderness experience, should make their itineraries and whereabouts known to someone who loves them before venturing into the park. Even though they may not love you, telling rangers of your plans is also a good idea. For more information, contact **British Columbia Parks Area Supervisor,** Box 118, Dease Lake, BC V0C 1L0 (604-771-4591).

Telegraph Creek

Lying 119km from Dease Lake on Telegraph Creek Rd., Telegraph Creek is the only remaining settlement along the Stikine River. As the highest navigable point on the Stikine, Telegraph Creek was an important rendezvous point for the coastal Tlingit and interior Tahltan people. While the Tlingit traded with the Russians in the late 18th century, the Tahltans eluded direct contact with Europeans until 1838, when Robert Campbell of the British Hudson's Bay Company arrived.

Today, Telegraph Creek has 300 residents, most of them Tahltan. The biggest attraction for the thrill-seeking tourist is 112km Telegraph Creek Road. The gravel road is well maintained, and offers magnificent views of the Grand Canyon of the Stikine. It is no place, however, to lug your clumsy RV or give your failed brake system a second chance. The second half of the road is worth the boredom of the first and features 20% grades and hairpin turns as the road clings perilously close to the steep obsidian outbanks of the Taya, Tahltan, and Stikine River canyons. Travelers should allow three hours to drive each way. The rest stop, 88km from Telegraph Creek, offers a gorgeous view of the Canyon and a chance to speak words of encouragement to your beleaguered transmission.

The "modern" village of Telegraph Creek revolves around the historic **Stikine Riversong** (235-3196). Originally the Hudson Bay Company building in the neighboring town of **Glenora,** 12 mi. from Dease Lake, the Riversong was disassembled in 1902 and moved to Telegraph Creek. In 1903, it was reassembled and reopened. Today, the jack-of-all-trades Riversong acts as Telegraph Creek's sole hotel, general store, and café. The staff is extremely helpful and can answer almost any question about the history of the area. Wash off 119km of road dust with a shower ($4; open daily 11am-7pm; winter closed Sun.). Hotel rooms at the Riversong are clean, with cedar finishing and a common kitchen (singles $46, doubles $50). The hotel also runs popular river charters on the Stikine which cost $100 but can take up to six people. Ask around to form a group.

There are no doctors in Telegraph Creek. There is, however, a **health clinic** with two nurses on duty (235-3211; follow signs for Glenora). The police can be reached at 235-3111. For **tire repair,** contact Henry Vance (235-3300). For light mechanical repair, ask around for Bob Jornsen.

Dease Lake To Jct. Alaska Hwy.

This stretch of highway follows the old Cassiar Gold Route, and tailings and still-used dredges can be seen along its length. Eighty-five km north of Dease Lake is **Moose Meadow Resort,** a roomy lakeside campground with access to canoe routes. Campsites are $11 per night, with two free showers. Lakeside log cabins for two are $30. Canoe rentals on the lake are $5 per hour with a two hour minimum, $25 per day. For campers willing to plug another 67km, **Boya Lake Provincial Park** (847-7320) is 152km north of Dease Lake, 2km east of the Cassiar Hwy. Campsites ($9.50) are on a turquoise lake with a boat launch and swimming dock. Shallow Boya Lake is warm by northcountry standards, but the water is still "refreshing."

At the end of this 733km odyssey, dirty, hungry, and weary travelers can grab showers, souvenirs, grub, groceries, and gas at the **PetroCan Station** (536-2794) at the junction of the Cassiar Hwy. and the Alaska Hwy. The PetroCan doubles daily as the office for the RV park and motel next door ($10, $15 with full hookup, singles and doubles $30). **Showers** are $1 with accommodations, $3 otherwise. They also operate a 24hr. **laundromat** (wash $1.25, 14-min. dry 25¢). Travelers can splurge on home cooking at the **Junction 37 Café** (536-2795) next door to the **PetroCan** (open daily May-Oct. 7am-10pm). **Whitehorse** lies another 435km west.

▓ Alaska Highway

Built during World War II, the Alaska Highway maps out an astonishing 2647km route between Dawson Creek, BC, and Fairbanks, AK. After the Japanese attack on Pearl Harbor in December 1941, worried War Department officials planned an overland route, out of range of carrier-based aircraft, to supply U.S. Army bases in Alaska. The U.S. Army Corps of Engineers completed the daunting task in just 34 weeks; the one-lane dirt trail curved around swamps and hills (landfill would come later). In recent years, the U.S. Army has been replaced by an annual army of over 250,000 tourists, the vast majority of them RV-borne senior citizens from the U.S. Travelers making the trip in July, the busiest month, will face crowded campgrounds and nearly impassable RV caravans.

In general, there's a trade-off between the excitement you'll find on the Alaska Hwy. and the speed with which you will reach Alaska. If you're willing to take the time, there are countless hiking, fishing, and wildlife viewing opportunities off the highway. If your priority is to beat the quickest path to the Alaska border, however, you're best off taking an alternate route.

A good beginning to any history of the highway and surrounding area is the one-hour video "Alaska Highway: 1942-1992" shown at the Dawson Creek Tourist Infocentre (see below). Before setting out on your epic Northwestern journey, pick up a copy of the free pamphlet *Help Along the Way* at a visitors bureau, or contact the Department of Health and Social Services, P.O. Box 110601, Juneau, AK 99811-0601 (907-465-3030); the pamphlet includes an exhaustive listing of emergency medical services and emergency phone numbers throughout Alaska, the Yukon, and British Columbia, plus tips on preparation and driving. Mileposts along the highway were put up in the 1940s and are still used as mailing addresses and reference points, although the highway has been reconstructed and rerouted so many times that they no longer reflect mileage accurately. Kilometer posts were installed in the mid-1970s and recalibrated in 1990; the distances they report are more accurate.

▓ Dawson Creek

Dawson Creek, BC (not to be confused with Dawson City, YT) is 590km northwest of Edmonton and is the Alaska Hwy.'s official starting point **(Mile 0.)** First settled in the 1890s, the small town of 10,000 has calmed down considerably since the heyday of construction. Sixty cases of dynamite exploded close to downtown on February 13, 1943, leveling the entire business district except the COOP building, which still provides a home to Bing's Furniture downtown. You can see the building across the street from the Mile 0 post.

Before the construction of the Alaska Hwy. (better known as the Alcan), Dawson Creek was a small town of 400-500 people that provided support and transport from the northern terminus of the railroad line to the surrounding farmland. When construction of the highway began, workers took "public transportation" to the end of the railroad line and began building the road from there. That meant that construction began in Dawson Creek. Its railroad link was what branded Dawson Creek forever as the start of the Alaska Hwy.

There are two ways to reach Dawson Creek from the south. Drive northwest from Edmonton along Hwy. 43, through Whitecourt to Valleyview. Turn left on Hwy. 34 to **Grande Prairie,** Alberta. From there, continue northwest on **Hwy. 2** to Dawson

Creek, for a total journey of 590km. Or start in Prince George and drive 402km north on the **Cariboo Hwy.** (Hwy. 97). Either drive takes most of a day.

Practical Information Before you head out on the Alcan, stop at the **Tourist Infocentre,** 900 Alaska Ave. (782-9595), in the old train station just off Hwy. 97. Also home to a small museum of the town and highway's history (open daily May 15-Sept. 5 8am-7pm, off season Tues.-Sat. 10am-noon and 1-4pm). **Greyhound,** 1201 Alaska Ave. (782-3131 or 800-661-8747), can bus you to Whitehorse, YT (July-Aug. 1 per day except Sun., winter 3 per week; $163), Prince George (2 per day, $48), and Edmonton, AB (2 per day, $66). The **King Koin Laundromat,** 1220 103rd Ave. (782-2395), has showers for $2.75 (no time limit!) and laundry (wash $2, 4-min. dry 25¢. Open daily 8am-9pm). The nearest **hospital** is Dawson Creek and District Hospital, located at 11100 13th St. (782-8501). In an **emergency,** call for an **ambulance** (782-2211) or contact the **police** (782-5211) at Alaska Ave. and 102nd Ave. The **post office** (782-2322) sits at 104th Ave. and 10th St. The **postal code** is V1G 4J8.

Accommodations and Camping Travelers willing to trade amenities for bargain prices, good location, and unique style should head straight for the **Alaska Hotel** (782-2625), on 10th St., 1½ blocks from the infocenter, upstairs from the Alaska Cafe & Pub. For a $25 single or a $30 double, you can bed down in a comfortable room decorated with pictures of Marilyn and Elvis. Toilets and showers are shared and rooms have no TVs or phones. The **Voyageur Motor Inn,** 801 111th Ave. (782-1020), offers refrigerators, cable TV, and phones. Singles $30, doubles $35. Campers can head for **Alahart RV Park,** 1725 Alaska Ave. (782-4702), which has free showers, a dump station, and coin-operated laundry (sites $8, full hook-up $16). Tenters can avoid some of the lumbering RVs at **Mile 0 City Campground** (782-2590), 1km west of Mile 0 on the Alaska Hwy., which offers showers and laundry (sites $10, RVs $16).

Food If foraging on your bug-splattered windshield has failed to satisfy you, a great place for a meal in Dawson Creek is the **Alaska Café & Pub** (782-7040), "55 paces south of the Mile 0 Post" on 10th St., which serves excellent burgers and fries for $7. The pub offers live music (mostly country) on Tues.-Sat. nights and homesick travelers can croon away their sorrows at Mon. night karaoke (open daily 11am-11pm). Inside Pioneer Village (see **Sights,** below) the **Mile 1 Café** (782-1456) serves up frontier-style food. Their best deal is the $7 buffet, served from 11:30am-2pm, which includes three kinds of salad (open daily 11:30am-7:30pm). Health-conscious travelers sick of fast food and Cheeze-Its can check out the **Organic Farms Bakery,** 1425 97th Ave. (782-6533), a short drive west on the Alaska Hwy. from the infocenter. Breads are made from organically grown local grain and start at $1.35 for a loaf of whole wheat; croissants and pastries are also available (open Mon. and Wed.-Fri. 10am-5:30pm, Sat. 9:30am-4pm). For those thirsting for a bit of Americana, **Chevy's Diner,** 330 Alaska Ave. (782-CHEV/2438), will satisfy. ($5 burgers, $3 "real fruit" shakes. Open daily 6am-10pm.)

Sights Dawson Creek's most inspiring sights have less to do with the town than with the highway that begins in it: the **Mile 0 Cairn,** on the edge of the rotary next to the infocenter, marks the beginning of the highway, and the **Mile 0 Post,** a block toward downtown at 10th and 102nd, commemorates its construction. **Pioneer Village,** 1km west of Mile 0 on the Alaska Hwy., is an excellent re-creation of Dawson Creek life from the 20s to the 40s. Admission is free and the village includes a restored schoolhouse and general store (open daily May 28-Aug. 31 9am-8pm). Chronically stressed travelers can take a dip in Dawson Creek's **Centennial Swimming Pool,** at 10th and 105th (782-7946). The pool houses a spiraling slide which plunks you down in the pool's center. ($3 per session, students and seniors $2.25; call for public swim times.)

ALASKA HIGHWAY: DAWSON CREEK, BC TO WHITEHORSE, YT

Fort St. John is the perfect pit stop for a weary traveler. The **Travel Infocentre,** 9323 100th St. (785-6037), in the museum complex, will quickly make it clear that there's really nothing to do or see in town (open daily July to Labor Day 8am-8pm, off season Mon.-Fri. 8am-5pm, Sat. 11am-4pm). Outside the city limits, however, things pick up considerably. Seven km north of town lies **Charlie Lake,** offering fishing and water-skiing and two provincial parks right off the highway. In early August, gold panners from across the globe pan for prizes and fame at the **World Invitational Gold Panning Championships,** held at Peace River Park, 20km south of town. For those who must spend the night, the **Esta Villa Motel** (785-6777), off the highway on the south end of town, has fully equipped rooms. Singles for $36 and doubles for $41. Just down the road is the **Roost Motel** (785-2906), featuring singles for $40 and doubles for $46; kitchenettes and cable (but no phones) included. **Centennial RV Park** is right behind the infocenter and is jam-packed with services: showers, laundry, horse-shoe pits, and a playground. Unfortunately, Centennial has all the ambience of a parking lot (sites $11, with electricity and water $16; phone the infocenter for reservations). **Charlie Lake Provincial Park,** 14km north on Hwy. 97, is a great choice if you can do without a hook-up; $9.50 gets you a grassy, secluded site near a picnic area, with hiking trails going down to the lake. **Busters,** 9720 100th St. (785-0770), is one of Fort St. John's few affordable departures from fast food boredom. A double burger with fries goes for $6 and the weekday luncheon buffet, served from noon to 2pm, fills you for $8 (open Mon.-Fri. 11am-11pm, Sat. 4-11pm, Sun. 10am-10pm).

    Fort Nelson, 480 (of the highway's most unexciting) km north of Dawson Creek, is the highway's next pit stop on the way to Whitehorse. The **Infocentre** (774-6400) hides itself in the Recreation Center on the western edge of town and provides a small brochure revealing a general lack of excitement (open daily 9am-7pm). The **Fort Nelson Heritage Museum** (774-3536), however, is an exception. Across the highway from the infocenter, the museum features an impressive, if unsettling, collection of taxidermy of all the game species in the area, as well as doodads of interest from the era of highway construction. The museum also possesses an unlikely collection of beautiful **vintage cars.** (Open in summer daily 8:30am-7:30pm; $2.50, children $1.25.) Rest up at the **Mini-Price Inn,** 5036 51st Ave. W. (774-2136), hidden a block off the highway (singles $37, doubles $42). Campers should head for the **Westend Campground** (774-2340) across from the infocenter. Westend boasts hot showers (25¢ per 3 min.), a laundromat ($2 wash, $1 for 30-min. dry), a free car wash, free firewood, an impressive wildlife display, and mini-golf to boot. A round of put-put might seem a bit more enticing after a fearsome local warns you not to hike without a gun or face certain death at the paws of a killer bear (sites $13, full hookups $18).

    Highway scenery improves dramatically after Fort Nelson. Small hotels, plain but expensive, pock the remainder of the highway every 80 to 160km on the way to Carcross, Whitehorse, and the Alaska border. Campers' needs·are satisfied by the provincial parks that spring up along the road. About 150km west of Fort Nelson, **Stone Mountain Provincial Park** presents some of the highway's best wildlife-viewing opportunities. Herds of Dall sheep frequently claim the right-of-way on the highway; deer and moose are common as well. The **Stone Mountain Campground,** set beside Summit Lake, makes an excellent starting point for hiking in the park (sites $9.50). Just outside the park boundary, at **One Fifteen Creek,** campers will find a provincial campground with rocky sites for $7.

    Forty km farther along the road lies **Toad River,** a booming town of 60. You may notice that downtown is made up of only a family home and a restaurant. The **Toad River Café** (232-5401) is a worthwhile stop just to peek up at the more than 4516 hats hanging from the ceiling. Tasty burgers from $4.25. (Open daily 6am-10pm, winter 6am-7pm.)

About 50km past Toad River, **Muncho Lake Provincial Park** dazzles even the road-weariest of drivers. **Strawberry Flats Provincial Campground,** at the southeast corner of Muncho Lake, is a spectacular place to camp (sites $9.50, pit toilets, water). If your head grows heavy and your sight grows dim and you have to stop for the night, head for the **Highland Glen Lodge** (774-2909), at Mile 462, where you can sack out in a room (singles $50, doubles $56) or a campsite ($20 for tents or RVs). Highland Glen also offers nightly boat tours of Muncho Lake ($10).

After winding its way along the beautiful Lake, the highway reaches the **Liard River Hot Springs** near the 800km mark. The naturally hot pools are a great place to soothe your weary driver's butt and ease your frazzled, dazed mind (free). The park service manages **campsites** ($12) and a free day-use area here. Come early if you want to spend the night—the campground is often full by midday.

Near the BC-Yukon border, the road winds through vast areas of land scorched by forest fires; gray arboreal skeletons mix with new growth and stretch in all directions as far as the eye can see. At night, this area offers prime viewing of the *aurora borealis,* as there are no city lights to pollute the view (beginning in late August with peak viewing in the winter months).

The Alaska Highway winds across the BC-Yukon border several times before it passes through Whitehorse. Just after it crosses into the Yukon for the second time, the highway runs through the small town of **Watson Lake** and the famed **"Sign Post Forest"** at Mile 635. The "forest" was born in 1942 when a homesick Army engineer erected a sign indicating the mileage to his hometown of Danville, Illinois. Today, more than 17,000 travelers have followed suit and almost every type of sign seems to have found a home here; if you look hard enough, you'll probably find the sign of a hometown near yours. The **infocenter** is hidden in the forest (open daily 8am-8pm). While in the Yukon, tune in for **road information** at **96.1 FM.**

Mile 626 marks the Alcan's junction with the **Cassiar Hwy.** (Hwy. 37; see page 254) leading south to **Yellowhead Hwy. 16** (see p. p.239). At Mile 804, the small and largely native community of **Teslin** is best known as the home of the excellent **George Johnston Museum** (390-2550). Born in Alaska in 1889, George Johnston was a Tlingit who made a living running a trap line and a general store. More important, however, was Johnston's interest in photography. The backbone of the museum's collection, Johnston's stunning photographs capture Tlingit life in Teslin Lake from 1910 to 1940, providing valuable insight into Native culture. (Open May 10am-6pm, June-Labor Day 8:30am-7pm; $2.50, seniors and students $2, children $1.)

YUKON TERRITORY

■ Whitehorse

Named for the once-perilous **Whitehorse Rapids,** whose crashing whitecaps were said to resemble a galloping herd of white mares before being tamed by a dam, Whitehorse marks the highest navigable point on the Yukon River and the starting point for the four-month trip along the length of the Yukon to Northeastern Alaska. The bone-weary Cheechako ("newcomer") of the 1898 Gold Rush often stopped here to wring themselves out after successfully navigating the rapids, and then continued on across Lake Laberge and down the Yukon along with the floating armada of expectant gold seekers headed for Dawson City and the Klondike.

Yukon's capital since 1953, Whitehorse has a cosmopolitan outlook though it remains aware and proud of its century-old Klondike history. In the warmer months, Whitehorse is a good base for exploring the vast surrounding wilderness.

PRACTICAL INFORMATION AND ORIENTATION

Visitors Information: Whitehorse Visitor Reception Centre (667-7545), is located in the new Tourism and Business Center at 100 Hansen St. Open Mon.-Sat. 8am-6pm, Sun. 10am-6pm. You can also get information by writing to **Tourism Yukon,** P.O. Box 2703, Whitehorse, YT Y1A 2C6.

Flights: Canadian Airlines (668-4466, for reservations 668-3535), **NWT Air** (800-661-0789), and **Royal Air** (800-663-9757). All airlines offer competitive prices. To: Calgary, AB (4 per day, $568); Edmonton, AB (4 per day, $568); and Vancouver, BC (5 per day, $466). Ask about youth standby fares (ages 12-24).

Buses: Greyhound, 2191 2nd Ave. (667-2223). To: Vancouver, BC ($292); Edmonton, AB ($228); and Dawson Creek, BC ($164). Prices are cheaper with 7-day advance purchase. Buses late June-Sept. Mon.-Sat.; winter Tues., Thurs., and Sat.; *no* Greyhound service to Alaska. Desk open Mon.-Fri. 8am-5:30pm, Sat. 10am-1pm, Sun. 4-8am. **Alaskon Express** (tickets at the Westmark Hotel, 668-3225), at 2nd Ave. and Wood St. Buses late May to mid-Sept. to: Anchorage (3 per week, US$190), Haines (3 per week, US$85), Fairbanks (3 per week, US$165), and Skagway (daily, US$54). **Norline** (668-3355), in the Greyhound depot. To Dawson City (3 per week, 2 per week in winter, $73).

Local Transportation: Whitehorse Transit (668-8381 for info line, Mon.-Fri. 8am-4pm). Limited service downtown and to surrounding areas. Buses arrive and depart downtown next to Canadian Tires on the northern edge of town. Runs Mon.-Thurs. 6:15am-7:15pm, Fri. 6:15am-10pm, Sat. 8am-7pm; $1.25, seniors 60¢, children and students $1.

Taxi: Yellow Cab, 668-4811. 24hr.

Car Rental: Norcan Leasing, Ltd. (668-2137 or 800-661-0445; 800-764-1234 from Alaska), on the Alaska Hwy. at Mile 917.4. Cars from $30 per day. 100km free; 15¢ per additional km. Must be 21 with credit card or $250 cash deposit.

Bike Rental: Element Sports, 4198 4th Ave. (393-3993). Mountain bikes $20 per day, $15 per ½ day, $5 per hr. Credit card required. Open Mon.-Sat. 9am-6pm.

Library: 2071 2nd Ave. (667-5239). Open Mon.-Fri. 10am-9pm, Sat. 10am-6pm, Sun. 1-9pm.

Laundromat: Norgetown, 4213 4th Ave. (667-6113), next to McDonald's at Ray St. Wash $1.90; dry 50¢ per 7½ min. Open daily 8am-9pm.

Public Showers: At the **Whitehorse Swimming Pool,** 4051 4th Ave. (668-7665) next to the High Country Inn. $5, $4 seniors, students, and children for pool and shower use. Call for swim times.

Pharmacy: Shoppers Drug Mart, 311 Main St. (667-2485). Open Mon.-Sat. 9am-9pm, Sun. 10am-9pm.

Hospital: (667-8700), on the east side of the Yukon River on Hospital Rd., just off Wickstrom Rd.

Emergency: 911. **Police:** 4th and Elliot.

Post Office: No main office. **General services** is 211 Main St. (668-5847). Open Mon.-Fri. 8am-6pm, Sat. 9am-5pm. **General delivery** is at 3rd and Wood, in the Yukon News Bldg. Open Mon.-Sat. 7am-7pm. **General Delivery Postal Code** for last names beginning with the letters A-L is Y1A 3S7; for M-Z it's Y1A 3S8.

Area Code: 403.

To reach Whitehorse by car, take the downtown exit off the Alaska Hwy. Once there, park the car. Downtown is compact. The airport is off the Alaska Hwy., just west of downtown, and the bus station is on the northeastern edge of town, a short walk from downtown.

ACCOMMODATIONS AND CAMPING

Call the **Northern Network of Bed and Breakfasts** (993-5649), in Dawson City, to reserve a room in a Klondike household. Singles start at $50 and doubles at $60. Camping in Whitehorse is limited; there is only one RV campground and one tenting park near the downtown area. Cash-strapped tenters who don't mind a 15-minute drive might head for the shores of Long Lake, where many a young wanderer has

camped for free. (Though illegal, camping in non-designated areas is reportedly toler-
ated for one night. If, however, the police decide not to tolerate you—which is
entirely within their rights—the fine is $500 and they may confiscate your camping
equipment.) To get there, cross the bridge off 2nd Ave. in the southeast corner of
town, turn left on Hospital Rd., turn left on Wickstrom Rd., and follow the winding
road until it ends at the lake.

High Country Inn (HI-C), 4051 4th Ave. (667-4471). Small, plain, clean. Shared
doubles are $25 per person, private singles start at $45, private quads for $115.
Roadhouse Inn, 2163 2nd Ave. (667-2594), adjacent to the Roadhouse Saloon.
Shared rooms at $19 per person, plus a $5 refundable deposit for sheets and towels. Private rooms $50, plus $5 for each additional person.
Robert Service Campground (668-3721), 1km from town on South Access Rd. on
the Yukon River. A convenient stop for tenting folk, but no RV sites. Home to many
of the college students who summer in Whitehorse, Robert Service has free firewood and pits, a playground, drinking water, toilets, metered showers, and a
knack for rhyming verse. Open late May to early Sept. 48 sites, $10.50.
High-Country RV Park (667-7445), at the intersection of the Alaska Hwy. and
South Access Rd., perched above town next to Yukon Gardens. Free showers, 2
coin-operated laundromats, mini-golf. Rest your rig for $18-21 for 2 people, $3
each additional person; tents $12.

FOOD

Get groceries at **Extra Foods** (667-6251), in the Quanlin Mall at 4th and Ogilvie (open
Mon.-Wed. 8:30am-7pm, Thurs.-Fri. 8:30am-9pm, Sat. 8:30am-6pm, Sun. 10am-6pm).

No Pop Sandwich Shop, 312 Steele (668-3227), at 4th Ave. This artsy alcove is popular with Whitehorse's small suit-and-tie crowd. Enjoy a Beltch (BLT and cheese,
$4.50) or a veggie sandwich ($4.25). A strictly fruit juice and milk joint. Open
Mon.-Thurs. 7:30am-8:30pm, Fri. 7:30am-9:30pm, Sat.-Sun. 10am-8:30pm.
Klondike Rib and Salmon Barbeque, 2116 2nd Ave. (667-7554). Lets you sample
northern salmon without breaking the bank. BBQ salmon salad on rye comes with
coleslaw for $5.95, although prices shoot up for other seafood selections. Hun-
dred-yr.-old Klondike era building's ambience is a welcome relief from the tedium
of hotel lounges and the Golden Arches. Open daily 6am-10pm.
Talisman Café, 2112 2nd Ave. (667-2736), next to Klondike Rib and Salmon Barbeque. Frequented by tourists and locals who sit and sip coffee for hours on end.
Burgers (from $5 with fries) and soup or pasta (from $9) are best bets for the poor
and hungry. Open daily 6am-10pm.
The Pasta Palace, 215 Main St. (667-6888). A full breakfast for $4.50, lunch entrees
for $5, and dinner entrees start at $9. Open Mon.-Fri. 10am-10pm, Sat. 11am-10pm,
Sun. 4-10pm.

SIGHTS AND ACTIVITIES

Considering the small size of the city, the Whitehorse welcoming committee has
assembled an astonishing array of scheduled tours and visitor activities. This can be
deceptive—most people do not come to Whitehorse because it is a destination unto
itself. It is the gateway to a stunning wilderness, and the swarms of students and travelers you see are just passing through on their way out. Beginning in late May, the
Yukon Historical and Museum Association, 3126 3rd Ave. (667-4704), sponsors
Heritage Walking Tours. The 45-minute tours leave from Donnenworth House, in
Lepage Park next to the infocenter (Mon.-Sat. 9am-4pm, every hr.; $2). The **Yukon
Conservation Society,** 302 Hawkins St. (668-5678), arranges free hikes Monday
through Friday during July and August (office open Mon.-Fri. 10am-2pm).

The restored *S. S. Klondike* (667-4511), on South Access Rd., is a dry-docked 1929
sternwheeler that recalls the days when the Yukon River was the city's sole means of
survival. Pick up a ticket from the information booth at the entrance to the parking
lot for a fascinating video and guided tour. ($3.25, children $2.25, families $7.50;

open June 1-Sept. 15 daily 9am-7:30pm.) The **Whitehorse Rapids Fishway** (633-5965), at the end of Nisutlin Drive, 2km southeast of town, allows salmon to bypass the dam and continue upstream in the **world's longest salmon migration** (open daily mid-June to mid-Sept. 8am-10pm; free). **Miles Canyon** lies 2km south of town on Miles Canyon Rd. off South Access Rd. Once the location of the feared Whitehorse rapids, this dammed stretch of the Yukon now swirls silently under the first bridge to span the river's banks. (Note: Large RVs may have trouble maneuvering on the small access road to the parking lot.)

Visitors hungry for a taste of local culture can feed their brains at the **MacBride Museum** (667-2709), at 1st Ave. and Wood St. The sod-roofed log cabin in the museum courtyard was built by Sam McGee in 1899. His demise has been immortalized by the Yukon Bard, Robert Service: "The Northern Lights have seen queer sights, but the queerest they ever did see, was that night on the marge of Lake Labarge I cremated Sam McGee." ($3.50, seniors and students $2.75, children $1.25, 6 and under free, families $8.50; open daily May and Sept. noon-4pm; June and Aug. 10am-6pm; July 9am-6pm.) If you're walking by 3rd Ave. and Lambert St., look up: those incredible three-story **log skyscrapers** were built singlehandedly in the 1970s by a local septuagenarian. Continuing on to the corner of 4th and Main, **Town & Mountain Hotel** (668-7644) has a bar inside that's popular with tourists and locals alike, offering live music and fairly inexpensive drinks (open daily noon-2am).

If you're in Whitehorse for a few days and want to see the country, pick up *Whitehorse Area Hikes and Bikes,* published by the Yukon Conservation Society ($18.95) or use the copy at the library or the visitors center. Options for getting out on the river range from two-hour tours to multi-day outfitted canoe trips. The **MV Schwatka** (668-4716), on Miles Canyon Rd. off South Access Rd., floats you through Miles Canyon for $17, kids 6-11 $8.50, and under 6 free (2-hr. cruises leave at 2pm and 7pm daily from June 15-Aug. 15, 2pm only in early June and Aug. 16-Sept. 10). **Taste of 98** (633-4767) also offers motorized raft trips of various lengths. **Up North Boat and Canoe Rentals,** 86 Wickstrom Rd. (667-7905), across the river from downtown, lets you paddle 25km to Jakkimi River for $20 per person (cost includes pick-up and return to Whitehorse; trip takes about 4hr.)

Traveling the full length of the Yukon River (also see p. 129) is increasingly popular, though it often takes four to five months. River travel is central to this region of Alaska and the Yukon. Hiking is extremely dangerous because the tree cover is thick, making it difficult to scan for and avoid bears. Locals recommend carrying a gun if you travel alone or in small groups for more than a few hours. In addition, roads are in constant need of repair and prone to washouts. On the river, you are safe from wildlife and your "road" has been a constant for thousands of years.

▨ Carcross

Carcross, short for "Caribou Crossing," sits on the narrows between Bennet and Nares Lakes, completely surrounded by snow-capped peaks and boasting a population of around 400. The native Tagish people hunted caribou at the crossing until the early 1900s when the herds were obliterated. Carcross also served as a link in the gold seekers' famous Chilcoot route from Skagway to the Yukon River and as a supply depot for the construction of the Alaska Highway. Since then, Carcross has survived off mining and tourism. Located in the Yukon's pristine southern lakes district, Carcross offers travelers a wonderful and unique look at what life in the Yukon was like at the gold-crazy turn of the century. On the Klondike Hwy. (Hwy. 2), Carcross is 74km south of Whitehorse and 106km north of Skagway, AK.

Practical Information Old photographs, displays, and a laser-disc presentation trace the history of the White Pass and Yukon Railroad at the **Carcross Visitor Reception Centre,** inside the depot (821-4431; open mid-May to mid-Sept. daily 8am-8pm). **Atlin Express** (604-651-7617) runs buses from Carcross to: Atlin, BC ($21, seniors $18, children 5-11 $10.50, under 5 free); Whitehorse ($26, seniors $20, children 5-11 $13, under 5 free); and Tagish ($15, seniors $13, children 5-11 $7.50, under 5 free). The two-story red building in Carcross houses the **health station** (821-4444). **Emergency numbers** include: **ambulance,** 821-3333; **fire,** 821-2222; and **police,** 821-5555 (if no answer call 667-5555). Suds your duds at **Montana Services** (see below; wash $2.25, 4-min. dry 25¢). **Public showers** also available here for $3. The **post office** is the white building with red trim on Bennett Ave. (open Mon., Wed., Fri. 8am-noon and 1-4pm, Tues. and Thurs. 10-11:45am; **postal code:** Y0B 1B0). Tune in to **visitors information** on **96.1 FM.** The **area code** is 403.

Accommodations, Camping, and Food History buffs will love the **Caribou Hotel** (821-4501), the **oldest operating hotel in the Yukon.** The original structure was destroyed in a 1909 fire; the present building was erected shortly thereafter. Insiders agree that "she was rebuilt after the fire, but she's still old enough to have a ghost." (No phones, no TVs, shared bath; singles and doubles $35.) **Spirit Lake Lodge** (821-4337), 7km north of town on Hwy. 2, maintains forested tent sites overlooking the lake (sites $6.50, showers $3, firewood $3 per bundle) and rooms (single $35, doubles $55, no TVs or phones). The **Spirit Lake Lounge** is also a popular after-hours spot for locals, particularly in winter. The Yukon Government maintains 14 secluded sites ($8) with drinking water, firewood, and pit toilets at **Carcross Campground,** 1km north of town on Hwy. 2.

The restaurant at the **Caribou Hotel** has standard food and prices (entrees $5-7; open daily 7am-8pm). Herbivores can get inexpensive meals for $5-9 at the **Spirit Lake Restaurant** (821-4337), in the Spirit Lake Lodge (open daily 8am-9:30pm). Groceries are available for cheap at **Montana Services** (821-3708), at the Chevron station on Hwy. 2 (open May-Sept. daily 7am-11pm, Oct.-April 8am-8pm).

Sights and Outdoors Hiking in the Carcross area is excellent. If you can, find a copy of *Whitehorse Area Hikes and Bikes* at the Carcross infocenter or in a Whitehorse bookstore before visiting. The most popular hike in the area is the **Chilkoot Trail,** a moderately difficult three-day adventure from Skagway over a formidable mountain pass that ends at the far end of Lake Bennet. The best approach is to take a bus from Carcross to Skagway, then arrange to have a boat pick you up at the far end of Lake Bennet (ask at the infocenter for details). The lake's 2-mi. sandy beach is understandably popular with locals in July and August.

South of town, a rough mining road reaches partway up Montana Mountain. It's a rough climb the rest of the way past lichen, snow, and boulders to a spectacular view. To get there follow Hwy. 2 south, take the first right after crossing the bridge, then the first left, and then follow until the road becomes impassable; from there, simply walk up to gain an astounding view of the Yukon. Anglers can cast for lake trout and grayling from the footbridge that spans the river, or check at the Reception Center for information on local lakes.

Visitors to the Yukon Territory should come to Carcross just to check out **The Barracks** (821-4372) and the **Chilcoot Trading Post** (821-3621), two shops which sell all Yukon-made crafts, clothing, and souvenirs, just across the railroad tracks from the Reception Center (open daily 9am-5pm). Part of the fun of Carcross is imagining the train of goldseekers who funneled over the Chilcoot trail and across Lake Bennett on makeshift rafts. Those who step inside the trading post are likely to be "mistaken" for **Claim-Jumpin' Jim** and thrown in the store's jail before they can browse through the local crafts and artwork.

Frontierland (667-1055), 1km north of the Carcross Desert (the exposed, sandy bottom of a glacial lake), presents a wildlife gallery of mounted animals in life-like settings, including the **largest bear ever mounted,** and Heritage Park, featuring live Yukon wildlife such as lynxes and Dall sheep. (Admission into the museum and the park $6 adults, $4 children; gallery or park alone $3.50 and $2.50; open mid-May to mid-Sept. daily 8am-5:30pm.)

The Chilkoot Trail

The winter of 1898 saw nine out of every 10 Klondike-bound stampeders slog through Skagway and Dyea on their way to Lake Bennett with at least 1000 lb. of provisions strapped to their (and their horses') backs. Canadian law demanded that each miner headed north bring this staggering amount of supplies. While the government's concern was touching, their demands were impractical. As one hiker puts it, "It's hard enough to do the trail with just yourself to look after. Imagine looking after yourself, plus a half a ton of mining supplies and beef jerky. And a horse."(The hiker at this point shakes his head in utter amazement.) The trail, besides acting as a thoroughfare for gold-hungry miners, was also a major trade route once controlled by the powerful Chilkat Tlingit nation. It extends 33 mi. from the ghost town of Dyea to the shores of **Lake Bennett** over the precipitous **Chilkoot Pass.** The 4-day hike (3 days for seasoned hikers) is littered with wagon wheels, horse bones, and plaques placed by the U.S. and Canadian National Park Services. In addition to these historic remnants, the trail also offers dramatic changes of climate, terrain, and vegetation through spectacular and rugged scenery, climbing above the treeline before descending into the forests of northern British Columbia. 4000 hikers ascend the demanding trail each summer. Most of them make it back alive.

■ Kluane National Park

On St. Elias's Day 1741, Vitus Bering, a Danish captain in the Russian service, sighted the mountains of what is now **Kluane National Park** (kloo-AH-nee). Kluane, a Tutchone Native word meaning "place of many fish," is Canadian wilderness at its most rugged, unspoiled, and beautiful. The "Green Belt" along the eastern park boundary, at the foot of the Kluane Range, has traditionally been a fruitful hunting ground for Athabaskan and Tlingit. One site on the Aishihik River contains evidence of a campfire that warmed bison hunters 8000 years ago. Today the Green Belt supports the greatest diversity of plant and animal species in northern Canada. Beyond the Kluane Range loom the glaciers of the Icefield Range, home to Canada's highest peaks, including the tallest, 19,850-ft. **Mt. Logan.** These glaciers and mountains cover nearly two-thirds of the park and are accessible only to the most intrepid alpinist and adventurer. However, the Alaska Hwy., near the northeastern boundary of the park, provides an easy way to see the park's eastern edge and glimpse a few of the spectacular peaks beyond.

Practical Information Pick up plenty of free information and take in a 25-minute slide show at the **Haines Junction Visitor Centre,** on Logan St. in Haines Junction (Canadian Park Service 634-7209; Tourism Yukon 634-2345; open mid-May to mid-Sept. daily 8am-8pm), or at the **Sheep Mountain Visitor Centre** (600/700-6116), at Alaska Hwy. Km 1707 (open June to mid-Sept. daily 9am-5pm). Sheep Mountain's outdoor telescopes let you scan the rocky slopes for sheep or gaze across Kluane Lake's turquoise waters. Visitors may also write to Kluane National Park and Preserve, Haines Junction, YT Y0B 1L0 for information.

Kluane's 22,015 sq. km are bounded by the Kluane Game Sanctuary and the Alaska Hwy. to the north, and the Haines Hwy. (Hwy. 3) to the east. The town of **Haines Junction** is at the eastern park boundary, 158km west of Whitehorse. **Alaska Direct** (800-770-6652, 668-4833 in Whitehorse) runs three buses per week from Haines Junction to Anchorage (US$125), Fairbanks (US$100), Whitehorse (US$20), and Skagway (US$55).

The **visitor radio** station (mostly tourism propaganda) is **FM 96.1. Emergency numbers** in Haines Junction include: **medical,** 634-4444; **fire,** 634-2222; **police,** 634-5555 (if no answer, call 1-403-667-5555); and **ambulance,** 634-4444. There is a **laundromat** in the Gateway Inn (see below; wash $2, 10-min. dry 25¢; open daily 7am-midnight). The **post office** (634-2706) is in Madley's General Store (open Mon., Wed., and Fri. 9-10am and 1-5pm, Tues. 9am-5pm, Thurs. 9am-noon and 1-5pm; store open Mon.-Fri. 9am-5pm). The **Postal Code** is Y0B 1L0. The **area code** is 403.

Camping, Accommodations, and Food Haine's Junction offers the standard array of clean-but-forgettable highway hotels; B&Bs and the several area campgrounds are the budget traveler's best options. **Kathleen Lake Campground** (634-2251), 27km south of Haines Jct. off Haines Rd., is close to good hiking and fishing and has water, flush toilets, fire pits, firewood, and "campfire talks" (sites $10; open June-Oct.). The Yukon government runs four campgrounds, all with water and pit toilets (sites $8; call Tourism Yukon at 634-2345 for more information). The closest by far to Haines Junction is beautiful **Pine Lake,** 7km east of Haines Jct. on the Alaska Hwy., featuring a sandy beach complete with a firepit for late night bonfires.

Seekers of an indoor bed should skip the motels and march straight to **Laughing Moose Bed and Breakfast,** 120 Alsek Crescent (634-2335), a four-block walk from the junction. Sparkling-clean kitchen facilities, spacious common room with TV and VCR, and view of the Auriol Mountains (single $55, double $65; shared bath). **The Gateway Inn** (634-2371) at the junction of the Alaska Hwy. and Haines Rd., offers clean, small rooms with private bath and TV (singles $70, doubles $75).

Haines Junction restaurants offer (yawn) standard highway cuisine. For groceries, head to **Madley's General Store** (634-2200) at Haines Rd. and Bates (open daily 8am-9pm; Oct.-April 8am-6:30pm). At the **Village Bakery and Deli** (634-2867), on Logan St. across from the visitors center, you can sate your sweet-tooth with a scrumptious $1.50 cinnamon bun (open May-Sept. daily 9am-9pm).

Outdoors in the Park Kluane has few developed trails, but the existing ones give ample opportunity to surround yourself with utter wilderness. It's best to stop at the visitors center to get **free maps** and find a day hike suited to your energy level. For a warm-up try the easy **Dezadeash River Loop** (DEZ-dee-ash), beginning at the Kluane RV Park just west of Haines Jct. The flat, forested 4km stroll includes a lookout deck where you can scope the valley for moose and bear. Rather than drive to the RV park, take the **Wetlands River Trail** which begins from the nearby day use area and hike through Ducks Unlimited protected wetlands to reach the **Dezadeash River Trail.** The 15km **Auriol Trail** can be completed in four to six hours but is also an excellent overnight hike. Starting from Haines Hwy., the trail cuts through boreal forest and leads to a subalpine bench just in front of the Auriol Range. The **King's Throne Route** and the **Sheep Mountain Ridge Walk** (starting near the Sheep Mountain Visitor Centre) offer steeper, more challenging terrain and the best views available on a day hike.

For mountain bikers, the **Alsek River Valley Trail** follows an old mining road 29km to Sugden Creek. The rocky road crosses several streams before climbing to a ridge with a stellar view of the Auriol Mountains. Be especially careful of bears on this trail. On the longer side, the **Cottonwood Trail** is a five- to seven-day trek beginning either 27 or 55km south of Haines Junction on the Haines Hwy. Cottonwood is an 83km loop trail offering 25km of trail above tree-line, and a short detour up an adjacent ridge provides a view of the Icefield Ranges and Mount Logan on clear days. The park also offers many **"routes"** that follow no formal trail and are not maintained by the park. These are reserved for more experienced hikers. Due to increased bear activity in this area, the park recommends the use of **bear-resistant food canisters** on all overnight trips, and mandates their use in the Slims River Area. These are available free with your backcountry permit at both of the park's visitor centers at Haines Junction and Sheep Mountain.

All overnight hikers are required to register at one of the visitors centers to pay user fees ($5 per person per night; a season pass is $50). The Sheep Mountain information center is responsible for hikes from the north end of the park and the Slims Valley. The park strongly encourages dayhikers to register, especially in the **north end** and **Slims Valley** section of the park where trails are not as well marked and bear activity is more frequent. For the less adventurous, the park offers shorter **dayhikes** and **walks** on specific themes, led by park interpreters, ranging from bear habitats to the park's wildflowers. The park also offers campfire talks at the Sheep Mountain and Haines Junction Park Information Centres.

The **Kluane Park Adventure Centre** (634-2313) is the central booking office for outdoor activities in and around the park (open daily 8am-8pm). The center rents **canoes** for $30 per day. For $100, travelers can ride the class III and IV rapids on the Tatshenshini River from Copper Mine, BC to Dalton Post, YT; the center also offers a two-hour scenic interpretive float trip illustrating the park's ecology, fauna, and geology for $25. For those interested in a drier, gentler ride, **Yukon Trail Rides** (634-2386) across from Petro-Canada just north of the junction, lets you trot, canter, and gallop through the forests and hills around Haines Junction on their guided trail rides ($15 per hour, $75 for full-day trips in the park, min. 3 people otherwise $100; ½-day rides $50 per person; open Mon.-Fri. 4-9pm). Flightseeing tours are increasingly popular in the park, but the prices can be steep. Shop around.

Anglers are invited to put the park's reputation to the test. **Kathleen Lake** (see above) is home to lake and rainbow trout, arctic grayling, and Kokanee salmon. Grayling abound in **Jarvis Creek,** halfway between Haines Jct. and Sheep Mountain. Visitors can obtain a National Parks fishing permit ($4 daily, $6 weekly, $13 annually) at Haines Junction Visitor's Center (see above) or at **Madley's General Store.** To maintain the natural stock, there are limits on both the size and number of fish which may be kept, and anglers are required to use barbless hooks. Those interested in fishing outside the park can purchase territorial licenses at Madley's and Kluane RV Park.

■ Alaska Highway: Kluane National Park to the Alaska border

BURWASH LANDING

Burwash Landing is home to the outstanding **Kluane Museum,** at Alaska Hwy. Mile 1093 (403-841-5561), which houses an extensive collection of native artifacts in addition to its famous wildlife exhibit ($3, seniors $2.75, children 6-12 $1.50; open daily 9am-9pm). Much to the delight of campers, Burwash Landing sits on immense **Kluane Lake,** and offers two stellar camping options. Kluane First Nation's **Dolan Campground** sports roomy, secluded sites on the lake with wood, water, and pit toilets ($10). You can camp for free on the grassy lawn at **Burwash Landing Resort** (403-841-4441), next to the museum, RV hookups $15. The resort, also on a choice lakeside plot, offers showers for $3, and a restaurant (open daily 7am-11pm). If you *must* have a roof over your head, the resort has rooms, some with lake views (singles $55, doubles $60). Restaurant has sandwiches for $5, hot meals for $8 and up.

BEAVER CREEK

176km north of Burwash Landing is **Beaver Creek,** where crews from Dawson Creek and Fairbanks met for the "final linkup" of the Alaska Highway in 1942. (For the Alaska Hwy. in Alaska, see p. 126). If you're coming from the south, savor the soothing hum of smooth pavement while you can; the Alaska Highway enters its most grueling, pothole-ridden stretch from here. The road was under construction in 1996 with no end in sight. The local *modus operandi* is to hit the lounge at **Beaver Creek Motor Inn** (862-7600; open until 2am) and nurse a hangover over breakfast at **Ida's Hotel and Cafe** (862-7223). Ida grills up eggs, hash browns, and toast ($4.95); for lunch, $7 will fetch you a mushroom burger and fries (open daily 24hr.). Travelers can **camp** cheaply at Ida's (tents $6 or $12 with showers; RVs free or $12 with showers). The **post office** (862-7211) is in the back of Community Hall (open Mon. 9am-noon and 1-5pm, Wed. 1-5pm, Fri. 1-5pm; **Postal Code:** Y0B 1A0). Going north on the highway, turn left immediately after the **visitor's center** (862-7321; open mid-May to mid-Sept. daily 8am-8pm). The adjacent **swimming pool** is open Tuesday through

Saturday in the afternoons and evenings (pick up a schedule there or at the post office; a day-pass is $3). The **health center** can be reached at 862-4444. In an **emergency,** call the police at 862-5555 or 403-667-5555.

■ Dawson City

Gold. Gold! Gold! Of all the insanity ever inspired by the lust for the dust, the creation of **Dawson City** must surely be ranked among the most amazing. For 12 glorious, crazy months, from July 1898 to July 1899, Dawson City, on the doorstep of the Arctic Circle and 1000 mi. from any other settlement, was the largest Canadian city west of Toronto and as cosmopolitan as present-day San Francisco or Seattle. Its 30,000-plus residents, with names like Swiftwater Bill, Skookum Jim, Arizona Charlie Meadows, and Evaporated Kid, had each lugged 1000 lbs of provisions—required by Canadian law for safely wintering in gold regions—over the treacherous Chilkoot Trail to the Yukon, all driven by the desire to be filthy, stinkin' rich.

After two years of frenzied claim-staking and legend-making, however, most of the once-eager Sourdoughs (Northwestern-speak for a prospector, now it conjures up images of lifelong Alaska residents) followed the Yukon River to Nome, and the city fizzled almost as quickly as it had exploded. It wasn't until the early 1960s that the Klondike Visitor's Association and the Canadian government, recognizing the historical importance of Dawson, set out to restore Dawson City and build it into the tourist destination that it is today. Each summer legions of RV travelers and a sizable international crowd come to Dawson, and a thousand or more college students migrate north for the natural setting and tourism-related jobs—all combining to triple the city's population and create a remarkably lively atmosphere. Almost 100 years after its moment in the midnight sun, Dawson City is again the jewel of the Yukon.

PRACTICAL INFORMATION AND ORIENTATION

Visitors Information: Visitor Reception Centre (993-5566), Front and King St. Historic movies and extensive information. Open mid-May to mid-Sept. daily 8am-8pm. For information, write Box 40, Dawson City, YT Y0B 1G0. The **Northwest Territories Visitors Centre** (993-6167) is across the street and has plenty of advice on driving the Dempster Hwy. Open daily late May-early Sept. 9am-9pm. **Tourist radio (96.1 FM)** broadcasts weather, road conditions, and events.

Buses: Norline Coaches Ltd. (993-6010), at the Gas Shack Chevron Station on 5th Ave. and Princess St. Service to Whitehorse 3 times per week (twice in winter) for $73. **Gold City Tours** (993-5175) runs buses up the Dempster Hwy. Tues. and Thurs. at 8am; (roundtrip to Inuvik $350).

River Travel: The **Yukon Queen** makes daily trips along the Yukon to and from Eagle, AK. The boat leaves Dawson daily in the morning. Call for times and reservations at **Yukon Queen River Cruises** (993-5599), on Front St. next to the dock (oneway US$74; roundtrip US$129).

Canoe and Bike Rental: At the hostel (see **Accommodations,** below). Bikes $15 per day, canoes $20 per day. Non-hostelers must present passport as deposit.

Library: 993-5571, at 5th Ave. and Princess St. Open summers Mon.-Thurs. 1-5pm and 6-8pm, Fri.-Sat. 1-5pm; in winter Tues.-Wed. and Fri. 9am-7pm, Thurs. 1-8pm, Sat. noon-5pm.

Laundromat and Showers: Laundry, at Front and York. Wash and dry each $2.50. 4-min. shower $2. Open daily 8am-11pm.

Pharmacy: No pharmacy in town, but **Arctic Drugs** (993-5331), on Front St. next to the visitors center, is the next best thing. Open June-Aug. Mon.-Sat. 9am-6pm, Sun. 9am-6pm.

Medical Emergency: Ambulance 993-4444; **fire** 993-2222; **poison control** 667-8700.

Crisis: Yukon crisis line 668-9111.

Police: Front St. and Turner St. (993-5555; if no answer 1-667-5555), in the southern part of town. **Royal Canadian Mounted Police (RCMP)** 993-5555.

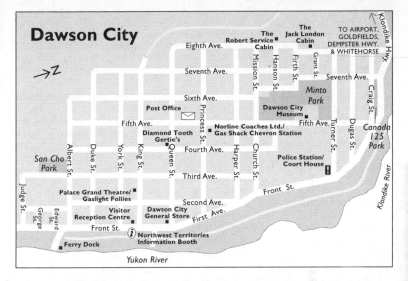

Dawson City

Eighth Ave.

The Robert Service Cabin

The Jack London Cabin

TO AIRPORT, GOLDFIELDS, DEMPSTER HWY. & WHITEHORSE

Klondike Hwy.

Seventh Ave.

Mission St.

Hanson St.

Firth St.

Grant St.

Seventh Ave.

Craig St.

Sixth Ave.

Minto Park

Post Office

Princess St.

Dawson City Museum

Fifth Ave.

Diamond Tooth Gertie's

Norline Coaches Ltd./ Gas Shack Chevron Station

Fifth Ave.

Turner St.

Dugas St.

Canada 125 Park

San Cho Park

Albert St.

Duke St.

York St.

King St.

Queen St.

Fourth Ave.

Harper St.

Church St.

Police Station/ Court House

Klondike River

Third Ave.

Front St.

Judge St.

Palace Grand Theatre/ Gaslight Follies

George St.

Edward St.

Visitor Reception Centre

Second Ave.

Dawson City General Store

First Ave.

Front St.

(i) Northwest Territories Information Booth

Ferry Dock

Yukon River

Post Office: 5th Ave. and Princess St. (993-5342). Open Mon.-Fri. 8:30am-5:30pm, Sat. 8:30am-12:30pm. Must register for general delivery service; photo ID required. Also check out the **Historical Post Office,** closer to downtown, at 3rd and King St., Mon.-Fri. noon-6pm. **Postal Code:** Y0B 1G0.
Area Code: 403.

To reach Dawson City, take the Klondike Hwy. 533km north from Whitehorse, or follow the **Top-of-the-World Hwy.** about 100km east from the Alaska border (see **Interior Alaska: Taylor Hwy.,** p. 128).

ACCOMMODATIONS AND CAMPING

The hostel and the campground on the west side of town are the cheapest options. The **ferry** across the Yukon River can be caught at the dock off Front St. and Albert. It is free and runs 24 hours. Although the government discourages camping in the woods west of the hostel, many squatters tent there undisturbed.

Dawson City River Hostel (HI-C) (993-6823). Across the Yukon river from downtown; take the 1st left when you come off the ferry. The best bargain in town. Brand-new bunks in brand-new log cabins, a wood-heated "prospector's bath," outdoor kitchen facilities, refreshingly icy showers (no soap allowed—it flows into the river), a cozy lounge with a wood stove and mini-library, and a beautiful hilltop view of the river and the city on the other side. Members $13, non-members $15, tent sites $8 for one person, $6 each additional person.

The Bunkhouse (993-6164), Front St. and Princess St. Brand new, very clean, and in a great location. Wood-planked rooms and tiny shared bathrooms. Singles $45. Doubles $50, with bath $60.

Dawson City Bed and Breakfast, 451 Craig St. (993-5649). Fantastic rooms and wonderfully accommodating management. Shared bath. Singles $69. Doubles $79. Make reservations at least a week in advance, 2 weeks in advance for weekend stays in July. If you're in the mood to splurge, this is worth it.

Yukon River Campground. Ride the ferry to the west side of Dawson City and take the 1st right. The roomy, secluded sites are a haven for budget travelers who want to nestle down in nature. Look for the peregrine falcons nesting across the river. Water and pit toilets. RVs welcome, but no hookups available. Sites $8.

Gold Rush Campground (993-5247), 5th and York St. Gold Rush has a monopoly on RV sites close to downtown, so it's wise to phone ahead. Parking lot-style landscape is a bummer for tenters; head across the river instead. Laundromat ($2.50 wash, about $1.25 dry), convenience store, shower ($1 for 4 min.), and dump station. Sites $11, electric hookups $16, full hookups $19.50. Open 24hr.

FOOD

On Thanksgiving Day in 1898, a single turkey cost over $100. Prices today are (thankfully) more reasonable, and there are quite a few good places to eat in town. Snag a bag of groceries at the **Dawson City General Store** (993-5475) at Front and Queen St. (open Mon.-Sat. 8am-8pm, Sun. 10am-6pm).

Klondike Kate's (993-6527), at 3rd and King St. Kate's breakfast special should satisfy even the hungriest Sourdoughs ($4 for 2 eggs, bacon or sausage, home fries, and toast). For lunch, kick back on the shady patio and sip the soup of the day ($3). Open mid-May to mid-Sept. daily 7am-11pm.

Nancy's (993-5633), at Front St. and Princess. Take in a view of the river and watch your fellow tourists wander by as you polish off a veggie sandwich on fresh, superthick bread or try the delicious German-style sausage. Both sausage and sandwich are $4.50 and come with hash browns. Open daily 7am-10pm, in winter until 8pm.

River West Food and Health (993-6339), on Front St. and Queen. The all-natural place to go for all-natural travelers. Muffins, snacks, and organic coffees ($1.25-3.50). Frozen yogurt for $2.25. Open Mon.-Sat. 7:30am-10:30pm, Sun. 10am-10:30pm, in winter until 5:30pm.

The Jack London Grill (993-5346), in the Downtown Hotel at 2nd and Queen St. A step up in price and quality—don't be scared off by the well-furnished dining room. Sandwiches start at $6 for lunch. Terrific dinners start at $13. Open daily 6-10pm, Fri.-Sat. in summer until 11pm.

Midnight Sun Hotel Restaurant (993-5495), 3rd and Queen. Burgers and fries go for $7. Great Chinese entrees, cooked by chefs invited from Vancouver for the summer, start at $10. (Open Sun.-Thurs. 6am-1am, Fri.-Sat. 6am-3am.)

SIGHTS AND ENTERTAINMENT

Perhaps the biggest reason for Dawson City's success in the tourism business is that it trounces the competition with a re-creation of Klondike culture that goes well beyond museums and restored buildings.

During the day, Dawson's cornucopia of museums and tours provide more information about gold mining and frontier life than the human mind can possibly hold. For the ravenously information-hungry, $10 buys a package of five not-to-be-missed attractions: the 90-minute **Town Walking Tour,** tours of **Dredge #4** and the **Bear Creek** historic mining community, the **Palace Grand Theater,** and the **Northwest Mounted Police** exhibit (ask at the visitor's center for times and meeting places). If you're short on time, start with the Town Walking Tour, which leaves from the reception center at 9am and 3:30pm daily. It costs $3 alone, as does each individual attraction. The guides are well-informed, and the tour is a great introduction to the city.

The **Dawson City Museum** (993-5291), on 5th St. south of Church, elaborates on regional history and exhibits the full range of Yukon history, from mastodons to sluice boxes to modern mining machinery. The museum hosts shows by local artists and has hourly events, including the half-hour documentary, *City of Gold* (which sparked Canada's interest in renovating Dawson City), showing daily at 10:30am and 4pm (museum admission $3.50, seniors $2.50, students and children $1; open daily 10am-6pm).

The two most interesting attractions in town relate to Dawson City's unrivalled claim to frontier-town literary genius. At the **Jack London Cabin,** on 8th Ave. and 5th, admission is free and the great Californian author's life and times in the Yukon are recounted daily during readings at noon and 2pm. Even if you can't catch a reading, it is worth a visit just to see the photos of a struggling young London. Be sure to catch the thoroughly entertaining **Robert Service readings** given at his nearby cabin. Performances of witty and unpretentious ballads by the Yukon Bard, including "The Cremation of Sam McGee" and "The Shooting of Dan McGrew," are given in front of the cabin where he penned them on 8th Ave. at Hanson ($6, under 8 $3; shows daily at 10am and 3pm).

Diamond Tooth Gertie's, at 4th and Queen, was Canada's first legal casino and should be proof enough that Dawson is no movie set: for a $4.75 cover you can try your hand at roulette, blackjack, and if you dare, play "Texas hold 'em" against local legends like Johnny Caribou and No Sleep Filippe. Or just take in one of three nightly floor shows at 8:30pm, 10:30pm, and 12:30am (open nightly 7pm-2am).

High-kicking dancers and audience participation delight the crowds at the **Gaslight Follies** (993-6217), at the Palace Grand Theater; an original vaudeville revue is shown Wednesday through Monday at 8pm ($13 and $16, children $6). Tickets available at the Expressions store next to the theater. Later in the evening, Dawson's youth show up at the **Sun Tavern and Lounge** (993-5495), at 3rd and Queen. Once Dawson's roughest bar, the Sun has calmed down but is still no place to sip fruity drinks (open daily noon-2:30am). Beers $3.50 during happy hour, Mon.-Fri. 5-7pm.

Further out of town, the goldfields of **Bonanza** and **Eldorado Creeks** yielded some of the richest lodes discovered in the Klondike. Nearly 16km of maintained gravel road follows Bonanza Creek to the former site of **Grand Forks,** chewed up when the dredges came through. Along the way are **Gold Dredge #4,** the huge machine used to thoroughly mine Bonanza Creek after the rush was over, and **Discovery Claim,** the site of the first discovery of gold by George Carmack on August 16, 1896. The Park Service also maintains **Bear Creek,** 13km south of town on the Klondike Hwy. Mining here suddenly halted in 1966, leaving behind a ghost town of tools and machinery.

For modern day fortune hunters, many businesses let you pan gold for around $5, but anyone can pan for free at the confluence of the Bonanza and Eldorado Creeks (you need your own pan, available at local hardware stores). Panning anywhere else along the creeks could lead to a *very* unpleasant encounter with the owner/miner of the claim you're jumping.

Pleasure Island Restaurant and **Yukon River Cruises** (993-5482), on Front St. between King and Queen, wrap several elements of Yukon culture into a single package: the three-hour cruise on the *Yukon Lou* includes an all-you-can-eat salmon barbecue on Pleasure Island and a chance to meet the owner's sled-dog team ($35; $17.50 children; departures vary). The *Yukon Lou* also makes a daily 1½-hr. cruise at 1pm ($15, children $7.50) and a "Midnight Sun" cruise perfect for insomniacs, departing nightly at 11pm ($20, children $10).

No, Ma'am, That's Not an Olive in Your Martini...

When some people run across amputated body parts, they take them to a hospital for surgical reattachment and a new career in the X-rated film industry. But for Capt. Dick Stevenson, the discovery of a **pickled human toe** in a cabin in the Yukon meant one thing: a damn fine cocktail. The drink became famous and spawned the **Sourtoe Cocktail Club,** an institution with a history as peculiar as its name. Aspiring initiates buy a drink of their choice and pay a small fee ($5) to Bill "Stillwater Willie" Boone (Dick's replacement as keeper of the sourtoe), who drops the chemically preserved (er, pickled) toe in the drink. Then it's bottoms up, and the moment the toe touches your lips, you've become one of the club's 12,000-plus proud members. "You can drink it fast, you can drink it slow—but the lips have gotta touch the toe." Listening to Stillwater Willie explain the club's sordid history and philosophize about life in the Yukon is itself worth the $5, but the fee includes a certificate, membership card, and pin. Inquire at the **Pleasure Island Restaurant** (993-5482), on Front St. between King and Queen, for initiation times and location.

■ Dempster Highway

The 741km **Dempster Hwy.** is named after Inspector W.J.D. Dempster, one of the most courageous officers to wear the Mountie redcoat. It is the sole access road to Canada's isolated Mackenzie River Delta communities of **Fort McPherson, Tsiige-htchic** (formerly known as **Arctic Red River**), and **Inuvik** (ih-NOO-vik), a flourishing and colorful city of 3200 people in the Northwest Territories. The Dempster Hwy. leads north from the Klondike River Lodge (41km east of Dawson City on the Klond-ike Loop) to Inuvik. The first 150km are spectacular, passing between the North and South Oglivie Mountain Ranges, both of which, like the Richardson Mountains farther north, remain hauntingly craggy, narrowly missed by glaciation during the last ice age. The road then descends back into forest and eventually tundra as it approaches the Arctic Circle. Halfway to Inuvik, 364km from Dawson City, gas, food, supplies, and accommodations are available at the well-kept **Eagle Plains Hotel.** You won't see eagles here, but you will witness monopoly pricing in action. Brace yourself (singles $100, doubles $120; winter singles and doubles $75; gas $1.90 per gallon). It's a good thing the **ferries** are free: they cross the Peel and Arctic Red Rivers, in the Northwest Territories roughly 550km and 600km north of Dawson City, about 15 times per day in summer (about mid-June to mid-Oct.). In winter, you can drive easily across the thick ice. **No crossing** is possible during fall freeze-in or spring thaw. Call 800-661-0752 for current ice status.

The Dempster is not to be taken lightly. If you drive, you can enjoy stunning views of Arctic wilderness virtually undisturbed. Hitching the route is a gamble; it's a long, isolated stretch of road, but a popular destination for hitchers. (*Let's Go* does not recommend hitchhiking.) For 4½ days each autumn, the **Porcupine Caribou herd** (150,000 caribou!) migrates across the highway. Before driving the Dempster, pick up the free **pamphlet** *The Dempster* at an information center in Whitehorse or Dawson City and consider buying *Along the Dempster: An Outdoor Guide to Canada's Northernmost Highway* ($11; available at Maximilian's at Front St. and Queen in Dawson City) or *The Western Arctic Travel Guide* by Daniela Talarico, $12. For conditions, **maps,** and information, contact the **Northwest Territories Visitors Centre** (993-6167), Front St. at King in Dawson City (open daily June-Sept. 9am-9pm). **Gold City Tours** (993-5175), on Front St. in Dawson City, provides **bus service** to Inuvik (Tues., Thurs.; $198, roundtrip $350).

Alberta

With its vast open prairie, oil-fired economy, and generally conservative political outlook, Alberta is the Texas of Canada. Petrodollars have fostered the growth of gleaming, modern cities on the prairie. At home in a vast wilderness, Calgary caught the world's eye when it hosted the Winter Olympics in 1988. It is also the annual stomping grounds for the wild Stampede, the world's largest rodeo. The Stampede brings together the most skilled cowboys from all over the West. Alberta's capitol, Edmonton, is slightly larger than its civic and hockey rival, and bravely shoulders a reputation for dullness.

Adventurous outdoor enthusiasts should have little trouble finding places to pursue their favorite activities. Hikers, mountaineers, and ice climbers will find the best terrain in the Canadian Rockies in Banff and Jasper National Parks and Kananaskis Country. Canoeing centers adjoin the lakes of northern Alberta and the Milk River in the south. The province boasts thousands of prime fishing holes, world-renowned fossil fields, and centers of indigenous Canadian culture. Some of Alberta's most fascinating attractions, such as Waterton Lakes National Park and Head-Smashed-In Buffalo Jump, are within easy traveling distance of the U.S. border.

PRACTICAL INFORMATION

Capital: Edmonton.
Visitors Information: Alberta Tourism, Commerce 10155 102 St., 3rd floor, Edmonton T5J 4L6 (427-4321 or 800-661-8888). Contact **Parks Canada,** 220 4th Ave. SE, Suite 552, Calgary T2G 4X3 (292-4401), for information on Waterton Lakes, Jasper, Banff, and Wood Buffalo provincial parks. **Alberta Wilderness Association,** P.O. Box 6398, Station D, Calgary T2P 2E1, (283-2025; fax 270-2743). Distributes info for off-highway adventurers.
Motto: *Fortis et Liber* (Strong and Free). **Provincial Bird:** Great Horned Owl. **Provincial Flower:** Wild Rose. **Provincial Tree:** Lodgepole Pine.
Emergency: 911 in most areas; some rural areas may not have 911 service.
Time Zone: Mountain (2hr. behind Eastern).
Postal Abbreviation: AB.
Provincial Sales Tax: None.
Drinking Age: 18.
Traffic Laws: Mandatory seatbelt law.
Area Code: 403.

GETTING AROUND

Hwy. 16 connects Jasper with Edmonton, while the **Trans-Canada Hwy.** (Hwy. 1) connects Banff with Calgary, 120km to the east. **Hwy. 3** runs from Medicine Hat to Vancouver, BC. The extensive highway system facilitates bus connections between major destinations. **Greyhound** runs from Calgary to Edmonton to Jasper, as well as from Calgary to Banff. **Brewster,** a subsidiary of Greyhound, runs an express bus between Banff and Jasper. Alberta's major **airports** are in Calgary and Edmonton.

■ Edmonton

When western Alberta's glitz and glamour were distributed, Edmonton was apparently last in line. Banff and Jasper won the spectacular scenery, Calgary got the Stampede, and Edmonton became the proud parent of…the provincial capital. Not one to wallow in its reputation for drabness, the city continues to improve its rank among other Albertan travel destinations. The perpetually competitive Oilers have made Edmonton a minor pilgrimage for hockey fans while an abundance of music, art, and performance festivals draws summer crowds. Add to the mix the largest mall in the world and a toy museum and Edmonton becomes a worthy urban oasis after the almost overpowering splendor of the nearby Rockies.

PRACTICAL INFORMATION AND ORIENTATION

Visitors Information: Edmonton Tourism, City Hall, 1 Sir Winston Churchill Sq. (496-8423), at 102A Ave. west of 99 St. Main floor. Info, maps, and directions. Open Victoria Day-Labor Day Mon.-Fri. 9am-4pm, Sat.-Sun. 11am-5pm, winter Mon.-Fri. 9am-4pm. Also at **Gateway Park** (496-8400 or 800-463-4667), on Hwy. 2 south of the city. Open daily 8am-9pm; winter Mon.-Fri. 8:30am-4:30pm, Sat.-Sun. 9am-5pm. For info about the rest of the province, head to **Alberta Tourism,** Commerce Place, 10155 102 St., Edmonton T5J 4L6 (800-661-8888), on the 3rd floor. Open Mon.-Fri. 8:15am-4:30pm. Info by phone Mon.-Fri. 9am-4:30pm.

Budget Travel: The Travel Shop, 10926 88 Ave. (travel 439-3096, retail 439-3089). Regional office for **Alberta Hostels.** A travel agency with camping and hiking gear, serving youth and student travelers. Will make international and local hostel reservations. Open Mon.-Wed. and Fri.-Sat. 9am-6pm, Thurs. 9am-8pm.

Buses: Greyhound, 10324 103 St. (420-2412). To: Calgary (nearly every hr. 8am-8pm, plus a milk run for die-hards at midnight, $33), Jasper (4 per day, $47), Vancouver (5 per day, $113), Yellowknife (1 per day Mon.-Fri.; winter 3 per week, $177). If you plan to travel extensively by bus, consider purchasing a 7- ($212), 15- ($277), 30- ($373), or 60-day Canada Pass ($480). Open daily 5:30am-midnight. Locker storage $1.50 per 24hr.

Trains: VIA Rail, 10004 104 Ave. (422-6032 for recorded info, 800-561-8630 for reservations), in the CN Tower, easily identified by the huge red letters on the front of the building. To: Jasper and Vancouver. No train service to Calgary.

Public Transportation: Edmonton Transit (496-1611 for schedule info). Buses and light rail transit **(LRT)** run frequently throughout the city. LRT is free in the downtown area Mon.-Fri. 9am-3pm and Sat. 9am-6pm (between Grandin Station at 110 St. and 98 Ave. and Churchill Station at 99 St. and 102 Ave.). Fare $1.60, over 65 and under 15 80¢. No bikes on LRT during peak hours (Mon.-Fri. 7:30-8:30am, 4-5pm). No bikes on buses. For info, stop by the **Downtown Information Centre,** 100 A St. and Jasper Ave. Open Mon.-Fri. 9:30am-5pm. Another info booth is in the Churchill LRT station. Open Mon.-Fri. 8:30am-4:30pm.

Taxis: Yellow Cab, 462-3456. **Alberta Co-op Taxi,** 425-8310. Both 24hr.

Car Rental: Tilden, 10133 100A St. (422-6097). Cars start at $35 per day, 12¢ per km after 200km. Must be 21 (open Mon.-Thurs. 7am-6pm, Fri. 7am-7pm, Sat.-Sun. 8am-4pm).

Bike Rental: The **Edmonton Hostel** (see **Accommodations** below) rents mountain bikes for $15 per day, $7.50 per ½ day.

Library: Edmonton Public Library, 7 Sir Winston Churchill Sq. Open Mon.-Fri. 9am-9pm, Sat. 9am-6pm, Sun. 1-5pm.

Gay and Lesbian Resources: Gay/Lesbian Community Centre, 10112 124th St. #104 (488-3234). Community listings, on-site peer counseling, and a library. Open Mon.-Fri. 7-10pm. Call 988-4188 for an events recording, 489-9661 for the gay youth line. **Womenspace** (425-0511), Edmonton lesbian group. Call for recording of local events.

Square Dancing: Edmonton and District Square Dance Assoc., 496-9136.

Weather Information: 468-4940.

Rape Crisis: Sexual Assault Centre, 423-4121. 24hr. **Distress Line:** 482-HELP/ 4357. 24hr.

Pharmacy: Shoppers Drug Mart, 11408 Jasper Ave. (482-1011). Open daily 24hr.

Hospital: Royal Alexandra Hospital, 10240 Kingsway Ave. (477-4111).

Emergency: 911. **Police:** 423-4567.

Post Office: 9808 103A Ave. (495-4105), adjacent to the CN Tower. Open Mon.-Fri. 8am-5:45pm. **Postal Code:** T5J 2G8.

Area Code: 403.

Although Edmonton is the northernmost major city in Canada, it's actually in the southern half of Alberta. Calgary is 294km south of Edmonton, an easy three-hour

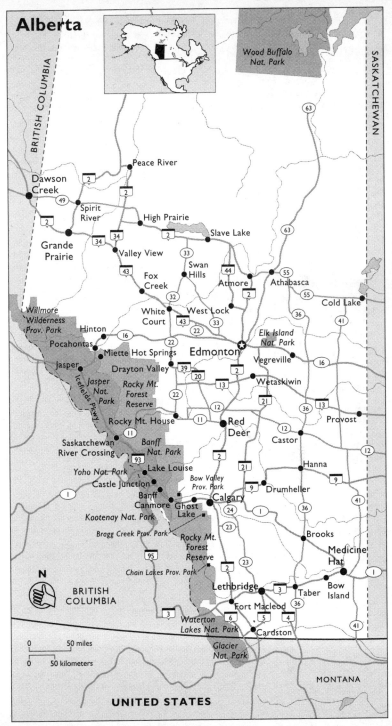

Alberta

WOOD BUFFALO Nat. Park

BRITISH COLUMBIA

SASKATCHEWAN

WESTERN CANADA

Peace River

Dawson Creek

Spirit River

High Prairie

Slave Lake

Grande Prairie

Valley View

Swan Hills

Atmore

Athabasca

Cold Lake

Fox Creek

White Court

West Lock

Willmore Wilderness Prov. Park

Hinton

Pocahontas

Miette Hot Springs

Elk Island Nat. Park

Edmonton

Vegreville

Jasper

Drayton Valley

Jasper Nat. Park

Rocky Mt. Forest Reserve

Wetaskiwin

Icefields Pkwy.

Rocky Mt. House

Red Deer

Provost

Saskatchewan River Crossing

Banff Nat. Park

Castor

Lake Louise

Yoho Nat. Park

Castle Junction

Bow Valley Prov. Park

Hanna

Banff

Canmore

Ghost Lake

Drumheller

Calgary

Kootenay Nat. Park

Bragg Creek Prov. Park

Rocky Mt. Forest Reserve

Brooks

Chain Lakes Prov. Park

Medicine Hat

N

BRITISH COLUMBIA

Lethbridge

Taber

Bow Island

Fort Macleod

Waterton Lakes Nat. Park

Cardston

Glacier Nat. Park

MONTANA

0   50 miles

0   50 kilometers

UNITED STATES

drive on **Hwy. 2.** Jasper lies 362km to the west, a four-hour drive on **Hwy. 16.** The **Greyhound** and **VIA Rail** stations are downtown. The **airport** sits 29km south of town, a prohibitively expensive cab fare away. The **Grey Goose Airporter Service** runs a shuttle to the downtown area for $11 ($18 roundtrip). Cheapskates are known to hop on an airport shuttle bus taking travelers to downtown hotels.

Edmonton's street system operates on a basic numerical system. Almost all streets and avenues are numbered, streets run north-south and avenues run east-west. Street numbers increase to the west, and avenues increase to the north. City Centre is quite off-center at 105 St. and 101 (Jasper) Ave. And beware of subset streets and avenues (101A St., etc.).

ACCOMMODATIONS

The liveliest place to stay in Edmonton is the hostel, though you'll have more privacy at St. Joseph's College or the University of Alberta. For **B&B** listings, call **Alberta Gem B&B Reservation Agency,** 11216 48 Ave. (434-6098), or **Edmonton Bed and Breakfast Reservation Agency,** 13824 110A Ave. (455-2297).

Edmonton International Youth Hostel (HI-C), 10422 91 St. (429-0140), off Jasper Ave. Take bus #1 or 2. A long walk from the bus station. The small building, low shower pressure, and no TV make this a rather rustic urban hostel. A/C, common room, snack bar, showers, kitchen, and laundry facilities. Family rooms available. Open daily 8am-midnight. $12.50, nonmembers $17.

St. Joseph's College (492-7681), on 89 Ave. at 114 St. near the University of Alberta. Take bus #43, or take the LRT and get off at University. The rooms here are smaller, quieter, less institutional, and cheaper than those at the university nearby. Shaded lawn out front. In summer, make reservations; rooms fill up fast. Library facilities, TV lounge, pool table. Check-in desk open Mon.-Fri. 8:30am-4pm. Full board plan available. Singles $21, weekly $130. Single with full board $34, or pay for meals separately: breakfast $3.25, lunch $4.50, dinner $6.50.

University of Alberta (492-4281), on 87 Ave. between 116 and 117 St. on the ground floor of Lister Hall. Rooms coincidentally decorated by the same person who designed every college dorm in Canada. Weight, steam, and game rooms, dry cleaning, and a convenience store. Check-in after 3pm. Singles $25, weekly $146. Doubles $17 per person, weekly $106. Suites $30-40 per night; shared bathroom.

YMCA, 10030 102A Ave. (421-9622), close to bus and rail stations. A lively, clean building with rooms available for both men and women. More secure rooms especially appropriate for women available on 4th floor. Free use of gym and pool facilities included with accommodation fee. Dorm bunk beds $15 per night, $12 with student ID. 3-night max. stay in dorm. Singles $27. Doubles $45. Student rates $85 per week, $235 per month.

FOOD

Little evidence can be found to support the theory that citizens of the self-labeled "City of Champions" kick off their day with a big bowl of Wheaties. Instead, the **coffee fever** that has spread like a rash across North America has concentrated a near-critical mass of cafés and coffee shops in Edmonton. The **Old Strathcona** area, a region along Whyte (82) Ave. between 102 and 105 St., exhibits both the dread coffee rash and a healthy number of reasonably priced eateries.

Carson's Cafe, 10331 Whyte (82) Ave. (432-7560). A classy but cozy restaurant in the middle of the Old Strathcona district. The selection is only slightly larger than the restaurant itself, but a range of daily specials and creative seasonings add diversity to the menu. Quesadilla Marrakesh $5.75, grilled chicken teriyaki sandwich $7. Burgers $5-6.25. Open 11am-11pm daily.

Chianti's, 10501 Whyte (82) Ave. (439-9829). Italian flavor oozes from this old Strathcona Post Office. Daily specialty wines and an expanse of pasta, veal, and seafood dishes. (Pastas $7-8, $6 Mon.-Tues.; veal $10-11.) Open Mon.-Thurs. 11am-11pm, Fri.-Sat. 11am-midnight, Sun. 4-11pm.

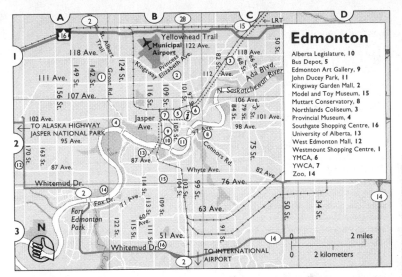

The Silk Hat, 10251 Jasper Ave. (428-1551), beside the Paramount theater. One of the oldest restaurants in Edmonton and it doesn't seem to have changed much over the years. Diner motif with Rock-Ola's (that's a jukebox to you and me) in every booth and prices from the Kennedy years. Two eggs with two monstrous pancakes ($2.50). Hamburger Deluxe with fries or potato salad ($4.95). Everything is 10% off after 5pm. Wacky tea leaf readings 1-7pm. Open Mon.-Fri. 6:30am-10pm, Sat. 8am-9pm, Sun. and holidays 11am-7pm.

The Next Act, 8224 104 St. (433-9345). A pub specializing in cheap red meat. Pints of draft beer $2.50 9-10pm daily. Gamblers can risk their arteries on the French concoction *poufine,* a heady mix of french fries, gravy, cheese, bacon and onions ($5). Open Mon.-Sat. 10:30am-2am, Sun. 10:30am-midnight.

The Mandarin, 11044 82 Ave. (433-8494) across from UBC. A standard-issue Chinese restaurant specializing in various regional dishes. Combination dinners $8.50-10, seafood entrees $11. Hours are baffling. Generally open several hours between 11:30am and 9pm.

SIGHTS

After worshiping at Edmonton's temple of commercialism, take a breather from the pace of the modern world with the refreshing **Fort Edmonton Park** (496-8787) on Whitemud Dr. at Fox Dr. Buses #32 and 39 stop near the park. At the far end of the park sits the fort, a 19th-century "office building" for Alberta's first entrepreneurs, ruthless whiskey traders. Between the fort and the park entrance are three long streets (1885 St., 1905 St., and 1920 St.), each bedecked with period buildings, including apothecaries, blacksmith shops, and barns, all keyed to the streets' respective years. Park volunteers dressed as schoolmarms and general-store owners greet visitors ($6.50, seniors and ages 13-17 $5; discounts for HI members; park open Victoria Day-late June, Mon.-Fri. 10am-4pm, Sat.-Sun. 10am-6pm; late June-Labor Day daily 10am-6pm).

After visiting the fort, stop at the **John Janzen Nature Centre** next door to pet the salamanders and take hikes through birch groves (free; Mon.-Fri. 9am-6pm, Sat.-Sun. 11am-6pm, winter Mon.-Fri. 9am-4pm, Sat.-Sun. 1-4pm). From the fauna of the Nature Centre, turn to the flora of the **Muttart Conservatory,** 9626 96A St. (496-8755). Bus #51 whisks you to Muttart. Plant species from around the world live here in the climate-controlled comfort of four ultramodern glass and steel pyramids. Palm trees and banana plants tower over orchids and hibiscus in the humid Tropical Pavilion ($4.25,

---

Capitalism's Mothership

The **West Edmonton Mall** (444-5200), envelops the general area of 170 St. and 87 Ave. When the Milky Way's largest assembly of retail stores first landed, its massive sprawl of boutiques and eateries seized 30% of Edmonton's retail business, choking the life out of the downtown shopping district. No ordinary collection of stores, the Über-mall boasts a water park, an amusement park, and dozens of pathetically caged exotic animals, as well as over 800 stores, 110 eating establishments, twice as many submarines as the Canadian Navy, a full-scale replica of Columbus's *Santa Maria,* a 14-story roller coaster, and an indoor bungee jumping facility (don't forget the golf course and ice skating rink). The World's Biggest Mall appears even bigger than It is, thanks to the mirrors plastered on nearly every wall. Take bus #10 to The Mall (open Mon.-Fri. 10am-9pm, Sat. 10am-6pm, Sun. noon-5pm). To tour Western Alberta without passing through its hallowed halls is almost as insulting as claiming that Canadians drink watery beer. On a last note, remember where you park. The world's largest mall has the world's largest parking lot.

---

seniors and youths $3.25, children $2; open Sun.-Wed. 11am-9pm, Thurs.-Sat. 11am-6pm).

Continue your provincial experience at the **Provincial Museum of Alberta,** 12845 102 Ave. (453-9100), which holds all kinds of Albertan relics. Take bus #21. The museum's collection of Alberta's plants, animals, and minerals is impressive. A boon to local taxidermists, the habitat exhibit is a better way to get up close and personal with Alberta's larger, more dangerous animals than surprising them in a forest or colliding with them on Hwy. 16. The museum's **Bug Room** is alive with a variety of insect species, some rodent-sized (yum!). ($5.50, youth $2.25; open Victoria Day-Labor Day Sun.-Wed. 9am-9pm, Thurs.-Sat. 9am-5pm; winter Tues.-Sun. 9am-5pm.)

Edmonton sports a number of smaller museums as well (telephone history, anyone?), but the most remarkable is the **Old Strathcona Model and Toy Museum,** McKenzie Historic House, 8603 104th St. (433-4512). Take bus #43. Examine over 200 paper reconstructions of monumental buildings and ships, including the Taj Mahal and the Titanic. The paper caricatures of Canadian Prime Ministers are particularly well done (free; open Mon.-Tues. 1-5pm, Wed.-Fri. noon-8pm, Sat. 10am-6pm, Sun. 1-5pm).

The **Edmonton Art Gallery,** 2 Sir Winston Churchill Sq. (422-6223), is a small gallery showcasing Canadian and Albertan art ($3, students and seniors $1.50, Thurs. after 4pm free; open Mon.-Wed. 10:30am-5pm, Thurs.-Fri. 10:30am-8pm, Sat.-Sun. and holidays 11am-5pm), close to the **Canadian Country Music Hall of Honour,** 9797 Jasper Ave., where visitors can figure out just how deep the similarities between Alberta and Texas really run.

NIGHTLIFE AND ENTERTAINMENT

Edmonton nightlife is fairly dead early in the week with rigor mortis settling in by Wednesday. Come Thursday, though, dead can dance. And drink.

Rebar, 10551 82nd Ave. (433-3600). Music ranges from alternative to dance with the requisite 80s night. Cheap drinks on weekends bring in some crowds. Open daily 8pm-2:30am.

Sherlock Holmes, 10341 82nd Ave. (453-9676). Also at 10012 101A Ave. (426-7784). Homesick Brits hold support groups over sing-alongs, cigars, and staple English Ales on tap. The 82nd Ave. location is younger and sharper while downtown is popular with the older crowd. Open Mon.-Sat. 11:30am-3am.

Cook County Saloon, 8010 103 St. (432-2665). Bring your hat and your best boots to Edmonton's liveliest country bar. Live music keeps 'em moseying nightly while Wednesday night dance lessons ensure that no one gets hurt in the process. Open Wed.-Sat. 7pm-2am.

For a more cerebral evening, buy tickets to the **Princess Theatre,** 10337 82 (Whyte) Ave. (433-0979 or 433-5785 for a recording). Watch for the Princess's **Grazing on Film** festival in June (tickets $7, seniors and children $3.25). Check the magazine *See* (free) for theater, film, and music listings. The "Live-Line" (424-5483) updates the performance scene.

Led by Wayne Gretzky, the NHL's **Edmonton Oilers** skated off with five Stanley Cups between 1984 and 1990. The Great One now scores his goals elsewhere, but true to form, Canadians are still as loyal to their team as they are to its hero. Hockey fans can still catch the Oilers from October through May in the **Edmonton Coliseum** (451-8000 for tickets).

EVENTS

Edmonton proclaims itself "Canada's Festival City" with celebrations of some kind going on year-round. The **International Jazz City Festival** packs 10 days with club dates and free performances by top international and Canadian jazz musicians (432-7166; June 27-July 6, 1997). This musical extravaganza coincides with a visual arts celebration called **The Works** (426-2122). The **International Street Performers Festival** (425-5162; July 11-20, 1997) fills downtown's Winston Churchill Square with a plethora of musical and acting talent. **Klondike Days** (426-4055 or 471-7210; July 17-26, 1997) are Edmonton's answer to the Stampede. The second week in August, Edmonton hosts its **Folk Music Festival** (429-1889; Aug. 7-10, 1997), considered one of the best in North America. The four-day celebration of blues, bluegrass, and world music takes over Gallagher Park. Only a week later, all the world's a stage on Whyte (82) Ave. for the **Fringe Theater Festival** (448-9000; Aug. 15-24, 1997). For ten days top alternative music and theater pours forth from area parks, theaters, and streets. Considered a high point of Edmonton's festival schedule, the Fringe Festival can warrant a visit in its own right.

■ Near Edmonton

Wilderness beckons a mere 35km to the east at **Elk Island National Park.** In 1906, civic concern prompted the creation of the park to protect endangered elk herds. Since then, all sorts of exotic mammals (plains bison, wood bison, moose, hikers) have moved in, along with 240 species of birds. Pick up your handy copy of *You Are in Bison Country* at the **Park Information Centre** (922-5790), just off Hwy. 16 (open Fri.-Sat. 10:30am-6pm, Sun. 9am-7pm). The shore of **Astotin Lake** is the center of activity in the park. The **Astotin Interpretive Centre** (992-6392) answers questions, screens films, and schedules activities (open Thurs.-Mon. noon-4pm). The information office at the south gate (922-5790; open Fri.-Sun. 8am-6pm) or the administration office for the park (992-2450) will also field questions. Admission to the park is $7 per vehicle. Backcountry **camping** is allowed in certain areas with a **free permit,** obtainable at the information center. The park features 12 well-marked **hiking trails,** most 3-17km in length, which double as cross-country and snowshoeing trails in the winter.

If possible, visitors should try to catch an extremely entertaining **small-town rodeo.** On any summer weekend there may be several near Edmonton; the $6-10 admission fee is negligible given the quality of competition. Nowhere else can one watch leather-clad contestants grip bleating, bucking sheep or narrowly escape being impaled by enraged bulls. Contact **Alberta Tourism Info** (800-661-8888) for a schedule of events and a list of cities and towns that hold rodeos.

▓ Yellowhead Highway 16

Yellowhead Hwy. 16 stretches 3185km across western Canada from Manitoba to the Pacific Coast, but the most interesting and scenic 999-km stretch connects Edmonton and Prince Rupert, BC. The highway is named after the Iroquois trapper and guide who led the European traders of the Hudson Bay Company across the Rockies and into the British Columbia interior in 1826. Lauded as the "less stress, more scenery" route, in Alberta and British Columbia, Hwy. 16 is uncongested and user-friendly. (For Hwy. 16 in British Columbia, see p. 239.) Drivers should pick up a free copy of *Yellowhead It,* a map showing distances between major points that also offers a complete listing of all radio stations along the way. The travel guidebook *The Legend of the Yellowhead,* also free, is more substantial, giving a province-by-province, city-by-city account of Hwy. 16's major, and not so major, tourist attractions. For **road conditions** along Hwy. 16 phone 800-222-6501. The **Yellow Emergency Shelter** offers confidential counseling and free accommodations and meals to women and children travelers in distress (800-661-0737, 24hr.).

In Alberta, the Yellowhead's two lanes, smooth surface, and 110kph (66 mph) speed limit makes for fast, easy driving. An hour west of Edmonton, amid the gentle undulations of the surrounding farmlands, is the town of **Fallis.** A massive radio tower here testifies to the appropriateness of the town's appellation. (*Let's Go* will not comment on the name Uren, Saskatchewan.) Hwy. 16 briefly acknowledges the sleepy town of **Edson** 189km west of Edmonton. Except for some good fishing in the surrounding lakes and rivers, the town has little to offer budget travelers.

Farther west, the many "Cold Beer" signs of downtown **Hinton** may distract travelers lacking the stamina necessary to complete the remaining 70km to Jasper. Plenty of pike, rainbow and cutthroat trout, dolly varden, and yellow perch lurk in nearby lakes and rivers for your angling pleasure. Consult the *Alberta Guide to Sportfishing* for a detailed listing of stocked lakes, licensing fees, and regulations. The guide and other tourist information is available at the **Tourist Information Centre,** 308 Gregg Ave. (865-2777), downtown (open Mon.-Sat. 10am-5:30pm).

Just west of Hinton, Hwy. 16 begins its long downward progression toward the floor of the **Athabaskan River Valley** and into **Jasper National Park.** Jasper's scenic splendor can loosen the jaw muscles of even the most seasoned mountaineer. Mesmerized drivers are cautioned to pay close attention to **wildlife warnings** in the park. Free to roam throughout the park's 10,878 sq. km, Jasper's animal inhabitants invariably choose to graze in roadside ditches. In 1993, 138 large animals were killed in collisions with vehicles. *Reduce your driving speed in the park, especially at night.*

CANADIAN ROCKIES

■ Jasper National Park

Before the Icefields Pkwy. was built, few travelers dared venture north from Banff into the untamed wilderness of Jasper. Those bushwhackers who returned came back with stunning reports, and the completion of the Parkway in 1940 paved the way for the masses to appreciate Jasper's astounding beauty. Jasper Townsite has managed to maintain the look and feel of a genuine small town. The houses of Jasper's permanent residents blend peacefully with the surrounding landscape, providing no distraction from the glorious Rocky Mountain environs. The only conspicuous traces of Jasper's tourist trade are the blue-and-white signs advertising "approved accommodations" and the imitation totem pole at the VIA Rail station. It thankfully keeps its back turned to the town in a gesture of good taste.

PRACTICAL INFORMATION AND ORIENTATION

Visitors Information: Park Information Centre, 500 Connaught Dr. (852-6176). Trail maps and info on all aspects of the park. Open daily 8:30am-7pm; early Sept. to late Oct. and late Dec. to mid-June 9am-5pm. For further info, write to **Park Headquarters,** Superintendent, Jasper National Park, 632 Patricia St., Box 10, Jasper T0E 1E0 (852-6200).

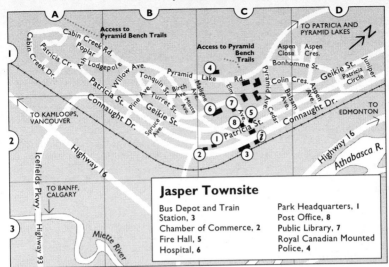

Jasper Townsite

Bus Depot and Train Station, **3**	Park Headquarters, **1**
Chamber of Commerce, **2**	Post Office, **8**
Fire Hall, **5**	Public Library, **7**
Hospital, **6**	Royal Canadian Mounted Police, **4**

Trains: VIA Rail (800-561-8630), on Connaught Dr. 3 per week to: Vancouver ($147), Edmonton ($87), and Winnipeg ($232). 10% discount for seniors and students, children 50%. Coin-operated lockers $1 for 24hr.

Buses: Greyhound (852-3926), in the VIA station. To: Edmonton (4 per day; $45); Kamloops ($47), and Vancouver ($86). **Brewster Transportation Tours**, (852-3332), in the VIA station. Daily to: Banff ($42) and Calgary ($56).

Taxi: Heritage Taxi, 611 Patricia (852-5558), offers a flat rate of $10 between town and Whistler's Hostel, and $16 to the Maligne Canyon Hostel.

Car Rental: Tilden Car Rental (852-4972), in the bus depot. $50 per day with 100 free km. Must be 21 with credit card. $300 insurance deductible for drivers under 25.

Bicycle Rental: Freewheel Cycle, 611 Patricia Ave. (852-3898). Mountain bikes $5 per hr., $15 per 6 hr., $20 per day. Open in summer daily 9am-8pm; spring and fall Tues.-Sun. 10am-6pm. **Whistlers Mountain Hostel** (see **Accommodations,** below) rents mountain bikes for $15 per day.

Laundry and Showers: Coin Clean, 607 Patricia St. (852-3852). Wash $1.75, 5-min. dry 25¢. Showers $2 for 10min. Open daily 8am-9:30pm.

Pharmacy: Whistler Drugs, 100 Miette Ave. (852-4411). Open daily 9am-10:30pm; early Sept. to mid-June 9am-9pm.

Women's Shelter: 800-661-0937.

AIDS Services: AIDS Society Jasper, 852-5274.

Hospital: 518 Robson St. (852-3344).

Local Police: 600 Pyramid Lake Rd. (852-4848). **RCMP Emergency:** 852-4848. **Ambulance and Fire:** 852-3100.

Post Office: 502 Patricia St. (852-3041), across from the townsite green. Open Mon.-Fri. 9am-5pm. **Postal Code:** T0E 1E0.

Area Code: 403.

All of the above addresses are found in **Jasper Townsite,** which is near the center of the park, 362km west of Edmonton and 287km northwest of Banff. **Hwy. 16** transports travelers through the northern reaches of the park, while the **Icefields Parkway** (Hwy. 93) connects to Banff National Park in the south. Buses run to the townsite daily from Edmonton, Calgary, Vancouver, and Banff. Trains arrive from Edmonton and Vancouver. Bikes can also be rented one way between Jasper and Banff. Hitching is both easy and popular along the Icefields Pkwy. (*Let's Go* would never even think of recommending hitchhiking.)

ACCOMMODATIONS

Hotels in Jasper Townsite are expensive. You may be able to stay cheaply at a **B&B** (singles $45-55, doubles $50-70). Most are located in town near the bus and train stations. Ask for the *Private Homes Accommodations List* at the park information center or the bus depot. Hostels are above all the most convenient and economical choice. A modern facility 5km outside of Jasper Townsite anchors a chain of hostels stretching from Jasper to Calgary. Rustic hostels are, not surprisingly, less laden with amenities than the main hostels, but they're also a lot closer to some of the park's best outdoor activities. HI-C runs a shuttle service connecting all the Rocky Mountain hostels and Calgary with rates from $9 to $59 depending on how far you're going. If you can't get a reservation by phone, you can try for a wait list bed (most become available at 6pm) or one of the six stand-by beds saved for shuttle arrivals. For reservations at any rustic hostel and information on winter availability, call **Jasper International Hostel** at 852-3215.

Jasper International Hostel (HI-C) (852-3215), on Sky Tram Rd., 5km south of the townsite off Hwy. 93. Closest to the townsite, this is the park's most modern (and crowded) hostel. Usually filled with gregarious travelers in summer. Bring your own food, leave your shoes at the front door, and play with the marmots who frequent the volleyball court. Accommodates 69. Curfew midnight. $15, nonmembers $20.

Maligne Canyon Hostel (HI-C), 11km east of the townsite on Maligne Canyon Rd. Small, recently renovated cabins on the bank of the Maligne River. Gas heat without electricity or running water. The manager is not only knowledgeable, he's on a first name basis with several local bears and is happy to lead guided hikes through nearby Maligne Canyon. Accommodates 24. $9, non-members $14.

Mt. Edith Cavell Hostel (HI-C), on Edith Cavell Rd., off Hwy. 93A. One of the more popular rustic hostels, Edith Cavell has propane light, pump water, and immediate access to Mt. Edith Cavell. The road is closed in winter, but the hostel welcomes anyone willing to ski 11km from Hwy. 93A. Accommodates 32. $9, nonmembers $14.

Athabasca Falls Hostel (HI-C) (852-5959), on Hwy. 93, 30km south of Jasper Townsite, 500m from Athabasca Falls. The only rustic hostel with electricity, but ironically no running water. Huge dining/recreation room with wood-burning stove. Accommodates 40. $9, nonmembers $14.

Beauty Creek Hostel (HI-C), on Hwy. 93, 87km south of Jasper Townsite. Next to the stunning Sunwapta River and close to the Columbia Icefields with several worthwhile hiking trails of its very own. Accommodates 24. Accessible through a "key system" in winter (groups only). $9, nonmembers $14.

CAMPING

The campsites below are listed from north to south. Most are primitive sites offering few facilities but ready outdoor access. They are also first-come, first-served, so get there early or sleep in the trees. For detailed information, call the park information center (852-6176).

Whistlers, on Whistlers Rd., 3km south of the townsite off Hwy. 93. The mother of all campgrounds and the only one in the park with full hook-ups and modern facilities available. If you're intimidated by wilderness, the occupants of the 781 neighboring sites will keep you company. Hot and cold running water, showers. Wheelchair access, public phone. Tent sites $14, full hookups $19. Open early May to mid-Oct.

Snaring River, 16km east of the townsite on Hwy. 16. Kitchen shelters, dry toilets, great view. 56 sites with 10 walk-in tent sites, $10. Open mid-May to early Sept.

Pocahontas, on Hwy. 16, at the northern edge of the park, 46km east of the townsite. Closest campground to Miette Hot Springs. Flush toilets, hot running water. Hookups available. Wheelchair access. 140 sites, $13. Open mid-May to early Oct.

Wapiti, on Hwy. 93, 2km south of Whistlers. With a nice balance between facilities and scenery, Wapiti has become an unofficial RV headquarters. But the plentiful brush offers tent campers plenty of protection from their land whale-driving neighbors. 366 sites. Hot running water, showers. Sites $15, with electricity $18. Open May 19-23 and early June to early Sept.

Wabasso, on Hwy. 93A, about 17km south of Jasper Townsite. Flush toilets, hot running water, showers, trailer sewage disposal. Wheelchair access. 238 sites, $13. Open May 19-23, late June to early Sept.

There are five campgrounds along the Icefields Parkway with fairly comparable facilities (kitchen shelters, dry toilets) for a comparable price ($10 during late May to early Oct.), making the main differences between them a matter of location. **Mount Kerkeslin**, about 35km south of Jasper Townsite, has 42 sites. **Honeymoon Lake,** about 52km south of town, sports its own swimming pool (but who wants to swim with the Sunwapta Falls only 3km away?). **Jonas Creek,** about 77km south of the townsite, is the smallest campground with only 13 sites along the Sunwapta River. The high point of the Parkway campgrounds is **Columbia Icefield,** on Hwy. 93, 109km south of the townsite. Close enough to the Athabasca Glacier to receive an icy breeze and even the occasional snowfall on a summer night. A difficult and steep access road makes it RV free, but crowded nonetheless. Two km down the highway, find **Wilcox Creek,** on Hwy. 93, at the southern park boundary (46 sites).

FOOD

Eating inexpensively in Jasper is easy—as long as you're willing to live on appetizers. Then again, between Alberta's hostel chain and endless outdoors activities, who needs restaurants? **Super A Foods,** 601 Patricia St. (852-3200), can satisfy all basic grocery needs (open Mon.-Sat. 8am-11pm, Sun. 9am-10pm). Groups, 10-day backpackers and the really hungry will love the selection of bulk foods available at **Nutter's,** 622 Patricia St. (852-5844), not to mention the deli meats, canned goods, and freshly ground coffee (open daily 9am-11pm).

Mountain Foods and Café, 606 Connaught Dr. (852-4050). An excellent stop for breakfast or lunch featuring an extensive selection of sandwiches and sandwich-like concoctions (bagelwich, anyone?) with a constantly shifting mix of ingredients. Even the martini menu is varied. Grilled foccacia sandwich $5.75. Burritos $4.50. Breakfast $4-5. Open daily 7am-11pm.

Scoops and Loops, 504 Patricia St. (852-4333). It doesn't take long before you begin to suspect that this is no ordinary ice cream parlor. Scoops dishes out sandwiches ($3.50-$5), pastries ($1.50), sushi ($2.50-6), udon noodles ($8), and ice cream. Open Mon.-Sat. 10am-11pm, Sun. 11am-10pm.

Mondi's, 632 Connaught Dr. (852-4070). Between 5:15pm and 6:15pm daily pasta entrees are 2-for-1 making Mondi's an ideal carbo-loading pit stop. While lunch serves pastas from $7-9, dinner prices rise considerably making earlier meals in this classy establishment the best deal. Open daily 7am-11pm.

OUTDOORS

An extensive network of trails weaves through Jasper, with many paths starting at the townsite itself. The trails cover the park's three different ecological zones. The **montane zone** blankets the valley bottoms with lodgepole pine, Douglas fir, white spruce, and aspen. Sub-alpine fir and Engelmann spruce inhabit the middle part of the canopy, called the **sub-alpine zone,** which makes up 40% of the park. Fragile plants and wildflowers struggle to subsist in the uppermost **alpine zone.** Hikers should not stray from trails in the alpine area to avoid trampling endangered plant species. Kick off any foray into the wilderness with a visit to the information center in the townsite. Experts there distribute free copies of *Day Hikes in Jasper National Park* and can direct you to appropriate hiking and mountain-biking trails. The **Icefield Centre,** on

Hwy. 93 at the southern entrance to the park (see **Icefields Pkwy.** on p. 287), provides similar services.

Named after an English nurse who was executed during World War I by the Germans for providing aid to the Allies, **Mt. Edith Cavell** will shake you to the bone with the thunderous roar of avalanches off the Angel Glacier. Take the 1.6km loop **Path of the Glacier** to the top or the hike through **Cavell Meadows.** Edith rears her enormous head 30km south of the townsite on Mt. Edith Cavell Rd. Because Mt. Edith Cavell has become one of Jasper's most popular attractions, the road to the top is now regulated. Check at the information center for times when you can travel up and down.

Not to be outdone by Banff, Jasper has a gondola of its own. The **Jasper Tramway** (852-3093) sits off Hwy. 93, 2km from Jasper. The longest and highest tramway in Canada offers a panoramic view of the park as it rises 2km up the side of **Whistlers Mountain.** The gondola draws crowds and packs the parking lot ($15, ages 5-14 $8.50, under 5 free; open April to Oct. 8:30am-10pm). The more rugged, adventurous, and economical way to the 8100 ft. peak is the steep 7km trail which starts from the Jasper International Hostel. Hike to the top, feel studly, and then take the tram ride down ($7.50) to spare your quadriceps. No matter how you go, be sure to bring along sunglasses and a warm jacket to protect against the bright sun and rapidly changing weather conditions at the summit.

Intrepid hikers should attempt the three-faced **Mystery Lake Trail,** leading east, uphill from the pools. The trail changes from a paved path into a dirt road, and then into a serious trek in the course of the 11km journey to Mystery Lake. Be warned that you will need to ford a major river that often becomes impassable after periods of heavy rainfall; contact the information center for a report on trail conditions.

Maligne Lake, the second largest glacier-fed lake in the Canadian Rockies, is located 48km southeast of the townsite at the end of Maligne Lake Rd. You can enjoy every water sport imaginable in Maligne's vivid turquoise waters. Reservations for boat cruises and whitewater rafting trips should be made through the **Maligne Tours** office, 626 Connaught Dr. (852-3370). Farther north in the valley and 30km east of the townsite, the Maligne River flows into **Medicine Lake,** but no river flows out. The water escapes underground through tunnels in the porous limestone, re-emerging 16km downstream in the **Maligne Canyon,** 11km east of the townsite on Maligne Canyon Rd. (This is the longest known underground river in North America. Pretty sneaky, eh?)

Whitewater Rafting (Jasper) Ltd. (852-7238) offers several rafting trips from $40; a two-hour trip down the Maligne River costs $48. Register by phone or stop at the Esso station in the townsite. **Rocky Mountain River Guides,** 600 Patricia St. (852-3777), in On-Line Sport and Tackle, offers a three-hour trip ($55) and a calmer Mile 5 ride ($35). **Sekani Mountain Tours** (852-5337) offers various trips for $40-80 with discounts to HI members. **Boat rental** is available at **Pyramid Lake** (852-4900; canoes $10 for 1hr., $7 each additional hr., $25 per day; $20 and a valid ID required for deposit) and **Maligne Lake,** 626 Connaught Dr. (852-3370; canoes $10 for 1hr., $45 per day; ID required for deposit). For a less strenuous tour of Maligne Lake, **Maligne Lake Scenic Cruises** offers narrated cruises in cozy, heated tour boats ($29, seniors $26, children $14.50; reservations recommended).

Fish aren't stocked in National Park waters, but diligent anglers won't go home empty-handed if they can find a spot that nobody else has. The key to finding a secluded **fishing** spot at Jasper is to go somewhere inaccessible by car. Rent equipment and get tips on good spots at **Currie's,** in **The Sports Shop,** 414 Connaught Dr. (852-3654; rod, reel, and line $10; one-day boat rental $25, $18 if rented after 2pm, $12 after 6 pm).

Warmer water can be found at **Miette Hot Springs** (866-3939), north of the townsite off Hwy. 16 along the clearly marked, 15km Miette Hotsprings Rd. The Hot Springs building contains lockers and two pools (one is wheelchair accessible; neither is especially mesmerizing). Spring water is pumped from the smelly source and journeys through a series of pipes to arrive, miraculously scentless, at the pools.

Unfortunately, the 40°C (104°F) water is off-limits in winter ($4, children $3.50; day passes $7.25, children $6.50; suit rental $1.25, towels $1, lockers 25¢; open May 15-June 20 daily 10:30am-9pm; June 21-Sept. 2 daily 8:30am-10:30pm; Sept. 3-Oct. 14 10:30am-9pm).

Winter may keep you away from the hot springs, but you can always warm up on the ski slopes of **Marmot Basin** (852-3816), near Jasper Townsite. A full-day lift ticket costs $35, youth $29, junior $14, seniors $24. Ski rental is available at **Totem's Ski Shop,** 408 Connaught Dr. (852-3078). A full rental package (skis, boots, and poles) runs $9 per day. Maligne Lake offers cross-country ski trails from late November through May.

The extra-adventurous who do not consider hiking, fishing, boating, skiing, and sightseeing stimulating enough will find Jasper a challenging site for feats of daredeviltry. The **Jasper Climbing School,** 806 Connaught Dr. (852-3964), offers an introductory three-hour rappelling class ($25) for those who want a closer look at the imposing cliffs which surround Jasper. **Caving** is a little-talked-about and extremely dangerous pursuit, and is not permitted in the national parks without a permit; one should try it only with an experienced guide. Ben Gadd (852-4012), author of *Handbook of the Canadian Rockies,* leads tours to the **Cadomin Caves** and charges a flat rate of $250 for 10-20 people. Because these caves are outside the National Park, a permit is not required.

■ Icefields Parkway

The Icefields Pkwy. (Hwy. 93), voted the most beautiful highway in North America, is a glacier-lined, 230km road connecting Jasper Townsite with Lake Louise in the south. Essentially a park in itself, the Parkway snakes past dozens of ominous peaks and glacial lakes. Pull over at the head of one of 17 **trails** into the wilderness, or stop at one of 22 **scenic points** to take in a spectacular view. The 10-minute trail to **Bow Summit** affords a magnificent view of **Peyto Lake,** with its unreal fluorescent blue-green coloring, especially vivid at the end of June. Marvel at the **Weeping Wall,** where water seems to seep from the rock, or at **Bridal Veil Falls'** beautiful series of cascades. Whether driving or biking, set aside at least three days for the parkway; its challenging hikes and endless vistas are never monotonous. Thanks to the extensive campground and hostel networks which line the parkway, extended trips down the entire length of Jasper and Banff National Parks are convenient and affordable. (See **Accommodations and Camping** under each park.)

Before setting your wheels on the road, pick up a free map of the *Icefields Parkway,* available at park information centers in Jasper and Banff. The pamphlet is also available at the **Icefield Centre** (852-6560), at the boundary between Banff and Jasper, 103km south of Jasper Townsite. The center is within view of the **Athabasca Glacier,** the most prominent of the eight major glaciers which flow from the 325 sq. km **Columbia Icefield.** The Columbia is the largest accumulation of ice and snow south of the Arctic Circle. Its meltwater runs into streams and rivers that terminate in three different oceans: north to the Arctic, east to the Atlantic, and west to the Pacific. Summer crowds have snowball fights on the vast icefields at the side of the road. **Brewster Transportation and Tours** (762-2241) carries visitors right onto the Athabasca Glacier in monster buses called "Snocoaches." This 75-minute trip costs $21.50 (ages 6-15 $5). Explore the icy expanse on your own from the parking lot (tours given May-Sept. daily 9am-5pm; Oct. daily 10am-5pm).

If you have a bone-chilling curiosity to know the geological history of glaciers, sign up for a guided **interpretive hike** on the mighty Athabasca (offered mid-June to mid-Sept.). A three-hour hike called "Ice Cubed" costs $27 (ages 7-17 $12), and the five-hour "Icewalk Deluxe" is $31 (ages 7-17 $14). Write **Athabasca Glacier Icewalks,** Attn.: Peter Lemieux, Box 2067, Banff T0L 0C0. A warmer alternative to journeying out onto the glacier is the 13-minute explanatory film inside the cozy Icefield Centre. (Open mid-June to Aug. daily 9am-7pm; mid-May to mid-June and Sept. 9am-4pm.)

Although the center is closed in winter, the parkway is closed only for plowing after heavy snowfalls.

If you only have time for a quickie, try the **Parker Ridge Trail.** The 2.4km hike (one way) guides you away from the parkway, past the treeline, and over Parker Ridge. At the end of the trail awaits an amazing view of the **Saskatchewan Glacier.** The trailhead is located 1km south of the **Hilda Creek Hostel,** which is located 8.5km south of the Icefields (see **Banff: Accommodations,** p. 290).

■ Lake Louise

Spectacular turquoise Lake Louise and its surrounding glaciers often serve North American filmmakers' need for "Swiss" scenery. Unfortunately, most visitors spend only enough time at the lake to snap photos. Few stay as long as explorer Tom Wilson did in the 1880s, when he wrote of its majesty, "I never in all my explorations...saw such a matchless scene."

The **Lake Louise Visitor Centre** (522-3833), at Samson Mall, swells with courteous staffpeople (open daily 8am-8pm, Sept. 8am-6pm, winter 9am-5pm). The brand-new $4.4 million complex is also a museum, with exhibits and a short film on the formation of the Rockies. Renting a canoe from the **Chateau Lake Louise Boat House** (522-3511) will give you the closest look at the lake ($25 per hr.; open daily 9am-8pm). Several hiking trails begin at the water; especially good are the 3.6km **Lake Agnes Trail** and the 5½km **Plain of Six Glaciers Trail.** The views only get better as you go farther along the trails, and you'll leave the shutterbugs behind at the end of the lake.

Many find nearby **Lake Moraine** to be even more impressive than its sister Lake Louise. The lake, also explorable by canoe or boat, lies in the awesome **Valley of the Ten Peaks,** including glacier-encrusted **Mount Temple.** Join the multitudes on the **Rockpile Trail** for an eye-popping view of the lake and valley, or stroll along the lake-hugging **Lakeshore Trail.** If you're looking for a longer route, try the trail to **Larch Valley.** Continue along the same trail to **Sentinel Pass** for some of the best views in the area. You can cross the pass and make a long loop, connecting with the **Paradise Valley Trail;** get further information at the Lake Louise Information Centre. If you don't get a chance to visit Lake Moraine, just get your hands on an old $20 bill; the Valley of Ten Peaks is pictured on the reverse.

Timberline Tours (522-3743), located off Lake Louise Dr. near Deer Lodge, offers guided horseback rides through the area. The 1½-hour tour costs $26; the daytrip, $70 (lunch included). The **Lake Louise Sightseeing Lift** (522-3555), which runs up Mt. Whitehorn across the Trans-Canada Hwy. from Lake Louise, provides another chance to gape at the landscape (open early June to late Sept. daily 8am-10pm; fare $9.50, seniors and students $8, ages 6-12 $6). Like Sulphur Mountain's, Lake Louise's lift offers a $13.25 breakfast deal at the peak-top café (seniors and students $12.25, ages 6-12 $9.25), which includes a lift ticket. Coupons worth $1 off appear in the lift's brochure, available locally and at the park Information Centres.

▩ Banff National Park

Banff is Canada's best-loved and best-known natural preserve. It offers 6600 sq. km (2543 sq. mi.) of peaks, canyons, white foaming rapids, brilliant turquoise lakes, dense forests, and open meadows. The glory of Banff lies in the awe-inspiring scale of its grandeur. Yet it was not a simple love of natural beauty that motivated Prime Minister Sir John MacDonald to establish Canada's first national park in 1885. Rather, officers of the Canadian Pacific Railroad convinced him of Banff's potential for "large pecuniary advantage," and were quick to add, "since we can't export the scenery, we shall have to import the tourists." Their plan worked with a vengeance. One of Canada's most popular vacation destinations, the town of Banff has exploded in a riot of Hard Rock Café Banff t-shirts. Fortunately, Banff's priceless beauty really does grow on trees, offering an expansive diversity of environments and experiences.

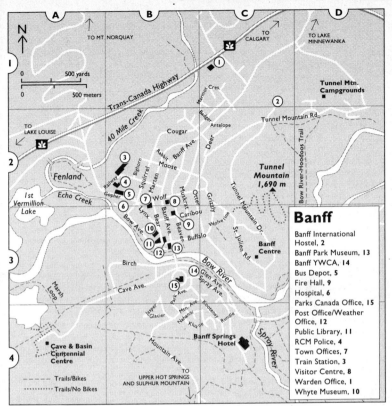

Banff

Banff International Hostel, 2
Banff Park Museum, 13
Banff YWCA, 14
Bus Depot, 5
Fire Hall, 9
Hospital, 6
Parks Canada Office, 15
Post Office/Weather Office, 12
Public Library, 11
RCM Police, 4
Town Offices, 7
Train Station, 3
Visitor Centre, 8
Warden Office, 1
Whyte Museum, 10

WESTERN CANADA

PRACTICAL INFORMATION AND ORIENTATION

Visitors Information: Banff Information Centre, 224 Banff Ave. Includes **Banff/ Lake Louise Tourism Bureau** (762-8421) and **Canadian Parks Service** (762-1550). The most efficient, informative, and well-organized info center in Western Canada. Open daily 8am-8pm; Oct.-May 9am-5pm. **Lake Louise Information Centre** (522-3833). Open mid-May to mid-June daily 10am-6pm; mid-June to Aug. 8am-8pm; Sept.-Oct. 10am-6pm; winter 9am-5pm. Both centers dispense detailed maps and brochures, and provide info on ski areas, restaurants, activities, accommodations, and cultural attractions.

American Express: Brewster Travel, 317 Banff Ave., Box 1140, Banff T0L 0C0 (762-3207). Holds mail free of charge for card members. Open Mon.-Fri. 8am-6pm, Sat. 9:30am-5pm.

Buses: Greyhound, 100 Gopher St. (800-661-8747). From the Brewster terminal. 4 per day to: Lake Louise ($10), Calgary ($18), and Vancouver ($97).

Tours: Brewster Transportation, 100 Gopher St. (762-6767), near the train depot. Monopoly on tours of the area; runs 1 express daily to Jasper ($42). To: Lake Louise (2 per day, $13) and Calgary (5 per day, $33). Does not honor Greyhound Ameripasses. Depot open daily 7:30am-10pm.

Public Transportation: Banff Explorer (760-8294), operated by the town, runs 2 routes. stretching from the Banff Springs Hotel ($1.50) to the hostel and Tunnel Mountain Campground ($1, children 50¢). Exact change required. Operates mid-June to mid-Sept. daily 9am-9pm.

Taxis: Legion Taxi, 762-3353. 24hr. **Lake Louise Taxi,** 522-2020.

Car Rental: Banff Used Car Rentals (762-3352), in the Shell Station at the junction of Wolf and Lynx. $36 per day, 100km free, 10¢ per additional km. Major credit card required.

Bike Rental: Bactrax Rentals, 337 Banff Ave. (762-8177), in the Ptarmigan Inn. Mountain bikes $6 per hr., $24 per day. HI member discount: $1 off per hr., $4 off per day. Open daily 8am-8pm.

Equipment Rental: Performance Ski and Sport, 208 Bear St. (762-8222). Rents everything from tents ($12 per day) to kayaks ($10 per hr.) to fishing gear ($10-20 per day). 10% discount for HI members.

Laundry: Cascade Coin Laundry, 317 Banff Ave. (762-0165), downstairs in the Cascade Mall. Wash $1.75, 5-min. dry 25¢. Open daily 7:30am-11pm. **Lake Louise Laundromat** (522-2143), Samson Mall. $2 wash, 7-min. dry 25¢. Showers $4. Open daily 9am-9pm.

Pharmacy: Harmony Drug, 111 Banff Ave. (762-5711). Open daily 9am-9pm.

Hospital: Mineral Springs, 316 Lynx St. (762-2222), near Wolf St.

Emergency: Banff Warden Office (762-4506), **Lake Louise Warden Office** (522-3866). Open 24hr. **Police:** (762-2226; non-emergency 762-2228), on Railway St. by the train depot.

Post Office: 204 Buffalo St. (762-2586). Open Mon.-Fri. 9am-5:30pm. **Postal Code:** T0L 0C0.

Area Code: 403.

Banff National Park hugs the Alberta-British Columbia border, 120km west of Calgary. The **Trans-Canada Hwy.** (Hwy. 1) runs east-west through the park connecting it to Yoho National Park to the west; **Icefields Parkway** (Hwy. 93) connects Banff with Jasper National Park to the north and Kootenay National Park to the southwest. Greyhound links the park to major points in Alberta and British Columbia. Civilization in the park centers around the towns of Banff and **Lake Louise,** 55km northwest of Banff on Hwy. 1. The **Bow Valley Pkwy.** (Hwy. 1A), parallels Hwy. 1 from Lake Louise to 8km west of Banff.

ACCOMMODATIONS

Finding a cheap place to stay in Banff is easy if you reserve ahead. Residents of the townsite offer rooms in their own homes, often at reasonable rates, especially in the off-season. Check the list in the back of the *Banff and Lake Louise Official Visitor's Guide,* available free at the Banff Townsite Information Centre. Mammoth modern hostels at Banff and Lake Louise anchor a chain of hostels stretching from Calgary to Jasper. The rustic hostels in the chain provide a more intense wilderness experience than the main hostels, as well as stone's-throw access to some of the best hiking and cross-country skiing in the park. HI-C runs a shuttle service connecting all the Rocky Mountain hostels and Calgary with rates from $9 to $59 depending on how far you're going. If you can't get a reservation by phone, you can try for a wait list bed (most become available at 6pm) or one of the six stand-by beds saved for shuttle arrivals. For reservations at any rustic hostel, call Banff International at 762-4122.

Banff International Hostel (BIH) (HI-C), Box 1358, Banff T0L 0C0 (762-4122), 3km from Banff Townsite on Tunnel Mountain Rd., among a nest of condominiums and lodges. BIH has the look and setting of a ski lodge. A large fireplace warms the lounge area in winter. Clean rooms with 2-4 bunk beds. Take the Banff Explorer from downtown, or join the many other hostelers hoofing it. Café, laundry facilities, hot showers. Wheelchair accessible. Accommodates 154. Linen free. Open all day. No curfew. $17, nonmembers $22.

Castle Mountain Hostel (HI-C) (762-4122), on Hwy. 1A, 1½km east of the junction of Hwy. 1 and Hwy. 93 between Banff and Lake Louise. Recently renovated. 36 beds. Common area has a general store and firepit; frequent bear sightings. The only rustic with running water and electricity. $11, nonmembers $16.

Lake Louise International Hostel (HI-C), Village Rd. (522-2200), ½km from Samson Mall in Lake Louise Townsite. More like a hotel than a hostel. 100 beds. Cafeteria, full service kitchen. Wheelchair accessible. The adjacent Canadian Alpine

Centre sponsors programs and events for hikers and skiers. $18.50-22.50, non-members $25-29.

Mosquito Creek Hostel (HI-C), 103km south of the Icefield Centre and 26km north of Lake Louise. Propane gas and heat. Babbling brook nearby. Close to Wapta Icefield. Accommodates 38. Fireplace, sauna, full-service kitchen. Call BIH for reservations. $11, nonmembers $16.

Rampart Creek Hostel (HI-C), 34km south of the Icefield Centre. Rampart's proximity to several world-famous ice climbs (including Weeping Wall, 17km north on Icefields Parkway) makes it a favorite of winter mountaineers. Accommodates 30 in rustic cabins. Sauna, full service kitchen, wood-heated bathtub. $10, nonmembers $15.

Hilda Creek Hostel (HI-C), 8½km south of the Icefield Centre on the Icefields Pkwy. Excellently situated at the base of Mt. Athabasca. Some of the Icefield's best hiking and skiing lie just behind the hostel on Parker Ridge. Wood-burning sauna, full service kitchen. Propane heat and light. $10, nonmembers $15.

CAMPING

As with the hostels, there is a chain of campgrounds connecting Banff to Jasper with large, fully hooked-up campgrounds as anchors. Try one of the primitive sites farther from the towns if you want to avoid RVs. The campgrounds don't take reservations, so showing up early is your best bet. The campgrounds below are listed from south to north. Proximity to the sights in the park that you wish to see should take precedence over amenities in your choice of campsite.

Tunnel Mountain Village, 1km past BIH, near Banff Townsite. The anchor of the Banff campground superstructure. 320 sites with full hookups, 188 with power only, and over 600 unserviced tent sites. Flush toilets, showers, trail to the Hoodoos, the works. Sites $19, full hookup $22. Open May-Sept. 30.

Two Jack Main, 13km northeast of Banff. 458 sites with 77 right by the lake. Canoeing and cycling nearby. Showers, flush toilets. Sites $13, lakeside $16. Open mid-May to Sept. 30.

Johnston Canyon, 26km northwest of Banff on Hwy. 1A. 132 sites with excellent trail access on the scenic route connecting Banff and Lake Louise. Flush toilets, showers. $16. Open mid-May to mid-Sept.

Castle Mountain, midway between Banff and Lake Louise along Hwy. 1A. Excellent and relatively uncrowded hiking within easy reach of these 43 sites. Flush toilets, no showers. $12. Open late June-early Sept.

Protection Mountain, 11km west of Castle Junction on Hwy. 1A. 89 spacious and wooded sites, on one of Banff's most primitive campgrounds. Cycling nearby. Pit toilets, no showers. $13. Open late June-early Sept.

Lake Louise. Separate tenting and trailer sites, no hook-ups. Not actually on the lake but there's hiking and fishing nearby. 216 tent sites $14, 189 trailer sites $18. Open mid-May to early Sept.

Mosquito Creek, 103km south of the Icefield Centre and 26km north of Lake Louise. 32 sites on the creek, immediate access to Icefields Parkway hiking. No facilities. $10; $8 in winter. Open year-round. Fully serviced mid-June to early Sept.

Waterfowl, 57km north of Hwy. 1 on Hwy. 93. 116 sites near the Waterfowl lakes. Hiking, canoeing, and fishing nearby. Flush toilets but no water. $13. Open early June to mid-Sept.

Rampart Creek, 147km north of Banff, 40km south of the Icefield Centre. 50 sites across the highway from the hostel. No showers or flush toilets. Interpretive hikes! Open mid-June to early Sept.

FOOD

Restaurants in Banff generally serve expensive, mediocre food. Luckily, the Banff **(Café Aspenglow)** and Lake Louise **(Peyto's Café)** International Hostels and the Banff YWCA serve affordable meals for $3-7. Shop at **Safeway** (762-5378), at Marten and Elk St., just off Banff Ave. (open daily 8am-10pm; winter 9am-9pm). Some of the bars offer reasonably priced daily specials.

Jump Start, 206 Buffalo St. (762-0332). Refuel with all varieties of coffee, home-made soups ($4.25), and fresh, tasty sandwiches ($5). For a heartier meal, try the veggie lasagna ($5.50) or the shepherd's pie ($5.40). Open Mon.-Fri. 7am-7pm, Sat.-Sun. 8am-8pm.

Aardvark's, 304A Caribou St. (762-5500). This small pizza place does big business after the bars close. Excellent pizza anytime. Slices $2.75. Small $6-8, large $12-19. Huge subs $4-6.50, buffalo wings ("mild" through "suicide"; $5.35 for 10). 10% discount with HI card. Open daily 11am-4am.

Laggan's Deli (522-3574), in Samson Mall at Lake Louise. Savor a thick sandwich on whole-wheat bread ($3.75) with a Greek salad ($1.75), or take home a freshly baked loaf ($2-2.25) for later. Excellent cappuccino ($2.50). Always crowded, there's nowhere better in Lake Louise Village. Open daily 6am-8pm.

Btfsplk's Diner, 221 Banff Ave. (762-5529). A clssc dnr, wth blck nd wht tl flr nd rd ptnt lthr. Meal-size Caesar salads ($7.25) and BBQ burgers ($7). Open daily 8am-10pm.

ENTERTAINMENT

Banff's bartenders maintain that the real wildlife in Banff is at the bars. Get the trail dust out of your throat along Banff Ave. where you can drink 'til you barff.

Rose and Crown, 202 Banff Ave. (762-2121). Comfy chairs and a welcoming fire make this a cozy place to drink a few even in mid-summer. Live music almost every night. Happy hour (Mon.-Fri. 4:30-7:30pm) has $3-3.50 drafts, $2.75 highballs. Sun. is local jam night from 9pm-2am. Open daily 11am-2am.

Barbary Coast, upstairs at 119 Banff Ave. (762-4616). Sports paraphernalia dominates the decor at this fashionable, laid-back bar. The kitchen could stand on its own as an excellent restaurant; the pasta dishes are particularly good. Look for specials at lunch ($6-7). Live music every night ranges from blues to rock. Mon. is pizza night ($7 for 10-in.); happy hour 4:30-7:30pm. Open daily 11am-2am.

Silver City, 110 Banff Ave. (762-3337). Once notorious for countless drunken brawls, this "Hall of Fame Sports Bar" has mellowed with age and an unforeseen 100% staff turnover, but it's still one of the most crowded in town. Billiards $1.25. Happy hour Mon.-Sat. 6-9pm, Sun. 6pm-2am. Dancing nightly 9pm-2am. Open daily 6pm-2:30am.

SIGHTS AND EVENTS

Every summer, the culture industry moves to the mountains bringing drama, ballet, opera, and the renowned Banff Festival of Mountain Films as part of the **Banff Festival of the Arts.** Pick up a brochure at the info centre or call 762-6300 for details. The palatial **Banff Springs Hotel** (762-2211), on Spray Ave., overlooks the town. In 1988, this 825-room castle celebrated its 100th birthday with a series of posh parties and its own special brand of beer (weakened at the request of hotel guests). You can enjoy a Centennial Ale, a basket of bread, and a fantastic view for $3.75 at the **Grapes Wine Bar** on the mezzanine level. Ride the guest elevator up to the 8th floor to see what kind of view you'd have if you could afford to stay here. In summer, the hotel offers guided tours of the grounds Monday to Saturday at 5pm ($5). The tour, good for a rainy day, offers a grand opportunity to view lavish architecture and museum-quality artifacts. The hotel also offers horseback riding (daily 9am-5pm; $25 for 1hr., $52 for 3hr.; for reservations call 762-2848).

Other rainy day attractions include Banff's small museums. The **Whyte Museum of the Canadian Rockies,** 111 Bear St. (762-2291), offers a look at the history of (surprise) the Canadian Rockies. Exhibits in the museum's **Heritage Gallery** explain how Banff developed: very rapidly, unchecked, and catering to the whims of wealthy guests at the Banff Springs Hotel. The galleries downstairs display local artists' paintings of the mountains and their inhabitants ($3, seniors and students $2, children free; open mid-May to mid-Sept. Sun.-Mon. 10am-6pm, Tues.-Sat. 10am-9pm; mid-Oct. to mid-May Tues.-Sun. 1-5pm, Thurs. 1-9pm). The **Banff Park Museum** (762-1558), on Banff Ave. near the bridge, is a taxidermist's dream. Clippings in the well stocked reading room recount in loving detail violent encounters between elk and automobiles. More impressive than the exhibits is the building itself, erected in 1903 before the heyday of electric light, and designed to maximize natural light with high windows ($2.25, seniors $1.75, children $1.25; open June-Aug. daily 10am-6pm; Sept.-May 1-5pm). A block away on the second floor of the Clock Tower Mall is the **Natural History Museum,** 112 Banff Ave. (762-4747). The amateur private collection focuses on geology, but contains a little of everything. The complete tour includes a thrilling 20-minute video documentary focusing on the eruption of Mount St. Helens. (Early 80s soundtrack not available for purchase.) On your way out, be sure to make faces at the 8-ft. "authentic" model of Sasquatch (free; open daily May-June 10am-8pm; July-Aug. 10am-10pm; Sept. 10am-8pm; winter 10am-6pm).

OUTDOORS

Hike to the **backcountry** for privacy, intense beauty, over **1600km** of trails, and trout that will bite anything. Pick up the complete *Backcountry Visitors' Guide* at information centers (see **Practical Information**). You need a **permit** to stay overnight; get one at the information centers for $6 per person per day, up to $30 per person, or $42 per year. Day hiking, on the other hand, does not require a permit. All litter must leave the backcountry with you, and no live trees may be chopped in the parks. Both the Banff International Hostel (see **Accommodations**) and the information centers will let you peruse the *Canadian Rockies Trail Guide,* with excellent information and maps. You can find your own copy in almost any bookstore or outdoors shop. The pamphlet *Drives and Walks* describes day hikes in the Lake Louise and Banff areas.

Two easy trails lie within walking distance of Banff. **Fenland** winds 2km through an area also frequented by beaver, muskrat, and waterfowl. Follow Mt. Norquay Rd. out of Banff and look for signs across the railroad tracks on the left side of the road (the trail is closed in late spring and early summer due to elk calving). The summit of **Tunnel Mountain** provides a spectacular view of the Bow Valley and Mt. Rundle. Follow Wolf St. east from Banff Ave. and turn right on St. Julien Rd. to reach the head of the steep 2.3-km trail.

About 25km out of Banff toward Lake Louise along the Bow Valley Parkway, **Johnston Canyon** is a popular half-day hike. The 1.1-km hike to the canyon's lower falls and the 2.7-km trip to the upper falls consist mostly of a catwalk along the edge of the canyon. Don't stop at the falls, though: keep on the more rugged trail for another 3.1km until you get to seven blue-green cold water springs known as the **Inkpots.** The trail is packed with tourists toting video cameras to the falls, but is relatively tourist-free beyond the upper falls.

If a strenuous day of hiking fails to entice you, take a drive on one of the many scenic routes in the Banff area. **Tunnel Mountain Drive** begins at the intersection of Banff Ave. and Buffalo St. and proceeds 9km past Bow Falls and up the side of Tunnel Mountain. Several markers along the way point to splendid views of the Banff Springs Hotel, Sulphur Mountain, and Mt. Rundle. Turn right onto Tunnel Mountain Rd. to see the **hoodoos,** long, finger-like projections of limestone once part of the cliff wall and thought by indigenous Canadians to encase sentinel spirits.

Bicycling is permitted on public roads and highways and on certain trails in the park. Spectacular scenery and the proximity to a number of hostels and campgrounds make the Bow Valley Parkway (Hwy. 1A) and the Icefields Parkway (Hwy. 93) perfect for extended cycling trips. The *Trail Bicycling Guide,* available at the information centers in Banff and Lake Louise, lists trails on which bikes are permitted. **Hammerhead Mountain Bike Tours** (547-1566) offers a great deal: a day-long guided off-road tour, including transport from Banff, bike and helmet rental, and picnic lunch, all for $44 (June-Sept. Mon., Wed., and Fri.). Trail cyclists should remember to dismount and stand to the downhill side if a horse approaches. Also be forewarned that a quick and quiet trail cycle is more prone to surprise a bear than is the tromping and yelling of hikers.

You Are In Bear Country

Bear sightings are common throughout the Canadian Rockies, but one black bear took it upon himself to remind the many residents of Banff whose park it really is. Affectionately known as **Bear 16,** this black furred beauty moved into town, and disrupted everyday activity by grazing on front lawns and laying in the road, unwittingly blocking traffic. Bear 16 crossed the line, though, when the smell from a bakery enticed him to take a closer look. At the behest of scared bakers, park staff removed Bear 16 from the park, had him castrated and placed in the Calgary Zoo.

While most travelers to the park are eager to see its wildlife, few want as intimate a contact as Bear 16 offered. As a defense, many hikers carry bear bells, ranging from mere jinglers to mighty sleigh bells. While such devices offer psychological security, park officials warn that the safest bet is simply to talk or sing loudly while hiking, especially near running water. One Banff official recommends regular yodelling as a way of warning nearby animals of your presence. The more self-conscious may opt to blow a whistle every so often or simply to travel in mid-sized groups of people with heavy boots.

The number of bear attacks ranks low among the total number of attacks by park wildlife. The most common animal attacks are committed by seemingly harmless squirrels scurrying across trails. Dozens of visitors are bitten each year by **pesky rodents** brought too close to food. Humans, however, are by far the most dangerous mammal in the park—road accidents are the most common cause of death within the park boundaries.

Banff National Park's original name was Hot Springs Reserve, and its featured attraction was the **Cave and Basin Hot Springs.** The **Cave and Basin National Historic Site** (762-1556), a refurbished resort built circa 1914, now screens documentaries and stages exhibits. Down the **Discovery Trail** you'll see the original spring discovered over 100 years ago by three Canadian Pacific Railway workers. The site is southwest of the city on Cave Ave. ($2.25, seniors $1.75, children $1.25; open daily 9am-6pm; winter 9am-5pm). The pool was closed in 1993 because its cracking tile posed a danger to the public. Guided tours meet out front at 11am.

Follow the rotten-egg smell to the **Upper Hot Springs pool** (762-1515), a 40°C (104°F) sulphurous cauldron up the hill on Mountain Ave. A soak in the pool is relaxing, but it will soak your wallet ($7, seniors and children $6; towel rental $1, lockers 25¢; open daily 9am-11pm; call for winter hr.).

After the steep 5.3km (and 2-3hr.) hike up **Sulfur Mountain,** you can enjoy a free ride down. Almost as a reward for those brave enough to tackle Banff's most popular hike, the **Sulfur Mountain Gondola** charges nothing for the trip downhill. The gondola runs trips to the top as well—for a price ($10, ages 5-11 $4, under 5 free, open daily 8am-9pm). The **Summit Restaurant** (762-2523) perched atop Sulfur Mountain, serves an "Early Morning Lift" breakfast special for $4. The gondola and the trail start from close to the Upper Hot Springs pool and travel 700m up to the summit.

Brewster Tours (762-6767) offers an extensive array of guided bus tours within the park. If you don't have a car, these tours may be the only way to see some of the main attractions, such as the Great Divide, the Athabasca Glacier, and the spiral railroad tunnel. The tour-guide drivers are professional, knowledgeable, and entertaining. If you are taking the regular Brewster bus from Banff to Jasper ($42), it's only $27 more to see the sights in between (one way 9½hr.; $69, roundtrip 2 days, $95; tour of the Columbia Icefields $21 extra; tickets available at the bus depot).

If you'd prefer to look up at the mountains rather than down from them, the nearby lakes provide a serene vantage point. **Fishing** is legal virtually anywhere you can find water, but you can't use bait (only lures) and you must hold a National Parks fishing permit, available at the Information Centre ($6 for a 7-day permit, $13 for an annual permit good in all Canadian National Parks). The 7km trail to **Borgeau Lake** offers both hiking and fishing with some privacy—and a particularly feisty breed of brook trout. Closer to the road, try **Herbert Lake,** off the Icefields Parkway between Lake Louise and the Columbia Icefield, or **Lake Minnewanka,** on Lake Minnewanka Rd. northeast of Banff Townsite, rumored to be the home of a half-human, half-fish Indian spirit. A 1½-hour guided tour sponsored by **Minnewanka Tours Ltd.** (762-3473; $22, children $11) will fill you in on the details of the life and times of said human/fish fellow. Lake Minnewanka Rd. also passes **Johnson Lake,** where the sun warms the shallow water to a swimmable temperature.

Raft the waters of the **Kootenay River. Kootenay River Runners** (604-347-9210) offers half- and full-day trips for $49 and $75 respectively, as well as a more boisterous full-day trip on the **Kicking Horse River** for $75. For tickets call 762-5385. The day-long trip offered by **Alpine Rafting Company** (800-663-7080; $75) includes a steak barbecue lunch. A full day of rafting on the Kicking Horse River (transportation included) for $45 is offered by the **Banff International Hostel** (see **Accommodations,** above).

Of course, the reason Banff is Western Canada's Rocky Mountain playland is that the fun doesn't stop when the snow starts. Wintery Banff offers more to do than just curling: activities range from dogsledding to mountaineering to ice fishing. The most obvious and popular activity is **skiing.** Those 1600km of summer hiking trails also provide exceptional cross-country skiing while **Sunshine Mountain, Mount Norquay,** and **Lake Louise** divide the downhill crowd among themselves. **Performance Ski and Sports,** 208 Bear St. (762-8222) rents downhill skis ($17 for 1 day, $45 for 3 days), cross-country skis ($11, $29), snowboards ($28, $74), telemarking skis and boots ($18, $48), and snowshoes ($8, $21).

▓ Kootenay National Park

Kootenay National Park hangs off the continental divide on the Southwest edge of British Columbia. Virtually all visitors to the park are traveling to or from Banff, and while the majestic Banff-Windermere Highway (a.k.a. the Trans-Canada Hwy.), running the length of the park, is a magnificent drive, it barely scratches the surface of Kootenay National Park. Stately conifers, lush alpine meadows, towering peaks, and rushing rivers afford a tremendous array of scenery and excellent outdoor recreation. Kootenay's best feature is what it doesn't have: people. Travelers who step even a short distance off the beaten path will leave the crowds behind and discover the solitude and beauty of the Canadian Rockies in a blessedly untouched state.

Practical Information The **West Gate Information Centre** (347-9505), on Hwy. 93 just inside the park boundary at Radium Hot Springs, hands out free maps and pamphlets as well as a $1 hiking guide (open daily 9am-7pm; call for off-season hours). The **Park Administration Office** (347-9615) is on the access road to Redstreak Campground (see below), or write Kootenay National Park, P.O. Box 220, Radium Hot Springs V0A 1M0 (open Mon.-Fri. 8am-noon and 1-4pm). **Greyhound** buses stop at the **Esso** station, 7507 W. Main St. (347-9726; open daily 7am-11pm), at the junction of Hwy. 93 and Hwy. 95 in the town of Radium Hot Springs just outside the park. Daily service to Banff ($18) and Calgary ($33) runs the length of the Banff-Windermere Hwy. through the park. For an **ambulance** call 342-2055. The nearest hospital is **Windermere District Hospital** (342-9201) in Windermere. Call the **police** in **Invermere** at 342-9292, and in **Radium Hot Springs** at 347-9393. The **post office** (347-9460) is on Radium St. in Radium Hot Springs (open Mon.-Fri. 8:30am-5pm; **Postal Code:** V0A 1M0). The **area code** is 604.

Kootenay National Park lies southwest of Banff and Yoho. Hwy. 93 runs through the park from the Trans-Canada Hwy. in Banff to Radium Hot Springs, at the southwest edge of the park, where it joins Hwy. 95 to run 143km south to Cranbrook.

Accommodations, Camping and Food The flagship campground of the park is **Redstreak,** with 242 sites, flush toilets, showers, firewood, playgrounds, and swarms of RVs. If you're looking for seclusion, look elsewhere: your only chance is the walk-in sites off **Loop "D."** To get there from BC, don't enter the park on Hwy. 93. Take the access road that departs Hwy. 95 near the south end of Radium Hot Springs (for reservations call 800-689-9025; sites $15, full hookup $20; open mid-May to mid-Sept.). More appealing from the solitude-seeker's point of view is **McLeod Meadows,** 27km north of the West Gate entrance on Highway 93. The 98 sites are wooded and better spaced than those at Redstreak, and RVs are rare (sites $12; open mid-May to mid-Sept.).

Marble Canyon, 86km north of the West Gate entrance, or 7km inside the park boundary with Banff, is similar to McLeod Meadows (61 sites; $12; open mid-June to early Sept.). In winter, free camping is available at the **Dolly Varden** picnic area, 36km north of the West Gate entrance. Firewood, water, toilets, and a kitchen shelter are provided. Camping outside the park is plentiful with an abundance of free camping in the nearby Invermere Forest district. Ask the staff at the info centre for more information. If you must have a bed, the **Columbia Motel,** 4886 St. Joseph St. (347-9557), offers clean, well-kept rooms with some of the lowest rates in town. Lots of seniors keep the place nice and quiet (rooms $45-50, $5 for kitchen).

There is no affordable food in the park; the town of Radium (insert radioactive food joke here) supports a few uninspiring eateries conveniently located within feet of each other on Main Street. If you love truck-stop food, the restaurant at the **Husky** station, 4918 Hwy. 93 (347-9811), offers the most cost-efficient food in town (measured in calories per dollar) short of a 5 lb. bag of sugar (open daily 7am-10:30pm). If you decide to go with the sugar, get it at **Radium Foods,** 7546 Main St. E (347-9600), which has a decent selection (open Mon.-Sat. 9am-8pm, Sun. 10am-7pm).

Outdoors Kootenay National Park's main attraction is **Radium Hot Springs** (347-9485), the complex of pools responsible for the congested traffic and towel-toting tourists just inside the West Gate entrance to the park. Be thankful this is the closest thing Kootenay has to a "townsite." The complex contains two pools, a hot pool for soaking (40°C; 104°F), and a cooler pool for swimming (27°C; 81°F). The deck overlooking the pools lets you check out the scene for free before you make any investment ($5, seniors and children $4.50; lockers 25¢; towel rental $1, suit rental $1.25; open daily 9am-10:30pm).

The 95-km **Banff-Windermere Hwy.** (Hwy. 93) forms the backbone of scoliosis-afflicted Kootenay. Stretching from Radium Hot Springs to Banff, the highway follows the **Kootenay** and **Vermilion Rivers,** with views of lofty glacier-enclosed peaks, dense stands of virgin forest, and rushing glacial-green rivers. When the route drops into the Kootenay River valley, feast your eyes on the vast, wild landscape. Except for the narrow ribbon of highway, this valley remains unblemished.

For most visitors, the experience of the park ends with the drive up Hwy. 93. With the exception of two short, photogenic trails, most travelers stalwartly refuse to leave their vehicle and experience nature intimately. One of the places they may stop is **Marble Canyon,** about 15km from the border with Banff, where a 1.6km trail leads along a remarkably deep, narrow gorge cut by Tokumm Creek. Despite the preponderance of video cameras, you won't want to miss this unique geologic feature or the voluminous falls at the end of the trail. Interpretive signs explain the processes that created this scenery.

The other tourist trail is the **Paint Pots Trail,** leaving Hwy. 93 3.2km south of Marble Canyon. This wheelchair-accessible trail leads to several springs rich in iron oxide. Local native Canadians quarried ochre from this oxide to make tipi and body paints. The trail winds through the **ochre flats,** where several early 20th-century mining operations produced the pigment commercially. Bounce on the suspension bridge over the Vermilion River. The 1.6km trail is a leisurely 30-minute stroll.

After the two self-guided trails, the myriad **hiking** trails in Kootenay are blissfully uncrowded. An easy dayhike, the **Stanley Glacier Trail** starts 2½km north of Marble Canyon and leads 4.8km into a glacier-carved valley, ending 1.6km from the foot of Stanley Glacier, which gouged out the valley. For the more adventurous day-hiker, the awe-inspiring hike over **Kindersley Pass** is an experience not soon forgotten. The

16½-km hike climbs more than 1km and is rough going, but the rewards are incredible **views** of the Columbia River Valley to the west and the crest of the Rockies to the east. The two trailheads at either end of the route, **Sinclair Creek** and **Kindersley Pass,** are less than 1km apart on Hwy. 93, about 15km inside the West Gate entrance.

Many longer backpacking routes cross the **backcountry.** One popular route is the four-day jaunt along the **Rockwall Trail** from **Floe Lake** to **Helmet Falls,** though there are many shorter and longer routes. Two fire roads, and the entire length of Hwy. 93, are open for **mountain biking.** In particular, the 32km **East Kootenay Trail,** a system of fire roads, parallels the Hwy. 93 through the Kootenay Valley, making a pleasant loop ride returning along the wide-shouldered highway. Rock flour from glaciers in the rivers makes for generally poor fishing.

Backcountry visitors should stop in at an information center and pick up a hiking guide for $1, which has useful maps, trail descriptions, and profiles. No permit is needed for dayhiking, but overnight backcountry camping requires a **Wilderness Pass,** $6 per person per night, or $35 for an entire season. Wilderness Passes are available from information centers. Both black and grizzly bears roam the woods, so hikers should use care on the trail, making noise (using your voice is best) to avoid surprising bears. Poles for suspending food out of bear-reach are provided at all backcountry campsites, and should be used religiously. Surface water is often inhabited by *giardia.* Treat or boil water before drinking (see **Common Ailments,** p. 14).

▓ Yoho National Park

Smaller and less glitzy than its neighbors, Yoho has the redeeming distinction of the best names in the Rockies. It also sports the Kicking Horse Pass, named when Captain John Hector, tired, hungry, and desperately trying to find a mountain pass for the Canada Pacific Railroad, was viciously kicked in the chest by his horse and rendered unconscious. Not only was the incident noteworthy enough to give the pass its name, the explorers were bold enough to rename the nearby Wapta (which is a native word meaning "river") River.

Yoho has one edge over its neighbors that doesn't involve nomenclature. Home to a number of scientific wonders, this spunky enclave boasts the largest waterfall in the Rockies, the Continental Divide, and the Burgess Shale, which found its way into paleontology textbooks in the early 20th century when it spewed forth valuable evidence of the complexity of pre-Cambrian life. Even if you leave your slide rule at home, it's easy to see that this quiet park and its highly inconspicuous village, Field, can match its bigger and badder neighbors in any contest of natural splendor.

Practical Information Visitor Information Centre (343-6783), in Field on Hwy. 1, houses park information, Tourism Alberta and Tourism BC (open daily 9am-7pm, winter 9am-4pm). For more information on the park, write to the **Park Superintendent,** Yoho National Park, PO Box 99, Field BC V0A 1G0. Ironically, a town founded by the railroad company is no longer accessible by rail and while Greyhound does stop in Field, it is not an actual Greyhound destination. Those without cars interested in exploring Yoho can try calling the bus company or hitching (although *Let's Go* does not recommend hitchhiking) the well-travelled Trans-Canada Hwy. In case of emergency, call the **warden office** at 343-6324 or the **RCMP** at 343-6316, although the scarcity of phones in the park makes it more efficient to just drive to Lake Louise for help. The area code is 250, but Yoho is still in Mountain Time. Yoho lies on Hwy. 1 (the Trans-Canada Hwy.), adjacent to Banff National Park. Lake Louise is 27km east of Field.

Accommodations, Camping and Food The best and most scenic deal in Yoho is the **Whiskey Jack Hostel,** 13km off the Trans-Canada on Yoho Valley Rd. Open from June to September, Whiskey Jack offers indoor plumbing, propane light, easy access to Yoho's best trails, and an excellent view of the Takakkaw Falls from the front porch. Unfortunately there is no phone, so make your highly recommended reservations by calling the Banff International Hostel at 403-762-3441 ($12, nonmembers $17). All frontcountry camping is operated on a first-come, first-served basis, but the abundance of backcountry camping keeps overcrowding from becoming a problem. The six frontcountry grounds offer a combined 350 sites, all easily accessible from the highway. The biggest is **Hoodoo Creek** at the west end of the park with 106 sites, kitchen shelters, running hot *and* cold water, a nearby river, a playground, and an outdoor theatre for presentations. The most popular campground, though, is **Kicking Horse** on Yoho Valley Rd. right off the highway. Imagine Hoodoo Creek with hot showers ($1) instead of a river. 86 sites, $17. Scenery hounds will love the **Takakkaw Falls** campground on Yoho Valley Rd. near the Takakkaw Falls. It may have only pump water and pit toilets, but it also has a gimmick—no cars are allowed on the campground, requiring residents to park in the falls parking lot and cart their gear 300m to the sites in free wheelbarrows available at the campground (35 sites for $12). The six **backcountry campgrounds** offer 48 sites total and an intense wilderness experience. Before heading down the trail, stop at the visitors center for a backcountry permit ($6) and a map.

Field's food options are incredibly diverse given its population and incredibly limited when compared with any other town in civilization. The most convenient locale is the **Siding General Store** on Stephen Ave. downtown. Basic foodstuffs line the walls, beer fills the cooler, and the friendly owners provide economic yet edible food across the counter. Sandwiches $4, breakfast $4.25-65, steak fajitas $3.25.

Outdoors Yoho's most distinctive traits are its most intellectually stimulating. **The Great Divide** is both the boundary between Alberta and British Columbia and the boundary of the Atlantic and Pacific watersheds. One stream forks, with one side flowing about 1500km to the Pacific Ocean, and the other flowing 2500km to the Atlantic. A large sign indicates its significance to the 19th-century railroad industry, while the number of people with cameras testifies to its importance in the 20th-century tourism industry. Bigger and yet more obscure is the **Burgess Shale.** Discovered in 1909 to hold the world's finest Cambrian-aged fossils, the Shale features imprints of the multitude of bizarre-looking soft-bodied organisms that inhabited the world's murky waters following the heyday of the tiny amoeba. Bigger, clumsier organisms known as people have required that the Shale be protected from excessive tourism. As a result, it is accessible only through guided day hikes. The hike to the **Mt. Stephen Fossil Beds** is a moderate, six-hour roundtrip, while the 20km roundtrip trek to **Walcott's Quarry** is recommended only for more advanced hikers. Call the **Yoho-Burgess Shale Foundation** (800-343-3006) for more information. Pay $1and pick up a copy of the *Backcountry Guide to Yoho National Park* at the information centre.

Yoho's most splendid lake is also its least accessible. **Lake O'Hara** in the northeast end of the park can be reached by a 13km pedestrian-only trail or through a park-operated bus. The bus requires reservations, an $11 roundtrip ticket, and a park permit, and provides the only means to the Lake O'Hara campground. High peaks, cirque and rock basin lakes, alpine larch stands, rock lichens and alpine plants in the area appreciate the restriction on tourism and reward those who do venture out there with an amazing spectacle of mountain life. (Call 343-6433 for reservations and more information.) In contrast, its most splendid waterfall is its most easily accessible. The **Takakkaw Falls** are visible for a good portion of the drive up Yoho Valley Rd. and the roadside vistas are often more spectacular than the view from the parking lot 14km off the Trans-Canada.

■ Calgary

The name Calgary is derived from Gaelic for "clear running water," but it was oil that built this city at Alberta's gateway to the Rockies. Founded in the 1870s by Mounties trying to stop the illegal whiskey trade, Calgary got its big break with the discovery of black gold, Texas tea. Suddenly the insignificant prairie cowtown became a signifi-

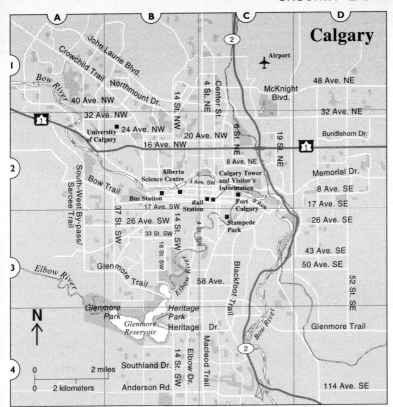

cant prairie cowtown. With the 1988 Winter Olympics, the Calgarian economy hit the big time again. Jobs, tourism, and a flock of young Canadians from the eastern provinces descended on Calgary and made it Alberta's liveliest city.

But no matter how urbane Alberta's largest city may become, it retains a close tie to its roots and its original claim to fame—the "Greatest Outdoor Show on Earth," the Calgary Stampede. Grown men and women don cowboy attire, horse and cattle art pops up everywhere, and the town lets out a collective "Yahoo!" every July for 10 days of world-class rodeo action, chuckwagon races, country music, rides, and pancake breakfasts. So put on yer jeans, yer best Western shirt, a 10-gallon hat, and come on down.

PRACTICAL INFORMATION AND ORIENTATION

Visitors Information: For drop-in info, go to the **Visitor Service Center** near the Calgary Tower at 131 9th Ave. SW (263-8510; open daily 8:30-5pm). For the cost of a local call, the **Talking Yellow Pages** provides a wide range of info, from local events and attractions to the latest in vomit-stain removal techniques (no joke). Dial 521-5222 and the appropriate 4-digit code, listed in the front of the Yellow Pages (general visitor's info is code 8950).

American Express: Canada Trust Tower, main floor, 421 7th Ave. SW, Calgary T2P 4K9 (261-5085).

Tours: Brewster Tours, 221-8242. Runs buses from the airport or downtown to: Banff (3 per day, $33); Lake Louise (3 per day, $38), and Jasper (1 per day, $59).

Buses: Greyhound, 877 Greyhound Way SW (265-9111 or 800-661-TRIP/8747). Frequent service to Edmonton (10 per day, $33), Banff (4 per day, $18), and Drumheller (3 per day, $19). Seniors 10% off. Free shuttle bus from C-Train at 7th Ave. and 10th St. to bus depot (almost every hr. on the ½hr., 6:30am-7:30pm).

Public Transportation: Calgary Transit. Downtown Information and Sales Centre, 240 7th Ave. SW. Bus schedules, passes, and maps. Open Mon.-Fri. 8:30am-5pm. Fare $1.50, ages 6-14 90¢, under 6 free. Exact change required. Day pass $4.50, children $2.50. Book of 10 tickets $12.50, children $8.50. **Information line** (262-1000) open Mon.-Fri. 6am-11pm, Sat.-Sun. 8:30am-9:30pm.

Taxi: Checker Cab, 299-9999. **Yellow Cab,** 974-1111. Both 24hr.

Car Rental: Rent-A-Wreck, 4201 MacLeod Trail SE (228-1660). Cars start at $40 per day, 200km free, 12¢ each additional km. Must be 21 with a credit card. Open Mon.-Fri. 8am-7:30pm, Sat.-Sun. 8am-7pm.

Bike Rental: Budget Car Rental, 140 6th Ave. SE (226-1550). $12 per day. Must be 18 with credit card. **Sports Rent,** 9250 Macleod Trail (292-0066). $20 per day.

Laundromat: Beacon Speed Wash & Dry, 1818 Centre St. N (230-9828). Open daily 8am-11pm.

Weather: Environment Canada, 299-7878. Calgary and Banff weather.

Calgary Gay Community Support Services: Call 234-9752 for a recording of events; call 234-8973 daily 7-10pm for peer counseling and info.

Women's Resource Centre: 325 10th St. NW (283-5994), 1 block west of the Sunnyside C-Train stop. Info and referrals for women of all ages seeking a range of services and assistance. Open Mon.-Fri. 9:30am-4:30pm.

Sexual Assault Centre: 403-1000 8th Ave. SW (237-5888). Office open Mon.-Fri. 8am-5pm. Phone 24hr.

Crisis Line: 266-1605. Open 24hr.

Poison Centre: 270-1414. Open 24hr.

Pharmacy: Shopper's Drug Mart, Chinook Centre, 6455 Macleod Trail S (253-2424). Open 24hr.

Hospital: Calgary General, 841 Centre Ave. E (268-9111).

Emergency: 911.

Police: 316 7th Ave. SE (266-1234).

Post Office: 207 9th Ave. SW (974-2078). Open Mon.-Fri. 8am-5:45pm. **Postal Code:** T2P 268.

Area Code: 403.

Calgary is 120km east of Banff along the **Trans-Canada Hwy.** (Hwy. 1). Planes fly into **Calgary International Airport,** about 5km northwest of the city centre. **Cab** fare from the airport to the city is about $20. Bus #57 provides sporadic service from the airport to downtown (call for schedule). Unless you take a cab or have impeccable timing, you will probably need the **Airporter Bus** (531-3907), which offers frequent service to major hotels in downtown Calgary for $8.50; if you ask nicely they may drop you off at an unscheduled stop.

Calgary is divided into quadrants: **Centre Street** is the east-west divide; the **Bow River** divides the north and south sections. The rest is simple: avenues run east-west, streets run north-south. Pay careful attention to the quadrant distinctions (NE, NW, SE, SW) at the end of each address. You can derive the street from an avenue address by disregarding the last two digits of the first number: thus 206 7th Ave. is at 2nd St., and 2339 Macleod Trail is at 23rd St.

Public transportation within the city is inexpensive and efficient. **Calgary Transit** (262-1000) operates both buses and streetcars ("C-Trains"). Buses ($1.50) run all over the city. Though they cover less territory, C-Trains are free in the downtown zone (along 7th Ave. S, between 10th St. SW and 3rd St. SE); you pay the $1.50 fare only when you leave downtown. The C-Train's free zone covers many lodgings, restaurants, and sights.

ACCOMMODATIONS

Lodging costs skyrocket when packs of tourists Stampede into the city's hotels. For stays in July, you cannot reserve too early. Contact the **B&B Association of Calgary**

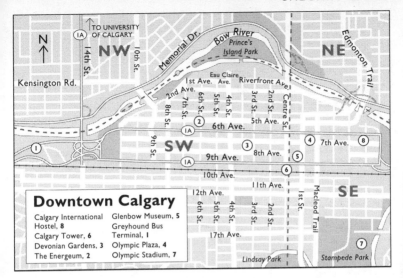

Downtown Calgary

Calgary International Hostel, **8**
Calgary Tower, **6**
Devonian Gardens, **3**
The Energeum, **2**

Glenbow Museum, **5**
Greyhound Bus Terminal, **1**
Olympic Plaza, **4**
Olympic Stadium, **7**

(531-0065) for information and availability on B&Bs. Prices for singles start around $35, doubles around $50.

Calgary International Hostel (HI-C), 520 7th Ave. SE (269-8239). Conveniently located several blocks east of downtown with access to the 3rd St. SE C-Train station and public buses. Pleasant, modern facility looks like a ski lodge. Snack bar, meeting rooms, barbecue facilities, and laundry. Employs an activities coordinator in summer, an invaluable resource for information about the city. Make reservations for the Stampede *far* in advance. Wheelchair accessible. Open 24hr. $14, nonmembers $19. Linen free.

University of Calgary, in the NW quadrant. Booking for all rooms coordinated through **Kananaskis Hall,** 3330 24th Ave. (220-3203), a 12-min. walk from the University C-Train stop (open 24hr.). The university is out of the way, but easily accessible via bus #9 or the C-Train. If you didn't make the Olympic squad, at least you can sleep in their beds; U of C was the Olympic Village home to competitors in 1988 and offers clean rooms at competitive prices. Rooms available May-Aug. only. 22 rooms are set aside for those with student ID: singles $30, doubles $38. More lavish suites with private bathrooms are approximately $35. Reservations recommended. Popular with conventioneers, U of C is often booked solid.

Regis Plaza Hotel, 124 7th Ave. SE (262-4641). Friendly management and clean, comfortable rooms. Rockin' country bar with live music downstairs. If you're feeling ascetic, try an inside room with no TV, bath, or windows for $31.35. Doubles from $55. Weekly rates $75-150.

FOOD

Downtown's offerings are concentrated in the **Stephen Avenue Mall,** 8th Ave. S between 1st St. SE and 3rd St. SW. Good, reasonably priced food is also readily available in the **"+15" Skyway System.** Designed to provide indoor passageways during bitter winter days, this futuristic mall-in-the-sky connects the second floors of dozens of buildings throughout downtown Calgary; look for the blue-and-white "+15" signs on street level.

Trendier, costlier restaurants litter the **Kensington District,** along Kensington Rd. and 10th and 11th St. NW. Take the C-train to Sunnyside or use the Louise Bridge to reach the area. Other lively café-restaurants are on 4th St. SW (take buses #3 and 53) and 17th Ave. SW (bus #7). Fresh fruits, vegetables, seafood, baked goods, and flowers grace the plaza-style, upscale **Eau Claire Market** (264-6450), on 3rd St. SW near Prince's Island Park.

Satay House, 206 Centre St. S (290-1927). Large portions of authentic Vietnamese cuisine make this one of the best deals in Chinatown. Several varieties of *Pho* (beef noodle soup) $3.50-4.50. The house special offers a taste of everything for only $5.50. Open Mon.-Fri. 11am-10pm, Sat.-Sun. 10am-11pm.

4th Street Rose, 2116 4th St. SW (228-5377). A fashionable, California-cool restaurant. The house specialty is the "pro-size" Caesar salad ($4.50), but the gourmet pizzas and pastas are excellent as well. Fajitas primavera $9. Open Mon.-Thurs. 11am-1am, Fri.-Sat. 11am-2am, Sun. 10am-midnight.

Island Experience, 314A 10th St. NW (270-4550). Specializes in Caribbean treats borrowed from India. *Roti* (flat bread filled with meat and curry) make for a fuller meal ($7.50-8.75), while meat and vegetable patties are excellent lighter fare ($2.25). Chutneys $1. Open Mon.-Wed. 11:30am-10pm, Sun. noon-8pm.

Take Ten Café, 304 10th St. NE (270-7010). Less trendy than other joints in the area, but the food is plentiful, tasty, and much less expensive. All burgers under $4, and the lunch specials are under $5.

Heartland Country Store, 920 2nd Ave. NW (270-4541). Sunny, white rooms in a Victorian-style nook. The light, veggie-laden menu offers soups, salads, and sandwiches for $4-$5. Open daily 7am-11pm.

SIGHTS

The **Olympic Oval** (220-7954) is the most impressive of the remaining arenas from Calgary's two weeks of glory in 1988. An enormous indoor speed-skating track on the University of Calgary campus, the oval remains a major international training facility, and sports the fastest ice in the world (open daily 7am-11pm, winter 9am-9:30pm). Speed skaters work out in early morning and late afternoon; you can sit in the bleachers and observe the action on the ice for free. Or try and haul some ice yourself during the public skate hours ($3.50, kids $2; hockey skate rental $3.20; speed skates $3.75). **Canada Olympic Park,** the site of the bobsled, luge, and ski jumping competitions, lies 10 minutes west of downtown on Hwy. 1. A guided one-hour bus tour of the Park costs $6.50 (seniors $5, students $3, children under 6 free). The bus tour of the facilities provides a view from atop the 90m ski jump tower and the chance to make like a Jamaican and stand in the bobsled track (hourly tours daily 10am-6pm and one at 7:30pm). The **Olympic Hall of Fame** (247-5452), also at Olympic Park, honors Olympic achievements with displays, films, and videos ($3.75, seniors $3, students $2.75, children under 6 free; open daily 9am-9pm). The Grand Olympic Tour includes the Park tour and the Hall of Fame for $9 (seniors $6.50, students $5). Discover the difference between **luging** and just sitting on a skateboard on a cruise through the last six turns of the Olympic luge course (open June-Aug. daily 11am-9pm, $12). You can always stroll the grounds for free.

For an Olympic atmosphere untainted by athleticism, downtown offers the **Olympic Plaza** on 7th Ave. SE just east of Centre Street. Once the site of medal presentations, this open-air park now hosts a variety of special events, including free concerts during the **Calgary Jazz Festival** in June. For an update on Olympic Plaza programming, call 268-3888 during business hours. One of the park's most interesting features, the **walkway** was constructed out of more than 20,000 bricks, each purchased for $20-30 and engraved with the name or personal message of the patron. The **Glenbow Museum,** 130 9th Ave. SE (268-4100), lies a few blocks south of the Plaza. From rocks and minerals, to exhibits of native Canadian lifestyles, to the art of Asia, to the history of the Canadian West, the Glenbow has it all ($5, seniors, students and children $3.50, under 7 free; open daily 9am-5pm).

Prince's Island Park can be reached by footbridges from either side of the Bow River. In true park-like tradition, the island is loaded with biking and running trails. Many evenings in summer at 7pm, Mount Royal College puts on free Shakespeare in the park (call 240-6359 for information). The park also hosts events such as the **Caribbean Cultural Festival** in June.

Calgary's other island park, **St. George's Island,** is accessible by the river walkway to the east and is home to the marvelous **Calgary Zoo** (232-9300). The Canadian Wilds exhibit re-creates the sights, sounds, and, yes, smells of Canada's wilderness. A pamphlet available at the zoo entrance gate lists animal feeding times; visitors are invited to watch big animals eat little animals. The squeamish may be content to stroll through the **botanical gardens** or visit the **children's zoo** ($7.50, seniors $5.50, children $3.75; seniors $2 on Tues.; gates open daily 9am-6:30pm, winter daily 9am-4pm; grounds open until 8:30pm, winter until 5:30pm).

For a botanical version of a zoo, explore the **Devonian Gardens,** 317 7th Ave. SW (263-3830), on the top floor of the Toronto Dominion Square retail center. A perfect refuge for anyone who prefers skylights to actual sky, this 2½-acre indoor garden contains sculptures, fountains, waterfalls, bridges, and over 20,000 plants representing 138 local and tropical species. Goldfish pools provide ample fodder for haiku (free; open daily 9am-9pm).

(To be sung to the tune of the *Beverly Hillbillies*.) Well this here's a story about the **Energeum,** a place about oil kinda like a museum. Play a game about drilling, watch a movie in the theater. And learn how Alberta puts the power in your heater. Energeum that is, 640 5th Ave. SW (297-4293; free; open Sun.-Fri. 10:30am-4:30pm).

ENTERTAINMENT

Nightclubs in Alberta became legal in 1990 and Calgary is making up for lost time. A proliferation of bars and clubs occasionally offer live music ranging from national acts to a dude with a guitar. For an easy-to-find good time, rock down to **"Electric Avenue,"** the stretch of 11th Ave. SW between 5th and 6th St., and pound back bottles of local brew with oodles of young Calgarians. Beware of Electric Avenue during hockey playoff time: the streets are closed and the lines for bars and clubs wind around the block. Last call in Calgary is 2am, and is strictly observed.

The King Edward Hotel, 438 9th Ave. SE (262-1680). With live music and dancing nightly, the Eddy brings in phenomenal bluesmen, including Buddy Guy, Clarence "Gatemouth" Brown and Matt "Guitar" Murphy. Cover depends on acts, but usually ranges $3-5. Great blues Mon.-Sat. 11am-2am and jazz on Sat. afternoons and Sun. 7pm-1am. Jam sessions Sat. 2:30pm-7pm and Sun. 7pm-1am.

REpublik, 219 17th Ave. SW (244-1884; events line 228-6163). Grungeoids slam and grind with their Gap-clad brethren in Calgary's loudest nuclear bunker and biggest party zone. On the harder side of alternative, a favorite stage for hungry up-and-coming bands (live music on Wed. and Fri. nights). The mosh pit likes its victims raw. Daily drink specials. Cover $2-7. Open Tues.-Sat. 7pm-2am.

Ranchman's Steak House, 9615 Macleod Trail SE (253-1100). One of Canada's greatest honky-tonks. Live C&W, line-dancing, and Stampede Beer. The $10 cover during the Stampede is a little steep but well worth the price for real cowboy junkies. Cover $6 Thurs.-Sat. Open Mon.-Sat. 10pm-2am.

Back Alley, 4630 MacLeod Trail SE (287-2500). A large, dark warehouse space filled with twentysomething locals and loud hard rock music. Guns 'N Roses fans will enjoy the weekend selection. Thurs. nights host live local bands. Cover around $2. Open Wed.-Sat. 7pm-2am.

Bottlescrew Bill's Pub, 10th Ave. SW (263-7900), and 1st St. Take refuge from Electric Avenue in the mellow atmosphere of this "Old English Pub." Bill's offers the widest selection of beers in Alberta ($3.30-20). If you feel bold, try a pint of Bill's own Buzzard Breath Ale ($3.50). Happy hour Mon.-Fri. 4-7pm, all day on Sun. Open daily 11am-2am.

THE STAMPEDE

It seems that the more cosmopolitan the city becomes, the more firmly it clings to its frontier origins. Drawing millions every summer from across Canada, and the world, the Stampede is worth a special visit. Make the short trip out to **Stampede Park,** just southeast of downtown, for steer wrestling, saddle bronc, bareback, and bull riding, pig racing, **wild cow milking,** and the famous chuckwagon races, involving four horses per wagon and nerves of steel. Visit an authentic Native Canadian encampment and a re-created Wild West town, ride the wild, thrashing roller coaster at the **Stampede Midway,** or try the gaming tables in the **Frontier Casino.**

Parking is ample and reasonably priced, but the crowd is more than reasonably sized. Instead of driving, take the C-Train from downtown to the Stampede stop. For information and ticket mail-order forms, write **Calgary Exhibition and Stampede,** Box 1860, Station M, Calgary T2P 2L8, or call 800-661-1260 (261-0101 in Calgary). Tickets are $16-42. Same-day rush tickets are $8 (youth $7, seniors and children $4). Plan now. The Stampede takes place July 4-13 in 1997.

■ Near Calgary: Alberta Badlands

You won't lose the crowds by going to the **Royal Tyrrell Museum of Paleontology** (TEER-ull; 403-823-7707), near Drumheller, but you will lose your sense of self-importance. The world's largest display of dinosaur specimens is a forceful reminder that humanity is a mere flyspeck on the giant windshield of life. From the Big Bang to the Quarternary Period (that's now), the museum covers it all with a dizzying array of displays and videos. The museum is guarded by one of the only Tyrannosaurus Rex skeletons in existence. If you're not slide-tackled by a hyperactive kindergartener on a class trip, you may get to build your own "Sillysaurus" on one of the museum's educational computers. A tour of every exhibit, video, and bone won't last as long as the Cretaceous Period but it will require a few hours ($6.50, ages 7-17 $3, under 7 free; winter Tues. half-price; open daily 9am-9pm; Labor Day-Victoria Day Tues.-Sun. 10am-5pm). To really get your hands on some fossils, participate in a **day dig.** These immensely popular day-long excursions include instruction in paleontology and excavation techniques and a chance to dig in a dinosaur quarry, all for $85 (ages 10-15 $55). The package includes lunch and transportation, but if you find anything, it goes to the museum (leaves July-Aug. daily at 8:30am; reservations recommended). If that's too expensive, consider a **Dig Watch,** a two-hour guided tour to the quarry, where you can watch the fortunate few digging ($12, ages 7-17 $8, under 7 free; July-Aug. daily 10am, noon, and 2pm). The museum is on **Secondary Hwy. 838,** or the **North Dinosaur Trail,** 11km from Drumheller. Drumheller lies 35km northeast of Calgary; get there by driving east on Hwy. 1 and northeast on Hwy. 9. Tyrrell isn't directly served by public transportation, but you can take Greyhound from Calgary to Drumheller (2-3 per day, one way $19). From Drumheller, rent a bike from the hostel (see below) —it's about a 20-minute ride.

Tyrrell lies in the heart of the Alberta **badlands,** where prehistoric wind, water, and ice carved a tortured landscape out of sedimentary rock. Free 90-minute guided walks run through the surrounding badlands (about 2-3 per day), but **Horseshoe Canyon,** about 20km west of Drumheller on Hwy. 9, offers the most accessible landscapes and a fairly good illustration of hell. Between the inhospitable terrain and the severely twisted rock formations, you can almost see souls suffering in purgatory. Carry at least one quart of water if you want to explore the badlands during hot weather. Horseshoe Canyon and the nearby provincial park are also favorite mountain biking locales, offering countless destinations as long as bikers don't hop fences onto nearby farmland. Ask for information and directions at the **Old Midland Mine Office,** on North Dinosaur Trail on the way to the Tyrell Museum.

Proof that Jurassic Park was not the last place where dinosaurs could reign supreme, **Drumheller** (home of the Jurassic Inn of course) is still overrun with the "terrible lizards," or at least their tackier younger cousins. Flee the dino-monsters at the **Alexandra Hostel (HI-C),** 30 Railway Ave. N (403-823-6337), which has 55 beds in a converted hotel built in the 1930s, a kitchen, and laundry. Check-in is from 9am to 11pm. ($13.65, nonmembers $17.65; bedding included.) The hostel also rents mountain bikes ($4 per hr., $15 per day). The **River Grove Campground,** off North Dinosaur Trail (823-6655, fax 823-3132), at the intersection with Hwy. 9, has flush toilets and showers. The majority of the 100 sites are tent sites ($16, full hook-up

$22.75). They also have cabins for 2 to 10 people with bathrooms, electricity, and cable TV for $40-70. Open Victoria Day to Labor Day 7am-11pm.

The **Field Station** (378-4342) for the Tyrrell Museum is located 48km east of **Brooks** in **Dinosaur Provincial Park.** The station contains a small museum that complements Tyrrell, but the main attraction is the **Badlands Bus Tour,** which runs two to eight times per day between Victoria Day and Thanksgiving. For $4.50 (youth $2.25, children free). You can be chauffeured into this restricted archaeological hot spot of dinosaur discoveries and fossil finds. Many fossils still lie within the eroding rock; if you make a discovery, however, all you can take home with you are memories, Polaroids, and a coveted "Fossil Finder Certificate," but not the actual goods. The **campground** (378-4342) in the park is shaded from the summer heat, and grassy plots cushion most campsites. Although it stays open year-round, the campground only has power and water in summer. (Sites $13, $15 with power. Field Station open Victoria Day-Labour Day daily 8:15am-9pm; call for winter hr.) For more information, contact the Field Station, Dinosaur Provincial Park, Box 60, Patricia T0J 2K0. To reach the field station from Drumheller, follow Hwy. 56 south for 65km, then take Hwy. 1 about 70km to Brooks. Once in Brooks, go north along the well-marked Hwy. 873 and east along Hwy. 544.

■ Kananaskis Country

Between Calgary and Banff lie 4000 sq. km of provincial parks and so-called "multi-use recreational areas," collectively known as Kananaskis Country. Although summer use can be heavy, the sheer size of Kananaskis and the dispersed nature of its attractions keep it tranquil and unspoiled.

Blessed with year-round attractions, Kananaskis offers skiing, snowmobiling, windsurfing, golfing, biking, and hiking. Eager staff members at the park information centers can help design itineraries. Expect to be showered with maps and elaborate brochures describing your activity of choice. The main visitor center is on Barrier Lake, 6km south of Hwy. 1 on Hwy. 40 (673-3985; open Sat.-Thurs. 9am-6pm, Fri. 9am-7pm, winter Wed.-Sun. 9am-4pm). There are also infocenters in and near the three provincial parks: the **Bow Valley** center (673-3663), north of Hwy. 1 between Seebe and Exshaw; **Elbow Valley** center (949-4261), on Hwy. 66 near **Bragg Creek;** the cozy, chalet-style center in **Peter Lougheed Park** (591-7222), complete with a fireplace, a wooden deck, and informative displays and videos on the Kananaskis Lakes Trail. Travel Alberta maintains a helpful office in **Canmore,** just off Hwy. 1A near the northwest border of K-Country (open daily 8am-8pm). In an emergency, call the **Canmore Police** (678-5516).

With over 337 hikes, K-country can accommodate anything from a 2km, one-hour quick fix to a full-blown Rocky Mountain High. For example, those with limited time or endurance can explore the 1.9km **Canadian Mt. Everest Expedition Trail** in Peter Lougheed Provincial Park, which provides a majestic view of both Upper and Lower Kananaskis Lakes. Meanwhile, more serious hikers will find Gillean Daffern's *Kananaskis Country Trail Guide* (published by Rocky Mountain Books) the definitive source on lengthier area trails. Bikers will find the park staff helpful in planning treks along the untraveled highways and trails. The **Canmore Nordic Centre** (678-2400), the 1988 Olympic Nordic skiing venue, offers world-class cross-country skiing in the winter and 60km of mountain bike trails in summer.

Greyhound buses stop at the **Rusticana Grocery,** 801 8th St. in Canmore (678-4465). Three buses pass each day bound for Calgary ($15) and Banff ($6). The Alberta hostels run a hostel-to-hostel shuttle connecting Calgary to Banff, including a stop in K-Country ($14). Call Banff International Hostel for reservations (762-4122).

No fewer than 3000 campsites are accessible via K-Country roads, and camping is unlimited in the backcountry as long as you set up camp at least 1km from a trail. Most established campsites in Kananaskis cost between $5.50 and $24 per night. The **Ribbon Creek Hostel,** near the Nakiska Ski Area, 24km south of the Trans-Canada Hwy. on Hwy. 40, accommodates 44 people. The hostel's private family rooms hold four beds each, and its living room has a fireplace ($12, nonmembers $17). For reservations call the Banff International Hostel at 762-4122.

SOUTHERN ALBERTA

■ Waterton Lakes National Park

Waterton Lakes National Park is only a fraction of the size of its Montana neighbor, Glacier National Park, but it offers spectacular scenery and activities, and is less crowded than Glacier during the peak months of July and August. Part of an "International Peace Park" symbolizing the lasting peace between Canada and the United States (apparently there were once conflicts), the park provides sanctuary for bears, bighorn sheep, mountain goats, moose, grey wolves, and lost Americans.

Practical Information The only road from Waterton's northern park entrance leads 5 mi. south to the town of **Waterton.** On the way, grab a copy of the *Waterton-Glacier Guide* at the **Waterton Visitor Centre, 215** Mountain View Rd. (859-2224), 5 mi. inside the park (open June to Labor Day daily 8am-8pm). Rent **bikes** from **Pat's Texaco and Cycle Rental,** Mount View Rd., Waterton Townsite (859-2266; mountain bikes $6 per hour or $30 per day, plus $20 damage deposit). In a medical **emergency,** call 859-2636. The **police station** (859-2044) is on Waterton Ave. at Cameron Falls Dr. Waterton's **post office** is on Fountain Ave. at Windflower, in Waterton town (open Mon., Wed., and Fri. 8:30am-4:30pm, Tues. and Thurs. 8:30am-4pm). The **postal code** is T0K 2M0. The **area code** is 403.

Accommodations, Camping, and Food Pitch a tent at one of the park's three campgrounds. **Crandell** (sites $13), on Red Rock Canyon Rd., and **Belly River** (sites $10), on Chief Mountain Hwy., are cheaper and further removed from the hustle and bustle characteristic of townsite life. **Backcountry camping** is plentiful and requires only a backcountry permit ($6 per person per night, $35 per person for an annual pass), available at the visitors center or from **Park Headquarters and Information,** Waterton Lakes National Park, 215 Mount View Rd., Waterton T0K 2M0 (859-2224; open Mon.-Fri. 8am-4pm). The backcountry campsites are rarely full, and several, including **Crandell Lake,** are less than an hour's walk from the trailhead.

If you prefer to stay indoors, head straight for the best B&B deal in North America, the **Mountain View Bed and Breakfast,** Box 82, Mountain View T0K 1N0 (653-1882), 20km east of the park on Hwy. 5, where you'll enjoy comfy beds, true downhome hospitality, and a hearty breakfast, including homemade bread. Singles are $25, doubles $45. Don Anderson, the owner, also runs a fishing guide service and can supply you with gear. Don will keep you entertained with stories from more than 50 years of living in the area. If you insist on having a bed in Waterton, drop by the **Waterton Pharmacy,** on Waterton Ave. (859-2335), and ask for one of the nine rooms in the **Stanley Hotel** (all rooms $45; no shower or private bath).

Waterton is sorely lacking in budget restaurants; the most attractive option in the townsite is **Zum's,** 116B Waterton Ave. (859-2388), which serves good cheeseburgers on a pleasant patio for $3.50 (open daily 8am-9pm). Stock up on dried meat and granola at the **Rocky Mountain Foodmart** (859-2526) on Windflower Ave. (open daily 8am-10pm). Nothing gets cheaper after being trucked out to Waterton. Buy your groceries outside the park for substantial savings.

Outdoors If you've brought only hiking boots to Waterton, you can set out on the **International Lakeside Hike,** which leads along the west shore of Upper Waterton Lake and delivers you to Montana about 5 mi. after leaving the town. The **Crypt Lake Trail,** voted Canada's best hike in 1981, leads past waterfalls in a narrow canyon, and through a 20m natural tunnel bored through the mountainside to arrive after 4 mi. at

Head-Smashed-In Buffalo Jump

Coveted as a source of fresh meat, sustenance, tools, and shelter, the buffalo was the victim of one of history's most innovative forms of mass slaughter: **the buffalo jump.** While warriors maneuvered the herd into position, a few extremely brave young men, disguised in coyote skins among the buffalo, would spook hundreds of nearly-blind bison into a fatal stampede over a 10m cliff. When successful, the buffalo jump created an instant all-you-can-eat-or-use buffet at the bottom of the cliff. Head-Smashed-In Buffalo Jump was named about 150 years ago in memory of a young thrill-seeking warrior who was crushed against the cliff by a pile of buffalo as he watched the event from below.

As this is a UN World Heritage site, UNESCO will fine you $50,000 if you forage for souvenirs in the 10m-deep beds of bone. But you can learn more than enough about buffalo jumps and local indigenous culture at the **Interpretive Centre** (553-2731), a $10-million, seven-story facility built into the cliff itself. The center screens an astounding film that reenacts the fatal plunge (filmed with real, but dead, buffalo). Extensive exhibits detail the lifestyle of the Native Canadians and the impact of their contact with Western civilization. Two km of walking trails lead to the top of the cliff and the kill site below. If all this talk of buffalo stirs your appetite, head to the café on the second floor, where you can munch Buffalo Burgers ($5) and "Buffalo Chips" ($1.80). The admission fee is steep, but well worth it ($6.50, seniors $5.50, youths $3, under 6 free; open daily 9am-8pm; Labor Day to Victoria Day 9am-5pm). Head-Smashed-In Buffalo Jump is west of Fort Macleod on Rte. 785, about 30km west of Hwy. 2.

icy, green Crypt Lake, which straddles the international border. To get to the trailhead, you must take the **water taxi** run by the **Waterton Shoreline Cruises** (859-2362). The boat shuttle runs regularly ($10, ages 4-12 $5). The marina also runs a two-hour boat tour of Upper Waterton Lake ($17, ages 13-17 $12, ages 4-12 $8; open mid-May to mid-Sept.).

Anglers will appreciate Waterton's **fishing,** which requires a **license** ($4 per day, $6 per week, $13 per year) available from the park offices, campgrounds, wardens, and service stations in the area. Lake trout cruise the depths of **Cameron** and **Waterton Lakes,** while northern pike prowl the weedy channels of **Lower Waterton Lake** and **Maskinonge Lake.** Most of the backcountry lakes and creeks support populations of rainbow and brook trout. Try the nameless creek that spills from Cameron Lake about 200m to the east of the parking lot, or hike 1½km in to Crandell Lake for plentiful, hungry fish. You can rent **rowboats, paddleboats, and canoes** at Cameron Lake for $8-12 per hour. **Alpine Stables,** 2½ mi. north of the townsite (859-2462, in winter 403-653-2449), conducts trail rides of varying lengths (1-hr. ride $15, all-day $77).

In the evening, take in a free **interpretive program** at the **Falls** or **Crandell Theatre.** These programs change yearly and have unbelievably witty titles, like *Bearying the Myths,* which offers straight talk about bears (daily in summer at 8:30pm; contact the visitor center for schedule information).

WASHINGTON AND OREGON

In the 1840s, Senator Stephen Douglas, chairman of the Committee on Boundaries, ran his cane down a map of the Oregon Territory tracing the spine of the Cascade Range. He argued, quite sensibly, that the mountains would make the perfect natural border between two new states. In the end, the Columbia River, running perpendicular to the Cascades and west into the Pacific Ocean, became the dominant geographic divider between Washington and Oregon. But even today it is the range, and not the Columbia, that serves as the region's most important landmark: to the west lie the microchip-, coffee-, and music-meccas of Portland and Seattle, and to the east lie vast tracks of farmland and an arid plateau. Over the course of the region's history, the Cascades have proven to be a powerful geographic—and cultural—divide.

Regionalism in the U.S. Northwest has undergone a revival in recent years, though it takes a self-protective form. While Californians draw attention to their irrigated, temperate paradise on the West Coast and New Englanders take pride in their historic sensibilities, inhabitants of the Pacific Northwest are eager to keep their blessings to themselves. Emmett Watson's "Lesser Seattle" movement has even gone so far as to publish negative (and often misleading) statistics concerning the city in an attempt to dissuade people from moving there. And with good reason: the region's cities are some of the most popular and fastest growing in the U.S., and invaders from California threaten to bring pollution and a cookie-cutter brand of urban planning with them.

The Northwest can be wonderful, but visitors should keep in mind that things are different in this corner of the nation. Drivers do not like to honk, and pedestrians do not jaywalk in major cities. In general, lines form themselves and tend to proceed just a little more strictly, and slowly, than in some other regions. Finally, residents of the Beaver state won't be especially friendly if they hear you call their home or-i-GAHN, but will be quick to welcome you to OR-i-gun.

Early History

Pacific Northwest natives discovered the influence of the Cascades long before Senator Douglas. Coast dwellers enjoyed a life of abundant resources: salmon was a staple food that easily supported the dense Indian population, old-growth forest provided an endless supply of timber for building, and plentiful rainfall guaranteed an array of edible plants. An affluent and complex society thrived and practiced the custom of the potlatch (also see p. 183). Plateau natives, in contrast, were on the move nine months of every year, hunting migratory herds across the flat, dry region east of the Cascades. Their semi-nomadic lifestyle kept tribal ties in flux, necessitating an egalitarian social system and consensual government. Even wider nomadism was encouraged by the arrival of wild horses around 1730.

The Fateful Expedition of Lewis and Clark

U.S. President Thomas Jefferson, eager to attain "geographical knowledge of our own continent" and strengthen American claims to the areas recently purchased from Napoleon, commissioned Meriwether Lewis and William Clark to explore the Northwest in 1803 (see also p. 433). These two proto-*Let's Go*-ers were accompanied by the inept Charbonneau and the indomitable Sacajawea, a Shoshone translator. The calming presence of her infant child helped Sacajawea convince those they encountered that Lewis and Clark's was a peaceful party. This was lucky, since Lewis' attempt to impress the Shoshone with his limited command of their language involved rushing an armed warrior, waving madly, and yelling "I am your enemy!"

The expedition traveled 4000 mi. from St. Louis to the mouth of the Columbia River and back, accumulating flora, fauna, and stronger claims to a region the U.S. still ostensibly shared with Britain. London, for its part, sent Captains James Cook and George Vancouver to map the coast and waterways. In 1818 the two nations hammered out an agreement that divided their claims as far west as the Rockies at the 49th parallel, but left the Oregon question unresolved.

Toward Statehood

The arrival of Europeans in the Northwest was devastating to the native population. The deliberate machinations of white settlers, as well as the unfamiliar diseases they inadvertently carried—measles, small pox, and influenza—wiped out as many as 90% of the natives by the late 1800s. Missionary fervor became an additional means of controlling and dispossessing Indians, and in some cases, brought tensions to a head. Crusaders such as Marcus and Narcissa Whitman rushed west to Walla Walla to "save" the natives. When an epidemic of measles broke out in the Cayuse tribe, natives blamed the missionaries. Marcus met his grisly end at the tomahawk of Chief Tilokaikt, and Narcissa and 10 others were killed shortly thereafter. The incident marked one of the first significant outbreaks of violence between Indians and whites in the Northwest. The indignation aroused by the incident was a crucial motivating factor in Oregon's transformation into an American territory. Those natives who survived the ensuing white invasion were herded, nation by nation, onto reservations on some of the worst land in the region.

Britain offered strong opposition to U.S. control of the Northwest, prompting James K. Polk to win the presidency with a manifest destiny platform and the jingoistic slogan, "54'40 or fight," a claim to the land west of the Rockies and north to present-day Prince George, BC. 1846 found Polk content with peace and the 49th parallel as the dividing line between British and American territories, leaving the Russian stake above the 54th parallel intact. The southern half of the Oregon territory became the state of Oregon in 1859, and the remaining territory to the north joined it 30 years later, reluctantly giving up the name "Columbia" (reserved for the congressional district back east) for "Washington."

Recent Events

With the pesky Brits long gone, present-day Oregon and Washington have found other problems to contend with. Oregonians have struggled with the birds and the bees in arenas as disparate as sexual harassment (witness the 1995 scandal surrounding Senator Bob Packwood) and gay rights legislation. Birds alone have also proven problematic, as the logging industry and environmentalists continue to butt heads over the endangered spotted owl. The Supreme Court, much to the chagrin of many timber industry groups, has upheld the Federal Government's broad (and, many would argue, anti-industry) interpretation of the 1973 Endangered Species Act. With the two states' once-lucrative timber and fishing industries on the downturn, many Oregonians and Washingtonians are looking to cities like Seattle for new economic leads. As computer software companies continue to boom and wealthy Pacific Rim nations strengthen ties to the West, many wonder if a slicker, more urban Northwest has forgotten its rural history as it acquires a taste for coffee.

Arts

The contemporary art scene in the Northwest maintains a generally convivial and public tone. On the first Thursday evening of each month, Portland and Seattle art galleries fling open their doors (and often their wine cellars) to browsers. The cities' 1% tax on capital improvements is funneled into the acquisition and creation of public art. Impressive collections of native art abound. The Northwest also offers imported artistic treasures, such as the Oregon Shakespeare Festival in Ashland, where an estimated annual audience of 450,000 spends a week every summer enjoying the world-renowned performances. A number of actors of note have performed here, including William Hurt in *Long Day's Journey into Night* and Kyle MacLachlan (of *Twin Peaks*

WASHINGTON

fame) as Romeo in *Romeo and Juliet*. Seattle, which has a repertory theater community second in size only to New York, offers a stunning assortment of new dramas in its many fine theaters.

In recent years, the Northwest has become famous for its musicians and billionaires. Seattle is home to Bill Gates and Kurt Cobain, and rock legends ranging from Jimi Hendrix to Soundgarden, Alice in Chains, Screaming Trees, and Pearl Jam have all emerged from the city. Hole and Bikini Kill hale from nearby Olympia. Bumbershoot, a blow-out festival of folk, street, classical, and rock is a great way to sample the music of Seattle. If rock isn't your cup of tea, orchestral music aficionados can trek down to the Bach Festival in Eugene, OR, where Helmut Rilling waves his exquisite Baroque baton. Make your way south for the Mt. Hood Jazz Festival in Gresham, OR; the event has played host to such greats as Wynton Marsalis and Ella Fitzgerald. The Seattle Opera puts on a show with classical and modern productions, and has earned an international reputation for its Wagner productions.

Literature and Film

A number of new writers and filmmakers have recently come out of the Northwest. Gus Van Sant, of *My Own Private Idaho* and *Drugstore Cowboy* fame is a Portland native. Matt Groening, also a Portland native and the tortured genius behind *The Simpsons*, Lynda Barry, Seattle native-cum-cartoonist, Gary Larson, and others can all point to a renaissance in the Northwest. David Lynch, after a boyhood in Spokane, produced the Oregon-based television series *Twin Peaks* and, later, the film *Twin Peaks: Fire Walk With Me* in Snoqualmie (see p. 336). Other films based on assorted misfits, losers, and residents of the Northwest include *Sleepless in Seattle, Reality Bites,* Cameron Crowe's *Singles, Say Anything,* Amy Heckerling's *Fast Times at Ridgemont High, One Flew Over the Cuckoo's Nest,* Robert Altman's *McCabe and Mrs. Miller, An Officer and a Gentleman, Immediate Family, Ice Station Zebra, Orca, Never Cry Wolf, Shoot to Kill,* and *Vision Quest.* You can even flip on the TV for reruns of *Northern Exposure,* which was shot in Washington (see **Roslyn,** p. 387).

Raymond Carver and Alice Munro write extensively about the area; E.B. White and Thomas Pynchon are from it; and John McPhee, John Muir, Ursula K. LeGuin and Jean M. Auel are inspired by it. What follows is a brief and idiosyncratic list of books by regional authors and about the region, from travel diaries to short fiction. Check your local bookstore or library for other suggestions: *Dharma Bums* by Jack Kerouac; *Where I'm Calling From* and *Fires* by Raymond Carver; *Sometimes a Great Notion* by Ken Kesey; *Journals of Lewis and Clark* by Meriwether Lewis and William Clark; *Undaunted Courage,* by Stephen E. Ambrose; *The Assistant* by novelist and former Oregon State University instructor Bernard Malamud; *Snow Falling on Cedars,* by David Guterson; *Another Roadside Attraction* and *Still Life with Woodpecker* by Tom Robbins; *The Lost Sun* by poet and former University of Washington instructor Theodore Roethke; *Sacajawea: American Pathfinder* by Flora Warren Seymour, and *Paul Bunyan* by James Stevens. The fearless Ramona, from the series of the same name by Beverly Clearly, has inspired many a middle child.

Washington

Deserts, volcanoes, farms, mountains, lakes, ocean beaches, and rainforests all lie within Washington's boundaries. You can raft on the Skagit and other wild rivers, sea kayak around the San Juan Islands, and build sand castles on the Strait of Juan de Fuca. Mount Rainier and the Olympic Peninsula have fantastic hiking, while the Cascades are perfect for winter skiing. Seattle, one of the country's great cosmopolitan cities, has superb food, a fantastic theater scene, and endless things to do. Best of all, Washington is a compact state by Western standards, and most destinations are within a day's travel.

Fed by wet Pacific storms, one of the world's only temperate rainforests thrives in western Washington's Olympic National Park. Low clouds and fog hang over Seattle, coloring the sky grayish-white and obscuring the view of Mt. Olympus, Mt. Rainier, and other huge peaks easily seen on clear days. It snows little in winter, but a constant drizzle falls in most months. To the east, minimal rainfall has made the area less inhabited, though the course of the Columbia River and irrigation have made the region productive in wheat, potatoes, apples, and other fruits. Most precipitation falls as winter snow.

The Cascade mountains truly divide Washington. Despite the fact that Spokane is a major trade center, "dry-siders" complain of being dominated by Puget Sound-controlled political interests. To them, a "wet-sider" might be a long-haired urban liberal pontificating endlessly about how those who make a living from the land should be thrown out of work. However, the animosity goes both ways. To "wet-siders"—the great majority of the state's population—the term "dry-siders" conjures images of rednecks tearing around in pickup trucks through wheat farms and ranches, rowdily kicking up clouds of dust. While these stereotypes are entertaining, they do no justice to a population as varied as Washington's landscape.

PRACTICAL INFORMATION

Capital: Olympia.
Visitor Information: Washington State Tourism, Department of Community, Trade, and Economic Development, P.O. Box 42500, Olympia 98504-2500 (360-586-2088 or 800-544-1800). Open Mon.-Fri. 9am-4pm. **Washington State Parks and Recreation Commission,** 7150 Cleanwater Ln., Olympia 98504 (360-902-8500 or 800-233-0321). Write to P.O. Box 42650 for an info and reservation packet. **Outdoor Recreation Information Center,** 2nd Ave., at Marion and Madison, 915 2nd Ave. Suite 442, Seattle 98174 (206-220-7450). Information on national parks and forests.
Fishing and Hunting: Department of Fish and Wildlife, 600 Capitol Way N., Olympia 98501-1091 (206-902-2200). Send away for complete guides to fishing and hunting regulations and licensing fees.
Population: 5,430,940. **State Motto:** *"Alki,"* a Salishan word meaning "by and by." **Nickname:** Evergreen State. **State Song:** "Washington, My Home." **State Flower:** Western Rhododendron. **State Rock:** Petrified Wood. **State Bird:** Willow Goldfinch. **State Fish:** Steelhead Trout. **State Tree:** Western Hemlock. **Land Area:** 70,637 sq. mi.
Emergency: 911.
Time Zone: Pacific (3hr. behind Eastern).
Postal Abbreviation: WA.
Sales Tax: 8.1%.
Drinking Age: 21.
Traffic Laws: Mandatory seatbelt law.
Area Codes: 206 in eastern Puget Sound from Tacoma north to Everett, 360 in the rest of western Washington, and 509 in eastern Washington.

GETTING AROUND

Taking **buses** remains the cheapest way to travel long distances in Washington. Greyhound (800-231-2222) serves the two main transportation centers, Spokane and Seattle, as well as towns in between. Local buses cover most of the remaining cities, although a few areas (such as the northwestern Olympic Peninsula) have no bus service. The **Amtrak** train line from Los Angeles to Vancouver makes many stops in western Washington; another line extends from Seattle to Spokane and on to Chicago. Amtrak serves most large cities along these two routes.

"No hitchhiking permitted" signs are posted on all highways. **Hitchhiking** in the San Juans, Whidbey Island, and Vashon Island is locally accepted though not legal. Opportunities for thumbing decrease as one goes east. *Let's Go* does not recommend hitchhiking as a safe means of transportation. Women traveling alone should *never* hitchhike.

ACCOMMODATIONS AND CAMPING

With the exception of those in Seattle, Washington's **hostels** are generally uncrowded, even in summer. Cheap motels exist in the downtown areas of most large cities, but safety is not assured.

State park **campgrounds** usually have less expensive, more secluded sites than private campgrounds and provide better access to trails, rivers, and lakes. Drivers will also find state park campgrounds more accessible than Department of Natural Resources (DNR) and National Forest campgrounds. Some parks allow self-registration, while others have rangers register campers at their sites in the evening. Expect long, slow lines if the campground requires office registration. Gates to state park campgrounds generally open at dawn and close at dusk. Pets must be leashed and accompanied by owners at all times.

Be aware that many state parks accept reservations from Memorial Day through Labor Day; campgrounds fill up weeks in advance, especially during July and August. Reservations can be made from January on, but they must be made at least two weeks in advance.

Campers may enjoy the solitude of the many National Forest and DNR sites. National Forest campsites cost up to $15 and are often free. Call 800-365-2267 to reserve campsites in national parks. National Park campgrounds accessible by road are generally in great settings. Olympic National Park has some free campgrounds accessible by car. Campgrounds accessible by trail are usually free.

■ Seattle

Seattle's serendipitous mix of mountain views, clean streets, espresso stands, and rainy weather is the magic formula of the 1990s, attracting migrants from across the U.S. Its seems that everyone living here today was born elsewhere. These newcomers come in droves, armed with college degrees and California license plates, hoping for job offers from Microsoft (in nearby Redmond) and a different lifestyle. Seattle has long been blessed with a magnificent setting and a vibrant artistic community, and the arrival of legions of energetic young people has made it one of the liveliest cities in the United States. A nearly epidemic fascination with coffee has also made it one of the most caffeinated.

Seattle sits on an isthmus, almost completely surrounded by water, with mountain ranges to the east and west. Every hilltop in Seattle offers an impressive view of Mt. Olympus, Mt. Baker, and Mt. Rainier. To the west, the waters of Puget Sound glint off downtown skyscrapers. The bright, watery light that reflects off Lake Washington and the Pacific Ocean highlights Seattle's spotless streets and graceful waterways. A day trip in any direction leads travelers into wild and scenic country. But even the city itself, built on nine hills (Rome, you ask?) and separated into distinct neighborhoods, begs for exploration.

WASHINGTON

Washington

National Parks

Mount Rainier, 5
Mount St. Helens
Volcanic Monument, 6
North Cascades, 10
Olympic, 4

National Forests

Colville, 14
Gifford Pinchot, 7
Mount Baker, 9
Mt. Baker-Snoqualmie, 11
Okanogan, 13
Olympic, 3
Umatilla, 17
Wenatchee, 12

Indian Reservations

Colville, 15
Makah, 1
Quinault, 2
Spokane, 16
Yakima, 8

IDAHO

CANADA
U.S.A.

Newport
Chewelah
Colville
Spokane
Davenport
Sprague
Ritzville
Moses Lake
Othello
Ephrata
Wenatchee
Ellensburg
Yakima
Toppenish
Goldendale
Vancouver
Portland
Astoria
Cathlamet
Kelso
Morton
Elbe
Chehalis
Olympia
Tacoma
Bellevue
Seattle
Everett
Bellingham
Mt. Vernon
Coupeville
Port Townsend
Port Angeles
Forks
Queets
Aberdeen
Montesano
Shelton
Bremerton
South Bend
Naselle
Long Beach
Victoria
Twisp
Brewster
Chelan
Wenatchee
Republic
Tonasket
Grand Coulee
Wilbur
Colville
Pomeroy
Colfax
Dayton
Walla Walla
Pasco
Pendleton
Prosser
Washtucna

Pasayten Wilderness

Lake Chelan

Columbia River

Strait of Juan De Fuca

Strait of Georgia

San Juan Islands

Vancouver Island

OREGON

CANADA
MEXICO
WA.

60 miles
60 kilometers

N

The city's artistic landscape is equally varied and exciting. *The New York Times* has complained that there is more good theatre in Seattle than on Broadway. Seattlites are also consummate music lovers. Opera performances consistently sell out, and the same city that produced Jimi Hendrix has again revitalized American rock and roll. Since Nirvana introduced the world to their disillusioned and discordant sensibility, the term "grunge" and Seattle have become inseparable: in a city that is home to entrepreneurs like Bill Gates of Microsoft and Howard Shultz of Starbucks, garage bands remain a major export. Night life in Seattle reaps the benefits; an army of good bands, waiting for a big break, perform in local nightclubs. With a number of successful micorbreweries and a coffee house renaissance, Seattle has become a mecca for grass roots, come as you are entertainment.

Regardless of its many successes, Seattle cannot make the rain go away. Two hundred days a year are shrouded in cloud cover and when the skies clear, Seattleites rejoice that "the mountain is out" and head for the country. The city's natives admit that they thrive on the drippy microclimate's moody feel, and they face their predicament with humor—Mayor Norm Rice was recently named America's funniest mayor in an HBO poll. (In case you were wondering, Rice is also an able politician. Seattle's first African-American mayor, he has won two electoral victories in a city that is only 10% black.) Whatever you do in Seattle, don't be dismayed by the drizzle and bag the umbrella. After all, you don't want to be tagged as an outsider.

PRACTICAL INFORMATION

Visitors Information: Seattle-King County Visitors Bureau (461-5840), 8th and Pike St., on the 1st floor of the **convention center**. Maps, brochures, newspapers, and transit and ferry schedules. Helpful staff. Open Nov.-March Mon.-Fri. 8:30am-5pm; May-Oct. Mon.-Fri. 8:30am-5pm, Sat. 10am-4pm; Memorial Day-Labor Day Mon.-Fri. 8:30am-5pm, Sat.-Sun. 10am-4pm.

Parks Information: Seattle Parks and Recreation Department, 5201 Green Lake Way N., Seattle 98103 (684-4075). Open Mon.-Fri. 8am-5pm. **National Park Service, Pacific Northwest Region,** 915 2nd Ave. #442 (220-7450). Will answer questions about area parks, give info on discounts and passes, and sell you a map to the National Park System ($1.20). Open Mon.-Fri. 8am-4:30pm.

Currency Exchange: Thomas Cook Foreign Exchange, 906 3rd Ave. (623-6203). Open Mon.-Fri. 9am-5pm. Also behind the Delta Airlines ticket counter, and at other locations in **Sea-Tac Airport,** as well as on the first floor of the Westlake Shopping Center (on Pine at Westlake Ave. N.).

Airport: Seattle-Tacoma International (Sea-Tac) (431-4444 for general info) on Federal Way, south of Seattle proper. Take the Metro #174 or 194 from downtown Seattle.

Trains: Amtrak (800-USA-RAIL/872-7245, 382-4125 for arrival/departure times), King St. Station, at 3rd and Jackson St., 1 block east of Pioneer Square, next to the King Dome. To: Portland (3 per day, $26), Tacoma (3 per day, $9), Spokane (4 per day, $67), San Francisco (1 per day, $161), Vancouver, BC (4 per day, $29). Check for cheaper winter rates and bus connections to smaller destinations. Open daily 6am-10:15pm.

Buses: Greyhound (628-5526 or 800-231-2222), 8th Ave. and Stewart St. Daily to Sea-Tac Airport (2 per day, $5), Spokane (4 per day, $25), Vancouver, BC (8 per day, $25), Portland (9 per day, $15), Tacoma (6 per day, $4). Ticket office open daily 6:15am-9pm and 12:15-2am. **Green Tortoise Bus Service** (800-227-4766). The cushion-seats on this bus-turned-lounge fold down into beds at night, and the bus makes frequent stops for barbecue dinners and saunas. A slow but friendly alternative to the frenzy of Greyhound. Buses leave from 9th Ave. and Stewart St. on Thurs. and Sun. at 8am. To: Portland, OR ($15), Eugene, OR ($25), Berkeley, CA ($49), San Francisco, CA ($49), Los Angeles, CA (Thurs. only, $69). Reservations suggested 5 days in advance.

Public Transportation: Metro Transit, Customer Assistance Office, 821 2nd Ave. (553-3000 for 24hr. info), in the Exchange Building downtown. Open Mon.-Fri. 8am-5pm. For 24hr. schedules and directions call 553-3000 or 800-542-7876. Fares are based on a 2-zone system. Zone 1 includes everything within the city limits

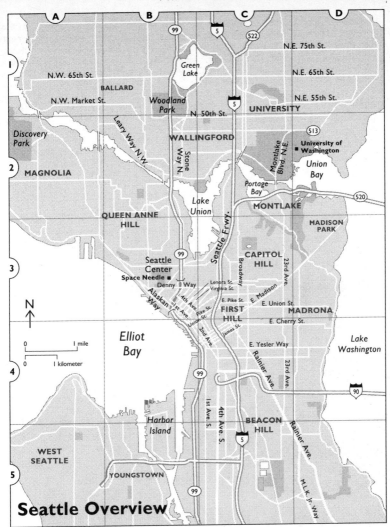

Seattle Overview

($1.10 during peak hours, 85¢ off peak). Zone 2 comprises anything outside the city limits ($1.60 peak, $1.10 off peak). Ages 5-18 always 75¢. Peak hours in both zones are Mon.-Fri. 6-9am and 3-6pm. Exact fare required. Transfers valid for 2hr. Weekend all-day passes $1.70. Ride free 5am-7pm daily in the downtown **ride free area**, bordered by S. Jackson St. on the south, 6th Ave. and I-5 on the east, Battery St. on the north, and the waterfront on the west. Always get a transfer. It can be used on any bus, including a return trip on the same bus within 2hr. All buses have free, easy-to-use **bike racks** and most are handicap accessible. See **Getting Around,** below, for more info.

Ferries: Washington State Ferries, Colman Dock, Pier 52, downtown (see p. 35 for schedule and fare info). Service from downtown to: Bainbridge Island, Bremerton in the Peninsula, and Vashon Island. Service from Fauntleroy in West Seattle to: Southworth in the Kitsap Peninsula and Vashon Island. Ferries leave daily, and frequently, 5am-2am. The **Victoria Line** (800-668-1167; 625-1880 for reservations), leaves Pier 48 daily at 1pm. This is the only auto ferry service available from Seattle to Victoria. One way: passengers $20.80, car and driver $46.15. Under 12 ½price.

Car Rental: A-19.95-Rent-A-Car, 804 N. 145th St. (365-1995). $20 per day ($25 if under 21); 10¢ per mi. after 100 mi. Free delivery. Under 21 must have verifiable auto insurance. Credit card required. Even cheaper, **Auto Driveaway** (235-0880) hires people to drive their cars to various locations across the U.S. (open Mon.-Fri. 9am-4:30pm).

Ride Board: 1st floor of the Husky Union Building (the HUB), behind Suzallo Library on the University of Washington main campus. Matches cars and riders for destinations across the country. Also check the board at the downtown AYH.

Bicycle Rentals: The Bicycle Center, 4529 Sand Point Way (523-8300). $3 per hr. (2-hr. min.), $15 per 24hr. period. Credit card or license required as deposit. Open Mon.-Fri. 10am-8pm, Sat.-Sun. 10am-5pm. **Gregg's Greenlake Cycle, Inc.,** 7007 Woodlawn Ave. NE (523-1822) is more expensive, but closer to Green Lake and Burke-Gilman bike trails ($18 for the day, $25 overnight). Photo I.D. and cash or credit card deposit required. Also rents in-line skates. Open Mon.-Fri. 9:30am-9pm, Sat.-Sun. 9:30am-6pm.

Seattle Public Library: 1000 4th Ave. (386-4636 for quick info, TDD 386-4697). Free newsletter with info on the library and local free lectures, films, and other programs. Free tours leave the info desk occasionally. A visitor's library card lasts for 3 months and costs $8 (with a temporary local address). Free 90-min. Internet access with a library card. Open Mon.-Thurs. 9am-9pm, Fri.-Sat. 9am-6pm; Sept.-May Sun. 1-5pm.

Ticket Agencies: Ticketmaster (628-0888, or 292-ARTS/2778) for plays, the symphony, and other fine arts events, in every Tower Records store; hr. depend on the store. **Ticket/Ticket,** 401 Broadway E. (324-2744), on the 2nd floor of the Broadway Market. ½-price day-of-show tickets to local theater, music, concerts, and dance performances. Cash only. Must purchase tickets in person. Open Tues.-Sun. 10am-7pm. Also in the Pike Place Market; open Tues.-Sun. noon-6pm.

Laundromat: Sit and Spin, 2219 4th St. (441-9484). Both a laundromat and a local hot spot (see **Clubs and Taverns** also). Wash $1.25, 10-min. dry 25¢. Open Sun.-Thurs. 9am-11pm, Fri.-Sat. 9am-2am. **Downtown-St. Regis,** 116 Stewart St., attached to the St. Regis Hotel. Wash $1.25, dry 75¢. Open 24hr.

Crisis Clinic: 461-3222. 24hr. **Seattle Rape Relief:** 1905 S. Jackson St., #102 (632-7273). Crisis counseling, advocacy, and prevention training. 24hr.

University of Washington Women's Information Center: (685-1090), Cunningham Hall, in the main campus. Community resource and referral for women's groups throughout the Seattle area. Open Mon.-Fri. 9am-5pm.

Senior Information and Assistance: 1601 2nd Ave. #800 (448-3110). Open Mon.-Fri. 9am-5pm.

Travelers' Aid: 909 4th Ave. #630 (461-3888), at Marion on the 6th floor of the YMCA. Free services for stranded travelers who have lost their wallets or their marbles. Open Mon.-Fri. 9am-4pm.

International District Emergency Center: 623-3321. Medics with multilingual assistance available. 24hr.

Poison Information: 800-732-6985. 24hr.

AIDS Information: AIDS Prevention Project, 296-4999.

Alcohol/Drug 24hr. Help Line: 722-3700.

Gay Counseling: 1820 E. Pine (323-0220). Open Mon.-Fri. noon-9pm. **Lesbian Resource Center:** 1808 Bellview Ave. #204 (322-3953). Support groups, drop-in center, lending library, and workshops. Open Mon.-Fri. 9am-7pm.

Health Care: Aradia Women's Health Center, 1300 Spring St. (323-9388). Urgent cases get priority. Staff will refer elsewhere when booked. Open Mon.-Fri. 10am-6pm. **Chec Medical Center,** 1151 Denny Way (682-7418). Walk-in.

Emergency: 911. **Police Department:** 610 3rd Ave. (583-2111).

Post Office: 442-6340, at Union St. and 3rd Ave. downtown. Open Mon.-Fri. 8am-5:30pm. **General Delivery ZIP Code:** 98101.

Area Code: 206.

GETTING THERE AND GETTING AROUND

Seattle is a long, skinny city, stretched north to south on an isthmus between **Puget Sound** to the west and **Lake Washington** to the east and linked by locks and canals. The city is easily accessible by **car** via **I-5,** which runs north-south through the city, east of downtown; and by **I-90** from the east, which ends at I-5 southeast of downtown. From I-5, get to **downtown** (including **Pioneer Square, Pike Place Market,** and the **waterfront)** by taking any of the exits from James St. to Stewart St. Take the Mercer St./Fairview Ave. exit to the **Seattle Center.** The Denny Way exit leads to **Capitol Hill,** and farther north, the 45th St. exit will take you to the **University District.** The less crowded **Rte. 99,** also called **Aurora Ave.** or the Aurora Hwy., runs parallel to I-5 and skirts the western side of downtown, with great views from the **Alaskan Way Viaduct.** Rte. 99 is often the better choice when driving downtown, to Queen Anne, Green Lake, Fremont, or to the northwestern part of the city.

Once there, navigating the city can seem daunting, but even the most road-weary of travelers can learn their way around the Emerald City like so many munchkins. Downtown, avenues run northwest to southeast and streets southwest to northeast. Outside downtown, everything is simplified: with few exceptions, avenues run north-south and streets east-west. The city is split into **quadrants:** 1000 1st Ave. NW is a long walk from 1000 1st Ave. SE.

When driving in Seattle, do as the natives do: yield to pedestrians. Not only do locals drive slowly, calmly, and politely, but police ticket frequently. Even jaywalking pedestrians rack up $50 fines for crossing against the light. Downtown driving can be nightmarish. Parking is expensive, hills are steep, and one way streets are ubiquitous. Parking is cheap, plentiful, and well-lit at the **Seattle Center,** near the Space Needle. Park there and take the **monorail** to the convenient **Westlake Center** downtown and walk or take a bus within the ride free zone, which covers most of downtown Seattle. See the **Metro** above in **Practical Information.**

Seattle is an extremely bicycle friendly city. All buses have free, easy-to-use **bike racks,** which hold two bikes. (Bike shops around town have sample racks for novices to practice on.) Check out Metro's *Bike & Ride* pamphlet, available at the visitors center and the hostel. One word of caution: between 6am and 7pm, bikes may only be loaded or unloaded at stops along the borders of the ride free zone. For a bicycle map of Seattle, call the **City of Seattle Bicycle Program** (684-7584).

The Metro covers King County east to North Bend and Carnation, south to Enumclaw, and north to Snohomish County, where Metro bus #6 hooks up with **Community Transit.** This line runs to Everett, Stanwood, and well into the Cascades. Metro bus #174 connects to Tacoma's Pierce County System in Federal Way.

PUBLICATIONS

The city's major newspaper, the *Seattle Times* (464-2121), lists upcoming events in its Thursday "Tempo" section. The *Seattle Weekly* offers a free, left-of-center, advertisement-stuffed alternative to the dominant daily, complete with a weekend event listing section every Wednesday. But the real pulse on the music and pop culture scene is the *Stranger,* which mysteriously materializes every Thursday at the door of any Seattle music store, coffee shop, or thrift store. This is the best place to start for the low-down on Seattle nightlife, or to read some entertaining personals (they say truth is stranger than fiction). *Arts Focus,* a free magazine available at most bookstores, carries information on the performing arts, while *Seattle Arts* published by the Seattle Arts Commission is especially good for events in the visual arts. Both are published monthly. *The Rocket* is another good source of information on the music scene. The established weekly *Seattle Gay News* has an excellent map and listings of gay owned and patronized business in Seattle, and sells like hot-cakes on Fridays at local newsstands (50¢). The *International Examiner* provides a free weekly news update of the local Asian-American community, and covers restaurants and upcoming community events.

TO DISCOVERY PARK

W. Mercer Pl.

W. Mercer St.

W. Republican St.

W. Harrison St.

W. Thomas St.

W. John St.

Denny Way

5th Ave. N.

Queen Anne Ave. N.

1st Ave. N.

Warren Ave. N.

2nd Ave. N.

3rd Ave. N.

4th Ave. N.

Valley St.

Roy St.

SEATTLE CENTER

5th Ave. W.

Taylor Ave. N.

Aurora Ave. N.

99

Elliott Ave. W.

Summer steamship to Victoria BC Pier 69

Pier 70

Broad St.

Clay St.

Cedar St.

Vine St.

Wall St.

Western Ave.

Elliott Ave.

2nd Ave.

Battery

Bell

Alaskan Way

1st Ave

Waterfront Streetcar

Pier 64-65

Pier 52

Waterfron
Par

Pie

Seattle

Getting Around

AAA Auto Club of Washington, 4
Central Bus Terminal, 11
King Street Station, 28
Monorail terminal, 3
Monorail terminal, 13
Municipal parking lot, 1
Port of Seattle General Offices
 Pier 66, 9
Trailways Bus Depot, 10
Union Station, 27
Washington State Ferry
 Terminal, 24

Things to See

Broadway Playfield, 12
Coliseum, 2
Elliott Bay Park, 7
Freeway Park, 14
Kingdome Stadium, 29
Myrtle Edwards Park, 8
Pacific Science Center, 6
Seattle Public Aquarium, 23
Smith Tower, 25
Space Needle, 5
State Convention and Trade
 Center, 15
Seattle Art Museum, 22

Your Tax Dollars at Work

Harborview Medical Center, 19
Post Office, 21
Post Office, 26
Public Library, 20
Seattle University, 17
Swedish Hospital Medical Ctr., 18
Virginia Mason Hospital, 16

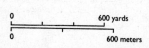

Passenger and auto ferry to Winslow, Pier 52

Passenger and auto ferry to Bremerton, Pier 52

Elliott Bay

N

0   600 yards
0   600 meters

LAKE UNION

TO
VOLUNTEER
PARK

E. Roy St.

12th Ave. E.

Dexter Ave. N.
8th Ave. N.
9th Ave. N.
Westlake Ave. N.
Terry Ave. N.
Boren Ave. N.
Fairview Ave. N.
Republican St.
Harrison St.
Pontius Ave. N.
Eastlake Ave. E.
Melrose Ave. E.
Bellevue Ave. E.
Summit Ave. E.
Belmont Ave. E.
Boylston Ave. E.
Harvard Ave. E.
Broadway East

E. Harrison St.

E. Thomas St.

John St.

E. John St.

E. Olive Way
E. Denny Way

Denny
Park

Denny Way

E. Howell St.
E. Howell St.

E. Olive St.
E. Olive St.

(12)

E. Pine St.
E. Pine St.

Monorail
Blanchard St.
9th Ave.
7th Ave.
Virginia St.
Stewart St.
Howell St.
Olive Way
Bellevue Ave.
E. Pike St.

E. Union St.

(11)
(10)
(i)
5th Ave.
4th Ave.
Lenora St.
Pine St.

E. Madison St.

12th Ave.

E. Spring St.

E. Marion St.

E. Columbia St.

E. Cherry St.

(13)
Pike St.

PIKE PLACE
MARKET

Union St.
(21)
University St.
(22)
8th Ave.
Hubble St.
Minor Ave.
Boren Ave.
Seneca St.
Terry Ave.
9th Ave.
(14)
(14)
(16)
(18)

Madison St.

Marion St.

Columbia St.

Cherry St.

(27)

Broadway

Pier 56
(23)
99
Western Ave.
Alaskan Way S.
Post Ave.
1st Ave.
2nd Ave.
3rd Ave.
Spring St.
Marion St.
6th Ave.
7th Ave.
4th Ave.
5th Ave.
(20)
(i)

James St.

Jefferson St.
Terry Ave.
(19)
Alder St.

E. Jefferson St.

E. Terrace

Alder St.

E. Spruce St.

Pier 54

(24)

(25)

E. Fir St.

E. Yesler Way

Yesler Way

S. Washington St.

S. Main St.

6th Ave. S.

S. Jackson St.

Pier 48

(28)
(27)
(26)

S. Jackson St.

Alaskan Freeway
E. Marginal Way S.
1st Ave. S.

Pier 46

S. King St.
S. Weller St.

8th Ave. S.

5

12th Ave. S.

S. King St.
S. Weller St.

S. Lane St.

PIONEER
SQUARE

S. Dearborn St.

S. Dearborn St.

Corwin Pl. S.

(29)

4th Ave. S.

99

S. Royal Brougham Way

Golf Dr. S.

ACCOMMODATIONS

The **Seattle International Hostel** is the best option for the budget traveler staying downtown, though not the least expensive. Those who are tired of the urban high-rise hostel scene should head for the **Vashon Island Hostel** (sometimes called the "Seattle B"; see p. 345). **Pacific Bed and Breakfast,** 701 NW 60th St., Seattle 98107 (784-0539), can set you up with a single room in a B&B in the $45-70 range (open Mon.-Fri. 9am-5pm).

Downtown

Seattle International Hostel (HI-AYH), 84 Union St. (622-5443), at Western Ave., right by the waterfront. Take bus #174, 184, or 194 from the airport (#194 from the north end of the baggage terminal is fastest), get off at Union St. and walk west. Free morning bagels and coffee, free linens, and a diverse, international crowd make up for the expanses of formica in this monstrously large hostel. The hostel boasts a palatial lounge and library/TV room. Amenities range from laundry facilities ($1 wash, 75¢ dry) to a ride board in the lobby. Offers discount tickets for Aquarium, Omnidome, and passenger ferry tickets. 7-day max. stay in summer. Front desk open 7am-2am. Checkout 11am. 24-hr. living room; no curfew. $16, nonmembers $19. Often full in summer; make reservations.

Green Tortoise Backpacker's Hostel, 1525 2nd Ave. (340-1222; fax 623-3207), between Pike St. and Pine St. Great location. 98 beds in 28 rooms plus 10 private rooms. Free breakfast and laundry. Pickup point for shuttle to Vancouver. No curfew. Beds $14, private rooms $30, private doubles $39.

Green Tortoise Garden Apartments, 715 2nd Ave. N. (282-1222; fax 282-9075) on the south slope of Queen Anne Hill, 3 blocks east from the Space Needle and the Seattle Center. Long-term accommodations for travelers staying over 30 days. Back yard, kitchens, garden, laundry, free breakfast. Beds $200 per month, private rooms $500 per month.

Commodore Hotel, 2013 2nd Ave. (448-8868), at Virginia. Take bus #174 or 194 from airport. Get off at 4th Ave. and Virginia. Many rooms have pleasant decor and walnut furniture (with a few broken baseboards). Not the best area of downtown, but the Commodore is a great deal and 24-hr. security keeps out the riff-raff. Singles $31, with bath $45. 2 beds and bath $52. 2 hostel-style rooms offer a bare-bones bunk room and shared bath for $12. Weekly single $134.

Moore Motel, 1926 2nd Ave. (448-4851 or 448-4852), at Virginia. 1 block east from Pike Place Market. Next to the historic Moore Theater. Big rooms include 2 beds, TV, and a slightly moldy bathroom. A 24-hr. diner located off the lobby and cavernous halls with gargantuan heavy wooden doors makes the Moore seem like it hasn't changed since the 20s. Singles $34. Doubles $39. For HI members when the hostel is full, singles $30, doubles $35.

Capitol Hill

Seattle American Backpacker's Hostel, 126 Broadway E. (720-2965 or 800-600-2965). Call for free airport, bus terminal, or train station pickup, or take bus #7 from downtown. Tucked away behind several buildings off Broadway in Capitol Hill, this hostel has one of Seattle's most entertaining neighborhoods at its doorstep, but a long list of rules and regulations at the desk suggests a history of wilder nights around the hostel. Free beer on Friday. Free bedding, free breakfast. No refunds; checkout by 11am. 3-day max. stay. HI-AYH members $14.50, nonmembers $15.50. Key deposit $5. Uncertain future, call ahead.

Vincent's Backpackers Guest House, 527 Malden Ave. E. (323-7849). Located in Capitol Hill between 14th and 15th Ave. Take bus #10 from downtown. Many a fisherman calls Vincent's home while anchored in Seattle. The house is clean, but both parking and living space is limited. Smoking is allowed inside the hostel. Desk open 9am-2am. Beds $12. Singles $30. Doubles $35.

Other Neighborhoods

For inexpensive motels a bit farther from downtown, drive north on Hwy. 99 (Aurora Ave.) or take bus #6 to the neighborhood of Fremont. Chain motels like the **Nites Inn**

(365-3216) line the highway north of the Aurora bridge, and many cater to the budget traveler, with rooms in the $30 range.

The College Inn, 4000 University Way NE (633-4441), at NE 40th St. For a place to crash near the University of Washington campus and its youthful environs, this is your best bet. Though singles are tiny and rooms have no TVs or private baths, turn-of-the-century bureaus and brass fixtures make a charming, if pricey, substitute. The TV is nestled in the 4th floor attic along with the kitchen, where breakfast materializes every morning (included in price of room) and guests loll on plush couches in front of the fireplace. Private singles from $42. Doubles $60-75. Rates higher in summer. Credit card required. No handicap access.

FOOD

Though Seattlites appear to subsist on espresso and steamed milk, they have to eat sometimes. When they do, they seek out healthy cuisine—especially seafood. The best fish, produce, and baked goods can be purchased from various vendors in Pike Place Market. Seattle's cheapest food is available on University Ave. in the University district, where food from around the world can be had for under $5. Or visit one of Seattle's active **food cooperatives,** at 6518 Fremont Ave. N. (in Green Lake) or at 6504 20th NE (in the Ravenna District north of the university). While in Ravenna look for fine produce at **Rising Sun Farms and Produce,** 6505 15th Ave. NE at 65th St. (524-9741; open daily 8am-8pm). Capitol Hill, the U District, and Fremont all close off main thoroughfares on summer Saturdays for their **farmer's markets.**

Pike Place Market

Farmers have been selling their produce here since 1907, when angry citizens demanded the elimination of the middle-merchant and local farmers sold produce from wagons by the waterfront. Not even the Great Depression slowed business at the market, which thrived until an enormous fire burned the building in 1941 and almost all of the market's 300 Japanese-American merchants were interned by the American government during WWII. But the early 1980s produced a Pike Place renaissance, and now hundreds of salivating tourists mob the market every day of the year. In the **Main Arcade,** which parallels the waterfront on the west side of Pike St., lunatic fish-mongers bellow at befuddled customers, competing for audiences and the contents of tourists' wallets by hurling fish from shelves to scales. The market's restaurants offer an escape from the crowded aisles to crowded tables, often with stellar views of the sound.

The best time to visit the market for shopping is between 7 and 9am, when the fish are still flopping and the fruit is freshest, though late in the day it's possible to score big discounts on produce. The monthly *Pike Place Market News,* available free in the market, has a **map** and the low-down on the market's latest events, new merchants, and old-timers. An information booth in front of the bike rack by the Main Arcade (at 1st Ave. and Pike St.) can give directions and answer questions (booth staffed Tues.-Sun. noon-6pm, with occasional coverage from 10am-noon; market open Mon.-Sat. 6:30am-6pm, Sun. 6:30am-5pm).

Soundview Café (623-5700), on the mezzanine level in the Main Arcade down Flower Row. This wholesome self-serve sandwich-and-salad bar offers fresh food, a spectacular view of Elliott Bay, and occasional poetry readings. Fill a $5 salad bar bowl with tabouli, pasta, salad, or fruit. Or bring a brown-bag lunch: the café offers the most pleasant and accessible public seating in the market. Open daily 7am-5pm, Sun. 9am-3pm.

Piroshki, Piroshki, 1908 Pike Pl. (441-6068). For an ample, high-fat, and heavenly hands-on meal, try this Russian specialty. Piroshki are made of a croissant-like dough, baked around anything from sausage and mushrooms ($2.85) to apples doused in cinnamon ($3.50). Watch the piroshki process in progress as you wait for your order. Open daily 8am-7pm.

WASHINGTON

> ## I'll Have A Double Decaf Espresso—with A Twist Of Lemon.
>
> Visiting Seattle without drinking the coffee would be like traveling to France without tasting the wine. The Emerald City's obsession with Italian-style espresso drinks has driven even gas stations to start pumping out thick, dark, soupy java. Espresso stands line streets and infiltrate office buildings, and "*Let's go* for coffee sometime" is a favorite local pick-up line. (*Let's Go* recommends using its trademark whenever it will get you a date.)
>
> It all started in the early 70s, when Starbucks started roasting its coffee on the spot in Pike Place Market. Soon, Stewart Brothers Coffee, now "Seattle's Best Coffee," presented Starbucks with a rival, and the race was on for the best cuppa joe. Today, hundreds of bean-brands compete for the local market, and Seattle coffee drinkers often claim undying allegiance to one or another. Follow this basic guide to the lingo when ordering espresso drinks:
>
> **Short:** 8oz.; **Tall:** 12oz.; **Grande:** 16oz.
>
> **Single:** one shot of espresso; **Double:** two—add shots (usually about 60¢) until you feel you've reached your caffeine saturation point.
>
> **Espresso:** the foundation of all espresso drinks—a small amount of coffee brewed by forcing steam through finely ground, dark-roasted coffee (pronounced es-PRESS-oh, not *ex*-PRESS-oh).
>
> **Cappuccino:** espresso topped by the foam from steamed milk. Order "wet" for more liquid milk and big bubbles, or "dry" for stiff foam.
>
> **Latté:** espresso with steamed milk and a little foam. More liquid than a "capp."
>
> **Americano:** espresso with hot water—an alternative to classic drip coffee.
>
> **Macciato:** steamed milk with a dollop of foam and espresso swirled onto the foam (not much coffee, but very pretty).
>
> With skim (nonfat) milk, any of these drinks is called **skinny**. If all you want is a plain ol' cuppa joe, say "drip coffee," otherwise, coffee shop workers will return your request for "coffee" with a blank stare.

The Alibi Room, 85 Pike St. (623-3180), across from the Market Cinema in the Post Alley. Created by a local producer, The Alibi Room proclaims itself a local "indie filmmaker" hangout. Turkey/brie sandwiches for $6.50. Racks of screenplays, live music after 8pm (21+ only), and chic decor get an Oscar for ambience. Open daily 11am-2am.

Delcambre's Ragin' Cajun, 1523 1st Ave. (624-2598). Good food, tremendous portions. Have a spicy dish of red beans and rice with *andouille* (a kind of sausage) for $6.95, the same dish the nearly-famous deaf chef served to President Clinton 2 years ago. Lunch $5-7. Open Tues.-Sat. 11am-3pm and 5:30-9pm.

Three Girls Bakery, 1514 Pike Pl. (622-1045), at Post. Order to go or sit in the café. The rows of bread and pastries will make you drool, as will the fresh bread aroma. Mammoth portions. 7 kinds of rye cost from $1.50-2.75 each. Sandwiches around $4. Open daily 6am-6pm.

Emmett Watson's Oyster Bar, 1916 Pike Pl. (448-7721). Watson is the local newspaper columnist and California-basher who founded the "Lesser Seattle" movement to keep away tourists and new residents. His plan includes the candid motto, "Keep the Bastards Out." You haven't really experienced a vitamin E high until you've tried the Oyster Bar Special ($5.75). Open Mon.-Sat. 11:30am-9pm, Sun. 10am-6pm. Closes 2hr. earlier in winter. No credit cards.

International District

Along King and Jackson St., between 5th and 8th Ave., directly east of the Kingdome, Seattle's International District is packed with great eateries. Fierce competition keeps prices low and quality high. Any choice here will probably be a good one, as three out of any four restaurants in the district have been named (at one time or another) the best in town by a *Seattle Times* reviewer. Locals often call these few blocks "Chinatown," but every kind of Asian food can be found. Don't shy away from a shabby exterior; the quality of the façade is often inversely proportional to the quality of the food. **Uwajimaya,** 519 6th Ave. S. (624-6248), is the largest East Asian retail store in the Pacific Northwest. A huge selection of Japanese staples, fresh seafood (often still swimming), a wide variety of dried and instant foods (great for camping), a sushi bar, and a bakery make this a Seattle institution. Take bus #7 (also sells toys, books, furniture, clothes, and jewelry; open daily 9am-8pm).

Phnom Penh Noodle Soup House, 414 Maynard Ave. S. (682-5690). Head to the tiny upstairs dining room for a view of the pagoda in Hing Hay Park. The menu will help you decipher what you order. Try the Phnom Penh Noodle Special; some people come here weekly and never order anything else (of course, there are only 6 items on the menu). Everything $3.90. Open daily 8:30am-7pm.

Tai Tung, 655 S. King St. (622-7372). A Chinese diner. The busiest hours at Tai Tung are 1-3am, when the munchies take hold of university students, who shuffle all the way from the U district for the Chinese version of fried chicken. It's roasted, not fried, but still greasy. Waiters here rise to the occasion; they're likely to learn your name by the second night you visit. 10-page, constantly-changing menu, entrees $7-8. Open Sun.-Thurs. 9:30am-11pm, Fri.-Sat. 9:30am-3:30am.

Ho Ho Seafood Restaurant, 653 S. Weller St. (382-9671). Fields of pink formica tables and friendly service. Watch the demise of your dinner as staff pluck live seafood from tanks. Generous portions of great seafood. Dinner from $7-9, lunch $3-5. Open Sun.-Thurs. 11am-1am, Fri.-Sat. 11am-3am.

House of Hong Restaurant, 409 8th Ave. S. (622-7997), at Jackson on the border of the International district. The most popular *dim sum* in town at $2 per dish; served daily 11am-5pm. Open Mon.-Thurs. 11am-10pm, Fri. 11am-midnight, Sat. 10:30am-midnight, Sun. 10:30am-10pm. Reservations recommended.

Viet My Restaurant, 129 Prefontaine Pl. S. (382-9923), near 4th and Washington. Consistently delicious Vietnamese food at great prices. Try *bo la lot* (beef in rice pancakes, $3.50) or shrimp curry ($4.25). Avoid the lunch rush. Open Mon.-Sat. 11am-9pm, closed between 3-5pm.

Pioneer Square and the Waterfront

Budget eaters beware of Pioneer Square: the Waterfront lures tourists with wharf-side fare that's better suited to the seagulls. The best option is a picnic in Waterfall Garden, on the corner of S. Main St. and 2nd Ave. S. in Pioneer Square.

Mae Phim Thai Restaurant, 94 Columbia St. (624-2979), a few blocks north of Pioneer Sq., between 1st Ave. and Alaskan Way. Local businesspeople who pack this tiny, unassuming restaurant at lunch attest to the glory of good, inexpensive take-out. Wait less than 5min. for an enormous meal of *pad thai*, then stroll one block west to the waterfront to enjoy your find. All dishes $4.

Ivar's Fish Bar, Pier 54 (624-6852), on the waterfront. One of a string of fast food seafood restaurants founded by and named for the late Seattle celebrity and shipping magnate Ivar Haglund. Fish and chips ($4.30), or the definitive Seattle clam chowder ($1.40). Dine with the gulls and pigeons in covered booths outside and avoid the adjoining "Ivar's Acres of Clams" restaurant, replete with expensive food and Winnebago-hauling tourists. Open daily 11am-11pm.

Capitol Hill

With bronze dance-step diagrams paved into the sidewalks and artsy, neon storefronts above, Capitol Hill offers a chance to escape from tourist traps to the espresso houses, imaginative shops, and elegant clubs of **Broadway Avenue.** At night, Broadway comes alive and Seattlites lollygag along in droves to see and be seen. Here, even the yuppies have noserings, and drag queens frequent grocery stores. The eclectic array of restaurants that line the avenue are prime people-watching venues. The food is some of the best in the city. **15th Street,** also on the hill, is more sedate. Bus #7 runs along Broadway; #10 runs through Capitol Hill along 15th St. Unless you're taking out, avoid the metered parking on Broadway and head east for the free angled spots behind the reservoir at Broadway Field, on 11th Ave.

Green Cat Café, 1514 E. Olive (726-8756), west of Broadway. This small coffee house is a favorite with locals for good reason. Sunny yellow walls and gilt-framed prints brighten up its already wonderful breakfast and lunch fare; healthy diner food with a twist. Get down with the hobo scramble ($4.25). Open Mon.-Fri. 7am-7pm, Sat. 7:30am-7pm, Sun. 9am-7pm.

The Gravity Bar, 415 Broadway E. (325-7186), in the Broadway Market. Neo-healthy, organic food and crazy fruit and vegetable juices. Stainless steel every-thing, and conical tables the Jetsons would die for fill this tiny room. Among the infamous fruit and vegetable drinks are Moonjuice (a melon/lime concoction, $3.50) and Mr. Rogers on Amino Acid (16 fl. oz., $5). Watch urban surfer employ-ees cram grass into a meat grinder to prepare shots of the trendy new health elixir, **wheat grass juice.** This green sludge is not satisfying unless the threat of oxidation terrifies you. Open Sun.-Thurs. 9am-10pm, Fri.-Sat. 10am-11pm.

HaNa, 219 Broadway Ave. E. (328-1187). Cramped quarters in this Japanese joint testify to the popularity of its sushi. Assorted sushi plate $8.25, large tempura lunch $5.95. Open Mon.-Sat.11am-10:30pm, Sun. 4:30-10pm.

Café Paradiso, 1005 E. Pike (322-6960). This proud-to-be-alternative café gives you your RDA of both caffeine and counterculture, but not much in the way of food. Muffin and croissant fare about does it. Espresso bars grace both floors, and angst-ridden artists exhibit their broodings on public chalkboard upstairs. Wear black. Smoke. Free musical performances (Sat. 8:30pm). Open Mon.-Thurs. 6am-1am, Fri. 6am-4am, Sat. 8am-4am, Sun. 8am-1am.

Dick's, 115 Broadway Ave. E. (323-1300). A Broadway institution, made famous in Sir Mix-A-Lot's rap "Broadway." This pink, 50s-style, drive-in burger chain also has locations in Wallingford, Queen Anne, and Lake City. Try Dick's Deluxe Burger ($1.60). Soft serve kiddie cones cost 50¢. Open daily 10:30am-2am.

Kokeb Restaurant, 926 12th Ave. (322-0485). Behind Seattle University at the far south end of Capitol Hill, near the First Hill neighborhood. This Ethiopian eatery was the first in the Northwest and serves hot and spicy meat or vegetable stews on spongy *injera* bread. Entrees $7-11. Open daily 5-10pm.

Dilettante Chocolates, 416 Broadway Ave. E. (329-6463). An alternative to the ubiquitous coffeehouse, this "cocoa lounge" has an extensive tea menu, the best cocoa in Seattle, and a repertoire of "adult milk shakes" for the 21+ chocolate lover (under $3).

University District

The immense **University of Washington** (colloquially known as "U-Dub"), north of downtown between Union Bay and Portage Bay, supports a colorful array of funky shops, international restaurants, and a slew of coffee houses. Most of the good restau-rants, cinemas, and cafés are within a few blocks of **University Way.** Due to the large student population it serves, this district offers more mileage for your food dollar than anywhere else in the city. A large meal can be had for under $5 at any one of the doz-ens of restaurants. Ask for "University Way," however, and be prepared for puzzled looks; it's known around here as **"Th'Ave."** To reach the University, take any one of buses #70-74 from downtown, or bus #7 from Capitol Hill.

Black Cat Café, 4113 Roosevelt Way NE (547-3887). Away from the fray, behind a dry cleaner. A sunny, non-smoking alternative to the Last Exit which exists in a vegan world of its own, without additives or preservatives. This student-run co-op is so laid back, it's almost asleep on the deck chairs out front. Eat outside in the gar-den or snuggle up next to the paperback "library" inside. Sandwiches and burritos $3-5. Open Tues.-Sat. 10:30am-8:30pm, Sun. 10:30am-3pm.

Flowers, 4247 University Way NE (633-1903). This local landmark has been here since the 20s, but spent its youth as a flower shop. Now a dark wood bar and mir-rored ceiling make a tasteful frame for the beautiful all-you-can-eat Mediterranean buffet ($5.50). Includes vegan options. Open Mon.-Sat. 11am-2am (kitchen closes at 10pm), Sun. 11am-5pm.

Pizzeria Pagliacci, 4529 University Way NE (632-0421). Voted Seattle's best pizza every year since 1986, at $1.20 a slice it's also one of the city's best values. Watch frat boys gobble up entire pizzas and attempt translating hundreds of Italian Holly-

> ### Pop Quiz
>
> What would you call a 12oz. espresso with an extra shot, steamed milk (skim, of course), and foam?

wood movie posters while you eat. Also on Capitol Hill. Open Sun.-Thurs. 11am-11pm, Fri.-Sat. 11am-1am.

Tandoor Restaurant, 5024 University Way (523-7477). Their all-you-can-eat lunch buffet ($5) is great deal. Dinner is more expensive. Grab a cushion on a back-room bench. Open Mon.-Sat. 11am-2:30pm and 4:30-10pm, Sun. 11am-3pm.

Last Exit, 5211 University Way NE (528-0522). One block west of University Way at NE 40th St. The Exit was established in 1967 and never quite outgrew the 60s; aging hippies watch aspiring chessmasters battle it out in a large smoky room. The Exit claims to be Seattle's first-ever coffee bar. Dirt-cheap espresso (90¢) and coffee ($1). Open daily 9am-midnight.

SIGHTS AND ACTIVITIES

The best way to take in the city skyline is from any one of the **ferries** that leave from the waterfront. The finest view of all of Seattle, however, is a bit of a secret, and an exclusively female privilege: the athletic club on the top floor of the **Columbia Tower** (the big black building at 201 5th Ave.) has floor-to-ceiling windows in the ladies' room that overlook the entire city. **Volunteer Park** in Capitol Hill (see below) has a view from the east that captures the entire skyline and the Sound.

It takes only two frenetic days to get a closer look at most of Seattle's major sights, as most are within walking distance of one another or are within the Metro's Free Zone (see **Getting Around**, above). Rumor has it that Seattle taxpayers spend more on the arts per capita than any other Americans. The investment pays off in the form of numerous galleries, free art tours, and the renovated Seattle Art Museum. But beyond its cosmopolitan downtown, Seattle also boasts over 300 parks and recreation areas where you can enjoy the well-watered greenery. Don't pass up spending some time out of doors: take a rowboat out on Lake Union, bicycle along Lake Washington, or hike through the wilds of Discovery Park.

Downtown

The new **Seattle Art Museum,** 100 University Way (654-3100 for a recording, TDD 654-3137), near 1st and University Way, boasts a stunning design by Philadelphian architect Robert Venturi. There's art *inside* the building, too. The museum has an entire floor dedicated to the art of Native Americans from the Pacific Northwest and houses an extensive collection of modern and contemporary Northwestern works. The impressive African collection boasts a coffin by Kane Kwei, the carpenter from Ghana who has recently found a niche in the art world with his theme coffins. Call for current information on films and lectures ($6, students and seniors $4, under 12 free; open Fri.-Wed. 10am-5pm, Thurs. 10am-9pm; free tours 12:30, 1, and 2pm; check for special tours at 7:15pm Thurs.). One block north of the museum on 1st Ave., inside the Alcade Plaza Building, is the free **Seattle Art Museum Gallery,** featuring current art, sculpture, and prints by local artists.

Westlake Park, with its Art Deco brick patterns and Wall of Water, is a good place to kick back and listen to steel drums. This small triangular park, on Pike St. between 5th and 4th Ave., is bordered by the original **Nordstrom's** and the gleaming new **Westlake Center,** where the monorail departs for the Seattle Center. Nordstrom's is an upscale department store emphasizing superlative customer service. (Travelers toting *Let's Go* may find **Nordstrom's Rack,** at 2nd and Pine, more appealing; see **Shopping**).

> ### Pop Quiz Answer
> A tall, skinny, double latté.

Many of the business-district high-rises warrant a closer look. **The Pacific First Center** at 5th and Pike displays a truly breathtaking collection of glass art commissioned from the prestigious Pilchuk School. Other notable buildings include the **Washington Mutual Tower** on 3rd Ave. and the buildings around 6th and Union.

Bristling with excitement, and only a short walk down Pike St., is the **Pike Place Market,** a public market frequented by tourists and natives in equal proportions. (See Pike Place Market in **Food,** above.) While downtown, trek a few blocks to **Freeway Park,** which straddles I-5 between Pike St. and Spring St., and marvel at a set of concrete waterfalls designed to mimic a natural gorge while simultaneously blocking freeway noise.

The Waterfront

The **Pike Place Hillclimb** descends from the south end of the Pike Place market down a set of staircases, past chic shops and ethnic restaurants to Alaskan Way and the **waterfront.** (An elevator is also available.) The ever-popular **Seattle Aquarium** (386-4330) sits at the base of the Hillclimb at Pier 59, near Union St. Outdoor tanks re-create the ecosystems of salt marshes and tide pools. The aquarium's star attraction, the underwater dome featuring the fish of the Puget Sound and some playful harbor seals, fur seals, and otters, is worth the admission price. See the world's only salmon ladder in an aquarium. Don't miss the daily 11:30am feeding ($7.15, seniors $5.70, ages 6-18 $4.70, ages 3-5 $2.45; limited hours on holidays. Open year-round, Memorial Day-Labor Day daily 10am-5pm).

Next to the aquarium is the **Omnidome** (622-1868). A unique theater experience, the Omnidome displays movies on a special rounded screen so that patrons actually feel they are in the movie. The booming sound system may scare small children ($7, seniors and students $6, ages 3-12 $5, second film $2; with admission to aquarium $11.95, seniors and ages 13-18 $9.25, ages 6-12 $8.50, under 12 $5.75. Films shown daily 9:30am-10pm).

Pier 59 and the aquarium sit smack in the middle of the waterfront district. Explore north or south by foot or by **streetcar.** The 1920s cars were imported from Melbourne in 1982 because Seattle sold its original streetcars to San Francisco, where they now enjoy fame as cable cars (85¢ for 1½hr. of unlimited travel. Metro passes are good on the streetcar; on Sun., children under 12 ride free if accompanied by 1 paying passenger; streetcars run every 20-30min. Mon.-Sat. 7am-11pm, Sun. 8am-11pm; winter until 6pm). Streetcars are fully handicap accessible and run from the Metro tunnel in Pioneer Square north to Pier 70 and Myrtle Edwards Park.

North of Pier 70's pricey shopping arcade, **Myrtle Edwards Park** stretches along the water to the granaries on Piers 90 and 91. Despite lovely grassy areas and equally good views, Myrtle Edwards affords more seclusion than other downtown parks. Boeing sponsors a spectacular 4th of July fireworks show off shore.

The Seattle Center

The 1962 World's Fair took place in Seattle, and the already entertainment-oriented city rose to the occasion by building the Seattle Center, where visitors can find anything from carnival rides to ballet. Although Seattlites generally disdain the Center (leaving it to tourists and suburbanites), there's actually a lot going on there. Take the **monorail** from the third floor of the Westlake Center; for 90¢ (ages 5-12 70¢, seniors 35¢) it will ferry passengers to the Seattle Center every 15 minutes from 9am to midnight. The center stretches between Denny Way and W. Mercer St., and 1st and 5th Ave., and has eight gates, each with a model of the Center and a **map** of its facilities. The **Pacific Science Center** (443-2001), within the park, houses a **laserium** (443-2850) and an **IMAX theater** (443-4629). Evening IMAX shows run Thurs. through Sun. (tickets to IMAX *and* the museum $9.50, seniors and ages 6-13 $7.50, ages 2-5 $5.50). The evening laser shows quake to music by groups like Led Zeppelin, Nine Inch Nails, and, of course, Nirvana (Tues. $3; Wed.-Sun. $6.75).

The renowned **Pacific Northwest Ballet Company,** the **Opera,** and the **Seattle Symphony** all perform at the Seattle Center (see **Entertainment: Music and Dance,** below) and the Center is also home to the **Bagley Wright Theater,** where the Seattle Repertory Theater performs, and the brand-new and beaming **Key Arena,** where the Seattle Supersonics basketball team played its way to recent fame as Western Conference Champions. For information regarding special events and permanent attractions at the Center, call 684-8582 for recorded information or 684-7200 for a speaking human. The Center has a customer service desk (684-8582) in the Center House (open 7am-5pm) and a visitor's info desk, also in the Center House (open 9am-6pm). See **Events,** below, for information on the ever-popular **Seafair,** the **Folklife Festival,** the **Seattle International Children's Festival,** and the **Bite of Seattle,** all held annually at the Center. Over Labor Day weekend, Seattlites demonstrate their partygoing endurance at the four-day **Bumbershoot,** a festival of folk, street, classical, and rock music. Free concerts are also held during the summer at the **Seattle Center Mural Amphitheater,** and feature a variety of local rock bands. Check the "Tempo" section of the *Seattle Times* for listings (see **Events**).

The **Space Needle** (443-2111), sometimes known as "the world's tackiest monument," is a useful landmark for the disoriented, and houses an observation tower and an expensive, 360° rotating restaurant. The Space Needle charges $8.50 (ages 5-12 $4) for a ride to its rotating top unless you have dinner reservations. (People have been known to make reservations with no intention of keeping them.)

Pioneer Square and Environs

From the waterfront or downtown, it's just a few blocks to historic Pioneer Square, at Yesler Way and 2nd Ave. The 19th-century warehouses and office buildings were restored in the 1970s and now house chic shops and trendy pubs. Pioneer Square today retains much of its historical intrigue, as well as suffocating tourist crowds.

Originally Seattle stood 12 ft. below the present-day streets. The **underground tours** (682-1511 for info or 682-4646 for reservations) take you into the subterranean rooms and passageways, explaining the sordid and soggy birth of Seattle. Be prepared for lots of tourists, comedy, and toilet jokes. Tours leave hourly from Doc Maynard's Pub, 610 1st Ave., and last 90 minutes ($6.50, seniors $5.50, students $5, and children $2.75; reservations recommended). The earliest Seattlites settled on the site of Pioneer Square. "Doc" Maynard, a notorious early resident, gave a plot of land here to one Henry Yesler on the condition that he build a steam-powered lumber mill. Logs were dragged down the steep grade of Yesler Way to feed the mill, earning that street the epithet **"Skid Row."** Years later, the center of activity moved north, precipitating the decline of Pioneer Square and giving the term "skid row" its present meaning as a neighborhood of poverty and despair.

Klondike Gold Rush National Historic Park, 117 S. Main St. (553-7220), is an antique interpretive center that depicts the lives and fortunes of miners. A slide show describes the role of Seattle in the Klondike gold rush. Daily walking tours of Pioneer Square leave the park at 10am. Unlike the underground tours, these are free. To add some levity to this history of shattered dreams, the park screens Charlie Chaplin's 1925 classic, *The Gold Rush,* on the first Sunday of every month at 3pm (free; open daily 9am-5pm).

The International District

Three blocks east of Pioneer Square, up Jackson on King St., is Seattle's International District. Though sometimes called "Chinatown" by Seattlites, this area is now home to immigrants from all over Asia and their descendants. Prominent members of Seattle's Asian community have recently made a push for the recognition of Asian-American cultures in Seattle.

Start your tour of the district by ducking into the **Wing Luke Memorial Museum,** 407 7th Ave. S (623-5124) to get a thorough description of life in an Asian-American community. This tiny museum houses a permanent exhibit on the different Asian nationalities in Seattle and temporary exhibits by local Asian artists. This was one of four museums to win the National Award for Museum Service in 1985 for its intergenerational and community emphasis. Thursdays are always free ($2.50, seniors and students $1.50, ages 5-12 75¢; open Tues.-Fri. 11am-4:30pm, Sat.-Sun. noon-4pm). Other landmarks of the International District include the **Tsutakawa sculpture** at the corner of S. Jackson and Maynard St. and the gigantic dragon mural and red-and-green pagoda in **Hing Hay Park** at S. King and Maynard St. The community gardens at Main and Maynard St. provide a peaceful and well tended retreat from the downtown sidewalks, though you may feel a bit like you're walking through someone else's back yard while you tiptoe through the turnips. Park next to the gardens in free three-hour angled parking to avoid meters.

Capitol Hill

Capitol Hill is, in many ways, the pinnacle of Seattle's art culture, where alternative lifestyles and mainstream capitalism converge seamlessly—crowds have recently attracted national chains like Ben & Jerry's and The Gap to join in the spend-happy atmosphere along Broadway Ave. The district's leftist and gay communities set the tone for its nightspots (see **Entertainment,** below), while the retail outlets include collectives and radical bookstores. Explore Broadway to window shop and experience the neighborhood, or walk a few blocks east and north for a stroll down the hill's residential streets, lined with well-maintained Victorian homes. Bus #10 runs along 15th Ave. and makes more frequent stops; the #7 cruises Broadway, which is a more lively ride.

Volunteer Park, between 11th and 17th Ave. at E. Ward St., north of the main Broadway activity, lures tourists away from the city center. Bus #10 runs parkward up 15th Ave. To get to the park, it's better to take the #10 than the 7; it runs more frequently and stops closer to the fun stuff. Named for the "brave volunteers who gave their lives to liberate the oppressed people of Cuba and the Philippines" during the Spanish-American War, the park boasts lovely lawns, an outdoor running track, a playground, and fields of rhododendrons in the spring and early summer. The outdoor stage often hosts free performances on summer Sundays. Climb the medieval-looking water tower at the 14th Ave. entrance for a stunning 360° panorama of the city and the Olympic Range. The views beat those from the Space Needle, and they're free. On rainy days, hide out amid the orchids inside the glass **conservatory** (free; open daily 10am-4pm, summer 10am-7pm). Be careful at night; the park has an unsavory reputation after dark. While in the park, visit the newly renovated **Seattle Asian Art Museum** (SAAM 654-3100). A tour through the world-renowned collection of Asian art reveals Ming vases and ancient kimonos at every turn, as well as a hands-on exhibit on the current practise of traditional arts. Suggested admission $6, seniors and students $4, under age 12 free. Open Tues.-Sun. 10am-5pm, Thurs. 10am-9pm, closed Mon. Take bus #7 or 10 from downtown.

The **University of Washington Arboretum** (543-8800), 10 blocks east of Volunteer Park, houses the Graham Visitors Center, with exhibits on local plant life (visitors center is open daily 10am-4pm; winter Mon.-Fri. 10am-4pm and Sat.-Sun. noon-4pm) and is located at the southern end of the arboretum at Lake Washington Blvd. Across the street, the tranquil and perfectly pruned **Japanese Tea Garden** (684-4725) offers a stroll through 3½ acres of sculpted gardens encompassing fruit trees, a reflecting pool, and a traditional tea house ($2.50; seniors, and ages 6-18 $1.50, disabled $1, under 6 free; open daily March-Nov.; garden hr. vary depending on sunset times; March-April open noon-4pm, May-Sept. 10am-8pm, Oct.-Nov. 11am-5pm). Take bus #11 from downtown. The Arboretum also shelters superb **walking** and **running** trails, and boasts 4000 species of trees and shrubs and 43 species of flowers. Swings and athletic facilities at the southern end lure families and frolickers. Tours of the arboretum leave Sat. and Sun. at 1pm from the visitors center (arboretum open dawn-dusk).

University District

With 33,000 students, the **University of Washington** is the state's cultural and educational center of gravity. The "U District" swarms with students year-round, and Seattlites of all ages take advantage of the area's many bohemian bookstores, shops, taverns, and restaurants. To reach the district, take buses #71-74 from downtown, or

#7, 43, or 48 from Capitol Hill. Stop by the friendly **visitors center,** 4014 University Way NE (543-9198), to pick up a campus **map,** a self-guided tour book, and obtain information about the University (open Mon.-Fri. 8am-5pm).

On the campus, visit the **Thomas Burke Memorial Washington State Museum** (543-5590), at NE 45th St. and 17th Ave. NE, in the northwest corner of the campus. The museum exhibits a superb collection on the Pacific Northwest's native nations, but it is slowly phasing out this collection to make room for its growing exhibit on Pacific Rim cultures. This is the only natural history museum in the area, so savor the chance to see the only dinosaur bones in the Northwest. In addition to Allosauri, they also display two beautiful Tiffany windows, a rare find outside of New York (suggested donation $3, seniors and students $2, ages 6-18 $1.50; open daily 10am-5pm). Across the street, the astronomy department's old stone **observatory** (543-0126) is open to the public for viewings on clear nights. Looming Gothic lecture halls, red brick, and rose gardens transform the campus into a bowery, fit for hours of strolling. The red concrete basin in the center of campus, known as **Red Square,** collects hundreds of students during the school year. The **UW Arts Ticket Office,** 4001 University Way NE (543-4880), has information and tickets for all events (open Mon.-Fri. 10:30am-4:30pm).

Students often cross town for drinks in **Queen Anne,** and the intervening neighborhood, **Fremont,** basks in the jovial atmosphere. Fremont residents pride themselves on their love of art, antiques, and for the liberal atmosphere of their self-declared "center of the world" under Hwy 99. The annual **Fremont Fair** and Solstice Parade in mid-June bring Fremont to a frenzy of music, frivolity, and craft booths. A statue entitled "Waiting for the Inner-city Urban" depicts several people waiting in bus-purgatory, and, in moments of inspiration and sympathy, is frequently dressed up by passers-by. The **troll,** who sits beneath the Aurora Bridge (on 35th St.) grasping a Volkswagen Bug, has a confounded expression on his broad cement face. Some say that kicking the Bug's tire brings good luck. Fremont is also the home of **Archie McPhee's,** 3510 Stone Way (545-8344), a shrine to pop culture and plastic absurdity. People of the punk and funk persuasion make pilgrimages from as far as the record stores of Greenwich Village in Manhattan just to handle the notorious **slug selection.** You can get to Archie's on the Aurora Hwy. (Rte. 99), or take bus #26. The store is east of the highway between 35th and 36th, two blocks north of Lake Union and Gasworks Park (see below; open Mon.-Sat. 9am-7pm, Sun. 10am-6pm).

WATERWAYS AND PARKS

A string of attractions festoon the waterways linking Lake Washington and Puget Sound. Houseboats and sailboats fill **Lake Union,** situated between Capitol Hill and the University District. Here, the **Center for Wooden Boats,** 1010 Valley St. (382-2628), maintains a moored flotilla of new and restored small craft for rent (rowboats $8-12 per hr., sailboats $10-15 per hr.; open daily 11am-6pm). **Gasworks Park,** a much-celebrated kite-flying spot at the north end of Lake Union, was recently converted to a park after its retirement from the oil refining business. **Gasworks Kite Shop,** 1915 N. 34th St. (633-4780), is one block north of the park (open Mon.-Fri. 10am-6pm, Sat. 10am-5pm, Sun. noon-5pm). To reach the park, take bus #26 from downtown to N. 35th St. and Wallingford Ave. N. If inspiration to go for a sail strikes while at the park, **Urban Surf,** across the street at 2100 N. Northlake Way (545-WIND/9463), rents windsurfing boards ($35 per day) and in-line skates ($5 per hr.).

Directly north of Lake Union, athletes run, ride, roller skate, and skateboard around **Green Lake.** Take bus #16 from downtown Seattle. The lake is also given high marks by windsurfers, but woe to those who lose their balance. Whoever named it Green Lake wasn't kidding; even a quick dunk results in gobs of green algae clinging to your body and hair. On sunny afternoons boat-renters, windsurfers, and scullers can make the lake feel like rush hour on I-5. Rent a bicycle from **Greg's Green Lake Cycle, Inc.** (see **Practical Information**), also on the east side across the street from Starbucks. Ask for directions to the **Burke-Gilman trail** for a longer ride.

Next to the lake is Woodland Park and the **Woodland Park Zoo,** 5500 Phinney Ave. N. (684-4800), best reached from Rte. 99 or N. 50th St. Take bus #5 from downtown. The park itself is shaggy, but the zoo habitats are realistic. The zoo specializes in conservation and research. The **elephant habitat** has enhanced the zoo's international reputation for creating natural settings. It's one of only three zoos in the U.S. to receive the Humane Society's highest standard of approval ($7.50; ages 6-17, seniors $5.75, students $5, ages 3-5 $4; parking $3, winter $1.50; open March 15-Oct. 15 daily 9:30am-6pm, Oct. 16-March 14 9:30am-4pm).

Farther west, the **Hiram M. Chittenden Locks** (783-7059) along the Lake Washington Ship Canal on NW St., crowds to watch Seattle's boaters jockey for position. A circus atmosphere develops as boats traveling between Puget Sound and Lake Washington try to cross over (June 1-Sept. 30 daily 7am-9pm). If listening to the cries of frustrated skippers ("Gilligan, you nitwit!") doesn't amuse you, climb over to the **fish ladder** to watch homesick salmon hurl themselves up 21 concrete steps. Take bus #43 from the U District or #17 from downtown. The busiest salmon runs occur from June to September. Free tours of the locks start at 1, 2, and 3pm on summer weekends (open daily 10am-7pm; Sept.-June Thurs.-Mon. 11am-5pm).

Discovery Park (386-4236), on a lonely point west of the Magnolia District and south of Golden Gardens Park, at 36th Ave. W. and Government Way W. (take bus #24.), comprises acres of minimally tended grassy fields and steep bluffs atop Puget Sound. Next door to the Chittenden Locks, the park is the largest in the Seattle area, with 534 bucolic acres. It provides a wonderful haven for birds forced over Puget Sound by the "bad-weather" Olympic Mountains. Possessing a wide range of habitats with easily distinguishable transitions, this park provides a fantastic introduction to the flora and fauna of the Pacific Northwest for those unable to make the trek to Olympic or Mt. Ranier National Parks. A **visitor's center** looms large at the entrance (3801 W. Government Way), waiting to sell you a cheap and handy map (75¢). Shuttles ferry the elderly and handicapped to the beach daily from 8:30am-5pm, June-Sept. At the park's northern end is the **Indian Cultural Center** (285-4425), operated by the United Indians of All Tribes Foundation, which houses the **Sacred Circle Gallery,** a rotating exhibit of Native American artwork (free; open Mon.-Fri. 9am-5pm, Sat.-Sun. noon-5pm). The tree walk that runs by the Center is a must-see, if only for the flocks of banana slugs that goo their way along the paths and leave happy trails of slime for passersby.

Seward Park is at the southern end of a string of beaches and forest preserves along the west shore of Lake Washington. Take bus #39. After a jaunt in the park, refresh yourself with a tour of the **Rainier Brewery Co.,** 3100 Airport Way S. (622-2600), off I-5 at the West Seattle Bridge. Beer (root beer for those under 21), cheese and crackers are all served free (30-min. tours on the hr., Mon.-Sat. 1-6pm).

Directly across town, on Puget Sound, is **Alki Beach Park,** a thin strip of beach wrapped around residential West Seattle. Take bus #36. The first white settlers of Seattle set up camp here in 1851, naming their new home New York Alki, meaning "New York By and By" in the local Native language. By the time the settlement moved to Pioneer Square, parvenu Doc Maynard suggested that perhaps "New York By and By" was too deferential a name and that the city should be named for his friend Chief Sealth. Because the Suquamish people did not believe in pronouncing the names of the deceased, the city's name became "Seattle." A monument to the city's birthplace is found along Alki Beach at 63rd Ave. SW, south of Alki. Just south of **Lincoln Park,** along Fauntleroy Way in Fauntleroy, is the departure point for **passenger and auto ferries** to **Vashon Island** and **Southworth** (see **Practical Information,** above). Take bus #18 to Lincoln Park.

SPORTS AND RECREATION

Pick up a copy of *Your Seattle Parks and Recreation Guide,* available at the visitors bureau or the Parks Department (see **Practical Information,** above), or the monthly *Sports Northwest,* available at most area sports outfitters (free). The paper has calendars of competitive events in the Northwest and recreation suggestions.

Swimming Upstream

The salmon's lot is not an easy one. After his birth in a small stream, he begins his long migration to the ocean. Along the way, he undergoes the process of smoltification, a series of changes which enable him to live in salt water. This journey oceanward has been significantly complicated by the massive hydroelectric dams and canal locks which dot the Pacific Northwest. Adolescent fish, known as fingerlings for their characteristic size, often must first evade predators in the slow waters of dammed lakes before they reach the sanctuary of the barges and trucks that await them at a collection zone to carry them to their salty new home. After feeding and gaining strength in the mighty Pacific, the salmon heeds the call of fate (and instinct) and begins his journey back home to mate. Benevolent humans have installed fish ladders along the dams and locks in order to aid the salmon in his quest. The "rungs" of a fish ladder are 3- to 4-ft. deep pools, each 1ft. higher than the last, designed to mimic a series of rapids. Though the fish used to leap dramatically from one pool to the next, recent innovations have hidden their acrobatics. Newly devised openings below the surface mean easier climbing, but no more photo ops.

The Seattle professional sports scene is truly odd. Uglier and less productive than the Boeing factory, the **Kingdome,** 201 S. King St. (622-3555 for info or 622-4487 for tickets), down 1st Ave., ranks second only to Houston's Astrodome as an insult to baseball. Seattle is the only city in America where fans might prefer to watch their home team (the **Mariners**) on TV rather than see them live, under poor, flat, purplish light, on artificial turf, amid unearthly echoes. In the fall of 1995, sections of the roof viciously attacked fans hoping to see Seattle make the World Series. Tickets for Mariners games are cheap: $15 on the 3rd base line (628-0888; open Mon.-Sat. 8am-9pm, Sun. 8am-6pm). Sunday is seniors discount day. The **Seahawks,** more of an afterthought than an NFL team, play football here.

On the other side of town (and at the other end of the aesthetic spectrum), the new and graceful Key Arena in the Seattle Center is packed to the brim whenever Seattle's pro basketball team, the **Supersonics** (281-5800) play. Last year, Seattlites danced in the streets as the Sonics ascended the NBA ranks, only to be defeated by the four-time champs, the Chicago Bulls. Undaunted by a recent NCAA post-season prohibition, the **University of Washington Huskies** football team has dominated the PAC-10. Call the Athletic Ticket Office (543-2200) for Husky schedules and price information.

Cyclists should gear up for the 192-mi., 1600-competitor **Seattle to Portland Race.** Call the **bike hotline** (522-2453) for more information. The Seattle Parks Department also holds a monthly **Bicycle Sunday** from May to September, when Lake Washington Blvd. is open only to cyclists from 10am to 6pm. Contact the Parks Department's Citywide Sports Office (684-7092) for more information.

Many **whitewater rafting** outfitters are based in the Seattle area. Though the rapids are hours away by car, over 50 companies compete for a growing market. A good way to secure an inexpensive trip is to call outfitters and quote competitors' prices; they are often willing to undercut one another. Two trade organizations, **PRO (Professional Rafters Organization)** (323-5485) and the **Washington State Outfitters and Guides Association** (392-6107), can provide advice and information. Whatever outfitter you use, be sure it lives up to basic safety standards.

The **Northwest Outdoor Center,** 2100 Westlake Ave. (281-9694), on Lake Union, holds instructional programs in **whitewater** and **sea kayaking** during the spring, summer, and fall (2-evening intro to sea kayaking, including equipment $45). The center also leads sea kayaking excursions through the San Juan Islands (open Mon.-Fri. 10am-8pm, Sat.-Sun. 9am-6pm).

Skiing near Seattle is every bit as good as the mountains make it look. **Alpental, Ski-Acres,** and **Snoqualmie** co-sponsor an information number (232-8182), which provides conditions and lift ticket rates for all three. **Crystal Mountain** (663-2265), the region's newest resort, can be reached by Rte. 410 south out of Seattle and offers ski rentals, lessons, and lift ticket packages.

Since the Klondike gold rush, Seattle has been one of the foremost cities in the world for outfitting wilderness expeditions. Besides Army-Navy surplus stores and campers' supply shops, the city is home to many world-class outfitters. **Recreational Equipment Inc. Coop (REI Coop),** 222 Yale Ave. is the largest of its kind in the world. This brand-new flagship store offers a 65ft. indoor climbing pinnacle, interactive pathways to test mountaineering equipment, and lessons on Northwest foliage. This paragon of woodsy wisdom (it also offers exploration and travel slide shows) can be seen from I-5. Take the Stewart St. exit. (Open Mon.-Sat. 10am-9pm, Sun. 11am-6pm. Rental area open 3hr. prior to store.)

Opening Day (the first Sat. in May) is a big spring **rowing** event in the University of Washington's Montlake Cut, the channel between Lake Washington and Portage Bay. Crowds flood the banks to watch streams of sailboats (usually gussied up to follow a theme), and, most importantly, to watch the Washington crews challenge competitors in 2km sprint races. Take the Bellevue exit off I-5.

ENTERTAINMENT

With one of the world's most notorious underground music scenes and the third largest theater community in the U.S. (only New York's and Chicago's are bigger), performances of all kinds take place in any Seattle building with four walls, from bars to bakeries. In the summertime, risers seem to grow out of asphalt during street fairs and farmers' markets, and outdoor theater springs up in most parks. High cost shows regularly sell half-price tickets, while alternative theaters offer high quality drama at low prices. During lunch hours in the summertime, the free **"Out to Lunch"** series (623-0340) brings everything from reggae to folk dancing to the parks, squares, and office buildings of downtown Seattle. Pick up a schedule at the visitors center (see **Practical Information**). The **Seattle Public Library** (386-4636) shows free films as part of the program, and has a daily schedule of other free events, such as poetry readings and children's book-reading competitions. *Events,* published every two months, is a calendar of goings-on hosted by the library.

Music and Dance

The **Seattle Opera** (389-7676, open Mon.-Fri. 9am-5pm, or Ticketmaster at 292-2787) performs at the Opera House in the Seattle Center throughout the year. The popularity of the program requires that you order tickets well in advance, although rush tickets are sometimes available (students and seniors receive ½price tickets day-of-performance, $15-30). Write to the Seattle Opera at P.O. Box 9248, Seattle 98109. The **Seattle Symphony Orchestra** (443-4747), also in Seattle Center's Opera House, performs a regular subscription series from September through June (rush tickets $6.50 and up) and a special popular and children's series. The symphony is moving in September 1998 from its home in the **Fifth Avenue Theater.** The **Pacific Northwest Ballet** (441-9411) starts its season at the Opera House in September. The spectacular Maurice Sendak-designed version of the *Nutcracker* always draws crowds, especially since this one of only two ballet companies on the West Coast (San Francisco's is the other). The season continues through May with six productions (tickets $10 and up). The **University of Washington** offers its own program of student recitals and concerts by visiting artists. Call the Meany Hall box office (543-4880, open Mon.-Fri. 10:30am-4:30pm).

Theater

The city hosts an exciting array of first-run plays and alternative works, particularly by the many talented amateur groups. You can often get **rush tickets** at nearly half price on the day of the show (with cash only) from **Ticket/Ticket** (324-2744). Watch for the popular, free, open-air Shakespeare in the summer put on by the **University of Washington School of Drama Theaters** (543-4880).

Seattle Repertory Theater, 155 W. Mercer St. (443-2222, open Mon. 10am-6pm, Tues.-Sat 10am-8pm), at the wonderful **Bagley Wright Theater** in Seattle Center. Their winter season combines contemporary and classic productions (usually including Shakespeare). *The Heidi Chronicles* and *Fences* got their start here, and later appeared on Broadway. Tickets $10-38. 30min. before each show senior and student rates are available at half price with ID (none on Sat.).

A Contemporary Theater (ACT), 100 W. Roy St. (285-5110), at the base of Queen Anne Hill. A summer season of modern and off-beat premieres. Tickets $14-26. Open Tues.-Thurs. noon-7:30pm, Fri.-Sat. noon-8pm, and Sun. noon-7pm.

Annex Theatre, 1916 4th Ave. (728-0933). Refreshing emphasis on company-generated material. Regular productions run 4 weeks. Shows usually Thurs.-Sat. at 8pm and Sun. at 7pm. Pay-what-you-can previews. Tickets $10-12.

The Empty Space Theatre, 3509 Fremont Ave. N. (547-7500), 1½ blocks north of the Fremont bridge. Comedies in this small theater attract the attention of the entire city. Season runs from mid-Nov.-late June. ½price rush tickets 10min. prior to curtain. Tickets $14-24, preview tickets (first 4 performances of any show) $10. Box office open daily 1-5pm.

Northwest Asian American Theater, 409 7th Ave. S (340-1049), in the International District. This excellent new theater offers theater by, for, and about Asian Americans. Tickets $12, students, seniors, and handicapped $9 (Thurs. $6).

Bathhouse Theater, 7312 W. Green Lake Dr. N. (524-9108), right by the lake. This small company is known for transplanting Shakespeare to unexpected locales (e.g. a Wild West *Macbeth,* Kabuki *King Lear,* and *Midsummer Night's Dream* in the 50s). Tickets $13-22. Rush tickets ($7.50) available Tues.-Thurs. before the show. Open Tues.-Sun. noon-7pm.

Seattle Group Theatre, 305 Harrison St. (441-1299), downstairs in the Seattle Center's center house. Home to **The Group,** one of Seattle's most innovative small theater ensembles, performing original, interactive, and avant-garde works, focusing on multi-ethnic issues. Tickets $14-20, seniors ½ price, students $6. Call Tues.-Sun. 11am-6pm.

Cinema

Seattle is a cinematic paradise. Most of the theaters that screen non-Hollywood films are on Capitol Hill and in the University District. Large, first-run theaters are everywhere. Most matinee shows cost $4; after 6pm, expect to pay $6.75. Seven Gables, a local company, has recently bought up the Egyptian, the Metro, the Neptune, and others. $20 buys admission to any five films at any of their theaters. Call 44-FILMS/34567 for local movie times and locations. Or, if you just want to feel like Tim Burton, try the Alibi Room (see p. 321).

The Egyptian, 801 E. Pine St. (32-EGYPT/34978), at Harvard Ave. on Capitol Hill. This handsome Art Deco theater shows artsy films and is best known for hosting the **Seattle International Film Festival** in the last week of May and the first week of June. The festival includes a retrospective of one director's work with a personal appearance by the featured director. Festival series tickets are available at a discount. Regular tickets $6.75, seniors and children $4, matinee $4.

The Harvard Exit, 807 E. Roy St. (323-8986), on Capitol Hill. Quality classic and foreign films. Half the fun of seeing a movie here is the theater, a converted residence that has its very own ghost (or so legend has it) and an enormous antique projector. The lobby was once someone's living room. Arrive early for a game of chess, checkers, or backgammon. $6.75, seniors and children $4, matinee $4.

Seven Gables Theater, 911 NE 50th St. (632-8820), in the U District, just off Roosevelt, a short walk west from University Way. Another cinema in an old house. Independent and classic films. $6.75, seniors and children $4, matinee $4.

Grand Illusion Cinema, 1403 NE 50th St. (523-3935), in the U District at University Way. A tiny theater attached to an espresso bar, showing films made on 1930s-type budgets. One of the last independent theaters in Seattle. $6, seniors and children $3, matinees $4.

United Artists Cinema, 2131 6th Ave. and Blanchard. Known around Seattle as the $2 theater. Tickets to fairly recent Hollywood flicks cost $2, except for "midnight madness" shows which cost $5, but come with popcorn or a drink.

Shopping

Seattle's younger set has created a wide demand for alternatives to massive retail chains, though a swiftly growing population has certainly lured "syndicated" stores to popular shopping areas as well. Downtown, trendy and fairly expensive clothing stores and boutiques line the avenues from 3rd east to 6th, between Seneca St. in the south and the **Westlake Center** in the north. You'll find the mega-**Nordstrom's** at 1051 5th Ave. (628-2111). The Westlake Center itself is an indoor conglomerate of mall chain stores and pricey gift shops.

For handmade crafts and jewelry, shop at **Pike Place Market** (see **Food**), where baubles are almost as plentiful as cherries and zucchini. **The Ave** (University Way) in the U. District caters to the college crowd, and promises good deals. **Used music stores** occupy almost every other storefront in this area and music-lovers glory in deals on all sorts of tunes. Capitol Hill also supports the used music market— **Orpheum** (618 Broadway E., 322-6370) has an inspiring collection of imports.

Thrift stores thrive in Seattle, especially on the Ave and between Pike and Pine Streets on Capitol Hill. Find astounding shops like **Rex and Angels Red Light Lounge and Cereal Bar** (4560 University Way NE, 545-4044) or **Righteous Rags** (506 E. Pine, 329-7847).

Bookstores

University Book Store, 4326 University Way NE (634-3400). Largest college book-store on the west coast, with 7 stores in the Seattle area. Open Mon.-Wed. and Fri.-Sat. 9am-6pm, Thurs. 9am-9pm, Sun. noon-5pm.

Left Bank Books, 92 Pike St. (622-0195), in the Pike Place Market. A leftist book-store, quietly awaiting the Revolution. Mostly political selection. Good prices on new and used books and an extensive women's literature section. Open Mon.-Sat. 10am-8pm, Sun. noon-6pm.

Elliott Bay Books, 101 S. Main St. (624-6600), in Pioneer Sq. Vast collection of 150,000 titles. The store sponsors frequent reading and lecture series. Coffee house in the basement. Open Mon.-Fri. 7am-10:30pm, Sat. 10am-10:30pm, Sun. 11am-5pm.

Red and Black Books, 432 15th Ave. E. (322-7323). Features multicultural, gay, and feminist literature, and frequent readings. Open Mon.-Thurs. 10am-8pm, Fri.-Sat. 10am-9pm, Sun. 11am-7pm.

Beyond the Closet, 1501 Belmont Ave. E. (322-4609). Exclusively gay and lesbian material. Open Sun.-Thurs. 10am-10pm, Fri.-Sat. 10am-11pm.

NIGHTLIFE

Seattle has moved beyond just beer to a new nightlife frontier: the café and bar. The popularity of espresso bars in Seattle might lead one to conclude that caffeine is more intoxicating than alcohol, but often an establishment poses as a diner by day, brings on a band, and breaks out the disco ball by night. The Northwest is famous for its microbrews and among the most popular are **Grant's, Red Hook, Ballard Bitter, Black Hook,** and **Yakima Cider.**

Many locals will tell you that the best spot to go for guaranteed good beer, live music, and big crowds is **Pioneer Square.** UW students from "frat row" tend to dom-inate the bar stools, while "real" Seattlites take their beer bucks downtown, to Capitol Hill, or up Hwy. 99 to Fremont. Most of the bars around the Square participate in a **joint cover** ($8) that will let you wander from bar to bar and sample the bands you like. **Fenix Café and Fenix Underground** (343-7740) and **Central Tavern** (622-0209) rock consistently, while **Larry's** (624-7665) and **New Orleans** (622-2563) fea-ture great jazz and blues nightly. **Kells** (728-1916) is a popular Irish pub with nightly celtic tunes. The **J and M Café** (624-1670) is in the center of Pioneer Square but has

WASHINGTON

no music. All the Pioneer Square clubs shut down at 2am Friday and Saturday nights, and around midnight during the week.

Downtown

Sit and Spin, 2219 4th St. This ain't no normal laundromat. Though the washers and dryers work, the real focus of this late-night café is the social scene. Furniture hangs from the walls and boardgames keep patrons busy while they sit waiting for their clothes to dry, or for bands with an alternative spin to play in the back room on Fri. and Sat. nights. The café sells everything from local microbrews on tap to urban style veggie bistro food (cashew chicken tarragon, $4.75) to boxes of laundry detergent. Artists recording in the Bad Animal recording studio down the street stop by every once in a while to play a game of checkers and bask in the plastic glow of 50s trailer park decor gone crazy. Open Sun.-Thurs. 9am-11pm, Fri.-Sat. 9am-2am. Kitchen opens daily at 11am.

Crocodile Café, 2200 2nd Ave. (448-2114) at Blanchard in Belltown. Another diner-turned-club. During the day, eat organic eggs and toast, and jam to popular local and national bands after dark. Only groovesters over 21 after 9pm, cover from $3-20. Open Tues.-Fri. 8am-midnight, Sat. 8am-2am, Sun. 9am-3pm for brunch.

Re-Bar, 1114 Howell (233-9873). A mixed gay and straight bar with a wide range of tunes and dancing on the wild side, depending on the night: Gay retro disco on Tues., hip-hop on Fri. Lots of acid jazz and **Greek Active** interactive theater on weekend nights. Cover $4. Open daily 9:30pm-2am.

Art Bar, 1516 2nd Ave. (622-4344). Exactly what the name says: a bar with walls like a gallery's and a small store, too! Lots of jazz and a clientele of all ages. Open Mon., Wed., Thurs. noon-1am, Tues., Fri. noon-2am, Sat. 2pm-2am, Sun. 2pm-1am.

Capitol Hill

Moe's Rockin' Café, 925 E. Pike St. (323-2373), 2 blocks east of Broadway. This new Seattle hotspot hosted Hootie and the Blowfish before they went big (don't worry, they have repented) and lures the best Seattle musicians to keep their corner of Capitol Hill hopping. Sun. and Mon. are dance nights—one floor R&B and one floor techno—and covers range from $4-12, depending on the show. Open daily 5pm-1:45am, and for brunch Sat.-Sun. 9am-3pm.

Kid Mohair, 1207 Pine St. (625-4444), south of Broadway on Capitol Hill. Dark wood and rich velvet in this new, cabaret-style gay club make for a glamorous scene. Dance to deejayed house music with sequin bedecked drag queens for a $5 weekend cover. Open Mon.-Sat. 4pm-2am, Sun. 6pm-2am.

Other Neighborhoods

Red Door Alehouse, 3401 Fremont Ave. N. (547-7521), at N. 34th St., across from the Inner-Urban Statue. Throbbing with yuppified university students who attest to the good local ale selection and a mile-long beer menu. A hint: try the Pyramid Wheaton or Widmer Hefeweizen with a slice of lemon. Open daily 11am-2am. Kitchen closes at 11pm Sun.-Weds. and at midnight Thurs.-Sat.

The Trolleyman Pub, 3400 Phinney Ave. N. (548-8000). Also in Fremont, west on N. 34th St. from the Red Door. In the back of the **Red Hook Ale Brewery,** which rolls the most popular kegs on campus. Early hours make it a mellow spot to listen to good acoustic music while lounging on one of the pub's couches and enjoying a fresh pint. Live blues on Sat. and jazz on Mon. Come back during the day for a $1 tour of the brewery and a generous sampling of all 4 beers currently on tap. Wear Birkenstocks. Brewery open in summer, daily noon-5pm; pub open Mon.-Thurs. 9am-11pm, Fri. 9am-midnight, Sat. 11am-midnight, Sun. noon-7pm.

OK Hotel, 212 Alaskan Way S. (621-7903; call 386-9934 for the coffee house). One café, one bar, one building. Just below Pioneer Square toward the waterfront. Lots of wood, lots of coffee. Live bands play everything from rock to reggae and draw equally diverse crowds. Bar art is "curated" monthly. Occasional cover charge up to $6. Café open Mon.-Wed. 11am-9pm, Thurs. 11am-10pm, Fri. 11am-11pm, Sat.-Sun. 8am-9pm. Bar open daily 4pm-2am.

EVENTS

Pick up a copy of the Seattle-King County visitors center's *Calendar of Events*, published every season, for event coupons and an exact listing of innumerable area happenings. The first Thursday evening of each month, the art community sponsors **First Thursday,** a free and well attended gallery walk. Watch for **street fairs** in the University District during mid to late May, the Pike Place Market over Memorial Day weekend, and the Fremont District in mid-June. The **International District** holds its annual two-day bash in mid-July, featuring arts and crafts booths, East Asian and Pacific food booths, and presentations by a range of groups from the Radical Women/Freedom Socialist Party to the Girl Scouts. For information call **Chinatown Discovery, Inc.,** at 236-0657 or 583-0460, or write P.O. Box 3406, Seattle 98114.

Puget Sound's **yachting** season begins in May. **Maritime Week** during the third week of May, and the **Seattle Boats Afloat Show** (634-0911) in mid-August, give area boaters a chance to show off their craft. At the beginning of July, the Center for Wooden Boats sponsors the free **Wooden Boat Show** (382-2628) on Lake Union. Blue blazers and deck shoes are *de rigeur.* Size up the entrants (over 100 wooden boats) and then watch a demonstration of boat-building skills. The year-end blow-out is the **Quick and Daring Boatbuilding Contest.** Hopefuls go overboard trying to build and sail wooden boats of their own design using a limited kit of tools and materials. Plenty of music, food, and alcohol make the sailing smooth.

The City Hall Park Concert Series presents free reggae, blues, jazz, and other concerts nearly every summer day. Call 781-3590 for information, or stop by the park at 516 3rd Ave, south of the King County Courthouse.

The Northwest Folklife Festival, one of the most notable Seattle events, is held on Memorial Day weekend at the Seattle Center. Artists, musicians, and dancers congregate to celebrate the heritage of the area.

Bon Odori, the Japanese community's traditional festival, is celebrated in the third week of July in the International District. Temples are opened to the public and dancing fills the streets.

The Bite of Seattle (232-2980) is a celebration of food, held in mid-July in the Seattle Center (free).

Bumbershoot (622-5123), a massive festival that caps off the summer, is held in the Seattle Center over Labor Day weekend. This fantastic four-day arts festival attracts big-name rock bands, street musicians, and a young, exuberant crowd ($25 for 4 days, $16 for any 2 days, $9 in advance or $10 at the door for a single day; seniors and children free on Fri., $4 other days).

The Seattle International Children's Festival, also held in the Seattle Center, is a week-long event in mid-May targeted to entertaining children, but its featured performers from Colombia, Ghana, China, and other countries have wide appeal. Call the Seattle Center (484-8582) or write 305 Harrison St., Seattle 98109-4695.

The Seattle Seafair (728-0123) is the biggest, baddest festival of them all. Spread over three weeks from mid-July to early August, all of the city's neighborhoods contribute with street fairs, parades large and small, balloon races, musical entertainment, and a seafood fest.

■ Near Seattle

EAST

Cross **Lake Washington** on the two floating bridges to arrive in a bikers' and picnickers' paradise. Unfortunately, this is also a suburbanites' paradise. Range Rovers and outdoor shopping plazas increasingly litter the landscape. Companies like Microsoft, which has nearly subsumed the suburb of Redmond, buy up expanses of East Sound land, smother them in sod and office complexes, and call them "campuses." But rapid growth has had its benefits; in the suburb of **Bellevue,** the July **Bellevue Jazz Festival** (455-6885) attracts both local cats and national acts. This wealthy and beautiful suburb is home to Bill Gates, among others.

Head farther out for wilder country excursions. Take I-90 east to **Lake Sammamish State Park,** off Exit 15, for swimming and water-skiing facilities, volleyball courts, and playing fields. In the town of **Snoqualmie,** 29 mi. east of Seattle, the **Northwest Railroad Museum,** 109 King St. (746-4025) on Rte. 202, dividing the two lanes of the town's main street, houses a small collection of functional early steam and electric trains in the old Snoqualmie Depot. One of its exhibits, the oldest running train in the state, runs 7 mi. to **North Bend,** offering views of **Snoqualmie Falls.** Trips run on the hour, and the roundtrip takes an hour. (Roundtrip rides $6.30, seniors $5.25, children $4.20. Open May-Sept. Sat.-Sun. 10am-5pm.)

From North Bend, take bus #210 or Rte. 202 north to view the astounding **Snoqualmie Falls.** Formerly a sacred place for the native Salish people, the 270-ft. wall of water has generated electricity for Puget Power since 1898. Five generators buried under the falls are hard at work, providing energy for 1600 homes. The falls were featured in David Lynch's cult TV series *Twin Peaks,* and the small town of Snoqualmie has been host to hordes of "Peaks freaks" (mostly Japanese) since the release three summers ago of the show's big-screen incarnation, *Fire Walk With Me.*

On the north end of **Woodinville** is the **Chateau Sainte Michelle Vintners,** 14111 145th St. NE (488-4633), a leader in the recent movement to popularize Washington **wines.** Tours of the facility, which resembles a French chateau, end with wine tasting (free; 45-min. tours daily 10am-5pm). To reach Woodinville from downtown Seattle, take bus #310 during peak hours only.

SOUTH

The Seattle area is surrounded by the vast factories of **Boeing,** Seattle's most prominent employer. At Boeing Field south of Seattle is the **Museum of Flight,** 9404 E. Marginal Way S. (764-5720). Take I-5 south to Exit 158 and turn north onto E. Marginal Way S., or take bus #123. A jaunt into the cavernous museum, where flying vehicles, from canvas biplanes to pitch-black fighter jets, hang from a three-story roof. A tribute to the Apollo space shuttle missions, which landed the first man on the moon, exhibits a life-sized replica of the command module. When tales of space-age technology become repetitive, explore the red barn, where William E. Boeing founded the company in 1916. Photographs and artifacts in the barn trace the history of flight from its beginnings through the 30s, including an operating replica of the Wright Brothers' wind tunnel. Tours with enthusiastic airforce veterans leave the entrance on the half hour from 10:30am-1:30pm ($8, seniors $7, ages 6-15 $4, under age 5 free; open Fri.-Wed. 10am-5pm, Thurs. 10am-9pm). The museum is fully wheelchair accessible.

TACOMA

Though spending time in Tacoma rather than Seattle is somewhat like hanging out in Newark instead of New York, Tacoma has a few worthwhile attractions suitable for a day trip. Tacoma is Washington's second largest city, and lies on I-5 about 35 mi. south of Seattle and 35 mi. east of Olympia. Rte. 7 offers quick access to Mt. Rainier, the Cowlitz Valley, and Mt. St. Helens. Get the skinny on Tacoma at the **Pierce County Visitor Information Center,** 906 Broadway (627-2836 or 800-272-2662), downtown at 9th St. (open Mon.-Fri. 9am-5pm). **Greyhound** (383-4621), at the corner of Pacific and 14th in downtown Tacoma, runs buses to and from Seattle (several per day, $4; station open daily 7:30am-2am). Some important numbers are: **emergency,** 911; **crisis line,** 759-6700; **rape relief,** 474-7273; **safeplace,** 279-8333. The Tacoma **post office** is on 11th at A St. (open Mon.-Fri. 8am-5:30pm; **General Delivery ZIP Code:** 98402). The **area code** is 206.

Make a jaunt to Tacoma's waterfront, home to **Point Defiance Park** (for Tacoma Parks Info call 305-1000), one of the most attractive parks in the Puget Sound area (free; open daily dawn-½hr. after dusk). Point Defiance is Tacoma's **ferry** terminal and the ferry runs regularly to Vashon Island (see p. 35 for schedule and fare information). To reach the park, take Hwy. 16 to the 6th Ave. exit, head east on 6th Ave., then north on Pearl St. A 5-mi. loop passes by all the park's attractions and offers postcard views of Puget Sound and access to miles of woodland **trails.** In the spring, stop to smell the flowers; a rhododendron garden lies nestled in the woods along the loop, and intricate fuschia, rose, and Japanese gardens make an Eden out of the park's entrance. **Owen Beach** looks across at **Vashon Island** and is a good starting place for a ramble down the beach. The loop then brushes by the spot where Captain Wilkes of the U.S. Navy proclaimed in 1841 that if he had guns on this and the opposite shore (Gig Harbor) he could defy the world: hence, "Point Defiance."

The park's prize possession is the **Point Defiance Zoo and Aquarium** (591-5337). Penguins, polar bears, beluga whales, and scary sharks populate the tanks of the aquarium. Kids and their distressed chaperones occupy the paths between them. A number of natural habitats are recreated within the zoo's boundaries. ($6.75, seniors $6.25, ages 5-17 $5, ages 3-4 $2.50, under 3 free; open daily 10am-7pm; Labor Day-Memorial Day 10am-4pm.) The meticulously restored **Fort Nisqually** (591-5339), in the park, also merits a visit. The Canadian Hudson's Bay Company built the fort in 1832 to offset growing commercial competition from Americans. The museum cloisters a compact but captivating exhibit on the lives of children, laborers, natives, and Hawaiians who worked there during the Hudson Bay years ($1.25, children 75¢; open June-Aug. daily 11am-6pm, Sept.-April Wed.-Sun. 1pm-4pm). **Camp Six Logging Museum** (752-0047), also in the park, retrieves an entire 19th-century logging camp from the dustbin of history. The camp also offers a 1-mi. ride on an original steam-powered logging engine (ride costs $2, seniors and children $1; open Wed., Sat., and Sun. 10am-4pm).

On your way out of the park, stop in at **Antique Sandwich Company,** 5102 N. Pearl St. (752-4069), near Point Defiance, for some great natural food, and an open mic on Tuesday nights. The "poor boy" sandwich ($6) will fill you for a week; espresso shakes are $3.50. The pies draw a faithful local following who come to spend sunny lunch hours among rose bushes in the sandwich company's "Garden of Eatin" (open Mon. and Wed.-Thurs. 7am-8pm, Tues. 7am-10pm, Fri. 7am-9pm, Sat. 7am-7pm, Sun. 8am-7pm).

BAINBRIDGE ISLAND

Ferries (see p. 315) depart from Colman Dock downtown for **Bainbridge Island,** a rural island homesteaded by late-19th-century Swedish and late-20th-century Californian immigrants. The ferry ride and a stroll through the town of Winslow make a relaxing escape from Seattle. Eat at the firecracker- and flower-festooned **Streamliner Diner,** 397 Winslow Way (842-8595), where natural foods and rich pies ($2.50) tempt (open Mon.-Fri. 7am-3pm, Sat.-Sun. 8am-2:30pm). Wash it down with a bottle of Ferry Boat White from the **Bainbridge Island Vineyards & Winery** (842-9463). You can sample the local grapes or tour the fields where they are grown; turn right at the first white trellis on Rte. 305 as you come from the ferry. Bottles range in price from $7.80 to $23.50 (open Wed.-Sun. noon-5pm, tours Sun. 2pm). Head for one of Bainbridge Island's state parks; **Fay-Bainbridge State Park** (842-3931), on the northeast tip of the island has good fishing, 26 trailer sites, and 35 **tent sites** with pay showers and flush toilets (trailer sites $11, tent sites $8).

WHIDBEY ISLAND

Clouds, wrung dry by the time they finally pass over Whidbey Island, release a scant 20 in. of rain each year over this slow-paced strip of land in Puget Sound. At the island's many forts (turned state parks), rocky beaches lead back to bluffs crawling with wild roses and blackberry brambles. Whidbey's points of interest are few and far between, and most of those who make the trek come in caravans of RVs to camp or visit grandparents who live in one of the island's retirement communities. Whidbey's beauty lies in its circle of beaches. Keep an eye out for **loganberries** and **Penn Cove Mussels,** Whidbey's biggest exports. The town of **Coupeville** is at the island's center and is a great place to start exploring its four major State Parks. Stay away from the towns of **Oak Harbor** and **Clinton**—they offer little more than KMarts, fast food, and busy streets.

Two **ferry** lines provide frequent service from the mainland to the island (for scheduling and fare information, see p. 35). One ferry connects **Mukilteo,** a tiny community just south of Everett, with **Clinton,** a town on the south end of Whidbey. The other connects **Port Townsend** on the Olympic peninsula with the terminal at **Keystone State Park,** at the "waist" of the island. You can drive onto the island on Rte. 20, which departs west from I-5 at Exit 230. Rte. 20 and Rte. 565 meet near Keystone and form the backbone of the island, linking all the significant towns and points of interest. **Island Transit** (678-7771 or 321-6688) provides free, hourly public transportation throughout the island, and gives information on connections to and from Seattle, but no service on Sundays and limited service on Saturdays.

Oak Harbor, on Rte. 20 facing Oak Harbor Bay at the northern end of the island, was named for the Garry Oaks that once dominated the landscape. Fast-food restaurants now dominate the town. At the north tip of the island, the **Deception Pass Bridge,** the nation's first suspension bridge, connects Whidbey Island to the Anacortes Islands, and has a secret cave at one end where 17th century prisoners were held and forced to make wicker furniture (Oh, the humanity!). See an example at the Island County Historical Museum.

When the Skagit lived and fished around Deception Pass, the area was often raided by the Haida from the north. A bear **totem** of the Haidas now occupies the Fidalgo Bay side of **Deception Pass State Park,** 5175 N. Rte. 20 (675-2417), at the northern tip of the island. The pass itself was named by veteran explorer Captain George Vancouver, who found the tangled geography of Puget Sound as confusing as most visitors do today. This is the most heavily used of Whidbey's four state parks, and its **views** are magnificent. A new **interpretive center** in the Bowman area, just north of the Works Progress Administration bridge on Rte. 20E, describes the army that built many of the parks in the Northwest during the Depression. There are camping facilities, a saltwater boat launch, and a freshwater lake for **swimming, fishing,** and **boating.** A **fishing license,** available at most hardware stores, is required for fishing in the lake; the season runs from mid-April to October. Thirty miles of trails link some of the best views of Puget Sound's shore line, and lure ambitious mid-summer crowds into this magnificent old-growth forest. 250 sites cost $11 apiece. Four rustic hiker/biker sites ($5) have limited facilities but make a pleasant alternative to the bustling but beautiful campground. Reservations are such a very, very good idea (800-452-5687, reservation fee $6).

For those who wish to remain indoors, the **Island County Historical Museum,** 908 NW Alexander St. (678-3310), in Coupeville offers a glimpse of the 19th century with displays of original tools, dress, and handicrafts (suggested donation $2; open May-Sept. daily 10am-5pm; Oct.-April Fri.-Mon. 11am-4pm). Have a cup of plain but perfect soup at Coupeville's **Knead and Feed,** 4 Front St. (678-5431). This small restaurant makes everything from scratch and has a serene view of the eastern waterfront. A lunch costs $3-7. (Open Mon.-Fri. 10:30am-3pm, Sat.-Sun. 8:30am-4pm). For a caffeine fix, stop in at **Great Times Espresso,** just south on Front Street, and chat with LaVonda, who makes some of the best scones this side of the UK and has all the local lowdown. Also in Coupeville are the **Whidbey General Hospital** (678-5151) at 1010 N. Main St. and the **post office** (678-5353) at 201 NW Coreland Rd. (open Mon.-Fri. 8:30am-5pm) The **General Delivery ZIP** code is 98239. In an **emergency** call 911. The **area code** is 360.

PUGET SOUND

According to Native American legend, Puget Sound was created when Ocean, wishing to keep his children Cloud and Rain close to home, gouged out a trough and molded the dirt into the Cascade Range. Since then, Cloud and Rain have stayed close to Ocean, rarely venturing east of the mountain wall. Millions of Washingtonians live along Puget Sound in the Everett-Seattle-Tacoma-Olympia belt, but with a pristine rural setting, a great hostel on Vashon Island, and the cycling trails of the Kitsap Peninsula, outdoor adventure is never far from urban sophistication.

■ Olympia

From the hilltop Capitol of Olympia, politicians can keep an eye on the college students, local fishermen, and tourists below. The Evergreen State College campus lies just a few miles from the city center, and the super-liberal, highly pierced student body spills into town, influencing local business and sometimes even local politics. But many locals scorn these "Greeners," nostalgic for a time when Olympia was a small industrial city with a thriving fishing industry. But newcomers keep pouring into Olympia, a testament to its spotless exterior and alluring diversity, and the capital of the Evergreen State continues to entice outsiders with more beautification projects, expanding local parks and wildlife refuges.

PRACTICAL INFORMATION

Visitors Information: Olympia State Capitol Visitors Center, P.O. Box 41020 (586-3460), on Capitol Way between 12th and 14th Ave. Signs on I-5 will direct you to this visitors center. Friendly volunteer staff helps navigate the center's plethora of free brochures and guides and provides detailed maps of both the capitol itself and the greater Olympia area. Open Mon.-Fri. 8am-5pm. **Olympia/Thurston Chamber,** 521 E. Legion Way (357-3362 or 800-753-8474). Less enthusiastically provides less enthusiastic information on local businesses, services, and festivals. Calling is best. Open Mon.-Fri. 9am-5pm. **Department of Natural Resources (DNR),** 1111 Washington St. (902-1000 or 800-562-6010). A maze of different offices in this building can provide information about outdoor activities on DNR land. The Maps Department, P.O. Box 47031 (902-1234), can provide any publication that includes a **DNR map,** including the *Guide to Camp and Picnic Sites* which points out free DNR sites statewide. The **Fish and Game** office down the hall offers recreational fishing licenses and information (902-2200). Open Mon.-Fri. 8:30am-4:30pm. For information on and reservations for state parks and facilities, call the **Washington State Parks and Recreation Commission Information Center** (800-233-0321).

Trains: Amtrak, 6600 Yelm Hwy. (800-872-7245). To: Seattle (3 per day, $15) and Portland (3 per day, $19).

Buses: Greyhound, 107 E. 7th Ave. at Capitol Way (357-8667). To: Seattle (6 per day, $8) *but check out the Olympia Express below,* Portland (7 per day, $15), and Spokane (3 per day, $29). Open daily 7:30am-8pm. Taxi dispatch next door.

Public Transportation: Intercity Transit (IT), (786-1881 or 800-BUS-ME-IT/287-6348). Visit the Customer Service Department at the Transit Center on State Ave. between Washington St. and Franklin St. to pick up maps and schedules. Olympians are very enthusiastic about the many benefits of public transportation and are the proud owners of an easy, reliable, and flexible transit system. Use it to get almost anywhere in Thurston County, even with a bike. The IT is open for information Mon.-Fri. 7am-7pm, Sat.-Sun. 8am-5pm. Fare 50¢, seniors and disabled 25¢. Day passes $1. The **Capitol Shuttle** is free. Buses run from the Capitol Campus to downtown or to the east side and west side, every 15min. between 6:30am and 6:15pm. For the standard fare, **Custom buses** continue on from where normal fixed routes stop Mon.-Sat. after 7pm; call 943-7777 for info during reservation hr. (Mon.-Sat. 6:30pm-9:30pm, Sun. 8:15am-5:30pm). Supplementary transport is provided for seniors and the disabled by Dial-A-Lift (754-9393 or 800-244-6846), with appropriate certification, available through the IT Business Office (786-8585).

Olympia Express (Intercity Transit) runs between Olympia and Tacoma Mon.-Fri. 5:50am-6pm. Buses leave every ½hr.; fare $1.50. Transferring to a Seattle bus in Tacoma costs an additional $3.

Taxi: Red Top Taxi, 357-3700. **Capitol City Taxi,** 357-4949. **DC Cab,** 786-5226. Handicap accessible. All 24hr.

WASHINGTON

Car Rental: U-Save Auto Rental, 3015 Pacific Ave. (786-8445). $26 per day plus 20¢ for each additional mi. over 150. Must be at least 21 with credit card.

Equipment and Bike Rental: Outdoor Adventure Center, 215 7th Ave. SW (705-1585), rents bikes ($12 per day), kayaks ($5 per hr., $25 per day), canoes ($5 per hr., $25 per day), and double kayaks ($10 per hr., $45 per day). This warehouse-turned-shop also houses a new climbing gym ($8 per day) and offers local kayaking, rafting, and climbing trips. Convenient to Capitol Lake. Open Mon.-Sat. 10am-9pm, Sun. 10am-6pm.

Olympia Timberland Library, 313 8th Ave. SE (352-0595), at Franklin St. Sign up for a free hour on the Internet. Open Mon.-Thurs. 10am-9pm, Fri.-Sat. 10am-5pm; winter Sun. 1-5pm also.

Laundromat: The Wash Tub, 2103 Harrison Ave. NW (943-9714). Wash $1.10, 8min. dry 25¢. Open Mon.-Sat. 7am-10pm, Sun. 8am-11pm.

Crisis Clinic: 352-2211 or 800-627-2211. 24-hr. hotline for info and referral.

Women's Shelter: Safeplace, 754-6300 or 800-562-6025. 24hr. counseling, housing referrals.

Emergency: 911. **Police:** 753-8300. **Fire:** 753-8348.

Post Office: 900 Jefferson SE (357-2286). Open Mon.-Fri. 7:30am-6pm, Sat. 9am-4pm. **General Delivery ZIP Code:** 98501.

Area Code: 360.

GETTING THERE AND GETTING AROUND

Olympia, located where I-5 meets U.S. 101, is an easy stopping point for those heading north to the Olympic Peninsula and Seattle, or south to the Cascade peaks and Portland. Exit 105 off I-5 leads to both the Capitol Campus and downtown Olympia. The west side of the downtown area borders freshwater Capitol Lake and West Bay, also known as Budd Bay. A bridge on 4th St. separates the two and leads to the city's northwest section, where fast food chains and plastic-happy shopping plazas sprawl.

Parking and Biking

Once in Olympia, parking lots designated for state employees will taunt the traveler, but parking is free for three hours per day in downtown "blue zones" and metered lots abound. Once parked, navigating Olympia on foot or on two wheels is less confusing than grappling with its one-way streets. Olympians love to cycle, and bike racks adorn every public bus. A new program called **The Bicycle Library** (786-0638) paints donated bikes pink and places them around the city for public use—just take one where you find it and leave it where you're finished.

ACCOMMODATIONS AND CAMPING

Because they cater to lobbyists and lawyers rather than budget tourists, motels in Olympia are generally pricey. Local universities never offer rooms to travelers, even in summer. Camping is the cheapest option.

Grays Harbor Hostel, 6 Ginny Ln. (482-3119), just off Rte. 8 in Elma, WA. Though this hostel lies 25 mi. west of Olympia, it is destination unto itself. This is also a great place to start a trip down the cost. Legends of the hosteling industry, Jay and Linda Klemp run this establishment as if it were their home. A bed in this joint costs $10 and comes replete a hot tub, a spacious, 24hr. common room and a 3-hole golf course. "Two-wheeled travellers" can park their bikes in a dry spot and camp on the lawn for $6. To find the Klemps, take the fairground exit off Rte.8 and make the first right. If you reach the fairgrounds, you've gone too far.

Motel 6, 400 W. Lee St. (754-7320; fax 705-0655), in Tumwater. Take Exit 102 off I-5 and follow signs. A left off Lee St. onto Capitol Way takes you to downtown Olympia in less than 5min. Reliably clean rooms. Cable TV, swimming pool, and weak coffee in the office. Singles $28. Doubles $34. Each additional person $3. Under 17 free with parent. AARP discount.

The Golden Gavel Motor Hotel, 909 Capitol Way (352-8533). Only a few blocks from the Capitol Campus. Immaculate, spacious rooms geared toward lower-budget businessmen. Cable TV, morning coffee, phones. Singles $42. Doubles, one bed, $45. Doubles, two beds, $49. AAA and senior discounts. On the seventh day, rest for free.

Millersylvania State Park, 12245 Tilly Rd. S. (753-1519), 10 mi. south of Olympia. Take Exit 99 off I-5, then follow signs on Rte. 121. 168 smallish, family-filled campsites nestled among the firs. The park also boasts 6 mi. of needle-carpeted trails and **Deep Lake**, which has two unguarded swimming areas. Pay showers 25¢ for 6min., flush toilets. Facilities for the disabled. Hiker-biker sites $5.50, standard sites $11, 48 RV hookups $16. Call 800-452-5687 for reservations (recommended on summer weekends or holidays). 10 day limit.

Capital Forest Multiple Use Area, 15mi. southwest of Olympia, Exit 95 off I-5. Administered by the DNR. 50 campsites on 6 campgrounds. Camping is free and requires no notification or permit. Pick up a forest **map** at the state DNR office (see **Practical Information**, above) or the Central Region DNR office (748-2383) in nearby Chehalis. The area is unsupervised, so lone women might be better off paying at Millersylvania. Grab a space early in the summertime; "free" is a magic word for many campers. Pit toilets. No showers.

FOOD

Nineties-style, vegi-intensive eateries line bohemian 4th Ave. east of Columbia. The waterfront tables at the **Bayview Deli & Bakery,** 516 W. 45h Ave. (352-4901) offer a pleasant view. When that 2am urge for carrot sticks hits you, try the 24-hr. **Top Foods & Drug,** 1313 Cooper Point Rd. SW (754-1428). The **Olympia Farmer's Market,** 401 N. Capital Way (352-9096), has a great selection of in-season fruits and berries and a brand new permanent building. You can buy a fantastic cheap lunch here. The grilled salmon burger ($3.75) is a local treat. Open Mar.-Apr. Sat.-Sun. 10am-3pm, May-Sep. Thurs.-Sun. 10am-3pm, Oct. Fri.-Sun. 10am-3pm.

Smithfield Café, 212 W. 4th Ave. (786-1725). The relaxed gay-friendly crowd digs the deluxe burrito ($4.50) and the vegetarian and vegan options. Try the "Eggs Espresso," ingeniously prepared fat-free by scrambling with an espresso machine steamer wand ($2.50 with toast and jam). Check the board inside for the word on local bands. Free condoms in the bathroom. Open Tues.-Fri. 7am-8pm, Sat.-Sun. 9am-8pm. Tues. is open mike night (no cover) which winds down around 11pm.

The Spar Café & Bar, 111 E. 4th Ave. (357-6444). Feel a touch of nostalgia as you down "Legislator Dip" ($5.50) or a Spar burger ($6) in this old logger haunt. Polished wood and a long counter send you back to the age of Bogart. Mellow bar in back, with live jazz Saturday nights 8pm-midnight (no cover). Burger Fest (Sun. 3-8pm) offers a 30-burger menu. Restaurant open Mon.-Sat. 6am-9pm, Sun. 7am-8pm; bar open daily 11am-2am.

Jo Mama's Restaurant, 120 N. Pear St. (943-9849), at State St. in an old house. Homemade pizza served in an all-wood, "old-tavern" atmosphere. The food is somewhat pricey (the 10-in. vegetarian pizza for $14.75 feeds two hungry travelers), but the family atmosphere and menus in Braille compensate. Cheerful, convivial staff, and a great porch swing to play on while you wait for a seat. Open Mon.-Thurs. 11am-10pm, Fri. 11am-11pm, Sat. 4-11pm, Sun. 4-10pm.

Santosh, 116 4th Ave. (943-3442). Northern Indian cuisine with an all-you-can-eat lunch buffet for $6, served Mon.-Fri. 11am-3:30pm. An immense clay Tandoor used to bake their traditional cuisine is on display in the hallway. Open for politician-priced dinners too, Mon.-Fri. 11am-9:30pm, Sat.-Sun. 11am-10pm.

The Dancing Goat, corner of 4th Ave. and N. Washington (754-8187). A corner café with a corner on the downtown, thirtysomething lunch market. Equipped with a rack of local and college publications and its locally roasted Batdorf and Bronson coffee, the Dancing Goat also caters to Greeners. Lunches vary according to chef's whims ($3-4), 88¢ for a cuppa joe and one refill. Open Mon.-Fri. 7am-11pm, Sat.-Sun. 9am-11pm.

WASHINGTON

SIGHTS, ACTIVITIES, AND EVENTS

The crowning glory of Olympia is the State Capitol Campus, the complex of state government buildings, meticulously manicured gardens, and veterans' monuments where (Madonna fans will be delighted to know) part of the movie *Body of Evidence* was filmed in 1991. Take a free tour of the **Legislative Building** (586-8677) to sneak a peek at the public sphere. Only tour guides can usher you into the legislative chambers, Jan.-Feb. on even years, and Jan.-April on odd years. The newly repainted and decorated interior boasts a six-ton Tiffany chandelier, and six two-ton bronze doors depicting the history of Washington.

Unfortunately, the building's spectacular **dome,** the fifth tallest stone dome in the world, is indefinitely closed to the public. Built for maintenance purposes only, the 262-step staircase was weakening under the tramping of tourists. Although the panoramic view of Olympia is no longer available, the rest of the magnificent building is certainly worth traversing. Tours leave from just inside the front steps daily on the hour 10am-3pm (building open Mon.-Fri. 8am-5:30pm, Sat.-Sun. 10am-4pm). The newly revamped **State Capitol Museum,** 211 W. 21st Ave. (753-2580), has historical and political exhibits (free, but donations encouraged; open Tues.-Fri. 10am-4pm, Sat.-Sun. noon-4pm). Several different tours of buildings on the capitol campus leave hourly on the weekdays. Call 586-TOUR/8687 for more information and accommodations for the disabled.

Every lunch hour, droves of state employees tumble forth from the capitol in spandex and sneakers and head for the various parks surrounding **Capitol Lake.** Trails begin in **Capitol Lake Park** at the west end of 7th Ave. and empty into the newly constructed **Heritage Park** with its $620,000 computerized, interactive fountain. Boats jam the Port in **Percival Landing Park** (743-8379), a reminder of Olympia's oyster-filled past. The 4th St. Bridge separates the freshwater lake from the saltwater West Bay, and is a perfect place to spot spawning salmon as they head for Tumwater Falls. The leaping lox-to-be cross the lake from late August through October. The **Yashiro Japanese Garden** (753-8380), at the intersection of Plum and Union, right next to City Hall, hoards hundreds of colorful plants behind its high walls, making it Olympia's very own secret garden. Open 10am-dusk for picnickers and ponderers.

Budget deals in Olympia come out after dark. The **State Theater,** 204 E. 4th Ave. (357-4010), shows recent movies for $1; Mon.-Fri. 6:45pm, Sat.-Sun. 1:45pm and 6:45pm. During the summer, the city schedules free jazz, ensemble, and symphony concerts at **Sylvester Park** (Fri. at noon; call 953-2375 for info). Local groovesters mosh and mingle at **The Backstage at Capitol Theater,** 206 E. 5th Ave. (754-5378). Three to five bands play on most weekend nights, usually for a $5 cover. Since 1985 the band Beat Happening and the label K Records have made Olympia a crucial pit-stop on the indie rock circuit. The **Kill Rock Stars** label, and their flagship feminist band Bikini Kill, live and work here too. Ask in record shops about shows or look for posters and flyers.

Capitol Lakefair is a not-to-be-missed bonanza the third week in July, with an overwhelming array of food, carnival rides, and booths staffed by non-profit organizations. Contact the Chamber of Commerce for more info (see **Practical Information**, above), and watch out for increased motel rates.

■ Near Olympia

Olympia Beer (754-5177) is actually brewed less than a mile south of the capital city on Capital Way in **Tumwater.** The brewery has been taken over by the Pabst Company, which now produces several different beers on the premises, including Hamm's and Olde English "800" (a.k.a. 8-Ball). You can tour the facility and have a brew on the house (free; open Mon.-Sat. 9am-4:30pm; tours at 9:30am, 11:30am, 1:30pm, 3:30pm). Olympia Beer, visible from I-5, can be reached from exit 103 in Tumwater and provides parking for nearby **Tumwater Falls Park.** This trail laden site, built by the Olympia Brewery, is perfect for salmon-watching, picnicking, or a midday run.

WASHINGTON

Ten mi. south of the city is **Wolfhaven,** 3111 Offut Lake Rd. (264-4695 or 800-448-9653). Take Exit 99 off I-5, turn east, and follow the brown signs. The haven now preserves 40 wolves that have been reclaimed from zoos or illegal owners. Take a guided tour of the grounds ($5, ages 5-12 $2.50; May-Sep. 10am-4pm, Oct.-Apr. 10am-3pm) and if you've lost that werewolf feelin' join the Howl-In ($6, children $4; May-Sept. Fri.-Sat. 7-9:30pm). Groups roast marshmallows and tell stories around a campfire to the accompaniment of the howling residents (open May-Sept. daily 10am-5pm; Oct.-April Wed.-Sun. 10am-4pm). The **Nisqually National Wildlife Refuge** (753-9467), off I-5 between Olympia and Tacoma at Exit 114, offers a safe haven to 500 species of plants and animals as well as miles of open trail for the I-5-weary traveler to stop and meander. The infamous spotted owls, bald eagles, and a plethora of shorebirds nest in the reserve. The trails are open daily during daylight hours, but are closed to cyclists ($2; office open Mon.-Fri. 7:30am-4pm).

■ Vashon Island

Only a short ferry ride from Seattle and an even shorter hop from Tacoma, Vashon (VASH-on) Island has remained inexplicably invisible to most Seattleites. With its forested hills and expansive sea views, the artists' colony of Vashon feels much like the San Juan Islands, but without the oppressive crowds of tourists. Vashon's wealth of natural beauty and the small-town lifestyle of its islanders are virtually unaffected by its proximity to city speedways. Most of the island is undeveloped and covered in forests of Douglas firs, rolling cherry orchards, wildflowers, and strawberry fields, and almost any Vashon road eventually winds its way to a rocky beach.

Practical Information Vashon Island stretches between Seattle and Tacoma on its east side and between Southworth and Gig Harbor on its west side. Four different **Washington State Ferries** can get you to Vashon Island. For more information on ferries, see **Planning Your Ferry Trips,** pg. 35. Ferries leave for the northern tip of Vashon Island from Fauntleroy in West Seattle, from downtown Seattle, and from Southworth in the Kitsap Peninsula; ferries leave for the southern tip from Point Defiance in Tacoma. Hostels give discounts on ferry tickets. To get to the ferry terminal from Seattle, drive south on I-5, take Exit 164 down to Western Ave. and the waterfront or take Exit 163A (West Seattle/Spokane St.) down Fauntleroy Way to the Fauntleroy Ferry Terminal. From Tacoma, take Exit 132 off I-5 (Bremerton/Gig Harbor) to Rte. 16. Get on 6th Ave. and turn right onto Pearl. Follow signs to Point Defiance Park and the ferry.

Buses #54, #118, and #119 pick up at 1st and Union and serve the island ferries from downtown Seattle (call 800-542-7876 for bus info), and #118 and #119 continue onto the island to the town of Vashon; buses also service the island, beginning their runs from the ferry landing. Both can be flagged down anywhere. Fares are the same as in the rest of the system: $1 for travel in one zone, $1.50 for two-zone travel. The island is all within one zone, but Seattle to Vashon is two zones. Only buses #54 and #55 from the Fauntleroy ferry to downtown Seattle run on Sunday. The steep hills on Vashon are a hindrance to hikers and bikers, though two wheels remain the recreational vehicle of choice on the island. You can pick up a map of Vashon at the local **Thriftway** (463-2100; open daily 8am-9pm) on 9740 SW Bank Rd., or call the **Vashon-Maury Chamber of Commerce** ahead of time (463-6217). Many locals and visitors resort to hitchhiking, which is reputed to be easier here than on the mainland. (*Let's Go* does not recommend hitchhiking.)

Feed your head at the **Vashon Library** (463-2069), 17210 Vashon Hwy. Wash your duds at **Joy's Village Cleaner and Laundry** (463-9933), 17318 Vashon Hwy. (wash and dry $1 each; open Mon.-Sat. 7am-8:30pm, Sun. 8am-8pm). Pick up your sunscreen at the **Vashon Pharmacy** (463-9118), 17617 Vashon Hwy. (open Mon.-Fri. 9am-7pm, Sat. 9am-6pm, Sun 11am-1pm). For **emergencies,** call 911. Reach the **police** at 463-3618 and the **coast guard** at 463-2951. Vashon's **post office** (463-9390) is on Bank Rd. (open Mon.-Fri. 9am-1pm and 2:30-4:30pm, Sat. 9-11:30am; **General Delivery ZIP code:** 98070). The **area code** is 206.

Accommodations and Food The **Vashon Island AYH Ranch Hostel (HI-AYH)** 12119 SW Cove Rd. west of Vashon Hwy. (463-2592), sometimes called the **"Seattle B,"** is the island's only real budget accommodation and one of the main reasons to trek to Vashon. It's easy to get to: jump on any bus at the ferry terminal, ride to **Thriftway Market,** and call from the free phone inside the store, marked with an HI-AYH label. Judy will come pick you up if the hour is reasonable, and she has never turned a hosteler away. A free pancake breakfast, free firewood, and a squadron of bikes for hostelers to borrow for free attract every sort of traveler, from road weary backpackers to couples escaping Seattle. Theme rooms (like the "Throne Room," a bathroom graced by a portrait of the Queen) add to the fun. The hostel accommodates 14 in bunk rooms. Hearty hostelers can also bed down under the stars in huge teepees or covered wagons. When all the beds are full, you can pitch a tent ($9, bicyclists $8, nonmembers $12; open May 1-Oct. 31).

Get creative in the hostel kitchen with supplies from the large and slightly offbeat, **Thriftway** downtown (see above). The deli sports good ol' artery-plugging fried chicken for $4.50/lb., and the bulk foods aisle is a health food buff's nirvana. All-purpose ATM in the front of the store. Options for cooking-phobes include **Sound Food** (463-3565) at Vashon Island SW at Valley Center, which offers exactly what its name suggests; $6.95 shrimp scampi and $4.50 sandwiches make Sound Food an island staple and their lilac-festooned garden in back is a lovely place to enjoy it. Finish off the experience with a truly inexpensive ($1.25!) cappuccino and wander over to the north end of the parking lot which boasts the "famous Vashon Island bike," a rusty kid's bike embedded in the bark of a fir tree.

For less formal take-out food, run to **Tatanka** for bison, bison, and more bison: bison burgers ($4.75), bison burritos ($3.50), and bison chili ($3). The much touted "meat of the 90s," bison has 10% the fat beef does, and requires half as much rangeland to graze. Hostelers get drinks for half price (open Mon.-Sat. 11am-7pm, Sun. noon-7pm). The **Dog Day Café and Juice Bar,** (463-6404) 17530 Vashon Hwy. on the Vashon Landing, is a café and restaurant that changes its menu daily and juices just about anything. Sandwiches run $3.50-5, entrees $5-7 (open Sun.-Thu. 10am-4pm, Fri. 10am-5pm, Sat. 9am-5pm).

Sights and Events The island is wonderful for **biking**, but don't be deceived by the short distances; Vashon's hills will turn even a short jaunt into an arduous affair. A sweaty exploration will be rewarded, however, with rapturous scenery. Unfortunately, no bike shop on Vashon rents bikes; if you're staying at the hostel, don't forget about the loaner bikes. **Point Robinson Park** is a gorgeous spot for a picnic (from Vashon Hwy. take Ellisburg Rd. to Dockton Rd. to Pt. Robinson Rd.); schedule a free tour of the 1885 **Coast Guard lighthouse** that faces off with Mt. Ranier (217-6123). On a calm day at **Tramp Harbor** (463-YAKS/9257) you can rent a sea kayak or rowboat for an hour from **Vashon Island Kayak Co.** (open Fri.-Sun. 10am-5pm). More than 500 acres of woods in the middle of the island are interlaced with mild hiking trails, and several woodsy walks start from the hostel. Call the Vashon Park District for more information (463-9602, daily 9am-1pm).

Count on some culture no matter when you visit—one in ten residents of Vashon is a professional artist. **Blue Heron Arts Center** (463-5131), 19704 Vashon Hwy., coordinates most activities, including free local gallery openings on the first Friday of every month (6-9pm). The **Strawberry Festival,** held during the second weekend in July, puts the spotlight on Vashon. Local and national bands inspire street dancing well into the night and art booths line the streets. Contact the Chamber of Commerce for more information (see **Practical Information** above).

■ Kitsap Peninsula

The Kitsap Peninsula occupies much of the area between the Olympic Peninsula and Seattle. With natural deep-water inlets, it is home to a major naval base, a fleet of nuclear-powered Trident submarines, and a rich maritime history. Even without top secret clearance, travelers can enjoy the area's forested and hilly terrain. The peninsula's back roads and campgrounds are a cycling paradise and, once outside of Bremerton, tiny coastal **hamlets** beckon tourists.

Bremerton is the hub of the Kitsap Peninsula. Once there, you'll swear you've stepped into a Tom Clancy novel; every third person has a Navy security pass swinging from his or her neck. The skyline of the Navy Yard rivals that of a small city, and when the **USS Nimitz** is home, the local barber works overtime providing crew cuts for all. For the Navy or military history buff, Bremerton is quite a find. For others, the city contains few sights other than dingy apartment buildings, but is a good base for exploring the peninsula and Hood Canal, which separates the Kitsap and Olympic peninsulas. **Kingston,** at the northern tip about 20 mi. from Bremerton on Rte. 3 and Rte. 104, is linked by ferry to **Edmonds** on the mainland. **Southworth,** about 10 mi. east of Bremerton on Rte. 16 and Rte. 160, is connected to West Seattle and Vashon Island by ferry. Rte. 3 and Rte. 104 lead north to the Olympic Peninsula across the **Hood Canal Bridge.** Rte. 16 leads south to Tacoma.

Practical Information The **Bremerton Area Chamber of Commerce,** 120 Washington St. (479-3579), is just up the hill from the ferry terminal in Bremerton and will help you navigate the area. A booth at the ferry dock is open on weekends when the office is not. The office puts out a flotilla of pamphlets on Bremerton and nearby towns and the lively staff tries hard to dress up the city's fundamental drabness. If on a bicycle, pick up the indispensable *Kitsap and Olympic Peninsula Bike Map* here (open Mon.-Fri. 9am-5pm).

Frequent **ferry service** to the Kitsap Peninsula arrives at three points. (For schedules and information, see **By Ferry,** p. 35.) From Bremerton, ferries run to downtown Seattle; from Southworth, to Fauntleroy in West Seattle and Vashon Island; and from Kingston to Edmonds on the mainland.

Once there, **Kitsap Transit,** 234 Wycoff St. (373-BUSS/2877), about 1½ blocks from the Bremerton Information Bureau, runs several bus lines. Call ahead for times, pick up schedules at the Winslow, Bremerton, or Kingston ferry terminals, or visit the customer service office at the ferry dock (Mon.-Fri. 6am-7pm, Sat.-Sun. 8am-4pm, open most holidays; 75¢ before 8am and between 4pm and 7pm, 50¢ off-peak times, seniors 25¢ off-peak). Buses serve most small communities on the Peninsula and Bainbridge Island, and generally run until 8pm. A bike will get you most places, but towns are spread out, so prepare for a strenuous, though pleasant, ride. Kitsap Transit has accommodations for bikes on almost all buses.

The **post office** (373-1456) is stationed at 602 Pacific Ave. (open Mon.-Fri. 9am-5pm; **General Delivery ZIP Code:** 98337).

Accommodations, Camping, and Food If you're intent on spending the night here, your best bet is to camp, though a day trip from Seattle or Vashon Island may make for a more rewarding experience. Those traveling by foot will find **Illahee State Park** (478-6460 or 800-452-5687 for reservations) convenient, if a bit cramped and close to Bremerton road noise. To get there, hop on bus #29 at the ferry terminal in Bremerton and take it to the corner of Perry St. and Sylvan Rd. From there, walk ¼ mi. up the hill on Sylvan until you reach the entrance. By car, drive north on Hwy. 303 from Bremerton to Sylvan Rd., turn right, and follow signs. The park has 25 campsites with water, restrooms, and hot showers (sites $10 with a vehicle, primitive sites without vehicle $5). Another possibility is **Scenic Beach State Park** (830-5079), near the village of Seabeck on the west coast of the peninsula. The park has 50 campsites with water and bathrooms (sites $10, walk-in sites $5). From Silverdale, take Anderson Hill Rd. or Newberry Hill Rd. west to Seabeck Hwy., and then follow the highway 7mi. south to the Scenic Beach turnoff. Cyclists should be prepared for the staggering hills along this route. Winter hours are limited, call for reservations.

Culinary choices in Bremerton are not very appealing. The Naval yuppies (officers) at **The Waterfront Café,** 112 Wash Ave. (792-1603) in Bremerton, are an amusing twist on the usual urban variety. Every meal comes with a gorgeous view of the docks and virtual buckets of free bread. Unfortunately, the kitchen often runs out of the lunchtime specials, which are around $6 for fair-sized portions (open daily 11am-4pm). For an enlisted man's meal, cross the street to **Emperor's Palace Chinese Restaurant** at 221 Wash. Ave. (377-8866), which serves predictable but tasty Mandarin and Szechuan dishes in a dark, vinyl-upholstered dining room. Any one of the eight lunch platters is $4.50 and a two-person family dinner starts at $9.95 (open Sun.-Thu. 11am-10pm, Fri-Sat. 11am-11pm).

Sights and Events Next to the Chamber of Commerce (see **Practical Information,** above), you'll find the dustily endearing **Bremerton Naval Museum** (479-7447). Friendly volunteers will explain the room full of patriotic gore with exhibits of World War II photos and transparent models of destroyers and aircraft carriers measuring up to 10ft. (free, donations requested; open Mon.-Sat. 10am-5pm, Sun. 1-5pm). In Bremerton, check out the destroyer **USS Turner Joy** (792-2457), before a stroll along the **Bremerton Boardwalk**. At the ferry dock, catch the **foot ferry** from the Bremerton terminal across the Sinclair Inlet to **Port Orchard** for an excellent view of the shipyards. The ferry leaves every hour on the ¼hr. Fare is 70¢, free on weekends May-Oct. If naval paraphernalia could keep you afloat all day, take Hwy. 303 north from Bremerton or the **Kitsap Fast Ferry** (passengers only, summers only, 396-4148) to the **Keyport Naval Station,** home of the **Naval Undersea Museum,** 610 Donell St. (396-4148), which exhibits artifacts salvaged from the oceans, including a K-10 torpedo and Japanese kamikaze aircraft (open June-Sept. daily 10am-4pm; Oct.-May Tues.-Sun. 10am-4pm).

Across Liberty Bay "fjord" from Keyport, Norwegian immigrants have made a tourist-luring shrine out of the town of **Poulsbo,** where various Scandinavian festivals take place year-round on streets with names like King Olav V. Contact the **Greater Poulsbo Chamber of Commerce** at 779-4848. While there, cross Hwy. 3 and take a short detour to the **Thomas Kemper Brewery,** 22381 Foss Rd. NE (697-7899), a local brewery that has won wide fame for its beers, cream soda, and root beer. Brewery tours are given on weekdays at 11 and 2:30pm, Sat.-Sun at 11am, 1,2,4, and 5pm. After putting back a couple, take to the beer garden outside for fun and company. Check for folk music in the afternoon on the first Sunday of every summer month. Sandwiches at the tap room go for $5 (open Mon.-Thurs. 11am-9pm, Fri.-Sat. 11am-10pm, Sun. 11am-9pm). North of Poulsbo, the **Historic Port Madison Indian Reservation** provides ample opportunity to learn about the history of Seattle-area Native Americans.

If you ask nicely, the driver of bus #90 will let you off at the Longhouse Convenience Store. Follow the road 1mi. to the fascinating **Suquamish Museum** (598-3311, ext. 422). The museum is on the north side of the **Agate Pass Bridge** on Rte. 305. Run by the **Port Madison Reservation**, this small museum is devoted entirely to the history and culture of the native Puget Sound Suquamish people. Striking photographs, artifacts, and quotations from respected elders piece together the lives of those who inhabited the peninsula before, during, and after the great invasion ($2.50, seniors $2, under 12 $1; open May-Sept. daily 10am-5pm; Oct.-April Fri.-Sun. 11am-4pm). **Chief Sealth's** grave is within driving distance of the town of Suquamish. The chief's memorial, constructed of cedar war canoes, is in the middle of a nearby Catholic cemetery. Pick up a map of the area at the museum.

▩ Bellingham

Strategically located between Seattle and Vancouver, Bellingham is a hub of Northwest transportation. The ferries of the **Alaska Marine Highway** serve Bellingham regularly, with connections once or twice a week in summer to Ketchikan, AK, and Prince Rupert, BC. Most travelers who stay the night in Bellingham are either winding their nautical way to or from Alaska, or visiting **Western Washington University** on the south side of town. Local students attract budget-oriented business, and a recent influx of young people has converted this former lumber town into a thriving, lively community with parks to ramble in and a boom-town atmosphere.

PRACTICAL INFORMATION AND ORIENTATION

Visitors Information: 904 Potter St. (671-3990). Take Exit 253 (Lakeway) from I-5. Prepare yourself for a flood of Whatcom County trivia. Extremely helpful staff. Open daily 8:30am-5:30pm.

Buses: Greyhound (733-5251), in the Greyhound/Amtrak station next to the ferry terminals. To: Seattle (6 per day, $12), Vancouver (5 per day, $13), Mt. Vernon (4 per day, $6). Open Mon.-Fri. 7:30am-5:30pm.

Public Transportation: Whatcom County Transit (676-7433). All buses originate at the terminal in the Railroad Ave. mall between Holly and Magnolia St., where **maps** and schedules are available. Fare 35¢, over 90 free; no free transfers. Buses run every 15-30min. Mon.-Fri. 7am-7pm, reduced service until 11pm and Sat.-Sun. 9am-6pm.

Ferries: Lummi Island Ferry (676-6730), at Gooseberry Pt. Take I-5 north to Slater Rd. (Exit 260), then take a left on Hackston Way. Frequent trips back and forth each day. Ferries depart every hr., more often during peak hr. The first leaves the island at 6:20am, 7am on weekends; the last departs the mainland at 12:10am. Departures from the mainland at 10min. after the hr., from the island on the hour. Roundtrip fare $1 per person, $2 per car.

Taxi: City Cab, 734-TAXI/8294 or 800-281-5430. Open 24hr.

Car Rental: U-Save Auto Rental, 1100 Iowa (671-3688). Cars from $20 per day; 15¢ per mi. after 100 mi. Must be 21 with credit card or $250 deposit. Open Mon.-Fri. 9am-5:30pm, Sat. 9am-4pm.

Laundromat: Bellingham Cleaning Center, 1010 Lakeway Dr. (734-3755). Wash $1.25, 10-min. dry 25¢. Open daily 7:30am-10pm.

Public Library: 210 Central (676-6860), on corner of Central and Commercial across from city hall downtown. A fountain and pristine lawn in back make for a great lazy afternoon picnic site; inside, the library offers free World Wide Web access. Open Mon.-Thurs. 10am-9pm, Fri.-Sat. 10am-6pm, Sun. 1-5pm.

City Parks Department: 3424 Guide Meridian Rd. (676-6985) by Cornwall Park. Pick up a map of Bellingham's miles of footpaths. Open Mon.-Fri. 9am-6pm.

Outdoor Supplies: The Great Adventure, 201 E. Chestnut St. (671-4615). Rents kayaks (from $20 per day), camping, climbing, and backpacking gear, and skis at reasonable rates. Deposit required. Open Mon.-Thurs. 10am-6pm, Fri. 10am-7pm, Sat. 9am-6pm, Sun. 11am-5pm.

Ride Board: Viking Union at Western Washington University. Rides often available to Seattle and eastern Washington.

Senior Services: 315 Halleck. Information and assistance 733-4033 (city) or 398-1995 (county). Take bus 10B to the corner of Ohio and Cornwall St. Open daily 8:30am-4pm.

Crisis: Bellingham (734-7271). Whatcom County (384-1485). Both 24hr.

Pharmacy: Payless Drug, 1400 Cornwall St. (733-0580). Open Mon.-Fri. 8am-7pm, Sat. 9am-6pm. Pharmacy opens and closes ½hr. before store.

Hospital: St. Joseph's General, 2901 Squalicum Pkwy. (734-5400). Open 24hr.

Post Office: 315 Prospect (676-8303). Open Mon.-Fri. 8am-5:30pm, Sat. 9:30am-2pm. **General Delivery ZIP Code:** 98225.

Area Code: 360.

Bellingham lies along I-5, 90 mi. north of Seattle and 57 mi. south of Vancouver, and is the only major city between the two. Downtown is a shopping and business area centered on Holly St. and Cornwall Ave., next to the Georgia Pacific pulp mill, accessible by Exits 252 and 253 off I-5. Western Washington University sits atop a hill to the south along Indian St. The South Side fronts the south end of the bay along S. State

St. A hundred and thirty acres of city parks encircle Bellingham. The town of Fairhaven lies directly south of Bellingham, and Whatcom County Transit provides service throughout the area.

ACCOMMODATIONS AND CAMPING

For both atmosphere and price, the hostel is the best bet. For help with other accommodations, try the **Bed & Breakfast Guild of Whatcom Co.** (676-4560). Many B&Bs offer rooms in the $60 neighborhood. If you're really in a jam, try the **YWCA** (734-4820).

Fairhaven Rose Garden Hostel (HI-AYH), 107 Chuckanut Dr. (671-1750), next to Fairhaven Park, about ¾ mi. from the ferry terminal. Take Exit 250 from I-5, west on Fairhaven Parkway to 12th St.; bear left onto Chuckanut Dr. From downtown Bellingham, take bus 1A or 1B. This tiny hostel is in the middle of the Fairhaven rose garden, though delinquent local deer have done their best to mow it down. The downstairs living quarters have been known to smell profoundly dank. Only 10 beds will fit in the clean bunk room, so be sure to call the management ahead of time, especially if you plan to stay a Wed. or Thurs. night, as Alaska-bound travelers fill the hostel quickly. All-you-can-eat pancakes $1, linens $2. No curfew, but living room closes at 10:30pm. Open Feb.-Nov. Check-in 5-10:30pm, check-out 9:30am. No wheelchair access. Reservations mandatory July-Aug.

Travelers Lodge, 202 E. Holly St. (734-1900). Take Exit 253 off I-5. Roll out of the lodge's big beds and clean rooms right into downtown Bellingham. Cable and coffee makers in the rooms make up for Bellingham's slight eau de paper plant and occasional 2am noise. Free local calls. Weekday singles $27, doubles $37. Prices increase a little bit on weekends.

Mac's Motel, 1215 E. Maple St. (734-7570), at Samish Way. Take Exit 252 from I-5. Large clean rooms. Pleasant management, cats, and exterior paint like an ice-cream sundae. Singles $26, 2 people $32, doubles $40. Open daily 7am-10pm.

Larrabee State Park (676-2093), on Chuckanut Dr., 7 mi. south of Bellingham. Eighty-six sites tucked in among the trees on Samish Bay, a half-hidden flatland outside the city. No handicap facilities. Check out the nearby tide pools or hike to alpine lakes. 8 walk-in tent sites are the best bet. Sites $11. Hookups $16. Park open daily 6:30am-dusk.

FOOD

The **Community Food Co-op,** 1220 N. Forest St. (734-8158), at Maple, has the essentials and a health food sit-down deli in the back. Buy in bulk (open daily 8am-9pm). If you're in town on a Saturday, head to the **Bellingham Farmer's Market,** at Chestnut St. and Railroad Ave., for the fruit and vegetable stands and homemade donuts (April-Oct., Sat. 10am-3pm). For information call 647-2060.

Casa Que Pasa, 1415 Railroad Ave. (738-TACO/8226). Bellingham's best burritos are a great deal. Huge burritos starting at $2.30 made with fresh vegetables purchased from local growers. Vegan and vegetarian options abound. Open Sat.-Thurs. 11am-9pm, Fri. 11am-midnight.

The Old Town Café, 316 West Holly St. (671-4431). Incredible breakfasts made with local ingredients from the farmer's market. Play a few songs on the piano in the adjoining art gallery and earn yourself a free drink to go with your buttermilk hotcakes ($3). Vegan and vegetarian options aplenty, and nothing on the menu is over $5. Open Mon.-Sat. 6:30am-3pm, Sun. 8am-2pm.

Tony's Coffees and Tea Shop, 1101 Harris Ave. (733-6319), in Fairhaven Village, just down the hill from S. 12th St. Dining garden complete with old railway car. Serves coffee, ice cream, bagels, and the infamous, high-voltage **Toxic Milkshake,** made with coffee and espresso grounds ($3.25). Open daily 7am-10pm. Same cinnamon rolls for ½ price at the **Great Harvest Bakery** (671-0873), in Sehome Village Mall on Samish Way. Bakery open Tues.-Sat. 9:30am-6pm.

WASHINGTON

Pepper Sisters, 1055 N. State (671-3414), ½ mi. north of Fairhaven. Mexican food served in turquoise booths under track lighting. Heaping portions (vegetarian burrito $5.50, pork and bean burrito $8.00) and cheap beer. Unfortunately, this room has no view, so don't opt for the outdoor seating. Open Tues.-Thurs. and Sun. 4:30-9pm, Fri.-Sat. 4:30-9:30pm.

SIGHTS, ACTIVITIES AND EVENTS

Western Washington University (650-3000) generates continuous cultural and artistic activity, as well as 7 mi. of hiking trails that reward explorers with views of Bellingham Bay and the San Juan Islands. Sixteen outdoor sculptures commissioned by local and nationally known artists stud the campus; a free brochure and headphones, available at the visitors information center, guide the wandering critic around campus from piece to piece. Friday nights during the academic year, a program of concerts called **Mama Sundays** heats up the Viking Union on campus. Topnotch folk and bluegrass are the norm ($3-5). In the summer, there are free weekday lunchtime concerts. The **Western Visitors Center** (650-3424) is at the entrance to the college on South College Dr. (open summer 7am-5pm, 7am-7pm during the academic year). Friendly staff will also give you the scoop on campus cultural events such as the **Summer Stock Theater** and the **Bellingham Music Festival.** Take bus 5A, 3B, 7B, 8A, or 9B from downtown to reach campus.

The **Whatcom Museum of History and Art,** 121 Prospect St. (676-6981), occupies four buildings along Prospect Street, most notably the looming old city hall. Find rotating exhibits on local topics ranging from native art to gardening history. Climb to the third floor of the old city hall to watch the clocktower innards at work (fully wheelchair accessible; open Tues.-Sun. noon-5pm).

Whatcom County hosts annual festivals that celebrate its modestly colorful past. Held on Gooseberry Point in the Lummi Island Reservation, the **Lummi Stommish Water Carnival** (734-8180) is entering its 48th year. The three-day carnival at the end of June stages traditional dances, war-canoe races, and a salmon barbecue.

In the second week of June, lumberjacks converge here from throughout the region to compete in axe-throwing, log-rolling, and speed-climbing at the **Deming Logging Show** (676-1089). To reach the Showgrounds, take Mt. Baker Hwy. 12 mi. east to Cedarville Rd. and head west. Signs lead you to the grounds. June sees the mother of all races, the **Ski to Sea Race.** This relay race starts at Mt. Baker and ends at the Bellingham Bay with participants skiing, running, biking, canoeing, biking, and sea kayaking to the finish line. Call 734-1330 for information, or write Ski to Sea, P.O. Box 958, Bellingham 98227. Bellingham is also home to the baseball greats the **Bellingham Giants,** a feeder team for the San Francisco Giants.

OUTDOORS

Hike up **Chuckanut Mountain** through a quiet forest for a view of the islands that fill the bay. You can occasionally spot Mt. Rainier to the south. A 2½-mi. hike uphill leaves from Old Samish Hwy. about 1 mi. south of the city limits. The beach at **Lake Padden Park,** 4882 Samish Way, delights those who find Puget Sound a little chilly; the water here is the warmest in the Sound. Take bus 10A 1 mi. south of downtown. A lifeguard keeps watch intermittently. The park also has miles of hiking trails, a boat launch (no motors allowed), tennis courts, playing fields, and fishing off the pier. The park is wheelchair-accessible (open daily 6am-10pm).

Whatcom Falls Park, 1401 Electric Ave., due east of town, also has fantastic hiking trails, picnic facilities, and tennis courts. The **Upper Whatcom Falls Trail** (1.6 mi.) leads to the falls themselves, converted into a waterslide by locals. Take bus 4A or 11A (park open daily 6am-dusk). The fishing is good in **Lake Samish** and **Silver Lake,** north of the town of Maple Falls off the Mt. Baker Hwy. The lake trout season opens on the third Sunday in April. **Fishing licenses** are available from the **Department of Fisheries** (902-2464), sporting goods stores, and some hardware stores.

Popular with South Side residents, the **Interurban Trail** runs 6.6 mi. from Fairhaven Park to Larrabee State Park along the route of the old Interurban Electric Railway. The trail is less developed than those at Padden and Whatcom Lakes and follows a creek through the forest. Occasional breaks in the trees permit a glimpse of the San Juan Islands; watch for divided paths and unmarked street crossings. Pick up a map from the **City Parks Department** (see **Practical Information,** above). Along the Interurban Trail you may stumble on **Teddy Bear Cove,** easily accessible from Chuckanut Drive, 2 mi. south of Fairhaven. This clothing-optional beach offers revealing views of the local wildlife. Recently converted to a public beach, this enclave has lost much of its scenic appeal, but still offers a relaxed haven for driftwood hunters and beachcombing romantics.

A hidden treasure in the residential area of Bellingham, **Big Rock Garden Park,** 2900 Sylvan (676-6801), is a 2.7-acre Japanese tea garden. Take Alabama St. east, then go left on Sylvan for several blocks. The garden doubles as an outdoor art gallery and numerous pieces hide in and around the trees and flowers. The park frequently hosts outdoor musical performances. Call ahead for a schedule. Open March-Nov., Wed.-Sun. 11am-5pm.

■ Near Bellingham

MT. BAKER

To reach the volcano, take Exit 255 off I-5, just north of Bellingham, to Rte. 542, better known as the **Mt. Baker Hwy.** Fifty-six miles of roadway traverse the foothills, affording spectacular views of Baker and the other peaks in the range. Crowning the Mt. Baker-Snoqualmie National Forest, Mt. Baker contains excellent downhill and cross-county skiing facilities as well as the best snowboarding in the state. The volcano packs more powder for longer than any other nearby area, so skiing facilities usually stay open from late October to early July. Stop by the Mt. Baker Ski Area office in Bellingham (734-6771, 1017 Iowa St.) for more information. On your way to the mountain, stop by **Carol's Coffee Cup,** 5415 Mt. Baker Hwy. (592-5441), for pre-skiing carbo-loading with the biggest cinnamon rolls on earth ($1.10).

Silver Lake Park, 9006 Silver Lake Rd. (599-2776), is 28 mi. east of Bellingham on the Mt. Baker Hwy. and 3 mi. north of Maple Falls on Silver Lake Road. The park tends 113 **campsites** near the lake with facilities for swimming, hiking, and fishing. Tent sites are $12, with hookups $14.

BLAINE

A border town 20 mi. north of Bellingham, Blaine is the busiest port of entry between Canada and the U.S. Those who get turned away from the Canadian border for insufficient identification or funds (you need CDN$500 per car and $50 per extra passenger if you're headed for Alaska) often head for Blaine, though the border patrol prides itself on catching these undesirables with blanket stop-checks. The **Blaine Visitors Center,** 215 Marine Dr., at Exit 276 off I-5, is a storehouse of information on Blaine as well as American and Canadian points of interest in the area (open daily 9am-5pm, winter Mon.-Fri. 9am-5pm).

The main attraction in Blaine is the **Peace Arch State Park** (332-8221; open daily 8am-dusk). Built in 1921 with donations from school children in Washington and British Columbia, the arch commemorates the 1814 signing of the Treaty of Ghent, which terminated the War of 1812 and inaugurated an era of peace between Canada and the U.S. The two legs of the arch, each containing pieces of wood from early Canadian and U.S. ships of discovery, straddle the international border. Summertime happenings include "hands across the border" events, complete with kids, balloons, and Rotarians. To reach the parking lot, take Exit 276 off I-5, then turn north onto 2nd St. (Open Oct. 16-March 1 8am-5pm; toilets, kitchen facilities).

The spit of land encompassing **Semiahmoo Park,** 5 mi. southwest of Blaine, was first inhabited by the coastal Salish people who harvested shellfish when the tide was low. Clam digging is still a popular activity. Buckets and shovels may be rented from the park; a license is required for fishing, digging for shellfish, and picking seaweed (licenses $3-20, depending on residency and type of activity). Take Drayton Harbor Rd. around to the southwestern side of Drayton Harbor (free; open mid-Feb. to Dec., Wed.-Sun. 1-5pm).

The **Birch Bay Hostel (HI-AYH),** 7467 Gemini St., building #630 on the former Blaine Air Force Base (371-2180; e-mail bbhostel@az.com), has lots of small rooms for more privacy than most hostels. Some have magnificent views of the marshes. Full kitchen facilities. Small, clean rooms and a woodstove sauna. Call or e-mail for more information on excursions and discounts. Take either the Birch Bay-Lynden Rd. exit or the Grandview Rd. exit off I-5 and head west. Blaine Rd. will take you to the Alderson Rd. entrance to the Air Force base (open April-Sept.; $10, nonmembers $13). The **Westview Motel,** 1300 Peace Portal Dr. (332-5501), also offers excellent lodgings (singles $29, two people $33, doubles $41).

Birch Bay State Park, 5105 Helwig Rd. (371-2800; 800-452-5687 for reservations), 10 mi. south of Blaine, operates 167 campsites near the water. The Semiahmoo Native people used this area and the marshland at the southern end of the park to harvest shellfish and hunt waterfowl; today, 300 species of birds live in the park's **Terrell Creek Estuary.** The park is also a good area for crabbing, scuba diving, water-skiing, and swimming. To reach the park, take the Birch Bay-Lynden exit off I-5 and turn south onto Blaine Rd. When you run out of road, turn east onto Bay Rd. Turn south on Jackson Rd. and take it to Helwig Rd. The way is well-marked from the freeway (open year-round; sites $11, with hookup $16; reservation fee $6; reservations recommended come summer).

The best seafood in town, fresh daily, is at the **Harbor Café,** on Marine Dr. (332-5176), halfway down the pier. The $7 fish and chips, salad bar or chowder included, is hard to resist (open Sun.-Thurs. 6am-10pm, Fri.-Sat. 6am-11pm).

SAN JUAN ISLANDS

If you're in pursuit of the picturesque Northwest, you'll find it in the lush San Juan Islands, where it rains half as much as in Seattle. The San Juans are home to an abundance of great horned owls, puffins, sea otters, sea lions, and more deer, raccoons, and rabbits than they can support. Pods of orcas ("killer whales") patrol the waters, keeping a protective eye on these glacier-carved islands. Today, pods of tourists mimic the whales, circling the islands in everything from yachts to kayaks in pursuit of cetacean encounters.

Although the population of San Juan, the main island in the chain, has doubled in the last five years, there are still fewer than 3000 permanent residents. The populations of the other inhabited islands are far lower, and endless parks and miles of coastline offer ample opportunity to commune with cedars and tidepools in relative seclusion. But over 1.5 million visitors come ashore the San Juans each year, usually in July and August; to avoid the rush but still enjoy good weather, try the islands in late spring or early fall. Although tension is building between locals and transplants from Seattle and California who are buying up huge chunks of the islands at exorbitant prices, well-behaved tourists and their dollars are still welcome. The islands particularly lure bikers and kayakers. Cheap biker/hiker sites in campgrounds are common, and most island roads are flat and well paved. The San Juans are a sea kayaker's dream, with hundreds of tiny islands to weave among, surrounded by diverse sea life; many locals consider their cars an alternative to their kayaks.

Two excellent guides to the area are *The San Juan Islands Afoot and Afloat* by Marge Mueller ($15) and *Emily's Guide,* a series of detailed descriptions of each island ($4, $11 for a set of three), available at bookstores and outfitting stores on the islands and in Seattle. *The San Juans Beckon* is published annually by the *Island Sounder,* the local paper, and includes maps and information on island recreation.

The *San Juanderer* also has useful information, including tide charts and ferry schedules. Both are free on ferries or at visitors centers.

GETTING THERE AND GETTING AROUND

Washington State Ferries serve the islands daily from **Anacortes** on the mainland. To reach Anacortes, take I-5 north from Seattle to Mt. Vernon. From there, Rte. 20 heads west to Anacortes. The way to the ferry is well-marked. The Bellingham Airporter (800-235-5247) makes eight trips to Anacortes on weekdays and six trips on weekends. The bus leaves from Seatac and costs $27.00 one way and $49.00 roundtrip.

Of the 172 islands in the San Juan archipelago, only four are accessible by ferry. **Washington State Ferries** depart Anacortes about nine times daily to **Lopez, Shaw, Orcas,** and **San Juan** (see p. 35 for fare and schedule information). Not every ferry services all the islands, and many provide service only among the islands without connections to Anacortes, so be sure to check the schedule. Ferries run from approximately 6am to midnight. The ferry system revises its schedule seasonally and there are no reservations. Puget Sound visitors centers have schedules aplenty.

You can purchase **ferry tickets** in Anacortes. Foot passengers travel in either direction between the islands free of charge. No charge is levied on eastbound traffic; pay for a vehicle only on **westbound** trips to or between the islands. **A money-saving tip:** to see more islands and save on ferry fares, travel directly to the westernmost island on your itinerary and then make your way eastward to the mainland island by island. The San Juan ferries are packed in summer, so get there early. On peak travel days, arrive with your vehicle at least one hour prior to departure. The ferry authorities accept only cash or in-state checks as payment, and no credit cards.

On the islands, short distances and good roads make the San Juans excellent for bicycle exploration. Island Transit provides bus service on San Juan and Orcas Islands (800-887-8387 or 376-8887). Hitchhiking is reputed to be easy on the islands. (*Let's Go* does not recommend hitchhiking.)

■ San Juan Island

The biggest of the San Juans, this island is also the most popular. **Lime Kiln State Park,** the only designated whale-watching park in the world, provides the best ocean vista for **whale-watching** of all of the island. San Juan is the last stop on the ferry route and is home to **Friday Harbor,** the largest town in the archipelago. It is also the easiest to explore, since the ferry docks right in town, the roads are fairly flat for bicyclists, and a shuttle bus runs throughout the island. But popularity has its price: Seattle weekenders flood the island throughout the summer, bringing fleets of undesirable traffic.

> **I Regret That I Have But One Life To Give For My Country.**
> Back in 1859, when Washington was officially part of "Oregon Country" and the San Juan Islands lay in a territorial no man's land between British Vancouver Island and the United States to the south, one brave swine gave his life for truth, justice, and the American Way. Twenty-five Americans lived and farmed on San Juan Island at a time when the British Hudson Bay Trading Co. claimed the island for Mother England. When Lyman Cutter caught a Hudson Bay pig making a royal mess of his potato patch on June 15th of that year, he understandably shot him dead. The Brits threatened to arrest him, and the Americans looked to Uncle Sam for protection. Three months, five British warships, and 14 American cannons later, war between the two nations seemed inevitable. Though the squabble cooled off, the **"Pig War"** lasted 12 years. Both countries occupied the island until 1872, when Kaiser Wilhelm of Germany was invited to settle the dispute and granted the U.S. the island. In the end, only the pig lost his life. But as we all know, everlasting fame is better than a life of wallowing in the mud any day.

PRACTICAL INFORMATION AND ORIENTATION

Visitors Information: Chamber of Commerce (468-3663), in a booth on East St. up from Cannery Landing. Open sporadically dawn-dusk daily. **San Juan Transit** (see below), located upstairs in the cannery landing next to the ferry dock, also distributes scores of San Juan-oriented brochures and maps. **National Park Service Information Center** (378-2240), on the corner of 1st and Spring, answers questions about San Juan National Historical Park. Open Mon.-Fri. 8:30am-5pm, off-season 8:30am-4pm.

Ferry Terminal: In Friday Harbor (378-4777 or 800-84-FERRY/843-3779). Information line open 24hr. Waiting room opens 30min. before scheduled departures.

Taxi: San Juan Taxi, 378-3550. 24hr.

Bus: San Juan Transit (800-887-8387 or 376-8887), circles the island every 35-55 min. Many convenient stops, but the driver will make additional stops upon request. Point to point $4. Day pass $10. Two-day pass (also good on Orcas Island) $17. If you plan to see San Juan Island only, it may be cheaper to leave your car in Anacortes and use the shuttle once you get to the islands.

Bike Rental: Island Bicycles, 380 Argyle St. (378-4941) in Friday Harbor. 6-speeds $15 per day, 12-speeds $20 per day, mountain bikes $25 per day. Locks and helmets included. Also rents child strollers ($5) and trailers ($15). Provides **maps** of the island and suggests bike routes. Credit card required. Open daily 10am-5:30pm; May 1-Sept. 30 Wed.-Sat. with more limited hours.

Moped Rental: Susie's Mopeds (800-532-0087 or 378-5244), one block above Landing. Mopeds $12 per hr., $45 per day, fuel included. Credit card required. Open March-Oct. daily 9am-6pm. Also available at Roche Harbor July 4-Labor Day.

Kayak Rental and Tours: Emerald Seas Kayaking (378-2772), on Spring St. next to the landing. 2hr. for $20, 4hr. for $35. Only plastic kayaks. Staff will give you introductory tips before you shove off. The only outfit on San Juan to rent kayaks without a guide. Open daily 9am-6pm. **Guided Tours: San Juan Safaris** (378-2155, ext. 258 or 800-451-8910, ext. 258), leaves from Roche Harbor on the north tip of the island, at the end of Roche Harbor Rd. A 3-hr. trip will set you back $35, but the scenery may be worth it.

Laundromat: Wash Tub Laundromat (378-2070), in the San Juan Inn on Spring St., ½ block from the ferry. Wash $2, 11-min. dry 25¢. Open daily 7:30am-9pm.

Senior Services: at the **Gray Top Inn** (378-2677). Open Mon.-Fri. 9am-4pm.

Red Tide Hotline: 800-562-5632 for info on safe shellfish-harvesting.

Pharmacy: Friday Harbor Drug, 210 Spring St. (378-4421). Open Mon.-Sat. 9am-7pm, Sun. 10am-4pm.

Medical Services: Inter-Island Medical Center, 550 Spring St. (378-2141). Open Mon.-Fri. 8:30am-5pm, Sat. 10am-noon.

Emergency: 911. **Sheriff:** 135 Rhone St. (non-emergency 378-4151), at Reed St.

Post Office: 378-4511, at Blair and Reed St. Open Mon.-Fri. 8:30am-4:30pm. **General Delivery ZIP Code:** 98250.

Area Code: 360.

With bicycle, car, and boat rentals all within a few blocks of the ferry terminal, Friday Harbor is a convenient base for exploring the islands. Miles of road make all corners of the island accessible, but the roads are poorly marked. It's smart to plot your course carefully on one of the free **maps** available at the information centers in town (see above), or stop at one of the island's real estate offices or gas stations. Or just grab one of the local publications for visitors.

ACCOMMODATIONS AND CAMPING

San Juan's campgrounds have become wildly popular; show up early in the afternoon to make sure you get a spot, or call ahead for a reservation. Outside of camping, cheap accommodations in the San Juans are an endangered species. You will not find great bargains in the busy season. If you plan to stay overnight and camping is not your style, try one of the many B&Bs: although expensive, they are often beautiful. The **Bed and Breakfast Association** (378-3030) can help you.

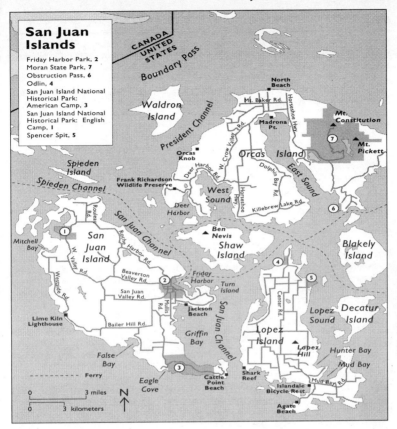

San Juan Islands

Friday Harbor Park, **2**
Moran State Park, **7**
Obstruction Pass, **6**
Odlin, **4**
San Juan Island National
Historical Park:
American Camp, **3**
San Juan Island National
Historical Park: English
Camp, **1**
Spencer Spit, **5**

The Orca Inn, 770 Mullis St. (378-2724) has converted a battalion of mobile homes into tiny, clean rooms. A bunk room holds 1-2 people and has a private bath, but no TV or phone ($36).

Lakedale Campgrounds, 2627 Roche Harbor Rd. (378-2350 or 800-617-CAMP/2267), 4 mi. from Friday Harbor. Very attractive grounds are surrounded by 50 acres of lakes. Hosts almost every imaginable water sport and rents almost every variety of water vessel. Lakes are stocked with trout, and fishing within the campground requires no permit. Pay showers ($1). Sites for 1-2 people with vehicle $16 (July-Aug. $19), each additional person $3.50 (July-Aug. $4.50). Day use $1.50. Hiker/biker sites $5 (July-Aug. $5.50). Open March15-Oct. 15. Reservations suggested, but management boast that they've never turned a camper away.

Pedal Inn, 1300 False Bay Dr. (378-3049). A campground designed for bikers and hikers. Very rustic, a bit ramshackle, quiet, and cheap. Hot water is only on during evening hours, but the self-described "mean old manager" Jim will negotiate. Sites $4.50. Any "accessories" like cars or vans cost $4.50 more. Open June-Sept.

San Juan County Park, 380 Westside Rd. (378-2992), 10 mi. west of Friday Harbor on Smallpox and Andrews Bays. Limited facilities, but very quiet, with excellent whale-watching and tide-pooling. Cold water, flush toilets, but no showers or RV hookups. Vehicle sites $15. Hiker/biker sites $5. Park open daily 7am-10pm. Office open 9am-7pm

FOOD

Stock up at **King's Market,** 160 Spring St. (378-4505; open Mon.-Sat. 7:30am-10pm, Sun. 8am-10pm). In addition to groceries, King's has the requisite deli and salad bar. Almost every restaurant on the island serves vegetarian food.

Katrina's, 135 2nd St. (378-7290), between Key Bank and Friday Harbor Drug. The tiny kitchen cooks up a different menu every day, invariably serving local organic salads, freshly baked bread, and gigantic cookies (70¢). What you would cook in your own kitchen if you could cook that well. Open Mon.-Sat. noon-5pm.

La Cieba, 395 Spring St. (378-8666). A small Mexican/Southwestern restaurant supported primarily by locals, but out-of-towners are welcome to join the feast. Super burritos ($4.50) and daily specials made of the freshest ingredients around. Open Mon.-Sat. 11am-8pm, daily July 8-Aug.

San Juan Bakery and Donut Shop, 225 Spring St. (378-2271). Cheap eats. Endless coffee refills, inexpensive breakfast, lunch sandwiches, and a tour of the local rumor mill. Coffee ($1). Grilled cheese, bacon and chips ($3.75). They will pack up a lunch if you call ahead. Open Mon.-Sat. 5am-4pm, Sun. 6am-3pm.

SIGHTS AND ACTIVITIES

Friday Harbor is crowded when the tourists are out in full force, but appealing at other times, especially in spring and fall. The **Whale Museum,** 62 1st St. (378-4710), exhibits skeletons, sculptures, and information on new research. The museum even operates a toll-free **whale hotline** (800-562-8832) to report sightings and strandings and posts a calendar of the most recent sightings and locations ($4, seniors $3.50, ages 5-18 $1, under 5 free; open daily 10am-5pm; Oct. 1-Memorial Day daily 11am-4pm). The **San Juan Historical Museum,** 405 Price St. (378-3949), in the old King House across from the St. Francis Catholic Church, explodes with exhibits, furnishings, and photographs from the late 1800s. A free pamphlets maps out a walking tour of Friday Harbor (open Wed.-Sat. 1-4:30pm; Labor Day-May Thurs.-Fri. 1-4pm).

A drive around the 35-mi. perimeter of the island takes about two hours, and the route is fairly flat for cyclists. The **West Side Rd.** traverses gorgeous scenery and provides the best chance for sighting **orcas** offshore. Three resident pods frolic in the nearby waters and at peak times orcas are sighted several times per day.

To begin a tour of the island, head south and west out of Friday Harbor on Mullis Rd. Bikers may want to take this "tour" in the opposite direction, as climbs heading counterclockwise around the island are much more gradual. Mulles Rd. merges with Cattle Point Rd. and takes you straight into **American Camp** (378-2902), on the south side of the island (open daily 8am-dusk). The camp dates to the Pig War of 1859. Two of the camp's buildings still stand. The visitors center explains the history of the conflict (open daily 8:30am-5pm). Guided walks leave the center at 11:30am and 2:30pm on Wed.-Fri. and Sat.-Sun. at 11:30am. A self-guided trail leads from the shelter through the buildings and past the site of a British sheep farm. Every Saturday (June-Sept. 12:30-3:30pm), volunteers in period costume reenact daily life at the camp (free). If the sky is clear, make the ½-mi. jaunt farther down the road to **Cattle Point** for views of the distant Olympic Mountains.

Returning north on Cattle Point Rd., the gravel False Bay Rd. to the west will guide you to **False Bay,** home to nesting **bald eagles** and a great spot for watching them. During the spring and summer, walk along the northwestern shore (to your right as you face the water) at low tide to see the nesting eagles. Continuing to the western part of the island, farther north on False Bay Rd., you'll run into **Bailer Hill Rd.,** which turns into West Side Rd. when it reaches Haro Straight.

Lime Kiln Point State Park, along West Side Rd., is known as the best whale-watching spot in the area as crowds of cliff-crawling visitors to the park can attest.

Before you head out, gauge your chances of actually seeing **orcas** by inquiring at the Whale Museum for day-to-day information on whale sightings. For those truly determined to see whales, a cruise may be best, but be prepared to shell out serious cash. Most operations charge about $40 for adults and $30 for children for a three- to four-hour boat ride. For information, pick up one of the many brochures at area businesses, the Chamber of Commerce, or the National Park Service Information Center (see **Practical Information,** above).

The Pig War casts its comic pallor over **British Camp,** the second half of the **San Juan National Historical Park.** The camp lies on West Valley Rd. on the sheltered **Garrison Bay** (take Mitchell Bay Rd. east from West Side Rd.). Here, four original buildings have been preserved, including the barracks, now used as an **interpretive center.** The center chronicles the "war" and sells guides to the island as well as leading walks Wed., Fri., and Sun. at 2:30pm. From the park, ascend the steep but short trail to "Mount" Young, the tallest hill on the island and a perfect place to take snapshots of Victoria and the Olympic Mountains (free; park open year-round; buildings open Memorial Day-Labor Day daily 8am-4:30pm).

Stop by the information kiosk in front of the **Hotel de Haro, the first hotel in Washington,** at the **Roche Harbor Resort,** Roche Harbor Rd. (378-2155), on the northern side of the island. The $1 brochure *A Walking Tour of Historic Roche Harbor* leads you through this old mining camp. Don't miss the bizarre mausoleum and the masonic symbolism that bedecks it.

If you're eager to **fish** or **clam,** pick up a copy of the Department of Fisheries pamphlet, *Salmon, Shellfish, Marine Fish Sport Fishing Guide,* for details on regulations and limits. The guide is available free at **Ace Hardware and Marine,** 270 Spring St. (378-4622). Hunting and fishing licenses are required, and can be obtained from the hardware store (open Mon.-Sat. 8am-6pm, Sun. 9am-5pm). Check with the **red tide hotline** (800-562-5632) if you'll be gathering shellfish.

The annual **San Juan Island Dixieland Jazz Festival** brings swing bands to Friday Harbor in late July. A $45 badge ($40 if purchased before July 1) gets you into all performances, but you'll have just as much fun for free if you join the crowds of revelers outside the clubs. Single performance tickets range from $15 to $25. For more information, contact San Juan Island Goodtime Classic Jazz Association, P.O. Box 1666, Friday Harbor 98250 (378-5509).

■ Orcas Island

Mt. Constitution overlooks much of Puget Sound from its 2409-ft. summit atop Orcas Island, the largest island of the San Juan chain. A small population of retirees, artists, and farmers dwell here in understated homes surrounded by the red bark of madrona trees and green shrubs. With the largest state park in Washington and a youth hostel, Orcas has the best budget tourist facilities of all the islands. Unfortunately, much of the beach access is occupied by private resorts and is closed to the public. The trail to **Obstruction Pass Beach** is the best of the few ways to clamber down to the rocky shores.

PRACTICAL INFORMATION AND ORIENTATION

Visitors Information: There is no visitors center, but the **Chamber of Commerce** (376-2273) returns phone calls. Your best bet is to pick up info about Orcas Island on San Juan Island or visit **Nature's Art** (376-4343), an embroidery shop on Horseshoe Hwy. in Eastsound that doubles as an informal information center.

Ferries: Washington State Ferry, 376-4389 or 376-2134. 24hr.

Taxi: Orcas Island Taxi, 376-TAXI/8294.

Transportation: San Juan Transit, 376-8887. Service about every 90 min. to most parts of the island. From the ferry to Eastsound $4, to Doe Bay $7.

Bike Rental: Wildlife Cycle (376-4708), at A St. and North Beach Rd., in Eastsound. 21-speeds $5 per hr., $20 per day. Open Mon.-Sat. 10:30am-5pm.

Kayak Tours: Shearwater Adventures (376-4699), at the corner of Northbeach Rd. and A St. in Eastsound. 3-hr. guided tours, $35.

Moped Rental: Key Moped Rentals (376-2474), just north of the fire station on Prune Alley in Eastsound. $12 per hr., $45 per 8-hr. day. Driver's license and $10 deposit required. Helmets, gas, and **maps** included. No pregnant women. Open May-Sept. daily 10am-6:30pm.

Library: 376-4985, at Rose and Pine in Eastsound. Open Tues.-Thurs. 10am-7pm, Fri.-Sat. 11am-4pm, Sun. 10am-3pm.

Senior Services Center: 376-2677, across from the museum on North Beach Rd. in Eastsound. Open Mon.-Fri. 9am-4pm.

Pharmacy: Ray's (376-2230, after-hours emergencies 376-3693), in Templin Center. Open Mon.-Sat. 9am-6pm, Sun. 10am-6pm.

Emergency: 911.

Post Office: 376-4121, on A St. in Eastsound Market Place. Open Mon.-Fri. 9am-4:30pm. **General Delivery ZIP Code:** 98245.

Area Code: 360.

Orcas is shaped like a horseshoe, which makes getting around a chore. The ferry lands on the southwest tip. Travel 9 mi. northeast to the top of the horseshoe to reach **Eastsound,** the island's main town. Olga and Doe Bay are an additional eight and 11 mi. from Eastsound, respectively, down the eastern side of the horseshoe. Stop in one of the four shops at the ferry landing to get a free **map.**

ACCOMMODATIONS AND CAMPING

Its a good idea to avoid the B&Bs on Orcas, which charge upwards of $60 per day; stay at the Doe Bay Resort or try a campground. Reservations help in summer.

Doe Bay Village Resort, Star Rte. 86, Olga 98279 (376-2291), off Horseshoe Hwy. on Pt. Lawrence Rd., 5 mi. out of Moran State Park. On a secluded bay. With its free-frolicking atmosphere, Doe Bay can be lots of fun. There's even a treehouse. Be prepared to sacrifice tidiness for atmosphere. The resort includes kitchen facilities, a health food store, an organic café, and extensive grounds for romping. The crowning attraction is the steam sauna and mineral bath ($3 per day, nonlodgers $6; bathing suits optional). Beds $12.50 for hostel-card carriers, $14.50 for others. Camping $16. Cottages from $41. Guided kayak trips twice daily; $35 for 3hr. (376-4755). Reservations recommended (only 8 bunks). Open year-round.

Moran State Park, Star Rte. 22, Eastsound 98245 (376-2326). Follow Horseshoe Hwy. straight into the park. The grandiose white arches tell you and hundreds of others like you that you're there. All the best of San Juan fun: swimming, fishing, and miles of hiking. Four campgrounds with a total of 151 sites. About 12 sites remain open year-round, as do the restrooms. Rowboats and paddleboats $10-13 for the 1st hr., $7 per hr. thereafter. Standard sites with hot showers $11. Hiker/biker sites $5. Reservations are strongly recommended May-Labor Day.

Obstruction Pass. Accessible only by boat or on foot. Just past Olga, turn off Horseshoe Hwy. and hang a right to head south on Obstruction Pass Rd. Soon you'll come to a dirt road marked "Obstruction Pass Trailhead"; if you reach the bay, you've gone too far. The sites are a ½-mi. hike from the end of the road. No water, so bring plenty. Pit toilets. A rocky but well maintained trail leads to a beach overhang, and, with patience, to a beach. 9 sites; free.

FOOD

All the essentials can be found at **Island Market,** on Langdell St. (376-6000; open Mon.-Sat. 8am-9pm, Sun. 10am-8pm). For all your natural needs, make a bee-line for **Orcas Homegrown Market** (376-2009), on Northbeach Rd. Large selection of groceries, medicines, and vegan cheeses. Try their deli for lunch, particularly the $5 vegetarian special (open daily 8am-11pm, winter 8am-9pm). For loads of fresh local produce, try the **Farmer's Market** in front of the museum (Sat. 10am-3pm).

> **Garden Cafe,** 10 Northbeach Rd. (376-5177), behind the Starfire gallery. Fresh, tasty Asian cuisine. The only seating is outside, but on a clear day, the peaceful garden and a plate of the cafe's *Panang* (a vegetable dish with coconut curry, $4.50) is a refreshing retreat from the bakery/café standard. Open Wed.-Sat. 11am-6pm.
>
> **Chimayo** (376-MEXI/6394), in the Our House Building on Northbeach Rd. A southwestern theme and comfy booths. Delve into a burrito-built-for-two ($2.75-3.50). Open Mon.-Tues. and Thurs.-Sun. 11am-7pm.
>
> **Rose's Bakery Café** (376-4220), in Eastsound Sq. on Northbeach Rd. Upbeat, offbeat staff serves up croissants ($1.25) and sandwiches ($6). Buy bags of day-old pastries at ½-price. Open Mon.-Sat. 8am-5pm.

SIGHTS AND ACTIVITIES

Trippers on Orcas Island don't need to travel with a destination in mind; at least half the fun lies in simply tramping about. Take advantage of the climbs on the hilliest of the San Juan Islands for inspiring views of the Sound and the rest of the archipelago. In between your meandering and meditations, stop by the island's numerous arts and crafts galleries.

Moran State Park is unquestionably Orcas's star outdoor attraction. Over 21 mi. of hiking trails cover the park, ranging in difficulty from a one-hour jaunt around Mountain Lake to a day-long constitutional up the south face of **Mt. Constitution,** the highest peak on the islands. Pick up a copy of the trail guide from the **registration station** (376-2326). From the summit of Constitution, you can see other islands in the group, the Olympic and Cascade Ranges, Vancouver Island, and Mt. Rainier. The stone tower at the top was built in 1936 by the Civilian Conservation Corps as an observation tower for tourists and a fire lookout. Though rental mopeds are not powerful enough to reach the summit, it is possible to drive to the top. The **Orcas Tortas** (800-967-1892) offers a slow ride on a green bus to the peak from Eastsound ($16). But the best way to go is by hiking—the most scenic route runs to Mountain Lake and then up the peak from there, a moderately taxing route which takes about 1½ hours. To shorten the hike, park your car at any one of the tree-lined lots along the road to the summit and proceed from there. For an abbreviated jaunt, drive up Mt. Constitution and hike part-way down to Cascade Falls, which is spectacular in the spring and early summer. Down below, you can swim in two freshwater lakes easily accessible from the highway or rent rowboats and paddleboats ($9 per hr.) from the park. Head from the lake to the lagoon for an oceanside picnic (park open daily 6:30am-dusk; Sept.-March 8am-dusk).

Continue along Horseshoe Hwy. to **Doe Bay Village Resorts** (376-2291), where you can soak in the natural mineral waters, sweat in the sauna, and have prophetic visions as you jump into the cold bath (bathing suits are the exception; see **Accommodations and Camping,** above). The **Sea Kayak Tour** (376-4699) of the surrounding islands, run by Shearwater Adventures, is a fascinating, albeit expensive, "waterhike" of the north end of Puget Sound. See bald eagles, seals, and blue herons up close ($35 per 3-hr. tour; tours include 30min. of dry-land training and also leave from Deer Harbor and Rosario Beach, see **Practical Information**). The resort grounds are secluded and make for good wandering.

■ Lopez Island

Smaller than either Orcas or San Juan, Lopez (or "Slow-pez") lacks some of the tourist facilities of the other islands. The island was settled largely by mutineers from ships charting Puget Sound who thrived in the secluded woods of the island. Today, Lopez Islanders still shy away from the mainland and maintain the age-old, if freakish, tradition of waving at every single car they pass.

Lopez Island is ideal for those seeking solitary beach-walking, bicycling, or a true small-town experience. It is, for the most part, free of both imposing inclines and heavy traffic. **Lopez Village,** the largest "town," is 3½ mi. from the ferry dock off Fisherman Bay Rd. To get there follow Ferry Rd. until it splits, then take a right. It's best to bring your own bicycle unless you're up for the hike. If you need to rent a bike or kayak, head to **Lopez Bicycle Works** (468-2847), south of the village next to the island's Marine Center. Even if you don't rent, the cheerful staff will give you a detailed **map** of island roads complete with mileage counts. This is the only outfit on the islands that rents real sea kayaks without guides (10-speeds and mountain bikes $5 per hr. and $23 per day; single kayaks $15 per hr., $50 per day, double kayaks $75 per day; guided tours $40 per person for half a day, $30 per person for "sunset paddle"; open June-Aug. daily 10am-6pm; call in winter).

Shark Reef and **Agate Beach County Parks** are two small parks on the south end of the island that offer a change from mainland campgrounds. Shark Reef has tranquil and well maintained hiking trails, and Agate's beaches are calm and deserted. The **Lopez Island Vineyards** (468-3644) on Fisherman's Bay Rd. are a must-see; for $1 you can sample all of their wines, and for $8-12 you can have a souvenir of your own (free equipment and tours of the grounds; open June 1-Sept. 7 Wed.-Sun. noon-5pm; Sept. 8-Dec. 23 and March 5-May 31 Fri.-Sat. noon-5pm).

If you decide to spend the night on the island, camping is your only hope for a good deal. **Spencer Spit State Park** (468-2251), on the northeast corner of the island about 3½ mi. from the ferry terminal, has 51 sites along 1 mi. of beachfront with good clamming in the late spring unless there is red tide. Some sites along the water, and pleasant wooded sites up the hill. Flush toilets, but no showers. Two lean-tos (called "Adirondacks") with eight bunks in each can be rented for $15, sites $11. No hookups. Call 800-452-5687 for reservations for summer weekends ($6 reservation fee). Park closed Nov. 1-Feb. 2; campers may enter until 10pm. **Odlin Park** (468-2496), is close to the ferry terminal, 1 mi. south along Ferry Rd. The park offers 30 sites and cold running water. There is a boat launch, volleyball net, baseball diamond, and pay phone on the grounds (sites for up to 5 people $13 with a vehicle, each additional person $2; hiker/biker sites $10). Stop by the park entrance on your way to the village to check out the Chamber of Commerce map. Or visit the "information booth" just west of the museum for free maps and clean pay showers.

Ferry transport has caused price inflation, so it's a good idea to bring a lunch to Lopez Island. **Village Market** has groceries (open Mon.-Thurs. 8am-7pm, Fri.-Sat. 8am-8pm, Sun. 9am-7pm). Sample fresh pastries, bread, and pizza at **Holly B's** (468-2133) in the village (from 85¢) or buy day-olds at a discount (open Wed.-Sat. 8am-5pm, Sun. and Mon. 8am-4pm). For a taxi, call **Angie's Cab** (468-2227). **Laundry** facilities lurk along Fisherman's Bay Road at **Keep It Clean,** 100 yards south of the winery (wash $1.75, 5-min. dry for 25¢; open Mon.-Sat. 8am-8pm, Sun. 9am-5pm). The **seniors' helpline** is 468-2421 (open Mon.-Fri. 9am-4pm). In an **emergency** call 911. The health clinic is **Lopez Clinic** (468-2245). You can find the **post office** (468-2282) in the Village on Weeks Rd. The **General Delivery ZIP Code** is 98261. The **area code** is 360.

■ Other Islands

Shaw Island is home to one store, 100 residents, wild turkeys, apple orchards and a bevy of Franciscan nuns. The convent lies on the water next to the ferry dock, and for the last 15 years, these women have been running the store/post office/gas station/ferry dock. Stop in for a couple of hours if only to take a walk, chat with a nun, or buy a postcard at the "Little Portion" store. The island's 11 mi. of public roads are endearing to hikers and bikers. **Shaw Island County Park,** on the south side of the island, has eight campsites ($10) that fill quickly despite the lack of running water. There is a also a shared camping site for hiker/bikers at $3, but space is limited. There are no other accommodations on the island.

Washington State Parks operates over 15 **marine parks** on some of the smaller islands in the archipelago. These islands, accessible by private transportation only, have anywhere from one to 51 mainly primitive campsites. The park system publishes a pamphlet on its marine facilities, available at parks or supply stores on the larger islands. One of the most popular destinations is tiny **Sucia Island,** which boasts gorgeous scenery and a few flopping seals. Canoes and kayaks can easily navigate the archipelago when the water is calm, but when the wind whips up the surf, only larger boats (at least 16 ft.) go out to sea. **Navigational maps** are essential to avoid the reefs and nasty hidden rocks that surround the islands. The Department of Natural Resources operates three parks; each has three to six free campsites with pit toilets but no drinking water. Cypress Head on **Cypress Island** has wheelchair-accessible facilities.

THE OLYMPIC PENINSULA

Due west of Seattle and its busy Puget Sound neighbors, the Olympic Peninsula is a remarkably different world. A smattering of logging and fishing communities and Indian reservations (along US Hwy. 101) lace the peninsula's coastline, but most of the ponderous land mass remains a remote backpacker's paradise. **Olympic National Park** dominates much of the peninsula and prevents the area's ferocious timber industry from threatening the glacier-capped mountains and temperate rainforests. However, the logging and fishing industries make living off the land the most common occupation on the peninsula. To the west the Pacific stretches to a distant horizon; to the north, the Strait of Juan de Fuca separates the Olympic Peninsula from Vancouver Island in Canada; and to the east, Hood Canal and the Kitsap Peninsula isolate this sparsely inhabited wilderness from the sprawl of Seattle.

GETTING THERE AND GETTING AROUND

Getting around the Peninsula is best done by car. Distances are great, and public transportation, while good for traveling to and between the Peninsula's small towns, does not serve the magnificent natural areas which are the main reason to come to the Peninsula. Most bus travel within the Peninsula itself is free or 75¢, and you can bring a bike. Public transportation heading into Olympic National Park, however, is sparse; hiking U.S. 101 to a trailhead can add many a paved and exhaust-filled mile to an otherwise tranquil trip. For a complete listing of how to get around the peninsula on public transportation, contact the **Rainforest Hostel,** 169312 U.S. 101, Forks 98331 (360-374-2270). The owners will be happy to help you navigate the various transit routes. Direct transfers between Greyhound, Grays Harbor Transit, West Jefferson Transit, Clallam Transit, and Port Angeles-Seattle Bus Lines can get you from Seattle, around the peninsula, and back for $16.75 on weekdays.

Bicycling on U.S. 101 is very dangerous. Long stretches have no shoulders and immense log trucks speed heedlessly along the winding road. Secondary roads on the Peninsula are often gravelly and poorly suited to cycling. Hitchhiking is poor in the Olympic Peninsula and illegal on most of U.S. 101.

■ Port Townsend

Unlike the salmon industry, the Victorian splendor of Port Townsend's buildings has survived the progression of time and weather. The town takes advantage of its 19th-century aura to keep its economy afloat and its facades freshly painted. The entire business district has been restored and declared a national landmark. You'll be lured in by countless cafés, art galleries, book shops, and an immense ice cream parlor on Water Street. Port Townsend is one of the few places on the Peninsula where espresso stands outnumber live bait shops.

Practical Information and Orientation The town's **Chamber of Commerce,** 2437 E. Sims Way, Port Townsend 98368 (385-2722), lies about 10 blocks from the center of town on Rte. 20. Ask the helpful staff for a free **map** and visitors guide (open Mon.-Fri. 9am-5pm, Sat. 10am-4pm, Sun. 11am-4pm). Find the **Public Library** at 1220 Lawrence (385-3181), uptown (open Mon. 11am-5pm, Tues.-Thurs. 11am-9pm, Fri.-Sat. 11am-5pm).

Jefferson County Transit (JCT), 1615 W. Sims Way (385-4777), operates Port Townsend's public transportation. You can easily reach Port Angeles, Poulsbo, Winslow, and Bremerton on JCT and connect with a neighboring transit system. Most buses do not run on Sunday (fares 50¢ and 25¢ per zone, seniors and disabled 25¢ per zone, ages 6-18 25¢; day passes $1.50). A Port Townsend **shuttle bus** loops around the town itself, and other service extends west along the strait to Sequim (50¢, seniors and students 25¢, under 6 free; day passes $1.50). For a **taxi,** call **Peninsula Taxi** (385-1872; open 24hr.).

P.T. Cyclery, 100 Tyler St. (385-6470), rents mountain bikes ($7 per hr., $25 per day; helmets, locks, and water bottles included; tandems and kid trailers available; open Mon.-Sat. 9am-6pm, Sun. by appointment). **Kayak P.T.,** 435 Water St. (385-6240), rents to kayakers with some experience (singles $25 for 4hr., doubles $45 for 4hr.; anyone over 84 rents for free; tours $39 for a ½-day, $68 for a day). **Sport Townsend,** 1044 Water St. (379-9711), rents out camping equipment (backpacks, pads, tents, and stoves; open Mon.-Sat. 10am-6pm, Sun. 11am-4pm). The local **Safeway pharmacy,** 442 Sims Way (385-2860), is open Mon.-Fri. 8:30am-7:30pm, Sat. 8:30am-6pm, Sun. 10:30am-6pm.

The Hospital is **Jefferson General,** 834 Sheridan (385-2200 or 800-244-8917). **Emergency Medical Care** (385-4622) is on the corner of Sheridan and 9th St. in the west end of town. In an **emergency,** call 911. The **police,** at 607 Water St., can be reached at 385-2322. The **Jefferson County Crisis Line** is 385-0321 (24hr.). **Poison control** is 800-732-6985. **Senior Assistance** (385-2552) is open Monday through Friday from 8:30am to 4:30pm. Port Townsend's **post office** is at 1322 Washington St. (385-1600; open Mon.-Fri. 9am-5pm. **General Delivery ZIP Code:** 98368). The **area code** is 360.

By land, Port Townsend can be reached from either **U.S. 101** or the **Kitsap Peninsula** across the Hood Canal Bridge. By water, take the **Washington State Ferry** (see p. 35 for scheduling and ticket information) from Seattle to Winslow on Bainbridge Island, and catch one of the Kitsap County Transit buses that meets every ferry and runs to Poulsbo. At Poulsbo, transfer to a Jefferson County Transit bus to Port Townsend. The Washington State Ferry also crosses frequently to and from Keystone on Whidbey Island. Ferries dock at Water St., west of downtown.

Accommodations and Camping The **Olympic Hostel (HI-AYH)** (385-0655), in Fort Worden State Park 1½ mi. from downtown (follow the signs), is situated right in the Fort in an old barrack with views of the ocean, plenty of space, and cushy hospital beds in the impeccable bunk room. Check out the Commanding Officer's house and Marine Science Center (see **Sights,** below). Kitchen facilities available ($11, nonmembers $14, cyclists $9-13; family rooms available; July-Sept. $12, nonmembers $15; check-in 5-10pm, check-out 9:30am; no curfew). The **Fort Flagler Hostel (HI-AYH),** in Fort Flagler State Park (385-1288), lies on handsome **Marrowstone Island,** 20 mi. from Port Townsend. From Port Townsend go south on Rte. 19, which connects to Rte. 116 East and leads directly into the park. Miles of pastoral bike routes wind over Marrowstone, and the hostel is less crowded than most. Another hostel in an old military haunt, the rooms are bright, clean and cheery, if a bit farther from local attractions. A storage and repair shed is open to bicyclists and has tools and a bike stand ($11, nonmembers $13, cyclists $9-12; open by reservation only; check in 5-10pm, lockout 10am-5pm).

Campers should try **Old Fort Townsend State Park** (385-4730), which has 40 beautiful but cramped sites and no potable water for $7 (hiker/biker sites $5). It is 5 mi. south of Port Townsend just off Rte. 20 (open mid-May to mid-Sept.). **Fort**

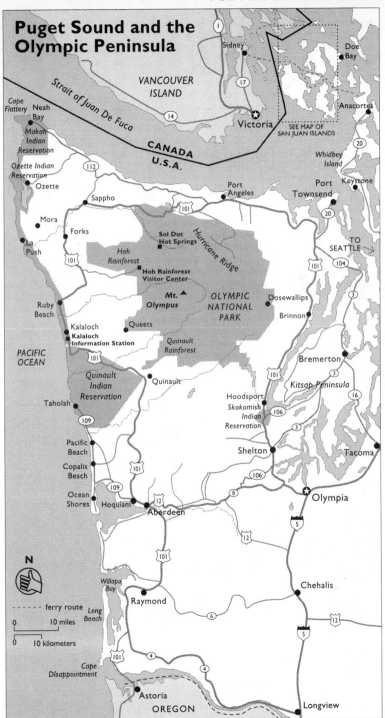

Puget Sound and the Olympic Peninsula

VANCOUVER ISLAND

Strait of Juan De Fuca

Sidney

Doe Bay

1

17

14

Cape Flattery

Neah Bay

Makah Indian Reservation

CANADA U.S.A.

Victoria

Anacortes

SEE MAP OF SAN JUAN ISLANDS

20

Whidbey Island

Keystone

Ozette Indian Reservation

Ozette

112

Port Angeles

Port Townsend

Mora

Forks

101

Sol Duc Hot Springs

Hurricane Ridge

20

La Push

101

Hoh Rainforest

Hoh Rainforest Visitor Center

TO SEATTLE

101

104

Ruby Beach

Mt. Olympus

OLYMPIC NATIONAL PARK

Dosewallips

3

Kalaloch

Queets

Brinnon

Kalaloch Information Station

101

Quinault Rainforest

Bremerton

PACIFIC OCEAN

Quinault Indian Reservation

Quinault

101

Kitsap Peninsula

3

Taholah

Hoodsport

16

109

Skokomish Indian Reservation

106

Pacific Beach

3

Shelton

Tacoma

Copalis Beach

101

106

Ocean Shores

109

Hoquiam

8

Olympia

12

Aberdeen

5

12

N

101

Willapa Bay

ferry route

Long Beach

Raymond

Chehalis

0   10 miles

6

12

0   10 kilometers

5

101

Cape Disappointment

4

4

5

Astoria

OREGON

Longview

WASHINGTON

Worden State Park (385-4730) has sites on the water for $15 ($16 April-Oct.). You can also camp on the beach at **Fort Flagler State Park** (385-1259; 116 sites; tents $11, RVs $16, hiker/biker sites $5). Reserve at both. Call parks directly.

Food   A huge **Safeway** at 442 Sims Way (385-2806), south of town along Rte. 20, serves any need. **Burrito Depot,** 609 Washington St. (385-5856), at Madison, offers quick, tasty Mexican food. Try the mouth-watering veggie fajita ($4.25), or fill up on big burritos from just $3 (open Mon.-Sat. 10:30am-8:30pm). For ridiculously healthy and entertaining food, try the **Coho Cafe and Juice Bar,** 1004 Lawrence St. (379-1030), at Polk St., uptown. A peppy paint job and local health nuts spice up the veggie roll-up ($4). Get your wheat grass shot here ($1). Open Tues.-Thurs. 7am-4pm, Fri.-Sat. 7am-8pm, Sun. 8am-4pm. The **Elevated Ice Cream Co.,** 627 Water St. (385-1156), is run by friendly folks receptive to the scruffy traveler. The Elevated serves delicious homemade ice cream and decent espresso (90¢). One scoop of ice cream or two mini-scoops of Italian ice costs $1.40 (open daily 9:30am-10pm; winter daily 11am-10pm).

Sights and Events   Port Townsend is full of huge Queen Anne and Victorian mansions. Of the more than 200 restored homes in the area, some have been converted into bed and breakfasts and are open for tours. The **Ann Starret Mansion,** 744 Clay St. (385-3205), has nationally renowned Victorian architecture, frescoed ceilings, and a free-hanging, three-tiered spiral staircase. Though it's now a bed and breakfast, people can take tours daily from noon-3pm ($2).

Go down the steps on Taylor St. to **Water Street,** the town's quaint main artery. Brick buildings from the1890s are interspersed with newer shops, art galleries, and cafés which have adopted the old-style motif. The **Jefferson County Museum** (385-1003), at Madison and Water St., showcases vestiges of the town's wild past. Highlights include a dazzling kayak parka made of seal intestines, jail cells in the basement (rumored to have held Jack London for a night), and an old-time pedal-powered dentist drill that will make your jaw hurt just looking at it (suggested donation $2; open Mon.-Sat. 11am-4pm, Sun. 1-4pm).

Point Hudson is the hub of the small shipbuilding area and forms the corner of Port Townsend, where Admiralty Inlet and Port Townsend Bay meet. North of Point Hudson are several miles of beach, **Chetzemolka Park,** and the larger **Fort Worden State Park** (open daily 6:30am-dusk). **Fort Worden** (385-4730), a strategic military post dating from the 1890s, guards the mouth of Puget Sound and commands views of Puget Sound. The fort went into service again in 1981 as a set for the movie *An Officer and a Gentleman.* History buffs should check out the **Commanding Officer's house** which, like practically every other building in Port Townsend, is stuffed to the rafters with Victorian furniture ($1; open daily April 1-Oct. 5 10am-5pm). Out on the pier at Fort Worden is the **Marine Science Center** (385-5582). Get up close and personal with the local sea life in several tanks. Daily interpretive events put an educational spin on the gawking ($2, children $1; open Tues.-Sun. noon-6pm; fall and spring Sat.-Sun. noon-4pm).

From mid-June to early September, **Centrum** sponsors a series of festivals in Fort Worden Park. The organization supports blues, jazz, folk, and classical music, along with poetry readings, dance performances, and workshops with artists-in-residence. Two of the most popular events are the **Festival of American Fiddle Tunes** in early July and **Jazz Port Townsend** later in the same month. Ticket prices vary; combination tickets can be purchased for all of each festival. For a schedule, write the Centrum Foundation, P.O. Box 1158, Port Townsend 98368 (385-3102 or 800-733-3608, ext. 1). Other annual attractions include the **Wooden Boat Festival,** held the first weekend after Labor Day, and the **House Tour,** held the following weekend, when many mansions are open to visitors free of charge. For more information, contact the Chamber of Commerce.

WASHINGTON

■ Port Angeles

Port Angeles is ideally situated between Olympic National Park and the gorgeous blue waters of the Strait of Juan de Fuca, but the town's character remains on the bland side of nebulous. An era of domination by paper and plywood mills has ended, and Port Angeles joins the legions of small towns hungering after the tourist dollar. Stop in town for information and transportation connections.

Practical Information Get visitors information at the **Chamber of Commerce,** 121 E. Railroad (452-2363), next to the ferry terminal, 1 block from the intersection of Lincoln and Front St. The office allows free local calls (open daily 8am-9pm; winter Mon.-Fri. 10am-4pm, Sat.-Sun. noon-4pm).

Port Angeles is served by **Greyhound,** 1115 E. Front (800-231-2222). Buses run to Seattle twice a day Monday through Saturday, once Sunday ($15, seniors $14). **The Coho Ferry,** 101 E. Railroad Ave. (457-4491), has service to Victoria ($6.50, $9.60 with bicycle, $26 with car, $3.25 for children). The **Clallam Transit System,** 830 W. Lauridsen Blvd. (800-858-3747 or 452-4511), serves the Port Angeles area and all of Clallam County, as far as Forks and Neah Bay (Mon.-Fri. 4:15am-11pm, Sat. 10am-6pm; fare within downtown 50¢, ages 6-19 35¢, disabled 25¢). **Car Rental** is available at **Evergreen Auto Rental,** 808 E. Front St. (452-8001). Low-end cars start from $29 per day, $170 per week with 50 mi. free, 20¢ per mile thereafter. Must be 21 yrs. old with proof of insurance. Every conceivable type of mountain equipment except sleeping bags can be rented from **Olympic Mountaineering, Inc.,** 221 S. Peabody St. (452-0240). Tents cost $20 per day; external frame packs are $13 per day, cross-country ski gear is $15 per day. The list goes on and on, and weekly rates are lower. Olympic Mountaineering also leads fairly inexpensive overnight (and longer) treks into the Olympic N.P. wilds. Call for more info. (Open Mon.-Sat. 9am-6pm, Sun. 10am-5pm.) **Pedal 'n' Paddle,** 120 E. Front St. (457-1240), rents mountain bikes ($8 per hr., $22 per day, helmets included).

The local **laundromat** is the **Peabody Street Coin Laundry,** 212 Peabody St. (452-6493; wash $1.25, 8min. dry 25¢; open 24hr.). The **post office** sits at 424 E. 1st St. (452-9275), at Vine (open Mon.-Fri. 8:30am-5pm, Sat. 9am-noon; **General Delivery ZIP Code: 98362**). **Area code:** 360.

Accommodations and Camping A night indoors in Port Angeles is costly, especially in the summer (winter rates drop $5-15). Budget believers should check out **The Spa,** 511 E. First St. (452-3257); get off the bus at Bonnie's Bakery. Everything you thought a Pacific Northwestern hostel would be. Everyone huddles down in the same room and breakfasts in the garden tea room. Reserve a matt or futon ahead of time. $15 per night including breakfast. The least expensive motel options line noisy U.S. 101. A few miles west of town, the **Fairmont Motel,** 1137 U.S. 101 W. (457-6113), has decent, cable-equipped rooms with a food mart next door (queen bed $37; winter rates lower). The **Royal Victorian Motel,** 521 First St. (452-2316), has newly remodeled rooms with microwaves, refrigerators, and wheelchair access. Managers provide limo service to and from the ferry dock. Lowest rate is a single by the street ($39). Check-in between 2pm and 11pm.

Heart o' the Hills is the closest campground (see **Olympic National Park: Northern Park Rim,** p. 370); unless you come after hours, you'll need to pay the $5 park entrance fee (good for 7 days) plus the $11 camping fee. The campground has no hook-ups, but does offer lush surroundings, handicap sites, and ranger-led programs on summer evenings. No reservations; open year-round. Or, try **Salt Creek County Park** (928-3441), a 20-min. drive east along Hwy. 112 from Port Angeles. Many of the park's 80 sites have waterfront views and the nearby tidepools are a treasure trove of sea stars and hermit crabs. Unlike National Park Campgrounds, Salt Creek has pay showers. No hook-ups or reservations. The closest free camping is **Boulder Creek Campground,** at the end of Elwha River Rd., 8 mi. past Altaire. Park at the end of the road, and hike 2 mi. along an abandoned road. Check out the natural hot springs while you're there (see **Olympic National Park: Northern Park Rim** p. 370). You'll need a free **backcountry permit,** available at the trailhead, to pitch at one of the 50 sites. Be sure to bring your own water.

Food Seafood is abundant, but grill the waiters to be sure it's fresh. An excellent place to sample the local catch is **La Casita,** 203 E. Front St. (452-2289). This Mexican restaurant stuffs its seafood burrito ($7) with generous amounts of crab, shrimp, and fish, and has free all-you-can-eat tortilla chips and salsa while you sip your $2 margarita (open Mon.-Thurs. 11am-9pm, Fri. 11am-10pm, Sat. 11am-10pm, Sun. noon-9pm). The new **Bella Italia** (457-5442) at 117B E. First St. gets rave reviews from Port Angelians. For $7, a hungry vegetarian can sit down to a hefty plate of veggie lasagna. The bustling **First Street Haven,** 107 E. 1st St. (457-0352) serves up strawberry Belgian waffles ($5.50), or the "Prospector," a huge shrimp sandwich (open Mon.-Fri. 7am-4pm, Sat. 8am-4pm, Sun. 8am-2pm). Picnickers can peruse the shelves of **Safeway,** (457-0788) 110 E. 3rd St. at Lincoln St. (open 24hr.).

Sights Port Angeles correctly bills itself as the "Gateway to the Olympics" but the city itself has little to offer. Before you go anywhere, stop by **Port Brook and News,** 104 E. 1st, which has a large **map** selection and can give you insider's advice on the best trails and campgrounds in the area. Find a book to weigh down your pack in their extensive used book section. For those without a vehicle and disinclined to ride a bike uphill for 20 mi., **Olympic Van Tours** (452-3858) runs three-hour or all-day excursions to Hurricane Ridge for $13-16 (see **Olympic National Park: Northern Park Rim** p. 370). The **Olympic National Park Visitors Center,** 3002 Mt. Angeles Rd. (452-0330), on Race St., dispenses free **maps** (open daily 9am-4pm, summers daily 8:30am-6pm). More accessible by foot is the **Arthur D. Feiro Marine Laboratory** (417-6254), offering a large classroom of touch tanks and aquariums with local marine life. The lab is operated by Peninsula College ($2, seniors and under 12 $1; open daily 7am-8pm; Oct.-June 14 Sat.-Sun. noon-4pm). Passing over the pier is the 6-mi. **Waterfront Trail,** a handicapped-accessible path that provides an overview of the city's portside activities.

The **Fine Arts Center,** 1203 E. 8th St. (457-3532), in the vicinity of the National Parks Visitors Center, offers great views of the water and small but excellent exhibits by regional artists. And hey, it's free (open Thurs.-Sun. 11am-5pm).

■ Olympic National Park

Olympic National Park is the centerpiece of the Olympic Peninsula, and contains perhaps the most diverse landscape of any national park. From the glacier-crusted peaks in the park's interior, to the lush and dripping **rainforests** in its western river valleys and the jagged shores of the Pacific Coast, the park appeals to the wide range of tastes of an even wider range of visitors. Roads lead to many interesting parts of Olympic National Park, but they only scratch the surface. Leave the pavement behind and delve into the backcountry to fully appreciate the many faces of the park, and avoid the hordes of tourists who descend annually. A day of salmon fishing on the Hoh River, an afternoon of shell hunting on miles of isolated beach, or a week of glacier-glazing from the tree line can be had with a little effort and planning.

The Olympic Mountains at the park's center wring huge quantities of moisture from the heavy Pacific air. Average precipitation in the park varies, but 12 ft. of rain and snow yearly is common; some areas average over 17 ft. The mountains take so much of the clouds' water that some areas northeast of the park get less than 1½ ft., making them among the driest in Washington. The rainforests lie on the west side of the park, along the coast, and in the **Hoh, Queets,** and **Quinault river valleys,** where moderate temperatures, lots of precipitation, and summer fogs support a fantastic Northwestern jungle dominated by Sitka spruce and western red cedar. The rest of the park is populated by Douglas fir and hemlock lowland forest, silver fir at higher elevations, and flower-filled mountain meadows which offer stunning views and are often accessible only by foot.

Sea stacks—bluffs left standing offshore—and ancient indian petroglyphs lend the beaches along the unspoiled coast a sense of mystery. Forests and rocky headlands edge the wide, driftwood-strewn beaches. During the off season, the only evidence of human existence you're likely to encounter is another hiker.

Visitors to the Peninsula may be stock by the extensive patches of naked mountainside left by **logging,** particularly on the western side. The National Park is totally protected from logging, and within the Park scarred views will disappear, but both the private land, and the National Forest surrounding it, are harvested by timber companies (see **Camping and the Outdoors,** p. 43). The State of Washington manages huge tracts along the Hoh and **Clearwater** Rivers, near the western shore. Until recently, private and state agencies pursued policies of "liquidation of old growth," a phrase illuminated by the western segment of U.S. 101. At times the highway is a corridor through clearcuts, with placards indicating the dates of harvest and replanting. Due to the spotted owl uproar and federal regulations banning logging on public land, the Forest Service stopped harvesting any Olympic timber in the late 1980s, and private and state harvesting has also slowed. Environmentally conscious travelers should avoid the issue with locals. Those who earn a living from forest resources dislike lectures on how to manage them. They will probably point out that the consumer of forest products is as responsible for clearcutting as the logging and paper industries themselves.

PRACTICAL INFORMATION AND ORIENTATION

Visitors Information: Olympic Visitors Center, 3002 Mt. Angeles Rd., Port Angeles (452-0330), off Race St. The Park's main information center. Fields questions about the whole park, including camping, backcountry hiking, and fishing. Look for the **map** of the locations of other park ranger stations. Also houses exhibits about the park, and a hands-on **Discovery Room** for children and adults (open daily 9am-4pm, June-Sep. 8:30am-6pm). **Park Headquarters,** 600 E. Park Ave., Port Angeles (452-4501, ext. 311), is just an administrative office but can answer phone questions. Open Mon.-Fri. 8am-4:30pm. **Olympic National Park Wilderness Center** (452-0300), just behind the Visitor's Center, has a helpful staff well versed in backcountry procedures. They will gladly sit down with backpackers and help design trips within the park. The Wilderness Center is the only place on the north end of the park to make reservations for the four Olympic NP backcountry areas that require reservations (see **Camping on the Peninsula,** below). Call 800-233-0321 for **State Parks Information.**

Entrance Fee: $5 per car and $3 per hiker or biker is charged during the day at the developed entrances, such as Hoh, Heart o' the Hills, Sol Duc, Staircase, and Elwha (all with paved roads and toilet facilities). The fee buys an entrance permit good for 7 days—keep that receipt!

Park Weather: 452-0329. 24hr.

Park Radio: 530 AM for road closures and general weather conditions, **610 AM** for general park rules and information.

Park Emergency: 452-4501. Daily 8am-5pm; at other times phone 911.

Area Code: 360.

Only a few hours from Seattle, Portland, and Victoria, the pristine rainforest wilderness of the **Olympic National Park** is most easily and safely reached by car. The roads that exist are accessible from U.S. 101 and serve as trailheads for over 600 mi. of hiking. No roads cross the entire park. There are a few outposts strewn about the interior of the park area, but **Port Angeles** and **Forks** are the only sizeable towns in which gas and food are always available. (For more information, see **Olympic Peninsula: Getting There and Getting Around,** p. 361.)

July, August, and September are the best months to visit Olympic National Park, since much of the backcountry remains snowed in until late June, and only summers are consistently rainless (which, of course, brings flocks of fellow sightseers; expect company). Coming from Seattle, the best place to start an exploration of the park is the **Olympic Visitor's Center** (see above), where cheerful rangers hand out park maps and give advice on all aspects of travel within the park. Hwy. 101 continues on in a U shape, with Port Angeles at the top. From Port Angeles, many visitors drive down the western leg of the U and through the park quickly in one day.

Explore the different climates of the park by driving to **Hurricane Ridge,** continuing on U.S. 101 southward, and detouring to the **Hoh Rain Forest Visitors Center** and then again southward on U.S. 101 to the pristine beaches near the **Klaloch Information Station.** While this whirlwind automobile tour gives a good overview of the park's potential, it in no way does it justice. There is much to be done along the way—trails to be hiked, beaches to be combed, photos to be taken. One could easily spend weeks here. The map distributed at the park gates and most ranger stations and information centers gives an excellent overview of the entire park as well as most of the peninsula. Robert Steelquist's *Olympic National Park and the Olympic Peninsula: A Traveler's Companion* gives wonderful, clear descriptions of the area with high quality photographs, and Robert Wood's *Olympic Mountains Trail Guide* is the best book for those planning to tackle the backcountry ($14.75 at any area bookstore or information center).

The perimeters of the park are well defined, but are surrounded by National Forest, Washington Department of Natural Resources, and other public land. The Park Service runs **interpretive programs** such as guided forest walks, **tidepool walks,** and campfire programs out of its ranger stations (all free). For a schedule of events, pick up a copy of the park newspaper from ranger stations or the visitors center.

Fishing within park boundaries does not require a permit, but you must obtain a state game department punch card for salmon and steelhead at local outfitting and hardware stores, or at the Fish and Game Department in Olympia. Though fishing is good in any of the park's 15 major rivers, the **Elwha River,** coursing through the northeastern part of the Park, is best for **trout.** The Hoh River, flowing west through the Park, is excellent for **salmon.** Ask at a fishing equipment store for current information.

CAMPING ON THE PENINSULA

Though motels are plentiful, you can camp for only a few bucks within walking distance of one of the world's three temperate rainforests. Olympic National Park, Olympic National Forest, and the State of Washington all maintain free campgrounds, and the Washington Department of Natural Resources (DNR) allows free backcountry camping off any state road on DNR land, as long as campers set up over 100 yards from the road. The majority of DNR land is near the Western shore along the Hoh and Clear Water Rivers, though they also manage smaller, individual campsites sprinkled around the peninsula. The DNR publishes a guide to all its Washington sites which can be obtained at visitors centers and ranger stations. Pick up a **map** of the park and area from a ranger station for comprehensive information. In summer, competition for campground space can be fierce, particularly on weekends. From late June to late September, most sites are taken by 2pm, so start hunting early; in the more popular areas and along the Hoh River, find a site before noon.

Camping by Car

Free **National Park campgrounds** include **Ozette** (with drinking water) and **Queets** (no water). In addition, the National Park has many standard campgrounds (sites $10). Fees in **National Forest Campgrounds** range from $4-12; six campgrounds in the Hood Canal Ranger District are free. Reservations can be made for three Forest Service campgrounds (Seal Rock, Falls View, and Klahowga) by calling 800-280-CAMP/2267. Any ranger station can provide information on Park and Forest Service Campgrounds. Several **State Parks** are scattered along Hood Canal and the eastern rim of the peninsula (sites generally $10-16; occasionally $4-5).

Backcountry Camping

To fully experience the diversity of the park—and to escape the oppressive crowds of summer—strap on your backpack, stock up on instant oatmeal, and hike to the backcountry. Whether in the rainforest, along the coast, or in the high country, certain general guidelines and rules apply: backcountry camping anywhere in the park requires a free backcountry permit, available at any ranger station and most trailheads. The purpose of the permit is to provide the park with information on internal traffic as well as your location in case of an emergency. Four destinations within the park issue a limited number of backcountry permits in response to the area's popularity. These are **North Beach** by Lake Ozette (452-0300), the **Soleduck District** and **Grand Valley** (327-3534), and **Lake Constance** and **Flapjack Lakes,** both overseen by the Hood Canal Ranger Station in Hoodsport (877-5254).

Reservations are crucial, especially at Lake Ozette and the campgrounds to the west which are 100% reservable (the rest are 50% first come, first served); call a few days in advance. Backpackers should be prepared for a mix of weather conditions at all times. Even in summer, the driest season, parts of the park are very wet. Always have a good waterproof jacket and waterproof hiking boots with good traction; trails can become rivers of slippery mud. Even in summer, layers of warm clothing and a wool hat are a good idea (see **Camping and Hiking Equipment,** p. 45). *Never* drink any **untreated water** in the park. *Giardia lamblia,* a nasty bacteria, lives in all these waters and causes severe diarrhea and abdominal cramps (see **Common Ailments,** p. 14). You can boil your water or buy water purification tablets at the visitors center and most camping supply stores. **Black bears** and **raccoons,** eager to share your granola and peanuts, are another potential hazard for backcountry campers. To prevent mishaps, ranger stations offer lessons on hanging food out of reach when they issue your backcountry permit. Some stations have free rope available, but don't count on it. Bring your own 50-100 ft. of thin, sturdy rope. A map and signs at the trailhead will tell you whether **open fires** are permitted in the backcountry area. For any backcountry trip, make sure to inquire at a ranger station about trail closures in advance. Winter weather has destroyed many a popular trail.

HOODSPORT AND EASTERN PARK RIM

The eastern and northern sections of the Park have the most heavily developed and used sites. Here the mountain canyons rise steeply and their jagged edges are breathtaking. A good source for information about this region is the joint Park/Forest Service **Hood Canal Ranger Station,** P.O. Box 68, Hoodsport 98548 (877-5254; open daily 8am-4:30pm; winters closed weekends). Hikers use these campgrounds as trailheads to the interior, parking their cars and hiking in. **Staircase Campground** (877-5569) is a major camping hub 16 mi. northwest of **Hoodsport** at the head of Lake Cushman (59 sites, $8 on top of the $5 Park entrance fee; RV accessible). To get there, turn west off U.S. 101 at Hoodsport, pass the Hood Canal Ranger Station, take a left after 9 mi. and follow the signs. **Lake Cushman State Park** (877-5491; 800-452-5687 for reservations), on the way to Staircase, is a popular base camp for extended backpacking trips into the National Forest and Park. Along with good swimming beaches, the park offers showers (3min. for 25¢) and flush toilets (80 sites for $11, 30 with full hookup $16).

Super-tough hikers should tackle the steep 3-mi. trail up **Mt. Ellnor,** 17 mi. east of Hoodsport. Get directions from the ranger station. On a clear day, the **view** from the top is spectacular: the Olympic range unfolds to the northwest, and Puget Sound, Seattle, Mt. Rainier, Mt. Adams, and the rim of Mt. St. Helens tower to the southeast. Back down at sea level, reward yourself with a giant ice cream cone at **Fuddy Duddy's** (877-9344), on U.S. 101, in Hoodsport. Hoodsport also has a few small **grocery stores;** it might be wise to stock up, because the next ones are 50 mi. north in Sequim. Drop by the **Hoodsport Winery,** 23501 U.S. 101 N. (877-9894), just south of town for tasting and tours (open daily 9am-7pm). Adjacent to the ranger station in Hoodsport is a **post office** (877-5552; open Mon.-Fri. 9am-5pm, Sat. 8:30am-11:30pm; **General Delivery ZIP Code:** 98548).

WASHINGTON

Dosewallips (doh-see-WALL-ups), on a road that leaves U.S. 101 27 mi. north of Hoodsport, has 32 less developed campsites ($8; not for RVs). A beautiful trail leads from Dosewallips across the park to **Hurricane Ridge** and a number of other popular backpacking trails, and takes several days. Thirty mi. north of Hoodsport, the **Quilcene Ranger Station,** 295142 U.S. 101 S. (765-3368) can point you to the **Mt. Walker View Point,** 5 mi. south of Quilcene on U.S. 101. A one-lane gravel road takes you four mi. to the lookout, the highest viewpoint accessible by car. The road is steep, has sheer drop-offs, and should not be attempted in foul weather or in a temperamental car. A phat view of Hood Canal, Puget Sound, Mt. Rainier, and Seattle awaits intrepid travelers on top. Picnic tables are provided on the east side; feast as you gaze at 7743-ft. **Mt. Constance** from the north side.

NORTHERN PARK RIM

The most developed part of Olympic National Park is along the northern rim near Port Angeles, where day trips to glaciers, rainforests, and sunsets over the Pacific are all possible. **Heart o' the Hills Campground** (452-2713), 5½ mi. from Port Angeles on Race Rd., is filled with vacationers poised to take **Hurricane Ridge** by storm the next day (105 sites; $10, plus the $5 entrance fee). The campground has no hookups or showers, but plenty of huge trees, fairly private sites, handicap access, and family-oriented evening campfire programs. The road up the ridge is an easy drive for those short on time, but the curves might make you queasy. Clear days bring splendid views of Mt. Olympus and Vancouver Island, with a foreground of snow and indigo lupine. The ridge can be crowded; the ideal time to go is sunrise. After the herds arrive, more seclusion can be found on the many short trails that originate here, including some designed for seniors and the disabled. Signs at the visitor's center give updates on visibility at the summit, but the best bet for camera-toters is to call ahead of time (452-0330) before tackling the 40 minute drive. On weekends from late Dec. to late March, the Park Service organizes free guided **snowshoe walks** atop the ridge. Call the visitors center (452-0330) for details.

For similarly stunning views without the company of Buicks and BMWs, drive up the spur to **Deer Park,** just east of Port Angeles, where trails are less crowded and vistas are just as plentiful. After hiking, breathe in the thin mountain air at the park's highest car-accessible camping (4500 ft.), **Deer Park campground** ($6, summer only). Come early and bring water—the campground's 14 sites have none. Trailers and RVs are prohibited. Farther west on U.S. 101, a short spur road to the south leads to two campgrounds along the waterfall-laced Elwha river: **Elwha Valley** (452-9191; 41 sites, $10), 5 mi. south off U.S. 101, and the nearby **Altaire** (452-9191; 30 sites, $10). Both have drinking water and flush toilets. Just past the Altaire campground, park at the Appleton Pass and Olympic Hotspring trailhead and hike 2½ mi. to the natural hotsprings. Intrepid bathers beware: it's possible to pick up a variety of infections in the warm, bacteria-friendly water. Follow the unmarked foot paths to more secluded, less used baths to stay on the safe side. The nearby backcountry camping area has 14 free primitive sites (with a backcountry permit).

Back on U.S. 101, head west to **Fairholm Campground** (928-3380), 30 mi. west of Port Angeles at the tip of **Lake Crescent,** which has sites—some handicap accessible—with drinking water (87 sites, $10). **The Storm King Ranger Station** (928-3380; hours vary because it is staffed by volunteers) runs evening interpretive programs at Fairholm Campground. Hikes around this glacier-scarred lake promise views of old-growth forests and the brilliantly blue waters of one of the only natural lakes in Washington (most exist because a river was dammed).

The **Marymere Falls Trail** (2-mi. roundtrip) through old-growth Douglas firs, western hemlock, and red cedar is great for those with kids or short on time. It leaves from the ranger station and the first ¼ mi. is wheelchair accessible. A number of more difficult and more scenic trails begin here; check at the ranger station for conditions. Farther west on U.S. 101, 13 mi. of paved road will get you to the **Sol Duc Hot Springs Campground** (327-3534), which has 80 sites with handicap-accessible restrooms right by the popular **Sol Duc Hot Springs Resort** (327-3583; open daily

9am-9pm, weekends in winter 9am-5pm, $6.25 per day, seniors $5.25), where retirees pay for a soak in the developed, chlorinated hotsprings and eat at the restaurant or snack bar inside the lodge. There are scheduled programs every evening except Friday. According to Native American legend, the source of the **Sol Duc Springs** and the **Olympic Springs** are two "lightning fish" who, after a long and indecisive battle, gave up the fight and crept into two caves, where they still weep hot tears of mortification. The Sol Duc trailhead is also a starting point for those heading for the heights; stop by the **Eagle Ranger Station** (327-3534; open June-Aug. daily 8am-5pm) for information and free backcountry permits. The **Sol Duc Trail** draws many tourists, but crowds thin dramatically above Sol Duc Falls.

EXPLORING THE RAINFOREST

Olympic National Park is home to one of the world's few temperate rainforests. Gigantic old-growth trees, ferns, and mosses blanket the valleys of the Hoh, Queets, and Quinault Rivers, along the west side of the Park. Although the forest floor is thickly carpeted with foliage and fallen trees, rangers keep the many walking trails clear and well-marked.

Many travelers seek out the **Hoh Rainforest Trail** which begins at the **Hoh Rainforest Visitor Center** (see below) and parallels the Hoh River for 18 mi. to Blue Glacier on the shoulder of Mount Olympus. Shy Roosevelt elk and northern spotted owl inhabit the area. The drive to the Hoh is stunning in some parts but some land belonging to the Department of Natural Resources has been, or is in the process of being, clear-cut. The first two campgrounds along the Hoh River Rd., which leaves U.S. 101 13 mi. south of Forks (see below), are administered by the DNR, accept no reservations, and are free. Drinking water is at the **Minnie Peterson** site only. DNR sites are uncrowded except in July and August; stay at one and drive to the Hoh trailhead to get a **map** and begin your rainforest exploration. You can obtain a separate **map** of the Hoh-Clearwater Multiple Use Area from the DNR main office, just off U.S. 101 on the north side of Forks.

The **Hoh Rainforest Visitor Center** (374-6925) provides posters and permits (open daily 9am-6:30pm; Sept.-June daily 9am-3:30pm). Once at the visitor's center (a good 45min. drive from U.S. 101), take the quick **Hall of Mosses Trail** (45min.) for a Cliff Notes version of rainforest vegetation or try the slightly longer, one-hour **Spruce Nature Trail.** The Spruce leads through lush forest and along the banks of the river with a smattering of educational panels to explain Mama Nature's bizarre details. Backcountry trails leading to **Mount Olympus** also begin here. Near the visitors center, the national park maintains 89 sometimes soggy sites ($10) with drinking water and flush toilets, but no handicap facilities.

Several other trailheads from U.S. 101 offer more solitude for the hiker and excellent opportunities to explore the **rainforest** amid surrounding ridges and mountains. The **Queets River Trail** follows the Queets River east from the free Queets Campground for 14 mi. The campground is at the end of a spur road that goes east from U.S. 101, 5 mi. south of the town of Queets (20 sites for tents only; open June-Sept.). The road is unpaved and unsuitable for RVs or large trailers. High river waters early in the summer can thwart a trek. Your best chance is in August, but there's still a risk that you'll be cut off. A shorter, 3-mi. loop is as much as most visitors can see of Queets. Elk are often spotted in fields along the trail, which passes a broad range of rainforest, lowland river ecosystems, and the park's largest Douglas fir. A ranger station at the trailhead can give you more information.

The Park and Forest Services and the Quinalt Reservation share the land surrounding **Quinault Lake and River,** a popular destination for vacationers coming from the southwestern corner of Washington. The Forest Service operates a day-use beach and an information center at the **Quinault Ranger Station,** South Shore Rd. (288-2444; open daily 9am-4:30pm; winter Mon.-Fri. 9am-4:30pm). From the Quinalt Ranger Station, it's 20 mi. to the North Fork trailhead, from which intrepid hikers can journey 44 mi. north across the entire park and finish at Whiskey Bend. Those with less time or energy have the day hike options of 1-8 -mi. trails leaving from the Graves Creek

Ranger Station. Between the coast and rainforest, the logging town of **Forks** on U.S. 101 offers cheap motels and food.

Forks is the only town to speak of on the western side of the park and is the perfect place to stop, stock up, and learn about timber culture from plaid-shirted, suspender-wearing locals. Get your dose of country music here—the only radio station plays nothing but Garth Brooks and Tammy Wynette. Forks lies a hefty two hours west of Port Angeles.

On the south end of town on U.S. 101, stop at the Forks Chamber of Commerce (374-02531 or 800-44-FORKS/36757; open daily 9am-4pm). Route 14 of **Clallam Transit** (452-4511 or 800-858-3747; see **The Olympic Peninsula: Getting There and Getting Around,** p. 361) serves Forks with trips to Port Angeles on every day but Sunday (50¢, seniors free, ages 6-19 35¢, disabled 25¢). The **post office** is on the corner of Spartan Ave. and A St., one block east of U.S. 101 (open Mon.-Fri. 9am-5pm, Sat. 10am-noon). Call the **police** at 374-2223 and the **hospital** at 674-6271. For emergencies, call 911. **General delivery ZIP code:** 98331. **Area code:** 360.

The closest budget accommodation to Forks is the **Rainforest Hostel,** 169312 U.S. 101 (374-2270). Owners Kay and Jim take any traveler into their home-turned-private-hostel (beds $10), but day-time passersby are welcome to stop in for a shower ($1.50). The house has animals and a fair amount of lovable clutter, but a trailer is available for those with allergies. The place is a font of information. To get there, follow the hostel signs off U.S. 101, 4 mi. north of Ruby Beach. In Forks itself, stay at the **Town Motel,** 1080 S. Forks Ave. (374-6231 or 800-742-2429), which has clean, well-kept rooms with lots of ruffles and a gardenful of dahlias (singles $34, doubles $46).

For good home-cooked food, drop in at the **Raindrop Café,** 111 E. A St. (374-6612), at S. Forks Ave., for a $6 gourmet burger. Play the "table topic" games while waiting for your food (open daily 6am-9pm, Sun. 6am-8pm; winter daily 5am-8pm). Grab groceries and a coffee at **Forks Thriftway** (374-6161), on U.S. 101 (open daily 8am-10pm; winter 8am-9pm). Make sure to get gas here, since there are few other stations further south.

EXPLORING THE BEACHES AND COAST

Fifty-seven mi. of pristine coastline await visitors on the Park's western coast. Piles of driftwood, sculptured arches, dripping caves, and abundant wildlife frame an often perfect sunset. **Sea stacks** (bits of coast stranded at sea after erosion swept away the surrounding land) jut from the waves and lend the coastline an eerie, rugged look. Bald eagles soar on windy days, and whales and seals speed through the sea. Between the Hoh and Quinault Reservations, U.S. 101 hugs the coast, with parking lots just a short walk from the sand. This 15-mi. stretch of beach begins in the north with **Ruby Beach** near Mile 165 on U.S. 101, where you can often see sea otters and eagles if you explore the excellent tide pools or sea stacks. Camping on this stretch of beach is not allowed; head north for beach camping. South of Ruby Beach at Mile 160 is Beach #6, a favorite whale-watching spot. Beach #4, three mi. south, has particularly abundant tidepools. South of Beaches #4 and #6 is **Kalaloch** (KLAY-lok) **Center,** a crowded campground with 177 sites near the ocean, including a lodge, a general store, a gas station, and a ranger station. Gather at low tide for talks on the tidepools; consult the park newspaper or bulletin boards at campgrounds for specific times.

The beach is a protected coastal wilderness for hiking and **backcountry camping.** Camping is permitted all along the beaches, except along the Kalaloch strip by U.S. 101. Those who camp along this stretch of beach can bask in the glory of easy, flat hiking, long evenings capped by resplendent sunsets reflected on the Pacific and a continually changing seascape. Before hiking or camping along the coast, pick up a required **permit**, a park map, a **tide table,** and the useful *Olympic Coastal Strip* brochure at a ranger station. Find the tide-line from the previous tide and use the tide table to calculate how many feet the tide will change while you are there. Then make camp well above where the next tide will be. The same common-sense approach applies to walking coastal trails: don't attempt a stretch of beach that could become submerged while you're walking it. Several stretches of beach lie within land belonging to the Makah, Ozette, Quileute, Hoh, and Quinault Native nations. A continuous 57-mi. beach trek is impossible; reservation land is private and may not be crossed by hikers without permission.

Farther north, between the Hoh and Quileute reservations, is a 17-mi. stretch dominated by rocky headlands. At the end of this strip, **Mora Beach** (374-5460), due west of Forks near the Quileute Reservation, has a drive-in campground (sites $10) and a ranger station. From **Rialto Beach** near Mora, you can hike 21 mi. north along the coast to a free campground and roadhead at **Ozette Lake** (by reservation only; call 452-0300) or just linger to absorb Rialto Beach's eccentric caves and sea stacks.

Day hikers or backpackers should not miss the 9-mi. loop that begins at Ozette Lake. The trail is a triangle with two 3-mi. legs along boardwalks through the rainforest. One heads toward the sea stacks at Cape Alava, the other to the gorgeous beach at Sand Point. A 3-mi. hike down the coast passes ancient native petroglyphs as it connects the two legs. While the entire area is relatively flat and the boardwalks are easy for children, slogging through the sand can still be tough going. Overnighters must make permit reservations in advance. The summer months fill up quickly. The **Ozette Ranger Station** (963-2725; open daily 8am-4:30pm) can offer further information. For permit reservations, call 452-0300.

■ Cape Flattery and Neah Bay

Trivial Pursuiters take heed: Cape Flattery is the northwesternmost point in the contiguous U.S., and possesses enough interest outside of geographical trivia to make it worth the hour-long drive off U.S. 101. In 1778, the area caught the attention of explorer James Cook, who named the tip Cape Flattery because it "flattered us with the hopes of finding a harbor." At the westernmost point on the strait is **Neah Bay,** the only town in the **Makah Reservation,** and home to a museum displaying finds from a 15th century village. Rte. 112 leads west from Port Angeles to Neah Bay; from the south, take the short road north from **Sappho.** The **Clallam Transit System** (800-858-3747 or 452-4511) reaches Neah Bay. Take bus #14 from Oak St. in Port Angeles to Sappho (75min.). Then take bus #16 to Neah Bay (60min.). Check schedules at the Port Angeles Greyhound Station to avoid long layovers (75¢, ages 6-19 60¢, seniors free). In case of **emergency,** call 911 (645-2236 in a **marine emergency**). The **area code** is 360.

Still teasing would-be explorers, **Cape Flattery** can only be reached through Neah Bay. Follow the road until it becomes dirt; stay on it for another 4 mi. until you reach a small, circular parking area. A trailhead then points you toward Cape Flattery. The half-hour hike rewards those willing to risk twisted ankles with bombastic views of Tatoosh Island just off the coast and Vancouver Island across the strait. A few miles south of Cape Flattery is **Hobuck Beach,** where camping and picnicking are within car's reach. Coming from Neah Bay, turn left just before you reach the Cape Flattery resort, cross the bridge, and take the first right to the **Hobuck Beach Park** (645-6422), with outhouses, running water, and camping space for $10 per night (no reservations). To the south, the beaches are more secluded, probably because they're available only to foot traffic. The beaches are property of the reservation and respectful visitors are welcome.

Back in Neah Bay, the **Makah Cultural and Research Center** (645-2711), on Hwy. 112, houses artifacts from an archaeological site at Cape Alava, where a huge mudslide 500 years ago buried and preserved a small Makah settlement. One exhibit expertly reproduces a room from a longhouse, complete with animal skins, cooking fire, and the smell of smoked salmon. Once inside the reservation, the museum is on the first left, directly across from the Coast Guard station ($4, seniors and students $3; open daily 10am-5pm; Sep.-May Wed.-Sun. 10am-5pm). The Makah nation, whose recorded history goes back 2000 years, still lives, fishes, and produces artwork on this land. During the weekend closest to Aug. 26, Native Americans from around the region come to participate in canoe races, traditional dances, and bone games (a form of gambling) during the **Makah Days.** Visitors are welcome and the delicious salmon bake is a definite highlight. Contact the museum for information.

THE PACIFIC COAST

■ Willapa Bay

The place to be for wildlife viewing is Willapa Bay, which divides the Long Beach peninsula from the mainland. U.S. 101 passes the bay as it winds along the border of the Olympic National Park and down the Washington Coast into Oregon. On its way out of the park it passes by Grays Harbor and through the industrial cities of **Aberdeen** and **Hoquiam** at the mouth of the Chehalis River. Unpleasant and grimy, these mid-sized cities have everything you'd expect in the way of malls, movie theaters, and motels. Aberdeen even sports a favorite son, Kurt Cobain, who (needless to say) got the hell out as soon as he could. U.S. 101 continues amid Willapa Bay's sparkling sloughs and pastoral farmlands, and more than compensates for the protected bay's ban on swimming and sunning. From the north, stop at the headquarters of the **Willapa National Wildlife Refuge** (484-3482), just off U.S. 101 on the left, the last unpolluted estuary in the U.S. and a sanctuary for seabirds and waterfowl. Check out the expertly stuffed birds inside the office—they'll help you know what to look for in the sanctuary.

No trails are directly accessible from the headquarters, but rangers can point out directions to several "units" scattered through the Willapa Bay region, including a unit at Leadbetter Point on the tip of the Long Beach Peninsula and one on **Long Island** in Willapa Bay accessible only by boat. The refuge offers a rare opportunity to observe Canada geese, loons, grebes, cormorants, trumpeter swans, and other birds. The greatest avian diversity descends upon the area during the fall and winter months; simultaneously, the greatest number of birdwatchers descend on the Leadbetter Point unit, about 45 minutes from headquarters. Long Island is Willapa Bay's most impressive attraction. The island teems with deer, bear, elk, beaver, otter, and grouse. It also supports a 274-acre cedar grove, one of the Northwest's last **climax forests,** still growing new trees after 4000 years. The cedars average 160 ft. in height; and some reach 11 ft. in diameter.

Long Island is home to five limited-use **campgrounds,** all inaccessible by car. Reaching the island is a problem; you'll have to find your own boat or bum a ride. Boats should be launched from the Wildlife Refuge Headquarters; the channel at this point is only about 100 yd. wide, though too muddy to swim. After reaching the island, hike 2½ mi. along the island's main road to reach the **Trail of Ancient Cedars.** The **office** at the Refuge furnishes advice on getting to the island and **maps** marked with campgrounds. Try your hand at digging **razor clams;** a two-day license costs $6. Morning low tides in spring and fall are best.

■ The Long Beach Peninsula

Long Beach Peninsula, with 28 mi. of unbroken beach accessible by U.S. 101 and Rte. 103 (which runs the length of the peninsula), is an overwhelming combination of kites, souvenir shops, and beaches. Fishing, swimming, boating, and kite-flying fill the warmer months, allowing residents to recuperate from the pounding winter storms. You can beachcomb for **glass balls** from Japanese fishing nets carried on a 10 year journey to Washington's shores by the Kuroshio current; locals say they have the most luck on the Ocean Park section of the beach. Permits are required for gathering **driftwood** in state parks.

During clamming season (usually from Oct. to mid-March; call 249-4628 to check with the **Washington Department of Fish and Wildlife** for season status), look for dimples or bubbles in the sand to find the notoriously fast-digging but succulent razor clams. If you're willing to shell out $10.50 for an annual non-resident license and spend a few days learning the ropes, you can harvest a seafood feast. (Be extra careful of the **red tide**.) Free tide tables are available at information centers and businesses. Access to the "world's longest beach" is easy to find; almost any east-west road to the peninsula ends in a parking lot by the sand.

Make Yogi Bear proud by **berry picking** in late summer. Wild varieties are an arm's reach away along the roadside. The peninsula contains nearly 500 acres of cranberry bogs, but be careful about picking on private property. This area is one of only four places in the U.S. where cranberries are grown. Most of the bogs are in Grayland along Cranberry Rd., parallel to Hwy. 105.

The **Long Beach Peninsula Visitors Bureau** (642-2400 or 800-451-2542), five minutes south of Long Beach on U.S. 101, has pamphlets galore on activities in Long Beach and the vicinity. **Pacific Transit** buses (in Raymond 642-9418, in Naselle 484-7136, farther north 875-9418) provide cheap local transportation. For 85¢ and a transfer, you can take a bus as far north as Aberdeen; exact change required. Buses run up and down the peninsula itself about 15 times per day. Schedules are available in post offices and visitors centers (service Mon.-Fri. 2-3 times per day).

The city of Long Beach invites kite flyers from Thailand, China, Japan, and Australia to the **International Kite Festival** (642-2400) during the third week of August. Late July brings the **Sand Castle Festival** to town. In 1989, a world record tumbled when participants built a 3-mi.-long fortress of sand. Call the Long Beach Peninsula visitors bureau (see above) for more information. If you're stopping in the town of Long Beach, check out **Marsh's Free Museum** (642-2188) along S. Pacific Way. Mechanical fortune tellers and "Jake," the amazing half man-half alligator featured in the *National Enquirer,* will win your dollars and your heart. Open (ironically) whenever tourists bring money. Alanis, eat your heart out.

THE COLUMBIA RIVER ESTUARY

Several miles south of Long Beach lies **Cape Disappointment** and the **Columbia River Estuary.** In 1788, bitter British fur trader and well-known grouchy-gus Captain John Meares, frustrated by repeated failures to cross the treacherous Columbia River sandbar, named the water now known as Baker Bay **Deception Bay,** and the large promontory guarding the river's mouth Cape Disappointment. Since then, more than 230 vessels have been wrecked, stranded, or sunk where the Columbia meets the ocean, a region aptly named "the graveyard of the Pacific."

Fort Columbia State Park (777-8221) lies on U.S. 101 northwest of the Astoria Megler Bridge, 1 mi. east of Chinook on the west side of the highway. The fort was built in 1896 and armed with huge guns to protect the mouth of the river from an enemy that never materialized (hence, even more disappointment). The park's **interpretive center** recreates life at the fort, and includes an exhibit on the indigenous Chinook people who once occupied this land. A wooded 1-mi. trail takes you past several historical sites (park open daily 6:30am-dusk; Oct. 16-March Wed.-Sun. 8am-dusk; center open Wed.-Sun. 9am-5pm). What was once the area's hospital is now the fantastic **Fort Columbia Youth Hostel,** P.O. Box 224, Chinook (777-8755; see p. 433).

In nearby **Ilwaco,** at the southern tip of the Peninsula, **Fort Canby State Park** (642-3078) offers camping and a megadose of Lewis and Clark. The Park was the dynamic duo's final destination and it boasts two lighthouses and a well-pruned campground packed with RVs and Adler trees. The sites fill up quickly in the summer months (180 tent sites $11, 86 RV hookup sites $16, and 5 hiker/biker sites $5. Full facilities include hot pay showers; call 800-452-5687 to make reservations, $6 fee). Enjoy models and working miniature trains at the fun, highly worthwhile **Ilwaco Museum,** 115 Lake St. (642-3446). Its four galleries take you through the history of the area. (Open summer Mon.-Sat. 9am-5pm, Sun. noon-4pm; winter Mon.-Sat. 9am-4pm, Sun. 10am-4pm. $2, under 12 75¢.)

At the end of the main road sits the **Lewis and Clark Interpretive Center,** above the ruins of the fort. Inside, a winding display documents the Lewis and Clark expedi-

WASHINGTON

tion from its Missouri origins to the party's arrival at the mouth of the Columbia, and the explorers' painstakingly detailed journal entries speak for themselves. The park is open daily from dawn to dusk and the center is open daily in the summer from 10am-5pm. The **North Head Lighthouse,** built in 1898, is in the northwest corner of the park and is accessible by a paved path. A clear day allows both a dizzying view of the Pacific cliffs and $1 tours between 10am and 6pm on the hour (summers only). The **Cape Disappointment Lighthouse,** built in 1856—the oldest in the Northwest—is in the southeast corner of the park and can be reached by puffing ¼ mi. up a steep hill from the Coast Guard station parking lot or by clambering half a mile along a narrow trail from the interpretive center (see above). For a magnificent beach-level view of the Cape Disappointment Lighthouse, drive through the campground area past **Waikiki Beach** on the **North Jetty.** Though not quite Honolulu, Waikiki Beach is ideal for swimming in summer, beachcombing after storms in winter, and year-round ship-watching.

The early 1990s is an era Ilwaco would like to forget. The 1993 Endangered Species Act and record-low salmon counts closed the commercial salmon season for two years. But salmon populations are on the rise, and gleeful local fishing companies are back on the water. Picking up a salmon steak from one of many fisheries along the Ilwaco waterfront is the budget way to sample the tasty fish, but many charter companies offer fishing trips for landlubbers who want to learn the art of fishing first hand. **Pacific Salmon Charters,** P.O. Box 519, Ilwaco 98624 (642-3466), in the Port of Ilwaco, leads eight-hour fishing tours (providing coffee and tackle), starting at $59 (trips run daily at 6am). Wander farther down the port of Ilwaco to **Smalley's Galley** (642-8700), which serves tasty clam chowder ($3.50), fish and chips ($6), and hamburgers with fries ($4; open Sun.-Mon. 4am-4pm, Wed. 5am-4pm, Thurs.-Fri. 4am-4pm, Sat. 4am-7pm).

Among the cheapest places to sleep on the Long Beach Peninsula is the **Sand-Lo-Motel,** 1910 Pacific Hwy., equipped with the added perk of coffee makers in each room (642-2600; singles and doubles $41, rates drop in winter; call early for reservations). Keep in mind that the beautiful and inexpensive Fort Columbia Youth Hostel lies just 15 minutes down the road in **Fort Canby State Park** (see **Astoria, OR,** p. 433). The friendly folks at **My Mom's Pie Kitchen** (642-2342), 4316 S. Pacific Hwy., make a meal that is an inexpensive and welcome respite from Long Beach's steak houses and greasy spoons. "My Mom's special," a half sandwich, soup or salad, and half a piece of pie costs a mere $7. Open Wed.-Mon. 11am-4pm.

For the best meal around, point your car down Rte. 103 to **Oysterville,** and purchase a dozen oysters for around $3.50. A tiny, whitewashed town, the featured attraction is the **Oysterville farm** (665-6585) which raises, cleans, packs, and dishes out the delicacy. They'll even let you check out the baby oysters (open daily March-Oct. 10am-5pm).

CASCADE RANGE

In 1859, an explorer making his way through the Cascade Range gushed: "Nowhere do the mountain masses and peaks present such strange, fantastic, dauntless, and startling outlines as here." Native people summed up their admiration more succinctly, dubbing the Cascades "Home of the Gods."

Intercepting the moist Pacific air, the Cascades divide Washington into the lush, wet green of the west and the low, dry plains of the east. The white-domed peaks of Mt. Baker, Vernon, Glacier, Rainier, Adams, and Mt. St. Helens are accessible by four major roads offering trailheads and impressive scenery. **U.S. 12** through White Pass approaches Mt. Rainier National Park and provides access to Mt. St. Helens from the north; **I-90** sends four lanes past the major ski resorts of Snoqualmie Pass; scenic **U.S. 2** leaves Everett for Stevens Pass and descends along the Wenatchee River, a favorite of whitewater rafters.

Rte. 20, better known as the **North Cascades Hwy.,** is the most breathtaking of the trans-Cascade highways and one of the most amazing drives in North America. From spring to fall it provides access to the wilderness of **North Cascades National Park.** Rte. 20 and U.S. 2 are often traveled in sequence as the **Cascade Loop.**

Greyhound runs on I-90 and U.S. 2 to and from Seattle, while **Amtrak** parallels I-90. Rainstorms and evening traffic can slow hitchhiking; locals warn against thumbing across Rte. 20. (*Let's Go* does not recommend hitchhiking.) The Cascades can only be explored properly with a car. The mountains are most accessible in the months of July, August, and September; many high mountain passes are snowed in during the rest of the year. The Cascade range is attractive primarily to serious backpackers. Crowds are usually deterred by the day's climb to most flat spots. The best source of general information on the Cascades is the joint **National Park/National Forest Information Service,** 915 2nd Ave., Seattle 98174 (206-220-7450).

▓ Mount St. Helens

In a single cataclysmic blast on May 18, 1980, the summit of Washington's Mt. St. Helens exploded into dust, creating a hole 2 mi. long and 1 mi. wide in what had been a perfect cone. The postcard-perfect peak that so many Washingtonians had camped, fished, and played upon suddenly ceased to exist. The force of the steam and ash-filled blast robbed the mountain of 1300 ft. in height and razed entire forests. Ash from the crater rocketed 15 mi. upward, blackening the sky for days and blanketing towns with black powder. Debris spewed from the volcano flooded Spirit Lake and choked rivers as far away as the Columbia. The explosion itself was three times the force of the atomic bomb dropped on Hiroshima.

The **Mount St. Helens National Volcanic Monument,** administered by the Forest Service, encompasses most of the "blast zone," the area around the volcano affected by the explosion. This ashy landscape, striking for its initially bleak expanses, is steadily recovering from the explosion that in minutes transformed 150 sq. mi. of prime forest into wasteland. The spectacle of disaster is now freckled by signs of life; saplings push their way up past denuded logs, and insects and small mammals are returning. Much of the monument is off-limits to the public because of ongoing delicate geological experiments and the fragile nature of the blossoming ecosystem. Like many other Cascade Peaks, the volcano still threatens to erupt, but probably won't do so again for several hundred years.

PRACTICAL INFORMATION AND ORIENTATION

Visitors Information: Because driving times around the Monument are long, a number of visitors centers and information stations line the highways surrounding the volcano, both inside and outside the monument itself. Plan the side you will approach the monument from, and find the most convenient visitors center.

Mount St. Helens National Volcanic Monument Visitor Center (206-274-2100 or 206-274-2103 for 24hr. recorded info). For most visitors, especially those coming from Seattle on I-5, this is the first stop on a tour of the volcano. The center is an excellent introduction to the mountain, with displays on eruption and regeneration and plenty of interactive exhibits for the gadget-lover or aspiring geologist. An infinitely patient staff help visitors find camping spots and navigate **maps.** Check for road closures. The free 22-min. film *The Eruption of Mount St. Helens,* with graphic footage of the eruption and its aftermath, is shown every hour on the hour daily mid-June to Aug. To reach the center (and the western side of the volcano), take Exit 49 off I-5 and follow signs along Rte. 504. The visitors center is 5 mi. east, across from Seaquest State Park. Open daily May-Sept. 9am-5pm; call for winter hr.

Coldwater Ridge Visitors Center (274-2131; fax 274-2129), follow Rte. 504 38 mi. from Monument Visitor Center. This sprawling glass and copper building has a superb view of the collapsed cavity and trails leading to a boardwalk along **Coldwater Lake,** which was created by the eruption. Emphasis on the recolonization of living things. Picnic areas, interpretive talks, and a gift shop/snack bar. Open daily 10am-6pm; Sept.-April 9am-5pm.

Johnson Ridge Observatory, a few miles east on Rte. 504. Scheduled to open in May of 1997. Named for David Johnson, a geologist who died in the eruption, this center focuses on the geology of the volcano. Call Coldwater Ridge (see above) for hr. and info.

Forest Learning Center (414-3439), outside the monument boundaries on Rte. 504, between the Mt. St. Helens visitor center and the Coldwater Ridge center. This massive propaganda machine houses impressive exhibits on the reclamation of the thousands of acres of Weyerhauser timber downed by the explosion. Open May-Oct. 10am-6pm.

Woods Creek Information Station, take Hwy. 12 on the north side of the volcano, go 6 mi. south of Randle on Rd. 25. An attendant answers your questions from the comfort of your car; info on hiking, camping, and Mt. Ranier. Pick up maps here. Open June-Sept. daily 9am-4pm, closed Wed. through June.

The Pine Creek Information Station, from Rd. 90 on the south side of the monument go 17 mi. east of Cougar. Shows a film of the eruption of Mt. St. Helens to prepare visitors for an excursion. Open June-Sept. daily 9am-6pm.

Apes' Headquarters, at Ape Cave on Rd. 8303, on the south side of the volcano, for questions on the lava tube. Open daily May 25-Sept. 30, 10am-5:30pm.

The Monument Headquarters (750-3900 or 750-3903 for 24hr. recorded info), 3 mi. north of Amboy on Rte. 503. Not a visitors center, but call for specific, detailed info on road conditions, and permits. They are in charge of **crater-climbing permits** (see below). Open Mon.-Fri. 7:30am-5pm.

Publications: *The Volcano Review,* a yearly publication available free at all visitors centers and ranger stations, is the tourist's Bible for Mt. St. Helens. Contains a **map** (you *will* get lost without it), copious info, and schedules concerning activities at the Monument. For a more thorough tour of the area, buy a copy of the *Road Guide to Mount St. Helens* for $5 at a visitors center.

Forest Information: Gifford Pinchot National Forest Headquarters, 6926 E. 4th Plain Blvd., P.O. Box 8944, Vancouver, WA 98668 (206-750-5000). Camping and hiking info within the forest. Additional **ranger stations** at: **Randle** (360-497-1100), north of the mountain on U.S. 12 and east of the Wood Creek visitors center; **Packwood** (360-494-0600), east on U.S. 12; **Wind River** (509-427-3200), south of the mountain on Forest Service Rd. 30 and north of the town of Carson in the Columbia River Gorge; and **Mt. Adams** (509-395-3400), at Trout Lake, southeast of the mountain on Rte. 141 and above White Salmon in the Columbia River Gorge. All stations are open Mon.-Fri. 8am-5pm; some open on weekends, but hours change season to season; call ahead.

Crater Climbing Permits: Between May 15 and Oct. 31, the Forest Service allows 100 people per day to hike to the crater rim. Reserve in person or write to **The Monument Headquarters,** 1hr. north of Portland off Rte. 503 at 42218 NE Yale Bridge Rd., Amboy 98601 (750-3900). 60 permits are available on reserve. The Forest Service begins accepting applications Feb. 1. Write early; weekends are usually booked before March, and weekdays often fill up as well. Climbers who procrastinate should head for **Jack's Restaurant and Country Store** (231-4276), Rte. 503, 5 mi. west of Cougar (I-5 Exit 21), where 40 unreserved permits are available each day. At 6pm the evening before the climb, a lottery is held outside of Jack's and 40 lucky adventurers get the go ahead for the following day. Any group larger than 4 must enter the lottery for a separate permit. All permits are free. Call the Monument Headquarters (750-3900) for more info. See **Climbing the Mount,** below.

Climbing Hotline: 247-5800. Info on snow, temperature, visibility, wind, and other vital factors that might affect climbing the volcano.

Radio Station: 530 AM. Road closures and station hours.

Emergency: 911.

Area Code: 360.

In order to have a blast at the volcano, visitors should do a fair amount of planning. The main **access routes** skirt the monument widely and views from different approaches to the volcano are drastically different. To explore all sides in a day would be impossible. Vigorous winter rains often decimate access roads making any long drive difficult. Check at a ranger station for **road closures** before heading out.

Visitors usually take one of three approaches to the Monument. From the **west,** many Seattlites and interstate travelers take Exit 40 off I-5 and travel Rte. 504, otherwise known as the **Spirit Lake Memorial Hwy.** The brand new 48-mi. road has wide shoulders and beautiful views of the crater. For most, this is the quickest and easiest day trip to the mountain, and the **Mount St. Helens Visitors Center,** the **Coldwater Ridge Visitors Center,** and the **Johnston Ridge Observatory** line the way to the volcano. This drive also lures the Winnebago battalions and summer crowds.

Along the **north** side, **U.S. 12** stretches from I-5 east, continuing to **Yakima.** The towns of **Mossyrock, Morton** and **Randle** line U.S. 12 and offer the closest major services to the popular Northeast part of the monument. Off U.S. 12 at Randle, Rte. 25 offers access to the **Iron Creek Campground, Windy Ridge,** and **Spirit Lake** (all laced with good hiking), and striking views of both the crater and the Blow Zone, where acres of blasted trees abut healthy forests.

Rte. 503 parallels the **south** side of the volcano until it connects with **Rd. 90.** The town of **Cougar** lies along Rte. 503, and Rd. 90 leads to the Climbers' Bivouac. The Ape Cave lava formations and visitors center, as well as several campgrounds are also located along Rd. 90. From the southern approach, Mt. St. Helens tricks the viewer with the illusion of pre-eruption serenity. Though views from this side don't highlight recent destruction, green glens and remnants of age-old explosions make this a better side for hiking and camping.

CAMPING

Although the monument itself contains no campgrounds, a number are scattered throughout the surrounding national forest. Free dispersed camping is allowed within the monument, meaning that if you stumble upon a site on an old forest service road you can camp out there, but finding a site is a matter of luck. The closest campsite to the scene of the explosion is the **Iron Creek Campground,** just south of the Woods Creek Information Center on Forest Service Rd. 25, near its junction with Rd. 76 (98 sites, $8). For reservations call 800-280-CAMP/2267. Only 15 sites can be reserved; the rest are first-come, first-camped. Farther south is **Swift Campground,** on Forest Service Rd. 90, just west of the Pine Creek Information Station. Swift is run by Pacific Power & Light (503-464-5023; 93 sites, $8; no reservations). Two other PP&L campgrounds lie west of Swift Campground on Yale Reservoir; both accept reservations and have toilets and showers. **Beaver Bay,** with 63 RV and tent sites ($8), sits 2 mi. east of **Cougar Campground,** which offers 45 sites ($8).

Seaquest State Park (274-8633), on Rte. 504, 5 mi. east of the town of Castle Rock at Exit 49 off I-5 and across from the visitors center, has 92 pleasant wooded sites ($10), four of which are primitive and reserved for hikers and bikers ($5). Full facilities include handicap sites and pay showers. No trails begin here, but this is one of the easiest campgrounds to reach on I-5 and the closest State Park with showers and hookups. Reservations in summer are a must. Call **Reservations Northwest** (the state park reservation system) to make one (800-452-5687).

OUTDOORS

The drive east on Rte. 504 offers plentiful views of the crater and blast devastation, but little opportunity for rigorous hiking. A network of dirt paths and wheelchair-accessible trails fan out over the area surrounding volcano-born Coldwater Lake below the visitors center. The ½ mi. "Winds of Change" trail has signposts aplenty to explain the eerie surrounding landscape. Another 10 mi. east, take a hike along Johnson Ridge, only 5½ mi. from the crater where geologist David Johnson died.

The first stop for visitors traveling south on Rd. 25 from Randle and U.S. 12 should be the **Woods Creek Information Station.** Viewpoints are listed on various handouts at the visitors center and include the **Quartz Creek Big Trees** and **Ryan Lake.** Continue south 9 mi. until you reach Rd. 99 going west. The newly paved, two-lane

Rd. 99 passes through 17 mi. of curves, clouds of ash, and cliffs. Trailer owners should leave their "crafts" in the **Wakepish Sno-Park,** the designated trailer drop at the junction of Rds. 25 and 99. Without stops it takes nearly one hour to travel out and back on Rd. 99, but the many talks, walks, and views along the way make stops worthwhile. Rd. 99 winds among the trees before opening onto the blast area where thousands of trees were felled in seconds. This area offers a chance to see the work of a volcano first hand. Unfortunately, torrents in the spring of 1996 ravaged many roads on the east side of the monument; make sure to check for road closures (listen to 530 AM) before heading to Rds. 25 or 99.

On the way west along Rd. 99, **Bear Meadow** provides the first interpretive stop, an excellent view of Mt. St. Helens, and the last restrooms before Rd. 99 ends at spectacular **Windy Ridge.** The monument begins just west of here, where Rd. 26 and Rd. 99 meet, at **Meta Lake.** Rangers lead 45-minute walks to this emerald lake from June through September (daily at 12:30pm and 3pm); meet at the old **miners' car** at the junction of Rds. 26 and 99. The trail around the lake is an easy ½ mi. jaunt, and illustrates the regenerative abilities of lake ecosystems.

Farther west along Rd. 99, frequent roadside turnouts offer information on the surroundings, unbeatable photo opportunities, and trailheads for hikers. These turnouts reveal the full effects of the blast, from trees felled like match sticks to pumice plains and the stump-choked waters of **Spirit Lake. Independence Pass Trail #227** (3½ mi., 4-hr. roundtrip) is a difficult hike with overlooks to Spirit Lake and superb views of the crater and dome that get only better as you go along. For a serious hike, continue along this trail to its intersection with the spectacular **Norway Pass Trail,** which ends on Rte. 26. The entire hike is 6 mi. long, takes about five and a half hours, and requires a vehicle at both ends. The trail lies within the Blast Zone and fans believe it is the best hike in the monument. Farther west, **Harmony Trail #224** (2 mi., 1½-hr. roundtrip) provides the only public access to Spirit Lake. Rangers lead a daily hike from the **Harmony Viewpoint** to Spirit Lake along this trail during the summer at 1:30pm. This trail is easy going down, but the return trip is tough.

Windy Ridge, at the end of Rd. 99, is worth the winding trip. From here, you can climb atop an ash hill for a magnificent view of the crater from 3½ mi. away. In summer, forest interpreters describe the eruption during talks held in the Windy Ridge amphitheater (every hr. on the ½hr., daily 11:30am-4:30pm). The **Truman Trail** leaves from Windy Ridge and meanders 7 mi. through the "Pumice Plain," where hot pyroclastic flows sterilized the land, leaving absolutely no life. Because the area is under constant scrutiny by biologists, its important to stay on the trails at all times.

Even inside "the beast," there are accessible places. The **Pine Creek Information Station** lies 25 mi. south of the Rd. 25-Rd. 99 junction. Take Rd. 90 12 mi. west and then continue 2 mi. north on Rd. 83 to **Ape Cave,** a broken 2½-mi.-long lava tube formed in an ancient eruption. To explore the cave, wear a jacket and sturdy shoes. Lanterns may be rented for $3, or bring your own flashlights or Coleman lanterns. Each expedition must have at least two.

Rd. 83 continues 9 mi. farther north, ending at **Lahar Viewpoint,** the site of terrible mudflows which followed the eruption. Nearby, **Lava Canyon Trail #184** offers three hikes with views of the **Muddy River Waterfall.**

Those with strong legs and a taste for conquest should scale the new, stunted version of the mountain to glimpse the lava dome from the crater's rim. Although not a technical climb, the route up the mountain is a steep pathway of ash strewn with boulders. Often the scree (a layer of loose shale) is so thick that one step forward includes a half-step back. (The trip down is often accomplished on the triumphant climber's ass.) The view from the top is magnificent. As you perch on the lip of the crater, listening to rumbling rockfalls, there are incredible views of Mt. Rainier, Mt. Adams, Mt. Hood, Spirit Lake, and the lava dome directly below. Average hiking time up is five hours and down is three hours. Bring sunglasses, sunscreen, sturdy climbing boots, foul-weather clothing, plenty of water, and gaiters to keep your boots from filling with ash. Free camping is available at the **Climber's Bivouac** (although water is

WASHINGTON

not), the trailhead area for the **Ptarmigan Trail #216A,** which starts the route up the mountain. For information on permits, see **Practical Information,** above.

■ Cowlitz Valley

The **Cowlitz River** originates from the tip of a Rainier glacier and cuts a long, deep divot west between Mt. Rainier and Mt. St. Helens, before turning south to flow into the Columbia River. Although your view of St. Helens and Rainier will be obscured when you sink into the Cowlitz Valley, your loss is compensated by miles of lush farmland. There is not much to do in this area besides traveling between Mt. Ranier and Mt. St. Helens, but the area contains the nearest major services to the parks.

The river forms part of the watershed for both the **Mt. Adams** and **Goat Rocks Wilderness Areas,** to the west and northwest of Mt. St. Helens. Both areas are excellent hiking country, accessible only by foot or horseback, and include sections of the **Pacific Crest Trail** among their extensive trail networks. The rugged Goat Rocks area is famous for its herd of mountain goats, and Mt. Adams seduces hundreds of climbers each year with its snow-capped summit (12,307 ft.). This area is particularly attractive because it receives less attention than neighboring wilderness areas. Two **ranger stations** in the valley are at 13068 U.S. 12, **Packwood** (494-0600), and at 10024 U.S. 12, **Randle** (497-1100). Contact the Forest Service at one of these locations for trail guides and other information.

The Cowlitz passes closest to Mt. St. Helens near the town of **Morton.** This logging town is accessed by U.S. 12 from the east and west (I-15 Exit 68), Rte. 508 from the west (I-5 Exit 71), and Rte. 7 from the north. The town's main festival is the **Loggers Jubilee** in mid-Aug., with beauty pageants, wood carving contests, races and a dance. The **Cody Café** (496-5787), on Main St., serves a mountainous stack of pancakes ($2.25). Lunches run from $3 to $5 (open Mon.-Fri. 4am-9pm, Sat. 5am-9pm Sun. 6am-2pm). If you are staying overnight in the area, head for the lime-green **Evergreen Motel** (496-5407), at Main and Front St. The rooms may be plain, but they're still cheap and clean (singles $27, 2 double beds $40). Morton's **post office** (496-5316) is on 2nd (open Mon.-Fri. 8am-5pm; **General Delivery ZIP code:** 98356). The **area code** is 360.

The Cowlitz River, once wild and treacherous, has been tamed considerably by a Tacoma City Light hydroelectric project. The **Mayfield** and **Mossyrock Dams** back up water into the river gorge to create two lakes, **Mayfield** and **Riffe,** both popular recreation areas. **Ike Kinswa State Park** and **Mayfield Lake County Park,** on Mayfield Lake off U.S. 12, offer camping and excellent **rainbow** and **silver trout** fishing year-round. Ike Kinswa (983-3402) has over 100 sites with showers (sites $11, full hookups $16). Mayfield Lake (985-2364) offers 54 tent and RV sites ($11). Public boat launches provide access to Mayfield, the lower of the two lakes.

■ Mount Rainier National Park

At 14,411 ft., Mt. Rainier (ray-NEER) presides over the Cascade Range. The Klickitat Native people called it *Tahoma,* "mountain of God," but Rainier is simply "the mountain" to most Washington residents. Due to its height and perpetually snow-capped peak, this active volcano draws visitors from around the globe. Because of its height, Rainier creates its own weather. It juts into warm, wet air, pulling down vast amounts of snow and rain. Clouds mask the mountain 200 days per year, frustrating visitors who come to see the summit. Seventy-six glaciers patch the slopes and combine with sharp ridges and steep gullies to make Rainier an inhospitable place for the thousands of determined climbers who attempt its summit each year.

Those who don't feel up to scaling the mountain can find much outdoor enjoyment in the old-growth forests and alpine meadows of Mt. Rainier National Park. With over 305 mi. of trails, whether you choose to hike past hot springs, across rivers, or alongside wildflowers, solitude is just a step away.

PRACTICAL INFORMATION AND ORIENTATION

Visitors Information: Each **visitors center** has displays, brochures on everything from hiking to natural history, postings on trail and road conditions, and rangers to point visitors in the right direction. Guided trips and talks, campfire programs, and slide presentations are given at the visitors centers and vehicle campgrounds throughout the park. Check at a visitors center or get a copy of the free guide, *Tahoma*. The **free map,** distributed at park entrances, is invaluable. The **Longmire Wilderness Center** (569-2211, ext. 3317) distributes **backcountry permits** and helps plan backpacking trips in the park. Open Sun.-Thurs. 8am-4:30pm, Fri. 8am-7pm, Sat. 7am-7pm; closed in winter. The **Paradise Visitors Center** (569-2211, ext. 2328) offers food, souvenirs, pay showers, and guided hikes. Open Sun.-Fri. 9am-6pm; late Sept. to mid-Oct. 9:30am-6pm; mid-Oct. to winter 10am-5pm. The **Sunrise Visitors Center** contains exhibits, snacks, and a gift shop. Open June 25-mid-Sept. Sun.-Fri. 9am-6pm, Sat. 9am-7pm. The **Ohanapecosh Visitors Center** offers info and wildlife displays. Open daily 9am-6pm; May-June Sat.-Sun. 9am-6pm; closed mid-Oct. to April. All centers can be contacted by writing c/o Superintendent, Mt. Rainier National Park, Ashford 98304, or by calling the park's central operator (569-2211). Obtain additional backpacking and camping info by writing or calling the **Backcountry Desk,** Mt. Rainier National Park, Tahoma Woods, Star Route, Ashford 98304 (569-2211 ext. 3317). **Park Administrative Headquarters,** Tahoma Woods, Star Route, Ashford 98304 (569-2211) are open Mon.-Fri. 8am-4:30pm. Not a visitors center, but good for phone inquiries.

Entrance Fee: $5 per car, $3 per hiker. Gates are open 24hr.; free evenings.

Backcountry Permits: Available at the **Paradise Ranger Station** (569-2211, ext. 2328). Sun.-Fri. 7:30am-3:30pm, Sat. 6am-3:30pm.

Buses: Gray Line Bus Service, 720 S. Forest St., Seattle 98134 (206-624-5077). Excursions daily from Seattle to Rainier May-Oct. 13 (single-day roundtrip $46, under 13 $17). Buses leave from the Sheraton Hotel in Seattle at 8:15am and return around 6pm, giving you about 1½hr. at Paradise and about 3½hr. total at the mountain. The **Ranier Shuttle,** P.O. Box 374, Ashford, 98304 (569-2331), runs daily between Sea-Tac Airport (Seattle) and park lodges or Ashford area lodges; also between Ashford and Paradise ($8 one way).

Hiking Supplies: Rainier Mountaineering Inc. (RMI) (569-2227), in Paradise. Rents ice axes ($8.50), crampons ($8.50), boots ($16.50), packs ($16.50), and helmets ($6) by the day. Expert RMI guides also lead summit climbs, seminars, and special schools and programs. Open May-Oct. daily 9am-5pm. Winter office: 535 Dock St. #209, Tacoma 98402 (206-627-6242). Beginners must buy a 3-day package that includes a day of teaching and 2 days of climbing ($425.50).

Ski Supplies: White Pass Sports Hut (494-7321), on U.S. 12 in Packwood. Alpine package $11.50 per day, Nordic package $9. Also rents snowshoes and snowboards and sells camping equipment. Open daily 8am-6pm; winter Mon.-Thurs. 8am-6pm, Fri.-Sun. 7am-6pm.

Park Emergency: 569-2211, ext. 2334 or 911. 24hr.

Post Office: In the **National Park Inn,** Longmire, and in the **Paradise Inn,** in Paradise. Both open Mon.-Fri. 8:30am-noon and 1-5pm. **General Delivery ZIP Code:** 98398 (Paradise), 98397 (Longmire).

Area Code: 360.

To reach Mt. Rainier from the **west,** drive south from Seattle on I-5 to Tacoma, then go east on Rte. 512, south on Rte. 7, and east on Rte. 706. This scenic road meanders through the town of **Ashford** and into the park by the Nisqually entrance. **Rte. 706** is the only access road open year-round; snow usually closes all other park roads from November to May. Mt. Rainier is 65 mi. from Tacoma and 90 mi. from Seattle.

The park covers over 350 sq. mi. **Longmire** does have a small store, but supplies are often limited and the distance from the Nisqually entrance to the first visitors center is considerable. Buy **gas** and groceries before entering the park.

A car tour is a good introduction to Rainier. All major roads offer scenic views of the mountain and have roadside lookouts for camera-clicking and general gawking. The roads to **Paradise** and **Sunrise** are especially picturesque. **Stevens Canyon Road** connects the southeast corner of the national park with Paradise, Longmire, and the Nisqually entrance, unfolding spectacular vistas of Rainier and the rugged Tatoosh Range.

Hitchhiking is technically illegal on National Park roads, though walking to a lookout point or parking lot and asking for a ride is not. However, many visitors say that hitchhiking opportunities along the mountain roads are exceptionally good. (*Let's Go* does not recommend hitchhiking.) Contrary to what rangers say, Park Service employees will sometimes give lifts to stranded hikers. Be careful to avoid getting marooned in the middle of nowhere. Those who need help should ask a ranger for assistance; park employees are helpful, especially on rare sunny days when the peak is visible and spirits are high.

Summer temperatures are warm during the day but drop sharply at night. Be prepared for changing weather. Pack warm clothes and cold-rated equipment. (See **Wilderness Concerns,** p. 47.) Before setting out, ask rangers for the two information sheets on **mountain-climbing** and **hiking** that contain helpful hints and a list of recommended equipment for the Rainier explorer. Party size is limited in many areas, and campers must carry all trash and waste out of the backcountry. Potable water is not available at most backcountry campsites. All stream and lake water should be treated for *giardia* with tablets, filters, or boiling before drinking (see **Common Ailments,** p. 14). Rangers can provide first aid. The nearest **medical facilities** are in **Morton** (40 mi. from Longmire) and **Enumclaw** (5 mi. from Sunrise).

The section of the **Mt. Baker-Snoqualmie National Forest** that adjoins Mt. Rainier is administered by **Wenatchee National Forest,** 301 Yakima St., Wenatchee 98807 (509-662-4314). The **Gifford Pinchot National Forest** is headquartered at 6926 E. Fourth Plain Blvd., P.O. Box 8944, Vancouver, WA 98668 (206-750-5000). Closer **ranger stations** are at 10061 U.S. 12, Naches 98937 (509-965-8005), and Packwood Ranger Station, P.O. Box 559 Packwood 98361 (206-494-5515).

ACCOMMODATIONS

Longmire, Paradise, and **Sunrise** offer accommodations that are usually too costly for the budget traveler. Stay in **Ashford** or **Packwood** if you must have a roof over your head. Otherwise, camp—isn't that what you're here for?

Whittaker's Bunkhouse, 30205 SR 706 E., P.O. Box E, Ashford 98304 (569-2439), owned by former Mt. Everest climber Lou Whittaker, offers spiffy bunk accommodations with firm mattresses, and sparkling clean showers (but no kitchen) for $18. The rooms are co-ed, though most of the clientele is male. Bring your own sleeping bag. The hotel also has traditional and more expensive rooms, as well as a homey espresso bar. Reservations strongly recommended.

Hotel Packwood, 102 Main St. (494-5431), in Packwood. A charming reminder of the Old West. Clean rooms with a mish-mash of antique furniture. Shared bathrooms. Singles $22, doubles from $25 (bunks). They do not accept credit cards.

Paradise Inn (reservations 569-2275), in Paradise. This rustic inn, built in 1917 from Alaskan cedar, offers gorgeous views of the mountain. Wake up early to hike the heavenly **Skyline Trail,** starting in the parking lot. Small but cheerful singles and doubles with shared bath from $65, each additional person $10. Open late May to early Oct. Reservations required in summer; call at least a month ahead.

FOOD

The general stores in the area sell only last-minute trifles like bug repellant and marshmallows, and items are charged an extra state park tax. Stock up before you go. **Blanton's Market** (494-6101) on Hwy. 123 in Packwood is the closest decent supermarket to the Park and has an ATM in front (open daily 5am-10pm).

Sweet Peaks, 38104 Hwy. 706 (569-2720), on the way to the Nisqually Entrance. Stop off for a "killer cinnamon roll" ($1.50) or a loaf of fresh bread ($1.25-2). The

WASHINGTON

bakery also sells an assortment of camping gear. Open daily in summer 7:30am-8pm; winter weekends and holidays 7:30am-8pm.

Wild Berry Restaurant (569-2628), in Ashford on Hwy. 706. An expensive local favorite. Fried foods are against their religion. The popular veggie lasagna goes for $7.95. Open daily 11am-9pm.

Ma & Pa Rucker's (494-2651), on Hwy. 12 in Packwood. Piping hot pizza (small $7, large $11) and typical roadhouse burgers. A single scoop of their peppermint candy ice cream is $1. Open Mon.-Thurs. 8am-9pm, Fri.-Sun. 7am-10pm.

CAMPING

Camping at auto-accessible campsites in the park between mid-June and late September is available on a first-come, first-camped basis ($6-10). National Park campgrounds all have facilities for the handicapped, but no hookups or showers. **Alpine** and **cross-country camping** require free permits year-round and are subject to certain restrictions. Be sure to contact a Wilderness Center for information on trail closures and permits before you set off. Alpine and cross-country access are strictly controlled to prevent forest damage, but permits for trail backpacking are available.

There are five campgrounds within the park. Drive to **Ohanapecosh** (205 sites) for the serene high canopy of **old-growth trees;** to **Cougar Rock** (200 sites), near Longmire, for the strictly maintained quiet hours (10pm-6am); to **Isput Creek** (29 sites) for the lush vegetation; and to both **White River** (117 sites) in the northeastern corner and **Sunshine Point** (18 sites) near the Nisqually entrance for the panoramas. Open on a first-come, first-camped basis, the grounds fill only on the busiest summer weekends. Sunshine Point is the only auto campground open year-round.

With a **backcountry permit** (see **Practical Information,** above), hikers can use any of the free, well established trailside camps scattered in the park's backcountry. Most camps have toilet facilities and a nearby water source, and some have shelters for groups of up to 12. Cross-country and alpine sites are high up the mountain on the glaciers and snow fields. Adventurous hikers can test their survival skills in the vast cross-country zone of the low forests if they know how to use a compass and map. *Fires are prohibited in all areas,* except front-country campgrounds, and there are limits to the number of members in a party. **Glacier climbers** and **mountain climbers** intending to go above 10,000 ft. must register in person at ranger stations to be granted permits.

The **national forests** outside Rainier Park provide developed sites (free-$5) and thousands of acres of freely campable countryside. Some developed sites cluster close to park entrances; rangers stations have a handout that lists these campgrounds. When free-camping, be sure to avoid eroded lakesides and riverbanks; flash floods and debris flows can catch unwary campers in their paths. Minimum-impact **campfire permits,** allowing hikers to burn small fires that don't sterilize the soil, are available at National Forest ranger stations (see **Practical Information**). Don't count on getting one, however, since the small number of backcountry sites limits the supply of permits.

OUTDOORS

Mt. Adams and Mt. St. Helens, not visible from the road, can be seen clearly from such mountain trails as **Paradise** (1½ mi.), **Pinnacle Peak** (2½ mi.), **Eagle Peak** (7 mi.), and **Van Trump Park** (5½ mi.). For more information on these trails, pick up *Viewing Mount St. Helens* at one of the visitors centers. The visitors centers have handouts for hiking in each of the park's sections, often including maps, travel time, and intensity for several hikes in one area.

Several less developed roads reach isolated regions, often meeting trailheads that cross the park or lead to the summit. Hiking and camping outside designated campsites is permissible in most regions of the park, but a permit is required for overnight backpacking trips. The **Wilderness Centers** at Carbon River and Longmire have information on day and backcountry hikes through the park, and supply camping permits (see **Practical Information** for hours). Most Ranger Stations can also give permits and all-important advice on trail conditions.

A segment of the **Pacific Crest Trail (PCT)**, which runs in its entirety from Mexico to the Canadian border, dodges in and out of the park's borders at the southeast corner of the park. Geared to hikers and horse riders, the PCT is maintained by the Forest Service. Primitive campsites and shelters line the trail but are not inside the park. All overnight camping is restricted to Forest Service land and a permit is required. Store food at designated food cache areas in the park. The trail, offering glimpses of the snow-covered peaks of the Cascades, leads through delightful wildlife areas. The **Wonderland Trail** winds 93 mi. up, down, and all around the Mountain. Hikers must get permits to make the arduous but stunning trek, and must complete the hike in 10-14 days. Call 569-2211, ext. 3317 for details on both hikes.

A trip to the **summit** of Mt. Rainier requires substantial preparation and expense. The ascent is a vertical rise of more than 9000 ft. over a distance of nine or more miles, usually taking two days and an overnight stay at **Camp Muir** on the south side (10,000 ft.) or **Camp Schurman** on the east side (9500 ft.). Each camp has a ranger station, rescue cache, and some form of toilet. To defray the costs of removing waste from the Mountain and employing rangers to patrol the area, permits for summit climbs now cost $15. Only experienced climbers should attempt the summit; Rainier claims lives regularly, and independent expeditions have a significantly worse safety record than organized trips. Novices can sign up for a summit climb with **Rainier Mountaineering, Inc. (RMI)** (see **Practical Information**, above), which offers a one-day basic-climbing course followed by a two-day guided climb. You must bring your own camping gear, and carry four meals to the camp. For more information, contact Park Headquarters or RMI (see above).

Less ambitious, ranger-led **interpretive hikes** delve into everything from area history to local wildflowers. Each visitors center (see **Practical Information**) conducts hikes on its own schedule and most of the campgrounds have evening talks. These free hikes complement evening campfire programs.

Longmire

Longmire's **museum,** near the visitors center, dwells on Rainier's past. The exhibit dutifully documents both natural history and the history of human encounters with the mountain. Mostly it shows that Rainier's most impressive lessons lie out of doors (open summer daily 9am-5:30pm; off-season daily 9am-4:30pm).

Programs run by the visitors center in the Longmire area typically include hikes into the surrounding forest and evening campfire programs. Join rangers for a morning cuppa joe at 7am (b.y.o. mug) at the Cougar Rock Amphitheater. The **Hikers Center** is an excellent source of info on all backcountry trips except summit attempts. Free info sheets about specific day and overnight hikes are available throughout the park. Check out the center's relief model of the mountain before plunging into the woods. A **permit** is required for backcountry camping.

The **Rampart Ridge Trail** (a 2½-hr., 4.6-mi. loop) has excellent views of the Nisqually Valley, Mount Rainier, and Tumtum Peak. The **Van Trump Park & Comet Falls Trail** (a steep 4-hr., 5-mi. hike) passes Comet Falls and, in early July, often a mountain goat or two. The trip to Comet Falls is only 1.6 mi. and the spectacular view of the 320-ft. drop is well worth the traffic on the trail. Unfortunately hikers also stray off the trail, cutting switchbacks and damaging the area; rangers will beg you to stay on the trail.

Longmire remains open during the winter as a center for snowshoeing, cross-country skiing, and other alpine activities. **Guest Services, Inc.** (569-2275) runs a **cross-country ski center** (rental $15 per day, $9.75 for children; lessons Sat.-Sun. 10am and 1:30pm; group lessons $16 per hr., private lessons $30; day tour $20, moonlight tour $12). The trails are difficult, but you can snowshoe eight months out of the year. Some diehards even enjoy winter hiking and climbing.

Paradise

One of the most visited places in the park, Paradise is perhaps the only place in Rainier where the sound of bubbling brooks and waterfalls might be drowned out by screaming children. Nevertheless, if you can manage to avoid the hustle and bustle and arrive on a clear, sunny weekday, the name Paradise will make sense. Above timberline, the sparkling snowfields can blind visitors looking out over forest canyons thousands of feet below, even in mid-June.

The road from the Nisqually entrance to Paradise is open year-round, but the road east through Stevens Canyon is open only from mid-June through October, weather permitting. The **Paradise Visitors Center** offers audio-visual programs, an observation deck, and all the requisite kitsch. From January to mid-April, park naturalists lead **snowshoe hikes** to explore winter ecology around Paradise (Sat.-Sun. at 10:30am, 12:30, and 2:30pm; snowshoe rental $1). In summer months, look for postings in the visitors center for ranger-led hikes, talks and wildflower walks.

Paradise is the starting point for several **trails** heading through the meadows to the nearby Nisqually Glacier or up the mountain to the summit. Many trails allow close-up views of Mt. Rainier's glaciers, especially the two closest to Paradise, the **Paradise** and the **Nisqually** glaciers. The 5-mi. **Skyline Trail** is the longest of the loop trails out of Paradise (4-hr. walk). The marked trail starts at the Paradise Inn, climbing above timberline. Skyline is probably the closest a casual hiker can come to climbing the mountain. The first leg of the trail is often hiked by climbing parties headed for **Camp Muir** (the base camp for most ascents to the summit). The trail turns off before reaching Camp Muir, rising to its highest elevation at **Panorama Point.** Although only halfway up the mountain, the point is within view of the glaciers, and the summit appears deceptively close.

The mildly strenuous, 2½-mi. half-day hike up to **Pinnacle Peak,** beginning across the road from Reflection Lake (just east of Paradise), features a clear view of Mt. Rainier, Mt. Adams, Mt. St. Helens, and Mt. Hood. One of the most striking aspects of hikes out of Paradise are the expanses of wildflower-strewn alpine meadows; they are some of the largest and most spectacular in the park.

Ohanapecosh and Carbon River

Though in opposite corners of the park, the Ohanapecosh and Carbon Rivers are in the same ranger district. The **Ohanapecosh Visitors Center** and campground snuggle under lush, old-growth cedars along a river valley in the park's southeast corner just a few miles north of Packwood. One of the oldest stands of trees in Washington, the **Grove of Patriarchs,** grows here. An easy 2-mi., one and a half hour walk will take you to these 500 to 1000-year-old Douglas firs, cedars, and hemlocks. The visitors center leads walks to the Grove, **Silver Falls,** and **Ohanapecosh Hot Springs,** a trickle of warm water in an area returning to the wild after development as a therapeutic resort in the 1920s. The **Summerland** and **Indian Bar Trails** are excellent for serious hiking—this is where rangers go on their days off.

Carbon River Valley, in the northwest corner of the park, is one of the only **rainforests** in the continental U.S., and its trails are on every ranger-in-the-know's top 10 list for hiking. **Spray Park** and **Mystic Camp** are superlative free backcountry campsites. Carbon River also has access to the **Wonderland Trail** (see **Sunrise,** below). Winter storms keep the road beyond the Carbon River entrance under constant distress. Because of floods in the spring of 1996, the road only reaches to the edge of the park. Check with rangers for updates and trip planning tips. Your time here will no doubt leave you hoping that Carbon River remains a secret.

Sunrise

The majority of Mt. Rainier's visitors head straight for Paradise, yet at Sunrise the views are equally spectacular without the crowds. The winding road to Sunrise, the highest of the four visitors centers, provides gorgeous views of the Pacific Ocean, Mt. Baker, and the heavily glaciated eastern side of Mt. Rainier.

Roslyn Exposed

A few years ago **Roslyn**, on Rte. 903 at the edge of Wenatchee National Forest was a sleepy little town. The mines responsible for the town's existence had closed, and no new source of income had yet emerged to take up the economic slack. Then came *Northern Exposure*, the wildly popular television show, which chose tiny Roslyn to play the fictitious town of **Cicely, Alaska** (the moose was imported). Tourists quickly followed, welcomed by most longtime residents as a source for much-needed revenue. Some curmudgeons, mostly recent transplants, curse the city folk who have spoiled their backwoods paradise.

While in town, fight your way through the crowd snapping pictures of the show's trademark mural at 2nd and Pennsylvania to eat some terrific food at the **Roslyn Café** (649-2763; open Mon.-Wed. 9:30am-4pm, Thurs.-Fri. 9:30am-8:30pm, Sat. 9am-8:30pm, Sun. 9am-8pm). You can sample the local brew, Roslyn Beer, at the **Brick Tavern,** 1 Pennsylvania Ave. (649-2643), the **oldest operating saloon in Washington** (open Mon.-Fri. noon-2am, Sat.-Sun. 10am-midnight or 2am). Or go straight to the source and visit the **Roslyn Brewing Company,** 33 Pennsylvania Ave. (649-2232; Fri.-Sun. noon-6pm).

Trails vary greatly in difficulty; the visitors center has details on hikes ranging from a ½ mi. to 13 mi. Two favorites are **Burrough's Mt. Trail,** a 5-mi., three-hour walk affording excellent views of the glaciers, and **Mt. Fremont Trail,** a 5.6-mi., four-hour hike with views of the Cascades, Grand Park, and quite possibly, mountain goats.

▓ Leavenworth

"Willkommen zu Leavenworth" proclaims the carved wooden sign at the entrance to this resort town/theme park. After the logging industry exhausted Leavenworth's natural resources and the railroad switching station moved to nearby Wenatchee, this rural mountain town was forced to invent a tourist gimmick to survive. By the mid-1960s, "Project Alpine" had painted a thick Bavarian veneer over Leavenworth. One can only wonder at the planners' *Weltanschauung*. Today, an estimated one million people visit this living Swiss Miss commercial annually, with massive influxes during the city's three annual festivals. Waiters in *Lederhosen* work in restaurants with comical, faux Anglo-German nomenclature. The sidewalks are lined with expensive stores, and loudspeakers pump the theme from the wedding scene of *Deerhunter* into the streets. Never mind that no one knows any German; this town is an experience in bizarre American vacation tackiness. Renting a bike and heading for the nearby mountain splendor may be the best way to take a vacation from your vacation in Leavenworth.

PRACTICAL INFORMATION AND ORIENTATION

Visitors Information: Chamber of Commerce, 894 U.S. 2 (548-5807), in the Clocktower Bldg. Helpful staff, many of whom see absolutely nothing amusing in their town's *töricht* gimmick. Open Mon.-Sat. 9am-6pm, Sun. 10am-4pm. **Ranger Station,** 600 Sherbourne (782-1413 or 548-4067), just off U.S. 2. The source for info on the mountains surrounding Leavenworth, especially the world-class rock climbing scene. Pick up a list of the 9 developed campgrounds within 20 mi. of Leavenworth. Open daily 7:45am-4:30pm; winter Mon.-Fri. 7:45am-4:30pm.

Buses: Greyhound (662-2183). Stops west of town on U.S. 2 at the Department of Transportation. 1 bus per day to Spokane ($32), and 3 to Seattle ($25).

Public Transportation: Link (662-1155 or 800-851-5465). Free bus service! Runs 20 buses per day Mon.-Sat. between Wenatchee and Leavenworth, with several stops around Leavenworth. The main stop is at the Park 'n' Ride lot, next to the ranger station. Pick up a schedule at the chamber. All buses have bike racks.

Bike Rental: Der Sportsmann, 837 Front St. (548-5623). Mountain bikes $6 per hr. or $20 per day, cross-country skis $12 per day. Also rents climbing shoes ($8) and

snow shoes ($2). Hiking and biking **maps** available. Open summer daily 9am-7pm; off season daily 10am-6pm.
Weather: 884-2982. **Cascade Snow Report:** 353-7440.
Senior Citizen Center: 423 Evans (548-6666), behind the chamber of commerce.
Pharmacy: Village Pharmacy, 821 Front St. (548-7731). Open Mon.-Fri. 8:30am-6:30pm, Sat. 9am-5:30pm, Sun. 11am-5pm.
Hospital: Cascade Medical Center, 817 Commercial St. (548-5815). Clinic open Mon.-Fri. 8am-7pm, Sat. 8am-5pm, Sun. 11am-5pm. Emergency room 24hr.
Emergency: 911.
Post Office: 960 U.S. 2 (548-7212). Open Mon.-Fri. 9am-5pm, Sat. 9-11am. **General Delivery ZIP Code:** 98826.
Area Code: 509.

Leavenworth is on the eastern slope of the Cascades, near Washington's geographic center. **U.S. 2** bisects Leavenworth in the main business district. The north-south route through the area is **U.S. 97,** intersecting U.S. 2 about 6 mi. southeast of town. Leavenworth is approximately 121 mi. east of Seattle and 190 mi. west of Spokane.

ACCOMMODATIONS AND CAMPING

Hotels start at $50 for singles and most cost even more. **Camping** is plentiful, inexpensive, and spectacular in the surrounding national forest. If you seek solitude, avoid weekend stays after Memorial Day. Otherwise, come early, or you may not find a spot at any of *die kampingplatzen.*

Wenatchee National Forest (782-1413). 10 mi. from town along **Icicle Creek Road,** a series of 7 Forest Service campgrounds squeeze between the creek and the road. The farther west the campground, the prettier the site—try the **Johnny Creek** campground for secluded forest sites or **Ida Creek** for proximity to the river. RVs and trailers may find the road difficult to maneuver. To get there, take the last left in town on U.S. 2 heading west. All have drinking water and pit toilets; the closest to town is $8, all others $7.

Tumwater, (800-280-2267) 10 mi. west of Leavenworth on U.S. 2. A forest service campground with water, flush toilets, and wheelchair access. 84 sites ($8).

FOOD

Predictably, Leavenworth's food mimics German cuisine; surprisingly, it often succeeds. Those who wish to avoid burgers and hot dogs and scarf some *schnitzel* should be prepared to pay at least $8-16 for a full dinner. If you're heading into the wilderness, shop at **Safeway,** 940 U.S. 2 (548-5435; open daily 7am-11pm). To find a German *Wurst,* just stop by any of the *wurst* booths tucked between buildings.

The Leavenworth Brewery, 636 Front St. (548-4545). This microbrewery justifies Leavenworth's Disneyfication of Bavaria by serving up tasty local ales (16 oz. $3) and pub fare (a potato stuffed with cheese, onions and peppers costs $4). The brewery also sponsors Sat. night performances and the occasional "Tacky Polyester Prom Night." Open Sun.-Thurs. 11am-10pm, Fri.-Sat. 11am-midnight.

Oberland Bakery and Café, 703 Front St. (548-7216). The "Europeans" painted on the wall keep you company as you nibble on your Bavarian almond pretzel. Generous subs $4.50. Lunch specials $5. Open daily 9am-5:30pm.

Casa Mia Restaurant, 703 U.S. 2 (548-5621). The food is great, and meals are preceded by chips and salsa. The lunch menu offers enchiladas and burritos from $5. The dinners are expensive, but authentic. *Arroz con pollo* is $10. Back window provides prime tourist watching. Lunch served daily noon-4pm. Open Sun.-Thurs. noon-9pm, Fri.-Sat noon-10pm.

Leavenworth Pizza Company, 892 U.S. 2 (548-7766). Located next to the visitor's center, this family-owned restaurant offers tasty pizzas as a respite from *schnitzel* and a mostly-locals atmosphere as a respite from *Deutsch*-crazed tourists. 2 person pizza runs $7-9. Open Sun.-Thurs. 11am-9pm, Fri.-Sat. 11am-10pm.

OUTDOORS

Except for tourist-watching, the most compelling reason to come to Leavenworth is for the extensive **hiking, mountain biking, and climbing** opportunities in the **Wenatchee National Forest.** The heavily visited **Alpine Lakes Wilderness** stretches south of town, as beautiful as it is clogged with hikers. The **ranger station** (782-1413) in Leavenworth hands out several brief, free descriptions of hikes near town. Families may wish to consult the page-long list of "relatively easy, short hikes," while the more experienced can check out the "moderate to difficult" list. The ranger station also sells an informative guide to all the area's trails for $3. The most complete hike descriptions can be found in the well written *100 Hikes in Washington's Alpine Lakes,* by Harvey Manning, on sale at the ranger station for $15 (or contact The Mountaineers Books; see p. 43). One pleasant day-hike is the moderately sloping 3½-mi. trail to picturesque **Eightmile Lake,** a great spot for a picnic or overnight backpacking. Mosey 9.4 mi. up Icicle Creek Rd., make a left onto Eightmile Rd., and continue 3 mi. uphill to the trailhead. On a hot day, stay near water and hike the 3½-mi. **Icicle Gorge Trail,** which starts just east of the Chatter Creek Campground on Icicle Rd. and moseys along beside the cool creek waters.

Although most trails in this area are unrestricted, permits are required to enter the popular **Stuart Lake, Colcheck Lake, Snow Lakes,** and **Enchantment Lakes** areas. If you're a day-hiker only, the permits are free and "self-issuing," meaning you just have to fill out a form, either at the ranger station or at trailheads. For overnights, obtaining a permit is tricky. Because of heavy hiker traffic, reservations ($6-7) are required for backcountry permits in the entire area. Dig out your Visa or Mastercard and call 800-735-2900 (Mon.-Fri. 8am-5pm; call at least 21 days in advance). For more spur of the moment types, the forest service holds a lottery for a limited number of **free permits** each morning at 7:45am (at the ranger station). A wide range of other restrictions governing fire use and pets apply in the Alpine Lakes Wilderness; contact the ranger station for details.

A labyrinth of fire roads and bike-friendly paths make the area a popular destination for mountain bikers and nordic skiing in the winter. Pick up a free copy of the *Wenatchee National Forest Guide to Mountain Bike Routes* and *Cross-Country Ski Guide* at the Ranger Station. The **Leavenworth Winter Sports Club,** P.O. Box 573, Leavenworth 98826 (548-5115), maintains the trail system. Day passes for the 23km of trails around Leavenworth cost $7 and are available at trailheads.

On your way up Icicle Rd., stop at the **Leavenworth National Fish Hatchery** (548-7641) and immerse yourself in exhibits about local river life. In the summer, adult chinook salmon, sometimes reaching 30lb., fill the holding ponds waiting to be caught and their eggs harvested. A 1-mi. self-guided interpretive trail explains the history and environment of the hatchery and Icicle Creek (open daily 8am-4pm). If you are in a riding mood, try the **Eagle Creek Ranch** (548-7798). The ranch offers horseback rides ($15 per hr.), hay rides ($12), and winter horse-drawn sleigh rides. To get there, go north on Rte. 209, turn right on Eagle Creek Rd. and go 5½ mi.

On your way south to the U.S. 97 junction, be sure to stop in **Cashmere** at the **Aplets and Cotlets Factory,** 117 Mission St. (782-2191; follow the signs from U.S. 2), for free tours of the plant and ample samples of their gooey candies. You have to wear a hat during the tour, but they'll give you a goofy paper one if you don't bring your own. (Open Mon.-Fri. 8am-5:30pm, Sat.-Sun. 9am-5pm; in winter Mon.-Fri. 9am-5pm, Sat. 10am-4pm., closed on weekends in Jan. and Feb.) The **Washington State Leaf Festival,** a celebration of autumn, lasts for nine days during the last week in September and the first week in October. It includes a Grand Parade, art shows, flea markets, and street dances. "Smooshing," a four-person race run on wooden two-by-fours, is the highlight of the **Great Bavarian Ice Fest,** held on the weekend of Martin Luther King, Jr. Day.

■ Lake Chelan

The serpentine body of Lake Chelan (sha-LAN) undulates over 50 mi. northwest from the Columbia River and U.S. 97 into the eastern Cascades. The resort town of **Chelan** perches at the south end of the lake amid brown bone dry hills and irrigated apple orchards. The town has developed a pricey tourist industry geared to the elderly and families with motor boats in tow. Up the lake, brown hills become vermilion mountains, and the North Cascades flaunt their awesome beauty. The lake, the third deepest in the U.S. and at points 1500 ft. deep, extends far into Wenatchee National Forest and pokes its northwesternmost tip into the **Lake Chelan National Recreation Area,** a section of **North Cascades National Park.** While Chelan has become an aquatic Disneyland, **Stehekin** (ste-HEE-kin), at the other end of the lake, offers solitude, space, and access to a vast wilderness.

Practical Information The **Chelan Ranger Station,** 428 W. Woodin Ave. (682-2576, or 682-2549 for the National Park Service), just south of town on the lakeshore, provides information on the area's forests and recreation areas (open daily 7:45am-4:30pm; Oct.-May Mon.-Fri. 7:45am-4:30pm). If you'll be in Chelan for a while, stop by the **Lake Chelan Chamber of Commerce,** 102 E. Johnson (682-3503 or 800-424-3526); it has plenty of information on Chelan and nearby Manson, but not much on the surrounding wilds (open Mon.-Fri. 9am-5pm, Sat. 10am-3pm; winter Mon.-Fri. 9am-5pm).

Link (800-851-5465), the local bus service, has hourly service to Wenatchee, where there is a Greyhound terminal. Rent a bike and just about anything from in-line skates to paragliding equipment at **Nature Gone Wild,** 109 S. Emerson (682-8680). Bikes go for $4 per hour or $20 per day (open Mon.-Fri. 9am-6pm, Sat. 8am-5pm). Chelan's pharmacy is **Green's Drugs,** 212 E. Woodin Ave. (682-2566; open Mon.-Sat. 9am-5:30pm, Sun. as posted). The **Lake Chelan Community Hospital,** 503 E. Highland St. (682-2531), is open 24hr. Important phone numbers: **emergency,** 911; **24hr. crisis line,** 662-7105; **police,** 207 N. Emerson St. (682-2588). Wash them clothes ($1.25 a load; 10-min. dry 25¢) at **Town Tub Laundry** on Woodin Ave. (open daily 8am-10pm). Mail from the **post office,** 144 E. Johnson (682-2625; open Mon.-Fri. 8:30am-5pm; **General Delivery ZIP Code:** 98816). The **area code** is 509.

Accommodations, Camping, and Food Most Chelan motels and resorts are too busy exploiting sun-starved visitors from Puget Sound to bother being affordable. An exception is **Mom's Montlake Motel,** 823 Wapato (682-5715) at Clifford, a mom-and-pop operation with clean, microwave-equipped rooms. Beds for one to two people start at $48 in the summer. Most campers head for **Lake Chelan State Park** (687-3710), a pleasant grassy campground 9 mi. from Chelan up the south shore of the lake with a beach and swimming area, a small store, and jet ski rentals. Open year-round, reservations are strongly recommended from April-Sept. (144 sites; $11, with hookup $16.) **Ramona Park,** a free, primitive campground, is reached by turning left onto Forest Rd. 5900 near the end of the South Shore Rd. (just beyond 25 Mile Creek), then left onto Forest Rd. 8410 after 2½ mi. Continue another ½ mi. Campers may also pitch tents for free anywhere they please in the National Forest and in this area. Fires must be kept in already established fire rings.

The cheapest eats in Chelan are at local fruit stands, the **Safeway** (106 W. Manson Rd., 682-2615; open daily 6am-11pm), or **Bear Foods,** 125 E. Woodin Ave. (682-5535), which sells a wide variety of natural foods and everything from Ben and Jerry's to books on tofu (open Mon.-Sat. 9am-7pm, Sun. noon-5pm). For an enlightening lunch, hunt down **Dagwood's International Kitchen,** at 246 W. Manson Way (682-8630). This unpretentious joint serves $6 Thai shrimp pizzas. Open daily from 11am until the after-dinner slow down. For the coffee addict, **Flying Saucers,** 116 S. Emerson (682-5129) offers lattés and aura galora in a converted 50s diner.

■ Stehekin

For less than the price of a motel room in touristy Chelan, you can take a ferry roundtrip from Chelan 50 mi. over sparkling turquoise waters to Stehekin, a tiny town at the mouth of a magnificent valley. Catch a shuttle bus a few miles up the valley, camp for free on the banks of a rushing, crystal green river and spend days exploring some of the most beautiful country in the Cascades.

The **Lake Chelan Boat Company,** 1418 W. Woodin (682-2224), about 1 mi. west of town, runs the Lady of the Lake II, a 350-person ferry which makes one roundtrip to Stehekin per day. For the same fare, you can catch the ferry at Chelan (daytime parking free, overnight $5) at 8:30am and return at 6pm, or at **Fields Point,** 16 mi. up the South Shore Rd. near Twenty-Five Mile Creek State Park (parking $3 per day, $17 per week) at 9:45am and return at 4:45pm. The *Lady Express* is a smaller boat that makes a faster, non-stop trip to Stehekin for a higher price ($41 roundtrip). Purchase tickets in advance on summer weekends; the boat often fills with eager tourists and backpackers, and the boat company will not accept credit cards on the day of travel. The scenery gets increasingly spectacular as the boat proceeds "uplake"; the views on the ride alone are worth the price. You may catch a glimpse of mountain goats or brown bears roaming the lakeside.

When the ferry arrives at Stehekin at 12:30pm, most people stay only until the boat's departure at 2pm. If that's your plan, the **Rainbow Falls Tour** ($5), leaving as soon as the *Lady* arrives, is a good way to see the valley and its major sights: the one-room **Stehekin School,** the **Stehekin Pastry Company,** a bakery in a log cabin in the woods, and **Rainbow Falls,** a misty 312-ft. waterfall. The narration on the bus tour includes healthy doses of the valley's natural and human history. Or, walk up the hill to the **Golden West Visitor Center,** (856-6055, ext. 14). Exuberant rangers can help plan anything from a one-hour jaunt to a 10-day backcountry trip.

Camping and Food To truly appreciate the Stehekin area, let the tourists take the boat back to Chelan and camp in the valley overnight. The Park Service maintains 12 primitive campgrounds along the **Stehekin Valley Road.** Get the free but required permit at the Ranger Station in Chelan or at the Golden West Visitor Center (open daily 8am-4:30pm). The closest campground is at Purple Point, right next to the ferry landing.

If you want a meal in the valley, you have a few options. The **grocery/convenience store** at the landing has hearty soups and chili ($1.50) and big, thick slices of pizza ($2). Next door, the **Lodge Restaurant** serves expensive burgers ($5-6) and dinners ($7-15) complete with tablecloths and vegetarian options. Or, you can catch a bus up to the **Stehekin Valley Ranch** (682-4677) for dinner. You'll need reservations, and the delicious country meal will set you back about $12. Bring groceries from Chelan; the store in Stehekin has only a small selection of fish bait and Fritos. Just a mile up the road (the only road), the **Stehekin Pastry Company** lures hikers out of the hills to snack on Rubenesque sticky buns ($1.85; open 7am-5pm).

Outdoors Some short but scenic day hikes surround the landing. The mellow **Lakeshore Trail** starts behind the visitors center, and follows the west shore of Lake Chelan for 17 mi. to Prince Creek, allowing you to wander as far as you like before retracing your steps. A more strenuous alternative follows the ¾-mi. **Imus Creek Trail,** a self-guided interpretive trail which also begins behind the Golden West Visitor Center. After passing fast-flowing Purple Creek, take a right turn up the switchbacks of the steep **Purple Creek Trail.** The 5500-ft. climb is tough, but the reward for the effort is a magnificent view of the lake and surrounding glaciers.

An unpaved road and many trails probe north into the North Cascades National park, where there are more secluded campgrounds. In the spring and summer, **Stehekin Transportation Services** runs a shuttle bus from Stehekin to **Highbridge,** where trails delve into the National Park. In the summer, the **Cascades Stehekin Lodge** (682-4494) runs the bus ($4, 4 per day). In the spring the National Parks Ser-

WASHINGTON

vice makes the trip ($5, 2 per day). Make reservations through the visitors center (856-5703, ext. 14). Either shuttle will drop you off anywhere along the way for full fare. You can rent a cruiser at the lodge ($3.50 per hour, $10 per day) or a mountain bike at **Discovery Bikes** (884-4844), just north of the ferry dock for $4 per hour or $15 per day (open June-Sept. 8am-5:30pm).

All walk-in campgrounds in **North Cascades National Park** are open May to October and are free (drinking water is not provided). **Backcountry permits** are mandatory in the park throughout the year and are available on a first-come, first-served basis. Pick one up at the visitors center or call the Chelan Ranger Station (see above). An excellent resource for the Stehekin Area is *The Stehekin Guidebook* (free), which you can pick up on the ferry or at the lodge.

Two **dayhikes** start from High Bridge. The mellow **Agnes Gorge Trail** begins 200 yd. beyond the bridge (2nd trail on the left), and travels a level 2½ mi. through forests and meadows with views of Agnes Mountain, ending where Agnes Creek takes a dramatic plunge into Agnes Gorge (oh, Agnes...). Behind the ranger cabin, the **McGregor Mountain Trail** is a straight shot up the side of the mountain (8124 ft. in elevation), climbing 6525 vertical ft. over a distance of 8 mi. The last ½ mi. is a scramble up ledges. This extremely difficult trail is often blocked by snow into July; check at the visitor center before starting out. The persevering hiker is rewarded with unsurpassed views of the high North Cascades peaks.

For **backpackers,** a good two-day, 17-mi. hike combines the **Purple Creek Trail,** beginning behind the Golden West Visitor Center, with the **Boulder Creek Trail.** The hike begins by climbing up 7 mi. of switchbacks to majestic Purple Pass before continuing through mountain forests and meadows on the Boulder Creek Trail. A longer, less-used loop combining the **Company Creek Trail** with the **Devore Creek Trail** begins and ends at the **Harlequin Group Campground.**

■ North Cascades (Rte. 20)

A favorite stomping ground for Jack Kerouac (*The Dharma Bums*), deer, mountain goats, black bears, and grizzlies, the North Cascades remain one of the most rugged expanses of land in the continental U.S. The dramatic peaks stretch north from Stevens Pass on U.S. 2 to the Canadian border and are preserved in pristine condition by several different government agencies. The centerpiece of the area is **North Cascades National Park,** which straddles the crest of the Cascades. Two designated wilderness areas attract backpackers and mountain climbers from around the world. **Rte. 20** (open April-Nov., weather permitting), a road designed for unadulterated driving pleasure, is the primary means of access to the area and awards jaw-dropping views around each curve.

Much of the wilderness is inaccessible without at least a day's uphill hike. Few are willing to spend the energy, but those who do will be rewarded with untrammeled land, views of jagged peaks, and an Eden of wildlife and flora. Ira Springs's *100 Hikes in the North Cascades* is among the most readable for recreational hikers, while Fred Beckley's *Cascade Alpine Guide* targets the more serious high-country traveler. Both are published by the Mountaineers Books (see p. 43).

Rte. 20 (Exit 230 on I-5) follows the Skagit River to the Skagit Dams and Lakes, whose hydroelectric energy powers Seattle. The highway then enters the **Ross Lake National Recreation Area,** a buffer zone between the highway and North Cascades National Park. After crossing Washington Pass (5477 ft.), Rte. 20 descends to the Methow River and the dry Okanogan rangeland of Eastern Washington. The North Cascades National Park complex is bordered on the west by **Mt. Baker/Snoqualmie National Forest,** on the east by **Okanogan National Forest,** and on the south by **Wenatchee National Forest.**

Greyhound stops in Burlington once per day on the Seattle-Bellingham route. The fare is about $15 from Seattle to the East Cascades. No public transportation lines run within the park boundaries or along Rte. 20.

SEDRO WOOLLEY TO MARBLEMOUNT

Though situated in the rich farmland of the lower Skagit Valley, **Sedro Woolley** is primarily a logging town. Stop by the **Chamber of Commerce,** 116 Woodsworth St. (360-855-0974), inside the train caboose. Open daily 9am-5pm. The main attraction of this village is the annual **Sedro Woolley Loggerodeo,** which takes place in late June and early August. The festivities are dominated by a carnival, parade, and rodeo queen contest. Axe-throwing, pole-climbing, and sawing competitions vie for center stage with rodeo events such as bronco-busting and calf-roping. Call or write Loggerodeo, P.O. Box 712, Sedro-Woolley 98284 (855-1841).

Sedro Woolley also houses the **North Cascades National Park Headquarters** at 2105 Rte. 20 (360-856-5700) and the headquarters for the **Mt. Baker/Snoqualmie National Forest.** Call 206-526-6677 for snow avalanche information. Seek out the **Wilderness Information Center** (360-873-4590), in Marblemount, for a mandatory backcountry permit. Rte. 9 leads north of Sedro Woolley, providing indirect access to **Mt. Baker** through the forks at the Nooksack River and Rte. 542.

As it continues east, Rte. 20 forks at **Baker Lake Road,** which dead-ends 25 mi. later at **Baker Lake.** There are several campgrounds along the way, but only **Horseshoe Cove** and **Panorama Point** offer toilets and potable water (sites $10, plus $6.50 for each additional vehicle). All other grounds are free. Call 800-280-CAMP/ 2267 for reservations.

Don't blink while heading east or you may miss the town of **Concrete,** where rows of businesses made of (yes) concrete pay homage to the now defunct local industry. On the western boundary of **Rockport State Park,** Sauk Mountain Road (a.k.a. Forest Service Rd. 1030) makes a stomach-scrambling climb up Sauk mountain, offering superb views of the North Cascades. For the intrepid driver willing to climb the peak (7 mi. up and a right turn at Rd. 1036) a view of Mt. Rainier, Puget Sound, and the San Juan Islands awaits. The **Sauk Mountain Trail** begins at the parking lot and winds 3½ mi. to backcountry campsites near Sauk Lake. The road promises pot holes galore and a thorough dust bath; trailers, RVs and the faint of heart should not attempt the ascent.

Rockport borders **Rockport State Park** (853-8461), which rests among an old growth forest of Douglas firs and ferns. The park has a trail that accommodates wheelchairs and 62 fully developed campsites ($10, with full hookup $15, each extra vehicle $5; Three-sided adirondack cabins with bunk beds for 8 are $15, no reservations). If Rockport is full, continue 1 mi. east to Skagit County's **Howard Miller Steelhead Park** (360-853-8808) on the Skagit River, where anglers come to catch the Park's tasty namesake (49 sites; tents $12, hookups $16, 3-sided Adirondack lean-tos $16). The surrounding **Snoqualmie National Forest** permits free camping closer to the high peaks.

At **Marblemount,** consider stopping at **Good Food** (873-2771), a small family diner at the east edge of town along Rte. 20. This pithy eatery boasts not only riverside picnic tables with incredible views and bikers to talk Harley's with, but also a great vegetarian sandwich ($3.25). Boost your caffeine level with a shot of espresso. Shakes ($2.25) are thick and tasty (open daily 9am-9pm).

From Marblemount, it's 22 mi. up Cascade River Rd. to the trailhead for a 3½-mi. hike to the amazing **Cascade Pass. Stehekin,** in the southeast and the north tip of Lake Chelan, is reachable only by boat, plane, or foot. This is a two day hike, and hikers must arrange for transportation to Stehekin (see p. 391). Call the **Golden West Visitor's Center** (856-6055. ext. 14) in Stehekin for detailed information on shuttle buses and trails, or stop by the **Marblemount Wilderness Information Center,** 728 Ranger Station Rd., Marblemount 98267 (873-4500, ext. 39), 1 mi. north of Marblemount on a well-marked road from the west end of town. This is the place to go for a backcountry permit for the National Park. Rangers will help plan a backpacking trip in detail and give updates on trail conditions (open summer Fri.-Sun. 7am-8pm, Mon.-Thurs. 7am-6pm; call for winter hr.).

WASHINGTON

ROSS LAKE & NORTH CASCADES NATIONAL PARK

Newhalem is the first town on Rte. 20 as you cross into the **Ross Lake National Recreation Area,** a buffer zone between the highway and North Cascades National Park. The newly rebuilt **North Cascades Visitors Center and Ranger Station** (206-386-4495), off Rte. 20 (open mid-April to mid-Nov. daily 8:30am-4:30pm; call for winter hr.), provides a peek at the diversity of flora and fauna in the Cascades. Take the 300-ft. boardwalk on the back side of the center to catch a glimpse of a characteristically treacherous North Cascades ridge. **Seattle City Light** (233-2709) operates a small visitors center on Hwy. 20. Open sporadically, it gives information on **Diablo Dam** and its operations. SCL also runs tours of the dam, one of which includes a 90-minute tour of the **Skagit hydroelectric project** with a 560-ft. ride up the **Incline Railway** and a walk across the dam ($5, summers only, Thurs.-Mon. 10am, 1pm, and 3pm).

The artificial and astoundingly blue expanse of **Ross Lake,** behind Ross Dam, snakes into the mountains as far as the Canadian border. The lake is ringed by 15 campgrounds, some accessible by trail, others only by boat. The National Park's **Goodell Creek Campground,** just south of Newhalem, has 22 leafy sites suitable for tents and trailers with drinking water and pit toilets, and a launch site for **whitewater rafting** on the Skagit River (sites $7; water turned off after Oct. when sites are free). **Colonial Creek Campground,** 10 mi. to the east, is a fully developed, wheelchair-accessible campground with flush toilets, a dump station, and campfire programs some evenings. Colonial Creek is also a trailhead for several hikes into the southern unit of the North Cascades National Park including the day-hike friendly **Thunder Creek Trail,** which extends through old growth cedar and fir forests and remains flat for 1½ mi. until it starts to climb. Serious hikers often use the trail as a starting point for longer treks (open mid-May to Oct.; 164 sites, $10). **Newhalem Creek Campground,** near the visitors center, is a similarly developed National Park facility with a less impressive forest of small pines, but brand new facilities, especially good for trailers and RVs (129 sites that rarely fill, $10). The **Skagit General Store** (386-4489), east of the visitors center, sells fishing licenses and basic groceries, and is the only store within miles.

EAST TO MAZAMA AND WINTHROP

Leaving the basin of Ross Lake, Rte. 20 begins to climb, exposing the jagged, snowy peaks of the North Cascades. Thirty miles of astounding views east, the **Pacific Crest Trail** crosses Rte. 20 at **Rainy Pass** on one of the most scenic and difficult legs of its 2500-mi. Canada-to-Mexico route. Near Rainy Pass, groomed **scenic trails** 1 to 3 mi. long can be hiked in sneakers, provided the snow has melted (about mid-July). Just off Rte. 20, an overlook at **Washington Pass** rewards a 5 mi. hike on a wheelchair accessible paved trail with one of the state's most dramatic panoramas, an astonishing view of the red rocks exposed by Early Winters Creek in **Copper Basin.** The area has many well-marked trailheads off Rte. 20 that lead into the desolate wilderness. The popular 2.2-mi. walk to **Blue Lake** begins just east of Washington Pass. The deep turquoise lake is surrounded by cliffs. An easier 2-mi. hike to **Cutthroat Lake** departs from an access road 4.6 mi. east of Washington Pass. From the lake, the trail continues 4 mi. farther (and almost 2,000 ft. higher) to **Cutthroat Pass,** giving the diligent a breathtaking view of towering, rugged peaks.

The hair-raising 23-mi. road to **Hart's Pass** begins at **Mazama,** on Rd. 1163, 10 mi. east of Washington Pass. The gravel road snakes up to the highest pass crossed by any road in the state. Breathtaking 360° views await the steel-nerved driver, both from the pass and from **Slate Peak,** the site of a lookout station 3 mi. beyond the pass. The road is open early July to late September and is **closed to trailers.**

The Forest Service maintains a string of dry but uncrowded campgrounds with pit toilets and water along Rte. 20 between Washington Pass and Mazama (sites $7). You may want to stop at the **Mazama Store,** 50 Lost River Rd. (996-2855), for gas, supplies, or an espresso. This unexpected eruption of bourgeois merchandising also rents mountain bikes, fly fishing equipment and makes a burly vegetarian sandwich. This is the last place to stock up for miles (open daily 7am-7pm). Explore the other, more remote campgrounds along the Forest Rd. northwest of Mazama. The **Pasayten Wilderness** is an area whose rugged terrain and mild climate endear it to hikers and equestrians (open daily 9am-5pm; usually closed after Labor Day).

The **Cedar Creek Trail** makes a fine day hike or overnight backpacking trip. Four mi. west of Mazama on Rte. 20, turn at a signed exit and drive along the gravel road to an old gravel pit. From there, trail #476 begins on the far left of the pit. The falls are about 2 mi. away on the wildflower strewn trail, although there are breathtaking views of several ridges 3 mi. beyond the falls, and Abernathy Pass is 9 mi. west from the trailhead. Walk as long as you like; there are campsites along the way.

WINTHROP TO TWISP

Farther east is the town of **Winthrop,** the child of an unholy marriage between the television series *Bonanza* and Long Island yuppies who would eagerly claim a rusty horseshoe as an antique. Find the **Winthrop Information Station** (996-2125), on the corner of Rte. 20 and Riverside, and the staff will laud the beauty of this "Old West" town (open early May-mid-Oct. daily 10am-5pm).

The summer is bounded by **rodeos** on Memorial and Labor Day weekends. Late July brings the top-notch **Winthrop Rhythm and Blues Festival** (996-2148), where big name blues bands flock to belt their tunes, endorse radio stations and play cowboy. Tickets for the three-day event cost $35. Take a guided trail ride at the **Rocking Horse Ranch** (996-2768), 9 mi. north of Winthrop on Rte. 20 ($20 per 1½hr.). Or rent a bike ($5 per hr., $20 per day) at **Winthrop Mountain Sports,** 257 Riverside Ave. (996-2886; open Mon.-Fri. 9am-6pm, Sat. 9am-7pm, Sun. 9am-5:30pm).

The shiny new **Methow** (MET-how) **Valley Visitors Center,** Building 49, Hwy. 20 (996-4000) hands out information on area camping, hiking and cross-country skiing which is tremendously popular during Methow Valley winters. Pick up the free, cassette-tape narration of the journey across Hwy 20. Open summers daily 8am-5pm; call for winter hours. For more in-depth skiing information, call the **Methow Valley Sports Trail Association** (996-03287), which grooms 175km of trails.

Between Winthrop and Twisp on East Country Rd. (#9129), the **North Cascades Smokejumper Base** (997-2031) is a center for folks who get their kicks by parachuting into forest fires in order to fight them. The courageous smokejumpers will give you a tour of the base and explain the procedures and equipment (open summers and early fall Mon.-Fri. 9am-6pm; call ahead).

Flee Winthrop's prohibitively expensive hotels and restaurants to sleep in **Twisp,** the town that should have been a breakfast cereal. It was actually named for the Native American word for yellow jacket, "T-wapsp." Nine mi. south of Winthrop on Rte. 20, this peaceful hamlet offers low prices and far fewer tourists than its neighbor. Stay at **The Sportsman Motel,** 1010 E. Rte. 20 (997-2911), a hidden jewel, where a barracks-like façade masks tastefully decorated rooms and kitchens (singles $31, with 2 people $36, doubles $39). If you are in town during lunch hour, head to the **Glover Street Café,** 104 N. Glover St. (997-1323). This café offers gourmet sandwiches that won't bust your budget ($5.25 with soup or salad) as well as special salads ($3.75; open Mon.-Fri. 8am-3pm). **The Bombers Restaurant,** 607 Canyon St. (997-2525), offers dinners named after famous airplanes. Locals come here to chow on burgers ($5 and up), stir-fry ($9), and other entrees ($7-10; open Mon.-Fri. 6am-8pm, Sat.-Sun. 6am-2pm).

The **Twisp Ranger Station,** 502 Glover St. (997-2131), employs a helpful staff ready to strafe you with trail and campground guides (open Mon.-Sat. 7:45am-4:30pm; winter Mon.-Fri. 7:45am-4:30pm). From Twisp, Rte. 20 continues east to Okanogan, and Rte. 153 runs south to **Lake Chelan.** There are many campgrounds and trails from 15 to 25 mi. up **Twisp River Road,** just off Rte. 20 in Twisp. Although the campsites are primitive, many are free. For camping closer to the highway, the **Riverbend RV Park,** 19951 Rte. 20 (997-3500), 2 mi. west of Twisp, is great. Don't let the letters "RV" scare you from this riverside campground. RVs and tents co-exist peacefully, mesmerized by the beauty of the mountains and sounds of rushing water (sites $14, with hookup $18, $2 per person over 2; office open 8am-10pm).

EASTERN WASHINGTON

In the rain-shadow of the Cascades, the hills and valleys of the Columbia River Basin once fostered little more than sagebrush and tumbleweed. The construction of 10 dams on the Columbia made irrigation possible, and the basin now yields bumper crops of fruit and high-quality wine. Sunshine defies the rainy Washington stereotype and ripens some of the world's best apples while bronzing flocks of visitors from Puget Sound. Agriculture gives the valley a calm beauty, visible in patchwork expanses from rimrock ledges in the Cascade foothills, and the region's rivers, lakes, and streams are well known for fishing and water sports. **Spokane** is the largest city east of the Cascades. **U.S. 97,** running north-south along the eastern edge of the Cascades, strings together the main fruit centers and mountain resorts of the Columbia River Basin. **I-90** emerges from Seattle and the Cascades to cut a route through Ellensburg, Moses Lake, and Spokane. **I-82** dips south from Ellensburg through Yakima and Richland to Hermiston, OR. **Greyhound** (509-624-5251) runs along both interstates. **Amtrak** (509-624-5144) runs its "Empire Builder" through Spokane and Richland to Portland, and through Ellensburg to Tacoma and Seattle.

■ Yakima

With 300 days of sunshine per year, volcanic soil, and a fresh groundwater supply, Yakima and the Yakima Valley have earned the title "fruit bowl of the nation" by producing the most apples, mint, and hops of any U.S. county. East of the Cascade range, Yakima is a convenient stop for fresh produce on your way to the mountains. Unfortunately, not everything in Yakima is peachy. Yakima has an extremely high crime rate. Visitors, especially women traveling alone, should keep this in mind, although the areas frequented by tourists are not usually dangerous, and Yakima residents are some of the friendliest in Washington. Most of the attractions of the Yakima Valley are wineries and orchards, and hence lie outside of the city proper.

Practical Information Yakima is on I-82, 145 mi. southeast of Seattle and 145 mi. northwest of Pendleton, OR. The Yakima Valley lies southeast of Yakima, along I-82. Pick up one of the local handouts at the **Yakima Valley Visitors and Convention Bureau,** 10 N. 8th St. (575-3010), at E. Yakima (open Mon.-Fri. 8am-5pm, Sat.-Sun.

Washington Wine Country

At one time, wine connoisseurs would have turned up their *nez* at pedestrian Washington labels, but the state is now the second-largest producer of wine in the nation, and local vineyards have been garnering international acclaim. The majority of wineries are situated in the Yakima, Walla Walla, and Columbia Valleys. These areas, just east of the Cascades, benefit from a rain shield that keeps the land naturally dry (and thus easily controlled by irrigation) and a mineral-rich soil bequeathed by ancient volcanoes. Sunlight produces grape sugars, and cool nights protect acids. And, as almost every wine brochure in the land points out, this region is at *exactly* the same latitude as Burgundy.

Wineries proliferate in the small towns between Yakima and Richland. Almost all offer tours and tastings, and many boast spectacular scenery right off I-82 that you don't have to be tipsy to appreciate. Hours vary, but most are open Monday through Saturday 10am-5pm, call ahead to see if they are open Sundays; call ahead for hours or make an appointment. The free guide *Yakima Valley Wine Tour*, available at visitor centers across the region, lists active wineries in the area, and has maps and information on tours and tastings.

9am-5pm; Nov.-Jan. closed Sat.-Sun.), or ask a local for tips on good car and bike loops. A beautiful path follows the Yakima River through the Yakima Greenway, a corridor of preserved land, from Robertson Landing (Exit 34 off I-82) to Harlan Landing in Selah Grove (Exit 31 off I-82).

Numbered streets are east of Front St., while numbered avenues are west of Front St. **Yakima Transit** (575-6175) buses trace 10 convenient routes (fare 50¢, ages 6-17 35¢, seniors 25¢; Mon.-Fri. 6:15am-7pm, Sat. 8:45am-6:30pm). **Greyhound,** 602 E. Yakima (457-5131; open Mon.-Fri. 8am-5pm), stops in Yakima on the way to and from Seattle (3 per day, $22 one way). There is no service from Yakima to Mt. Rainier. For a taxi, call **Diamond Cab** at (453-3113), open 24hr. It's worth renting a car to see the Cascades. Get a great deal at **Savemore Auto Rentals,** 615 S. 1st St. (575-5400; $16 per day with 100 free mi., 15¢ each additional mi.; must be 21). For **senior information and assistance** call 574-1080 (Mon.-Fri. 8:30am-5pm). The **crisis line** is 575-4200 (24hr.). Seniors get a discount on all prescriptions at **Medicine Mart Downtown,** 306 E. Yakima Ave. (248-9061; open Mon.-Fri. 9am-6pm). Yakima has two **hospitals,** both open 24hr.: **Yakima Valley Memorial,** 2811 Tieton Dr. (575-8000), and **Providence Medical Center,** 110 S. 9th Ave. (575-5000). In an **emergency,** call 911. The **police** are at 200 S. 3rd St. (575-6200). Rinse your rags at **K's Coin Laundry,** at the corner of N. 6th and Fruitvale (452-5335; open daily 7am-9pm). The **post office** (454-2450) is at 205 W. Washington Ave. at 3rd Ave. (open Mon.-Fri. 8:30am-5pm; **General Delivery Zip Code:** 98903). The **area code** is 509.

Accommodations The "fruit bowl" is full of reasonably priced, run-of-the-mill motels. A good bet for clean and comfortable rooms is the **Red Apple Motel,** 416 N. 1st St. (248-7150), where the friendly management does its best to keep out the rotten ones (21 and over; A/C, cable TV, apple-shaped pool; singles $42, doubles $46, on weekdays $36 and $42). **Motel 6,** 1104 N. 1st St. (454-0080), a 20 minute walk from downtown, is more reliable and professional than most of the budget motels along 1st St. The pool provides welcome relief from the scorching Yakima heat (singles $39, doubles $45).

Yakima's few **campgrounds** are overcrowded and noisy. The **Yakama Nation RV Park,** 280 Buster Rd. (865-2000 or 800-874-3087), in Toppenish, 20 mi. southeast of Yakima on U.S. 97, is the exception. Though primarily an RV park, there are tepees to sleep in and a pool set in a field on the reservation (sites $12, RV $18). Cheaper, more pleasant campgrounds lie on U.S. 12, about 30 mi. west of town on the way to Mt. Rainier. Sites with drinking water are $5; those without are free.

Food A cluster of boxcars-turned-tourist-bait on W. Yakima Ave. houses a number of mid-cost, mid-quality restaurants. **Ruben's Tortillería y Panadería,** 1518 1st St. (454-5357) sells freshly baked Mexican pastries for around 35¢ apiece and packages of 10 tortillas for $1. Open daily 8am-10pm. For a hearty Italian dinner, call **Deli da Pasta,** 7 N. Front St. (453-0571) and make the often necessary reservation. At lunch, "pick a pasta" and one of seven sauces for $7. At dinner, pay $8 for the same deal and splurge on their *tiramisu* for dessert. (Open Mon.-Sat. 11:30am to when the customers leave.) Stop in for a beer just across the street at **Grant's Brewery Pub,** 32 N. Front St. (575-2922), on the north end of the train station. Call to arrange a tour of the microbrewery, the oldest in the Northwest and still a great place to have a good time (575-1900). A pint of Grant's Scottish Ale costs $3, Yakima cider goes for $3. The small lunch menu varies, but usually includes fish and chips ($6.25). Live jazz, blues, and folk bands play on weekends (open Mon.-Thurs. 11:30am-11pm, Fri.-Sat. 11:30am-midnight, Sun. 11:30am-8pm).

Sights and Events The *Yakima Valley Farm Products Guide,* distributed at the visitors bureau and at regional hotels and stores, lists local fruit sellers and u-pick farms. Pounds of peaches often cost less here in season than do single peaches in other parts of the country. Fruit stands are common on the outskirts of town, particularly on 1st St. and near interstate interchanges. A good fruit stop for interstate trav-

---

Grand Coulee

Eighteen thousand years ago, the weather warmed and a little glacier blocking a lake in Montana slowly melted and gave way. The resulting flood swept across eastern Washington, gouging out layers of loess and basalt to expose the granite below. The washout, believed to have taken a little over a month, carved massive canyons called "coulees" out of a region now known as the **Channeled Scab Lands.** The largest of these coulees is appropriately named **Grand Coulee.**

The construction of the Grand Coulee Dam was a local cure for the economic woes of the Great Depression. From 1934 to 1942, 7000 workers were employed in constructing the nearly mile-long behemoth. The dam is the **world's largest solid concrete structure** and irrigates the previously parched Columbia River Basin while generating more power than any other hydroelectric plant in the United States. The backed-up Columbia River formed both the massive Franklin D. Roosevelt Lake and Banks Lake. "Wet siders" flock from western Washington for the hot, dry weather and some lakeside recreation. Go with the flow and visit the rotund **Visitors Arrival Center** (633-9265), on Rte. 155 just north of Grand Coulee, filled to the brim with exhibits on the construction, operation, and legacy of the dam, all set to a Woody Guthrie soundtrack. The dam is the place to be when night falls during the summer. A spectacular, multicolored laser show is projected on the dam's tremendous face (late May-late July 10pm, Aug. 9:30pm, Sept. 8:30pm; free).

---

elers is the **Donald Fruit and Mercantile,** 4461 Yakima Valley Hwy. (877-3115), in Wapato, 11 mi. southeast of Yakima, at Exit 44 off I-82 (open May-Oct. Mon.-Sat. 9am-6pm, Sun. 10am-6pm). **Johnson Orchards,** 4906 Summitview Ave. (966-7479), is the u-pick farm closest to town, specializing in tree-ripened cherries (June-July) and apples (Aug.-Nov.).

A slightly longer jaunt can yield a wider range of **u-pick** produce, from cantaloupes to jalapeño peppers. Farms generally stay open in summer from 8am to 5pm, but check in the *Farm Products Guide* or call ahead to be sure. Wear gloves and sturdy shoes, and bring as many empty containers as you can. U-picks are good deals and fun, but you can save almost as much by buying directly from the farms. While exploring the fruitful possibilities, stop by **Washington's Fruit Place Visitor Center,** 105 S. 18th (576-3090) to push buttons and pull levers on exhibits that explain and illustrate the area's crop productions. Your labors will be rewarded with free apple juice. (Open Mon.-Fri. 9am-5pm, Sat. 10am-5pm, Sun. noon-4pm.)

Toppenish, 19 mi. southeast of Yakima, is the jumping-off town for the **Yakama Reservation** (the tribe recently changed the official spelling of its name). The **Yakama Nation Cultural Center** (865-2800), 22 mi. south on U.S. 97 in Toppenish, presents exhibits on the culture of the 14 tribes and bands that inhabit the Yakima Valley. The phenomenal museum concentrates on the oral tradition of the Yakama Natives, and houses a small bookstore as well. The rest of the cultural center surrounds the museum and includes a public library and a restaurant which serves native dishes. The entire complex is well worth a visit ($4, students and seniors $2; open Mon.-Sat. 9am-6pm, Sun. 9am-5pm). The **Toppenish Powwow Rodeo and Pioneer Fair** (865-3262) occurs during the first weekend of July on Division Ave. in Toppenish, and features games, dancing, live music, a rodeo, and fair food (fair admission $2, rodeo $10). The **Central Washington State Fair** is held in Yakima in late September. The nine-day event includes agricultural displays, rodeos, big-name entertainers, and horse racing (call 248-7160 for more info).

■ Spokane

Spokane was established as an agricultural and logging hub in 1871, and has a long history of surmounting seemingly overwhelming obstacles. A gigantic fire ravaged the city in 1889 but the citizens, prosperous from the silver mines in northern Idaho,

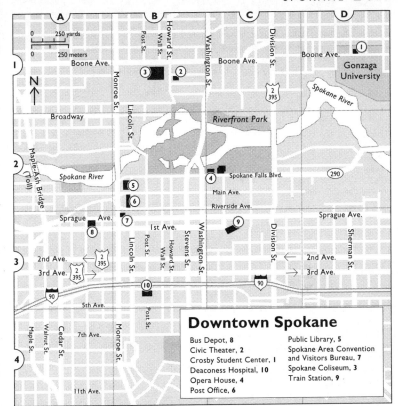

Downtown Spokane

Bus Depot, **8**
Civic Theater, **2**
Crosby Student Center, **I**
Deaconess Hospital, **10**
Opera House, **4**
Post Office, **6**

Public Library, **5**
Spokane Area Convention
and Visitors Bureau, **7**
Spokane Coliseum, **3**
Train Station, **9**

WASHINGTON

rebuilt on a grander scale. However, after decades of prosperity as a center of commerce fueled by agriculture, mining, logging, manufacturing, and a central rail link, Spokane's economy stumbled. The city recovered by hosting the 1974 World's Fair. Defunct rail yards were torn up to make room for the 100-acre fairgrounds, and much of the city received a make-over in preparation for hordes of visitors from all over the world. Expo '74 was a huge success, and gave Spokane an opera house, Imax theater, and amusement park. Today Spokane is the hub of a vast land-locked portion of the Pacific Northwest, and supports a thriving service industry. Downtown, enormous department stores linked by covered skyways mix with nameless burger joints for a comfortable suburban atmosphere. Still, despite its inexpensive motels and massive quantities of cheap food, Spokane is still more of a gateway than a destination for most travelers.

PRACTICAL INFORMATION AND ORIENTATION

Visitors Information: Spokane Area Convention and Visitors Bureau, 201 W. Main St. (747-3230 or 800-248-3230), Exit 281 off I-90. Overflowing with literature extolling every aspect of Spokane. Open Mon.-Fri. 8:30am-5pm; summers Sat. 8am-4pm, Sun. 9am-2pm. The **Spokane River Rest Area Visitor Center** (226-3322), at the Idaho state line, Exit 299 off I-90, offers similar pamphlets and enthusiasm. Open daily May-Sept. 8:30am-4:30pm.

Airport: Spokane International (624-3218 for automated info), off I-90 8 mi. southwest of town. Most major carriers with flights to Seattle, Portland and beyond.

Trains: Amtrak, W. 221 1st St. (624-5144, after business hours 800-USA-RAIL/872-7245), at Bernard St., downtown. To: Chicago (1 per day, $219); Seattle (1 per day, $67); Portland (1 per day, $67). Amtrak counter open Mon.-Fri. 11am-5:30am, Sat.-Sun. 7:15pm-5:30am.

Buses: Greyhound, W. 221 1st St. (624-5251 for tickets; 624-5252 for info), at Bernard St., downtown in the beautiful new depot. **Northwestern Trailways** (838-5262 or 800-366-3830) shares the terminal with Greyhound, serving other parts of Washington, Oregon, Idaho, and Montana. Greyhound to Seattle (5 per day, $25), to Portland (3 per day, $35). Ticket office open daily 7:30am-9pm, midnight-2:30am. Student and military discounts.

Local Transit: Spokane Transit System, W. 1229 Boone Ave. (328-RIDE/7433). Serves all of Spokane, including Eastern Washington University in Cheney. Fare 75¢, over 64 and travelers with disabilities 65¢. Operates until 12:15am downtown, 9:45pm in the valley along E. Sprague Ave. All buses have bike racks.

Taxi: Checker Cab, 624-4171. **Yellow Cab,** 624-4321. Both open 24hr.

Car Rental: U-Save Auto Rental, W. 918 3rd St. (455-8018), at Monroe. Cars from $21.95 per day; 20¢ per mi. after 200 mi. Must be over 21 and have a major credit card. Open Mon.-Fri. 7am-7pm, Sat. 8am-5pm, Sun. 10am-5pm.

Camping Equipment: White Elephant, N. 1730 Division St. (328-3100) and E. 12614 Sprague (924-3006). Every imaginable piece of equipment sandwiched between dolls and shotguns. Open Mon.-Thurs. and Sat. 9am-6pm, Fri. 9am-9pm.

Public Library: W. 906 Main St. (626-5336). Open Mon.-Thurs. 10am-9pm, Fri.-Sat. 10am-6pm.

Laundromat: Ye Olde Wash House Laundry and Dry Cleaners, E. 4224 Sprague (534-9859). Washe ye olde clothes for 75¢, 12-min. drye 25¢.

Gay & Lesbian Community Services: 489-2206.

Travelers Aid Service, W. 1017 1st (456-7164), at Madison, near the bus depot. Open Mon.-Fri. 7am-11:30am, 1-5pm. If they can't help, try the **Salvation Army** (325-6813).

Crisis Hotline: 838-4428. 24hr.

Poison Information: 800-732-6985. 24hr.

Senior Center: W. 1124 Sinto (327-2861). Open Mon.-Fri. 8:30am-4:30pm, Sat. 9am-1:30pm. **Elderly Services Information and Assistance:** 458-7450.

Pharmacy: Hart and Dilatush, W. 501 Sprague (624-2111), at Stevens. Open Mon.-Fri. 8am-10pm, Sat.-Sun. noon-8pm.

Urgent Care Center: Rockwood Clinic, E. 400 5th Ave. (838-2531). Open 8am-8pm. Walk-in. **Hospital: Deaconess Medical Center,** W. 800 5th (emergency, 458-7100; info, 458-5800), at Lincoln. 24hr. emergency room.

Emergency: 911. **Police:** W. 1100 Mallon (456-2233), at Monroe.

Post Office: W. 904 Riverside (626-6860), at Lincoln. Open Mon.-Fri. 6am-5pm. **General Delivery ZIP Code:** 99210.

Area Code: 509.

Spokane lies 280 mi. east of Seattle on I-90. Avenues run east-west parallel to the river, streets north-south, and both alternate one way. The city is divided north and south by **Sprague Ave.,** and east and west by **Division St.** Downtown is the quadrant north of Sprague and west of Division, wedged between I-90 and the Spokane River. I-90 Exits 279 to 282 gives access to Spokane. As in many western cities, street addresses begin with the compass point first, list the number second, and the street name third (e.g., W. 1200 Division). All Spokane Transit System buses start and finish their routes at the bus station at the intersection of Riverside and Wall.

ACCOMMODATIONS AND CAMPING

Don't try to sleep in Riverfront Park; the Spokane police *don't* like it. Stay indoors. Spokane is good to budget travelers.

Rodeway Inn City Center, W. 827 1st (838-8271 or 800-4-CHOICE/24-6423), at Lincoln. Elevated pool in the middle of the parking lot, great location, and pristine rooms. Free continental breakfast, evening snack, and 24-hr. coffee in the office.

Indoor sauna and spa, A/C, cable TV (no movie channels), 10% AAA discount in advance. Singles $44. Double $54. Rates fall by $10 in the off season.

Suntree 8 Inn, S. 123 Post St. (838-8504), at 1st St.; look for the rainbow balloon perched atop the inn. Clean, comfortable rooms hide behind this motel's drab exterior. If you're feeling tolerant, you can save $7 by taking a room (identical to the others) on the 3rd floor or next to the railroad tracks. Join the "V.I.P. Club" for $4, and you can pay with CDN$ at par. Communal jacuzzi, cable with movie channels, and free continental breakfast. Singles $45, $5 each additional guest.

Riverside State Park (456-3964, 800-452-5687 for reservations), 6 mi. northwest of downtown on Rifle Club Rd., off Rte. 291 or Nine Mile Rd. Take Division St. north and turn left on Francis, then follow the signs. 101 standard sites in sparse, dry Ponderosa forest next to the river. Showers. Wheelchair access. Sites $11.

Park Washington Ponderosa Hill, (747-9415 or 800-494-7275), 5 mi. west of the city. Take I-90 to Exit 272. Follow the signs along Hallett Rd. east to Thomas-Mallon Rd., then 1 mi. south. Friendly hosts run a campground so big (168 full hookup sites) it deserves its own ZIP code. Showers, laundry facilities, phone and cable hookups. RVs $23, tents $14, tents with electricity $15. AAA 10% off.

FOOD

Spokane is a great place for fresh produce. The **Spokane County Market** (482-2627), on the north end of Riverside Park just East of the Flour Mill, sells fresh fruit, vegetables, and baked goods (open May-Oct. Wed., Fri. and Sat. 9am-5pm, Sun 10am-4pm). The **Green Bluff Growers Cooperative,** E. 9423 Green Bluff Rd., Colbert 99005, is an organization of 20-odd fruit and vegetable farms, marked with the big red apple sign 16 mi. northwest of town off Day-Mountain Spokane Rd. Many farms have u-pick arrangements and are near free picnic areas. To tank up on **caffeine** downtown, dash into Nordstroms and up the escalator to the third floor, where the café serves 25¢ coffee with unlimited refills.

Dick's, E. 10 3rd Ave. (747-2481), at Division. Look for the huge pink, er, panda sign near I-90 and "buy burgers by the bagful." This takeout burger phenomenon is a time warp: customers eat in their parked cars and pay prices straight out of the 50s (burgers 55¢, fries 49¢, sundaes 67¢, soft drinks 53-73¢). Since there's no breakfast menu, start off your day with a "Whammy" ($1.07), which has twice the meat and double the cheese. Dick's proves that Spokane is not just an apple and potatoes town. The joint is always crowded, but battalions of workers move things along quickly. Open daily 9am-1am.

Europa Pizzaria, S. 125 Wall St. (455-4051). Located in the **Atrium**, a small brick building containing several restaurants and stores on Wall St. near 1st Ave. A remarkably classy spot. Cheap dishes on the medium-to-high priced menu: a good 6 in. pizza ($3), sandwiches ($5), and calzones ($6). Plenty of vegetarian choices. Open daily 11am-midnight.

Milford's Fish House and Oyster Bar, N. 719 Monroe (326-7251). While the neighborhood isn't great, Milford's is one of the finest restaurants in the Pacific Northwest. And though it may sink your budget, the freshest seafood in town will certainly buoy your spirits. Choose from a placard of fresh specials ($13-19) rotated daily; each includes a bowl of clam chowder or a dinner salad along with bread and vegetables. Open Sun-Mon. 4-9pm, Tues.-Sat 5-10pm. Reservations recommended, especially on weekends.

The Il Moon Café at the Mars Hotel, W. 300 Sprague (747-MARS/6277). The amazing interior of this bizarre restaurant overshadows the gourmet food. Movie set experts crafted large trees and gigantic rocks, complete with vegetation and a waterfall. There's even a casino upstairs. Though breakfast and dinner are pricey, lunch is reasonable: salads, sandwiches, vegetarian and chicken dishes are $6-7. Your best bet is to soak up the atmosphere over dessert and gourmet coffee ($1.25). 24hr. Lunch served Mon.-Sat. 11:30am-2:30pm.

WASHINGTON

SIGHTS

Spokane is too down-to-earth to bother with flashy art. The city's best attractions concentrate on local history and culture. The **Cheney Cowles Memorial Museum,** W. 2316 1st Ave. (456-3931, ext. 101), houses displays on the history of the area, from the Lewis and Clark expedition to Expo '74. Follow 2nd Ave. west out of town, turn right onto Poplar, and in two blocks you're there. Included in the price of admission is a tour of the **Campbell House,** a throwback to Spokane's "Age of Elegance." The museum also hosts the annual **Art Fest** on the last day of May and the first of June. (Open Tues.-Sat. 10am-5pm, Wed. 10am-9pm, Sun. 1-5pm; admission $4, students and seniors $3, ½-price Wed. 10am-5pm, free Wed. 5pm-9pm.)

    Riverfront Park, N. 507 Howard St. (625-6600 or 800-336-PARK/7275), just north of downtown, is Spokane's civic center and greatest asset. Developed for the 1974 World's Fair, the park's 100 acres are divided by the roaring rapids that culminate in Spokane Falls. The **IMAX Theater** (625-6686) holds a five-story movie screen and a projector the size of a Volkswagen. (Open Sun.-Thurs. 11am-8pm; Fri.-Sat. 11am-9pm; shows on the hr.; $5.25, seniors $4.75, under 18, $4.25; $3 on Mon.) Another section of the park offers a full range of kiddie rides, including the exquisitely hand-carved **Looff Carousel** (open summers daily 11am-8pm, Fri.-Sat. 11am-10pm; $1 a whirl). A one-day pass ($10) covers both these attractions, plus the ferris wheel, park train, sky ride and others. If that's not enough, you can rent in-line skates and bikes from **Quinn's** (456-6545) in the park for $5 per hour with pads and a helmet. The park also offers ice-skating in the winter.

    Manito Park, 4 W. 21st Ave. (625-6622), has four sections for both hard-core botanists and those just wishing to spend time in one of the most beautiful spots in Spokane. Check out the carp in the Nishinomiya Japanese Garden, overdose on roses on Rosehill (they bloom in late June here), relax in the elegant Duncan Garden, or sniff the flowers in the David Graiser Conservatory. From downtown, go south on Stevens St. and turn left on 21st Ave. (free; open daily 8am-8pm).

    Don't leave Spokane without tasting eastern Washington wine. If the spectacular views don't make your head spin, the wine at the **Arbor Crest Estate,** N. 4705 Fruithill Rd. (927-9894), will. After a self-guided tour that explores stunning vistas overlooking the valley below, sip excellent wine (both free). Take I-90 to Exit 287, travel north on Argonne over the Spokane River, turn right on Upriver Dr., proceed 1 mi., and then bear left onto Fruithill Rd. Take a sharp left at the top of the hill. The Chamber of Commerce (see **Practical Information**) hands out various publications on area wineries. Stop by for a copy of the *Washington Winery Tour.*

    Hard-core Bing Crosby devotees and other obsessive types will be drawn to the **Crosby Student Center,** E. 502 Boone St. (school operator, 328-4220), at Gonzaga University. Here, in the tiny Crosbyana Room in the White Student Center, the faithful exhibit the Bingmeister's relics and gold records. The Oscar is a replica. Amusing. (Free; open Mon.-Fri. 8:30am-4:30pm.)

ENTERTAINMENT AND EVENTS

The *Spokane Spokesman-Review*'s Friday "Weekend" section, the *Spokane Chronicle*'s Friday "Empire" section, and the *Inlander* (a free local publication) give the lowdown on area happenings.

    Spokane's **Indians** play single A baseball in the Seafirst Stadium at N. 602 Havana (535-2922) from June to August (tickets $3.50-5.50), while the **Chiefs** skate at the **Veteran's Memorial Arena** (better known as "the Arena"), 720 W. Mallon Ave. (328-0450 for Chiefs tickets and info, 325-SEAT/7328 for other events). The arena has enough seating for 12,500 Chiefs fans or concert goers, and hosts musical talents from James Taylor to Garth Brooks. To get to the Arena, follow signs on the Maple St. exit off I-5. Box office open Mon.-Fri. 10am-6pm. All city-sponsored events are ticketed by Select-A-Seat. Call 325-7469 for recorded information or 325-7328 for tickets Mon.-Fri. 8am-5pm.

Spokane also has its share of cultural institutions. **The Opera House,** W. 334 Spokane Falls Blvd. (353-6500), is home to the Spokane Symphony Orchestra and traveling Broadway shows, as well as staging special performances ranging from rock concerts to chamber music to G. Gordon Liddy (open Mon.-Fri. 8am-5pm). The **Civic Theater,** N. 1020 Howard St. (325-2507; for calendar info, 800-248-3230 or 747-3230), is opposite the Arena. It is known for locally produced shows, and has a downstairs theater for more experimental productions. (Tickets for musicals Fri.-Sat. $15, $12 seniors and students. Tickets for plays Fri.-Sat. $12, seniors $10, students $7, discounted on Thurs. and Sun.) The **Spokane Interplayers Ensemble,** S. 174 Howard (455-7529), is a resident professional theater which performs a broad range of plays (Sept.-June, Tues.-Sat; tickets $12.50-16).

The city is also home to a treasure trove of budget movie theatres. The **Fox Theatre,** W. 1005 Sprague, (624-0105), is the most convenient of several theatres with grand old 20s decor and shows major releases anywhere from one month to a year after mainstream release ($1). The box office opens at 5pm, noon in summer. The **Magic Lantern Theatre,** S. 123 Wall St. (838-4919), shows foreign, independent, and art films with the occasional major release. It is blessed with a lobby full of café tables and Lautrec prints that make this a Friday night place to be ($5.50, seniors and students $4.50, and $3 for matinees and *Rocky Horror,* Fri.-Sat. at midnight).

Residents of Washington's dry-side capitol know good beer as well as their Seattle cousins. At the **Fort Spokane Brewery,** W. 401 Spokane Falls Blvd. (838-3809), try the house specialty, Border Run, or sample five microbrews for $4. The kitchen is open for lunch and dinner, serving burgers for under $5 (closes at 10pm). Live blues on Friday and Saturday, and occasional big names on Thursday nights. (Open Mon.-Thurs. 11am-midnight, Fri.-Sat. 11am-2am, Sun. noon-midnight. Happy hour, daily 4pm-7pm, features $2 microbrew pints.)

Outback Jack's, W. 321 Sprague (624-4549), is also fit for any competition with Seattle. Home to thrashing live music (Tues., Fri., Sat.), DJ dancing (Wed., Thurs., Sun.), and pool tournaments (Mon.), the self-proclaimed "Party Capital" has hosted such legends as Quiet Riot and is painted floor to ceiling an absosmurfely aggravating blue. Draft pints are $1.25 and up. (Beware of Schlitz!) (Open daily noon-2am.) **Dempsey's Brass Rail,** W. 909 1st. (747-5362), has a good dance floor and a lounge featuring big screen Nintendo games on the second floor. Dempsey's proclaims itself "the place to be gay." Draft pints are $1.50-3.25. (Open daily 3pm-2am.)

The "Lilac City" celebrates May with two grand events. The **Bloomsday Road Race,** on May 1, features 60,000 runners and strollers going the 10km distance before a crowd of 100,000. The third week of May brings the **Lilac Festival,** a week-long hoopla culminating with the Torchlight Parade, which includes floats from as far as California.

■ Near Spokane: Coeur d'Alene, Idaho

When French and English fur traders passed through northern Idaho in the late 1800s, they attempted to trade with uninterested local Native Americans. The trappers' French-speaking Iroquois guides dubbed the dismissive natives "people with pointed hearts," which the trappers shortened to "hearts of awls"—Coeur d'Alene (kur-duh-Lane). The gaggle of tourists can do little to mar the rustic beauty of this town 20 minutes from Spokane and known as CDA to locals. No matter how many people clutter the beaches near the tastefully developed resort town, the deep blue waters of Lake Coeur d'Alene offer a serene escape.

Practical Information Get info at the **visitors center,** 414½ Mullan Ave. (667-4990; open Sun.-Tues. 9am-5pm, Wed.-Sat. 9am-7pm). The **bus station** lies at 1527 Northwest Blvd. (664-3343), 1 mi. north of the lake (open daily 8am-8pm). **Greyhound** serves Boise (1 per day, 11hr., $65), Spokane (3 per day, 45min., $9), Lewiston (2 per day, 3hr., $30), and Missoula (3 per day, 4hr., $31). **U-Save Auto Rental,** 501 Northwest Blvd. (664-1712), does the car rental thang. ($30 per day with

200 free mi., 20¢ per additional mi. Open Mon.-Fri. 9am-4pm, Sat. 8am-3pm, Sun. 10am-4pm.) **Crisis Services** can be reached at 664-1443 (24hr.). Coeur d'Alene's **post office,** is at 111 N. 7th St. (664-8126), 5 blocks east of the Chamber of Commerce (open Mon.-Fri. 8:30am-5pm); **ZIP code:** 83814; **area code:** 208.

Accommodations, Camping

Cheap lodgings are hard to find in this resort town. Try the motels on Sherman Ave., on the eastern outskirts of the city. **Star Motel,** 1516 E. Sherman Ave. (664-5035), fits phones and TVs with HBO in its tidy cubicles (singles $40, doubles $45). Across the street, **Budget Saver Motel,** 1519 Sherman Ave. (667-9505), competes with roomier accommodations (singles $35, doubles $42-47; late Sept.-early June $30/$37-40). For a list of B&Bs, stop by the Chamber of Commerce or call the B&B information center at 667-5081 or 800-773-0323. Some are fairly reasonable at about $60 a night.

Camping is the way to go for cheap lodging in Coeur d'Alene. There are five **campgrounds** within 20 mi. of town. **Robin Hood RV Park,** 703 Lincoln Way (664-2306, 800-280-CAMP/2267), lies within walking distance of downtown and just a few blocks from a swimmable beach (sites $7.50 for two; showers, laundry, hookups, no evil sheriffs). There are a few first-come, first-served national forest campgrounds in the area: popular **Beauty Creek,** 10 mi. south from Robin Hood along the lake, boasts the trailhead to the much acclaimed Caribou Ridge Trail #79, and **Bell Bay,** on Lake Coeur d'Alene (off U.S. 95 south, then 14 mi. to Forest Service Rd. 545), with 26 sites and good fishing. All sites cost $9 and have access to potable water and pit toilets; the campgrounds are generally open May through September. Call the **Fernan Ranger District Office,** 2502 E. Sherman (769-3000), for details on these and other forest campgrounds (open Mon.-Fri. 7:30am-4pm).

Food

Coeur d'Alene has oysters aplenty. For the best and most entertaining shellfish slurp, go to **Cricket's Restaurant and Oyster Bar,** (765-1990) on Sherman Ave., with the car on the roof, to sup on six oysters for $7.50 and watch the toy train chug by on raised tracks. (Open Mon.-Fri. 11am-10pm, Sat. and Sun. 11am-11pm.) If you like your snacks without shells, "Wake up and Live" at the **Java Café,** 324 Sherman Ave. (667-0010). Sip gourmet coffee, eat confetti eggs for breakfast ($4), or gourmet pizza for lunch ($4-5; open daily 7am-10pm). Revere the scorching power of the chile and the heroism of **Taco Dude,** 415 Sherman Ave. (666-9043). Check your e-mail among fellow spice-loving neophytes—only $4 for half an hour, or free with a purchase. (Everything on the menu is $1.25-$5. Open Sun.-Thurs. 11am-9pm, Fri.-Sat. 11am-10pm.)

Get a dose of Thai flavor and hilarious marketing at **Mad Mary's,** 1801 Sherman Ave. (667-3267), where Mary chops, dices, yells and generally makes herself heard. Let her "light your fire" with her $7.50 spicy chicken livers or more traditional Pad Thai ($8.50-11.95). Huge portions. (Open Tues.-Thurs. 11am-9pm, Fri. 11am-10pm, Sat.-Sun. noon-whenever. Handicap accessible.) Or head north and turn right at 313 Coeur d'Alene Lake Dr. for **Tubs Coffee House,** where locals munch on 7-in. pesto pizzas ($4) and sip perfect espresso. The tubs in question are private, cedar-enclosed outdoor hot tubs ($15 per hr.). Open daily 6am-10pm.

Sights and Activities

The lake is Coeur d'Alene's *raison d'être*. Hike 2 mi. up **Tubbs Hill** to a scenic vantage point, or head for the **Coeur d'Alene Resort** and walk along the **world's longest floating boardwalk** (3300 ft.). You can tour the lake on a **Lake Coeur d'Alene Cruise** (765-4000) and see the world's only floating golf green. (Departs from the downtown dock May-Sept. 1:30, 3:30, and 5:30pm; 90min.; $10.75, seniors $9.75, kids $5.75.) Rent a canoe or a pedal boat at the city dock, and explore the lake ($7 per hr., $20 per ½day, $35 first whole day, $15 per day thereafter). A 3-mi. bike/foot path follows the lake shore. **Four Seasons Outfitting,** 200 Sherman Ave. (765-2863), organizes horse rides ($13 first 45min., $36 for 3hr.) and a variety of other expensive outdoor activities. Call in advance.

▓ Pullman

Pullman's two main attractions are the undulating wheat and lentil-carpeted hills of the Palouse (puh-LOOZ) region and the enormous **Washington State University (WSU)** campus. With WSU Cougar banners on every street light—the university is home to PAC 10 football and basketball teams—the college *is* the town. Once a sleepy farming town, the fast pace of a large university propels Pullman today.

PRACTICAL INFORMATION

Visitors Information: The **Pullman Chamber of Commerce,** N 415 Grand Ave. (334-3565 or 800-365-6948), doles out free maps and will tell you *all* about Pullman's favorite vegetable, the lentil. Open Mon.-Fri. 9am-5pm, Sat. 10am-2pm during the school year.

Buses: Northwestern Trailways, NW 1002 Nye (334-1412), runs buses to Boise (1 per day; $39), Seattle (2 per day; $35 and $39), and Spokane (2 per day; $13 and $22.75). Open Mon.-Fri. 8am-4:30pm.

Public Transportation: The two lines of **Pullman Transit,** NW 775 Guy St. (332-6535), run between the WSU campus and the downtown area. 35¢, seniors and under 18 20¢. Operates Mon.-Fri. 6:50am-5:50pm.

Taxi: Moscow Pullman Cab (208-883-4744) runs Sun.-Thurs. 7am-midnight, Fri.-Sat. 7am-2am.

Car Rental: U-Save Car Rental, S 1115 Grand Ave. (334-5195), rents cars for $32 per day, 20¢ per mi. after 150 mi. Must be 21 with a major credit card. Open Mon.-Fri. 8am-5:30pm, Sat. 9am-4:30pm.

Laundromat: Betty's Brite and White, N 1235 Grand Ave. (332-3477).

Senior Services: Pullman Senior Center, SE 325 Paradise St. (332-1933), in City Hall. Open Mon.-Sat. 11am-4pm.

Hospital: Pullman Memorial Hospital, NE 1125 Washington Ave. (332-2541).

Pharmacy: Corner Drug Store, E 255 Main St. (334-1565), at Kamiaken.

Rape Crisis: Rape Resource (332-4357). 24hr.

Emergency: 911. **Ambulance and Police:** 332-2521. The **Police Station** is behind City Hall.

Post Office: S 1135 Grand Ave. (334-3212). Open Mon.-Fri. 8:30am-5pm, Sat. 8:30-11:30am. **General Delivery ZIP Code:** 99163.

Area Code: 509.

Pullman lies at the junction of Rte. 27 and 272. U.S. 195, running from Spokane south to Lewiston, bypasses the city to the west. Spokane lies 70 mi. north. Pullman lies 8 mi. *zapad* of Moscow, Idaho on Washington Hwy. 270.

ACCOMMODATIONS AND CAMPING

The steady stream of students through Pullman fosters a decent selection of moderately priced, no-frills motels. Rooms are easy to find, except on home football weekends and during commencement (the first week of May).

The American Travel Inn Motel, S 515 Grand Ave. (334-3500) on U.S. 195, has 35 spacious, spic-and-span rooms, with A/C, cable TV, laundry facilities, and a nice pool. Singles $38. Doubles $42.

The Manor Lodge Motel, SE 455 Paradise (334-2511), at Main. The pleasant innkeepers offer clean rooms with cable TV, refrigerators, and microwaves. The decor is Brady Bunch chic. Office open 7am-11pm, after hours ring night bell. Singles $35. Doubles $40.

Kamiak Butte Park, 11 mi. north of Pullman on U.S. 27, offers 10 forested campsites with water, toilets, and a stunning view of the Palouse for $5.

FOOD

The university has spawned a thriving gaggle of cheap eateries. Take your pick between hip cafés, a university-run dairy, and a classic drive-in.

Basilios, E 337 Main St. (334-7663). There has been no end to business in this joint since they opened their doors. Order a plate of pesto and penne ($4.25) or just about any other Italian dish. Open Mon.-Thurs. 7am-10pm, Fri. 7am-11pm, Sat. 11am-11pm, Sun. 11am-10pm.

The Combine, E 215 Main St. (332-1774), in the Combine Mall. Dodge low hanging lamps and shelves of tea to order fabulous, healthy sandwiches ($4.50). Plenty of tables, students reading lit crit, and goodies galore. Live bands and poetry readings during the school year. Open Mon.-Sat. 7am-midnight, Sun. 9am-10pm.

Ferdinand's (335-4014) on the WSU campus. They make everything with milk from WSU's dairy. From Stadium Way, turn toward the tennis courts onto South Fairway and follow it to the Food Quality Building. Ferdinand's Cougar Gold cheese ($11 for a 30-oz. tin) may be Pullman's biggest attraction. One of their excellent ice cream cones ($1) and a large glass of milk will do your body good. Open Mon.-Fri. 9:30am-4:30pm.

Cougar Country Drive-In, N 760 Grand Ave. (332-7829). A 10-min. walk from downtown. Motor to the drive-through or slide into one of the booths inside. This popular student hangout offers burgers wider than Whoppers with their own special sauce ($2.39). They've also got shakes as thick as mud ("dozens of flavors," $1.49). Open daily 10am-11pm.

Rancho Viejos, S 170 Grand Ave. (332-4301). The $5 lunch special and "Best North of the Border" burritos ($4.65-$7.95) should keep budget travelers happy. Also a bar in the evening. Open Sun.-Thurs. 11am-10pm, Fri.-Sat. 11am-11pm.

SIGHTS AND ENTERTAINMENT

There are nearly as many bars as there are Cougar signs in the Palouse. Two local favorites are **Rico's,** E 200 Main (332-6566; open Mon.-Sat. 11:30am-2am), and **Pete's Bar and Grill,** SE 1100 Johnson Ave. (334-4200; open Mon.-Sat. 11am-9pm, Sun. 4-9pm). Near the end of August of each year, the **National Lentil Festival** explodes onto the Pullman scene with a parade, live music, a 5km fun run, and so much more. The centerpiece of the festival remains the lentil food fair, showcasing lentil pancakes and lentil ice cream. The festival gained national recognition a few years back when it became the first engagement ever cancelled by Jerry Seinfeld. The festival remains a small-town tribute to a major player in the local economy (nearly all the lentils grown in the U.S. come from the Palouse). For more information, write National Lentil Festival, N 415 Grand Ave., Pullman 99163, or call the Chamber of Commerce at 334-3565 or 800-365-6948.

OUTDOORS

Pullman's gentle surrounding terrain and the broad, sweeping vistas of Washington's majestic Palouse region make the area ideal for exploration by bicycle or automobile. **Kamiak** and **Steptoe Buttes,** north of town off Rte. 27, both make enjoyable day trips. Pack a picnic lunch and head for the hills.

In the midst of baking summer temperatures, a glimpse of the **Blue Mountains** 25 mi. south of Pullman may spark a yearning for high, cool forests. A good approach is along Rte. 128 from the town of **Pomeroy,** a 40 mi. drive southwest. Follow U.S. 195 south to Clarkston, and then proceed on U.S. 12 west. This area, including the vast, remote **Wenaha-Tucannon Wilderness,** is administered by the **Pomeroy Ranger District** of Umatilla National Forest, Rte. 1, Box 53-F, Pomeroy 99347 (843-1891; open Mon.-Fri. 7:45am-4:30pm). Information is also available at the **Walla Walla Ranger District** office at W 1415 Rose St., Walla Walla 98362 (522-6290; open Mon.-Fri. 7:45am-4:30pm).

■ Near Pullman: Moscow, Idaho

Imagine Moscow as Pullman's conjoined twin, fused at the spinal column by Hwy. 8. This town does not offer hair-raising excitement. Moscovites are proud of their sense of small town community. When asked what to do in Moscow (MOS-ko) for only two hours, one resident answers, "I'd just walk down Main Street." The helpful **Moscow Chamber of Commerce,** 411 S. Main (882-1800 or 800-380-1801), is open Mon.-Fri. 9am-5pm.

As one might expect, **The Beanery,** 602 S. Main (882-7646), has great coffee and serves all three meals. You can get a full breakfast for $5, or a hefty Belgian waffle for $3, from 6:30am-11am. After 11am, it's sandwich time ($3.50-4); add $1.50 for soup or salad and coffee or Coke. Dinners are more expensive. (Open Mon.-Sat. 6:30am-7pm, Sun. 8am-3pm.) This local hangout serves more than the "liberal, commie, hippy fringe" and sponsors live jazz every Thursday at lunch. **Mikey's Gyros,** 527 S. Main (882-0780), serves up Greek grub for under $4. (Open Sun.-Thurs. 11am-8pm, Fri.-Sat. 11am-9pm; in summer closed Sun.) **Casa d'Oro,** 415 S. Main (883-0536), is a cantina that somehow avoids cheesiness, even though pinatas and sombreros hang from the walls. Dinner entrees range from $7-9, and locals come here for their margaritas. For a good deal, split a two-burrito meal, or just order an appetizer. Open Sun.-Thurs. 11am-10pm, Fri. and Sat. 11am-11pm.

Two events exemplify why Moscovites calls their town the **Heart of the Arts. The Lionel Hampton Jazz Festival** sizzles during the third week in February. Concerts and workshops are given by some of the country's best jazz musicians, including Lou Rawls and, of course, Lionel Hampton. Call 885-7212 or 800-345-7402 for more information. On the first weekend of May, the **Renaissance Fair** brings out the 16th-century Italian courtesan in everyone. Call the Chamber of Commerce for more information.

The Camas Winery, 110 S. Main (882-0214 or 800-616-0214), has free tastings and an informative display. The winery is open Tuesday-Saturday, noon-6pm (except during University of Idaho's spring break). **Mingles Bar and Grill,** 102 S. Main (882-2050), is cool, dark, and full of pool tables. Their extensive bar food collection (pizza, burgers, chili, and salads) is reasonably priced ($4.50-6). Domestic pitchers are $4.50. The restaurant is open Monday through Friday 11am-2am, Saturday and Sunday 9:30am-12am. The bar is open daily 11am-2am.

WASHINGTON

Oregon

One hundred years ago, entire families liquidated their possessions and sank their life savings into covered wagons, corn meal, and oxen. They hightailed it to Oregon in droves with little more than the shirts on their backs. Today, thousands of visitors are drawn each year by Oregon's remarkable natural beauty. While the coastal towns of Seaside and Cannon Beach are enticing, the waves and cliffs of Oregon's gorgeous Pacific should not blind the enterprising tourist to everything else the state has to offer. Don't miss out on the full Oregonian experience by clinging to the coast; venture inland to see other fabulous attractions—majestic Mt. Hood, the volcanic cindercones near Crater Lake, and the Shakespeare festival in Ashland. North America's deepest gorge and the towering Wallowa Mountains clash in the northeast, and the forested peaks of the Cascade Range stun visitors with their splendor. Both town and country are worth a closer look; Oregon's cities are as exciting and challenging as its wilderness. Portland is a casual and idiosyncratic city whose name was determined by a coin toss (one more turn of a coin and it would have been "Boston, Oregon"), while Eugene is a diverse college town with an attitude. Bend, a small interior city with an athletic, youthful crowd, is one of the liveliest towns in the state. Everything from excellent microbrews to accessible snow-capped peaks and lush forests make this state a seductive destination.

PRACTICAL INFORMATION

Capital: Salem.

Visitors Information: Oregon Tourism Commission, 775 Summer St. NE, Salem 97310 (800-547-7842; fax 503-986-0001). **Oregon State Parks,** 1115 Commercial St. NE, Salem 97310-1001 (503-378-6305; fax 378-6447). For **reservations** in most state parks, call 800-452-5687. **Department of Fish and Wildlife,** P.O. Box 59, Portland 97207 (503-229-5222 for a recording of fishing seasons and legal sites). For a complete list of licensing restrictions and fees, send away for the *Sport Fishing Regulations, Ocean Salmon Sport Fishing Regulations, Game Bird Regulations,* and *Big Game Regulations.* Contact the **Oregon State Marine Board,** 435 Commercial St. NE, Salem 97310 (503-378-8587; fax 378-4597) for info on boating permits. **Statewide Road Conditions:** 541-889-3999.

Population: 3,140,585. **State Motto:** "She flies with her own wings." **Nickname:** Beaver State. **State Song:** "Oregon, My Oregon." **State Flower:** Oregon Grape. **State Animal:** Beaver. **State Fish:** Chinook Salmon. **State Stone:** Thunderegg. **Land Area:** 97,093 sq. mi.

Emergency: 911.

Time Zone: Mostly Pacific (1hr. behind Mountain, 2 behind Central, 3 behind Eastern). A small southeastern section is Mountain (1hr. ahead of Pacific, 1hr. behind Central, 2 behind Eastern).

Postal Abbreviation: OR.

Sales Tax: None.

Drinking Age: 21.

Traffic Laws: Seatbelts required. Also, state law prohibits self-serve gas stations.

Area Codes: Portland and the Willamette Valley 503, everywhere else 541.

▇ Portland

The quietest and mellowest big city on the West Coast, Portland is in no hurry to be discovered. Downtown is a spotless, uncongested, pedestrian paradise. Like the popular poster depicting local tavern-owner "Bud" Clark in a trenchcoat flashing a public sculpture (he was shortly thereafter elected mayor), Portland has nothing to hide. Building height is regulated to preserve views, and zoning laws require all new buildings to have street-level retail space, thereby preventing that oh-so-common feeling of

OREGON

Oregon

National Forests
Crater Lake Ntl. Pk., 12
Deschutes, 17
Fremont, 18
Hells Canyon Ntl.
  Rec. Area, 21
Malheur, 23
Malheur Ntl. Wildlife
  Refuge, 25
Mt. Hood, 15
Ochoco, 19
Oregon Dunes Ntl.
  Rec. Area, 9
Siskiyou, 11
Siuslaw, 8
Three Sisters Wilderness
  Area, 13
Wallowa Whitman, 14
Willamette, 22

State Parks
Beverly Beach, 7
Cape Kiwanda, 6
Cape Lookout, 5
Cape Meares, 4
Fort Stevens, 1
Saddle Mountain, 2
Shore Acres, 10
Tillamook St. Forest, 3

Indian Reservations
Burns, 24
Fort McDermitt, 26
Umatilla, 20
Warm Springs, 16

N

PACIFIC
OCEAN

0   60 miles
0   60 kilometers

IDAHO
NEVADA
CALIFORNIA
WASHINGTON

Boise

CASCADE RANGE

Columbia R.
Snake River
Steens Mountain
Alvord Desert

Labels on map:
Astoria, Seaside, Cannon Beach, Manzanita, Nehalem, Garibaldi, Tillamook, Hebo, Pacific City, Lincoln City, Depoe Bay, Newport, Waldport, Florence, Winchester Bay, Reedsport, Charleston, North Bend, Coos Bay, Bandon, Port Orford, Gold Beach, Brookings

Portland, Oregon City, Mt. Hood, Hood River, The Dalles, Maupin, Carlton, McMinnville, Salem, Albany, Corvallis, Eugene, Roseburg, Grants Pass, Jacksonville, Medford, Ashland, Klamath Falls, Upper Klamath Lake

Sisters, Redmond, Bend, Prineville, Madras, Dayville, Condor, Prineville, La Pine, Crater Lake, Silver Lake, Summer Lake, Lake Abert, Valley Falls, Lakeview, Beatty

John Day Fossil Beds Nat. Mon., John Day, Long Creek, Burns, Crane, Malheur Lake, Harney Lake, Frenchglen, Burns Junction

Milton-Freewater, Stanfield, Pendleton, Enterprise, Joseph, La Grande, Halfway, Baker City, Ontario

Newberry Crater National Volcanic Monument
Umatilla National Forest
Willamette Pass

Highway numbers: 1, 3, 5, 7, 11, 19, 20, 26, 30, 58, 62, 74, 78, 82, 84, 86, 95, 97, 101, 126, 138, 140, 197, 199, 205, 205, 216, 219, 226, 230, 234, 395 urban alienation. Indeed, despite its substantial size, Portland maintains the feel of an overgrown town.

Driven indoors for the better part of the year by the persistent winter rains, the people of Portland have developed a love of art and music, and a keen taste for good beer. It is these common pursuits that bring the community together in theaters and pubs across the city. Funded by a one-percent tax on new construction, Portland has fostered a growing body of outdoor sculpture and a series of outdoor jazz concerts. The work of local artists fill galleries, cafés, muralled walls, and streets. Improvisational theaters are in constant production, and the Center for the Performing Arts is widely known for its talent. The varied artistic scene is anchored by Portland's venerable symphony orchestra, the oldest in the western United States.

Knowing that good beverages are essential to the full enjoyment of any event, the city's first-rate flock of small breweries pump out barrels of the nation's finest ale. Beer in hand, Portlanders browse the stuffed interior of Powell's Books, the largest bookstore in the country. Though there is plenty to do in the city, Portlanders also take full advantage of their area's natural endowments. Drawn by a common need to escape the urban, they are consummate hikers, bikers, and runners. The Willamette River and its wide park border the downtown, and dense forests at the city's edge cloak miles of well-maintained hiking trails. On any July day you can ski Mt. Hood in the morning, watch the sun drop into the Pacific Ocean from the cool sand of an empty beach, and still return to town in time to catch live blues.

PRACTICAL INFORMATION

Visitors Information: Portland/Oregon Visitors Association, 25 SW Salmon St. (222-2223 or 800-345-3214), at Front St. in the Two World Trade Center complex. From I-5, follow the signs for City Center. Extensive info on the city and surrounding area available; worker bees will point out the spots you're looking for on the free *Powell's Books Walking Map*. The free *Portland Book* contains maps, historic trivia, and comprehensive info on local attractions. Open Mon.-Fri. 8:30am-6:30pm, Sat. 9am-5pm; winter Mon.-Fri. 8:30am-5pm, Sat. 9am-4pm. **Portland Parks and Recreation,** 1120 SW 5th Ave. #1302 (823-2223) offers information on hiking and tennis opportunities in Portland's parks. Open Mon.-Fri. 8am-5pm.

Airport: Portland International Airport, 7000 NE Airport Way (335-1234). For transportation to and from the airport, see **Orientation and Getting Around.**

Train: Amtrak, 800 NW 6th Ave. (273-4866 for info recording; 800-USA-RAIL/872-7245 for national reservation line; Union Station 273-4865), at Hoyt St. To: Seattle (4 per day, $26), Eugene (2 per day, $20), Spokane (1 per day, $67), and Boise (3 days a week, $104). Open daily 6:45am-6pm.

Buses: Greyhound, 550 NW 6th Ave. (243-2357 or 800-231-2222), at Glisan in Fareless Sq. (see below). To: Seattle (9 per day, $15), Eugene (8 per day, $13), Spokane (6 per day, $35), and Boise (2 per day, $29). Lockers $2 for 6 hr. Ticket window open daily 5am-11:45pm. Station open daily 5am-1am. **Amtrak,** 200 yds from Greyhound, runs buses to Eugene (3 per day, $20) and a bus-train combo to Boise via Seattle ($51). **Green Tortoise** (800-867-8647 for reservations) picks up at 616 SW College Ave. at 6th Ave. Confirm 2 days in advance. To: Seattle (Tues. and Sat., 4pm, $15) and San Francisco (Sun. and Thurs., 12:30pm, $39).

Public Transportation: Tri-Met, Customer Service Center, #1 Pioneer Courthouse Sq., 701 SW 6th Ave. (238-7433; open Mon.-Fri. 7:30am-5:30pm). Several 24hr. recorded information numbers available: **Call-A-Bus** information system (231-3199); fare information (231-3198); updates, changes, and weather-related problems (231-3197); TDD information (238-5811); senior and disabled services (238-4952; open Mon.-Fri. 7:30am-5:30pm); lost and found (238-4855; open Mon.-Fri. 9am-5pm). Service generally 5am-midnight, reduced weekends. Fare 95¢-$1.25, ages 7-18 70¢, over 65 and disabled 45¢; no fare in Fareless Square downtown. All-day pass $3.25. All buses have bike racks (a $5 1-year permit can be obtained at area bike stores) and are wheelchair accessible. **MAX** (228-7246) is an efficient, light-rail train running between Gresham to the east and downtown, stopping at points along the way. MAX, based at the Customer Service Center, has the same

Portland

Sights

City Hall, 13
Civic Auditorium, 12
Civic Stadium, 14
Pacific Northwest
College, 10
Pioneer Courthouse
Square, 7
Portland Building, 11
Portland State
University, 9
Powell's Book Store, 4
Rose Garden Arena, 15
Skidmore Fountain, 5

Essentials

Ben Stark Hostel, 8
Bus Station, 2
Library, 6
Post Office, 1
Union Station (Amtrak), 3

Parks
Fareless
Square
MAX

Portland State University is
bounded by Route 405 to the
west and south, Market St. to
the north, and 6th Ave. to the
east.

TO YOUTH HOSTEL →

TO REED COLLEGE →

OREGON

12th Ave.
Everett St.
Burnside St.
Stark St.
7th Ave.
Grand Ave.
Martin Luther King Jr. Blvd.
3rd Ave.
2nd Ave.
Morrison St.
Belmont St.
Yamhill St.
Taylor St.
Salmon St.
Main St.
Madison St.
Hawthorne Blvd.

TO COLUMBIA RIVER GORGE
TO AIRPORT
Sandy Blvd

Lloyd Blvd
Hassalo

TO OREGON MUSEUM OF SCIENCE AND INDUSTRY →

Willamette River
Burnside Bridge
Morrison Bridge
Hawthorne Bridge
Steel Bridge

Front Ave.

1st Ave.
2nd Ave.
3rd Ave.
4th Ave.
5th Ave.
6th Ave.
Broadway Ave.
Park Ave.
10th Ave.
14th Ave.
Burnside St.
17th Ave.
19th Ave.
21st Ave.
23rd Ave.

Kearney St.
Johnson St.
Irving St.
Hoyt St.
Glisan St.
Flanders St.
Everett St.
Davis St.
Couch St.
Ankeny St.
Stark St.
Washington St.
Alder St.
Morrison St.
Yamhill St.
Park Ave.
9th Ave.
Broadway
Main St.
Jefferson St.
Columbia St.
Clay St.
Market St.
Oak St.
Front Ave.
Transit Mall
1st Ave.
2nd Ave.
3rd Ave.
4th Ave.
Taylor St.
Salmon St.
Madison St.
6th Ave.

TO LEWIS AND CLARK COLLEGE
TO ONDINE
TO DOWNTOWN INN 4TH AVE MOTEL
TO WASHINGTON PARK ZOO

1/2 mile
1/2 kilometer

N

fares as Tri-Met and runs 4:30am-11:30pm toward downtown and 5:30am-12:30am toward Gresham on weekdays (starts slightly later on weekends). More MAX lines toward Beaverton planned and under construction.

Taxi: Broadway Cab, 227-1234. **Radio Cab,** 227-1212. Airport to downtown $20-23. Airport to Portland International Hostel $17-20. Both 24hr.

Car Rental: Avis Rent-A-Car (800-331-1212 or 249-4950), at airport. Starting at $28 per day, $195 weekly rate with unlimited free mileage. Must be 25 or older with credit card. Reserve in advance for lowest rates. Open 24hr. **Practical Rent-A-Car,** 1315 NE Sandy Blvd. (224-8110). Transport from airport can be arranged. From $24 per day, 15¢ per mi. after 100 mi, or $27 per day with unlimited mileage. Must be 21 or older with credit card. Open Mon.-Fri. 8am-5:30pm, Sat. 9am-4pm; winter Mon.-Fri. 8am-5:30pm, Sat. 9am-noon.

Car Club: AAA Automobile Club of Oregon, 600 SW Market St., 97201 (222-6734). Open Mon.-Fri. 8am-5pm.

Library: 801 SW 10th Ave. (248-5123). Open Mon.-Thurs. 10am-8pm, Fri-Sat 10am-5:30pm, Sun. 1-5pm.

Tickets: Ticketmaster (224-4400), for Oregon and Washington events only. Also **Fastixx,** 224-8499.

Laundromat: Springtime Thrifty Cleaners and Laundry, 2942 SE Hawthorne Blvd. (232-4353), across from the hostel. Wash $1, 10-min. dry 25¢. Open Mon.-Fri. 7:30am-10pm, Sat.-Sun. 8am-10pm. **City Laundry** (224-4204), at NW 14th and Glisan. Attendant always on duty, same day wash and fold (85¢ a lb.). Wash $1, 10 min. dry 25¢. Open daily 7am-10pm.

Ski Conditions: Timberline, 222-2211. **Ski Bowl,** 222-2695. **Mt. Hood Meadows,** 227-7669.

Weather/Road Conditions: 541-889-3999.

Crisis Line: 223-6161. 24hr.

Women's Services: West Women's Hotel Shelter, 2010 NW Kearney St. (224-7718). **Women's Crisis Line:** 235-5333. 24hr.

AIDS Hotline: 223-2437.

Gay and Lesbian Information: Phoenix Rising, 620 SW 5th Ave. #710 (223-8299). Counseling and referral for gays and lesbians. Open Mon.-Sat. 9am-9pm.

Senior Services: Senior Helpline, 248-3646, Mon.-Fri. 8am-5pm. **Oregon Retired Persons' Pharmacy,** 9800 SW Nimbus Ave., Beaverton (800-456-2277 for orders, 646-3500 for information). Open Mon.-Fri. 8am-5:30pm, Sat. 9am-1pm.

Suicide Hotline: 223-6161.

Emergency: 911. **Police:** 1111 SW 2nd Ave. (230-2121 for non-emergency response, 823-4636 for info). **Fire:** 55 SW Ash St. (823-3700).

Post Office: 715 NW Hoyt St. (294-2300). **General Delivery ZIP Code:** 97208-9999. Open Mon.-Fri. 7am-6:30pm, Sat. 8:30am-5pm.

Area Code: 503.

GETTING THERE AND GETTING AROUND

Portland is in the northwest corner of Oregon, where the Willamette (wi-LAM-it) River flows into the Columbia River. I-5 connects Portland with San Francisco and Seattle; I-84 follows the route of the Oregon Trail through the Columbia River Gorge toward Boise. West of Portland, U.S. 30 follows the Columbia downstream to Astoria, but U.S. 26 is the fastest way to reach the coast. I-405 runs just west of downtown to link I-5 with U.S. 30 and 26.

The cheapest way to reach downtown from the **Portland International Airport** is to take Tri-Met bus #12 (a 45-min. ride, leaving 4 times per hour), which passes through town going south on SW 5th Ave. (95¢). **Raz Tranz** (246-3301 for taped information) provides an airport shuttle twice per hour, which stops at most major hotels downtown. Fare $8.50, ages 6-12 $2.

Portland is divided into five districts. **Burnside St.** divides the city into north and south, while east and west are separated by the Willamette River. **Williams Ave.** cuts off a corner of the northeast sector, called simply "North." All street signs are labeled by their districts: N., NE, NW, SE, and SW. **Southwest Portland** is known as **downtown,** but also includes the southern end of historic **Old Town** and a slice of the wealthier **West Hills.** In the middle of downtown, between SW 5th and 6th Ave., lies the **transit mall,** the center of an extensive bus network closed to all but pedestrian and bus traffic. Almost all downtown streets are one-way, and they are riddled with "no turn" signs. Two-way streets are so rare in some parts of downtown that they are specially marked. Parking is plentiful but expensive: meters are 85¢ per hour, and usually limited to one to three hours total. The City of Portland's **Smart Park** decks are well marked and all over downtown. Rates are 75¢ per hour for the first four hours but jump to $2 per hour after that, making Tri-Met the best choice when spending the day downtown. For walkers, jaywalking is risky: cars will definitely stop for you, but the police may ticket you. It's a bit like using an umbrella—everyone will know you're not from Portland.

Old Town, in **Northwest Portland,** encompasses most of the historic part of the city. The southernmost blocks of the quarter, around W. Burnside, are best walked in groups at night. Overlapping with Old Town and stretching further north is the up-and-coming **Pearl District,** an industrial zone in the process of revitalization. Further north and west, Northwest Portland also offers metropolitan trendiness: NW 21st and NW 23rd St., collectively known as **Nob Hill,** are hot-spots for upscale and yuppie boutique shopping. **Southeast Portland** is home to residential areas of all classes, parks, factories, and local businesses. The wide green quads and brick halls of beautiful Reed College lie deep within Southeast Portland. But perhaps the best known part of Southeast is **Hawthorne Blvd.** with its rich collection of cafés, stores, theaters, and restaurants. **North** and **Northeast Portland** are chiefly residential, punctuated by a few small, quiet parks, though North Portland is also the site of the **University of Portland.** Drug traffickers base their operations in Northeast Portland; parts of the area are dangerous and there is almost no reason to go there.

The award-winning **Tri-Met bus system** weaves together Portland's districts and suburbs. Its logical organization makes it one of the most rider-friendly public transportation systems in America. In the transit mall, 31 covered passenger shelters serve as stops and information centers. Southbound buses pick up passengers along SW 5th Ave.; northbound passengers board on SW 6th Ave. Bus routes fall into seven regional service areas, each with its own individual "Lucky Charm": orange deer, yellow rose, green leaf, brown beaver, blue snow, red salmon, and purple raindrop. Shelters and buses are color-coded for their region. A few buses with black numbers on white backgrounds cut through town north-south or east-west.

Most of downtown, from NW Hoyt St. in the north to I-405 in the west and south and the Willamette River in the east, constitutes **"Fareless Square."** As the name suggests, buses and MAX are free in this zone. For fares outside this zone, see **Practical Information.** Pick up monthly passes, **bus maps,** and schedules at the Tri-Met Customer Assistance Office in Pioneer Courthouse Square.

ACCOMMODATIONS AND CAMPING

Although downtown is studded with Marriott-esque hotels and the smaller motels are steadily raising their prices, Portland is still great for the budget traveler, especially for those willing to share a room. The **Portland Hostel** is an old standby, and a number of other hostels and smaller establishments offer pleasant, low-cost housing. It's always wise to make reservations early because places can fill in a flash, especially during the Rose Festival and conventions. Camping spots are distant, but nature abounds; there are no gravel RV-only sites around Portland.

Hosteling International—Portland (HI-AYH), 3031 SE Hawthorne Blvd. (236-3380), at 31st Ave. Take bus #14 (brown beaver). Cool people come to Portland and this is the place to meet them. Cheerful, clean, and crowded. Kitchen facilities; laundromat across the street. Fills up early in the summer (particularly the women's rooms), so make reservations (credit card required) or plan to arrive at 5pm to get one of the 12-15 beds saved for walk-ins. Don't miss the all-you-can-eat pancakes every morning (a paltry $1). Open daily 7:30-11am and 4-11pm. 34 beds. No curfew. $13, nonmembers $16. Members only July-Aug.

McMenamins Edgefield Hostel, 2126 SW Halsey St., Troutdale (669-8610 or 800-669-8610), 20min. east of Portland off I-84. McMenamins converted this farm into its crown jewel. The lodge shares the estate with a winery (wine tasting!), brewery (beer tasting!), movie theater, and two restaurants (food tasting!). Elegant dark wood bunks and vast rooms. Two single-sex dorm-style rooms, each with 12 beds. Shower facilities down the hall include two claw-footed tubs. The restaurants offer good food at reasonable prices, but you can save money by bringing food. $18 per night.

Ben Stark International Hostel, 1022 SW Stark St. (274-1223; fax 274-1033). This old building is charming but run-down. Ascend the imposing, dark staircase to find 6 well kept hostel rooms, 2 bathrooms, and a sunny—if "stark"—common room down the hall. Laundry and lockers downstairs. No curfew; 24hr. desk service. Convenient location, but take note: there are some shady characters around, and the club across the street is noisy on weekends. Reservations and passport or hostel membership required. $15 per night, $12 Nov.-May. Private rooms $36-45.

YWCA, 1111 SW 10th Ave. at Main Street (294-7400, ext. 0; fax 294-7399). Women only, youth and Christianity optional. Two min. walk from the center of town. Rooms are small, but clean, quiet, and safe. Laundry and a bare-bones kitchen down the hall. Sleep in hostel-like room (quad $16.35), share a room with a stranger ($19.52), or opt for a single ($23.98, with private bath $28.34) or a double ($30.52, with private bath $33.79). Key deposit $2. Space limited.

Ondine, 1912 SW 6th Ave. (725-4336), between College St. and Hall St. If you are in town on business with Portland State University, you are eligible for the budget travel experience of a lifetime! 24 big, clean rooms, each with 2 twin beds. Linen and towels provided. Private bathrooms. Microwaves available; no kitchen. Coin laundry facilities. Excellent views. Close to downtown (within Fareless Square). Parking nightmarish. Reservations required, at least 1-2 wks. in advance. Cash or checks accepted. Singles $25, doubles $30.

Fourth Avenue Motel, 1889 SW 4th Ave. (226-7646). Location, location, location. Unremarkable rooms with dim lighting, but just blocks from the center of downtown. A/C and TV. Mandatory 10:30am wake-up call, and you have to be out by 11am. Singles from $35, doubles from $40.

Motel 6, 3104 SE Powell Blvd. (238-0600; fax 238-7167). Take bus #9 (brown beaver) from 5th Ave. Everything you'd expect from a Motel 6. Clean rooms without the color-coordinated watercolors. Sparkling outdoor pool. $47 if you're solo, $54 for 2 people, $57 for 3, or $60 for 4. Always full; call in advance, or show up at 6pm to catch a room that's been cancelled. Wheelchair access.

Downtown Value Inn, 415 SW Montgomery St. (226-4751). These rooms don't sparkle, but they are secluded safely from the street. Excellent location, blocks from town. A/C, TV, free local calls. Parking available. Singles $45, doubles $55.

Champoeg State Park, 8239 NE Champoeg Rd. (678-1251). Take I-5 south 20 mi. to Exit 278, then follow the signs west for 6 mi. more. Play along miles of paved bikeway or hike by the Willamette River. Nineteen shady RV sites ($19) have water and electricity. Tent sites ($15) do not afford much privacy. Two-day advance reservation required.

Ainsworth State Park, 37mi. east of Portland, at Exit 35 off I-84, in the Columbia Gorge. Proximity to expressway makes it convenient but noisy. Hardly a natural get-away, but the drive into Portland through the gorge is beautiful. Hot showers, flush toilets, hiking trails, and full hookup. All sites $19.

FOOD

Portland has more restaurants per capita than any other American city. Family establishments and quirky cafés, scattered most heavily across the NW and SE quadrants, offer great food at reasonable prices. You'll never get tired of eating out in Portland, and if you're careful, you won't go broke. Get your caffeine quotient from the comfort of your car at one of Coffee People's **Motor Mokas.** Coincidentally, they also serve Portland's best milkshakes. Natives recommend the Cappucino Borgia or the Black Tiger, each $3.45 for 20oz.

Northwest

If lunch or dinner time finds you prowling NW 21st and 23rd St., you are not alone. In a city full of wonderful, cheap food, the trendy, pricey eateries on this thoroughfare are mobbed. **Food Front,** a small cooperative grocery at 2375 NW Thurman St. (223-6819), has a superb deli selection amid a wonderland of natural foods, fruit, and baked goods (open daily 9am-9pm, summer daily 9am-10pm).

Garbonzo's, 922 NW 21st (227-4196), at Lovejoy. Seek refuge from the mad boutique-seekers on the street at this quiet, delicious falafel bar. Tasty, healthy food at excellent prices. The falafel pita ($3.50) is a superb choice. Good hummus ($3), baba ghanoush ($3.50), and mouthwatering baklava ($1.25). Only 2 items over $7. Open Sun.-Thurs. 11:30am-1:30am, Fri.-Sat. 11:30am-3am.

Accaurdi's Old Town Pizza, 226 NW Davis St. (222-9999). Relax on a couch, or at a table in this former whorehouse. Reported ghost sightings by the staff have not affected their pizza-crafting abilities (small cheese, $4.55). The lunch special lasagna can be meaty or veggie ($4.75). Open daily 11:30am-11:30pm.

Kornblatt's, 628 NW 23rd Ave. (242-0055). Take bus #15 (red salmon). The only one of its kind in Portland, this New York-style deli is an overdone sight for sore eastern eyes. "What, you're not eating? You look so thin!" Menu includes matzoh-ball soup ($3.25), knishes ($2.25), and latkes ($1.25). Sandwiches are expensive but huge ($6). Open Sun.-Wed. 7am-9pm, Thurs.-Sat. 7am-10pm.

Giant Steps, 1208 NW Glisan St. (226-2547). This chic Pearl District coffeehouse is a local favorite, with art from seven surrounding galleries and shots of wheat grass juice ($1.25). Named after John Coltrane's classic album, Giant Steps plays (you guessed it) great jazz. Open Mon.-Fri. 7am-7pm, Sat.-Sun. 8am-5pm.

Torrefazione Italia, 838 NW 23rd Ave. (800-727-9692). *Willamette Week*'s "Best Coffee in Portland" is the headliner at this crowded Nob Hill institution. When it's nice out, the giant windows slide open to let in fresh air, and allow for conversations with the hipsters on the street. Single espressos $1-3. Or try the marionberry granita ($2) for a refreshing kick. Open Mon.-Thurs. 6am-10pm, Fri. 6am-11pm, Sat. 7am-11pm, Sun. 8am-9pm.

Southwest

Streetcars downtown provide an array of portable food, but the best deals are found indoors. Usually an expensive place to eat, a row of fast and cheap ethnic restaurants downtown can be found between 10th and 11th Ave. on Morrison.

Chang's Mongolian Grill, 1 SW 3rd St. (243-1991), at Burnside. After one of their all-you-can-eat lunches ($6) or dinners ($9), you too will feel fit to conquer Asia. Select your meal from a buffet of fresh vegetables, meat, and fish, mix your own sauce to taste, and watch your chef make a wild show of cooking it on a domed grill the size of a Volkswagen Beetle. Rice, soup, and pancakes included. Open Mon.-Fri. 11:30am-2:30pm and 5-10pm, Sat.-Sun. noon-2:30pm and 5-10pm.

Rocco's Café, 949 SW Oak St. (223-9835), at W. Burnside Blvd. Gigantic slices of good thick pizza ($2) in a funky 90s pizza joint. Five wise-cracking signs remind you to tip before you take your pie to a psychedelic booth. Open Mon.-Thurs. 11am-11pm, Fri.-Sat. 11am-4am, Sun. noon-9pm.

Western Culinary Institute Chef's Corner, 1239 SW Jefferson (242-2422 or 800-666-0312). The testing ground for the cooking school's creative adventures. Sit on stools while cheerful students in tall white hats taste and discuss food. Sandwiches ($3.50) are small; the best bet is a hearty, homemade loaf of bread ($1) or a mouth-watering pastry ($1.25). All lunches under $6. Dinners are about $15 per person, but are spectacular seven course affairs. Call ahead. Open Mon. 8am-2:30pm, Tues.-Fri. 8am-6pm.

Good Dog/Bad Dog, 708 SW Alder at Broadway (222-3410). Only the choicest meats and seasonings go into the 10 types of sausages made here, and served on a

OREGON

fresh french roll. Try the local favorite Oregon Smokey ($4) or, for the veggie dog lover, there's a garden Sausage (also $4). Open Mon.-Sat. 11am-7pm.

Macheezmo Mouse, 723 SW Salmon St. (228-3491) between Broadway and Park. Fast, cheap Tex-Mex for the health-nut or finicky eater. Whether it's a $1.50 plate of beans and rice, a chicken quesadilla ($3.25), or a crazy Thai burrito with peanut sauce ($4.50), they do it fresh and to your specifications. Look for this Mouse's compadres on SE Hawthorne or NW 23rd if you're in need of a nibble. Open Mon.-Fri. 11am-9pm, Sat. 11am-8pm, Sun. noon-8pm.

Heathman Bakery & Pub, 901 SW Salmon St. (227-5700). The finest fresh fish in the city is grilled to perfection amidst museums and theaters. It comes at quite a price ($14-17), so you may just opt for the ever-popular seafood chowder ($3.25), house salad ($1.50), and all the homebaked bread your heart desires. Open Sun.-Thurs. 7am-11pm, Fri.-Sat. 8am-midnight.

Mayas Tacqueria, 1000 SW Morrison (226-1946). Have a veggie taco ($2.25) while examining the colorful pseudo-Mayan art. The main dishes are reasonable: super burritos are $6 and combo plates $7-8, but watch out for the $1.95 side of sour cream. The loud Latin tunes may agitate. Open Sun.-Thurs. 11am-10pm, Fri.-Sat. 11am-11pm.

Brasserie Montmartre, 626 SW Park Ave. (224-5552). This elegant, expensive restaurant has a subtle funny bone. Paper tablecloths, crayons, marauding magicians and nightly live jazz offer diversions for dull dates. The bistro section is slightly less expensive than the rest of the restaurant. Pasta and chicken $10, seafood and steak dishes $10-15, burgers $5. Open Mon.-Thurs. 11:30-2am, Fri. 11:30-3am, Sat. 10am-3am, Sun. 10am-2am.

Southeast and Northeast

Anchored by the happening Hawthorne Blvd., Southeast is a great place to head—day or night—to pass the time and fill your tummy. Eclectic restaurants with exotic decor and economical menus are hidden throughout residential and industrial neighborhoods alike. Granola seekers will be glad to find the **People's Food Store,** 3029 SE 21st, which runs an all-organic farmer's market on Wednesdays in the summer (open daily 9am-9pm), and the larger, more equipped **Nature's,** 3061 Division St. (open daily 9am-10pm).

Café Lena, 2239 SE Hawthorne Blvd. (238-7087). Take bus #5 (brown beaver). The Portland intelligentsia reverently frequent this café, known for its open-mike poetry every Tues. at 9:30pm, and its sumptuous homemade bread. Local art on the wall. An eclectic menu features Thai, Italian, and American ($7-10). Vegetarian soup or salad with half a gargantuan sandwich is a good bet for $5.50-6.50. Spoken word or acoustic music every night. Breakfast served until 4pm. Open Tues.-Thurs. 7am-11pm, Fri.-Sat. 7am-midnight, Sun. 8am-3pm.

Montage, 301 SE Morrison St. (234-1324). Take bus #15 (brown beaver) to the end of the Morrison Bridge and walk back toward the river. An oasis of Louisiana style and cooking. Unbelievable mac and cheese ($3), and gumbo you wish your mama made ($3). Open for lunch Mon.-Fri. 11am-2pm, dinner daily 6pm-2am.

Nicholas' Restaurant, 318 SE Grand Ave. (235-5123), across from Miller Paint. Take bus #6 (red salmon) to the Andy and Bax stop. Don't be fooled by the unassuming facade. Nicholas serves tantalizing Lebanese and Mediterranean food at incredibly inexpensive prices. Try the Meezza (the "I'll-try-a-little-bit-of-everything") platter ($6) or the Phoenician pizza ($2). Mediterranean sandwiches ($2.75-3). Open Mon.-Thurs. 10am-6pm, Fri.-Sat. 11am-7pm.

Delta Café, 4607 SE Woodstock Blvd. Take bus #19 (brown beaver) from 5th Ave.; look left 2 or 3 blocks after you pass Reed. Boasting dishes like fried okra and fried egg sandwiches (both $2), the food is decidedly soul, and the colorful ambience Portland. Decor is adamantly free-spirited. Worth the trek to Woodstock. Open daily 10am-10pm.

Tony's, 2932 SE Division St. (238-4785). Bus #4 (brown beaver) just before Nature's. This snappy new neighborhood hangout offers a classic array of hoagies and pizzas, but the masterpiece is the Philly cheesesteak ($4.50). Tony is serious about his East Coast-ness, and you can taste it. Tip as you will, but save enough change for a go at shuffleboard bowling. Open Tues.-Thurs. 11am-11pm, Fri.-Sat. 11am-midnight, Sun. noon-9pm.

Pied Cow Coffeehouse, 3244 SE Belmont St. (230-4866). Take bus #15 (brown beaver) right to the front door. Bring that hot date from the nearby hostel for latte and chocolate cake by the light of tiki torches in the outdoor garden. When it starts raining you can pet the fuzzy tiger-print walls inside the Victorian parlor. Espresso drinks $1-2. Open Tues.-Thurs. 6pm-midnight, Fri. 6pm-1am, Sat. 10am-1am, Sun. 10am-11pm. Closed January.

Saigon Kitchen, 835 NE Broadway (281-3669). Take bus #9 (purple raindrop). Quite possibly the best Vietnamese restaurant in town, with no pretensions of finery. The *chazio* rolls, deep fried and served with fresh herbs and sauce ($3.50), are a perennial favorite. Vegetarians are not neglected by this menu. Most entrees $6-8. Open Mon.-Fri. 11am-10pm, Sat.-Sun. noon-10pm.

PaRaDoX Palace Café, 3439 SE Belmont St. (232-7508). Classic 1950s greasy-spoon decor—complete with obligatory turquoise vinyl seats—but the food is strictly 90s. One lonely hamburger sits on a menu of vegetarian and vegan options like the veggie haystack ($3.50) or the tofu burrito ($5). Open daily 8am-9pm.

Rimsky-Korsakoffee House, 707 SE 12th Ave. (232-2640). Take bus #15 (brown beaver) to 12th, then walk 2 blocks north. Big red Victorian house converted into a cozy salon. Bacchanalian frenzy of desserts in a casually threatening atmosphere. Ask for a mystery table. Live classical music nightly. Open Sun.-Thurs. 7pm-midnight, Fri.-Sat. 7pm-1am.

Thanh Thao Restaurant, 4005 SE Hawthorne Blvd. (238-6232). Take bus #14 (brown beaver). You'll come back to Portland just for a second helping of this fabulous Thai cuisine. The long menu, ranging from cashew beef ($6.75) to eggplant in black bean sauce ($6.25), makes up for what they lack in decor. Salad rolls ($3) are a successful mutation of spring rolls. There's often a wait for dinner. Open Mon. and Wed.-Fri. 11am-2:30pm and 5-10pm, Sat.-Sun. 11am-10pm.

Cup & Saucer, 3566 SE Hawthorne Blvd. (236-6001). Take bus #5 (brown beaver). Friendly, frantic neighborhood restaurant famous for its pancakes ($3.50) and scrumptious grilled veggie sandwich ($4.75). The world's biggest blocks of coffee cake, brownies, and rice krispy treats are made there daily, and go for $.85-$1.50. Open daily 7am-8pm.

Hawthorne Street Café, 3354 SE Hawthorne Blvd. (232-4982). In yet another converted Victorian house, this café has perfected a relaxed elegance, with huge windows and light-strewn bistro tables. Lunch features enticing experimental sandwiches ($5). Some come in just for the marionberry coffee cake ($3). For dinner try the honey-mustard chicken salad ($6). Discount of 20% if you are staying at the hostel. Open Mon.-Fri. 7:30am-2:30pm; dinner Wed.-Fri. 5-10pm, Sat.-Sun. 7:30am-10pm.

SIGHTS AND ACTIVITIES

Shaded parks, magnificent gardens, innumerable museums and galleries, and bustling open-air markets beckon Portland's tourists and residents alike. For 95¢, bus #63 (orange deer or brown beaver) will deliver you to 13 different tourist attractions. You can catch the best of Portland's dizzying dramatic and visual arts scene on the **First Thursday** of each month when the small galleries in the Southwest and Northwest all stay open until 9pm. For information contact the **Metropolitan Arts Commission,** 1120 SW 5th Ave. (823-5111). Grab the *Art Gallery Guide* at the visitors center which pinpoints 65 art hot spots on a map. Or go to the **Portland Art Museum,** 1219 SW Park Ave. (226-2811), to latch onto a **Public Art Walking Tour.**

Downtown

Portland's downtown is centered around the **pedestrian and bus mall,** running north-south on 5th and 6th Ave., between W. Burnside Blvd. at the north end and SW Madison St. to the south. At 5th Ave. and Morrison St. sits **Pioneer Courthouse,** a downtown landmark. This monument is still a Federal courthouse and is the centerpiece of **Pioneer Courthouse Square,** 701 SW 6th Ave. (223-1613), which opened in 1983, and has since earned the affectionate name "Portland's Living Room." Portland-

OREGON

Don't Expect to Play Frisbee in This Park

No one knew that a hole cut through the sidewalk at the corner of SW Taylor St. and SW Front St. in 1948 was destined for greatness. Indeed, it was expected to accommodate an inglorious lamp post. But the post was never installed, and the 24-in. circle of earth was left empty until Dick Fagan, a columnist for the *Oregon Journal,* noticed it. Fagan used his column, called "Mill Ends," to publicize the patch of dirt, pointing out that it would make a great, though microscopic, park. After years of lobbying, the park was officially added to the city's roster in 1976. At 452.16 sq. in., **Mill Ends Park** is recognized by the *Guiness Book of World Records* as the **world's smallest park.** Locals have enthusiastically adopted the park, planting flowers and hosting a hotly contested **snail race** on St. Patrick's Day. Imagine all the things you can do there: eat your lunch (alone), wave at passing cars, read Habermas, meditate, develop a national healthcare plan everyone will accept, or just stand (in the place where you are).

---

ers of every ilk hang out in this massive brick quadrangle, complete with a Starbucks in one corner and the travel branch of Powell's in the other. With Tri-Met's Customer Service Office at its center and plenty of places to sit, the square is a shrine to the pedestrian. At the time it was built, area citizens purchased personalized bricks to support the construction of an amphitheater that hosts live jazz and folk music. During the summer, the **Peanut Butter and Jam Sessions** draw thousands of music lovers (Tues. and Thurs. noon-1pm). During the **Rose Festival** (see **Events**), the square blooms with a colorful but temporary array of flowers.

Certainly the most controversial building in the downtown area is Michael Graves' postmodern **Portland Building,** 1120 SW 5th Ave., on the mall. The building's 1984 opening was attended by King Kong (full-sized and inflatable), who perched on the roof. Since then, this confection of pastel tile and concrete has been vigorously praised and condemned as an overgrown jukebox. On a niche outside the building's second floor, *Portlandia* reaches down to crowds below. This immense bronze statue portrays the trident-bearing woman of the state seal, but to many she looks like a man with breasts brandishing a large salad fork. The **Standard Insurance Center,** nearby at 900 SW 5th Ave., has also engendered controversy for *The Quest,* the white marble sculpture out front. The sculpture is more commonly known to locals as *Three Groins in the Fountain.*

Anyone who doubts that mega-corporations will soon rule the world need only visit **Niketown,** 930 SW 6th Ave. at Salmon (221-6453). TVs in the floor, life-size Andre Agassi and Michael Jordan sculptures, and hypnotic signs have tourists wandering around this overgrown store glassy eyed. Sports fans will enjoy the various artifacts: jerseys and shoes worn by famous athletes, the balls they've played with, and even an autographed Jordan Wheaties Box. (Open Mon.-Thurs. and Sat. 10am-7pm, Fri. 10am-8pm, Sun. 11:30am-6:30pm.)

There is room for romping just west of the mall on the **South Park Blocks,** a series of cool, shaded parks down the middle of Park Ave., enclosed on the west side by **Portland State University (PSU).** Also on the west side of the park sits the **Portland Art Museum,** 1219 SW Park (226-2811), at Jefferson St., which houses Western painting and sculpture from the 1350s to the 1950s, as well as prints, photos, contemporary works, and a collection of art from cultures as diverse as Cameroon and China. The excellent Pacific Northwest Native American exhibit includes masks, textiles, and sacred objects ($6, seniors and students over 16 $4.50, under 16 $2.50; open Tues.-Sun. 11am-5pm; 2 for 1 AAA discount). The **Pacific Northwest College of Art** (226-4391) and the **Northwest Film Center** (221-1156) share space with the museum in the two buildings along the park. The Film Center shows classics, documentaries, and off-beat flicks Thurs.-Sun. Tickets are available at the box office for $6. **Museum After Hours** is a jazz and blues concert series held in the museum's ballroom, popular with the after-work crowd (Oct.-April 5:30-9pm; prices vary; call the Museum).

Across the park, the **Oregon Historical Society Museum and Library,** 1200 SW Park Ave. (222-1741), stores photographs, artifacts, and records of Oregon's last two centuries. Recent refurbishments of the exhibits on Oregon, Willamette County, and Portland have made them more interactive ($6, students $3; open Tues.-Sat. 10am-5pm, Sun. noon-5pm; Thurs. seniors free; 2 for 1 AAA discount). If the kiddies get bored, take them to the **Portland Children's Museum,** 3037 SW 2nd Ave. (823-2227), at Wood St. (not in downtown; take bus #1, 12, 40, 41, 43, 45, or 55, all yellow rose), which schedules games, arts activities, and hands-on exhibits, including the ever-popular grocery store where plastic celery and bananas are the currency of fun. (Open daily 9am-5pm; $3.50 for all ages over 1. Infants admitted free.)

The part of downtown just south of the Burnside Bridge and along the river is considered the gateway to **Old Town.** In the past two years, it has been revived by the large-scale restoration of store fronts, new "old brick," polished iron and brass, and a bevy of recently opened shops and restaurants. A popular people-watching spot, the **Skidmore Fountain,** at SW 1st Ave. and SW Ankeny St., marks the entrance to the quarter. Had the city accepted resident brewmeister Henry Weinhard's offer to run draft beer through the fountain, it would have been a truly cordial watering hole indeed (and much more popular). The fountain also marks the end of **Waterfront Park.** This 20-block-long swath of grass and flowers along the Willamette River provides locals with an excellent place to picnic, fish, stroll, and enjoy major community events.

The eclectic, and festive **Saturday Market,** 108 W. Burnside St. (222-6072), by the Skidmore Fountain between 1st and Front St., is overrun with street musicians, artists, craftspeople, chefs, and greengrocers clogging the largest open-air crafts market in the country. Many of these artists sell their work in the city's studios and galleries during the week. (March-Dec. Sat. 10am-5pm, Sun. 11am-4:30pm.) The **New Market Village,** 120 SW Ankeney, is in a restored old port building that's listed in the National Register of Historic Places. Inside, check out the living gallery courtyard, a veritable Noah's Ark of "chia" animals. Grass sprouts instead of fur and feathers on this life-size menagerie of lions, bears, birds, and more. Nineteen **fountains** decorate the city and Portland's inhabitants get some serious frolicking done in them. Cool your feet in **Ira's Fountain** (between 3rd and 4th and Market and Clay; in front of the Civic Auditorium) as 13,000 gallons cascade down cobblestoned terraces and platforms every minute. Pick up the free *Portland's Municipal Fountains* guide at the visitors center, and as you do, watch **Salmon St. Springs** (in Waterfront Park, at SW Salmon St.) rocket high into the air and change form as an underground computer manipulates the fountain's 185 jets.

Downtown's waterfront district is laced with a complex web of underground passages, known as the "Shanghai" tunnels. Urban lore has it that seamen would get their victims drunk, drag them down to the tunnels, and store them there till their ship sailed. Forced aboard and taken out to sea, these hapless Portlanders would provide a free crew to the lucky ship. North of Burnside lies what was once a thriving **Chinatown,** but only its arched gateway remains today. (Look for red street signs indicating Chinatown and black and white ones for Old Town.) The area has been recycled again, this time as the **Pearl District.** Stretching north from Burnside to I-405 along the river, the old industrial zone is packed with art galleries, loft apartments, and warehouse-turned-office buildings. Storefronts and cafés have made the area more welcoming, but the boxy architectural identity of the area, like the mild lawlessness of its curbless streets, has been preserved.

For a dose of fun that might go over youngsters' heads, pay a visit to the first and only 24hr. coin-operated **Church of Elvis,** 720 SW Ankeny St. (226-3671). Listen to synthetic oracles, witness satirical miracles, and, if you're lucky, experience a tour in the church's Art-o-Mobile.

Portland is the uncontested **microbrewery** capital of the United States and possibly the world, and Portlanders are proud of their beery city. The visitors center can give you a list of 26 metro area breweries, most of which will be happy to show you

OREGON

around their facilities. Henry Weinhard, a German brewmaster, started this tradition when he established the first brewery in the Northwest, outside of Fort Vancouver, in 1856. Today **"Henry's"** has become an Oregon standard, outgrowing its status as a microbrew. Visit the **Blitz Weinhard Brewery**, 1133 W. Burnside (222-4351), for a ½hr. tour and samples in the hospitality room (free; open weekday afternoons).

Northwest, North, and Northeast

From Washington Park (see **Parks**, below), you have easy access by car or on foot to sprawling **Forest Hills Park**, a favorite of hikers and bikers, and the largest park located completely within the confines of an American city. The 5000 acre park is laced with trails and scenic picnic areas. The **Pittock Mansion**, 3229 NW Pittock Dr. (823-3624), within Forest Park, was built by Henry L. Pittock, the founder of Portland's daily, the *Oregonian*. From the lawn of the 80-year-old, 16,000 square foot French Renaissance mansion, you can take in a striking panorama of the city. To reach the mansion from downtown, take crosstown bus #20 (orange deer) to NW Barnes and W. Burnside St., and walk ½mi. up steeply sloped Pittock Ave. (house tours $4.25, seniors $3.75, 6-18 $2; open daily noon-4pm; closed the first 3 weeks of Jan. for maintenance).

Downtown on the edge of the Northwest district is **Powell's City of Books**, 1005 W. Burnside St. (228-4651 or 800-878-7323; http://www.powells.portland.or.us), a cavernous establishment with close to a million new and used volumes, more than any other bookstore in the U.S. If you like to dawdle in bookstores, bring a sleeping bag and rations. It's so huge, they even provide a map of the store; you'll need it. Seven color-coded rooms house books on everything from Criminology to Cooking. The **Anne Hughes Coffee Room**, inside Powell's, is a haven for the hungry. Enjoy bagels and cookies and sip coffee while devouring a book. Powell's also features frequent poetry and fiction readings in the afternoons and an extensive travel section on Portland and the Northwest (open Mon.-Sat. 9am-11pm, Sun. 9am-9pm).

The **American Advertising Museum**, 50 SW 2nd Ave. (226-0000) at the Skidmore stop on MAX, chronicles the fast-paced world of advertising. The gallery shows temporary exhibits; summer 1996 showcased a fascinating and informative retrospective on images of women in advertising. ($3, seniors and under 12 $1.50; open Wed.-Sun. 11am-5pm.)

Southeast

Southeast Portland is a largely residential district scattered with pockets of activity. To the south, **Reed College**, 3203 SE Woodstock (771-1112), a small liberal arts college founded in 1909, sponsors a number of cultural events. The ivy-draped grounds, encompassing a lake and a state wildlife refuge, make up one of the most attractive college campuses in the country. Ironically, in 1968, this enclave of progressive politics became the first undergraduate college to open its own nuclear reactor. But some students consider the gigantic and still mounting college-wide compost heap more ominous, even, than nuclear activity. One-hour tours, geared mainly to prospective students, leave Eliot Hall #220, 3203 Woodstock Blvd. at SE 28th, twice per day (Mon.-Fri. 10am and 2pm; individual tours are available by appointment in summer; call 777-7511 or 800-547-4750).

The **Chamber Music Northwest Summer Festival** (294-6400 or 223-3202) holds concerts at the college and at the Catlin Gabel School in Portland every summer from late June to late July (Mon.-Tues. and Thurs.-Sat. at 8pm). Concerts sell out quickly; call ahead for tickets ($12-17). Open, free rehearsals are held in July at the Reed College Commons; call 223-3202 for full details. Across the street from the Commons, in the **Crystal Springs Rhododendron Test Gardens**, SE 28th Ave., at Woodstock (take bus #19), 2500 rhododendrons of countless varieties surround a lake. Unwind among ducks, man-made waterfalls and 90-year-old rhododendrons. Azaleas and rhododendron flowers are in full bloom late April and early May ($2; gates open daily 6am-10pm; March-Sept. Thurs.-Mon. 10am-6pm).

The **Oregon Museum of Science and Industry (OMSI),** 1945 SE Water Ave. (797-4000), at SE Clay, will keep children mesmerized with do-it-yourself science exhibits, including an earthquake-simulator chamber. A noisy romper room when school groups visit, the museum's theater is more likely to interest adults ($6, seniors and children 4-13, $4.50). The impressive **Omnimax** theater, located near OMSI, under Marquam bridge (797-4640 for recorded hours and rates), routinely awes visitors. ($7, seniors $6, ages 3-17 $4.50; shows start on the hour, daily 11am-4pm and Tues.-Wed. 7-8pm, Thurs.-Sat. 6-9pm.) The same theater rocks with **laser light music shows** (797-4646 for recorded hours and rates) like Lazervana and Lazed and Confused (daily matinees $4.50, seniors $4, ages 3-17 $2.00; evening shows Tues.-Sun. $6.50). While at OMSI, check out the *U.S.S. Blueback* (797-4624), the Navy's last diesel submarine. This amazing sub set a record by traversing the Pacific Ocean underwater. She never failed to complete a mission, and starred in the 1990 film *The Hunt for Red October.* The sub is now open for exploration ($3.50; open daily 10am-6pm; departure times for the 35-min. tour vary).

Hawthorne Boulevard has a high concentration of quiet cafés, antique shops, used book stores, and theaters useful for dodging unpredictable Portland rainfall. It's a hip strip where prices aren't yet too high and parking can still be found on weekends. It ends at the bottom of **Mt. Tabor Park,** one of two city parks in the world on the site of an extinct volcano. To get to the area, take bus #15 (brown beaver) from downtown, or hunt it down at SE 60th Ave. and Belmont Ave. Shops have also sprouted on **Belmont Ave.** (a few avenues north), which some have touted as the new Hawthorne, though locals are still waiting for the rest of Belmont to sprout.

Parks

Portland has more park area than any other U.S. city. **Forest Park,** the 5,000 acre splotch of wilderness in the city's northwest, might have something to do with this. Less than 2 mi. west of downtown, the posh neighborhoods of **West Hills** form a manicured buffer zone between soul-soothing parks and the turmoil of the city below. In the middle of West Hills, mammoth **Washington Park** and its nearby attractions typify the blend of urbanity and natural bounty which Portland has perfected. To get there, take the animated "zoo bus" (#63) on SW Main St. or drive up SW Broadway to Clay St., turn right onto U.S. 26, and get off at the zoo exit.

The park's gates are only open until 9pm in order to keep out lawless types. Sketchy after 9pm, by day Washington Park is beautiful. **Maps** are available at the information stand near the parking lot of the arboretum, or refer to those posted on the windows. **Hoyt Arboretum,** 4000 SW Fairview Blvd. (228-8733 or 823-3655), at the crest of the hill above the other gardens, features 200 acres of trees and trails, including the charming—and wheelchair accessible—**Bristlecone Pine Trail.** Free nature walks (April-Nov. Sat.-Sun. at 2pm) last 90min. and cover 1-2 mi. The 26-mi. **"Wildwood" Trail,** which winds through Washington and Forest Park, connects the arboretum to the zoo in the south (trails open daily 6am-10pm; Washington Park visitors center open Mon.-Fri. 9am-3pm, Sat.-Sun. 10am-2pm).

Below the Hoyt Arboretum lie many of Portland's most popular assets. The **International Rose Test Garden** (better known as the Rose Garden), 400 SW Kingston Ave. (823-3636), on the way to the zoo entrance, is packed with flora and is a gorgeous place to stroll on a lazy day or cool evening (open daily 7am-9pm). Clear days afford splendid views of the city and distant **Mount Hood.** The spectacular **Japanese Gardens,** 611 SW Kingston Ave. (223-4070), are reputed to be the most authentic outside Japan. ($5, seniors and students $2.50; open daily, April-May and Sept. 10am-6pm; June-Aug. 9am-8pm; Oct.-March 10am-4pm.) Although they can be crowded on hot summer days, both gardens are worth seeing.

The **Washington Park Zoo,** 4001 SW Canyon Rd. (226-1561 or 226-7627), is renowned for its successful elephant-breeding and its scrupulous re-creation of natural habitats. Whimsical murals decorate the #63 "zoo bus," which connects the park to SW Main St. in the downtown mall. A steam engine pulls passengers on a mini rail-

OREGON

way out to Washington Park gardens and back, giving a better view of flowers and animals (½hr. tour $2.75, seniors and ages 3-11 $2). The zoo features a number of interesting "animal talks" on weekends and has a pet-the-animals **children's zoo.** If you have time, pull up a seat in the grassy theater and watch as huge birds of prey swoop down over you in a demonstration. ($5.50, seniors $4, children under 12 $3.50, 2nd Tues. of each month free 3-6pm; open June-Aug. daily 9:30am-6pm; Sept.-May 9am-4pm.) If you're around in late June, July, or August, grab your picnic basket and head to the zoo's sculpture garden to catch live outdoor jazz at **Your Zoo and All That Jazz** (234-9695), Wed. nights. On Thurs. nights, the **Rhythm and Zoo Concerts** (234-9694) host a diverse range of international styles. Both events are free with zoo admission.

ENTERTAINMENT

Once an uncouth and rowdy port town, Portland manages to maintain an irreverent attitude. Nightclubs cater to everyone from the casual college student to the hard-core rocker. Upon request, the Portland Oregon Visitors Association will hand over a thick packet outlining that month's events. The best shows will drain your pocket, but the community also sponsors many well attended free events. The best entertainment listings are in the Friday edition of the *Oregonian* and in a number of free hand-outs. The town's favorite cultural reader, the **Willamette Week** (put out each evening), the *Main Event, Clinton St. Quarterly, Just Out* (catering to gay and lesbian interests), the *Portland Guide,* and the *Downtowner* (friend of the upwardly mobile) are available on street corners and in restaurants downtown.

Music

Portland has its share of excellent concerts, but why bother with admission fees when you can find exciting talent playing for free in various public facilities around the city? Check the *Oregonian's* A&E (Arts and Entertainment) section or pick up a *Willamette Week* for up to date information (see above). For the best local rock, visit the **Satyricon** and **Laluna** (see **Nightlife** below).

Oregon Symphony Orchestra, 1111 SW Broadway Ave. (800-228-7343 or 228-1353), in the Arlene Schnitzer Concert Hall, plays a classical and pop series Sept.-June. Tickets $10-50. "Symphony Sunday" afternoon concerts $9-12. Student tickets (½price) available 1hr. before showtime. One ticket per student ID.

Portland Civic Auditorium, 222 SW Clay St. (796-9293 for info line; call Ticketmaster for most tickets). Attracts the usual hard rockin' arena acts and a few jazz and opera stars. Ticket prices vary ($8-30).

Sack Lunch Concerts, 1422 SW 11th Ave. (222-2031), at Clay St. at the Old Church. Free concert every Wed. at noon; sometimes organ, sometimes acoustic guitar— you never know what you'll find.

Chamber Music Northwest, 522 SW 5th Ave. #725 (294-6400). Performs summer concerts from late June-July at Reed College Commons. Classical music Mon., Tues., and Thurs.-Sat. at 8pm. $12-26, ages 7-14 $5.

Starbucks by Starlight (223-1613), at Pioneer Courthouse Square, hosts blues and jazz Fri. 5:30-7pm during the month of Aug.

Peanut Butter and Jam Sessions (223-1613) at Pioneer Courthouse Square from noon-1pm every Tues. and Thurs. during the summer. A potpourri of rock, jazz, folk, and world music. Always jammed.

Aladdin Theatre, 3017 SE Milwaukee Ave., just off SE Powell by the Ross Island Bridge (233-1994). A popular gig for a wide range of talent from alternative to country. The atmosphere depends on the band but people seldom get up out of the 800 seats to dance.

Theater

Theater in Portland covers all tastes, ages, and budgets. The **Portland Center for the Performing Arts (PCPA)** (796-9293 for tickets) is the largest arts center in the U.S. that receives no government support, though the City of Portland owns the actual theaters. Friends of the Performing Arts Center puts on the **Brown Bag Lunch series** which gives free glances at professional productions (occasional weekdays at lunchtime; check the *Oregonian*). Tickets for most productions can also be charged by phone at Ticketmaster or Fastixx (see **Practical Information**).

Portland Center Stage (248-6309), at the Intermediate Theater of PCPA, at SW Broadway and SW Main. 5-play series of classics and modern adaptations runs Oct.-April. Tickets: Fri.-Sat. $12.50-35, Sun. and Tues.-Thurs. $11-30.50. Half-price tickets sometimes available at the Intermediate Theater 1hr. before showtime.

Portland Repertory Theater, 25 SW Salmon St. (224-4491), in Two World Trade Center, Bridge level. Five plays per year. Intimate 223-seat theater. Professionally done with prices to match. Tickets start at $25, ½price tickets sold ½hr. prior to curtain.

Oregon Ballet Theater, 1120 SW 10th Ave. (241-8316 or 241-8316). Performs at the Civic Auditorium at 3rd and Clay and at the Intermediate Theater at Main and Broadway. Four creative ballet productions per season Oct.-May. The 1996-97 season includes an American choreographers' showcase. Tickets $10-65, student rush 1hr. before curtain.

Artists Repertory Theater (294-7373), corner of 10th Ave. and Main St., on the 3rd floor of the YMCA. This theater puts on excellent low-budget and experimental productions. Tickets $15.

Portland State University Summer Festival Theater (229-4440), at the Lincoln Hall Auditorium. Schedules at the box office or the Portland Public Library. Performances mid-June to mid-July. Tickets $8-15.

Portland Civic Auditorium, 222 SW Clay St. (274-6560). Occasional big splashy opera, touring shows, and small rock concerts. Part of the PCPA. Tickets $25-55.

Cinema

Most of Portland's countless movie theaters have half-price days or matinee shows. With the help of the *Oregonian*, it is sometimes possible to dodge the $7.25 ticket price for a "major motion picture." McMenamins runs two **theater/pubs** (Bahgdad and Mission) where you can sit in sofas or at tables and order food and brew while you watch. No minors are admitted to these theaters.

Mission Theatre and Pub, 1624 NW Glisan (223-4031). Serves excellent homebrewed ales, and delicious sandwiches and burgers ($4-6). Watch recent, out-of-first-run movies while lounging on couches, sitting at tables, or perched in the old-style balcony. Showtimes 5:30, 8:05, 10:30pm. All you can watch for a buck.

Baghdad Theater and Pub, 3702 SE Hawthorne Blvd. (230-0895). Take bus #14 (brown beaver). Built in 1921 for vaudeville, this magnificently renovated theater shows second-run movies and boasts an excellent beer menu ($2.90 a pint). Have a pricy pizza delivered to you right in the theater. Doors open 5pm. $1.

Cinema 21, 616 NW 21st, at Hoyt St. (223-4515). Clean and pistachio green. Showing mostly documentary, independent, and foreign films. Highly acclaimed student haunt; plenty of progressive literature in the lobby. Tickets $5; students $4; seniors, under 12, and matinee $2.

Northwest Film Center, 1219 SW Park Ave. (221-1156), in the Berg Swann Auditorium at the Portland Art Museum. Mostly documentary films on little-known peoples and places. Also foreign independents and premieres. Films rotated every three months on a thematic basis; also hosts a film and video festival in early November. Tickets $6, seniors $5.50. Box office opens 30min. before each show.

Clinton Street Theater, 2522 SE Clinton St. (238-8899). This multimedia theater hosts meetings, cabaret, and even Sunday night theater sports ($5). Do the time-warp again with the *Rocky Horror Picture Show* every Sat. at midnight ($4).

Lloyd Cinema (225-5555 ext. 4600), across the street from the Lloyd Center mall. On the off chance you want to pay big bucks to see a first-run movie, this 10-screen, ultra-modern neon wonderland should be just what you're looking for.

OREGON

Shopping

For some, shopping is a religious experience in the **Nob Hill** district. Fashionable boutiques run from Burnside to Thurman St., between NW 21st and NW 24th Ave., mostly on 23rd. Or make the pilgrimage to NE Broadway and 15th Ave. to shop at Portland's mega-mall **Lloyd Center** (282-2511). While you're there, slide over to the indoor **ice-skating rink** (288-6073; $7, under 17 $6, skate rental included; open year round though hours vary) and do your impression of Portland's very own Tonya Harding. Parking can be a hassle in both spots on the weekends, but Lloyd Center is on the MAX line, and Nob Hill can be reached by bus #15 (red salmon) or the cross town bus #77.

    Nordstrom's (224-6666), 701 SW Broadway, downtown in Pioneer Courthouse Square, is a department store mecca for its many loyal patrons. Upscale shops can also be found up and down **Newberry St.,** where moneyed hipsters roam for their rags. For those without a hefty wad, check out **Hawthorne** between 30th and 40th; women's bookstores and music stores abound. If books are what you're after, check out **Powell's** in **Sights,** above. Portland is also home to a thriving thrift-store culture, especially by **Dot's Café** on Clinton St. (see **Nightlife** below) and the **Clinton Street Theater** (see **Cinema** above).

Sports

When Bill Walton led the **Trailblazers** (234-9291) to the 1979 NBA Championship, Portland went crazy. Portland views the landing and supporting of an NBA team as a substantial accomplishment for this overgrown town. Residents even go bonkers when a former Trailblazer wins with another team, as they did when Clyde "The Glide" Drexler helped lead the Houston Rockets to the 1995 Championship. The Trailblazers play in the sparkling new **Rose Garden Arena,** by the Steel Bridge in the northeast quadrant of the city, fully equipped with is own stop on the MAX line. The season lasts from November to May (or June if they make the playoffs). From June-Sept., the city's indoor soccer team, **Portland Pride,** takes over the Rose Garden Arena. (Call 644-8478 for schedule info and tickets.) The **Winter Hawks** (238-6366) of the Western Hockey League play both at the Rose Garden and next-door at the **Coliseum** in the winter, Sept.-March. Take bus #9 (brown beaver) or MAX. The Civic Stadium, 1844 SW Morrison St., on the other side of town is home to the **Portland Rockies** (223-2837), Colorado's AAA farm team, who played their inaugural season in 1995. Reserved tickets cost $6.50, general admission $5.50, seniors and children 12 and under $4.50.

    Contact the **Portland Parks and Recreation Bureau,** 1120 SW 5th Ave., #1302 (823-2223), for a guide to Portland's parks, chock full of hiking and cycling trails and lakes for swimming and sailing. Forty parks have outdoor **tennis courts,** many lighted for night play and free to the public. The following parks have **swimming pools:** Columbia, Creston, Dishman, Grant, Mt. Scott, Montavilla, Peninsula, Pier, Wilson, and Sellwood. Special facilities and programs are provided for seniors and the disabled (call Portland's **Aquatics Office** at 823-5130 for specifics).

NIGHTLIFE

The best clubs in Portland are the hardest ones to find. Neighborhood taverns and pubs may be hidden, but they usually have the most character and best music. The clubs in Northwest Portland are easily accessible from downtown. It is wise to park close by or come with a friend since walking alone at night can be dangerous. Flyers advertising upcoming shows are always plastered on telephone poles around town, especially on SE Hawthorne and NW 23rd. Pubs are plentiful and half of them are owned by McMenamins. Mischievous minors be warned: the drinking age is strictly enforced in Portland. When it comes down to their liquor license or your fake ID, bars know which choice to make.

Southwest

Berbati, 231 SW Ankeny St. (248-4570). This ever-expanding nightspot started as a small Greek restaurant on 2nd Ave. Now the upscale dining room, 3-table pool room, venue, bar, dance hall, and 24hr. café wind all the way back to 3rd. While the stage belongs to jazz on Tuesdays, any other night it could be ska, acid blues, funk, or rock. Authentic Greek dishes will run you $6-7, or stick with a burger for $4.50. Club and pool room open daily 11am-4am; bar closes at 2:30am.

Lotus Card Room and Café, 932 SW 3rd Ave. (227-6185), at SW Salmon St. Grooviest dance floor in the city has a movie screen with trippy projections, glowing cartoon paintings, and a cage. Packed with twentysomethings on the weekend, the Lotus also has a room full of tables. Jambalaya ($7). Dance floor open 9pm-2am. Cover $2-4, sometimes free. Happy hour (Wed.-Sun.4-6:30pm) features micro-pints ($2). Open daily 11am-2am.

Panorama, Briggs, and **Boxes,** 341 SW 10th St. (221-RAMA/7262), form a network of interconnected clubs along Stark St. between 10th and 11th. Dance till you drop on Panorama's cavernous dance floor amid a thriving gay and straight crowd. (Open Thurs. and Sun. 9pm-2:30am, Fri.-Sat. 9pm-4am, with a $3 cover on Fri.-Sat., $2 on Thurs.) After 11:30 pm, you can wander over to the smaller Briggs, where the majority of the crowd is gay (open daily 9pm-2:30am). Or push on farther into Boxes, an all-gay video bar (open daily noon-2:30am). Fridays are disco night, but the norm is techno. Dance yourself silly into the wee hours.

Caribou Café, 503 W. Burnside St. (227-0245). Two caribou oversee this bar and six more appear on the brightly muralled walls. 125 drinks for $1 each and $2 pints Thurs.-Sat. Eclectic clientele on weekends and varied music make for one loud and crowded fiesta. Private security always on hand. Try the Caribou fries ($4.25). Live music Mon.-Wed., DJ Thurs.-Sat. Cover $2-3 on weekends. Open Mon and Sat 5pm-1am, Tues.-Fri. 11:30am-1am.

Southeast

Biddy McGraw's, 3518 SE Hawthorne Blvd. (233-1178). Take bus #14 (brown beaver). You couldn't get more authentically Irish in Belfast. With live Irish tunes and raucous dancing, weekends are always boisterous. If you don't want to bother, come in Mon. or Tues. when neither music nor table service will impose. Imports go for $3.25 a pint, micros $3, Henry's $2. (20 kegs of Guiness are consumed here a week.) Hours not set in stone, but should be open Mon. 6:30pm-2am, Tues.-Fri. 10am-2:30am, Sat.-Sun. 2pm-2:30am.

Produce Row Café, 204 SE Oak St. (232-8355). Take bus #6 (red salmon) to SE Oak and SE Grand, then walk west along Oak toward the river. Though they remodelled 2 years ago, none of this 30-year-old hangout's character was lost. 27 beers on tap, over 200 bottled domestic and imported beers. Soak in the summer starlight and industrial ambience from the walled-off deck out back. Live music: Sat. rock ($2), Sun. jazz ($2), Mon. jam ($1), free Bluegrass Tues. Domestic bottles $1.25, domestic pints $1.75. Open Mon.-Fri. 11am-1am, Sat.-Sun. noon-1am.

La Luna, 215 SE 9th Ave. (241-LUNA/5862). Take bus #20 (purple raindrop), get off at 9th, walk 2 blocks south. One of the hipper venues in town. Plays host to many of the more prominent bands that come to Portland. Music generally 4 times a week. Mon. night is queer night ($3) with dancing. The non-smoking coffee room is open every night (except Sun.) to an anything goes crowd. All ages admitted, except to the bars. Call ahead for concert listings. Pints $2-3.50.

The Space Room, 4800 SE Hawthorne Blvd. (235-8303). Take bus #14 (brown beaver). Judy Jetson smoked way too many cigarettes inside this space-age joint. The cutting-edge compress themselves into dark booths and contemplate the vintage-clothing possibilities. One Bloody Mary ($3.75) will put you over the edge. Open daily 6am-2:30am.

Barley Mill Pub, 1629 SE Hawthorne Blvd. (231-1492). This smoky temple to counterculture hero and guitar genius Jerry Garcia has not been the same since the bandleader's untimely death. Bring your bootlegs on Wed. nights and let the music live on. Full of fantastic murals, and long bench tables that may land you next to a stranger. Upbeat but mellow atmosphere. McMenamins beer on tap ($2.55 a pint). Open Mon.-Sat. 11am-1am, Sun. noon-midnight.

Dot's Café, 2521 SE Clinton St. (235-0203). Take bus #4 (brown beaver) to 26th, and walk 3 blocks south. Though the place burned down in 1993, today only Dot's business is aflame. Can be crowded and smoky. Dotted with alternative artifacts like the treasured velvet Elvis. Pool table. Caters more to musician types and their bohemian brethren than to college frat boys. Lunch too: burgers, sandwiches and a killer burrito go for $4-6. Vegan Vavoom $4. Open daily 11am-2am.

Other Neighborhoods

Satyricon, 121 NW 6th Ave. (243-2380). Alternarock rumbles in the glowing back room every night. Old bar and a chic new sister restaurant, **Felini.** Step into this madly mosaiced space to rest your ears and taste the innovative cuisine. Veggie entrees start at $3, and **Liberace's Libido** goes for $7.50. No cover Mon. for New Band Night, otherwise $2-6. Food daily noon-2:30am; music 3pm-2:30am.

Bridgeport Brew Pub, 1313 NW Marshall (241-7179). The zenith of beer and pizza joints in a now defunct wood-beamed rope factory. The pizza is locally famous, and though pricey ($18 for a 5 topping pie), it can feed a family of four. Lotsa space for lotsa people. Tables cut from old bowling allies. The outdoor patio is surprisingly pleasant, and fills up during happy hour. Brews are all Bridgeport; $1.65 for a 10oz pint, $2.75 for a 20oz. Open Mon.-Thurs. 11am-11pm, Fri. 11:30am-midnight, Sat. noon-midnight, Sun. 1-9pm.

The Laurelthurst Public House, 2958 NE Glisan (232-1504). The neighborhood crowd gets their yayas out to the tune of local acoustic and electric acts in this mellow joint. The upscale kitchen serves breakfast until 3pm. Burgers and sandwiches $4-5. Microbrew pints $3, domestic $2. Cover $2 nightly. Free pool all day Sun., Mon.-Thurs. before 7pm. Open daily 9am-2:30am.

Embers, 110 NW Broadway at Couch St. (222-3082). Follow the rainbows all the way onto a hopping dance floor and bustling bar. Mostly gay clientele; retro and house music. Nightly drag show at 10pm. Domestic bottled beer $2.25, mixed drinks $2.50. Open daily 11am-3am.

Jazz de Opus, 33 NW 2nd Ave. (222-6077). Sit and soak it up or get down and boogie. Tables are inches from the live jazz (Tues.-Sun. 8:30pm-12:30am), but there's still room for conversation. Dinners on the pricey side. No covers, just a 50¢ surcharge on drinks while the music plays. Open for lunch Mon.-Fri. 11:30am-3pm; for dinner Mon.-Fri. 5-11pm, Sat.-Sun. 5pm-midnight; bar open daily 3pm-close, happy hour 4-7pm.

Gypsy, 625 NW 21st Ave. at Hoyt St. (796-1859). Take bus #17 (red salmon). With sparkley red vinyl circular booths, the restaurant looks like a 1950s experiment gone awry. Bring your cool friends for moral support. Groovy hour Mon.-Fri. 4-6:30pm and Sat.-Sun. 3-5:30pm features mixed drinks and domestics for $1.50, appetizers at ½price. Pass through padded doors to the lounge where black lights and video poker rule the night. Open Mon.-Fri. 9am-2am, Sat.-Sun. 8am-2am.

EVENTS

Cinco de Mayo Festival (292-5752). May 5th. Mexican Independence Day celebration with sister city Guadalajara complete with fiery food, entertainment, and crafts at SW Front and Salmon.

Rose Festival, 220 NW 2nd Ave. (248-7923 for recording, 277-2681 for the offices). During the first three weeks of June, U.S. Navy sailors flood the street while the city decks itself in all its finery for Portland's premier summer event. Waterfront concerts, art festivals, celebrity entertainment, auto racing, parades, an air show, Navy ships, and the largest children's parade in the world (the Rose Junior Parade). Great during the day, at night women should exercise caution. Many of the events require tickets; call 224-4400 to order.

Waterfront Blues Festival (282-0555). Early July. Outrageously good. International celebrities and some of the finest regional blues artists participate in this three-day event. Admission $3 and 2 cans of food.

Oregon Brewers Festival (778-5917). Late July. The continent's largest gathering of independent brewers makes for one incredible party at Waterfront Park. Brew expensive and admission charged.

Mt. Hood Festival of Jazz (666-3810), first weekend in Aug. at Mt. Hood Community College in Gresham. Expensive (tickets start at $27.50 per night and even more when you buy them by calling Ticketmaster at 224-4400), but this is the premier jazz festival of the Pacific Northwest, with 20hr. of music over the course of a weekend. Wynton Marsalis and the late Stan Getz have been regulars in the past. Reserve tickets well in advance. Write Mt. Hood Festival of Jazz, P.O. Box 3024, Gresham 97030. To reach the festival, take I-84 to Wood Village-Gresham exit and follow the signs, or follow the crowd on MAX to the end of the line.

The Bite—A Taste of Portland (248-0600). Second week in August in Waterfront Park. Food and music abound. Pricey, but Portland natives swear by it.

Artquake (227-2787). Labor Day weekend. Music, mime, food, and neo-situationist hoopla in and around Pioneer Courthouse Square.

Portland Marathon (226-1111). Late Sept. If you're in shape, join the thousands who run this 26.2-mi. race. Many shorter runs and walks also held (thank god).

■ Near Portland

Few Portland residents would consider relocating—not only is the city a cultural giant, but it is near some of America's most fantastic natural attractions. The burned-out, truncated shell of Mount St. Helens is a short drive north into Washington State; the Columbia River Gorge, full of world-class windsurfers and breathtaking views, is only a 30-minute drive up I-84; Mt. Hood, is one and a half hours away and is a nearly year-round host to skiers. You can retrace the footsteps of early pioneers east along the Oregon Trail in the Mount Hood National Forest. A two-hour jaunt west from Portland will take you to the rugged rocks and cliffs lining the Pacific; a pleasant drive will land you in such coastal towns as Cannon Beach, Astoria, or Tillamook.

SAUVIE ISLAND

Twenty minutes northwest of downtown Portland on U.S. 30 (follow signs to Mt. Saint Helens from 405, Vaughn, or Yeon Ave.), Sauvie Island is a peaceful rural hideaway at the confluence of the Columbia and Willamette Rivers. The island offers great views of the city from its vast sandy stretches. On winter mornings, eagles and geese congregate along the roads, and in spring and summer, berries are everywhere. For many Portlanders, a summer trip to the island's **u-pick farms** (family operations announced by hand-lettered signs along the roads) is an annual tradition.

The island's beaches are another star attraction, and on the south side many visitors soak up the rays. Although some people bring their fishing rods, some their bathing suits, and some their dogs, none make contact with the Willamette's lovely waters. Factories and imperfect sewage systems upstream tell a sad tale. The best inland beach area is **Oak Island** on the south side of Sturgeon Lake, a 10-minute drive once you reach the island. After turning west onto Sauvie Island Rd. from the Sauvie Island Bridge, take the first major right onto Reeder Rd. After a left-hand curve, continue straight onto Oak Island Rd. which ends after 2 mi. in a gravel parking lot. Wander the weedy road from there. A $3 parking permit is required for the whole island and efficiently enforced. You can pick one up at Sam's Cracker Barrel Grocery, along with a free map of the island and any supplies you might need. Plan ahead; **Sam's** is the only one you'll find and it's right by the bridge, a backtrack of several miles from the beaches.

MOUNT HOOD

Magnificent, glacier-topped Mt. Hood is at the junction of U.S. 26 and Rte. 35, 90 minutes east of Portland and one hour from the Hood River. The 11,235-ft. active volcano doesn't steam, has no crater, and appears dormant because open vents keep internal pressure low. Though Mt. Bachelor (see **Bend,** p. 493) is known as Oregon's best skiing, three decent resorts are closer: **Timberline** and **Mt. Hood Ski Bowl,** off U.S. 26 at Government Camp, and **Mt. Hood Meadows,** nine miles away on Rte. 35. All three offer night skiing. **Timberline** (272-3311 or 231-7979) a largely beginner and intermediate area, has the longest ski season in Oregon (until Labor Day). Rental equipment costs around $19. Snowboard rental is $33 with boots, $26 without. Lift tickets cost $29 (seniors and ages 7-12 $18). Winter night skiing, daily 4-10pm. **Mount Hood Ski Bowl,** 87000 E. U.S. 26 (272-3206), in Government Camp, 2 mi. west of the junction with Hwy. 35, is smaller, but considered the best of the three. It has varied terrain at lower altitude which limits its season from Nov. to April. Ski equipment rentals go for $17, juniors (ages 7-12) $11. Snowboards are $25 with boots, $20 without. Lift tickets cost $18 for the day, $13 for the night, $29 for both (80-90% of the trails are lit for night skiing Sun.-Thurs. 4:30 -10pm, and Fri.-Sat. 4:30-11pm). **Mount Hood Meadows** (337-2222), 9 mi. west of Government Camp on Hwy. 35, is the largest resort in the area and offers largely intermediate terrain. At a medium elevation, it is able to stay open through July 4th weekend. Ski equipment rentals are $18, juniors $13; lift tickets are $34, juniors $20 (night skiing Wed.-Sun. 4-10pm). All three areas offer ski lessons averaging $35 per hour or $15 per person for group lessons. Special packages including rentals, lessons, and lift tickets are often available at a much-reduced price; call for current deals.

For adventurers who wish to tackle the mountain on foot, **Timberline Mountain Guides,** P.O. Box 23214, Portland (636-7704), offers mountain, snow, and ice climbing courses led by experts. Climbs last one to three days, with one-day trips starting at $80. Or give your feet a break and take Timberline's **Magic Mile,** a lift that carries non-skiers up above the clouds for spectacular views of the Cascades ($6, children $3; discounts with a coupon that just about any employee will be happy to turn over). Even if you decide to ski at Ski Bowl or Mt. Hood Meadows, turn up the 6-mi. road just past **Government Camp** to the Depression-era **Timberline Lodge** (231-5400; for reservations 800-547-1406), the outdoor filming location for Stanley Kubrick's *The Shining*. The road to the lodge also offers arresting views of the valley below, and the high Cascades to the south. Next door is the **Wy'east Day Lodge,** where skiers can store equipment without staying overnight, and the **Wy'east Kitchen,** a cafeteria alternative to Timberline's expensive dining (entrees $2-6; open daily 7am-3pm in summer; 7:30am-4pm in winter; 7:30-10pm when there is night skiing). If you're there in the summer and the snow seems too soggy, Mount Hood Ski Bowl offers an **Action Park,** complete with Indy Karts ($5 for 5min.), **bungee jumping** ($25), and an alpine slide ($5 a go, and don't worry, they'll show you how to brake). Also at the Ski Bowl (on the west side), **Hurricane Racing** (272-0240), where you can rent mountain bikes ($28 a day and up, $40 with unlimited rides on chair lift) from mid-June to late November. If the prices seem steep, wait 'til you see the trails. The rental cost includes a $4 U.S. forest trail permit, required all over the mountain.

In addition, **hiking** trails circle the mountain. Simple maps are posted on a number of signs around Government Camp. The most popular is **Mirror Lake,** a 4-mi. loop open June to Oct. which starts from a parking lot off U.S. 26, 1 mi. west of Government Camp, and ends with a reflection of Mount Hood's peak in the glassy lake.

Stop by the **Hood River District Ranger Station,** 67805 Rte. 35, Parkdok 97041 (352-6002), or the **Zigzag District Ranger Station,** 70220 E. U.S. 26 (622-3191, or 666-0704 from Portland) for more detailed information. Another source for permits is the well-stocked **Mt. Hood Visitors Information Center,** 65000 E. U.S. 26, Welches 97067 (666-0704, ext. 684; 30min. west of Mt. Hood). It is a part of the **Mt. Hood Village** (622-4011, 253-9445 from Portland, or 800-255-3069) a giant complex (420 sites and a weekend recreation schedule), with everything from a dance hall to tournament horse shoe pits to a heated pool (Jan.-May tents $20, RV $20, full hookup $22; June-Dec. tents and RV $23, full hookup $25).

Camping spots in the Mt. Hood National Forest cluster near the junction of U.S. 26 and Rte. 35. Less than 1 mi. below Timberline is **Alpine** (800-547-1406, or 231-5400 in Portland) accessible only in the summer. Choose one of 16 sites, all with water and toilets. Reservations are essential ($7). **Trillium Lake Campground,** two miles east of the Timberline turnoff on U.S. 26, has scenic trails around the clear lake, and 55

You Won't Find the Hendersons Here

John Lithgow thankfully has a new day job and **"Sasquatch"** fever has subsided of late, but the mystery members of this hominid family, their existence shrouded in murky lore, remain inscrutable to the scientific community. Mt. Hood marks the southern boundary of the Dark Divide, the area most associated with the sightings of these large, hirsute creatures who lurk in the forests and eat nuts and twigs. This fearsome beast was known even before the white man got his grubby hands on the New World. The Salish called the creature *saskehavas*, from which comes the English term "Sasquatch." Many dismiss the possibility of any such mysterious **ape-man.** Why, they query, hasn't conclusive evidence of its existence been adduced? Cryptozoologists (scientists who study undiscovered species) know better. They reply that numerous sightings and photographs *are* conclusive, and that naysayers are deluded by their own skepticism. If you do chance upon a **Bigfoot,** it will be easy to recognize. The big galoot stands roughly six to ten feet tall, weighs about 400 pounds, is covered in dark fur, and leaves behind a strong, fetid **odor.**

paved sites equipped with water and toilets. Plenty of people in the summer, but pine trees offer some privacy (sites $10 plus a $3 parking fee). Just a mile west of Trillium Lake, **Still Creek Campgrounds** has a quieter, more woodsy feel, with unpaved sites, underbrush and no glitzy lake ($9). On the other side of the action, 10 mi. north of the 35-26 junction on Rte. 35, **Sherwood and Robinwood Campgrounds,** both $10 per night, lie between a running creek and a well-traveled road. All Mt. Hood National Forest campground reservations should be made by calling 800-280-CAMP/ 2267.

■ Columbia River Gorge

Only an hour from Portland, the spectacular Columbia River Gorge stretches for 70 miles. The Columbia River has carved a canyon 1000 ft. deep through rumpled hills and sheer, rocky cliffs. Mt. Hood and Mt. Adams loom nearby while waterfalls plunge hundreds of feet over cliffs toward the Columbia. Traveling eastward along the gorge, heavily forested peaks give way to broad, sheer, bronze cliffs and golden hills. The river widens out and the wind picks up at the town of **Hood River.**

The gorge is the confluence of Oregon's various identities. Once "as fast as a waterfall turned on its side," and so full of fish that Lewis and Clark joked that they could drive their wagons over the backs of them, the Columbia's waters are now slower and emptier due to dams and fishing. On one side lies the desert, and on the other, the rain-soaked Western coast. Not far from the gorge, mountains and alpine zones tower over their surroundings.

Practical Information To follow the gorge, which divides Oregon and Washington, take I-84 east to Exit 22. Continue east up the hill on the only road possible, and you will find yourself on Hwy.30, a.k.a. the **Columbia River Scenic Highway.** This road follows the crest of the gorge walls and affords unforgettable views.

The largest town in the gorge is Hood River, at the junction of I-84 and Rte. 35. Take **Greyhound** from Portland ($11) or Seattle ($37) to Hood River; the **station** (386-1212) is at 1205 B Ave., between 12th and 13th St. (open Mon.-Sat. and sometimes on Sun. 8:30am-7pm). **Amtrak** also runs trains from Portland to the station at Cascade and 1st St. ($14). This **windsurfing** mecca is crammed with board-rental shops. Boards are available for a range of abilities; contact the **Hood River County Chamber of Commerce,** 405 Portway Ave. (386-2000 or 800-366-3530) just off the City Center exit (#63), for information on Hood River (open Mon.-Thurs. 9am-5pm; mid-April-mid-Oct. Fri. 9am-4pm, Sat.-Sun. 10am-4pm; mid-Oct.-mid-April Fri. 9am-5pm). Free publications, including *Gorge Vistas, The Visitor's Guide to Gorge Fun,* and for windsurfers, *Northwest Sailboard,* offer excellent information on local sights, camping, accommodations, history, and events. Also useful for backpackers is the $2 US Forest Service **map** of the Columbia Wilderness. These are available at visitor centers along the gorge. The **Post office** is at 408 Cascade Ave. (open Mon.-Fri. 8:30am-5pm).

Accommodations and Camping Crash with the boardsailers at the outdoorsy **Bingen School Inn Hostel** (509-493-3363), three minutes from Hood River across the Singing Bridge in Bingen, WA. Take your third left after the yellow blinking light and it's one block up the hill on Humbolt. Sleep, this time without guilt, in front of the blackboards at this converted school house. Forty-eight hostel beds ($11 per night) and five private bedrooms ($40 per night). Significant discounts for longer stays. **Mountain bikes** ($15 per day) and **sailboards** ($40 per day for a complete rig) are available for rent.

The **Gorge View Bed and Breakfast,** 1009 Columbia St. (386-5770), is a comfortable, elegant old house with a giant porch (complete with swing) overlooking the gorge. Usually filled with boardsailers, it has a relaxed, sporty feel (and an outdoor shower). Two rooms with queen-sized beds go for $59-69, or claim one of four bunks in the sunny back room for $32. A communal breakfast is included in the room rates (open only in summer; fills frequently; call ahead for a reservation).

Beacon Rock, across the Bridge of the Gods (Exit 44) then 7 mi. west on Washington Hwy. 14, has secluded sites for $10. The entrance to the park, directly across from the rock, is hard to miss. If you don't mind camping in a crowded yard, the **Cascade Locks Marina,** ½ mi. off the bridge on the Oregon side, has a nice lawn on the river. They pack as many RVs and tents on it as they can but offer showers as compensation (space goes for $10). Campgrounds surround Hood River, but the state parks tend to be expensive. **Ainsworth** (695-2301), at exit 35 off I-84, is conveniently located and well-equipped, with 45 full hook-up sites (all sites $18).

Sights and Outdoors The wide Columbia and its 30mph winds make Hood River a **windsurfing** paradise. Vibrantly colored sailboards decorate the Gorge, and engage in obsessive, zany competitions like the "Killer Loop Classic." Everything stops in town on windy days and folks gets antsy during calm stretches. To fully experience Hood River, rent a board or take a lesson. At **Duck Jibe Pete's,** 1st and Oak St. (386-9434 or 386-1699), you can rent a high-quality sailboard including a car rack for $40 a day (open 9am-8pm daily). Beginners will want to sail at the **hook,** a shallow, sandy cove, and experts might try the **Spring Creek Fish Hatchery** on the Washington side. If the wind is up, the Hatchery is the place to watch the best in the business. The Event Center, toward the water off Exit 63, is another hub of activity. Parking all day is $3, but it's free if you just sit and watch. If you catch windsurfing mania, a 2½-3 hour class at **Rhonda Smith Port Marina Park** (386-WIND/9463)—take Exit 64 under the bridge and to the left—will get you started or bump you up a notch ($65-75). Rentals (right on the water) start at $25-35 for a half-day, with discounts for longer periods. The gorge also has excellent mountain biking. **Discover Bicycles,** 1020 Wasco St. (386-4820), rents mountain bikes for $5 per hour and $25 a day, and can suggest routes. If you're staying at the hostel, try the **Hospital Hill Trail,** which starts behind the hospital parking lot in White Salmon.

The gorge also offers a panoply of sights that you don't have to get wet or dirty to enjoy. The famous **Vista House** (695-2230), completed in 1917 as a memorial to Oregon's pioneers, is now a visitors center in Crown Point State Park (open May 1-Oct. 15th 9am-6pm daily). The first point of intrigue along scenic Hwy. 30, it is a prime place to stop and check out the road ahead. A three dimensional model of the area illuminates various trails and waterfalls along the gorge, and maps are there for the taking. The house hangs on the edge of an outcropping high above the river. A trail leaves the road a few yards down from the house, ending in a secluded view of both the house and the gorge. Crown Point is 3 mi. east of eastbound Exit 22 off I-84. For an even loftier view, drive up the **Larch Mountain Road,** which splits from Hwy. 30

just above the Vista House and winds up 4000 ft. over 14 mi. to a picnic area that has views of Mt. St. Helens and Mt. Rainier on a clear day.

A string of waterfalls adorns the scenic highway east of Crown Point. At **Latourell Falls,** 2½ mi. east of Crown Point, a jaunt down a paved path is sure to get you sprayed. Five miles farther east, **Wahkeena Falls** is visible from the road, winding 242 feet down a narrow gorge. A short, steep scramble over loose rock, or a ¼-mi. trip up a paved walk will put you right in the middle. Another mile east of Hwy. 30 is the granddaddy of them all, **Multnomah Falls,** which attracts two million visitors annually. From a viewing platform (just past the espresso cart) you can watch the falls crash 620 ft. into a tiny pool and then drain under the gracefully arching Benson Bridge into a lower falls. Exit 31, on I-84, takes you to an island in the middle of the freeway from which you can only see the upper falls. You will have access to the falls through a pedestrian subway. A quick hike that takes you to Benson Bridge shouldn't be missed. Those who push up the trail past the top will be rewarded with relative solitude and a series of smaller waterfalls. Hikers can follow other paths into **Mt. Hood National Forest** (including one that links up with Lorch Mountain); the **information center** at the base of Multnomah Falls has excellent free maps and great suggestions. **Oneonta Falls,** 2 mi. east, is a 1.1-mi. hike through Cold Creek in Oneonta Gorge (the trail *is* the creek). **Horsetail Falls,** another mile east, drops 221 ft.; a steep ½-mi. hike affords a closer look.

Two longer, sublime **hiking** experiences are the medium-length **Wyeth Trail** near the hamlet of Wyeth (Exit 51), and the long (13 mi.) but incredible **Eagle Creek Trail,** chiseled into cliffs high above Eagle Creek, passing four waterfalls before joining the Pacific Crest Trail. For information on trails and a friendly earful of local lore, call the Columbia Gorge National Scenic Area Headquarters (386-2333).

Forty-four mi. east of Portland is the oldest of the Columbia River hydroelectric projects, the **Bonneville Dam** (Exit 40 off I-84). Woody Guthrie was working for the Bonneville Power Co. when he wrote "Roll On Columbia," a salute to river development: "Your power is turning our darkness to dawn, so roll on Columbia, roll on." You can make your way across one section of the river atop turbine powerhouses to the **Bradford Island Visitors Center** (374-8820), which has self-guided tours of the locks and fish hatcheries (open daily 9am-5pm). In the summer months, when the spillway is open, the riotous flow of water will take your breath away.

One exit down off I-84 (#44), in Cascade Locks, you will come upon the **Bridge of the Gods** (75¢ toll). The bridge was constructed at the site where, according to native legend, a natural bridge once stood. It collapsed when the two warrior gods, Klickitat (Mt. Adams) and Wy'east (Mt. Hood), erupted in a fight for the honor of Sleeping Beauty Mountain. (Mt. Adams, at 12,307 ft., is easy to spot north of the town of White Salmon, WA; Sleeping Beauty is 4568 ft. high). The bridge seems fragile even now; if you drive slowly, you can see through the grating to the river below.

About 7 mi. west of the bridge on the Washington side is **Beacon Rock,** the 848-ft.-high neck of an old volcano, the largest monolith in the U.S. (across the river from Exit 35 off I-84). You will know it when you see it, and you may long to climb it, but alas, it is not only a tough technical climb requiring a permit (contact the National Scenic Area Headquarters in Hood River at 541-386-2333), it is also closed to climbers in the summer, while the falcons roost at its crown.

If you're up for an assertive incline, amazing views of the gorge and, in June and July, an explosion of wildflowers, look for signs to **Dog Mountain.** This 2250-ft., 3½-mi. hike starts in a well marked parking lot just east of Beacon Rock.

In Stevenson, WA, 3 mi. east of the bridge, is the snazzy **Columbia Gorge Interpretive Center,** Box 396 (427-8211). The highlights include an actual-size replica of the now illegal fish wheels used to harvest millions of pounds of salmon, an enormous antique steam engine (that now runs on electricity), and a 12-min. multimedia show on the formation of the gorge ($6, seniors and students $5, ages 6-12 $4, under age 6 free; open daily 10am-5pm).

Thirty miles east of Hood River, the **Mary Hill Museum of Art,** 35 Maryhill Museum Dr. (509-773-3733), sits high above the Columbia on the Washington side. I-84 to Biggs or the slightly more scenic Hwy. 14 both follow the river and will get you close enough to follow signs. Peacocks stroll through the garden. Built by Sam Hill in the 1920s, the mansion is named for his daughter. European and American paintings, a collection of drawings and sculptures by Rodin, works by Native Americans, and nearly 150 hand-made chess sets from around the world make the museum an interesting visit ($5, seniors $4.50, ages 6-16 $1.50; open mid-March through mid-Nov. daily 9am-5pm).

Nineteen mi. east of Hood River on I-84, **The Dalles** (DALZ) was the last stop on the agonizing Oregon Trail. Lewis and Clark camped here at Fort Rock on Bargeway Rd. in 1805. French trappers named the area *Le Dalle* (the trough) after the rapids around that section of the river. For a free **map** and a walking tour of historical spots in town, go to the **Convention and Visitor's Bureau,** 404 W. 2nd St. (296-6616 or 800-255-3385; open Mon.-Fri. 9am-5pm, Sat. 10am-4pm). It's on your right, half a mile down Exit 84 off I-84. Up the hill, the **Fort Dalles Museum,** 500 W. 15th (296-4547), at 15th and Garrison, is housed in the original 1856 surgeon's quarters and displays memorabilia of the pioneer and military history of the region. Highlighting the dusty collection of old buggies and cars are an eight passenger horse-drawn "bus" and two hearse carriages ($3, under 18 free; open daily 10am-5pm; winter Thurs.-Mon. 10am-4pm). The visitors center at the **Dalles Lock and Dam** (296-1181), the longest concrete dam in America, offers free one hour tours that include a train ride to the dam, a view of the fish ladder, a glimpse of the generator, and a look at old Indian petroglyphs (open April, May, and Sept., daily 10am-4pm; June-Aug. daily 9am-5pm; tours leave every ½hr.).

OREGON COAST

A renowned coastal highway, **U.S. 101** hugs the shore, occasionally rising to lofty viewpoints. From Astoria in the north to Brookings in the south, the highway laces together the resorts and fishing villages that cluster around the mouths of the rivers that feed into the Pacific. Its most breathtaking stretches lie between coastal towns, where hundreds of miles of state and national parks allow direct access to the beach. Wherever the highway leaves the coast, look for a beach loop road. Stop and wander along the long stretches of unspoiled beach and observe the ocean's diverse sealife: seals, sea lions, and waterfowl lounging on rocks just offshore.

GETTING AROUND

Travel down the coast by bike can be both rewarding and exhausting. Cyclists should write to the **Oregon Tourism Commission** (see p. 408), or to virtually any visitors center or chamber of commerce on the coast for the free *Oregon Coast Bike Route Map;* it provides invaluable information on campsites, hostels, bike repair facilities, temperatures, and wind conditions. Remember that Portlanders head down-road to vacation, so most traffic flows south of the city. In summer, the prevailing winds will be at your back if you **cycle** south.

Gasoline and grocery **prices** on the coast are about 20% higher than in the inland cities. Motorists should try to stock up and fill up before reaching the coastal highways. When searching for a site to pull in for the night, look to the small villages, as they tend to be both the most interesting and the cheapest places to stay. From north to south, Nehalem, Wheeler, Depoe Bay, Winchester Bay, Charleston, Bandon, and Port Orford offer escape from the larger and more commercialized towns of Seaside, Tillamook, Lincoln City, Newport, and Coos Bay. State parks along the coast offer 17 major campgrounds with electricity and showers.

Lewis and Clark

Along the Columbia River Gorge, Merriweather Lewis and William Clark are the stuff of tourism legend. Lewis and Clark mania reaches near frenzy and profiles of the intrepid Easterners adorn road signs, restaurants, and any nook or cranny historians think the explorers might have touched. In 1804, U.S. President Thomas Jefferson made a lasting contribution to the "Age of Enlightenment" by commissioning Merriweather Lewis to follow the Missouri River to its source in hopes of finding a waterway to the Pacific Ocean. Lewis asked his friend William Clark to accompany him, and on May 14, 45 men in three boats set off from St. Louis. They were instructed to record in intricate detail all aspects of the geography, biology, ecology, and native culture along the way. Tagging along were Toussaint Charbonneau, a French-Native American interpreter and guide, his Shoshone wife Sacagawea, and their infant son.

A year and a half and many a mosquito-bitten, rain-drenched adventure later, the expedition sighted the Pacific near the town of McGowan, WA, on the Columbia River. Lewis and Clark had changed the course of American history by establishing the United States' presence in the Northwest and Oregon territories and maintaining peaceful communication with natives along their route. The expedition also spawned a phalanx of American heroes: from the fearless white guys to the courageous native mother, this expedition turned out more role models than the *Apollo 13*.

■ Astoria

Lewis and Clark arrived in Astoria in 1805 at the end of their transcontinental trek; six years later, John Astor, scion of a famously wealthy 19th-century family, established a fur-trading post, making Astoria the first permanent U.S. settlement west of the Rockies. After more than a century, Astorians still make their livings at fishing.

Rows of Victorian homes (painted in candy-coated hues, perhaps to combat the area's perseverant cloudcover), plenty of espresso bars and fast food, and a comfortable, working class atmosphere make this smallish town a Hollywood favorite: *Kindergarten Cop*, with Arnold Schwarzenegger, was filmed here. Movies like *Goonies*, *Free Willy*, and *Teenage Mutant Ninja Turtles III* also use Astoria's panoramic view of the Columbia River and Pacific Ocean.

PRACTICAL INFORMATION AND ORIENTATION

Visitors Information: Astoria/Warrenton Area Chamber of Commerce, 111 W. Marine Dr. (325-6311; fax 325-9767), just east of the bridge to Washington. P.O. Box 176, Astoria 97103. Stocked with info on Astoria, the Coast, and southwest Washington. Open Mon.-Sat. 8am-6pm, Sun. 9am-5pm; Oct..-May Mon.-Fri. 8am-5pm, Sat.-Sun. 11am-4pm.

Buses: Pierce Pacific Stages, Inc. (692-4437). Pick-up at Video City, 95 W. Marine Dr., across from the Chamber of Commerce. To Portland (1 per day, $15 one way) and Seaside (1 per day, $5 one way). **Sunset Empire Transit** (325-0563), pick-up at the Greyhound bus station, Duane St. at 9th. To Seaside (5 per day, $2.75, seniors and disabled $2) and Cannon Beach (5 per day, $3.50, seniors and disabled $2.50).

Public Transportation: Astoria Transit System, 364 9th St. (325-0563 or 800-452-2085). Local bus service. Makes a full city loop every 20min. (75¢, students 50¢). Service Mon.-Fri. 6:50am-6:30pm, Sat. 9am-6:30pm.

Taxi: Yellow Cab, 325-313 or 861-26261. 24hr.

Car Club: AAA, 5 N. U.S. 101 (861-3118), Warrenton. Open Mon.-Fri. 8am-5pm.

Laundromat: Coin Laundry, 823 W. Marine Dr. (325-2027), next to Dairy Queen. Wash $1, 8½min. dry 25¢. Open daily 7:30am-10pm.

Crisis Line: 325-3426. Open Mon.-Fri. 9am-5pm.

Women's Resource Center: 10 6th St. #104 (325-5735), at Marine Dr. 24hr.

Seniors Information Service: 800 Exchange St. (325-0123). Legal services and community center. Open Mon.-Fri. 8:30am-noon and 1-3pm.

Pharmacy: Astoria Pharmacy, 840 Exchange St. (325-1123), in the Astoria Family Clinic Building. Open Mon.-Fri. 9:30am-5:30pm, Sat. 9:30am-12:30pm.

Hospital: Columbia Memorial, 2111 Exchange St. (325-4321 or 800-962-2407).

Emergency: 911. **Police:** 555 30th St. (325-4411). **Clatsop County Sheriff:** 911 Center St. (325-2061). **Coast Guard:** 861-6228.

Post Office: 750 Commercial St. (325-2141), in the Federal Bldg. at 8th St. Open Mon.-Fri. 8:30am-5pm. **General Delivery ZIP Code:** 97103.

Area Code: 503.

Astoria is the most convenient connection between the Oregon coast and Washington. Two bridges run from the city: the **Youngs Bay Bridge,** to the southwest, on which Marine Drive becomes U.S. 101, and the **Astoria Bridge,** a scenic 4-mi. span over the Columbia River into Washington. The Astoria Bridge has narrow and hazardous bike lanes. Motorists might prefer to drive you across rather than swerve around you on the bridge. Streets in downtown Astoria are all one way. Pick up a map from the Chamber of Commerce (see above) before exploring downtown. Even-numbered streets run toward the hills, odd streets toward the water. All streets parallel to the water are in alphabetical order except for the first one (Marine Dr.).

Warrenton lies a few miles west of Astoria. U.S. 30 runs to Portland, 100 mi. east. Astoria can also be reached from Portland via U.S. 26 and U.S. 101 at Seaside.

ACCOMMODATIONS AND CAMPING

Motels in the area cater to tourists heading south to Oregon's coastal resort towns; rooms can be expensive and hard to come by during the summer. The area has a great, almost unknown hostel, though, and U.S. 101, south of Astoria, is littered with excellent campgrounds. **Fort Stevens State Park** is by far the best.

Fort Columbia State Park Hostel (HI-AYH), Fort Columbia, Chinook, WA (360-777-8755), within the park boundaries. Across the 4-mi. bridge into Washington, then 3 mi. north on U.S. 10, take a sharp left just after exiting the tunnel. Take the 75¢ Astoria Transit System bus on weekdays and Saturday (see **Practical Information**). This 1896 military hospital-turned-hostel pampers with flowered bedsheets, wooden floors, and a cozy living room. The friendly atmosphere and 50¢ pancake breakfasts make leaving a chore. Despite all this and laundry facilities, the hostel rarely fills up. Lockout 10am-5pm, check-in 5-10pm. $10, nonmembers $13, bicyclists $8, under 18 (with parent) $5. Open Apr. 1-Sept. 31.

Grandview Bed and Breakfast, 1574 Grand Ave. (325-0000 or 800-488-3250). Cheery rooms with shared bath (unless you've got $70 to spare). "Continental breakfast plus" includes fresh muffins, smoked salmon, bagels, and more. The only catch to the otherwise charming B&B is that, according to management, "unmarried couples will be uncomfortable." Cheapest room $39, the rest start at $55. Off season, second night is free.

Lamplighter Motel, 131 W. Marine (325-4051). Next to the Pig'n Pancake diner. Attractive rooms with multiple amenities and large bathrooms. Coffee in lobby, cable TV. Singles $48. Doubles $58. Winter rates $15 less. Senior discounts. Reserve at least a week in advance.

Fort Stevens State Park (861-1671), over Youngs Bay Bridge on U.S. 101 S., 10 mi. west of Astoria. A mammoth park with rugged, empty beaches, and bike trails. This is the closest major campground to the resort towns of Seaside and Cannon Beach. 603 sites with hot showers. Facilities for the disabled. Call 800-452-5687 to make reservations for summer weekends ($6). Sites $17, $20 with full hookups. Hiker/biker $4. The park also has yurts—domed tents with sloping dirt walls and plywood floors—for $25.

Drinking with Paul

One block up from the Maritime Museum, Paul van der Veldt, the eccentric owner of the **Shallon Winery,** 1598 Duane St. (325-5978), holds court. He will give you a tour of his small viniculture facilities, provide his interpretation of the area's history, and proudly display his extraordinary repertoire of wines, none made with grapes. A self-proclaimed connoisseur of fine food, he insists you call him "anytime of day or night" before you consider eating at any restaurant within a 50-mi. radius. He'll treat you to a taste of wines made from local berries and the only commercially produced **whey wines** (from Tillamook cheese) in the world. Approach the cranberry and whey wine with caution; their fruity taste belies their high alcohol content. Sampling **lemon meringue pie wine** is likely to be the highlight of any trip to the Oregon Coast and not to be missed is his **chocolate orange** wine, which others have spent millions trying to reproduce without success (of course you must be 21 to drink; gratuities appreciated; open almost every afternoon).

FOOD

Escape the expensive seafood and chain restaurants at **Sentry Supermarket,** 3300 Leif Erickson Rd. (325-1931), and have the ultimate seaside experience. Barking sea lions can often be heard from the market. Grab a latte ($1.75) at the drive-through and sit on the rocks to watch the animals (open daily 7am-10pm). A limited selection of natural foods and organic produce is available at the tiny **Community Store,** 1389 Duane St. (325-0027; open Mon.-Sat. 10am-6pm).

Columbian Café, 1114 Marine Dr. (325-2233). The crêpe-flipping action of the lively, charismatic chef is the best show in town. The pasta dishes ($8-9) and crêpes ($5-7) are divine. Dinner is too popular for the café's tiny size; waits for a meal can be long, but listening to local banter or just perusing the microbrew menu makes up for lost time. Dinners $12.50-$14. At breakfast or lunch, order "Mercy Food"—the chef chooses your meal for you; you say how spicy ($6). One local has so much faith that he has ordered Mercy Food over 1200 times. Open Mon.-Fri. 8am-2pm, Sat. 10am-2pm; for dinner Wed.-Thurs. 5-8pm, Fri.-Sat. 5-9pm.

Someplace Else, 965 Commercial St. (325-3500). A family-style Italian restaurant which offers more than the Italian standards ($4.50-10). Every month the regulars get to vote on what specials they want. The chick-peas in tamarind sauce gets rave reviews. Open Wed.-Mon. 11:30am-2pm and 4-9pm.

Ship Inn, 1 2nd St. (325-0033). A harbor for seafood lovers, this popular restaurant admirably replicates an English fish and chips establishment. No wimpy fries here, "potato planks" are heaped high with your order. The squid is tender and delicious; half an entree ($6-7) will fill you up. Open daily 11:30am-9:30pm.

Ricardi Gallery, 108 10th St. (325-5450). The town's hip coffee house doubles as an art gallery. Café fare, with salads, soups and copies of the *New Yorker* to boot. Open Mon.-Fri. 7:30am-5:30pm, Sat. 8am-5:30pm, Sun. 9am-4:30pm.

SIGHTS AND EVENTS

Astoria's prime location is best appreciated from the top of the **Astoria Column,** on Coxcomb Hill Rd. There is a view of Saddle Mtn. and lush forests to the south, and the Columbia River estuary to the north. Completed in 1926, the column is wrapped by 166 steps on the exterior, passing newly repainted friezes which depict the history of the area. Tableaux of historic Astoria include the discovery of the Columbia River by intrepid English sea captain Robert Grey, the arrival of Lewis and Clark, and the settling of Astoria. To get there, follow the tower icons painted on Astoria's streets (free; open from dawn to 10pm).

Astoria's most unique attraction is the wave-shaped **Columbia River Maritime Museum,** 1792 Marine Dr. (325-2323), on the waterfront. The prize of the model boat collection is Robert Grey's 1792 vessel, in which he "discovered" the mouth of

OREGON

the Columbia River. The large museum is packed with marine lore, including displays on the salmon fisheries that once dominated Astoria. Tours of the *Columbia*, the last lightship to see active duty at the mouth of the Columbia, are self-guided ($5, seniors $4, ages 6-17 $2, under 6 free; museum open daily 9:30am-5pm).

The **Astoria Regatta** (325-0285), held the second week in August, is one of the longest running events in the Northwest, dating back to 1894. The tradition is running strong and features food and craft booths, a watershow, scenic boat rides, fireworks, dances, and even a sailboat race or two. The **Scandinavian Festival** on the second weekend in June attracts a large following to enjoy the crafts, dancing, and Scandinavian food. Contact the Chamber of Commerce (325-6311) for information.

■ Near Astoria

Five mi. south of Astoria, the **Fort Clatsop National Memorial** (861-2471) reconstructs the winter headquarters of the Lewis and Clark expedition, based on descriptions in their detailed journal. The log fort housed Lewis, Clark, their interpreter Sacajawea, Clark's servant York, three officers, 24 enlisted men, several Northwest natives, and plenty of fleas. To find Ft. Clatsop, take the old Hwy. 101 exit (now the bus route) before the Youngs Bay bridge and make a left on Fort Clatsop Rd. Talks and demonstrations by historically clothed rangers are delivered daily, including a demonstration of the fragile-looking muzzle-loading guns the expedition relied on for hunting and defense ($2, under 17 free, family $4; open mid-June to Labor Day daily 8am-6pm; winter 8am-5pm).

Fort Stevens State Park (campground 861-1671, historical area 861-2000), off U.S. 101 on a narrow peninsula 10 mi. west of Astoria, has excellent swimming, fishing, boating facilities, beaches, and hiking trails. Fort Stevens was constructed in 1864 to prevent Confederate naval raiders from entering the Columbia. It also demonstrated American military strength in the Northwest and prevented the more threatening British from taking advantage of the U.S. preoccupation with the war back east. From 1897 to 1904, during the Spanish-American War, the fort underwent a massive development program, including the construction of eight concrete gun batteries. Although the guns have all been removed, nearly all the batteries remain and are the primary focus of a self-guided walking tour (about 2hr.), which begins up the road from the day-use and campground areas. Daily between Memorial Day and Labor Day, a restored 1954 Army cargo truck takes visitors on narrated tours at 11am, 12:30, 2:30, and 4pm ($2.50, ages 12 and under $1.25). The tours leave from the **Fort Stevens Military Museum and Interpretive Center** (861-2000), which contains displays and artifacts spanning the history of the fort (open daily 10am-6pm; winter Wed.-Sun. 10am-4pm).

Battery Russell (861-2471), in the park ½ mi. south of the historical area, bears the dubious distinction of being the only mainland American fort to see active defensive duty since the War of 1812. At 11:30pm on June 21, 1942, a Japanese submarine surfaced offshore and shelled the fort with 17 rounds. The fort was undamaged and did not return fire. Today it is a military monument, and allows free access to visitors. Colorful kites offset the gloomy skeletal remains of the British schooner *Peter Iredale*, which ran aground in 1906.

Bike paths weave through the park. If a dip in the ocean sounds a bit icy, try **Coffenbury Lake,** a warmer spot for swimming and fishing. The fee is only $3, and encompasses both the interpretive center and the lake.

■ Seaside

In the winter of 1805-6, explorers Lewis and Clark made their westernmost camp near Seaside. They'd be appalled to see what has become of the area. If baby strollers, bumper cars, and fried dough don't appeal, you too may feel the urge to turn and head back up the Columbia. Built into a resort in the 1870s, years and tourists have eroded Seaside's charm. With crowds, fast food, video arcades, and a developed beach, Seaside has ambitions to be the Jersey shore; it lacks only sunshine, warm water, and a Trump casino.

For the budget traveler, however, Seaside makes a good base for exploring the popular northern Oregon coast. Prices are lower than in neighboring Cannon Beach, and the hostel here is one of the best in the northwest.

PRACTICAL INFORMATION AND ORIENTATION

Visitors Information: Chamber of Commerce, 7 N. Roosevelt St. (738-6391 or 800-444-6740), on U.S. 101 and Broadway. Well-versed staff. Also a referral service for all local motels; make reservations on a free phone. Open Mon.-Sat. 8am-6pm, Sun. 9am-5pm.; Oct.-May Mon.-Fri. 9am-5pm, Sat.-Sun. 10am-4pm.

Buses: Pierce Pacific Stages (a Greyhound affiliate, makes Greyhound connections; 717-1651). Runs out of the hostel. To Portland (1 daily, $20) and Seattle (1 daily, $31). Buy tickets at the hostel too.

Public Transit: Sunset Empire Transit (325-0563). Runs between Astoria and Cannon Beach; stops at the hostel. Five runs daily (each way) on weekdays only ($1.25-$5, senior/disabled $1-$2.50, ages 6-12 $.65-1.75). Tickets and info available at the hostel.

Taxi: Yellow Cab, 738-3131. 24hr.

Bike Rental: Prom Bike Shop, 622 12th Ave. (738-8251), at 12th and Holladay; also at 80 Ave. A, downtown. Bikes, roller skates, in-line skates, and beach tricycles $6 per hr. and $25 per day; tandem bicycles $8 per hr. ID held during rental. Open daily 10am-6pm. Ave. A location open daily 7am-9pm. Also operates **Seaside Surry,** a rental shop at 153 Ave. A (same hours).

Library: 60 N. Roosevelt Dr. (738-6742). Open Tues.-Thurs. 9am-8pm, Fri.-Sat. 9am-5pm, Sun. 1-5pm.

Senior Citizen's Information Service: 1225 Ave. A (738-7393). Info and referral. Open Mon.-Fri. 8:30am-4:30pm.

Women's Crisis Service: 325-5735. 24hr.

Hospital: Providence Seaside Hospital, 725 S. Wahanna Rd. (738-8463).

Emergency: 911. **Police:** 1091 S. Holladay Dr. (738-6311). **Coast Guard:** 861-6228.

Post Office: 300 Ave. A (738-5462). Open Mon.-Fri. 8:30am-5pm, Sat. (for pickup only) 8-10:30am. **General Delivery ZIP Code:** 97138.

Area Code: 503.

Seaside lies 17 mi. south of Astoria and 8 mi. north of **Cannon Beach** along U.S. 101. The most direct route between Seaside and Portland is U.S. 26, which intersects U.S. 101 just south of Seaside along Saddle Mountain State Park. The **Necanicum River** runs north-south through Seaside, approximately two blocks from the coastline, paralleled by U.S. 101 and Holladay Dr. to the east. All three are bisected by **Broadway,** the main street. "The Promenade" is a paved path that parallels the beach and is open to cyclists, roller skaters, and pedestrians. Broadway is usually clogged with tourists because all of Seaside's attractions are within easy walking distance.

ACCOMMODATIONS AND CAMPING

Seaside's dismally expensive motel scene has been greatly remedied by the opening of a large hostel. Reservations are essential. The prices of motels are directly proportional to their proximity to the beach. Though the town is teeming with motels, the cheapest hover near $40 per night (cheaper during the off-season). Rooms are invariably full by 5pm; get ahead of the game and ask the Chamber of Commerce for availability listings. They won't reserve a room for you, but they'll offer advice.

Get ready to drive if you aim to camp. The closest state parks are **Fort Stevens,** 21 mi. north (see **Astoria: Accommodations,** p. 434) and **Saddle Mountain** (861-1671), 14 mi. southeast of Seaside off U.S. 26, 8 mi. northeast of Necanicum Junction (10 primitive campsites, $9). Closer to Seaside is **Kloochie Creek,** about 300 yd. off U.S. 26, 6 mi. southeast of town (9 sites, $6). Sleeping on the beach in Seaside is illegal, and police enforce this rule.

Seaside International Hostel (HI-AYH), 930 N. Holladay Dr. (738-7911). This new hostel sprang up in 1994 from the remains of an old hotel and a law office. Where attornies once scribbled, friendly hostel employees serve up lattés and cookies at the espresso bar. The hostel is just 4 blocks from the beach and the main drag, but ask the management about the less frequented areas "Off Broadway." Employees can recommend hikes or loan one of two canoes (for a small donation) to those who want to escape the tourist craze. Free movies shown nightly, a well-equipped kitchen, and a grassy back yard along the river. 48 large bunks $13, non-members $16; private rooms $34, nonmembers $45. Call ahead.

Mariner Motel, 429 S. Holladay Dr. (738-8254). Fine rooms, many newly recar-peted, with TVs and phones. Free coffee (8:30-10am) in the office. Pool. Singles $45. Doubles $56. Call for reservations in summer. Sept. 15-June 11, $6 lower.

Riverside Inn, 430 S. Holladay Dr. (738-8254 or 800-826-6151). Small bedrooms, with bookshelves, fresh flowers, and raftered ceilings make this B&B a charming alternative to Seaside motel-madness. All rooms have private bath and TV. Take your breakfast on the riverfront deck (included). Singles from $49, $45 in winter.

FOOD

Broadway, especially toward the beach, becomes a madhouse at lunchtime. For the lowest prices, try **Safeway,** 401 S. Roosevelt (738-7122; open daily 6am-midnight).

The Stand, 220 Ave. U. (738-6592), has the cheapest meals around and is fre-quented by locals—a good sign. Don't come for the unassuming decor, but expect plenty of delicious food and enthusiastic service (burritos $1.50-$3.25). Open Mon.-Sat. 11am-8pm.

Planet Zoe's Deli, 846 Ave. C (738-5286). A refuge for vegetarians and vegans, this shiny, happy deli serves a mean veggie lasagna ($4) and juiced anything. Small por-tions, but congo drums on the sound system make up for it. Open Tues. 11am-6pm, Wed.-Sat. 11am-7pm, Sun. 11am-4pm.

Evergreen Lanes Coffee Shop, 3518 Hwy. 101 N. (738-5333) also in Gearhart. Don't let the aura à la Denny's and the attached bowling alley scare you away from this local seafood favorite. The fish here is just as fresh and plentiful as on Broad-way, but less expensive (halibut fish and chips $8.50). Again, locals swear by it. We promise. Bowl a few frames afterwards. Open daily 6:30am-10pm.

Café Espresso, 600 Broadway #7 on the Necanicum Walkway (738-6169), makes a sublime cappuccino and hosts the only palatable—if limited—nightlife scene in Seaside. Come Saturday nights at 8pm for live local jazz, blues, and acoustic rock; minimal cover. Open daily 9am-6pm.

SIGHTS AND EVENTS

Seaside revolves around **Broadway,** a garish strip of arcades, shops, and salt water taffy joints running the ½ mi. from Roosevelt (U.S. 101) to the beach. Indoor minia-ture golf, bumper cars, and video games are some of the highlights. The **Turnaround** at the end of Broadway signals the "official" (read: arbitrary) end of the Lewis and Clark Trail. In 1986, the Turnaround underwent a facelift, and a statue of Lewis and Clark was erected at the end of the Trail. The tiny **Seaside Museum,** 570 Necanicum Dr. (738-7065), brims with tasty tidbits about Lewis and Clark, as well as other arti-facts and displays. Open daily 10:30am-4:30pm during summer months.

Seaside's beach front is large, but crowded nonetheless. Lifeguards are on duty from Memorial Day to Labor Day (daily 10am-6pm), even though the water is always too cold for swimming. Don't even think about taking a dip on "red flag" days: the surf is too rough. Exercise caution at all times; there are strong undertows. For a qui-eter beach, head to **Gearhart,** approximately 2 mi. north of downtown off U.S. 101. Explore the long stretch of sand and dunes on foot or by car. The beach has no life-guard, and town officials strongly discourage swimming.

The **Seaside Beach Run, Promenade Walk, and Sand Games** are held toward the end of July. The 8-mi. beach race leaves from Seaside's Turnaround. Contact Sunset

Empire Park & Recreation, 1140 E. Broadway (738-3311), for more information. This organization also oversees **"Where the Stars Play,"** a free concert series every Saturday in July and August. Everything from folk to Caribbean is blasted at Quatat Marine Park at 2pm. The real kicker comes at the end of August, when the **Hood to Coast Race** finishes in Seaside to the cheers of 25,000 spectators. Some 750 12-person teams run this two-day relay race from Mt. Hood in 5-mi. shifts. Contact Bob Foote (292-4626) for more info. Seaside also hides little-known natural wonders behind its beach bungalows and cotton candy stands. The Necanicum River estuary picks up where the north end of the promenade ends and makes a dune-covered, bird-filled loop back into town. From the Seaside beach, head south to the **Tillamook Head** (see Cannon Beach) for a day-long hike amid uncrowded forests and along vertigo-inducing cliffs. This is the cheapest way to see Tillamook Head and the lighthouse, since the Cannon Beach entrance charges a fee.

■ Cannon Beach

A rusty cannon from the shipwrecked schooner *Shark* washed ashore at Arch Cape, giving this town its name. Now the only artillery in this beachfront town is its battery of boutiques, bakeries, and galleries. Nothing in Cannon Beach is cheap, but a traveler resigned to window shopping and gallery hopping can actually spend an enjoyable day dodging Saabs and drinking espresso with local surfers and Portland escapees. When the credit-card flashing crowds reach critical mass, head to the tide pools or trails of Ezola State Park.

PRACTICAL INFORMATION AND ORIENTATION

Visitors Information: Cannon Beach Chamber of Commerce, 207 N. Spruce St., P.O. Box 64, Cannon Beach, 97110 (436-2623), at 2nd St. Emblematic of the city, this visitors center stocks T-shirts, postcards, and brochures. Open Mon.-Sat. 10am-5:30pm, Sun. 11am-5pm.

Bus: Sunset Transit System (325-0563). To: Seaside ($1.25) and Astoria ($3.50).

Public Transportation: Cannon Beach Shuttle, a **free** natural-gas powered bus service. Traverses the downtown area; board at any point. Service daily 10am-6pm. Ask the Chamber of Commerce for the schedule.

Bike Rental: Mike's Bike Shop, 248 N. Spruce St. (436-1266 or 800-492-1266), around the corner from the Chamber of Commerce. Offers **maps** of routes along old logging roads. Mountain bikes ($5-7 for the 1st hr., $35 every hr. after), beach tricycles ($6 per 90min). Credit card deposit required. Open daily 10am-6pm.

Lifeguard Service: 436-2345. July-Aug. daily 10am-8pm.

Weather: 861-2722.

Hospital: Providence Seaside Hospital, 725 S. Wahanna Rd. (738-8463), in Seaside. **Cannon Beach,** 171 Larch St. (436-1142), in Sandpiper Sq. Walk-in clinic Mon.-Fri. 9am-midnight.

Emergency: 911. **Police:** 163 Gower St. (436-2811). **Fire Dept.:** 436-2949.

Post Office: 155 N. Hemlock St. (436-2822). Open Mon.-Fri. 9am-5pm. **General Delivery ZIP Code:** 97110.

Area Code: 503.

Cannon Beach lies 7 mi. south of Seaside and 42 mi. north of Tillamook on U.S. 101. Hemlock, Cannon Beach's main drag, connects with U.S. 101 in four places. Cannon Beach is 79 mi. from Portland via U.S. 26.

ACCOMMODATIONS AND CAMPING

Pleasant motels line Hemlock St., none of which cost under $40 in the summer, though family units are sometimes available for less. Book early on summer weekends. In the winter, inquire about specials; most motels offer "two nights for one" deals in an effort to stay afloat. Real budget deals are only a short drive away. The Seaside International Hostel is a 7 mi. drive north (see **Seaside**), and **Oswald West State**

Park (see **Cannon Beach to Tillamook,** below), 10 mi. south of town, has a stunning campground.

The Sandtrap Inn, 539 S. Hemlock St. (436-0247 or 800-400-4106 from Portland). Picturesque, tastefully furnished rooms. Working fireplaces, cable TV. Prices start at $55, $45 off season. 3 nights for the price of 2 off-season special.

Blue Gull Inn, 487 S. Hemlock St. (436-2714 or 800-507-2714). Big, clean rooms with cable TV and laundry facilities. Set back from the street. Singles and doubles from $60 in summer; in winter from $50. Ask about winter specials; the family units, which sleep 4, are a good bulk deal.

Sea Ranch RV Park, 415 N. Hemlock St., P.O. Box 214 (436-2815). 55 tent sites and over 30 hookup sights in a safe field and tree-studded area, right on the north edge of town. Showers included. Sites $16, with full hookup $18, any extra person over 2, $2. Also offers a 1hr. horse ride for $25. Reservations recommended, one-night's deposit required.

FOOD

Soups, salads, and sandwiches have infected Cannon Beach eateries like a plague. For the best deals on food, avoid the strip and head farther down Hemlock to the mid-town area. For the basics, **Mariner Market,** 139 N. Hemlock St. (436-2442), has groceries. (Open Sun.-Thurs. 8am-10pm, Fri.-Sat. 9am-11pm; Oct.-April Sun.-Thurs. 8am-9pm, Fri.-Sat. 8am-10pm.)

Knoodlz, 171 Sunset Blvd. (436-0123). Global dining for the next millennium, Knoodlz serves (you guessed it) noodles, in 30 different combinations. Vegetarians can fill their tofu quota here, though the diverse and inexpensive menu (most lunches $5 and dinners $7) appeals to all sorts of noodle-slurping fans. The juice bar selection is equally varied. Open Wed.-Sat. 11:30am-8pm.

Midtown Café, 1235 S. Hemlock St. (436-1016) in the Haystack Sq. Relax with a tub of potatoes deluxe ($5) in the morning, or have a lunchtime lentil burger ($7). The huge, popular waffle breakfasts could fill you for a week ($3.50). Open Mon. and Wed.-Sat. 8am-2:30pm, Sun. 8am-2pm.

The Homegrown Café, 3301 S. Hemlock (436-1803) at the south end of Hemlock, just before the last exit back to U.S. 101. Have a seat in front of the fireplace and gobble down the ever-popular Homegrown burrito ($5) at any time of day. Excellent veggie fare. Open Fri.-Mon. 8am-8pm, Tues. 11am-2pm.

Bill's Tavern, 188 N. Hemlock (436-2202). If you're 21-plus in Cannon Beach, Bill's is the place to be. Down-home pub grub ranges from $3-5, pints $1.75-2.75. Open Thurs.-Tues. 11:30am-midnight.

SIGHTS, EVENTS, AND OUTDOORS

Browse at your leisure through elegant, expensive art galleries and gift shops. Or slip away for a more pedestrian (ha!) morning stroll along the 7-mi. stretch of flat, bluff-framed beach. Picnickers and hikers can follow the narrow, winding road to **Ecola State Park** (436-2844; $3 entrance fee). Ecola Point offers a spectacular view of hulking **Haystack Rock,** which is spotted with (and splattered by) gulls, puffins, barnacles, anemones, and the occasional sea lion. The Rock's **tide pools** teem with colorful and fragile sea life. Digging for mussels and clams is now prohibited by the city police. In an effort to educate the public about the Rock's remarkable self-contained ecosystem, guides are present on weekends during unusually low tides.

Ecola Point also affords views of the Bay's centerpiece, the **Tillamook Lighthouse,** which clings like a barnacle to a wave-swept rock. Construction of the lighthouse began in 1879 and continued for years in Sisyphean fashion as storms washed the foundations away. Decommissioned in 1957 because of damage from the storm tossed rocks, the now privately owned lighthouse can only be reached by helicopter for the purpose of depositing the ashes of the dead. From Ecola State Park, take the 12-mi. roundtrip hike to **Tillamook Head,** the miniature cape that divides Seaside

Beach from Cannon Beach, where you can sometimes glimpse migrating whales. The trail is open year-round, and the top provides an excellent view of the coast. If you want to tear up the water, **Cleanline Surf,** 171 Sunset Blvd. (436-9726), rents surfing gear for $35 per day. Indian Beach, in Ecola State Park, is a favorite with surfers. Cleanline also rents other watercraft (kayaks, boogieboards).

Saddle Mountain State Park, 14 mi. east of Cannon Beach on U.S. 26, is named for the highest peak in the Coast Range. A 6-mi., four-hour hike to Saddle Mountain's 3283-ft. summit rewards the fit with an astounding view of Nehalem Bay and the Pacific to the west and the Cascades to the north (summit trail open March-Dec.).

If you hunger for culture, try the **Coaster Theater,** 1087 N. Hemlock St. (436-1242), which stages theater productions, concerts, ballet and modern dance performances, comedy, and musical revues year-round. Write to Coaster Theater, P.O. Box 643, Cannon Beach 97110 for information (tickets $12-15; by phone with a Visa or MasterCard at the box office Tues.-Sat. 1-5pm, or an hour before showtime).

In late spring, catch the annual **Sand Castle Competition.** Contestants pour in from hundreds of miles away and begin early in the morning, creating ornate sculptures from wet sand. By evening the high tide washes everything away, leaving people's photographs as the sole testimony to the staggering creative energy expended during the day. Call the Chamber of Commerce (436-2623) for more info.

■ Cannon Beach to Tillamook

In the summer of 1933, the "Tillamook Burn" reduced 500 sq. mi. of forest to charcoal. While nature has restored Tillamook State Forest to health, the coastal towns teem with espresso bars and dime-a-dozen gift shops. The coastline that these tiny towns flirt with, however, is much less crowded than Seaside and Cannon Beaches and attracts those in search of less populous beaches. Tourist information for the area is available at the visitors information bureau in Tillamook (see **Tillamook: Practical Information**) or the **Rockaway Beach Chamber of Commerce,** 405 S. U.S. 101 (355-8108; open Mon.-Fri. 9am-noon, 1-4pm).

Oswald West State Park, 10 mi. south of Cannon Beach, is a tiny headland **rainforest** with huge spruce and cedar trees. Locals call this park "Short Sand Beach"; calling it Oswald West will blow your cover. The park is accessible only on foot by a ¼-mi. trail off U.S. 101. This doesn't quite qualify as "roughing it," as the park provides hulking, wooden wheelbarrows for transporting gear from the parking area to the 37 primitive campsites near the beach and the 11 woodsy ones (open mid-May to Oct.; sites $9). The sites are beautiful and secluded, just minutes away from the beach. Surfers occupy every other campsite. Fall asleep to the sound of gently babbling water. Arrive early, even on a summer weekday; these are the cheapest sites around. From the park, take the 4-mi. **Cape Falcon** hiking trail over the headland, or just follow the path from the campground to one of Oregon's few surfing beaches.

Five mi. south of Oswald West State Park, the consciously quaint town of **Manzanita** reclines across a long expanse of uncrowded beach. The **San Dune Motel,** 428 Dorcas Lane (368-5163), just off Laneda St., the main drag through town, has pleasant rooms a mere five blocks from the shore. Ask for the newly remodeled rooms (singles $50, winter $35). Scenic coastal hiking trails are close to Cannon Beach. The **Tillamook Head Trail,** 6 mi. north near Ecola State Park, is a 1000-ft. climb up a huge promontory, and provides incredible photo opportunities.

Nehalem, a few mi. south of Manzanita, consists of little more than a handful of "made in Oregon" shops marshalled along U.S. 101. Stop in at the **Bayway Eatery,** 25870 7th St. (368-6495), for an excellent fish and chips meal ($5.50) or an enormous order of fries ($1.50). This well-worn diner is a favorite Nehalem hangout. (Open Sun.-Thurs. 6am-9pm, Fri.-Sat. 6am-10pm.) Three mi. away, south on U.S. 101 to Rte. 53, is Nehalem's resident ongoing party. The **Nehalem Bay Winery,** 34965 Rte. 53 (368-WINE/9463), offers tastes of the local specialties, including cranberry and blackberry wines, and is a major center of activity in the area, with frequent performances in a small theater, and an annual bluegrass festival. Even if you're not up to tasting, stop in to chat with owner Ray, who adores travelers and gives all sorts of valuable tips on free camping, local swimming holes, and the merits of a good time. Open daily 9am-6pm; winter 10am-5pm.

■ Tillamook

Though the word Tillamook translates as "land of many waters," to Oregonians it means one thing: cheese. The land around Tillamook is densely populated by grazing dairy cows and devoted consumers of the region's famous cheddar. You can stop at the Tillamook Cheese Factory on your way through town and take your pick of sharp, medium, or mild. Since it's only 3 mi. from the coast, Tillamook gets its share of tourist traffic, but its shortage of dining and lodging options won't let you forget that it is still a small farming town.

PRACTICAL INFORMATION AND ORIENTATION

Visitors Information: Tillamook Chamber of Commerce, 3705 U.S. 101 N. (842-7525), in the big red barn across the parking lot from the Tillamook Cheese Factory. Friendly folks, free **maps,** and a complete listing of places to camp in Tillamook County. Open Mon.-Fri. 9am-5pm, Sat. 10am-4:30pm, Sun. 10am-2pm.
Taxi: Tillamook Taxi (842-4567). 24hr.
Seniors' Information: 842-7988. Open daily 8am-5pm.
Tillamook Women's Crisis Center: 2215 11th St. (842-9486). 24hr.
Laundromat: Little Cheese Coin-Op, on the corner of 3rd and Pacific. $1.50 wash, 7½-min. dry 25¢. 24hr.
Hospital: Tillamook County General Hospital, 1000 3rd St. (842-4444).
Emergency: 911. **Police:** 842-2522, in City Hall. **Fire:** 2310 4th St. (842-7587). **County Sheriff:** 201 Laurel St. (842-2561), in the courthouse.
Post Office: 2200 1st St. (842-4711). Open Mon.-Fri. 8:30am-5pm. **General Delivery ZIP Code:** 97141.
Area Code: 503.

Tillamook lies 49 mi. south of Seaside and 44 mi. north of Lincoln City on U.S. 101. The most direct route from Portland is to take U.S. 26 to Rte. 6. U.S. 101 is the main drag, and splits into two one way streets, Pacific and Main, in the downtown area. The Tillamook Cheese Factory lies a mile or two north of the town proper.

ACCOMMODATIONS AND CAMPING

Severe floods in February of 1996 meant full-scale renovations for most businesses in the area, so while some motels may look washed-out on the outside, you'll find new beds and carpets on the inside. The water's back down, but rates are still high enough to send you sailing into the area's finest campgrounds.

Tillamook Inn, 1810 U.S. 101 N. (842-4413 or 800-742-2087), between the center of town and the Tillamook Cheese Factory. New carpets, and cable with HBO. Singles $35. Doubles $45. Winter rates $3-5 lower. Call a few days ahead.
MarClair Inn, 11 Main Ave. (842-7571 or 800-331-6857). Convenient location at the junction of Rte. 6 and Hwy. 101. Large, newly remodeled, tastefully decorated rooms and pool, jacuzzi, and sauna that are well shielded from the road. $4 AAA discount. Singles $56. Doubles $64. Off season $44 and $54.
Cape Lookout State Park, 13000 Whiskey Creek Rd. (842-4981), 15 mi. southwest of Tillamook on the Three Capes Loop. Some of these 201 sites are only 20yd. from the beach, while others offer more privacy and shade. Showers. Tents $16, full hook-ups $20. Reserve with Oregon State Parks (800-452-5687).
Kilchis River Park (842-6694), 8 mi. northeast of Tillamook at the end of Kilchis River Rd., which meets U.S. 101 1 mi. north of the factory. 35 primitive sites nestle between a varied forest of tall mossy trees and a small baseball field. Nifty swingset. Water, flush toilets, sinks. Tent sites $10. Hiker/biker $2.

FOOD

If you like cheese and ice cream, you're in paradise. You might as well go to the source because Tillamook is weak on other dining options. Collect picnic supplies at **Safeway,** 955 U.S. 101 (842-4831; open daily 6am-midnight).

Tillamook Cheese Factory, 4175 U.S. 101 N. (842-4481). Fun just to see. More than just cheese cubes and pepperoni by the yard ($2.25). Deli sandwiches featuring you-know-what $2-5. Breakfasts 8-11am. Divine melty ice cream $1.25. Mid-June to Aug. open daily 8am-8pm; Sept. to mid-June 8am-6pm.

Blue Heron French Cheese Company, 2001 Blue Heron Dr. (842-8281), 1 mi. south of the Tillamook factory on U.S. 101 (but north of town). While the Tillamook Cheese Factory makes mostly cheddar, the focus at the Blue Heron is decidedly on brie. Deli serves up gourmet sandwiches ($5.50), fresh soups, and salads. Open daily 8am-8pm, winter 9am-5pm.

La Casa Medello, 1160 U.S. 101 N. (842-5768). Eat like a *conquistador* under bull horns, a sombrero, and two mounted machetes. Good family dining, with mild Mexican food prepared to order. Diminutive lunch specials $4-5. Massive 12-in. tacos ($6) and burritos ($5). Dinners ($6-9) come with rice, beans, and chips. Always hopping. Open Tues.-Sat. 4-8:30pm.

SIGHTS AND ACTIVITIES

The **Tillamook Cheese Factory** (see **Food,** above), is a temple to dairy delights, and a surprisingly entertaining experience. The free self-guided tour starts off with displays of antique churns and a short video. **Learn** about the modern cowbell, a computer chip which monitors the cow's every move. **Watch** as a milking machine goes to work on a plastic cow. **See** the whole factory from upstairs (with the help of more videos). **Find** the poor soul who has to wear a net on his beard while he watches blocks of cheese for eight hours a day. **Taste** a tidbit at the gift shop.

West of the highway, downtown, the **Tillamook County Pioneer Museum,** 2106 2nd St. (842-4553), features all manner of household and industrial goods from the pioneer era, set in mannequin-rich dioramas. The museum's prized treasure, however, is an impressive collection of animals, considered the best in the state, and preserved by taxidermist Alex Walker (not to be confused with novelist Alice Walker, who is *not* a licensed taxidermist). See a head of oryx, horn of kudu, a pouncing bobcat, and an unborn fawn ($2, seniors $1.50, ages 12-17 50¢, under 12 free, families $5; open Mon.-Sat. 8am-5pm, Sun. 11am-5pm; Oct.-Feb. closed Mon.).

Tillamook's largest attraction is the **Tillamook Naval Air Station Museum,** 6030 Hangar Rd. (842-1130), 2 mi. south of Tillamook. This hulking hangar is the largest wooden clear span structure in the world, covers seven acres, and is the only one of 16 built by the Navy in the 1940s that has survived to the present. The chilly cavern contains functional World War II planes including a German ME-109 Messerschmidt, an RAF MK-8 Spitfire, and a P-51 Mustang used by the U.S. The admission price is high ($5, ages 7-12 $2.50), but the museum is entertaining if you're into planes (open summer daily 9am-6pm; winter 10am-5pm).

■ Tillamook to Lincoln City

Between Tillamook and Lincoln City, U.S. 101 wanders eastward into wooded land, losing contact with the coast. Instead of staying on the highway, consider taking the **Three Capes Loop,** a 35-mi. circle to the west that connects a trio of spectacular promontories: **Cape Meares, Cape Lookout,** and **Cape Kiwanda State Parks.** The beaches are quieter than some stretches to the south, and the scenery makes the uncrowded drive worthwhile. Cyclists should beware the narrow twists and poor condition of the roads and drivers should be aware of the occasional cyclist.

Cape Meares State Park, at the tip of the promontory jutting out from Tillamook, is home to the tree-climber's ultimate fantasy known as the **Octopus Tree,** a gnarled Sitka spruce with several trunks. The **Cape Meares Lighthouse** (842-4981), built in

1890, also stands in the park and operates as an illuminating on-site interpretive center. Struggle up a story and a half's worth of tiny stairs for sweeping views and a peek at the original lens of the big light (free; open May-Sept. daily 11am-4pm; Oct., March, April Fri.-Sat. 11am-4pm). From Cape Meares, you can make out the three lonely **Arch Rocks** in the distance. Rising out of the water like the humps of a ghastly sea monster, the Arch Rocks are a federal refuge for sea lions and birds. You can gain a better view of the sea lions a bit farther south, toward **Netarts Bay.**

Continue 12 mi. southwest to **Cape Lookout State Park** (842-4981), where a free day use area accompanies the well used campground and offers picnic tables and access to the beach (see **Tillamook: Accommodations**). Start here on a 2½-mi. trail to the end of the lookout with a spectacular 360° view of **Tillamook Head, Three Arches Rock,** and **Haystack Rock.**

South of Cape Lookout, the road undulates through sand dunes, where the sound of the rushing wind battles the roar of all-terrain vehicles. Alongside this sandy playground lies the U.S. Forest Service's popular **Sandbeach Campground** (follow signs to Sand Lake), where you might feel left out if you don't have an ATV. Arrive early in the summer or make a reservation at 800-280-CAMP/2267 (101 sites with toilets and potable water $10). Or, camp in the sand at the edge of giant parking lots at **East Dunes** and **West Winds** ($5) just down the road.

Cape Kiwanda State Park, the third promontory on the loop, is for day use only (open 8am-dusk). On sunny, windy days, hang gliders gather to soar over the wave-carved sandstone cliffs. The sheltered cape also draws skin divers and beachcombers. On the cape, barely north of Pacific City, massive rock outcroppings in a small bay mark the launching pad of the flat-bottomed **dory fleet,** one of the few fishing fleets in the world that launches beachside, directly onto the surf. If you bring your own fishing gear down to the cape most mornings around 5am, you can probably convince someone to take you on board; the fee will probably be lower than that of a commercial outfitter.

Pacific City, a delightful town missed by most travelers on U.S. 101, is home to another **Haystack Rock,** just as impressive as its sibling to the north. The **Anchorage Motel,** 6585 Pacific Ave. (965-6773) offers homey rooms. Singles start at $33, doubles at $37. Rates drop significantly in winter. All rooms have cable TV and coffee, some have kitchens, none have phones.

For so small a town, Pacific City has some remarkably good restaurants. The **Pelican Pub and Brewery,** 33180 Cape Kiwanda Dr. (965-7007) is the hands-down victor in any location battle. On the breezy patio, you can see the sun setting between Cape Kiwanis and Haystack Rock. Pack away a generously stacked "Ham I Am sandwich" ($5.25) or salad ($3), and then clamor up the sandy flank of the cape to improve your view. For more memorable food in an intimate setting, head away from the salt water to the **Riverhouse Restaurant,** 34450 Brooten Rd. (965-6722), a tiny white house overlooking the Nescutta River. Come here for the excellent seafood ($13-19) and homemade desserts ($3-6) that have earned the Riverhouse its reputation as the best restaurant in town (open Sun.-Thurs. 11am-9pm, Fri.-Sat. 11am-10pm). Coming in close as a new town favorite is the **Grateful Bread Bakery,** 34805 Brooten Rd. (965-7337), where you can get anything from a black bean chili omelette ($6) and fresh squeezed OJ ($2) to a grilled salmon fillet with sauteed vegetable ($10) between 8am and 6pm.

Back on U.S. 101 and 6 mi. north in **Hebo,** the ranger district operates a **ranger station** for the **Siuslaw National Forest** at 31525 Rte. 22 (392-3161), ½ mi. from U.S. 101. Lists of hiking and camping options are available (open Mon.-Fri. 7:30am-4:30pm). Five mi. up steep and twisty Forest Service Road #14 is **Hebo Lake Campground,** with 16 gorgeous, outhouse- and water-equipped sites bordering **Small Hebo Lake** ($6; open mid-April to mid-Oct.). Three and a half mi. farther up the road, commune with microwave transmission towers on the summit of **Mt. Hebo** for excellent views of the coastline and, on clear days, Mt. Hood to the east. Other Forest Service campgrounds in the area include the **Mt. Hebo Campground,** 2 mi. beyond the summit on Forest Rd. 14 (free, 3 primitive sites, breezy, no drinking water) and the **Rocky Bend Campground,** 15 mi. east of Beaver on paved Nestuccca River Rd. (free; primitive; no drinking water).

About 1¼ mi. east of where Rte. 18 crosses 101 is the minuscule town of **Otis** (don't blink), where the famed **Otis Café** (994-2813), across from the BP station, serves excellent home-style strawberry-rhubarb pie for $2 à slice. The café often has a line out the door. Your patience will be rewarded with sinful breakfast specials ($2.50-6). The two eggs and two rich waffles are a delicious value at $4.25. They talk about the Otis cheese-covered German potatoes ($4.95) as far away as Paris, for Pete's sake (open Mon.-Thurs. 7am-3pm, Fri.-Sat. 7am-9pm, Sun. 8am-9pm).

A dozen wineries line Rte. 18 on the way to Portland. A 9-mi. detour via Rte. 99 W and Rte. 47 will take you far from the coast to **Carlton,** home of the **Chateau Benoit Winery** (864-2991), on Mineral Springs Rd. From Rte. 99 W near Lafayette turn north on Mineral Spring for 1¼ mi. Bring your own picnic for complimentary tasting at tables overlooking the vineyard (open daily 10am-5pm).

▓ Lincoln City

Lincoln City is actually five towns, all forcing you to crawl at 30 mph past a 7-mi. strip of motels, gas stations, and tourist traps on U.S. 101. Bicyclists will find Lincoln City hellish, and hikers should cut three blocks west to the seashore. Although it is perhaps the most commercialized town on the Oregon coast (boasting more than 1000 ocean-front motel rooms), Lincoln City is a convenient place to seek shelter and extra kite-string while exploring nearby capes, beaches, and waterways.

PRACTICAL INFORMATION AND ORIENTATION

Visitors Information: Lincoln City Visitor and Convention Bureau, 801 SW U.S. 101 #1 (800-452-2151 or 994-8378), across from the Burger King. Offers brochures covering Lincoln City and beyond. Sporty new 24hr. telephone board can connect you with local motels and restaurants at the (free) push of a button. Open Mon.-Fri. 8am-5pm, Sat. 9am-5pm, Sun. 10am-4pm.

Buses: Greyhound (265-2253 in Newport), S. 14th St. at U.S. 101, behind the bowling alley. To: Portland (2 per day, $12) and Newport (2 per day, $6). A stop only; no depot.

Taxi: Lincoln Cab Company, 996-2003. 24hr.

Car Rental: Robben-Rent-A-Car, 3232 NE U.S. 101 (994-5530). $25 per day plus 15¢ per mi. after 50 mi. Must be 21 with a major credit card. Reserve ahead. Office open Mon.-Sat. 8am-5pm.

Laundry: Coin Laundry, 2164 NE U.S. 101. Wash $1, 10-min. dry 25¢. Open daily 9am-10pm.

Library: Driftwood Library, 801 SW U.S. 101 (996-2277), near the visitors center. Open Mon.-Thurs. 9am-9pm, Fri.-Sat. 9am-5pm.

Swimming and Showers: Community Pool, 2150 NE Oar Place (994-5208). Pool $1.75, teens $1.25, 12 and under free, families $5; showers 75¢. Open Mon.-Sat. 1-3:30pm and 7-9pm, Sun. 1-3:30pm; call for winter hours.

Senior Citizen Center: 2150 NE Oar Place (994-2722).

Hospital: North Lincoln Hospital, 3043 NE 28th St. (994-3661).

Emergency: 911. **Police:** 1503 E. Devils Lake Rd. (994-3636). **Fire:** 2525 NW U.S. 101 (994-3100). **Coast Guard:** 765-2124, in Depoe Bay.

Post Office: 1501 SE Devils Lake Rd. (994-2148), 2 blocks east of U.S. 101. Open Mon.-Fri. 9am-5pm. **General Delivery ZIP Code:** 97367.

Area Code: 541.

Lincoln City, situated 38 mi. south of Tillamook, 30 mi. north of Newport, and 93 mi. southwest of Portland, is a long, narrow strip of civilization between the ocean and Devils Lake. In spite of its oblong shape, Lincoln City follows the quadrant system. The middle of town is marked by D River Wayside Park, a popular kite-flying spot on the beach. The east-west divide is Hwy. 101.

ACCOMMODATIONS

Camping near Lincoln City can be crowded; this may be a good time to opt for a roof over your head. Saturated by the Chinook Winds Casino crowds, the motel market yields nice rooms off the water along Hwy. 101. (For more options, see **Tillamook to Lincoln City** and **Lincoln City to Newport**.)

Captain Cook Inn, 26 NE U.S. 101 (994-2522 or 800-994-2522). This well maintained motel features gracious, remodeled rooms with beautiful new checkered furniture. Rooms start at $39. Reserve 2 weeks in advance.

Sea Echo Motel, 3510 NE U.S. 101 (994-2575). A single story, stone-fronted building set back from the highway atop a steep slope. Snippets of the ocean visible over the tops of the trees. Pink sinks! Standard rooms, phones, cable TV. Singles and doubles $35; 2 beds $45.

Budget Inn, 1713 NW 21st St. (994-5281). A big pale blue complex with fairly large, clean rooms. The second floor seems inches from the highway, but the third floor has a balcony. Only 3 blocks from the beach. Singles $33 ($46 on weekends). Doubles $46 ($60 on weekends). Reserve at least 2 weeks in advance.

Ester Lee Motel, 3803 SW Hwy. 101 (996-3606), 2.2 mi. south of D River State Park. If you must be oceanfront and you're down with the Brady Bunch school of interior decoration, look no further. Beach access and excellent views. Rooms $59 in peak season; cabins $65-115. Call ahead.

FOOD

Head down to Depoe Bay or Newport for good seafood. Lincoln City has a few classy spots, if you can navigate the fast-food shoals. Zip north to **Price Chopper Foods** (open daily 7am-11pm) in Lighthouse Square for basic food items. **The Family Store,** 3321 NW U.S. 101 (996-3433) is the place for fresh fruits and veggies. Pick up a 15¢ orange or some freshly squeezed juice (name the victim and they'll juice it for $5.50 a quart; open Mon.-Thurs. 9am-6pm, Sat. 9am-5pm, Sun. 10am-4pm).

Lighthouse Brew Pub, 4157 NE U.S. 101 (994-7238), in Lighthouse Sq. at the north end of town. Fresh-cut fries, phenomenal brews, and a low-key atmosphere upstairs and down. The food is cheap and good—try a Communication Breakdown Burger ($5). It's even cheaper after 9pm, when selected prices drop a dollar or two (cold sandwiches are $2.75) for late night specials. Open Mon.-Sat. 11am-1am, Sun. 11am-midnight.

Foon Hing Yuen, Inc., 3138 SE U.S. 101 (996-3831). Generous portions of good Chinese food. Lunches cost about $4; specials will run you $6-9. Despite its name, the *pork chow yuk* ($6.50) is delicious. This is one of few restaurants in town that doesn't close before 10pm. Take-out available. Bar and restaurant open Sun.-Thurs. noon-midnight, Fri.-Sat. noon-1:30am.

Kyllo's, 1110 NW First Ct. (994-3179), next to the D River Park; turn on NW 2nd. The town's biggest restaurant uses iron, wood, and stone to its artful advantage to achieve maximum sunset surface area and an elegant ambience. Elevated prices for well-dressed but average food. Try the Manilla clams in white wine ($9), but skip the forgettable crab cake and grilled vegetables ($9). Open daily noon-dark.

SIGHTS, ACTIVITIES, AND EVENTS

The windy beaches of Lincoln City are so fantastic for kite-flying, that they play host to three annual kite festivals. The largest one is the **Fall International Kite Festival** in the beginning of October at D River Park, but the spring and summer festivals in early May and July cause their own stir in the sky with competitions like "best train." Check out the hand-made wind toys at **Catch the Wind,** 266 SE U.S. 101 (994-9500). The folks here are rabid kite fans—just ask them about Wei Fang, Lincoln City's kite-flying sister city in China.

You can enjoy coffee, food, and Oregon wines at the **Chateau Benoit Wine & Food Center,** 1524 E. Devils Lake Rd. (996-3981), in the Factory Stores (open Mon.-

Sat. 9am-8pm, Sun. 9am-6pm). Brave the crowded parking lots at the corner of E. Devils Lake Rd. and Hwy. 101 for a chance to hunt bargains at 69 outlet stores.

The top-notch **Cascade Music Festival** comes to Lincoln City the first three weekends in July. The international classical concerts ($15) take place at St. Peter the Fisherman Lutheran Church, 1126 SW 13th (994-5333).

The latest addition to Lincoln City's list of attraction is the **Chinook Winds Siletz Tribal Gaming Convention Center** (1755 NW 44th St.; 888-CHINOOK/244-6665), known around town as the "the casino." Check your budget at the door; whether your money goes down the nickel slot or into the pond by the escalator, it won't stay in your pocket. Still, this Oregonian Vegas with glowing whales and cartoon wilderness is the perfect way to spend a rainy afternoon. Turn west on NW 40th St. and look to your right; it's the hulking yellow stucco structure with suspiciously glamorous-looking tribal markings (open 24hr.).

■ Lincoln City to Newport

Between Lincoln City and Newport, there are rest stops and beach access parking lots every few miles, one with overnight camping. The free **North Creek Campground,** a small area within the Siuslaw National Forest with no drinking water, is off County Rte. 229 on Forest Service Rd. 19.

A few miles south on U.S. 101, diminutive **Depoe Bay** boasts excellent **gray whale viewing** along the seawall in town, at the **Depoe Bay State Park Wayside,** and at the **Observatory Lookout,** 4½ mi. south of town. Go out early in the morning on a cloudy, calm day between December and May for the best chance of spotting the huge grays. Several outfitters charter fishing trips from Depoe Bay. **Tradewinds Charters** (765-2345), on U.S. 101 downtown, has two five-hour ($47 per person) and seven-hour ($58 per person) trips a day, the first leaving at dawn (call for reservations and information on other trips). **Dockside Charters** (765-2545 or 800-733-8915) offers similar trips for $47 (1-hr. whale-watching trip $10, teenagers $8, under 13 $6).

Just south of Depoe Bay, take a detour from U.S. 101 to the famous **Otter Crest Loop,** a twisting 4-mi. drive high above the shore which affords spectacular vistas at every bend. A lookout over **Cape Foulweather** has telescopes (25¢) for spotting sea lions on the rocks below. Captain James Cook first saw the North American mainland here in 1778 when it greeted him with gale-force winds. Wind-speeds at this 500-ft. elevation often reach 100 mph. Also on the loop, the **Devils Punchbowl** formed when two seaside caves collapsed leaving a round hole in the sandstone terrace. The resulting "bowl" fills with ocean water when the tide comes in through a hole in its side. The best viewing is at high tide, when the heavy waves form a frothing cauldron beneath your feet.

Just south of the Punchbowl, the road returns to U.S. 101 and brings eager campers to the much-trafficked **Beverly Beach State Park,** 198 NE 123rd St. (265-9278), 7 mi. north of Newport, a year-round campground in gorgeous, rugged terrain. Cold water and frequent riptides should discourage even the most daring swimmers. Beverly Beach was one of the first parks in Oregon to sport the latest in outdoor accommodations, **YURTS** (Year-round Universal Recreational Tents), round tents with bunk beds modelled after Mongolian huts ($26.50; reserve ahead by calling 800-452-5687). Hot showers, facilities for the disabled, and a few hiker/biker spots are available (sites $16, hiker/biker $4.25, electrical $19, full $20; non-camper showers $2). Reservations are strongly advised in summer.

Just south of Beverly Beach is the **Yaquina Head Lighthouse** (265-2863), a photogenic coastal landmark. More spectacular is the **seabird colony** on the offshore rocks below. Large decks provide good views of western gulls, cormorants, murres, and if you're lucky, the colorful **tufted puffin.** The tide pools along the low, flat rock to the south of the headland are home to harbor seals, sea lions, and many small pebbles. Gray whales are sometimes spotted in the waters beyond. The top of the seven-story lighthouse itself can be reached only through free tours (daily June to mid-Sept. every ½hr. 9-11:30am). The first 15 people get to go; arrive early to ensure a spot. The public can guide themselves through the ground-level kiosk of the lighthouse daily noon-4pm, but the top is closed.

■ Newport

Newport is one part fishing village, one part logging town, and two parts tourist mill with a few idyllic campgrounds nearby. The recently renovated waterfront area gives Newport a refreshingly well defined center of activity after the miles of malls and gas stations of U.S. 101. The best escape from the kitschy shops and high admission fees near the port is Nye Beach, a historic and relatively unspoiled strip of sand just north of the busy harbor.

PRACTICAL INFORMATION AND ORIENTATION

Visitors Information: Chamber of Commerce, 555 SW Coast Hwy. (265-8801 or 800-262-7844). Large new office with bus and theater schedules, free **maps,** guides, and an on-the-ball staff. Open Mon.-Fri. 8:30am-5pm, Sat.-Sun. 10am-4pm; Oct.-April Mon.-Fri. 8:30am-5pm. **Newport Parks and Recreation Office,** 169 SW Coast Hwy. (265-7783), Room 5. Open Mon.-Fri. 7:30am-5:30pm.

Buses: Greyhound, 956 SW 10th St. (265-2253) at Bailey St. To: Portland (3 per day, $17), Seattle (3 per day, $38), and San Francisco (5 per day, $65). Open Mon.-Fri. 8-10am and 12:30-4:15pm, Sat. 8am-1pm.

Taxi: Yaquina Cab Company, 265-9552. 24hr.

Car Rental: Sunwest Motors, 1030 N Coast Hwy. (265-8547). All cars $25 with 50 free miles per day, 15¢ per extra mi. Must be 25 with $500 or 21 with a major credit card. Reservations advised.

Bike Rental: Embarcadero, 1000 SE Bay Blvd. (265-5435). $4 per hour, $25 per day; $25 deposit or major credit card held. No helmets. Also rents crab rings ($6 per day), clam shovels ($3.50 per day), and skiffs ($12.50 per hr., 3-hr. min.).

Public Library: 34 NW Nye (265-2153). Open Mon.-Thurs. 10am-9pm, Fri.-Sat. 10am-6pm, Sun. 1-4pm.

Laundry: Eileen's Coin Laundry, 1078 N. Coast Hwy. Wash $1, 10-min. dry 25¢. Open daily 6:30am-11pm.

Weather and Sea Conditions: 265-5511.

Crisis Line: Contact, 133 SE Cape St. (265-9234). Advice, referrals, and assistance for stranded travelers.

Senior Services: Senior Center, 20 SE 2nd St. (265-9617).

Hospital: Pacific Communities Hospital, 930 SW Abbey (265-2244).

Emergency: 911. **Police:** 810 SW Alder (265-5331). **Fire:** 245 NW 10th St. (265-9461). **Coast Guard:** 925 Naterlin Rd. (265-5381).

Post Office: 310 SW 2nd St. (265-5542). Open Mon.-Fri. 8:30am-5pm. **General Delivery ZIP Code:** 97365-9999.

Area Code: 541.

U.S. 101, known as the Coast Hwy. in town, divides East and West Newport, while U.S. 20 (Olive St.) bisects North and South. Corvallis lies 50 mi. east on U.S. 20. Newport is bordered on the west by the foggy Pacific Ocean, and on the south by Yaquina Bay. A suspension bridge ferries U.S. 101 travelers across the bay. Just north of the bridge, Bay Blvd. wraps around the bay and is the heart of the port.

ACCOMMODATIONS AND CAMPING

The strip along U.S. 101 provides plenty of affordable motels with predictably noisy consequences. Weekend rates generally rise a couple of dollars, and winter rates improve the already good deals. Campers should escape to the many state campgrounds along U.S. 101, where access to both the beach and city is plentiful. **South Beach State Park,** 5580 S. Coast Hwy., South Beach 97366 (867-4715), 2 mi. south of town, has a few yurts ($27), 25 electrical hookup sites ($19), several hiker/biker sites ($4.25), and showers. Just north of town lies the best option, **Beverly Beach State**

Park, 198 N. 123rd St. (265-9278), which has 151 sites specifically for tents ($16) and 53 full hookup sites ($20).

Brown Squirrel Hostel, 44 SW Brook St. (265-3729) off W. Olive St. This converted church has a few resident kittens and lively hosts. Basement has a bountiful kitchen and casually kept common space, complete with TV. You can be out the door and on the beach in 2min. Laundry. 22 beds; continued construction will yield 22 more. Beds $12, couples $20 (couples should call ahead).

City Center Motel, 538 SW Coast Hwy. (265-7381), across from the visitors center. Lovely sparkling exterior. Little rooms with prices to match. Singles start at $36, doubles at $48.

Summerwind Budget Motel, 728 N. Coast Hwy. (265-8076). All rooms have HBO. Old rooms are smallish, clean bathrooms, brown furniture. Singles $30. Doubles $39. New rooms somewhat bigger, but audibly closer to the road. Singles $34. Doubles $43. Winter rates significantly reduced.

The Newport Motor Inn, 1311 N. Coast Hwy. (265-8516). Clean, comfortable rooms with some old furniture and the region's requisite maritime decor. Cable with HBO. Laundry. Summer rates: singles $40, doubles $50.

FOOD

Food in Newport is decent, particularly along the bay, where tourists cluster. **Oceana Natural Foods Coop,** 159 SE 2nd St. (265-8285), has a small selection of reasonably priced natural foods and produce (open daily 9am-7pm). **J.C. Sentry,** 107 N. Coast Hwy. (265-6641), sells standard supermarket stock; open 24hr.

Mo's Restaurant, 622 SW Bay Blvd. (265-2979). Share a large wooden table in this small local favorite for the best clam chowder on the coast (with fish 'n' chips $7). Open daily 11am-9pm.

Cosmos Café, 740 W. Olive St. (265-7511). Great omelettes ($5.95) in a swirly purple atmosphere that's off the beaten tourist path. Sumptuous black bean burrito $5.95, fresh pie $2.50. Muffin flavors like rhubarb-applesauce and cranberry-peach. Open Mon.-Sat. 8am-9pm, Sun. 8am-8pm.

Nye Beach Hotel and Café, 219 NW Cliff St. (265-3334), off W. Olive. Stylishly simple with high ceilings and a splendid view of the ocean. Fish-centric menu ($10-17) is not aimed at the budget traveler, but the escape from tackiness and fried food may be worth the extra bucks. Breakfast until 2pm features Belgian waffles ($3.75). Phenomenal crabcakes $7.95. Open daily 7:30am-10:30pm; winter Sun.-Thurs. 7:30am-9:30pm, Fri.-Sat. 7:30am-10:30pm.

Rogue Ale & Public House, 748 SW Bay Blvd. (265-3188). All hail the local ale: plenty of brew on tap, ale-brewed chili, and beer bread ($1.50) to boot. Walls explore beer as art. Pizza ($7-21) is delicious, but everyone orders the fish and chips ($6). Open daily 11am-11pm or midnight.

SIGHTS, ACTIVITIES, AND EVENTS

The **Oregon Coast Aquarium,** 2820 SE Ferry Slip Rd. (867-3474) at the south end of the bridge, is at the top of Newport's greatest hits list. This world class aquarium is still celebrating the recent arrival of Keiko, the killer whale of *Free Willy* fame (and 15 years of theme park stardom before that). This vast, well designed complex features 2½ acres of wet and wild indoor and outdoor exhibits. Stroll through the galleries, where anemones "stick" to your hands, and the "New Currents" changing exhibit...umm, changes. Admire the jellyfish or slip into the whale theater where a 10-minute video on different denizens of the deep will fascinate adults as well as children. The sea otters and seals ham it up for the crowd. And, of course, make your way to Keiko's tank, though you won't be alone in your moment with the great orca. Admission to the aquarium is a slightly swollen $8.50 (seniors $7.50, ages 4-13 $4.25) and lines are long—if speedy. Tickets may be purchased ahead at the Embarcadero Resort, 1000 SE Bay Blvd. (265-8521). Aquarium open daily 9am-6pm; winter 10am-5pm.

Unless you're up for gaudy thrills, outdated special effects, and the molestation of marine creatures, save your $5.75 (children 5-11 $3.50) and avoid the tourist-trap trio of **Ripley's Believe It or Not, Undersea Gardens,** and **The Wax Works** at the gift shop-fortified Mariner Square, 250 SW Bay Blvd. (265-2206; open daily 9am-8pm; winter 10am-5pm).

To sample local beer, cross the bay bridge, follow the signs to the Hatfield Center and turn off into the **Rogue Ale Brewery,** 2320 SE Oregon State University Dr. (867-3663). Their line of 12 brews, which can also be tasted at the pub on the bay (see **Food**), includes the favorite Oregon Golden, American Amber, and Maierbock Ales. Unfortunately, the brewery found free tasting unprofitable and began charging 50¢ for a 3oz. glass of brew (open daily 11am-6pm; sometimes later in the summer).

If you have time and money, try **bottom-fishing** with one of Newport's numerous charter companies. Salmon and halibut are no longer plentiful, but you can try to net some tuna with **Newport Tradewinds,** 653 SW Bay Blvd. (265-2101), which runs five, six, and eight-hour trips for $10 per hour. A three-hour crabbing trip in the bay costs $30; a two and a half-hour whale-watching trip is $20.

Observe more refined culture in the many elegant **art galleries** which populate Bay Blvd. by the harbor. Ask the Chamber of Commerce for help in locating them, and while you're there, pick up a schedule for the **Newport Performing Arts Center,** 777 W. Olive (265-2787). Theater and dance performances, film festivals, and some excellent orchestral and band concerts usually happen on weekends. Tickets range from $4-13 with a few freebies. The box office is at the Center, across from the Cosmos Café, and is open Mon.-Fri. 9am-5pm and an hour before showtime.

Popular festivals in Newport include the **Newport Seafood and Wine Festival** on the third full weekend in February, which showcases Oregon wines, food, music, and crafts in over 100 booths, drawing 25,000 people (admission around $5); and **Newport Loyalty Days and Sea Fair Festival,** the first weekend in May, with rides, parades, and sailboat races. The second week in October, the **Microbrew Festival** features the tiniest beers in the Northwest for 50¢ apiece on top of $5 admission. The third week of July brings the three-day **Lincoln County Fair and Rodeo** (265-6237) to the Newport Fairgrounds ($6). Contact the Newport Chamber of Commerce (see **Practical Information,** above) for information on all seasonal events.

■ Newport to Reedsport

From Newport to Reedsport, U.S. 101 slides through a string of small towns, passing beautiful campgrounds, spectacular stretches of Oregon beach, and a fair number of unsightly tourist snares failing in their game. The **Waldport Ranger District Office,** 1049 SW Pacific Hwy. (563-3211), in **Waldport,** is not far from U.S. 101 and worth a stop if you're considering **hiking** in the **Siuslaw National Forest,** a patchwork of three wilderness areas along the Oregon Coast. The office sells detailed **maps** of the area for $3, on which they can point out the several campgrounds and trails in the forest (open Mon.-Fri. 8am-4pm).

Continuing south, U.S. 101 passes through Yachats, a town not particularly notable except for the **New Morning Coffeehouse** (547-3848), at 4th and U.S. 101. This subtly refined place is a favorite coffee-stop for U.S. 101 travelers. Tantalizing pastries are a little fancier than budget travel affords ($2-2.50) but if you come at dinner time (Thurs.-Sun.) the pasta and pizza dishes will prove worth the $7-8.50 (open Wed. 9am-4pm, Thurs.-Sun. 9am-9pm).

Cape Perpetua, 3 mi. south of Yachats, combines the highest point on the coast, at 803 ft., with a few exciting sea level trails. Take a break from the highway and drive 2 mi. up to the **view point** for a heavenly vista overlooking the coast below. The **Cape Perpetua Visitors Center,** 2400 S U.S. 101 (547-3289), just south of the view point turnoff, has informative exhibits about the phenomenal surrounding land, including a 16-minute video which shows how Oregon emerged volcanically from the sea (free; plays every ½hr.; open daily 9am-5pm, winter 10am-4pm). Before you go, grab a free visitors guide which lists the many trails that lead up through the hills and down to the rocks. Well worn sites off the coast sport names like **Devils Churn** (½ mi. north of the visitors center) and **Spouting Horn** (½ mi. west of it down Captain Cook Trail), and demonstrate the tremendous power of the waves hitting solid basalt.

Cape Perpetua Campground, at the view point turn off, has 32 sites that run straight back into a narrow valley along a tiny, fern-banked creek. It has drinking water, vault toilets, and can accommodate up to 30-ft. rigs (all sites $11). The **Rock Creek Campground,** 7½ mi. south, has 16 sites under tall mossy spruces by Rock Creek. A ½-mi. walk on the highway puts you at the soothingly unspoiled **Ocean Beach** day-use park (drinking water, vault toilets, $11). Five mi. farther south, the **Sea Lion Caves,** 91560 U.S. 101 (547-3111) are a product of the a 65-year-old clash of nature and capitalism. Visitors come here at all times of year to watch fellow mammals (sea lions, seals, and the like) as they engage in highly personal activities such as breeding. In the fall and winter, visitors can peep through a subterranean hole to watch the several hundred California seals who populate the caves. In the spring and summer, tourists bring binoculars to watch the stellar rookery (that's a breeding ground) on the rocks over 200 ft. below. This area is home to **the largest sea cave in America,** as well as many **stellar** and **California sea lions.**

Florence is a far-too-long strip of fast-food joints and expensive motels. Fifteen mi. east of Florence, at the junction of U.S. 36 and U.S. 126 (to Eugene) is **Mapleton,** a tiny community with a **Ranger Station,** 10692 U.S. 126 (268-4473), which can offer tips to prospective **hikers** or **bikers** in the **Siuslaw National Forest** (open Mon.-Fri. 8am-4:30pm). Road-trip-induced hunger can be assuaged at the **Alpha Bits Café** (268-4311), on U.S. 126, just beyond the ranger station. Owned and staffed by members of a commune, the store is part café, part book store (open Mon.-Thurs. and Sat. 10am-6pm, Fri. 10am-9pm). For a complete, free experience in community living, push 30 minutes east to **Alpha Farm** (964-5102), 7 mi. up Deadwood Creek Rd. The farm, in scenic Nowheresville, offers an unusual, distinctively communal alternative to the bourgeois tourism of the coast. In exchange for a day of labor on the farm, visitors can camp out or stay in the sparse but comfortable bedrooms. Visitors are welcome from Monday to Friday for stays of up to three days; call ahead. Be prepared to kiss the hands of your fellow diners in a warm pre-supper ritual.

■ Reedsport and the Dunes

For 50 mi. between Florence and Coos Bay, millennia of wind and water flow have formed the **Oregon Dunes National Recreation Area.** Shifting mounds of sand rise to 500 ft. and extend up to 3 mi. inland (often to the shoulder of U.S. 101), clogging mountain streams and forming small lakes. Hiking trails wind around the lakes, through the coastal forests, and up to the dunes themselves. In many places, no grasses or shrubs grow, and the vista holds only sand, sky, and a few tire tracks. Campgrounds fill up early with dune buggy and motorcycle junkies, especially on summer weekends. The blaring radios, thrumming engines, and staggering swarms of tipsy tourists might drive you to the sands in (often vain) search of quiet. The dune-buggy invasion grows increasingly controversial, but the **National Recreation Area Headquarters** in Reedsport refuses to take sides.

PRACTICAL INFORMATION AND ORIENTATION

Visitors Information: Oregon Dunes National Recreation Area Information Center, 855 U.S. 101 (271-3611), in Reedsport just south of the Umpqua River Bridge. The Forest Service runs this center and will happily answer your questions on fees, regulations, and hiking and camping, or provide you with *Sand Tracks,* the area recreation guide. Map $3. They can also run a 20-min. filmstrip about the dunes. Open Sat.-Thurs. 8am-4:30pm, Fri. 8am-6pm; Sept.-May Mon.-Fri. 8am-4:30pm. **Reedsport Chamber of Commerce** (271-3495 or 800-247-2155 from OR), P.O. Box 11, at U.S. 101 and Rte. 38, a pointy log shack across the street from

OREGON

the recreation area office. Dune buggy rental info and motel listings. Open daily 8:30am-5:30pm; Oct.-May daily 9am-4pm.

Buses: Greyhound (276-4436 in Coos Bay) runs 3 buses per day from Reedsport to Portland ($24), 4 to Eugene ($20), and 3 to San Francisco ($58).

Taxi: Coastal Cab, 139 N. 3rd St. (271-2690). About $7 to Winchester Bay, $3 more to the beach. Service daily 6am-3am.

Sand Buggy/Bicycle Rentals: Rent-All Center, 75303 U.S. 101 (271-4011), in Winchester Bay. Tandems and mountain bikes ($4 per hr., $16 per 8-hr. day), single-speed bikes ($3), buggies ($30 first hr., $25 each additional hr.; $50 deposit). It may prove easier to rent at the dune-access sites (see **Outdoors,** below). Open daily 8am-5:30pm; Nov.-Feb. Thurs.-Tues. 8am-5:30pm.

Laundromat: Coin Laundry, 420 N. 14th St. (271-3587) next to the Umpqua Shopping Center in Reedsport. Wash $1, 7½-min. dry 25¢, Open daily 8am-9pm.

Library: 395 Winchester Ave. (271-3500). Open Mon. and Thurs. 2-8:30pm, Tues.-Wed. and Fri. 10am-6pm, Sat. 10am-1pm.

Emergency: 911. **Police:** 136 N. 4th St. (271-2109 or 271-2100), in Reedsport.

Coast Guard: 271-2137, near the end of the harbor, in Winchester Bay.

Post Office: 301 Fir Ave. (271-2521), off Rte. 38. Open Mon.-Fri. 8:30am-5pm. **General Delivery ZIP Code:** 97467.

Area Code: 541.

The dunes' shifting grip on the coastline is broken only once along the expanse, where the Umpqua and Smith Rivers empty into Winchester Bay at Reedsport. Twenty-one mi. south of Florence, at the junction of Rte. 38 and U.S. 101, Reedsport is a typical highway town of motels, banks, and flashy restaurants. The older part of town flanks Rte. 38, just east of Hwy. 101 and south of the river.

ACCOMMODATIONS

The town of **Winchester Bay,** just south of Reedsport, has rooms for $30 or under, while those in Reedsport average about $40.

Harbor View Motel (271-3352), U.S. 101 in Winchester Bay. Spitting distance from the boats. The turquoise and white exterior gives it a buoyant appearance reminiscent of pool floaties, but rooms are nice and tidy and they all have small refrigerators. Singles $28. Doubles $34. Off-season rates $2 lower.

Fir Grove Motel, 2178 U.S. 101 (271-4848), in Reedsport. Attractive rooms with plaster walls and arched doorways. Outdoor heated pool is clean and lovely, but only inches from 101. Geraniums everywhere, cable TV, coffee, donuts, and fruit in the lobby from 7-9:30am. Singles $36, doubles $55; $10 less in winter. $4-8 senior discount.

Tropicana Motel, 1593 U.S. 101 (271-3671), in Reedsport off the parking lot of the Umpqua Shopping Center. A respectable, clean motel with comfortable rooms; no tropical fruit in evidence. Arrive early, when the parking lot is less than ½ full, and play "let's make a deal." Continental breakfast, TV with HBO. Singles $37, doubles $45; $2-3 AAA discount.

CAMPING

The national recreation area is administered by Siuslaw National Forest. The campgrounds that allow dune buggy access, **Spinreel** (36 sites), parking-lot style **Driftwood II** (69 sites), and **Horsfall** (69 sites, showers), are generally loud and rowdy in the summer (all have flush toilets and $10 sites). Limited reservations for summer weekends are available; call 800-280-CAMP/2267 more than five days prior to arrival. **Carter Lake** (23 sites) and **Tah Kenitch** (34 sites), both $10, are quieter sites designed for tenters and small RVs. The sites closest to Reedsport are in Winchester Bay and are either ugly, RV-infested, or both.

During the summer, RVs dominate all the campsites around Reedsport and Winchester Bay. Dispersed camping is allowed on public lands, but only if you are 200 yd. from any road or trail and equipped to extinguish a fire. Summer campers with tents don't have much hope of finding a legal campground free of screaming children or screaming sand vehicles. Flee to Eel Creek and Carter Lake. At Eel Creek, at least you can slip away into the dunes (see **Outdoors,** below).

Carter Lake Campground, 12 mi. north of Reedsport on U.S. 101. Boat access to Carter Lake, but more importantly some sites are stream side. Sites are well screened and as quiet as it gets north of Reedsport; 23 pleasant sites with nice bathrooms, but no showers. No ATVs. Sites $10.

William H. Tugman State Park (759-3604), 8 mi. south of Reedsport on U.S. 101. A manicured park with 115 shady sites and pleasant smatterings of sand. Most of the sites are kept separate by high bushes, but hiker/biker camp is the most private. Very close to gorgeous Eel Lake. All sites have water and electricity. Showers and facilities for campers with disabilities. Sites $17, hiker/biker $4.

North Eel Creek Campground, 10 mi. south of Reedsport on U.S. 101. The 52 very sandy sites are well hidden from the road and each other by the tall brush. Quiet dunal adventures may begin here at the trailhead to the 2½-mi. **Umpqua Dunes Trail.** Sites $10.

FOOD

Cheap, greasy options prevail in Winchester Bay and Reedsport; vegophiles should blaze a trail to **Safeway** (open daily 7am-11pm), in the Umpqua Shopping Center or the **Price 'n' Pride** (6am-midnight) across the street, both in Reedsport.

Back to the Best (271-2619), U.S. 101 at 10th St. The turquoise and yellow exterior shrieks tacky tourist zone, but this is actually one of the classiest spots in town. Sandwiches ($4.25) are piled high with fresh cut fineries like smoked gouda and home roasted ham. Swedish fish $4.95 per pound. Open Mon.-Sat. 10:30am-6:30pm, Sun. 11am-6:30pm.

Seafood Grotto and Restaurant, 115 8th St. (271-4250), at Broadway in Winchester Bay. An unexpected find: excellent seafood in an average looking dining room. If you're sick of clam chowder, their cioppino soup ($5.45) is incredible, but prices float up after that. Lunches $4-11. Open daily 11am-9pm.

OUTDOORS

Romp in the dunes. Why else are you here? Those with little time or low noise tolerance should at least stop at the **Oregon Dunes Overlook,** off U.S. 101, about halfway between Reedsport and Florence. Wooden ramps lead through the bushes for a peak at some untrammeled dunes and a glimpse of the ocean. The **Tahkenitch Creek Loop** covers 2½ mi. from the overlook through forest, dunes, wetlands, and beach, and is marked by blue-ringed posts. The *Sand Tracks* brochure (available at the Information Center) has a free detailed **map** of the dunes. The overlook is staffed daily from Memorial Day to Labor Day between 10am and 3pm. Guided hikes, brochures, and talks are available.

A pamphlet on trails for dune-bound **hikers** is also available at the information center. An excellent walk is through the Umpqua Dunes 2 mi. to the ocean. From the trailhead at the North Eel Creek Campground (see **Camping,** above), walk on or around the massive Oblique Dunes in bare feet. Be careful in the low, wet areas since there may be some quicksand.

For an authentically silence-shattering dune experience, venture out on wheels. Plenty of places between Florence and Coos Bay rent and offer tours (see **Practical Information,** above). **Pacific Coast Recreation,** 4121 U.S. 101 (756-7183), in Hauser, has direct dune access and restored World War II army vehicles out front. Take a **sand dune tour** in an old transport ($12, under 14 $8) or rent ATVs ($25 per hr.). **Spinreel Dune Buggy Rentals,** 9122 Wild Wood Dr. (759-3313), on U.S. 101, 7 mi. south of Reedsport, rents Honda Odysseys ($20 ½hr., $30 1st hr., $25 2nd hr.). They also have dune buggy rides, a good alternative to the monster dune tours ($15 ½hr., $25 per person per hr.). Family tours in a "VW Thing" are $35 for a half hour, $55 per hour. Or rent from the **Rent-All Center,** in Winchester Bay (see **Practical Information,** above). A host of other dune-buggy hot spots will be glad to rent their vehicles; ask at the Reedsport Chamber of Commerce.

When you tire of dune dawdling, you could try **deep-sea fishing** with one of the many charter companies that operate out of **Salmon Harbor,** in Winchester Bay. Like everywhere else on the coast, you can forget salmon fishing, but tuna and bottom-fishing are still available for die-hard enthusiasts. **Gee Gee Charters, Inc.** offers five-hour bottom-fishing trips ($50) daily at 6am and 1pm. Call the 24-hr. phone service several days before you wish to go for a reservation (271-3152). The required one-day license ($6.75) may be purchased at any of the charter offices. Three-hour crabbing trips are also available for $30.

The Umpqua Lighthouse State Park has an excellent **gray whale viewing station.** Unfortunately, dune buggies cause a racket underneath this 100-ft.-high overlook. The best times to see these massive creatures are during their migrations; they head north in two waves, first in March, then in late May and June. They head south in late December and early January.

Bird watching is also popular in the area around Reedsport. Lists of rare and common species and their seasons are available at the National Recreation Area headquarters (see **Practical Information,** above). If you would rather catch animals than watch them, you can rent huge nets to nab crabs in Salmon Harbor. Around Labor Day every summer, Winchester Bay merchants sponsor a crabbing contest. A $3000 reward goes out for catching the legendary **Cleo the crab.** More likely prizes are $50-100 for tagged crabs.

■ Coos Bay, North Bend, and Charleston

The largest city on the Oregon Coast, Coos Bay is making an economic turnaround in the face of the environmental regulations which decimated the local lumber industry. The tourist trade has expanded economic opportunity, and businesses are returning to the once-deserted pedestrian shopping mall. Huge iron-sided tankers have begun to replace quaint fishing boats, and U.S. 101 passes through a bustling strip of shops and espresso bars. The nearby town of North Bend blends immutably into Coos Bay, while Charleston sits peacefully a few miles west on the coast.

PRACTICAL INFORMATION AND ORIENTATION

Visitors Information: Bay Area Chamber of Commerce, 50 E. Central Ave. (269-0215 or 800-824-8486), off Commercial Ave. in Coos Bay, between the one way thoroughfares of U.S. 101. Plenty of free brochures; comprehensive bay area maps are $1.50. Open Mon.-Fri. 8:30am-7pm, Sat. 10am-4pm, Sun. noon-4pm; mid-Sept. to May Mon.-Fri. 9am-5pm, Sat. 10am-4pm. **North Bend Information Center,** 1380 Sherman Ave. (756-4613), on U.S. 101, just south of the harbor bridge in North Bend. Open Mon.-Fri. 9am-5pm, Sat. 10am-4pm. **Charleston Information Center** (888-2311), at Boat Basin Dr. and Cape Arago Hwy. Open May-Oct. daily 9am-5pm. **Oregon State Parks Information,** 365 N. 4th St., Coos Bay (888-8867). Open Mon.-Fri. 8am-5pm.

Buses: Greyhound, 2007 Union St. (267-4436). 3 per day to Portland ($26), 2 per day to San Francisco ($58). Open Mon.-Thurs. 9am-5pm, Fri. 9am-4pm, Sat. 9am-3pm.

Car Rental: Verger, 1400 Ocean Blvd. (888-5594; ask for the rental department). Cars from $23 per day, 20¢ per mi. after 100 mi. Open Mon.-Fri. 8am-5:30pm, Sat. 9am-5pm. Must be 22 or older and have a credit card.

Taxi: Yellow Cab (267-3111). 24hr. Senior discount.

Laundromat: Wash-A-Lot, 1921 Virginia Ave. (756-5439), in North Bend. Wash $1, 10-min. dry 25¢. 24hr.

Public Library: 525 W. Anderson (269-1101), in Coos Bay. Open Mon.-Thurs. 10am-8pm, Fri.-Sat. 10am-5:30pm.

Crisis Line: 888-5911. 24-hr. information and referral.

Women's Crisis Service: 756-7000. 24hr.
Hospital: Bay Area Hospital, 1775 Thompson Rd. (269-8111), in Coos Bay. **Medical Emergency:** 269-8085.
Emergency: 911. **Police:** 500 Central Ave. (269-8911). **Fire:** 150 S. 4th St. (269-1191). **Coast Guard:** 4645 Eel Ave. (888-3266), in Charleston.
Post Office: 470 Golden Ave. (267-4514), at 4th St. Open Mon.-Fri. 8:30am-5pm. **General Delivery ZIP Code:** 97420.
Area Code: 541.

U.S. 101 jogs inland south of Coos Bay, rejoining the coast at Bandon. From Coos Bay, Rte. 42 heads east 85 mi. to I-5, and U.S. 101 continues north into dune territory. U.S. 101 skirts the east side of both Coos Bay and North Bend, and the Cape Arago Hwy. continues west to **Charleston,** at the mouth of the bay. Newark St. heads west from U.S. 101 and leads into the Cape Arago Hwy.

ACCOMMODATIONS AND CAMPING

Non-camper types should consider the wonderful Sea Star Hostel, 23 mi. south on U.S. 101 in **Bandon** (347-9632; see p. 457). Campers, rejoice. The state-run and private campgrounds allow you to take full advantage of the breathtaking coast.

2310 Lombard, guess where (756-3857), at the corner of Cedar St. in North Bend. Two small, pleasant rooms with a smattering of African and Korean art on the walls, one with two twin beds, one with a double bed; shared bath. Full breakfast from a wonderful hostess. Singles $35. Doubles $40. Reservations recommended.

Itty Bitty Inn Motel Bed and Breakfast, 1504 Sherman Ave. (756-6398), which is the stretch of U.S. 101 running through North Bend. Eensy-weensy refurbished 5-room motel doesn't look like a B&B, but rates include a $5 breakfast at the Virginia St. diner. Rooms are small and cozy, with purple doors, cable TV, refrigerators, and microwaves (for an extra dollar). Singles $39. Doubles $52.

Sunset Bay State Park 10965 Cape Arago Hwy. (888-4902; 800-452-5687 for reservations), 12 mi. south of Coos Bay and 3½ mi. west of Charleston. Akin to camping in a well landscaped parking lot; when it's full the park is a zoo. Fabulous Sunset Beach makes it all worthwhile. Camping here will win you a free entrance to Shore Acres State Park. 138 sites with hot showers and wheelchair-accessible facilities. Non-camper showers $2. Hiker/biker sites $4, tent sites $15. Electrical hookup $18, full hookup $19, yurts $25. Open mid-April through Oct.

Bluebill Campground, off U.S. 101, 3 mi. just north of North Bend. Follow the signs to the Horsfall Beach area. A U.S. Forest Service campground with flush toilets and 19 sites. Road leads ½ mi. to the ocean and dunes. Sites $10.

FOOD

The Blue Heron Bistro, 100 Commercial St. (267-3933), at U.S. 101 in Coos Bay. Almost upscale atmosphere affected by numerous skylights and a shiny tile floor. A tad more expensive than most places, but the food's a tad better, too. Cajun and Tex-Mex dinners average $11-12, but you can have a Mexican grilled cheese with black beans for $6, and the $5 cold sandwiches include a delectable super-veggie with herbed cheese. Long beer list. Open daily 10am-10pm; winter 10am-9pm.

Virginia Street Diner, 1430 Virginia St. (756-3475), 4 or 5 blocks north of 101 on North Bend. The booths are a festive, sparkly red, and the carpet is just wrong, but the prices are right. A 75¢ coffee at breakfast means the whole pot. The reliable tuna melt comes with a cup of soup ($4), and entrees come with veggies, a biscuit, and potatoes or rice. Try the homemade meatloaf or Virginia cured ham (both $5.95). Open daily 6am-10pm.

Cheryn's Seafood Restaurant and Pie House (888-3251), at the east end of Charleston Bridge in Charleston. The menu boasts the widest selection of seafood in town. Any grilled or fried combo platter you could imagine is on there for $7-10, including a $9 salmon steak. Diffuse awkward silences by staring at the rotating case of pre-cut pie slices. Open daily 8am-9pm; winter daily 8am-8pm.

Kaffe 101, 134 S. Broadway St. (267-5894), in Coos Bay, next to the visitos center. The fireplace, comfortable chintz chairs, and book-strewn shelves echo an English tea house. Food is limited to the likes of fireside nibblettes like bagels ($1.35 with cream cheese), but there is plenty of espresso ($1.25). Live music once a week. Open Mon.-Thurs. 6am-9pm, Fri. 6am-10pm, Sat. 8am-10pm; winter Mon.-Thurs. 7am-8pm, Fri. 7am-10pm, Sat. 8am-10pm.

Basin Café, 4555 King Fisher Dr. (888-5227), across the parking lot from the boats toward the end of the Charleston harbor. You can smell the sea breeze in the front, you can hear the grease spit in the back, and you can sit down to a $2.65 stack of 3 pancakes at 4:30am. Blow it all on the veggie omelette ($4.50), or save a dollar and take the burger basket ($3.50) spilling over with fries. Open Sun.-Thurs. 4:30am-8:30pm; Fri. and Sat. 4:30am-9pm; winter 5am-8pm.

SIGHTS AND ACTIVITIES

Those who need to fill a rainy day or are simply tired of water should make a beeline for **Cranberry Sweets,** 1005 Newmark (888-9824), in Coos Bay. This sucrose wonderland is half-factory, half-shop. Free candy samples are tiny but abundant; nibble as you watch amorphous chocolate sludge miraculously transformed into shapely pieces of candy (open Mon.-Sat. 9am-5:30pm, Sun. 11am-4pm).

Coos Bay is one of the few places on the coast where life slows down as you near the shore. Escape the industrial chaos by following Cape Arago Hwy. from the west end of Newmark St. in Coos Bay to **Charleston,** a more pleasantly rustic place to stay for an extended period than its two bigger neighbors.

Ocean fanatics should hop on board with **Bob's Sportfishing,** P.O. Box 5018 (888-4241 or 800-628-9633), operating out of a small building at the west end of the Charleston Boat Basin, or **Betty Kay Charters,** P.O. Box 5020 (888-9021 or 800-752-6303), a stone's throw away on the water's edge, both of which run six-hour bottom fishing trips daily at 6am and noon for $55 with a $6.75 daily license. Betty Kay will also rent you crab rings for $4 each (with a $15 deposit).

OUTDOORS

Sunset Bay, 3½ mi. west of Bastendorff Beach, on Cape Arago State Hwy., has been rated one of the top ten American beaches, and for good reason. The beach is nestled between two low dirt cliffs which hook around to shelter the bay. The remaining ocean front is calmed by natural rock outcroppings. Water temperatures heat up a bit from the frigid North Pacific, making Sunset Bay popular for swimming.

A mile beyond Sunset Bay on the Cape Arago Hwy. is beautiful **Shore Acres State Park** (888-3732). Once the estate of local lumber lord Louis J. Simpson, the park contains elaborate botanical gardens that survived when the mansion was razed. The egret sculptures are a more recent addition, courtesy of some artistically inclined inmates from the state penitentiary. A lovely rose garden boasting rows of award winning strains lies hidden in the back. For the entire month of December, the flowers are festooned with strings of over 150,000 lights, and the park serves complimentary cocoa and hot cider (open daily 8am-9pm; winter 8am-dusk. $3 per car. Wheelchair access).

Farther south at the end of the highway is breezy **Cape Arago,** the dramatic culmination of this 5-mi. stretch of craggy shoreline notable mainly for its creature-encrusted **tide pools.** Paved paths lead out toward the tip of the cape, and provide an excellent view of wildlife on **Shell Island,** ¼ mi. off shore. The island is a rookery for elephant and harbor seals. The paths may be closed in the spring to prevent habitat destruction, but the island can still be spotted from a pull-off ½ mi. before the cape. Bring binoculars. Blue whales, sea lions, and a number of noteworthy seabirds are also known to make appearances.

Four mi. south of Charleston up Seven Devils Rd., the **South Slough National Estuarine Research Reserve** (888-5558) is one of the most dramatic and underappreciated spots on the central coast. Spreading out from a small interpretive visitors center are almost 7 sq. mi. of protected estuaries, where salt and fresh waters mix. The slough teems with wildlife, from sand shrimp to deer. **Hiking trails** weave through the sanctuary; take a lunch and commune with the blue heron. The trails are usually quiet, but during the academic year, schools of children on field trips swarm into the reserve. Maps are free at the visitors center and guided walks are given in the summer (Fri. 2-4pm). Canoe tours ($5) are available, if you have your own canoe. For a summer calendar, write P.O. Box 5417, Charleston 97420 (open daily June-Aug. 8:30am-4:30pm; Sept.-May Mon.-Fri.; trails open daily dawn to dusk).

EVENTS

The **Oregon Coast Maritime Festival** hits Coos Bay in mid-July, during the opening weekend of the **Oregon Coast Music Festival,** P.O. Box 663, Coos Bay 97420 (267-0938), which is itself the most popular event on the coast. Art exhibits, vessel tours, and a free classical concert in Mingus Park triple the cultural options in Coos Bay. The two-week music festival draws a variety of musical performances (ranging from Baroque to country but skipping over rock and roll) to Coos Bay, North Bend, Bandon and Reedsport. Tickets cost $11-15, or charge by phone for a few extra bucks (269-2720 or 800-676-7563). Ask at the Chamber of Commerce (see **Practical Information,** above) about unreserved ticket outlets.

In the second week of August, Charleston hosts a refined but nevertheless decadent **Seafood and Wine Festival** in the Boat Basin. In late August, Coos Bay celebrates a native fruit with the **Blackberry Arts Festival.** Downtown rocks with square dancing, wine tasting, concerts, and crafts. In September, Oregon remembers one of its favorite sons in the **Steve Prefontaine 10K Road Race,** named after the great Olympic athlete who died in an automobile accident. The race draws dozens of world-class runners to the area (entrance $12-15). For information on these events, contact the Bay Area Fun Festival, P.O. Box 481, Coos Bay (269-7514).

■ Coos Bay to Brookings

BANDON

In spite of the steady flow of tourists in the summer, the small fishing town of Bandon (24 mi. south of Coos Bay on U.S. 101), has refrained from hauling out the pink and turquoise paint and making itself up like Disneyland. **Greyhound** (267-4436) stops twice daily by **McKay's Market** on U.S. 101, once going north and once going south. The **Bandon Chamber of Commerce,** 300 SE 2nd St., P.O. Box 1515 (347-9616), in the old town next to U.S. 101, has departure times and plenty of brochures and assistance (open daily June-Aug. 10am-5pm; Sept.-May 10am-4pm). The **post office** in Bandon is at 105 12th St. (347-3406; open Mon.-Fri. 8:30am-4:30pm). The **General Delivery ZIP Code** is 97411.

The rambling **Sea Star Hostel (HI-AYH),** 375 2nd St. (347-9632), on the right as you enter old-town from the north, adds a budget element to town accommodations. Comfortable bunkrooms, kitchen, laundry room, and an open-24hr. policy combine to make this hostel a relaxed and right-rocking place to pass a night ($12, nonmembers $15, under 12 ½price, but can only stay in the family rooms; $26 for 2 members, $32 nonmembers, $12 additional person). Alternatively, find your way to the **Bandon Wayside Motel** (347-3421) on Hwy. 42, just off 101 (singles $30; significantly larger doubles $44). Two mi. north of town, and across the bridge, lies **Bullard's Beach State Park** (347-2209), home to the **Coquille River Lighthouse,** built in 1896. The park has 192 sites (all $19, except yurts $25, and hiker/biker $4), tucked into the sand and pines. Although it is technically reserved for those with horses, llamas, elephants and such, the base camp, set off from the other sites, may be a peaceful place to park a tent. Campfire talks are given Tues.-Sat. nights in the summer.

For a tasty and healthy morsel, step into **Mother's Natural Grocery and Deli**, 975 U.S. 101 (347-4086), near the junction with Rte. 425, where you can pick up four vegetarian nori rolls for $3 or a well stuffed carrot hummus pita pocket ($3.50; open Mon.-Sat. 10am-6pm). The best seafood in town can be had at **Bandon Boatwork,** 275 Lincoln SW. (347-2111) through old town and out South Jetty Rd. The dining room may be simple, but the splendid view of the ocean and the menu of sauteed, baked, and fried fish speak for themselves. Lunches ($6-8) are more affordable than dinners ($10-15) when they bring out the wine glasses for a fancier affair.

Outdoor activities near Bandon abound. Strolling around old town is picturesque and pleasant, as is exploring the beaches on a horse from **Bandon Beach Riding Stables** (347-3423; 1-hr. trip $20). Or drive the beach loop road which leaves from old town and joins U.S. 101 5 mi. south. The loop is well marked and goes by **Table Rock, Elephant Rock,** and **Face Rock,** some of the most impressive offshore rock outcroppings along the coast.

PORT ORFORD

Tiny Port Orford is several miles south of **Cape Blanco,** the westernmost point in Oregon. **The Cape Blanco State Park,** 5 mi. west of U.S. 101, has a campground high on the hill and a road leading down to the cape's beach. The very tip of the cape is capped with a functional lighthouse, and sadly the grounds are closed to the public. Port Orford is 45 mi. south of Bandon and 30 mi. north of **Gold Beach.** Some of the best views in the area are from Battle Rock, a seaside park in town where the whales pass close by during December and spring migrations. The beautiful beaches are littered with agate, easy to find at low tide when they sparkle in the sun. The **Chamber of Commerce,** P.O. Box 637 (332-8055), lazes year-round in the parking lot overlooking the bay (open Mon.-Fri. 9am-5pm, Sat. and Sun. 10am-5pm). **Greyhound** (247-7710) stops at the Circle K, across from the Port Orford Motel, with one bus to Portland ($33) and two to San Francisco ($55). The **post office** is at 311 W. 7th St. (332-4251), at Jackson (open daily Mon.-Fri. 8:30am-1pm and 2-5pm; **General Delivery ZIP Code:** 97465). The **area code** is 541.

For those traveling by bus, the **Port Orford Motel,** 1034 Oregon St. (332-1685; fax 332-3306), at U.S. 101, with its fluorescent green trim and convenient location is hard to miss. Rooms sport sofas and wacky wallpaper, and are billed by the person (one $28, two $35, three $40). Several blocks south and around the bend, the **Shoreline Motel,** P.O. Box 26 (332-2903), on U.S. 101, sits across the road from dramatic Battle Rock and the bay. The bathrooms are small, but the rooms are big and well cared for (TV, cable; singles $38, doubles $42, winter rates drop $10). If you must stay on the beach, two nearby campgrounds, one to the north and one to the south, offer the most peaceful and convenient access. Six mi. south of Port Orford, where the highway ducks back behind mountains, **Humbug Mountain State Park** (332-6774) has 108 tightly packed sites in the crisp green shade of deciduous trees (all sites, some with hookups, $18). **Cape Blanco State Park** (332-6774), 6 mi. north of Port Orford and 5 mi. west of U.S. 101, in a grove of pines just south of the lighthouse dominated cape, has 58 sites ($16 tent, $18 with water and electricity, hiker/biker $4; call 800-452-5687 for reservations). Survivors of the 3-mi. hike up the mountain win a tremendous panorama of the entire area.

Health food nuts are in luck in Port Orford. Beside the greasy seafood and breakfast joints stands **Sisters Natural Grocery and Café,** 832 Hwy. 101 (332-3640), where four eclectic tables find room in back by the pastry case. Come in the morning (8-11am) for garden sausage and a couple eggs from the chickens next door ($3, chickens not included) or have a vegetable sandwich on fresh sourdough rye ($3.75) at lunch time. Café open Tues.-Fri. 8am-3pm; grocery Mon.-Fri. 10am-6pm and Sat. 10am-5pm.

■ Brookings

The southernmost stop before California, Brookings is one of the few coastal towns that has remained relatively tourist-free. Here, trinket shops do not elbow out hardware stores and warehouses. Although beaches and parks surround Brookings, it has a residential feel that makes it more of a stopover than a destination in itself. The beaches are among the most unspoiled on the Oregon Coast, but the restaurant and lodging scene leaves something to be desired. Brookings sits in a region often called the "banana belt" due to its mild climate: warm weather is not rare in January, and Brookings' beautiful blossoms bloom early. Strictly speaking, there are two towns here, separated by the Chetco River: **Brookings,** on the north side, and **Harbor,** to the south. They share virtually everything, including a Chamber of Commerce, and are referred to collectively as Brookings. Go figure.

Practical Information The **Brookings State Welcome Center,** 1650 U.S. 101 (469-4117), maintains an office just north of Brookings (open May-Sept. Mon.-Sat. 8am-6pm, Sun. 9am-5pm; April and Oct. Mon.-Sat. 8am-5pm). The town's **Chamber of Commerce,** 16330 Lower Harbor Rd. (469-3181 or 800-535-9469; fax 469-4094), is across the bridge to the south, a short distance off the highway. City maps are $1; if you're one of those rare budget travellers with several hundred thousand dollars to spare, the seaside real estate map is free (open Mon.-Fri. 9am-5pm). The **Chetco Ranger Station,** 555 5th St. (469-2196), distributes information on this part of the **Siskiyou National Forest** (open Mon.-Fri. 8am-4:30pm).

The **Greyhound** station, 601 Railroad Ave. (469-3326), at Tanburk, sends two buses north and two south each day. (To: Portland, $35; San Francisco, $45; open Mon.-Fri. 8:30am-6:30pm, Sat. 8:30am-noon.) The **Maytag Laundry** (469-3975), is known to locals as "The Old Wash House"; you'll find it in the Brookings Harbor Shopping Center (wash $1, 10-min. dry 25¢; open daily 7am-11pm). The **post office** (469-2318), is at 711 Spruce St. (open Mon.-Fri. 9am-4:30pm). The **General Delivery ZIP Code** is 97415, and the **area code** is 541.

Accommodations and Camping Motel rooms and campsites alike are costly in Brookings except in winter, when motel rates tend to drop about $10. The **Bonn Motel,** 1216 Hwy. 101 (469-2161), is basic budget bedding. Its three low buildings have a row of hydrangeas lurking behind each room and a somewhat distant view of the ocean out front. Singles go for $38 in the summer, doubles for $45. Down the road, the **Beaver State Motel,** 437 Hwy. 101 (469-5361), provides spiffier accommodations for a few dollars more. Bedspreads actually match the curtains in both singles ($39, winter $30) and doubles ($49, winter $36).

Harris Beach State Park (469-2021), at the north edge of Brookings, has 68 tent sites amid a grand natural setting. The beach looks across a narrow waterway toward a 21-acre hunk of uninhabited rock and pines known as **Goat Island.** The campground, set back in the trees behind the beach, is equipped with showers, hiker/biker sites ($4), and facilities for people with disabilities (sites $16, with full hookup $19; open year-round). Make reservations (800-452-5687) for stays between Memorial Day and Labor Day. For campsites off the beaten path, travel 15 mi. east of Brookings on Chetco River Rd. to the charming **Little Redwood** campground. In an impressive forest alongside a burbling, salamander-filled creek, the campground has 15 sites ($6), with drinking water and pit toilets. Several other campgrounds along that road are free but have no water. For information contact the **Chetco Ranger District** (see **Practical Information,** above).

Food A fishing town at heart, Brookings can batter up a good piece of flounder with the best of 'em. A number of salty seafood spots can be found heading out toward the harbor, among them the local favorite **Marty's Pelican Bay Seafood,** 16403 Lower Harbor Rd. (469-7971), just down the hill from the highway. Loggers and fisherfolk alike come in for coffee and french toast ($2.20) when the hours can appropriately be classified "wee." Sandwiches are big (tuna melt $4.75) and come with shoestring fries (dinners $6.50-9). For a delicious, if somewhat morbid-sounding treat, try the $2 bowl of graveyard stew. (Open Mon.-Sat. 4am-9pm, Sun. 5am-9pm.) For some serious

OREGON

Mexican food, stick to the highway and head for **Los Amigos**, 541 Hwy. 101, (469-4102). Its plain, baby-blue exterior may not catch your eye immediately, but the $4 super burrito, $2.50 pork tamale, and 30¢ corn tortillas made fresh to order are not to be missed. (Open Mon.-Sat. 11am-8pm, Sun. noon-8pm.)

Sights, Activities, and Events Brookings is known statewide for its beautiful flowers. In **Azalea Park,** downtown, lawns are encircled by large native azaleas, some of which are more than 300 years old (bloom-time is April-June). Two rare weeping spruce trees also grace the park's grounds. The pride of Brookings is its annual **Azalea Festival** (469-3181), held in Azalea Park during Memorial Day weekend. The **Chetco Valley Historical Society Museum,** 15461 Museum Rd. (469-6651), 2½ mi. south of the Chetco River, occupies the oldest building in Brookings. Exhibits include the patchwork quilts of settlers and Native American basketwork. The museum is hard to miss; just look for the **nation's largest cypress tree** in front ($1, children 50¢; open Wed.-Sun. noon-5pm).

If you're heading north from Brookings by bicycle, take scenic **Carpenterville Rd.,** the only highway out of town before U.S. 101 was built. The twisty, 13½-mi. road features beautiful ocean views. **Boardman State Park** enfolds U.S. 101 for 8 mi. north of Brookings; overlooks and picnic sites provide fantastic views of the coast. Thirty mi. north of Brookings in Gold Beach, you can ride a mail boat up the **Rogue River. Mail Boat Hydro-Jets** (247-7033 or 800-458-3511) offers 64-, 80-, and 104-mi. daytrips. Whitewater trips last six to seven and a half hours and start at $30, children age 4-11 start at $12.

▓ Redwood National Park

Redwood National Forest, along the northern California coast a scant 20 mi. from Brookings, is home to the unique and massive redwood. The famous trees in this park are the last-remaining stretch of the old-growth forest which used to blanket 2 million acres of Northern California and Oregon. The park gives new meaning to the word lush. The ferns grow the height of humans and the redwood trees the size of skyscrapers. You almost expect a dinosaur to tromp by at any moment. You will probably catch a glimpse of the plentiful Roosevelt Elk, though the park's black bears and mountain lions retire in the backwoods. While a short tour of the big sights and the Drive-thru Tree will certainly give visitors a few thrills and ample photo ops, it will also provide an overdose of fellow tourists. A more memorable way to experience the redwoods is to head down one of the solitary hiking paths into the quiet of the forest. Here you'll find trees as they have been for thousands of years. The extraordinary forest is well worth the brief trip to Cali.

PRACTICAL INFORMATION

Visitor Information:

Redwood National Park Headquarters and Information Center, 1111 2nd St. (464-6101), in Crescent City. Open daily 9am-5pm. This is the headquarters of the entire national park, but the ranger stations are just as well-informed. Offers 1- to 3-day field seminars on everything from the ecology of the spotted owl to scenic photography ($10-75, advance registration essential).

Redwood Information Center (488-3461), on U.S. 101, 1 mi. south of Orick. Shows free films about park and wildlife on request. Mountain bike trail information. Free map of the park and brochures on trails and campsites. Enthusiastic and extremely helpful rangers (open daily 9am-5pm).

Crescent City Chamber of Commerce, 1001 Front St. (464-3174), in Crescent City provides plenty of information. Open Mon.-Fri. 8am-7pm, Sat.-Sun. 9am-5pm; Labor Day-Memorial Day Mon.-Fri. 9am-5pm.

Prairie Creek Ranger Station (488-2171), on U.S. 101, in Prairie Creek Redwood State Park. Open daily 9am-5pm, summer only.

OREGON

Hiouchi Ranger Station (458-3134), on U.S. 199, across from Jedediah Smith Redwoods State Park. Open May-Oct. daily 9am-5pm.

Jedediah Smith State Park Information Center (458-3310), on U.S. 199 across from the Hiouchi Ranger Station. Open daily 9am-5pm.

Park Entrance Fee: The national park is free, but there's a $6 per carload fee for use of Redwood State Park facilities, such as beaches and picnic tables.

Greyhound: 1125 Northcrest Dr. (464-2807), in Crescent City. 2 buses per day going north and 2 going south, to San Francisco ($51) and Portland ($52). Buses can supposedly be flagged down at 3 places within the park: at the **Shoreline Deli** (488-5761), 1 mi. south of Orick, CA on U.S. 101 ($10 to Crescent City); at **Paul's Cannery** in Klamath, CA on U.S. 101 ($7 to Crescent City, CA); and in front of the **Redwood Hostel** ($5 to Crescent City). Beware capricious bus drivers who may decide to ignore you. Call the Greyhound station directly preceding your stop and ask the attendant to make the driver aware of your presence. Open Mon.-Fri. 7-10am and 5-7:35pm, Sat. 7-9am and 9pm.

Road Conditions: 800-427-7623. **Highway Patrol:** 464-3117.

AAA Emergency Road Service: (464-5626). Open 24hr.

Laundromat: Econ-o-wash, 601 H St., Crescent City (464-9935). Open 7am-11pm. Wash 75¢-$2. Dry 25¢ for 10min.

Rape Crisis: 465-2851. 24hr.

Disabled Information: *Access Brochure,* available by mail or at the ranger's station. If notified in advance, rangers can help you make the most of your stay.

Hospital: Sutter Coast, 800 E. Washington Blvd. (464-8511), Crescent City, CA.

Emergency: 911.

Post Office: 751 2nd St. (464-2151), in **Crescent City.** Open Mon.-Fri. 8:30am-5pm, Sat. noon-3pm. **ZIP Code:** 95531. Another office at 121147 U.S. 101 in **Orick.** Open Mon.-Fri. 8:30am-noon and 1-5pm. **ZIP Code:** 95555.

Area Code: 707.

ORIENTATION

Redwood National Park is only one of four parks where the redwoods grow between The Northern California towns of **Klamath,** 30 mi. from the Oregon border on U.S. 101, and **Orick,** 45 mi. from the border. The others are **Jedediah Smith State Park, Del Norte Coast Redwoods State Park,** and **Prairie Creek Redwoods State Park.** The name Redwood National Park is an umbrella term for all four parks. **Crescent City,** with park headquarters and a few basic services, stands at the park's northern end. The small town of Orick is situated at the southern limit and harbors an extremely helpful ranger station, a state park headquarters, and a handful of motels. Klamath and **Crescent City** also have basic services and a few motels. **Rte. 101** connects the two, traversing most of the park. The slower, but more scenic **Newton Drury Pkwy.** runs parallel to Rte. 101 from Klamath to Prairie Creek.

Fruits and berries can be gathered in the park for personal consumption; however, all other plants and animals are protected; even feathers dropped by birds of prey are off limits. **Fishing licenses** are required for fresh and saltwater fishing, and there are minimum-weight and maximum-catch requirements for both. One-day licenses range from $5-8. Call the ranger station or the License and Revenue Office at 916-739-3380.

ACCOMMODATIONS

The most pleasant pad is the **Redwood Youth Hostel (HI-AYH),** 14480 U.S. 101, Klamath (482-8265), at Wilson Creek Rd. *Quelle location!* Overlooking the crashing Pacific surf and housed in the historic Victorian DeMartin House, this hostel combines ultramodern facilities with a certain ruggedness. Its 30 beds, kitchen, and laundry facilities are all wheelchair accessible. There's a separate vegetarian stove, 12 recycling bins, two sundecks overlooking the ocean, staple foods for sale, and a laundry service ($1.25 per load, free for passing cyclists). The hostel simply asks you to take your shoes off when inside the building and let the caretakers rest when the office is closed. (Check-in 4:30-9:30pm. Curfew 11pm. Closed 9:30am-4:30pm, so you'll have to be an early riser. $10-12. Linen $1. Couples rooms available. Reservations recommended. You must pay in advance by check or credit card.)

The well-kept, woodsy cabins of **Camp Marigold,** 16101 U.S. 101 (482-3585 or 800-621-8513), in Klamath are a pleasant alternative to the mundane budget-motel look ($34 for 2 people). Each is handily equipped with a kitchen. The **Park Woods Motel,** 121440 Rte. 101 (488-5175), in Orick, has clean, bare-bones rooms for the lowest prices in town ($35 for 1 or 2 people, and a 2-bedroom unit with full kitchen is only $40). **El Patio,** 655 H St. (464-5114), in Crescent City, offers decent rooms with wood-paneled early-70s look for a modest price. Some rooms have kitchenettes ($5 extra); all have TVs (singles are $30, doubles $37; $2 key deposit).

CAMPING

Redwood National Park offers several backcountry campsites. All are free and accessible by hiking only a short distance from roads or parking lots. **Demartin Campsite** is on a redwood prairie and can be reached by parking at Hwy. 101, mile marker 14.42, and hiking ½ mi. **Nickel Creek Campground,** off the end of Enderts Beach Rd., outside of Crescent City, has five sites with toilets but no showers or water. **Flint Ridge,** off Klamath Beach Rd., has water and toilets but no showers. The remote **Little Bald Hills Horse/Backpack Camp** is at the end of a 4½-mi. hike at the east end of Howland Hill Rd. Remote. **State Park Campsites** (464-9533) are all fully developed and easily accessible. The fee is $16 and reservations (necessary in the winter) can be made by calling DESTINET (800-436-7275). North of Crescent City on Rte. 199 is the **Jedediah Smith State Park.** Amenities include showers, water, restrooms, picnic tables, and grills. They also offer campfire programs and nature walks. In the **Del Norte Coast State Park,** camping is at **Mill Creek Campground.** It comes equipped with all the same goods as the Jedediah Smith, and the ocean view is magnificent. Camping in **Prairie Creek State Park** is possible at **Elk Prairie** and **Gold Bluffs Beach.** There are also several campgrounds in **Six Rivers National Park** (457-3131). **Big Flat Campground** is 14 mi. up South Fork Rd. off Hwy. 199. There are no hookups, but it's near the Smith River and it's free. **Grass Flat** is 4 mi. east on Hwy. 199 and has vault toilets and water.

FOOD

There are more picnic table sites in the area than there are restaurants, so the best option for eating is probably to stop by the reasonably priced **Orick Market** (488-3225; open Mon.-Sat. 8am-7pm, Sun. 9am-7pm), to stock up on supplies, and then find a spot by the ocean or the trees. In Crescent City, head to the 24hr. **Safeway** in the shopping center on Hwy. 101 (M St.) between 2nd and 5th St. **Alias Jones,** 983 3rd St. (465-6987), is known for serving hearty portions. For breakfast, try a cinnamon roll the size of a cake ($1.75) or a fruity muffin ($1.45). Tasty and unusual sandwiches with salad are $4-6 (open Mon.-Fri. 7am-5:30pm, Sat. 7am-3pm). Another popular spot is the **Good Harvest Cafe,** 700 Northeast St. (465-6028), which serves up healthy sandwiches and gooey baklava (95¢). (Open Mon.-Sat. 7am-3pm, Sun. 8am-1pm.) The **Palm Café,** Rte. 101 in Orick (488-3381), dishes out basic diner food to local boys in rattlesnake cowboy hats (head and tail attached, of course), but outsiders are also welcome. Old Maid Plate with 2 eggs and a stack of pancakes ($5). Homemade fruit pies ($2) are positively delicious. Open daily 4:45am-8pm.

SIGHTS

Driving at breakneck speed, you can see Redwood National Park in just over an hour, but the best way to experience the park is on foot. The park is divided into several regions, each of which have unique attractions and information centers. The National Park Service conducts a symphony of organized activities for all ages. Pick up a detailed list of Junior Ranger programs and nature walks at any of the park's ranger stations (see **Practical Information**) or call the **Redwood Information Center** (488-

3461) for details. Be on the lookout for black bears and mountain lions. Hikers should take particular care to wear protective clothing—**ticks** and **poison oak** thrive in these deep, dark places. After hiking, inspect your body, particularly your lower legs, scalp, and any area covered by tightly-fitting garments, like socks, for ticks (see **Common Ailments,** p. 14). If you suspect you've been exposed to poison oak, remove and wash your clothes and wash your skin immediately. If you're really worried, call the TeleNurse at 445-3121 and God have mercy on you! Before setting out, get the *Redwood National Park Trail Guide* ($2) at the visitor center. It has great advice on different trails and a detailed map.

Orick Area

The Orick Area covers the southernmost section of the park. Its **visitor center** lies about 1 mi. south of Orick on U.S. 101 and ½ mi. south of the Shoreline Deli (the Greyhound bus stop). The main attraction is the **tall trees grove,** a 2½-mi. trail which begins 6 mi. from the ranger station. If you're driving, you'll need a permit (available at the visitor center; free). A minimum of three to four hours should be allowed for the trip. From the trailhead at the end of Tall Trees Access Rd. (which is accessible by Bald Hills Rd. off Hwy 101 just north of Orick), it's a 1.3-mi. hike down to the tallest redwoods in the park and, in fact, to the **tallest known tree in the world** (367.8 ft., one-third the height of the World Trade Center).

Orick itself (pop. 650) is a friendly town, overrun with souvenir stores selling "burl sculptures" (wood carvings pleasing to neither eye nor wallet). Nevertheless, the town provides some useful amenities, like a **post office** and some motels.

Patrick's Point State Park lies 15 mi. south of Orick along U.S. 101 and offers one of the most spectacular views on the California coast. Campers, boaters, and nature enthusiasts may want to spend a day or two at Patrick's Point before heading north to the redwoods (camping $16). During **whale-watching** season (Oct.-Dec., March-May), the towering cliffs and rocky geography of the point provide the best seats in the house for observing migration of these mammoth mammals.

Prairie Creek Area

The Prairie Creek Area, equipped with a **ranger station** and **state park campgrounds,** is perfect for hikers, who can experience 75 mi. of trails in the park's 14,000 acres. Bring a map along because some trails are not well marked. The **James Irvine Trail** (4½ mi. one way) winds through magnificent redwoods, around clear and cold creeks, past grazing elk, through **Fern Canyon** (famed for its 50-ft. fern walls and crystalline stretch), and by the Pacific (wear shoes you don't mind getting wet). The trail starts at the Prairie Creek visitor center. The less ambitious can elk-watch too—the beasts love to graze on the meadow in front of the ranger station.

The **Elk Prairie Trail** (1.4 mi. one way) skirts the prairie and can be made into a loop by joining the nature trail. Elk may look peaceful, but they are best left unapproached. **Revelation** and **Redwood Access Trails** were designed to accommodate people with disabilities. **Big Tree Trail** is an easy walk, and its 306-ft. behemoth is a substitute for those who don't want to make the long trek to the tallest tree in the world (see **Orick,** above).

Klamath Area

To the north, the Klamath Area consists of a thin stretch of park land connecting Prairie Creek with Del Norte State Park. The main attraction here is the ruggedly spectacular coastline. The **Klamath Overlook,** where Requa Rd. meets the Coastal Trail, is an excellent **whale-watching site.** Even when the whales are not migrating north (March-May), the view from this cliff is worth the trip.

The mouth of the **Klamath River** is a popular fishing spot (permit required) during the fall and spring, when salmon spawn, and during the winter when steelhead trout do the same. The town of Klamath has gone so far as to name itself the "Salmon and Steelhead Capital of the World." Sea lions in the spring and harbor seals in the summer congregate near the **Douglas Memorial Bridge,** or the part that survived a 1964 flood. Two golden bears guard each end of the bridge. **Coastal Drive** passes by the bridge and then continues along the ocean for 8 mi. of incredible views. The **Yurok Loop** (1 mi.), a self-guided trail near the Klamath Falls Cove, is short and easy (like John Wayne Bobbit) but with great views of the shoreline.

Crescent City Area

Crescent City calls itself the city "where the redwoods meet the sea." In 1964, a wrathful Mother Nature took this literally, when a *tsunami* caused by oceanic quakes caused 500-mph winds and leveled the city. Nine blocks into the town, the powerful wave was still two stories high. Today the rebuilt city offers an outstanding location from which to explore the national park, but don't linger too long lest you become the first person to actually die of boredom.

The **Battery Point Lighthouse** (464-3089), on a causeway jutting off Front St., houses a **museum** open only during low tide (open Wed.-Sun. 10am-4pm, tide permitting; $2, children 50¢). Ask museum guides about the resident **ghost.** From June through August, the national park offers two-hour **tidepool walks** (1 mi.) at the end of Endert's Beach Rd. (turn off 4 mi. south of Crescent City). The fascinating walks will bring you close to starfish, sea urchins, sea anemone, and crabs in their natural setting. Call 464-6101 for details and times.

The **Coastal Trail** runs from Endert in the north part of the park to Tall Tree Grove in the south, passing cliffs, beaches, forests, and prairie along the way. Much of the trail is difficult, but the section near Endert Beach (there called the **Crescent Beach Trail**) is relatively easy. Perfect for **birdwatchers.** The trailhead is at the **Crescent Beach Information Center** on Endert Beach Rd., just off Hwy. 101.

A scenic drive from Crescent City along **Pebble Beach Drive** to **Point St. George** snakes past a stretch of coastline that looks transplanted from New England. Craggy cliffs, lush prairies, and an old lighthouse complete the postcard view.

Annual highlights include the **World Championship Crab Races** (800-343-8300) which feature races and crab feasts on the third Sunday in February. During **Easter in July** (487-8400), the lily's biennial bloom is celebrated. The **Weekend in Bear Country** (464-7441), is a mid-August beachfront park festival.

Hiouchi Area

This inland region sits in the northern part of the park along Rte. 199 and contains some excellent hiking trails, most of which lie in Jedediah Smith State Park. The best trails lie off Howland Hill Rd., a dirt road easily accessible from both Hwy. 101 and 199. From 199, turn onto South Fork Road in Hiouchi and turn right onto Douglas Park Rd., which then turns into Howland Hill Rd. From Crescent City, go south on Hwy. 101, turn left onto Elk Valley Rd. and right onto Howland Hill. The handicap-accessible **Stout Grove Trail** is a short (½ mi.) jaunt through the lush redwoods. The trailhead is near the Hiouchi end of Howland Hill Rd. The **Mill Creek Trail** is a moderate hike with excellent swimming and fishing opportunities. This 2.6-mi. trail is accessible from the Mill Creek Bridge on Howland Hill and from the Jedediah Smith Campground. The more strenuous (wimpy sounding) **Boy Scout Trail** splits after 3 mi.; one path goes to the monstrous Boy Scout Tree and the other ends at Fern Falls, but we're not gonna tell you which is which. Two mi. west of Jedediah State Park on U.S. 199 lie the **Simpson-Reed and Peterson Trails,** both of which are disabled-accessible. A tour map (25¢ from the ranger station) will guide you.

Six Rivers National Forest (457-3131) lies directly east of Hiouchi. The Smith River rushes through rocky gorges as it winds its way from the mountains to the coast. This last wild and scenic river in California is the state's only major undammed river (that's why you're going to Alaska and the Pacific Northwest, of course) and the salmon, trout, and steelhead fishing is heavenly. There are also numerous hiking trails throughout the enormous forest. Call the ranger station for more information.

INLAND VALLEYS

While the jagged cliffs and coastal surf draw tourists and nature lovers to the Oregon coast, Oregonians themselves choose the lush Willamette and Rogue River Valleys. Vast tracts of fertile land support productive agriculture. For decades, the immense forest resources also supported a healthy timber industry, but in recent years a call to save what's left of the nation's forest and wildlife has divided the population of Oregon. A few years ago, Congress passed legislation to protect the endangered northern spotted owl, and a federal court injunction banned logging in the public forests of the Pacific Northwest. Idle mills, unemployed loggers, and crippled local economies pushed the issue back into Congress in June 1994, and limited logging resumed under a complex new forest-use-and-protection plan created by the Clinton Administration. The issue of the spotted owl is still a tense one in western Oregon. Environmental groups and timber interests will likely contest the forest plan in court. But while the fortunes of the timber industry are uncertain, tourism is definitely a growth industry in southern Oregon.

I-5, which runs north-south through Oregon to the west of the Cascades, traverses rolling agricultural and forest land punctuated by a few urban centers. Farthest south, the **Rogue River Valley,** from Ashland to Grants Pass, is generally hot and dry in the summer, which brings a lucrative business to the whitewater rafting and kayaking outfitters. **Eugene,** Oregon's second-largest city and bawdiest college town, rests at the southern end of the temperate **Willamette Valley.** This carpet of agricultural land extends 20 mi. on either side of the river and runs 80 mi. north until it bumps into Portland's bedroom communities. It is possible to drive Oregon's 305-mi. stretch of I-5 from tip to toe in less than six hours, but lead-footed out-of-staters should be wary—most Oregonians obey speed limits, and fines for speeding have recently skyrocketed.

■ Ashland

With a casual, rural setting near the California border, Ashland mixes hippies and history, making it the perfect locale for the world-famous **Shakespeare Festival** (see below). From mid-February to October, drama devotees can choose from a repertoire of 11 plays performed in Ashland's three elegant theaters. Over the 60-year course of the festival's history, the town has evolved with it, giving rise to business names like "All's Well Drugstore," highway signs that display the remaining mileage to the Shakespeare Center, and a vibrant population of artists, actors, and food lovers. The extravagant Shakespearean and contemporary productions impress connoisseurs and casual observers alike, and draw internationally famous theater companies into the fray. Though Ashland can be crowded with visitors in the summer, the town has not sold its soul to the tourist trade. Culture comes with a price, but low-cost accommodations and tickets reward those who investigate. If it is known only for the festival by the rest of the world, Oregonians know Ashland as a cultural magnet, rife with fabulous restaurants, art galleries, concerts, and a well-attended lecture series in Lithia Park.

PRACTICAL INFORMATION AND ORIENTATION

Visitors Information: Chamber of Commerce, 110 E. Main St. (482-3486). A busy (but friendly) staff frantically answers phones and dishes out free play schedules and brochures, several of which contain small but adequate **maps.** (Oddly, the best maps of Ashland are in the to-go menu at **Omar's,** 1380 Siskiyou Blvd., 482-1281). The chamber does *not* sell tickets to performances. Open Mon.-Fri. 9am-5pm. The chamber also staffs an info booth in the center of the plaza that is open in the summer daily 9am-5pm. **Ashland District Ranger Station,** 645 Washington St. (482-3333), off Rte. 66 by Exit 14 on I-5. Hiking, mountain biking, and other outdoor info, including the Pacific Crest Trail and certain camping restrictions. Open Mon.-Fri. 8am-4:30pm.

Tickets: Oregon Shakespearean Festival Box Office, 15 S. Pioneer St., P.O. Box 158, Ashland 97520 (482-4331; fax 482-8045), next to the Elizabethan Theater. Rush tickets (½price) occasionally available ½hr. before performances not already sold out. Ask at the box office for more options; the staff is full of tips for desperate theatergoers.

Buses: Greyhound (779-2103 in Medford). No depot in Ashland. Pick-up and drop-off at the BP station, 2073 Hwy. 99N, at the north end of town. To: Portland (4 per day, $36), Sacramento (3 per day, $40), and San Francisco (3 per day, $47). Call 800-231-2222 for departure times. **Green Tortoise** (800-867-8647) comes through at 4 inconvenient times per week, stopping at safeway, 585 Siskiyou Blvd. Northbound Tues. and Sat. 5:15am (to Portland $29, to Seattle $39); southbound Sun. and Thurs. 11:45 pm (to San Francisco $39).

Public Transportation: Rogue Valley Transportation (779-2877, 776-4444, ext. 2877 for schedules), in Medford. Schedules available at the Chamber of Commerce. Base fare $1. Over 62 and ages 10-17 ½price, under 10 free. The #10 bus serving Ashland runs daily every ½hr. 4:30am-7pm between the transfer station at 200 S. Front St. in Medford and the Plaza in Ashland. Also to Jacksonville (on bus #30, $1). Local buses loop through Ashland every 15min. (25¢).

Taxi: Ashland Taxi (482-3065). 24hr.

Car Rental: Budget, 2525 Ashland St. (488-7741 for reservations, phone or fax 482-0626 for information), at the Windmill Ashland Hills Inn on Rte. 66. Economy cars are $31 per day, $179 per week, with unlimited mileage. 5% AARP discount, $2 off for *Let's Go* users. Under 25 $7.50 per day extra. Must be 21. Accepts all major credit cards.

Library: Ashland Branch Library, 410 Siskiyou Blvd. (482-1197), at Gresham St. Occupies an historic building with stone fireplace. Open Mon.-Tues. 10am-8pm, Wed.-Thurs. 10am-6pm, Fri.-Sat. 10am-5pm.

Laundromat: Main St. Laundromat, 370 E. Main St. (482-8042). Wash $1, 9-min. dry 25¢. Double and triple loaders and Ms. Pac-Man. Open daily 9am-9pm.

Equipment Rental: Ashland Mountain Supply, 31 N. Main St. (488-2749). Internal frame backpacks $7.50 per day ($100 deposit). External frame backpacks $5 per day ($50 deposit). Mountain bikes $10 for 2hr., $25 per day. Discounts for longer rentals. **The Adventure Center,** 40 N. Main St. (488-2819). Mountain bikes ½day $20, one day $25. Guided bike tours ($59 for ½day with lunch) and raft trips (see **Outdoors**) also offered.

Crisis Intervention Services: 779-4357. 24hr.

Emergency: 911. **Police:** 1155 E. Main St. (482-5211). **Fire:** 422 Siskiyou Dr. (482-2770).

Post Office: 120 N. 1st St. (482-3986), at Lithia Way. Open Mon.-Fri. 9am-5pm. **General Delivery ZIP Code:** 97520.

Area Code: 541.

Ashland is 15 mi. north of the California border, near the junction of I-5 and Rte. 66, which traverses 64 mi. of stunning scenery between Klamath Falls and Ashland. Hwy. 99 cuts through the middle of town on a northwest-southwest axis. Its local name changes from N. Main St. to E. Main at the triangular plaza, where a medley of shops and restaurants form Ashland's downtown, and then to Siskiyou Blvd. a mile farther south. **Southern Oregon State College** (SOSC), another few blocks down Siskiyou, is flanked by affordable motels and several less than inspiring restaurants.

ACCOMMODATIONS AND CAMPING

> *"Now spurs the lated traveler apace to gain the timely inn"*
> Macbeth, III.iii.6.

In winter, Ashland is a budget traveler's paradise of vacancy and low rates; in summer, hotel and B&B rates practically double, and the hostel is overflows with travelers. Only rogues and strumpets arrive without reservations. Midsummer nights see vacant accommodations only in nearby Medford. Note: the bathroom in your hotel or accommodation may (or may not) smell strongly of rotten eggs. At least part of Ashland's water supply contains dissolved sulfurous compounds. It is perfectly safe to drink and bathe in but lends some bathrooms a repugnant, and nearly permanent, odor. If you're a desperate traveler during the crowded Shakespeare festival, seek shelter in Jacksonville or Medford (see **Medford: Accomodations,** p. 472, and **Jacksonville: Accommodations,** p. 474).

Ashland Hostel, 150 N. Main St. (482-9217). Well kept and cheery, this hostel has an air of elegance worthy of the Bard himself. The Victorian parlor, sturdy bunks, and a front porch swing play host to a mixed crowd of budget travelers and theater-bound families wise to the ways of saving money in Ashland. Laundry facilities and kitchen. Check-in 5-11pm. Curfew at midnight. Lockout 10am-5pm. $12, non-members $14. $1 discounts for Pacific Crest Trail hikers or touring cyclists. Two private rooms (can sleep 4 each, $35). Reservations advised March-Oct.

Columbia Hotel, 262½ E. Main St. (482-3726 or 800-718-2530). A European-style home, 1½ blocks from the theaters. Rooms are spacious, with wood panelling, old pictures, and muted colors. No TVs. Bathroom and pay phone down the hall. Singles $52, doubles $59; Nov.-Feb. singles $30, doubles $34; March-May singles $32, doubles $45. 10% discount for HI-AYH members in the off season, children under 12 free. Call ahead.

Vista Motel, 535 Clover Lane (482-4423), on I-5 at the Rte. 66 exit (#14). Small rooms in a low red, white, and blue building resembling a Lego. Not center-stage for main attractions, but there is TV, A/C, a small pool, and an amiable staff. Singles $37. Doubles $45. Winter and spring discounts of about $10.

Ashland Motel, 1145 Siskiyou Blvd. (482-2561), across from the college. Fresh and tidy with a pale pink façade and an interior that puts little to no unique spin on the ubiquitous "motel brown" motif. Laundry, phones, TV, A/C, and a good sized pool. Singles $43, doubles $58. Off-season rates $12-13 lower.

Jackson Hot Springs, 2253 Hwy. 99 N. (482-3776), 2 mi. north of Ashland on Hwy. 99; from I-5 go west ½ mi from Exit 19 and turn right on 99. Not the most natural setting, but the nearest campground to downtown. Separate tent area in a grassy, open field encircled by RV sites. Laundry facilities, hot showers, and indoor mineral baths ($6 per person, $9 per couple). Tent sites $13, RV sites $16, with full hookup $18.

Mt. Ashland Campground, 9 mi. west of I-5 at Exit 6. Follow signs up to Mt. Ashland Ski Area and take the high road from the far west end of the lot. Exquisitely placed on the side of a mountaintop, looking south across the valley to Mt. Shasta. Seven primitive sites set in the high grass. Fire pits and vault toilets, but **no drinking water.** Free.

FOOD

> *"Give them great meals of beef and iron and steel, they will eat like wolves and fight like devils"*
> Henry V, III.vii.166.

The incredible selection of delectable food available on North and East Main St. has earned the plaza a reputation independent of the festival. Even the ticketless come from miles around to dine in Ashland's fine restaurants. Beware the pre-show rush—a downtown dinner planned for 6:30pm can easily become a late affair. Also, note that many businesses close at 8:30 or 9pm, when the rush has passed. **Ashland Community Food Store COOP,** 237 N. 1st St. (482-2237), at A St., has a lively spirit and a great selection of organic produce and natural foods, ideal to supply a picnic or a home-cooked meal at the hostel (5% discount for seniors; open Mon.-Sat. 8am-9pm, Sun. 9am-9pm). Standard, less expensive groceries are available at **Safeway,** 585 Siskiyou Blvd. (482-4495; open daily 6am-midnight).

Geppetto's, 345 E. Main St. (482-1138). A local favorite, Geppetto's is the place for that late-night nosh. The staff is fun, the walls inexplicably covered in baskets, and the menu conversational, offering you 6 infamous feta and spinach wontons for $3.25. $15 dinner specials are enticing, but there are smaller ticket options, like a pile of sauteed vegetables for $2.50 or a $3.25 super cheese sandwich. Loosely Italian and decidedly innovative cuisine, with burgers randomly included. Mostly healthy; fantastic eggplant veggie burger on a bun $4. Lunches $4-6, breakfasts slightly more. Try the Milano omelette ($7). Open daily 8am-midnight.

Thai Pepper, 84 N. Main St. (482-8052), one level below the street. A hotspot, in the coolest area of town, with decks in the leafy green shade over Ashland Creek. Entrees are deliciously exotic and reasonably priced for Ashland ($10-13). The best deal is lunch, when you don't have to wait for a seat outside, and your choice of 3 small dishes (including curry, rolls, and saté among other) is a steal for $6.50. Open Tues.-Sat. 11:30am-2pm, Wed.-Sat. 5:30-9:30pm, Sun. 5:30-8:30pm.

Rain Forest Café, 120 E. Main St. (482-9463). Great Mexican and Oriental vegetarian fare in a semi-bohemian setting. Unwind on the streetside deck with tofu spinach enchiladas ($5.95). Most items on the wall-sized menu are $5-6 and contain some form of tofu, with the exception of the absurdly tasty bean burrito ($4). Open Mon.-Fri. 11am-8pm, Sat.-Sun. 11am-9:30pm.

Five Rivers, 139 E. Main St. (488-1883), one flight up from street level. Slip upstairs to the warm smells of eastern spices and delicious Indian cuisine. Elegant Indian artwork and music set an intimate tone. Entrees $5.50-11.50; vegetarian options all below $6.50. Daily lunch buffet $5.50. Open daily 11am-2:30pm and 5-10pm.

Greenleaf Restaurant, 49 N. Main St. (482-2808). Healthy, delicious food, right on the plaza with creekside seating out back. Omelettes and frittatas are a bargain in the morning for $4.50-6. Tremendous array of salads ($2.50-9), stir fry ($7), and pastas ($5-9), and a spanakopita that's a meal in itself. Chomp inside or take it down the block for a picnic in nearby Lithia Park. Open Tues.-Sun. 8am-9pm, off season 8am-8pm. Closed January.

Brothers Restaurant and Delicatessen, 95 N. Main St. (482-9671) A block off the trampled tourist beat, this New York-style deli and café feeds more locals than most. Some offbeat selections like the zucchini burger ($4) join the meat ($5.25) and double meat ($6.50) sandwiches on the menu. Open Mon. and Wed.-Fri. 7am-2pm, Tues. 7am-8pm, Sat. and Sun. 7am-3pm.

THE SHAKESPEARE FESTIVAL

"This is very midsummer madness"

Twelfth Night, III.iv.62.

The **Shakespeare Festival,** the 1935 brainchild of local college teacher Angus Bowmer, began with two plays performed in the Chautauqua theater by schoolchildren as an evening complement to daytime boxing matches. Today, professional actors perform 11 plays in repertory. As the selections have become more modern, Shakespeare's share has shrunk to four plays; the other seven are classical and contemporary dramas. Performances run on the three Ashland stages from mid-February through October, and any boxing now is over the extremely scarce tickets ("Lay on, Macduff! And damned be him that first cries, 'Hold, enough!'" *Macbeth,* V.vii.62). On the side of the Chautauqua theater stands the **Elizabethan Stage,** an outdoor theater modeled after one in 18th-century London. Open only from mid-June through early October, the Elizabethan hosts three Shakespeare plays per season. The **Angus Bowmer** is a 600-seat indoor theater that stages one Shakespeare play and several classical dramas. The newest of the theaters is the intimate **Black Swan,** home to small, offbeat productions. The house is dark on Mondays.

Due to the tremendous popularity of the productions, ticket purchases are recommended six months in advance. General mail-order ticket sales begin in January, but phone orders are not taken until February ($19-37 spring and fall, $22-42 in summer, plus a $3.50 handling fee per order for phone, fax, or mail orders; children under 5 not admitted to any of the shows). For complete ticket information, write Oregon

Shakespeare Festival, P.O. Box 158, Ashland 97520 (482-4331; fax 482-8045). Though obtaining tickets can be difficult in the summertime, spontaneous theatergoers should not abandon hope. The **box office** at 15 S. Pioneer St. opens at 9:30am on theater days; prudence demands arriving a few hours early. Local patrons have been known to leave their shoes to hold their places in line, and you should respect this tradition. At 9:30am, the box office releases any unsold tickets for the day's performances. If no tickets are available, a limited amount of priority numbers will be given out. These entitle their holders to a designated place in line when the precious few tickets that festival members have returned are released (12:30pm for matinees, and 5:30pm for evening performances). At these times, the box office also sells twenty clear-view standing room tickets for sold-out shows on the Elizabethan Stage ($10, obtained on the day of the show).

Unofficial ticket transactions also take place just outside the box office, "on the bricks," though scalping is illegal. ("Off with his head!"—*Richard III,* III.iv.75). Ticket officials advise those buying on the bricks to check the date and time on the ticket carefully, to pay only the face value, and to check with the box office before purchasing any tickets that have been altered. From March to May, half-price rush tickets are often available an hour before every performance that is not sold out. Additionally, in the spring and October, some half-price student-senior matinees are offered. Spring and summer previews (pre-critic, full-performance shows) are offered early in each play's run at the Black Swan and Elizabethan Stage for a discounted price ($15-24).

Backstage tours provide a wonderful glimpse of the festival from behind the curtain. Tour guides (usually actors or technicians) divulge all kinds of anecdotes—from bird songs during an outdoor *Hamlet* to the ghastly events which take place every time they do "that Scottish play." Tours last almost two hours and usually leave from the Black Swan ($8-9, ages 5-17 $6-6.75, children under 5 not admitted; Tues.-Sun. 10am). Admission fee includes a trip to the **Exhibit Center** for a close-up look at sets and costumes (otherwise $2, children 5-17 $1.50; open Tues.-Sun. 10am-4pm, fall and spring 10:30am-1:30pm). Further immersion in Shakespeare can be had at two-hour discussion **seminars** offered every Friday between Memorial and Labor Day (9:30-11:30am) by Southern Oregon State College ($5). Call 552-6331 for more information. The Shakespeare festival also includes special events, such as the **Feast of Will** in mid-June, a celebration honoring the annual opening of the Elizabethan Theater. Dinner and merry madness are held in Lithia Park starting at 6pm (tickets $16; call 482-4331 for exact date).

SIGHTS AND ACTIVITIES

> "Matador pants make everyone look big."
>
> Albert Einstein

Before it imported Shakespeare, Ashland was naturally blessed with lithia water—water containing dissolved lithium salts, reputed to have miraculous healing powers. The mineral springs have given their name to the well tended **Lithia Park,** west of the plaza off Main St. To quaff the vaunted water itself, hold your nose (the water contains dissolved sulfur salts) and head for the circle of fountains in the center of the plaza. Free concerts, readings, and educational nature walks happen early every day there, in and around the park's hiking trails, Japanese garden, and the swan ponds by Ashland Creek. Events are listed in brochures at the Chamber of Commerce (see **Practical Information,** above).

If the park and mineral waters fail to refresh you, find your way to the **Chateulin Selections,** 52 E. Main St. (488-WINE/9463), for free wine tasting. Since a sip is never enough, the wines are available for sale (open daily 11am-6pm; winter Tues.-Sun. 11am-6pm). Or duck into **Garo's Java House,** 376 E. Main St. (482-2267) for a bowl of coffee ($1) or a Zaffiro Smoothie (blackberries, blueberries, and OJ $2.25) and relax among the college students. The local art that decks the halls of this little house

OREGON

changes every month. Live jazz every Sun. night attracts a crowd (open Mon. and Wed.-Fri. 7am-8pm, Tues. 7am-noon, Sat. 8am-8pm, Sun. 8am-10pm).

If you have not yet perished from cultural overload then hang around Ashland. ("Give me excess of it, that, surfeiting, the appetite may sicken and so die"—*Twelfth Night*, I.i.2-3). Artists love to play to the town's characteristically enthused audiences, so there is always something to attend. The **Oregon Cabaret Theater**, P.O. Box 1149 (488-2902), at 1st and Hagarcline, stages light musicals in a pink former church with drinks and hors d'oeuvres (tickets $9-16; box office open Mon. and Wed.-Sat. 11am-6:30pm, Sun. 3-6:30pm). Small groups, such as **Actor's Theater of Ashland, Studio X,** and the theater department at **Southern Oregon State College** (552-6346) also raise the curtains sporadically throughout the summer. The travelling **Rogue Valley Symphony** and the **State Ballet of Oregon** perform at the Music Recital Hall at SOSC and, of course, in Lithia Park, when they are in town. In July and August, the ballet strikes the stage on Mondays at 7:30pm; the Ashland City Band (488-5340) fires itself up at the same time on Thursdays in Lithia Park. The **Palo Alto Chamber Orchestra** (482-4331) performances in late June ($13) are also a hit. Contact the Chamber of Commerce (see **Practical Information,** above) for a current schedule of events.

The **Schneider Museum of Art** (552-6245), 1250 Siskiyou Blvd. on the Southern Oregon State campus, is too small to house a permanent collection, but its travelling contemporary art exhibits are definitely worth a visit (free; open Tues.-Sat. 11am-5pm). The much-heralded **Pacific Northwest Museum of Natural History,** 1500 E. Main St. (488-1084), is a splendid if expensive diversion. Bringing together computers, fabulously detailed models, and hands-on activities, it educates and raises political issues about the ecology of Oregon ($6, ages 5-15 $4.50; open April-Oct. 9am-5pm, Nov.-March 10am-4pm).

If your muscles are demanding a little abuse after all this R&R, you can join the **Pacific Crest Trail** at Grouse Gap where it passes near Ashland. Take Exit 6 off I-5 and follow the signs along the Mt. Ashland Access Rd. At the top of the 9 mi. road is **Mount Ashland,** a small community-owned ski area on the north face of the mountain, with 23 runs. (Day ticket weekdays $20, children 9-12 and seniors $14; weekends $25, children and seniors $18; full rental $15; snowboard and boots $25; open Thanksgiving Day-April, daily 9am-4pm; night skiing Thurs.-Sat. 4-10pm.) Contact **Ski Ashland,** P.O. Box 220, Ashland 97520 (482-2897). For **snow conditions,** call 482-2754. Over 100 mi. of cross-country trails surround Mt. Ashland and are free to the public. **Bull Gap Trail,** which starts from the ski area's parking lot, is good for skiing and for biking after the snow has melted. It winds 2½ mi. down 1100 ft. to paved Tollman Creek Rd., 15.6 mi. south of where it crosses Siskiyou Blvd.

Join flocks of kids to get wet'n'wild on the double-flumed, 280-ft. **waterslide** at **Emigrant Lake Park** (776-7001; 10 slides for $4 plus a $3 entry fee), or just practice your freestyle in the man-made lake for free. Although it is only 6 mi. east of town on Rte. 66, the lake is in a different geological region from Ashland. The parched hills that surround it are part of the Great Basin, where cows graze freely and render the lake water unsuitable to drink. **Jackson Hot Springs** (482-3776), 2 mi. north of Ashland on Rte. 99, offers swimming in a pool filled by the hot springs ($3, under 14 $2; and 6pm-8pm $2, under 14 $1) and private hot mineral baths ($5, $8 per couple; both open daily June-Oct.; noon-4pm).

BARS AND CLUBS

The Black Sheep, 51 N. Main St. (482-6414), upstairs on the Plaza. Brew is in bulk: all pints are imperial (20 oz.) and cost $4. Food is fabulous. Scones ($3.50) are baked to order, fries are fresh cut, and herbs are grown in the British owner's backyard. Open daily 11am-1am; minors welcome (to eat) until 11pm.

Rogue Brewery and Public House, 31B Water St. (488-5061), down the outdoor steps to the left. About 10 homebrews on tap and fresh pizza with an herbed beer crust draw an unpretentious, older crowd. Play darts or chess in the smallish inside section, or troop past rows of kegs to the wide deck out back. Rogue and Siskiyou micros $3 a pint; slices of veggie or pepperoni pie $1.75. Live local music on Tuesdays. Open Mon. 4-10pm, Tues.-Thurs. 4-11pm, Fri. 4pm-midnight, Sat. 11:30am-midnight, Sun 11:30am-10pm.

Mark Antony Hotel, 212 E. Main St. (482-1721). You can depend on "The Mark" if the nightclub scene is your style. Small and spare, with booths and a prominent stage. Live acts every day but Sun. have a $3-5 cover and include Mon. night blues jams and comedy Tues. Weekend dancing. Daily happy hour brings microbrews and imports down from $3 to $2.25. Domestics always $1.75. Open Mon.-Thurs. 3pm-1am, Fri.-Sat. 3pm-2am, Sun. 3-9pm.

Cook's Tavern, 66 E. Main St. (482-4626) on the plaza. Gay and straight crowds have flocked to Cook's for 15 years for DJ-ed dancing Thurs. and Sat. nights. Friends hang out and play pool the rest of the week. Micro pints $3.25, domestic $2.25. Open Sun.-Wed. 4pm-2am, Thurs.-Sat. 4pm-2:30am.

▓ Medford

Once a mere satellite to Jacksonville, Medford lured the 19th-century railroad barons with $25,000 in under-the-table cash. Medford got the railroad lines and the county seat, while Jacksonville was left in the dust with outmoded horse-and-buggy transport. Today, Medford is a rapidly expanding but nondescript community. The visitor's center motto is "We Hug Visitors in Medford"—though the town is not known to embrace diversity, accept your hug, rest up in an inexpensive motel, and then slip off to nearby Jacksonville or Ashland for some real action.

PRACTICAL INFORMATION

Visitors Information: 1314 Center Dr., Suite E. (776-4012 or 800-231-2222), in the Harry and David Country Village, just off I-5 at exit 27. A plethora of free brochures. The volunteer staff is armed with fluorescent highlighters, the better to mark up the maps they will give you. Open daily June-Sept. 9am-6pm, Oct.-May Mon.-Sat. 9am-5pm.

Buses: Greyhound, 212 N. Bartlett St. (779-2103), at 5th St. To: Portland (8 per day; $32), Sacramento (7 per day; $41), and San Francisco (6 per day; $48). Open daily 5:30am-7:30pm. Call 800-231-2222 for departure times.

Public Transportation: Rogue Valley Transportation (RVTD), 3200 Crater Lake Ave. (779-2877). Connects Medford with Jacksonville, Ashland, and other cities. Buses leave from 200 S. Front St., at 10th St., Mon.-Fri. 4:30am-7pm, Sat. 8am-6pm. Service to Ashland every ½ hr., hourly service to all other destinations. Fare $1, seniors and under 18 pay ½ price, under 10 free.

Taxi: Metro Cab Co., 773-6665. 24hr.

Car Rental: Budget (773-7023 at the airport or 779-0488 at 3038 Biddle Rd.). Cars from $35 per day (on weekends), $37 per day mid-week, $7.50 per day extra for drivers under 25, unlimited mi. 5% AAA, AARP discounts. Must be at least 21 with credit card. Open Mon.-Fri. 7am-11pm.

Equipment Rental: McKenzie Outfitters, 130 E. 8th St. (773-5145 or 683-2038 for central office in Eugene), off Central Ave. 3-day backpack rental: internal frame ($15 per day, $25 per week) or external frame ($10 per day, $15 per week); crampons $5 per day. Open Mon.-Sat. 10am-6pm, Sun. 11am-4pm.

Public Library: 413 W. Main St. (776-7281), at Oakdale Ave. Open Mon.-Thurs. 9:30am-8pm, Fri.-Sat. 9:30am-5pm.

Crisis Intervention Services Helpline: 779-4357. 24hr.

Hospital: Providence Medfor Medical Center, 1111 Crater Lake Ave. (773-6611). Emergency care 24hr.

Emergency: 911. **Police and Fire:** City Hall, 411 W. 8th St. (770-4783), at 8th and Oakdale.

Post Office: 333 W. 8th (776-1326), at Holly St. Open Mon.-Fri. 8:30am-5:30pm. **General Delivery ZIP Code:** 97501-9998

Area Code: 541.

Medford straddles I-5 at its intersection with Rte. 238 in Southern Oregon, and is known as Main St. in town. Main St. intersects Central in the heart of the city and then proceeds west to Jacksonville. Grants Pass is 30 mi. northwest, Ashland 12 mi. to the southeast. Central Ave. and Riverside Ave., both one way, have a number of cheap motels. Find food near E. Main St., on the other side of I-5.

ACCOMMODATIONS AND CAMPING

The small motels that line Central Ave. and Riverside Ave. are depressingly similar, but the prices will cheer up the weary visitor from overpriced Ashland or Jacksonville. Motels along the highway are kept in better condition, but tend to charge $8-10 more. If you're willing to drive 30 or 40 mi. to one of the campgrounds listed below, you'll be camping in style. If not, check out Valley of the Rogue State Park, just 10 mi. away. Ask at the visitors center for directions

Capri Motel, 250 Barnett Rd. (773-7796), just off I-5 exit 27. Blue building with small, clean rooms. Bean shaped pool wedged in the middle. Quiet. A/C, phones, and cable. Hot pot with instant coffee in each room. (That's how you really know you've made it in life.) Singles $29. Doubles $35.

Cedar Lodge, 518 N. Riverside Ave. (773-7361 or 800-282-3419; fax 776-1033). Spacious rooms, with complimentary coffee and fruit served in the office in the morning. Spiffy new section in back has microwaves and fridges but cost an extra $8. Singles $40. Doubles $45. 15% AAA and senior discounts make prices even more reasonable.

Village Inn, 722 N. Riverside (773-5373). Clean, well-kept rooms with new red carpets. It's an old building but a good price, and there are roses in the parking lot to boot. Singles $32. Doubles $42.

North Fork Campground, 30 mi. northeast of Medford on Rte. 140. Take the Crater Lake Hwy. (Exit 30) north 5 mi. to 140 east in White City. Nine lovely sites sit snuggly in the woods at the west end of Fish Lake. No cost, no crowd, no drinking water, but you can fill up at any one of the pay campgrounds down the road.

Joseph H. Stewart State Park, (560-33340) 35 mi. northeast of Medford on Rte. 62. Follow signs to Crater Lake. An RV friendly behemoth of a campground on the bank of the Lost Creek Reservoir, a damned section of the Rogue. 199 well-groomed sites, 2 playgrounds, and a network of trails keep the campers happy; showers keep them clean. Open May-Sept. Tents $12, electric $13, $2 more on Fri. and Sat.

FOOD

For a rapidly expanding city, Medford has surprisingly few attractive eating options. Other than the "downtown deli" concept, there aren't many other dominant paradigms for cuisine in Medford. Locals make the 12 mi. drive to Ashland when they want to eat something special. **Food 4 Less,** (779-0171) on Biddle Rd. near I-5 exit 30, has mass quantities of every food imaginable (stacked warehouse style) and sells it for cheap (open 24 hrs.).

Squeeze-Inn Sandwich Shop, 616 Crater Lake Ave. (772-7489), in the second strip of Shamrock Square. Not downtown, so you know the crowd came on purpose. Cheap deli-style sandwiches ($4 whole, $2 half) served deli-style make it a haven for salami and cheese lovers. There's often a short line around lunch time, but the Squeeze-Inn is not as cramped as its name would imply. Light and airy with an amiable staff and a high ratio of plants to people. Don't miss the fresh cookies ($1). Open Mon.-Sat. 10am-5pm.

C.K. Tiffins, 226 E. Main St. (779-0480). "Naturally good" health food and pastries served cafeteria-style space that just barely resembles the alley-way it once was. Great place to bring your newspaper for breakfast ($2-3.50). Downtown business crowds partake of $5 Daily lunch specials that run the lowfat gamut from potato cakes and grilled chicken to Greek spinach and artichoke pasta. The albacore tuna burger ($4.50) will rock your world. No red meat. Open Mon.-Fri. 7am-3pm.

Las Margaritas, 12 N. Riverside (779-7628). Feast on large portions of Mexican food amid Mediterranean murals and Corona beer flags. Burritos range in price from the burrito vallarta ($8.50) down to the refried bean burrito ($2.50). Enchiladas come large ($4) and small ($2.50). One of the few decent dinner places in town, serving nightly specials like Tuesday's tasty chicken carnitas ($7.50), and festive cocktails like the Singapore Sling ($3.50). Open Sun.-Tues. 11am-10pm, Fri.-Sat. 11am-11pm.

Deli Down, 406 E. Main St. (772-4520), in the Main St. Market downstairs from Country Things. This bustling, underground deli constructs sandwiches from your blueprint ($4.75). The full veggie sandwich comes with soup, salad, or pasta ($4). All-you-can-eat hot pasta bar ($4.25) comes with fantastic garlic bread and 2 choices of homemade noodles and sauce. Open Mon.-Fri. 10am-4pm.

SIGHTS AND ACTIVITIES

Medford's location on I-5 between Grants Pass and Ashland makes it the hub of southern Oregon. Many visitors use it as a gateway to the Shakespeare festival or Jacksonville, but the town has little appeal on its own. If you didn't get enough packaged history in Jacksonville, try the **Medford Railroad Park** (770-4586), on Berrydale Ave. by the fire station between I-5 and Table Rock Rd. It offers Medford's closest brush with Disneyworld; for no charge, you can chug around in cars pulled by a miniature steam engine. (Open April-Oct. 2nd and 4th Sun. each month, 11am-3pm). More glimpses of the past can be had at the **South Oregon History Center,** 106 N. Central Ave. (773-6536), at 6th St., where a new exhibit lets you walk through mine shafts and wooden tree cut-outs from 1850 to the present ($3, seniors and children 6-12 $2; open Mon.-Fri. 9am-5pm, Sat. noon-5pm).

In April, the **Pear Blossom Festival,** P.O. Box 339 (776-0064), lures runners to its 10km race. Other activities include a street fair in Alba Park, a band festival near the armory on S. Pacific Hwy, a golf tournament and, of course, a parade. A more recent addition to the Medford social calendar is the **Medford Jazz Jubilee** (770-6972), held for three days in early October. Bands come from across the nation to blow their horns in Medford, giving over 100 performances in venues all over town. The Flipper contest and the Big Band Dance are a smash hit, Medford style ($15-20 per day, ages 18 and under $5).

Harry and David's Original Country Store, 1314 Center Dr. Suite A (776-2277), in Harry and David's Country Village at exit 27 of I-5, is the fruit and nut capital of the known universe. This L.L. Bean of the vegetable world sells produce, nuts, candies, and gift items (open Mon.-Sat. 11am-5pm, Sun. 10am-6pm). Next door is the most prolific rose grower in the world, **Jackson & Perkins,** 1310 Center Dr., Suite J (776-2388). Get your hands on a "ready-plant bare root" of a rose bush for your garden-happy grandma ($13; open Mon.-Thurs 9am-8pm, Fri.-Sun. 9am-6pm, winter Mon.-Sat. 9am-7pm and Sun. 10am-6pm). Second hand shoppers will be delighted by the **Value Village** in Bear Creak Plaza on Biddle Rd.

▓ Jacksonville

The biggest of Oregon's gold boomtowns, Jacksonville played the role of rich and rowdy frontier outpost with appropriate licentious zeal. But the gold dwindled, the railroad and stagecoach lines took Jacksonville off their routes, and, in the final *coup de (dis)grâce,* the city lost the county seat to nearby Medford. On the brink of oblivion, Jacksonville was revitalized by nostalgia. The town was rehabilitated in the 50s and today, it is the only town in Oregon designated a "National Historic Landmark City" by the National Park Service. A stroll through downtown passes balustraded, century-old buildings: the United States Hotel, the Methodist-Episcopal Church, the old courthouse, and others.

Practical Information To reach Jacksonville (or "J-ville," as residents affectionately call it), take Rte. 238, also called the Jacksonville Hwy., southwest from Medford or catch the #30 bus at 200 S. Front St. at 10th in Medford (**Rogue Valley Transpor-**

OREGON

tation runs buses out of Medford Mon.-Fri. 4:30am-7pm, Sat. 8am-6pm. Fare $1, seniors and under 18 ½price, under 10 free. See **Medford: Practical Information,** p. 471). Jacksonville can be reached by bus from Ashland only via Medford. Rte. 238 comes into town as 5th St. and hangs a right on California.

Drop by the **visitors center** in the old railway station at 185 N. Oregon St. (899-8118), at C St., where you will be vigorously supplied with directions and pamphlets (open daily 10am-4pm). The **post office** (899-1563) is next door at 175 N. Oregon St. (open Mon.-Fri. 8:30am-5pm; **General Delivery ZIP Code:** 97530-9999). The **area code** is 541.

Accommodations
A bed in Jacksonville is decidedly pricey. **The Stage Lodge,** 830 N. 5th St. (899-3953 or 800-253-8254), though charming and less expensive than the $100 luxury B&Bs in town, is still nowhere near budget. The recently built Lodge captures the Jacksonville mood with fine furniture and ornate exterior trim. Rooms are spacious and luxuriantly decorated. Rates start at $65, but drop $12 in the winter.

A number of campgrounds lie 25-30 mi. southwest of Jacksonville in the **Red Butte Wilderness.** Take Rte. 238 8 mi. west to Ruch and turn left on Applegate Rd. The **Star Ranger Station,** 6941 Upper Applegate Rd. (899-1812), about 10 mi. past the turn, can fill you in on specific fees and the amenities, but the campgrounds are another 7-12 mi. farther. **Latagawa Cove** requires a short hike and the fore-thought to bring water, but it's free and right on the edge of Applegate Lake.

Food
For a classy but casual dining experience, head for the **Bella Union,** 170 W. California St. (899-1770). This revamped saloon serves American favorites like pizza, pasta, and chicken, at relatively high prices ($9-15), but the opportunity to dine beneath a canopy of vines out back is worth the extra buck. A fine array of sandwiches ($6-8) come with salad, and appetizers include scrumptious chorizo quesadillas ($5.50). The attached Bella Union **saloon** hosts live bands Thursday through Saturday nights (open Mon.-Fri. 11:30am-10pm, Sat. 11am-10pm, Sun. 10am-10pm). A cheaper and even more casual dining experience can be had at **The Mustard Seed,** 130 N. 5th St. (899-1958), a tiny café that made it past the turn of the century but got stuck in the 50s. Cushy red stools lined up at the speckled counter are ideal spots for sipping milk shakes made for two ($2.45). Veggie burgers ($3.50) may suit your fancy if the ½lb. bacon cheeseburger ($3.25) isn't your style. Open Mon.-Fri. 7am-6pm, Sat.-Sun. 8am-5pm. Closed at 3pm in winter.

Sights and Events
A walk down California St. is an instant flashback to the 19th century. The Beekman Bank, at the corner of 3rd and California, has not been touched since Cornelius Beekman, the town's most prominent figure, died in 1915. Down the street you can meet his "family" at the **Beekman House** (773-6536), on the corner of Laurelwood St. and California St., where hosts, in character and costume, will be quite charmed, my dear, to guide you through the residence. The delightful interactive tour lasts 35 minutes ($3, ages 6-12 $2; open Memorial Day-Labor Day 1-5pm). If you see a well-dressed 19th-century gentleman in the middle of the street, it isn't a history-induced hallucination; "Mr. Beekman" often gets the urge to wander the streets of Jacksonville.

The **Jacksonville Museum** (773-6536) in the Old County Courthouse at 206 N. 5th St., is a treasure trove of history. As you explore the museum's fantastic collection of artifacts and historical photographs, leave the kids locked up in the jail next door (now the **Children's Museum**). Delightful, hands-on exhibits make it hard to obey the "no running" rule. It's hard to resist an antique dentist's chair or a life-size set of Lincoln Logs. The kids may head straight for the exhibit on **Bozo the Clown,** an authentic Jacksonville native (born 1892). Each museum charges $3 ($2 for seniors and children 6-12) and both are open in summer daily 10am-5pm; in winter they are closed Monday. **Stan the Trolley Man** (535-5617), a community legend, runs a 50-minute trolley-tour, which provides an excellent overview of the town's attractions

Eves in the Trees

If you're in the market for a decidedly unusual night's stay, head for **Out 'n' About,** a not-quite B&B in the town of Takilma, OR. The remnants of a commune built in the trees, the sturdy arboreal dwellings did not receive the county stamp of approval. The reticent county authorities may not have trusted the former community, which celebrated its heyday in the 70s. Marijuana busts in the early 80s cast enough bad publicity on the area to put an end to the hippy utopia. Though they once held 66 people, three dogs and a cat, the tree houses were not sanctioned as official pay accommodations. There is hope, however. If you buy a $70-125 T-shirt and take an oath to "protect the treehouses and the trees," you will be made an official **Tree Musketeer.** An invitation to spend the night will undoubtedly follow suit. Call 541-592-2208 or 800-200-5484 for information and directions.

and a chance to sit down ($4, under 12 $2; runs daily Memorial Day-Labor Day from 3rd and California St. 10am-4pm on the hr.).

Jacksonville is the place to be every summer (mid-June to early Sept.) when it is taken over by the **Peter Britt Music Festivals,** P.O. Box 1124, Medford 97501 (773-6077 or 800-882-7488; fax 503-776-3712), named after the pioneer photographer whose hillside estate is the site of the fest. Now in its 34th year, the festivals feature jazz, classical, folk, country, and pop acts, as well as dance theater, and musicals. 1996 saw the Oak Ridge Boys, Nancy Griffith, and Johnny Cash perform for the crowded outdoor amphitheater (tickets for single events $10-$30, 12 and under $6-10; you can order tickets early in May; on performance days, tickets are available at the Main Britt Pavilion at 1st and Fir St. in Jacksonville; advance purchase discounts available for groups of 15 or more; $2 senior discounts for classical events). Many people bring picnic dinners to eat as they watch.

■ Grants Pass

Workers building a road through the Oregon mountains in 1863 were so overjoyed by the news of General Ulysses Grant's victory at Vicksburg that they named the town after the burly President-to-be. Grants Pass is a base to discover the Rogue River Valley and the Illinois Valley regions. The city itself sprawls awkwardly to fill the hot, flat valley with espresso stands, auto parts stores, and parking lots. Lofty mountains beckon from just beyond the city limits: heed their call.

PRACTICAL INFORMATION AND ORIENTATION

Visitors Information: Visitor and Convention Bureau, 1501 NE 6th St. (476-7717 or 800-547-5927), at 6th and Midland. Loads of brochures covering all of Josephine County. Air conditioning and a list of 50 things to do in Grants Pass. Open Mon.-Fri. 8am-5pm, Sat.-Sun. 9am-5pm; winter closed weekends.

Buses: Greyhound, 460 NE Agness Ave. (476-4513), at the east end of town. To: Portland (5 per day; $34), Sacramento (4 per day; $42), and San Francisco (4 per day; $48). A few storage lockers (75¢ per 24hr.). Open Mon.-Fri. 6:30am-6:30pm, Sat. 6:30am-3:30pm; winter closed Sat. at noon. Closed holidays.

Taxi: Grants Pass Cab (476-6444). 24hr.

Car Rental: Discount Rent-a-Car, 1470 NE 7th St. (471-6411). Cars from $27 per day and unlimited mileage. Open Mon.-Fri. 7:30am-5:30pm.

Laundromat: MayBelle's Washtub, 306 SE I St. (471-1317), at 8th St. Wash 75¢, 10-min. dry 25¢. Open Mon.-Fri. 7am-9pm, Sat.-Sun. 8am-8pm.

Crisis Hotline: 479-4357. 24hr. Helpline referral services.

Seniors' Information: Senior Community Center, 317 NW B St. (474-5440). **Senior Citizen Helpline** (479-4357). 24hr.

Information for Travelers with Disabilities: Independent Abilities Center, 290 NE C St. (479-4275). Open Mon.-Thurs. 9am-3pm, Fri. 9am-1pm.

OREGON

Hospital: Riverside City Medical Clinic, 1215 NE 7th St., Suite C (476-2804). Open Mon.-Fri. 9am-7pm, Sat. 9am-3pm.
Emergency: 911. **Police:** Justice Building at 101 NW A St. (474-6370) at 6th St. **Josephine County Sheriff:** 474-5123. **Oregon State Police:** 474-3174.
Post Office: 132 NW 6th St. (479-7526). Open Mon.-Fri. 9am-5pm. **General Delivery ZIP Code:** 97526.
Area Code: 541.

I-5 curves around the northeast edge of Grants Pass on its way north to Portland. The Rogue River lies just south of the old downtown area which is linked to both northbound Exit 58 off the highway by 7th St., and Sixth St., the main southbound artery. Sixth St. is the divider between streets labeled East and West, and the railroad tracks (between G and F St.) divide North and South addresses. U.S. 199 runs along the Rogue River before making the 30-mi. trip south to Cave Junction.

ACCOMMODATIONS AND CAMPING

Grants Pass supports one of every pricey franchise motel you've ever seen. The one-of-a-kind cheapo motels are farther back from the interstate on 6th near A St. Since Grants Pass is a favorite highway stop, rooms fill up quickly, especially on weekends and in August, when rates hit their peak. A few convenient campgrounds provide a pleasant alternative, but even they are hardly cheap.

Fordson Home Hostel (HI-AYH), 250 Robinson Rd., Cave Junction 97523 (592-3203), 37 mi. southwest of Grants Pass on U.S. 199. Accessible only by car; call for directions. This rambling old house is the headquarters of Nowhere, but you won't be lonely. Companions include at least 20 antique tractors, a saw mill, a few other hostel guests, and the eccentric owner who regularly gives tours of his 20 acres. Comfortable accommodations (2 double beds and a pull-out couch). Free bicycle loans. 33% discounted admission to the Oregon Caves National Monument. Camping available. $8, nonmembers $10.

Hawk's Inn, 1464 NW 6th St. (497-4057), across the street from the visitors center. The building is old, but the sparkling pool out front is a blessed sight and it's the nicest $30 room you'll find in summer. Singles $30, doubles $45.

Knight's Inn Motel, 104 SE 7th St. (479-5595 or 800-826-6835), by the railroad tracks. Huge rooms are clean and freshly carpeted. Furniture is well aged. Cable TV (plus HBO), A/C, and kitschy knight shields on the railings. One person $38, two people $42. Prices drop $12-20 in winter. Reservations advised.

Valley of the Rogues State Park, (582-1118), 12 mi. east of Grant's pass, off I-5 Exit 45B. Separate loops for tents ($15), electric ($17), and full hookups ($18) spread out along a mile-long stretch between the highway and river. Happy campers enjoy the thick green grass and the shade. Hot showers and flush toilets.

River RV Park, 2956 Rogue River Hwy. (479-0046 or 800-677-8857), 2 mi. south on Rte. 99. On the shady bank of the Rogue River. Welcome to suburbia. This manicured RV haven has hot showers, free cable hookups, and flowers in the bathrooms. 47 sites with hookup $20; 2 tent sites $16.

Schroeder Campgrounds, 605 Schroeder Ln. (474-5285), run by the county 4 mi. south of town; take U.S. 199 southwest, angle right on Redwood Ave., turn right onto Willow Ln., then follow the signs 1 mi. to the campground. Flat grassy field shaded by an awkward variety of planted trees. A trail at the far right corner leads to a good swimming spot on the Rogue. Playground. Showers 25¢. Sites $12, with hookups $17.

FOOD

Dining in Grants Pass is, if not inspiring, at least better than you'd expect. For groceries, try the **Safeway,** 115 SE 7th at G St. (479-4276; open daily 6am-midnight). **The Growers' Market** (476-5375) on C St. between 4th and 5th is the largest open-air market in the state, vending everything a produce-lover could imagine (open Tues. 4-9pm, and Sat. 9am-1pm).

OREGON

The Square Nail, 2185 Rogue River Hwy. (479-5132). A down-home local favorite for low prices and large portions. Check the special board for the bargain of the moment, or stick with Hawaiian Chicken, soup, salad, rice pilaf, and dessert, all for $5.75. Lunches hover around $4. Good diner breakfasts. Open Sun.-Mon. and Thurs. 5am-8pm, Tues.-Wed. 5am-3pm, Fri.-Sat. 5am-9pm.

Matsukaze, 1675 NE 7th St. (479-2961). Japanese food Americans will recognize in a simple and tasteful setting. Bonding opportunities in booths sunk into the floor. Daily lunch specials are $3.75-4.75—try the vegetable Tempura. California rolls (4 for $3.75) with crab and avocado are an ever-tasty item. Light dinners $5-6, full entrees like the specially spiced Kalbi Ribs $8-13. Open Mon.-Fri. 11am-2pm; also open Mon.-Thurs. 5-9pm and Fri.-Sat. 5-9:30pm; winter closed ½hr. earlier.

Pongsri's, 1571 NE 6th St. (479-1345). Sunlight struggles in through the hanging plants and trellises to illuminate a lengthy menu. 21 vegetarian dishes are the cheapest of the ($6.50-9) entrees. The spring rolls are greasy, but shirt-licking good (4 for $4.95). Lunch special $4. Open Tues.-Sun. 11am-3pm and 5-9pm.

SIGHTS AND OUTDOORS

The Rogue River is Grant's Pass' greatest attraction. One of the few federally protected rivers designated as a "Wild and Scenic River," you can enjoy it by raft, jetboat, mail boat, or simply by fishing or walking along its banks. If you fish, you'll be in good company: Zane Grey and Clark Gable once roamed the Rogue River with tackle and bait. Enterprising (and affluent) souls can hop on a two-hour scenic tour given by **Hellgate Excursions, Inc.** (479-7204; $22, ages 4-11 $12). Those in search of longer trips can try four-hour "Cruise and brunch" ($32, ages 4-11 $19) or the two-hour "Whitewater adventure" ($39, ages 4-11 $25) which run May-Sept. If you want to paddle the river yourself, head west off I-5 Exit 61 toward Merlin and Galice where the outfitting companies cluster. A 35-mi. stretch of class III and IV rapids starting just north of Galice is the whitest water on the rogue. It's a restricted area; to get on it, you have to go with guides and pay about $55 per person. Try **Rogue River Raft Trips,** 8500 Galice Rd. (476-3825 or 800-826-1963) in Merlin, for a full day trip ($55) with the best guides and equipment. **Orange Torpedo Trips,** 209 Merlin Rd. (479-5061 or 800-635-2925), runs more adventurous guided tours down the river in inflatable orange kayaks for a reasonable price (full day $50 per person, ½ day $35 per person; under 12 15% off).

While **Gold Hill** (20 mi. south on I-5) is famous for the large cave of bat guano kept under constant watch by local police, it also houses the **Oregon Vortex/House of Mystery,** 4303 Sardine Creek Rd. (855-1543), follow signs 5 mi. east from Exit 40. Here, balls roll uphill, pendulums hang at an angle, and people seem to vary in height depending on where they stand. The bizarre phenomena are supposedly due to a local perturbation of the earth's magnetic field. The owners apologize for any crude imitations of this house that tourists may have seen across the country, and assure visitors that this is the *real* thing. Decide for yourself. ($6, ages 5-11 $4.50; 50¢ off each ticket for groups of 15 or more; open June-Aug. daily 9am-6pm, March-May and Sept.-Oct. 9am-4:30pm.)

The **Oregon Caves National Monument** (592-3400) can be reached by heading 30 mi. south along U.S. 199 to Cave Junction, and then following Rte. 46 as it slowly winds east for 20 mi. Here in the belly of the ancient Siskiyous, acidic waters carved out limestone later compressed into marble. Dissolved and redeposited, the limestone fills cavernous chambers with exotic formations, the slow growth of which is nurtured by the constant 41°F (5°C) climate. Bring a jacket. If you've seen stalactites and flow-stones before, you may want to bypass this large but unspectacular series of caverns. Tours last 90 minutes and are fairly strenuous, involving some ducking and twisting and 500 stairs; they are conducted in groups of 16 ($6, ages 6-11 $3.75, under 6 $3; tours given May-mid.-Sept. daily 8am-7pm; mid-Sept.-mid.-Oct. 8:30am-5pm; mid-Oct. to April at 9:30, 11:30am, and 1, 2:30, and 4pm). Children must be over 42 in. (107cm) tall and pass an ability test to take a tour.

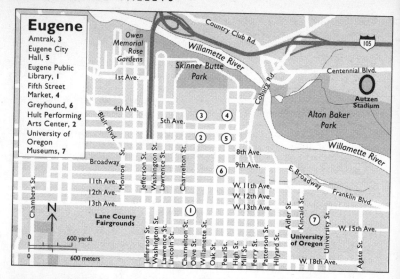

Eugene

Amtrak, 3
Eugene City Hall, 5
Eugene Public Library, 1
Fifth Street Market, 4
Greyhound, 6
Hult Performing Arts Center, 2
University of Oregon Museums, 7

■ Eugene

Eugene is a blender set to "liquefy," with rednecks wearing hunting boots, students riding mountain bikes, former Deadheads eating organically-grown food and searching for new purpose, outfitters making a killing off tourists, and amateur and elite runners dodging each other on the streets. Tolerance defines Oregon's second-largest city, which sits astride the Willamette River and between the Siuslaw and Willamette National Forests. It is home to the University of Oregon (U of O).

Eugene is trying hard to shake a reputation for being stuck in the 70s, but it doesn't seem to know where to go next. Unregulated diversity rules the city. Eugene is teeming with art museums, pizza joints, and all the other trappings of a college town. Nevertheless, city slickers can shop and dine in the downtown pedestrian mall or **Fifth St. Market** or head to **WOW Hall** for an evening of entertainment. Outdoor types can raft the river, bike and run on its banks, or hike in one of the large parks near the city.

The fleet of foot and free of spirit have dubbed Eugene the "running capital of the universe." Only in this city could the annual **Bach Festival,** in late June, be accompanied by the "Bach Run," a 5km dash through the city's downtown area. The Nike running shoe company, founded in Eugene, sponsors the event, which culminates in a performance of the so-called "Sports Cantata" (based on Bach's "*Weinen, Klagen, Laufen,*" or "Weeping, Lamenting, Running").

PRACTICAL INFORMATION AND ORIENTATION

Visitors Information: Eugene-Springfield Convention and Visitors Bureau, 115 W. 8th, but the door is on Olive St. (484-5307; outside OR 800-547-5445). **Maps** and brochures line this office staffed by knowledgeable people and equipped with a courtesy phone. Open Mon.-Fri. 8:30am-5pm, Sat.-Sun. 10am-4pm; Sept.-April Mon.-Sat. 8:30am-5pm, closed Sun. **Willamette National Forest,** 211 E. 7th Ave. (465-6522) in the federal building. If you make it past the metal detectors, you can ask about the campgrounds, recreational areas, and wilderness areas in the National Forest or invest in a **forest map** ($3). Open Mon.-Fri. 8am-4:30pm. **University of Oregon Switchboard,** in Oregon Hall at 1585 E. 13th Ave. (346-3111). Referral for almost anything—rides, housing, emergency services. Open Mon.-Fri. 7am-6pm.

Trains: Amtrak, 433 Willamette St. (800-872-7245), at 4th St. To: Seattle (2 per day; $44), Portland (2 per day; $20), Emeryville (1 per day; $109, with service to San Francisco). 15% discount for seniors and people with disabilities. No lockers, but you can check bags ($1.50 each per 24hr.).

Buses: Greyhound, 987 Pearl St. (344-6265 or 800-231-2222) at 9th St. To: Seattle ($32), San Francisco ($71), Portland ($15). Open daily 6am-10pm. Storage lockers $1 per day. **Green Tortoise** (937-3603), drop-off and pick-up at 14th and Kincaid. To: San Francisco ($39), Portland ($10), and Seattle ($25). Reservations required. Open daily 8am-8pm.

Public Transportation: Lane Transit District (LTD) (687-5555), at 10th and Willamette St. Provides bus service throughout Eugene. Pick up a **map** and timetables at the Convention and Visitors Bureau, or the LTD Service Center. All routes are wheelchair-accessible. Fares 80¢, 50¢ Mon.-Fri. after 7pm and Sat.-Sun.; 40¢ seniors and children. Main route service Mon.-Fri. 5am-11:30pm, Sat. 7:30am-11:30pm, Sun. 8:30am-8:30pm.

Ride Board: Erb Memorial Union (EMU) Basement, University of Oregon. One block east of Kincaid, on the pedestrian section of 13th Street in the middle of campus. Housing bulletin board, too (toward the back). Open Mon.-Thurs. 7am-7pm, Fri. 7am-5pm.

Taxi: Yellow Cab (746-1234). 24 hr.

Car Rental: Enterprise Rent-a-Car, 810 W. 6th St. (683-0874). $30 per day; unlimited mileage. 10% county tax. Must be 21. Cash rentals accepted. Open Mon.-Fri. 7:30am-6pm, Sat. 9am-noon.

AAA Office, 983 Willagillespie Rd. (484-0661 or 800-RENTACAR/736-8222, 800-736-8222), near Valley River Center Mall, 2 mi. north of the Univeristy of Oregon campus. Only members get goodies like maps. Open Mon.-Fri. 8am-5pm.

Laundromat: Club Wash, 595 E. 13th St. (431-1039), at Patterson. Open daily 7am-1am. Wash 75¢, 10min. dry 25¢.

Bike Rental: Paul's Bicycle Way of Life, 152 W. 5th Ave. (344-4105). Friendly staff offers city/mountain bikes for $20 per day, $8 for 4hr., $2 per additional hr. Tandems $30 per day, $12 per ½day. Major credit card or $100 deposit required. Open Mon.-Fri. 9am-7pm, Sat.-Sun. 10am-5pm. **Pedal Power,** 535 High St. (687-1775), downtown. 21-speeds $5 per hr., $20 per day. Off-road mountain bikes $25 for 4hr., $40 per day. Tandems $10 per hr., $50 per day. Open Mon.-Fri. 9am-7pm, Sat. 9am-6pm, Sun. 10am-5pm.

Crisis Line: White Bird Clinic, 341 E. 12th Ave. (800-422-7558). Free crisis counseling and low-cost medical care. Open Mon.-Fri. 8am-5pm. 24hr. crisis hotline.

Rape Crisis: Sexual Assault Support Services, 630 Lincoln St. (485-6700). Open Mon.-Fri. 8:30am-5pm. Hotline and counselling service 24hr.

Emergency: 911. **Police/Fire:** 777 Pearl St. (687-5111), Room 107 at City Hall.

Post Office: Main office at 520 Williamette (341-3611), at 5th. Open Mon.-Fri. 8:30am-5:30pm, Sat. 10am-2pm. **General Delivery ZIP Code:** 97401-9999.

Area Code: 541.

Eugene is 111 mi. south of Portland on the I-5 corridor, just east of the town of **Springfield.** The **University of Oregon** campus lies in the southeastern corner of Eugene, bordered on the north by Franklin Blvd., which runs from the city center to I-5. First Ave. runs alongside the winding Willamette River. **Willamette Ave.,** Eugene's main drag, intersects the river, dividing the city into east and west Willamette. It is interrupted by the pedestrian mall on 7th, 8th, and Broadway downtown. The city is a motorist's nightmare of one way streets, and free parking is virtually nonexistent in the downtown area. The most convenient way to get around town is by bike—the roads are flat and there are plenty of bike paths.

Most park hours are officially 6am-11pm, and while the University of Oregon has recently attempted to increase safety with ingenious schemes like the "yellow duck path" signifying better lit areas, locals still maintain that lone women should avoid the university campus at night. Whittaker, the area around Blair Blvd. near 6th St., is another place to be wary of.

ACCOMMODATIONS

Eugene's cheapest motels are on E. Broadway and W. 7th St. and tend toward the seedy side. Make reservations early; motels are packed on big football weekends. The closest legal camping is 7 mi. away, but people have been known to camp by the river (especially in the wild and woolly northeastern side, near Springfield). Your best bet may be to camp in the surrounding **Willamette National Forest** or the meadow at Lost Valley and make day trips into Eugene.

Lost Valley Educational Center (HI-AYH), 81868 Lost Valley Lane, Dexter 97431 (937-3351). Take Rte. 58 east for 9 mi. toward Oakridge, turn right on S. Rattle-snake Rd., turn right after 4 mi. onto Lost Valley Lane. Follow Lost Valley Ln. for 1 mi. to the gravel driveway. Or, take bus #92 from Eugene to Dexter and call to arrange pick-up. The hostel accommodations are rustic and a little cramped, but there's no lockout, no curfew and you're welcome to camp in the meadow. Write or call for info about the ongoing workshops on such subjects as sustainable living and Siberian shamanism. Arrive between 5-9pm. Phenomenal organic dinner served Mon.-Fri. ($6). 12 beds and a kitchen. Members $9, non-members $10. Approximately 7 camping spaces at $6 per person. Reservations required.

Downtown Motel, 361 W. 7th Ave. (345-8739 or 800-648-4366). Spacious and beautiful rooms under a green terra-cotta roof. Deco-tile and plaster walls enhance the architecture. The Downtown is one of the few motels in the area that doesn't jack up prices during the summer season, so make reservations early (credit card required). Cable TV, A/C, and free coffee in the morning. Singles $33. Doubles $46. Prices include tax.

Executive House Inn, 1040 W. 6th Ave. (683-4000). All rooms are not created equal; you're lucky if you get one with new carpet or a fridge (no extra charge). Rooms in back are cooled by fans instead of A/C and aren't quite as nice as the front. Proximity to country fairground causes prices to rise $5-10 when there are events. TV, phones, and showers. Singles $30. Doubles $36. Prices include tax.

66 Motel, 755 E. Broadway (342-5041), convenient to the interstate. Its lifeless blue exterior hides clean and colorful rooms. The bathrooms are old, the TVs are new, and the train tracks are inches away. Pets allowed. Cable, A/C, and phones (with $20 deposit). Checks not accepted. Singles $33. Doubles $41.

CAMPING

Unfortunately, KOAs (Kampgrounds of America) and RV-only parks monopolize the camping scene around Eugene; Lost Valley (see **Accommodations,** above) is the closest pleasant spot. Farther east on Rte. 58 and 126, the immense **Willamette National Forest** is packed with forested campsites ($3-16). You can gather info from the ranger station (see **Practical Information,** above) first, but ample signs make things easy to find. Around the beautiful, mysterious **Black Canyon** campground 28 mi. east of Eugene on Hwy. 58 ($8-16), a swamp gives the tree bark and ferns an eerie phosphorescence.

Eugene Mobile Village, 4750 Franklin Blvd. (747-2257). 3 mi. from downtown Eugene. RV-only park where the few young trees look lost amid the gravel. 30 spaces, showers. $17 per night for 2 with full hookup; $1 per additional person, 50¢ per dog. Reserve 3 nights ahead in summer.

Sherwood Forest Campground KOA, I-5 Exit 182 (895-4110 or 800-KOA-4110/562-4110), 9 mi. south of Eugene. An RV town where Maid Marian Lane is reserved for tents. The big clean pool, showers, and laundry facilities may explain the high prices. Tents ($17) and RVs ($18, with full hookup $21).

Pine Meadows, (942-8657), go east 3½ mi. off Exit 174, turn left on Cottage Grove Reservoir Rd., and go 2 mi. On the marshy shore of the lake. Plenty of RV and jet ski traffic. Showers, shade, and 92 sites ($12).

Shwarz Park (942-1418), 4 mi. east off Exit 174 just below the dam of swimmable Dorena Lake. Flat and quiet, with dry yellow grass and pine trees. Showers, flush toilets and drinking water. The better sites (all $10) are toward the back.

FOOD

Cheap ethnic food and hamburger joints are tough to find in this down-to-earth "track city." Outdoor café dining and veggi-centric menus are common all over. The downtown area specializes in trendy, gourmet food; the university hang-out zone at 13th St. and Kincaid has more grab-and-go options, and regular grocery stores circle the city. The leaf and twig crowd does its shopping at **Sundance Natural Foods,** 748 E. 24th Ave. (343-9142), at 24th and Hilyard. You can create a salad for $3.89 per pound (open daily 7am-11pm). Right in town, **Kiva,** 125 W. 11th (342-8666), supplies a smaller array of organic produce and natural foods (open Mon.-Sat. 9am-8pm, Sun. 10am-5pm). For American cheese singles and ground beef, head to the **Safeway,** 145 18th St. at Oak (485-3664; open daily 6am-2am).

Keystone Café, 395 W. 5th St. (342-2075). Cool and calm with a creatively accommodating menu and a strong local following, the Keystone is a true taste of Eugene. Their incredible food is mostly meatless, some of it wheatless; all bread is home-baked and organic. A small kitchen makes for slow service, but one mouthful of their famous plate-sized pancakes ($2.25, fruit or seeds on top 75¢) and all will be forgiven. Vegetarian burgers, sandwiches, and chili served after 11am, breakfast served all day. Open daily 7am-3pm.

Café Navarro, 454 Willamette St. (344-0943). The mood is casual but the Caribbean and Latin cuisine is served with a gourmet flare. Vegetarian and seafood specialties complement a selection of dishes from Jamaica, Ethiopia, and Peru. Have Pozole ($7.50), or another lunch for only $5-6.50. Open Tues.-Fri. 11am-2pm and 5-9:30pm. Also breakfast Sat.-Sun. 9am-2pm.

New Day Bakery, 345 Van Buren St. (345-1695), at the corner of 3rd and Blair. Far enough from downtown and the university that you won't end up there by accident, but definitely worth the trip. Heaps of goodies like raspberry hazelnut rolls fill the case in this quiet, sunlit café. Four kinds of soup ($2.75) that are perfect with fresh bread. Day old bread is 75¢. Open Mon.-Sat. 5am-7pm, Sun. 5am-3pm.

West Bros. Bar-B-Que, 844 Olive St. (345-8489). Grab a seat in the polished interior and relax with a beer ($3 per pint) from their micro-brewery downstairs. B-B-Q recipes collected on a journey across the USA; menu items like Memphis "dry-rubbed" baby-backs and blown-up photos tell the tale. Except for the $1.50 cheese grits, it's not cheap. Lunch is $6-11 and dinner is $7-14. Open Sun.-Thurs. 11:30am-9:30pm, Fri.-Sat. 11:30am-10pm. Delivery available.

Sy's Pizza, 1211 Alder St. (686-9598), off 13th. Where students go for good greasy pizza by the slice ($1.70, deep dish Sicilian $1.85). This nifty little joint would only be called a hole-in-the-wall with the utmost affection. Whole pizzas $9-25. Open Mon.-Sat. 11:30am-midnight, Sun. 3:30pm-midnight.

Zenon Café, 898 Pearl St. (343-3005). If you have one night to splurge, this is the place to do it. The Mediterranean and Northwest regional food is light and flavorful. The attitude chic. Small plates are a trusty $6.25 while entrees climb to a peak of $15.75 for dinner. If for nothing else, though, come for dessert ($4); the array is astounding and the quality superb. Open Mon.-Thurs. 8am-11pm, Fri.-Sat. 8am-midnight, Sun 10:00am-11pm.

Glenwood Campus Café, 1340 Alder (687-0355), off 13th St. Locals relax on the brick patio, sipping their coffee (drinks only, 3-6am) and trying new tofu creations. The Blue Corn Waffles ($2.70) and Tomato Cheese Soup ($1.35/2.35) rival each other in local fame, and the Eggs Benedict ($5.35) is captioned "please forgive us if we sell out." Dinners $4.50-6. Only *closed* Sun. 10pm-Mon. 7am.

China Blue, 879 E. 13th Ave. (343-2832), upstairs. Sizable portions of Chinese food at college-kid prices. The mandarin chicken ($6.95) is tried and true. If you want it all, the combination plates ($5-6.50) will rescue you from indecision. Open Mon.-Fri. 11am-10pm, Sat. 5-10pm, Sun. dim sum, 11am-3pm, dinner 5-9:30pm.

Newman's Fish Company, 1545 Willamette St. (344-2371). A novel approach to dining in the Eugenest of Styles. Through this walk-up, bike-up, drive-up window is delivered the finest fish and chips (salmon $5, cod $3.50, or halibut $5) east of the Cascades. Fries by themselves are $1. Show up on Sat. afternoon (noon-5pm) for sushi by the piece ($1-2). Open Mon.-Fri. 11am-7pm, Sat. 11am-6:30pm.

Prince Puckler's Ice Cream Parlor, 861 Willamette St. (343-2621) on the pedestrian mall. They churn their own from all-natural ingredients and go crazy with flavors like Bittersweet Nugget and Tiger Velvet Hammer. Hefty single scoops ($1.50), doubles ($2.50), and minis that are small but worth the 75¢. Open Mon.-Thurs. 7am-6pm, Fri.-Sat. 7am-9pm, Sun. 10am-9pm.

SIGHTS AND ACTIVITIES

If you hanker to get closer to nature, **River Runner Supply,** 2222 Centennial Blvd. (343-6883 or 800-223-4326), organizes outdoor experiences from fishing to whitewater rafting on the Willamette River. A four-hour rafting trip costs $40 per person on the Wilamette and $45 on the McKenzie (lunch included, 4-person min.), two- to three-hour trips run $30 per person. They also rent out kayaks ($25 per day), canoes ($20 per day), and rafts ($40 per day). The visitors information center can supply a list of several other outfitters. Reservations recommended on weekends. Check local river conditions and **maps,** since there are some rough areas on the Willamette near Eugene, especially when the water is high.

If you just have an afternoon hour to spare, canoe or kayak the **Millrace Canal,** which parallels the Willamette for 3 mi. This shallow waterway passes under many small foot bridges and through a tunnel under the road. Rent water craft from **The Water Works Canoe Company,** 1395 Franklin Blvd. (346-4386), which is run by University of Oregon students. (Open summer Mon.-Fri. 3pm-dusk, Sat.-Sun. noon-dusk; $4 per hr.; $14 for 24hr.; $30 deposit.) Or join the ranks of cyclists and joggers at **Amazon Park.** Head south on Pearl St. and it will become Amazon Dr. just beyond E. 19th St. This small, peaceful park has paved and dirt trails along the river. To the northwest of the city just after the I-5 overpass, the **Owen Memorial Rose Garden** is perfect for a picnic accompanied by the sweet strains of rumbling traffic. Any frolicking should take place in full daylight, because the surrounding Whittaker neighborhood is considered unsafe.

High-brow culture can be found at the $26-million **Hult Performing Arts Center,** the city's crown jewel, One Eugene Center, at 7th and Willamette St. The two theater halls host a wide variety of music from the blues to Bartók. (Free tours Thurs. and Sat. at 1pm and should be arranged in the lobby; call 687-5087 or fax 687-5426 for info, 687-5000 for the ticket office, and 342-5746 for 24hr. event info.) Locals young and old leave the Hult to the society types who can afford tickets, and instead head to the Community Center for the Performing Arts, better known as **WOW Hall,** 291 W. 8th St. (687-2746). For years WOW Hall, an old Wobblie (International Workers of the World) meeting hall, has sponsored concerts by lesser-known artists. Flyers announcing these offbeat acts are plastered everywhere. Tickets available at WOW Hall (open Tues.-Fri. 3-6pm), CD World (3215 W. 11th St.), and various other locations. Tickets are occasionally available at the door for less raging acts. Another favorite in the **Bijou Art Cinema,** 492 East 13th at Ferry St., where obscure films are screened in the sanctuary of an old Spanish church ($2-5).

The University of Oregon is the centerpiece of Eugene. The people at the reception centers at **Oregon Hall** (346-3014), E. 13th Ave. and Agate St., and at the visitors parking and information booth, just left of the main entrance on Franklin Blvd., give tours and hand out **campus maps.** Take time to admire the ivy-covered halls that set the scene for National Lampoon's *Animal House.* Also on campus, just off the pedestrian section of 13th St. between Kincaid and University St., the **University Museum of Art** (346-3027) houses a changing repertoire of Northwestern and American pieces, and an extensive permanent collection from Southeast Asia (free; open Wed.-Sun. noon-5pm; tours Sat. by appointment and Sun. at 2pm). A few blocks away, the **Museum of Natural History,** 1680 E. 15th Ave. (346-3024), at Agate, shows a collection of relics from indigenous cultures worldwide that includes a 7000-year-old pair of shoes (opportunistically billed by Nike as sneakers). A primitive "swoosh" logo is still visible (free; open Wed.-Sun. noon-5pm).

On the edge of town lurks the highly acclaimed **Fifth Street Market** (484-0383), at 5th and High St., a historical building that's been refurbished and ushered into mall-hood (open Mon.-Sat. 10am-7pm, Sun. 10am-6pm). This collection of exorbitantly priced boutiques and eateries (one under the mystifying impression that British cuisine is "gourmet") brings joy to the monied and a lingering sense of dissatisfaction to the poor. If your timing is right, you can easily find cheaper (and often better) nourishment around the array of artists' wares at the **Saturday Market** (686-8885), at 8th and Oak, held weekly April to November, 10am-5pm.

CLUBS AND BARS

According to some, the nightlife in Eugene is the best in Oregon, and there's always plenty for everyone. Not surprisingly, the string of establishments by the university along 13th St. can be dominated by fraternity beer bashes. Refugees from this scene will find an amazingly diverse cross-section of nightlife elsewhere. Things pick up after 10pm. Check out the *Eugene Weekly* for current bands.

Sam Bond's Garage, 407 Blair Blvd. (343-2635), at 4th. Supremely laid back gem of an establishment in a soulful but not-so-great neighborhood. Entertainment every night and an ever-changing selection of Northwest microbrews ($2.25 per pint). Rusting car parts in the haphazard flowerbeds speak the history of the 1928 garage. 10% beer discount for *Let's Go* users. Open daily 7am-1am.

Doc's Pad, 165 W. 11th St. (683-8101). The drinks are strong, the music is loud, and the place can be packed and smoky—take a deep breath and unbuckle your seat belt. Timothy Leary used to hang out at this converted drive-thru. Classic rock until 9pm; "alternative" rock after. Happy hour sees $1.75 wells and $2 micros, Mon.-Fri. 4-7pm. Open daily 7am-3am.

High St. Brewery Café, 1234 High St. (345-4905). Proudly sells McMenamins and seasonal fruit ale. Toss on a pair of jeans and relax in this oriental rug-bedecked Victorian house. Backyard deck and patio catch the overflow in this popular spot. Excellent ales brewed in the basement are $2.55 a pint. Open Mon.-Sat. 11am-1am, Sun. noon-midnight.

Jo Federigo's, 259 E. 5th St. (343-8488). A snazzy and somewhat pricey restaurant with New Orleans flair. Jazz 6 nights a week at 9:30pm. Wednesday gets the blues and the whole place rattles when the train goes by. Happy hour is 4:30-6:30pm. No cover, but $5 drink minimum and after 7:30pm an additional surcharge of 50¢ per drink. Open Mon.-Thurs. 2pm-midnight, Fri. 2pm-2am, Sat. 5pm-2am, Sun. 5pm-midnight.

Rainy Day Café, 50 E. 11th Ave. (343-8108). A casual sandwich shop by day, this place gets serious about local music at night. Open mike Tues. night (free); Wed.-Sat. nights see folk and rock bands for a $1-3 cover. Microbrew is $2.50 a pint. The ½ order of fresh-cut fries are under a dollar. Open Mon. 11am-5pm, Tues.-Thurs. 11am-11pm, Fri.-Sat. 11am-midnight.

Club Arena, 959 Pearl St. (683-2360). The only gay dance club in town. The huge, checkered dance floor gets kicking every night at 11pm to house and techno tunes. Sun. nights are retro, Mon. is men's night, Wed. is women's night, and Thurs. are packed for the $1 mixed drinks. Fri.-Sat. $2.50, Thurs. $1. Open daily 7pm-2:30am.

East 19th Street Café, 1485 19th St. (342-4025). Situated on the athletic edge of campus, about 3 blocks from the track, this branch of McMenamins draws a healthy U of O sports crowd. Hammerhead and Terminator Stout are favorites on the rotating list of homebrews. Tasty food specials. Happy hour daily 4-6pm has $2 pints. Open Mon.-Sat. 11am-1am, Sun. noon-midnight.

John Henry's, 136 E. 11th St. (342-3358). In the heart of downtown, this warehouse style venue hosts headliners and smaller potatoes. Anything from alternative rock to country swing. Bits of abstract art give the high walls color; plenty of bar booths to hide in, but the action is on the dance floor. Cover usually $3-7. Call for a schedule. Free pool until 9pm. Open daily 4pm-1am.

EVENTS

The two-week **Oregon Bach Festival** (346-5666), at the Hult and the University of Oregon's Beall Concert Hall beginning the last week of June, brings Helmuth Rilling, a world-renowned authority on Baroque music, to lead some of the country's finest musicians in performances of Bach's cantatas and concerti. (Contact the Hult Center Ticket Office, listed above, for info; tickets $23-35, senior and student discounts for selected events.) Next to come is **Art and the Vineyard** (345-1571), a four day celebration of food, wine, and culture around the 4th of July. Alton Baker Park, on the northern bank of the Willamette east of Coburg Rd., is taken over by West Coast artisans, food, and live music (suggested donation $4).

By far the biggest event of the summer is the **Oregon Country Fair** (343-6554). It actually takes place in Veneta, west of town on Rte. 126, but it can be clearly felt 13 mi. away in Eugene. For the three days in mid-July, a third of the city's population drops everything to go to the Fair. These wooded acres have been the annual gathering grounds for artists, musicians, misfits, and activists for 27 years. Now the 300 art and food booths and the six stages worth of show after show are only a backdrop to the unique experience of the Country Fair. Drums, parades of painted bodies, dancing 12-ft. dolls, and the smell of wacky tobacky successfully invoke a temporary return to the early 70s. Word of this wonder has gotten out; some 23,000 other people will be partying with you. To alleviate the yearly traffic jams, free bus service between a free parking area in Eugene is provided (take Jackson St. south to 13th) and the fairgrounds in Veneta. Buses run every 15 minutes starting around 9 or 10am and continuing until the fairgrounds close at 7pm. For the past two years, the limited number of tickets available at the gate have sold out around 1pm. Purchase in advance through Fastixx (800-992-8499), at the Hult Center, or at EMU (see **Practical Information,** above) on campus. No public camping or overnight parking. (Advance tickets Fri. $7, Sat. $12, Sun. $8; day of Fri. and Sun. $10, Sat. $15.)

Next in the summer line-up is the **Oregon Festival of American Music** (687-6526), which has a different theme every year. It takes place during one week in mid-August and often combines free youth recitals, exhibits, and features performances by big-name musicians. (Tickets range from $11.50-25.30, depending on the event. 5% discount for tickets bought before June 21.)

OUTDOORS

The Willamette Valley attracted waves of 19th-century pioneers with its fertile floor and richly forested hills. To see country that hasn't noticeably changed since human invasion, take Rte. 126 east from Eugene. The highway runs adjacent to the beautiful McKenzie River, and on a clear day the mighty snowcapped **Three Sisters** of the Cascades are visible. Just past the town of McKenzie Bridge, the road splits into a "scenic byway" loop; Rte. 242 climbs east to the breathtakingly vast lava fields of **McKenzie Pass** while Rte. 126 turns north over Santiam Pass and meets Rte. 242 in Sisters. This stretch of Rte. 242 is an incredible drive, tunnelling its narrow, winding way between the Mt. Washington and Three Sisters Wilderness areas before rising to the high plateau of McKenzie Pass, where lava outcroppings served as a training site for astronauts preparing for **lunar landings.** Decades before, the Civilian Conservation Corps left their mark on the land with a lava block lookout tower for all the world to use on clear days. Learn which of the peaks is which by squinting through the dozen square holes, each labelled with the mountain they frame.

Rte. 242 is often blocked by snow until the end of June. Wide enough for two cars to pass in places and kinked with tight turns in others, Rte. 242 is off-limits to all vehicles over 35 ft. in length. Trucks with trailers should not even try it. They have been known to get stuck.

Along the curviest section of Rte. 242, about 15 mi. east of where it branches off Rte. 126, a number of trails begin that will carry you above the treeline. As with all Oregon wilderness areas, biking is not allowed and permits are required. These permits are, happily, free and available at the trailheads. For groups over 12, call the **McKenzie Ranger Station** (822-3381; open daily 8am-4:30pm), which is located 3 mi. east of McKenzie Bridge on Rte. 126. On the other side of the loop, the **McKenzie River Trail** winds 26 mi. parallel to Rte. 126 and the river, through thick, lush forest draped in moss. It starts about 1½ mi. west of the McKenzie Ranger Station (where you can pick up an excellent map of the trail for $1) and ends up north at Old Santiam Road near the Fish Lake Old Growth Grove. The entire trail is now open to mountain bikers. The two most accessible parts of the trail are its first 6 mi., sandwiched between the highway and the river, and the spectacular 2-mi. section between **Koosah Falls, Sahalie Falls,** and **Clear Lake**. Camp at **Ice Cap Creek**, along the river, just below Koosah Falls (8 tent sites, 14 tent/trailer sites, drinking water faucets, $8) or the more picturesque **Coldwater Cove,** 1 mi. up the road at Clear Lake (35 tent/trailer sites, one hand-pump for drinking water, $9). No motorized boats are allowed on this cold, crystalline lake. The remarkable clarity of its water reveals 3000-year-old trees preserved on the lake bottom. A number of other Forest Service campgrounds cluster along this stretch of Rte. 126, including the riverside **Olallie** (11 mi. northeast of McKenzie Bridge, $6) and **Trail Bridge** (13 mi. northeast of McKenzie Bridge, $8). More ambitious hikers can sign up for an overnight permit at the McKenzie Ranger Station and head for the high country. Rte. 242 branches off 126 about 3 mi. beyond the ranger station and winds into the Three Sisters Wilderness. Trails that will carry you above treeline begin about 15 mi. up the road. Ask for advice at the McKenzie Ranger Station (see above) when you're signing up for the permit.

West of McKenzie Bridge, an easy 40 mi. east out of Eugene., **Blue River Lake** and **Cougar Lake,** river valleys dammed by the Army Corps of Engineers in the 60s, rest between heavily forested, steep mountain ridges. They are officially reservoirs and are only completely full April to mid-August. Tucked back in the woods along the north edge of the Blue River Lake are the 25 secluded sites of the **Mona Campground** ($9). If you're not partial to shade, you can save some money by parking your tent at **Lookout Campground** ($2), a dry, grassy field between the road and the boat landing. Both campgrounds have drinking water.

The larger and more popular Cougar Lake features the free pleasure of Terwilliger Hot Springs, known fondly by all as **Cougar Hot Springs.** To get there, go 6 mi. east of Blue River on Rte. 126, turn right onto Auderheide Drive (Forest Service Rd. #19), and follow the road for 7.3 mi. as it winds on the right side of Cougar Reservoir. These two lovely rock pools have become the Willamette Forest's hippie hotspot. By convention, the springs (and the cove of the lake down the hill from them) are clothing-optional hangouts—not for the timid. There is no regular attendant at the springs; however, rangers do show up at dusk to enforce the area's **day-use only** policy. Other hot springs are scattered through the area; the Forest Service can suggest clothing-compulsory sulfur baths for the more modest. Continue down the road to camp on the other side of the lake at **Slide Creek** (16 sites, drinking water, $9) or along the south fork of the McKenzie at **French Pete** (17 sites, drinking water, $9). For information or free maps, stop in at the Blue River District ranger station (822-3317; open Mon.-Fri. 7:45am-4:30pm) off Hwy. 126 in Blue River.

■ Corvallis

This peaceful residential community, 15 mi. east of I-5 in the northern Willamette Valley, does not pretend to be "historic." Home to **Oregon State University (OSU)** and a giant Hewlett-Packard plant, this unassuming town lives in the present, particularly when it comes to outdoor frolicking. Mountain bikes dominate the roads, and those without wheels enjoy several parks scattered throughout the city. Most importantly, Corvallis is the hometown of the Maraschino cherry. As in any college town, the pace mellows in Corvallis during the summer. Aside from a few choice festivals, there's not too much to do but relax and hang with your OSU friends.

PRACTICAL INFORMATION

Visitors Information: Chamber of Commerce (757-1505) and **Convention and Visitors Bureau** (757-1544 or 800-334-8118), both at 420 NW 2nd St., the first right past the bridge if you're coming from the east. City **maps** $1. Open Mon.-Fri. 8am-5pm. **Oregon State University** (737-0123). Main entrance and information booth at Jefferson and 15th St. (737-6445 for campus events info). Get a free **map** here.

Buses: Greyhound, 153 NW 4th St. (757-1797). To: Portland (4 per day, $12), Seattle (4 per day, $39), Newport (3 per day, $10), and Eugene (4 per day, $7). Lockers $1 for 24hr. Open Mon.-Fri. 7am-6:30pm, Sat. 7am-3pm, Sun. 7am-7pm.

Public Transportation: Corvallis Transit System (757-6998). Fare 50¢; ages 5-17, seniors, and disabled 25¢. Service Mon.-Fri. 6:45am-6:45pm, Sat. 9:45am-3:45pm. Bus schedule available free from Chamber of Commerce or City Hall.

Taxi: A-1 Taxi, 754-1111. 24hr. $5 min.

Laundromat: Campbell's Laundry, 1120 NW 9th St. Wash $1, 10-min. dry 25¢. Open daily 7am-1am.

Library: 645 NW Monroe (757-6927 for recording, 757-6426 for further questions). Open Mon.-Fri. 9am-9pm, Sat. 9am-6pm, Sun. noon-6pm.

Emergency: 911. **Police:** 180 NW 5th St., 757-6924.

Post Office: 311 SW 2nd St. (758-1412). Open Mon.-Fri. 8am-5:30pm, Sat. 9am-4pm. **General Delivery Zip Code:** 97333.

Area Code: 541.

Corvallis is laid out in a checkerboard fashion that degenerates away from downtown; numbered streets run north-south and streets named for lesser-known presidents (Van Buren, Polk, Buchanan) run east-west. College students and residents of the numerous Greek houses hang out along SW Monroe St. and the surrounding area when they aren't hitting the trails.

ACCOMMODATIONS AND CAMPING

A couple of easily accessible campgrounds, which are *not* RV mini-cities, give the budget conscious traveler a break. Motels are reasonably priced, but scattered and few. They fill fast in the summer with those pesky conventioneers.

C.E.W. Motel, 1705 NW 9th St. (753-8823; fax 753-7830). Rooms are clean with soft beds and textured chairs. An eclectic statue garden graces the parking lot. Upstairs rooms have tubs. Singles $35.50. Doubles $49.

Budget Inn, 1480 SW 3rd St. (752-8756), take 4th under the bridges. Bathrooms big enough to waltz in. Singles $35. Doubles $42. Senior/AAA discount $2. Reserve 2 weeks ahead.

Benton County Fairgrounds, 110 SW 53rd St. Follow Harrison west through Corvallis, and turn left onto 53rd St. about 1 mi. out. A pleasant, tree-lined campspot with showers. First-come, first-served. Closed for fair and other events for much of July. Sites $5. Full hookup $10.

Willamette Park (757-6918), on SE Goodnight Rd. Follow Rte. 99W toward Eugene, after 2 mi. turn left on Goodnight Rd. 15 lovely camping sites on a tree-lined field close to the Willamette River. Sites $7. No hookups or reservations.

FOOD AND ENTERTAINMENT

Corvallis has a selection of collegiate pizza parlors and several different variations on the Mexican theme. OSU students usually prowl Monroe St. for grub. Prices are marvelously cheap for tasty, filling food. The natural foods connection is **First Alternative Inc.,** 1007 SE 3rd St. (753-3115). Run by volunteers, this store stocks a range of well priced produce, baked goods, and bountiful bulk food (open Mon.-Sat. 9am-9pm, Sun. 10am-8pm). The **Safeway,** 450 SW 3rd (753-5502), is, as usual, an option (open daily 6am-2am).

Nearly Normal's, 109 NW 15th (753-0791). This adorable wooden house holds large portions of nearly everything but meat for $3-7.50. Arboreal aura. Dine under a live canopy of branches out back. The sunflower seed burgers are about as hearty as their cow-nterparts. Open Mon.-Fri. 8am-9pm, Sat. 9am-9pm.

McMenamins, 420 NW 3rd St. (758-6044). Some of the best pub fare in town, made from scratch and reasonably priced ($3-7). Fresh-cut fries ($2-4) are worth a trip themselves. All pints $2.55. Open Mon.-Sat. 11am-1am, Sun. noon-midnight.

Bombs Away Café, 2527 NW Monroe (757-7221). Where Mexican food and multi-colored geometric art collide and combust. Adventures in anti-authenticity succeed with a ricotta enchilada and a duck confit chimichanga. Most still slurp down the enormous "Wet Burrito," though, or slip back to the tiny bar for a shot of tequila. Open Mon.-Fri. 11am-midnight, Sat. 4pm-midnight, Sun. 4-9pm.

Clubs and Bars

Murphy's Tavern, 2740 SW 3rd Ave. a.k.a. 99W (754-3508). OSU students and loggers get their drinking done at this roadhouse. Live country music Fri. and Sat.; brave the crowds for Mr. Bill's Traveling Trivia Night on Thurs. Domestic pints $1.80. Beers 25¢ every Wed. 7-8pm. Open Mon.-Thurs. 10:30am-midnight, Fri.-Sat. 10:30am-1:30am, Sun. noon-8pm.

The Museum II, 137 SW 3rd St. (758-6641). An upscale sports bar where the average bar food is cheap and has a sporty name like "The Superstar" ($4 burger with sauteed mushrooms), or "The Bench Warm" ($4 barbecue chicken sandwich with provolone). Pints $1.75-3. Open Mon.-Wed. 10am-1am, Thurs.-Sat. 10am-2am, Sun. 10am-11pm.

Peacock Tavern, 125 SW 2nd (754-8522). Low ceilings and 6 pool tables. Draws as many locals as students. Features live R&B Wed.-Sun. for a price ($2-5 cover). Live acts have included such superstars as Curtis Salgado. Also see frat boys playing pool (no extra charge). Happy hour, weekdays 5-7pm, has domestic pints for $1.25. Open Sun.-Tues. 7am-1am, Wed.-Sat. 7am-2am.

EVENTS AND OUTDOORS

Mountain-biking is a way of life in Corvallis. Set off in any direction and you're bound to hit a trail. Many people head for the **McDonald Forest** owned by OSU; just drive west out of town on Harrison about 2 mi., and angle right on Oak Creek Rd. The road dead ends at OSU's Lab, and multiple trails lead from there into the forest. **Mary's Peak,** 14 mi. east of Corvallis off Rte. 34, is also a popular area that can be reached by car. **Peak Sports,** 129 NW 2nd St. (754-6444), rents out bikes for $15 per day (open Mon.-Thurs. and Sat. 9am-6pm, Fri. 9am-8pm, Sun. noon-5pm).

City parks are well maintained, and are fantastic areas for a hike along a trail, a mosey, or a picnic. Seventy four-acre **Avery Park,** just south of the city off 99W, draws frisbee players, sun bathers, and kids who clamber on the full-size locomotive model. The vast campus of **Oregon State University,** marked by buildings of widely varying architectural styles, is worth exploring. Anyone can arrange a tour in advance through the admissions office (737-2626). Parking is available behind the information booth at Jefferson and 15th (ask at the booth for a free permit).

The third weekend in July, the heart rate of sleepy Corvallis picks up 50 beats with the **da Vinci Days Festival** (800-334-8118). The main event is the **Kinetic Sculpture Race,** in which man-powered, all-terrain works of art compete in several different races for the overall crown. If your interest in technology extends only to stereo equipment, don't despair: the festival brings in nationally known bands, from jazz and folk to Cajun and rock ($5, ages 4-12 $3). The **Fall Festival,** held in Avery Park during the third weekend in September, combines food with music in one of the best arts and crafts fairs in Oregon.

Fifteen mi. east in **Albany** (at the junction of US 20 and I-5), thousands of people gather from mid-July through August each Thursday night for the **River Rhythms** concert series. The music varies drastically from week to week, but concerts are always free, always at 7pm, and always held in the Monteith River Park. A new tradition on the make is the Monday night show each week in July that features local per-

OREGON

formers, also free at 7pm in Monteith River Park. Call the Albany Visitors Center (928-0911) for further information.

■ Salem

Despite state-capital status and the presence of Willamette University, Salem seems barely able to register a pulse. Travelers stopping or staying in Salem might check out the impressive Capitol, but the city offers few options for budget travelers.

Practical Information and Orientation The **Visitors Association and Salem Convention Center,** 1313 Mill St. SE (581-4325 or 800-874-7012), part of the Mission Mill Village complex, stocks brochures on Salem and other parts of the state (open Mon.-Fri. 8:30am-5pm, Sat.-Sun. 10am-4pm).

Amtrak, 500 13th St. SE (588-1551 or 800-872-7245), is at 12th and Mill St. SE, across from the visitors center. Trains run daily to Portland ($11), Seattle ($33), and San Francisco ($88). Open daily 6:30am-4:45pm. **Greyhound,** 450 Church St. NE (362-2428), at Center St., run buses north and south, with service eight times daily to Portland ($7). Lockers are $1 for 24hr. Station open daily 6am-8pm. **Cherriots Customer Service Office,** 183 High St. NE (588-BUSS/2877), provides maps and multiple-day passes. Twenty different routes originate from High St. between State and Court St. in front of the courthouse. (Fare 75¢, under 18 50¢, seniors and disabled 35¢. Service Mon.-Fri. 6:15am-10pm about every ½hr., Sat. 7:45am-5:45pm hourly.) For a taxi, call **Salem Yellow Cab Co.** (362-2411; 24hr.).

The **library** is at 585 Liberty St. SE (588-6315; open Mon., Fri., and Sat. 10am-6pm, Tues.-Thurs. 10am-9pm, in winter also Sun. 1-5pm). Wash your clothes at the **Suds City Depot,** 1785 Lancaster Dr. NE (362-9845), at Market St. Wash 75¢, $1 on weekends, 17-min. dry 25¢ (open daily 7:30am-9pm). Reach the **Women's Crisis Center** at 399-7722 (24hr.). The **Human Services Crisis and Info Hotline** is 581-5535 (24hr.). In an **emergency,** dial 911 or find the **police** at 555 Liberty St. SE (588-6123), in City Hall. The **post office** is at 1050 25th St. SE (370-4700; open Mon.-Fri. 8:30am-5:30pm. **General Delivery ZIP Code:** 97301). The **area code** is 503.

Salem is bordered on the west by the Willamette River and on the east by I-5, 47 mi. south of Portland. Willamette University occupies a central portion of the city just behind the Capitol, but the heart of downtown lies several blocks west around Court St. Street addresses are arranged by the quadrant system, with State St. as the north-south divider, and Summer St. as the east-west divider.

Accommodations and Camping In the far, far away galaxy of Northwestern budget travel, Salem is the Dark Side. For camping, struggle valiantly against the tractor beam of KOA and stay at Silver Falls. Rent is high in Salem, which pushes the price of even the most modest motel rooms up to $40 and $50. B&Bs are about as affordable here as anywhere else in the state (starting at $55 per room), so spending the extra $10 might not be a bad idea. The visitors center has a list of area B&Bs. The **City Center Motel,** 510 Liberty St. SE (364-0121 or 800-289-0121; fax 581-0554), set between the downtown library and a tree-lined neighborhood, is the most pleasant and convenient motel you may find in Salem. The rooms are somewhat worn, but clean and spacious (singles $40, doubles $48). The **Cottonwood Cottage,** 960 E. St. NE (362-3979), follow Capitol St. north from town two blocks and turn left on E St., is a charming old house in a peaceful neighborhood close to downtown. Two sunny and recently renovated bedrooms are available starting at $55 with cable TV, A/C, and shared bath. Seek out Jedi instruction at **Silver Falls State Park,** 20024 Silver Falls SE (Rte. 214) (873-8681), 26 mi. east of Salem via Rte. 20 and 214 across rolling farmland. Oregon's largest inland state park offers swimming, hiking, storytelling, and views of waterfalls, including a trail leading behind one of the falls. The tallest, spectacular Double Falls, crashes 178 ft. (tent sites $15; improved sites $20; showers, water, recycling center).

Food A global array of ethnic restaurants on Court St. catch yuppie dollars by day but shut down at night when pedestrian traffic slows to a trickle. On the other hand, the busiest road in Oregon, Lancaster Dr. (just east of and parallel to I-5), is lit with fast food signs into the night. For those with a market in mind, the local **Safeway** on 12th and Center is open daily 6am-midnight. Alternatively, **Heliotrope Natural Food,** 2060 Market St. NE (362-5487), has a good selection of bread and produce (open Mon.-Fri. 9am-9pm, Sat. 9am-7pm, Sun. 10am-7pm).

The **Off-Center Café,** 1741 Center NE (363-9245), in the long blue building, has a leftist approach and generally delicious food. Start the morning off with a hearty dose of "bibble and squib" ($4) or scrambled tofu ($5.25). The boysenberry milkshake is better than Ezra ($2.50; open Tues.-Fri. 7am-2:30pm, Sat.-Sun. 8am-2pm; dinner Thurs.-Sat. 6-9pm). Join the locals at the low orange vinyl counter or booths at the **Court Street Dairy,** 347 Court St. NE (363-6433), for a taste of the 30s. Try old-fashioned burgers ($2.90) or shakes ($2.50) made from Curly's hard ice cream. Old photos of Depression-era Salem cover the walls and prove it used to be worse (open Mon.-Fri. 7am-2pm). **The Daily Planet,** 1667 Center St. (391-9369), is Salem's utterly unpretentious answer to the couch-equipped coffeehouse. Espresso starts at $1, pinball at 25¢, and spots on the carpet are free (open daily 6am-midnight).

Sights and Events The **State Capitol,** 900 Court St. NE (986-1388), on Court St. between W. Summer and E. Summer St., is capped by a 23-ft. gold-leaf statue of the quintessential "Oregon Pioneer," giving the building an imposing, temple-like appearance. Murals and sculptures depicting the great westward push through the frontier ornament the interior. The Capitol's rotunda was closed off for two and a half years due to damage inflicted by a 5.6 earthquake in March, 1993. Now that it's open again, you can climb the 121 steps to its top with a free tour that leaves every half hour (Memorial-Labor Day only). If you aim for weekday mornings, you can count on seeing some action in the legislative chamber in the spring of 1997 (open Mon.-Fri. 7:30am-5:30pm, Sat. 9am-4pm, Sun. noon-4pm).

Across the street is the beautiful campus of **Willamette** (Wil-AM-it) **University,** 900 State St. (370-6303). Founded by Methodist missionaries in 1842, this private school is the oldest university west of the Mississippi. **The Historic Deepwood Estate,** 1116 Mission St. SE (363-1825), gives house tours ($3, senior and students $2.50, ages 6-12 $1; open Sun.-Fri. noon-4:30pm; winter Sun.-Fri. 1-4pm; used for weddings on Sat.), but the real joy of Deepwood comes in wandering through the six acres of formal English gardens that surround the mansion.

The **Honeywood Winery,** 1350 Hines St. SE (362-4111), just six blocks south of the visitors center, is Salem's only urban winery and Oregon's oldest (open for free tastings Mon.-Fri. 9am-5pm, Sat. 10am-5pm, Sun. 1pm-5pm). The winery also offers tours by appointment for groups of 20 or more ($1 per person). Many other wineries lie just west of Salem and can be found by contacting visitors information.

Check out the **Bush Barn Art Center and Museum,** 600 Mission St. SE (581-2228 or 800-874-7012), one of the finest sights in Salem. You can tour the house museum ($2.50, seniors and students $2, 6-12 $1, under 6 free) or stroll through the rose garden, greenhouse and art center (free). The collection of art is extensive and includes some interesting off-beat exhibits. The Bush Barn hosts the free **Salem Art Fair and Festival,** held during the third full weekend of July in Bush's **Pasture Park.** The festival showcases the works of Northwestern artists. Bands strum away the afternoons, and anyone with extra energy can join the 5K **Run for the Arts,** held during the festival (entrance $5; contact the Bush Barn for more information).

Salem gears up for the annual **Oregon State Fair** (378-3247 or 800-833-0011), 12 days in late August ending on Labor Day, when people, farm animals, and chaos come hurtling into the city. In 1996, Steve Miller, Sawyer Brown, and Nancy Griffith performed at this statewide show (concert tickets $15-25; call 503-224-4400).

OREGON

To keep up with regularly scheduled cultural events in Salem, contact the **Mid-Valley Arts Council,** 170 High St. SE (370-7469). Or visit their office downtown next to the almost completely restored Elsinore Theatre, a magnificent cathedral-like structure with two double balconies and a yawning, three-story lobby. **Stage,** an in-house theater group, performs nearly every month. The theater also hosts occasional concerts and silent movie series. The lower balcony has the comfiest seats.

CENTRAL AND EASTERN OREGON

Most people picture Oregon as a verdant land of sweeping rains and rich forests. This is true enough of western Oregon, where most Oregonians live, but Oregon's eastern half is better characterized as a high desert region. The low evergreen Coast Range and the high, jagged, volcanic Cascades are natural rain barriers, trapping moisture from Pacific winds. The western coast and valleys are consequently densely wooded and green, while the eastern basin is hot and arid.

For generations, this arid region has challenged its human inhabitants, from the Cayuse, Shoshone, Nez Perce, and others who first occupied it, to the pioneers who crossed it on foot and in wagons, to the modern farmers, ranchers, and loggers who live there today. Eastern Oregon today is known as the High Desert, but the term "desert" is somewhat misleading. The area known as Central Oregon on the eastern slope of the Cascades is full of life, with high peaks, world-class skiing, volcanic flows, Crater Lake, and the energetic town of **Bend,** an outdoor mecca. The southeastern region near **Burns** is the driest, full of beautiful, desolate country: dramatic mountains, expansive skies, vast grasslands, lava beds, desert, and its own share of marshes and lakes. Northeastern Oregon, near **Pendleton** and **Baker City,** offers the Wallowa Mountains, pine and fir forests, fossil beds, 8000-ft.-deep Hells Canyon, and a heap of Oregon Trail history. But despite all the possibilities for outdoor activity, eastern Oregon is sparsely populated and seldom visited. In this vast and largely undeveloped region, a car is almost a must. Distances are great, and the few buses take roundabout routes.

■ Crater Lake and Klamath Falls

Mirror-blue Crater Lake, the namesake of **Oregon's only national park,** was regarded as sacred by Native American shamans, who forbade their people to look upon it. Iceless in winter, though snowbanked until late July, the flawlessly circular lake plunges from its 6176-ft. elevation to a depth of nearly 2000 ft., making it the nation's deepest lake. Klamath (kuh-LAH-math) Falls offers a few diversions for those making a pit stop, but time and money are better spent at Crater Lake.

PRACTICAL INFORMATION AND ORIENTATION

Visitors Information: William G. Steel Center (594-2211, ext. 402), 1 mi. from the south entrance of the park. Pick up backcountry camping **permits** here or at Rim Village (free). Check out the model of Crater Lake or the free 18min. movie on its formation every ½hr. 9am-4:30pm. Open daily 9am-5pm. **Crater Lake National Park Visitors Center** (594-2211, ext. 415), on the lake shore at **Rim Village.** A smaller center with pamphlets and advice regarding trails and campsites. Open daily June-Sept. 8:30am-6pm. The **Klamath County Department of Tourism** runs a visitor information center at 1451 Main St. (884-0666 or 800-445-6728) in Klamath Falls. Open June-Sept. Mon.-Sat. 9am-5:30pm; Oct.-May Mon.-Sat. 8am-4:30pm.

Park Admission: Call for schedule. Cars $5, hikers and bikers $3, free with Golden Age Passport or Golden Eagle Passport. Free in winter.

Trains: Amtrak (884-2822 or 800-USA-RAIL/872-7245 for reservations), S. Spring St. depot, Klamath Falls at the east end of Main Street. 1 train per day north, 1 per day south. To: Portland ($64). Open daily 6:45-10:15am and 9-10:30pm.

Buses: Greyhound, 1200 Klamath Ave., Klamath Falls (882-4616). To: Bend (1 per day, $21), Redding, CA (1 per day, $27), Eugene (1 per day, $24), Ashland (1 per day, $42). Lockers $1 per 24hr. Open Mon.-Fri. 6-10am and 11:30am-5:30pm, Sat. 6am-3pm.

Public Transportation: Basin Transit Service (883-2877), runs 5 routes around Klamath Falls Mon.-Fri. 6am-9pm, Sat. 10am-5pm. 80¢, seniors and disabled 40¢.

Taxi: AB Taxi (885-5607). 24hr. 10% senior discount.

Car Rental: Budget (885-5421), at the airport. Take S. 6th St. and turn right on Altamonta. $34 per day on weekends, $50 weekdays. Open Mon.-Fri. 7:30am-7:30pm, Sat. 8am-3pm, Sun. 10am-5pm.

Laundromat: Main Street Laundromat, 1711 Main St. (883-1784). Clean and cool inside. Wash $1.25, 12-min. dry 25¢. Open daily 10am-7pm.

Weather and Road Conditions: Park information, including weather and road conditions, is broadcast continuously on **1610 AM** in Crater Lake.

Crisis: Poison Control (800-452-7165). **Rape Crisis** (884-0390). **Suicide/ Mental Health** (800-452-3669).

Hospital: Merle West Medical Center, 2865 Doggett St. (883-6176), from U.S. 97 northbound, turn right on Campus Dr., then right on Doggett.

Emergency: 911. Police: Klamath Falls, 425 Walnut St. (883-5336). **Fire:** 143 N. Broad St. (non-emergency 885-2056).

Post Office: Klamath Falls, 317 S. 7th St. (884-9226). Open Mon.-Fri. 7:30am-5:30pm, Sat. 9am-noon. **Zip Code:** 97601. **Crater Lake,** in the Steel Center. Open Mon.-Fri. 10am-4pm, Sat. 10am-2pm. **Zip Code:** 97604.

Area Code: 541.

Crater Lake National Park is reachable throughout the year off Rte. 62 and the south access road that leads up to the Caldera's Rim, but the park is not completely open until after the snow has melted. Crater Lake averages over 44 ft. of snow per year, and some roads could be closed as late as July; call the Steel Center for road conditions (see above). Rte. 62 skirts the southwestern edge of the park, as it makes a 130 mi. arch northeast from Medford and back south to Klamath Falls. To reach the park from Portland, take I-5 to Eugene, then Rte. 58 east to U.S. 97 south. During the summer you can take Rte. 138 west from U.S. 97 and approach the lake from the park's north entrance, but this route is one of the last to be cleared. Before July, stay on Hwy. 97 south to Rte. 62. *All of Crater Lake's services and operating hours are based on changing funding levels, which are not determined until April. Call the Steel Center to verify services and hours.*

ACCOMMODATIONS AND CAMPING

Klamath Falls has several affordable hotels; it is wise to sack out in town and make your forays to Crater Lake from there. The national park contains **Mazama Campground,** and the smaller **Lost Creek Campground,** both of which are closed each year until roads are passable. Backcountry camping is allowed within the park; pick up free permits from Rim Village Visitors Center or at the Steel Center.

Fort Klamath Lodge Motel, 52851 Rte. 62 (381-2234), 6 mi. from the southern entrance to Crater Lake National Park. The closest motel to the lake, the 6-unit lodge is in historic Fort Klamath, which consists of little more than a grocery store, post office, restaurant, and wildflowers in the spring. Cozy but aging countrified motel rooms with knotted-pine walls and orange carpet. TV; no phones in the rooms. 24hr. coin laundry. Singles $32. Doubles $42. Closed Nov.-April.

Townhouse Motel, 5323 S. 6th St. (882-0924). 3 mi. south of Main, deep in the heart of strip development land. The price can't be beat. None of the 16 units have phones. One double bed $25. Two bedrooms $30.

Maverick Motel, 1220 Main St. (882-6688 or 800-404-6690; fax 885-4095), around the corner from Greyhound in Klamath Falls. Clean, unremarkable rooms. Ask the manager about rides to Crater Lake. Phones, cable TV, A/C, and a postage stamp-sized pool. Singles $29, doubles $33.

Mazama Campground (594-2511), by the south entrance to Crater Lake National Park. RVs swarm into the 194 sites in this monster facility in midsummer, but fortunately a sprinkling of sites throughout are reserved for tents only. **Loop G** has denser timber and more spacious sites, offering greater seclusion. Firewood for sale. No hookups, but flush toilets, and showers. Pay laundry and telephone by the convenience store where you can get your frozen burritos. Wheelchair accessible. Tents $11, RVs $12. No reservations. Open June- mid-Oct.

Lost Creek Campground (594-2211 ext. 402), Crater Lake National Park. 3 mi. off Rim Dr. on a paved road, hidden at the southwest corner of the park. Set amid thin, young pines, this campground has only 16 sites. Try to secure a spot in the morning. Drinking water and pit toilets. Usually open by mid-July. Tents only, sites $10. No reservations.

FOOD

Eatin' cheap ain't easy in Crater Lake. The Crater Lake Lodge has a small dining room, and Rim Village establishments charge high prices for a skimpy array of food. There are several affordable restaurants in Klamath Falls and a number of large grocery stores, including a **Safeway** (882-2660) at Pine and 8th St., one block north of Main (open daily 6am-11pm). Stock up in Klamath Falls; selection and prices only get worse from there. If you're coming from the south, **Fort Klamath** is the final food frontier before you trek into the park. If you forgot the sweet gherkins, try the **Old Fort Store** (381-2345; open summer daily 9am-7pm).

Hobo Junction, 636 Main St. (882-8013), at 7th St. This quiet, corner café in the center of Klamath Falls is working on its railroad motif. Sandwiches are on the slim side, but the chili is hearty, and there are 9 varieties of hot dogs. The poor Buff Dog ($1.50) has no bun. Double scoop of ice-cream only $1.25. Open Mon.-Fri. 9am-4pm, Sat. 10am-3pm.

Cattle Crossing Café, (381-9801) on Hwy. 62 in Fort Klamath. Step over the silver-plated cow pie into this cool, spare restaurant. A perfect stop on your way to or from the park. Get a rib-sticking breakfast ($4.25-5.10) or burger ($4-5.25). Great selection of homemade pies ($2.25). Open April-Oct. daily 6am-9pm.

SIGHTS

Crater Lake's first impression is unremarkable. As you ascend, however, the lake's placid, reflected blue becomes almost unreal. The fantastic depth of the lake (1932 ft.), combined with the extreme clarity of its waters, creates the amazingly serene and intensely blue effect. About 7700 years ago, Mt. Mazama created this pacific scene in a massive eruption that buried thousands of square miles of the western U.S. under a thick layer of ash. The cataclysmic eruption left a deep caldera which filled gradually with centuries of rain. The clear, reflective lake has become the center of activity in the park.

Rim Drive, which does not open entirely until mid-July, is a 33-mi. loop around the rim of the caldera, high above the lake. The Park Service has carefully placed pull-outs at every point where a view of the lake might cause an awe-struck tourist to drive right off the road. A vast majority of visitors stay in their vehicles as they tour the lake, so it's relatively easy to get away from the shifting crowds. Just stop at any of the trailheads scattered around the rim, and hike away from the road for the real view. Most spectacular are **Garfield Peak Trail** (1.7 mi. one way) which starts at the lodge, and **Watchman Lookout** (.8 mi. one way) on the west side of the lake. The Steel Center has a handy photocopied map of the trails around the lake.

The hike up **Mt. Scott,** the park's highest peak (a tad under 9000 ft.), begins from the drive near the lake's eastern edge. Although steep, the 2½-mi. trail to the top gives the persevering hiker a unique view of the lake and its surroundings that justifies the sweaty ascent. The steep **Cleetwood Trail,** a 1-mi. switchback on the lake's north edge, is the only route down to the water. From here, the **Lodge Company** (594-2511) offers two-hour boat tours on the lake. (Fare $11.75, under 12 $6.50; tour schedule varies; 3-9 tours per day June 18-Sept. 17; take Rim Drive clockwise from either park entrance to get there.) Both **Wizard Island,** a cinder cone 760 ft. above lake level, and **Phantom Ship Rock** are fragile, tiny specks when viewed from above, but are surprisingly large when viewed from the surface of the water. If you take an early tour, you can be left on Wizard Island and picked up later. Picnics and fishing are allowed, as is swimming, but surface temperature reaches a maximum of only 50°F (10°C). Six species of fish have been introduced artificially into the lake, but the water is too pure to support much life; only rainbow trout and kokanee have survived. Park rangers lead free walking tours daily in the summer and periodically during the winter (on snowshoes). Call the Steel Center for schedules (see **Practical Information,** above).

If pressed for time, walk the easy 100 yd. from the visitors center at the rim down to the **Sinnott Memorial Overlook,** a stone enclave built into the slope. The view is the area's most panoramic and accessible, and in the summer, a ranger gives hourly talks on the area's geology and history. A similar talk is given nightly (July-Labor Day at 9pm) at the **Mazama Campground Amphitheater** or catch the 18- minute film, refreshing for its Native American perspective, at the Steel Center.

A few hundred yards east of Sinnott Memorial Overlook stands the Crater Lake Lodge, reopened July 7, 1995, after four seasons and $18 million worth of renovation. Rooms are booked a year in advance and start at $100, but you can have some fun in the lodge for free. Make a quick visit to the rustic "great hall" rebuilt from its original materials, and the observation deck, which affords great views where you can sit back in a rocking chair, fantasizing about actually staying in the lodge.

After you've seen the lake from every possible angle, consider a **hiking** trip into the park's vast **backcountry.** No fewer than 99.7% of Crater Lake's visitors stick to the Rim Drive during their visits. Leave all the exhaust and tourists behind and explore the Pacific Crest Trail where it passes through the park, or any of the other trails that cross the terrain. One excellent route starts at the **Red Cone** trailhead (on the north access road) and makes a 12 mi. loop of the Crater Springs, Oasis Butte, and Boundary Springs trails. Get information and permits (free) at the Steel Center.

▦ Bend

Nestled against the east slope of the Cascades, Bend is at the epicenter of a region with a kickin' array of accessible summertime activities. The area is defined by dramatic volcanic features to the South, Mt. Bachelor and the fish-rich Cascades to the west, and the Deschutes River through its heart. Heavy snowfalls at Mt. Bachelor, a major ski resort, keep the tourist industry fires burning in the winter.

Bend was settled as "Farewell Bend" in the early 19th century, a way station on a pioneer trail that paralleled the Deschutes river. The turn of the century town of 250 has since become the state's largest urban center east of the Cascades (30,000) and offers a wider array of cultural, culinary, and athletic options than its neighbors. Although the endless strip malls and chain stores along 3rd. St. (U.S. 97) make a bad first impression, the city's self-contained downtown area wins over most visitors with an extensive variety of restaurants and shops. For a long time Oregon's biggest little city in the east, Bend is losing its small town feel to a stream of Californian refugees in search of the perfect blend of urban attitude and pristine wilderness. Cheap eats and a place to stay are still easy to find in Bend, and a young, athletic crowd make the town one of the liveliest in the state.

PRACTICAL INFORMATION AND ORIENTATION

Visitors Information: Central Oregon Welcome Center, 63085 N. U.S. 97 (382-3221). In a spacious new building. Read the State Park Guide, Events Calendar, National Forest info, and free **maps** while you drink a complimentary cup of steaming coffee. The *Attractions and Activities Guide* has a clear area map. Open Mon.-Sat. 9am-5pm, Sun. 11am-3pm. **Deschutes National Forest Headquarters,** 1645 E. U.S. 20 (388-2715). General forest, recreation, and wilderness info. Peruse the *Recreation Opportunity Guide* for each of the four ranger districts. Open Mon.-Fri. 7:45am-4:30pm. **Bend/Fort Rock District Ranger Station,** 1230 NE 3rd St. #A262 (388-5664), has more specific info on parts of Deschutes National Forest. **Fish and Wildlife,** 61374 Parrell Rd. (388-6363), can fill you in on local regulations and permit requirements. Open daily 7:45am-4:30pm.

Buses: Greyhound, 2045 E. U.S. 20 (382-2151), 1½ mi. east of town. One bus per day to: Portland ($21) and Klamath Falls ($20). Open Mon.-Fri. 7:30-11:30am and 12:30-5:30pm, Sat. 7:30am-noon, Sun. 8-11:30am. Several other bus and van lines stop here, with different destinations; call the above number for info.

Taxi: Owl Taxi, 1917 NE 2nd St. (382-3311). 24hr.

Bicycle Rental: Hutch's Bicycles, 725 NW Columbia Ave. (382-9253). Mountain bikes $15 per day or $50 per week. Open Mon.-Fri. 9am-7pm, Sat.-Sun. 9am-6pm.

Laundromat: Nelson's, 738 NW Columbia Ave. (382-7087). Attendant on duty 8:30am-9:30pm. Wash $1, 10-min. dry 25¢. Open 6am-9:30pm.

Library: Deschutes County Library, 507 NW Wall (388-6679). Open Mon., Wed., Fri. 10am-6pm, Tues. and Thurs. 10am-8pm, Sat. 10am-5pm.

Ben and Jerry's Peace Pops: Don't even think of buying them in this town. None to be found anywhere. This is a Peace Pop wasteland.

Central Oregon Battering and Rape Alliance (COBRA): 800-356-2369.

Poison Control: 800-452-7165.

Alcohol and Drug Help Line: 800-621-1646.

Hospital: St. Charles Medical Center, 2500 NE Neff Rd. (382-4321), for major emergencies only. For routine cuts, scrapes, fractures, and illnesses, go to **Mountain Medical Immediate Care Center,** 1302 NE U.S. 97 (388-7799; open Mon.-Sat. 8am-8pm, Sun. 10am-6pm).

Emergency: 911. **Police:** 711 NW Bond (388-5550). **Fire:** 388-5533.

Post Office: 2300 NE 4th St. (388-1971), at Webster. Open Mon.-Fri. 8:30am-5:30pm, Sat. 10am-1pm. **General Delivery ZIP Code:** 97701.

Area Code: 541.

Bend is bisected by U.S. 97 (3rd St.). The downtown area lies to the west along the Deschutes River; Wall and Bond St. are the two main arteries. Watch out for curving streets with shifting names. From east to west, Franklin becomes Riverside, then Galveston, then Skyliner; Greenwood becomes Newport; and 14th St. becomes Century Dr. and is the first leg of the Cascade Lakes Hwy.

ACCOMMODATIONS AND CAMPING

Bend treats budget travelers right; the hostel and B&B provide phenomenal deals for tired travelers. Most of the cheapest motels are just outside town on 3rd St., and rates are surprisingly low. **Deschutes National Forest** maintains a *huge* number of lakeside campgrounds along the Cascade Lakes Highway to the west of town. All have toilets; those with drinking water cost $8-12 per night; those on paved roads without water are free. Contact the **Bend/Ft. Rock Ranger District Office** (see above) for more information.

Mill Inn, 642 NW Colorado (389-9198), on the corner of Bond St., 4 blocks from downtown. This B&B in a recently rebuilt hotel and boarding house is a labor of love for Ev and Carol Stiles, who keep the place sparkling clean. Hearty home-cooked breakfast served in the open dining room. Free laundry and plenty of storage for outdoor gear. $15 gets you a bunk in the dorm-style "Locker Room" (capacity 4), or spring for a trim, elegant private room (single $32, double $40, with shared bath). Rooms with private baths more expensive.

Bend Cascade Hostel, 19 SW Century Dr. (14th St.), Bend 97702 (389-3813 or 800-299-3813). From 3rd St., take Franklin west, and follow the Cascade Lakes Tour signs to Century Drive (14th St.); just past the Circle-K. Foosball and a healthy community atmosphere. Two blocks from ski and bike rentals and the free shuttle to

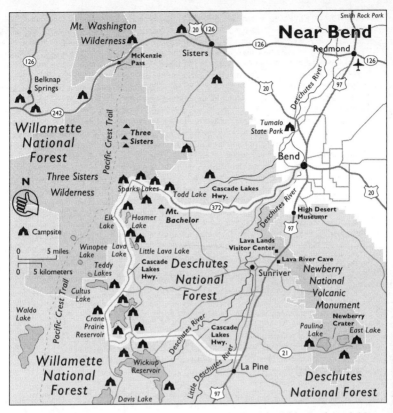

Mt. Bachelor. Coin laundry and kitchen, linen rental available. Lockout 9:30am-4:30pm, curfew 11pm. 4 private rooms available. 55 beds. $14. Seniors, students, cyclists, and members $13. Under 18 $7.

Royal Gateway Motel, 475 SE 3rd (382-5631). Clean and comfy, if close to the road. The bathrooms are not actually larger than the bedrooms; it's just a clever optical illusion. Free local phone calls and cable TV. Microwaves and fridges available. Singles $26, doubles $38. Rates $2-3 lower in winter.

Edelweiss Motel, 2346 NE Division St. (382-6222), at Xerxes St. near the northern intersection with 3rd St. A worn building, with a hint of German heritage. No phones or A/C, but clean, and you won't find a cheaper room in Bend. Singles $25. Doubles $36.

Cultus Lake Campground, 40 mi. west of Bend, 2 mi. off the Cascade Lakes Hwy. You can get anything you need at the little resort across the lake—including boat rentals. Well shaded campground slopes to the shore. A slightly longer drive than other nearby spots, it is slower to fill up. Drinking water and vault toilets. $9.

FOOD

The diversity of food in Bend breaks the surrounding beef-and-potatoes monotony. You won't go hungry here; restaurants generally maintain high standards, and there are a number to choose from. The most interesting and exceptional cafés are generally found downtown. No fewer than four mega-markets line the east side of 3rd St. **Devore's Good Food Store and Wine Shop,** 1124 NW Newport (389-6588) peddles anything organic, as well as excellent wine, beer, and cheese.

West Side Bakery and Café, 1005 NW Galveston (382-3426). Locally famous for its breakfasts, the West Side Café's lunches should soon extend its reputation. Healthy and delish sandwiches ($5.25) are served amid plastic dinosaur heads and Disney figures while a toy train circles overhead. Virtually everything here is homemade, including the bread ($2 per loaf). Open daily 7am-3pm.

Taqueria Los Jalapeños, 601 NE Greenwood Ave. (382-1402). Narrow and delightfully simple space with a steady stream of devoted locals coming through the screen door. A bean and cheese burrito costs a piddly $1.50 and the chimichanga plate ($4.75) is the priciest item on the menu. Open Mon.-Sat. 7:30am-8pm.

Deschutes Brewery and Public House, 1044 NW Bond St. (382-9242). The homemade sausage sandwich ($5) and smoked vegetable sandwich ($5) are always a good option, but 6 or 7 new specials a day ($5-7) render the menu moot. Imperial pints (20oz.) of ale, bitters, or stout brewed on the premises ($2.50). Their Black Butte Porter is found on tap in bars all over Oregon. Live music many weekends. Wheelchair accessible. Open Mon.-Thurs. 11am-11:30pm, Fri.-Sat. 11am-12:30am, Sun. 11am-10pm. Minors not allowed after 8:30pm.

JoOl's Bento Bar, 114 NW Minnesota St. (385-9194), between Wall and Bond. Fax in your order or make a personal appearance at this snappy little spot. Do the chicken, tofu, or vegetable skewer with rice ($3.75-4.15) or opt for a heap of Yaki Soba Noodles ($2.90); both come with any or all of 4 savory sauces. Open Mon.-Fri. 11am-7pm, Sat. 11am-4pm.

SIGHTS AND OUTDOORS

In Bend, you can get up close and personal with Canada geese, or just enjoy a picnic lunch, on the lawns of beautiful **Drake Park.** The park is sandwiched between Mirror Pond, a dammed part of the Deschutes River, and Franklin St., a block from downtown. The park is host to a number of events and festivals, most significantly the **Cascade Festival of Music** (383-2202), a 10-day series of concerts held each year in late August under a tent by the river. The music is primarily classical, though there is an occasional pops or jazz night. Tickets are $12, or you can try for a $3 student rush ticket 10 minutes before showtime. Call the festival office (382-8381) or write 842 NW Wall St. #6, Bend 97701.

Baseball fans bemoaning the departure of the Bend Rockies for Portland can still catch a professional baseball game. The **Bend Bandits** (383-1983), in an independent league, play at Vince Genna Stadium, 401 SE Roosevelt, just off 3rd St., from mid-May to early September (box seats $6, general admission $4, kids and seniors $3). Weekends sell out on occasion, so it may be wise to call ahead or swing by the office to pick out your seat. Six mi. south of Bend on U.S. 97, the exceptional **High Desert Museum** (382-4754) is one of the premier natural history museums in the Pacific Northwest. In the "Spirit of the West," visitors walk through stunning life-size dioramas of life in the Old West, including mining tunnels straight out of Indiana Jones. The indoor "desertarium" presents seldom-seen animals like burrowing owls, collared lizards, and even endangered trout in a simulated desert habitat. Outside, paved paths wind past playful otters and docile porcupines, plus exhibits on birds of prey, a settler's cabin, sheepherder's wagon, and an old-time sawmill. The museum attracts about 1200 visitors daily in mid-summer, so come early to beat the crowds. The price of admission is high, but it's entirely worth it ($6.25, seniors and ages 13-18 $5.75, ages 5-12 $3, under 5 free; open daily 9am-5pm).

In November 1990, **Newberry National Volcanic Monument** was established to link together and preserve the volcanic features south of Bend. For an introduction to the area, visit the **Lava Lands Visitor Center** (593-2421), 5 mi. south of the High Desert Museum on U.S. 97 (open March to mid-Oct., Wed.-Sun. 10am-4pm, late June-Labor Day daily 9:30am-5pm; off-season dates subject to weather and annual budget decisions).

Immediately behind the visitors center is **Lava Butte,** a 500-ft. cinder cone from which much of the nearby lava flows. Between Memorial Day and Labor Day, you can take a shuttle bus ($1.75, seniors and children $1, under 6 free) or walk the 1½-mi.

road. In the off season, individuals may drive their own cars up the spiralled incline. From the top lookout point, you can see the 10-sq. mi. area leveled by the lava that flowed from the butte, and the relatively rapid regeneration of life within the area. On clear days, the point affords vistas of Mt. Bachelor, South Sister, and other Cascade peaks.

One mi. south of the Visitor Center on U.S. 97 is **Lava River Cave** (593-1456), a 100,000-year-old, 1-mi.-long subterranean lava tube. The entrance to the cave is in a stand of gigantic ponderosa pines, perfect for a picnic. The rocky path smooths out after about five minutes of hiking into the cavernous tunnel, which is 50 ft. high in places. Bundle up before you descend and either bring a lantern or rent one at the cave for $1.50 (entrance $2.50, ages 13-17 $2, under 13 free; open mid-May to mid-Oct. 9am-6pm).

The central component of the monument is **Newberry Crater,** 18 mi. south of Lava Butte on U.S. 97, then about 13 steep miles eastward and upward on Rte. 21. This diverse volcanic region was formed by the eruptions of Newberry Volcano over millions of years (Newberry is one of three volcanoes in Oregon most likely to erupt again "soon"). The caldera, or center of the volcano, covers about 500 sq. mi. and contains two lakes, **Paulina Lake** and **East Lake.** The most scenic campground is **Little Crater,** with close to 50 sites between Rte. 21 and the lakeshore strung along Paulina Lake. Over 150 mi. of trails cross the area, including a short walk up to an enormous **obsidian flow** deposited by an eruption 1300 years ago, a 21-mi. loop that circumnavigates the caldera rim, and a 7-mi. loop around Paulina Lake ($11; premier sites $13). For a great view of the crater, drive up **Paulina's Peak** (June-Sept., weather conditions permitting).

If you can ski the 9075-ft. **Mt. Bachelor** with its 3100-ft. vertical drop, you're in good company; Mt. Bachelor is one of the home mountains of the U.S. Ski Team. The ski season often extends to the 4th of July. From Christmas through Easter, a free morning and afternoon shuttle bus service is offered for the 22 mi. between the parking lot at the corner of Simpson and Columbia in Bend and the West Village Guest Services Building at the mountain. (Daily lift passes $35, ages 7-12 $19, or ski by a "point system" where you pay only for the runs you ski. Many nearby lodges offer 5-night ski packages. Call 800-800-8334 or 382-8334 to make reservations. For general information call 800-829-2442; for a daily updated ski report and summer events call 382-7888.) Chairlifts are open for sightseers during the summer, and you can hike back down the mountain or ride both ways ($9.50, kids $4.75, seniors $6.50; open 10am-4pm). It can be a chilly ride, even in August. A U.S. Forest Service naturalist gives free presentations on local natural history at the summit in summer daily at 11am and 1pm.

The **Three Sisters Wilderness Area,** north and west of the Cascade Lakes Highway, is one of Oregon's largest and most popular wilderness areas. A permit (free) is required to go into the wilderness, but day-hikers can issue themselves permits at most trailheads. Bikes are not allowed in the wilderness. Permits and information are available at Bend Ranger District Office or Central Oregon Welcome Center (see **Practical Information,** above).

Mountain biking is the favorite sport of Benders. Many roads have bike lanes or wide shoulders. Hutch's (see **Practical Information,** above) will rent you a bike. Try **Phil's Trail** for an zesty 11-mi. ride through young ponderosa pine forests on easy to moderate terrain. To reach this single-track trail, follow Skyliner Rd. (a.k.a. Galveston) west 2.7 mi. from the last stop sign, then turn left on paved Forest Rd. 220 and follow for half a mile to the gate at the trailhead (at Forest Rd. 4606). This one's a little hard to find; when in doubt, follow the bike tracks in the dirt. For a difficult, technical ride, try the **Shevlin Park Loop** in Shevlin Park, 5 mi. west of downtown on Newport Ave. (which becomes N. Shevlin). The 5½-mi. loop crosses Tumalo Creek and climbs the canyon wall before returning. A slick new guide to the vast array of mountain bike trails around Bend is available for $7 at the Bend Ranger District Office and most bike shops in the area, but the hottest trails aren't on the maps. You have to talk to locals or find them yourself.

Would-be cowpokes can get their fix on **horseback rides** offered by local resorts. **Nora Stables** (389-6152, ask for the stables), at Inn of the Seventh Mountain, several miles west of Bend on Century Dr., leads trail rides (1½hr. $17, each additional ½hr. $5; 4hr. $50, 8hr. $70). **Whitewater rafting,** although costly, is one of the most popular local recreational activities. Half-day trips usually last three hours and cover the fairly tame waters of the Upper Deschutes, while full-day trips require a one-hour ride to Maupin to run the class I-IV rapids of the lower Deschutes. **Cascade River Adventures** and **Sun Country Tours** (call 389-8370 or 800-770-2161 for both) run half-day ($34; under 12 $28) and full-day ($80; under 12 $70) trips out of the Sun River Resort (15 mi. south of Bend off U.S. 97) and out of an office in Bend (61115 S. Hwy. 97). For the longer trip, however, you might try **Blazing Paddle Whitewater Adventures** (388-0145). Their full day trip is $70 per person and they'll pick you up anywhere in town.

Smith Rock State Park, equidistant from **Prineville, Sisters,** and Bend (located 9 mi. north of Redmond, off U.S. 97), is a remarkable gorge whose sheer cliffs make it a rock climber's paradise. Over the years, the Crooked River has carved into the high plain east of the Cascades, leaving a gorge of iridescent pinkish-yellow walls and immense rocky spires. World class climbers hang above the river like spiders. A number of trails wind along the river and to the top of several of the formations, where panoramic views of the Cascades and surrounding rock formations unfold. The campground is cheap ($4) because it's a 200-yd. commute from the parking lot (flush toilets; showers $2 for noncampers).

■ Near Bend: Sisters

Twenty mi. northwest of Bend on U.S. 20, the restored western village of Sisters nestles against the Cascades. The tiny town has managed to adopt an Old West look to attract tourist dollars without falling victim to tacky commercialism (yet). The plan seems to have worked, and Sisters can be overrun in midsummer by camera-snapping and souvenir-buying crowds. While Cascade St. (Sisters' main drag) is good for a stroll or snack, the real reason to come to this corner of central Oregon is the massive mountains to the west, where dense forest is interspersed with spring-fed creeks, alpine lakes, and the sizable Metolius River. Although this is a popular part of the Cascades, it isn't hard to find somewhere to be alone, if that's your fancy.

Practical Information From Sisters, Rte. 126 heads east to Redmond (20 mi.) and Prineville (39 mi.), and joins U.S. 20 for the trip over the Cascades. Rte. 242 heads southwest out of town and over McKenzie Pass to rejoin Rte. 126 on the other side of the Cascades. In town, the highways all blend into Cascade St. The **Sisters Ranger District Station** (Deschutes National Forest), P.O. Box 249 (549-2111), on the corner of Cascade and Pine at the west edge of town, is the place to go for all kinds of recreation information, including a list of nearby campgrounds and the *Day Hike Guide* (free), a catalogue of five nearby hikes from 2 to 10 mi. long (hr. vary, call ahead; if they do not plan on being open, they will leave brochures and maps in the drop box).

Accommodations, Camping, and Food A cheap bed is hard to find in Sisters. At the **Sisters Motor Lodge,** 600 W. Cascade (549-2551), on the highway at the west end of town, you get your money's worth with individually-themed rooms like "Grandma's Cottage" or "Picket Fence" that are pulled off gracefully with handmade quilts and antique accents (also with phones, coffee makers and cable TV). Rooms start around $55 in the summer. If cheap is what you're after, the **Silver Spur Motel,** 540 W. Cascade (549-6591), next to Sisters Motor Lodge, is perfect. The old building has dim, undistinguished rooms (some with free kitchens), cable TV, and no phones (1 bed $35, 2 beds $45).

Camping is plentiful and spectacular near Sisters. The Sisters Ranger District (see above) maintains 26 campgrounds in the area. Many of these cluster near **Camp Sherman,** a small community on the Metolius River, 15 mi. northwest of Sisters. The Metolius River campgrounds tend to be the most crowded, and virtually all charge a $9 fee. One noteworthy exception is **Riverside,** a walk-in tent ground where you can escape from motorized vehicles and pump your own water ($5). **Link Creek,** at the end of a 3-mi. road which circles Suttle Lake (14 mi. northwest of Sisters on Hwy. 20) is one of six campgrounds open year round. Although the lake can fill up with fishing boats and the occasional windsurfer, it is a serene spot on weekdays ($10; premium sites $12). For a free and less frequented camping spot, cruise 14 mi. west on Rte. 242 and a bumpy ½ mi. on a red dirt road to **Lava Camp Lake,** a magnificently isolated campground just off the lava fields of McKenzie Pass.

Plan on breezing through Sisters during the daylight hours; things are slow at six and dead by dark. Overpriced seafood and bar food can be had anytime, but the best bets for the palette and the purse are the delis that close by 5 or 6pm. For exquisite specialty salads and carefully assembled gourmet sandwiches ($4.50-5.25), head for **Seasons Café and Wine Shop,** 310 E. Hood (549-8911) one block south of Cascade along a little brook (open daily 11am-6pm; mid-Oct. to mid-May 11am-3pm). The **Sisters Bakery,** 120 E. Cascade St. (549-0361), has big front windows and all kinds of delectable baked goods, including small, scrumptiously sweet marionberry scones ($1.25). The bakery is also a good place to stock up on loaves of top-quality specialty bread ($1.80-4.25; open daily 6am-6pm).

Events and Outdoors The **Sisters Rodeo,** the "Biggest Little Show in the World," takes place annually on the second weekend in June and packs an astonishing purse: a total of $170,000 attracts big-time wranglers for three days and nights of saddle bronco-riding, calf-roping, and steer-wrestling, among other events. Keep your gender stereotypes in order by watching the Pepsi Girls, Dodge Pickup Guys, and some excellent rodeo clowning. Tickets are $8-12, and the show usually sells out. (Write the Sisters Rodeo Association, P.O. Box 1018, Sisters 97759, or call 549-0121 for more information, or call 800-827-7522 for tickets.)

Hundreds of miles of **hiking** trails loop through the forests and mountains around Sisters. An easy, level walk along the **Metolius River** will give you time to ponder the debate over the origin of the river's name (some say "metolius" means "white fish," some, "spawning salmon," and others, "stinking water"). Drive past Camp Sherman to the Wizard Falls Fish Hatchery to catch the trail. A slightly more challenging hike is the 4-mi. roundtrip up **Black Butte,** a near-perfect cone which looms over the west end of town. To get to the trailhead, go 6 mi. west from Sisters on U.S. 20, turn right onto Forest Rd. 11, then turn onto Forest Rd. 1110 after 4 mi. The trailhead is another 4 mi. up the road. Deeper in the mountains, the strenuous 7.6 mi. roundtrip hike up **Black Crater** offers unsurpassed views of snow-capped peaks and lava flows on McKenzie Pass and an intimate experience with volcanic debris. The trail departs from the left-hand side of Rte. 242 about 11 mi. west of Sisters.

The Metolius River is ground zero for **fishing** in the area, with a top notch fishery for rainbow and brook trout, kokanee, and the woefully underappreciated whitefish. Special regulations allow only catch-and-release and fly-fishing in certain areas. Stream fishing is not allowed so that fish may spawn in peace and privacy. Contact the Sisters Ranger District Office (see **Practical Information,** above) for details. **Suttle Lake,** a jewel of a lake 12 mi. northwest of Sisters off U.S. 20, supports a warm-water fishery, including bass.

McKenzie Pass, 15 mi. west of Sisters on Rte. 242, was the site of a relatively recent lava flow, creating ranging, barren fields of black *aa* (AH-ah) lava. Look for the hill the lava flowed around, creating an island. A tall, quasi-medieval tower built of lava chunks affords a panoramic view of the high Cascades. A ½-mi. paved trail winds among the basalt boulders, cracks, and crevices.

OREGON

Mountain biking opportunities abound near Sisters. Although no bikes or motorized vehicles are allowed in designated wilderness areas, some trails are open to bikes, as are the many miles of little-used dirt roads in the area. Ask at the ranger station for details. **Eurosports,** 115 W. Hood (P.O. Box 1421; 549-2471) rents mountain bikes for $10 per 24hr., $50 per week (open daily 9am-5:30pm).

■ John Day Fossil Beds National Monument

The small town of **John Day,** known for the fossil beds nearby and found at the junction of U.S. 26 and U.S. 395, is the largest for miles around, and the best place near the monument to find a bed or a meal. The AAA-approved **Dreamer's Lodge,** 144 N. Canyon Blvd. (575-0526, reservations 800-654-2849), is a great place to relax. The clean, comfortable rooms all have La-Z-Boy recliners, and huge pictures of tropical landscapes over the beds. A/C, refrigerators, and cable TV with movie channels (singles $40, doubles $44, two kitchen units are available). The **Travelers Motel and Mini-mart,** 755 S. Canyon Blvd. (575-2076) has the best rates in town and a laudromat on the premises (75¢ wash, 50¢ dry). Though the rooms have TV, A/C, microwaves, and refrigerators, none are non-smoking, and the decor reflects the inexpensive price ($22 single, $27 double). Seven mi. west of John Day on U.S. 26, the flat, neatly-mowed grass of **Clyde Holliday State Park** (575-2773) has a slightly suburban aura (30 campsites with electricity and showers cost $17; hiker/biker sites $4 per person).

With four microbrews and all-you-can-drink Coke, **The Cave Inn,** 830 S. Canyon Blvd. (575-1083) is the happening local hangout (open Sat.-Thurs. 11:30am-10pm, Fri. 11:30am-11pm). At **The Bite,** 150 E. Main St. (575-0835), choose from seven meats, six breads, and eight cheeses to create a solid sandwich that comes with soup, salad, or chips ($15). The 32oz. milkshake, made from hard-packed Oregon-made ice cream ($2.50), is too thick for a straw. Open Mon.-Fri. 8am-5:30pm, Sat. 10am-5pm. The best watering hole in town, the **Dirty Shame Tavern and Pizza,** 145 Main St. (575-1935), sports a fancy wooden bar, pool table, dance floor, dart board, and TV. They claim to have the "best pizza in town"—you decide (open Mon.-Sat. 10:30am-midnight, Sun. noon-8pm).

Ferdinand's, 128 W. Front St. (820-4455) a lovely 13 mi. drive from John Day in **Prairie City,** offers a surprising array of gourmet food and imported beers. With homemade crust on the pizzas (large, $10-15.95), fresh sauces on all the pasta (try the pesto), and a remarkable selection of items from the grill, including fresh Oregon sturgeon, Ferdinand's will shock and impress the most discerning of palates. Grilled chicken with porcini mushroom sauce $8.95. Open Sun.-Mon. 7am-9pm, Sat. 7am-10pm.

The **John Day Fossil Beds National Monument** records the history of life before the Cascade Range was formed, depicting a land of lush, tropical vegetation and ambling dinosaurs. The park exists in three isolated parts, each representing a different epoch, each at least as impressive for its scenery as for its fossils. **Clarno,** the oldest, is on Rte. 218 (accessible by U.S. 97 to the west and Rte. 19 to the east), 20 mi. west of the town of **Fossil.** You will be humbled by the embarrassing insignificance of our species in the grand geological scheme. **Painted Hills,** 3 mi. west of Mitchell off U.S. 26, focuses on an epoch 30 million years ago, when the land was in geologic transition. Its smooth mounds of colored sediment are particularly vivid at sunset and dawn, or after a rain when the whole gorge glistens. The ½-mi. trail to the overlook is a good leg stretcher.

Sheep Rock, 25 mi. east of Mitchell and 5 mi. west of Dayville at the junction of U.S. 26-Rte. 19, houses the monument's **visitors center** and will satiate all cravings for fossils you can see and touch. The center displays rocks and fossils from all layers of history, exhibits on early mammals, and an award-winning 17-minute video explaining the history of the fossil beds (you'd never guess high school students put it together). After a stop in the visitor center, don't miss the **Island in Time Trail,** 3 mi. up the road. The unfortunately named "Island in Time" is a ½-mi. trail that leads into the middle of Blue Basin, a fossil-rich and strikingly beautiful canyon of eroded badland spires. (Park always open; **visitors center** open March-Aug. daily 8:30am-6pm; Sept.-Nov. daily 8:30-5pm; Dec.-Feb. Mon.-Fri. 8:30am-5pm.)

The town of John Day is surrounded on three sides by the massive **Malheur** (mal-HERE) **National Forest.** Malheur ranges in elevation from 4000 to 9038 ft., and contains sagebrush-and-juniper grasslands and forests of pine and fir. Information is available at the Malheur National Forest Supervisor's Office, 431 Patterson Bridge Rd. (575-1731) in John Day or the Bear Valley/Long Creek District Ranger Station, 528 E. Main St. (575-2110; both open Mon.-Fri. 7:15am-5pm). Most of the time, this vast, wild region of timbered hills and jagged ridges gets little use, and there are prime opportunities for solitude and great hiking, particularly in the Forest's two designated wilderness areas, **Strawberry Mountain** and **Monument Rock.** By far the most popular area in the forest is the **Eastern Lakes Basin,** in the Strawberry area. Three campgrounds—McNaughton (4 sites), Slide Creek (3 sites), and Strawberry (11 sites)—are near the **Strawberry Trailhead,** a main access point for the Strawberry Mountain area. From the Strawberry Trailhead, you can hike 1 mi. to Strawberry Lake, climb Strawberry Mountain, the forest's highest peak, or take a 12-mi. loop hike past several other lakes. The trailhead is located south of Prairie City on Forest Rd. 6001. **Magone Lake** (Mah-GOON) is another popular free campground, with beaches, fishing, and hiking trails. The campground has 25 sites and nice bathrooms. From Mt. Vernon, west of John Day, take U.S. 395 north, and go east on Forest Rd. 36, which becomes 3620 and leads to the campground. You can also camp wherever you please in the forest, except, of course, near "No Trespassing" signs.

▓ Burns

Burns is the seat of Harney County, a county larger than Vermont in area with fewer residents than the city of Montpelier. Tiny Burns and its even tinier neighbor Hines serve as way-stations and supply centers for travelers. Ideally situated between the **Ochoco** and **Malheur National Forests,** and the **Malheur National Wildlife Refuge, Steens Mountain,** and the **Alvord Desert,** there's plenty of open country around Burns. Stock up on gas, water, information, and supplies in Burns, and head for the unspoiled, virtually uninhabited wilderness that fills southeastern Oregon.

Practical Information and Orientation For information on the public lands surrounding Burns, head to the **Burns Ranger District (Malheur National Forest)** and **Snow Mountain Ranger District (Ochoco National Forest),** HC 74, Box 12870, Hines 97738 (573-4300). On the main drag, about 4½ mi. south of the center of Burns, these two share the same office and provide information on hiking, fishing, and camping (open Mon.-Fri. 8am-4:30pm). The **Burns District Office (BLM),** HC 74-12533 U.S. 20 W., Hines 97738 (573-4400), a few miles west of Hines, is rife with information on public lands administered by the BLM around Burns. (Open Mon.-Fri. 8am-4:30pm.) A makeshift **visitors center** in the Tuning Studio and Gallery, 21 N. Broadway (573-2435) at Monroe, has **maps** and information on the town itself (open Mon.-Sat. 9am-6pm).

After a messy romp across the land, clean up your gear at **Jiffy Wash,** S. Diamond St., one block south of W. Monroe (wash $1, 12½-min. dry 25¢; open daily 7am-10pm). Ease your aching muscles with remedies from **Payless Drug,** 629 N. U.S. 20 (573-1525), in Hines (open Mon.-Fri. 9am-9pm, Sat. 9am-8pm, Sun. 10am-6pm). The **crisis hotline** in the area is **H Hope Hotline** (573-7176). For a daily recording on **road conditions** call 1-889-3999. The local hospital is **Harney District Hospital,** 557 W. Washington St. (573-7281). In an **emergency** call 911. The **police** are at 242 S. Broadway (573-6028), or call the **Harney County Sheriff** (573-6136). The **post office** is at 100 S. Broadway (573-2931; open Mon.-Fri. 8:30am-5pm; **ZIP code:** 97720). The **area code** is 541.

U.S. 20 from Ontario and U.S. 395 from John Day converge about 2 mi. north of Burns, and continue through Burns and Hines as one highway (known as Broadway, Monroe, and Oregon Ave. through town), and diverge about 30 mi. to the west. U.S. 20 continues west to Bend and the Cascade Range; U.S. 395 south to Lakeview, OR, and California. Although buses and vans can get you to and from some towns in the area, there is no transportation to the most interesting outdoor areas in the vicinity.

Accommodations and Camping Though Burns provides several good budget motels, the **Malheur Field Station** (See **Outdoors,** below) provides a unique way to experience the natural beauty of southeastern Oregon. If you must have a roof, head down Rte. 205 south to The **Frenchglen Hotel.** The hotel, Rte. 205, Frenchglen 97736 (493-2825), serves up almost ridiculously good homemade food in a quaint, historic building owned by Oregon State Parks. The enormous breakfasts ($3-5.75) will keep you going all day, and the "family-style" dinner is not to be forgotten ($10.50-15). Trim, cozy rooms with wood-frame full beds, patchwork quilts, and shared bath go for $45; two single beds $49. Reservations are essential in the summer. Whether you come to eat, sleep, or both, hotel operator John Ross will make you feel right at home (open March 15-Nov. 15; breakfast 7:30am-9:30am, lunch 11:30am-2:30pm, dinner by reservation).

The **Bontemps Motel,** 74 W. Monroe (573-2037 or 800-735-2037), at the center of Burns, is a good deal, with small, spare rooms which look better when you find out what they cost (no phone in rooms; pay phone on premises; TV, A/C, garage, refrigerators; kitchenettes available for $3-5; singles $27.25, doubles $31.60; pets $1 extra). Camping is the cheapest way to enjoy the breathtaking open country around Burns. About 10 mi. north of town, within earshot of U.S. 395, is **Idlewild,** the only official campground that could be called convenient to town. It has 24 sites sprinkled through sparse pines, and a solitary bench carved out of a single log. Although there are relatively few campgrounds around Burns, the public lands are vast and dispersed camping is allowed. Certain restrictions apply when the risk of wildfire is high. Contact the U.S. Forest Service and BLM offices in Hines (see **Practical Information,** above) for more information.

About 4 mi. east of Frenchglen, along the first bit of the loop, two easy-to-find campgrounds provide more primitive sleeping arrangements. The privately-owned **Steens Mountain Resort** (also called the **Camper Corral;** 493-2415 or 800-542-3765 for reservations), set atop a low hill, offers groceries, showers, and a 24hr. laundry, but not much shade or privacy (tent site $10, RV hookup $14, open year-round). Just down the road, by the side of the Blitzen River, the BLM-administered **Page Springs** campground has 30 sites of varying seclusion and cover, drinking water, and pit toilets. (No reservations, $4.)

Food Beef is king here; with few exceptions, restaurants serve traditional, uninspired American fare in dining rooms with even less flavor. Groceries can be had at **Safeway,** 246 W. Monroe (573-6767; open daily 5am-11pm). The best food in the area can be had at the Frenchglen Hotel (see **Accommodations,** above), but an equally appealing alternative is the **Frenchglen Mercantile,** just two doors down on Rte. 205 (493-2738), which covers all the bases. A functional gas station, grocery store, bar, and café, the Mercantile has all you need to stockpile for impending biological disaster. The menu choices are all between $4.50-7.50, and they have several microbrews on tap. (Open March 1-Nov. 15 daily 7am-11pm.)

Outdoors The surrounding open country beckons to any soul seeking adventure, fresh air, and solitude. Rte. 205 provides passage to the intriguing terrain south of Burns. The wide, dry land is home only to sagebrush until it gives way to the rich grasslands and marshes of **Harney** and **Malheur Lakes.** Thousands of birds abandon their migratory flight paths each year to make **Malheur National Wildlife Refuge** their home. Protecting both lakes and stretching 35 mi. south along Rte. 205, the refuge covers 185,000 acres and is home to 300 species of birds. It contains enough grebes, ibis, plovers, shrikes, owls, goatsuckers, and wigeons to satisfy the most serious bird-watchers and photographers. The refuge headquarters, 5 mi. east of 205 on a well marked turnoff, includes a **visitors center** (493-2612; open Mon.-Fri. 7am-4:30pm) which helps provide a valuable orientation to the area. The refuge is open year-round during daylight hours. The **Malheur Field Station,** HC 72 Box 260, Princeton 97721 (493-2629), run by a consortium of universities and located 2 mi. short of the headquarters, offers room and board to visitors staying overnight in the refuge. Accommodations are undeniably spartan, but clean and inexpensive; $18 for dorm or private accommodations. You can also rent your own mobile home for $27. Meals cost $6-7. Cooking facilities are available. Bring a sleeping bag or bedroll. (Reservations strongly encouraged in the spring and fall, when the place is packed with school groups.)

Geology buffs will want to turn off toward **Diamond Craters,** where a series of basaltic burps by the earth's mantle have created a landscape of diverse volcanic features. But if you go, be careful, or "you might spend some time stuck in loose cinder, volcanic ash, or clay," warns a BLM publication. Rattlesnakes should also be avoided, as they are notoriously intolerant of humans, particularly tourists. Pick up a self-guided auto tour of the area, along with other information, at the Burns District BLM office in Hines, or the refuge visitors center.

About 70 mi. southeast of Burns, and a few miles from Frenchglen, is **Steens Mountain,** a 30-mi.-long fault-block whose east face rises a dramatic vertical mile above the surrounding desert. At 9773 ft. in elevation, Steens is the highest mountain in southeastern Oregon, and the view from the top includes parts of four states. The **Steens Mountain Loop Road** is a 66-mi. dirt road which climbs the gradual west slope of the mountain to several viewpoints above deep glacier-carved gorges. The road is only open when clear of snow, typically July 1 to Oct. 31, and even then is rough, but the view is magnificent. The mountain offers many recreational opportunities, including wildlife watching (notably bighorn sheep and pronghorn antelope) and hiking. The mountain's remoteness keeps it relatively uncrowded, and nearly all visitors are vehicle-shackled sightseers; a willingness to walk even a short distance from the road brings solitude. The loop road heads east from Rte. 205 just south of Frenchglen and, though marked, is not obvious. It comes back into Rte. 205 8 mi. farther south. Contact the Burns District BLM office (see **Practical Information**) for up-to-date road information and advice on recreational opportunities.

The bone-dry, mirror-flat **Alvord Desert** stretches east of Steens. The mountain blocks virtually all moisture from reaching the Alvord, which receives less than 6in. of precipitation a year. The driest and emptiest part of the Pacific Northwest, this ocean of sand is the playground of desert hikers, glider pilots, and land-sailors. To get to this Oregonian Sahara, head south from Frenchglen for about 50 mi. to the small town of Fields, and turn left onto the dirt road toward Andrews.

Winding its way north from Nevada through the Alvord Desert and up Steens Mountain is the **Desert Trail,** an arid hiking route which runs from the Mexican border to the Canadian border on the desert lands east of the Sierras and Cascades. This little-known trail stretches 150 mi. through southeastern Oregon, offering some beautifully desolate exploration. Trail guides and information are available from the **Desert Trails Association.** Contact the Membership and Hike Chairman Keith Sheerer at P.O. Box 346, Madras 97741 (475-2960).

▓ Pendleton

This small town was named in 1868 after George Hunt Pendleton, a vice-presidential candidate from Ohio. He had nothing to do with Oregon, but someone liked the ring of his name and the town was born. In spite of this honor, he never visited Pendleton and fatefully lost the election. If you find yourself on these quiet streets, you'll be easily spotted as the only tourist. If you come in mid-September with the 50,000 other cowboys and horsey hipsters for the **Pendleton Round-Up,** you can witness Pendleton's annual transformation into a macho town, and join the rodeo party of a lifetime.

PRACTICAL INFORMATION AND ORIENTATION

Visitors Information: Pendleton Chamber of Commerce, 25 SE Dorion Ave. (276-7411 or 800-547-8911), across from City Hall. Open Mon.-Fri. 8am-5pm.

Greyhound, 320 SW Court Ave. (276-1551), a few blocks west of the city center. To: Portland (2 per day, $30); Boise, ID (2 per day, $35); Walla Walla (2 per day; $9). Open Mon-Fri. 9:30am-6pm, Sat. 10am-6pm, later only to meet the buses. Call 800-231-2222 for up-to-date fare and schedule info.

Amtrak: Unstaffed shelter and boarding area at 108 S. Frazer. To: Portland (Tues., Thurs., and Sat., $50) and Denver (Mon., Wed., and Sat., $194). Call 800-872-7245 for prices and additional info.

Taxi: Elite Taxi (276-8294). Open Mon.-Sat. 4:30am-3am, Sun. 7am-3am.

Car Rental: Ugly Duckling Rent-A-Car, 309 SW Emigrant Ave. (276-1498). The only way to enjoy the Blue or Wallowa Mts. from Pendleton without your own car. $20 per day with 50 free mi., 15¢ each additional mi. Unlimited free mileage for weekly rental ($140). Must be over 25 and have a major credit card. Open Mon.-Fri. 8am-5pm, Sat. 8am-1pm.

Hospital: St. Anthony's, 1601 SE Court Ave. (276-5121).

Emergency: 911. **Police:** 109 SW Court Ave. (276-4411). **Fire:** 911 SW Court (276-1442). **Poison:** 800-452-7165. **Mental Health Services:** 800-452-5413.

Post Office: 104 SW Dorion Ave. (278-0203), in the Federal Building at SW 1st. Open Mon.-Fri. 9am-5pm, Sat. 10am-1pm. **General Delivery ZIP Code:** 97801. **Area Code:** 541.

Pendleton is at the junction of I-84 and Rte. 11, just south of the Washington border, roughly equidistant (200-230 mi.) from Portland, Spokane, and Boise. While cool, green **Raley Park**—humming year-round with the latent life of the Round-Up Grounds next door—may be the spiritual center of town, Main Street is Pendleton's geographic hub.

The town's streets were named to facilitate navigation for airmen from a nearby base (now closed). The east-west streets are named in alphabetical order. From Main St., north-south streets are numbered, increasing in both directions (there are two 2nd Streets, for example, 2nd SE and 2nd SW, parallel to each other).

ACCOMMODATIONS AND CAMPING

Most of the time, lodging in Pendleton is inexpensive. To stay here during the Round-Up, however, you must reserve rooms *up to two years* in advance. Rates double, and prices on everything from hamburgers to commemorative cowboy hats are jacked up. The nearest decent camping is 25 mi. away, though the Round-Up provides 1500 camping spots at schools around town (RVs $13, tents $9). Call the Chamber of Commerce after April 1 for reservations.

Longhorn Motel, 411 SW Dorion Ave. (276-7531), around the corner from the bus station. Clean, comfy rooms and a light blue and white exterior reminiscent of beach houses. Right in downtown Pendleton. Upstairs rooms have HBO. Downstairs rooms have wheelchair access. Singles $28. Doubles $34.

7 Inn (276-4711), 6 mi. west of town at exit 202 off I-84 (outside the reach of the city's motel tax). Horribly inconvenient for travelers without a car, but the sublime rolling farmlands which can be seen from the third level walkway, make it worth the trek. Large, clean rooms with cable TV, A/C, and VCRs. $2 movie rentals at the front desk. 24hr. Ranch Café down the hill. One bed $39, two $42.

Tapadera Budget Inn, 105 SE Court (276-3231 or 800-722-8277 for reservations), near the center of town. Lounge and eat on the premises. Singles $36, doubles $48. 10% AAA and senior discount available.

Emigrant Springs State Park (983-2277), 26 mi. southeast of Pendleton off Exit 234 on I-84. 51 sites (18 with hookup, disabled access) in a shady grove of evergreens at a historic Oregon Trail camp. Smell the pines and hear the highway. Hot showers. Sites $13, with hookup $17. Call ahead, budget cuts loom menacingly.

There are four campgrounds along this route. The most convenient are Woodward ($4 per night) and Woodland (free), two tiny campgrounds just off Rte. 204. Better bets are **Target Meadows** ($3 per night), an isolated spot only 2 mi. off the highway, or continue 12 mi. up the gravel road to **Jubilee Lake** ($5-7 per night), a developed (and crowded) wheelchair-accessible campground. To reach these two, turn north onto Forest Rd. 64 at Tollgate, 22 mi. east of the Rte. 204-Rte. 11 junction, and follow the signs.

FOOD

Vegetarians will have more luck grazing in the outlying wheat fields than in local restaurants. This is steak country. Exceptions are **Cakreations** and **The Great Pacific Café** (see below) and, for staples, the huge **Albertson's** on SW Court across from the Round-Up grounds (276-1362, open daily 6am-11pm).

Cakreations, 16 SE Court (276-7978). Originally started as a specialty cake bakery, now expanded to include a full line of bakery products, deli sandwiches, and soups. You can watch the activity, or enjoy the new patio. Food is healthy and delicious and the sandwiches ($3.45-3.85) come on fresh bakery bread. The "vegi" sandwich has an entire garden in it, add $1.25 for soup or salad. Finish up with a pastry from the case ($0.70-1.55). Open Mon.-Sat. 7:30am-6pm.

The Great Pacific Café, 403 S. Main (276-1350). *The* chill establishment in Pendleton hosts free wine tastings every two weeks and jazz concerts off and on during the summer. While their dishes are slightly more expensive than Pendleton's other restaurants, open-faced baked sandwiches run $3-5 and the veggie bagel is $3.95. Extensive beer list; the Black Butte Beer ($2.50 a pint) is fabulous. Open Mon.-Thurs. 8:30am-6pm, Fri. 8:30am-7pm, Sat. 8:30-6pm.

The Circle S., 210 SE 5th St. (276-9637). Don't let the 3-ft. axe door-handle scare you away from this Western barbecue restaurant. Sit in huge, wrap-around, faux-leather booths and drink from Mason jars while eating a teriyaki burger and fries ($5.25) and a *creme de menthe* sundae ($1.75). If you can eat the 72-oz. sirloin ($45) in an hour, like John Candy in *The Great Outdoors,* it's free (weekdays only before 8pm). Thankfully, smaller portions also available. Open Tues.-Thurs. 7am-9pm, Fri. and Sat. 7pm-10pm, Sun. 7am-2pm.

Bread Board, 141 S. Main St. (276-4520). Floral wallpaper, plastic-covered tablecloths, and quilts hanging on the walls make it feel like lunch at Grandma's. Great $3-4 sandwiches and huge cookies for 70¢. For breakfast try the ham, egg, and cheese croissant with a cup of fruit ($2.75). If it's not too busy, they'll make it for lunch, too. Open Mon.-Fri. 8am-3pm.

SIGHTS AND ACTIVITIES

Pendleton Underground Tours, 37 SW Emigrant (276-0730) is the town's greatest year-round attraction. It retells Pendleton's wild history from the height of activity, when it claimed 32 bars and 18 bordellos, to when they unscrewed the last red lightbulb. Pendleton did not have a sheriff until 1912, and even after that, many actually lived underground. The first half of the tour explains how Chinese and German immigrants prospered amid persecution. The second half describes the debauchery of the bordellos and speakeasies. They charge $10 for the full hour-and-a-half tour, or you can just attend the first or second half for $5. AAA members get a $1 discount. Open daily, call for times.

Pendleton is also a good stop-off point if you're on your way to explore the northern **Blue Mountains** or **Umatilla National Forest** (yoo-ma-TILL-uh). The **Forest Headquarters** in Pendleton, 2517 SW Hailey Ave. (278-3716), has the friendliest, most helpful staff you could ever want in a land management agency. Go there for

> ### Yeeeeee-haw!
>
> The **Pendleton Round-Up** (276-2553 or 800-457-6336), one of the premier events on the nation's rodeo circuit, draws ranchers from all over the U.S. for "four glorious days and nights" (always the second full week in Sept.; Sept. 16-19, 1997; Sept. 10-13, 1998). Steer-roping, saddle-bronc riding, bulldogging, and bareback riding barely over-shadow the buffalo-chip tosses, wild cow milking, and greased-pig chases. Yippee-kai-yay! The **Round-Up Hall of Fame** (278-0815), under the south grandstand area at SW Court Ave. and SW 13th St., has captured some of the rodeo's action for all eternity, including Pendleton's best preserved Round-Up hero, a stuffed horse named "War Paint." A lifetime membership to the Hall of Fame ($100) includes nominating power and an invitation to the annual banquet during the Round-Up. Call to arrange a tour (open April-Sept. daily 10am-5pm). For tickets to the Round-Up ($8-17.50 per event), write to the Pendleton Round-Up Association, P.O. Box 609, Pendleton 97801. While the 1997 event is already sold out and tickets for 1998 will probably be gone by the fall of 1997, have no fear: tickets for 1999 go on sale in November of 1997.

information on hiking, camping, fishing, and biking in the vast forested plateaus and canyons of the Blues. The red brick building is up the hill from exit 209 off I-84, just above the Burger King on the right (open Mon.-Fri. 7:45am-4:30pm). The main access to the area is found at Rte. 204, reached by heading north out of Pendleton on Rte. 11 for 21 mi. After a 41-mi. loop over the Blue Mountains, 204 meets Rte. 82 at Elgin on the east side of the mountains. Along the way, the road winds through dense timber, past campgrounds, creeks, and lakes, near two wilderness areas, the small **North Fork Umatilla** and the larger, more remote **Wenaha-Tucannon** wilderness. Both are little-used and offer real solitude, though Wenaha-Tucannon offers more challenging hiking.

■ Baker City

When Oregon Trail pioneers discovered gold, they decided to settle down and build a city at the base of the Blue Mountains. Tossing their tents aside, Baker City's first residents poured their riches into Victorian houses and grand hotels. Convenient to the Wallowa-Whitman National Forest and Hells Canyon, Baker City still claims the tallest building in Oregon east of the Cascades (Hotel Baker is an astounding 10 stories high). Even with a sizable population of 10,000, Baker City feels more like a town than its name lets on. Wonderful museums celebrate Baker's roots in the Oregon Trail.

PRACTICAL INFORMATION AND ORIENTATION

Visitors Information: Baker County Visitor Center and Convention Bureau, 490 Campbell St. (523-3356 or 800-523-1235), just off Exit 304 of I-84. Everything a visitors center should be. Stockpiled with enough brochures for three states, and the upper level is a museum of antique furniture and photos. Open Mon.-Fri. 8am-6pm, Sat. 8am-4pm, Sun. 9am-2pm; winter Mon.-Fri. 8am-5pm.

Buses: Greyhound, 515 Campbell St. (523-5011), by the interstate in the Truck Corral Café. Buses east to Boise (2 per day; $22) and west to Portland (2 per day; $35). Open daily 7-9:30am and 5-8pm; 800-231-2222 has up-to-date info.

Taxi: Baker Cab Co., 990 Elm St. (523-6070). Up to $3.75 within Baker City, $1 per mi. outside city limits. 24hr.

Laundromat: Baker City Laundry, 815 Cambell St. (523-9817). The mother of all laundromats, with untimed showers ($3.95), the cheapest fountain drinks around (32oz. 69¢), and a **Subway** sub shop next door. What more could you want? Wash $1, 12-min. dry 25¢. Open daily 7am-10pm.

Senior Services: Community Connection (523-6591). Open Mon.-Fri. 8am-5pm.

Women's Crisis: Mayday (523-4134).

Emergency: 911. **Police:** 1655 1st St. (523-3644).
Hospital: St. Elizabeth, 3325 Pocahontas Rd. (523-6461). Open 24hr.
Post Office: 1550 Dewey Ave. (523-4237). Open Mon.-Fri. 8:30am-5pm. **General Delivery ZIP Code:** 97814.
Area Code: 541.

Baker City lies 43 mi. southeast of La Grande and 137 mi. northwest of Boise, ID, on I-84 in northeastern Oregon. Rte. 86 leads east from Baker to Hells Canyon and Rte. 7 leads west, connecting with U.S. 26 to John Day and Prineville. Campbell and Main St. are the principal thoroughfares: Main runs parallel to I-84, and Campbell intersects I-84 just east of the city. Other important streets are Broadway Ave., which intersects Main St. downtown, 10th St., which crosses Broadway in the west, and Bridge St., an offshoot of Main St. to the southeast.

ACCOMMODATIONS AND CAMPING

Baker City has several reasonably priced motels. Generally, the deals get better the farther you get from the interstate.

Bruno Ranch Bed and Breakfast, Box 51, Bridgeport (call ahead, 446-3468). From Baker City, 9 mi. south on Rte. 7, then left onto Rte. 245. After 14 mi., turn left onto Bridgeport Rd.; it's the first house on the right. Bruno Ranch is rustic and comfortable, but not exceptional. Stay for the hospitality of Maria Bruno, an engaging Italian woman who, in return for company, cares for her guests like a grandmother. She cooks an excellent, hearty hunter's breakfast and will show you around the extensive ranch and surrounding terrain. If you're lucky, you can help feed the chickens. Popular with hunters in season. Single $25. Double $30. Camping $3 for tents, $8 for vehicles.

Eldorado Motel, 695 Campbell St. (523-6494 or 800-537-5756), right next to Greyhound. A friendly, gleaming motel, with neo-conquistador architecture. Big, refurbished rooms, Mexican tile bathrooms, and matador paintings. Indoor pool and jacuzzi, cable TV, refrigerators, A/C. 10% senior discounts. Singles $36. Two people $39. Two beds $49.

Royal Motor Inn, 2205 Broadway (523-6324 or 800-547-5827) at 3rd St. Clean, thickly carpeted rooms have hard beds. Cable TV, A/C, outdoor pool, $2-3. AAA discount. Singles $33. Doubles $39.

Green Gables, 2533 10th St. (523-5588) at Campbell. Unfortunately, the interior of these green and white cabins does not match the exterior. The rooms are somewhat cramped, but adjoining kitchens and low weekly rates make it a good choice for longer stays. 10% senior and commercial discount. Singles $31. Doubles $34. Weekly $135 and up.

Anthony Lake Campground: Take Rte. 30 north, past Haines and turn west onto Country Rd. 1146, which becomes Forest Rd. 73. Look for signs. Bored after his stint at the White House, the U.S.'s beloved national security advisor nabbed a position with the forest service. Despite its elevation (7100ft.), Lake's place draws large weekend crowds to its 37 sites on the shores of a lake. Closed until early July. Call Rangers for details. Wheelchair accessible. $5 per vehicle. If it's too crowded, try **Mud Creek,** a more primitive camping ground across the road.

Union Creek Campground, Box 54, Baker (894-2210), at Phillips Lake. Follow Rte. 7 west 20 mi. (toward Sumpter). High grasses and sparse pines make for high RV visibility in some parts. The tent grounds are woodsier. Beach with swimming area and boat ramp, flush toilets, but no showers. 58 sites. Tent area $10. Sites $12. Full hookup $14. Heater or A/C $1 per day. Senior citizen discount.

FOOD

Compared to the towns around it, Baker City is a delight to the downtrodden diner. While big breakfasts and burgers may still be had on 10th St., there are a number of great cafés along Main St. that offer a touch of big city ambiance and an alternative to the ubiquitous Oregon meat-and-potatoes fare. Take time to grab Mexican food or gourmet pizza while you can.

El Erradero, 2100 Broadway (523-2327). Where the locals go for giant Mexican meals. From free chips and delectable salsa to the espresso burrito with everything on it ($6.50), this place serves Mex without the Tex. The chicken enchilada ($4) comes with rice and beans. Two enchiladas $6.25. Open Sun.-Thurs. 11am-9:30pm, Fri. and Sat. 11am-10pm.

Baker City Café-Pizza à Fetta, 1915 Washington Ave. (523-3641). This elegant and friendly café makes everything from scratch, including their phenomenal gourmet pizza. The prices may look steep: slices go for $2-2.50, small pies for $10, but are well worth it. Besides, 2 thick, wide slices will fill most people. Open Mon.–Sat. 9am-8pm.

Front Street Coffee Co., 1840 Main St. (523-7536). An old-time Main Street soda shop done up with electric-lavender trim. Square up to John Wayne as you walk in, admire their lunch box collection as you sit at the counter, or play checkers on the hand-painted wooden tables. Choose from 30 different espresso drinks ($1-3) or 4 daily coffees (75¢). The finest charbroiled, lemon pepper chicken breast sandwich in town ($5). Open Mon.-Tues. 7am-2:30pm, Weds.-Sat. 7am-8pm; Oct.-mid-June Mon.-Sat. 7am-2:30pm.

Klondike's Pizza, 1726 Campbell St. (523-7105). Cheap pizza in what looks like a reclaimed bordello, with gold tassels on the heavy curtains and red velveteen walls. Cutely named pizzas, including Pyrite Pete's Pleaser and the Ace of Spades. Pies come in 4 sizes from the microscopic "mini" to the gargantuan "giant," and range in price from $2.35-19.15. The "super saver special" pizza, costs $7 for a medium, $8 for a giant. Many lunch specials under $5. Open daily 11am-11pm.

ENTERTAINMENT, SIGHTS AND EVENTS

As far as **nightlife** goes in Baker City, the nightly 7:30 movie at the **Eltrym Theater** at 1st and Valley Ave., is a staple. Other options include **Main Event,** 1929 Main St. (523-6988), a classic sports bar with a full sized hang glider, sailboard, and five TVs hanging from its high ceilings (open daily 9am-2:30am, unless there's nobody there). Otherwise, **Sunny's Bar and Grill,** a spiffy little hotel bar at the Sunridge Best Western (off Campbell next to I-84) is where it's at.

The hills 6 mi. east of Baker City have been recently invaded by the multi-million-dollar **National Historic Oregon Trail Interpretive Center** at Flagstaff Hill. Volunteers in pioneer vesture will greet you at the door, ushering you on to a tour that recreates the trek with closed-caption videos, life-size models, and more. The tour depicts the trials and tribulations of life on the trail, not only for the pioneers, but for the miners, fur traders, and Native Americans who lived here. You can load up a model wagon with your choice of supplies and they'll tell how far you'd get. Demonstrations of pioneer arts and skills are held outside. Over 4 mi. of trails, some accessible to the disabled, lead to scenic overlooks and interpretive sites. In some places you can actually walk alongside the wagon ruts of the original trail. Highly recommended; set aside at least a few hours for this informative and exceptionally rendered look at the past. Call 523-1843 for information and current admission prices. Open daily 9am-6pm; Nov.-March 9am-4pm.

Across the street from the Oregon Trail Regional Museum, the **Geiser Pollman Park** on Campbell St., is a big lawn with a playground, two blocks from Main St. along the river. On the other side of the park, the **public library** (523-6419), on Resort St., has a huge selection of children's books (open Mon. and Thurs. 10am-8pm, Tues.-Wed. 10am-6pm, Fri. 10am-5pm, Sat. 10am-4pm). The festivities at the **Miners' Jubilee,** on the 3rd weekend of July, include the hotly-contested mining competition **single-jack,** where one man pounds a chisel as many as seven inches through solid granite in five minutes, and "Arts in the Park," a show and sale of arts with live music. Call the visitors' center (see **Practical Information,** above) for information.

Elkhorn Ridge, towering steeply over Baker City to the west, is the local manifestation of the Blue Mountains. While this jagged line of peaks was avoided by Oregon Trail pioneers, today a paved loop, designated a national scenic byway, leads over the range, providing drivers of the 106 mi. route with lofty views and hiking and fishing opportunities. A ¼-mi. hike follows a ridge from a parking lot on Forest Rd. 210 (off Rd. 73) to a great vista at **Lakes Lookout.** On the south portion of the loop, the 3 mi. climb up 8321-ft. Mt. Ireland offers spectacular 360° views. From Rd. 73, take 7370 near the forest boundary and park at **Grizzly Mine.** If you want to make it a longer trip, there's plenty to keep you occupied. Fish in any of the numerous high mountain lakes and creeks, and set up camp in Anthony Lakes campground (see **Accommodations**) or any place that looks good to you (provided it's 200 yards from the shoreline). Check out plenty of well-maintained trails, or take on the challenging **Elkhorn Crest Trail,** which winds through alpine and sub-alpine climates for 22.6 mi. between Anthony Lake in the north and Marble Creek in the south. For more information on the Elkhorns and current conditions or restrictions, stop at the **Wallowa National Forest Ranger Station,** 3165 10th St. (523-4476), open Mon.-Fri. 7:45am-4:30pm. If they're closed, the *Anthony Lakes Recreation Area* brochure (available in the foyer) should tell you all you need to know.

If you're heading west on I-84, a wonderful complement to the Oregon Trail Interpretive Center in Baker City is the **Blue Mountain Crossing.** A ½ mi., paved, wheelchair-accessible path leads through the open forest to the original ruts of the Oregon Trail. Signs provide excerpts from emigrant diaries and commentary on the sights. Two self-guided paths afford a longer look at the trail. On summer weekends, a pioneer encampment offers a living-history glimpse of life on the trail. It's all free, and highly recommended. To reach the site, leave I-84 at Exit 248 (12 mi. west of La Grande; nearly 60 mi. from Baker City) and follow the signs 3 mi. up the hill (open daily Memorial Day-Labor Day, 8am-8pm).

■ Hells Canyon and The Wallowa Mountains

The northeast corner of Oregon is the state's most rugged, remote, and arresting country, with jagged granite peaks, glacier-gouged valleys, and azure lakes. East of La Grande, the Wallowa Mountains (Wa-lá-wah) rise abruptly, towering over the plains from elevations of over 9000 ft. Thirty mi. farther east, the deepest gorge in North America plunges 5500 ft. to the Snake River below. The barren and dusty slopes, lack of water, and scorching heat give credence to the name Hells Canyon. It may take a four-wheel-drive vehicle and some real initiative to get off the beaten path, but you will be rewarded.

PRACTICAL INFORMATION AND ORIENTATION

Visitor Information: The Wallowa Mountains Visitor Center, 88401 Rte. 82 (426-5546), just outside Enterprise to the west, is a Forest Service Information extraordinaire, packed with info and fabulous displays about the Wallowas and Hells Canyon. The $3 **forest map** is a virtual necessity for navigating the elaborate network of roads in the area. Competent, friendly staff can help you plan everything from an afternoon's drive to a week-long backpacking trek. Movies and slide shows of the Wallowa Mountains and Hells Canyon are shown upon request. Open Mon.-Sat. 8am-5pm; Labor Day-Memorial Day 8am-5pm. **The Wallowa County Chamber of Commerce,** P.O. Box 427 (426-4622 or 800-585-4121), is a well-stocked counter in the Mall at SW 1st St. and W. Greenwood Ave., in Enterprise, and offers both general tourist info with an emphasis on local business establishments and the comprehensive and free *Wallowa County Visitor's Guide* ($1). Also gives info on **road and trail conditions.** Open Mon.-Fri. 10am-3pm. The **Hells Canyon Chamber of Commerce,** P.O. Box 841, Halfway, OR 97834 (742-5722), in the office of Halfway Motels, provides info on accommodations, outfitters, and guides; a welcome orientation to the area when approaching from the south.

Bus Line: Moffit Brothers Transportation, P.O. Box 156, Lostine, OR 97857 (569-2284), runs the **Wallowa Valley Stage Line,** which makes one roundtrip run from Joseph to La Grande, Mon.-Sat. Pick-up at the Chevron station on 82 in Joseph, the Texaco station on 82 in Enterprise, and the Greyhound terminal in La Grande. Will stop at Wallowa Lake if you ask. Will also pick you up there if you call the day before. One way fare from La Grande to: Enterprise ($8.10), Joseph ($8.80), Wallowa Lake ($12.50). Reservations recommended.

Bike Rental: Crosstown Traffic, 102 W. McCully (432-2453), in Joseph. $15 per day, discounts for multiple-day rentals. Open Mon.-Sat. 10am-6pm. Knowledgeable staffers can suggest biking routes.

Laundromat: Enterprise Homestyle Laundromat and Car Wash, on Rte. 82 in Joseph, across from the Indian Lodge Motel. $1 wash, 25¢ for 10min. dry. Open daily 6am-10pm.

Hospital: Wallowa Memorial, 401 NE 1st St. (426-3111), in Enterprise.

Emergency: 911. **Police:** State Police, (963-7175). **County Sheriff's Office,** (426-3131), in the back of the Court House. **Enterprise Police Department** (426-3136), at the corner of North St. and NE 1st on S. River St. (Rte. 82).

Post Office: 101 NE 1st (426-3555), on Rte. 82 in Enterprise. Open Mon.-Fri. 9am-4:30pm. **General Delivery ZIP Code:** 97828.

Area Code: 541.

Hells Canyon and the Eagle Cap Wilderness lie on either side of the Wallowa Valley, which can be reached in three ways. From Baker City, Rte. 86 heads east through Halfway to connect with Forest Rd. 39, which winds north over the southern end of the Wallowas, meeting Rte. 350 8 mi. east of Joseph. From La Grande, Rte. 82 arcs around the north end of the Wallowas, through the small towns of **Elgin, Minam, Wallowa,** and **Lostine,** continuing through Enterprise and Joseph, and terminating at Wallowa Lake. From Clarkston, WA, Rte. 129 heads south, taking a plunge through the valley of the Grande Ronde River, becoming Rte. 3 in Oregon, to end at Rte. 82 in Enterprise. Within the area, the only two major roads are Rte. 350, a paved route from Joseph northeast 30 mi. to the tiny town of Imnaha, and Forest Rd. 3955 (a.k.a. 727), or the Imnaha River Rd., a good gravel road which runs south from Imnaha to reconnect with Forest Service 39 about 50 mi. southeast of Joseph. The free pamphlet *Look Into Hells Canyon,* available in information centers and ranger stations in most of northeastern Oregon, is invaluable. It includes a clear map of area roadways showing campgrounds and points of interest.

ACCOMMODATIONS

Most of the towns along Rte. 82 have motels with welcoming vacancy signs during the week. On weekends, things get more crowded and rooms are scarce.

Country Inn Motel (426-4022), on Rte. 82 in Enterprise. This friendly motel's frilly decorations suggest a county farm. The lack of A/C is not a problem—even on the hottest summer days the rooms stay remarkably cool. Cable TV, coffee makers, and refrigerators. Singles $30. Doubles $40, kitchens $4 extra.

Indian Lodge Motel, 201 S. Main (432-2651), on Rte. 82 in Joseph. A one-story roadsider with terracotta roofing and elegant rooms: recently renovated, and tastefully decorated with lots of dark wood. Air conditioning, cable TV, coffee makers, and refrigerators. Singles $35. Doubles $45 (rates $5 lower in winter).

Halfway Motels, 170 S. Main (742-5722), just off Rte. 86 in Halfway. Verging on a monopoly, this dynasty includes three separate locations. The units in the "old" part of the motel have no phones and are worn with age, but clean. Singles $35. Doubles $42. For shiny "new" rooms in a two-story building with an indoor hallway, TVs, and matching furniture ensembles, singles $40, doubles $52.

Outbound Inn & Breakfast House, 507 S. River St. (426-6457), on Rte. 82 in Enterprise. For a few dollars more than a motel in town, you can settle into the spacious

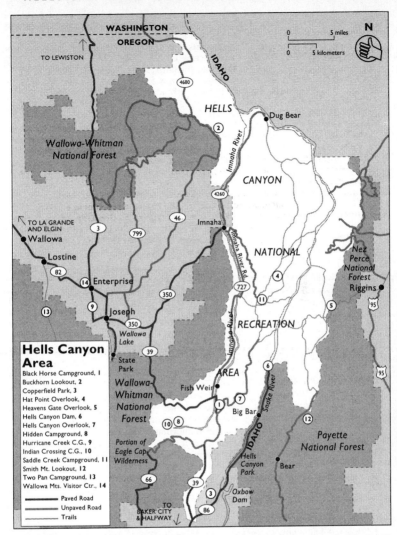

WASHINGTON
OREGON

TO LEWISTON

IDAHO

4680

HELLS

*Wallowa-Whitman
National Forest*

Dug Bear

2

CANYON

Imnaha River

4260

TO LA GRANDE
AND ELGIN
● Wallowa

3

46

Imnaha

799

NATIONAL

Nez
Perce
National
Forest
Riggins

● Lostine

82

14 Enterprise

350

727

11

4

5

95

13

9

Joseph

350

RECREATION

Wallowa
Lake

Hells Canyon Area

Black Horse Campground, 1
Buckhorn Lookout, 2
Copperfield Park, 3
Hat Point Overlook, 4
Heavens Gate Overlook, 5
Hells Canyon Dam, 6
Hells Canyon Overlook, 7
Hidden Campground, 8
Hurricane Creek C.G., 9
Indian Crossing C.G., 10
Saddle Creek Campground, 11
Smith Mt. Lookout, 12
Two Pan Campground, 13
Wallowa Mts. Visitor Ctr., 14

━━━━ Paved Road
──── Unpaved Road
──── Trails

State
Park

39

*Wallowa-
Whitman
National
Forest*

Fish Weir

AREA

6

7

1

Big Bar

10 8

Snake River

*Portion of
Eagle Cap
Wilderness*

12

*Payette
National Forest*

66

39

Hells
Canyon
Park

Bear

95

3

Oxbow
Dam

86

TO
BAKER CITY
& HALFWAY

N

0   5 miles
0   5 kilometers

rooms of this old farmhouse. The farm is long gone, but the sunny kitchen still overlooks a neat row of vegetables and a small rock garden. $55-58 per couple.

CAMPING

There's no reason to come to the Wallowa Valley if you don't love nature. Campgrounds here are plentiful, inexpensive, and sublime. At the Wallowa Mountains Visitor Center, pick up the green *Campground Information* pamphlet for a complete listing of campgrounds in the area. Due to budget constraints, only certain campgrounds are fully serviced—check beforehand at the visitor center whether a campground has potable water.

Saddle Creek Campground, 7 spectacular sites perched right on the lip of Hells Canyon. Unbelievable views of the canyon, especially at dusk and dawn. To get there, drive 18 mi. up the rough, steep narrow road to Hat Point from Imnaha. Bring your own water. Pit toilets. Free.

Hurricane Creek Campground, a quiet, if sometimes unkempt, campground by Hurricane Creek is the closest free camping. Take the well-marked Hurricane Creek road from Rte. 82 in Enterprise, or from Main St. in Joseph follow the large green sign onto W. Wallowa Rd. After about 2 mi. make a sharp left at a white grange and a red barn. The gravel road turns into pavement in 1½ mi. and the campground lies ½ mi. farther down a dirt road labeled "100" to the left. Bring your own water. 14 free and secluded sites.

Hidden Campground, shaded by giant conifers and bordered by the clear, cool South Fork of the Inmaha River, from which you may be able to pull a trout for your dinner. Head southwest of Joseph on Forest Rd. 39 for about 40 mi., then turn up Forest Rd. 3960 toward Indian Crossing for 9 mi. (gravel). 13 sites, pit toilets, drinking water, $4.

Indian Crossing Campground, a little past Hidden, has great secluded sites across the river. This is the farthest out of any campsite on Forest Rd. 3960, and is worth the extra few miles. 14 sites, pit toilets, drinking water, $4.

Two Pan Campground, with 8 pleasant sites, some right on the Lostine River. From Lostine, follow the Lostine River Rd. (Forest Rd. 8210) to its end after 18 mi. The last 5 mi. are on a rough gravel road. Bring your own water. Free.

FOOD

A few affordable restaurants hide out in the small towns of the Wallowa Valley. If you're heading out onto the chassis-shaking roads of Hells Canyon, bring along some provisions. You never know when a flat or breakdown will leave you stranded. Stock up at **Safeway,** 601 W. North St. (462-3722), on Rte. 82 in Enterprise (open daily 6am-10pm).

Vali's Alpine Delicatessen Restaurant, 59811 Wallowa Lake Hwy. (432-5691), in Wallowa Lake. Ask any local where to get a good meal and they will unhesitatingly tell you "Vali's." Mr. Vali cooks one authentic European dish each night and the endearing Mrs. Vali serves it in this one-room, alpinesque cottage. Reservations are required, and the offerings increase in cost from Hungarian Kettle Goulash on Wednesday ($7.50) to schnitzel on Sunday ($12). No reservations are necessary for the daily continental breakfast, where homemade donuts (50-65¢) are available by the pound. Breakfast daily 10am-noon. Dinner Tues.-Sun. 5:30pm-8pm; winter Sat. and Sun. only.

The Common Good Marketplace, 100 W. Main (426-4125), in Enterprise. An orange-carpeted establishment which sells bulk food, herbal extracts, and books on holistic living. Take a seat at someone's old dining room table and order up a triple-decker deli sandwich on homemade bread (around $4; ½ for $3), suck down a steaming espresso, or sip a tall carrot-beet juice ($3) from the full-service juice bar. Open Mon.-Sat. 9:30am-5:30pm, lunch served 10:30am-3pm.

Embers Brew House, 204 N. Main St. (432-BREW/2739) in Joseph. The ambience of this new white house needs some time to age, but the 13 microbrews on tap are perfect the way they are. Snack on the breaded brew fries ($1.50) or be healthy with a loaded vegetarian sandwich ($4.95). Draws a younger crowd. Open daily 7am-11pm.

OUTDOORS

The Wallowa Mountains

Without a catchy, federally-approved name like "Hells Canyon National Recreation Area," the Wallowas often take second place to the canyon in the minds of tourists. This is a shame; the mountains possess a scenic beauty as magnificent as that of Hells Canyon. The jagged peaks, towering in stately splendor over the Wallowa Valley are a sharp contrast to the dry canyons. **Wallowa Lake** is a brilliantly blue, deep body of water that starts within a mile of Joseph and stretches south to a resort area. Wallowa

Lake State Park and resort, at the south end of the lake, is the center of tourist activity in the Wallowa Valley. Unless you want to try your luck for the rainbow or brook trout, kokanee, or dolly varden cruising the lake, the view is better, the swimming is as good, and the crowds are gone at the north end of the lake.

While there are lots of **fish** in the lake, there are even more anglers. If you want to join the fray, the **Wallowa Lake Marina** (432-9115) is open daily 8am-8pm and rents rods to beginners ($5 a day, plus a $10 deposit) as well as paddleboats ($6 per hr.), canoes and rowboats ($5 per hr., $15 for 5hrs.), and six-horsepower motorboats ($10 per hr., $30 for 5hrs.). If you're short on time, you can catch a ride on the **Wallowa Lake Tramway** (432-5331), which will whisk you up 3700 feet in 15 minutes on North America's steepest gondola. The **views** on the ride up, and at the top of 8250 ft. Mt. Howard, can't be beat. On a clear day you can see four states. Two mi. of walking trails at the top lead to different viewpoints. Unfortunately, the lofty views come with a lofty price ($12.75, seniors $11, under 11 $7; open June-Sept. daily 10am-4pm).

Over 500 mi. of hiking trails cross the **Eagle Cap Wilderness** and are free of snow mid-July to October. Deep glacial valleys and high granite passes make hiking this wilderness tough going; it often takes more than a day to get into the most picturesque and remote areas. Still, several high alpine lakes are accessible to the dayhiker. The 5-mi. hike to **Chimney Lake**, from the Boruman Trail head on the Lostine River Rd. (#8210), traverses fields of granite boulders with a few small meadows. Just a little farther lie the serene Laverty, Hobo, and Wood Lakes, where the path is less beaten. The **Two Pan** trailhead at the end of the Lostine River Road is the start of the forested 6 mi. hike to popular **Minam Lake**. Minam Lake is a good jumping off point for other back country spots like Blue Lake (a mile above Minam) which features views of jagged granite peaks. Or, hike the 6 mi. from the **Wallowa Lake** trailhead, behind the little powerhouse at the dead end of Rte. 82, up the East Fork of the Wallowa River to **Aneroid Lake.** From Aneroid the summit hikes to Pete's Point and Aneroid Mountain offer great vistas.

By far the most popular area in the Eagle Cap Wilderness is the **Lakes Basin,** where one can find unsurpassed scenery, hiking to Eagle Cap Peak, good fishing, and camping. While it is possible to escape the crowds in the basin during the week, on weekends it is like a mountainous Central Park. **Steamboat, Long,** and **Swamp Lakes** are as magnificent as the Lakes Basin but with only half as many people. The trailheads for both areas are on the Lostine River Road. Rangers at the visitor's center can also recommend alternative, secluded routes. Fishing in the alpine lakes of the Eagle Cap Wilderness is incredible, but it is important to be familiar with current restrictions. It is *illegal* even to catch and release if you don't have a permit, and some fish, such as the Bull Trout, are entirely protected. Pick up a permit (about $6 a day or $40 for the year) and the annual *Oregon Sport Fishing Regulations* booklet at any local sporting store. **Wallowa Outdoors,** 110 S. River St. (426-3493) on Rte. 82 in Enterprise is a good bet. (Open Mon.-Fri. 9:30am-5:30pm, Sat. 9am-4pm.) With all the tackle and gear you might need, Mac will set you on the way to your limit of golden, rainbow, and brook trout. Or, for a sizeable sum (starting at $90 a person) he'll take you out himself.

Many excellent day hikes to **Lookingglass, Culver, Bear, Eagle, Cashed, Arrow,** and **Heart Lakes** start from the Main Eagle Trailhead (on Forest Rd. 7755 from 77) on the southern side of the Eagle Cap Wilderness (accessible from Baker City and Halfway). An amazing overnight expedition would tour the loop of all or some of these lakes. For a hefty fee, you can hire a **llama** to carry your supplies. **Hurricane Creek Llama Treks** (432-4455) offers a range of trips into the Wallowa Mountains and Hells Canyon.

Hells Canyon

As one early white settler said, "The government bet you 160 acres that you couldn't live there three years without starving to death." Hells Canyon's endearing name

OREGON

comes from its legendary inaccessibility and hostility to human habitation. The Grand Canyon's big sister, it is North America's deepest gorge: in some places the walls drop over 8000 ft. to the **Snake River** below. The fault and fold lines in the canyon walls cause the cliffs to melt into great wrinkles of grass and rock.

Accessing the area without a vehicle or horse is difficult. Some people hitchhike in from the gateway towns of Joseph or Halfway, and talk it up with people at campsites to get back out. (*Let's Go* does not recommend hitchhiking.) The **Area Headquarters,** 88401 Rte. 82 (426-5564), is on the west side of Enterprise. This is a good place to start, as the rangers can provide extensive information on the area and tips on the best things to see. Detailed **maps** are worth the $3 price tag (open Mon.-Sat. 8am-5pm). There are also Recreation Area offices in Riggins, ID (208-628-3916), and Clarkston, WA (509-758-0616).

Inaccessibility poses a problem when exploring Hells Canyon. The few roads are notoriously poor and most Forest Roads are snowed in Oct.-June. The only way to get close to the canyon without taking at least a full day is to drive the **Hells Canyon National Scenic Loop Drive,** which will only give you the vaguest idea of what Hells Canyon is all about. The drive begins and ends in Baker City, following Rte. 86, Forest Rd. 39 and 350, Rte. 82, and finally I-84. Even this paved route takes six hours to two days to drive.

Lookout points provide dramatic views of the rugged canyons. **Hells Canyon Overlook,** the most accessible (though least impressive), is reachable by driving up Forest Rd. 3965, 3 mi. of the smoothest, most luxurious pavement in Wallowa County. Enjoy it while you can. The road departs Rd. 39 about 5 mi. south of the Imnaha River crossing. The broadest and most eye-popping **views** are from the **Hat Point Overlook,** where visitors can climb a 90-ft. wooden fire lookout to vastly improve the view. The price you pay for this sensational vista is a 24-mi. drive up a steep, but well-maintained gravel road from Imnaha (Forest Road 4320, then turn off onto 315; watch the signs). There are pit toilets at the overlook and six primitive campsites just over the hill. The **Buckhorn Lookout** lies far off the beaten path, 42 mi. northeast of Joseph, and offers lofty views of the Imnaha River Valley. To get there, take Rte. 82 north 3 mi. out of Joseph or south 3 mi. out of Enterprise. You'll see the green sign for Buckhorn. Turn off and follow Zumwalt Rd. (a.k.a. Forest Road 26) approximately 40 mi. to Buckhorn. The rough ride takes a full day to drive roundtrip, or you can camp at the lookout.

Campers should stock up on food, drinking water, and gas, and remember that there are no showers or flush toilets anywhere. If you plan to hike down into the canyon and around the high lakes, insect repellent is a must in the summer. Weather can make extreme shifts in a short time, so be prepared for any condition. There are a plethora of potential campsites out there for the taking, but because of adverse road conditions, most campsites are only open from July to September. **Copperfield, McCormick,** and **Woodland** (all owned by Idaho Power) have tent and RV sites and restrooms, and are the only campgrounds open year round. These manicured campgrounds are located near Oxbow and Brownlee Dams, on Rte. 86 and Rte. 71 on the Snake (tent fee $6, RV fee $8).

Also at that end of the canyon, the immense **Hells Canyon Dam** lies 23 mi. north of Oxbow on Rte. 86. The Snake's-eye views from the winding road become increasingly dramatic as you travel north. This drive is the only way to get near the bottom of the canyon by car, and the dam is the only place to cross.

The easiest way to see a lot of the canyon is to zip through on a jet boat tour or float through on a raft. A panoply of outfitters operate out of Oxbow and the dam area and run trips through the canyon. The Wallowa Mountains Visitor Center (see page 509) has a list of all the permittees, or pick up a brochure at any Chamber of Commerce office (see page 509). **Hells Canyon Adventures,** (785-3352, outside Oregon 800-422-3568), 1½ mi. from the Hells Canyon Dam in Oxbow, runs a wide range of jet boat and raft trips through the Canyon. You can take a full day ($70) or three hour

($30) jet boat tour. A full day of whitewater rafting ($90) includes a jet boat ride back upstream.

Hells Canyon Bicycle Tours, P.O. Box 483, Joseph OR 97846 (432-2453), operates out of the Crosstown Traffic Bike Shop in Joseph (see **Practical Information,** page 509). With the encouraging motto "We bring 'em back alive," the outfit offers one- to four-day tours of the National Recreation Area. Day rides ($75) include transportation and lunch, while overnight trips ($75/day) include everything but sleeping bags and personal gear. Rides of varying difficulty can be arranged, though mountain biking experience is necessary for rides which drop into the canyon. Most canyon-bottom rides are in spring or fall.

Hiking is perhaps the best way to fully comprehend the vast emptiness of Hells Canyon, but to really get into the canyon requires a backpacking trip of at least a few days. There are over 1000 mi. of trails in the canyon, only a fraction of which are maintained regularly by the Forest Service. A wide array of dangers lurks below the rim: huge elevation gains and losses can catch your body off guard, as well as poison oak, rattlesnakes, blistering heat, and lack of water, to name a few. Still, if you're prepared, a backpacking trip into the Canyon can provide an incredible one-on-one experience with the land.

The dramatic 56 mi. **Snake River Trail** runs beside the river for the length of the canyon. At times the trail is cut into the side of the rock with just enough clearance for a horse's head. Come prepared for all the hazards (see above), but, should you need help, the outfitters and rangers that patrol the river by boat are never too far. You can follow this trail from **Dug Bar** in the north clear down to the Hells Canyon Dam, or you can access it from treacherously steep trails along the way. From north to south, **Hat Point, Battle Creek,** and **P.O. Saddle** are possible access points. To reach Dug Bar take Forest Road 4240 (a steep and sometimes slippery trek recommended only for four-wheel-drive or high-clearance vehicles) 27 mi. northeast from Imnaha. Discuss your plans with rangers before heading out.

Appendix

▓ Weather

City	Avg. High/Low Temperatures in °F			
	Jan.	April	July	Oct.
Anchorage, AK	20/8	42/28	65/50	40/29
Denali National Park, AK (entrance)	10/-8	38/15	67/42	32/13
Vancouver, BC	40/32	55/42	70/55	56/43
Victoria, BC	43/32	55/39	72/52	57/43
Whitehorse, YT	13/-3	41/22	67/45	41/28
Banff, AB	19/3	46/25	72/45	50/30
Calgary, AB	21/0	48/27	73/48	54/30
Olympic Peninsula, WA (Port Angeles)	42/34	53/41	62/51	54/45
Seattle, WA	45/32	58/40	74/54	60/45
Eugene, OR	45/31	60/38	81/50	65/40
Portland, OR	30/10	52/32	79/59	60/39

▓ Holidays and Festivals

OFFICIAL U.S. HOLIDAYS IN 1997

New Year's Day, Wed. Jan. 1; **Martin Luther King, Jr.'s Birthday,** Mon. Jan. 20; **Presidents Day,** Mon. Feb. 17 (observed); **Memorial Day,** Mon. May 26; **Independence Day,** Fri. July 4; **Labor Day,** Mon. Sept. 1; **Columbus Day,** Mon. Oct. 13; **Veterans Day (Armistice Day),** Tues. Nov. 11 (observed); **Thanksgiving,** Thurs. Nov. 27; **Christmas Day,** Thurs. Dec. 25.

OFFICIAL CANADIAN HOLIDAYS IN 1997

New Year's Day, Wed. Jan.1; **Easter Monday,** Mon. March 31; **Victoria Day,** Mon. May 19; **Canada Day,** Tues. July 1; **Thanksgiving,** Mon. Oct. 13; **Remembrance Day,** Tues. Nov. 11; **Christmas Day,** Thurs. Dec. 25; **Boxing Day,** Fri. Dec. 26.

WHERE'S THE PARTY?

Festival/event	City	Approximate dates
Bumbershoot	Seattle, WA	late July
Canada Day	. anywhere in Canada	July 1
Folk Music Festival	Vancouver, BC	mid-July
Iditarod	Anchorage to Nome, AK	1st-3rd weeks in March
Independence Day	anywhere in the U.S.	July 4
Rose Festival	Portland, OR	first three weeks of June
Oregon County Fair	Eugene, OR	2nd week of July
Rhythm & Blues Festival	Winthrop, WA	late July
Round-Up	Pendleton, OR	2nd week in Sept.
Stampede	Calgary, AB	July 4-13

Mileage

	Anch.	Boise	Calg.	Daws. City	Edm.	Fairb.	Port.	Prince Geo.	Prince Rupert	Prud. Bay	Seattle	Spok.	Vanc.	White-horse	NYC	Chic.	San F.
Anch.		2934	2160	515	1975	358	2610	1678	1605	847	2435	2578	2145	724	4649	3818	3153
Boise	62 hr.		828	2537	1011	2930	439	1128	2079	3419	499	379	642	2210	2451	1650	649
Calg.	47½ hr.	17 hr.		1747	184	2038	859	493	950	2527	738	443	609	1436	2490	1658	1514
Daws. City	15½ hr.	53½ hr.	43½ hr.		1562	393	2197	1390	1192	882	2022	2200	1764	327	4236	3405	2830
Edm.	47½ hr.	34½ hr.	3½ hr.	33 hr.		1853	1043	461	906	2342	790	628	722	1251	2674	1953	1698
Fairb.	8 hr.	59½ hr.	45 hr.	9½ hr.	45 hr.		2455	1668	1483	489	2313	2456	2137	602	4527	3696	3121
Port.	55½ hr.	8½ hr.	18 hr.	49 hr.	21 hr.	53 hr.		733	1208	2977	175	400	318	1886	2950	2229	655
Prince Geo.	37½ hr.	24½ hr.	10 hr.	31 hr.	10 hr.	3 hr.	14½ hr.		434	2074	558	663	486	983	3553	2174	1437
Prince Rupert	35½ hr.	32½ hr.	19½ hr.	26½ hr.	18 hr.	33 hr.	24 hr.	9½ hr.		1972	1033	1230	901	881	3440	2608	1880
Prud. Bay	27½ hr.	79 hr.	64½ hr.	29 hr.	64½ hr.	19½ hr.	72½ hr.	52 hr.	49 hr.		2802	2975	2541	1091	5016	4185	3610
Seattle	52 hr.	10 hr.	14½ hr.	43½ hr.	17 hr.	49½ hr.	3½ hr.	14½ hr.	22½ hr.	69 hr.		282	143	1711	2924	2113	808
Spok.	57½ hr.	8 hr.	9 hr.	49 hr.	12½ hr.	55 hr.	7½ hr.	15 hr.	24½ hr.	74½ hr.	5½ hr.		400	1987	2642	1837	1055
Vanc.	49½ hr.	12½ hr.	13 hr.	41 hr.	14½ hr.	47 hr.	6 hr.	12 hr.	20 hr.	66½ hr.	2½ hr.	8 hr.		1450	3067	2255	973
White-horse	16 hr.	46 hr.	31½ hr.	7½ hr.	31½ hr.	13½ hr.	39½ hr.	21½ hr.	19½ hr.	33 hr.	36 hr.	41½ hr.	33½ hr.		3925	3094	2519
NYC	99 hr.	49 hr.	50 hr.	85 hr.	53½ hr.	90½ hr.	59 hr.	71 hr.	68½ hr.	109 hr.	55 hr.	53 hr.	61½ hr.	78½ hr.		831	2945
Chic.	76 hr.	33 hr.	33 hr.	68 hr.	39 hr.	74 hr.	44½ hr.	43½ hr.	52 hr.	93½ hr.	39½ hr.	37 hr.	45 hr.	17 hr.	15½ hr.		2151
San F.	63 hr.	13 hr.	30 hr.	56½ hr.	34 hr.	62½ hr.	12½ hr.	29 hr.	38 hr.	82 hr.	15½ hr.	21 hr.	18½ hr.	51 hr.	55½ hr.	40½ hr.	

■ Time Zones

Oregon, Washington, British Columbia, and the Yukon Territory are in the **Pacific Time Zone,** three hours earlier than Eastern Standard Time. Most of Alaska is in **Alaska Time,** one hour earlier than Pacific, four hours earlier than Eastern. Alberta is on **Mountain Time,** one hour later than Pacific, two hours earlier than Eastern.

■ Measurements

Although the metric system has made considerable inroads into American business and science, the British system of weights and measures continues to prevail in the U.S. The following is a list of U.S. units and their metric equivalents:

1 inch = 25 millimeter (mm)	1mm = 0.04 inch (in.)
1 foot (ft.) = 0.30 meter (m)	1m = 3.33 foot (ft.)
1 yard (yd.) = 0.91m	1m = 1.1 yard (yd.)
1 mile = 1.61kilometer (km)	1km = 0.62 mile (mi.)
1 ounce = 25 gram (g)	1g = 0.04 ounce (oz.)
1 pound (lb.) = 0.45 kilogram (kg)	1kg = 2.22 pound (lb.)
1 quart = 0.94 liter (L)	1 liter = 1.06 quart (qt.)

COMPARATIVE VALUES OF U.S. UNITS OF MEASUREMENT:

1 foot	= 12 inches
1 yard	= 3 feet
1 mile	= 5280 feet
1 pound	= 16 ounces (weight)
1 cup	= 8 ounces (volume)
1 pint	= 2 cups
1 quart	= 2 pints
1 gallon	= 4 quarts

It should be noted that gallons in the U.S. are not identical to those across the Atlantic; one U.S. gallon equals 0.83 Imperial gallons.

The U.S. uses the Fahrenheit **temperature scale.** To convert Fahrenheit to Centigrade temperatures, subtract 32, then multiply by 5/9. To convert from Centigrade to Fahrenheit, multiply by 9/5 and then add 32. Or, just remember that 32°F is the freezing point of water, 212°F its boiling point, normal human body temperature is 98.6°F, and room temperature hovers around 70°F.

■ The Juice

Electricity is 110V AC in the U.S. and Canada, only half as much as that of most European countries. Visit a hardware store for an **adapter** (which changes the shape of the plug) and a **converter** (which changes the voltage). Do not make the mistake of using only an adapter, or you'll fry your appliances. Travelers who heat-disinfect their **contact lenses** should consider switching to a chemical disinfection system.

Index

Numerics

100 Mile House, BC 236
15,000 bald eagles 131
150,000 caribou 274
22,000 gray whales 215
5,000 rubber duckies 242

A

AAA (American Automobile
  Association) 30
AIDS 15
Air Canada 25
air passes 25
air travel 25
  charter flights 27
  from Asia 27
  within North America 25
Alaska 54–182
  Anchorage 60
  arts and crafts 67
  Athabascan Natives 107
  Bush 170
  current events 58
  Fairbanks 117
  geography 54
  getting around 59
  history 55
  Interior Alaska 107,
  practical information 59
  Southcentral Alaska 60
  Southeastern Alaska 131
  statehood 55
Alaska Airlines 25
Alaska Day 150
Alaska Dept. of Fish & Game
  50, 146
Alaska Division of Tourism 1
Alaska Hwy. 59
  Dawson Creek, BC to
    Whitehorse, YT 261
  introduction 259
  Kluane Nat'l Park, YT to
    the YT/AK border 269
Alaska Marine Highway 35,
  98
Alaska Maritime Nat'l Wildlife
  Refuge 83
Alaska Native Claims Settle-
  ment Act (ANCSA) of 1971
  55, 107
Alaska Northwest Travel Ser-

vice, Inc. 35
Alaska Panhandle. See South-
  eastern Alaska
Alaska Public Lands Informa-
  tion Center
  APLIC Anchorage 59
  APLIC Fairbanks 117
Alaska Raptor Rehabilitation
  Center 150
Alaska State Division of Parks
  59
Alaska State Museum 156
Alaska Wildland Adventures
  79
Alaskan National Park Ser-
  vice, 59
AlaskaPass 35, 60
Alberta 275–307
  Alberta Badlands 304
  Banff Nat'l Park 288
  Calgary 298
  Edmonton 275
  getting around 275
  Jasper Nat'l Park 282
  practical information 275
Alert Bay, BC 220
Aleutian Islands, AK 179
Alexander Mackenzie Heri-
  tage Trail, BC 236
Along the Cassiar
  Glenora 258
  Stikine Riversong 258
altitude 14
Alvord Desert, OR 501
America West Airlines 25
American Airlines 26
American Bald Eagle Associa-
  tion Center 163
American Express 11, 30
American Foundation for the
  Blind 22
American Motorcyclist Asso-
  ciation 34
AMOCO Motor Club 30, 31
Amtrak 29
an expensive fish 77
Anacortes, WA 353
Anaktuvuk Pass, AK 174
Anan Bear Observatory 142
Anchorage Music Festival 68
Anchorage, AK 60–73

accommodations 64
  International Airport 62
  camping 65
  entertainment 67
  events 68
  food 65
  nightlife 68
  outdoors 69
  practical information 61
  sights and activities 66
animals, obscure
  ankoli 226
  aoudads 226
  burrowing owls 496
  collared lizards 496
  gnus 226
  musk ox 72
  reindeer 72
  rhinoceros 226
  Sasquatch 233, 429
  Shag-ra 228
  whiskered auklet 180
APEX 25
Archie McPhee's 329
Arctic Circle, AK 171
Arctic Nat'l Wildlife Refuge,
  AK 58, 118
area codes 52
Ashland, OR 465
  Ashland Shakespeare
    Festival 468
Astoria, OR 433
ATM cards 12
aurora borealis 117
auto transport companies 32
automobile renting 32

B

Bainbridge Island, WA 338
Baker City, OR 506
Bandon, OR 457
Banff Nat'l Park, AB 288
  accommodations 290
  camping 291
  entertainment 292
  food 291
  outdoors 293
  practical information 289
  sights and events 292
bathtub races
  Nanaimo, BC 213

★Let's Go 1997 Reader Questionnaire ★

Please fill this out and return it to us at **Let's Go, St. Martin's Press,** 175 5th Ave. NY, NY 10010

Name: _____ **What book did you use?**_____

Address: _____

City: _____ **State:** _____ **Zip Code:** _____

How old are you? under 19   19-24   25-34   35-44   45-54   55 or over

Are you (circle one) in high school   in college   in grad school   employed   retired   between jobs

Have you used Let's Go before? yes   no

Would you use Let's Go again? yes   no

How did you first hear about Let's Go? friend   store clerk   CNN   bookstore display   advertisement/promotion   review   other

Why did you choose Let's Go (circle up to two)? annual updating   reputation   budget focus   price   writing style   other: _____

Which other guides have you used, if any? Frommer's $-a-day   Fodor's   Rough Guides   Lonely Planet   Berkeley   Rick Steves   other: _____

Is Let's Go the best guidebook? yes   no

If not, which do you prefer? _____

Which part of Let's Go do you feel needs most to be improved, if any (circle up to two)? packaging/cover   practical information   accommodations   food   cultural introduction   sights   practical introduction ("Essentials")   directions   entertainment   gay/lesbian information   maps   other: _____

How would you like to see these things improved?

_____

_____

How long was your trip? one week   two weeks   three weeks   one month   two months or more

Have you traveled extensively before? yes   no

Do you buy a separate map when you visit a foreign city? yes   no

Have you seen the Let's Go Map Guides? yes   no

Have you used a Let's Go Map Guide? yes   no

If you have, would you recommend them to others? yes   no

Did you use the internet to plan your trip? yes   no

Would you buy a Let's Go phrasebook   adventure/trekking guide   gay/lesbian guide

Which of the following destinations do you hope to visit in the next three to five years (circle one)? Australia   China   South America   Russia   other: _____

Where did you buy your guidebook? internet   chain bookstore   independent bookstore   college bookstore   travel store   other: _____